Population Density
Persons per Square Mile

Under 5
5 to 100
101 to 250
Over 250

WHITE
SEA

•Archangel

N. Dvina R.

URAL MOUNTAINS

LAKE
ONEGA

LAKE
LADOGA

R U S S I A

•St. Petersburg

IA

•Moscow

Samara

Volga R.

Oral

Zhayyq R. (Ural R.)

K A Z A K H S T A N

vina R.

•Smolensk

Saratov

•Minsk

ARUS

Kursk

PRIPET
MARSHES

ARAL
SEA

Kiev

Dnieper R.

Kkarkiv

Volgograd

U B E K I S T A N

U K R A I N E

Dnipropetrovsk

Astrakhan

ster R.

MOLDOVA

Don R.

Prut R.

Chisinau

Rostov

•Odessa

BESSARABIA

SEA OF
AZOV

C A S P I A N   S E A

T U R K M E N I S T A N

IA

CRIMEA

Grozny

Krasnowodsk
(Balkhan)

Ashkhabad

DOBRUJA

Sevastopol

CAUCASUS MTS.

HIA

GEORGIA

Baku

BLACK SEA

Tbilisi

ube R.

Sinop

Batumi

AZERBAIJAN

GARIA

•Varna

Ardahan

ARMENIA

AFGHANISTAN

Kars

Bosporus

Yerevan

•Istanbul

AZERBAIJAN

Dardanelles

T U R K E Y

Lake
Van

Tabriz

Ankara

Lake
Urmia

•Teheran

AN

Lake
Tuz

A S I A

•Izmir

Adana

Tigris R.

Kirkuk

I R A N

Antalya

Aleppo

Isfahan

Euphrates R.

Nicosia

SYRIA

Baghdad

CYPRUS

Beirut

Damascus

I R A Q

Abadan

LEBANON

GOLAN
HEIGHTS

Basra

Bandar-e Bushehr

RETE
eece)

ISRAEL

Tel Aviv

Amman

S E A

Jerusalem

WEST
BANK

KUWAIT

PERSIAN GULF

OMAN

GAZA STRIP

JORDAN

Alexandria

NILE DELTA

SINAI
PENINSULA

Suez Canal

BAHRAIN

UNITED
ARAB
EMIRATES

OMAN

El Alamein

Nile

Cairo

GULF OF
SUEZ

Aqaba

GULF OF
AQABA

S A U D I   A R A B I A

QATAR

E G Y P T

A History
of the
Modern
World

EIGHTH EDITION

A HISTORY OF THE MODERN WORLD

R. R. Palmer
Joel Colton

McGraw-Hill, Inc.
New York   St. Louis   San Francisco   Auckland   Bogotá   Caracas
Lisbon   London   Madrid   Mexico City   Milan   Montreal   New Delhi
San Juan   Singapore   Sydney   Tokyo   Toronto

A HISTORY OF THE MODERN WORLD

This book is printed on acid-free paper.

4 5 6 7 8 9 0   VNH VNH   9 0 9 8 7 6

ISBN 0-07-040826-2

This book was set in Times Roman by Monotype Composition Company.
The editors were Pamela Gordon and Caroline Izzo;
the production supervisor was Annette Mayeski.
The cover was designed by Rafael Hernandez.
The photo editor was Kathy Bendo.
Von Hoffmann Press, Inc., was printer and binder.

Maps of Contemporary Europe and Contemporary Asia were prepared by
Mapping Specialists Limited.

Acknowledgment is hereby made for permission to quote from the following works: *P. 48:* M. K. Bennett, *The World's Food.* Copyright ©1954 by Harper & Brothers, renewed ©1982 by Helen B. Lucine, Stephen W. Bennett, and John F. Bennett. Reprinted by permission of HarperCollins Publishers, Inc. *P. 462:* P. Deane and W. A. Cole, *British Economic Growth, 1688–1959,* Cambridge, Eng.: Cambridge University Press, 1962, pp. 166–167. Reprinted with the permission of Cambridge University Press. *P. 588:* A. N. Carr-Saunders, *World Population,* 1936. Reprinted by permission of Oxford University Press. *PP. 593, 594:* W. Woodruff, *The Impact of Western Man,* 1966, pp. 106, 108. Reprinted by permission of St. Martin's Press, Inc. *P. 650:* "The White Man's Burden," from *The Five Nations,* by Rudyard Kipling. Reprinted by permission of the National Trust and Doubleday & Company, Inc. *P. 769:* B. R. Mitchell, *European Historical Statistics: 1750–1970,* 1975, pp. 319 and 396. Reprinted by permission of Macmillan Press, Ltd. *P. 961:* The World Bank, *World Tables, 1992.* The Johns Hopkins University Press, Baltimore/London, 1993 *P. 1016:* Soviet Census of 1989.

Library of Congress Cataloging-in-Publication Data

Palmer, R. R. (Robert Roswell), (date).
    A history of the modern world / R. R. Palmer, Joel Colton. — 8th ed.
      p.   cm.
    Includes bibliographical references and index.
    ISBN 0-07-040826-2 (hard)
    1. History, Modern.   I. Colton, Joel, (date).   II. Title.
D209.P26   1995
909.82—dc20   94-14758

ABOUT THE
AUTHORS

R. R. PALMER was born in Chicago. After graduating from the University of Chicago he received his doctorate from Cornell University in 1934. From 1936 to 1963 he taught at Princeton University, was then at Washington University in St. Louis from 1963 to 1966, and at Yale from 1969 until his retirement in 1977. He now resides in Princeton, where he is affiliated with the Institute for Advanced Study. His books include *Twelve Who Ruled: The Year of the Terror in the French Revolution* (1941, 1989), and the two-volume *Age of the Democratic Revolution* (1959 and 1964), both volumes of which were History Book Club selections, and the first of which won the Bancroft Prize in 1960. He has likewise written *The World of the French Revolution* (1970) and *The Improvement of Humanity: Education and the French Revolution* (1985), and has edited the *Rand McNally Atlas of World History* (1957). He is the translator of Georges Lefebvre's *Coming of the French Revolution* (1947, 1989), Louis Bergeron's *France under Napoleon* (1981), and Jean-Paul Bertaud's *Army of the French Revolution: From Citizen-Soldiers to Instrument of Power* (1988), and editor-translator of *From Jacobin to Liberal: Marc-Antoine Jullien, 1775–1848* (1993). He was president of the American Historical Association in 1970. He has received honorary degrees from the Universities of Uppsala and Toulouse, and was awarded the Antonio Feltrinelli International Prize for History in Rome in 1990.

JOEL COLTON was born in New York City. He graduated from the City College of New York, served as a military intelligence officer in Europe in World War II, and received his Ph.D. from Columbia University in 1950. He joined the Department of History at Duke University in 1947, chaired the department from 1967 to 1974, received a Distinguished Teaching Award in 1986, and became emeritus professor in 1989. From 1974 to 1981, on leave from Duke University, he served with the Rockefeller Foundation in New York as director of its research and fellowship program in the humanities. In 1979 he was elected a Fellow of the American Academy of Arts and Sciences and was named a national Phi Beta Kappa lecturer in 1983–1984. He has received Guggenheim, Rockefeller Foundation, and National Endowment for the Humanities fellowships. He has served on the editorial board of the *Journal of Modern History* and of *French Historical Studies,* and on the advisory board of *Historical Abstracts.* He has been vice-president of the Society of French Historical Studies and co-president of the International Commission on the History of Social Movements and Social Structures. His writings include *Compulsory Labor Arbitration in France, 1936–1939* (1951); *Léon Blum: Humanist in Politics* (1966, 1987), for which he received a Mayflower Award; *Twentieth Century* (1968, 1980), in the *Time-Life Great Ages of Man* series; and numerous contributions to journals, encyclopedias, and collaborative volumes.

CONTENTS

ILLUSTRATIONS

MAPS, CHARTS, AND TABLES

PREFACE

THE EXTRAORDINARY events of the last few years have made this eighth edition come sooner than usual after its predecessor. It is of course too early to assess the magnitude and consequences of what has happened, but we have done much new writing, rewriting, rewording, and rearrangement to present the upheavals in Eastern Europe, the disintegration of the former Soviet Union, the reunification of Germany, the end of the Cold War, the Islamic fundamentalist movement, changes in Latin America, and much else. We now have four chapters on the half-century since the Second World War. This is more than for the similar time span from Bismarck's unification of Germany in 1871 to the First World War, or from the beginnings of the American Revolution to the fall of Napoleon in 1815. There are adjustments to maps and tables, some alterations made in response to readers' comments, and various emendations in many places. The bibliography has always been a special feature of the book. It has been brought up to date; and although reviewed and pruned, it remains very extensive, containing about 5,000 titles classified by subject according to the plan of the book as a whole. In general, we have done what we could to make so long and complex a volume more manageable and digestible. The whole structure of chapters, sections and subsections, the frequent cross-references, the chronological tables, and the detailed index are intended for this purpose. A student's Study Guide is also available for those who may wish to use it.

Since its first edition the book has been designed as a history both of Europe and of the "modern world." Given this objective, it is a source of satisfaction that the book since its second edition has been translated into seven languages, of which three are non-European. It is gratifying also that such a work, written as a textbook for American colleges and universities, has found readers not only outside the United States but in both public and private secondary schools in this country and among the general reading public.

To obtain breadth, emphasis falls on situations and movements of international scope, on what Europeans and their descendants in other continents have done in common, and on the gradual convergence of the European and non-European worlds into a global economy and an interdependent political system. National histories are therefore somewhat subordinated, and in each national history the points of contact with a larger civilization are emphasized. Historic regional differences within Europe, as between western and eastern Europe, are brought out, and the history of the Americas is woven into the story at various points, as are developments of the past two centuries in Asia and Africa. A good deal of institutional history is included. Considerable space is given to the history of ideas, not only in special sections devoted to ideas, but throughout the book in close connection with the account of institutions and events. Social and economic development bulks rather large, as does the impact of wars and revolutions. Since our own age is one in which much depends on political decision, we think of this volume as political history in the broadest sense, in that matters of many kinds, such as religion, economics, social welfare, and international relations, have presented themselves as public questions requiring public action by responsible citizens or governments. It seems to us that many subjects of current research interest, such as women's history, family history, the history of the laboring classes, the history of minorities, or demographic and quantitative studies, are best understood when seen within a wider framework such as this book attempts to provide.

We are again pleased to thank all those who have helped with the book over the years. We are indebted to McGraw-Hill, Inc., and its staff, publisher of the book since its seventh edition, and especially to Pamela Gordon, Caroline Izzo, Nancy Blaine, and Sarah Touborg, who have provided invaluable assistance in making this edition possible. We are grateful also to Alfred A. Knopf, Inc., our earlier publisher, for continuing to make the book available in a trade edition for the general public. Since they have left the important decisions to us, and all the actual writing is ours, we assume all responsibility for errors, imperfections, questionable judgments, and other possible shortcomings. Esther Howard Palmer and Shirley Baron Colton have contributed in innumerable ways to the newest edition of this history, which can stand as some kind of continuing monument to marriage, friendship, and intellectual collaboration.

R. R. PALMER
JOEL COLTON

A FEW
WORDS ON
GEOGRAPHY

HISTORY IS THE experience of human beings in time, but it takes place also in space, on the planet Earth, so that geography always underlies it. It is the business of geography not merely to describe and map the earth and its various areas, but to study the changing relationships between human activities and the surrounding environment.

The earth is over four billion years old. The entire history of mankind since the Middle Stone Age has occupied less than a hundred-thousandth of the time in which the earthly habitat has been developed. Some minerals now put to human use were formed in the earliest ages of the planet, others such as coal and petroleum were not laid down until a few hundred million years ago, but none that are now being consumed in a flicker of geologic time can ever be replaced. Oceans and continents have moved about, changing in size, shape, and location with respect to one another and to the North and South Poles. There was a time when dinosaurs could walk from North America to Europe (as we now call them) on solid land in a warm climate. The continents as we now know them became fully distinct less than a hundred million years ago. It is only a few thousand years since the end of the most recent glacial age, which may not be the last. The melting back into the ocean of water frozen over a mile thick in Antarctica and in large parts of North America and Europe produced the coastlines, offshore islands, inland seas, straits, bays, and harbors that we see on a map today, as well as some of the largest river systems and lakes. It is only about three hundred years since the first French explorers saw Niagara Falls, which then looked quite different, because by eating away the underlying rock the falls have receded several hundred feet since that time.

At present, the oceans cover more than two-thirds of the surface of the globe. By no means is all the remaining third suited for occupation by human beings, or indeed by most other animal or vegetable organisms, for much of the land still lies under perpetual ice in Antarctica and Greenland, much is tundra, much is desert, and some is along the windswept ridges of high mountains. Like the oceans, these desolate regions have been important in human history, first in earlier times by acting as barriers. Man, as the anthropologists call him (and her), is now thought to have originated in Africa. He (and she) eventually spread to every continent except Antarctica. In doing so, human groups became isolated from each other for thousands of years, separated by oceans, deserts, or mountains, and so became differentiated into the modern races, though all are derived from the same source and belong to the same species. The same is true of cultures or civilizations over a time period measured in centuries rather than millennia. It is such separation that accounts for the historic cultural differences between Africa, pre-Columbian America, China, India, the Middle East, and Europe. On a smaller scale it explains the differences in languages and dialects.

Separation has also produced differences in flora and fauna, and hence in the plants and animals by which humans live. Wheat became the most usual cereal in the Middle East and Europe, millet and rice in East Asia, sorghum in tropical Africa, maize in pre-Columbian America. The horse, first domesticated in central Asia, was for centuries a mainstay of Europe for muscle power, transportation, and combat, while the less versatile camel was adopted later and more slowly in the Middle East, and America had no beasts of burden except the llama. Not until Europeans began to cross the oceans, taking plants and animals with them, and bringing others back, did these great differences begin to diminish.

The present book is concerned primarily with Europe, and with the last few hundred years. And as a traveler setting out on a journey may obtain a map, study it, and keep its contents as much as possible in mind, so the reader is invited to examine the map of Europe on pages 4 and 5, and keep it in mind while reading the following history. The map shows the topographical features that have remained unchanged in historic times.

Europe is physically separated from Africa by the Mediterranean Sea, which however has been as much a passageway as a barrier. A more effective barrier was created when the Sahara Desert dried up only a few thousand years ago. The physical separation of Europe from Asia has always been less clear; the conventional boundary has long been the Ural Mountains in Russia, but the Russians recognize no such official distinction. The Urals are in any case low and wide, and it can be argued that Europe is not a continent at all, but a cultural conception arising from felt differences from Asia and Africa. Europe, even with European Russia, contains hardly more than 6 percent of the land surface of the earth. It has about the same area as the United States including Alaska. It is a little larger than Australia, and a little smaller than Antarctica.

If we consider only its physical features, Europe is indeed one of several peninsulas jutting off from Asia. It is altogether different, however, from the Arabian and Indian peninsulas, which also extend from the mass of Asia, as shown on the back end papers of the present book. For one thing, the Mediterranean Sea is unique among the world's bodies of water. Closed in by the Strait of Gibraltar, which is only eight miles wide, it is more shielded than the Caribbean or East Asian seas from the open ocean. Hence it has very little tide, and is protected from the most violent ocean storms. Though over two thousand miles long, it is subdivided by islands and peninsulas into lesser seas with an identity of their own, such as the Aegean and the Adriatic, and it gives access also to the Black Sea. It is possible to travel for great distances without being far from land, so that navigation developed from early times, and one of the first civilizations appeared on the island of Crete. It is possible also to cross between Europe and Asia at the Bosporus and between Europe and Africa at Gibraltar, so that populations became mixed by early migrations, and various historic empires—Carthaginian, Roman, Byzantine, Arabic, Spanish, Venetian, and Turkish—have used the Mediterranean as an avenue between their component parts. After the Suez Canal was built the Mediterranean became a segment in the "lifeline of empire" for the British Empire in its heyday.

In southern Europe, north of the Mediterranean and running for its whole length, is a series of mountains, produced geologically by the pushing of the gigantic mass of Africa against this smaller Eurasian peninsula. The Pyrenees shut off Spain from the north, as the Alps do Italy; the Balkan Mountains have always been difficult to penetrate; and the only place where one can go at water level from the Mediterranean to the north is by the valley of the Rhone River, so that France, since it came together in the Middle Ages, is the only country that clearly belongs both to the Mediterranean and to northern Europe. North of the mountains is a great plain, with branches in England and Sweden, extending from western France through Germany and Poland into Russia and on into Asia, passing south of the Urals through what is called the Caspian Gate, north of the landlocked Caspian Sea. One might draw a straight line from Amsterdam eastward through the Caspian Gate as far as the borders of western China, and although this line would reach the distance from New York to a point five hundred miles west of San Francisco, one would never in traveling along it be higher above sea level than central Kansas. The continuity of this level plain has at various times opened Europe to Mongol and other invasions, enabled the Russians to move east and create a huge empire, and made Poland a troubled intermediary between Western Europe and the Russians and other peoples.

The rivers as shown on the map are worth particular attention. Until quite recent times rivers offered an easier means of transportation than any form of carriage by land. The principal rivers also give access to the sea. Most are navigable, especially in the north European plains. With their valleys, whether in level country or confined between mountains, they provided areas where intensive local development could take place. Thus we see that some of the most important older cities of Europe are on rivers—London on the Thames, Paris on the Seine, Vienna and Budapest on the Danube, Warsaw on the Vistula. In northern Europe it was often possible to move goods from one river to another, and then in the eighteenth century to connect them by canals; and the networks of rivers and canals still carry much heavy traffic by barges. The importance of water is shown again by the location of Copenhagen, Stockholm, and St. Petersburg (formerly Leningrad) on the Baltic, which is a kind of inland lake, and of Amsterdam and Lisbon, which grew up after the ocean could be traversed by Europeans.

There are many important geographical conditions that a topographic map cannot show. One is climate, which depends on latitude, ocean currents, and winds that bring or withhold rainfall. In latitude Europe lies as far north as the northern United States and southern Canada, with Madrid and Rome in the latitude of New York, and with Stockholm and St. Petersburg as far north as the middle of Hudson Bay. All Europe thus is within what is called the temperate zone, somewhat misleadingly, since the temperate zone is by definition the region of pronounced difference between winter and summer. But the parts of Europe that are near the sea have less extreme temperatures than the corresponding northerly regions of America, and the Mediterranean countries have more sunshine and less severe winters than either northern Europe or the northern

ICELAND

NORWEGIAN SEA

SCANDINAVIAN
PENINSULA

FAEROE I.

GULF OF BOTHNIA

KJÖLEN MOUNTAINS

SHETLAND I.

Dal R.

FI
L
R

ALAND
I.

Helsinki

GULF O

Oslo

HEBRIDES

ORKNEY I.

L. Vanern

Stockholm

ATLANTIC OCEAN

BRITISH
ISLES

GRAMPIANS

SCOTTISH
LOWLANDS

Edinburgh

NORTH
SEA

Skagerrak

L. Vattern

GOTLAND

ÖLAND

BALTIC SEA

Kattegat

Copenhagen

Niemer

PENNINE CHAIN

JUTLAND
PENINSULA

IRISH
CENTRAL
PLAIN

Dublin

IRISH SEA

St. George's
Channel

THE
WASH

HELIGOLAND
FRISIAN I.

Weser R.

Elbe R.

Danzig

Masu
Lake

NORTH GERMAN PLAIN

Bristol Channel

MIDLAND
PLAIN

Thames R.

Amsterdam

IJsselmeer

HARZ
MTS.

Berlin

Warta R.

Vistula R.

Warsa

SCILLY I.

London

Maas R.

Oder R.

Neisse R.

Bre

LAND'S END

ENGLISH CHANNEL

Strait of Dover

Scheldt R.

Rhine R.

Main R.

ERZ MTS.

SUDETEN MTS.

USHANT I.

BRITTANY
PENINSULA

PLAIN OF FRANCE

Meuse R.

ARDENNES

Moselle R.

VOSGES MTS.

BLACK FOREST

Prague

BOHEMIAN
PLAIN

CA

Marne R.

Paris

Seine R.

Loire R.

Danube R.

Inn R.

BOHEMIAN FOREST

Vienna

Tisz

BAY OF
BISCAY

JURA MTS.

L. Constance

Budapest

PLAIN OF
HUNGARY

L.
Balaton

CAPE FINISTERRE

Garonne R.

MASSIF
CENTRAL

CÉVENNES

Rhone R.

L. Geneva

ALPS

Drave R.

Save R.

IRON

CANTABRIAN MTS.

PYRENEES

PLAIN OF
LOMBARDY

Adige R.

Trieste

ISTRIA

DALMATIAN

DINARIC ALPS

Belgrade

IBERIAN
PENINSULA

SPANISH

Douro R.

GUADARRAMAS

Ebro R.

Po R.

Arno R.

APENNINES

ADRIATIC SEA

BALKAN
PENINSULA

Madrid

Tagus R.

ELBA

CORSICA

Rome

PIN

Lisbon

PLATEAU

Guadiana R.

SIERRA MORENA

BALEARIC I.

MINORCA

ITALIAN
PENINSULA

Mt. Vesuvius

IONIAN I.

Guadalquivir R.

IVIZA

MAJORCA

SARDINIA

TYRRHENIAN
SEA

MOR
PENIN

SIERRA NEVADA

CAPE TRAFALGAR

Strait of Gibraltar

Gibraltar

Algiers

Mt. Etna

SICILY

IONIAN
SEA

Strait of Messina

Fez

LITTLE ATLAS MOUNTAINS

Tunis

PANTELLERIA

MIDDLE ATLAS MOUNTAINS

SAHARAN ATLAS MOUNTAINS

MALTA

MEDITERRANEAN S

GREAT ATLAS MOUNTAINS

ALGERIAN SAHARA

Tripoli

GULF OF
SIDRA

WHITE SEA

N. Dvina R.

L. Onega

.. Ladoga

Petersburg

NORTH RUSSIAN PLAIN

CENTRAL RUSSIAN HIGHLANDS

Moscow

Oka R.

Volga R.

Kama R.

URAL MOUNTAINS

Tobol R.

Ishim R.

Areas Below Sea Level

0   100   200   300 miles

KIRGHIZ   STEPPE

Syr Darya

VOLGA HEIGHTS

Ural R.

BLACK EARTH REGION

ARAL SEA

TURANIAN PLAIN

Amu Darya

et R.

ET
SHES

Kiev

Dnieper R.

Donets R.

Don R.

CASPIAN DEPRESSION

Volga R.

Bug R.

DONETS HEIGHTS

CASPIAN SEA

Dniester R.

Pruth R.

Odessa

CRIMEA

SEA OF AZOV

CAUCASUS   MOUNTAINS

ALPS

Bucharest

BLACK SEA

Araxes R.

ARMENIAN HIGHLANDS

ELBURZ MTS.

MTS.

Bosporus

Istanbul

Ankara

Kizilirmak

L. Van

L. Urmia

Teheran

sa R.

PE

SEA OF MARMARA

ASIA MINOR
(ANATOLIAN PENINSULA)

ZAGROS

Dardanelles

Meander R.

TAURUS MOUNTAINS

MESOPOTAMIAN PLAINS

Tigris R.

MTS.

Euphrates R.

Baghdad

SEA

DODECANESE I.

RHODES

CYPRUS

SYRIAN

DESERT

PERSIAN   GULF

CRETE

SEA OF GALILEE

Jordan R.

Jerusalem

DEAD SEA

Alexandria

NILE DELTA

Suez Canal

SINAI PENINSULA

Cairo

Nile R.

GULF OF SUEZ

GULF OF AQABA

NEFUD   DESERT

United States. Everywhere, however, the winters are cold enough to keep out certain diseases by which warmer countries are afflicted. They have also obliged the inhabitants to expend more effort on clothing, housing, and heating. Warm summers with their growing seasons have produced an annual cycle of agriculture, for which rainfall has been adequate but not excessive. Although the Spanish plateau is arid, and the Mediterranean shores are subject to seasonal variations of rainfall, Europe is the only continent that has no actual desert. Thanks to a combination of causes, including rainfall, ground water, deposits left by retreating glaciers, the character of the underlying rock, and the alternate freezing and thawing, Europe is also for the most part a region of fertile soils. In short, since the end of the Ice Age, or since humans learned how to survive the winters, Europe has been one of the most favored places on the globe for human habitation. In recent times it has been, as shown by the insets of the two endpaper maps in this book, one of the few large regions, along with China and India, of very high density of population.

Climate itself can change. The Roman ruins in the interior of Morocco and Tunisia remind us that the climate there was once more favorable. Studies of tree rings, fossil plants, and alpine glaciers show that average temperatures were warmer from the end of the Ice Age throughout ancient and medieval times, and then fell during what is called the "little Ice Age" from about 1400 to 1850, when the winters lengthened and the growing season shortened, without drastic consequences for the people, who by that time could simply wear more wool, so that sheep raising and the woolen trade became a main staple of European commerce.

There is no geographical determinism. Climate and the environment not only set limits but provide opportunities for what human beings can do. What happens depends on the application of knowledge and abilities in any particular time and place. A broad river is an obstruction and hence a good boundary under simple conditions; it is less so after bridges connect the two sides. The oceans that long divided mankind became a highway for the Portuguese, Spanish, Dutch, French, and English, and later for others. Distance, which any good map will show by its scale, also varies in its effects according to the means of transportation; it must be remembered that for most of human history neither persons, information, nor commands could travel much more than thirty miles a day, so that localism prevailed, and large organizations, in trade or government, were hard to create and to maintain. For most of its history Europe was in fact made up of a diversity of small local units, pockets of territory each having its own customs, way of life, and manner of speech, each largely unknown to the others and looking inward upon itself, rather than of the blocks called "Germany" or "France" that we take for granted on a map today. A "foreigner" might come from a thousand miles away, or from only ten.

What constitutes a natural resource varies with the state of technology and the possibilities of exchange. The tin of Cornwall at the western tip of Britain became an important resource as long ago as the early Bronze Age, when despite its remoteness it gave rise to some of the first long-distance European trade. Deposits of coal were not massively exploited until the nineteenth century, and petroleum was of no significance, nor even known, until about a century ago. It is a big fact of human history, rather than of geologic history, that some of the world's greatest coal beds happened to be in northwestern Europe and the United States, which could be more readily industrialized because they had easy access to abundant fuel, over which they had control, an advantage that was lost as they became more dependent on natural gas and oil. If the future is like the past, it will see a similar conversion of natural materials into natural resources.

The Mediterranean coasts were more wooded three thousand years ago than they are today. It was not only the change of climate that changed their appearance. Many human generations spent in cutting timber, pasturing goats, and planting vines and olives brought about erosion and depletion of the soil. Europe north of the mountains was heavily forested before human intervention. Trees were cut down and burned there as in America centuries later, so that the landscape slowly became an orderly expanse of carefully tended fields, still interrupted by woodlands. The state of agriculture obviously depends on natural conditions. But it depends historically also on the invention and improvement of the plow, the finding of appropriate crops, the rotation of fields to prevent soil exhaustion, and the introduction of livestock from which manure can be obtained as a fertilizer. Socially, agriculture benefits from the existence of stable village communities, and is affected by demographic changes; if a population falls as a result of war or epidemics, some fields will be abandoned and return to "nature"; if population grows, new and less fertile or more distant areas will be brought under cultivation. Nor can agriculture be improved without the building of roads, a division of labor between town and country, and some degree of regional specialization, so that some areas may grow cereals, others raise livestock, and still others be devoted to orchards and vineyards. Basic to agriculture, as to other enterprises, is elementary security. Farming cannot proceed, nor food be stored over the winter, unless the men and women who work the fields can be protected from attack by marauders, brigands, barbarian invaders, warring chiefs, or hostile armies. Such protection, or what might be called the normalcy of peace, was for several centuries imposed by the Roman Empire, in more recent times (barring wars) by the national state, and in between by barons who at least protected the peasants who worked for them, and by kings attempting to pacify their kingdoms.

For maps with exact detail, or extensive coverage, it is best to consult a good historical atlas, of which several are listed in the bibliography at the end of this book. Over fifty maps are included in the present volume, but some are only diagrams rather than true maps; all are intended to supplement the written text, by showing the location and geographical spread of matters under discussion. Many of the maps are mainly designed to show political boundaries at particular dates. Readers in looking at them can use their imagination to fill in the mountains and rivers that these maps cannot show but which can be important for an understanding of the extent of political power. Readers can also, by using their imaginations and consulting the scale, convert space into time, remembering that until the invention of the railroad both people and news traveled far more slowly than today, or that at a rate of thirty miles a day it would take three weeks to travel from London to Venice, and at least six weeks for an exchange of letters. In human terms Europe has not been such a small place after all.

I.
THE RISE OF
EUROPE

IT MAY SEEM strange for a history of the modern world to begin with the European Middle Ages, for Europe is not the world and the Middle Ages were not modern. But most of what is now meant by "modern" made its first appearance in Europe, and to understand modern Europe it is necessary to reach fairly far back in time. To understand the modern world it is likewise necessary to begin by looking at Europe.

Over the centuries Europe created the most powerful combination of political, military, economic, technological, and scientific apparatus that the world had ever seen. In doing so, Europe radically transformed itself, and also developed an overwhelming impact on other continents and other cultures in America, Africa, and Asia, sometimes destroying them, sometimes stimulating or enlivening them, and always presenting them with problems of resistance or adaptation. This European ascendancy became apparent about 300 years ago. It reached its zenith with the European colonial empires at the beginning of the twentieth century. Since then, the position of Europe has relatively declined, partly because of conflicts within Europe itself, but mainly because the apparatus which had made Europe so dominant can now be found in other countries. Some, like the United States, are essentially offshoots of Europe. Others have very different and ancient backgrounds. But whatever their backgrounds, and willingly or not, all peoples in the twentieth century are caught up in the process of modernization or "development," which usually turns out to mean acquiring some of the skills and powers first exhibited by Europeans.

There is thus in our time a kind of uniform modern civilization which overlies

Chapter Emblem: The symbolic Chi-Rho, or crossed X and P, standing for the first two letters of the Greek Khristos. *From a Roman sarcophagus. "P" is the Greek letter* rho, *for small "r," so that the symbol stands for Christ.*

or penetrates the traditional cultures of the world. This civilization is an interlocking unity, in that conditions on one side of the globe have repercussions on the other. Communications are almost instantaneous and news travels everywhere. If the air is polluted in one country, neighboring countries are affected; if oil ceases to flow from the Middle East, the life of Europe, North America, and Japan may become very difficult. The modern world depends on elaborate means of transportation, on science, industry, and machines, on new sources of energy to meet insatiable demands, on scientific medicine, public hygiene, and methods of raising food. States and nations fight wars by advanced methods, and negotiate or maintain peace by diplomacy. There is an earth-encompassing network of finance and trade, loans and debts, investments and bank accounts, with resulting fluctuations in monetary exchanges and balances of payments. Over 180 very unequal and disunited members compose the United Nations. The very concept of the nation, as represented in that body, is derived from Europe.

In most modern countries there have been pressures for increased democracy, and all modern governments, democratic or not, must seek to arouse the energies and support of their populations. In a modern society old customs loosen, and ancestral religions are questioned. There is a demand for individual liberation, and an expectation of a higher standard of living. Everywhere there is a drive for more equality in a bewildering variety of meanings—for more equality between sexes and races, between high and low incomes, between adherents of different religions, or between different parts of the same country. Movements for social change may be slow and gradual, or revolutionary and catastrophic, but movement of some kind is universal.

Such are a few of the indexes of modernity. Since they appeared first in the history of Europe, or of the European world in the extended sense in which the United States is included, the present book deals mainly with the growth of European society and civilization, with increasing attention, in the later chapters, to the earth as a whole. There have also been antimodern movements and protests; when they occur in Asia or Africa, as in the recent Islamic revival, they are called anti-Western, as if to show that Europe and the "West" have been at the heart of the problem.

If "modern" refers especially to a certain complicated way of living, it has also another sense, meaning merely what is recent or current. As a time span the word "modern" is purely relative. It depends on what we are talking about. A modern kitchen may be as much as 5 years old, modern physics is less than 100 years old, modern science over 300, the modern European languages about 1,000. Modern civilization, the current civilization in which we are living, and which may be passing, is in one sense a product of the twentieth century, but in other senses it is much older. In general, it is agreed that modern times began in Europe about the year 1500. Modern times were preceded by a period of 1,000 years called the Middle Ages, which set in about A.D. 500, and which were in turn preceded by another 1,000 years of classical Greco-Roman civilization. Before that reached the long histories of Egypt and Mesopotamia, and, further east, of the Indus Valley and of China. All times prior to the European Middle Ages are commonly called "ancient." But the whole framework—ancient, medieval, and modern—is largely a matter of words and convention, without meaning except for Europe. We shall begin our history with a running start, and slow down the pace, surveying the scene more fully in proportion as the times grow more "modern."

1. Ancient Times: Greece, Rome, and Christianity

Europeans were by no means the pioneers of human civilization. Half of recorded history had passed before anyone in Europe could read or write. The priests of Egypt began to keep written records between 4000 and 3000 B.C., but two thousand years later the poems of Homer were still being circulated in the Greek city-states by word of mouth. Shortly after 3000 B.C., while the pharaohs were building the pyramids, Europeans were laboriously setting up the huge, unwrought stones called megaliths, of which Stonehenge is the best-known example. In a word, until after 2000 B.C., Europe was in the Neolithic or New Stone Age. This was in truth a great age in human history, the age in which human beings learned to make and use sharp tools, weave cloth, build living quarters, domesticate animals, plant seeds, harvest crops, and sense the returning cycles of the months and years. But the Near East—Egypt, the Euphrates and Tigris valley, the island of Crete, and the shores of the Aegean Sea (which belonged more to Asia than to Europe)—had reached its Neolithic Age two thousand years before Europe. By about 4000 B.C. the Near East was already moving into the Bronze Age.

After about 2000 B.C., in the dim, dark continent that Europe then was, there began to be great changes that are now difficult to trace. Europeans, too, learned how to smelt and forge metals, with the Bronze Age setting in about 2000 B.C. and the Iron Age about 1000 B.C. There was also a steady infusion of new peoples into Europe. They spoke languages related to languages now spoken in India and Iran, to which similar peoples migrated at about the same time. All these languages (whose interconnection was not known until the nineteenth century) are now referred to as Indo-European, and the people who spoke them, merging with and imposing their speech upon older European stocks, became the ancestors both of the classical Greeks and Romans and of the Europeans of modern times. All European languages today are Indo-European with the exceptions of Basque, which is thought to be a survival from before the Indo-European invasion, and of Finnish and Hungarian, which were brought into Europe from Asia some centuries later. It was these invading Indo-Europeans who diffused over Europe the kind of speech from which the Latin, Greek, Germanic, Slavic, Celtic, and Baltic languages were later derived.[1]

The Greek World

The first Indo-Europeans to emerge into the clear light of history, in what is now Europe, were the Greeks. They filtered down through the Balkan peninsula to

---

[1] Formerly the term "Aryan" was sometimes used to denote Indo-European. In Germany, under Adolf Hitler, much nonsense was written about an Aryan race, and the term Aryan was made in practice to mean simply non-Jewish. The grain of truth in all this was simply that Hebrew is not an Indo-European but a Semitic language, closely related to Arabic (which is also Semitic) and less closely to the language of the ancient Egyptians. There is no Indo-European (Aryan) or Semitic "race"; persons speaking these languages no more had to be of one physical descent than are persons who speak English today.

the shores of the Aegean Sea about 1900 B.C., undermining the older Cretan civilization, and occupying most of what has since been called Greece by 1300 B.C. Beginning about 1150 B.C., other Greek-speaking tribes invaded from the north in successive waves. The newcomers consisted of separate barbaric tribes and their coming ushered in several centuries of chaos and unrest before a gradual stabilization and revival began in the ninth century. The *Iliad* and the *Odyssey*, written down about 800 B.C., but composed and recited much earlier, probably refer to wars between the Greeks and other centers of civilization, of which one was at Troy in Asia Minor. The siege of Troy is thought to have occurred about 1200 B.C.

The Greeks proved to be as gifted a people as mankind has ever produced, achieving supreme heights in thought and letters. They absorbed the knowledge of the, to them, mysterious East, the mathematical lore of the ancient Chaldeans, the arts and crafts that they found in Asia Minor and on voyages to Egypt. They added immediately to everything that they learned. It was the Greeks of the fifth and fourth centuries B.C. who first became fully conscious of the powers of the human mind, who formulated what the Western world long meant by the beautiful, and who first speculated on political freedom.

As they settled down, the Greeks formed tiny city-states, all independent and often at war with one another, each only a few miles across, and typically including a coastal city and its adjoining farmlands. Athens, Corinth, Sparta were such city-states. Many were democratic; all citizens (i.e., all grown men except slaves and "metics," or outsiders) congregated in the marketplace to elect officials and discuss their public business. Politics was turbulent in the small Greek states. Democracy alternated with aristocracy, oligarchy, despotism, and tyranny. From this rich fund of experience was born systematic political science as set forth in the unwritten speculations of Socrates and in the *Republic* of Plato and the *Politics* of Aristotle in the fourth century before Christ. The Greeks also were the first to write history as a subject distinct from myth and legend. Herodotus, "the Father of History," traveled throughout the Greek world and far beyond, ferreting out all he could learn of the past; and Thucydides, in his account of the wars between Athens and Sparta, presented history as a guide to enlightened citizenship and constructive statecraft.

Perhaps because they were a restless and vehement people, the Greeks came to prize the "classical" virtues, which they were the first to define. For them, the ideal lay in moderation, or a golden mean. They valued order, balance, symmetry, clarity, and control. Their statues revealed their conception of what man ought to be—a noble creature, dignified, poised, unterrified by life or death, master of himself and of his feelings. Their architecture, as in the Parthenon, made use of exactly measured angles and rows of columns. The classical "order," or set of carefully wrought pillars placed in a straight line at specified intervals, represented the firm impress of human reason on the brute materials of nature. The same sense of form was thrown over the torrent of human words. Written language became contrived, carefully planned, organized for effect. The epic poem, the lyric, the drama, the oration, along with history and the philosophic dialogue, each with its own rules and principles of composition, became the "forms" within which, in Western civilization, writers long continued to express their thoughts.

Reflecting on the world about them, the Greeks concluded that something more fundamental existed beyond the world of appearances, that true reality was not what met the eye. With other peoples, and with the Greeks themselves in earlier times, this same realization had led to the formation of myths, dealing with invisible but mighty beings known as gods and with faraway places on the tops of mountains, beneath the earth, or in a world that followed death. Greek thinkers set to criticizing the web of myth. They looked for rational or natural explanations of what was at work behind the variety and confusion that they saw. Some, observing human sickness, said that disease was not a demonic possession, but a natural sequence of conditions in the body, which could be identified, understood, foreseen, and even treated in a natural way. Others, turning to physical nature, said that all matter was in reality composed of a very few things—of atoms or elements—which they usually designated as fire, water, earth, and air. Some said that change was a kind of illusion, all basic reality being uniform; some, that only change was real, and that the world was a flux. Some, like Pythagoras, found the enduring reality in "number," or mathematics. The Greeks, in short, laid the foundations for science. Studying also the way in which the mind worked, or ought to work if it was to reach truthful conclusions, they developed the science of logic. The great codifier of Greek thought on almost all subjects in the classical period was Aristotle, who lived in Athens from 384 to 322 B.C.

Greek influence spread widely and rapidly. Hardly were some of the city-states founded when their people, crowded within their narrow bounds, sent off some of their number with equipment and provisions to establish colonies. In this way Greek cities were very early established in south Italy, in Sicily, and even in the western Mediterranean, where Marseilles was founded about 600 B.C. Later the Greek city-states, unable to unite, succumbed to conquest by Philip of Macedon, who came from the relatively crude northern part of the Greek world, and whose son, Alexander the Great (356–323 B.C.), led a phenomenal and conquering march into Asia, across Persia, and on as far as India itself. Alexander's empire did not hold together, but Greek civilization, after having penetrated the raw world of the western Mediterranean, now began to revivify the ancient peoples of Egypt and the Near East. Greek thought, Greek art, and the Greek language spread far and wide. The most famous "Greeks" after the fourth century B.C. and on into the early centuries of the Christian era usually did not come from Greece but from the Hellenized Near East, and especially from Alexandria in Egypt. Among these later Greeks were the great summarizers or writers of encyclopedias in which ancient science was passed on to later generations—Strabo in geography, Galen in medicine, Ptolemy in astronomy. All three lived in the first and second centuries after Christ.

The Roman World

In 146 B.C. the Greeks of Greece were conquered by a new people, the Romans. The Romans, while keeping their own Latin language, rapidly absorbed what they could of the intellectual and aristic culture of the Greeks. Over a period of two or three centuries they assembled an empire in which the whole world of ancient civilization (west of Persia) was included. Egypt, Greece, Asia Minor, Syria all became Roman provinces, but in them the Romans had hardly any deep influence except in a political sense. In the West—in what are now Tunisia, Algeria, Morocco, Spain, Portugal, France, Switzerland, Belgium, and England— the Romans, though ruthless in their methods of conquest, in the long run acted as civilizing agents, transmitting to these hitherto backward countries the age-old achievements of the East and the more recent culture of Greece and of Rome itself. So thorough was the Romanization that in the West Latin even became the currently spoken language. It was later wiped out in Africa by Arabic but survives to this day, transformed by time, in the languages of France, Italy, Spain, Portugal, and Romania.

In the Roman Empire, which lasted with many vicissitudes from about 31 B.C. to the latter part of the fifth century A.D., virtually the entire civilized world of the ancient West was politically united and enjoyed generations of internal peace. Rome was the center, around which in all directions lay the "circle of lands," the *orbis terrarum,* the known world—that is, as known in the West, for the Han Empire at the same time in China was also a highly organized cultural and political entity. The Roman Empire consisted essentially of the coasts of the Mediterranean Sea, which provided the great artery of transport and communication, and from which no part of the empire, except northern Gaul (France), Britain, and the Rhineland, was more than a couple of hundred miles away. Civilization was uniform; there were no distinct nationalities; the only significant cultural difference was that east of Italy the predominant language was Greek, in Italy and west of it, Latin. Cities grew up everywhere, engaged in a busy commercial life and exchange of ideas with one another. They remained most numerous in the east, where most of the manufacturing crafts and the densest population were still concentrated, but they sprang up also in the west—indeed, most of the older cities of France, Spain, England, and western and southern Germany boast of some kind of origin under the Romans.

The distinctive aptitude of the Romans lay in organization, administration, government, and law. Never before had armies been so systematically formed, maintained over such long periods, dispatched at a word of command over such distances, or maneuvered so effectively on the field of battle. Never had so many peoples been governed from a single center. The Romans had at first possessed self-governing and republican institutions, but they lost them in the process of conquest, and the governing talents which they displayed in the days of the empire were of an authoritarian character—talents, not for self-government, but for managing, coordinating, and ruling the manifold and scattered parts of one enormous system. Locally, cities and city-states enjoyed a good deal of autonomy. But above them all rose a pyramid of imperial officials and provincial governors, culminating in the emperor at the top. The empire kept peace, the *pax Romana,* and even provided a certain justice as between its many peoples. Lawyers worked on the body of principles known ever afterward as Roman law.

Roman judges had somehow to settle disputes between persons of different regions, with conflicting local customs, for example, two merchants of Spain and Egypt. The Roman law came therefore to hold that no custom is necessarily right, that there is a higher or universal law by which fair decisions may be made, and that this higher, universal, or "natural" law, or "law of nature," will be understandable or acceptable to all men, since it arises from human nature and reason. Here the lawyers drew on Greek philosophy for support. They held also that law derives its force from being enacted by a proper authority (not merely from custom, usage, or former legal cases); this authority to make law they called *majestas,* or sovereign power, and they attributed it to the emperor. Thus the Romans emancipated the idea of law from mere custom on the one hand and mere caprice on the other; they regarded it as something to be formed by enlightened intelligence, consistently with reason and the nature of things; and they associated it with the solemn action of official power. It must be added that Roman law favored the state, or the public interest as seen by the government, rather than the interests or liberties of individual persons. These principles, together with more specific ideas on property, debt, marriage, wills, etc., were in later centuries to have a great effect in Europe.

The Coming of Christianity

The thousand years during which Greco-Roman civilization arose and flourished were notable in another way even more momentous for all the later history of mankind. It was in this period that the great world religions came into being. Within the time bracket 700 B.C.–A.D. 700 the lives of Confucius and Buddha, of the major Jewish prophets, and of Muhammad are all included. At the very midpoint (probably about 4 B.C.), in Palestine in the Roman Empire, was born a man named Jesus, believed by his followers to be the Son of God. The first Christians were Jews; but both under the impulse of its own doctrine, which held that all men were alike in spirit, and under the strong leadership of Paul, a man of Jewish birth, Roman citizenship, and Greek culture, Christianity began to make converts without regard to former belief. There were certainly a few Christians in Rome by the middle of the first century. Both Paul and the elder apostle, Peter, according to church tradition, died as martyrs at Rome in the time of the Emperor Nero about A.D. 67.

The Christian teaching spread at first among the poor, the people at the bottom of society, those whom Greek glories and Roman splendors had passed over or enslaved, and who had the least to delight in or to hope for in the existing world. Gradually it reached other classes; a few classically educated and well-to-do people became Christians; in the second century Christian bishops and writers were at work publicly in various parts of the empire. In the third century the Roman government, with the empire falling into turmoil, and blaming the social troubles on the Christians, subjected them to wholesale persecution. In the fourth century (possibly in A.D. 312) the Emperor Constantine accepted Christianity. By the fifth century the entire Roman world was formally Christian; no other religion was officially tolerated; and the deepest thinkers were also Christians, men who combined Christian beliefs with the now thousand-year-old tradition of Greco-Roman thought and philosophy.

It is impossible to exaggerate the importance of the coming of Christianity. It brought with it, for one thing, an altogether new sense of human life. Where the Greeks had demonstrated the powers of the mind, the Christians explored the soul, and they taught that in the sight of God all souls were equal, that every human life was sacrosanct and inviolate, and that all worldly distinctions of greatness, beauty, and brilliancy were in the last analysis superficial. Where the

Greeks had identified the beautiful and the good, had thought ugliness to be bad, and had shrunk from disease as an imperfection and from everything misshapen as horrible and repulsive, the Christians resolutely saw a spiritual beauty even in the plainest or most unpleasant exterior and sought out the diseased, the crippled, and the mutilated to give them help. Love, for the ancients, was never quite distinguished from Venus; for the Christians, who held that God was love, it took on deep overtones of sacrifice and compassion. Suffering itself was proclaimed by Christians to be in a way divine, since God himself had suffered on the Cross in human form. A new dignity was thus found for suffering that the world could not cure. At the same time the Christians worked to relieve suffering as none had worked before. They protested against the massacre of prisoners of war, against the mistreatment and degradation of slaves, against the sending of gladiators to kill each other in the arena for another's pleasure. In place of the Greek and pagan self-satisfaction with human accomplishments they taught humility in the face of an almighty Providence, and in place of proud distinctions between high and low, slave and free, civilized and barbarian, they held that all men were brothers because all were children of the same God.

On an intellectual level Christianity also marked a revolution. It was Christianity, not rational philosophy, that dispelled the swarm of greater and lesser gods and goddesses, the blood sacrifices and self-immolation, or the frantic resort to magic, fortune-telling, and divination. The Christians taught that since there was only one God, the pagan gods must be at best lesser demons, and even this idea was gradually given up. The pagan conception of local, tribal, or national gods disappeared. It was now held that for all the world there was only one God, one plan of Salvation, and one Providence, and that all mankind took its origin from one source. The idea of the world as one thing, a "universe," was thus affirmed with a new depth of meaning. The very intolerance of Christianity (which was new to the ancient world) came from this overwhelming sense of human unity, in which it was thought that all men should have, and deserved to have, the one true and saving religion.

It was for their political ideas that the Christians were most often denounced and persecuted. The Roman Empire was a world state; there was no other state but it; no living human being except the emperor was sovereign; no one anywhere on earth was his equal. Between gods and human beings, in the pagan view, there was moreover no clear distinction. Some gods behaved very humanly, and some human creatures were more like gods than others. The emperor was held to be veritably a god, *divus Caesar, semper Augustus*. A cult of Caesar was established, regarded as necessary to maintain the state, which was the world itself. All this the Christians firmly refused to accept. It was because they would not worship Caesar that the Roman officials regarded them as monstrous social incendiaries who must be persecuted and stamped out.

The Christian doctrine on this point went back to the saying gathered from Jesus, that one should render to Caesar the things that were Caesar's, and to God those that were God's. The same dualism was presented more systematically by St. Augustine about A.D. 420 in his *City of God*. Few books have been more influential in shaping the later development of Western civilization.

The "world," the world of Caesar, in the time of St. Augustine, was going to ruin. Rome itself was plundered in 410 by heathen barbarians. Augustine wrote the *City of God* with this event obsessing his imagination. He wrote to show that though the world itself perished there was yet another world that was more enduring and more important.

There were, he said, really two "cities," the earthly and the heavenly, the temporal and the eternal, the city of man and the City of God. The earthly city was the domain of state and empire, of political authority and political obedience. It was a good thing, as part of God's providential scheme for human life, but it had no inherently divine character of its own. The emperor was a man. The state was not absolute; it could be judged, amended, or corrected from sources outside itself. It was, for all its majesty and splendor, really subordinate in some way to a higher and spiritual power. This power lay in the City of God. By the City of God Augustine meant many things, and all sorts of meanings were found by readers in later ages. The heavenly city might mean heaven itself, the abode of God and of blessed spirits enjoying life after death. It might mean certain elect spirits of this world, the good people as opposed to the bad. It might, more theoretically, be a system of ideal values or ideal justice, as opposed to the crude approximations of the actual world. Or it was later thought, by some, to mean the organized church and its clergy.

In any case, with this Christian dualism the Western world escaped from what is called Caesaropapism, the holding by one man of the powers of ruler and of pontiff. Instead, the spiritual and the political power were held to be separate and independent. In later times popes and kings often quarreled with each other; the clergy often struggled for worldly power, and governments at various times (including the twentieth century with its totalitarian systems) have attempted to dictate what men should believe, or love, or hope for. But speaking in general of European history neither side has ever won out, and in the sharp distinction between the spiritual and the temporal has lain the germ of many liberties in the West. At the same time the idea that no ruler, no government, and no institution is too mighty to rise above moral criticism opened the way to a dynamic and progressive way of living in the West.

As for Augustine himself, he lived to see the world grow worse. He died in A.D. 430. In 429 the Roman province of Africa, where he had been a bishop, was pillaged by a wild Germanic tribe called the Vandals.

2. The Early Middle Ages: The Formation of Europe

There was really no Europe in ancient times. In the Roman Empire we may see a Mediterranean world, or even a West and an East in the Latin- and Greek-speaking portions. But the West included parts of Africa as well as of Europe, and Europe as we know it was divided by the Rhine-Danube frontier, south and west of which lay the civilized provinces of the empire, and north and east the "barbarians" of whom the civilized world knew almost nothing. To the Romans "Africa" meant Tunisia-Algeria, "Asia" meant the Asia Minor peninsula; and the word "Europe," since it meant little, was scarcely used by them at all. It was in the half-millennium from the fifth to the tenth centuries that Europe as such for the first time emerged with its peoples brought together in a life of their own, clearly set off from that of Asia or Africa.

The Disintegration of the Roman Empire

First of all the Roman Empire went to pieces, especially in the West. The Christianizing of the empire did nothing to impede its decline. The Emperor Constantine, who in embracing Christianity undoubtedly hoped to strengthen the imperial system, also took one other significant step. In A.D. 330 he founded a new capital at the old Greek city of Byzantium, which he renamed Constantinople. (It is now Istanbul.) Thereafter the Roman Empire had two capitals, Rome and Constantinople, and was administered in two halves. Increasingly the center of gravity moved eastward, as if returning to the more ancient centers in the Near East, as if the "modern" experiment of civilizing the West were to be given up as a failure.

Throughout its long life the empire had been surrounded on almost all sides by barbarians—wild Celts in Wales and Scotland, Germans in the heart of Europe, Persians or Parthians in the East ("barbarian" only in the ancient sense of speaking neither Greek nor Latin), and, in the southeast, the Arabs. (In the south the empire simply faded off into the Sahara.) These barbarians, always with the exception of Persia, had never been brought within the pale of ancient civilization. Somewhat like the Chinese, who about 200 B.C. built the Great Wall to solve the same problem, the Romans simply drew a line beyond which they themselves rarely ventured and would not allow the barbarians to pass. Nevertheless the barbarians filtered in. As early as the third century A.D. emperors and generals recruited bands of them to serve in the Roman armies. Their service over, they would receive farmlands, settle down, marry, and mingle with the population. By the fourth and fifth centuries a good many individuals of barbarian birth were even reaching high positions of state. At the same time, in the West, for reasons that are not fully understood, the activity of the Roman cities began to falter, commerce began to decay, local governments became paralyzed, taxes became more ruinous, and free farmers were bound to the soil. The army seated and unseated emperors. Rival generals fought with each other. Gradually the West fell into decrepitude and an internal barbarization so that the old line between the Roman provinces and the barbarian world made less and less difference.

After some centuries of relative stability, the barbarians themselves, pressed by more distant peoples from Asia, rather suddenly began to move. Sometimes they first sought peaceable access to the empire, attracted by the warmer Mediterranean climate, or desiring to share in the advantages of Roman civilization. More often, tribes consisting of a few tens of thousands, men, women, and children, moved swiftly and by force, plundering, fighting, and killing as they went. At first most of the barbarians threatening the empire were Germanic, going under many names. The Angles and Saxons overran Britain about 450, the Franks invaded Gaul at the same time, the Vandals reached as far as Roman Africa in 429, the East Goths appeared in Asia Minor in 382 and in Italy in 493, the West Goths lunged toward Constantinople about 380, tore through Greece in 396, sacked Rome itself in 410, and reached Spain about the year 420. In 476 the last Roman emperor in the West was deposed by a barbarian chieftain. Sometimes in the general upheaval wild Turkman peoples fresh from Asia were intermixed. Of these the most famous were the Huns, who cut through central Europe and France about 450 under their leader Attila, the "scourge of God"—and then disappeared. Nor were these invasions all. Two centuries later new irruptions burst upon the Greco-Roman world on its opposite side, where hitherto outlying peoples poured in from the Arabian deserts. The Arabs, aroused by the new faith of Islam (Muhammad died in 632), fell as conquerors upon Syria, Mesopotamia, Persia, occupied Egypt about 640, the old Roman Africa about 700, and in 711 reached Spain, where they destroyed the Germanic kingdom set up there by the West Goths.

Beneath these blows the old unity of the Greco-Roman or Mediterranean world was broken. The "circle of lands" divided into three segments. Three types of civilization now confronted each other across the inland sea.

The Byzantine World, the Arabic World, and the West about A.D. 700

One was the Eastern Roman, Later Roman, Greek, or Byzantine Empire (all names for the same thing) with its capital at Constantinople, and now including only the Asia Minor peninsula, the Balkan peninsula, and parts of Italy. It represented the most direct continuation of the immemorial civilization of the Near East. It was Christian in religion and Greek in culture and language. Its people felt themselves to be the truest heirs both of early Christianity and of the Greeks of the golden age. Art and architecture, trades and crafts, commerce and navigation, thought and writing, government and law, while not so creative or flexible as in the classical age, were still carried on actively in the eastern Empire, on much the same level as in the closing centuries of ancient times. For all Christians, and for heathen barbarians in Europe, the emperor of the East stood out as the world's supreme ruler, and Constantinople as the world's preeminent and almost fabulous city.

The second segment, and the most extensive, was the Arabic and Islamic. It reached from the neighborhood of the Pyrenees through Spain and all North Africa into Arabia, Syria, and the East. Arabic was its language; it became, and still remains, the common speech from Morocco to the Persian Gulf. Islam was its religion. It was organized in the caliphate in which all Muslims were included, and the caliph was regarded as the true religious and military successor to Muhammad himself. The Arabic world, like the Byzantine, built directly upon the heritage of the Greco-Romans. In religion, the early Muslims regarded themselves as successors to the Jewish and Christian traditions. They considered the line of Jewish prophets to be spokesmen of the true God, and they put Jesus in this line. But they added that Muhammad was the last and greatest of the prophets, that the Koran set forth a revelation replacing that of the Jewish Bible, that the New Testament of the Christians was mistaken because Christ was not divine, and that the Christian belief in a Trinity was erroneous because there was in the strictest and most rigid sense only One True God. To the Muslim Arabs, therefore, all Christians were contemptible infidels.

In mundane matters, the Arabs speedily took over the civilization of the lands they conquered. In the caliphate, as in the Byzantine Empire, the civilization of the ancient world went its way without serious interruption. Huge buildings and magnificent palaces were constructed; ships plied the Mediterranean; merchants ventured over the deserts and traversed the Indian Ocean; holy or learned men corresponded over thousands of miles; taxes were collected, laws were enforced, and provinces were kept in order. In the sciences the Arabs not only learned from but went beyond the Greeks. The Greek scientific literature was translated: some of it is known today only through these medieval Arabic versions. Arab geographers had a wider knowledge of the world than anyone had possessed up to their time. Arab mathematicians developed algebra so far beyond the Greeks as almost to be its creator (''algebra'' is an Arabic word), and in introducing the ''Arabic'' numerals (through their contacts with India) they made arithmetic, which in Roman numerals had been a formidably difficult science, into something that every schoolchild can be taught.

The third segment was Latin Christendom, which about A.D. 700 did not look very promising. It was what was left over from the other two—what the Byzantines were unable to hold, and the Arabs unable to conquer. It included only Italy (shared in part with the Byzantines), France, Belgium, the Rhineland, and Britain. Barbarian kings were doing their best to rule small kingdoms, but in truth all government had fallen to pieces. Strange and uncouth peoples milled about. Usually the invading barbarians remained a minority, eventually to be absorbed. Only in England, and in the region immediately west of the Rhine, did the Germanic element supersede the older Celtic and Latin. But the presence of the invaders, armed and fierce amid peasants and city dwellers reduced to passivity by Roman rule, together with the disintegration of Roman institutions that had gone on even before the invasions, left this region in chaos.

The Western barbarians, as noted, were Germanic; and the Germanic influence was to be a distinctive contribution to the making of Europe. Some Germans were Christian by the fourth century, but most were still heathen when they burst into the Roman Empire. Their languages had not been written down, but they possessed an intricate folklore and religion, in which fighting and heroic valor were much esteemed. Though now in a migratory phase, they were an agricultural people who knew how to work iron, and they had a rudimentary knowledge of the crafts of the Romans. They were organized in small tribes, and had a strong sense of tribal kinship, which (as with many primitive peoples) dominated their ideas of leadership and law. They enjoyed more freedom in their affairs than did the citizens of the Roman Empire. Many of the tribes were roughly self-governing in that all free men, those entitled to bear arms, met in open fields to hold council;

THE MEDITERRANEAN WORLD ABOUT A.D. 400, 800, AND 1250

Greco-Roman civilization, centered about the Mediterranean, was officially Christian and politically unified under the Roman Empire in A.D. 400, but broke apart into three segments in the early Middle Ages. Each segment developed its own type of life. Each segment also expanded beyond the limits of the ancient Mediterranean culture. By 1250 Latin Christendom reached to the Baltic and beyond, to include Iceland and even an outpost in Greenland. Greek Christendom penetrated north of the Black Sea, to include the Russians. The Muslim world spread into inner Asia and black Africa. In 1250, and until 1492, the Muslims, or Moors, still held the southern tip of Spain. There continued to be Greek, Armenian, and other Christians under Muslim rule in the eastern Mediterranean, and Jews in varying numbers in each of the three segments.

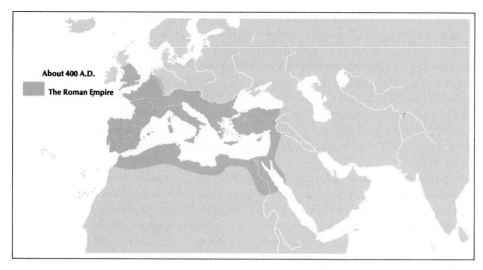

About 400 A.D.

The Roman Empire

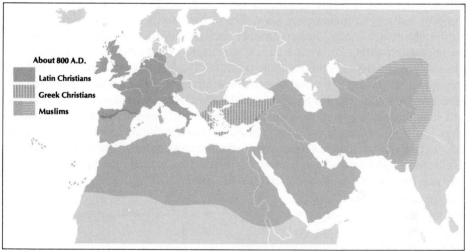

About 800 A.D.

Latin Christians

Greek Christians

Muslims

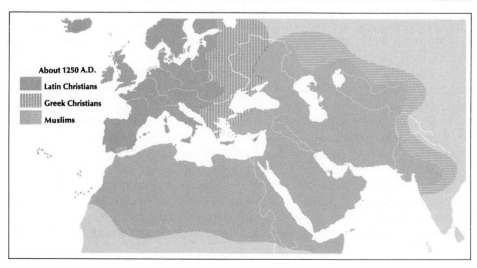

About 1250 A.D.

Latin Christians

Greek Christians

Muslims

and often the tribe itself elected its leader or king. They had a strong sense of loyalty to persons, of fealty to the acknowledged king or chief; but they had no sense of loyalty to large or general institutions. They had no sense of the state—of any distant, impersonal, and continuing source of law and rule. Law they regarded as the inflexible custom of each tribe. In the absence of abstract jurisprudence or trained judges, they settled disputes by rough and ready methods. In the ordeal, for example, a person who obstinately floated when thrown into water was adjudged guilty. In trial by battle, the winner of a kind of ritualistic duel was regarded as innocent. The gods, it was thought, would not allow wrong to prevail.

The Germans who overran the old Roman provinces found it difficult to maintain any political organization at more than a local level. Security and civil order all but disappeared. Peasant communities were at the mercy of wandering bands of habitual fighters. Fighters often captured peasant villages, took them under their protection, guarded them from further marauders, and lived off their produce. Sometimes the same great fighting man came to possess many such villages, moving with his retinue of horsemen from one village to another to support himself throughout the year. Thus originated a new distinction between lord and servant, noble and commoner, martial and menial class. Life became local and self-sufficient. People ate, wore, used, and dwelled in only what they themselves and their neighbors could produce. Trade died down, the cities became depopulated, money went out of circulation, almost nothing was bought or sold. The Roman roads fell into neglect; people often used them as quarries for ready-cut building blocks for their own crude purposes. The West not only broke up into localized villages, but also ceased to have habitual contacts across the Mediterranean. It became isolated from the eastern centers from which its former civilization had always been drawn. The West was reverting. From roughly A.D. 500 on, Europe was in the so-called Dark Ages.

The Church and the Rise of the Papacy

Only one organized institution maintained a tie with the civilized past. Only one institution, reaching over the whole West, could receive news or dispatch its agents over the whole area. This institution was the Christian church. Its framework still stood; its network of bishoprics, as built up in late Roman times, remained intact except in places like England where the barbarian conquest was complete.

In addition, a new type of religious institution was rapidly spreading with the growth of monasteries. The serious and the sensitive, both men and women (though not together, to be sure), rejected the savagery about them and retired into communities of their own. Usually they were left unmolested by rough neighbors who held them in religious awe. In a world of violence they formed islands of quiet and of peace. In a society of burly barbarians they lived the life of contemplation. Their prayers, it was believed, were of use to all the world, and their example might at the least arouse in obstreperous worldlings the pangs of shame. The monastic houses generally adopted the rule of St. Benedict (*c.* 480–543), and were generally governed by an abbot. Dedicated to the same ideals, they formed unifying filaments throughout the chaos of the Latin West.

Bishops, abbots, and monks looked with veneration to Rome as the spot where St. Peter, the first apostle, had been martyred. The bishop of Rome corresponded with other bishops, sent out missionaries (to England, for example), gave advice on doctrine when he could, and attempted to keep in mind the situation throughout the Latin world as a whole. Moreover, with no emperor any longer in Rome, the bishop took over the government and public affairs of the city. Thus the bishop of Rome, while claiming a primacy over all Christians, was not dominated by any secular power. In the East the great church functionaries, the patriarchs, fell under the influence of the emperor who continued to rule at Constantinople, so that a tradition of Caesaropapism grew up in the East; but in the West the independence of the bishop of Rome now confirmed in practice a principle always maintained by the great churchmen of the West—the independence of the spiritual power from the political or temporal.

In this way was built up the authority of the popes. It was fortified by various arguments. St. Peter, it was held, had imparted the spiritual authority given to him by Christ himself to the Roman bishops who were his successors. This doctrine of the "Petrine supremacy" was based on two verses in the Bible, according to which Christ designated Peter as the head of the church, giving him the "power of the keys," to open and close the doors of eternal salvation.[2] As for the pope's temporal rule in Rome, it was affirmed that the Emperor Constantine had endowed the bishop with the government of the city. This "Donation of Constantine" was accepted as historical fact from the eighth century to the fifteenth, when it was proved to be a forgery.

It was the church which incorporated the barbarians into a higher way of life, and when a barbarian embraced a more civilized way of living it was the church that he entered. As early as about A.D. 340, the church sent out Ulfilas to convert the Goths; his translation of the Bible represents the first writing down of any Germanic language. About 496 the king of the Franks, Clovis, was converted to Christianity. A hundred years later, in 597, the king of Kent in southeast England yielded to the persuasions of Augustine of Canterbury, a missionary dispatched from Rome, and the Christianization of the Anglo-Saxons gradually followed. Missionaries from Ireland also, to which Christians of the Roman Empire had fled before the heathen barbarians, now returned to both Britain and the Continent to spread the gospel. By some such year as A.D. 700, after three centuries of turmoil, the borders of Christianity in the West were again roughly what they had been in late Roman times. Then in 711, as we have seen, the Arabs conquered Spain. They crossed the Pyrenees and raced toward central Europe, but were stopped by a Christian and Frankish army in 732 at Tours on the river Loire. Islam was not destined to reach beyond Spain.

---

[2] "Thou art Peter, and upon this rock I will build my church; and the gates of hell shall not prevail against it. And I will give unto thee the keys of the kingdom of heaven, and whatsoever thou shalt bind on earth shall be bound in heaven; and whatsoever thou shalt loose on earth shall be loosed in heaven." Matthew xvi, 18–19. In Greek the name Peter meant a "rock"; a play upon words was involved. The pun is still evident in some modern languages, as in French, where *pierre,* a rock, is the same as *Pierre,* Peter.

The Empire of Charlemagne, A.D. 800

Among the Franks, in what is now northern France and the German Rhineland, there had meanwhile arisen a line of capable rulers of whom the greatest was Charlemagne. The Frankish kings made it their policy to cooperate with the pope. The pope needed a protector against depredations by his barbarian neighbors and against the political claims of the Byzantine Empire upon the city of Rome. The Frankish kings, in return for protection thus offered, won papal support to their side. This made it easier for them to control their own bishops, who were more often seen on horseback than in the episcopal chair, and was of use in pacifying their own domains and in wars of conquest against the heathen. In the year 800, in Rome, the pope crowned Charlemagne as emperor of the West. Frankish king and Roman bishop both believed that if only the Roman Empire could be restored peace and order might once more reign. Church and empire, the spirit and the state, were to be as two mighty swords employed in the same holy cause.

Charlemagne crossed the Pyrenees and won back the northeastern corner of Spain to Christian rule. He overthrew and subordinated the barbarian kings who had set themselves up in Italy. He sent forces down the Danube, penetrated into Bohemia, and proceeded against some of the still heathen Germans (the Saxons) who lived along the river Elbe, and whom he either massacred or converted to Christianity. All these regions he brought within his new empire. Except for England and Ireland, which remained outside, the borders of his empire were coextensive with those of the Latin Christian world.

Once more, to a degree, the West was united. But a momentous change had occurred. Its capital was now not Rome and did not lie in the ancient world of the Mediterranean. Its capital was at Aix-la-Chapelle, or Aachen, near the mouth of the Rhine. Its ruler, Charlemagne, was a German of an ethnic group which ancient civilization had left outside. Its people were Germans, French, and Italians, or the ancestors from whom these nationalities were to be developed. In the Greco-Roman world the north had always been at best provincial. Now the north became a center in its own right. Charlemagne dispatched embassies to the emperor at Constantinople, and to Harun al-Rashid, the great caliph at Baghdad. In intellectual matters, too, the north now became a capital. Centuries of violence and confusion had left ignorance very widespread. Charlemagne himself, though he understood Latin, could barely read and never learned to write. He used his authority to revive the all but forgotten ancient learning and to spread education at least among the clergy. To his palace school came scholars from England, Germany, France, Italy, Spain. They wrote and spoke in Latin, the only Western language in which any complicated ideas could at the time be expressed. Disintegrating ancient manuscripts were copied and recopied to assure a more abundant supply for study—always by hand, but in a more rapid script than had before been used, the so-called Carolingian minuscule, from which come the small letters of the modern Western alphabet, only the capitals being Roman. Commerce also, which had virtually disappeared, Charlemagne undertook to foster. He created a new and more reliable coinage, which was based on silver, the gold coins of the Roman Empire having long since vanished. A pound of silver was divided into 20 *solidi* or 240 pennies. This scheme of values, though long used in many parts of Europe, survived longest in the country that remained outside Charlemagne's empire, namely, in England, the last country to replace it with a decimal currency, and then not until the twentieth century.

Ninth-Century Invasions; Europe by A.D. 1000

It is in Charlemagne's empire that we can first see the shape of Europe as a unit of society and culture distinct from the Mediterranean world of antiquity. The empire did not last. The troubled era was not yet over. New hordes of barbarians assailed Western Christendom in the ninth century. The Magyars (called in Latin "Hungarians") terrified various parts of Europe until they settled down on the middle Danube about the year 900. New Germanic tribes uprooted themselves, coming this time from Scandinavia, and variously known as Norsemen, Vikings, or Danes. Bursting out in all directions, they reached Kiev in Russia in 864, discovered Iceland in 874, and even touched America in 1000. In the Christian world they assaulted the coasts and pushed up the rivers but settled in considerable numbers only in the Danelaw in England and in Normandy in France. Meanwhile the Arabs raided the shores of France and Italy and occupied Sicily. Nowhere was the power of government strong enough to ward off such attacks. Everywhere the harassed local population found its own means of defense or, that failing, was slaughtered, robbed, or carried off into slavery.

Gradually the second wave of barbarians was incorporated as the first had been, by the same process of conversion to Christianity. By the year 1000 the process was nearly complete. In 1001 the pope sent a golden crown to the Magyars to crown St. Stephen as their first king, thus bringing Hungary within the orbit of the Latin West. Poland, Bohemia, and the Scandinavian homelands of the Norsemen were being rapidly Christianized. In older Christian countries, such as France, the last remote and isolated rustics—the "heathen" who lived in the "heath"—were finally ferreted out by missionaries and brought within the Christian fold. In Christian countries Christianity now permeated to every corner, and the historic peoples of western Europe had come together within the spreading system of the Latin church.

Meanwhile West and East continued to drift apart. The refusal of Greek patriarchs at Constantinople to recognize the claims to primacy of the bishop of Rome, whom they regarded as a kind of Western barbarian, and the refusal of the Roman pontiff to acknowledge the political pretensions of the Byzantine Empire, led to the Great Schism of East and West. This schism, after developing for three centuries, became definite in 1054. It divided the Christian world into the Latin or Roman Catholic and the Greek Orthodox churches. It was from Constantinople that Christianity reached the peoples of Russia. The Russians, like the Balkan peoples, remained out of contact with the West during the centuries when spiritual and intellectual contacts were carried through the clergy. They believed, indeed, that the Latin West was evil, heretical, contumacious, and unholy. The Latin West, at the same time, by the schism, cut one more of its ties with antiquity and emerged the more clearly as an independent center of its own civilization.

By the year 1000, or soon thereafter, the entity that we call Europe had been brought into existence. From the turbulence that followed the collapse of the Greco-Roman civilization had issued the peoples and the countries of modern

Europe. A kingdom of France was in being, adjoining the great ill-defined bulk of Germany to the east. There were small Christian kingdoms in northern Spain and a number of city-states in the Italian peninsula. In the north there were now a kingdom of England and a kingdom of Scotland; Denmark, Norway, and Sweden had also taken form. In the east rose the three great kingdoms of Poland, Bohemia, and Hungary, the first two predominantly Slavic, Hungary predominantly Magyar, but all Latin and Catholic in culture and religion, and Western in orientation. The east Slavs, or Russians, and the Slavs and other peoples of the Balkan peninsula also formed kingdoms of their own. Their way was diverging from the West. Christianized by Byzantine missionaries, they were Greek and Orthodox in culture and religion and oriented toward Constantinople.

The civilization of the West, in the year 1000, was still not much to boast of in the more polished circles of Byzantium or Baghdad. It might still seem that the West would suffer more than the East from their separation. But the West began at this time to experience a remarkable activity, ushering in the European civilization of the High Middle Ages.

3. The High Middle Ages: Secular Civilization

Changes after A.D. 1000

Some historical periods are so dynamic that a person who lives to be fifty years old can remember sweeping changes that have come in one's own lifetime. Such a time has been the last century of the modern age. Such a time, also, began in Europe in the eleventh century. People could see new towns rise and grow before their eyes. They could observe new undertakings in commerce or government. It is hardly too much to say that all the cities that Europe was to know before the modern industrial era sprang up between about 1050 and 1200. The population of western Europe, which had been sparse even in Roman days, and which was even more sparse after 500, suddenly began to grow more dense about the year 1000, and expanded steadily for two or three hundred years. The people of the High Middle Ages did not develop the conception of progress, because their minds were set upon timeless values and personal salvation in another world, but the period was nevertheless one of rapid progress in nonreligious or "secular" things. It was a period in which much was created that remained fundamental far into modern times.

The new era was made possible by the process of growth in population which went along with agricultural changes. After the Norse and Magyar inroads had stopped, Europe was spared the assaults of barbarians. There came to be more security of life and limb. A farmer could plant with more confidence that he would reap. A man could build a house and expect to live his life in it and pass it on to his children. Hence there was more planting and building. Sometime before the year 1000 a heavier plow had been invented, which cut a deeper furrow. Better methods of harnessing horses had been found than the ancients had ever known. The Romans had continued simply to throw a yoke over a horse's neck, so that the animal in pulling a weight easily choked. Europeans, before the year 1000, began to use a horse collar that rested on the animal's shoulders. The single horse could pull a greater load, or several horses could now for the first time be hitched in tandem. The amount of available animal power was thus multiplied, at a time when animals were the main source of power other than human muscle. Windmills also, unknown to the ancients, were developed in the Low Countries about this time. They too offered a new source of power. Thus at the very beginning of a specifically "European" history, one may detect a characteristic of European civilization—a faculty for invention, a quest for new sources of energy.

With such labor-saving devices people continued to work very hard, but they obtained more results by their efforts. Probably the use of such inventions, together with the influence of the Christian clergy, accounts for the gradual disappearance of slavery from Europe and its replacement by the less abject and less degrading status of serfdom. It is true that medieval Christians, when they could, continued to enslave whites as they were later to do with blacks. Usually such slaves were captives in war, taken from tribes not yet converted to Christianity, and sometimes exported as a form of merchandise to the Byzantine and Muslim worlds. As the successive European peoples became Christianized, the supply of slaves dried up. Medieval Christians did not enslave each other, nor was slavery essential to any important form of production.

Not only did population increase, and work become more productive, but groups of people became less isolated from one another. Communications improved. The roads remained poor or nonexistent, but bridges were built across the many European rivers, and settlers filled in the wildernesses that had formerly separated the inhabited areas. Trees were felled and land cleared, as they would be long afterward in the United States during the westward movement. But where the forest gave way in America to an agricultural world of detached individual farmsteads, in medieval Europe the rural population clustered in village communities. The "nucleated" village gave more security, more contact between families, and readier access to the blacksmith or the priest. It also made possible a communally organized agriculture.

Better ways of using land were introduced in the "three-field" system, which spread almost everywhere where cereal crops were the staple. In this "system" the peasant village divided its arable fields into three parts. In a given year one part was sown with one crop, such as wheat, a second part with another, such as barley, and the third was left to lie fallow. The three parts were rotated from year to year. Thus soil exhaustion was avoided at a time when fertilizers were unknown. Formerly half or less of the available fields had been cultivated at any one time. With the three-field system two-thirds of the land came into annual use. This fact, reinforced by better plowing and more effective employment of animals, led to a huge increase in the supply of food.

The peace and personal security necessary to agriculture were also advanced, in the absence of effective public authority, by the growth of institutions that we know as "feudalism." Feudalism was intricate and diverse, but in essence it was a means of carrying on some kind of government on a local basis where no organized state existed. After the collapse of Charlemagne's empire the real authority fell into the hands of persons who were most often called "counts." The count was the most important man of a region covering a few hundred square miles. To build up his own position, and strengthen himself for war against other counts, he tried to keep the peace and maintain control over the lesser lords in his county, those whose possessions extended over a few hundred or a few thousand acres. These lesser lords accepted or were forced to accept his protection. They became his vassals, and he became their "lord." The lord and vassal relation was one of reciprocal duties. The lord protected the vassal and assured him justice and firm tenure of his land. If two vassals of the same lord disputed the possession of the same village, the lord decided the case, sitting in council (or "court") with all his vassals assembled, and judging according to the common memory or customary law of the district. If a vassal died young, leaving only small children, the lord took the family under his "wardship" or guardianship, guaranteeing that the rightful heirs would inherit in due time. Correspondingly the vassal agreed to serve the lord as a fighting man for a certain number of days in the year. From other "unauthorized" fighting and squabbling the vassal was supposed to refrain. The vassal also owed it to the lord to attend and advise him, to sit in his court in the judging of disputes. Usually he owed no money or material payment; but if the lord had to be ransomed from captivity, or when his children married, the vassal paid a fee. The vassal also paid a fee on inheriting an estate, and the income of estates under wardship went to the lord. Thus the lord collected sporadic revenues with which to finance his somewhat primitive government.

This feudal scheme, which probably originated locally, gradually spread. Lords at the level of counts became in turn the vassals of dukes. In the year 987 the great lords of France chose Hugh Capet as their king, and became his vassals. The kings of France enjoyed little real power for another two hundred years, but the descendants of Hugh occupied their throne for eight centuries, until the French Revolution. Similarly the magnates of Germany elected a king in 911; in 962 the German king was crowned emperor, as Charlemagne had been before him; thus originated the Holy Roman Empire of which much will be heard in the following chapters.

To England, in these formative centuries, it was not given to choose a king by election. England was conquered in 1066 by the Duke of Normandy, William. The Normans (the old Norsemen reshaped by a century of Christian and French influence) imposed upon England a centralized and efficient type of feudalism which they had developed in Normandy. In England, from an early date, the king and his central officials therefore had considerable power. In England there was more civil peace and personal security than on the Continent. Within the framework of a strong monarchy self-governing institutions could eventually develop with a minimum of disorder.

The notable feature of feudalism was its mutual or reciprocal character. In this it differed from the old Roman imperial principle, by which the emperor had been a majestic and all-powerful sovereign. Under feudalism no one was sovereign. King and people, lord and vassal, were joined in a kind of contract. Each owed something to the other. If one defaulted, the obligation ceased. If a vassal refused his due services, the king had the right to enforce compliance. If the king violated the rights of the vassal, the vassals could join together against him. The king was supposed to act with the advice of the vassals, who formed his council or court. If the vassals believed the king to be exceeding his lawful powers, they could impose terms upon him. It was out of this mutual or contractual character of feudalism that ideas of constitutional government later developed.

Feudalism applied in the strict sense only to the military or noble class. Below the feudal world lay the vast mass of the peasantry. Here, in the village, the lowliest vassal of a higher noble was lord over his own subjects. The village, with its people and surrounding farmlands, constituted a "manor," the estate of a lord. In the eleventh century most people of the manor were serfs. They were "bound to the soil" in that they could not leave the manor without the lord's permission. Few wanted to leave anyway, at a time when the world beyond the village was unknown and dangerous, and filled at best only with other similar manors in which opportunities were no different. The lord, for his part, could not expropriate the villagers or drive them away. He owed them protection and the administration of justice. They in turn worked his fields and gave him part of the produce of their own. No money changed hands, because there was virtually no money in circulation. The manorial system was the agricultural base on which a ruling class was supported. It supported also the clergy, for the church held much land in the form of manors. It gave the protection from physical violence and the framework of communal living without which the peasants could not grow crops or tend livestock.

Many consequences flowed from the rise of agricultural productivity. Lords and even a few peasants could produce a surplus, which they might sell if only they could find a market. The country was able to produce enough food for a town population to live on. And since population grew with the increase of the food supply, and since not all the new people were needed in agriculture, a surplus of population also began to exist. Restless spirits among the peasants now wanted to get away from the manor. And many went off to the new towns.

The Rise of Towns and Commerce

We have seen how the ancient cities had decayed. In the ninth and tenth centuries, with few exceptions, there were none left in western Europe. Here and there one would find a cluster of population around the headquarters of a bishop, a great count, or a king. But there were no commercial centers. There was no merchant class. The simple crafts—weaving, metalworking, harness making—were carried on locally on the manors. Rarely, an itinerant trader might appear with such semiprecious goods as he could carry for long distances on donkeys—Eastern silks, or a few spices for the wealthy. Among these early traders Jews were often important, because Judaism, penetrating the Byzantine and Arabic worlds as well as the Western, offered one of the few channels of distant communication that were open.

Long-distance trading was the first to develop. The city of Venice was founded about A.D. 570 when refugees from the barbarians settled in its islands. The Venetians, as time went on, brought Eastern goods up the Adriatic and sold them to traders coming down from central Europe. In Flanders in the north, in what is now Belgium, there developed manufacturers of woolen cloth. Flemish woolens were of a unique quality, owing to peculiarities of the atmosphere and the skill of the weavers. They could not be duplicated elsewhere. Nor could Eastern goods be procured except through the Venetians—or the Genoese or Pisans. Such goods could not possibly be produced locally, yet they were in demand wherever they became known. Merchants traveled in increasing numbers to disseminate them.

Money came back into more general circulation; where it came from is not quite clear, since there was little mining of gold or silver until the end of the Middle Ages. Merchants began to establish permanent headquarters, settling within the deserted walls of ghostly Roman towns or near the seat of a lord or ecclesiastic, whose throngs of retainers might become customers. Craftsmen moved from the overpopulated manors to these same growing centers, where they might produce wares that the lords or merchants would wish to buy. The process once started tended to snowball: the more people settled in such an agglomeration the more they needed food brought to them from the country, and the more craftsmen left the villages the more the country people, lords and serfs, had to obtain clothing and simple tools and utensils from the towns. Hence a busy local trade developed also.

By 1100, or not long thereafter, such centers existed all over Europe, from the Baltic to Italy, from England as far east as Bohemia. Usually there was one about every twenty or thirty miles. The smallest towns had only a few hundred inhabitants, the larger ones two or three thousand, or sometimes more. Each carried on a local exchange with its immediate countryside and purveyed goods of more distant origin to local consumers. But their importance was by no means merely economic. What made them "towns" in the full sense of the word was their acquisition of political rights.

The merchants and craftsmen who lived in the towns did not wish to remain, like the country people, subject to neighboring feudal lords. At worst, the feudal lords regarded merchants as fat possessors of ready money; they might hold them up on the road, plunder their mule trains, collect tolls at river crossings, or extort cash by offering "protection." At best, the most well-meaning feudal lord could not supervise the affairs of merchants, for the feudal and customary law knew nothing of commercial problems. The traders in the course of their business developed a "law merchant" of their own, having to do with money and moneychanging, debt and bankruptcy, contracts, invoices, and bills of lading. They wished to have their own means of apprehending thieves, runaway debtors, or sellers of fraudulent goods. They strove, therefore, to get recognition for their own law, their own courts, their own judges and magistrates. They wished, too, to govern their towns themselves and to avoid payment of fees or taxes to nearby nobles.

Everywhere in Latin Christendom, along about 1100, the new towns struggled to free themselves from the encircling feudalism and to set themselves up as self-governing little republics. Where the towns were largest and closest together— along the highly urbanized arteries of the trade routes, in north Italy, on the upper Danube and Rhine rivers, in Flanders, or on the Baltic coast—they emancipated themselves the most fully. Venice, Genoa, Pisa, Florence, Milan became virtually independent city-states, each governing a substantial tract of its surrounding country. In Flanders also, towns like Bruges and Ghent dominated their localities. Along the upper Danube, the Rhine, the North Sea, the Baltic, many towns became imperial free cities within the Holy Roman Empire, each a kind of small republic owing allegiance to no one except the distant and usually ineffectual emperor. Nuremberg, Frankfurt, Augsburg, Strasbourg, Hamburg, and Lübeck were free cities of this kind. In France and England, where the towns in the twelfth century were somewhat less powerful, they obtained less independence but received charters of liberties from the king. By these charters they were assured the right to have their own town governments and officials, their own courts and law, and to pay their own kind of taxes to the king in lieu of ordinary feudal obligations.

Often towns formed leagues or urban federations, joining forces to repress banditry or piracy or to deal with ambitious monarchs or predatory nobles. The most famous such league was the Hanse; it was formed mainly of German towns, fought wars under its own banner, and dominated the commerce of the North Sea and the Baltic until after 1300. Similar tendencies of the towns to form political leagues, or to act independently in war and diplomacy, were suppressed by the kings in England, France, and Spain.

The fact that Italy, Germany, and the Netherlands were commercially more advanced than the Atlantic countries in the Middle Ages, and so had a more intensive town life, was to be one cause (out of many) preventing political unification. Not until 1860 or 1870 were nationwide states created in this region. In the west, where towns also grew up, but where more of a balance was kept between town and country, the towns were absorbed into nationwide monarchies that were arising under the kings. This difference between central and western Europe was to shape all the subsequent history of modern times.

The liberties won by the towns were corporate liberties. Each town was a collective thing. The townsman did not possess individual rights, but only the rights which followed from being a resident of a particular town. Among these were personal liberty; no townsman could be a serf, and fugitive serfs who lived over a year in a town were generally deemed to be free. But no townsman wanted individual liberty in the modern sense. The world was still too unsettled for the individual to act alone. The citizens wanted to join together in a compact body, and to protect themselves by all sorts of regulations and controls. The most obvious evidence of this communal solidarity was the wall within which most towns were enclosed. The citizens in time of trouble looked to their own defense. As the towns grew they built new walls farther out. Today, in Paris or Cologne, one may still see remains of different walls in use from the tenth to the thirteenth centuries.

Economic solidarity was of more day-to-day importance. The towns required neighboring peasants to sell foodstuffs only in the town marketplace. They thus protected their food supply against competition from other towns. Or they forbade the carrying on of certain trades in the country; this was to oblige peasants to make purchases in town, and protect the jobs and livelihood of the town craftsmen. They put up tariffs and tolls on the goods of other towns brought within their own walls. Or they levied special fees on merchants from outside who did business in the town. In Italy and Germany they often coined their own money; and the typical town fixed the rates at which various moneys should be exchanged. The medieval towns, in short, at the time of their greatest liberty, followed in a local way the same policies of protectionism and exclusiveness which national governments were often to follow in modern times.

Within each town merchants and craftsmen formed associations, or "guilds," for collective supervision of their affairs. Merchants formed a merchant guild.

Stonemasons, carpenters, barbers, dyers, goldsmiths, coppersmiths, weavers, hatters, tailors, shoemakers, grocers, apothecaries, etc., formed craft guilds of their own. The guilds served a public purpose, for they provided that work should be done by reliable and experienced persons, and so protected people from the pitfalls of shoddy garments, clumsy barbers, poisonous drugs, or crooked and flimsy houses. They also provided a means of vocational education and marked out a career for young men. Typically a boy became an apprentice to some master, learned the trade, and lived with and was supported by the master's family for a term of years, such as seven. Then he became a journeyman, a qualified and recognized worker, who might work for any master at a stated wage. If lucky, he might become a master himself, open his own shop, hire journeymen, and take apprentices. So long as the towns were growing, a boy had some chance to become a master himself; but as early as 1300 many guilds were becoming frozen, and the masters were increasingly chary of admitting new persons to their own status. From the beginning, in any case, it was an important function of the guilds to protect their own members. The masters, assembled together, preserved their reputation by regulating the quality of their product. They divided work among themselves, fixed the terms of apprenticeship, the wages to be paid to journeymen, and the prices at which their goods must be sold. Or they took collective steps to meet or keep out the competition of the same trade in nearby towns.

Whether among individuals within the town itself, or as between town and country, or between town and town, the spirit of the medieval economy was to prevent competition. Risk, adventure, and speculation were not wanted. Almost no one thought it proper to work for monetary profit. The few who did, big merchants trading over large areas, met with suspicion and disapproval wherever they went.

The towns, although in many ways they tried to subject the peasants' interests to their own, nevertheless had an emancipating influence on the country. A rustic by settling in town might escape from serfdom. But the town influence was more widespread, and far out of proportion to the relatively small number of people who could become town dwellers. The growth of towns increased the demand for foods. Lords began to clear new lands. All western Europe set about developing a kind of internal frontier. Formerly villages had been separated by dark tracts of roadless woods, in which wolves roamed freely shadowed by the gnomes, elves, and fairies of popular folklore. Now pioneers with axes cleared farmlands and built villages in these immemorial forests. The lords who usually supervised such operations (since their serfs were not slaves, and could not be moved at will) offered freer terms to entice peasants to go and settle on the new lands. It was less easy for the lord of an old village to hold his people in serfdom when in an adjacent village, within a few hours' walk, the people were free. The peasants, moreover, were now able to obtain a little money by selling produce in town. The lords now wanted money because the towns were producing more articles which money could buy. It became very common for peasants to obtain personal freedom, holding their own lands, in return for an annual money payment to the lord for an indefinite period into the future. As early as the twelfth century serfdom began to disappear in northern France and southern England, and by the fifteenth century it had disappeared from most of western Europe. The peasant could now, in law, move freely about. But the manorial organization remained; the peasant owed dues and fees to the lord, and was still under his legal jurisdiction.

The Growth of National Monarchies

Meanwhile the kings were busy, each trying to build his kingdom into an organized monarchy that would outlast his life.[3] Monarchy became hereditary; the king inherited his position like any other feudal lord or possessor of an estate. Inheritance of the crown made for peace and order, for elections under conditions of the time were usually turbulent and disputed, and where the older Germanic principle of elective monarchy remained alive, as in the Holy Roman Empire, there was periodic commotion. The kings sent out executive officers to supervise their interests throughout their kingdoms. The kings of England, adopting an old Anglo-Saxon practice, had a sheriff in each of the forty shires; the kings of France created similar officers who were called bailiffs. The kings likewise instituted royal courts, under royal justices, to decide property disputes and repress crime. This assertion of legal jurisdiction, together with the military might necessary to enforce judgments upon obstinate nobles, became a main pillar of the royal power. In England especially, and in lesser degree elsewhere, the kings required local inhabitants to assist royal judges in the discovery of relevant facts in particular cases. They put men on oath to declare what they knew of events in their own neighborhood. It is from this enforced association of private persons with royal officers that the jury developed.

The kings needed money to pay for their governmental machinery or to carry on war with other kings. Taxation, as known in the Roman Empire, was quite unknown to the Germanic and feudal tradition. In the feudal scheme each person was responsible only for the customary fees which arose on stated occasions. The king, like other lords, was supposed to live on his own income—on the revenue of manors that he owned himself, the proceeds of estates temporarily under his wardship, or the occasional fees paid to him by his vassals. No king, even for the best of reasons, could simply decree a new tax and collect it. At the same time, as the use of money became more common, the kings had to assure themselves of a money income. In England, in the twelfth century, the customary obligation of the vassal to render military service to the king was being converted into a money payment, called "scutage" or shield money. As the towns grew up, with a new kind of wealth and a new source of money income, they agreed to make certain payments in return for their royal charters.

The royal demands for money, the royal claims to exercise jurisdiction, were regarded as innovations. They were constantly growing and sometimes were a source of abuse. They met with frequent resistance in all countries. A famous case historically (though somewhat commonplace in its own day) was that of Magna Carta in England in 1215, when a group of English lords and high churchmen, joined by representatives of the city of London, required King John to confirm and guarantee their historic liberties.

The king, as has been said, like any lord, was supposed to act in council or

---

[3] See p. 28.

"court" with his vassals. The royal council became the egg out of which departments of government were hatched—such as the royal judiciary, exchequer, and military command. From it also was hatched the institution of parliaments. The kings had always, in a rough sort of way, held great parleys or "talks" (the Latin *parliamentum* meant simply a "talking") with their chief retainers. In the twelfth and thirteenth centuries the growth of towns added a new element to European life. To the lords and bishops was now added a burgher class, which, if of far inferior dignity, was too stubborn, free-spirited, and well furnished with money to be overlooked. When representatives of the towns began to be normally summoned to the king's great "talks," along with lords and clergy, parliaments may be said to have come into being.

Parliaments, in this sense, sprouted all over Europe in the thirteenth century. Nothing shows better the similarity of institutions in Latin Christendom, or the inadequacy of tracing the history of any one country by itself. The new assemblies were called *cortes* in Spain, diets in Germany, Estates General or provincial estates in France, parliaments in the British Isles. Usually they are referred to generically as "estates," the word "parliament" being reserved for Britain, but in origin they were all essentially the same.

The kings called these assemblies as a means of publicizing and strengthening the royal rule. They found it more convenient to explain their policies, or to ask for money, to a large gathering brought together for that purpose than to have a hundred officials make local explanations and strike local bargains in a hundred different places. The kings did not recognize, nor did the assemblies claim, any right of the parliament to dictate to the king and his government. But usually the king invited the parliament to state grievances; his action upon them was the beginning of parliamentary legislation.

The parliaments were considered to represent not the "nation" nor "people" nor yet the individual citizen, but the "estates of the realm," the great collective interests of the country. The first and highest estate was the clergy, the second the landed or noble class; to these older ruling groups were added, as a "third estate," the burghers of the chartered towns. Quite commonly these three types of people sat separately as three distinct chambers. But the pattern varied from country to country. In England, Poland, and Hungary the clergy as a whole ceased to be represented; only the bishops came, sitting with lay magnates in an upper house. Eventually the burghers dropped out in Poland, Bohemia, and Hungary, leaving the landed aristocracy in triumph in eastern Europe. In Castile and Württemberg, on the other hand, the noble estate eventually refused to attend parliament, leaving the townspeople and clergy in the assemblies. In some countries—in Scandinavia, Switzerland, and in the French Estates General—even peasants were allowed to have delegates.

In England the Parliament developed eventually in a distinctive way. After a long period of uncertainty there came to be two houses, known as the Lords and the Commons. The Lords, as in Hungary or Poland, included both great prelates and lay magnates. The House of Commons developed features not found on the Continent. Lesser landholders, the people who elsewhere counted as small nobles, sat in the same House of Commons with representatives of the towns. The Commons was made up of "knights and burgesses," or gentry and townsmen together, a fact which greatly added to its strength, for the middle class of the towns long remained too weak to act alone. The mingling of classes in England, the willingness of townsmen to follow the leadership of the gentry, and of the gentry to respect the interests of townsmen, helped to root representative institutions in England more deeply than in other countries, in many of which the parliaments tended to die out in later times, in part because of class conflict. Moreover, England was a small country in the Middle Ages, even smaller than it looked on the map because the north was almost wild. There were no provincial or local parliamentary bodies (as in France, the Holy Roman Empire, or Poland) which might jealousy cut into the powers of the central body or with which the king could make local arrangements without violating the principle of representative government. And finally, as a reason for the strength of Parliament in England, the elected members of the House of Commons very early obtained the power to *commit* their constituents. If they voted a tax, those who elected them had to pay it. The king, in order to get matters decided, insisted that the votes be binding. Constituents were not allowed to repudiate the vote of their deputy, nor to punish or harass him when he came home, as often happened in other countries. Parliament thus exercised power as well as rights.

In summary, the three centuries of the High Middle Ages laid foundations both for order and for freedom. Slavery was defunct and serfdom expiring. Politically, the multitude of free chartered towns, the growth of juries in some places, the rise of parliaments everywhere, provided means by which peoples could take some part in their governments. The ancient civilizations had never created a free political unit larger than the city-state. The Greeks had never carried democracy beyond the confines within which people could meet in person, nor had the Romans devised means by which, in a large state, the governed could share any responsibilities with an official bureaucracy. The ancients had never developed the idea of representative government, or of government by duly elected and authorized representatives acting at a distance from home. The idea is by no means as obvious or simple as it looks. It first appeared in the medieval monarchies of the West.

4. The High Middle Ages: The Church

So far in our account of the High Middle Ages we have told the story of Hamlet without speaking of the Prince of Denmark, for we have left aside the church, except, indeed, when some mention of it could not be avoided. In the real life of the time the church was omnipresent. Religion permeated every pore. In feudalism the mutual duties of lord and vassal were confirmed by religious oaths, and bishops and abbots, as holders of lands, became feudal personages themselves. In the monarchies, the king was crowned by the chief churchman of his kingdom, adjured to rule with justice and piety, and anointed with holy oils. In the towns, guilds served as lay religious brotherhoods; each guild chose a patron saint and marched in the streets on holy days. For amusement the townspeople watched religious dramas, the morality and miracle plays in which religious themes were enacted. The rising town, if it harbored a bishop, took especial care to erect a new cathedral. Years of effort and of religious fervor produced the Gothic cathedrals which still stand as the best known memorials of medieval civilization.

The Development of the Medieval Church and Papacy

If, however, we turn back to the tenth century, the troubled years before 1000, we find the church in as dubious a condition as everything else. The church reflected the life about it. It was fragmented and localized. Every bishop went his own way. Though the clergy was the only literate class, many of the clergy themselves could not read and write. Christian belief was mixed with the old pagan magic and superstition. The monasteries were in decay. Priests often lived in a concubinage that was generally condoned. It was customary for them to marry, so that they had recognized children, to whom they intrigued to pass on their churchly position. Often rough laymen dominated their ecclesiastical neighbors, with the big lords appointing the bishops, and the little ones the parish priests. When people thought about Rome at all, they sensed a vague respect for something legendary and far away; but the bishop of Rome, or pope, had no influence and was treated in unseemly fashion in his own city. The popes of the tenth century were the creatures of the unruly Roman nobles. Marozia, daughter of a Roman "senator," became the mistress of one pope, by whom she had a son who became pope in turn, until she imprisoned him so that another son, by another father, could claim the papacy also.

The Roman Catholic church is in fact unrecognizable in the jumble of the tenth century. So far at least as human effort was concerned, it was virtually created in the eleventh century along with the other institutions of the High Middle Ages.

The impulse to reform came from many quarters. Sometimes a secular ruler undertook to correct conditions in his own domains. For this purpose he asserted a strict control over his clergy. In 962 the Holy Roman Empire was proclaimed. This Empire, like the Carolingian and Roman empires which it was supposed to continue, was in theory coterminous with Latin Christendom itself, and endowed with a special mission of preserving and extending the Christian faith. Neither in France nor in England (nor, when they became Christian states, in Spain, Hungary, Poland, or Scandinavia) was this claim of the Holy Roman Empire ever acknowledged. But the Empire did for a time embrace Italy as well as Germany. The first emperors, in the tenth and eleventh centuries, denouncing the outrageous conditions in Rome, strove to make the pope into their appointee.

At the same time a reform movement arose from spiritual sources. Serious Christians took matters into their own hands. They founded a new monastery at Cluny in France, which soon had many daughter houses. It was their purpose to purify monastic life and to set a higher Christian ideal to which all clergy and laity might look up. To rid themselves of immediate local pressures, the greed, narrowness, ignorance, family ambition, and self-satisfied inertia that were the main causes of corruption, the Cluniacs refused to recognize any authority except that of Rome itself. Thus, at the very time when conditions in Rome were at their worst, Christians throughout Europe built up the prestige of Rome, of the idea of Rome, as a means to raise all Latin Christendom from its depths.

As for the popes in Rome, those who preserved any independence of judgment or respect for their own office, it was their general plan to free themselves from the Roman mobs and aristocrats without falling into dependence upon the Holy Roman Emperor. In 1059 Pope Nicholas II issued a decree providing that future popes should be elected by the cardinals. The cardinals, at that time, were the priests of churches in the city of Rome or bishops of neighboring dioceses. By entrusting the choice of future popes to them, Pope Nicholas hoped to exclude all influence from outside the clergy itself. Popes have been elected by cardinals ever since, though not always without influence from outside.

One of the first popes so elected was Gregory VII, known also as Hildebrand, a dynamic and strong-willed man who was pope from 1073 to 1085. He had been in touch with the Cluniac reformers, and dreamed of a reformed and reinvigorated Europe under the universal guidance of the Roman pontiff.

To understand what followed, readers must exert their imagination. In their mind's eye they must see a world in which all political barriers have dropped away. In this world people have no nationality. They do not live in the state, as in modern times; they live in the church. Society itself is a great religious community. Its leaders are the clergy, to which all educated persons belong. The public personage with whom people come into most frequent contact is the priest, and the most important public official is the bishop. The chief public buildings are churches, abbeys, and cathedrals. Secular interests, those of kings and dukes, of merchants and artisans, are earthbound and shortsighted. All persons, even kings, in addition to secular interests, have a higher concern. All are living in the religious community and preparing their souls for eternal life. The religious community, or church, reaches in principle as far as the borders of the known world. It is universal, for all must be saved. At its head stands the bishop of Rome, the Vicar of Christ, the successor to Peter, the keeper of the keys, the *servus servorum Dei,* the servant of the servants of God.

Some such vision filled the mind of Gregory VII, and with it he founded the papal supremacy of the high Middle Ages. He believed that the church should stand apart from worldly society, that it should judge and guide all human actions, and that a pope could judge and punish kings and emperors if he deemed them sinful. His ideal was not a "world state," but its spiritual counterpart, a world church officered by a single-minded and disciplined clergy, centralized under a single authority. He began by insisting that the clergy free itself of worldly involvements. He required married priests to put aside their wives and families. Celibacy of the clergy, never generally established in the Greek Orthodox church, and later rejected by Protestants in the West, became and remained the rule for the Roman Catholic priesthood. Gregory insisted also that no ecclesiastic might receive office through appointment by a layman. In his view only clergy might institute or influence clergy, for the clergy must be independent and self-contained.

Gregory soon faced a battle with that other aspirant to universal supremacy and a sacred mission, the Holy Roman Emperor, who at this time was Henry IV. In Germany the bishops and abbots possessed a great deal of the land, which they held and governed under the emperor as feudal magnates in their own right. To the emperor it was vitally important to have his own men, as reliable vassals, in these great positions. Hence in Germany "lay investiture" had become very common. "Lay investiture" meant the practice by which a layman, the emperor, conferred upon the new bishop the signs of his spiritual authority, the ring and the staff. Gregory prohibited lay investiture. He supported the German bishops and nobles when they rebelled against Henry. Henry proving obstinate, Gregory excommunicated him, i.e., outlawed him from Christian society by forbidding any priest to give him the sacraments. Henry, baffled, sought out the pope at Canossa in Italy to do penance. "To go to Canossa" in later times became a byword for submission to the will of Rome.

In 1122, after both original contenders had died, a compromise on the matter of lay investiture was effected by which bishops recognized the emperor as their feudal head but looked to Rome for spiritual authority. But the struggle between popes and emperors went on unabated. The magnates of Germany, lay lords as well as bishops, often allied with the pope to preserve their own feudal liberties from the emperor. The emperor in Germany was never able to consolidate his domains as did the kings in England and France. In Italy, too, the popes and emperors quarreled, the foes of each commonly siding with the other. The unwillingness of lords and churchmen (and of towns also, as we have seen) to let the emperors build up an effectual government left its mark permanently upon Europe in two ways. It contributed to the centralization of Latin Christendom under Rome, while it blocked national unity in central Europe.

The height of the medieval papacy came with Innocent III, whose pontificate lasted from 1198 to 1216. Innocent virtually realized Gregory's dream of a unified Christian world. He intervened in politics everywhere. He was recognized as a supreme arbiter. At his word, a king of France took a wife, a king of England accepted an unwanted archbishop, a king of León put aside the cousin whom he had married, and a claimant to the crown of Hungary deferred to his rival. Innocent advised the kings of Bohemia, Poland, and Denmark on weighty matters, and the kings of England, Aragon, and Portugal acknowledged him as feudal overlord within their realms. Huge revenues now flowed to Rome from all over Latin Christendom, and an enormous bureaucracy worked there to dispatch the voluminous business of the papal court. As kings struggled to repress civil rebellion, so Innocent and his successors struggled to repress heresy, which, defined as doctrine at variance with that of the church at large, was becoming alarmingly common among the Albigensians of southern France.

In 1215 Innocent called a great church council, the greatest since antiquity, attended by 500 bishops and even by the patriarchs of Constantinople and Jerusalem. The council labored at the perplexing task of keeping the clergy from worldly temptations. By forbidding priests to officiate at ordeals or trials by battle, it virtually ended these survivals of barbarism. It attempted to regularize belief in the supernatural by controlling the superstitious traffic in relics. It declared the sacraments to be the channel of God's saving grace and defined them authoritatively.[4] In the chief sacrament, the Eucharist or Mass, it promulgated the dogma of transubstantiation, which held that, in the Mass, the priest converts the substance of bread and wine into the substance of Christ's body and blood.

---

[4] A sacrament is understood to be the outward sign of an inward grace. In Catholic doctrine the sacraments were and are seven in number: baptism, confirmation, penance, the Eucharist, extreme unction, marriage, and holy orders. Except for baptism, a sacrament may be administered only by a priest. A dogma is the common belief of the church, in which all the faithful share and must share so long as they are members of the church. Dogmas are regarded as implicitly the same in all ages; they cannot be invented or developed, but may from time to time be clarified, defined, promulgated, or proclaimed.

Except for heretics, who were suppressed, the acts of the Fourth Lateran Council were accepted with satisfaction throughout Latin Europe.

Intellectual Life: The Universities, Scholasticism

Under the auspices of the church, as rising governments gave more civil security, and as the economy of town and country became able to support men devoted to a life of thought, the intellectual horizon of Europeans began to open. The twelfth and thirteenth centuries saw the founding of the first universities. These originated in the natural and spontaneous coming together of teachers and pupils which had never wholly disappeared even in the Dark Ages. By 1200 there was a center of medical studies at Salerno in south Italy, of legal studies at Bologna in north Italy, of theological studies at Paris. Oxford was founded about 1200 by a secession of disgruntled students and professors from Paris, Cambridge shortly thereafter. By 1300 there were a dozen such universities in Latin Europe, by 1500 almost a hundred.

As the early agglomerations of traders developed into organized towns, so the informal concourses of students and teachers developed into organized institutions of learning, receiving the sharp corporate stamp that was characteristic of the High Middle Ages. It was in having this corporate identity that medieval universities resemble our own and differed from the schools of Athens or Alexandria in ancient times. A university, the early University of Paris, for example, was a body of men, young and old, interested in learning and endowed by law with a communal name and being. It possessed definite liberties under some kind of charter, regulated its own affairs through its own officials, and kept its own order among its often boisterous population. It gave, and even advertised, courses and lectures, and it decided collectively which professors were the best qualified to teach. It might consist of distinct schools or "faculties"—the combination of theology, law, and medicine, as at Paris, was the most usual. It held examinations and awarded degrees, whose meaning and value were recognized throughout the Latin West. The degree, which originated as a license to teach, admitted its holder to certain honors or privileges such as those of a craft guild. With it, a professor might readily move from one university to another. Students moved easily also, the language being everywhere Latin and the curriculum much the same. The university, moreover, though typically it began in poverty, was as a corporate body capable of holding property; and the benefactions of pious donors, as the years went on, often built up substantial endowments in lands and manors. So organized, free from outside control, and enjoying an income from property, the university lived on as an institution beyond the lifetime of all living men, through good times and bad.

The queen of the sciences was theology, the intellectual study of religion. Many in Europe, by the eleventh century, were beginning to reflect upon their beliefs. They continued to believe but could no longer believe with naïve or unthinking acceptance. It was accepted as a fact, for example, that the Son of God had been incarnated as a man in Jesus Christ. But in the eleventh century an Italian named Anselm, who became archbishop of Canterbury, wrote a treatise called *Cur Deus Homo?*—"Why Did God Become Man?"—giving reasoned explanations to show why God had taken human form to save mankind.[5] Soon afterward Abelard, who taught at Paris, wrote his *Sic et Non*—"Yes and No" or "Pro and Con"—a collection of inconsistent statements made by St. Augustine and other Fathers of the Church. Abelard's purpose was to apply logic to the inherited mass of patristic writings, show wherein the truth of Christian doctrine really lay, and so make the faith consistent with reason and reflection.

Meanwhile, in the twelfth century a great stream of new knowledge poured into Europe, bringing about a veritable intellectual revolution. It was derived from the Arabs, with whom Christians were in contact in Sicily and Spain. The Arabs, as has been seen, had taken over the ancient Greek science, translated Greek writings into Arabic, and in many ways added further refinements of their own. Bilingual Christians (assisted by numerous learned Jews who passed readily between the Christian and Muslim worlds) translated these works into Latin. Above all, they translated Aristotle, the great codifier of Greek knowledge who had lived and written in the fourth century B.C. The Europeans, barely emerging from barbarism, were overwhelmed by this sudden disclosure of an undreamed of universe of knowledge. Aristotle became The Philosopher, the unparalleled authority on all branches of knowledge other than religious.

The great problem for Europeans was how to digest the gigantic bulk of Aristotle, or, in more general terms, how to assimilate or reconcile the body of Greek and Arabic learning to the Christian faith. The universities, with their "scholastic" philosophers or "schoolmen," performed this useful social function. Most eminent of scholastics was Thomas Aquinas (1225–1274), the Angelic

---

[5] It may be useful to note that the Latin *homo* refers to all members of the human race, male and female, children and adults, the word for an adult male being *vir*. In English "man" is often used in both senses. Thus in modern biology and anthropology all members of the genus *homo*, of which *homo sapiens* is the only living species, are "man." In the present book the use of "man" in this generic sense will occur from time to time. In such contexts the pronouns "he," "his," and "him" are of indeterminate gender.

THE MEETING OF ST. ANTHONY AND ST. PAUL
by Sassetta (Italian, 1392–1450)

Here we can see something of the medieval way of thinking. The picture tells a religious story. St. Anthony appears in three places, walking alone, converting a centaur, and meeting and embracing St. Paul. There is no attempt to present him as a unique individual person; his head and features disappear behind those of St. Paul in the principal scene. The picture gives the "idea" of the story. The two figures are typical saints, with the halos which conventionally designated sacred persons. The artist has painted the "idea" or "essence" of a forest, i.e., many trees; he has not shown the actual appearance of a particular forest, with underbrush, shadows, trees of different sizes, and foliage of different kinds. His hills are hills in general, i.e., mounds of earth; his cave is a cave in general, i.e., a dark hole. When the two saints embrace, their arms and legs are placed where the mind knows that they ought to be, not where the eye would see them concretely in any particular situation. The picture thus illustrates, on a simple level, what is meant by the abstractness or "realism" (the realism of ideas) of medieval thought. A child today, or an artistically untrained adult, draws in the same way, portraying the idea rather than the physical actuality. The idea of a forest is, after all, "many trees"; all else is special or incidental, not of the essence. Courtesy of the National Gallery of Art, Washington, D.C., Samuel H. Kress Collection.

Doctor, known also to his own contemporaries as the Dumb Ox from the slow deliberation of his speech. His chief work, appropriately called the *Summa Theologica,* was a survey of all knowledge. The thought of Aquinas, as recently as 1879, was pronounced by Pope Leo XIII to be the foundation of official Catholic philosophy.

The chief accomplishment of Thomas Aquinas was his demonstration that faith and reason could not be in conflict. By reason he meant a severely logical method, with exact definition of words and concepts, deducing step by step what follows and must follow if certain premises are accepted. His philosophy is classified as a form of "realism." It holds, that is, that the general idea is more "real" than the particular—that "man" is more real than this or that man or woman, that "law" as such is more real and binding than this or that particular law. He derived his philosophy from what he took to be the nature of God, of man, of law, of reason, of beings in general. He taught a hierarchic view of the universe and of society, of which God was the apex, and in which all things and all men were subordinated to God in a descending order, each bound to fulfill the role set by its own place and nature. It was the emphasis on the superior reality of abstractions that enabled men in the Middle Ages to believe steadfastly in the church while freely attacking individual churchmen, to have faith in the papacy while denouncing the popes as scoundrels—or to accept without difficulty the mystery of transubstantiation, which declared that what admittedly looked and tasted like bread and wine was, in real inner substance, the body of Christ.

The scholastic philosophy, as perfected by Thomas Aquinas, was not very favorable to the growth of natural science, because, in its emphasis on an inner reality, it drew attention away from the actual details and behavior of concrete things. On the other hand, the scholastic philosophy laid foundations on which later European thought was to be reared. It habituated Europeans to great exactness, to careful distinctions, even to the splitting of hairs. It called for disciplined thinking. And it made the world safe for reason. If any historical generalization may be made safely, it may be safely said that any society that believes reason to threaten its foundations will suppress reason. In Thomas' time, there were some who said that Aristotle and the Arabs were infidels, dangerous influences that must be silenced. Any reasoning about the faith, they warned, was a form of weakness. Thomas' doctrine that faith could not be endangered by reason gave a freedom to thinkers to go on thinking. Here Latin Christendom may be contrasted with the Muslim world. It was ruled, in about the time of Thomas Aquinas, that valid interpretation of the Koran had ended with the Four Great Doctors of early Islam. As Muslims said, the Gate was closed. Arabic thought, so brilliant for several centuries, went into decline.

The Crusades; New Invasions; Europe by 1300

Meanwhile, the West was expanding. Europe in the eleventh century took the offensive against Islam. All Latin Christendom went on the Crusades. War itself was subordinated to the purposes of religion.

The most ambitious, best remembered, and least successful of such expeditions were the Crusades to win back the Holy Land. The First Crusade was preached in 1095 by Pope Urban II, who hoped thereby to advance the peace of God by draining off bellicose nobles to fight the infidels, and to build up the leadership of Rome, just asserted by Gregory VII, through raising a universal cause of which the pope might be the head. Crusades to the Holy Land, with varying success, and sometimes departing woefully from their religious aims, went on intermittently for two hundred years. It was the growth of Italian shipping in the Mediterranean, the rise of more orderly feudal monarchies, the increasing sense of a Europe-wide common purpose, that made possible the assembly and transport of considerable forces over a great distance. It is sometimes said that the Crusades, by bringing contacts with the East, stimulated the development of civilization in the West, but it seems more likely that, as Europe's counterthrust against Islam, the Crusades were the consequence of Europe's own growing strength. For a century the Latin Christians occupied parts of Palestine and Syria. But in the thirteenth century they had to withdraw, and the Muslims remained in possession.

Other crusades (for such they were) had more lasting results. A party of Normans won Sicily from the Arabs about 1100. Iberian Christians, descending from the mountains of northern Spain, carried on a *reconquista* of two centuries against the Moors. By 1250 they had staked out the Christian kingdoms of Portugal, León, Castile, Aragon, and Valencia, leaving the Muslims only Granada in the extreme south, which was conquered much later, in 1492. In southern France, an Albigensian crusade in the thirteenth century put down the heretics, those born in the faith but erring from it. Against remaining European heathen, those born in ignorance of the faith, of whom a few were still found along the Baltic coast, crusading expeditions were also launched. The Teutonic Order, a military-religious society of knights founded originally to fight in the Holy Land, transferred its operations to the north. Christianity, and with it the civilization of the Latin West, was brought by the sword to primitive Prussia and the east Baltic regions.

About the year 1250 there developed a new threat of invasion from Asia. As the Huns had burst out of Asia in the fifth century, and the Magyars in the ninth, so now the Tartars appeared in the thirteenth century, to be followed in the fourteenth by the Ottoman Turks. We shall see how the Turks long continued to press upon central Europe. But, on the whole, by the thirteenth century, Europe was capable of resistance. Always until then it had lain open, an outlying, backward, thinly populated protuberance from the Eurasian land mass. It had lain open in the remote past to wandering Indo-Europeans, then to Roman imperial conquerors, to Germanic barbarians, to Huns, Magyars, and, in part, the Arabs. All these were assimilated. The blood of all flowed in European veins. In spirit all were assimilated by the Roman church, the Latin language, the common institutions of feudalism, monarchy, a free town life, parliamentary assemblies, and scholastic learning, which ran as an almost seamless web from England to Sicily and from Portugal to Poland.

By 1300 the "rise of Europe" was an accomplished fact. The third of the three segments into which the Greco-Roman world had divided, the one which in A.D. 700 had been the most barbarous, now some six hundred years later had a civilization of its own. It was still only one among the several great cultures of the world, such as the Islamic, Byzantine, Indian, and Chinese. It enjoyed no preeminence. The Chinese empire, for example, in the thirteenth century, had cities whose population reached into millions. It had an affluent merchant class,

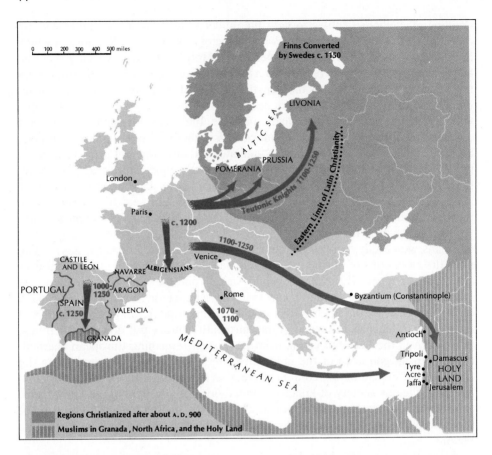

0 100 200 300 400 500 miles

Finns Converted
by Swedes c. 1150

LIVONIA

BALTIC SEA

PRUSSIA

POMERANIA

London

Paris

c. 1200

Teutonic Knights 1100–1250

Eastern Limit of Latin Christianity

1100–1250

Venice

CASTILE
AND LEÓN

NAVARRE ALBIGENSIANS

PORTUGAL

1000–
1250 ARAGON

Rome

Byzantium (Constantinople)

SPAIN

c. 1250

VALENCIA

1070–
1100

GRANADA

MEDITERRANEAN SEA

Antioch

Tripoli   Damascus
Tyre   HOLY
Acre   LAND
Jaffa   Jerusalem

▓ Regions Christianized after about A.D. 900
▒ Muslims in Granada, North Africa, and the Holy Land

CRUSADING ACTIVITY, 1100–1250

Medieval Christendom expanded geographically until about A.D. 1250. Darker regions are those Christianized shortly before and after A.D. 1000. Arrows indicate organized military-religious expeditions, which by 1250 had recovered most of Spain from Muslim control, but had failed to do so in the Holy Land. Dates are rounded and very rough.

great textile manufacturers, and an iron industry that produced over 100,000 tons a year. The arts and sciences were assiduously pursued. Government was centralized and complex; it issued paper money, and employed a civil service recruited by competitive examinations. Books on religious, technical, and agricultural subjects, including whole multivolume encyclopedias, were printed in enormous numbers, even though the lack of an alphabet and use of thousands of characters made it difficult for literacy to become widely spread. The Venetian Marco Polo was dazzled by the China that he lived in from 1275 to 1292.

Many have asked why China did not generate, as Europe did in these centuries, the forces that ultimately led to the modern scientific and industrial world. One answer is suggested by the fact that it was Europeans like Marco Polo who went to China, not Chinese who went to Europe. It was the Chinese who invented printing, but it was Europe that was revolutionized by printed books. The Chinese knew of gunpowder, but the Europeans developed more effective guns. Chinese merchant vessels traded with India in the twelfth century, but did not pursue the advantage; Europeans did so three centuries later, and they also discovered America. Somehow Europe was more enterprising and restless. It was already on the alert for something new. In Europe there was no all-embracing empire as in China, but kings, lords, and towns that competed with each other. Conformity was not one of the primary virtues. With religion and the church kept distinct from the state, the questions of what one should do with one's life were less dependent on the political powers than in China. Europe was disorderly and full of conflict—rivalries and wars between kings, quarrels between kings and their barons, disputes between church and state, clashes between lords and their peasant workers. In such disorder there was also a kind of freedom, and a dynamism which promoted change.

II.
THE UPHEAVAL IN CHRISTENDOM, 1300–1560

IN THE TRANSITION from a traditional to a more modern form of society all the old civilizations have had to reexamine their religious base. Today we can observe this process at work everywhere: the Chinese reconsider the age-old teachings of Confucius, the Muslims enter into wider activities than those known to the Koran, and the peoples of India attempt to found a society in which historic Hindu practices no longer form the dominant pattern. It is not necessarily that peoples reject their ancestral religion. They may even reaffirm it, but they try also to modernize it, to adapt it, to make room for new and nonreligious interests. The process of developing a variety of activities outside the sphere of religion is called "secularization."

Latin Christendom was the first of the world's major civilizations to become "secularized." In the very long run it was those aspects of European civilization that were least associated with Christianity, such as natural science and industrial technology, or military and economic power, that the "non-European" world from Islam to East Asia proved to be most willing to adopt. If in our own time there has come to be such a thing as a world civilization, it is because all the world's great traditional cultures have been increasingly secularized.

The Europe which by the thirteenth century was so triumphantly Christian soon entered upon a series of disasters. The Mongols after about 1240 held Russia in subjugation for two hundred years. The Ottoman Turks, who had originated in central Asia, penetrated the Byzantine Empire, crushed the medieval Serbian kingdom at the battle of Kosovo in 1389, and spread over the Balkans. They took

Chapter Emblem: A medal struck in honor of Pico della Mirandola, Florentine humanist of the fifteenth century.

Constantinople itself in 1453. Eastern Christianity continued to exist, but under alien political domination. Latin Christianity, reaching from Poland and Hungary to the Atlantic, remained independent but was beset with troubles. The authority of the papacy and of the Roman Catholic church was called into question. Eventually the Protestant churches emerged. The whole of medieval civilization was undermined. Yet new forces also asserted themselves, alongside or outside the religious tradition. Government, law, philosophy, science, the arts, material and economic activities were pursued with less regard for Christian values. Power, order, beauty, wealth, knowledge, and control of nature were regarded as desirable in themselves.

In this mixture of decline and revival, of religious revolution and secularization, medieval Christendom began to take on the outlines of modern Europe.

5. Disasters of the Fourteenth Century

The Black Death and Its Consequences

During the fourteenth century, and quite abruptly, almost half the population of Europe was wiped out. Some died in sporadic local famines that began to appear after 1300. The great killer, however, was the bubonic plague, or Black Death, which first struck Europe in 1348. Since the plague recurred at irregular and unpredictable intervals, and killed off the young as well as the old, it disrupted marriage and family life and made it impossible for many years for Europe to regain the former level of population. In some places whole villages disappeared. Cultivated fields were abandoned for want of able-bodied men and women to work them. The towns were especially vulnerable, since the plague bacillus was carried by rats, which infested the dark houses crowded within town walls. Trade and exchange were obstructed; prices, wages, and incomes moved erratically; famine made its victims more susceptible to disease, and deaths from the plague contributed to famine. The living were preoccupied with the burial of the dead and with fears for their own future.

There were immediate social and political repercussions. For the survivors, at least, there were some advantages in that labor became scarce and so could expect higher wages. On the other hand, in the general disorganization, and with landowners and urban employers decimated also, many of the poor could find no work, or took to vagabondage and begging. The upper classes, acting through governments, attempted to control wages and prices, as in the English Statute of Laborers of 1351. Rebellions of workers broke out in various towns, especially in Flanders. There were massive insurrections of peasants in many parts of Europe. In France these were called "jacqueries" (from "Jacques," a nickname for a peasant), of which the first was in 1358. In England a similar large-scale uprising in 1381 came to be known as Wat Tyler's rebellion. Sometimes the spokesmen for these movements went beyond their immediate grievances to question the whole class structure, asking why some should be rich and others poor. It was in Wat Tyler's rebellion that the famous couplet was coined:

> *When Adam delved and Eve span*
> *Who was then a gentleman?*

Governments and the upper classes replied to this menace with ferocious repression. The peasants generally returned to their usual labors. Yet something was gained for the rural workers, at least in the long run, as underlying economic and demographic forces continued to assert themselves. The landowners, or feudal class, in order to get the work done on their manors, and assure their own incomes, had to offer more favorable terms. These included, for example, the giving of lifetime tenures to peasant families, in return for fixed payment of sums of money. Over the years many of these peasant holdings became hereditary and the value of money decreased, so that payment of a shilling, for example, which in 1400 represented a significant amount, became much less burdensome for the

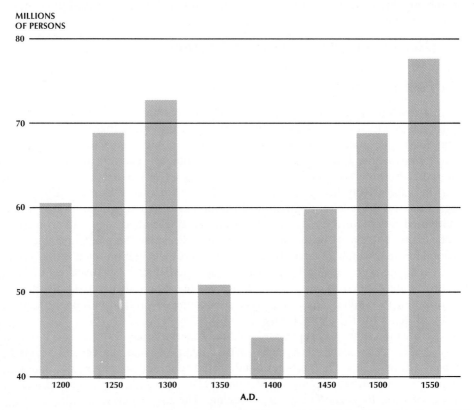

Source: M. K. Bennett, *The World's Food* (New York: Harper, 1954).

rural worker by 1600. In effect, a class of small peasant property owners began to emerge in much of Europe.

The kings also, who had been building up their position against the church and the feudal lords since the eleventh century, found their problems complicated by the disasters of the fourteenth. They still had their governments to maintain, and their ambitions to satisfy, even if death removed large fractions of their subjects. They even had to increase their incomes, as it became usual for kings to employ royal armies of foot soldiers against the recurring possibility of feudal resistance. Various means of increasing the royal spending power were devised. Currency was debased; that is, the king ordered a given weight of gold or silver to represent a larger number of monetary units. Thus he temporarily had more money, but the result was inflation and higher prices, that is, the declining value of money already mentioned. New taxes were introduced. About 1300 the kings of both England and France undertook to tax the clergy of their respective kingdoms, in both of which the clergy were substantial owners of land. The impact on the church was violent and dramatic, as will shortly be seen. The kings made increasing demands as well on great noble landholders and urban merchants. These demands were resisted, or made subject to bargains by the representative bodies whose origin was described in the last chapter, so that the fourteenth century, and still more the fifteenth, has been called the "golden age" of the medieval parliaments.

In 1337 the Hundred Years' War began between England and France. The battles all took place in France, which was internally divided, some parts, like Aquitaine, having long belonged to the English crown. France was ravaged by marauding bands of English soldiers and their French adherents, until it began to recover in the days of Joan of Arc, who was burned at Rouen in 1431. In England the effects of the long and intermittent war were less divisive. As English soldiers with their longbows defeated the mounted French knights, a kind of popular patriotism arose in England. Parliament widened its powers as the kings needed money for their campaigns. But the great barons also became more unruly. They deposed Richard II in 1399, then quarreled among themselves, in a confusion punctuated by invasion from Scotland and revolt in Wales. Disorder became worse in the fifteenth century. Dukes and earls and their followers formed private armies and fought with each other; they defied the royal law courts and intimidated juries, used Parliament and government for their own purposes, and exploited their peasants. In 1450 a movement known as Jack Cade's rebellion called for reform without success. From then until 1485 England was beset by the upper-class turmoil of the Wars of the Roses.

Troubles of the Medieval Church

Meanwhile similar calamities afflicted the church. In 1300, the church of the High Middle Ages, centralized in the papacy, stood at its zenith. But the church was weakened by its very successes. It faced the danger that besets every successful institution—a form of government or a university, to choose modern examples—the danger of believing that the institution exists for the benefit of those who conduct its affairs. The papacy, being at the top, was the most liable to this danger. It became "corrupt," set in its ways, out of touch with public opinion, and controlled by a self-perpetuating bureaucracy. It was unable to reform itself, and unwilling to let anyone else reform it.

Both Edward I of England and Philip the Fair of France, in the 1290s, assessed taxes on the landed estates belonging to the great abbeys, bishoprics, and other components of the church. The pope, Boniface VIII, prohibited the taxation of clergy by the civil ruler. In the ensuing altercation, in 1302, he issued the famous bull, *Unam Sanctam,* the most extreme of all assertions of papal supremacy, which declared that outside the Roman church there was no salvation, and that "every human creature" was "subject to the Roman pontiff."[1] The French king retorted by sending soldiers to arrest Boniface, who soon died. French influence in the College of Cardinals brought about the election of a pope who was subservient to Philip, and who took up his residence, with his court and officials, at Avignon on the lower Rhone river, on the then borders of France. Thus began the "Babylonian Captivity" of the church. The rest of Europe regarded the popes at Avignon throughout the century as tools of France. The prestige of the papacy as a universal institution was badly dimmed.

Attempts to correct the situation made matters worse. In 1378 the College of Cardinals, torn by French and anti-French factions within it, elected two popes. Both were equally legitimate, being chosen by cardinals, but one lived at Rome, one at Avignon, and neither would resign. The French and their supporters recognized the Avignon pope, England and most of Germany, the Roman. For forty years both lines were perpetuated. There were now two papacies, estranged by the Great Schism of the West.

Never had the papacy been so externally magnificent as in the days of the Captivity and the Schism. The papal court at Avignon surpassed the courts of kings in splendor. The papal officialdom grew in numbers, ignoring the deeper problems while busily transacting each day's business. Papal revenues mounted, and new papal taxes were devised, for example, the "annates," by which every bishop or abbot in Christendom had to transmit to Rome most of the first year's income of his office. In the continuing movement of funds from all over Europe to the papal court, from the thirteenth century on, a new class of international bankers rose and prospered.

But the papacy, never so sumptuous, had never since the tenth century rested on such shaky foundations. People pay willingly for institutions in which they believe, and admire magnificence in leaders whom they respect. But before 1378, with the pope submissive to France, and after 1378, with two popes and two papacies to support, there was growing complaint at the extravagance and worldliness of papal rule. It must be remembered that all this happened in a Europe traumatized by the plague, and with a declining number of people expected to bear increasing burdens. The most pious Christians were the most shocked. To them the behavior of the cardinals was disgraceful. Earnest souls were worried in conscience. They recognized the vital necessity of obtaining God's grace, but with two churches under two popes, each claiming to hold the keys of Peter, how could anyone be certain that his church gave true salvation? In a society that was

---

[1] Bulls are known by their first one or two Latin words, which in this case mean "one holy (Catholic church)"; a "bull," while the most solemn form of papal edict, does not as such embody a dogma; and it is not Catholic practice today to affirm this policy of Boniface VIII.

still primarily a religious community, this sense of religious insecurity was a source of uneasiness and dread.

The old moorings were weakened, the wrath of God seemed to be raining upon mankind, and no one had the slightest notion of how the world was going to turn out. Symptoms of mass neurosis appeared. Some people sought refuge in a hectic merriment or luxury and self-indulgence. Others became preoccupied with grisly subjects. Some frantically performed the Dance of Death in the cemeteries, while others furtively celebrated the Black Mass, parodying religion in a mad desire to appease the devil. The Order of Flagellants grew up; its members went through the streets, two by two, beating each other with chains and whips. It was at this time that the great witchcraft delusion, which was to reach its height in the fifteenth and sixteenth centuries, first became important.

Disaffection with the church, or the thought that it might not be the true or the only way to salvation, spread in all ranks of society. It was not only kings who disputed the claims of the clergy. Obscure parish priests, close to the distress of ordinary people, began to doubt the powers of their ecclesiastical superiors. One of these humble clerics was William Langland, who in his *Piers Plowman,* in the 1360s, contrasted the sufferings of the honest poor with the hypocrisy and corruption in high places. Such unsettling ideas spread very widely; in England those who held them were known as Lollards. Since the actual poor left no records, it is hard to say exactly what their ideas consisted of, but something like them was also expressed by John Wyclif, who taught at Oxford. About 1380, Wyclif was saying that the true church could do without elaborate possessions, and even that an organized church might not be necessary for salvation, since ordinary, devout persons could do without priests and obtain salvation by reading the Bible, which he translated into English. Similar ideas appeared in Bohemia in central Europe, with John Huss as their spokesman. Here they became a national movement, for the Hussites were both a religious party and at the same time a Slavic or Czech party protesting against the supremacy of the Germans who lived in Bohemia. The Hussite wars ravaged central Europe for decades in the fifteenth century. The ideas of the Lollards and of Huss and Wyclif were branded as heresy, or unacceptable deviations from the true doctrine of the church.

Influential and established persons did not yet turn to heresy, and still less to witchcraft or flagellation. Their answer to the needs of the day was to assemble a great Europe-wide or general council of the church, in which reforms could be pressed by the whole body of Christians upon the reluctant and rival popes.

The Conciliar Movement

In 1409 such a church council met at Pisa. All parts of the Latin West were represented. The council declared both reigning popes deposed, and obtained the due election of another, but since the first two refused to resign there were now three. In 1414 an even greater and more fully attended council met at Constance. Its aims were three: to end the now threefold schism, to extirpate heresy, and to reform the church "in head and members," or from top to bottom. Not much was accomplished in reform. To discourage heresy, John Huss was interrogated, condemned, and burned at the stake. The schism was ended. All three popes were at last persuaded or compelled to withdraw, and another, Martin V, was elected. The unity of the church, under the papacy, was at last restored.

The majority of the Council of Constance wished to make general councils part of the permanent apparatus of the church for all time in the future. They regarded the pope as, so to speak, a constitutional monarch, and the council as a representative body for all Christians. Martin V, however, no sooner elected pope, reaffirmed the prerogatives of the papal office. He dissolved the Council of Constance, and repudiated its decrees. The next thirty years saw a continuing contest of wills between successive popes and successive councils.

In this battle for jurisdiction few reforms could be adopted, and fewer still enforced. Increasingly the life of the church was corrupted by money. No one believed in bribery; but everyone knew that many high churchmen (like many high civil officials of the day) could be bribed. To buy or sell a church office was a crime in the canon law, known as "simony," but it was a crime which in the fifteenth century could not be suppressed. For churchmen to live with mistresses was considered understandable, if unseemly; the standards of laymen in such matters were not high; but for a bishop or other ecclesiastic to give lucrative church positions to his own children (or other relatives) was the abuse known as nepotism, and it, too, could not be eradicated. To sell divine grace for money, all agreed, was not only wrong but impossible. But in 1300 Boniface VIII had given encouragement to the practice of "indulgences." A person, if properly confessed, absolved, and truly repentant, might, by obtaining an indulgence, be spared certain of the temporal punishments of purgatory. One obtained such an indulgence, almost always, in return for a donation of money. The practice proved to be a fatally easy method of fund raising, despite complaints against the sale of indulgences.

Gradually the popes prevailed over the councils. The conciliar movement was greatly weakened for Christendom as a whole when the powerful French element secured its aims by a local national arrangement. In the Pragmatic Sanction of Bourges, in 1438, the Gallican (or French) church affirmed the supremacy of councils over popes, declared its administrative independence from the Holy See, suppressed the payment of annates to Rome, and forbade papal intervention in the appointment of French prelates. The papacy thus lost influence in France, but the conciliarists themselves were divided. In 1449, with the dissolution of the Council of Basel, the conciliar movement came to an end. In 1450 a great Jubilee was held to celebrate the papal triumph.

The papacy, its prestige and freedom of action thus secured, now passed into the hands of a series of cultivated gentlemen, men of the world, men of "modern" outlook in tune with their times—the famous popes of the Renaissance. Some, like Nicholas V (1447–1455) or Pius II (1458–1464), were accomplished scholars and connoisseurs of books. Some were like Innocent VIII (1484–1492), a pleasant man who was the first pope to dine in public with ladies. Alexander VI (1492–1503), of the Spanish Borgia family, exploited his office for the benefit of his relatives, trying to make his son Cesare Borgia the ruler of all Italy, while his daughter, Lucretia Borgia, gathered literary men and artists about her, and developed a perhaps exaggerated reputation for depravity. Alexander VI's successor, Julius II (1503–1513), was a capable general, and Leo X (1513–1521) was a superb patron of architects and painters. But we must now describe the

Italian Renaissance, in which worthies of this kind were elevated to the Holy See.

6. The Renaissance in Italy

In Italy in the fifteenth century, and especially at Florence, we observe not merely a decay of medieval certainties but the appearance of a new and constructive attitude toward the world. The Renaissance, a French word meaning "rebirth," first received its name from those who thought of the Middle Ages as a dark time from which the human spirit had to be awakened. It was called a *re*birth in the belief that men now, after a long interruption, took up and resumed a civilization like that of the Greco-Romans. Medieval people had thought of the times of Aristotle or Cicero as not sharply distinct from their own. In the Renaissance, with a new historical sense, arose the conception of "modern" and "ancient" times, separated by a long period with a different life style and appropriately called the Middle Ages.

A few useful distinctions can be made. The basic institutions of Europe, the very languages and nationalities, the great frameworks of collective action in law, government, and economic production, all originated in the Middle Ages. But the Renaissance marked a new era in thought and feeling, by which Europe and its institutions were in the long run to be transformed. The origins of modern natural science can be traced more to the medieval universities than to the Renaissance thinkers. But it was in the Italy of the Quattrocento (as Italians call the fifteenth century) that other fields of thought and expression were first cultivated. The Italian influence in other countries, in these respects, remained very strong for at least 200 years. It pertained to high culture, and hence to a limited number of persons, but extended over the whole area represented by literature and the arts—literature meaning all kinds of writing, and the arts including all products of human skill. The effects of the Italian Renaissance, though much modified with the passage of time, were evident in the books and art galleries of Europe and America, and in the architecture of their cities, until the revolution of "modern" art in the early twentieth century. They involved the whole area of culture which is neither theological nor scientific but concerns essentially moral and civic questions, asking what man ought to be or ought to do, and is reflected in matters of taste, style, propriety, decorum, personal character, and education. In particular, it was in Renaissance Italy that an almost purely secular attitude first appeared, in which life was no longer seen by leading thinkers as a brief preparation for the hereafter.

The Italian Cities and the New Conception of Life

The towns of Italy, so long as trade converged in the Mediterranean, were the biggest and most bustling of all the towns that rose in Europe in the Middle Ages. The crafts of Italy included many refined trades such as those of the goldsmith or stonecarver, which were so zealously pursued that artisanship turned into art, and a delight in the beautiful became common among all classes. Merchants made fortunes in commerce; they lent their money to popes or princes, and so made further fortunes as bankers. They bought the wares of the craftsmen-artists. They rejoiced, not so much in money or the making of money, as in the beautiful things and psychological satisfactions that money could buy; and if they forgot the things that money could not buy, this is only to say again that their outlook was "secular."

The towns were independent city-states. There was no king to build up a government for Italy as a whole, and for several generations the popes were either absent at Avignon or engaged in disputes arising from the Great Schism, so that the influence of Rome was unimportant. The merchant oligarchies, each in its own city, enjoyed an unhampered stage on which to pursue interests other than those of business. In some, as at Milan, they succumbed to or worked with a local prince or despot. In others, as at Florence, Venice, and Genoa, they continued to govern themselves as republics. They had the experience of contending for public office, of suppressing popular revolt or winning popular favor, of producing works of public munificence, of making alliances, hiring armies, outwitting rivals, and conducting affairs of state. In short, Italy offered an environment in which many facets of human personality could be developed.

All this was most especially true in Florence, the chief city of Tuscany. In the fifteenth century it had a population of about 60,000, which made it only moderately large as Italian cities went.[2] Yet, like ancient Athens, Florence produced an extraordinary sequence of gifted men in a short period. From the days of Dante, Petrarch, and Boccaccio, who all died before 1375, to those of Machiavelli, who lived until 1527, an amazing number of the leading figures of the Italian Renaissance were Florentines. Like Athens also, Florence lost its republican liberty as well as its creative powers. Its history can be summarized in that of the Medici family. The founder of the family fortunes was Giovanni (d. 1429), a merchant and banker of Florence. His son, Cosimo de' Medici (1389–1464), allying himself with the popular element against some of the leading families of the republic, soon became unofficial ruler himself. Cosimo's grandson, Lorenzo the Magnificent (1449–1492), also used his great wealth to govern but is chiefly remembered as a poet, connoisseur, and lavish benefactor of art and learning. In the next century Tuscany became a grand duchy, of which the Medici were hereditary grand dukes until the family died out in 1737. Thus established, they furnished numerous cardinals and two popes to the church, and two Medici women became queens of France.

What arose in Italy, in these surroundings, was no less than a new conception of life. The world was so exciting that another world need not be kept in mind. It seemed very doubtful whether a quiet, cloistered, or celibate life was on a higher plane than an active gregarious life, or family life, or even a life of promiscuity and adventure. It was hard to believe that clergy were any better than laity, or that life led to a stern divine judgment in the end. That human will and intelligence might prove misleading seemed a gloomy doctrine. That man was a frail creature, in need of God's grace and salvation, though perhaps said with the lips, was not felt in the heart. Instead, what captivated the Italians of the Renaissance was a sense of the vast range of human powers.

Formerly, the ideal had been seen in renunciation, in a certain disdain for the

[2] See the picture essay, pp. 95–105.

concerns of this world. Now a life of involvement was also prized. Formerly, poverty had been greatly respected, at least in Christian doctrine. Now voices were heard in praise of a proper enjoyment of wealth. In the past, men had admired a life of contemplation, or meditative withdrawal. Now the humanist Leonardo Bruni could write, in 1433, "The whole glory of man lies in activity." Often, to be sure, the two attitudes existed in the same person. Sometimes they divided different groups within the same city. As always, the old persisted along with the new. The result might be psychological stress and civil conflict.

The new esteem for human activity took both a social and an individualistic turn. In cities maintaining their republican forms, as at Florence in the early fifteenth century, a new civic consciousness or sense of public duty was expressed. For this purpose the writings of Cicero and other ancients were found to be highly relevant, since they provided an ethics independent of the Christian and medieval tradition. There was also a kind of cult of the great individual, hardly known to the ancients, and one which gave little attention to collective responsibility. Renaissance individualism put its emphasis on outstanding attainments. The great individual shaped his own destiny in a world governed by fortune. He had *virtù*, the quality of being a man (*vir*, "man"), and although women might also exhibit *virtù*, it was a quality which in the society of the day was more to be expected in the most aggressive adult males. It meant the successful demonstration of human powers. A man of *virtù*, in the arts, in war, or in statecraft, was a man who knew what he was doing, who, from resources within himself, made the best use of his opportunities, hewing his way through the world, and excelling in all that he did. For the arts, such a spirit is preserved in the autobiography of Benvenuto Cellini.

The growing preoccupation with things human can be traced in new forms of painting, sculpture, and architecture that arose in Italy at this time. These arts likewise reflected an increasing this-worldliness, a new sense of reality and a new sense of space, of a kind different from that of the Middle Ages, and which was to underlie European thinking almost to our own time. Space was no longer indeterminate, unknowable, or divine; it was a zone occupied by physical human beings, or one in which human beings might at least imagine themselves moving about. Reality meant visible and tangible persons or objects in this space, "objective" in the sense that they looked or felt the same to all normal persons who perceived them. It was a function of the arts to convey this reality, however idealized or suffused by the artist's individual feeling, in such a way that observers could recognize in the image the identity of the thing portrayed.

Architecture reflected the new tendencies. Though the Gothic cathedral at Milan was built as late as 1386, at Florence and elsewhere architects preferred to adapt Greco-Roman principles of design, such as symmetrical arrangements of doors and windows, the classical column, the arch and the dome. More public buildings of a nonreligious character were built, and more substantial town houses were put up by wealthy merchants, in style meant to represent grandeur, or civic importance, or availability and convenience for human use. Gardens and terraces were added to many such buildings.

Sculpture, confined in the Middle Ages to the niches and portals of cathedrals, now emerged as an independent and free-standing art. Its favored subjects were human beings, now presented so that the viewer could walk around the object and see it from all directions, thus bringing it securely into his own world. The difference from the religious figures carved on medieval churches was very great. Like the architects, the sculptors in parting from the immediate past found much in the Greek and Roman tradition that was modern and useful to their purpose. They produced portrait busts of eminent contemporaries, or figures of great leaders sometimes on horseback, or statues depicting characters from Greco-Roman history and mythology. The use of the nude, in mythological or allegorical subjects, likewise showed a conception of humanity that was more in keeping with the Greek than with the Christian tradition.

Painting was less influenced by the ancients, since the little of ancient painting that had survived was unknown during the Renaissance. The invention of painting in oils opened new pathways for the art. Merchants, ecclesiastics, and princes provided a mounting demand. In subject matter painting remained conservative, dealing most often with religious themes. It was the conception and presentation that were new. The new feeling for space became evident. With the discovery of the mathematics of perspective, space was presented in exact relation to the beholder's eye. The viewer, in a sense, entered into the world of the painting. A three-dimensional effect was achieved, with careful representation of distance through variation of size, and techniques of shading or chiaroscuro added to the illusion of physical volume. Human figures were often placed in a setting of painted architecture, or against a background of landscape or scenery, showing castles or hills, which though supposedly far away yet closed in the composition with a knowable boundary. In such a painting everything was localized in place and time; a part of the real world was caught and put in the picture. The idea was not to suggest eternity, as in earlier religious painting, nor yet to express private fantasy or the workings of the unconscious, as sometimes in "postmodern" art, but to present a familiar theme in an understandable setting, often with a narrative content, that is, by the telling of a story.

Painters were able also, like the sculptors, by a close study of human anatomy, to show people in distinctive and living attitudes. Faces took on more expression; individual personality was depicted. Differences among men were shown, not merely abstract characteristics that all men or certain kinds of men, such as kings or saints, had in common. Painting became less symbolic, less an intimation of general truths, more a portrayal of concrete realities as they met the eye. In the portrait by Bellini of a *condottiere* the reader can see for himself, though who the man was is not known, how a strong, real, and vivid personality looks out from the canvas.[3] Similarly, the great religious paintings were peopled with human beings. In Leonardo da Vinci's *Last Supper* Christ and his disciples are seen as a group of men each with his own characteristics. Raphael's Madonnas seem to be young Italian women, and in the mighty figures of Michelangelo the attributes of humanity invade heaven itself.

There were always countercurrents that make such generalizations debatable. The main tone of the arts in Renaissance Italy was to take satisfaction in beauty, to present the world as desirable, to be clear-cut, lucid, and finite. But many Florentines were troubled by the worldliness and even paganism that had grown up about them. Their anxieties were expressed in a movement for religious

[3] See p. 64.

reforms led by the priest Savonarola. As it ran its course it became involved in political questions, until Savonarola was tried and burned at the stake in 1498.

Humanism: The Birth of "Literature"

The literary movement in Renaissance Italy is called humanism because of the rising interest in humane letters, *litterae humaniores*. There had indeed been much writing in the later Middle Ages. Much of it had been of a technical character, as in theology, philosophy, or law; some of it had been meant to convey information, as in chronicles, histories, and cosmographical descriptions of the world. Great hymns had been composed, lively student songs had been heard at the universities, plays had been performed in cathedrals, the old legends of King Arthur and Roland had been written down, and occasionally a monk would try his hand at a long narrative poem. Yet it is hardly too much to say that literature, in the modern sense, first appeared in the fourteenth and fifteenth centuries in Italy. There came to be a class of men who looked upon writing as their main life's work, who wrote for each other and for a somewhat larger public, and who used writing to deal with general questions, or to examine their own states of mind, or resolve their own difficulties, or used words to achieve artistic effects, or simply to please and amuse their readers.

The Italian humanists, like their predecessors, wrote a good deal in Latin. They differed from earlier literate persons in that they were not, for the most part, members of the clergy. They complained that Latin had become monkish, barbaric, and "scholastic," a jargon of the schools and universities, and they greatly preferred the classic style of a Cicero or a Livy. In all this there was much that was unfair, much that was merely literary, and something that anticipated the famous twentieth-century problem of the "two cultures," or failure of understanding between persons of humanistic interests and those of more scientific concerns. Medieval Latin was a vigorous living language that used words in new senses, many of which have passed into English and the Romance languages as perfectly normal expressions. Yet in the ancient writers the humanists found qualities that medieval writing did not have. They discovered a new range of interests, a new sensibility, discussion of political and civic questions, a world presented without the overarching framework of religious belief. In addition, the Greeks and Romans unquestionably had style—a sense of form, a taste for the elegant and the epigrammatic. They had often also written for practical ends, in dialogues, orations, or treatises that were designed for purposes of persuasion.

If the humanists therefore made a cult of antiquity it was because they saw kindred spirits in it. They sensed a relevancy for their own time. The classical influence, never wholly absent in the Middle Ages, now reentered as a main force in the higher civilization of Europe. The humanists polished their Latin, and increasingly they learned Greek. They made assiduous searches for classical texts hitherto unknown. Many were found; they had of course been copied and preserved by the monks of preceding times.

But while an especial dignity attached to writing in Latin, known throughout Europe, most of the humanists wrote in Italian also. Or rather, they used the mode of speech current in Florence. This had also been the language of Dante in the *Divine Comedy*. To this vast poem the humanists now added many writings in Florentine or Tuscan prose. The result was that Florentine became the standard form of modern Italian. It was the first time that a European vernacular—that is, the common spoken tongue as opposed to Latin—became thus standardized amid the variety of its dialects and adapted in structure and vocabulary to the more complex requirements of a written language. French and English soon followed, and most of the other European languages somewhat later.

The Florentine exile, Francesco Petrarca, or Petrarch, has been called the first man of letters. The son of a merchant, he spent his life in travel throughout France and Italy. Trained for the law, and ordained to the clergy, he became a somewhat rootless critic of these two esteemed professions, which he denounced for their "scholasticism." He lived in the generation after Dante, dying in 1374, and he anticipated the more fully developed humanism that was to come. His voluminous writings show him to have been the prey of contrary attitudes. He was attracted by life, love, beauty, travel, and connections with men of importance in church and state; he could also spurn all these things as ephemeral and deceptive. He loved Cicero for his common sense and his commitment to political liberty; indeed, he discovered a manuscript of Cicero's letters in 1345. He loved St. Augustine for his otherworldly vision of the City of God. But in Cicero's writings he also found a deep religious concern, and in St. Augustine he esteemed the active man who had been a bishop, a writer heavily engaged in the controversies of his time, and one who taught that for true Christians the world is not evil.

Petrarch wrote sonnets in Italian, an epic in Latin, an introspective study of himself, and a great many letters which he clearly meant to be literary productions. He aspired to literary fame. In all this we see a new kind of writer, who uses language not merely as a practical tool but as a medium of more subtle expression, to commune with himself, to convey moods of discouragement or satisfaction, to clarify doubts, to improve his own understanding of the choices and options that life affords. With Petrarch, in short, literature became a kind of calling, and also a consideration of moral philosophy, still related but no longer subordinate to religion. It was moral philosophy in the widest sense, raising questions of how human beings should adjust to the world, what a good life could be or ought to be, or where the genuine and ultimate rewards of living were to be found.

Petrarch was an indication of things to come. Boccaccio, his contemporary and also a Florentine, wrote the *Decameron* in Italian, a series of tales designed both to entertain and to impart a certain wisdom about human character and behavior. They were followed by the main group of humanists, far more numerous but less well remembered. Men of letters began to take part in public life, to gather pupils and found schools, to serve as secretaries to governing bodies or princes, and even to occupy office themselves. Thus the humanist Coluccio Salutati became chancellor of Florence in 1375. During the following decades Florence was threatened by the expansive ambitions of Milan, where the princely despotism of the Visconti family had established itself. Against such dangers a new and intense civic consciousness asserted itself. Salutati, in addition to the usual duties of chancellor, served the state with his pen, glorifying Florentine liberty, identifying it with the liberties of ancient republican Rome before they were undermined by the Caesars. He was succeeded as chancellor by two other humanists, Bruni and Poggio. Bruni wrote a history of Florence which marked a new achievement in historical writing, when compared with the annals and chronicles of the Middle Ages. He saw the past as clearly past, different from but relevant to the present; and he introduced a new division of historical periods. On the model of such ancient writers as Livy, he adopted a flowing narrative form. And he used history for a practical political purpose, to show that Florence had a long tradition of liberty and possessed values and attainments worth fighting for against menacing neighbors. History took on a utility that it had had for the Greeks and Romans and was to retain in the future in Europe and eventually America: the function of heightening a sentiment, not yet of nationalism, but of collective civic consciousness or group identity. It was meant to arouse its readers to a life of commitment and participation.

All this literary activity was of a scholarly type, in which authors broadened their understanding as much by reading as by personal experience of the world. And scholarly activity, the habit of attending closely to what a page really said, had consequences that went beyond either pure literature or local patriotism. A new critical attitude developed. Bruni, in his history, showed a new sense of the need for authentic sources. Lorenzo Valla became one of the founders of textual criticism. Gaining a historical sense for the Latin language, he observed that its characteristic words and expressions varied from one time to another. He put this knowledge to the service of the king of Naples in a dispute with the pope. Valla showed, by analysis of the language used in the document, that the Donation of Constantine, on which the papacy then based its temporal claims, could not have been written in Constantine's time in the fourth century, and so was a forgery. Pico della Mirandola and others looked for aspects of truth not revealed in the Christian Scriptures. As men of letters, they put their faith in books, but as men of the Renaissance they were receptive to anything written by men anywhere. A group at the Academy of Florence took a serious interest in the study of Plato. The enthusiastic and very learned young Pico, at the age of twenty-three, in 1486, offered to expatiate publicly on all human knowledge in 900 theses, to be drawn from "the Chaldaic, Arabic, Hebrew, Grecian, Egyptian and Latin sages."

Schooling and Manners

While Italian humanism thus contributed much to literature and scholarship, to classical learning, and to the formation of modern national languages, it also had tangible and lasting effects in education. Here its impact remained in all regions of European civilization until the twentieth century. The medieval universities were essentially places for professional training in theology, medicine, and law. Except in England this continued to be their primary function. What came to be known as secondary education, the preparation of young men either for the universities or for "life," owes more to the Renaissance. The organized education of women came much later.

Medieval schooling had been chaotic and repetitious. Youngsters of all ages sat together with a teacher, each absorbing from the confusion whatever he could of Latin rules and vocabulary. The Renaissance launched the idea of putting different age groups or levels of accomplishment into separate classes, in separate rooms, each with its own teacher, with periodic promotion of the pupil from one level to the next. Latin remained the principal subject, with Greek now added. But many new purposes were seen in the study of Latin. It was intended to give skill in the use of language, including the pupil's native tongue. Rhetoric was the art of using language to influence others. It heightened communication. Knowledge alone was not enough, said the historian and chancellor Bruni, who also wrote a short work on education—"to make effectual use of what we know we must add the power of expression." Nor was Latin merely the necessary professional tool for the priest, the physician, the lawyer, or the government servant. The student learned Latin (and Greek) in order to read the ancient writings—epics, lyrics, orations, letters, histories, dialogues, and philosophical treatises—and these writings, especially at a time when the modern literatures were undeveloped, opened his horizons in all directions. They had a practical application; and at least as late as the American and French revolutions readers found useful lessons in the rise and decline of the Roman republic and the troubles of the Greek city-states. The classics were meant also to have a moral impact, to produce a balanced personality, and to form character. Not everyone could be important or gifted, said the humanist Vittorino, but we all face a life of "social duty," and "all are responsible for the personal influence which goes forth from us." These aims built themselves permanently into the educational system of modern Europe.

Young men were trained also for a more civilized deportment in everyday social living. Personal style in the upper classes became somewhat more studied. Hitherto Europeans had generally acted like big children; they spat, belched, and blew their noses without inhibition, snatched at food with their fingers, bawled at each other when aroused, or sulked when their feelings were offended. It was Italians of the Renaissance who first taught more polite habits. Books of etiquette began to appear, of which the most successful was Castiglione's *Book of the Courtier*. The "courtier" was ancestor to the "gentleman"; "courtesy" was originally the kind of behavior suited to princely courts.

The "courtier," according to Castiglione, should be a man of good birth but is chiefly the product of training. His education in youth, and his efforts in mature years, should be directed toward mixing agreeably in the company of his equals. His clothes should be neat, his movements graceful, his approach to other people perfectly poised. He must converse with facility, be proficient in sports and arms, and know how to dance and appreciate music. He should know Latin and Greek. With literary and other subjects he should show a certain familiarity but never become too engrossed. For the well-bred man speaks with "a certain carelessness, to hide his art, and show that what he says or does comes from him without effort or deliberation." Pedantry and heaviness must yield to a certain air of effortless superiority, so that even if the "courtier" knows or does something seriously, he must treat it lightly as one of many accomplishments. At its best, the code taught a certain considerateness for the feelings of others, and incorporated some of the moral ideas of the humanists, aiming at a creditable life in active society. Castiglione's book was translated into numerous languages, and a hundred editions were printed before 1600. Its ideal was inculcated for centuries by private tutors and in the schools.

Politics and the Italian Renaissance

The Italian Renaissance, for all its accomplishments, produced no institution or great idea by which masses of men living in society could be held together. Indeed, the greatest of Europe's institutions, the Roman church, in which Europeans had lived for centuries, and without which they did not see how they could live at all, fell into sheer neglect under the Renaissance popes. Nor did Italy develop any effectual political institutions. Florence during the fifteenth century passed from a high-spirited republicanism to acceptance of one-man rule. Throughout the peninsula the merchants, bankers, connoisseurs, and courtly classes who controlled the city-states could not fight for themselves, nor arouse their citizens to fight for them. They therefore hired professional fighting men, *condottieri,* private leaders of armed bands, who contracted with the various city-states to carry on warfare, and often raised their price or changed sides during hostilities. Italian politics became a tangled web, a labyrinth of subterfuge and conspiracy, a platform on which great individuals might exhibit their *virtù.* "Italian cunning" became a byword throughout Europe. Dictators rose and fell. The Medici became dukes in Florence, the Sforza in Milan, while in Venice and Genoa, where the republics were kept, narrow oligarchies held the rule. These states, along with the states of the church, jockeyed about like pugilists in a ring, held within an intricate, shifting, and purely local balance of power.

Italy was the despair of its patriots, or of such few as remained. One of these was Niccolò Machiavelli, who, in *The Prince* (1513), wrote the most lasting work of the Italian Renaissance. He dreamed of the day when the citizens of his native Florence, or indeed of all Italy, should behave like early Romans—show virility in their politics, fight in citizen armies for patriotic causes, and uphold their dignity before Europe. It was outside Italy, in kings Ferdinand of Aragon, Louis XI of France, and Henry VII of England, that Machiavelli was obliged to find his heroes. He admired them because they were successful builders of states. In *The Prince* he produced a handbook of statecraft which he hoped Italy might find useful. He produced also the first purely secular treatise on politics.

Medieval writings on politics, those of Thomas Aquinas or Marsiglio of Padua, for example, had always talked of God's will for the government of men, with such accompanying matters as justice and right, or divine and natural law. All this Machiavelli put aside. He "emancipated" politics from theology and moral philosophy. He undertook to describe simply what rulers actually did, and thus anticipated what was later called the scientific spirit, in which questions of good and bad are excluded, and the observer attempts to discover only what really happens. What really happens, said Machiavelli, is that effective rulers and governments act only in their own political interest. They keep faith or break it, observe treaties or repudiate them, are merciful or ruthless, forthright or sly, peaceable or aggressive, according to their estimates of their political needs. Machiavelli was prepared to admit that such behavior was bad; he only insisted that it was in this way, however regrettably, that successful rulers behaved. He was thought unduly cynical even in an age not characterized by political delicacy. He had nevertheless diagnosed the new era with considerable insight. It was an age when politics was in fact becoming more secular, breaking off from religion, with the building up of states and with state authority emerging as a goal requiring no other justification.

But the most successful states of the time, as Machiavelli saw, were not in Italy. They were what history knows as the New Monarchies, and they owed their strength to something more than princely craft, for they enjoyed a measure of spontaneous loyalty from their own peoples. Italy was politically helpless. Politics in Italy was not about anything vital; it was an affair of *virtù;* and the people of Italy lost interest in politics, as they did in war, becoming "effeminate" in the eyes of outsiders.

So Italy, the sunny land of balmy Mediterranean skies, rich in the busy life of its cities, its moneyed wealth, its gorgeous works of art, lay helplessly open to the depredations of less easygoing peoples, from Spain and the north, who possessed institutions in which men could act together in large numbers. In a new age of rising national monarchies the city-states of Italy were too small to compete. In 1494 a French army crossed the Alps. Italy became a bone of contention between France and Spain. In 1527 a horde of undisciplined Spanish and German mercenaries, joined by foot-loose Italians, fell upon Rome itself. Never, not even from the Goths of the fifth century, had Rome experienced anything so horrible and degrading. The city was sacked, thousands were killed, soldiers milled about for a week in an orgy of rape and loot, the pope was imprisoned, and cardinals were mockingly paraded through the streets facing backward on the backs of mules. By this time religious passions were aroused; we are encroaching on the story of the Reformation.

After the sack of Rome the Renaissance faded away. Politically, for over three hundred years, Italy remained divided, the passive object of the ambitions of outside powers. Meanwhile its culture permeated the rest of Europe.

7. *The Renaissance outside Italy*

Outside Italy people were much less conscious of any sudden break with the Middle Ages. Developments north of the Alps, and in Spain, were more an outgrowth of what had gone before. There was indeed a Renaissance in the Italian sense. In some of the innovations in painting the Flemish masters preceded those of Italy. In the north also, as in Italy a little sooner, writers favored a neoclassical Latin, but the modern written languages also began to develop.

But the northern Renaissance was more a blend of the old and the new. In it, above all, the religious element was stronger than in Italy. The most important northern humanists were men like Thomas More in England and the Dutch Erasmus. The French humanism that produced Rabelais also produced John Calvin.

Religious Scholarship and Science

It is customary to distinguish between the "pagan" humanism of Italy and the Christian humanism of the north. In the north, Christian humanists studied the Hebrew and Greek texts of the Bible and read the Church Fathers, both Latin and Greek, in order to deepen their understanding of Christianity and to restore its moral vitality. Among lesser people, too, without pretense to humanistic learning, religion remained a force. Medieval intellectual interests persisted. This is apparent from the continuing foundation of universities. The humanists generally regarded universities as centers of a pedantic, monkish, and "scholastic" learning. Concentrating upon theology, or upon medicine and law, the universities gave little encouragement to experimental science and still less to purely literary studies. In Italy in the fifteenth century no new universities were established. But in Spain, in France, in Scotland, in Scandinavia, and above all in Germany, new universities sprouted up. Between 1386 and 1506 no less than fourteen universities were established in Germany. At one of the newest, Wittenberg, founded in 1502, Martin Luther was to launch the Protestant Reformation.

Germany at this time, on the eve of the great religious upheaval, and before the shift of the commercial artery from central Europe to the Atlantic seaboard, was a main center of European life. Politically, the German-speaking world was an ill-defined and ill-organized region, composed of many diverse parts, from which the Netherlands and Switzerland were not yet differentiated. Parts of it were infested by robber knights, picturesque in legend, but unpleasant for those who had to live with them in reality. Economically, nevertheless, western and southern Germany enjoyed a lead; the towns traded busily, and German banking families, like the famous Fugger, controlled more capital than any others in Europe. Technical inventiveness was alive; mining was developing; and it was in the Rhineland, at Mainz, that Gutenberg, about 1450, produced the first books printed with movable type. In painting, the western fringe of the Germanic world produced the Flemish masters, and south Germany gave birth to Dürer and the Holbeins.

Intellectually, Germany shared in the Latin culture of Europe, a fact often obscured by the Latinizing of German names. Regiomontanus (the Latin name of Johann Müller) laid the foundations during his short lifetime (1436–1476) for a mathematical conception of the universe. He was probably the most influential scientific worker of the fifteenth century, especially since Leonardo da Vinci's scientific labors remained unknown. Nicholas of Cusa (1401?–1464), a Rhinelander, was a churchman whose mystical philosophy entered into the later development of mathematics and science. From such a background of mathematical interests came Copernicus (Niklas Koppernigk, 1473–1543), who believed that the earth moved about the sun; he was indeed a Pole, but he originated in the mixed German-Polish region of East Prussia. Fortified by the same mathematical interests, Europe's best-known cartographers were also Germans, such as Behaim and Schöner, whose world maps the reader may see on pages 302–303. Paracelsus (Latin for Hohenheim) undertook to revolutionize medicine at the University of Basel. His wild prophecies made him a mixture of scientist and charlatan; but, in truth, science was not yet clearly distinguished from the occult, with which it shared the idea of control over natural forces. A similar figure, remembered in literature and the arts, was the celebrated Dr. Faustus. In real life, Faust, or Faustus, was perhaps a learned German of the first part of the sixteenth century. He was rumored to have sold his soul to the devil in return for knowledge and power. The Faust story was dramatized in England as early as 1593 by Christopher Marlowe, and, much later, by Goethe in poetry and by Gounod in the opera. In the legend of Faust later generations

were to see a symbol of the inordinate striving of modern man. Oswald Spengler published his *Decline of the West* in 1918. Needing a name for the European civilization whose doom he prophesied, he called it "Faustian."

The idea of human powers to understand and control physical nature, as developed most especially north of the Alps, corresponded in many ways to the more purely Italian and humanistic idea of the infinite richness of human personality. Together, they constituted the new Renaissance spirit, for both emphasized the emancipation of humanity's limitless potentialities. The two ideas constantly interacted; in fact, most of the scientific workers just mentioned— Regiomontanus, Nicholas of Cusa, Copernicus—spent many years in Italy, receiving the stimulus of Italian thought.[4]

Mysticism and Lay Religion

In the north a genuine religious impulse, in addition to religious humanistic scholarship, also remained alive. Where in Italy the religious sense, if not extinct, seemed to pass into the aesthetic, into a joyous and public cult in which God was glorified by works of art, in the north it took on a more mystical and a more soberly moral tone. Germany in the fourteenth century produced a series of mystics. The mystic tendencies of Nicholas of Cusa have been mentioned. More typical mystics were Meister Eckhart (d. 1327) and Thomas à Kempis (d. 1471), author of the *Imitation of Christ*. The essence of mysticism lay in the belief, or experience, that the individual soul could in perfect solitude commune directly with God. The mystic had no need of reason, nor of words, nor of joining with other people in open worship, nor even of the sacraments administered by the priests—nor even of the church. The mystics did not rebel against the church; they accepted its pattern of salvation; but at bottom they offered, to those who could follow, a deeper religion in which the church as a social institution had no place. All social institutions, in fact, were transcended in mysticism by the individual soul; and on this doctrine, both profound and socially disruptive, Martin Luther was later to draw.

For the church, it was significant also that religion was felt deeply outside the clergy. Persons stirred by religion, who in the Middle Ages would have taken holy orders, now frequently remained laymen. In the past the church had often

---

[4] On da Vinci, Copernicus, and the rise of modern science in general, see Chapter VII.

PORTRAIT OF A CONDOTTIERE
by Giovanni Bellini (Italian, 1430–1516)

An emphatic portrayal of Renaissance individualism. Note the artist's ability to present a concrete human being, one who is not merely an abstract type. For the *condottieri* see p. 61. The name of this particular *condottiere* is not known. But the hard expression and set features, the firm lines about the mouth and chin, the bull neck and the unflinching gaze suggest an aggressive character of considerable *virtù*. The face is thoughtful and intelligent but devoid of spirituality. The man is clearly in the habit of depending on himself alone. The artist has heightened the sense of his subject's independence and self-sufficiency by making him stand out from a dark and entirely vacant background. Courtesy of the National Gallery of Art, Washington, D.C., Samuel H. Kress Collection.

needed reform. But in the past, in the bad times of the tenth century, for example, the clergy had found reformers within their own ranks. The church had thus been repeatedly reformed and renewed without revolution. Now, in the fifteenth and early sixteenth centuries an ominous line seemed to be increasingly drawn: between the clergy as an established interest, inert and set in its ways, merely living, and living well, off the church; and groups of people outside the clergy—religious lay persons, religiously inclined humanists and writers, impatient and headstrong rulers—who were more influential than ever before, and more critical of ecclesiastical abuses.

Lay religion was especially active in the Netherlands. A lay preacher, Gerard Groote, attracted followers by his sermons on spiritual regeneration. In 1374 he founded a religious sisterhood, which was followed by establishments for religiously minded men. They called themselves, respectively, the Sisters and the Brothers of the Common Life, and they eventually received papal approval. They lived communally, but not as monks and nuns, for they took no vows, wore ordinary clothing, and were free to leave at will. They worked at relieving the poor, and in teaching. The schools of the Brothers, since some of them came to have as many as a thousand boys, were the first to be organized in separate classes, each with its own room and its own teacher, according to the pupil's age or level of advancement. The Sisters maintained similar though less elaborate schools for girls. Reading and writing were of course taught, but the emphasis was on a Christian ideal of character and conduct, to instill such qualities as humility, tolerance, reverence, love of one's neighbor, and conscientiousness in the performance of duty. This Modern Devotion, as it was called, spread widely in the Netherlands and adjoining parts of Germany.

Erasmus of Rotterdam

In this atmosphere grew up the greatest of all the northern humanists, and indeed the most notable figure of the entire humanist movement, Erasmus of Rotterdam (1466–1536). Like all the humanists, Erasmus chose to write in a "purified" and usually intricate Latin style. He regarded the Middle Ages as benighted, ridiculed the scholastic philosophers, and studied deeply the classical writers of antiquity. He had the strength and the limitations of the pure man of letters. To the hard questions of serious philosophy he was largely indifferent; he feared the unenlightened excitability of the common people, and he was almost wholly unpolitical in his outlook. He rarely thought in terms of worldly power or advantage and made too little allowance for those who did. An exact contemporary to the most notorious of the worldly Renaissance popes, Erasmus was keenly aware of the need of a reform of the clergy. He put his faith in education, enlightened discussion, and gradual moral improvement. He led no burning crusade and counseled against all violence or fanaticism. He prepared new Greek and Latin editions of the New Testament. Urging also the reading of the New Testament in the vernacular languages, he hoped that with a better understanding of Christ's teaching people might turn from their evil ways. In his *Praise of Folly* he satirized all wordly pretensions and ambitions, those of the clergy most emphatically. In his *Handbook of a Christian Knight* he showed how a man might take part in the affairs of the world while remaining a devout Christian. Mildness, reasonableness, tolerance, restraint, scholarly understanding, a love of peace, a critical and reforming zeal which, hating nobody, worked through trying to make people think, a subdued and controlled tone from which shouting and bad temper were always excluded—such were the Erasmian virtues.

Erasmus achieved an international eminence such as no one of purely intellectual attainments has ever enjoyed. He corresponded with the great of Europe. He lectured at Cambridge and edited books for a publisher at Basel. The king of Spain named him a councilor, the king of France called him to Paris, Pope Leo X assisted him when he was in trouble. Theologians found fault with Erasmus' ideas (in which, indeed, the supernatural had little importance), but among the chief practical men of the church, the popes and prelates, he had many admirers. Erasmus, it must be noted, attacked only the abuses in the church, the ignorance or sloth of the clergy, the moral or financial corruption of their lives. The essence and principle of the Roman Catholic church he never called into question. Whether the Erasmian spirit, so widely diffused about 1520, would have sufficed to restore the church without the revolutionary impact of Protestantism is one of the many unanswerable questions of history.

8. The New Monarchies

Meanwhile, in Europe outside Italy, kings were actively building up the institutions of the modern state. It was these states, more than any other single factor, that were to determine the course of the religious revolution. Whether a country turned Protestant, remained Catholic, or divided into separate religious communities was to depend very largely upon political considerations.

War, civil war, class war, feudal rebellion, and plain banditry afflicted a good deal of Europe in the middle of the fifteenth century. In this formless violence central governments had become very weak. Various rulers now tried to impose a kind of civil peace. They have been conveniently called the New Monarchs, but they were not really very new, because they resumed the interrupted labors of kings in the High Middle Ages.[5] They thus laid foundations for the national, or at least territorial, states.

The New Monarchs offered the institution of monarchy as a guarantee of law and order. Arousing latent sentiments of loyalty to the reigning dynasty, they proclaimed that hereditary monarchy was the legitimate form of public power, which all should accept without turmoil or resistance. They especially enlisted the support of middle-class people in the towns, who were tired of the private wars and marauding habits of the feudal nobles. Townspeople were willing to let parliaments be dominated or even ignored by the king, for parliaments had proved too often to be strongholds of unruly barons, or had merely accentuated class conflict. The king, receiving money in taxes, was able to organize armies with which to control the nobles. The use of the pike and the longbow, which enabled the foot soldier to stand against the horseman, was here of great potential value. The king, if only he could get his monarchy sufficiently organized, and his finances into reliable order, could hire large numbers of foot soldiers, who generally came

[5] See pp. 33–35.

from the endless ranks of plebeians, unlike the knightly horsemen. But to organize his monarchy, the king had to break down the mass of feudal, inherited, customary, or "common" law in which the rights of the feudal classes were entrenched. For this purpose, at least on the Continent, the New Monarch made use of Roman law, which was now actively studied in the universities.[6] He called himself a "sovereign"—it was at this time that kings began to be addressed as "majesty." The king, said the experts in Roman law, incorporated the will and welfare of the people in his own person—and they would cite the principle *salus populi suprema lex*, "the welfare of the people is the highest law." The king, they added, could *make* law, enact it by his own authority, regardless of previous custom or even of historic liberties—and they would quote, *quod principi placuit legis habet vigorem*, or "what pleases the prince has the force of law."

The New Monarchy in England, France, and Spain

The New Monarchy came to England with the dynasty of the Tudors (1485–1603), whose first king, Henry VII (1485–1509), after gaining the throne by force, put an end to the civil turbulence of the Wars of the Roses. In these wars the great English baronial families had seriously weakened each other, to the great convenience of the king and the bulk of the citizenry. Henry VII passed laws against "livery and maintenance," the practice by which great lords maintained private armies wearing their own livery or insignia. Since ordinary procedures had recently failed to give security, with witnesses afraid to testify and juries afraid to offend the mighty, Henry VII used his royal council as a new court to deal with property disputes and infractions of the public peace. It met in a room decorated with stars, whence its name, the Star Chamber. It represented the authority of the king and his council, and it operated without a jury. Later denounced as an instrument of despotism, it was popular enough at first, because it preserved order and rendered substantial justice. Henry VII, though miserly and unpleasant in person, was accepted as a good ruler. National feeling in England consolidated around the house of Tudor.

In France the New Monarchy was represented by Louis XI (1461–1483), of the Valois line, and his successors. In the five centuries since the first French king had been crowned, the royal domain had steadily expanded from its original

[6] See p. 14.

ERASMUS OF ROTTERDAM
by Hans Holbein, the Younger (German, 1497–1543)
The classic portrayal of humanism at its best. The portrait was painted in 1523, when Erasmus was fifty-six, and the Lutheran Reformation had already begun in Germany. Holbein has conveyed the mood of tight-lipped calm, or of saddened humanity, felt by a lifelong reforming writer who has lived to see violent revolution. The face, finely delineated, and highlighted against the deeper tones of the cap and cloak, is concentrated upon Erasmus' only weapon, the pen. The picture captures the life of thought; it is a picture of the human mind, as Bellini's *Condottiere* is a picture of the will. Courtesy of the Louvre (Giraudon).

small nucleus around Paris through a combination of inheritance, marriage, war, intrigue, and conquest. Louis XI continued to round out the French borders. Internally, he built up a royal army, suppressed brigands, and subdued rebellious nobles. He acquired far greater powers than the English Tudors to raise taxation without parliamentary consent. The Estates General of France met only once in his reign. On that occasion, remembering the anarchy of the past, they requested the king to govern without them in the future. The French monarchy also enlarged its powers over the clergy. We have seen how, by the Pragmatic Sanction of 1438, the Gallican church had won considerable national independence.[7] In 1516 King Francis I reached an agreement with Pope Leo X, the Concordat of Bologna. By this agreement the Pragmatic Sanction was rescinded; the pope received his "annates," or money income, from French ecclesiastics; the king appointed the bishops and abbots. The fact that, after 1516, the kings of France already controlled their own national clergy was one reason why, in later years, they were never tempted to turn Protestant.

Strictly speaking, there was no kingdom of Spain. Various Spanish kingdoms had combined into two, Aragon and Castile. To Aragon, which lay along the Mediterranean side of the peninsula, belonged the Balearic Islands, Sardinia, Sicily, and the south Italian kingdom of Naples. To Castile, after 1492, belonged the newly discovered Americas. The two were joined in a personal union by the marriage of Ferdinand of Aragon and Isabella of Castile in 1469. The union was personal only; that is, both kingdoms recognized the two monarchs, but they had no common political, judicial, or administrative institutions. There was little or no Spanish national feeling; indeed, the Catalans in northern Aragon spoke a language quite different from Castilian Spanish. The common feeling throughout Spain was the sense of belonging to the Spanish Catholic church. The common memory was the memory of the Christian crusade against the Moors. The one common institution, whose officials had equal authority and equal access to all the kingdoms, was a church court, the Inquisition. The church in Spain was in vigorous condition. Cardinal Ximenes, shortly before 1500, managed to rid it of the abuses and the inertia which debilitated the church in the rest of Europe. The *reconquista* was at last completed. In 1492 Granada, the southern tip of Spain, was conquered from the Moors. Its annexation added to the heterogeneous and undigested character of the Spanish dominions.

In these circumstances the New Monarchy in Spain followed a religious bent. Unification took place around the church. The rulers, though they made efforts at political centralization, worked largely through facilities offered by the church, notably the Inquisition. They insisted on religious conformity. National feeling was church feeling; the sense of "Spanishness" was a sense of Catholicity. Formerly the Spanish had been among the most tolerant of Europeans; Christians, Muslims, and Jews had managed to live together. But in the wave of national (or religious) excitement that accompanied the conquest of Granada both the Jews and the Moors were expelled. The expulsion of the Jews by a decree of 1492 was actually a sign of former toleration in Spain, for the Jews had been similarly expelled from England in 1290 and from France in 1306. They were not again legally allowed in England until the mid–seventeenth century, nor in France (with

[7] See p. 52.

great exceptions) until the French Revolution. It would appear that in the history of many European peoples the attainment of a certain degree of national consciousness brought a feeling against Jews as "outsiders."[8]

All persons in Spain were now supposed to be Christians. In fact, however, Spain was the one country in Europe where a person's Christianity could not be taken for granted, because many Spanish families had been Jewish or Muslim for centuries, and had only accepted Christianity to avoid expulsion. Hence arose a fear of false Christians, of an unassimilated element secretly hostile to the foundations of Spanish life. It was feared that Moriscos (Christians of Moorish background) and Marranos (Christians of Jewish background) retained a clandestine sympathy for the religion of their forebears. A distaste for eating pork, or an inclination not to work on Saturday, was enough to arouse suspicion. Thousands of such persons were haled before the Inquisition, where, as in the civil courts under Roman procedure, torture could be employed to extort confessions. Spanish life became rigidly and ostentatiously orthodox. It was safest to be profuse in one's external devotions. It was the way of proving oneself to be a good Spaniard. The national and the Catholic were fused.

The life of Spain remained a great crusade, a crusade within Spain against Moriscos and Marranos, a crusade carried against the Moors into Africa itself, which the Spanish invaded immediately after the conquest of Granada. The crusade crossed the ocean into the Americas, where the Spanish church set about gathering the Indians into the fold. And it was soon to spread to Europe also. Spain was ready, before Protestantism ever appeared, to play its role in the Reformation, to be the avenging angel to extirpate heresy, and the stern apostle demanding Catholic reform.

The Holy Roman Empire and the Habsburg Supremacy

Ideas of the New Monarchy were at work even in Germany, which is to say, in the Holy Roman Empire. There were three kinds of states in the Empire. There were the princely states—duchies, margraviates, etc.—each a little hereditary dynastic monarchy in itself, such as Saxony, Brandenburg, or Bavaria. There were ecclesiastical states—bishoprics, abbacies, etc.—in which the bishop or abbot, whose rule was of course not hereditary, conducted the government. A large portion of the area of the Empire consisted of these church-states, as may be seen from the map on pages 72–73. Third, there were the imperial free cities, some fifty in number; their collective area was not large, but they dominated the commercial and financial life of the country. There was in truth also a fourth category, made up of some thousands of imperial knights, noblemen of minor consequence who possessed a few manors, but who belonged to no state, recognizing the supremacy of none but the emperor.

The states, over the centuries, had prevented the emperor from infringing upon their local liberties. They had taken care to keep the emperorship an elective

---

[8] The Jews who left Spain (the Sephardic Jews) went to North Africa and the Near East, and in smaller numbers to the Dutch Netherlands and even to southwestern France (one of the exceptions noted above). Those who left England two centuries earlier generally went to Germany, the great center of Ashkenazic Jewry in the Middle Ages. Driven from Germany in the fourteenth century they concentrated in Poland, which remained the great center of European Jewry until the Nazi massacres of the 1940s. See map, p. 858.

Habsburg Dominions
Church Lands
Boundary of Holy Roman Empire

od

Moscow

R U S S I A
(MUSCOVY)

YEDISAN

KHANATE OF THE CRIMEA

CRIMEA

BLACK SEA

Constantinople

E M P I R E

na

RHODES (Turkish)

CYPRUS
(Venice)

0   100   200   300 miles

EUROPE, 1526

The main feature of the political map of Europe about 1526 is the predominance of the house of Habsburg. Much of Europe was ruled by the Habsburg Emperor Charles V, who was at the same time King Charles I of Spain. As is explained in this and the following chapter, Charles left his possessions in Austria, Hungary, and Bohemia to his brother, those in Spain, the Netherlands, Italy, and America to his son. He thus established the Austrian and Spanish branches of the Habsburg dynasty. France was nearly encircled by Habsburg dominions and habitually formed alliances with various German princes and with Sweden, Poland, and Turkey. The Habsburgs remained the principal power in Europe until after the Thirty Years' War, which ended in 1648.

office, so that with each election local liberties could be reaffirmed. After 1356 the right of electing an emperor was vested in seven electors—namely, four of the princely lords, the Count Palatine, Duke of Saxony, Margrave of Brandenburg, and King of Bohemia (the one king in the Empire), and in three ecclesiastical lords, the archbishops of Mainz, Trier, and Cologne. In 1452 the electors chose the Archduke of Austria to be emperor. His family name was Habsburg. The Habsburgs, by using the resources of their hereditary possessions in Austria (and later elsewhere) and by delicately balancing and bribing the numerous political forces within Germany, managed to get themselves consistently reelected to the Holy Roman Emperorship in every generation, with one exception, from 1452 until 1806.

The principles of New Monarchy were successful mainly in the hereditary princely states of reasonable size. Here the rulers went through the familiar process of quelling their own feudal subordinates, increasing their revenues, enforcing local peace, and letting their own parliamentary bodies fall into abeyance. Thus Brandenburg, Saxony, Bavaria, Württemberg, and a few others, though small, began to take on the semblance of modern states.

The Habsburg emperors also tried to introduce the centralizing principles of the New Monarchy in the Empire as a whole. Under Maximilian I (1493–1519) there seemed to be progress in this direction: the Empire was divided into administrative "circles," and an Imperial Chamber and Council were created, but they were all doomed to failure before the immovable obstacle of states' rights. Maximilian was the author of the Habsburg family fortunes in a quite different way. *Bella gerunt alii; tu, felix Austria, nubes*—"where others have to fight wars, you, fortunate Austria, marry!" Maximilian himself married the heiress of the dukes of Burgundy, who, over the past century, had acquired a number of provinces in the western extremities of the Empire—the Netherlands and the Free County of Burgundy, which bordered upon France. Maximilian by this marriage had a son Philip, whom he married to Joanna, heiress to Ferdinand and Isabella of Spain. Philip and Joanna produced a son Charles. Charles combined the inheritances of his four grandparents: Austria from Maximilian, the Netherlands and Free County from Mary of Burgundy, Castile and Spanish America from Isabella, Aragon and its Mediterranean and Italian possessions from Ferdinand. In addition, in 1519, he was elected Holy Roman Emperor and so became the symbolic head of all Germany.

Charles V of the Empire (he was known as Charles I in Spain) was thus beyond all comparison the most powerful ruler of his day. But still other fortunes awaited the house of Habsburg. The Turks, who had occupied Constantinople in 1453, were at this time pushing through Hungary and menacing central Europe. In 1526 they defeated the Hungarians at the battle of Mohacs. The parliaments of Hungary, and of the adjoining kingdom of Bohemia, hoping to gain allies in the face of the Turkish peril, thereupon elected Charles V's brother Ferdinand as their king. The Habsburg family was now entrenched in central Europe, in the Netherlands, in Spain, in the Mediterranean, in south Italy, in America. No one since Charlemagne had stood so far above all rivals. Contemporaries cried that Europe was threatened with "universal monarchy," with a kind of world-state in which no people could preserve its independence.

The reader who wishes to understand the religious revolution, and consequent emergence of Protestantism, to which we shall now turn, must bear in mind the extraordinarily intricate interplay of the factors that have now been outlined: the decline of the church, the growth of secular and humanistic feeling, the spread of lay religion outside the official clergy, the rise of monarchs who wished to control everything in their kingdoms, including the church, the resistance of feudal elements to these same monarchs, the lassitude of the popes and their fear of church councils, the atomistic division of Germany, the Turkish peril, the zeal of Spain, the preeminence of Charles V, and the fears felt in the rest of Europe, especially in France, of absorption or suffocation by the amazing empire of the Habsburgs.

9. *The Protestant Reformation*

Three streams contributed to the religious upheaval of the sixteenth century. First, among simple people, or the laboring poor, who might find their spokesmen among local priests, there was an endemic dissatisfaction with all the grand apparatus of the church, or a belief that its bishops and abbots were part of a wealthy and oppressive ruling class. For such people, religious ideas were mixed with protest against the whole social order. They found expression in the great peasant rebellion in Germany in the 1520s. The sects which emerged are known historically as Anabaptists, and the modern Baptists, Mennonites, and Moravian Brothers are among their descendants. Second, and forming a group generally more educated and with broader views of the world, were the middle classes of various European cities, especially of cities that were almost like autonomous little republics, as in Germany, Switzerland, and the Netherlands. They might wish to manage their own religious affairs as they did their other business, believing that the church hierarchy was too much embedded in a feudal, baronial, and monarchical system with which they had little in common. The modern churches of Calvinist origin came in large part from this stream. Third, there were the kings and ruling princes, who had long disputed with the church on matters of property, taxes, legal jurisdiction, and political influence. Each such ruler wanted to be master in his own territory. In the end it was the power of such rulers that determined which form of religion should officially prevail. The Lutheran and Anglican churches were in this tradition, and to some extent the Gallican church, as the French branch of the Roman Catholic church was called. As it turned out, by 1600, the second and third streams had won many successes, but the first was suppressed. Socio-religious radicalism was reduced to an undercurrent in countries where Anglican, Lutheran, Calvinist, or Roman Catholic churches were established.

Since northern Europe became Protestant while the south remained Catholic, it may look as if the north had broken off in a body from a once solid Roman church. The reality was not so simple. Let us for a moment put aside the term "Protestant," and think of the adherents of the new religion as religious revolutionaries.[9] Their ideas were revolutionary because they held, not merely

---

[9] The word "Protestant" arose as an incident in the struggle, at first denoting certain Lutherans who drew up a formal protest against an action of the diet of the Empire in 1529. Only very gradually did the various groups of anti-Roman reformers think of themselves as collectively Protestant.

that "abuses" in the church must be corrected, but that the Roman church itself was wrong in principle. Even so, there were many who hoped, for years, that old and new ideas of the church might be combined. Many deplored the extremes but gradually in the heat of struggle had to choose one side or the other. The issues became drawn, and each side aspired to destroy its adversary. For over a century the revolutionaries maintained the hope that "popery" would everywhere fall. For over a century the upholders of the old order worked to annihilate or reconvert "heretics." Only slowly did Catholics and Protestants come to accept each other's existence as an established fact of European society. Though the religious frontier that was to prove permanent appeared as early as 1560, it was not generally accepted until after the Thirty Years' War, which closed in 1648.

Luther and Lutheranism

The first who successfully defied the older church authorities was Martin Luther. He was a monk, and an earnest one, until he was almost forty years old. A vehement and spiritually uneasy man, with many dark and introspective recesses in his personality, Luther was terrified by the thought of the awful omnipotence of God, distressed by his own littleness, apprehensive of the devil, and suffering from the chronic conviction that he was damned. The means offered by the church to allay such spiritual anguish—the sacraments, prayer, attendance at Mass—gave him no satisfaction. From a reading and pondering of St. Paul (Romans i, 17)—"the just shall live by faith"—there dawned upon him a new realization and sense of peace. He developed the doctrine of justification by faith alone. This held that what "justifies" a man is not what the church knew as "works" (prayer, alms, the sacraments, holy living) but "faith alone," an inward bent of spirit given to each soul directly by God. Good works, Luther thought, were the consequence and external evidence of this inner grace, but in no way its cause. A man did not "earn" grace by doing good; he did the good because he possessed the grace of God. With this idea Luther for some years lived content. Even years later some high-placed churchmen believed that in Luther's doctrine of justification by faith there was nothing contrary to the teachings of the Catholic church.

Luther, now a professor at Wittenberg, was brought out of seclusion by an incident of 1517. A friar named Tetzel was traveling through Germany distributing indulgences, authorized by the pope to finance the building of St. Peter's in Rome.[10] In return for them the faithful paid certain stipulated sums of money. Luther thought that people were being deluded, that no one could in this way obtain grace for himself, or ease the pains of relatives in purgatory, as was officially claimed. In the usual academic manner of the day, he posted ninety-five theses on the door of the castle church at Wittenberg. In them he reviewed the Catholic sacrament of penance. Luther held that, after confession, the sinner is freed of his burden not by the priest's absolution, but by inner grace and faith alone. Increasingly, it seemed that the priesthood performed no necessary function in the relation between man and God.

Luther at first appealed to the pope, Leo X, to correct the abuse of indulgences

---

[10] On indulgences, see p. 52.

in Germany. When the pope refused action Luther (like many before him) urged the assembly of a general church council as an authority higher even than the pope. He was obliged, however, to admit in public debate that even the decision of a general council might be mistaken. The Council of Constance, he said, had in fact erred in its condemnation of John Huss. But if neither the pope, nor yet a council, had authority to define true Christian belief, where was such authority to be found? Luther's answer was, in effect: There is no such authority. He held that each individual might read the Bible and freely make his own interpretation according to his own conscience. This idea was as revolutionary, for the church, as would be the assertion today that neither the Supreme Court nor any other body may authoritatively interpret or enforce the Constitution of the United States, since each citizen may interpret the Constitution in his own way.

From his first public appearance Luther won ardent supporters, for there was a good deal of resentment in Germany against Rome. In 1519 and 1520 he rallied public opinion in a series of tracts, setting forth his main beliefs. He declared that the claim of the clergy to be different from the laity was an imposture. He urged people to find Christian truth in the Bible for themselves, and in the Bible only. He denounced the reliance on fasts, pilgrimages, saints, and Masses. He rejected the belief in purgatory. He reduced the seven sacraments to two— baptism and the communion, as he called the Mass. In the latter he repudiated the new and "modern" doctrine of transubstantiation, while affirming that God was still somehow mysteriously present in the bread and wine.[11] He declared that the clergy should marry, upbraided the prelates for their luxury, and demanded that monasticism be eliminated. To drive through such reforms, while depriving the clergy of their pretensions, he called upon the temporal power, the princes of Germany. He thus issued an invitation to the state to assume control over religion, an invitation which, in the days of the New Monarchy, a good many rulers were enthusiastically willing to accept.

Threatened by a papal bull with excommunication unless he recanted, Luther solemnly and publicly burned the bull. Excommunication followed. To the emperor, Charles V, now fell the duty of apprehending the heretic and repressing the heresy. Luther was summoned to appear before a diet of the Empire, held at Worms in the Rhineland. He declared that he could be convinced only by Scripture or right reason; otherwise—"I neither can nor will recant anything, since it is neither right nor safe to act against conscience. God help me! Amen." He was placed under the ban of the Empire. But the Elector of Saxony and other north German princes took him under their protection. In safe seclusion, he began to translate the Bible into German.

Luther's excitable obstinacy, intemperate language, and sweeping repudiation of existing authorities antagonized many who had at first looked upon him with favor, and who still hoped for a reform of the church without revolution. Among these was Erasmus, who, as often happens to those who find themselves in the middle, was in his last years looked upon by both sides, Lutheran and Catholic, as a meddlesome friend of the opposition.

Lutheranism, or at least anti-Romanism, swept over Germany, assuming the proportions of a national upheaval. It became mixed with all sorts of political and

[11] See pp. 38, 42.

social revolution. A league of imperial knights, adopting Lutheranism, attacked their neighbors, the church-states of the Rhineland, hoping by annexations to enlarge their own meager territories. In 1524 the peasants of a large part of Germany revolted. They were stirred by new religious ideas, worked upon by preachers who went beyond Luther in asserting that anyone could see for himself what was right. Their aims, however, were social and economic; they demanded a regulation of rents and security of common village rights and complained of exorbitant exactions and oppressive rule by their manorial overlords. Luther repudiated all connection with the peasants, called them filthy swine, and urged the princes to suppress them by the sword. The peasants were unmercifully put down, but popular unrest continued to stir the country, expressing itself, in a religious age, in various forms of extreme religious frenzy. Various leaders had various followings, known collectively as Anabaptists. Some said that all the world needed was love, some that Christ would soon come again, some that they were saints and could do no wrong, and some that infant baptism was useless, immersion of full-grown adults being required, as described in the Bible. The roads of Germany were alive with obscure zealots, of whom some tens of thousands converged in 1534 on the city of Münster. There they proclaimed the reign of the saints, abolished property, and introduced polygamy as authorized in the Old Testament. A Dutch tailor, John of Leyden, claimed authority from God himself, and, hemmed in by besieging armies, ruled Münster by a revolutionary terror. Luther advised his followers to join even with Catholics to repress such an appalling menace. After a full year Münster was relieved. The "saints" were pitilessly rooted out; John of Leyden died in torture.

Luther, horrified at the way in which religious revolution became confused with social revolution, defined his own position more conservatively. He restricted, while never denying, the right of private judgment in matters of conscience, and he made a larger place for an established clergy, Lutheranized, to be sure, but still established as teachers over the laity. Always well disposed to temporal rulers, having called upon the princes to act as religious reformers, he was thrown by the peasant and Anabaptist uprisings into an even closer alliance with them. Lutheranism took on a character of submissiveness to the state. Christian liberty, Luther insisted, was an internal freedom, purely spiritual, known only to God. In worldly matters, he said, the good Christian owed perfect obedience to established authority. Lutheranism, more than Catholicism and more than the Calvinism which soon arose, came to hold the state in a kind of religious awe as an institution almost sacred in its own right.

In the revolution that was rocking Germany it was not the uprising of imperial knights, nor that of peasants or tailors and journeymen, that was successful, but the rebellion of the higher orders of the Empire against the emperor. Charles V, as Holy Roman Emperor, was bound to uphold Catholicism because only in a Catholic world did the Holy Empire have any meaning. The states of the Empire, always fearing the loss of local liberty, saw in Charles' efforts to repress Luther a threat to their own freedom. Many imperial free cities, and most of the dynastic states of north Germany, now insisted on adding to their other rights and liberties the right, or liberty, to determine their own religion. The *ius reformandi,* they said, the right or power to reform, belonged to member states, not to the Empire itself. They became Lutheran, locally, introducing Lutheran bishops, doctrines, and forms of worship. Where a state turned Lutheran it usually "secularized" (i.e., confiscated) the church properties within its borders, a process which considerably enriched some of the Lutheran princes and gave them a strong material interest in the success of the Lutheran movement. In most of the church-states, since the Catholic archbishop or bishop was himself the government, Catholicism prevailed. But a few church-states turned Lutheran. A good example of the secularization of a church-state was afforded in East Prussia, just outside the Empire. This territory belonged to the Teutonic Order, a Catholic organization of which the grand commander, an elective official, was at this time Albert of Brandenburg. In 1525 Albert declared for Luther and converted East Prussia into a secular duchy, of which he and his descendants became hereditary dukes.

Against the emperor, a group of Lutheran princes and free cities formed the League of Schmalkald. The king of France, Francis I, though a Catholic in good standing, allied with and supported the League. Political interests overrode religious ones. Against the "universal monarchy" of the swollen Habsburgs the French found alliances where they could, allying with the Turks as with the Lutherans, building up a balance of power against their mighty foe. It became the studied policy of Catholic France to maintain the religious division of Germany.

Charles V strove to find some basis of agreement by which the permanent religious division of Germany could be avoided. He was at war with France over certain disputed territories and with the Turks, who in 1529 besieged Vienna itself. Though the Lutheran princes did render a little help at the last moment, it seemed on the whole that the infidels might overrun Germany before the German states would yield their liberties to their own emperor.

Charles appealed to the pope, urging him to assemble a Europe-wide council in which all disputed matters could be considered, the Protestants heard, compromises effected, and church unity and German unity (such as it was) restored. The king of France schemed at Rome to prevent the pope from calling any such council. The kings of both France and England urged national councils instead, in which religious questions could be settled on a national basis. Pope after pope delayed. The papacy feared that a council of all Latin Christendom might get out of control, since Catholics as much as Protestants demanded reform. At the very rumor of a council the price of salable offices in Rome abruptly fell. To the papacy, remembering the Council of Constance, nothing was more upsetting than the thought of a council, not even the Protestants, not even the Turks. So the popes procrastinated, no council met, years passed, and a new generation grew up in Lutheranism. Desperately, in 1548, Charles tried to settle matters himself, issuing the *Interim*, to guide religion in all Germany until a general church council could complete its work. The *Interim* upheld the main Catholic doctrines, but, to attract the Protestants, allowed marriage of the clergy and one or two other minor concessions. Neither side would accept it: Protestants found that it gave too little, and Catholics refused to have their religion tampered with by the temporal power.

Meanwhile the Schmalkaldic League, allied with France, had actually gone to war with the emperor in 1546. Germany fell into an anarchy of civil struggle between Catholic and Protestant states, the latter aided by France. The war was ended by the Peace of Augsburg of 1555.

The terms set at Augsburg signified a complete victory for the cause of Lutheranism and states' rights. Each state of the Empire received the liberty to be either Lutheran or Catholic as it chose—*cuius regio eius religio,* "whose the region, his the religion." No individual freedom of religion was permitted; if a ruler or a free city decided for Lutheranism, then all persons had to be Lutheran. Similarly in Catholic states all had to be Catholic. The Peace of Augsburg provided also, by the so-called Ecclesiastical Reservation, that any Catholic bishop or other churchman who turned Lutheran in the future (or who had turned Lutheran as recently as 1552) should not carry his territory with him, but should turn Lutheran as an individual and move away, leaving his land and its inhabitants Catholic. Since the issues in Germany were still far from stabilized, this proviso was often disregarded in later years.

The Peace of Augsburg was thus, in religion, a great victory for Protestantism, and at the same time, in German politics and constitutional matters, a step in the disintegration of Germany into a mosaic of increasingly separate states. Lutheranism prevailed in the north, and in the south in the duchy of Württemberg and various detached islands formed by Lutheranized free cities. Catholicism prevailed in the south (except in Württemberg and certain cities), in the Rhine valley, and in the direct possessions of the house of Habsburg, which in 1555 reached as far north as the Netherlands. The Germans, because of conditions in the Holy Roman Empire, were the one large European people to emerge from the religious conflict almost evenly divided between Catholic and Protestant.

No rights were granted by the Peace of Augsburg to another group of religious revolutionaries which neither Lutherans nor Catholics were willing to tolerate, namely, the followers of John Calvin.

Lutheranism, it must be pointed out, was adopted by the kings of Denmark and Sweden as early as the 1520s. Since Denmark controlled Norway, and Sweden ruled Finland and the eastern Baltic, all Scandinavia and the Baltic regions became, like north Germany, Lutheran. Beyond this area Lutheranism failed to take root. Like Anglicanism in England (to be described shortly) Lutheranism was too closely associated with established states to spread easily as an international movement. The most successful international form of the Protestant movement was Calvinism.

Calvin and Calvinism

John Calvin was a Frenchman, born Jean Cauvin, who called himself Calvinus in Latin. Born in 1509, he was a full generation younger than Luther. He was trained both as a priest and as a lawyer, and had a humanist's knowledge of Latin and Greek, as well as Hebrew. At the age of twenty-four, experiencing a sudden conversion, or fresh insight into the meaning of Christianity, he joined forces with the religious revolutionaries of whom the best known was then Luther. Three years later, in 1536, he published, in the international language, Latin, his *Institutes of the Christian Religion.* Where Luther had aimed much of his writing either at the existing rulers of Germany, or at the German national feeling against Rome, Calvin addressed his *Institutes* to all the world. He seemed to appeal to human reason itself; he wrote in the severe, logical style of the trained lawyer; he dealt firmly, lucidly, and convincingly with the most basic issues. In the

Institutes people in all countries, if dissatisfied with the existing Roman church, could find cogent expression of universal propositions, which they could apply to their own local circumstances as they required.

With Luther's criticisms of the Roman church, and with most of Luther's fundamental religious ideas, such as justification by faith and not by works, Calvin agreed. In what they retained of the Catholic Mass, the communion or Lord's Supper as they called it, Luther and Calvin developed certain doctrinal differences. Both rejected transubstantiation, but where Luther insisted that God was somehow actually present in the bread and wine used in the service (''consubstantiation''), Calvin and his followers tended more to regard it as a pious act of symbolic or commemorative character.

The chief differences between Calvin and Luther were two. Calvin made far more of the idea of predestination. Both, drawing heavily on St. Augustine, held that man by his own actions could earn no merit in the sight of divine justice, that any grace which anyone possessed came from the free action of God alone. God, being Almighty, knew and willed in advance all things that happened, including the way in which every life would turn out. He knew and willed, from all eternity, that some were saved and some were damned. Calvin, a severe critic of human nature, felt that those who had grace were relatively few. They were the ''elect,'' the ''godly,'' the little band chosen without merit of their own, from all eternity, for salvation. A person could feel in his own mind that he was among the saved, God's chosen few, if throughout all trials and temptations he persisted in a saintly life. Thus the idea of predestination, of God's omnipotence, instead of turning to fatalism and resignation, became a challenge to unrelenting effort, a sense of burning conviction, a conviction of being on the side of that Almighty Power which must in the end be everlastingly triumphant. It was the most resolute spirits that were attracted to Calvinism. Calvinists, in all countries, were militant, uncompromising, perfectionist—or Puritan, as they were called first in England and later in America.

The second way in which Calvinism differed from Lutheranism was in its attitude to society and to the state. Calvinists refused to recognize the subordination of church to state, or the right of any government—king, parliament, or civic magistracy—to lay down laws for religion. On the contrary, they insisted that true Christians, the elect or godly, should Christianize the state. They wished to remake society itself into the image of a religious community. They rejected the institution of bishops (which both the Lutheran and Anglican churches retained), and provided instead that the church should be governed by presbyteries, elected bodies made up of ministers and devout laymen. By thus bringing an element of lay control into church affairs, they broke the monopoly of priestly power and so promoted secularization. On the other hand, they were the reverse of secular, for they wished to Christianize all society.

Calvin, called in by earlier reformers who had driven out their bishop, was able to set up his model Christian community at Geneva in Switzerland. A body of ministers ruled the church; a consistory of ministers and elders ruled the town. The rule was strict; all loose, light, or frivolous living was suppressed; disaffected persons were driven into exile. The form of worship was severe, and favored the intellectual rather than the emotional or the aesthetic. The service was devoted largely to long sermons elucidating Christian doctrine, and all appeals to the senses—color, music, incense—were rigidly subdued. The black gown of Geneva replaced brighter clerical vestments. Images, representing the saints, Mary, or Christ, were taken down and destroyed. Candles went the way of incense. Chanting was replaced by the singing of hymns. Instrumental music was frowned upon, and many Calvinists thought even bells to be a survival of "popery." In all things Calvin undertook to regulate his church by the Bible. Nor was he more willing than Luther to countenance any doctrine more radical than his own. When a Spanish refugee, Michael Servetus, who denied the Trinity, i.e., the divinity of Christ, sought asylum at Geneva, Calvin pronounced him a heretic and burned him at the stake.

To Geneva flocked reformers of all nationalities, Englishmen, Scots, Frenchmen, Netherlanders, Germans, Poles, and Hungarians, to see and study a true scriptural community so that they might reproduce it in their own countries. Geneva became the Protestant Rome, the one great international center of Reformed doctrine. Everywhere Calvinists made their teachings heard (even in Spain and Italy in isolated cases), and everywhere, or almost everywhere, little groups which had locally and spontaneously broken with the old church found in Calvin's *Institutes* a reasoned statement of doctrine and a suggested method of organization. Thus Calvinism spread, or was adopted, very widely. In Hungary and Bohemia large elements turned Protestant, and usually Calvinist, partly as a way of opposing the Habsburg rule. In Poland there were many Calvinists, along with less organized Anabaptists and Unitarians, or Socinians, as those who denied the Trinity were then called. Calvinists spread in Germany, where, opposing both Lutheran and Catholic churches as ungodly impositions of worldly power, they were disliked equally by both. In France the Huguenots were Calvinist, as were the Protestants of the Netherlands. John Knox in the 1550s brought Calvinism to Scotland, where Presbyterianism became and remained the established religion. At the same time Calvinism began to penetrate England, from which it was later to reach British America, giving birth to the Presbyterian and Congregationalist churches of the United States.

Calvinism was far from democratic in any modern sense, being rather of an almost aristocratic outlook, in that those who sensed themselves to be God's chosen few felt free to dictate to the common run of mankind. Yet in many ways Calvinism entered into the development of what became democracy. For one thing, Calvinists never venerated the state; they always held that the sphere of the state and of public life was subject to moral judgment. For another, the Calvinist doctrine of the "calling" taught that a man's labor had a religious dignity, and that any form of honest work was pleasing in the sight of God. In the conduct of their own affairs Calvinists developed a type of self-government. They formed "covenants" with one another, and devised machinery for the election of presbyteries. They refused to believe that authority was transmitted downward through bishops or through kings. They were inclined also to a democratic outlook by the circumstance that in most countries they remained an unofficial minority. Only at Geneva, in the Dutch Netherlands, in Scotland, and in New England (and for a few years in England in the seventeenth century) were Calvinists ever able to prescribe the mode of life and religion of a whole country. In England, France, and Germany, Calvinists remained in opposition to the established authorities of church and state and hence were disposed to favor limitations upon established power. In Poland and Hungary many Calvinists were nobles who disliked royal authority.

The Reformation in England

England was peculiar in that its government broke with the Roman church before adopting any Protestant principles. Henry VIII (1509–1547) in fact prided himself on his orthodoxy. When a few obscure persons, about 1520, began to whisper Luther's ideas in England, Henry himself wrote a *Defense of the Seven Sacraments* in refutation, for which a grateful pope conferred upon him the title of "Defender of the Faith." But the king had no male heir. Recalling the anarchy from which the Tudor dynasty had extricated England, and determined as a New Monarch to build up a durable monarchy, he felt, or said, that before all else he must have a son. In order to remarry, he requested the pope to annul his existing marriage to Catherine of Aragon. Popes in the past had obliged monarchs similarly pressed. The pope now, however, was embarrassed by the fact that Catherine, who objected, was the aunt of the Emperor Charles V, whom the pope was in no position to offend. Henry, not a patient man, drove matters forward. He put in a new archbishop of Canterbury, repudiated the Roman connection, and married the youthful Anne Boleyn. The fact that only three years later he put to death the unfortunate Anne, and thereafter in quick succession married four more wives, for a total of six, threw considerable doubt on the original character of his motives.

Henry acted through Parliament, believing, as he said, that a king was never stronger than when united with representatives of his kingdom. In 1534 Parliament passed the Act of Supremacy, which declared the English king to be the "Protector and Only Supreme Head of the Church and Clergy of England." All subjects were required, if asked, to take the oath of supremacy acknowledging the religious headship of Henry and rejecting that of the pope. For refusing this oath Sir Thomas More, a statesman and humanist best known as the author of *Utopia,* was executed for treason. He received a somewhat delayed reward four centuries later when the Roman church pronounced him to be a saint. Henry, in the next few years, closed all the monasteries in England. The extensive monastic lands, accumulated by never-dying corporations from gifts made over the centuries, were seized by the king, who passed them out to numerous followers, thus strengthening and reconstituting a landed aristocracy which had been seriously weakened in the Wars of the Roses. The new landed gentry remained firm supporters of the house of Tudor and the English national church, whatever its doctrines.

It was Henry's intent not to change the doctrines at all. He simply wished to be the supreme head of an English Catholic church. On the one hand, in 1536, he forcibly suppressed a predominantly Catholic rebellion, and, on the other, in 1539, through the Six Articles, required everybody to believe in transubstantiation, the celibacy of the clergy, the need of confession, and a few other test items of Catholic faith and practice. But it proved impossible to maintain this position, for a great many people in England began to favor one or another of the ideas of Continental Reformers, and a small minority were willing to accept the entire Protestant position.

For three decades the government veered about. Henry died in 1547 and was succeeded by his ten-year-old son, Edward VI, under whom the Protestant party came to the fore. But Edward died in 1553 and was succeeded by his much older half-sister, Mary, the daughter of Catherine of Aragon and a devout Roman Catholic whose whole life had been embittered by the break with Rome. Mary tried to re-Catholicize England, but she actually made Catholicism more unpopular with the English. In 1554 she married Philip of Spain, who became king of England, though only nominally. The English did not like Philip, nor the Spanish, nor the intense Spanish Catholicism that Philip represented. Under Mary, moreover, some three hundred persons were burned at the stake, as heretics, in public mass executions. It was the first (and last) time that such a thing had happened in England, and it set up a wave of horror. In any event, Mary did not live long. She was succeeded in 1558 by Henry's younger daughter, Elizabeth, the child of Anne Boleyn. Whatever Elizabeth's real views in religion might be (she concealed them successfully and was rumored to have none), she could not be a Roman Catholic. For Catholics she was illegitimate and so unable to be queen.

Under Elizabeth the English became Protestant, gradually and in their own way. The Church of England took on a form of its own. Organizationally, it resembled a Lutheran church. It was a state church, for its existence and doctrines were determined by the temporal power, in this case the monarch acting through Parliament. All English subjects were obliged to belong to it, and laws were passed against "recusants," a term used to cover both the Roman Catholics and the more advanced Calvinists who refused to acknowledge it. With the exception of monasteries and certain other church foundations, the Church of England retained the physical possessions, buildings, and internal organization of the medieval church—the bishops and the archbishops, who continued to sit in the House of Lords, the episcopal courts with their jurisdiction over marriage and wills, the tithes or church taxes paid by all landowners, the parish structure, the universities of Oxford and Cambridge. In religious practice, the Church of England was definitely Protestant: English replaced Latin as the language of the liturgy, there was no cult of the saints, and the clergy married, though Elizabeth confessed to some embarrassment at the thought of an archbishop having a wife. In doctrine, it was Elizabeth's policy to make the dogmas broad and ambiguous, so that persons of all shades of belief could be more readily accommodated. The Thirty-nine Articles (1563), composed by a committee of bishops, defined the creed of the Anglican church. In the light of the burning issues of the day many of the articles were evasive, though Protestant in tone. All but one of the Anglican bishops had been newly appointed by Elizabeth at her accession; many had lived in exile among Continental Protestants in the reign of Mary Tudor; and except on the matter of church government through bishops (known as episcopacy) a strong Calvinist impress was set upon Anglican belief in the time of Elizabeth. Anglicans, for a century or more, generally considered themselves closer to Geneva than to Rome, the seat of "popery," and regarded Lutherans as "semipapist." There remained, however, a High Church element, emphasizing the Catholic rather than the Protestant character of Anglicanism.

The same ecclesiastical settlement was prescribed for Ireland, where English or rather Anglo-Norman conquerors had settled since the twelfth century, shortly after the Norman conquest of England. A replica of the Church of England was now established, called the Church of Ireland, which took over the properties and position of the Roman church in the lesser island. The native Irish remained almost solidly Roman Catholic. As in Hungary or Bohemia people who resented the Habsburgs were likely to turn Protestant rather than share in the ruler's religion, so in Ireland the fact that the ruling English were Protestant only confirmed the Irish in their attachment to the Roman church. The Catholic priests, deprived of status, income, and church buildings, and often in hiding, became national leaders of a discontented people.

The Religious Situation by 1560

Neither in England, nor in Germany, nor in a Europe at large penetrated by international Calvinism were the issues regarded as settled in 1560. Nor had the Roman church accepted the new situation. But by 1560 the chief Protestant doctrines had been affirmed, and geographically Protestantism had made many conquests. The unity of Latin Christendom had been broken. Christendom was disintegrating into a purely intangible ideal. A world of separate states and nations was taking its place.

Protestants differed with one another, yet there was much that all had in common. All rejected the papal authority. None participated in any effective international organization; the ascendancy of Geneva was spiritual only and proved to be temporary. All Protestants rejected the special, sacerdotal, or supernatural character of the priesthood; indeed, the movement was perhaps most fundamentally a revolt against the medieval position of the clergy. Protestants generally called their clergy ministers, not priests. All Protestant clergy could marry. There were no Protestant monks, nuns, or friars. All Protestant churches replaced Latin with the vernacular in religious services—English, French, German, Czech, as the case might be. All Protestants reduced the number of sacraments, usually to two or three; such sacraments as they retained they regarded more as symbols than as actual carriers of divine grace; all believed, in one way or another, in justification by faith. All denied transubstantiation, or the miracle of the Mass. All gave up the obligatory confessional, and with it priestly absolution. All gave up the idea of purgatory as a kind of temporal zone between heaven and hell and hence abandoned the practice of saying prayers and Masses for the dead. It need hardly be added that nothing like indulgences remained. All gave up the cult of the saints and of the Virgin Mary, whose intercession in heaven was no longer expected. All declared that the one true source of Christian belief was the Holy Scripture. And while all established Protestant churches, in the sixteenth century, insisted on conformity to their own doctrines, allowing no individual freedom, all Protestants still had some small spark of the spirit first ignited by Luther, so that none flatly repudiated the right of private judgment in matters of conscience.

It has sometimes been maintained that one of the motivations in Protestantism was economic—that a new acquisitive, aggressive, dynamic, progressive, capitalistic impulse shook off the restrictions imposed by medieval religion. The fact that Protestant England and Holland soon underwent a rapid capitalistic development gives added likelihood to this idea. The alacrity with which Protestant governments confiscated church lands shows a keen material interest; but in truth, both before and after the Reformation, governments confiscated church properties without breaking with the Roman church. That profound economic changes were occurring at the time will become apparent in the following chapter. Yet it seems that economic conditions were far less decisive than religious convictions and political circumstances. Calvinism won followers not only in cities, but in agrarian countries such as Scotland, Poland, and Hungary. Lutheranism spread more successfully in the economically retarded north Germany than in the busy south. The English were for years no more inclined to Protestantism than the French, and in France, while many lords and peasants turned Protestant, Paris and many other towns remained as steadfastly Catholic. It is possible that Protestantism,

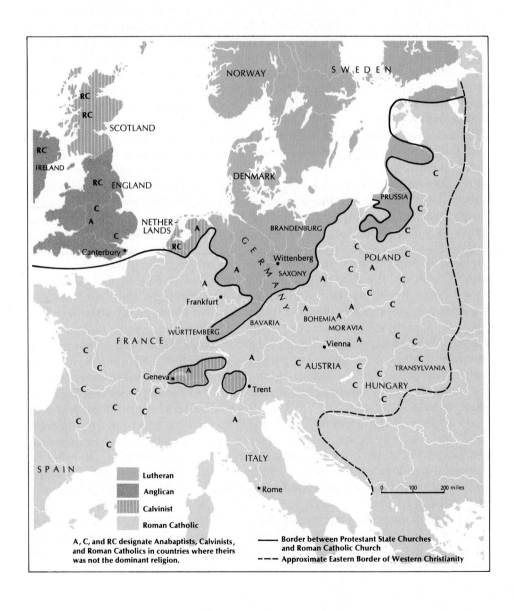

Lutheran

Anglican

Calvinist

Roman Catholic

A, C, and RC designate Anabaptists, Calvinists, and Roman Catholics in countries where theirs was not the dominant religion.

——— Border between Protestant State Churches and Roman Catholic Church

– – – Approximate Eastern Border of Western Christianity

by casting a glow of religious righteousness over a man's daily business and material prosperity, later contributed to the economic success of Protestant peoples, but it does not seem that economic forces were of any distinctive importance in the first stages of Protestantism.

10. *Catholicism Reformed and Reorganized*

The Catholic movement corresponding to the rise of Protestantism is known as the Catholic Reformation or the Counter Reformation, the former term being preferred by Catholics, the latter by Protestants. Both are applicable. On the one hand the Catholic church underwent a genuine reform, which might have worked itself out in one way or another even if the stimulus of revolutionary Protestantism had been absent. On the other hand the character of the reform, the decisions made, and the measures adopted were shaped by the need of responding explicitly to the Protestant challenge; and certainly, also, there was a good deal of purely "counter" activity aimed at the elimination of Protestantism as such.

The demand for reform was as old as the abuses against which it was directed. Characteristically, it had expressed itself in the demand for a general or ecumenical church council. The conciliar movement, defeated by the popes about 1450, showed signs of revival after 1500.[12] But it was almost as hard, even then, to assemble a general council as it is today to create an international body possessing any effective authority.

Several years before Luther had been heard of, Europe's two most important secular rulers, the king of France and the Holy Roman Emperor, jointly convened on their own authority a council at Pisa in 1511. It was their purpose to force reforms upon Pope Julius II, and if necessary depose him. But no delegates from other countries attended; the five cardinals and handful of bishops who came to

---

[12] On the conciliar movement, see pp. 51–52.

STATE RELIGIONS IN EUROPE ABOUT 1560

It is not possible to draw an accurate religious map of Europe during the Reformation, because in many countries persons of different religions were intermixed. What the map shows is the legally authorized, established, or territorial churches about 1560. Many Catholics lived north of the heavy line, and many Protestants south of it. Most widely dispersed were the Calvinists and the more radical Protestants or Anabaptists. Calvinism was established in various Swiss cantons, the Dutch provinces, and Scotland, but there were many Calvinist congregations elsewhere, especially in southern France and in Poland and Hungary. Radical Protestants, who rejected the principle of the state church, could be found in both Protestant and Catholic countries; they were most numerous in parts of Germany and in Bohemia-Moravia, but included the first American Pilgrims. In Germany, under the Holy Roman Empire, each principality and free city chose its own religion; hence, the Germans were the only large European nationality to emerge from the Reformation almost evenly divided between Catholics and Protestants. In other large countries in the century after 1560 one side or the other, Protestant or Catholic, was reduced to a small minority. Such minorities were either persecuted, barely tolerated, or at least out of favor with their respective governments until the French Revolution.

Pisa were regarded as minions of the two rulers who sent them. The council thus lacked moral authority, no one listened to it, and it accomplished nothing, never even attaining historically the name of a council. The pope, however, to ward off the danger of a council under secular auspices, himself assembled the Fifth Lateran Council at Rome in 1512. It was supposed to be general, ecumenical, Europe-wide, representing that "spiritual unity" sometimes imagined to have existed in Europe before Luther. In fact, few took it seriously, because it was composed mainly of Italian prelates, who began by denouncing the doctrines of the Council of Constance and ended by making a few tame resolutions on miscellaneous topics.

Then came the Lutheran upheaval, and the attempts of Charles V, in the interests of German unity, to persuade the pope to assemble a true and adequately empowered council, so that removal of abuses in the church, which no one really defended, would take away the grounds upon which many Germans were turning to Lutheranism. But meanwhile the king of France found reason to favor the pope and to oppose the emperor. The French king, Francis I (1515–1547), could support the pope because he had obtained from the papacy what he wanted, namely, control over the Gallican church, as acquired in the Concordat of Bologna of 1516.[13] And he had reason to oppose Charles V, because Charles V ruled not only in Germany but in the Netherlands, Spain, and much of Italy, thus encircling France and threatening Europe with what contemporaries called "universal monarchy." Francis I therefore actively encouraged the Protestants of Germany, as a means of maintaining dissension there, and used his influence at Rome against the calling of a council by which the troubles of the Catholic world might be relieved.

Gradually, in the curia, there arose a party of reforming cardinals who concluded that the need of reform was so urgent that all dangers of a council must be risked. The pope summoned a council to meet in 1537, but the wars between France and the Empire forced its abandonment. Then a council was called for 1542, but no one came except a few Italians so that it had to be suspended. Finally, in 1545, a council did assemble and begin operations. It met at Trent, on the Alpine borders of Germany and Italy. The Council of Trent, which shaped the destiny of modern Catholicism, sat at irregular intervals for almost twenty years—in 1545–1547, 1551–1552, and 1562–1563. It was not until the Second Vatican Council in the 1960s that some of the main decisions made at Trent were substantially modified.

The Council of Trent

The council was beset by difficulties of a political nature, which seemed to show that under troubled conditions an international council was no longer a suitable means of regulating Catholic affairs. For one thing, it was poorly attended. Whereas at the Fourth Lateran Council of 1215, and at Constance in 1415, some five hundred prelates had assembled, the attendance at Trent was never nearly so great; it sometimes fell as low as twenty or thirty, and the important decree on "justification," the prime issue raised by Luther, and one on which some

[13] See p. 70.

good Catholics had until then believed a compromise to be possible, was passed at a session where only sixty prelates were present. The most regular in attendance were the Italians and Spanish; the French and Germans came erratically and in smaller numbers. Even with the small attendance, the old conciliar issue was raised. A party of bishops believed that the bishops of the Catholic church, when assembled in council from all parts of the Catholic world, collectively constituted an authority superior to that of the pope. To stave off this "episcopal" movement was one of the chief duties of the cardinal legates deputed by the pope to preside over the sessions.

The popes managed successfully to resist the idea of limiting the papal power. In the end they triumphed, through a final ruling, voted by the council, that no act of the council should be valid unless accepted by the Holy See. It is possible that had the conciliar theory won out, the Catholic church might have become as disunited in modern times as the Protestant. It was clear, at Trent, that the various bishops tended to see matters in a national way, in the light of their own problems at home, and to be frequently under strong influence from their respective secular monarchs. In any case, the papal party prevailed, which is to say that the centralizing element, not the national, triumphed. The Council of Trent in fact marked an important step in the movement which issued, three hundred years later, in the promulgation of the infallibility of the pope when speaking *ex cathedra* on matters of faith and morals. After 1563 no council met at all until the Vatican Council of 1870 at which this papal infallibility was proclaimed.[14] The Council of Trent thus preserved the papacy as a center of unity for the Catholic church and helped prevent the very real threat of its dissolution into state churches. Even so, the council's success was not immediate, for in every important country the secular rulers at first accepted only what they chose of its work, and only gradually did its influence prevail.

Questions of national politics and of church politics apart, the Council of Trent addressed itself to two kinds of labors—to a statement of Catholic doctrine and to a reform of abuses in the church. When the council began to meet, in 1545, the Protestant movement had already gone so far that any reconciliation was probably impossible: Protestants, especially Calvinists, simply did not wish to belong to the church of Rome under any conditions. In any case, the Council of Trent made no concessions.

It declared justification to be by works and faith combined. It enumerated and defined the seven sacraments, which were held to be vehicles of grace independent of the spiritual state of those who received them.[15] The priesthood was declared to be a special estate set apart from the laity by the sacrament of holy orders. The procedures of the confessional and of absolution were clarified. Transubstantiation was reaffirmed. As sources of Catholic faith, the council put Scripture and tradition on an equal footing. It thus rejected the Protestant claim to find true faith in the Bible alone and reasserted the validity of church development since New Testament times. The Vulgate, a translation of the Bible into Latin made by St. Jerome in the fourth century, was declared to be the only version on which authoritative teaching could be based. The right of individuals

[14] See p. 634.
[15] See p. 38.

to believe that their own interpretation of Scripture was more true than that of church authorities (private judgment) was denied. Latin, as against the national languages, was prescribed as the language of religious worship—a requirement abolished by the Second Vatican Council in the 1960s. Celibacy of the clergy was maintained. Monasticism was upheld. The existence of purgatory was reaffirmed. The theory and correct practice of indulgences were restated. The veneration of saints, the cult of the Virgin, and the use of images, relics, and pilgrimages were approved as spiritually useful and pious actions.

It was easier for a council to define doctrines than to reform abuses, since the latter consisted in the rooted habits of thousands and millions of people's lives. The council decreed, however, a drastic reform of the monastic orders. It acted against the abuse of indulgences while upholding the principle. It ruled that bishops should reside habitually in their dioceses and attend more carefully to their proper duties. It gave bishops more administrative control over clergy in their own dioceses, such as mendicant friars, who in the past had been exempt from episcopal jurisdiction, and whose presence had often caused disturbance, or indeed scandal, among the local people. The abuse by which one man had held numerous church offices at the same time (pluralism) was checked, and steps were taken to assure that church officials should be competent. To provide an educated clergy, the council ordered that a seminary should be set up in each diocese for the training of priests.

The Counter Crusade

As laws in general have little force unless sustained by opinion, so the reform decrees of the Council of Trent would have remained ineffectual had not a renewed sense of religious seriousness been growing at the same time. Herein lay the inner force of the Catholic Reform. In Italy, as the Renaissance became more undeniably pagan, and as the sack of Rome, in 1527, showed the depths of hatred felt even by Catholics toward the Roman clergy, the voices of severer moralists began to be heeded. The line of Renaissance popes was succeeded by a line of reforming popes, of whom the first was Paul III (1534–1549). The reforming popes insisted on the primacy of the papal office, but they regarded this office, unlike their predecessors, as a moral and religious force. In many dioceses the bishops began on their own initiative to be more strict. The new Catholic religious sense, more than the Protestant, centered in a reverence for the sacraments and a mystical awe for the church itself as a divine institution. Both men and women founded many new religious orders, of which the Jesuits became the most famous. Others were the Oratorians for men and the Ursulines for women. The new orders dedicated themselves to a variety of educational and philanthropic activities. Missionary fervor for a long time was more characteristic of Catholics than of Protestants. It reached into Asia and the Americas, and in Europe expressed itself as an intense desire for the reconversion of Protestants. It showed itself, too, in missions among the poor, as in the work of St. Vincent de Paul among the human wreckage of Paris, for which the established Protestant churches failed to produce anything comparable. In America, as colonies developed in the sixteenth and seventeenth centuries, the Protestant clergy tended to take the layman's view of the Indians, while Catholic clergy labored to convert and preserve them; and the Catholic church generally worked to mitigate the brutality of Negro slavery, to which the pastors in English and Dutch colonies, perhaps because they were more dependent upon the laity, remained largely indifferent.

We have seen how in Spain, where the Renaissance had never taken much hold, the very life of the country was a boundless Christian crusade.[16] It was in Spain that much of the new Catholic feeling first developed, and from Spain that much of the missionary spirit first went out. It was Spain that gave birth to St. Ignatius Loyola (1491–1556). A soldier in youth, he too, like Luther and Calvin, had a religious "experience" or "conversion," which occurred in 1521, before he had heard of Luther, and while Calvin was still a boy. Loyola resolved to become a soldier of the church, a militant crusader for the pope and the Holy See. On this principle he established the Society of Jesus, commonly known as the Jesuits. Authorized by Paul III in 1540, the Jesuits constituted a monastic order of a new type, less attached to the cloister, more directed toward active participation in the affairs of the world. Only men of proven strength of character and intellectual force were admitted. Each Jesuit had to undergo an arduous and even horrifying mystical training, set forth by Loyola in his *Spiritual Exercises*. The order was ruled by an iron discipline, which required each member to see in his immediate superior the infallibility of Holy Church. If, said Loyola, the church teaches to be black what the eye sees as white, the mind will believe it to be black. Aside from demanding absolute submission in matters of faith, the Jesuits generally favored rationality and a measure of liberty in the religious life. For two hundred years they were the most famous schoolmasters of Catholic Europe, eventually conducting some five hundred schools for boys of the upper and middle classes. In them they taught, besides the faith, the principles of gentlemanly deportment (their teaching of dancing and dramatics became a scandal to more puritanical Catholics), and they carried over the Renaissance and humanist idea of the Latin classics as the main substance of adolescent education. The Jesuits made a specialty of work among the ruling classes. They became confessors to kings and hence involved in political intrigue. In an age when Protestants subordinated an organized church either to the state or to an individual conscience, and when even Catholics frequently thought of the church within a national framework, the Jesuits seemed almost to worship the church itself as a divine institution, the Church Militant and the Church Universal, internationally organized and governed by the Roman pontiff. All full-fledged Jesuits took a special vow of obedience to the pope. Jesuits in the later sessions of the Council of Trent fought obstinately, and successfully, to uphold the position of Rome against that of the national bishops. The high papalism of the Jesuits (later called "ultramontanism") for centuries made them as obnoxious to many Catholics as they were to the Protestants.

By 1560 the Catholic church, renewed by a deepening of its religious life, and by an uncompromising restatement of its dogmas and discipline, had devised also the practical machinery for a counteroffensive against Protestantism. The Jesuits acted as an international missionary force. They recruited members from all countries, including those in which the governments had turned Protestant.

[16] See pp. 70–71.

English Catholics, for example, trained as Jesuits on the Continent, returned to England to overthrow the heretic usurper, Elizabeth, seeing in the universal church a higher cause than national independence in religion. Jesuits poured also into the most hotly disputed regions where the issue still swayed in the balance—France, Germany, Bohemia, Poland, Hungary. As after every great revolution, many people after an initial burst of Protestantism were inclined to turn back to the old order, especially as the more crying evils within the Catholic church were corrected. The Jesuits reconverted many who thus hesitated.

For the more recalcitrant other machinery was provided. All countries censored books; Protestant authorities labored to keep "papist" works from the eyes of the faithful, and Catholic authorities took the same pains to suppress all knowledge of "heretics." All bishops, Anglican, Lutheran, and Catholic, regulated reading matter within their dioceses. In the Catholic world, with the trend toward centralization under the pope, a special importance attached to the list published by the bishop of Rome, the papal Index of Prohibited Books. Only with special permission, granted to reliable persons for special study, could Catholics read books listed on the Index, on which most of the significant works written in Europe since the Reformation have been included.

All countries, Protestant and Catholic, also set up judicial and police machinery to enforce conformity to the accepted church. In England, for example, Elizabeth established the High Commission to bring "recusants" into the Church of England. All bishops, Protestant and Catholic, likewise possessed machinery of enforcement in their episcopal courts. But no court made itself so dreaded as the Inquisition. In reality two distinct organizations went under this name, the word itself being simply an old term of the Roman law, signifying a court of inquest or inquiry. One was the Spanish Inquisition, established originally, about 1480, to ferret out Jewish and Muslim survivals in Spain. It was then introduced into all countries ruled by the Spanish crown and employed against Protestantism, particularly in the Spanish Netherlands, which was an important center of Calvinism. The other was the Roman or papal Inquisition, established at Rome in 1542 under a permanent committee of cardinals called the Holy Office; it was in a sense a revival of the famous medieval tribunal established in the thirteenth century for the detection and repression of heresy. Both the Spanish and the Roman Inquisition employed torture, for heresy was regarded as the supreme crime, and all persons charged with crime could be tortured, in civil as well as ecclesiastical courts, under the existing laws. In the use of torture, as in the imposition of the harshest sentence, burning alive, the Roman Inquisition was milder than the Spanish. With the growth of papal centralization the Roman Inquisition in principle offered a court to protect purity of faith in all parts of the Catholic world. But the national resistance of Catholic countries proved too strong; few Catholics wished the agents of Rome inquiring locally into their opinions; and the Roman Inquisition never functioned for any length of time outside of Italy. In France no form of the Inquisition was admitted either then or later.

In the "machinery" of enforcing religious belief, however, no engine was to be so powerful as the apparatus of state, of political sovereignty. Where Protestants won control of government, people became Protestant. Where Catholics retained control of governments, Protestants became in time small minorities. And it was in the clash of governments, which is to say in war, for about a century after 1560, that the fate of European religion was worked out. In 1560 the strongest powers of Europe—Spain, France, Austria—were all officially Catholic. The Protestant states were all small or at most middle-sized. The Lutheran states of Germany, like all German states, were individually of little weight. The Scandinavian monarchies were far away. England, the most considerable of Protestant kingdoms, was a country of only four million people, with an independent and hostile Scotland to the north, and with no sign of colonial empire yet in existence. In the precedence of monarchs, as arranged in the earlier part of the century, the king of England ranked just below the king of Portugal, and next above the king of Sicily. Clearly, had a great combined Catholic crusade ever developed, Protestantism could have been wiped out. To launch such a crusade was the dream of the king of Spain. It never succeeded; why, will be seen in the next chapter.

THE FLORENCE OF
THE RENAISSANCE

The supreme site of the Italian Renaissance, Florence was both a city lying on either side of the river Arno and an independent republic, with a territory extending, by 1500, for about fifty miles in most directions from Florence itself. The city had grown wealthy in the later Middle Ages from the production of woolens. It developed also an intense civic spirit in its conflicts with other Italian cities. It became a home of merchant princes, of whom the Medici were the most famous. Such families, enriched in earlier generations by the woolen trade, then passing into banking, emerged as an urban patriciate or governing class, the more easily because there was no royalty to overshadow them, and the feudal nobility in the surrounding country was very weak.

Patricians were sometimes opposed by the populace, and sometimes, like the early Medici, they had popular followings of their own. Outbursts of factionalism were therefore very common, compounded by the rivalry with other Italian cities, and by the increasing involvement of the Holy Roman Emperor, the king of France, and the pope. The Medici became dominant in the fifteenth century, were expelled in 1494, restored in 1512, expelled again in 1527, then again restored in 1530, this time permanently, since they remained as hereditary grand dukes of Tuscany until 1737. The following pages suggest something of the wealth, the civic life, and the political crises of Florence until the end of the republic in the 1530s.

More interesting to outsiders than the civil turmoil were Florentine literature and works of art. Writers of a new kind, the humanists, abounded in the city. Reflecting the new interests of the Renaissance, they rejected the church-centered and university-oriented learning of the Middle Ages, and they brought a new spirit to the study of the Latin and Greek classics, in which they found a keen significance for their own times. Of these writers, the best remembered is Machiavelli, who worked to strengthen Florentine republicanism during the period of the Medici exile from 1494 to 1512.

Also born in Florence, either in the city or in the republic, were Michelangelo, Leonardo da Vinci, Masaccio, Donatello, Brunelleschi, Botticelli, and Benvenuto Cellini, to name only the most eminent painters and sculptors, in addition to such lesser lights as the historian Guicciardini and the explorer Amerigo Vespucci, Latinized as Americus Vespucius, after whom America was named. Never since ancient Athens had so much talent appeared in so small a place within the short span of three or four generations. Patronage by the ruling elite was reinforced by a high degree of literacy in the general population; a chronicler reports that as early as 1338 there were 8,000 boys and girls in the schools. Such conditions promoted a degree of taste and understanding in which architecture, painting, sculpture, literature, and intellectual discussion could flourish.

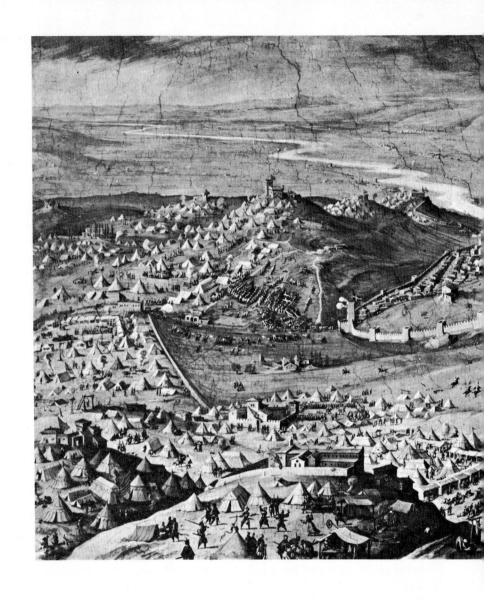

This view of Florence shows the river Arno bisecting it and flowing on into the Tuscan plain. In the right center is the Duomo, or cathedral, dominating the city. The scene, painted by Vasari, shows the situation in 1530, when the city was besieged by the Holy Roman Emperor, Charles V. The defenses were strong, and Michelangelo himself served as one of nine citizens in charge of engineering and fortifications. The Imperial army, shown encamped outside the walls, eventually overcame the resistance and restored the exiled Medici to power.

At the extreme left is the sign of the wool guild of Florence, in which a sheep is appropriately displayed. The near left shows the modest establishment of a fifteenth-century banker, engaged in the actual counting or changing of money.

Above, Lorenzo de' Medici, the "Magnificent," examines a model for a villa built for him about 1480 on the outskirts of the city. The Medici town house, or "palace," appears on the last page of the present essay.

At the left is a part of a huge fresco executed for the chapel of the Medici town house by Benozzo Gozzoli in 1469. It is called the Procession of the Three Kings to Bethlehem, but what it really represents is the important personages of Florence at their most resplendent. The presence of an African servant in Italy at this early date is to be noted. He wears his hair in African style and carries a bow. To the right of him is Cosimo de' Medici on a white horse, followed by a throng whose varied complexions and miscellaneous headgear, including the miter of a Greek patriarch, suggest the cosmopolitanism of the city.

The three figures at the left are from a painting by Domenico Ghirlandaio, done about 1490 for a chapel in memory of a woman who had died in childbirth. The theme is Zacharias in the Temple, *but the three heads are actually portraits of contemporary Florentine humanists. The painting thus illustrates, like the one by Gozzoli on the preceding pages, the use of religious themes to convey secular subjects, or of everyday observation to convey religious ideas.*

Above, the governing council, or signoria, *deliberates on going to war against the neighboring city of Pisa, during the period of republican revival after expulsion of the Medici in 1494. A Nemesis floats over the councilors' heads.*

Valse el c° della lana a g° contanty 26 ɣ 13 ß 4 ɖ di pl̄

Upper left: Detail of the fall of Troy, enacted in Florentine costume in the streets of Florence. The building at the left is the Medici palace (see the next page). At the right, the African warrior wielding a large bow is Memnon, King of the Ethiopians, who according to an ancient legend fought at Troy on the side of the Trojans.

Lower left: Two wool merchants with their goods, from a book of 1492 on arithmetic. Arabic numerals are visible above, but the bags of wool are marked "CLX" or 160 in Roman numerals.

Above: The Piazza della Signoria showing the burning of Savonarola. The dome of the cathedral is half in view at the left. The arcade at the right is the loggia dei lanzi, *built about 1380 as an open but sheltered place for public assemblies. The* palazzo della signoria, *or town hall, the large square building, very dark in this picture, dates from 1298 and so reflects the medieval fortress-like style, with small windows, crenelated roof lines, and high towers that characterized this part of Italy before the classicizing features of Renaissance architecture were adopted.*

These are town houses, or palazzi, of Florentine patricians. At the right is the Palazzo Medici, built for Cosimo de' Medici in the 1440s. At the left is the slightly later Palazzo Rucellai. Architects such as Brunelleschi transformed the old fortress-like dwellings of an earlier day into these massive and elegant residences. The new style is evident in the horizontal composition, the long rows of wide, closely spaced, identical windows, the pilasters, and the cornices under the overhanging roof. The interiors were often even more classical, with arches and columns enclosing an open courtyard.

It was in the Medici Palace that Lorenzo the Magnificent received his following of artists and humanists, and that Pope Leo X (born 1475; pope, 1513–1521) and Catherine de' Medici (born 1519; queen of France, 1547–1559; queen mother, 1559–1589) spent their youth.

III.
ECONOMIC
RENEWAL AND
WARS OF RELIGION,
1560–1648

It IS CONVENIENT to think of the period of about a century following 1560 as the age of the Wars of Religion, which may be said to have ended with the Peace of Westphalia in 1648. France, England, the Netherlands, and the Holy Roman Empire fell into internal struggles in which religion was the most burning issue, but in which political, constitutional, economic, and social questions were also involved. They, and other powers, also fought in international wars in which the conflict between Catholics and Protestants was a main source of contention but in which other interests were at work too. Often the ideological lines became blurred, as Catholics lent aid to Protestants, or vice versa, somewhat as ideological issues in our own day tend to be confused.

The time of the long, drawn-out Wars of Religion was also a time of economic renewal. From the beginning of the sixteenth century society was transformed by contacts with a newly discovered overseas world, by expanded trade routes, an emergent capitalism, and the formation of new social classes. The effects of these profound changes, however, were obscured and delayed by the politico-religious struggles. In the present chapter we must first examine the geographical discoveries, then survey the broad new economic and social developments under way, and finally trace the impact of the religious wars on various parts of Europe. The wars, as we shall see, left Spain and Germany very much weakened, and

Chapter Emblem: A mariner's, or simplified, astrolabe that could be taken to sea and used in determination of latitude.

opened the way for the English, Dutch, and French to profit from the economic changes and play leading roles in the drama of early modern times.

11. *The Opening of the Atlantic*

Always until about 1500 the Atlantic Ocean had been a barrier, an end. About 1500 it became a bridge, a starting place. The consequences were enormous for all concerned. In general, they were favorable for Europeans but devastating for peoples elsewhere—in America through massive depopulation by diseases such as smallpox brought from Europe, in Africa through the transatlantic slave trade, and ultimately as far away as Australia and New Zealand. By 1992, as Native American and African American voices were increasingly heard, the fifth centennial of Columbus's first voyage was seen as little to celebrate. But no one could doubt that the association of the Old and New Worlds, as Europeans called them, was a momentous event in the history of the human race.

Europeans had skirted their Atlantic coast since prehistoric times. Vikings had settled in Iceland in the ninth century, and even reached North America soon thereafter. In 1317 Venetians had established the Flanders galleys, commercial flotillas that regularly made the passage between the Adriatic and North seas. In the fifteenth century, improvements in shipbuilding, the rigging of sails, and the adoption of the mariner's compass made it feasible to sail on the open ocean out of sight of land. When the Portuguese about 1450 settled in the Azores Islands, in the mid-Atlantic, they found steady westerly winds to assure a safe return to Europe. It seemed that the ocean might even lead to Asia.

For centuries Asia had been a source for Europe of many highly valued commodities, partly manufactures in which Europe could not compete, such as silk and cotton fabrics, rugs, jewelry, porcelains, and fine steel, and partly raw or semimanufactured drugs and foodstuffs, such as sugar and above all spices. Europeans had never themselves gone to the sources of supply of Eastern goods. Somewhere, east of Suez, barely known to Europeans, was another world of other merchants, who moved the wares of China, India, and the East Indies Spice Islands by caravan over land and by boat through the Red Sea or Persian Gulf to the markets of the eastern Mediterranean. Traders of the two worlds met and did business at such thriving centers as Alexandria or Beirut or Constantinople.

The Portuguese in the East

In 1498 the Portuguese navigator Vasco da Gama, having rounded Africa in the wake of other intrepid explorers, found himself in the midst of the unknown world of Arab commerce. He landed on the Malabar Coast (the southwest coast of India), where he found a busy commercial population of heterogeneous religious background. These people knew at least as much about Europe as Europeans did about India (one Jew was able to act as da Gama's interpreter) and they realized that the coming of the Portuguese would disturb their established channels of commerce. Da Gama, playing upon local rivalries, was able to load his ships with the coveted wares, but on his second voyage, in 1502, he came better prepared, bringing a fighting fleet of no less than twenty-one vessels. A ferocious war broke out between the Portuguese and Arab merchants, the latter supported

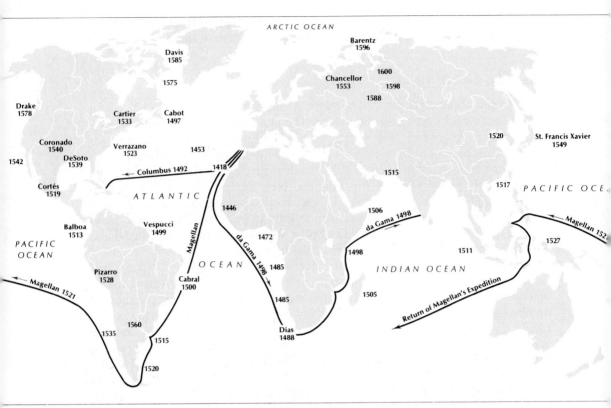

EUROPEAN DISCOVERIES, 1450–1600

Since very remote times the human race has occupied all the continents—except Antarctica—and most of the islands, and between A.D. 1000 and 1450 Norsemen reached Greenland and North America, various Europeans traveled overland to China, and Genoese sailors visited the Azores and the Canary Islands. "Discovery," however, means the bringing of newly found countries within the habitual knowledge of the society from which the discoverer comes. It was the Europeans who thus "discovered" the rest of the world between about 1450 and 1600. They did so by using maritime skills and geographical knowledge developed in the Mediterranean; hence many of the first discoverers— Columbus, Cabot, Vespucci, Verrazano—were Italians, though in the service respectively of Spain, England, Portugal, and France. Two of the greatest, however, da Gama and Magellan, were Portuguese, although Magellan sailed under the Spanish flag. Dates on the map show the years of first significant European arrival at the points indicated. With a few exceptions, as for Coronado and the Russian penetration of Siberia, these dates mark the explorers' arrival by sea across the open ocean. Still unknown to Europeans in 1600 were most of the interior of both Americas and of Africa, northeastern Asia, and the very existence of Australia and New Zealand. (See also maps on pp. 302–303, and the picture essay, pp. 151–159.)

Europeans were not the first to make long-distance voyages. Long before Columbus, the Indian Ocean had been crossed by Arab and even by Chinese sailors, and Polynesians had spread to many south Pacific islands. The north Atlantic presented greater hazards in its high latitude, long freezing winters, and turbulent winds.

in one way or another by the Egyptians, the Turks, and even the distant Venetians, all of whom had an interest in maintaining the old routes of trade. For the Portuguese, trained like the Spaniards in long wars against the Moors at home, no atrocities were too horrible to commit against the infidel competitors whom they found at the end of their heroic quest. Cities were devastated, ships burned at their docks, prisoners butchered and their dismembered hands, noses, and ears sent back as derisive trophies. One Brahmin, mutilated in this way, was left alive to bear them to his people. Such, unfortunately, was India's introduction to the West.

In the following years, under the first governor general, Albuquerque, the Portuguese built permanent fortified stations at Goa on the Malabar Coast, at Aden near the mouth of the Red Sea, at Hormuz near the mouth of the Persian Gulf, and in East Africa. In 1509 they reached Malacca, near modern Singapore, from which they passed northward into China itself, and eastward to Amboina, the heart of the Spice Islands, just west of New Guinea. Thus an empire was created, the first of Europe's commercial-colonial empires, maintained by superiority of firearms and sea power and with trade alternating with war and plunder. Albuquerque died in 1515, dreaming grandiose and preposterous dreams—to deflect the course of the Nile and so destroy Egypt and Egyptian commerce, and to capture Mecca and exchange it for the Holy Land. It should be added that bold Jesuits soon arrived, led by St. Francis Xavier, who, by 1550, had baptized thousands of souls in India, Indonesia, and even Japan.

By the new route the cost of Eastern goods for Europeans was much reduced, for the old route had involved many transshipments, unloadings, and reloadings, movements by sea and by land, through the hands of many merchants. In 1504 spices could be bought in Lisbon for only a fifth of the price demanded in Venice. The Venetians (who in their desperation even talked of digging a Suez canal) were hopelessly undersold; their trade thereafter was confined to products of the Near East itself. As for the Portuguese, never was a commercial monopoly built so fast. The lower prices added enormously to European demand and consumption. Beginning in 1504, only five years after da Gama's first return, an average of twelve ships a year left Lisbon for the East.

The Discovery of America

Meanwhile, as every American schoolchild can tell, the same quest for a route to the East had led to the somewhat disappointing discovery of America. Like most such discoveries, this was no chance hit of a queer or isolated genius. Behaim's globe, constructed in 1492,[1] the very year of Columbus's first voyage, could hardly fail to suggest the idea of sailing westward. Nevertheless, it was Christopher Columbus who had the persistence and daring to undertake the unprecedented westward voyage. Before the invention of sufficiently accurate clocks (in the eighteenth century) mariners had no way of determining longitude, i.e., their east-west position, and learned geographers, as may be seen from Behaim's map, greatly underestimated the probable distance from Europe westward to Asia. When Columbus struck land, he naturally supposed it to be an

[1] See p. 302.

outlying part of the Indies. The people were soon called Indians, and the islands where Columbus landed, the West Indies.

Columbus had sailed with the backing of Queen Isabella of Castile, and the new lands became part of the composite dominions of the crown of Spain. The Spaniards, hoping to beat the Portuguese to the East (which da Gama had not yet reached), received Columbus' first reports with enthusiasm. For his second voyage they gave him seventeen ships, filled with 1,500 workmen and artisans. Columbus himself, until his death in 1506, kept probing about in the Caribbean, baffled and frustrated, hoping to find something that looked like the fabulous East. Others were more willing to accept the new land for what it was. Churchmen, powerful in Spain, regarded it as a new field for crusading and conversion. The government saw it as a source of gold and silver for the royal exchequer. Footloose gentry of warlike habits, left idle by the end of war with the Moors, turned to it to make their fortunes. The *conquistadores* fell upon the new lands. Cortés conquered the Aztecs in Mexico, Pizarro the Incas in Peru. They despoiled the native empires. Mines for precious metals were opened almost immediately. The Indians were put to forced labor, in which many died. The attempts of the church to protect its Indian converts, and restrictions set by the royal authorities on their exploitation, led almost immediately to the importation of African slaves, of whom, it was estimated, 100,000 had been brought to America by 1560.

Explorers began to feel their way along the vast dim bulk that barred them from Asia. A Spanish expedition, led by Magellan, found a southwestern passage in 1520, sailed from the Atlantic into the Pacific, crossed the Pacific, discovered the Philippine Islands, and fought its way through hostile Portuguese across the Indian Ocean back to Spain. The globe was thus circumnavigated for the first time, and an idea of the true size and interconnection of the oceans was brought back to Europe. Geographical experts immediately incorporated the new knowledge, as in the map drawn by Schöner in 1523.[2] Meanwhile others sailing for Spain, the Cabots sailing for England, Jacques Cartier for France, began the long and fruitless search for a northwest passage. An English expedition, looking for a northeast passage, discovered the White Sea in 1553. English merchants immediately began to take the ocean route to Russia. Archangel became an ocean port.

For a century it was only the Spanish and Portuguese who followed up the new ocean routes to America and the East. These two peoples, in a treaty of 1494, divided the globe between them by an imaginary north-and-south line that

[2] See p. 302.

THE GEOGRAPHER
by Jan Vermeer (Dutch, 1632–1675)
The impact on Europe of the opening of the Atlantic may be seen in this painting and the following one. For the first time in human history it became possible to conceive, with some accuracy, of the relationships of the oceans and continents throughout the globe. The wonder aroused by the Age of Discovery is evident in this painting by Vermeer. By the seventeenth century the Dutch had built up a large ocean-going trade, and many of the leading instrument makers and cartographers lived in the Netherlands. For Vermeer and Dutch painting, see p. 164. Courtesy of the Städelsches Kunstinstitut, Frankfurt.

III

ran from a point in the middle of the North Atlantic Ocean through the north pole and so on across eastern Asia. Spain claimed all the Americas by this treaty, and Portugal, all rights of trade in Africa, Asia, and the East Indies. But when Brazil was discovered in 1500 by Pedro Cabral it was found to be far enough east to lie within the Portuguese area, and when the Philippine Islands were discovered by Magellan in 1521 they were claimed to be in the Spanish zone.

In the populous and civilized East the Portuguese were never more than a handful of outsiders who could not impose their language, their religion, or their way of life. It was otherwise in the Americas.

The Spanish Empire in America

In South America, Mexico, and the Caribbean, after the first ferocity of the *conquista,* the Spanish established their own civilization. In Protestant countries, and also in France, as the years went on there arose an extremely unfavorable idea of the Spanish regime in America, where, it was noted, the Inquisition was presently established and the native peoples were reduced to servitude by the conquerors. The Spanish themselves came to dismiss this grim picture as a Black Legend concocted by their rivals. The true character of the Spanish empire in America is not easy to portray. The Spanish government (like the home governments of all colonial empires until the American Revolution, and even later) regarded its empire as existing for the benefit of the mother country. The Indians were put into servitude, to work in mines or in agriculture. They also died off in large numbers from infections brought by Europeans to which Europeans had developed immunities but against which the native American peoples had no such protection. The same was true farther north in what later became the United States. The Spanish government made efforts to moderate the exploitation of Indian labor. It introduced the encomienda, by which Indians were required to work for an owner a certain number of days in the week, while retaining parcels of land on which to work for themselves. How much the royal regulations were enforced on remote encomiendas is another question, to which answers vary. Black African slavery became less important in most of Spanish America than it later became in some of the Dutch, French, and English colonies or in Portuguese Brazil. But the white population remained relatively small. Castilian Spaniards looked down on American-born whites, called creoles. Since fewer women than men emigrated from Spain, there arose a large class of mestizos, of mixed white and Indian descent.

STUDY OF TWO BLACK HEADS
by Rembrandt van Rijn (Dutch, 1606-1669)
One consequence of the new intercontinental travel was the mass transportation to the Americas of black Africans as slaves. Some appeared also in Europe, where they attracted a great deal of personal curiosity and produced much speculation on the diversity of human races. Rembrandt, though he never traveled more than twenty miles from his native Leyden, painted all types of persons who streamed into the Netherlands. The greatest of the Dutch painters, and a profound observer of human beings, he was no doubt fascinated by the dark color tones, rugged features, and secret inner feelings of these two men in the strange world into which they had been cast. Courtesy of the Mauritshuis, The Hague (A. Dingjan).

The mestizos, along with many pure Indians, adopted to a considerable degree the Spanish language and the faith of the Spanish church. The Indians, while unfree, had usually been unfree under their own tribal chiefs; they were spared from tribal war; and the rigors of the Inquisition were mild compared with the sheer physical cruelty of the Aztecs or Incas. The printing press was brought to Mexico in 1544. By the middle of the sixteenth century Spanish America consisted of two great viceroyalties, those of Mexico and Peru, with twenty-two bishoprics, and with a university in each viceroyalty, the University of Lima established in 1551, that of Mexico in 1553. When Harvard College was founded in New England (in 1636) there were five universities on the European model in Spanish America.

In 1545 a great discovery was made, the prodigiously rich silver deposits at Potosí in Peru. (It is now in Bolivia.) Almost simultaneously, better methods of extracting silver from the ore by the use of mercury were developed. American production of precious metals shot up suddenly and portentously. For years, after the mid-century, half a million pounds of silver flowed annually from America to Spain, and ten thousand pounds of gold. The riches of Potosí financed the European projects of the king of Spain. Peruvian ores, Indian labor, and Spanish management combined to make possible the militant and anti-Protestant phase of the Counter Reformation.

The opening of the Atlantic reoriented Europe. In an age of oceanic communications Europe became a center from which America, Africa, and Asia could all be reached. In Europe itself, the Atlantic coast enjoyed great advantages over the center. No sooner did the Portuguese begin to bring spices from the East Indies than Antwerp began to flourish as the point of redistribution for northern Europe. But for a century after the great discoveries the northern peoples did not take to the oceans. French corsairs did indeed put out from Bayonne or Saint-Malo, and Dutch prowlers and English "sea dogs" followed at the close of the century, all bent upon plundering the Iberian treasure ships. Still the Spanish and Portuguese kept their monopoly. No organized effort, backed by governments, came from the north until about 1600. For it is by no means geography alone that determines economic development, and the English, Dutch, and French could not make use of the opportunities with which the opening of the Atlantic provided them until they had cleared up domestic troubles at home and survived the perils and hazards of the Wars of Religion.

12. The Commercial Revolution

In the great economic readjustment that was taking place in Europe, the opening of ocean trade routes was important, but it was by no means the only factor. Two others were the growth of population and a long, gradual rise in prices, or a slow inflation.

European population again grew rapidly, as in the High Middle Ages, reaching about 90 million in 1600, of which 20 million represented the growth during the sixteenth century. The increase took place in all countries, though it is well to remember that distribution was quite different from what we have known in more recent times. England in 1600 had no more than five million inhabitants. France had almost four times as many, and the German states altogether about as many as France. Italy and Spain had fewer than France, and distant Russia, within its then boundaries, may have had no more than ten million people. Some cities grew substantially, with London and Paris approaching 200,000; Antwerp, Lisbon, and Seville, thanks to the ocean trade, jumped to 100,000 by 1600. But smaller towns remained much the same; Europe as a whole was probably no more urbanized than in the later Middle Ages. Most of the population growth represented increasing density in the rural regions.[3]

The steady rise in prices, which is to say the steady decline in value of a given unit of money (such as a shilling), constituted a gradual inflation. It has been called a "price revolution," but it was so slow as to be hardly comparable to the kinds of inflation known in the twentieth century. One cause seems to have lain in the growth of population itself, which set up an increasing demand for food. This meant that new land was brought under cultivation, land that was less fertile, more inaccessible or more difficult to work than the fields that had been cultivated previously. With increasing costs of production, agricultural prices rose; in England, for example, they about quadrupled during the sixteenth century. Prices were also pushed upward by the increase in the volume of money. The royal habit of debasing the currency brought a larger amount of money into circulation, since larger numbers of florins, *reals,* or *livres* were obtained from the same amount of bullion. The flow of gold and silver from America also made money more plentiful, but the impact of Peruvian and Mexican mines can easily be exaggerated. Even before the discovery of America, the development of gold and silver mines had augmented the European money supply. In any case, an increase of money supply is inflationary only if it runs ahead of the volume of monetary transactions. The expansion of both population and commerce thus checked the inflationary forces. Nevertheless, the long trend of prices was upward. It affected all prices, including rents and other payments that were set in money values, but it seems that the price of hired labor, i.e., wages, rose the least. The price changes thus had different effects on the well-being of social classes.

Commercial undertakings were favored by rising prices and growing population. Merchants could count on increasing numbers of customers, new men could enter trade with hope of success, stocks of goods rose in value with the passage of time, and borrowed money could more easily be repaid. Governments benefited also, so far as kings could count on having more taxpayers and more soldiers.

The economic changes in Europe in the early modern period have been called the "Commercial Revolution," which in general signifies the rise of a capitalistic economy and the transition from a town-centered to a nation-centered economic system. This "revolution" was an exceptionally slow and protracted one, for it began at least as early as the fourteenth century and lasted until machine industry began to overshadow commerce.

Changes in Commerce and Production

In the Middle Ages the town and its adjoining country formed an economic unit.[4] Craftsmen, organized in guilds, produced common articles for local use. Peasants and lords sold their agricultural products to the local town, from which they

---

[3] See Appendix III for estimates of population of selected cities and countries at various dates.
[4] See pp. 31–32.

bought what the craftsmen produced. The town protected itself by its own tariffs and regulations. In the workshop the master both owned his "capital"—his house, workbench, tools, and materials—and acted as a workman himself along with half a dozen journeymen and apprentices. The masters owned a modest capital, but they were hardly capitalists. They produced only upon order, or at least for customers whose tastes and number were known in advance. There was little profit, little risk of loss, and not much innovation.

All this changed with the widening of the trading area, or market. Even in the Middle Ages, as we have seen, there was a certain amount of long-distance trading in articles that could not be produced as well in one place as in another. Gradually more articles came within this category. Where goods were produced to be sold at some time in the future, in faraway places, to persons unknown, the local guildmaster could not manage the operation. He lacked the money (or "capital") to tie up in stocks of unsold wares; he lacked the knowledge of what distant customers wanted, or where, in what quantities, and at what price people would buy. In this type of business a new type of man developed. Economists call him the "enterpriser," or *entrepreneur*. He usually started out as a merchant working in an extensive market, and ended up as a banker. The Italian Medici family has been mentioned.[5] Equally typical were the German Fuggers.

The first of this family, Johann Fugger, a small-town weaver, came to Augsburg in 1368. He established a business in a new kind of cloth, called fustian, in which cotton was mixed, and which had certain advantages over the woolens and linens in which people then clothed themselves. He thus enjoyed a more than local market, and made trips to Venice to obtain the cotton imported from the Near East. Gradually the family began to deal also in spices, silks, and other Eastern goods obtained at Venice. They made large profits, which were invested in other enterprises, notably mining. They lent money to the Renaissance popes. They lent Charles V the money which he spent to obtain election as Holy Roman Emperor in 1519. They became bankers to the Habsburgs in both Germany and Spain. Together with other German and Flemish bankers, the Fuggers financed the Portuguese trade with Asia, either by outright loans or by providing in advance, on credit, the cargoes which the Portuguese traded for spices. The wealth of the Fuggers became proverbial and declined only through repeated Habsburg bankruptcies and with the general economic decline that beset Germany in the sixteenth century.

Other dealers in cloth, less spectacular than the first Fugger, broke away from the town-and-guild framework in other ways. England until the fifteenth century was an exporter of raw wool and an importer of finished woolens from Flanders. In the fifteenth century certain Englishmen began to develop the spinning, weaving, and dyeing of wool in England. To avoid the restrictive practices of the towns and guilds they "put out" the work to people in the country, providing them with looms and other equipment for the purpose, of which they generally retained the ownership themselves. This "putting out" or "domestic" system spread very widely. In France the cloth dealers of Rouen, feeling the competition of the new silk trade, developed a lighter, cheaper, and more simply made type

[5] See pp. 54, 104.

of woolen cloth. Various guild regulations in Rouen, to protect the workers there, prohibited the manufacture of this cheaper cloth. The Rouen dealers, in 1496, took the industry into the country, installed looms in peasant cottages, and farmed out the work to the peasants.

Capital and Labor

This domestic system, or system of rural household industry, remained typical of production in many lines (cloth, hardware, etc.) in western Europe until the introduction of factories in the late eighteenth century. It signified a new divergence between capital and labor.[6] On the one hand were the workers, people who worked as the employer needed them, received wages for what they did, and had no interest in or knowledge of more than their own task. Living both by agriculture and by cottage industry, they formed an expansible labor force, available when labor was needed, left to live by farming or local charity when times were bad. On the other hand was the man who managed the whole affair. He had no personal acquaintance with the workers. Estimating how much of his product, let us say woolens, he could sell in a national or even international market, he purchased the needed raw materials, passed out wool to be spun by one group of peasants, took the yarn to another group for weaving, collected the cloth and took it still elsewhere to be dyed, paying wages on all sides for services rendered, while retaining ownership of the materials and the equipment and keeping the coordination and management of the whole enterprise in his own head. Much larger business enterprises could be established in this way than within the municipal framework of guild and town. Indeed, the very master weavers of the guilds often sank to the status of subcontractors, hardly different from wage employees, of the great "clothiers" and "drapers" by whom the business was dominated. The latter, with the widening market, became personages of national or even international repute. And, of course, the bigger the business the more of a capital investment it represented.

Certain other industries, new or virtually new in the fifteenth and sixteenth centuries, could by their nature never fit into a town-centered system and were capitalistic from the start, in that they required a large initial outlay before any income could be received. One such was mining. Another was printing and the book trade. Books had a national and even international market, being mainly in Latin; and no ordinary craftsman could afford the outlay required for a printing press, for fonts of type, supplies of paper, and stocks of books on hand. Printers therefore borrowed from capitalists, or shared with them an interest in business. Shipbuilding was so stimulated by the shift to the oceans as almost to be a new industry, and still another was the manufacture of cannons and muskets. For the latter the chief demand came from the state, from the New Monarchies which were organizing national armies. In the rise of capitalism the needs of the military were in fact fundamentally important. Armies, which started out by requiring thousands of weapons, in the seventeenth century required thousands of uniforms, and in the eighteenth century many solidly built barracks and fortifications. These

[6] On capitalism, see also pp. 257–258, 268–272.

were the first demands for mass production; and where governments themselves did not take the initiative, private organizers stepped in as middlemen between these huge requirements and the myriads of small handicraft workers by whom, before the industrial age, the actual product was still manufactured.

The new sea route to the East and the discovery of America brought a vast increase in trade not only of luxury items but of bulk commodities like rice, sugar, tea, and other consumer goods. Older commercial activities were transformed by the widening of markets. Spain increasingly drew cereals from Sicily. The Netherlands were fed from Poland, the French wine districts lived on food brought from northern France. With the growth of shipping, the timber, tar, pitch, and other "naval stores" of Russia and the Baltic came upon the commercial scene. There was thus an ever growing movement of heavy staple commodities, in which again only men controlling large funds of capital could normally take part.

Not all capital was invested; some was simply lent, either to the church, or to governments, or to impecunious nobles, or, though perhaps this was the least common type of lending in the sixteenth century, to persons engaged in trade and commerce. Bankers and others who lent money expected to receive back, after a time, a larger sum than that of the loan. They expected "interest"; and they sometimes received as much as 30 percent a year. In the Middle Ages the taking of interest had been frowned upon as usury, denounced as avarice, and forbidden in the canon law. It was still frowned upon in the sixteenth century by almost all but the lenders themselves. The Catholic church maintained its prohibitions. The theologians of the University of Paris ruled against it in 1530. Luther, who hated "Fuggerism," continued to preach against usury. Calvin made allowances, but as late as 1640, in capitalist Holland itself, the stricter Calvinist ministers still denounced lending at interest. Nothing could stop the practice. Borrowers compounded with lenders to evade prohibitions, and theologians of all churches began to distinguish between "usury" and a "legitimate return." Gradually, as interest rates fell, as banking became more established, and as loans were made for economically productive uses rather than to sustain ecclesiastics, princes, and nobles in their personal habits, the feeling against a "reasonable" interest died down, and interest became an accepted feature of capitalism. The Bank of Amsterdam, in the seventeenth century, because depositors knew that their money was safe and could be withdrawn at will, was able to attract deposits from all countries by offering a very low rate of interest, which enabled it in turn to make loans, at a low rate, to finance commercial activities.

The net effect of all these developments was a "commercialization of industry." The great man of business was the merchant. Industry, the actual processes of production, still in an essentially handicraft stage, was subordinate to the buyers and sellers. Producers—weavers, hatters, metalworkers, gunsmiths, glassworkers, etc.—worked to fill the orders of the merchants, and often with capital which the merchants supplied and owned. The man who knew where the article could be sold prevailed over the man who simply knew how to produce it. This commercial capitalism remained the typical form of capitalism until after 1800, when, with the introduction of power machinery, it yielded to industrial capitalism, and merchants became dependent on industrialists, who owned, understood, and organized the machines.

Mercantilism

There was still another aspect of the commercial revolution, namely, the various government policies that go historically under the name of "mercantilism." Rulers, as we have seen, were hard pressed for money, and needed more of it as it fell in value. The desire of kings and their advisers to force gold and silver to flow into their own kingdoms was one of the first impulses leading to mercantilist regulation. Gradually this "bullionist" idea was replaced by the more general idea of building up a strong and self-sufficient economy. The means adopted, in either case, was to "set the poor on work," as they said in England, to turn the country into a hive of industry, to discourage idleness, begging, vagabondage, and unemployment. New crafts and manufactures were introduced, and favors were given to merchants who provided work for "the poor" and who sold the country's products abroad. It was thought desirable to raise the export of finished goods and reduce the export of unprocessed raw materials, to curtail all imports except of needed raw materials, and thus obtain a "favorable" balance of trade so that other countries would have to pay their debts in bullion. Since all this was done by a royal or nationwide system of regulations, mercantilism became in the economic sphere what the state building of the New Monarchies was in the political, signifying the transition from town to national units of social living.[7]

Mercantilists frowned upon the localistic and conservative outlook of the guilds. In England the guilds ceased to have any importance. Parliament, in the time of Elizabeth, did on a national scale what guilds had once done locally when it enacted the Statute of Artificers of 1563, regulating the admission to apprenticeship and level of wages in various trades. In France the royal government kept the guilds in being, because they were convenient bodies to tax, but it deprived them of most of their old independence and used them as organizations through which royal control of industry could be enforced. In both countries the government assisted merchants who wished to set up domestic or cottage industry in the country, against the protests of the town guilds, which in their heyday had forbidden rural people to engage in crafts. Governments generally tried to suppress idleness. The famous English Poor Law of 1601 (which remained in effect, with amendments, until 1834) was designed both to force people to work and to relieve absolute destitution.

Governments likewise took steps to introduce new industries. The silk industry was brought from Italy to France under royal protection, to the dismay of French woolen and linen interests. The English government assisted in turning England from a producer of raw wool into a producer of finished woolens, supervising the immigration of skilled Flemish weavers, and even fetching from faraway Turkey, about 1582, two youths who understood the more advanced dyeing arts of the Near East. Generally, under mercantilism, governments fought to steal skilled workers from each other while prohibiting or discouraging the emigration of their own skilled workers, who might take their trade secrets and "mysteries" to foreign parts.

By such means governments helped to create a national market and an industrious nationwide labor supply for their great merchants. Without such

---

[7] On the New Monarchies, see pp. 67–75.

government support the great merchants, such as the drapers or clothiers, could never have risen and prospered. The same help was given to merchants operating in foreign markets. Henry VII of England in 1496 negotiated a commercial treaty with Flanders, known as the Intercursus Magnus; and in the next century the kings of France signed a number of treaties with the Ottoman Empire by which French merchants obtained privileges in the Near East. A merchant backed by a national monarchy was in a much stronger position than one backed merely by a city, such as Augsburg or Venice. This backing on a national scale was again given when national governments subsidized exports, paying bounties for goods whose production they wished to encourage, or when they erected tariff barriers against imports to protect their own producers from competition. Thus a national tariff system was superimposed on the old network of provincial and municipal tariffs. These latter were now thought of as "internal tariffs," and mercantilists usually wished to abolish them, in order to create an area of free trade within the state as a whole. But local interests were so strong, and a sense of interprovincial and intertown unity was so slow to develop, that for centuries they were unable to get rid of local tariffs except in England.

In wild or distant parts of the world, or in exotic regions nearer home, such as the Muslim Near East or Russia, it was not possible for individual merchants to act by merely private initiative. Merchants trading with such countries needed a good deal of capital, they often had to obtain special privileges and protection from native rulers, and they had to arm their ships against Barbary or Malay pirates or against hostile Europeans. Merchants and their respective governments came together to found official companies for the transocean trade. In England, soon after the English discovery of the White Sea in 1553, a Russia Company was established. A Turkey Company soon followed. Shortly after 1600 a great many such companies were operating out of England, Holland, and France. The most famous of all were the East India Companies, which the English founded in 1600, the Dutch in 1602, the French not until 1664. Each of these companies was a state-supported organization, with special rights. Each was a monopoly in that only merchants who belonged to the company could legally engage in trade in the region for which the company had a charter. Each was expected to find markets for the national manufactures, and most of them were expected to bring home gold or silver. With these companies the northern peoples began to encroach on the Spanish and Portuguese monopoly in America and the East. With them new commercial-colonial empires were to be launched. But, as has been already observed, before this could happen it was necessary for certain domestic and purely European conflicts and controversies to be settled.

13. Changing Social Structures

Social structure, for present purposes, refers to the composition, functions, and interrelationships of social classes. Because changes in social structure are slow, they are hard to identify with any particular period of time. In general, however, with the effects of the commercial revolution, population growth, and the falling value of money, the classes of Europe, broadly defined, took on forms that were to last until the industrial era of the nineteenth and twentieth centuries. These classes were the landed aristocracy, the peasantry or mass of agricultural workers, the miscellaneous middle classes, and the urban poor.

While all prices rose in the sixteenth century, it was agricultural prices that rose the most. Anyone who had agricultural products to sell was likely to benefit. Among such beneficiaries were peasants who held bits of land in return for payments to a manorial lord set in unchangeable sums of money, in the old values of the fourteenth or even thirteenth century. Such peasants in effect paid much less to the lord than in the past. Other rural workers, however, either held no land of their own or produced only at a subsistence level with nothing to sell in the market. Such peasants, and hired hands dependent on wages, found their situation worsened. Village life became less equalitarian than it had been in the Middle Ages. In England a class of small freeholders (the ''yeomanry'') developed between the landed gentry and the rural poor. On the Continent, at least in France, western Germany, and the Netherlands, some peasants acquired more secure property rights, resembling those of small freeholders in England. But both in England and on the Continent a large class of unpropertied rural workers remained in poverty.

Land rents went up as agricultural prices rose, and inflation and population growth drove up rentals for housing in the towns. Owners of real property (i.e., land and buildings) were favored by such changes, but within the former class of feudal lords the effects were mixed. If one's great-grandfather had let out land in earlier times in exchange for fixed sums of money, the value of the income received had actually declined. But those who received payments in kind from their tenants, for example, in bushels of wheat or barley, or who managed their estates themselves, could sell their actual agricultural products at current prices and so increase their money income.

Basic Social Classes

The former feudal class, or nobles, thus turned into a more modern kind of aristocracy. If income from their estates declined, they sought service in the king's army or government or appointment to the more prestigious offices in the church. If landed income increased, they were more wealthy. In either case they became more concerned with civilian pursuits, and were likely to develop more refined tastes and pay more attention to the education of their children. Like the peasants, the landowning class became more heterogeneous, ranging from the small gentry to the great peers of England, and from small or impoverished nobles to the *grands seigneurs* of France. Some led a life of leisure; others were eager to work in the higher reaches of organized government. The most impoverished nobles sometimes had the longest pedigrees. As their social functions changed, and as persons of more recent family background competed for education, government employment, and even military service, there came to be an increasing importance set upon ancestry as a badge of status. Among the upper class, there was more insistence on high birth and distinguished forebears in the seventeenth and eighteenth centuries than there had been before.

Below the aristocracy were the ''middle classes,'' or ''bourgeoisie.'' *Bourgeois* was a French word, which, like the English ''burgher,'' originally meant a person living in a chartered town or borough and enjoying its liberties. The bourgeoisie was the whole social class made up of individual bourgeois. In a much later sense of the word, derived from Karl Marx, the term "bourgeoisie" was applied to the class of owners of capital. This sense must be kept distinct from the earlier meaning, which is usually adopted in this book. In this latter sense, the word refers to the middle levels of society between the aristocracy on the one hand, which drew its income from land, and the laboring poor on the other, who depended on wages or charity, or who often went hungry. Class lines tended to blur as aristocratic families formed the habit of living in towns, and middle-class burghers began to buy land in the country. Some bourgeois thus came to live on landed rents, while some of the gentry and aristocracy, most notably in England, bought shares in the great overseas trading companies or engaged in other forms of business enterprise. Aristocrats possessing large agricultural estates, timberlands, or mines increasingly brought their products to market to be sold at a profit. But even when aristocrat and bourgeois became economically more alike, a consciousness of social difference between them remained.

The middle class became more numerous in the sixteenth century, and increasingly so thereafter. It was an indefinite category, since the countries of Europe were very different in the size and importance of their middle classes, in the kinds of persons that made them up, and in the types of occupations pursued. Near the top were the urban elites who governed the towns; they might draw their incomes from rural property, from commerce, or from the emoluments of government itself, and they sometimes intermarried with persons of noble status. Especially where the towns were strong or broad royal government was lacking, as in the Netherlands, the German free cities, or north Italy, such urban patriciates formed virtual aristocracies in themselves. But in a larger perspective the families of merchants, bankers, and shipowners were middle-class, as were those of the traditional learned professions, law and medicine. So in general were judges, tax officials, and other employees of governments, except in the highest ranks. In the professions and in government service the younger sons of the aristocracy might be found alongside the offspring of the middle classes, most commonly in England, less so in France, and even less as one moved into Germany or Spain. The clergy was drawn from all classes; there were poor parish priests, who might be the sons of peasants, and noblemen among the bishops and abbots; but the bulk of the clergy was recruited from middle-class families. In Protestant countries, where the clergy married, their sons and daughters became an important element in the middle class. Members of trade guilds were middle class, though the guilds differed widely in social status, from those of the great wholesale merchants or the goldsmiths, down through the guilds of such humble occupations as the tanners and barrel makers. At the bottom the middle class faded into the world of small retail shopkeepers, innkeepers, owners of workshops in which ordinary articles were manufactured by hand, the lesser skilled tradespeople and their employees, journeymen, and apprentices.

The mass of the population in all countries was composed of the working poor. These included not only the unskilled wage laborers but the unemployed, unemployable, and paupers, with a large fringe that turned to vagabondage and begging. They were unable to read or write, and were often given to irregular habits which distressed both middle-class persons and government officials. The efforts of mercantilist governments to put the poor to work, or make them

every Local gov. was responsible for their poor

contribute to the wealth of the country, have already been mentioned. Charitable relief also developed toward the end of the sixteenth century, as shown in the English Poor Law of 1601 and in similar efforts on the Continent. The idea gained ground that begging was a public nuisance, and that the poor should be segregated in workhouses or hospices from the rest of society. Most of the poor were of course not recipients of such relief. They were the people who tilled the fields, tended the livestock, dug in the mines, went to sea as fishermen or common sailors, found work in the towns as casual laborers, porters, water carriers, or removers of excrement, or entered the domestic service of noble and upper middle-class families, whose rising standard of living required a growing number of chambermaids, washerwomen, footmen, lackeys, coachmen, and stable boys. It has already been remarked that wages rose less than prices in the sixteenth century. The poor, if not positively worse off than in former times, gained the least from the great developments with which much history is concerned. The very growth of social differentiation, the fact that the middle and upper classes made such advances, left the condition of the poor correspondingly worse.[8]

Social Roles of Education and Government

Education in the latter part of the sixteenth century took on an altogether new importance for the social system. One consequence of the Reformation, in both Protestant and Catholic countries, was the attempt to put a serious and effective pastor in each parish. This set up a demand for a more educated clergy. The growth of commerce made it necessary to have literate clerks and agents. Governments wanted men from both the noble and middle classes who could cooperate in large organizations, be reliable, understand finance, keep records, and draft proposals. There was also a widespread need for lawyers.

The new demand for education was met by an outburst of philanthropy, which reached a high point in both England and France between about 1580 and 1640. Many endowed scholarships were established. At what would now be called a secondary level, hundreds of "grammar schools" were founded at this time in England. In France the *collèges* combined the work of the English grammar school with what corresponded to the first year or two of university work at Oxford or Cambridge. Of the 167 most important French colleges still existing at the time of the Revolution in 1789, only 36 had been founded in the centuries before 1560, and 92 were established in the years between 1560 and 1650. Provision for girls' schools was more sporadic, but the Ursuline sisters, for example, founded in Italy in 1535, by the year 1700 had about 350 convents in Catholic Europe and even in Canada, in most of which the education of girls was a principal occupation of the sisters. Mme. de Maintenon, the morganatic wife of Louis XIV, founded and closely supervised a school for the daughters of the French gentry and lesser nobility.

education

Dutch and Swiss Protestants founded the universities of Leyden and Geneva. New universities, both Protestant and Catholic, appeared in Germany. In Spain the multiplication of universities was phenomenal. Castile, with only two universities dating from the Middle Ages, had twenty by the early seventeenth

[8] See pp. 251–256.

century; Salamanca was enrolling over 5,000 students a year. Five universities also existed in Spanish America by 1600. In England, new colleges were founded at Oxford and Cambridge, and it was especially in these years that some of the Oxford and Cambridge colleges became very wealthy. Annual freshman admissions at Oxford, barely 100 in 1550, rose to over 500 in the 1630s, a figure not exceeded, or even equaled, during the following two hundred years. If this fivefold increase seems small, compared with figures for Spain or other countries, it must be remembered that England was not very populous, that English grammar schools did some of the teaching offered by universities elsewhere, and that the study of law, important in Continental universities, was carried on in England outside the universities, at the Inns of Court.

The schools, colleges, and universities drew their students from a wide range of social classes. For girls less organized schooling was offered, but an intelligent and lucky boy of poor family had perhaps a better chance for education than at any time in Europe until very recently. In Spain most of the students seem to have been nobles, or "hidalgos," aspiring to positions in the church or the royal government; but hidalgos were very numerous in Spain, overlapping with what might be called the middle class in other countries. The French colleges, including those operated by the Jesuits, recruited their students very widely, taking in the sons of nobles, merchants, shopkeepers, artisans, and even, more rarely, of peasants. English grammar schools did likewise; it was in later times that a few of them, like Eton and Harrow, became more exclusive Public Schools. As for universities, we have detailed knowledge for Oxford, which recorded the status of its students at matriculation, classifying them as "esquires," "gentlemen," "clergy," and "plebeians." From 1560 to 1660 about half of the Oxford students were "plebeians," which in the language of that time could embrace the whole middle class from big merchants down to quite modest levels. It seems certain that Oxford and Cambridge were more widely representative of the English people in 1660 than in 1900.

Social classes were formed not only by economic forces, and not only by education, but also by the action of governments. Government could inhibit economic growth, as in Spain, or promote it, as in England. Kings contributed to the rise of capitalism and a business class by granting monopolies, borrowing from bankers, and issuing charters to trading companies. In many countries, and notably in France, many families owed their middle-class position to the holding of government offices, some of which might become a form of inheritable property. It might also be the action of governments, as much as economic conditions, that kept alive a distinction between nobles and commoners, or "privileged" and "unprivileged" classes, of which more will be heard.[9] Where peasants suffered heavily from royal taxes, it was more from political than from economic causes. The king, by "making" nobles—that is, by conferring titles of nobility on persons who did not inherit them—could raise a few in the middle class to higher status. Tax exemption could be a sign of high social standing. The king was also the fountain of honor, at the top of "society" in the more frivolous sense of the word. The royal court formed the apex of a pyramid of social rank, in which each class looked up to or down upon the others. Those favored with the royal presence

[9] See pp. 187, 363, 368.

disdained the plain country nobility, who sniffed at the middle classes, who patronized or disparaged the hired servants, day laborers, and the poor. Looking upward, people were expected to show deference for their betters.

Eastern and Western Europe

One other remark may be made on social structure. It was in the sixteenth century that a great difference developed between eastern and western Europe. In the west, the commercial revolution and the declining value of money were advantageous to the middle class and to many of the peasantry for whom the old burdens of the manorial system were lightened. In eastern Europe, it was the lords who benefited from rising prices and the growing market for grain and forest products. Here too the institution of the manor existed; but the peasants' land tenures were more precarious than in the west, more dependent on accidents of death or on the wishes of the lord, and the lord worked a larger part of the manor with his own work force for his own use or profit.

The rise of prices and expansion of Baltic shipping gave the lord the incentive to increase his output. In northeast Germany (where such lords were called Junkers), in Poland, and as time went on in Russia, Bohemia, and Hungary, beginning in the sixteenth century and continuing into the eighteenth, a vast process set in by which the mass of the peasantry sank into serfdom. It was hastened in many regions by the violence and insecurity engendered by the religious wars. Typically, peasants lost their individual parcels of land, or received them back on condition that they render unpaid labor services to the lord. Usually peasants owed three or four days a week of such forced labor (called *robot* in Bohemia and adjoining territories), remaining free to work during the remainder of the week on their own parcels. Often the number of days of *robot* exacted by the lord was greater, since in eastern Europe, where central monarchy was weak and centralized legal systems almost unknown, the lord himself was the final court of appeal for his people. His people were in fact his "subjects." Serfdom in Germany was not called serfdom, an ill-sounding word, but "hereditary subjection." By whatever name they were known throughout eastern Europe, serfs, or hereditary subjects of the manorial lord, could not leave the manor, marry, or learn a trade without the lord's express permission. The lord, drawing on this large reserve of compulsory labor, using most of it for agriculture but teaching some quick-minded youths the various handicrafts that were needed on the estate, worked the land as his own venture, sold the produce, and retained the profit.

Thus, in eastern Europe at the beginning of modern times, the rural masses lost personal freedom and lived in a poverty unknown among the peasants to the west, poor as the latter were. In western Europe there were peasants who were already on the way to becoming small proprietors. They were free people under the law. They could migrate, marry, and learn trades as opportunity offered. Those who held land could defend it in the royal courts, and raise crops and take part in the market economy on their own account. They owed the lord no forced labor—or virtually none, for the ten days a year of corvée still found in parts of France hardly compared with the almost full-time *robot* of the peasant of eastern Europe.

The landlord in the east, from the sixteenth century onward, was solidly entrenched in his own domain, monarch of all he surveyed, with no troublesome bourgeoisie to annoy him (for towns were few), and with kings and territorial rulers solicitous of his wishes. Travelers from the west were impressed with the lavishness of great Polish and Lithuanian magnates, with their palatial homes, private art galleries, well-stocked libraries, collections of jewels, swarms of servants, trains of dependent lesser gentry, gargantuan dinners, and barbaric hospitality. The Junkers of northeast Germany lived more modestly, but enjoyed the same kind of independence and social superiority. The importance of all this will become evident when, in later chapters, we turn to Prussia, Poland, Russia, and the Austrian lands.

But meanwhile, with all the economic growth and social development that has been sketched in the preceding pages, Europe was torn by the destructive ferocity of the Wars of Religion.

14. The Crusade of Catholic Spain: The Dutch and English

The Ambitions of Philip II

Charles V, having tried in vain for thirty-five years to preserve religious unity in Germany, abdicated his many crowns and retired to a monastery in 1556, the year after the Peace of Augsburg.[10] He left Austria, Bohemia, and Hungary (or the small part of it not occupied by the Turks) to his brother Ferdinand, who was soon elected Holy Roman Emperor.[11] All his other possessions Charles left to his son Philip, who became Philip II of Spain. The Habsburg dynasty remained thereafter divided into two branches, the Austrian and the Spanish. The two cooperated in European affairs. The Spanish branch for a century was the more important. Philip II (1556–1598) not only possessed the Spanish kingdoms but in 1580 inherited Portugal, so that the whole Iberian peninsula was brought under his rule. He possessed the seventeen provinces of the Netherlands and the Free County of Burgundy, which were member states of the Holy Roman Empire, lying on its western border, adjacent to France. Milan in north Italy and Naples in the south belonged to Philip, and since he also held the chief islands, as well as Tunis, he enjoyed a naval ascendancy in the western Mediterranean which was threatened only by the Turks. For five years, until 1558, he was titular king of England, and in 1589, in the name of his daughter, he laid claim to the throne of France. All America belonged to Philip II, and after 1580 all the Portuguese empire as well, so that except for a few nautical daredevils all ships plying the open ocean were the Spanish king's.

Philip II therefore naturally regarded himself as an international figure, and the more so because he thought in terms not of nationality but of religion. Before all else he was a Catholic, fervid and fanatical, committed to upholding the sway of the universal church, within which all nations were no more than minorities and

[10] See p. 80.
[11] See map, pp. 72–73.

all heretics no more than rebels. A grave and sober man, of abstemious personal habits, sharing in the moral severity of the Catholic Reform, and in the dark, brooding, and tormented inner world of the Spanish mystics, he took upon himself the headship of a far-flung Catholic counteroffensive, into which he was willing to pour with grim persistence the blood and treasure of all his kingdoms. To economic and material interests he gave no thought, and in such matters Spanish society began to deteriorate in his reign; but for all material problems the wealth of Potosí provided a facile solution, and meanwhile Spain entered upon the Golden Age of its culture.

In this period, the *siglo de oro,* running in round dates from 1550 to 1650, Cervantes wrote his *Don Quixote* and Lope de Vega his seven hundred dramas, while El Greco, Murillo, and Velázquez painted their pictures, and the Jesuit Suarez composed works on philosophy and law that were read even in Protestant countries. But the essence of Spanish life was its peculiarly intensive Catholicism. The church was vitally present at every social level, from the archbishop of Toledo, who ranked above grandees and could address the king as an equal, down to a host of penniless and mendicant friars, who mixed with the poorest and most disinherited of the people. It is said that about 1600 a third of the population of Spain was in one way or another in the service of the church. Spain, whose whole history had been a crusade, was ideally suited to be Philip's instrument in the re-Catholicizing of Europe.[12]

Philip II built himself a new royal residence ("palace" is hardly the word), the Escorial, which well expressed in solid stone its creator's inner spirit. Madrid itself was a new town, merely a government center, far from the worldly distractions of Toledo or Valladolid. But it was thirty miles from Madrid, on the bleak arid plateau of central Castile, overlooked by the jagged Sierra, that Philip chose to erect the Escorial. He built it in honor of St. Lawrence, on whose feast day he had won a battle against the French. The great pile of connecting buildings was laid out in the shape of a grill, since, according to martyrologists, St. Lawrence, in the year 258, had been roasted alive on a grill over burning coals. Somber and vast, angular and unrelieved, made of blocks of granite meant to last forever, and with its highest spire rising three hundred feet from the ground, the Escorial was designed not only as a palace but as a monastery and a mausoleum. The monks moved in before the king, who, when he installed himself, brought with him eight coffins, those of his father, his dead wives, and his children, to remind him of his own. Here, in an atmosphere that could be painted only by El Greco, the king of Spain worked and lived, a slim figure dressed almost like a monk himself, always industrious, avid for detail, dispatching his couriers to Mexico, to Manila, to Vienna, to Milan, his troops and his bars of bullion to Italy and the Netherlands, his diplomats to all courts, and his spies to all countries, wholly and utterly absorbed in his one consuming project.

Let us try to see the events of the time internationally, for though it may be confusing to try to see all nations together, it is distorting to look at only one of them alone. The first years of Philip's reign were also the first years of Elizabeth's reign in England, where the religious issue was still in flux; they were years in which Calvinism agitated the Netherlands, and when France, ruled by teen-aged

[12] See pp. 69–71.

boys, fell apart into implacable civil war. Religious loyalties that knew no frontiers overlapped all political boundaries. Everywhere there were people who looked for guidance outside their own countries. Calvinists in England, France, and the Netherlands felt closer to one another than to their own monarchs or their own neighbors. Zealous Catholics, in all three countries, welcomed the support of international Catholic forces—the Jesuits, the king of Spain, the pope. National unity threatened to dissolve or was not yet formed. The sense of mutual trust between people who lived side by side was eaten away; and people who lived not only in the same country, but in the same town, on the same street, or even in the same house, turned against each other in the name of a higher cause.

For about five years, beginning in 1567, it seemed that the Catholic cause might prevail. The great crusade took the offensive on all fronts. In 1567 Philip sent a new and firmer governor general to the Netherlands, the Duke of Alva, with 20,000 Spanish soldiers; the duke proceeded to suppress religious and political dissidents by establishing a Council of Troubles. In 1569 Philip put down a revolt of the Moriscos in Spain. In the same year the Catholics of northern England, led by the Duke of Norfolk, and sewing the cross of crusaders on their garments, rose in armed rebellion against their heretic queen. In the next year, 1570, the pope excommunicated Elizabeth, and absolved her subjects from allegiance to her, so that English Catholics, if they wished, could henceforth in good conscience conspire to overthrow her. In 1571 the Spanish won a great naval battle against the Turks, at Lepanto off the coast of Greece; on their sails they wove the same cross that had been raised at the other corner of Europe, by the Duke of Norfolk in England; and they themselves believed that they were carrying on the crusades of the Middle Ages. In the next year, 1572, the Catholic leaders of France, with the advice of the pope and of Philip II, decided to make an end of the Huguenots, or French Protestants. Over three thousand were seized and put to death on the eve of St. Bartholomew's Day in Paris alone; and this massacre was followed by lesser liquidations throughout the provinces.

But none of these victories proved enduring. The Turkish power was not seriously damaged at Lepanto. In fact, the Turks took Tunis from Philip two years later. The Moriscos were not assimilated. The English Catholic rebellion was stamped out; eight hundred persons were put to death by Elizabeth's government. The revolt in the Netherlands remained very much alive, as did the French Huguenots. Twenty years later England was Protestant, the Dutch were winning independence, a Huguenot had become king of France, and the Spanish fleet had gone to ruin in northern waters. Let us see how these events came to pass.

The Revolt of the Netherlands

The Netherlands, or Low Countries (they had no other name), roughly comprised the area of the modern kingdoms of the Netherlands and Belgium and the grand duchy of Luxembourg. They consisted of seventeen provinces, which in the fifteenth century, one by one, had been inherited, purchased, or conquered by the dukes of Burgundy, from whom they were inherited by Charles V and his son, Philip II. In the mid–sixteenth century neither a Dutch nor a Belgian nationality yet existed. In the northern provinces the people spoke German dialects; in the southern provinces they spoke dialects of French; but neither here, nor elsewhere in Europe, was it felt that language boundaries had anything to do with political borders. The southern provinces had for centuries been busy commercial centers, and we have seen how Antwerp, having once flourished on trade with Venice, now flourished on trade with Lisbon. The northern provinces, or rather the two of them which were most open to the sea, the counties of Holland and Zeeland, had developed rapidly in the fifteenth century. They had a popular literature of their own, written in their own kind of German, which came to be called Dutch. The lay piety of the Brothers of the Common Life had originated in this region, and here Erasmus of Rotterdam had been born. The wealth of the northern provinces was drawn from deep-sea fishing. Amsterdam was said to be built on herring bones, and the Dutch, when they added trading to fishing, still lived by the sea.

The northern provinces felt no tie with each other and no sense of difference from the southern. Each of the seventeen provinces was a small state or country in itself. Each province enjoyed typical medieval liberties, privileges, and immunities, including the right to preserve its own law and consent to its own taxes. This constitution of the Netherlands, for such it was, went under the name of the *Joyeuse Entrée,* from the "joyous entry" made by the reigning duke into Brussels in 1355 after a solemn promise to recognize the liberties of the province of Brabant. The common bond of all seventeen provinces was simply that beginning with the dukes of Burgundy they had the same ruler; but since they had the same ruler they were called upon from time to time to send delegates to an estates general, and so developed an embryonic sense of federal collaboration. The feeling of Netherlandish identity was heightened with the accession of Philip II, for Philip, unlike his father, was thought of as foreign, a Spaniard who lived in Spain; and after 1560 Spanish governors general, Spanish officials, and Spanish troops were seen more frequently in the Netherlands. Moreover, since the Netherlands was the crossroads of Europe, with a tradition of earnestness in religion, Protestant ideas took root very early, and after 1560, when the religious wars began in France, a great many French Calvinists fled across the borders. At first, there were probably more Calvinists in the southern provinces than in the northern, more among the people that we now call Belgians than among those that we now call Dutch.

The revolt against Philip II was inextricably political and religious at the same time, and it became increasingly an economic struggle as the years went by. It began in 1566, when some 200 nobles of the various provinces founded a league to check the "foreign" or Spanish influence in the Netherlands. The league, to which both Catholic and Protestant nobles belonged, petitioned Philip II not to employ the Spanish Inquisition in the Netherlands. They feared the trouble it would stir up; they feared it as a foreign court; they feared that in the enforcement of its rulings the liberties of their provinces would be crushed. Philip's agents in the Netherlands refused the petition. A mass revolt now broke out. Within a week fanatical Calvinists pillaged 400 churches, pulling down images, breaking stained-glass windows, defacing paintings and tapestries, making off with gold chalices, destroying with a fierce contempt the symbols of "popery" and "idolatry." The fury spread from town to town, to Antwerp, to Amsterdam, to Armentières (now in France, but then in the Netherlands); it was chiefly journeymen wage earners, numerous in the industrial Netherlands, and aroused by social and economic grievances as well as religious belief, who formed the rank and file for these anti-Catholic and anti-Spanish demonstrations. Before such vandalism many of the petitioning nobles recoiled; the Catholics among them, as well as less militant Protestants, unable to control their revolutionary followers, began to look upon the Spanish authorities with less disfavor.

Philip II, appalled at the sacrilege, forthwith sent in the Inquisition, the Duke of Alva, and reinforcements of Spanish troops. Alva's Council of Troubles, nicknamed the Council of Blood, sentenced some thousands to death, levied new taxes, and confiscated the estates of a number of important nobles. These measures united people of all classes in opposition. What might have been primarily a class conflict took on the character of a national opposition. At its head emerged one of the noblemen whose estates had been confiscated, William of Orange (called William the Silent), Philip II's "stadholder" or lieutenant in the County of Holland. Beginning to claim the authority of a sovereign, he issued letters of marque, or authorizations to ship captains—Dutch, Danes, Scots, English—to make war at sea. Fishing crews, "sea dogs," and downright pirates began to raid the small port towns of the Netherlands and France, descending upon them without warning, desecrating the churches, looting, torturing, and killing, in a wild combination of religious rage, political hatred, and lust for booty. The Spanish reciprocated by renewing their confiscations, their inquisitorial

THE LOW COUNTRIES, 1648

This group of towns and provinces, along the lower reaches of the Rhine, Meuse, and Scheldt rivers, originated in the Middle Ages as part of the Holy Roman Empire. The northern or Dutch provinces were recognized as independent of the Empire in 1648. Early in the seventeenth century a political frontier emerged between the "Dutch" and "Belgian" parts, but the word "Belgium" was not used until much later, the southern or Habsburg provinces being called the Spanish Netherlands in the seventeenth century and the Austrian Netherlands in the eighteenth. The large bishopric of Liège remained a separate church-state until the French Revolution. The language frontier, then as now, ran roughly east and west somewhat south of Brussels, with French to the south and Flemish (a form of Dutch, and hence Germanic) to the north of the line.

tortures, and their burnings and hangings. The Netherlands was torn by anarchy, revolution, and civil war. No lines were clear, either political or religious. But in 1576 the anti-Spanish feeling prevailed over religious difference. Representatives of all seventeen provinces, putting aside the religious question, formed a union to drive out the Spanish at any cost.

The Involvement of England

But the Netherlands revolution, though it was a national revolution with political independence as its first aim, was only part of the international politico-religious struggle. All sorts of other interests became involved in it. Queen Elizabeth of England lent aid to the Netherlands, though for many years surreptitiously, not wishing to provoke a war with Spain, in which it was feared that English Catholics might side with the Spaniards. Elizabeth was troubled by having on her hands an unwanted guest, Mary Queen of Scots, a Catholic who had been queen of France until her husband's premature death, and queen of Scotland until driven out by irate Calvinist lords, and who—if the pope, the king of Spain, the Society of Jesus, and many English Catholics were to have their way—would also be queen of England instead of the usurper Elizabeth.[13] Elizabeth under these circumstances kept Mary Stuart imprisoned. Many intrigues were afoot to put Mary on the English throne, some with, and some without, Mary's knowledge.

In 1576 Don Juan, hero of Lepanto, and half-brother of Philip II, became governor general of the embattled Netherlands. It was his grandiose idea, formed after consultations in Rome, not merely to subdue the Netherlands but to use that country as a base for an invasion of England, and after overthrowing Elizabeth with Spanish troops, to put Mary Stuart on the throne, marry her himself, and so become king of a re-Catholicized England. Thus the security of Elizabethan and Protestant England was coming to depend on the outcome of fighting in the Netherlands. Elizabeth signed an alliance with the Netherlands patriots.

Don Juan died in 1578 and was succeeded as governor general of the Netherlands by the prince of Parma. A diplomat as well as a soldier, Parma broke the solid front of the seventeen provinces by a mixture of force and persuasion. He promised that the historic liberties of the *Joyeuse Entrée* would be respected, and he appealed not only to the more zealous Catholics but to moderates who were wearying of the struggle and repelled by mob violence and religious vandalism. On this basis he rallied the southernmost provinces to his side. The seven northern provinces, led by Holland and Zeeland, responded by forming the Union of Utrecht in 1579. In 1581 they formally declared their independence from the king of Spain, calling themselves the United Provinces of the Netherlands. Thus originated what was more commonly called the Dutch Republic, or simply "Holland" in view of the predominance of that county among the seven. The great Flemish towns—Antwerp, Ghent, and Bruges—at first sided with the Union.

Where formerly all had been turmoil, a geographical line was now drawn. The south rallying to Philip II now faced a still rebellious north. But neither side accepted any such partition. Parma still fought to reconquer the north, and the

---

[13] Mary Stuart, a great-granddaughter of Henry VII, was the next lawful heir to the English throne after Elizabeth, since Elizabeth had no children.

Dutch, led by William the Silent, still struggled to clear the Spanish out of all seventeen provinces. Meanwhile the two sides fought to capture the intermediate Flemish cities. When Parma moved upon Antwerp, still the leading port of the North Sea, and one from which an invasion of England could best be mounted, Elizabeth at last openly entered the war on the side of the rebels, sending 6,000 English troops to the Netherlands under the Earl of Leicester in 1585.

England was now clearly emerging as the chief bulwark of Protestantism and of anti-Spanish feeling in northwestern Europe. In England itself, the popular fears of Spain, the popular resentment against Catholic plots revolving about Mary Stuart, and the popular indignation at "foreign" and "outside" meddling in English matters produced an unprecedented sense of national solidarity. The country rallied to Protestantism and to Elizabeth, and even the Catholic minority for the most part disowned the conspiracies against her. The English were now openly and defiantly allied with the Protestant Dutch. Not only were they fighting together in the Netherlands, but both English and Dutch sea raiders fell upon Spanish shipping, captured the treasure ships, and even pillaged the Spanish Main, the mainland coast of northern South America. The Dutch were beginning to penetrate East Indian waters. Elizabeth was negotiating with Scotland, with German Calvinists and French Huguenots. At the Escorial it was said that the Netherlands could only be rewon by an invasion of England, that the queen of the heretics must be at last dethroned, that in any case it was cheaper to launch a gigantic attack upon England than to pay the cost of protecting Spanish galleons, year after year, against the depredations of piratical sea dogs.

Philip II therefore prepared to invade England. The English retorted with vigor. Mary Stuart, after almost twenty years' imprisonment, was executed in 1587; an aroused Parliament, more than Elizabeth herself, demanded her life on the eve of foreign attack. Sir Francis Drake, most spectacular of the sea dogs, sailed into the port of Cádiz and burnt the very ships assembling there to join the Armada. This was jocosely described as singeing the beard of the king of Spain.

The great Armada, the *armada católica,* was ready early in 1588. With crosses on the sails and banners bearing the image of the Holy Virgin, it went forth as to a new Lepanto against the Turks of the north. It consisted of 130 ships, weighing 58,000 tons, carrying 30,000 men and 2,400 pieces of artillery—the most prodigious assemblage of naval power that the world had ever seen. In Spain only the pessimistic observed that its commander was no seaman, that some of its ships were too cumbersome, and some too frail, to weather the gales of the north, that orders had to be issued to its crews in six languages, and the antagonisms of Portuguese, Catalans, Castilians, Irishmen, and émigré English Catholics some-how appeased. The plan was for the fleet to sail to the Netherlands, from which it was to escort the prince of Parma's army across the straits to the English coast. In the Channel the Armada was met by some two hundred English vessels, with Sir Francis Drake as vice-admiral under Lord Howard of Effingham. The English craft—lighter, smaller, and faster, though well furnished with guns—harried the lumbering mass of the Armada, broke up its formations, attacked its great vessels one by one. It found no refuge at Calais, where English fireships drove it out again to sea. Then arose a great storm, the famous "Protestant wind," which blew the broken Armada northward, into seas that to southerners seemed almost polar, around the tip of Scotland, the Orkneys, the Hebrides, and northern

Ireland, forbidding coasts which the Spaniards had to skirt without charts or pilots, and which they strewed with their wreckage and their bones.

The Results of the Struggle

The war went on for several years. Philip died in 1598, after a long and horrible illness, a frustrated and broken man. In the wars with Spain the English had, above all else, assured their national independence. They had acquired an intense national spirit, a love of "this other Eden, demi-paradise," "this precious stone set in the silver sea," as Shakespeare wrote; and they had become more solidly Protestant, almost unanimously set against "popery." With the ruin of the Armada, they were more free to take to the sea; we have seen how the English East India Company was founded in 1600.[14]

In the Netherlands, the battle lines swayed back and forth until 1609. In that year a Twelve Years' Truce was agreed to. By this truce the Netherlands were partitioned. The line of partition ran somewhat farther north than it had in Parma's time, for the Spaniards had retaken Antwerp and other cities in the middle zone. The seven provinces north of the line, those that had formed the Union of Utrecht in 1579, were henceforth known as Dutch. The ten provinces south of the line were known as the Spanish Netherlands. Protestants in the south either became Catholics or fled to the north, so that the south (the modern Belgium) became solidly Catholic, while the number of Protestants in the north was increased. Even so, the Dutch were not a completely Protestant people, for probably as many as a third of them remained Catholic. Calvinism was the religion of most Dutch burghers and the religion favored by the state; but in the face of an exceptionally large religious minority the Dutch Netherlands adopted a policy of toleration. The southern Netherlands were ruined by almost forty years of war. The Dutch, moreover, occupied the mouth of the Scheldt and refused to allow ocean-going vessels to proceed upstream to Antwerp or to Ghent. The Scheldt remained "closed" for two centuries, and the Flemish cities never recovered their old position. Amsterdam became the commercial and financial center of northern Europe; it retained its commercial supremacy for a century and its financial supremacy for two centuries. For the Dutch, as for the English, the weakening of Spanish naval power opened the way to the sea. The Dutch East India Company was organized in 1602. Both Dutch and English began to found overseas colonies. The English settled in Virginia in 1607, the Dutch at New York in 1612.

As for Spain, while it remained the most formidable military power of Europe for another half-century, its internal decline had already begun. At the death of Philip II the monarchy was living from hand to mouth, habitually depending on the next arrival of treasure from the Indies. The productive forces of the country were weakened by inflation, by taxation, by emigration, by depopulation. At Seville, for example, only 400 looms were in operation in 1621, where there had been 16,000 a century earlier. Spain suffered from the very circumstances that made it great. The qualities most useful in leading the Counter Reformation were not those on which a modern society could most easily be built. The generations

---

[14] See above, p. 120.

of crusading against infidels, heathen, and heretics had produced an exceptionally large number of minor aristocrats, chevaliers, dons, and hidalgos, who as a class were contemptuous of work, and who were numerous enough and close enough to the common people to impress their haughty indifference upon the country as a whole. With the extreme concentration on religion the ablest men entered the church, and so great was the popular admiration for saints and mystics, missionaries and crusaders, theologians, archbishops, ascetics, and begging friars, that more secular activities offered little psychological satisfaction or reward.

The very unity accomplished under Ferdinand and Isabella threatened to dissolve. After more than a century of the Inquisition people were still afraid of false Christians and crypto-Muslims. The question of the Moriscos rose again in 1608.[15] The Moriscos included some of the best farmers and most skilled artisans in the country. They lived in almost all parts of Spain and were in no sense a "foreign" element, since they were simply the descendants of those Spaniards who, in the Muslim period, which had begun 900 years before, had adopted the Muslim religion and Arabic language and culture. They were now supposedly Christian, but the true and pure Christians accused them of preserving in secret the rites of Islam and of sympathy for the Barbary pirates. They were thought to be clannish, marrying among themselves; and they were so efficient, sober, and hard working that they outdistanced other Spaniards in competition. In 1609 some 150,000 Moriscos were driven out of Valencia; in 1610 some 64,000 were driven from Aragon; in 1611 an unknown number were expelled from Castile. All were simply put on boats and sent off with what they could carry. Spain, whose total population was rapidly falling in any case, thus lost one of the most socially valuable, if not religiously orthodox, of all its minorities.

Nor could the Christian kingdoms hold peaceably together. In 1640 Portugal, which had been joined to the Spanish crown since 1580 when its own ruling line had run out, reestablished its independence. That same year Catalonia rose in open rebellion. The Catalan war, in which the French streamed across the Pyrenees to aid the rebels, lasted for almost twenty years. Catalonia was at last reconquered, but it managed to preserve its old privileges and separate identity. Catalan and Castilian viewed each other with increased repugnance. The Spanish kingdoms were almost as disunited, in spirit and in institutions, as in the days of Isabella and Ferdinand. They suffered, too, during the seventeenth century from a line of kings whose mental peculiarities reached the point of positive imbecility. Meanwhile, however, the might of Spain was still to be felt in both Germany and France.

15. *The Disintegration and Reconstruction of France*

Both France and Germany, in the so-called Wars of Religion, fell into an advanced state of decomposition, France in almost forty years of civil war between 1562 and 1598, Germany in a long period of civil troubles culminating in the Thirty

---

[15] See p. 71.

Years' War between 1618 and 1648. From this decomposition France recovered in the seventeenth century, but Germany did not.

Political and Religious Disunity

The Wars of Religion in France, despite the religious savagery shown by partisans of both sides, were no more religious than they were political and were essentially a new form of the old phenomenon of feudal rebellion against a higher central authority. "Feudal," in this postmedieval sense, generally refers not to nobles only, but to all sorts of component groups having rights within the state, and so includes towns and provinces, and even craft guilds and courts of law, in addition to the church and the noble class. It remained to be seen whether all these elements could be welded into one body politic.

In France the New Monarchy, resuming the work of medieval kings, had imposed a certain unity on the country.[16] Normally, or apart from civil war, the country acted as a unit in foreign affairs. The king alone made treaties, and in war his subjects all fought on his side, if they fought at all. Internally, the royal centralization was largely administrative; that is, the king and those who worked for him dealt with subordinate bodies of all kinds, while these subordinate bodies remained in existence with their own functions and personnel. France by the ideas of the time was a very large country. It was three times as large as England and five times as populous. At a time when the traveler could move hardly thirty miles a day it took three weeks of steady plodding to cross the kingdom. Local influence was therefore very strong. Beneath the platform of royalty there was almost as little substantial unity in France as in the Holy Roman Empire. When the Empire had three hundred "states," France had some three hundred areas with their own legal systems. Where the Empire had free cities, France had *bonnes villes,* the king's "good towns," each with its stubbornly defended corporate rights. Where the Empire had middle-sized states like Bavaria, France had provinces as great as some European kingdoms—Brittany, Burgundy, Provence, Languedoc—each ruled by the French king, to be sure, but each with its own identity, autonomy, laws, courts, tariffs, taxes, and parliament or provincial estates. To all this diversity, in France as in Germany, was now added diversity of religion. Calvin himself was by birth and upbringing a Frenchman. Calvinism spread in France very rapidly.

Nor was France much attached to a papal, Rome-centered, or international Catholicism. The French clergy had long struggled for its national or Gallican liberties; the French kings had dealt rudely with popes, ignored the Council of Trent, and allied for political reasons with both the Lutherans and the Turks. Since 1516 the king of France had the right to nominate the French bishops.[17] The fact that both the monarchy and the clergy felt already independent of Rome held them back from the revolutionary solutions of Protestantism. The Protestantism which did spread in France was of the most clear-cut and radical kind, namely, Calvinism, which preached at kings, attacked bishops, and smashed religious images and desecrated the churches. Even in countries that became

[16] See p. 69.
[17] See above, pp. 52, 70.

Protestant—England, north Germany, even the Netherlands—this extreme Protestantism was the doctrine of a minority. In France there was no middle-of-the-road Protestanism, no broad and comfortable Anglicanism, no halfway Lutheranism inspired by governments, and in the long run, as will be seen, the middle of the road was occupied by Catholics.

At first, however, the Huguenots, as the French Calvinists were called, though always a minority, were neither a small one nor modest in their demands. In a class analysis, it is clear that it was chiefly the nobility that was attracted to Protestantism, though of course it does not follow that most French Protestants were nobles, since the nobility was a small class. More than a third, and possibly almost a half, of the French nobility was Protestant in the 1560s or 1570s. Frequently the seigneur, or lord of one or more manors, believed that he should have the *ius reformandi,* or right to regulate religion on his own estates, as the princes of Germany decided the religion of their own territories. It thus happened that a lord might defy the local bishop, put a Calvinist minister in his village church, throw out the images, simplify the sacraments, and have the service conducted in French. In this way peasants also became Huguenots. Occasionally peasants turned Huguenot without encouragement by the lord. It was chiefly in southwestern France that Protestantism spread as a general movement affecting whole areas. But in all parts of the country, north as well as south, many towns converted to Protestantism. Usually this meant that the bourgeois oligarchy, into whose hands town government had generally fallen, went over to Calvinism and thereupon banned Catholic services, of which the sequel might be either that the journeymen wage earners followed along, or that, estranged by the class differences whose development has been described above, they remained attached to their old priests.[18] In general, the unskilled laboring mass probably remained the least touched of all classes by Calvinist doctrine.

Both Francis I and Henry II opposed the spread of Calvinism—as did Lutheran and Anglican rulers—for Calvinism, a kind of grassroots movement in religion, rising spontaneously among laity and reforming ministers, seemed to threaten not only the powers of monarchy but the very idea of a nationally established church. The fact that in France the nobility, a traditionally ungovernable class, figured prominently in the movement only made it look the more like political or feudal rebellion. Persecution of Huguenots, with burnings at the stake, began in the 1550s.

Then in 1559 King Henry II was accidentally killed in a tournament. He left three sons, of whom the eldest in 1559 was only fifteen. Their mother, Henry's widow, was Catherine de' Medici, an Italian woman who brought to France some of the polish of Renaissance Italy, along with some of its taste for political intrigue, with which she attempted to govern a distracted country for her royal sons. (Their names were Francis II, who died in 1560, Charles IX, who died in 1574, and Henry III, who lasted until 1589.) The trouble was that, with no firm hand in control of the monarchy, the country fell apart, and that in the ensuing chaos various powerful factions tried to get control of the youthful monarchs for their own purposes. Among these factions were both Huguenots and Catholics. The Huguenots, under persecution, were too strong a minority to go into hiding.

[18] See pp. 121–125.

Counting among their number a third or more of the professional warrior class, the nobles, they took naturally and aggressively to arms.

The Civil and Religious Wars

Exact history distinguishes no less than nine civil wars in the concluding four decades of the sixteenth century in France, but in this history they will be telescoped together. They were not civil wars of the kind where one region of a country takes up arms against another, each retaining some apparatus of government, as in the American Civil War or the civil wars of the seventeenth century in England. They were civil wars of the kind fought in the absence of government. Roving bands of armed men, without territorial base or regular means of subsistence, wandered about the country, fighting and plundering, joining or separating from other similar bands, in shifting hosts that were quickly formed or quickly dissolved. The underlying social conditions detached many people from their old routines and threw them into a life of adventure. The more prominent leaders could thus easily obtain followers, and at the coming of such cohorts the peasants usually took to the woods, while bourgeois would lock the gates of their cities. Or else peasants would form protective leagues, like vigilantes; and even small towns maintained diminutive armies.

The Huguenots were led by various personages of rank, such as Admiral de Coligny and Henry of Bourbon, king of Navarre, a small independent kingdom at the foot of the Pyrenees between Spain and France. A pronounced Catholic party arose under the Guise family, headed by the Duke of Guise and the Cardinal of Lorraine. Catherine de' Medici was left in the middle, opposed like all monarchs to Calvinism, but unwilling to fall under the domination of the Guises. While the Guises wished to extirpate heresy they wished even more to govern France. Among the Huguenots some fought for local liberties in religion, while the more ardent spirits hoped to drive "idolatry" and "popery" out of all France, and indeed out of the world itself. Catherine de' Medici for a time tried to play the two parties against each other. But in 1572, fearing the growing influence of Coligny over the king, and taking advantage of a great concourse of leading Huguenots in Paris to celebrate the marriage of Henry of Navarre, she decided to rid herself of the heads of the Huguenot party at a single blow. In the resulting massacre of St. Bartholomew's Day some thousands of Huguenots were dragged from their beds after midnight and unceremoniously murdered. Coligny was killed; Henry of Navarre escaped by temporarily changing his religion.

This outrage only aroused Huguenot fury and led to a renewal of civil war, with mounting atrocities committed by both sides. The armed bands slaughtered each other and terrorized noncombatants. Both parties hired companies of mercenary soldiers, mainly from Germany. Spanish troops invaded France at the invitation of the Guises. Protestant towns, like Rouen and La Rochelle, appealed to Elizabeth of England, reminding her that kings of England had once reigned over their parts of France, inviting English invasion and a renewal of the horrors of the Hundred Years' War; but Elizabeth was too preoccupied with her own problems to give more than very sporadic and insignificant assistance. Neither side could subdue the other, and hence there were numerous truces, during which fighting still flared up, since no one had the power to impose peace. The truces usually acknowledged the status quo, allowing Protestant worship locally in places where it was actually going on; but the Protestants felt no security in such terms, nor were Catholics satisfied at such recognition of heresy, so that each truce expired in further war.

Gradually, mainly among the more perfunctory Catholics, but also among moderate Protestants, there developed still another group, who thought of themselves as the "politicals" or *politiques*. The *politiques* were men who concluded that too much was being made of religion, that no doctrine was important enough to justify everlasting war, that perhaps after all there might be room for two churches, and that what the country needed above all else was civil order. Theirs was the secular not the religious view. They believed that men lived primarily in the state, not in the church. They were willing to overlook a man's ideas if only he would obey the king and go peaceably about his business. To escape anarchy they put their hopes in the institution of monarchy. Henry of Navarre, now again a Protestant, was at heart a *politique*. Another was the political philosopher Jean Bodin (1530–1596), the first thinker to develop the modern theory of sovereignty. He held that in every society there must be one power strong enough to give law to all others, with their consent if possible, without their consent if necessary. Thus from the disorders of the religious wars in France was germinated the idea of royal absolutism and of the sovereign state.

The End of the Wars: Reconstruction under Henry IV

In 1589 both Henry III, the reigning king, and Henry of Guise, the Catholic party chief who was trying to depose him, were assassinated, each by a partisan of the other. The throne now came by legal inheritance to the third of the three Henrys, Henry of Navarre, the Huguenot chieftain. He reigned as Henry IV. Most popular and most amiably remembered of all French kings, except for medieval St. Louis, he was the first of the Bourbon dynasty, which was to last until the French Revolution.

The civil wars did not end with the accession of Henry IV. The Catholic party refused to recognize him, set up a pretender against him, and called in the Spaniards. Henry, the *politique,* sensed that the majority of the French people were still Catholic, and that the Huguenots were not only a minority but after thirty years of civil strife an increasingly unpopular minority kept going as a political party by obstinate nobles. Paris especially, Catholic throughout the wars, refused to admit the heretic king within its gates. Supposedly remarking that "Paris is well worth a Mass," Henry IV in 1593 abjured the Calvinist faith, and subjected himself to the elaborate processes of papal absolution. Thereupon the *politiques* and less excitable Catholics consented to work with him. The Huguenots, at first elated that their leader should become king, were now not only outraged by Henry's abjuration but alarmed for their own safety. They demanded not only religious liberty, but positive guarantees.

Henry IV in 1598 responded by issuing the Edict of Nantes. The Edict granted to every seigneur, or noble who was also manorial lord, the right to hold Protestant services in his own household. It allowed Protestantism in towns where it was in fact the prevailing form of worship, and in any case in one town of each *bailliage* (a unit corresponding somewhat to the English shire) throughout the country; but it barred it from Catholic episcopal towns and from a zone surrounding and including the city of Paris. It promised that Protestants should enjoy the same civil rights as Catholics, the same chance for public office, and access to the Catholic universities. In certain of the superior law courts it created "mixed chambers" of both Protestants and Catholics—somewhat as if a stated minority representation were to be legally required in United States federal courts today. The Edict also gave Protestants their own means of defense, granting them about 100 fortified towns to be held by Protestant garrisons under Protestant command.

The Huguenot minority, reassured by the Edict of Nantes, became less of a rebellious element within the state. The majority of the French people viewed the Edict with suspicion. The parlements, or supreme law courts, of Paris, Bordeaux, Toulouse, Aix, and Rennes all refused to recognize it as the law of the land. It was the king who forced toleration upon the country. He silenced the parlements, and subdued Catholic opposition by doing favors for the Jesuits. France's chief minority was thus protected by the central government, not by popular wishes. Where in England the Catholic minority had no rights at all, and in Germany the religious question was settled only by cutting the country into small and hostile fragments, in France a compromise was effected, by which the Protestant minority had both individual and territorial rights. A considerable number of French statesmen, generals, and other important persons in the seventeenth century were Protestants.

Henry IV, having appeased the religious controversy, did everything that he could to let the country gradually recover, to replant, rebuild, transact business, and rediscover the arts of peace. His ideal, as he breezily put it, was a "chicken in the pot" for every Frenchman. He worked also to put the ruined government back together, to collect taxes, pay officials, discipline the army, and supervise the administration of justice. Roads and bridges were repaired and new manufactures were introduced under mercantilist principles. Never throughout his reign of twenty-one years did he summon the Estates General. A country that had just hacked itself to pieces in civil war was scarcely able to govern itself, and so, under Henry IV, the foundations of the later royal absolutism of the Bourbons were laid down.

Henry IV was assassinated in 1610 by a crazed fanatic who believed him a menace to the Catholic church. Under his widow, Marie de' Medici, the nobility and upper Catholic clergy again grew restless and forced the summoning of the Estates General, in which so many conflicting and mutually distrustful interests were represented that no program could be adopted, and Marie dismissed them in 1615 to the general relief of all concerned. No Estates General of the kingdom as a whole thereafter met until the French Revolution. National government was to be conducted by and through the king.

Cardinal Richelieu

In the name of Marie de' Medici and her young son, Louis XIII, the control of affairs gradually came into the hands of an ecclesiastic, Cardinal Richelieu. In the preceding generation Richelieu might have been called a *politique*. It was the state, not the church, whose interests he worked to further. He tried to strengthen the state economically by mercantilist edicts. He attempted to draw impoverished gentlemen into trade by allowing them to engage in maritime commerce without loss of noble status. For wholesale merchants, as an incentive, he made it possible to become nobles, in return for payments into the royal exchequer. He founded and supported many commercial companies on the Anglo-Dutch model.

For a time it seemed that civil war might break out again. Nobles still feuded with each other and evaded the royal jurisdiction. Richelieu prohibited private warfare and ordered the destruction of all fortified castles not manned and needed by the king himself. He even prohibited dueling, a custom much favored by the d'Artagnans of the day, but regarded by Richelieu as a mere remnant of private war. The Huguenots, too, with their own towns and their own armed forces under the Edict of Nantes, had become something of a state within the state. In 1627 the Duke of Rohan led a Huguenot rebellion, based on the city of La Rochelle, which received military support from the English. Richelieu after a year suppressed the rebellion, and in 1629, by the Peace of Alais, amended the Edict of Nantes. For this highly secularized cardinal of the Catholic church it was agreeable for the Protestants to keep their religion, but not for them to share in the instruments of political power. The Huguenots lost, in 1629, their fortified cities, their Protestant armies, and all their military and territorial rights, but in their religious and civil rights they were not officially molested for another fifty years.

The French monarchy no sooner reestablished itself after the civil wars than it began to recur to the old foreign policy of Francis I, who had opposed on every front the European supremacy of the house of Habsburg.[19] The Spanish power still encircled France at the Pyrenees, in the Mediterranean, in the Free County of Burgundy (the Franche-Comté), and in Belgium. The Austrian branch had pretensions to supremacy in Germany and all central Europe. Richelieu found his opportunity to assail the Habsburgs in the civil struggles which now began to afflict Germany.

16. The Thirty Years' War, 1618–1648: The Disintegration of Germany

The Holy Roman Empire extended from France on the west to Poland and Hungary on the east. It included the Czechs of Bohemia, and sizable French-speaking populations in what are now Belgium, Lorraine, eastern Burgundy, and western Switzerland; but with these exceptions the Empire was made up of Germans.[20] Language, however, was far less important than religion as the tie which people felt to be basic to a community; and in religion the Empire was almost evenly divided. Where in England, after stabilization set in, Roman Catholics sank to a minority of some 3 percent, and in France the Huguenots fell to not much over 5 percent, in Germany there was no true minority, and hence no majority, and religion gave no ground for national concentration. Possibly there were more Protestants than Catholics in the Empire in 1600, for not only was Protestantism the state religion in many of the 300 states, but individual Protestants were exceedingly numerous in the legally Catholic states of the

[19] See map, pp. 72–73; and p. 79.
[20] See maps, pp. 72–73, 146–147.

Austrian Habsburgs. Bohemia had a Protestant majority, rooted in the Czech people, and even in Austria, in meetings of the estates, the Protestants sometimes prevailed. Farther east, outside the Holy Roman Empire, the Hungarian nobles were mainly Protestant, and Transylvania, in the elbow of the Carpathian Mountains, was an active center of Calvinism.

In 1500 Germany had led in the life of Europe, but in 1600 it showed evidences of backwardness and provincialism. Literature had declined, and the language itself became barbarized and ungainly. Where both Catholics and Calvinists recognized international affiliations and read with interest books written in other countries, Lutherans were suspicious of the world outside the Lutheran states of Germany and Scandinavia, and hence suffered from a cultural isolation. The German universities, both Lutheran and Catholic, attracted fewer students than formerly, and their intellectual effort was consumed in combative dogmatics, each side demonstrating the truth of its own ideas. More witches were burned in Germany than in the west, the popular fairy tales were more gruesome, and the educated were more fascinated by astrology. The commerce of south Germany and the Rhineland was in decay, both because of the shift of trade to the Atlantic and because the Dutch controlled the mouth of the Rhine in their own interests. German bankers, such as the Fuggers, were of slight importance after 1600. It was now in the West that capital was being formed.

Background of the Thirty Years' War

The Peace of Augsburg in 1555, with its principle of *cuius regio eius religio,* had provided that in each state the government could prescribe the religion of its subjects.[21] In some states a bishop himself constituted the government. In these cases, whenever an incumbent died, there was a race to name his successor, to secure the territory as Lutheran or Catholic. In 1593 a small war was fought for the control of Aachen, in 1600 another for the control of Cologne. In general, in the decades following the Peace of Augsburg, the Lutherans made considerable gains, putting Lutheran administrators into the church states, or "secularizing" them and converting them into lay principalities. The Catholics did not accept this constant attrition, which violated the Ecclesiastical Reservation of the Peace of Augsburg. In addition, Calvinism spread into Germany. Though Calvinists had no rights under the Peace of Augsburg, a number of states became Calvinist. One of these was the Palatinate, important because it was strategically placed across the middle Rhine, and because its ruler, the Elector Palatine, was one of the seven persons who elected the Holy Roman Emperor. In 1608 the Protestant states, urged on by the Elector Palatine, formed a Protestant union to defend their gains. To obtain support, they negotiated with the Dutch, with the English, and with Henry IV of France. In 1609 a league of Catholic German states was organized by Bavaria. It looked for help from Spain.

The Germans were thus falling apart, or rather coming together, into two parties in anticipation of a religious war, and each party solicited foreign assistance against the other. Other issues were also maturing. The Twelve Years' Truce between Spain and the Dutch, signed in 1609, was due to expire in 1621. The

[21] See pp. 79–80.

Spanish (whose military power was still unaffected by internal decline) were again preparing to crush the Dutch Republic, or, at the very least, to open the mouth of the Scheldt and to get Dutch traders out of the East Indies. Since the Dutch insisted on independence, and were in any case unwilling to leave the Indies or to remove their stranglehold on the port of Antwerp, a renewal of the Dutch-Spanish war appeared to be inevitable. The Spanish also wished to consolidate the Habsburg position in central Europe. From Milan in north Italy they proposed to build up a fork of territory, one of whose prongs would lead through the easternmost of the Swiss cantons directly to Habsburg Austria, the other through the westernmost Swiss cantons to the valley of the Rhine. There, on and near the Rhine, if they could conquer a few states like the Calvinistic Palatinate, they might join the Netherlands and Franche-Comté (the Free County of Burgundy, ruled by Spain) into a large and continuous territorial block.[22] These Spanish designs in the Rhineland and Switzerland naturally aroused the opposition of France. Moreover, the Austrian branch of the Habsburg family was slowly bestirring itself to eradicate Protestantism in its own domains and even to turn the Holy Roman Empire into a more modern and national type of state. The idea of a strong power in Germany was abhorrent to the French. France, through opposition to the Habsburgs, was again put in the position of chief protector of Protestantism. France, as we have observed, was a giant of Europe, five times as populous as England, over ten times as populous as Sweden or the Dutch Republic, incomparably more populous than any single German state. And France after 1600 was at last unified within—at least relatively. As a French writer has observed, speaking of these years, the appearance of the fleur-de-lis upon the Rhine would tumble to the ground the vast projects of the Counter Reformation.

The Thirty Years' War, resulting from all these pressures, was therefore exceedingly complex. It was a German civil war fought over the Catholic-Protestant issue. It was also a German civil war fought over constitutional issues, between the emperor striving to build up the central power of the Empire and the member states struggling to maintain independence. These two civil wars by no means coincided, for Catholic and Protestant states were alike in objecting to imperial control. It was also an international war, between France and the Habsburgs, between Spain and the Dutch, with the kings of Denmark and Sweden and the prince of Transylvania becoming involved, and with all these outsiders finding allies within Germany, on whose soil most of the battles were fought. The wars were further complicated by the fact that many of the generals were soldiers of fortune, who aspired to create principalities of their own, and who fought or refused to fight to suit their own convenience.

The Four Phases of the War

The fighting began in Bohemia. It is in fact customary to divide the war into four phases, the Bohemian (1618–1625), the Danish (1625–1629), the Swedish (1630–1635), and the Swedish-French (1635–1648).

In 1618 the Bohemians, or Czechs, fearing the loss of their Protestant liberties, dealt with two emissaries from the Habsburg Holy Roman Emperor, Matthias

---

[22] See map, pp. 146–147.

(who was also their king), by a method occasionally used in that country—throwing them out of the window. After this "defenestration of Prague" the king-emperor sent troops to restore his authority, whereupon the Bohemians deposed him and elected a new king. In order to obtain Protestant assistance, they chose the Calvinist Elector Palatine, the head of the Protestant Union. This young man proceeded to Bohemia, where he assumed the title of Frederick V. He brought aid to the Bohemians from the Protestant Union, the Dutch sent money, and the prince of Transylvania harried the Habsburg rear. The Emperor Ferdinand, Matthias' successor, assisted by money from the pope, Spanish troops sent up from Milan, and the forces of Catholic Bavaria, managed to overwhelm the Bohemians at the battle of the White Mountain in 1620. Frederick fled, jeered or pitied as the "winter king." His ancestral domains in the Palatinate were overrun by the Spaniards.

Two facts emerged in consequence of the Bohemian war. First, the Spaniards were entrenching themselves in the Rhineland, building up their position against the French and the Dutch. Second, Bohemia was reconquered and revolutionized by the Habsburgs. Ferdinand got himself elected again as king. He confiscated the estates of almost half the Bohemian nobles. He granted these lands as endowments for Catholic churches, orders, and monasteries, or gave them out to a swarm of adventurers of all nationalities who had entered his service, and who now became the new landed aristocracy of Bohemia. Jesuits streamed in, and through missions and schools, as well as court proceedings and executions, the re-Catholicization of Bohemia began. In Austria also, which had at first joined Bohemia in rebellion, Protestantism was stamped out.

With Protestant fortunes at a low ebb, and the Protestant Union itself dissolved in 1621, the lead in Protestant affairs was now taken by the king of Denmark, who was also Duke of Holstein, a state of the Holy Roman Empire. His aims were well mixed with politics, for he hoped by acquiring a few bishoprics in Germany to construct a kingdom for his younger son. With a little aid from the Dutch and English, and with promises from Richelieu, he entered the fray. Against him the Emperor Ferdinand raised another army, or, rather, commissioned Albert of Wallenstein to raise one on his own private initiative. Wallenstein assembled a force of professional fighters, of all nationalities, who lived by pillage rather than by pay. His army was his personal instrument, not the emperor's, and he therefore followed a policy of his own, which was so tortuous and well concealed that the name of Wallenstein has always remained an enigma. Possibly he dreamed of a united empire and a revived Germany from which foreigners should be expelled; certainly he dreamed of creating a sizable principality for himself. Wallenstein and other imperial generals soon defeated the king of Denmark, reached the Baltic coast, and even invaded the Danish peninsula.

The full tide of the Counter Reformation now flowed over Germany. Not only was Catholicism again seeping into the Palatinate, and again flooding Bohemia, but it rolled northward into the inner recesses of the Lutheran states. By the Edict of Restitution, in 1629, the emperor declared all church territories secularized since 1552 automatically restored to the Catholic church. Two archbishoprics, twelve bishoprics, and over a hundred small territories formerly belonging to monasteries and religious orders were involved. Some, like the bishopric of Lübeck, were as far north as the Baltic. Some had been Protestant since the oldest person could remember. Terror swept over Protestant Germany. It seemed that the whole Protestant Reformation, now a century old, might be undone.

Among those to be alarmed were the French and the Swedes. Richelieu, however, was still putting down fractious nobles and Huguenots. He had not yet consolidated France to his satisfaction and believed that France, without fighting itself, could counter the Habsburg ambitions through the use of allies. He sent diplomats to help extricate the king of Sweden from a war with Poland, and he promised him financial assistance, which soon rose to a million livres a year in return for the maintenance in Germany of 40,000 Swedish troops. The Dutch subsidized the Swedes with some 50,000 florins a month.

The king of Sweden was Gustavus Adolphus, a ruler of superlative ability, who had conciliated all parties in Sweden and thus created a base from which he could safely conduct overseas operations. He had extended Swedish holdings on the east shore of the Baltic. Using Dutch and other military experts, he had created the most modern army of the times, noted for its firm discipline, high courage, and mobile cannon. Himself a religious man, he had his troops march to battle singing Lutheran hymns. He was ideally suited to be the Protestant champion, a role he now willingly took up, landing in Germany in 1630. Richelieu, besides giving financial help, negotiated with the Catholic states of Germany, playing on their fears of imperial centralization and so sowing discord among German Catholics and isolating the emperor, against whom the Swedish war machine was now hurled.

The Swedes, with military aid from Saxony, won a number of spectacular victories, at Breitenfeld in 1631 and Lützen in 1632, where, however, Gustavus Adolphus was killed. His chancellor, Oxenstierna, carried on. The Swedish army penetrated into Bohemia, and as far south as the Danube. What those in the higher counsels of Sweden were aiming at is not clear. Perhaps they dreamed of a great federal Protestant empire, to include Scandinavia and north Germany, a Lutheran empire confronting a Catholic and Habsburg empire in the south. But the brilliant Swedish victories came to little. Both sides were weakened by disagreement. Wallenstein, who disliked the Spanish influence in Germany, virtually ceased to fight the Swedes and Saxons, with whom he even entered into private talks, hoping to create an independent position for himself. He was finally disgraced by the emperor and assassinated by one of his own staff. On the Swedish-Saxon side, the Saxons decided to make a separate peace. Saxony therefore signed with the emperor the Peace of Prague of 1635. The other German Protestant states concurred in it and withdrew their support from the Swedes. The emperor, by largely annulling the Edict of Restitution, allayed Protestant apprehensions. The Swedes were left isolated in Germany. It seemed that the German states were coming together, that the religious wars might be nearing an end. But, in fact, in 1635, the Thirty Years' War was only well begun. Neither France nor Spain wished peace or reconciliation in Germany.

Richelieu renewed his assurances to the Swedes, paid subsidies even to the wealthy Dutch, hired a German princeling, Bernard of Saxe-Weimar, to maintain an army of Germans in the French service, and, cardinal of the Roman church though he was, at last came out openly and plainly in favor of the German Protestants.

So the fleur-de-lis at last moved toward the Rhine, though not at first with the success for which Frenchmen or Protestants might hope. The Spanish, from their bases in Belgium and Franche-Comté, drove instead deep into France. Champagne and Burgundy were ravaged, and Paris itself was seized with panic. The Spanish also raided the south. The French had a taste of the plunder, murder, burnings, and stealing of cattle by which Germany had been afflicted. But the French soon turned the tables. When Portugal and Catalonia rebelled against Philip IV, France immediately recognized the independence of Portugal under the new royal house of Braganza—as did England, Holland, and Sweden with equal alacrity. French troops streamed over the Pyrenees into Catalonia, spreading the usual devastation. Richelieu even recognized a Catalan republic.

In Germany the last or Swedish-French phase of the war was not so much a civil war among Germans as an international struggle on German soil. Few German states now sided with the French and Swedes. A feeling of national resentment against foreign invasion even seemed to develop.

The Peace of Westphalia, 1648

Peace talks began in 1644 in Westphalia, at the two towns of Münster and Osnabrück. The German states were crying for peace, for a final religious settlement, and for "reform" of the Holy Roman Empire. France and Sweden insisted that the German states should individually take part in the negotiations, a disintegrating principle that the German princes eagerly welcomed and which the emperor vainly resisted. To Westphalia, therefore, hundreds of diplomats and negotiators now repaired, representing the Empire, its member states, Spain, France, Sweden, the Dutch, the Swiss, the Portuguese, the Venetians, many other Italians, and the pope. There had been no such European congress since the Council of Constance, and the fact that a European assemblage had in 1415 dealt with affairs of the church, and now in the 1640s dealt with affairs of the state, war, and power, was a measure of the secularization that had come over Europe. The papal nuncio, it may be remarked, was barely listened to at Westphalia, and the pope never signed the treaties.

The negotiations dragged on, because the armies were still fighting, and after each battle one side or the other raised its terms. France and Spain refused to make peace with each other at all and in fact remained at war until 1659. But for the Holy Roman Empire a settlement was agreed to, incorporated in 1648 in the two treaties of Münster and Osnabrück, and commonly known as the Peace of Westphalia.

The Peace of Westphalia represented a general checkmate to the Counter Reformation in Germany. It not only renewed the terms of the Peace of Augsburg, granting each German state the right to determine its own religion, but it added Calvinism to Lutheranism and Catholicism as an acceptable faith. On the controversial issue of church territories secularized after 1552 the Protestants won a complete victory.

The dissolution of the Holy Roman Empire, which had been advanced by the drawing of internal religious frontiers in the days of Luther, was now confirmed in politics and international law. Borderlands of the Empire fell away. The Dutch and Swiss ceased to belong to it, both the United Provinces and Swiss cantons (or Helvetic Body) being recognized as sovereign and independent. The Dutch,

Austrian Habsburgs

Spanish Habsburgs

Swedish Dominions

Brandenburg-Prussia

Church Lands

—— Boundary of the Holy Roman Empire

0   100   200   300 miles

SHETLAND I.

SWEDEN

NORWAY

Bergen

Helsingfo

ORKNEY I.

Stockholm

SCOTLAND

KINGDOM OF
DENMARK AND NORWAY

Edinburgh

NORTH SEA

DENMARK

(TO SWEDEN, 1658)

BALTIC SEA

COURI

Belfast

IRELAND

Copenhagen

SCHLESWIG

SWEDISH
POMERANIA

Danzig

DUCHY
OF
PRUSSIA

Dublin   Liverpool

ENGLAND
(COMMONWEALTH 1649-1660
UNITED KINGDOM 1707)

HOLSTEIN

Hamburg

Lübeck   Stralsund

Stettin

BRANDENBURG-PRUSSIA

POMERANIA

Vistula R.

Bristol

UNITED
PROVINCES

Elbe R.

Bremen

BRANDENBURG

GREAT
POLAND

Warsaw

Amsterdam   HANOVER   Verden

Berlin

Ryswick   Osnabrück   Magdeburg

Oder R.

London

Utrecht   Münster

Leipzig
SAXONY

Breslau
SILESIA

LITTLE
POLAND

ENGLISH CHANNEL

SPANISH
NETH.

Brussels   MINOR
GERMAN STATES

Dresden

Cracow

CA

Cologne   Prague

ATLANTIC OCEAN

Rouen

Trier   Mainz

BOHEMIA

MORAVIA

Paris

Metz   PALATINATE

AUSTRIA

KINGDOM OF HUNGARY

Rennes

LORRAINE
ALSACE

Strassbourg   BAVARIA

Vienna

Budapest

Nantes   Orléans

Augsburg

HUNGAR

FRANCE

FRANCHE-
COMTÉ

SWISS CANTONS

SLAVONIA

OTT

Bordeaux   Lyons

SAVOY

Venice

REPUBLIC OF VENICE

BOSNIA

Belgrade

PIEDMONT

Milan

ADRIATIC SEA

Zara

SERBIA

LaCoruña

PYRENEES

Avignon

Parma

Genoa

Florence

MONTENE

Oporto

León

Montauban

Marseilles

TUSCANY

PAPAL
STATES

ALBANIA

Sa

PORTUGAL
(TO SPAIN
1580-1640)

Valladolid

NAVARRE

SPAIN

Saragossa

CATALONIA

Rome

Aquila

Bari

Lisbon

Escorial   Madrid

CASTILE

ARAGON

Barcelona

CORSICA
(Genoa)

Naples   NAPLES

Mérida   Toledo

Valencia

BALEARIC I.

MINORCA

SARDINIA

KINGDOM OF THE
TWO SICILIES

IONIAN I.
(Venice)

Seville   Murcia

MAJORCA

Cadiz   Malaga

Palermo

Tangier   Ceuta
(Portugal)

MEDITERRANEAN

SICILY

Algiers

Oran (Spain)

Tunis

SEA

FEZ AND MOROCCO

ALGERIA

TUNISIA

MALTA
(Knights of St. John)

B A R B A R Y   S T A T E S

Moscow

R U S S I A

A N I A

N D

Kiev

AVIA   YEDISAN

BESSARABIA   CRIMEA

DOBRUJA

R

BLACK SEA

Constantinople

E M P I R E

Smyrna

RHODES
(Turkish)

CYPRUS
(Turkish)

EUROPE, 1648

The map shows the European states at the time of the Peace of Westphalia. The main feature of the Peace of Westphalia was that the threat of domination of Europe by the Catholic Habsburgs was averted. A plurality of independent sovereign states was henceforth considered normal. The plurality of religions was also henceforth taken for granted for Europe as a whole, though each state continued to require, or at least to favor, religious uniformity within its own borders. By weakening the Habsburgs, and furthering the disintegration of Germany, the Peace of Westphalia opened the way for the political ascendancy of France.

in addition, were confirmed in their conquest of both banks of the lower Scheldt, the closure of that river to ocean-going vessels, and hence the commercial destruction of Antwerp. They likewise received, from Portugal, the right to have outposts in Brazil and Indonesia.

From the disintegrating western frontier of the Holy Empire the French cut off small pieces, receiving sovereignty over three Lorraine bishoprics, which they had occupied for a century, and certain rights in Alsace which were so confused that they later led to trouble. The king of Sweden received the bishoprics of Bremen and Verden and the western half of Pomerania, including the city of Stettin. Sweden thus added to its trans-Baltic possessions. The mouths of the German rivers were now controlled by non-Germans, the Oder, Elbe, and Weser by Sweden, the Rhine and the Scheldt by the Dutch. In the interior of the Empire Brandenburg received eastern Pomerania, the large archbishopric of Magdeburg, and two smaller bishoprics, while Bavaria also increased its stature, obtaining part of the Palatinate and a seat in the electoral college, so that the Empire now had eight electors.

It was in the new constitution of the Empire itself, not in territorial changes, that the greatest victory of the French and their Swedish and Dutch allies was to be found. The German states, over three hundred in number, became virtually sovereign. Each received the right to conduct diplomacy and make treaties with foreign powers. The Peace of Westphalia further stipulated that no laws could be made by the Empire, no taxes raised, no soldiers recruited, no war declared or peace terms ratified except with the consent of the imperial estates, the 300-odd princes, ecclesiastics, and free cities in the Reichstag assembled. Since it was well known that agreement on any such matters was impossible, the principle of self-government, or of medieval constitutional liberties, was used to destroy the Empire itself as an effective political entity. While most other European countries were consolidating under royal absolutism, Germany sank back into "feudal chaos."

Not only did the Peace of Westphalia block the Counter Reformation, and not only did it frustrate the Austrian Habsburgs and forestall for almost two centuries any movement toward German national unification, but it also marked the advent in international law of the modern European *Staatensystem,* or system of sovereign states. The diplomats who assembled at Westphalia represented independent powers which recognized no superior or common tie. No one any longer pretended that Europe had any significant unity, religious, political, or other. Statesmen delighted in the absence of any such unity, in which they sensed the menace of "universal monarchy." Europe was understood to consist of a large number of unconnected sovereignties, free and detached atoms, or states, which acted according to their own laws, following their own political interests, forming and dissolving alliances, exchanging embassies and legations, alternating between war and peace, shifting position with a shifting balance of power.

Physically Germany was wrecked by the Thirty Years' War. Cities were sacked by mercenary soldiers with a rapacity that their commanders could not control; or the commanders themselves, drawing no supplies from their home governments, systematically looted whole areas to maintain their armies. Magdeburg was besieged ten times, Leipzig five. In one woolen town of Bohemia, with a population of 6,000 before the wars, the citizens fled and disappeared, the houses collapsed, and eight years after the peace only 850 persons were found there. On the site of another small town Swedish cavalry found nothing but wolves. The peasants, murdered, put to flight, or tortured by soldiers to reveal their few valuables, ceased to give attention to farming; agriculture was ruined, so that starvation followed, and with it came pestilence. Even revised modern estimates allow that in many extensive parts of Germany as much as a third of the population may have perished. The effects of fire, disease, undernourishment, homelessness, and exposure in the seventeenth century were the more terrible because of the lack of means to combat them. The horrors of modern war are not wholly different from horrors that men and women have experienced in the past.

Germany as such, physically wrecked and politically cut into small pieces, ceased for a long time to play any part in European affairs. A kind of political and cultural vacuum existed in central Europe. On the one hand, the western or Atlantic peoples—French, English, Dutch—began in the seventeenth century to take the lead in European affairs. On the other hand, in eastern Germany, around Berlin and Vienna, new and only half-German power complexes began to form. These themes will be traced in the two following chapters.

With the close of the Thirty Years' War the Wars of Religion came to an end. While in some later conflicts, as in Hungary or in Ireland and Scotland, religion remained an issue, it was never again an important issue in the political affairs of Europe as a whole. In general, by the close of the seventeenth century, the division between Protestant and Catholic had become stabilized. Neither side any longer expected to make territorial gains at the expense of the other. Both the Protestant and the Catholic reformations were accomplished facts.

THE WORLD OVERSEAS

With the Age of Discovery, Europe entered into habitual communication with the "Indies," as Asia, Africa, and America were at first vaguely and collectively called.

Europeans found some peoples in these countries less civilized than themselves, and others whom they considered equally civilized or more so, as in India and China. From Asia, while the Europeans at first sought spices, they soon imported manufactures of a more refined kind than Europe could then produce, such as Indian cottons and Chinese porcelains. In Asia, as in Africa, the Europeans were transients—traders, sailors, missionaries, and officials sent to govern small outposts. There was no lasting settlement of European families except at the Cape of Good Hope. The interior of Africa remained unknown. The Mogul empire in India until after 1700, and the Ming empire in China, succeeded by the Ch'ing or Manchu empire about 1650, long commanded the awe and respect of Europeans. China exerted a special fascination. During the European Enlightenment, in the eighteenth century, China was admired as a huge empire that had no clergy, and was governed by an enlightened literary class, the mandarins, recruited by competitive examination rather than by noble birth.

The native Americans and the black Africans were regarded by Europeans as barbarous or savage peoples, who in any case could not defend themselves against European organization and weapons. The spread of Old World diseases, to which Europeans and Africans had developed immunities, had devastating effects on the populations of the Americas. The surviving American Indians, especially in North America, were either killed off, subjugated, or pushed aside. To exploit the resources of America the Europeans brought in Africans as slaves. The number of Africans reaching America, including the two continents and the West Indies, was far greater than the number of Europeans who settled there before 1800. Spaniards emigrated permanently to New Spain and Portuguese to Brazil, but by the time of the American Revolution the most "European" region was the Atlantic coast of North America from Savannah to Quebec, where about 2 million whites lived with half a million blacks and a few Indians.

Europe itself was transformed by these overseas ventures. A wealthy commercial class grew up in northwestern Europe. Naval power became decisive. The inflow of American gold and silver affected currency values and hence the relationship between social classes. Population grew with the adoption of the American potato. Europeans took increasing pride in their understanding of the world. There was much speculation on the diversity of human races and cultures, which sometimes led to a new kind of race consciousness on the part of Europeans, and sometimes to a cultural relativism in which European ways were seen as only one variant of human behavior as a whole.

Right: Our Lady of the Navigators, *painted about 1535 by Alejo Fernandez for the Casa de Contratacion, or Trade House, at Seville. The figures to whom the Virgin extends her protection, with their sharply individualized features, are thought to represent various actual explorers; the one to the left may be Columbus. The picture evokes the combination of religious spirit with adventure and gold-seeking that motivated the early expeditions.*

The Spaniards stamped out much of the Indian religion as idolatrous, yet it is to Spanish priests that we owe the preservation of much of our knowledge of the pre-Conquest culture. The page at the right above is from a book in which a Spaniard wrote down the Aztec language in the Latin alphabet. A human sacrifice is also depicted.

At the left above is a page from a book published in England, translated from the Dutch. The author, Johannes Nieuhoff, spent three years in Java and nine in Brazil, where the Dutch had a settlement in the 1640s. He was thus well qualified to write on the "West and East Indies," whose wonders are suggested by palms, parasols, and elephants. The aerial creature is probably a "flying squirrel" of a kind that is common in Indonesia.

An Episode in the Conquest of America, *by Jan Mostaert of Haarlem in Holland. An early visualization of the New World by a painter who died in 1555. The multitude of busy small figures suggests the style of the Flemish Breughel, and the placid livestock is Dutch. The American Indians are seen as naked, helpless, and confused—and very different from Europeans.*

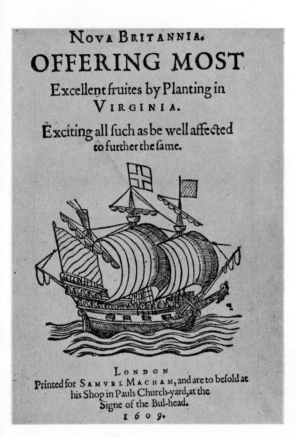

NOVA BRITANNIA.
OFFERING MOST
Excellent fruites by Planting in
VIRGINIA.

Exciting all fuch as be well affected
to further the fame.

LONDON
Printed for SAMVEL MACHAM, and are to befold at
his Shop in Pauls Church-yard, at the
Signe of the Bul-head.
1609.

Opposite, above: Europeans negotiate with an African chief and his council on the Guinea coast. The Europeans have guns, the Africans only spears, but the Africans, in contrast to the American Indians on the preceding page, are fully clothed and seated with dignity in an organized situation. They may be discussing the sale of slaves.

Above, right: Black slaves are stooped over in a diamond-processing operation in Brazil, while overseers watch with whips. The slaves seem to be sifting material in water made to flow through the little compartments.

Above, left: An early advertisement to attract European immigration to what eventually became the United States. This one was published in London two years after the founding of Jamestown, the first permanent English settlement in America. "Planting" meant settling in the seventeenth century.

Right: The headquarters of the Dutch East India Company in 1665 in Bengal, long before the British predominance there. It is wholly walled off from the Indian life around it, with offices, living quarters, and spacious gardens for the employees of the Company. A large Dutch flag flies at the corner of the enclosure, and others can be seen on the ships in the Hooghly River (in the Ganges delta); these ships kept the Dutch traders in continual touch with Holland, though the voyage took almost a year.

The outside of the Lodg

These two prints suggest some results of three centuries of European experience with the world overseas. In China, no Europeans had as yet any territorial foothold. China was seen by Europe as a kind of counterpart civilization to itself. Confucius is shown here in a library of suspiciously European appearance, but holding a book in which Chinese characters are represented. He symbolized for Europeans the great teacher of virtue and wisdom, of social harmony and civic duty, far removed from the theological bickering of European religions.

Meanwhile the settlement at Jamestown had grown into a string of populous colonies. Above, we see Boston Common in 1768. The town seems rural, but has substantial houses with fences and rows of planted trees. British troops have just moved in, because of rising political troubles. They have pitched their tents on the common, where they march and drill in full sight of the citizens. The first fighting of the American Revolution was soon to begin here.

159

IV.
THE
ESTABLISHMENT OF
WEST-EUROPEAN
LEADERSHIP

IF THE READER were to take a map of Europe, set a compass on the city of Paris, and draw a circle with a radius of five hundred miles, a zone would be marked out from which much of modern or "Western" civilization has radiated since about 1650. It was within this zone that a secular society, modern natural science, a developed capitalism, the modern state, parliamentary government, democratic ideas, machine industry, and much else either originated or received their first full expression. The extreme western parts of Europe—Ireland, Portugal, and Spain—were mainly outside the circle. But within it were England, southern Scotland, France, the Low Countries, Switzerland, western and central Germany, and northern Italy. This area, for over two hundred years beginning in the seventeenth century, was the earth's principal center of what anthropologists might call cultural diffusion. Western Europe, as a dynamic cultural area, was to have a tremendous impact on the rest of Europe, the Americas, and ultimately the whole world.

This leadership of western Europe became established in the half-century following the Peace of Westphalia. The fading out of the Italian Renaissance, the subsiding of religious wars, the ruin of the Holy Roman Empire, and the decay of Spain all cleared the stage on which the Dutch, English, and French were to be the principal actors. But the Dutch were few in number, and the English during

Chapter Emblem: A commemorative medal, in which Louis XIV receives the homage of Tournai and Courtrai, Flemish towns temporarily annexed in 1667.

most of the seventeenth century were weakened by domestic discord. It was France that for a time played the most imposing role. The whole half-century following the Peace of Westphalia is in fact often called the Age of Louis XIV.

17. *The* Grand Monarque *and the Balance of Power*

This king of France inherited his throne in 1643 at the age of five, assumed the personal direction of affairs in 1661 at the age of twenty-three, and reigned for seventy-two years until his death in 1715. No one else in modern history has held so powerful a position for so long a time. Louis XIV was more than a figurehead. For over half a century, during his whole adult life, he was the actual and working head of the French government. Inheriting the achievement of Richelieu,[1] he made France the strongest country in Europe. Using French money, by bribes or other inducements, he built up a pro-French interest in virtually every country from England to Turkey. His policies and the counterpolicies that others adopted against him set the pace of public events, and his methods of government and administration, war and diplomacy, became a model for other rulers to copy. During this time the French language, French thought and literature, French architecture and landscape gardens, French styles in clothes, cooking, and etiquette became the accepted standard for Europe. France seemed to be the land of light, and Louis XIV was called by his fascinated admirers Louis the Great, the *Grand Monarque*, and the Sun King. To the internal achievements of France we shall shortly return.

Internationally, the consuming political question of the last decades of the seventeenth century (at least in western Europe—eastern Europe we shall reserve for the next chapter) was the fate of the still vast possessions of the Spanish crown. Spain was what Turkey was later called, "the sick man of Europe." To its social and economic decline[2] was added hereditary physical deterioration of its rulers. In 1665 the Spanish throne was inherited by Charles II, an unfortunate afflicted by many ills of mind and body, impotent, even imbecile, the pitiable product of generations of inbreeding in the Habsburg house. His rule was irresolute and feeble. It was known from the moment of his accession that he could have no children, and that the Spanish branch of the Habsburg family would die out with his own death. The whole future not only of Spain but of the Spanish Netherlands, the Spanish holdings in Italy, and all Spanish America was therefore in question. Charles II dragged out his miserable days until 1700, the object of jealousy and outright assault during his lifetime, and precipitating a new European war by his death.

Louis XIV, who in his youth married a sister of Charles II, intended to benefit from the debility of his royal brother-in-law. His expansionist policies followed two main lines. One was to push the French borders eastward to the Rhine, annexing the Spanish Netherlands (or Belgium) and the Franche-Comté or Free County of Burgundy, a French-speaking region lying between ducal Burgundy

---

[1] See pp. 139–140.
[2] See pp. 133–134.

and Switzerland.[3] Such a policy involved the further dismemberment of the Holy Roman Empire. The other line of Louis XIV's ambitions, increasingly clear as time went on, was his hope of obtaining the entire Spanish inheritance for himself. By combining the resources of France and Spain he would make France supreme in Europe, in America, and on the sea. To promote these ends Louis XIV intrigued with the smaller and middle-sized powers of Europe. He took various princes of Germany, and for a time a king of England, into his pay. He supported, with complete disregard of ideology, the republicans in Holland against their prince, and the royalists in England against the parliamentary opposition, knowing that in Holland it was the republicans, and in England the partisans of high monarchy, who were most dependent on foreign assistance.

Were Louis XIV to succeed in his aims, he would create the "universal monarchy" dreaded by diplomats, that is to say, a political situation in which one state might subordinate all others to its will. The technique used against universal monarchy was the balance of power. Universal monarchy had formerly been almost achieved by the Austro-Spanish Habsburgs. The Habsburg supremacy had been blocked mainly by a balance of power headed by France, of which the Thirty Years' War and the Peace of Westphalia were the outstanding triumphs. Now the danger of universal monarchy came from France, and it was against France that the balance of power was directed.

The Idea of the Balance of Power

It will be useful to explain what a balance of power was and was not meant to be. The phrase itself, which came into general use at this time, has been employed ever since in different though related senses. In one sense it refers to a condition of equilibrium, or of even balance, in which power is distributed among many separate states. The second sense arises when this equilibrium is disturbed. If one state preponderates, and if others then form a coalition against it, then the coalition itself may be called the "balance," though it is actually the counterweight by which balance or equilibrium is to be restored. In a third sense one speaks of "holding" or "controlling" the balance of power; here the balance refers to that decisive increment of weight or power which one state may bring to bear. Thus if a state is a vitally necessary member of a coalition, more needed by its allies than it is in need of them, it may be said to "hold" the balance. Or if it belongs to no coalition at all, but tries to keep all other states in a condition of equilibrium, so that its own intervention on one side or the other would be decisive, it may also be said to "hold" the balance, although strictly speaking not participating in the balance at all.

The aim of statesmen pursuing policies of balance of power in the seventeenth and eighteenth centuries was generally to preserve their own independence of action to the utmost. Hence the basic rule was to ally against any state threatening domination. If one state seemed to dictate too much, others would shun alliance with it unless they were willing (from ideological sympathy or other reasons) to become its puppets. They would seek alliance with the other weaker states instead. They would thus create a balance or counterweight, or "restore the

---

[3] See map, pp. 146–147.

balance," against the state whose ascendancy they feared. Another more subtle reason for preferring alliance with the weak rather than with the strong was that in such an alliance each member could feel his own contribution to be necessary and valued, hence could preserve his own dignity and prestige, and by threatening to withdraw his support could win consideration of his own policies. Indeed, the balance of power may be defined as a system in which each state tends to throw its weight where it is most needed, so that its own importance may be enhanced.

The purpose of balance-of-power politics was not to preserve peace, but to preserve the sovereignty and independence of the states of Europe, or the "liberties of Europe," as they were called, against potential aggressors. The system was effective as a means to this end in the seventeenth and eighteenth centuries. Combinations were intricate, and alliances were readily made and unmade to deal with emerging situations. One reason for the effectiveness of the system lay in the great number of states capable of pursuing an independent foreign policy. These included not only the greater and middle-sized states of Austria, Spain, France, England, Holland, Sweden, and Bavaria, but a great number of small independent states, such as Denmark, the German principalities, Portugal after 1640, and Savoy, Venice, Genoa, and Tuscany. States moved easily from one alliance to another, or from one side of the balance to another. They were held back by no ideologies or sympathies, especially after the religious wars subsided, but could freely choose or reject allies, aiming only to protect their own independence or enlarge their own interests. Moreover, owing to the military technology of the day, small states might count as important military partners in an alliance. By controlling a strategic location, like the king of Denmark, or by making a contribution of ships or money, like the Dutch Republic, they might add just enough strength to an alliance to balance and overbalance the opposing great power and its allies.

As the ambitions of Louis XIV became bolder, and as the capacity of Spain to resist them withered away, the prevention of universal monarchy under France depended increasingly on combining the states of Europe into a balance of power against him. The balance against Louis XIV was engineered mainly by the Dutch. The most tireless of his enemies, and the man who did more than any other to checkmate him, was the Dutchman William III, the prince of Orange, who in his later years was king of England and Scotland as well.

Let us, after first surveying the Dutch in the seventeenth century, turn to the British Isles, where a momentous conflict occurred between Parliament and king. We shall then examine the French absolute monarchy under Louis XIV and conclude the present chapter with the wars of Louis XIV, particularly the War of the Spanish Succession, in which the great international issues of the time conflicted and were resolved.

18. The Dutch Republic

Dutch Civilization and Government

The ambassadors of kings, strolling beside a canal at The Hague, might on occasion observe a number of burghers in plain black garments step out of a boat and proceed to make a meal of cheese and herring on the lawn, and they would recognize in these portly figures Their High Mightinesses the Estates General of the United Provinces, as the Dutch government was known in the diplomatic language of the day. Though noblemen lived in the country, the Dutch were the most bourgeois of all peoples. They were not the only republicans in Europe, since the Swiss cantons, Venice, Genoa, and even England for a few years were republics, but of all republics the United Provinces was by far the most wealthy, the most flourishing, and the most preeminently civilized.

The Dutch acquired a nationality of their own in the long struggle against Spain, and with it a pride in their own freedom and independence. In the later phases of the war with Spain, notably during the Thirty Years' War, they were able to rely more on their wealth, ready money, shipping, and diplomacy than on actual fighting, so that during the whole seventeenth century they enjoyed a degree of comfort, and of intellectual, artistic, and commercial achievement unexcelled in Europe. The classic Dutch poets and dramatists wrote at this time, making a literary language of what had formerly been a dialect of Low German. Hugo Grotius produced, in his *Law of War and Peace*, a pioneering treatise on international law. Baruch Spinoza, of a family of refugee Portuguese Jews, quietly turned out works of philosophy, examining the fundamentals of reality, of human conduct, and of church and state. Spinoza made his living by grinding lenses; there were many other lens grinders in Holland; some of them developed the microscope, and some of these, in turn—Leeuwenhoek, Swammerdam, and others—peering through their microscopes and beholding for the first time the world of microscopic life, became founders of modern biological science. The greatest Dutch scientist was Christian Huyghens (1629-1695), who worked mainly in physics and mathematics; he improved the telescope (a Dutch invention), made clocks move with pendulums, discovered the rings of Saturn, and launched the wave theory of light. A less famous writer, Balthasar Bekker, in his *World Bewitched* (1691) delivered a decisive blow against the expiring superstition of witchcraft.

But the most eternally fresh of the Dutch creations, suffering from no barrier of time or language, were the superb canvases of the painters. Frans Hals produced bluff portraits of the common people. Jan Vermeer threw a spell of magic and quiet dignity over men, and especially women, of the burgher class. Rembrandt conveyed the mystery of human consciousness itself. In Rembrandt's *Masters of the Cloth Hall* (see illustration) we face a group of men who seem about to speak from the canvas, inclined slightly forward, as intent on their business as judges on the proceedings in a courtroom; men of the kind who conducted the affairs of Holland, in both commerce and government; intelligent men, calculating but not cunning, honest but determined to drive a hard bargain, stern rather than mild; and the sober black cloaks, with the clean white collars, set against the carved woodwork and rich table covering of the Cloth Hall, seem to suggest that personal vanity must yield to collective undertakings, and personal simplicity be maintained in the midst of material opulence. And in Vermeer's *Geographer,* painted in 1669 (also reproduced in this book—see p. 111), there appears not only an immaculately scrubbed and dusted Dutch interior, but something of a symbol of the modern world in its youth—the pale northern sunlight streaming through the window, the globe and the map, the dividers in

THE MASTERS OF THE CLOTH HALL
by Rembrandt van Rijn (Dutch, 1606–1669)

This painting was done on commission for the Cloth Hall of Amsterdam, that is, the guild of "clothiers" or "drapers" such as are described on p. 117 in connection with the Commercial Revolution. The men shown are the heads of the guild. Over a period of forty years Rembrandt produced some 600 paintings, in addition to etchings and drawings, in which he conveyed all types of experience, from the commercial practicality of the present group to the deeply mystical and religious. The vitality of Dutch culture in the seventeenth century is shown also in the pictures on pp. 111, 113, and 292. Courtesy of the Rijksmuseum, Amsterdam.

the scholar's right hand, instrument of science and mathematics, the tapestry flung over the table (or is it an Oriental rug brought from the East?), the head lifted in thought, and eyes resting on an invisible world of fresh discoveries and opening horizons.

In religion, after initial disputes, the Dutch Republic adopted toleration. Early in the seventeenth century the Dutch Calvinists divided. One group favored a modification of Calvinism, with a toning down of the doctrine of absolute and unconditional predestination; it drew its main support from the comfortable burghers and its doctrines from a theologian of Leyden named Arminius. To deal with this Arminian heresy a great international Calvinist synod met in 1618 at Dordrecht in Holland. Of the hundred delegates almost a third came from Scotland, England, Germany, Switzerland, and France. The orthodox party won out at the synod; one old man was put to death; the philosopher Grotius fled to France for safety. But beginning in 1632 the Arminians were tolerated. Rights were granted to the large Catholic minority. Jews had long been welcomed in the republic; and Christian sects despised everywhere else, such as the Mennonites, found a refuge in it. Although none of these people had as many political or economic rights as the Calvinists, the resulting mixture stimulated both the intellectual life and the commercial enterprise of the country.

The Dutch as early as 1600 had 10,000 ships, and throughout the seventeenth century they owned most of the shipping of northern Europe. They were the carriers between Spain, France, England, and the Baltic. Much coastwise shipping between ports of France was in Dutch hands. They settled in Bordeaux to buy wines, lent money to vintners, and soon owned many vineyards in France itself. They sailed on every sea. They explored the waters around Spitzbergen and almost monopolized Arctic whaling. They entered the Pacific by way of South America, where they rounded Cape Horn and named it after Hoorn in Holland. Organized in the East India Company of 1602, their merchants increasingly replaced the Portuguese in India and the Far East. In Java, in 1619, they founded the city of Batavia—the Latin name for Holland. (It is now called Jakarta.) Finding some Englishmen in 1623 at Amboina, in the midst of the Spice Islands, they tortured and killed them. The English did not return until the days of Napoleon. Not long after 1600 the Dutch reached Japan. But the Japanese, fearing the political consequences of Christian penetration, in 1641 expelled all other Europeans and confined the Dutch to limited operations on an island near Nagasaki. The Dutch remained for over two centuries the sole link of the West with Japan. In 1612 the Dutch founded their first settlement on Manhattan Island, and in 1621 they established a Dutch West India Company to exploit the loosely held riches of Spanish and Portuguese America. They founded colonies at Pernambuco and Bahia in Brazil (lost soon thereafter) and at Caracas, Curaçao, and in Guiana in the Caribbean. In 1652 the Dutch captured the Cape of Good Hope in South Africa from the Portuguese. Dutch settlers soon appeared—men, women, and children. From these settlers and from French Huguenots and others have come the modern Afrikaner people, whose language and religion still reflect their mainly Dutch origins.

In 1609 the Dutch founded the Bank of Amsterdam. European money was a chaos; coins were minted not only by great monarchs but by small states and cities in Germany and Italy, and even by private persons. In addition, under inflationary pressures, kings and others habitually debased their coins by adding more alloy, while leaving the old coins in circulation along with the new. Anyone handling money thus accumulated a miscellany of uncertain value. The Bank of Amsterdam accepted deposts of such mixed money from all persons and from all countries, assessed the gold and silver content, and, at rates of exchange fixed by itself, allowed depositors to withdraw equivalent values in gold florins minted by the Bank of Amsterdam. These were of known and unchanging weight and purity. They thus became an internationally sought money, an international measure of value, acceptable everywhere. Depositors were also allowed to draw checks against their accounts. These conveniences, plus a safety of deposits guaranteed by the Dutch government, attracted capital from all quarters and made possible loans for a wide range of purposes. Amsterdam remained the financial center of Europe until the French Revolution.

Under their republican government the Dutch enjoyed great freedom, but it can hardly be said that their form of government met all the requirements of a state. Their High Mightinesses (the *Hooge Moogende*), who made up the estates general, were only delegates from their respective seven provinces and could act only as the estates of the provinces gave instructions. The seven provinces, like the states of the Holy Roman Empire in which they had originated, were jealous of their own independence. Each province had, as its executive, an elected stadholder, but there was no stadholder for the United Provinces as a whole. This difficulty was overcome by the fact that most of the various provinces usually elected the same man as stadholder. The stadholder in most provinces was usually the head of the house of Orange, which since the days of William the Silent and the wars for independence had enjoyed exceptional prestige in the republic. The prince of Orange, apart from being stadholder, was simply one of the feudal noblemen of the country. But the noble class had been outdistanced by the commercial, and affairs were generally managed by the burghers. The burghers, intent on making money and enjoying comfort, rarely worried over military questions and hated taxes.

Politics in the Dutch Republic was a seesaw between the burghers, pacifistic and absorbed with business, and the princes of Orange, to whom the country owed most of its military security. When foreigners threatened invasion, the power of the stadholder increased. When all was calm, the stadholder could do little. The Peace of Westphalia produced a mood of confidence in the burghers, followed by a constitutional crisis, in the course of which the stadholder William II died, in 1650. No new stadholder was elected for twenty-two years. The burgher, civilian, and decentralizing tendencies prevailed.

In 1650, eight days after his father's death, was born the third William of the house of Orange, seemingly fated never to be stadholder and to pass his life as a private nobleman on his own estates. William III grew up to be a grave and reserved young man, small and rather stocky, with thin compressed lips and a determined spirit. He learned to speak Dutch, German, English, and French with equal facility, and to understand Italian, Spanish, and Latin. He observed the requirements of his religion, which was Dutch Calvinism, with sober regularity. He had a strong dislike, Dutch and Calvinistic, for everything magnificent or pompous; he lived plainly, hated flattery, and took no pleasure in social conversation. In these respects he was the opposite of his life-long enemy the

Sun King, whom he resembled only in his diligent preoccupation with affairs. In 1677 he married the king of England's niece, Mary.

Foreign Affairs: Conflict with the English and French

Meanwhile matters were not going favorably for the Dutch Republic. In 1651 the revolutionary government then ruling England passed a Navigation Act. This act may be considered the first of a long series of political measures by which the British colonial empire was built up. It was aimed against the Dutch carrying trade. It provided that goods imported into England and its dependencies must be brought in English ships, or in ships belonging to the country exporting the goods. Since the Dutch were too small a people to be great producers and exporters themselves, and lived largely by carrying the goods of others, they saw in the new English policy a threat to their economic existence. The English likewise, claiming sovereignty of the "narrow seas," demanded that Dutch ships salute the English flag in the Channel. Three wars between the Dutch and English followed, running with interruptions from 1652 to 1674 and generally indecisive, though the English annexed New York.

While thus assaulted at sea by the English, the Dutch were menaced on land by the French. Louis XIV made his first aggressive move in 1667, claiming the Spanish Netherlands and Franche-Comté by alleging certain rights of his Spanish wife, and overrunning the Spanish Netherlands with his army. The Dutch, to whom the Spanish Netherlands were a buffer against France, set into motion the mechanism of the balance of power. Dropping temporarily their disputes with the English, they allied with them instead; and since they were able also to secure the adherence of Sweden, the resulting Triple Alliance was sufficient to give pause to Louis XIV, who withdrew from the Spanish Netherlands. But in 1672 Louis XIV again rapidly crossed the Spanish Netherlands, attacked with forces five times as large as the Dutch, and occupied three of the seven Dutch provinces.

A popular clamor now arose among the Dutch for William of Orange, demanding that the young prince, who was now twenty-two years of age, be installed in the old office of stadholder, in which his ancestors had defended them against Spain. He was duly elected stadholder in six provinces. In 1673 these six provinces voted to make the stadholderate hereditary in the house of Orange. William, during his whole tenure or "reign" in the Netherlands, attempted to centralize and consolidate his government, put down the feudal liberties of the provinces, and free himself from constitutional checks, moving generally in the direction of absolute monarchy, which by the tests of power and under French example was the successful form of government at the time. He was unable, however, to go far in this course, and the United Provinces remained a decentralized patrician republic until 1795. Meanwhile, to stave off the immediate menace of Louis XIV, William resorted to a new manipulation of the balance of power. He formed an alliance this time with the minor powers of Denmark and Brandenburg (the German margraviate around Berlin) and with the Austrian and Spanish Habsburgs. Nothing could indicate more clearly the new balance of power precipitated by the rise of France than this coming over of the Dutch to the Habsburg side. The alliance was successful to the extent at least of wearying Louis XIV of the war. Peace was signed in 1678 (treaty of Nimwegen), but only at the expense of Spain and the Holy Roman Empire, from which Louis XIV took the long coveted Franche-Comté, together with another batch of towns in Flanders. The Dutch preserved their territory intact.

In the next ten years came the great windfall of William's life. In 1689 he became king of England. He was now able to bring the British Isles into his perpetual combinations against France. Since the real impact of France was yet to be felt, and the real bid of Louis XIV for universal monarchy was yet to be made, and since the English at this time were rapidly gaining in strength, the entrance of England was a decisive addition to the balance formed against French expansion. In this way the constitutional troubles of England, by bringing a determined Dutchman to the English throne, entered into the general stream of European affairs and helped to assure that western Europe and its overseas offshoots should not be dominated totally by France.

19. Britain: The Puritan Revolution

After the defeat of the Spanish Armada and recession of the Spanish threat the English were for a time less closely involved with the affairs of the Continent. They played no significant part in the Thirty Years' War, and were almost the only European people, west of Poland, who were not represented at the Congress of Westphalia. At the time of the Westphalia negotiations in the 1640s they were in fact engaged in a civil war of their own. This English civil war was a milder variant of the Wars of Religion which desolated France, Germany, and the Netherlands. It was fought not between Protestants and Catholics as on the Continent, but between the more extreme or Calvinistic Protestants called Puritans and the more moderate Protestants, or Anglicans, adhering to the established Church of England. As in the wars on the Continent, religious differences were mixed indistinguishably with political and constitutional issues. As the Huguenots represented to some extent feudal rebelliousness against the French monarchy, as German Protestants fought for states' rights against imperial centralization, and the Calvinists of the Netherlands for provincial liberties against the king of Spain, so the Puritans asserted the rights of Parliament against the mounting claims of royalty in England.

The civil war in England was relatively so mild that England itself can be said to have escaped the horrors of the Wars of Religion. The same was not true of the British Isles as a whole. After 1603 the kingdoms of England and Scotland, while otherwise separate, were ruled by the same king; the kingdom of Ireland remained, as before, a dependency of the English crown. Between England and Presbyterian Scotland there was constant friction, but the worst trouble was between England and Catholic Ireland, which was the scene of religious warfare as savage as that on the Continent.

England in the Seventeenth Century

For the English the seventeenth century was an age of great achievement, during which they made their debut as one of the chief peoples of modern Europe. In 1600 only four or five million persons, in England and Lowland Scotland, spoke the English language. The number did not rise rapidly for another century and a half. But the population began to spread. Religious discontents, reinforced by economic pressures, led to considerable emigration. Twenty thousand Puritans settled in New England between 1630 and 1640, and about the same number went to Barbados and other West India islands during the same years. A third stream, again roughly of the same size, but made up mainly of Scottish Presbyterians, settled in northern Ireland under government auspices, driving away or expropriating the native Celts. English Catholics were allowed by the home government to settle in Maryland. A great many Anglicans went to Virginia in the mid-century, adding to the small settlement made at Jamestown in 1607. Except for the movement to northern Ireland, called the "plantation of Ulster," these migrations took place without much attention on the part of the government, through private initiative organized in commercial companies. After the middle of the century the government began deliberately to build an empire. New York was conquered from the Dutch, Jamaica from the Spanish, and Pennsylvania and the Carolinas were established. All the Thirteen Colonies except Georgia were founded before 1700, and there were at that time perhaps half a million people in British North America. Relative to the home population, it was as if the United States should in three generations build up a distant colonial appendage with fifteen million inhabitants.

The English also, like the Dutch, French, and Spanish at the time, were creating their national culture. Throughout western Europe the national languages, encroaching upon international Latin on the one hand and local dialects on the other, were becoming adequate vehicles for the expression of thought and feeling. Shakespeare and Milton projected their mighty conceptions with overwhelming power of words, not since equaled in English or in any other tongue. The English classical literature, rugged in form but deep in content, vigorous yet subtle in insight, majestic, abundant, and sonorous in expression, was almost the reverse of French classical writing, with its virtues of order, economy, propriety, and graceful precision. The English could never thereafter quite yield to French standards, nor be dazzled or dumbfounded, as some peoples were, by the cultural glories of the Age of Louis XIV. There were no painters at all comparable to those on the Continent, but in music it was the age of Campion and Purcell, and in architecture the century closed with the great buildings of Christopher Wren.

Economically the English were enterprising and affluent, though in 1600 far outdistanced by the Dutch. They had a larger and more productive country than the Dutch, and were therefore not as limited to purely mercantile and seafaring occupations. Coal was mined around Newcastle, and was increasingly used, but was not yet a leading source of English wealth. The great industry was the growing of sheep and manufacture of woolens, which were the main export. Weaving was done to a large extent in the country, under the putting-out system, and organized by merchants according to the methods of commercial capitalism.[4] Since 1553 the English had traded with Russia by way of the White Sea; they were increasingly active in the Baltic and eastern Mediterranean; and with the founding of the East India Company, in 1600, they competed with the Dutch in assaulting the old Portuguese monopoly in India and East Asia. But profitable as

4 See p. 118.

such overseas operations were, the main wealth of England was still in the land. The richest men were not merchants but landlords, and the landed aristocracy formed the richest class.

Background to the Civil War: Parliament and the Stuart Kings

In England, as elsewhere in the seventeenth century, the kings clashed with their old medieval representative bodies. In England the old body, Parliament, won out against the king. But this was not the unique feature in the English development. In Germany the estates of the Holy Roman Empire triumphed against the emperor, and much the same thing, as will be seen, occurred in Poland. But on the Continent the triumph of the old representative bodies generally meant political dissolution or even anarchy. Successful governments were generally those in which kingly powers increased; this was the strong tendency of the time, evident even in the Dutch Republic after 1672 under William of Orange. The unique thing about England was that Parliament, in defeating the king, arrived at a workable form of government. Government remained strong but came under parliamentary control. This determined the character of modern England and launched into the history of Europe and of the world the great movement of liberalism and representative institutions.

What happened was somewhat as follows. In 1603, on the death of Queen Elizabeth, the English crown was inherited by the son of Mary Stuart, James VI of Scotland. As a descendant of Henry VII he became king of England also, taking there the title of James I. James was a philosopher of royal absolutism. He had even written a book on the subject, *The True Law of Free Monarchy*. By a "free" monarchy James meant a monarchy free from control by Parliament, churchmen, or laws and customs of the past. It was a monarchy in which the king, as father to his people, looked after their welfare as he saw fit, standing above all parties, private interests, and pressure groups. He even declared that kings drew their authority from God, and were responsible to God alone. The doctrine which he represented is known as the divine right of kings.[5]

Probably any ruler succeeding Elizabeth would have had trouble with Parliament, which had shown signs of restlessness in the last years of her reign, but had deferred to her as an aging woman and a national symbol. She had maintained peace within the country and fought off the Spaniards, but these very accomplishments persuaded many people that they could safely bring their grievances into the open. James I was a foreigner, a Scot, who lacked the touch for dealing with the English, and who was moreover a royal pedant, the "wisest fool in Christendom," as he was uncharitably called. Not content with the actualities of control, as Elizabeth had been, he read the Parliament tiresome lectures on the royal rights. He also was in constant need of money. The wars against Spain had left a considerable debt. James was far from economical, and, in any case, in an age of rising prices, he could not live within the fixed and customary revenues of the English crown. These were of a medieval character, increasingly quaint under the new conditions—rights of wardship and marriage, escheats, franc-fiefs and fees for the distraint of knighthood, together with

[5] See p. 185.

"tunnage and poundage," or rights given to the king by Parliament at his accession (and normally unchanged during his reign) to collect specified duties on exports and imports, according to quantity, not value, and hence not rising in proportion to prices.

Neither to James I nor to his son Charles I, who succeeded him in 1625, would Parliament grant adequate revenue, because it distrusted them both. Many members of Parliament were Puritans, dissatisfied with the organization and doctrine of the Church of England.[6] Elizabeth had tried to hush up religious troubles, but James threatened to "harry the Puritans out of the land," and Charles supported the Anglican hierarchy which, under Archbishop Laud, sought to enforce religious conformity. Many members of Parliament were also lawyers, who feared that the common law of England, the historic or customary law, was in danger. They disliked the prerogative courts, the Star Chamber set up by Henry VII, the High Commission set up by Elizabeth.[7] They heard with trepidation the modern doctrine that the sovereign king could make laws and decide cases at his own discretion.[8] Last but not least, practically all members of Parliament were property owners. Landowners, supported by the merchants, feared that if the king succeeded in raising taxes on his own authority their wealth would be insecure. Hence there were strong grounds for resistance.

In England the Parliament was so organized as to make resistance effective.[9] There was only one Parliament for the whole country. There were no provincial or local estates, as in the Dutch Republic, Spain, France, Germany, and Poland. Hence all parliamentary opposition was concentrated in one place. In this one place, the one and only Parliament, there were only two houses, the House of Lords and the House of Commons. The landed interest dominated in both houses, the noblemen in the Lords and the gentry in the Commons. In the Commons the gentry, who formed the bulk of the aristocracy, mixed with representatives of the merchants and the towns. Indeed the towns frequently chose country gentlemen to represent them. Hence the houses of Parliament did not accentuate, as did the estates on the Continent, the class division within the country. Nor was the church present in Parliament as a separate force. Before Henry VIII's break with Rome the bishops and abbots together had formed a large majority in the House of Lords. Now there were no abbots left, for there were no monasteries. The House of Lords was now predominantly secular; in the first Parliament of James I there were eighty-two lay peers and twenty-six bishops. The great landowners had captured the House of Lords. The smaller landowners of the Commons had been enriched by receiving former monastic lands and had prospered by raising wool. The merchants had likewise grown up under mercantilistic protection. Parliament was strong not only in organization but in the social interests and wealth that it represented. No king could long govern against its will.

In 1629 king and Parliament came to a deadlock. Charles I attempted to rule without Parliament, which could legally meet only at the royal summons. He

[6] See pp. 83–85.
[7] See pp. 69, 92.
[8] See p. 69.
[9] See pp. 34–35.

intended to give England a good and efficient government. Had he succeeded, the course of English constitutional development would have paralleled that of France. But by certain reforms in Ireland he antagonized the English landlords who had interests in that country. By supporting the High Anglicans he made enemies of the Puritans. By attempting to modernize the navy with funds raised without parliamentary consent (called "ship money") he alarmed all property owners, whose opposition was typified in the famous lawsuit of a country gentleman, John Hampden, in 1637.

The ship-money case illustrates the best arguments of both sides. It was the old custom in England for coastal towns to provide ships for the king's service in time of war. More recently, these coastal towns had provided money instead. Charles I wished to maintain a navy in time of peace and to have ship money paid by the country as a whole, including the inland counties. In the old or medieval view it was the function of the towns which were directly affected to maintain a fleet. In the new view, sponsored by the king, the whole nation was the unit on which a navy should be based. The country gentlemen whom Parliament mainly represented, and most of whom lived in inland counties, had less interest in the navy, and in any case were unwilling to pay for it unless they could control the foreign policies for which a navy might be used. The parliamentary class represented the idea, derived from the Middle Ages, that taxes should be authorized by Parliament. The king represented the newer ideas of monarchy that were developing on the Continent. John Hampden lost his case in court, but he won the sympathy of the politically significant classes of the country. Until the king could govern with the confidence of Parliament, or until Parliament itself was willing, not merely to keep down taxes, but to assume the responsibilities of government under modern conditions, neither a navy nor any effectual government could be maintained.

The Scots were the first to rebel. In 1637 they rioted in Edinburgh against attempts to impose the Anglican religion in Scotland. Charles, to raise funds to put down the Scottish rebellion, convoked the English Parliament in 1640, for the first time in eleven years. When it proved hostile to him he dissolved it and called for new elections. The same men were returned. The resulting body, since it sat theoretically for twenty years without new elections, from 1640 to 1660, is known historically as the Long Parliament. Its principal leaders—men like John Hampden, John Pym, and Oliver Cromwell—were small or moderately well-to-do land-owning gentry. The merchant class, while furnishing no leaders, lent its support.

The Long Parliament, far from assisting the king against the Scots, used the Scottish rebellion as a means of pressing its own demands. These were revolutionary from the outset. Parliament insisted that the chief royal advisers be not merely removed but impeached and put to death. It abolished the Star Chamber and the High Commission. The most extreme Calvinist element, the "root and branch" men or "radicals," drove through a bill for the abolition of bishops, revolutionizing the Anglican church. In 1642 Parliament and king came to open war, the king drawing followers mainly from the north and west, the Parliament from the commercially and agriculturally more advanced counties of the south and east. During the war, as the price of support from the Scottish army, Parliament adopted the Solemn League and Covenant. This prescribed that religion in England, Scotland, and Ireland should be made uniform "according to the word

of God and the example of the best reformed churches." Thus Presbyterianism
became the established legal religion of the three kingdoms.

The Emergence of Cromwell

The parliamentary forces, called Roundheads from the close haircuts favored by
Puritans, gradually defeated the royalists. The wars brought a hitherto unknown
gentleman named Oliver Cromwell to the foreground. A devout Puritan, he
organized a new and more effective military force, the Ironsides, in which extreme
Protestant exaltation provided the basis for morale, discipline, and the will to
fight. Parliament had no sooner defeated the king than it fell out with its own
army. The army, in which a more popular class was represented than in the
Parliament, became the center of advanced democratic ideas. Many of the soldiers
objected to Presbyterianism as much as to Anglicanism. They favored a free
toleration for all "godly" forms of religion, with no superior church organization
above local groups of like-minded spirits.

Cromwell concluded that the defeated king, Charles I, could not be trusted,
that "ungodly" persons of all kinds put their hopes in him (what later ages would
call counterrevolution), and that he must be put to death. Since Parliament
hesitated, Cromwell with the support of the army broke Parliament up. The Long
Parliament, having started in 1640 with some 500 members, had sunk by 1649 to
about 150 (for this revolution, like others, was pushed through by a minority); of
these Cromwell now drove out almost 100, leaving a Rump of 50 or 60. This
operation was called Pride's Purge, after Colonel Pride who commanded the
soldiers by whom Parliament was intimidated; and in subsequent revolutions such
excisions have been commonly known as purges, and the residues, sometimes,
as rumps. The Rump put King Charles to death on the scaffold in 1649.

England, or rather the whole British Isles, was now declared a republic. It was
named the Commonwealth. Cromwell tried to govern as best he could. Religious
toleration was decreed except for Unitarians and atheists on the one hand, and
except for Roman Catholics and the most obstinate Anglicans on the other—a
considerable exception. Cromwell had to subdue both Scotland and Ireland by
force. In Scotland the execution of the king, violating the ancient national Scottish
monarchy of the Stuarts, had swung the country back into the royalist camp.
Cromwell crushed the Scots in 1650. Meanwhile the Protestant and Calvinist fury
swept over Ireland. A massacre of newly settled Protestants in Ulster in 1641
had left bitter memories which were now avenged. The Irish garrisons of Drogheda
and Wexford were defeated and massacred. Thousands of Catholics were killed;
priests were put to the sword, and women and small children dispatched in cold
blood. Where formerly, in the "plantation" of Ulster, a whole Protestant
population had been settled in northern Ireland, bodily replacing the native Irish,
now Protestant landlords were scattered over the country as a whole, replacing
the Catholic landlords and retaining the Catholic peasantry as their tenants. What
now happened in Ireland was a close parallel to what had happened thirty years
before in Bohemia, except that Protestant and Catholic roles were reversed.[10]
For the Irish, as for the Czechs, the native religion and clergy were driven

[10] See pp. 142–143, 224.

underground, a foreign and detested church was established, and a new and foreign landed aristocracy, originally recruited in large measure from military adventurers, was settled upon the country, in which, as soon as it assured the payment of its rents, it soon ceased to reside.

In England itself Cromwell ruled with great difficulty. In external affairs his regime was successful enough, for he not only completed the subjugation of Ireland, but in the Navigation Act of 1651[11] he opened the English attack on the Dutch maritime supremacy, and in a war with Spain, in which the English acquired Jamaica, he opened the English bidding for the inheritance of the Spanish Habsburgs. But he failed to gain the support of a majority of the English. The Puritan Revolution, like others, produced its extremists. It failed to satisfy the most ardent and could not win over the truly conservative, so that Cromwell found himself reluctantly more autocratic, and more alone.

A party arose called the Levellers, who were in fact what later times would call advanced political democrats. They were numerous in the Puritan army, though their chief spokesman, John Lilburne, was a civilian. Appealing to natural rights and to the rights of Englishmen, they asked for a nearly universal manhood suffrage, equality of representation, a written constitution, and subordination of Parliament to a reformed body of voters. They thus anticipated many ideas of the American and French revolutions over a century later. There were others in whom religious and social radicalism were indistinguishably mixed. George Fox, going beyond Calvinism or Presbyterianism, founded the Society of Friends, or "Quakers," who caused consternation by rejecting various social amenities in the name of the Spirit. A more ephemeral group, the "Diggers," proceeded to occupy and cultivate common lands, or lands privately owned, in a general repudiation of property. The Fifth Monarchy Men were a millennial group who felt that the end of the world was at hand. They were so called from their belief, as they read the Bible, that history has seen four empires, those of Assyria, Persia, Alexander, and Caesar; and that the existing world was still "Caesar's" but would soon give way to the fifth monarchy, of Christ, in which justice would at last rule.

Cromwell opposed such movements, by which all established persons in society felt threatened. As a regicide and a Puritan, however, he could not turn to the royalist and Anglican interests. Unable to agree even with the Rump, he abolished it also in 1653, and thereafter vainly attempted to govern, as Lord Protector, through representative bodies devised by himself and his followers, under a written constitution, the Instrument of Government. Actually, he was driven to place England under military rule, the regime of the "major generals." These officials, each in his district, repressed malcontents, vagabonds, and "bandits," closed ale houses, and prohibited cockfighting, in a mixture of moral puritanism and political dictatorship. Cromwell died in 1658; and his son was unable to maintain the Protectorate. Two years later, with all but universal assent, royalty was restored. Charles II, son of the dead Charles I, became king of England and of Scotland.

Cromwell, by beheading a king and keeping his successor off the throne for eleven years, had left a lesson which was not forgotten. Though he favored

[11] See pp. 168–169.

constitutional and parliamentary government and had granted a measure of religious toleration, he had in fact ruled as a dictator in behalf of a stern Puritan minority. The English people now began to blot from their memories the fact that they had ever had a real revolution. The fervid dream of a "godly" England was dissipated forever. What was remembered was a nightmare of standing armies and major generals, of grim Puritans and overwrought religious enthusiasts. The English lower classes ceased to have any political consciousness for over a century, except in sporadic rioting over food shortages or outbursts against the dangers of "popery." Democratic ideas were generally rejected as "levelling." They were generally abandoned in England after 1660 or were cherished by obscure individuals who could not make themselves heard. Such ideas, indeed, had a more continuous history in the English colonies in America, where some leaders of the discredited revolution took refuge.

20. Britain: The Triumph of Parliament

The Restoration, 1660–1688: The Later Stuarts

What was restored in 1660 was not only the monarchy, in the person of Charles II, but also the Church of England and the Parliament. Everything, legally, was supposed to be as it had been in 1640. The difference was that Charles II, knowing the fate of his father, was careful not to provoke Parliament to extremes, and that the classes represented in Parliament, frightened by the disturbances of the past twenty years, were for some time more warmly loyal to the king than they had been before 1640 and more willing to uphold the established church.

Parliament during the Restoration enacted some far-reaching legislation. It changed the legal basis of land tenure, abolishing certain old feudal payments owed by landholders to the king. The possession of land thus came to resemble private property of modern type, and the landowning class became more definitely a propertied aristocracy. In place of the feudal dues to the king, which had been automatically payable, Parliament arranged for the king to receive income in the form of taxation, which Parliament could raise or reduce in amount. This gave a new power to Parliament and a new flexibility to government. The aristocracy, in short, cleared their property of customary restrictions and obligations, and at the same time undertook to support the state by imposing taxes on themselves. The English aristocracy proved more willing than the corresponding classes on the Continent to pay a large share of the expenses of government. Its reward was that, for a century and a half, it virtually ran the government to the exclusion of everyone else. Landowners in this period directed not only national affairs through Parliament, but also local affairs as justices of the peace. The justices, drawn from the gentry of each country, decided small lawsuits, punished misdemeanors, and supervised the parish officials charged with poor relief and care of the roads. The regime of the landlord-justices came to be called the "squirearchy."

Other classes drew less immediate advantage from the Restoration. The Navigation Act of 1651 was renewed and even added to, so that commercial, shipping, and manufacturing interests were well protected. But in other ways the landed classes now in power showed themselves unsympathetic to the business classes of the towns. Many people in the towns were Dissenters, of the element formerly called Puritan, and now refusing to accept the restored Church of England. Parliament excluded Dissenters from the town "corporations," or governing bodies, forbade any dissenting clergymen to teach school or come within five miles of an incorporated town, and prohibited all religious meetings, called "conventicles," not held according to the forms and by the authority of the Church of England. The effect was that many middle-class townspeople found it difficult or impossible to follow their preferred religion, to obtain an education for their children, either elementary or advanced (for Oxford and Cambridge were a part of the established church), to take part in local affairs through the town corporations, or to sit in the House of Commons, since the corporations in many cases chose the burgesses who represented the towns. The lowest classes, the very poor, were discouraged by the same laws from following sectarian and visionary preachers. Another enactment fell upon them alone, the Act of Settlement of 1662, which decentralized the administration of the Poor Law, making each parish responsible only for its own paupers. Poor people, who were very numerous, were condemned to remain in the parishes where they lived. A large section of the English population was immobilized.

But it was not long after the Restoration that Parliament and king were again at odds. The issue was again religion. There was at this time a tendency throughout Europe for Protestants to return voluntarily to Roman Catholicism, a tendency naturally dreaded by the Protestant churches. It was most conspicuously illustrated when the daughter of Gustavus Adolphus himself, Queen Christina of Sweden, to the consternation of the Protestant world, abdicated her throne and was received into the Roman church. In England the national feeling was excitedly anti-Catholic. No measures were more popular than those against "popery"; and the squires in Parliament, stiffly loyal to the Church of England, dreaded papists even more than Dissenters. The king, Charles II, was personally inclined to Catholicism. He admired the magnificent monarchy of Louis XIV, which he would have liked to duplicate, so far as possible, in England. At odds with his Parliament, Charles II made overtures to Louis XIV. The secret treaty of Dover of 1670 was the outcome. Charles thereby agreed to join Louis XIV in his expected war against the Dutch; and Louis agreed to pay the king of England three million livres a year during the war. He hoped also that Charles II would soon find it opportune to rejoin the Roman church.

While these arrangements were unknown in detail in England, it was known that Charles II was well disposed to the French and to Roman Catholicism. England went to war again with the Dutch. The king's brother and heir, James, Duke of York, publicly announced his conversion to Rome. Charles II, in a "declaration of indulgence," announced the nonenforcement of laws against Dissenters. The king declared that he favored general toleration, but it was rightly feared that his real aim was to promote Roman Catholicism in England, and that his policy might be the opening wedge for the Counter Reformation, which had already swept Protestantism out of Bohemia and Poland and was at this very moment menacing it in France. Parliament retorted in 1673 by passing the Test Act, which required all officeholders to take communion in the Church of England. The Test Act renewed the legislation against Dissenters and also made it impossible for Catholics to serve in the government or in the army and navy. The Test Act remained on the statute books until 1828.

While Charles' pro-French and pro-Catholic policies were extremely unpopular, both among the country gentry who disliked Frenchmen from prejudice, and the merchants who found them increasingly pressing competitors, still the situation might not have come to a head except for the avowed Catholicism and French orientation of Charles' brother James, due to be the next king since Charles had no legitimate children. A strong movement developed in Parliament to exclude James by law from the throne. The exclusionists—and those generally who were most suspicious of the king, Catholics, and Frenchmen—received the nickname of Whigs. The king's supporters were popularly called Tories. The Whigs, while backed by the middle class and merchants of London, drew their main strength from the upper aristocracy, especially certain great noblemen who might expect, if the king's power were weakened, to play a prominent part in ruling the country themselves. The Tories were the party of the lesser aristocracy and gentry, those who were suspicious of the "moneyed interest" of London, and felt a strong loyalty to church and king. These two parties, or at least their names, became permanently established in English public life. But all the Whigs and Tories together, at this time, did not number more than a few thousand persons.

The Revolution of 1688

James II, despite Whig vexation, became king in 1685. He soon antagonized even the Tories. The Tories were strong Anglicans or Church of England men. As landowners they appointed most of the parish clergy, who imparted Tory sentiments to the rural population, and from their ranks were drawn the bishops, archdeacons, university functionaries, and other high personnel of the church. The laws keeping Dissenters and Catholics from office had given Anglicans a monopoly in local and national government and in the army and navy. James II acted as if there were no Test Act, claiming the right to suspend its operation in individual cases, and appointed a good many Catholics to influential and lucrative positions. He offered a program, as his brother had done, of general religious toleration, to allow Protestant Dissenters as well as Roman Catholics to participate in public life. Such a program, whether frankly meant as a secularizing of politics or indirectly intended as favoritism to Catholics, was equally repugnant to the Church of England. Seven bishops refused to endorse it. They were prosecuted for disobedience to the king but were acquitted by the jury. James, by these actions, violated the liberties of the established church, threatened the Anglican monopoly of church and state, and aroused the popular terrors of "popery." He was also forced to take the position philosophically set forth by his grandfather James I, that a king of England could make and unmake the law by his own will. The Tories joined the Whigs in opposition. In 1688, a son was born to James II and baptised into the Catholic faith. The prospect now opened up of an indefinite line of Catholic rulers in England. Leading men of both parties thereupon abandoned James II. They offered the throne to his grown daughter Mary, born and brought up a Protestant before her father's conversion to Rome.

Mary was the wife of William of Orange. William, it will be recalled, had spent his adult life in blocking the ambitions of the king of France, who, it should be recalled, likewise threatened Europe with a "universal monarchy" by absorbing or inheriting the world of Spain. To William III it would be a mere distraction to be husband to a queen of England, or even to be king in his own name, unless England could be brought to serve his own purposes. He was immutably Dutch; his purpose was to save Holland and hence to ruin Louis XIV. His chief interest in England was to bring the English into his balance of power against France. Since the English were generally anti-French, and had chafed under the pro-French tendencies of their kings, William without difficulty reached an understanding with the discontented Whigs and Tories. Protected by a written invitation from prominent Englishmen, he invaded England with a considerable army. James II fled, and William was proclaimed co-ruler with Mary over England and Scotland. In the next year, 1690, at the Boyne River in Ireland, a motley army of Dutchmen, Germans, Scots, and French Huguenots under William III defeated a French and Irish force led by James II. Thus the liberties of England were saved. James II fled to France.

Louis XIV of course refused to recognize his inveterate enemy as ruler of England. He maintained James at the French court with all the honors due the English king. It was thereafter one of his principal war aims to restore the Catholic and Stuart dynasty across the Channel. The English, contrariwise, had added reason to fight the French. French victory would mean counterrevolution and royal absolutism in England. The whole Revolution of 1688 was at stake in the French wars.

In 1689, Parliament enacted a Bill of Rights, stipulating that no law could be suspended by the king (as the Test Act had been), no taxes raised or army maintained except by parliamentary consent, and no subject (however poor) arrested and detained without legal process. William III accepted these articles as conditions to receiving the crown. Thereafter the relation between king and people was a kind of contract. It was further provided, by the Act of Settlement of 1701, that no Catholic could be king of England; this excluded the descendants of James II, known in the following century as the Pretenders. Parliament also passed the Toleration Act of 1689, which allowed Protestant Dissenters to practice their religion but still excluded them from political life and public service. Since ways of evading these restrictions were soon found, and since even Catholics were not molested unless they supported the Pretenders, there was thereafter no serious trouble over religion in England and Lowland Scotland.

The English Parliament could make no laws for Scotland, and it was to be feared that James II might some day be restored in his northern kingdom. The securing of the parliamentary revolution in England, and of the island's defenses against France, required that the two kingdoms be organically joined. There was little sentiment in Scotland, however, for a merger with the English. The English tempted the Scots with economic advantages. The Scots still had no rights in the English East India Company, nor in the English colonies, nor within the English system of mercantilism and Navigation Acts. They obtained such rights by consenting to a union. In 1707 the United Kingdom of Great Britain was created. The Scots retained their own legal system and established Presbyterian church, but their government and parliament were merged with those of England. The term "British" came into use to refer to both English and Scots.

As for Ireland, it was now feared as a center of Stuart and French intrigue.

The Revolution of 1688 marked the climax of a long record of trouble. Ireland had never been simply "conquered" by England, though certain English or rather Anglo-Norman families had carved out estates there since the twelfth century. By the end of the Middle Ages Ireland was organized as a separate kingdom with its own parliament, subordinate to the English crown. During the Reformation the Irish remained Catholic while England turned Protestant, but the monasteries were dissolved in Ireland as in England; and the organized church as such, the established Church of Ireland, with its apparatus of bishoprics, parishes, and tithes, became an Anglican communion in which the mass of native Irish had no interest. Next came the plantation of Ulster, already mentioned, in which a mass of newcomers, mainly Scottish and Presbyterian, settled in the northern part of the island.[12] Then in Cromwell's time, as just seen, English landlords spread through the rest of the country; or rather, a new Anglo-Irish upper class developed, in which English landowning families, residing most often in England, added the income from Irish estates to their miscellaneous revenues. Ireland therefore by the close of the seventeenth century was a very mixed country. Probably two-thirds of its population was Catholic, of generally Celtic ethnic background; perhaps a fifth was Presbyterian, with recent Scottish connections; the small remainder was made up of Anglicans, largely Anglo-Irish of recent or distant origin in England, who controlled most of the land, manned the official church, and were influential in the Irish parliament. It was essentially a landlord and peasant society, in which the Presbyterian as well as the Catholic mass was overwhelmingly agricultural; towns were small, and the middle class scarcely developed.

After the Revolution of 1688, in which the final overthrow of James II took place at the Boyne River, the English feared Ireland as a source of danger to the postrevolutionary arrangements in England. Resistance of the subjugated Catholics had also to be prevented. Hence to the burden of an alien church and absentee landlordism was now added the "penal code." Catholic clergy were banished, and Catholics were forbidden to vote or to sit in the Irish parliament. Catholic teachers were forbidden to teach, and Catholic parents were forbidden to send children overseas to be educated in Catholic schools. No Catholic could take a degree at Trinity College (Dublin University), an Anglican institution. Catholic Irishmen were forbidden to purchase land, to lease it for more than thirty-one years, to inherit it from a Protestant, or to own a horse worth more than £5. A Catholic whose son turned Protestant found his own property rights limited in his son's favor. Catholics were forbidden to be attorneys, to serve as constables, or, in most trades, to have more than two apprentices. Some disabilities fell on the Protestant Irish also. Thus Irish shipping was excluded from the British colonies, nor could the Irish import colonial goods except through England. Export of Irish woolens and glass manufactures was prohibited. No import tariff on English manufactures could be levied by the Irish parliament. About all that was left to the Irish, in international trade, was the export of agricultural produce; and the foreign exchange acquired in this way went very largely to pay the rents of absentee landlords.

The purpose of the penal code was in part strategic, to weaken Ireland as a

---

[12] See pp. 84–85, 169–170, 174–175.

potentially hostile country during a long period of wars with France. In part it was commercial, to favor English manufactures by removing Irish competition. And in part it was social, to confirm the position of the Anglican interest, or "ascendancy" as it came to be called. Parts of the code were removed piecemeal in the following decades, and a Catholic merchant class grew up in the eighteenth century; but much remained in effect for a long time, so that, for example, a Catholic could not vote for members of the Irish parliament until 1793, and even then could not be elected to it. In general, the Irish emerged from the seventeenth century as the most repressed people of western Europe.

England, immediately after the expulsion of James II, joined William III's coalition against France. To the alliance England brought a highly competent naval force, together with very considerable wealth. William's government, to finance the war, borrowed £1,200,000 from a syndicate of private lenders, who in return for holding government bonds were given the privilege of operating a bank. Thus originated, in 1694, both the Bank of England and the British national debt. Owners of liquid assets, merchants of London and Whig aristocrats with fat rent rolls, having lent their money to the new regime, had a compelling reason to defend it against the French and James II. And having at last a government whose policies they could control, they were willing to entrust it with money in large amounts. The national debt rapidly rose, while the credit of the government held consistently good; and for many years the Continent was astonished at the wealth that the British government could tap at will, and the quantities of money that it could pour into the wars of Europe.

The events of 1688 came to be known to the English as the Glorious Revolution. The Revolution was considered to have vindicated the principles of parliamentary government, the rule of law, and even the right of rebellion against tyranny. It has often been depicted as the climax in the growth of English constitutional self-government. Political writers like John Locke, shortly after the events, helped to give wide currency to these ideas.[13] There was in truth some justification for these views even though in more recent times some writers have "deglorified" the Revolution of 1688. They point out that it was a class movement, promoted and maintained by the landed aristocracy. The Parliament which boldly asserted itself against the king was at the same time closing itself to large segments of the people. Where in the Middle Ages members of the House of Commons had usually received pay for their services, this custom disappeared in the seventeenth century, so that thereafter only men with independent incomes could sit. After the parliamentary triumph of 1688 this tendency became a matter of law. An act of 1710 required members of the House of Commons to possess private incomes at such a level that only a few thousand persons could legally qualify. This income had to come from the ownership of land. England from 1688 to 1832 was the best example in modern times of a true aristocracy, i.e., of a country in which the aristocratic landowning class not only enjoyed privileges but also conducted the government. But the landowning interest was then the only class sufficiently wealthy, numerous, educated, and self-conscious to stand on its own feet. The rule of the "gentlemen of England" was within its limits a regime of political liberty.

---

[13] On John Locke and the philosophy of the Glorious Revolution, see pp. 311–313.

21. The France of Louis XIV, 1643–1715: The Triumph of Absolutism

French Civilization in the Seventeenth Century

Having traveled in the outer orbits of the European political system, we come now to its radiant and mighty center, the domain of the Sun King himself, the France against which the rest of Europe felt obliged to combine, and on whose push and pull depended the course of the lesser bodies—the future of the Spanish possessions, the independence of Holland, the maintenance in England of the parliamentary revolution. The France of Louis XIV owed much of its ascendancy to the quantity and quality of its people. Population was stabilized or possibly even falling in the seventeenth century, the last century in which France was seriously disturbed by famine, pestilence, and peasant rebellion. With 19 million inhabitants in 1700 France was still over three times as populous as England and twice as populous as Spain. Its fertile soil, in an agricultural age, made it a wealthy country, though the wealth was very unevenly distributed. France was big enough to harbor many contradictions. Millions of its people lived in poverty, yet the number in comfortable or even luxurious circumstances was very large. There were both modest country nobles and cosmopolitan *grands seigneurs*. The middle class included an inordinate number of lawyers, officeholders, and bureaucrats, and the country was less commercial than Holland or England, yet in sheer numbers there may have been more merchants in France than in either of the other two countries. Protestants were a declining minority, yet in the mid–seventeenth century there were still more French Huguenots than Dutch Calvinists. It was a self-sufficient country, yet the French in this century began trading in India and Madagascar, founded Canada, penetrated the Great Lakes and the Mississippi valley, set up plantations in the West Indies, expanded their ancient commerce with the Levant, enlarged their mercantile marine, and for a time had the leading navy of Europe.

The dominance of France meant the dominance not merely of power, but of a people generally admitted to be in the forefront of civilization. They carried over the versatility of the Italy of the Renaissance. In Poussin and Claude Lorrain they produced a notable school of painters, their architecture was emulated throughout Europe, and they excelled in military fortification and general engineering. Much of their literature, though often written by bourgeois writers, was designed for an aristocratic and courtly audience, which had put aside the uncouth manners of an earlier day and prided itself on the refinement of its tastes and perceptions. Corneille and Racine wrote austere tragedies on the fundamental situations of human life. Molière, in his comedies, ridiculed bumbling doctors, new-rich bourgeois, and foppish aristocrats, making the word "marquis" almost a joke in the French language. La Fontaine gave the world his animal fables, and La Rochefoucauld, in his witty and sardonic maxims, a great nobleman's candid judgment on human nature. In Descartes the French produced a great mathematician and scientific thinker, in Pascal a scientist who was also a profound spokesman for Christianity, in Bayle the father of modern skeptics. It was French thought and the French language, not merely the armies of Louis XIV, which in the seventeenth century were sweeping the European world.

The Development of Absolutism in France

This ascendancy of French culture went along with a regime in which political liberties were at a discount. It was an embellishment to the absolute monarchy of Louis XIV. France had a tradition of political freedom in the feudal sense. It had the same kind of background of feudal liberties as did the other countries of Europe. It had an Estates General, which had not met since 1615 but was not legally abolished. In some regions Provincial Estates, still meeting frequently, retained a measure of self-government and of power over taxation. There were about a dozen bodies known as parlements,[14] which, unlike the English Parliament, had developed as courts of law, each being the supreme court for a certain area of the country. The parlements upheld certain "fundamental laws" which they said the king could not overstep, and they often refused to enforce royal edicts which they declared to be unconstitutional. We have already observed how France, beneath the surface, was almost as composite as Germany.[15] French towns had won charters of acknowledged rights, and many of the great provinces enjoyed liberties written into old agreements with the crown. These local liberties were the main reason for a good deal of institutional complication. There were some 300 "customs" or regional systems of law; it was observed that a traveler sometimes changed laws more often than he changed horses. Internal tariffs ran along the old provincial borders. Tolls were levied by manorial lords. The king's taxes fell less heavily on some regions than on others. Neither coinage nor weights and measures were uniform throughout the country. France was a bundle of territories held together by allegiance to the king.

This older kind of freedom discredited itself in France at the very time when by triumphing in Germany it pulled the Holy Roman Empire to pieces, and when in England it successfully made the transition to a more modern form of political liberty, embodied in the parliamentary though aristocratic state. In France the old medieval, feudal, or local type of liberty became associated with disorder. It has already been related how after the disorders of the sixteenth-century religious wars people had turned with relief to the monarchy and how Henry IV and then Richelieu had begun to make the monarchy strong.[16] The troubles of the Fronde provided additional incentive for absolutism in France.

The Fronde broke out immediately after the Peace of Westphalia, while Louis XIV was still a child, and was directed against Cardinal Mazarin, who was governing in his name. It was an abortive revolution, led by the same elements, the parlements and the nobility, which were to initiate the great French Revolution in 1789. The parlements, especially the Parlement of Paris, insisted in 1648 on their right to pronounce certain edicts unconstitutional. Barricades were thrown up and street fighting broke out in Paris. The nobility rebelled, as it had often in the past. Leadership was assumed by certain prominent noblemen who, roughly

---

[14] Spelled *parlements* in French, to distinguish from the English Parliament.
[15] See p. 135 and map, p. 188.
[16] See pp. 138–140.

like the great Whigs of England, had enough wealth and influence to believe that, if the king's power were kept down, they might govern the country themselves. The nobility demanded a calling of the Estates General, expecting to dominate over the bourgeoisie and the clergy in that body. Armed bands of soldiers, unemployed since the Peace of Westphalia and led by nobles, roamed about the country terrorizing the peasants. If the nobles had their way, it was probable that the manorial system would fall on the peasants more heavily, as in eastern Europe, where triumphant lords were at this very time exacting increased labor services from the peasants. Finally the rebellious nobles called in Spanish troops, though France was at war with Spain. By this time the bourgeoisie, together with the parlements, had withdrawn support from the rebellious nobles. The agitation subsided in total failure, because bourgeoisie and aristocracy could not work together, because the nobles outraged the loyalty of many Frenchmen by joining with a power with which France was at war, and because the *frondeurs*, especially after the parlements deserted them, had no systematic or constructive program, aiming only at the overthrow of the unpopular Cardinal Mazarin and at obtaining offices and favors for themselves.

After the Fronde, as after the religious wars, the bourgeoisie and peasantry of France, to protect themselves against the claims of the aristocracy, were in a mood to welcome the exercise of strong power by the kings. And in the young Louis XIV they had a man more than willing to grasp all the power he could get. Louis, on Mazarin's death in 1661, announced that he would govern the country himself. He was the third king of the Bourbon line. It was the Bourbon tradition, established by Henry IV and by Richelieu, to draw the teeth from the feudal aristocrats, and this tradition Louis XIV followed. He was not a man of any transcendent abilities, though he had the capacity, often found among successful executives, of learning a good deal from conversation with experts. His education was not very good, having been made purposely easy; but he had the ability to see and stick to definite lines of policy, and he was extremely methodical and industrious in his daily habits, scrupulously loading himself with administrative business throughout his reign. He was extremely fond of himself and his position of kingship, with an insatiable appetite for admiration and flattery; he loved magnificent display and elaborate etiquette, though to some extent he simply adopted them as instruments of policy rather than as a personal whim.

With the reign of Louis XIV the "state" in its modern form took a long step forward. The state in the abstract has always seemed theoretical to the English-speaking world. Let us say, for simplicity, that the state represents a fusion of justice and power. A sovereign state possesses, within its territory, a monopoly over the administration of justice and the use of force. Private persons neither pass legal judgments on others nor control private armies of their own. For private and unauthorized persons to do so, in an orderly state, constitutes rebellion. This was in contrast to the older feudal practice, by which feudal lords maintained manorial courts and led their own followers into battle. Against these feudal practices Louis XIV energetically worked, though not with complete success, claiming to possess in his own person, a sovereign ruler, a monopoly over the lawmaking processes and the armed forces of the kingdom. This is the deeper meaning of his reputed boast, *L'état, c'est moi*—"the state is myself." In the

France of the seventeenth century, divided by classes and by regions, there was in fact no means of consolidating the powers of state except in a single man.

The state, however, while representing law and order within its borders, has generally stood in a lawless and disorderly relation to other states, since no higher monopoly of law and force has existed. Louis XIV, personifying the French state, had no particular regard for the claims of other states or rulers. He was constantly either at war or prepared for war with his neighbors. The modern state, indeed, was created by the needs of peace at home and war abroad. Machinery of government, as devised by Louis XIV and others, was a means of giving order and security within the territory of the state, and of raising, supporting, and controlling armies for use against other states.

The idea that law and force within a country should be monopolized by the lawful king was the essence of the seventeenth-century doctrine of absolutism. Its principal theorist in the time of Louis XIV was Bishop Bossuet. Bossuet advanced the old Christian teaching that all power comes from God, and that all who hold power are responsible to God for the way they use it. He held that kings were God's representatives in the political affairs of earth. Royal power, according to Bossuet, was absolute but not arbitrary: not arbitrary because it must be reasonable and just, like the will of God which it reflected; absolute in that it was free from dictation by parlements, estates, or other subordinate elements within the country. Law, therefore, was the will of the sovereign king, so long as it conformed to the higher law which was the will of God. This doctrine, affirming the divine right of kings, was popularly held in France at the time and was taught in the churches. "Absolutism" and "absolute monarchy" became the prevailing forms of government on the European continent in the seventeenth and eighteenth centuries. It must be remembered, however, that these terms, if not historians' clichés, referred more to legal principle than to facts. A ruler was "absolute" because he was not legally bound by any other persons or institutions in the country. In reality he became dependent upon a host of advisers and bureaucrats, he often had to compromise with vested interests, and he could be thwarted by the sheer weight of local custom, or meet resistance from lawyers, ecclesiastics, nobles, grandees, hereditary officeholders, and miscellaneous dignitaries.

Government and Administration

Possibly the most fundamental step taken by Louis XIV was to assure himself of control of the army. Armed forces had formerly been almost a private enterprise. Specialists in fighting, leading their own troops, worked for governments more or less as they chose, either in return for money or to pursue political aims of their own. This was especially common in central Europe, but even in France great noblemen had strong private influence over the troops, and in times of disorder nobles led armed retainers about the country. Colonels were virtually on their own. Provided with a general commission and with funds by some government, they recruited, trained, and equipped their own regiments, and likewise fed and supplied them, often by preying upon bourgeois and peasants in the vicinity. In these circumstances it was often difficult to say on whose side soldiers were fighting. It was hard for governments to set armies into motion and equally hard to make them stop fighting, for commanders fought for their own interests and on their own momentum. War was not a "continuation of policy"; it was not an act of the state; it easily degenerated, as in the Thirty Years' War, into a kind of aimless and perpetual violence.

Louis XIV made war an activity of state. He saw to it that all armed persons in France fought only for him. This produced peace and order in France, while strengthening the fighting power of France against other states. Under the older conditions there was also little integration among different units and arms of the army. Infantry regiments and cavalry went largely their own way, and the artillery was supplied by civilian technicians under contract. Louis XIV created a stronger unity of control, put the artillery organically into the army, systematized the military ranks and grades, and clarified the chain of command, placing himself at the top. The government supervised recruiting, required colonels to prove that they were maintaining the proper number of soldiers, and assumed most of the responsibility for equipping, provisioning, clothing, and housing the troops. Higher officers, thus becoming dependent on the government, could be subjected to discipline. The soldiers were put into uniforms, taught to march in step, and housed in barracks; thus they too became more susceptible to discipline and control. Armed forces became less of a terror to their own people and a more effective weapon in the hands of government. They were employed usually against other governments but sometimes to suppress rebellion at home. Louis XIV also increased the French army in size, raising it from about 100,000 to about 400,000. These changes, both in size and in degree of government control, were made possible by the growth of a large civilian administration. The heads of this administration under Louis XIV were civilians. They were in effect the first ministers of war, and their assistants, officials, inspectors, and clerks constituted the first organized war ministry.

Louis XIV was not only a vain man, but made it a political principle to overawe the country with his own grandeur. He built himself a whole new city at the old village of Versailles about ten miles from Paris. Where the Escorial had the atmosphere of a monastery, Versailles was a monument to worldly splendor. Tremendous in size alone, fitted out with polished mirrors, gleaming chandeliers, and magnificent tapestries, opening on to a formal park with fountains and shaded walks, the palace of Versailles was the marvel of Europe and the envy of lesser kings. It was virtually a public building, much of it used for government offices, with nobles, churchmen, notable bourgeois, and servants milling about on the king's affairs. The more exclusive honors of the château were reserved for the higher aristocrats. The king surrounded his daily routine of rising, eating, and going to bed (known as the *lever, dîner,* and *coucher*) with an infinite series of ceremonial acts, so minute and so formalized that there were, for example, six different entries of persons at the *lever,* and a certain gentleman at a specified moment held the right sleeve of the king's nightshirt as he took it off. The most exalted persons thought themselves the greater for thus waiting on so august a being. In this way, and by more material favors, many great lords were induced to live habitually at court. Here, under the royal eye, they might engage in palace intrigue but were kept away from real political mischief. Versailles had a debilitating effect on the French aristocracy.

For positions in the government, as distinguished from his personal entourage, Louis XIV preferred to use men whose upper-class status was recent. Such men, unlike hereditary nobles, could aspire to no independent political influence of their own. He never called the Estates General, which in any case no one except some of the nobility wanted. Some of the Provincial Estates, because of local and aristocratic pressures, he allowed to remain functioning. He temporarily destroyed the independence of the parlements, commanding them to accept his orders, as Henry IV had commanded them to accept the Edict of Nantes.[17] He developed a strong system of administrative coordination, centering in a number of councils of state, which he attended in person, and in "intendants" who represented these councils throughout the country. Councilors of state and intendants were generally of bourgeois origin or newly ennobled. Each intendant, within his district, embodied all aspects of the royal government, supervising the flow of taxes and recruiting of soldiers, keeping an eye on the local nobility, dealing with towns and guilds, controlling the more or less hereditary officeholders, stamping out bandits, smugglers, and wolves, policing the marketplaces, relieving famine, watching the local law courts, and often deciding cases himself. In this way a firm and uniform administration was superimposed upon the heterogeneous mass of the old France. In contrast to England, many local questions were handled by agents of the central government, usually honest and often efficient, but essentially bureaucrats constantly instructed by, and referring back to, their superiors at Versailles.

Economic and Financial Policies: Colbert

To support the reorganized and enlarged army, the panoply of Versailles, and the growing civil administration, the king needed a good deal of money. Finance was always the weak spot in the French monarchy. Methods of collecting taxes were costly and inefficient. Direct taxes passed through the hands of many intermediate officials; indirect taxes were collected by private concessionaries called tax farmers, who made a substantial profit. The state always received far less than what the taxpayers actually paid. But the main weakness arose from an old bargain between the French crown and nobility; the king might raise taxes without consent if only he refrained from taxing the nobles. Only the "unprivileged" classes paid direct taxes, and these came almost to mean the peasants only, since many bourgeois in one way or another obtained exemptions. The system was outrageously unjust in throwing a heavy tax burden on the poor and helpless. Louis XIV was willing enough to tax the nobles but was unwilling to fall under their control, and only toward the close of his reign, under extreme stress of war, was he able, for the first time in French history, to impose direct taxes on the aristocratic elements of the population. This was a step toward equality before the law and toward sound public finance, but so many concessions and exemptions were won by nobles and bourgeois that the reform lost much of its value.

Like his predecessors, Louis resorted to all manner of expedients to increase his revenues. He raised the tax rates, always with disappointing results. He

[17] See pp. 138–139.

devalued the currency. He sold patents of nobility to ambitious bourgeois. He sold government offices, judgeships, and commissions in the army and navy. For both financial and political reasons the king used his sovereign authority to annul the town charters, then sell back reduced rights at a price; this produced a little income but demoralized local government and civic spirit. The need for money, arising from the fundamental inability to tax the wealthy, which in turn reflected the weakness of absolutism, of a government which would not or could not share its rule with the propertied classes, corrupted much of the public life and political aptitude of the French people.

Louis XIV wished, if only for his own purposes, to make France economically powerful. His great minister Colbert worked for twenty years to do so. Colbert went beyond Richelieu in the application of mercantilism, aiming to make France a self-sufficing economic unit and to increase the wealth from which government income was drawn.[18] There was not much that he could do for agriculture, the principal industry of the kingdom, which remained less developed than in England and the Netherlands. But he managed to reduce internal tariffs in a large part of central France, where he set up a tariff union oddly entitled the Five Great Farms (since the remaining tolls were collected by tax farmers); and although vested interests and provincial liberties remained too strong for him to do away with all internal tariffs, the area of the Five Great Farms was in itself one of the largest free-trade areas in Europe, being about the size of England. For the convenience

[18] On mercantilism in general, see pp. 119–120. On taxation, see pp. 329–330.

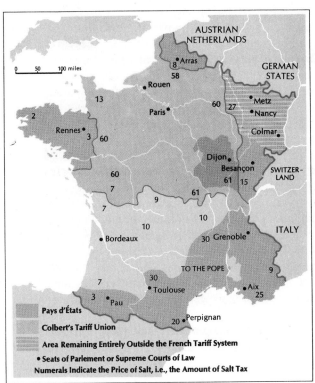

FRANCE FROM THE LAST YEARS OF LOUIS XIV TO THE REVOLUTION OF 1789

The map gives an idea of the diversity of law and administration before the Revolution. Dark areas are "pays d'états," provinces in which representative bodies ("estates") continued to meet. Cities named are the seats of what the French called parlements (see p. 183). The key indicates Colbert's tariff union, the Five Great Farms (see above). The area marked with hatching remained outside the French tariff system entirely; it continued to trade with the states of the Holy Roman Empire (from which it had been annexed) without interference by the French government. Numerals indicate the price of salt, i.e., the varying burden of the salt tax, in various regions. In general, it will be seen that regions farthest from Paris enjoyed the most "privileges" or "liberties," preserving their legal and judicial identity, Provincial Estates, local tariffs, and a favored position in national taxation.

of business Colbert promulgated a Commercial Code, replacing much of the local customary law, and long a model of business practice and regulation. He improved communications by building roads and canals, of which the most famous was one joining the Bay of Biscay with the Mediterranean. Working through the guilds, he required the handicraft manufacturers to produce goods of specified kind and quality, believing that foreigners, if assured of quality by the government, would purchase French products more freely. He gave subsidies, tax exemptions, and monopolies to expand the manufacture of silks, tapestries, glassware, and woolens. He helped to found colonies, built up the navy, and established the French East India Company. Export of some goods, notably foodstuffs, was forbidden, for the government wished to keep the populace quiet by holding down the price of bread. Export of other goods, mainly manufactures, was encouraged, partly as a means of bringing money into the country, where it could be funneled into the royal treasury. The growth of the army, and the fact that under Louis XIV the government clothed and equipped the soldiers and hence placed unprecedentedly large orders for uniforms, overcoats, weapons, and ammunition, greatly stimulated the employment of weavers, tailors, and gunsmiths and advanced the commercial capitalism by which such labors were organized. In general, trade and manufacture developed in France under more direct government guidance than in England. They long gave the English an extremely brisk competition. Not until the age of iron and coal did France begin economically to lag.

In general, the system elaborated in the two centuries of Bourbon rule, known in retrospect as the Old Regime, was a society in which groups of many kinds could identify their own special interests with those of the "absolute" monarchy. But it rested on a precarious inconsistency. On the one hand, the royal government, through its intendants and bureaucracy, worked to restrict the privileges of provinces, nobles, and others. On the other hand, it multiplied and protected these and other privileges in its perpetual need for money. The inconsistency was not resolved until the Revolution of 1789, when the principle of equality of rights replaced the regime of privilege.

Religion: The Revocation of the Edict of Nantes, 1685

The consolidation of France under Louis XIV reached its high point in his policies toward religion. For the Catholics, Louis backed the old claims of the Gallican church to enjoy a certain national independence from Rome. He repressed the movement known as Jansenism, a kind of Calvinism within the Catholic church, which persisted for almost two centuries. But it was the Protestants who suffered most.

France, in the early years of Louis XIV's reign, still allowed more religious toleration than any other large state in Europe. The Huguenots had lost their separate political status under Richelieu, but they continued to live in relative security and contentment, protected by the Edict of Nantes of 1598.[19] From the beginning, however, toleration had been a royal rather than a popular policy, and under Louis XIV the royal policy changed. The fate of Catholics at the hands of

[19] See pp. 138–139.

a triumphant Parliament in England suggests that the Protestants in France would have been no better off under more popular institutions.

Bending all else to his will, Louis XIV resented the presence of heretics among his subjects. He considered religious unity necessary to the strength and dignity of his rule. He perhaps envied the right claimed by most governments at the time, Protestant as well as Catholic, to determine the religion of their respective peoples. He fell under the influence of certain Catholic advisers, who, not content with the attrition by which some Protestants were turning back to Catholicism in any case, wished to hasten the process to the greater glory of themselves. Systematic conversion of Huguenots was begun. Life for Protestant families was gradually made unbearable. Finally they were literally "dragooned," mounted infantrymen being quartered in Huguenot homes to reinforce the persuasions of missionaries. In 1685 Louis revoked the Edict of Nantes. During the persecutions a good many Protestants left France, migrating to Holland, Germany, and America. Their loss was a blow to French economic life, for although Protestants were found in all levels of French society, those of the commercial and industrial classes were the most mobile. With the revocation of the Edict of Nantes France embarked on a century of official intolerance (slowly mitigated in practice), under which Protestants in France were in much the same position as Catholics in the British Isles. The fact that a hundred years later, when Protestants were again tolerated, many of them were found to be both commercially prosperous and politically loyal indicates that they fared far better than the Catholic Irish.

All things considered, the reign of Louis XIV brought considerable advantages to the French middle and lower classes. His most bitter critics, with the natural exception of Protestants, were disgruntled nobles such as the duke of Saint-Simon, who thought that he showed too many favors to persons of inferior social rank. Since Protestants were an unpopular minority, his repression of them won much approval. Colbert's system of economic regulation, and perpetuation of the guilds, meant that innovation and private enterprise developed less fully than in England, but France was economically stronger in 1700 than in 1650. Peasants were heavily taxed, but they did not sink into the serfdom that was rising in eastern Europe. Compared to later times, France was still a hodgepodge of competing jurisdictions, special privilege, and bureaucratic ineptitude. The king was in truth far from "absolute" but France was nevertheless the best organized of the large monarchies on the Continent. Louis XIV, in turning both high and low into dutiful subjects, put an end to civil war and even advanced the cause of civil equality. For a long time he was generally popular. What finally turned his people against him in his last years was the strain of his incessant wars.

22. The Wars of Louis XIV: The Peace of Utrecht, 1713

Before 1700

From the outset of his reign Louis pursued a vigorous foreign policy. The quarrel between the house of France and the house of Habsburg had gone on for more than a century. The Austrian branch of the Habsburgs had been checkmated at the Peace of Westphalia. With the Spanish branch the French remained at war for another decade, until the Peace of the Pyrenees in 1659. When, two years later, Louis XIV assumed his personal rule, Spanish territories still faced France on three sides, northeast, east, and south; but so weakened was Spain that this fact was no longer a menace to France so much as a temptation to French expansion. Louis XIV could count on popular national feeling to support him, for the dream of a frontier on the Rhine and the Alps was captivating to Frenchmen. He struck in 1667. (The war was called the "War of Devolution," from a legal term used in the preliminary demands.) He was blocked, as noted above, by a Triple Alliance engineered by the Dutch.[20] With strength renewed by reforms at home, and in alliance with Charles II of England, he struck again in 1672 (the "Dutch War"), invading the Dutch provinces on the lower Rhine, and this time raising up his great adversary and inveterate enemy, the prince of Orange.[21] William III, bringing the Austrian and Spanish Habsburgs, Brandenburg, and Denmark into alliance with the Dutch Republic, forced Louis to sign the treaty of Nimwegen in 1678. The French gave up their ambitions against Holland but took from Spain the rich province of Franche-Comté, which outflanked Alsace on the south, and brought French power to the borders of Switzerland.

In the very next year, 1679, Louis further infiltrated the dissolving frontier of the Holy Roman Empire, this time in Lorraine and Alsace. By the Peace of Westphalia the French king had rights in this region, but the terms of that treaty were so ambiguous, and the local feudal law so confusing, that claims could be made in contrary directions. Louis XIV now set up *chambres de réunion*, as he called them, law courts in which French judges examined the claims to various parcels of territory and pronounced in favor of the king of France. French troops thereupon moved in. In 1681 French troops occupied the city of Strasbourg, which, as a free city of the Holy Roman Empire, regarded itself as an independent little republic. A protest went up throughout Germany against this undeclared invasion. But Germany was not a political unity. Since 1648 each German state conducted its own foreign policy, and at this very moment, in 1681, Louis XIV had an ally in the Elector of Brandenburg (forerunner of the kings of Prussia); and the electors of the Rhineland church-states—the archbishops of Cologne, Trier, and Mainz—were on the French payroll, receiving "subsidies" from the French king. The diet of the Holy Roman Empire was divided between an anti-French and a pro-French party. The emperor, Leopold I, was distracted by developments in the East. The Hungarians, incited and financed by Louis XIV, were again rebelling against the Habsburgs. They appealed to the Turks, and the Turks in 1683 moved up the Danube and actually besieged Vienna—as in 1529. Louis XIV, if he did not on this occasion positively assist the Turks, ostentatiously declined to join the proposed crusade against them.

The emperor, with Polish assistance, succeeded in getting the Turkish host out of Austria.[22] Returning to western problems, observing the western border of the Empire constantly crumbling, Franche-Comté already lost, the Spanish Netherlands constantly threatened, Lorraine and Alsace absorbed bit by bit, and

[20] See p. 168.
[21] See pp. 168, 178.
[22] See pp. 221–223.

the Rhineland archbishops reduced to the status of French puppets, and not forgetting that Louis XIV had designs on the whole of Habsburg Spain, the Emperor Leopold gathered the Catholic powers into a combination against the French. The Protestant states at the same time, aroused by Louis' revocation of the Edict of Nantes in 1685 and by Huguenot émigrés who called down the wrath of God on the perfidious Sun King, began to ally the more readily with William of Orange. Catholic and Protestant enemies of Louis XIV came together in 1686 in the League of Augsburg, which comprised the Holy Roman Emperor, the kings of Spain and of Sweden, the electors of Bavaria, Saxony, and the Palatinate, and the Dutch Republic. In 1686 the king of England was still a protégé of France, but three years later, when William became king in England, that country too joined the League.

The War of the League of Augsburg broke out in 1688. The French armies won battles but could not drive so many enemies from the field. The French navy could not overpower the combined fleets of the Dutch and English. Louis XIV found himself badly strained (it was at this time that he first imposed direct taxes on the French nobles) and finally made peace at Ryswick in the Netherlands in 1697. The Peace of Ryswick, terminating the long "War of the League of Augsburg," left matters about where they had been when the war began.

In all the warring and negotiating the question had not been merely the fate of this or that piece of territory, nor even the French thrust to the east, but the eventual disposition of the whole empire of Spain. The Spanish king, Charles II, prematurely senile, momentarily expected to die, yet lived on year after year. He was still alive at the time of the Peace of Ryswick. The greatest diplomatic issue of the day was still unsettled.

The War of the Spanish Succession

The War of the Spanish Succession lasted eleven years, from 1702 to 1713. It was less destructive than the Thirty Years' War, for armies were now supplied in more orderly fashion, subject to more orderly discipline and command, and could be stopped from fighting at the will of their governments. Except for the effects of civil war in Spain and of starvation in France, the civilian populations were generally spared, and in this respect the war foreshadowed the typical warfare of the eighteenth century, fought by professional armies rather than by whole peoples. Among wars of the largest scale, the War of the Spanish Succession was the first in which religion counted for little, the first in which commerce and sea power were the principal stakes, the first in which English money was liberally used in Continental politics, and the first that can be called a "world war," because it involved the overseas world together with the leading powers of Europe.

The struggle had long been foreseen. The two main aspirants to the Spanish inheritance were the king of France and the Holy Roman Emperor, each of whom had married a sister of the perpetually moribund Charles II, and each of whom could hope to place a younger member of his family on the throne of Spain. During the last decades of the seventeenth century the powers had made various treaties agreeing to "partition" the Spanish possessions. The idea was, by dividing the Spanish heritage between the two claimants, to preserve the balance of power in Europe.[23] But when Charles II finally died, in 1700, it was found that he had made a will, in which he stipulated that the world of Spain should be kept intact, that all Spanish territories without exception should go to the grandson of Louis XIV, and that if Louis XIV refused to accept in the name of his seventeen-year-old grandson, the entire inheritance should pass to the son of the Habsburg emperor in Vienna. Louis XIV decided to accept. With Bourbons reigning in Versailles and Madrid, even if the two thrones were never united, French influence would run from Belgium to the Straits of Gibraltar, and from Milan to Mexico and Manila. At Versailles the word went out: "The Pyrenees exist no longer."

Never, at least in almost two centuries, had the political balance within Europe been so threatened. Never had the other states faced such a prospect of relegation to the sidelines. William III acted at once; he gathered the stunned or hesitant diplomats into the last of his coalitions, the Grand Alliance of 1701. He died the next year, before hostilities began, and with Louis XIV at the seeming apex of his grandeur, but he had in fact launched the engine that was to crush the Sun King. The Grand Alliance included England, Holland, and the emperor, supported by Brandenburg and eventually by Portugal and the Italian duchy of Savoy. Louis XIV could count on Spain, which was generally loyal to the late king's will. Otherwise his only ally was Bavaria, whose rivalry with Austria made it a habitual satellite of France. The Bavarian alliance gave the French armies an advanced position toward Vienna and maintained that internal division, balance of power, or cancellation of forces within Germany which was fundamental to the politics of the time, and of a long time to come.

The war was long, mainly because each side no sooner gained a temporary advantage than it raised its demands on the other. The English, though they sent relatively few troops to the Continent, produced in John Churchill, Duke of Marlborough, a preeminent military commander for the Allied forces. The Austrians were led by Prince Eugene of Savoy. The Allies won notable battles at Blenheim in Bavaria (1704), and at Ramillies (1706), Oudenarde (1708), and Malplaquet (1709) in the Spanish Netherlands. The French were routed; Louis XIV asked for peace but would not agree to it because the Allied terms were so enormous. Louis fought to hold the two crowns, to conquer Belgium, to get French merchants into Spanish America, and at the worst in self-defense. After minor successes in 1710 he again insisted on controlling the crown of Spain. The Spanish fought to uphold the will of the deceased king, the unity of the Spanish possessions, and even the integrity of Spain itself—for the English moved in at Gibraltar and made a menacing treaty with Portugal, while the Austrians landed at Barcelona and invaded Catalonia, which (as in 1640) again rose in rebellion, recognizing the Austrian claimant, so that all Spain fell into civil war.

The Austrians fought to keep Spain in the Habsburg family, to crush Bavaria, and to carry Austrian influence across the Alps into Italy. The Dutch fought as always for their security, to keep the French out of Belgium, and to close the river Scheldt. The English fought for these same reasons and also to keep the French-supported Catholic Stuarts out of England and preserve the Revolution of 1688. It was to be expected that the Stuarts, if they returned, would ruin the Bank of England and repudiate the National Debt. Both maritime powers, England

---

[23] On the idea of the balance of power, see pp. 162–163.

and Holland, fought to keep French merchants out of Spanish America and to advance their own commercial position in America and the Mediterranean. These being the war aims, the Whigs were the implacable war party in England, the vaguely pro-Stuart and anticommercial Tories being quite willing to make peace at an early date. As for the minor allies, Brandenburg and Savoy, their rulers had simply entered the alliance to gain such advantages as might turn up.

The Peace of Utrecht

Peace was finally made at the treaties of Utrecht and Rastadt of 1713 and 1714. So fierce was the Whig war spirit in England that ratification of the treaty of Utrecht incidentally marked a step in English constitutional history. The Whigs thought the treaty insufficiently favorable to England. The Tories, pledged to peace, had won the House of Commons in 1710, but the Whigs continued to control the House of Lords. Queen Anne, at the request of Tory leaders and in the interests of peace, raised twelve Tory commoners to the peerage, the number required to give a Tory majority in the Lords and hence to obtain ratification of the treaty. This established itself as a precedent; it became an unwritten article of the British constitution that when the Lords blocked the Commons on an issue of fundamental importance, enough new Lords of appropriate views would be created to make a majority in that House.[24]

The treaty of Utrecht, with its allied instruments, in fact partitioned the world of Spain. But it did not divide it between the two legal claimants only. The British remained at Gibraltar, to the great irritation of the Spaniards, and likewise annexed the island of Minorca. The Duke of Savoy was granted the former Spanish island of Sardinia in return for his contribution to the Allied cause.[25] The rest of the Spanish Mediterranean holdings—Milan, Naples, and Sicily—passed to the Austrian Habsburgs, as did the Spanish Netherlands (or Belgium), subsequently referred to as the Austrian Netherlands—except that the tiny region of Spanish Guelderland was handed over to the Elector of Brandenburg for his pains. In Spain itself, shorn of its European possessions but retaining America, the grandson of Louis XIV was confirmed as king (Philip V of Spain), on the understanding that the French and Spanish thrones should never be inherited by the same person. The Bourbons reigned in Spain, with interruptions, from Philip V to the republican revolution of 1931. French influence was strong in the eighteenth century, for a good many French courtiers, advisers, administrators, and businessmen crossed the Pyrenees with Philip V. They helped somewhat to revive the Spanish monarchy by applying the methods of Louis XIV, and they passed a swelling volume of French manufactures through Seville into Spanish America.

[24] The precedent was invoked in 1832 and 1911, but never since 1713 have the Lords allowed themselves to be swamped by newcomers. They have yielded at the threat.

[25] By the terms of 1713 Sardinia was awarded to Austria and Sicily to Savoy, but Sardinia and Sicily were exchanged in 1720. The kingdom of the Two Sicilies (Naples and Sicily) was thereby reconstituted. Savoy was originally a small region in the high Alps, whose ruler acquired the lowland area around Turin in the Middle Ages, with the title of Duke of Savoy. His domains were thereafter also called Piedmont because some of them lay at the foot of the Alps. After 1720 the Duke of Savoy became the King of Sardinia, because that island, though the least important of his possessions, provided a less controversial basis for a royal title. See the map on p. 328.

The old objective of William III, to prevent domination by France, was realized at last. The war itself was the main cause of French loss of strength. It produced poverty, misery, and depopulation, exposed Louis XIV to severe criticism at home, and led to a revival of aristocratic and parliamentary opposition. By the peace treaties the French abandoned, for the time being, their efforts to conquer Belgium. They ceased to recognize the Stuart pretender as king of Great Britain. They surrendered to the British two of their colonies. Newfoundland and Nova Scotia (called Acadia), and recognized British sovereignty in the disputed American northwest, known as the Hudson Bay territory. But the French were only checked, not downed. They retained the conquests of Louis XIV in Alsace and the Franche-Comté. Their influence was strong in Spain. Their deeper strength and capacity for recovery were soon evident in renewed economic expansion. Their language and civilization continued to spread throughout Europe.

The Dutch received guarantees of their security. They were granted the right to garrison the "Dutch Barrier," a string of forts in Belgium on the side toward France. With Belgium transferred to Austria, which was not expected to stimulate Belgian commerce, and with the closure of the river Scheldt reconfirmed at Utrecht, the Dutch could comfortably expect a minimum of competition from their southern neighbors. But the Dutch, strained by the war and outdistanced by England, never again played a primary role in European political affairs. Two other small states ascended over the diplomatic horizon, Savoy and Brandenburg. The rulers of both, for having sided with the victors, were recognized as "kings" by the treaty of Utrecht. Savoy came to be known as "Sardinia," and Brandenburg as "Prussia." More is said of Prussia in the next chapter.

The greatest winners were the British. Great Britain made its appearance as a great power. Union of England and Scotland had taken place during the war. Based at Gibraltar and Minorca, Britain was now a power in the Mediterranean. Belgium, the "pistol pointed at the heart of England," was in the innocuous hands of the Austrians. The Austrians had not especially wanted Belgium because it was too distant from Vienna and too likely to embroil them with France. They had taken it largely at the instigation of the maritime states, Britain and Holland, which saw in transfer to Austria a good solution to the problem. The British added to their American holdings at the expense of France. Far more valuable than Newfoundland or Nova Scotia, won from France, was the *asiento* extorted from Spain. The *asiento* granted the lucrative privilege (which the French had sought) of providing Spanish America with African slaves. Much of the wealth of Bristol and Liverpool in the following decades was to be built upon the slave trade. The *asiento*, by permitting one shipload of British goods to be brought each year to Porto Bello in Panama, also provided opportunities for illicit trade in nonhuman cargoes. The Spanish empire was pried open, and British merchants entered on an era of wholesale smuggling into Spanish America, competing strenuously with the French, who because of their favored position in Spain were usually able to go through more legal channels. Moreover, the British, by defeating France, assured themselves of a line of Protestant kings and of the maintenance of constitutional and parliamentary government. The landed aristocracy and their merchant allies could now govern as they saw fit. The result was a rapid increase of wealth in England, precipitating within a few generations a veritable Industrial Revolution.

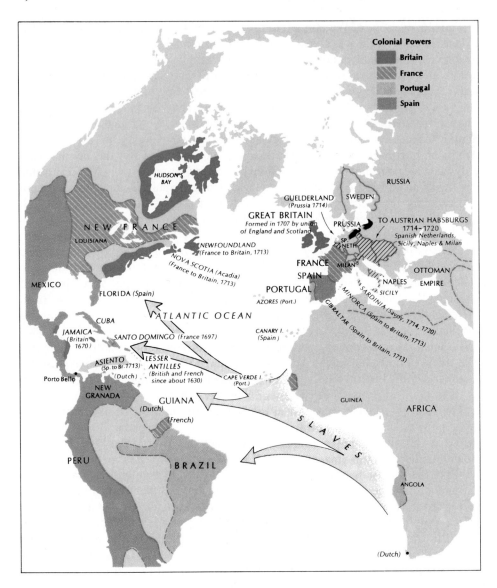

THE ATLANTIC WORLD AFTER THE PEACE OF UTRECHT, 1713

The map shows the partitioning of the Spanish empire and the rise of the British. Spain and its American possessions went to the Bourbon Philip V; the European possessions of Spain—the Netherlands, Milan, Naples, and Sicily—went to the Austrian Habsburgs. Britain meanwhile was strengthened by the union of England and Scotland, the acquisition of Minorca, Gibraltar, and the commercial privilege of the "asiento" from Spain, and of Newfoundland and Nova Scotia from France. (See also map, p. 328.)

Except for the addition of England, the same powers were parties to the treaty of Utrecht in 1713 as to the Peace of Westphalia in 1648, and they now confirmed the system of international relations established by Westphalia. The powers accepted each other as members of the European system, recognized each other as sovereign states connected only by free negotiation, war, and treaty, and adjusted their differences through rather facile exchanges of territory, made in the interests of a balance of power, and without regard to the nationality or presumed wishes of the peoples affected. With Germany still in its "feudal chaos," Italy negligible, and Spain subordinated to France, the treaty of Utrecht left France and Great Britain as the two most vigorous powers of Europe and as the two principal carriers and exporters of the type of civilization most characteristic of the modern world. In the next chapter we turn to central and eastern Europe, to see how these regions developed along lines of their own, though under strong influence from the West.

THE AGE OF GRANDEUR

The seventeenth century was an age of high monarchy, or royal absolutism, of which the great exemplar was France. A style of life that developed first in Italy during the Renaissance, and which set high value on patronage of the arts, courtly manners, elaborate clothing, and elegant speech, was taken over in France (with some influence from the two Medici queens), and from France was diffused throughout much of Europe. It was especially suited to monarchies, since the kings, with their increasingly organized governments, could afford the necessary expense and even required a palatial atmosphere in which to impress their often unruly subjects. The same applies in a way to the papal monarchy of the church, and the new ideas came as much from papal Rome as from ducal Florence. The result is best illustrated by architecture, to which the following pages are devoted.

It was an architecture derived from classical elements of design, but it soon went beyond the Greeks and Romans. The baroque, as it is called, delighted in arches and colonnades, domes and entablatures, and ornamented windows and cornices. Indoors and outdoors flowed together in complexes of façades, staircases, terraces, balustrades, gardens, fountains, and formal vistas. Statuary was distributed inside and out. Mirrors, paintings, and tapestries adorned the interiors. Great halls were built for state receptions, and paved courtyards for troops of soldiers, throngs of retainers, the arrival of coaches, or simply to provide open views.

Architecture passed over into city planning. Versailles was a new city; the plan of modern Paris also dates from Louis XIV; and Washington, D.C., planned by a Frenchman, with its diagonal streets and circles, punctuated by statues, still reflects these traditions of neoclassical monumentality. On the other hand it was the kings who initiated a movement to the suburbs. Versailles was built ten miles from Paris, away from the clamor and restlessness of the city, and where the king already owned enough land for a new spacious development. When other monarchs imitated Louis XIV they often did likewise. The Habsburgs built Schönbrunn outside Vienna, and the Hohenzollern Frederick II built Sans Souci at Potsdam about twenty miles from Berlin.

The Russian tsars, in their new city of St. Petersburg, and the kings of Sweden, in their new royal palace at Stockholm, joined the host of German princes in emulating the royal grandeur of France. It was different where royalty counted for less. The Dutch had no king and cared little for public magnificence. Sans Souci was hardly more than a wealthy gentleman's home. The English, with their antimonarchical revolutions, built no grandiose royal palaces at this time. But they built Blenheim Palace and presented it to John Churchill, the first Duke of Marlborough, as a reward for his services in the last great war against the *Grand Monarque*.

*Above: The Emperor Constantine (d. 337)
discusses with Pope Julius II (d. 1513) the
building of a new church of St. Peter's in
Rome. An older church, of which parts went
back to Constantine's time, was torn down
to make room for the new one.*

*The new St. Peter's, seen here in a seven-
teenth-century print, required a century and
a half for completion. The great dome of the
church is the work of Michelangelo. The pair
of immense semicircular arcades, each four
columns thick, was built about a hundred
years later by Bernini, one of the great masters of the baroque.*

The château of Versailles was mainly built by Louis XIV in the 1670s, on a site used by his predecessor as a hunting lodge. Thirty thousand workmen were employed at one time in the building operations, which are shown in a painting of the period at the left above. The painting below it shows the château and its adjacent buildings about a hundred years later, shortly before the Revolution. The twin structures in the foreground, left and right of the vast court, were assigned to government offices. The château proper is in the middle distance, with the gardens invisible behind it, except that the long rectangular basin of the Grand Canal can be seen reaching to the horizon.

At Versailles, for thirty years, the Sun King received visitors from all countries in overwhelming splendor. The memorable arrival in 1684 of ambassadors from far-off Siam (now Thailand) is recorded in the print below.

Louis XIV gave sponsorship and subsidies to cultural activities of many kinds, usually organized as academies. At the left, he appears on a visit to the Academy of Sciences, founded in 1666. A scientific gentleman is explaining the "philosophical apparatus" to the king.

AMBASSADEURS DE SIAM

204

The opera developed as an art form in the seventeenth century and was characteristic of the baroque in its simultaneous use of different arts, its ostentation, and general staginess. At the left, below, Lully's "Alceste" is performed for Louis XIV in the courtyard of a lesser palace before the building of Versailles.

Left, above: Frederick the Great's Sans Souci. The young Frederick had been disciplined by his drill sergeant father for writing poetry and corresponding with Frenchmen, but after becoming king, in 1740, at the age of twenty-eight, he gave full rein to his French tastes, and after the first Silesian War built this residence, whose name means "carefree." Here he met with Voltaire and other intellectual companions.

Above: There were many buildings in St. Petersburg on the model of European palaces of the day, but here we have signs of the Western influences penetrating to Moscow. If the structures seem dreamy and evanescent, it is because they are only temporary pavilions set up in 1775 to celebrate the end of a victorious war with Turkey.

Above: Schönbrunn Palace, near Vienna. The Habsburg monarchs, as the Turkish menace receded, planned this great edifice to compete with their Bourbon rivals. The plan was never completed, partly because the sensible Maria Theresa (1740–1780) thought that what is seen here was enough. It was here that the six-year-old Mozart astonished the court with his precocious virtuosity.

At the right: Blenheim Palace in Oxfordshire, presented to the Duke of Marlborough for his victories over Louis XIV. Built in the 1720s with funds voted by Parliament, a monument in a way to England's rising greatness, it has always been thought by the English to be a little exaggerated. The architect, Vanbrugh, left everyone dissatisfied. He sacrificed interiors to external splendor, putting the kitchen 400 yards from the dining room. Voltaire said that if only the rooms were as wide as the walls were thick, it would be a convenient little château.

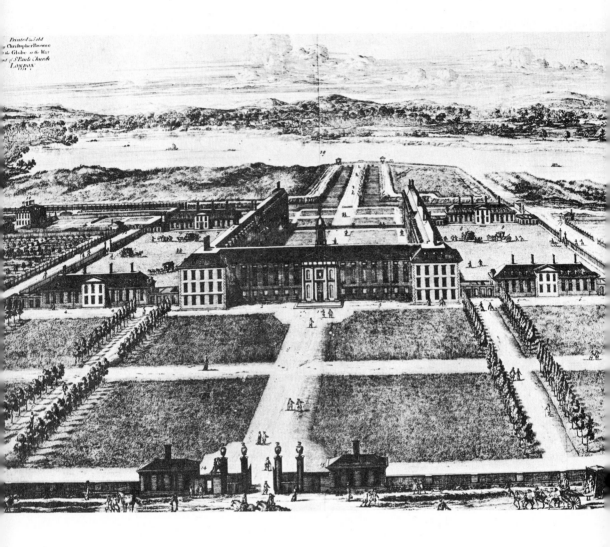

These two buildings were built at the same time for the same purpose, as homes for old and retired soldiers. It was a sign of the growth of royal government to have professional standing armies, in which men might spend their whole lives apart from the civilian population.

Above is Chelsea Royal Hospital, founded by Charles II; at the right, the Invalides, founded by Louis XIV. The much greater size and imposing dome of the French establishment contrast with the simplicity of the English, and reflect the far greater power of France at that time. The broad avenues radiating beyond the Invalides, then in open country, are now boulevards of central Paris.

208

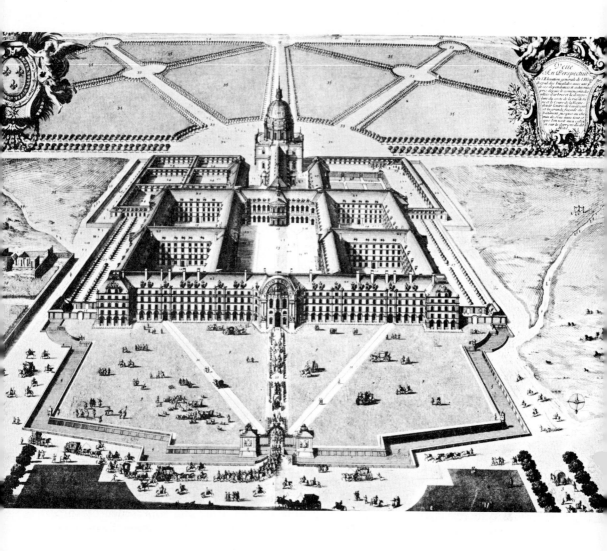

V.
THE
TRANSFORMATION
OF EASTERN
EUROPE, 1648–1740

IN EASTERN EUROPE, in the century after the Peace of Westphalia of 1648, it became apparent that political systems that failed to become more "modern" might be in danger of going out of existence. In the mid–seventeenth century most parts of Eastern Europe belonged to one or another of three old-fashioned political organizations—the Holy Roman Empire, the Republic of Poland, and the empire of the Ottoman Turks.[1] All three were loose, sprawling, and increasingly ineffective. They were pushed aside and superseded by three new and stronger powers—Prussia, Austria, and Russia. These three, by overrunning the intermediate ground of Poland, came to adjoin one another and cover all Eastern Europe except the Balkans. It was in this same period that Russia expanded territorially, adopted some of the technical and administrative apparatus of Western Europe, and became an active participant in European affairs.

East and West are of course relative terms. For the Russians Germany and even Poland were "western." But for Europe as a whole a real though indefinite line ran along the Elbe and the Bohemian mountains to the head of the Adriatic Sea. East of this line towns were fewer than in the West, human labor less productive, the middle classes less strong. Above all, the peasants were governed by their landlords.[2] From the sixteenth to the eighteenth century, in eastern Europe in contrast to what happened in the West, the peasant mass increasingly lost its freedom. The commercial revolution and widening of the market, which

---

[1] See maps, pp. 212 and 216.
[2] See pp. 125–126.

Chapter Emblem: A Russian medal commemorating the capture of Narva from the Swedes in 1704, and hence the establishment of Russian power on the Baltic.

in the West raised up a strong merchant class and tended to turn working people into a legally free and mobile labor force, in eastern Europe strengthened the great landlords who produced for export, and who secured their labor force by the institutions of serfdom and "hereditary subjection." The main social unit was the agricultural estate, which the lord exploited with uncompensated compulsory labor (or *robot*) furnished by his people, who could neither migrate, marry, nor learn a trade except as he permitted, and who, until the eighteenth century, had no legal protector or court of appeal other than himself. In the East, therefore, the landlords were exceedingly powerful. They were the only significant political class. And the three new states that grew up—Prussia, Austria, Russia—were alike in being landlord states.

23. *Three Aging Empires*

In 1648 the whole mainland of Europe from the French border almost to Moscow was occupied by the three large and loosely built structures that have been mentioned—the Holy Roman Empire, the Republic of Poland, and the empire of the Ottoman Turks.[3] The Turkish power reached to about fifty miles from Vienna, extended over what is now Romania, and prevailed over the Tartars on the north shore of the Black Sea. Even so, its European holdings were but a projection from the main mass in Asia and Africa. Poland extended roughly from a hundred miles east of Berlin to a hundred miles west of Moscow, and virtually from "sea to sea" in the old phrase of its patriots, from the Baltic around Riga almost to the Black Sea coast, which, however, was held by Tartar Khans under the overlordship of the Turkish sultan at Constantinople. The Holy Roman Empire extended from Poland and Hungary to the North Sea.

These three empires were by no means alike. The Holy Empire bore some of the oldest traditions of Christendom. Poland too had old connections with the West. Turkey was a Muslim power, strange to Europe and contemptuous of it. Yet in some ways the three resembled each other. In all of them central authority had become weak, consisting largely of understandings between a nominal head and outlying dignitaries or potentates. All lacked efficient systems of administration and government. All were being put out of date by newer types of state of which France was the leading example. All, but especially Poland and Turkey, were made up of diverse ethnic or language groups.[4] None of these peoples, nor any combination of them—neither the dominant Germans, Poles, and Turks, nor the submerged Lithuanians, Byelorussians, Ukrainians, Czechs, Slovaks, Romanians, Croats, Magyars, Serbs, Bulgars, or Greeks—had been formed into a compact organization. The whole immense area was politically soft. It was malleable in the hands of whoever might become a little stronger than his neighbor. We must try to see in what this softness consisted, and then how newer and harder "state forms" (as the Germans would say) were created.

[3] For the origins of the Holy Roman and Ottoman Empires, see pp. 28 and 46.
[4] For language groups, see map, p. 470.

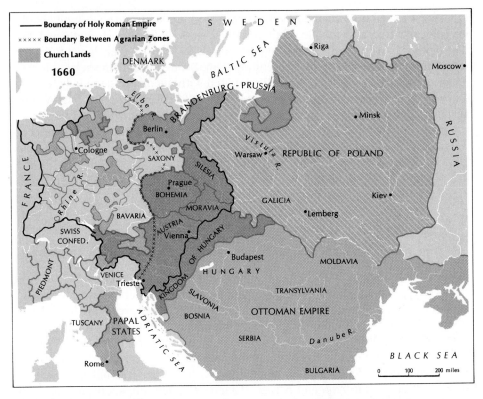

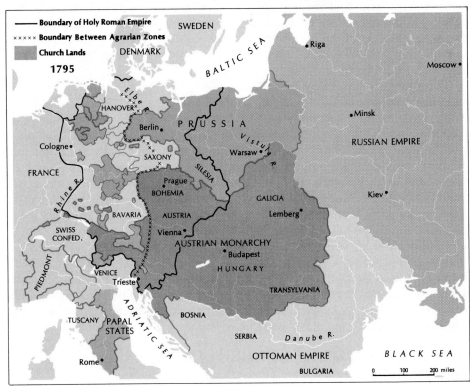

The Holy Roman Empire after 1648

With the Holy Roman Empire the reader is already familiar.[5] It was an empire, especially after the Peace of Westphalia, with next to no army, revenues, or working organs of government. Voltaire called it neither holy, Roman, nor an empire. As the seventeenth-century German jurist Pufendorf put it, it was somewhat of an abortion and a monstrosity. Created in the Middle Ages, it was Roman in that it was then believed to continue the imperial sway of the Rome of antiquity, and it was holy in being the secular counterpart to the spiritual empire of the pope. It had been ruined by the Reformation, which left the Germans divided almost evenly between Protestant and Catholic, with each side thereafter demanding special safeguards against the other. The Empire continued, however, to be universal in principle, having no relation to nationality, and theoretically being a form of government suitable to all peoples, although it had never made good this theoretical claim and had shown no expansionist tendency since the Middle Ages. In actuality, the Empire was roughly coterminous with the German states and the region of the German language, except that it excluded after 1648 the Dutch and Swiss, who no longer considered themselves German; and it likewise excluded those Germans who since the fourteenth century had settled along the eastern shores of the Baltic.

Large parts of the Empire had suffered repeatedly from the Thirty Years' War. Yet the war, and the peace terms which followed it, only accentuated a situation which had long been unfavorable. Postwar revival was difficult; the breakup of commercial connections and the wartime losses of savings and capital were hard to overcome. Germany fell increasingly out of step with western Europe. The burgher class, its ambitions blocked, lost much of its old vitality. No overseas colonies could be founded, for want of strong enough government backing, as was shown when a colonial venture of Brandenburg came to nothing. There was no stock exchange in Germany until one was established at Vienna in 1771, half a century after those of London, Paris, and Amsterdam. Laws, tariffs, tolls, and coinage were more variegated than in France. Even the calendar varied. It varied, indeed, throughout Europe as a whole, since Protestant states long declined to accept the corrected calendar issued by Pope Gregory XIII in 1582, but in parts of divided Germany the holidays, the date of the month, and the day of the week changed every few miles. The arts and letters, flourishing in western Europe as

[5] See pp. 24, 28, 36, 71–75, 145–149.

CENTRAL AND EASTERN EUROPE, 1660–1795

This complex area is shown in simplified form on p. 216. The upper panel of the present map indicates boundaries as of 1660, the lower panel those of 1795. Both panels show the border between the eastern and western agrarian zones, running from the mouth of the Elbe River into central Germany and down to Trieste. East of this line, from the sixteenth to the eighteenth centuries, the mass of people sank into a kind of serfdom in which they rendered forced labor to their lords on large farms. West of the line the peasants owed little or no forced labor and tilled small farms which they owned or rented. This line is one of the most important sociological boundaries in the history of modern Europe.

never before, were at a low ebb in Germany in the seventeenth century. In science the Germans during and after the Thirty Years' War did less than the English, Dutch, French, or Italians, despite the great mathematician and philosopher Leibniz, one of the great minds of the age. Only in music, as in the work of the Bach family, did the Germans at this time excel. But music was not then much heard beyond the place of its origin. Germany for the rest of the world was a mute country, a byway in the higher civilization of Europe.

After the Thirty Years' War each German state had sovereign rights. These "states" numbered some 300 or 2,000, depending on how they were counted. The higher figure included the "knights of the Empire," found in south Germany and the Rhineland. They were persons who acknowledged no overlordship except that of the emperor himself. The knights had tiny estates of their own, averaging not over a hundred acres apiece, consisting of a castle and a manor or two, enclosed by the territory of a larger state but not forming a part of it. These free knights had arisen in various ways; in Württemberg, for example, the lords simply ceased to attend the diet, won exemption from the duke's jurisdiction, and retired to their own domains, leaving the surface of Württemberg pockmarked with small units politically independent of it. It was as if, in England, the peers had lost interest in the House of Lords and had set up independently, each on his own estates. Since the emperor, whom the knights regarded as their only superior, had in fact no authority, the knights were in effect private persons enjoying sovereign status—the last anomaly of bizarre neofeudalism and distorted freedom.

But even without the knights there were about three hundred states capable of some independence of action—free cities, abbots without subjects, archbishops and bishops ruling with temporal power, landgraves, margraves and dukes, and one king, the king of Bohemia. The highest ranking were called electors, who had the privilege of electing the emperor. By the Golden Bull of 1356 there were seven electors—three ecclesiastics (the archbishops of Cologne, Mainz, and Trier) and four laymen, the Count Palatine of the Rhine, the Duke of Saxony, the Margrave of Brandenburg, and the King of Bohemia. Bavaria was made an electorate at the Peace of Westphalia, and Hanover at the end of the century, so that finally there were nine electors. The fact that nearly half the electors were Protestants after the Reformation, whereas the Holy Empire had meaning only in a Catholic world, added to the internal confusion and general oddity of the system.

All these states were intent on preserving what were called the "Germanic liberties." They were gladly assisted by outside powers, notably but not exclusively France. The Germanic liberties meant freedom of the member states from control by emperor or Empire. The electors, at each election of an emperor, required the candidate to accept certain "capitulations," in which he promised to safeguard all the privileges and immunities of the states. The Habsburgs, though consistently elected after 1438, had none of the advantages of hereditary rulers, each having to bargain away in turn any gains made by his predecessor. The elective principle meant that imperial power could not be accumulated and transmitted from one generation to the next. It opened the doors to foreign intrigue, since the electors were willing to consider whichever candidate would promise them most. The French repeatedly supported a rival candidate to the Habsburgs. After 1648 they had a party in the electoral college, Bavaria and

Cologne being the most consistently pro-French. Cardinal Mazarin in 1658 even entertained the thought of making the young Louis XIV Holy Roman Emperor. He had to accept election of a Habsburg, despite liberal use of French money, but the new emperor, Leopold I, undertook not to engage the Empire in any war supporting the Spanish Habsburgs against France. In 1742 the French obtained the elevation of their Bavarian ally to the imperial throne. The office of emperor became the political football of Germans and non-Germans working together.

Nor would the German states, after the Thirty Years' War, allow any authority to the imperial diet. The diet possessed the power to raise troops and taxes for the whole Empire, but the power remained unused. On matters affecting religion, after 1648, either Protestants or Catholics could demand the *ius eundi in partes*, or "right of sitting apart." Each religious group then constituted itself as a chamber, Protestant or Catholic, and since agreement of the two was required, each possessed a veto. The deliberations of the diet became notorious for their wordiness and futility. Many sessions were spent, for example, in attempts to fix for all Germany a common date for Easter, on which the whole calendar depended. In 1663 a diet met to consider measures against a new Turkish advance on the Danube. It was the last diet ever to be convoked, for it lasted "forever," i.e., until the end of the Holy Empire in 1806. It became the "perpetual diet" of Regensburg, never dismissed or renewed, unresponsive to events or issues, the states simply replacing their representatives individually, generation after generation, as at an endless congress of diplomats.

The states which insisted with such obstinacy on their liberties from the Empire gave few liberties to their subjects. The free cities were closed oligarchies, as indeed were most cities in other countries, but in Germany the burgher oligarchs of the free cities were virtually sovereign also. Most of the other states, large or small, developed in the direction of absolutism. Absolutism was checked for Germany as a whole, only to reappear in miniature in hundreds of different places. Each ruler thought himself a little Louis XIV, each court a small Versailles. Subjects became attached by ties of sentiment to their rulers, who almost always lived in the neighborhood and could be readily seen by passers-by. People liked the little courts, the toy armies, the gossipy politics, and the familiar officials of their tiny states.

The Empire, for all its faults, had the merit of holding this conglomeration of states in a lawful relation to one another. It was a kind of miniature league of nations. For a century and a half after the Peace of Westphalia infinitesimally small states existed alongside larger ones, or often totally enclosed within them, without serious fear for their security and without losing their independence. Only in power politics and in European or world affairs was the Empire a shadow. For the Germans it was a reality, a world in itself, which no one for a long time dreamed of violating or even reforming, for its existence assured a way of life which most Germans were glad to keep.

Yet there were many ambitious rulers in Germany after the Peace of Westphalia. They had won recognition of their sovereignty in 1648. They were busily building absolutist monarchies over their subjects. They aspired also to extend their dominions and cut a greater figure in the world. There were other ways of doing this than by devouring their smaller neighbors outright. One was by marriage and inheritance. The Empire in this respect was a paradise of fortune hunters; the variety of possible marriages was enormous because of the great number of ruling families. Another outlet for ambition lay in the high politics of the Empire. The Wittelsbach family, which ruled in Bavaria, managed to win an electorate in the Thirty Years' War; they consistently placed members of the family as archbishop of Cologne and in the other great Rhineland sees, and with the interest thus built up were able to sell their influence to France, which in turn backed them against the Habsburgs. The Guelph family, ruling in Hanover, schemed for years to obtain an electorate, which they finally extorted from the emperor in 1692; in 1714 they inherited the throne of Great Britain, preferred by the British as Protestants to their Catholic Stuart cousins. Two electors of Saxony in these years got themselves crowned king of Poland. The Hohenzollerns, electors of Brandenburg, were extremely fortunate in the seventeenth century in inheriting territories as far apart as the Rhine and the Vistula. The Habsburgs, hereditary rulers in Austria, a mere archduchy, were confirmed by the Peace of Westphalia as hereditary kings of Bohemia, where they had formerly depended on election.

The half-century after the Peace of Westphalia was a highly critical period in central Europe. The situation in Germany was fluid. No one could tell which, if

AGING EMPIRES AND NEW POWERS

The left panel shows the "three aging empires" which occupied much of central and eastern Europe in the seventeenth century. (See pp. 211–221.) Though maintaining themselves with growing difficulty under modern conditions, the Polish Republic lasted until 1795, the Holy Roman Empire until 1806, the Ottoman Empire until 1923. Meanwhile, beginning in the seventeenth century, the political leadership in this area was assumed by three states of more modern type, organized around the institutions of monarchy, the standing army, and the professional bureaucracy or civil service—the reorganized Austrian Empire of the Habsburgs, the Hohenzollern kingdom of Prussia, and the Russian empire of the Romanovs. These are shown in the right panel. All three figured prominently in the affairs of Europe for over two hundred years; all perished in the First World War, 1914–1918.

any, of the half-dozen chief German states would emerge in the lead. Nothing was crystallized; anything might happen. Two states definitely came forward after 1700, built by the skill and persistence of their rulers—Austria and Prussia. It is a curious and revealing fact that neither really had a name of its own. They were for a long time known most commonly as "houses"—the house of Austria or Habsburg and the house of Brandenburg or Hohenzollern. Each house put together a certain combination of territories. Each would have been as willing to possess any other combination had the course of events been different. By extension of meaning, one came to be called "Austria," which for centuries had been simply an archduchy on the upper Danube, and the other "Prussia," which for centuries had meant only a certain stretch of the Baltic coast. To the development of these two states we shall shortly turn.

The Republic of Poland about 1650

Running almost a thousand miles eastward from the Holy Roman Empire in the middle of the seventeenth century lay the vast tract of the Republic of Poland, called a republic because its king was elected, and because the political classes took pride in their constitutional liberties. Its vast size was one cause of its internal peculiarities. No administrative system could have kept up with the expansion of its frontiers, so that a large degree of freedom had always been left to outlying lords. In addition, the population was heterogeneous.

The Polish state was a far more recent and less substantial creation than the Holy Roman Empire. It was made up of two main parts, Poland proper (the Kingdom of Poland) in the west and the Grand Duchy of Lithuania in the east. They had been joined by a union of their crowns.[6] Only in the west was there a mass of Polish population. The Duchy of Prussia, a fief of the Polish crown, was peopled mainly by Germans. Further east a Byelorussian and Ukrainian peasantry was subject to a scattering of Polish and Lithuanian landlords. Even in Poland itself the town population was not generally Polish, being largely Germans and Jews. The latter spoke Yiddish, derived from German, and were very numerous because a king of Poland in the later Middle Ages had welcomed Jewish refugees fleeing from Germany.[7] They lived in separate communities with their own law, language, and religion, islands of Orthodox Jewish life in the Gentile ocean. The Germans too held aloof, resisting assimilation to their less advanced surroundings. An unsurpassable barrier thus existed between town and country. There was no national middle class. The official and political language was Latin. Roman Catholicism was the leading religion.

Poland is interesting as the region in which the landed aristocracy won over all other groups in the country, neither allowing the consolidation of the state on absolutist lines, nor yet creating an effective constitutional or parliamentary government. The Polish aristocracy, or *szlachta*, made up some 8 percent of the population, a far higher proportion than the aristocracy of any country of western Europe. On this ground the old Polish kingdom has sometimes been considered, especially by later Polish nationalists, as the possessor of an early form of

[6] See maps, pp. 212 and 216.
[7] See p. 71, note.

democracy. The aristocracy were sticklers for their liberties, called the "Polish liberties," which resembled the German liberties in consisting largely of a fierce suspicion of central authority and in being a perpetual invitation to foreign interference. As in the Holy Roman Empire, the monarchy was elective, and the king upon election had to accept certain contractual agreements, which, like the German "capitulations," made impossible the accumulation of authority by the crown. As in the Empire, the royal elections were a cockpit of foreign influence, bribery, and intrigue. The Poles were too factious to accept one of their own number as king. They were divided into pro-French, pro-Sweden, and other parties. From 1572 to the extinction of Poland over two centuries later there were only two native Polish kings who reigned for any length of time, and one of these was the discarded lover of a Russian empress. The other was the national hero John Sobieski, whose decisive action against the Turks is noted below.

As in Germany, also, the central diet was ineffective and the nuclei of political action were local. The aristocracy met in fifty or sixty regional diets, turbulent assemblages of warlike gentry, in which the great lords used the little ones for their own purposes. The central diet, from which the towns were excluded, was a periodic meeting of emissaries, under binding instructions, from the regional diets. It came to be recognized, as one of the liberties of the country, that the central diet could take no action to which any member objected. Any member, by stating his unalterable opposition, could oblige a diet to disband. This was the famous *liberum veto*, the free veto, and to use it to break up a diet was called "exploding" the diet. The first diet was exploded in 1652. Of fifty-five diets held from that year to 1764, forty-eight were exploded.

Government became a fiasco. The monopoly of law and force, characteristic of the modern state, failed to develop in Poland. The king of Poland had practically no army, no law courts, no officials, and no income. The nobility paid no taxes. By 1750 the revenues of the king of Poland were about one-thirteenth those of the tsar of Russia and one seventy-fifty those of the king of France. Armed force was in the hands of a dozen or so aristocratic leaders, who also conducted their own individual foreign policies, pursuing their own adventures against the Turks, or bringing in Russians, French, or Swedes to help them against other Poles. The landlords became local monarchs on their manorial estates, and the mass of the rural population fell deeper into a serfdom scarcely different from slavery, bound to compulsory labor on estates resembling plantations, with police and disciplinary powers in the hands of the lords, and with no outside legal or administrative system to set the limits of exploitation. Some Polish aristocrats, hiring architects or buying libraries from Germany and western Europe, traveling with trains of servants to Italy or France, masters of many languages and habitually associating with the great, became among the most accomplished and cosmopolitan people in Europe. A great Polish nobleman could boast of more territory and subjects, and of more international consideration, than many a sovereign princeling of Germany. But the mass of the aristocracy became an unruly body of decayed gentry, dependent on their connections with the powerful families, and indifferent to western Europe.

The huge expanse comprised under the name of Poland was, in short, a power vacuum, an area of low political pressure; and as centers of higher pressure developed, notably around Berlin and Moscow, the push against the Polish frontiers became steadily stronger. It was facilitated by the centrifugal habits of the Poles themselves. As early as 1660 the East Prussian fief became independent of the Polish crown. As early as 1667 the Muscovites reconquered Smolensk and Kiev. Already there was confidential talk of partitioning Poland, which, however, was deferred for a century. The history of the world would have been different had the Poland of the seventeenth century held together. There would have been no kingdom of Prussia and no Prussian influence in Germany; nor would Russia have become the chief Slavic power or reached so far into central Europe.

The Ottoman Empire about 1650

The Ottoman state, the third of the three empires which together spread over so much of Europe, was larger than either of the others, and in the seventeenth century was more solidly organized. In 1529 the Turks had attacked Vienna and seemed about to burst into Germany.[8] To the Christian world the Turks were a mystery as well as a terror. They had formerly been among the rougher of the Muslim peoples, who had erupted from central Asia only a few centuries before and owed most of their higher civilization to the Arabs and the Persians. Their dominions extended, about 1650, from the Hungarian plain and the south Russian steppes as far as Algeria, the upper Nile, and the Persian Gulf. The empire was based to a large degree on military proficiency. Long before Europe the Turks had a standing army, of which the main striking force was the janissaries. The janissaries were originally recruited from Christian children taken from their families in early childhood, brought up as Muslims, reared in military surroundings, and forbidden to marry; without background or ties, interests, or ambition outside the military organization to which they belonged, they were an ideal fighting material in the hands of political leaders. The Turkish forces were long as well equipped as the Christian, being especially strong in heavy artillery. But by the mid–seventeenth century they were falling behind. They had changed little, or for the worse, since the days of Suleiman the Magnificent a century before, whereas in the better organized Christian states discipline and military administration had been improved, and firearms, land mines, and siegecraft had become more effective.

The Turks cared little about assimilating subject peoples to their language or institutions. Law was religious law derived from the Koran. Law courts and judges were hard to distinguish from religious authorities, for there was no separation between religious and secular spheres. The sultan was also the caliph, the commander of the faithful, and while on the one hand there was no clergy in the European sense, on the other hand religious influences affected all aspects of life. The Turks, for the most part, applied the Muslim law only to Muslims.

The Ottoman government left its non-Muslim subjects to settle their own affairs in their own way, not according to nationality, which was generally indistinguishable, but according to religious groupings. The Greek Orthodox church, to which most Christians in the empire belonged, thus became an almost autonomous intermediary between the sultan and a large fraction of its subjects. Armenian Christians and Jews formed other separate bodies. Except in the

[8] See pp. 43, 74–75, and 79.

western Balkans (Albania and Bosnia) there was no general conversion of Christians to Islam during the Turkish rule, although there were many individual cases of Christians turning Muslim to obtain the privileges of the ruling faith. North of the Danube the Christian princes of Transylvania, Wallachia, and Moldavia (later combined in the modern Romania) continued to rule over Christian subjects. They were kept in office for that purpose by the sultan, to whom they paid tribute. In general, since their subjects were more profitable to them as Christians, the Turks were not eager to proselytize for Islam.

The Ottoman Empire was therefore a relatively tolerant empire, far more so than the states of Europe. Christians in the Turkish empire fared better than Muslims would have fared in Christendom or than the Moors had in fact fared in Spain. Christians were less disturbed in Turkey than were Protestants in France, after 1685, or Catholics in Ireland. The empire was tolerant because it was composite, an aggregation of peoples, religions, and laws, having no drive, as did the Western states, toward internal unity and complete legal sovereignty. The same was evident in the attitude toward foreign merchants.

The king of France had had treaty arrangements with Turkey since 1535, and many traders from Marseilles had spread over the port towns of the Near East. They were exempted by treaty from the laws of the Ottoman Empire and were liable to trial only by their own judges, who though residing in Turkey were appointed by the king of France. They were free to exercise their Roman Catholic religion, and if disputes with Muslims arose, they appeared in special courts where the word of an infidel received equal weight with that of a follower of the prophet. Similar rights in Turkey were obtained by other European states. Thus began "extraterritorial" privileges of the kind obtained by Europeans in later centuries in China and elsewhere, wherever the local laws were regarded as backward. To the Turks of the seventeenth century there was nothing exceptional about such arrangements. Only much later, under Western influence, did the Turks learn to resent these "capitulations" as impairments of their own sovereignty.

Yet the Turkish rule was oppressive, and the "terrible Turk" was with reason the nightmare of eastern Europe. Ottoman rule was oppressive to Christians if only because it relegated them to a despised position, and because everything they held holy was viewed by the Turks with violent contempt. But it was oppressive also in that it was arbitrary and brutal even by the none too sensitive standards of Europeans. It was worse in these respects in the seventeenth century than formerly, for the central authority of the sultans had become corrupt, and the outlying governors, or pashas, had a virtual free hand with their subjects.

Those parts of the Ottoman Empire which adjoined the Christian states were among the least firmly attached to Constantinople. The Tartar Khans of south Russia, like the Christian princes of the Danubian principalities, were simply protégés who paid tribute. Hungary was occupied but was more a battlefield than a province. These regions were disputed by Germans, Poles, and Russians. It seemed in the middle of the seventeenth century as if the grip of the Turks might be relaxing. But a series of capable grand viziers, of the Kiuprili family, came to power and retained it contrary to Turkish customs for fifty years. Under them the empire again put forth a mighty effort. By 1663 the janissaries were again mobilizing in Hungary. Tartar horsemen were on the move. Central Europe again felt the old terror. The pope feared that the dreaded enemy might break into Italy.

Throughout Germany by the emperor's order special "Turk bells" sounded the alarm. The states of the Empire assembled in 1663 as a diet at Regensburg. They voted to raise a small imperial army. The Holy Roman Empire, even in its senility, bestirred itself temporarily against the historic enemy of the Christians. However, it was not the Empire, but the house of Austria, under whose auspices the Turks were to be repelled.

24. *The Formation of an Austrian Monarchy*

Having now surveyed the three very different empires whose occupancy of most of Europe from France to Muscovy kept the whole area politically malleable and soft, we turn to the three new states which consolidated themselves in this region, namely, Austria, Prussia, and Russia.

The Recovery and Growth of Habsburg Power, 1648–1740

The Austria which appeared by 1700 was in truth a new creation, though not as obviously so as the two others. The Austrian Habsburgs had long enjoyed an eminent role. Formerly their position had rested on their headship of the Holy Roman Empire and on their family connection with the more wealthy Habsburgs of Spain. In the seventeenth century these two supports collapsed. The hope for an effective Habsburg empire in Germany disappeared in the Thirty Years' War. The connection with Spain lost its value as Spain declined, and vanished when in 1700 Spain passed to the house of France. The Austrian family in the latter half of the seventeenth century stood at the great turning point of its fortunes. It successfully made a difficult transition, emerging from the husk of the Holy Empire and building an empire of its own. At the same time the Habsburgs continued to be Holy Roman Emperors and remained active in German affairs, using resources drawn from outside Germany to maintain their influence over the German princes. The relation of Austria to the rest of Germany became a political conundrum, forcibly solved by Bismarck in 1866 by the exclusion of Austria, only to be raised again by Adolf Hitler in the twentieth century.

The dominions considered by the house of Austria to be its own direct possessions were in three parts. The oldest were the "hereditary provinces"— Upper and Lower Austria, with the adjoining Tyrol, Styria, Carinthia, and Carniola. Second, there was the kingdom of Bohemia—Bohemia, Moravia, and Silesia joined under the crown of St. Wenceslas. Third, there was the kingdom of Hungary—Hungary, Transylvania, and Croatia joined under the crown of St. Stephen. Nothing held all these regions together except the fact that the Austrian Habsburg dynasty, in the seventeenth century, reaffirmed its grip upon them all. During the Thirty Years' War the dynasty rooted Protestantism and feudal rebelliousness out of Austria and the hereditary provinces, and reconquered and re-Catholicized Bohemia. And in the following decades it conquered Hungary also.

Since 1526 most of Hungary had been occupied by the Turks. For generations the Hungarian plain was a theater of intermittent warfare between the armies of Vienna and Constantinople. The struggle flared up again in 1663, when the Kiuprili vizier started Turkish armies moving up the Danube. A mixed force, assembled from the Empire and from all Christendom, obliged the Turks in 1664 to accept a twenty-year truce. But Louis XIV, who in these years was busily dismembering the western frontier of the Empire, stood to profit greatly from a diversion on the Danube. He incited the Turks (old allies of France through common hostility to the Habsburgs) to resume their assaults, which they did as the twenty-year truce came to a close.

In 1683 a vast Turkish host reached the city of Vienna and besieged it. The

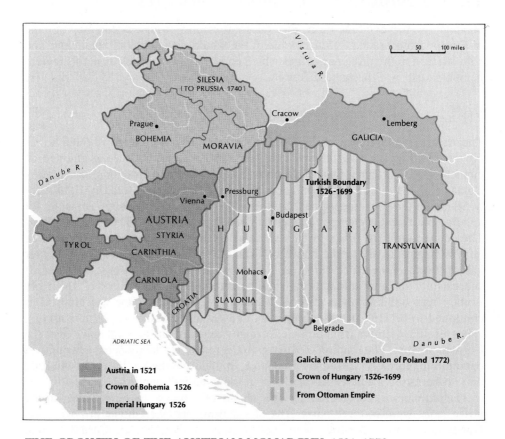

THE GROWTH OF THE AUSTRIAN MONARCHY, 1521–1772

The map shows the main body of the Austrian monarchy as it came to be in the eighteenth century and continued until the collapse of the empire in 1918. There were three main parts: (1) a nucleus, composed of Austria and adjoining duchies, often called the "hereditary provinces"; (2) the lands of the Bohemian crown, which became Habsburg in 1526 and where the Habsburgs reasserted their power during the Bohemian phase of the Thirty Years' War; and (3) the lands of the Hungarian crown, where at first the Habsburgs held only the segment called Imperial Hungary, the rest remaining Turkish until reconquered by the Habsburgs in 1699. In the first partition of Poland the Habsburgs annexed Galicia. Silesia was lost to Prussia in 1740. Outlying parts of the empire in the eighteenth century, not shown on the map, were most of what is now Belgium (then the Austrian Netherlands) and the duchy of Milan in Italy. The Italian duchy of Tuscany, where the Medici family died out in 1737, was thereafter ruled as a separate state by a Habsburg archduke.

Turks again, as in 1529, peered into the very inner chambers of Europe. The garrison and people of Vienna, greatly outnumbered, held off the besiegers for two months, enough time for a defending force to arrive. Both sides showed the composite or "international" character of the conflict. The Turkish army included some Christians—Romanian and Hungarian— the latter being in rebellion against Habsburg rule in Hungary. The Christian force was composed mainly of Poles, Austrian dynastic troops, and Germans from various states of the Empire. It was financed largely by Pope Innocent XI; it was commanded in the field by the Habsburg general, Duke Charles of Lorraine, who hoped to protect his inheritance from annexation by France; and its higher command was entrusted to John Sobieski, king of Poland. Sobieski contributed greatly to the relief of Vienna, and his bold action represented the last great military effort of the moribund Republic of Poland. When the Turks abandoned the siege, a general anti-Turkish counteroffensive developed. Forces of the pope, Poland, Russia, and the republic of Venice joined with the Habsburgs. It was in this war, in fighting between Turks and Venetians, that the Parthenon at Athens, which had survived for two thousand years but was now used as an ammunition dump by the Turks, was blown to ruins.

The Habsburgs had the good fortune to obtain the services of a man of remarkable talent, Prince Eugene of Savoy. Eugene, like many other servants of the Austrian house, was not Austrian at all; he was in fact French by origin and education but like many of the aristocratic class of the time was an international personage. More than anyone else he was the founder of the modern Austrian state. Distinguished both as a military administrator and as a commander in the field, he reformed the supply, equipment, training, and command of the Habsburg forces, along lines laid out by Louis XIV, and in 1697 he won the battle of Zenta, driving the Turks out of Hungary. At the Peace of Karlowitz (1699) the Turks yielded most of Hungary, together with Transylvania and Croatia, to the Habsburg house.

The Habsburgs were now free to pursue their designs in the west. They entered the War of the Spanish Succession to win the Spanish crown, but although an Austrian archduke campaigned in Spain for years, assisted by the English, they had to content themselves at the treaty of Rastadt in 1714 with the annexation of the old Spanish Netherlands and with Milan and Naples. Prince Eugene, freed now in the west, again turned eastward. Never before or afterward were the Austrians so brilliantly successful. Eugene captured Belgrade and pushed through the Iron Gate into Wallachia. But the Turks were not yet helpless; and by the Peace of Belgrade (1739) a frontier was drawn which on the Austrian side remained unchanged until the twentieth century. The Turks continued to hold Romania and the whole Balkan peninsula except Catholic Croatia, which, incorporated in the Habsburg empire, was again faced toward Europe. The Habsburg government, to open a window on the Mediterranean, developed a seaport at Trieste.

The Austrian Monarchy by 1740

Thus the house of Austria, in two or three generations after its humiliation at the Peace of Westphalia, acquired a new empire of very considerable proportions. Though installed in Belgium and Italy, it was essentially an empire of the middle

Danube, with its headquarters at Vienna in Austria proper, but possessing the sizable kingdoms of Hungary and Bohemia, and so filling the basin enclosed by the Alpine, Bohemian, and Carpathian mountain systems. Though German influence was strong, the empire was international or nonnational. At the Habsburg court, and in the Habsburg government and army, the names of Czech, Hungarian, Croatian, and Italian noblemen were very common. It is hard today to see this empire as it was, because it is hard to see it except through the eyes of its enemies. It made enemies of all Protestants. Democrats came to hate it. When the nationalistic movement swept over Europe in the nineteenth century, the empire was denounced as tyrannical by Hungarians, Croats, Serbs, Romanians, Czechs, Poles, Italians, and even some Germans, whose national ambitions were blocked by its existence. Later, disillusioned by nationalism in central and eastern Europe, some tended to romanticize unduly the old Danubian monarchy, noting that it had at least the merit of holding many discordant peoples together.

The empire was from the first international, based on a cosmopolitan aristocracy of landowners who felt closer to each other, despite differences of language, than to the laboring masses who worked on their estates. Not for many years, until after 1848, did the Habsburg government really touch these rural masses; it dealt with the landed class and with the relatively few cities, and left the landlords to control the peasants. The old diets remained in being in Bohemia, Hungary, and the Austrian provinces. No diet was created for the empire as a whole. The diets were essentially assemblages of landlords; and though they no longer enjoyed their medieval freedom, they retained certain powers over taxation and administration and a sense of constitutional liberty against the crown, like the Provincial Estates in France. So long as they produced taxes and soldiers as needed, and accepted the wars amd foreign policy of the ruling house, no questions were asked at Vienna. The peasants remained in, or reverted to, serfdom.[9]

The Habsburgs were determined to make their new empire unmistakably hereditary and Catholic. The first to feel the blow had been Bohemia. The Czech rebellion had been crushed, as we have seen, at the battle of the White Mountain in 1620.[10] This ended, until 1918, the national independence of a people who had greatly prospered in the Middle Ages. The reigning Habsburg, Ferdinand II, abrogated the elective Bohemian monarchy and declared the kingdom hereditary. He poured Catholic missionaries into the country. He confiscated the estates of the rebel nobles and granted them to a host of adventurers of many nationalities, mostly colonels and generals of the Thirty Years' War. A few of these were Czechs, but most were ignorant of the languages and customs of the people, and they owed their position entirely to the Habsburgs. Bohemia remained an entirely separate kingdom. Its new aristocracy, while remaining apart from the native peasantry and the towns, soon developed a sense of Bohemian autonomy and a desire to be let alone by the central government at Vienna.

Somewhat the same happened in Hungary after its reconquest from the Turks in 1699. Protestanism was widespread in Hungary, where it formed part of the famous Hungarian liberties. Every Hungarian magnate, like princes of the Holy Roman Empire, possessed the *ius reformandi,* or right to reform religion on his

[9] See pp. 125–126.
[10] See pp. 142–143.

own estates. There was thus religious disorder, and religion and politics were mixed. The Turks, during their occupation, favored the Protestants, knowing that Protestants would have no longing for a Catholic Habsburg king. In Hungary, therefore, as in Bohemia, the first step following the reconquest was to repress Protestanism, which was not only detested as heretical but feared as pro-Turkish. The elective monarchy was done away with; the crown of St. Stephen[11] became the hereditary possession of the Habsburgs. The Hungarian nobles lost their constitutional right of armed rebellion. German veterans were settled in the country, the Croats given privileges, and even Serbs imported from across the Danube, all to weaken the grip of the Magyar aristocracy; the effect was to scramble the nationalities in an already heterogeneous region. Hardly had Eugene's armies entered Turkish Hungary when a rebellion against the Habsburgs broke out in 1703, led by Prince Francis Rakoczy, who received help from Louis XIV but was finally crushed by 1711 and spent the rest of his life in France and Turkey. The Hungarians, proud and stubborn, became nationalistic before the era of nationalism. And for all that the Habsburgs could do, Hungary remained a distinct kingdom, and the magnates of Hungary remained the most free-handed aristocracy in Europe, except for the Poles.

Thus, despite the efforts of the Habsburgs, the Austrian monarchy remained a collection of territories held together by a personal union. Inhabitants of Austria proper considered their ruler as archduke, Bohemians saw in him the king of Bohemia, Magyars the apostolic king of Hungary. Each country retained its own law, diet, and political life. No feeling in the people held these regions together, and even the several aristocracies were joined only by common service to the house. For the empire to exist, all crowns had to be inherited by the same person.

After the reconquest of Hungary the king-archduke, Charles VI (1711–1740), devised a form of insurance to guarantee such an undivided succession. This took the form of a document called the Pragmatic Sanction, first issued in 1713. By it every diet in the empire and the various archdukes of the Habsburg family were to agree to regard the Habsburg territories as indivisible and to recognize only one specified line of heirs. The matter became urgent when it developed that Charles would have no children except a daughter, Maria Theresa, and that the direct male line of the Austrian Habsburgs, as of the Spanish a few years before, was about to become extinct. Charles VI gradually won acceptance of the Pragmatic Sanction by all parts of his empire and all members of his family. He then set about having foreign powers guarantee it, knowing that Bavaria, Prussia, or others might well put in claims for this or that part of the inheritance. This process took years, and was accomplished at the cost of many damaging concessions. Charles VI had attempted, for example, to revive Belgium commercially by founding an overseas trading company at Ostend. The British government, before agreeing to guarantee the Pragmatic Sanction, demanded and obtained the abandonment of this commercial project. Finally all powers signed. Charles VI died in 1740, having done all that could be done, by domestic law and international treaty, to assure the continuation of the Austrian empire.

He was scarcely dead when armed "heirs" presented themselves. A great war broke out to partition the Austrian empire, as the Spanish empire had been

[11] See p. 25.

partitioned shortly before. Bohemia threw off its allegiance. Hungary almost did the same. But these events belong later in the story.[12] At the moment it is enough to know that by 1740 a populous empire, of great military strength, had been founded on the Danube.

25. The Formation of Prussia

It was characteristic of the seventeenth century that very small states were able to play an influential part in European affairs, seemingly out of all proportion to their size. The main reason why small states could act as great powers was that armies were small and weapons simple. Difficulties of supply and communications, the poor state of the roads, the lack of maps, the absence of general staffs, together with many other administrative and technical difficulties, held down the number of soldiers who could be successfully managed in a campaign. The battles of the Thirty Years' War, on the average, were fought by armies of less than 20,000 men. And while Louis XIV, by the last years of his reign, built up a military establishment aggregating some 400,000, the actual field armies in the wars of Louis XIV did not exceed, on the average, 40,000. Armies of this size were well within the reach of smaller powers. If especially well trained, disciplined, and equipped, and if ably commanded and economically employed, the armies of small powers could defeat those of much larger neighbors. On this fact, fundamentally, the German state of Prussia was to be built. But Prussia was not the first to exploit the opportunity with spectacular consequences. The first, it may be said, was Sweden.

Sweden's Short-Lived Empire

Sweden almost, but not quite, formed an empire out of the malleable matter of central and eastern Europe in the seventeenth century. The population of Sweden at the time was not over a million; it was smaller than that of the Dutch Republic. But the Swedes produced a line of extraordinary rulers, ranging from genius in Gustavus Adolphus (1611–1632) through the brilliantly erratic Queen Christina (1632–1654) to the amazing military exploits of Charles XII (1697–1718). The elective Swedish kingship was made definitely hereditary, the royal power freed from control by the estates, craftsmen and experts brought from the west, notably Holland, war industries subsidized by the government, and an army created with many novel features in weapons, organization, and tactics.

With this army Gustavus Adolphus crossed the Baltic in the Thirty Years' War, made alliances with Protestant German princes, cut through the yielding mass of the Holy Roman Empire, and helped to ward off unification of Germany by the Habsburgs.[13] The Swedish crown, by the Peace of Westphalia, received certain coastal regions of Germany—western Pomerania, including the city of Stettin, and the former bishoprics of Bremen and Verden on the North Sea. Subsequently, in a confused series of wars, in which a Polish king claimed to be

[12] See pp. 273–285.
[13] See pp. 143–148.

king of Sweden, and a Swedish king claimed to be king of Poland, the Swedes won control of virtually all the shores and cities of the Baltic. Only Denmark at the mouth of that sea and the territories of the house of Brandenburg, which had almost no ports, remained independent. For a time the Baltic was a Swedish lake. The Russians were shut off from it, and the Poles and even the Germans, who lived on its shores, could reach it only on Swedish terms.

The final Swedish effort was made by the meteoric Charles XII. As a young man he found his dominions attacked by Denmark, Poland, and Russia; he won victories over them but would not make peace; he then led an army back and forth across the East European plain, only to be ruined by the Russians, and spend more long years as a guest and protégé of the Turks.[14] With the death of Charles XII in 1718 the Swedish sphere contracted to Sweden itself, except that Finland and reduced holdings in northern Germany remained Swedish for a century more. The Swedes in time proved themselves exceptional among European peoples in not harping on their former greatness. They successfully and peaceably made the transition from the role of a great power to that of a small one.

The Territorial Growth of Brandenburg-Prussia

In the long run it was to be Prussia that dominated this part of Europe. Prussia also became famous for its "militarism," which may be said to exist when military needs and military values permeate all other spheres of life. Through its influence on Germany over a period of two centuries it played a momentous part in the modern world. The south coast of the Baltic, where Prussia was to arise, was an unpromising site for the creation of a strong political power. It was an uninviting country, thinly populated, with poor soil and without mineral resources, more backward than Saxony or Bohemia, not to mention the busy centers of south Germany and western Europe. It was a flat open plain, merging imperceptibly into Poland, without prominent physical features or natural frontiers.[15] The coastal region directly south from Sweden was known as Pomerania. Inland from it, shut off from the sea, was the electoral margraviate of Brandenburg, centering about Berlin. Brandenburg had been founded in the Middle Ages as a border state, a "mark" or "march" of the Holy Roman Empire, to fight the battles of the Holy Empire against the then heathen Slavs. Its ruler, the margrave, was one of the seven princes who elected the Holy Roman Emperor. Hence he was commonly called the Elector of Brandenburg. After 1415 the electors were always of the Hohenzollern family.

All Germany east of the Elbe, including Brandenburg, represented a medieval conquest by the German-speaking peoples— the German *Drang nach Osten*, or drive to the East. From the Elbe to Poland, German conquerors and settlers had replaced the Slavs, eliminating them or absorbing them by intermarriage. Eastward from Brandenburg, and outside the Holy Roman Empire, stretched a region inhabited by Slavic peoples and known historically as Pomerelia. Next to the east came "Prussia," which eventually was to give its name to all territories of the

[14] See p. 240.
[15] See maps, pp. 4–5, 146–147, 212, 216.

Hohenzollern monarchy. This original Prussia formed part of the lands of the Teutonic Knights, a military crusading order which had conquered and Christianized the native peoples in the thirteenth century.[16] Except for its seacoast along the Baltic, the duchy of Prussia was totally enclosed by the Polish kingdom. To the north, along the Baltic, as far as the Gulf of Finland, German minorities lived among undeveloped Lithuanians, Latvians (or Letts), and Estonians. The towns were German, founded as German commercial colonies in the Middle Ages, and many of the landlords were German also, descendants of the Teutonic Knights, and later known as the "Baltic barons." These Germans at that time, since nationalist sentiment scarcely existed, felt no affiliation with the main block of Germans farther west, but they retained their German language and traditions.

Modern Prussia began to appear in the seventeenth century when a number of territories came together in the hands of the Hohenzollerns of Brandenburg, who, we have noted, had ruled in Brandenburg since 1415. In 1618 the Elector of Brandenburg inherited the duchy of Prussia. Another important development occurred when the old ruling line in Pomerania expired during the Thirty Years' War. Although the Swedes succeeded in taking the better part of Pomerania, including the city of Stettin, the Elector of Brandenburg received at the Peace of Westphalia eastern or Farther Pomerania. Barren, rural, and harborless though it was, it at least had the advantage of connecting Brandenburg with the Baltic. The Hohenzollerns no sooner obtained it than they began to dream of joining it to the duchy of Prussia, a task which required the absorption of the intermediate and predominantly Slavic Pomerelia, which was part of Poland. (This task was accomplished in 1772. The Hohenzollern administrators then called the old duchy "East Prussia" and the old Pomerelia "West Prussia"; but by that time, in a general confusion of nomenclature, "Prussia" also referred to all the Hohenzollern provinces taken together.)

Had the duchy of Prussia and Farther Pomerania been the only acquisitions of the Hohenzollerns, their state would have been oriented almost exclusively toward eastern Europe. But at the Peace of Westphalia they received, in addition to Farther Pomerania, the large bishopric of Halberstadt and the still larger archbishopric of Magdeburg, which lay on the west bank of the Elbe. Moreover, through the play of inheritance so common in the Holy Roman Empire, the Hohenzollerns had earlier fallen heir, in 1614, to the small state of Cleves on the Rhine at the Dutch border and a few other small territories also in western Germany. These were separated from the main mass around Brandenburg by many intermediate German principalities. But they gave the Hohenzollerns a direct contact with the more advanced regions of western Europe, and a base from which larger holdings in the Rhineland were eventually to be built up.

In the seventeenth century, meanwhile, the dominions of the house of Brandenburg were in three disconnected masses. The main mass was Brandenburg, with the adjoining Pomerania and Elbe bishoprics. There was a detached eastern mass in ducal Prussia and a small detached western mass on and near the Rhine. The middle and western masses were within the Holy Roman Empire. The eastern mass was outside the Empire, and until 1660, a fief of Poland. To

[16] See p. 43.

connect and unify the three masses became the underlying long-range policy of the Brandenburg house.

In the midst of the Thirty Years' War, in 1640, a young man of twenty, named Frederick William, succeeded to these diverse possessions. Known later as the Great Elector, he was the first of the men who made modern Prussia. He had grown up under trying conditions. Brandenburg was one of the parts of Germany to suffer most heavily from the war. Its location made it the stamping ground of Swedish and Habsburg armies. In 1640, in the twenty-two years since the beginning of the war, the population of Berlin had fallen from about 14,000 to about 6,000. Hundreds of villages had been wiped out. Wolves roamed over the countryside.

Frederick William concluded that in his position, ruling a small and open territory, without natural frontiers or possibility of defense in depth, he must put his main reliance on a competent army. With an effective army, even if small, he could oblige the stronger states to take him into their calculations and so could enter with some hope of advantage into the politics of the balance of power. This long remained the program of the Brandenburgers—to have an army but not to use it, to conserve it with loving and even miserly care, to keep an "army in being," and to gain their ends by diplomatic maneuver. They did so by siding with France against the Habsburgs, or with Sweden against Poland. They aspired also to the title not merely of margrave or elector, but king. The opportunity came in 1701, when the Habsburg emperor was preparing to enter the War of the Spanish Succession. The emperor requested the elector of Brandenburg, who was then Frederick III, to support him with 8,000 troops. The elector named his price: recognition of himself, by the emperor, as king "in Prussia." The emperor yielded; the title, at first explicitly limited to the less honorable king *in* Prussia, soon became king *of* Prussia. The elector Frederick III of Brandenburg became King Frederick I of Prussia. Another rent was made in the old fabric of the Holy Empire. There was now a German king above all the other German princes.

The Prussian Military State

The preoccupation of Prussia with its army was unquestionably defensive in origin, arising from the horrors of the Thirty Years' War. But it outlasted its cause, and became the settled habit and character of the country. Prussia was not unique, in a world of Bourbons and Habsburgs, Swedes, Russians, Turks, and the growing British navy, in the attention it paid to its armed forces. The unique thing about Prussia was the disproportion between the size of the army and the size of the resources on which the army was based. The government, to maintain the army, had to direct and plan the life of the country for this purpose. Nor was Prussia the originator of the "standing" army, kept active in time of peace, and always preparing for war. Most governments imitated Louis XIV in establishing standing armies, not merely to promote foreign ambitions but to keep armed forces out of the hands of nobles and military adventurers, and under control by the state.

But Prussia was unique in that, more than in any other country, the army developed a life of its own, almost independent of the life of the state. It was

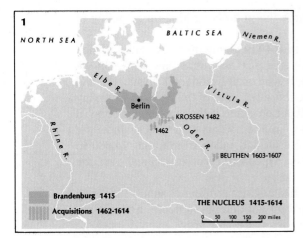

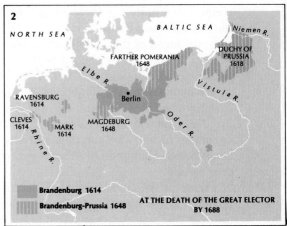

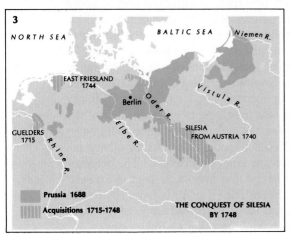

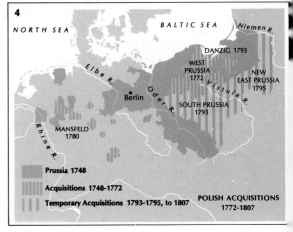

THE GROWTH OF PRUSSIA, 1415–1918

The maps shown here give a conspectus of Prussian history from the time when Brandenburg began to expand in the seventeenth century. One may see, by looking at all the panels together, how Prussia was really an east-European state until 1815; its center of gravity shifted westward, in significant degree, only in the nineteenth century. Panel 2 shows the early formation of three unconnected masses; Panel 3, the huge bulk of Silesia relative to the small kingdom that annexed it (pp. 275–278); Panel 4, the fruits of the partitions of Poland (p. 248); Panel 5, Napoleon pared Prussia down (pp. 421–422). The main crisis at the Congress of Vienna, and its resolution, are shown in Panels 6 and 7 (pp. 447–450). Bismarck's enlargement of Prussia appears in Panel 8 (pp. 557–558). The boundaries established by Bismarck remained unchanged until the fall of the monarchy in 1918.

older than the Prussian state. In 1657 the Great Elector fought a great battle at Warsaw with soldiers from all parts of his dominions. It was the first time that men from Cleves, Brandenburg, and ducal Prussia had ever done anything together. The army was the first "all Prussian" institution. Institutions of civilian government developed later and largely to meet the needs of the army. And in

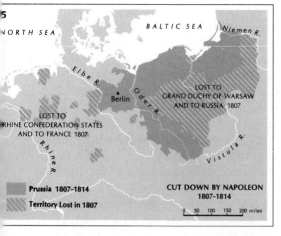

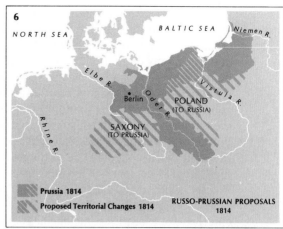

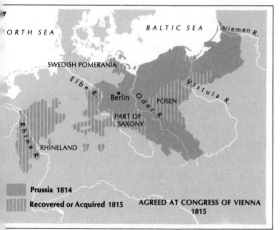

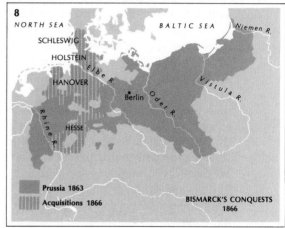

later generations the army proved more durable than the state. When Prussia collapsed before Napoleon in 1806, the spirit and morale of the Prussian army carried on; and when the Hohenzollern empire finally crashed in 1918, the army still maintained its life and traditions on into the Republic, which again it survived.[17]

In all countries, to some extent, the machinery of the modern state developed as a means of supporting armed forces, but in Prussia the process was exceptionally clear and simple. In Prussia the rulers drew roughly half their income from the crown domain and only about half from taxes. The crown domain, consisting of manors and other productive enterprises owned directly by the ruler as lord, was in effect a kind of government property, for the Prussian rulers used their income almost entirely for state purposes, being personally men of simple and even Spartan habits. The rulers of Prussia, until a century after the accession of the Great Elector, were able to pay the whole cost of their civil government from their own income, the proceeds of the crown domain. But to maintain an army

[17] See pp. 439–441, 717–718, 784.

they had to make the domain more productive, and also find a new income derived from taxes. To develop the domain and account for and transfer the funds, they created a large body of civilian officials. The domain bulked so large that much of the economy of the country was not in private hands but consisted of enterprises owned and administered by the state. For additional income the Great Elector introduced taxes of the kind used in France, such as excise taxes on consumers' goods and a government monopoly on the sale of salt. These taxes, together with the old land tax, began to be collected during the disorders of the Thirty Years' War by war commissioners, later organized into a general commissariat. In effect, the army itself collected the taxes and determined the purposes for which the funds should be spent. All taxes, for a century after the accession of the Great Elector, were levied for the use of the army.

Economic life grew up under government sponsorship, rather than by the enterprise of a venturesome business class. This was because, for a rural country to maintain an organized army, productive and technical skills had to be imported, mainly from the West. The Great Elector in his youth spent a number of years in Holland, where he was impressed by the wealth and prosperity that he saw. After becoming elector he settled Swiss and Frisians in Brandenburg (the Frisians were almost Dutch); he welcomed Jews from Poland; and when Louis XIV began to persecute the French Protestants, he provided funds and special officials to assist the immigration of 20,000 Huguenots to Brandenburg. Frenchmen for a time formed a sixth of the population of Berlin and were the most advanced element of that comparatively primitive city. The government, as in France under Colbert, initiated and helped to finance various industries; but the importance of such government participation was greater than in France, because the amount of privately owned capital available for investment was incomparably less. Military needs, more than elsewhere, dominated the market for goods, because civilian demand, in so poor a country, was relatively low; so that the army, in its requirements for food, uniforms, and weapons, was a strong force in shaping the economic growth of the country.

The army had a profound effect also on the social development and class structure of Prussia. The civilian middle class remained submissive, and it became the policy of the rulers to absorb practically the whole landed aristocracy, the Junkers, into military service. They used the army, with conscious purpose, as a means of implementing an "all Prussian" psychology in the landed families of Cleves, Brandenburg, Pomerania, and the former dominions of the Teutonic Knights. The sense of service to the king or state was exalted as the supreme human virtue. The fact that Prussia was a very recent and artificial combination of territories, so that loyalty to it was not at first a natural sentiment, made it all the more necessary to instill it by obvious and martial means. Emphasis fell on duty, obedience, service, and sacrifice. That military virtues became characteristic of the whole Prussian aristocracy was also due, like so much else, to the small size of the population. In France, for example, with perhaps 50,000 male adult nobles, only a small minority served habitually as army officers. In Prussia there were few Junker families that did not have some of their members in uniform.

Moreover, the Great Elector and his successors, like all absolutist rulers, repressed the estates or parliamentary assemblages in which the landed aristocracy was the main element. To mollify the squires, the rulers promised commissions in the army to men of their class. They promised them also a free hand over their peasants. The Prussian monarchy was largely based on an understanding between the ruler and the landlord gentry—the latter agreed to accept the ruler's government and to serve in his army, in return for holding their own peasants in hereditary subjection. Serfdom spread in Prussia as elsewhere in eastern Europe.[18] In East Prussia the condition of the peasants became as deplorable as in Poland.

The Prussian rulers believed that the Junkers made better army officers because they were brought up in the habit of commanding their own peasants. Bourgeois officers, a minority in all armies, were of the utmost rarity in Prussia. To preserve the officer class, legislation forbade the sale of "noble" lands, i.e., manors, to persons not noble. In France, again by way of contrast, where manorial rights had become simply a form of property, bourgeois and even peasants could legally acquire manors and enjoy a lordly or "seigneurial" income. In Prussia this was not possible; classes were frozen by owning nonexchangeable forms of property. It was thus harder for middle-class persons to enter the aristocracy by setting up as landed gentry. The bourgeois class in any case had little spirit of independence. Few of the old towns of Germany were in Prussia. The Prussian middle class was not wealthy. It was not strong by the possession of private property. The typical middle-class man was an official, who worked for the government as an employee or leaseholder of the large crown domain, or in an enterprise subsidized by the state. The civil service in Prussia, from the days of the Great Elector, became notable for its honesty and efficiency. But the middle class, more than elsewhere, deferred to the nobles, served the state, and stood in awe of the army.

These peculiar features of Prussia developed especially under Frederick William I, who was king from 1713 to 1740. He was an earthy, uncouth man, who, were the matter less serious, might almost be regarded as a comical character. He disdained whatever savored of "culture," to which his father and grandfather (the Great Elector) and also his son (Frederick the Great) were all strongly attracted. He begrudged every penny not spent on the army. He cut the expense of the royal household by three-fourths. On his coronation journey to Königsberg he spent 2,547 thalers, where his father had spent five million. He ruled the country in a fatherly German way, supervising it like a private estate, prowling the streets of Berlin in an old seedy uniform, and disciplining negligent citizens with blows of his walking stick. He worked all the time, and expected everyone else to do likewise. He loved the army, which all his policies were designed to serve. He was the first Prussian king to appear always in uniform. He rearranged the order of courtly precedence, pushing army officers up and civilians down. His love of tall soldiers is famous; he collected a special unit, men between six and seven feet high, from all over Europe, and indeed Peter the Great sent him some from Asia. He devised new forms of discipline and maneuver, founded a cadet corps to train the sons of the Junkers, and invented a new system of recruiting (the canton system, long the most effective in Europe), by which each regiment had a particular district or canton assigned to it as a source of soldiers. He raised the size of the army from 40,000 at his accession to 83,000 at his death. During his reign Berlin grew to be a city of 100,000, of whom 20,000 were soldiers, a proportion probably matched in no other city of Europe. He likewise left to his

[18] See pp. 125–126, 210–211, 218, 224, 235.

successor (for he fought practically no wars himself) a war chest of 7,000,000 thalers.

With this army and war chest Frederick II, later called the Great, who became king in 1740, startled Europe. Charles VI of Austria had just died. His daughter Maria Theresa entered upon her manifold inheritance. All Europe was hedging on its guarantee of the Pragmatic Sanction. While others waited, Frederick struck. Serving no notice, he moved his forces into Silesia, to which the Hohenzollerns had an old though doubtful claim. Silesia was a part of the kingdom of Bohemia on the side toward Poland, lying in the upper valley of the Oder River, and adjoining Brandenburg on the north. The addition of Silesia to the kingdom of Prussia almost doubled the population and added valuable industries, so that Prussia now, with 6,000,000 people and an army which Frederick raised to 200,000, at last established itself as a great power. It must be added that, judged simply as a human accomplishment, Prussia was a remarkable creation, a state made on a shoestring, a triumph of work and duty.

26. The "Westernizing" of Russia

The affairs of central and eastern Europe, from Sweden to Turkey and from Germany to the Caspian Sea, were profoundly interconnected. The underlying theme of the present chapter, it may be recalled, is that this whole great area was fluid, occupied by the flabby bodies of the Holy Roman Empire, Poland, and Turkey, and that in this fluid area three harder masses developed—the modern Austrian monarchy, the kingdom of Prussia, and the Russian empire. All, too, in varying degree, were modernized by borrowings from the West.

In the century after 1650 the old tsardom of Muscovy turned into modern Russia. Moving out from the region around Moscow, the Russians not only established themselves across northern Asia, reaching the Bering Sea about 1700, but also entered into closer relations with Europe, undergoing especially in the time of Tsar Peter the Great (1682–1725) a rapid process of Europeanization. To what extent Russia became truly European has always been an open question, disputed both by western Europeans and by Russians themselves. In some ways the Russians have been European from as far back as Europe itself can be said to have existed, i.e., from the early Middle Ages. Ancient Russia had been colonized by Vikings, and the Russians had become Christians long before the Swedes, the Lithuanians, or the Finns. But Russia had not been part of the general development of Europe for a number of reasons. For one thing, Russia had been converted to the Greek Orthodox branch of Christianity; therefore, the religious and cultural influence of Constantinople, not of Rome, had predominated. Second, the Mongol invasions and conquest about 1240 had kept Russia under Asiatic domination for about two hundred and fifty years, until 1480 when a grand duke of Muscovy, Ivan III (1462–1505), was able to throw off the Mongol overlordship and cease payment of tribute.[19] Last, Russian geography, especially the lack of warm-water or ice-free seaports, had made commerce and communciation with the West difficult. For these reasons Russia had not shared in the general

[19] See pp. 26, 43.

European development after about 1100, and the changes that took place in the seventeenth and eighteenth centuries may accurately be called Europeanization, or at least a wholesale borrowing of the apparatus of civilization from the West. The Europeanizing or westernizing of Russia was by no means a unique thing. It was a step in the expansion of the European type of civilization and hence in the formation of the modern world as we have known it in the last three hundred years.

In some ways the new Russian empire resembled the new kingdom of Prussia. Both took form in the great plain which runs uninterruptedly from the North Sea into inner Asia. Both lacked natural frontiers and grew by addition of territories to an original nucleus. In both countries the state arose primarily as a means of supporting a modern army. In both the government developed autocratically, in conjunction with a landlord class which was impressed into state service and which in turn held the peasantry in serfdom. Neither Russia nor Prussia had a native commercial class of any political importance. In neither country could the modern state and army have been created without the importation of skills from western Europe. Yet Prussia, with its German connections, its Protestant religion, its universities, and its nearness to the busy commercial artery of the Baltic, was far more "European" than Russia, and the Europeanization of Russia may perhaps better be compared with the later westernization of Japan.[20] In the Russia of 1700, as in the Japan of 1870, the main purpose of the westernizers was to obtain scientific, technical, and military knowledge from the West, in part with a view to strengthening their own countries against penetration or conquest by Europeans. Yet here too the parallel must not be pushed too far. Russia became more fully Europeanized than did the peoples of Asia. In time, its upper classes intermarried with Europeans, and Russian music and literature became part of the culture of Europe. Russia developed a unique blend of European and non-European traits.

Russia before Peter the Great

The Russians in the seventeenth century, as today, were a medley of peoples distinguished by their language, which was of the Slavic family, of the great Indo-European language group.[21] The Great Russians or Muscovites lived around Moscow. Moving out from that area, they had penetrated the northern forests and had also settled in the southern steppes and along the Volga, where they had assimilated various Asiatic peoples known as Tartars. After two centuries of expansion, from roughly 1450 to 1650, the Russians had almost but not quite reached the Baltic and the Black seas. The Baltic shore was held by Sweden. The Black Sea coast was still held by Tartar Khans under the protection of Turkey. In the rough borderlands betwen Tartar and Russia lived the semi-independent cowboylike Cossacks, largely recruited from migratory Russians. West of Muscovy were the White Russians (or Byelorussians) and southwest of Muscovy the Little Russians (or Ruthenians or Ukranians), both in the seventeenth century under the rule of Poland, which was then the leading Slavic power.

[20] See pp. 577–582.
[21] See p. 11, and the language map, p. 470.

The energies of the Great Russians were directed principally eastward. They conquered the Volga Tartars in the sixteenth century, thus reaching the Ural Mountains, which they immediately crossed. Muscovite pioneers, settlers, and townbuilders streamed along the river systems of Siberia, felling timber and trading in furs as they went. In the 1630s, while the English were building Boston and the Dutch New York, the Russians were establishing towns in the vast Asiatic stretches of Siberia, reaching to the Pacific itself. A whole string of settlements, remote, small, and isolated—Tomsk and Tobolsk, Irkutsk and Yakutsk—extended for 5,000 miles across northern Asia.

It was toward the vast heartland of central Asia that Muscovy really faced, looking out upon Persia and China across the deserts. The bazaars of Moscow and Astrakhan were frequented by Persians, Afghans, Kirkhiz, Indians, and Chinese. The Caspian Sea, into which flowed the Volga, the greatest of Russian rivers, was better known than was the Baltic. Europe as sensed from Moscow was in the rear. During most of the seventeenth century even Smolensk and Kiev belonged to Poland. Yet the Russians were not totally shut off from Europe. In 1552, when Ivan the Terrible conquered Kazan from the Tartars, he had a German engineer in his army. In the next year, 1553, Richard Chancellor arrived in Moscow from England by the roundabout way of Archangel on the White Sea.[22] Thereafter trade between England and Muscovy was continuous. The tsars valued Archangel as their only inlet from the West, through which military materials could be imported. The English valued it as a means of reaching the wares of Persia.

Russia in the seventeenth century reflected its long estrangement from Europe and its long association with the peoples of Asia. Women of the upper classes were secluded and often wore veils. Men wore beards and skirted garments that seemed exotic to Europeans. Customs were crude, wild drunkenness and revelry alternating with spasms of repentance and religious prostration. Dwarfs and fools, no longer the fashion in the West, still amused the tsar and his retainers. Superstition infected the highest classes of church and state. Life counted for little; murder, kidnapping, torture, and elaborate physical cruelty were common. The Russian church supported no such educational or charitable institutions as did the Catholic and Protestant churches of Europe and had developed no such respect for learning or sentiments of humanity. Churchmen feared the incipient Western influences. "Abhorred of God," declared a Russian bishop, "is any who loves geometry; it is a spiritual sin." Even arithmetic was hardly understood in Russia. Arabic numerals were not used, and merchants computed with the abacus. The calendar was dated from the creation of the world. Ability to predict an eclipse seemed a form of magic. Clocks, brought in by Europeans, seemed as wonderful in Russia as they did in China, where they were brought in by Jesuits at about the same time.

Yet this great barbarous Russia, which fronted on inner Asia, was European in some of its fundamental social institutions. It possessed a variant of the manorial and feudal systems. It felt the same wave of constitutional crises that was sweeping over Europe at the same time. Russia had a duma or council of retainers and advisers to the tsar, and the rudiments of a national assembly

22 See p. 110.

corresponding to meetings of the estates in western Europe. In Russia as in Europe the question was whether power should remain in the hands of these bodies or become concentrated in the hands of the ruler. Ivan the Terrible, who ruled from 1533 to 1584 and was the first grand duke of Muscovy to assume the title of tsar,[23] was a shrewd observer of contemporary events in Poland. He saw the dissolution that was overtaking the Polish state and was determined to avoid it in Muscovy. His ferocity toward those who opposed him made him literally terrible, but though his methods were not used in Europe, his aims were the aims of his European contemporaries. Not long after his death Russia passed into a period known as the Time of Troubles (1604–1613), during which the Russian nobles elected a series of tsars and demanded certain assurances of their own liberties. But the country was racked by contending factions and civil war, like the religious wars in France or the Thirty Years' War in central Europe.

In 1613 a national assembly, hoping to settle the troubles, elected a seventeen-year-old boy as tsar, or emperor, believing him young enough to have no connection with any of the warring factions. The new boy tsar was Michael Romanov, of a gentry family, related by marriage to the old line of Ivan the Terrible. Thus was established, by vote of the political classes of the day, the Romanov dynasty which ruled in Russia until 1917. The early Romanovs, aware of the fate of elective monarchy in Poland and elsewhere, soon began to repress the representative institutions of Russia and set up as absolute monarchs. Here again, though they were more lawless and violent than any European king, they followed the general pattern of contemporary Europe.

Nor can it be said that the main social development of the seventeenth century in Russia, the sinking of the peasantry into an abyss of helpless serfdom, was exclusively a Russian phenomenon. The same generally took place in eastern Europe.[24] Serfdom had long been overtaking the older free peasantry of Russia. In Russia, as in the American colonies, land was abundant and labor scarce. The natural tendency of labor was to migrate over the great plain, to run off to the Cossacks, or to go to Siberia. In the Time of Troubles, especially, there was a good deal of moving about. The landlords wished to assure themselves of their labor force. To this end they obtained the support of the Romanov tsars. The manor, or what corresponded to it in Russia, came to resemble the slave plantation of the New World.[25] Laws against fugitive serfs were strengthened; lords won the right to recover fugitives up to fifteen years after their flight, and finally the time limit was abolished altogether. Peasants came to be so little regarded that a law of 1625 authorized anyone killing another man's peasant simply to give him another peasant in return. Lords exercised police and judicial powers. By a law of 1646 landowners were required to enter the names of all their peasants in government registers; peasants once so entered, together with their descendants, were regarded as attached to the estate on which they were registered. Thus the peasant lost the freedom to move at his own will. For a time he was supposed to have secure tenure of his land; but a law of 1675 allowed the lords to sell peasants

---

[23] The Slavic word *tsar*, like the German *Kaiser*, derives from *Caesar*, a title used as a synonym for *emperor* in the Roman, the Holy Roman, and the Byzantine (or Eastern Roman) empires. The spelling *czar*, also common in English, reveals the etymology and the current English-language pronunciation, *zar*.

[24] See pp. 125–126, 210–211, 233–234.

[25] See pp. 260–261.

without the land, and thus to move peasants like chattels at the will of the owner. This sale of serfs without land, which made their condition more like slavery as practiced in America, became indeed a distinctive feature of serfdom in Russia, since in Poland, Prussia, Bohemia, and other regions of serfdom, the serf was generally regarded as "bound to the soil," inseparable from the land.

Against the loss of their freedom the rural population of Russia protested as best it could, murdering landlords, fleeing to the Cossacks, taking refuge in a vagrant existence, countered by wholesale government-organized manhunts and by renewed and more stringent legislation. A tremendous uprising was led in 1667 by Stephen Razin, who gathered a host of fugitive serfs, Cossacks, and adventurers, outfitted a fleet on the Caspian Sea, plundered Russian vessels, defeated a Persian squadron, and invaded Persia itself. He then turned back, ascended the Volga, killing and burning as he went and proclaiming a war against landlords, nobles, and priests. Cities opened their gates to him; an army sent against him went over to his side. He was caught and put to death in 1671. The consequence of the rebellion, for over a century, was that serfdom was clamped on the country more firmly than ever.

Even from the church the increasingly wretched rural people drew little comfort. The Russian Orthodox church at this time went through a great internal crisis, and ended up as hardly more than a department of the tsardom, useful to the government in instilling a superstitious reverence for Holy Russia. The Russian church had historically looked to the Patriarch of Constantinople as its head. But the conquest of Constantinople by the Turks made the head of the Greek Orthodox church a merely tolerated inferior to the Muslim sultan-caliph, so that the Russians in 1589 set up an independent Russian patriarch of their own. In the following generations the Russian patriarchate first became dependent on, then was destroyed by, the tsarist government.

In the 1650s the Russian patriarch undertook certain church reforms, mainly to correct mistranslations in Russian versions of the Bible and other sacred writings. The changes aroused the horror and indignation of the general body of believers. Superstitiously attached to the mere form of the written word, believing the faith itself to depend on the customary spelling of the name of Jesus, the malcontents saw in the reformers a band of cunning Greek scholars perpetrating the work of Antichrist and the devil. The patriarch and higher church officials forced through the reforms but only with the help of the government and the army. Those who rejected the reforms came be called Old Believers. More ignorant and fanatical than the established church, agitated by visionary preachers, dividing into innumerable sects, the Old Believers became very numerous, especially among the peasants. Old Believers were active in Stephen Razin's rebellion and in all the sporadic peasant uprisings that followed. The peasants, already put by serfdom outside the protection of law, were also largely estranged from the established religion. A distrust of all organized authority settled over the Russian masses, to whom both church and government seemed mere engines of repression.

But while willing enough to modernize to the extent of correcting mistranslations from the Greek, the church officials resisted the kind of modernization that was coming in from western Europe. They therefore opposed Peter the Great at the end of the century. After 1700 no new patriarch was appointed. Peter put the church under a committee of bishops called the Holy Synod, and to the Synod he attached a civil official called the Procurator of the Holy Synod, who was not a churchman but head of a government bureau, and whose task was to see that the church did nothing displeasing to the tsar. Peter thus secularized the church, making himself in effect its head. But while the consequences were more extreme in Russia than elsewhere, it must again be noted that this action of Peter's followed the general pattern of Europe. Secular supervision of religion had become the rule almost everywhere, especially in Protestant countries. Indeed an Englishman of the time thought that Peter the Great, in doing away with the patriarchate and putting the church under his own control, was wisely imitating England, which he visited in his youth.

Peter the Great: Foreign Affairs and Territorial Expansion

The Russia in which Peter the Great became tsar, in 1682, was in short European in some ways and had in any case been in contact with Westerners for over a century. Without Peter, Russia would have developed its European connections more gradually. Peter, by his tempo and methods, made the process a social revolution.

Peter obtained his first knowledge of the West in Moscow itself, where a part of the city known as the German quarter was inhabited by Europeans of various nationalities, whom Peter often visited as a boy. Peter also in his early years mixed with Westerners at Archangel, still Russia's only port, for he was fascinated by the sea and took lessons in navigation on the White Sea from Dutch and English ship captains. Like the Great Elector of Brandenburg, Peter as a young man spent over a year in western Europe, especially Holland and England, where he was profoundly impressed with the backwardness of his own country. He had considerable talents as a mechanic and organizer. He labored with his own hands as a ship's carpenter in Amsterdam and talked with political and business leaders on means of introducing Western organization and technology into Russia. He visited workshops, mines, commercial offices, art galleries, hospitals, and forts. Europeans saw in him a barbarian of genius, a giant of a man standing a head above most others, bursting with physical vitality and plying all he met with interminable questions on their manner of working and living. He had neither the refinement nor the pretension of Western monarchs; he mixed easily with workmen and technical people, dressed cheaply and carelessly, loved horseplay and crude practical jokes, and dismayed his hosts by the squalid disorder in which he and his companions left the rooms put at their disposal. A man of acute practical mind, he was as little troubled by appearances as by moral scruples.

Peter on his visit to Europe in 1697-1698 recruited almost 1,000 experts for service in Russia, and many more followed later. He cared nothing for the civilization of Europe except as a means to an end, and this end was to create an army and a state which could stand against those of the West. His aim from the beginning was in part defensive, to ward off the Poles, Swedes, and Turks who had long pushed against Russia; and in part expansionist, to obtain seaports or "windows on the West," warm-water ports on the Baltic and Black seas, free from the shortcomings of Archangel, which was frozen a good part of the year and in any case offered only a roundabout route to Europe. For all but two years of his long reign Peter was at war.

The Poles were a receding danger. A Polish prince had indeed been elected tsar of Muscovy during the Time of Troubles, and for a while the Poles aspired to conquer and Catholicize the Great Russians, but in 1667 the Russians had regained Smolensk and Kiev, and the growing anarchy in Poland made that country no longer a menace, except as the Swedes or others might install themselves in it. The Turks and their feudatories the Tartars, though no longer expanding, were still obstinate foes. Peter before going to Europe managed in 1696 to capture Azov at the mouth of the Don, but he was unable to hold any of the Black Sea coast and learned in these campaigns to know the inferiority of the Russian army. The Swedes were the main enemy of Russia. Their army, for its size, was still probably the best in Europe. By occupying Finland, Karelia, and Livonia they controlled the whole eastern shore of the Baltic including the Gulf of Finland. In 1697, the Swedish king having died, Peter entered into an alliance with Poland and Denmark to partition the overseas possessions of the Swedish house.

The new king of Sweden, the youthful Charles XII, though descended from civilized enough forebears, was in some ways as crude as Peter (as an adolescent he had sheep driven into his rooms in the palace in order to enjoy the warlike pleasure of killing them), but he proved also to have remarkable aptitude as a general. In 1700, at the battle of Narva, with an army of 8,000 men, he routed Peter's 40,000 Russians. The tsar thus learned another lesson on the need of westernizing his state and army. Fortunately for the Russians Charles XII, instead of immediately pressing his advantage in Russia, spent the following years in furthering Swedish interests in Poland, where he forced the Poles to elect the Swedish candidate as their king. Peter meanwhile, with his imported officers and technicians, reformed the training, discipline, and weapons of the Russian army. Finally Charles XII invaded Russia with a large and well-prepared force. Peter used against him the strategy later used by the Russians against Napoleon and Adolf Hitler; he drew the Swedes into the endless plains, exposing them to the Russian winter, which happened to be an exceptionally severe one, and in 1709, at Poltava in south Russia, he met and overwhelmed the demoralized remainder. The entire Swedish army was destroyed at Poltava, only the king and a few hundred fugitives managing to escape across the Turkish frontier. Peter in the next years conquered Livonia and part of eastern Finland. He landed troops near Stockholm itself. He campaigned in Pomerania almost as far west as the Elbe. Never before had Russian influence reached so deeply into Europe. The imperial day of Sweden was now over, terminated by Russia. Peter had won for Russia a piece of the Baltic shore and with it warm-water outlets. These significant developments ending the great Northern War (1700–1721) were confirmed in the treaty of Nystadt in 1721.

War is surely not the father of all things, as has been sometimes claimed, but these wars did a good deal to father imperial Russia. The army was transformed from an Asiatic horde into a professional force of the kind maintained by Sweden, France, or Prussia. The elite of the old army had been the *streltsi*, a kind of Moscow guard, composed of nobles and constantly active in politics. A rebellion of the *streltsi* in 1698 had cut short Peter's tour of Europe; he had returned and quelled the mutiny by ferocious use of torture and execution, killing five of the rebels with his own hands. The *streltsi* were liquidated only two years before the great Russian defeat at Narva. Peter then rebuilt the army from the ground up. He employed European officers of many nationalities, paying them half again as much as native Russians of the same grades. He filled his ranks with soldiers supplied by districts on a territorial basis, somewhat as in Prussia. He put the troops into uniforms resembling those of the West and organized them in regiments of standardized composition. He armed them with muskets and artillery of the kind used in Europe and tried to create a service of supply. With this army he had not only driven the Swedes back into Sweden, but also dominated Russia itself. At the very time of the Swedish invasion large parts of the country were in rebellion, as in the days of Stephen Razin, for the whole middle and lower Volga, together with the Cossacks of the Don and Dnieper, rose against the tsar and rallied behind slogans of class war and hatred of the tsar's foreign experts. Peter crushed these disturbances with the usual ruthlessness. The Russian empire, loose and heterogeneous, was held together by military might.

While the war was still in progress, even before the decisive battle of Poltava, Peter laid the foundations of a wholly new city in territory conquered from the Swedes and inhabited not by Russians but by various Baltic peoples. Peter named it St. Petersburg after himself and his patron saint. From the beginning it was more truly a city than Louis' spectacular creation at Versailles established at almost the same time. Standing at the head of the Gulf of Finland, it was Peter's chief window on the West. Here he established the offices of government, required noblemen to build town houses, and gave favorable terms to foreign merchants and craftsmen to settle. Peter meant to make St. Petersburg a symbol of the new Russia, a new city facing toward Europe and drawing the minds of the Russians westward, replacing the old capital, Moscow, which faced toward Asia and was the stronghold of opposition to his westernizing program. St. Petersburg soon became one of the leading cities of northern Europe. It remained the capital of Russia until the Revolution of 1917 when Moscow resumed its old place. After the Revolution, until late in the twentieth century, St. Petersburg was called Leningrad.

Internal Changes under Peter the Great

The new army, the new city, the new and expanding government offices all required money, which in Russia was very scarce. Taxes were imposed on an inconceivable variety of objects—on heads, as poll taxes; on land; on inns, mills, hats, leather, cellars, and coffins; on the right to marry, sell meat, wear a beard, or be an Old Believer. The tax burden fell mainly on the peasants; and to assure the payment of taxes the mobility of peasants was further restricted, and borderline individuals were classified as peasants in the government records, so that serfdom became both more onerous and more nearly universal. To raise government revenues and to stimulate production Peter adopted the mercantilist policies exemplified by Colbert in France. He encouraged exports, built a fleet on the Baltic, and developed mining, metallurgy, and textiles, which were indispensable to the army. He organized mixed groups of Russians and foreigners into commercial companies, provided them with capital from government funds (little private capital being available), and gave them a labor supply by assigning them

THE GROWTH OF RUSSIA IN THE WEST

At the accession of Peter the Great in 1682 the Russian empire, expanding from the old grand duchy of Muscovy, had almost but not quite reached the Black and Baltic seas. Most of Peter's conquests were in the Baltic region where he pushed back the Swedes and built St. Petersburg. Under Catherine the Great (1762–1796) Russia took part in the three partitions of Poland and also reached the Black Sea. Tsar Alexander I (1801–1825), thanks largely to the Napoleonic wars, was able to acquire still more of Poland and annex Finland and Bessarabia; he also made conquests in the Caucasus. In the nineteenth century the western boundary of Russia remained stabilized but additional gains were made in the Caucasus. Russia also spread over northern Asia in the seventeenth century, first reaching the Pacific as early as 1630. (See also map, pp. 758–759.)

the use of serfs in a given locality. Serfdom, in origin mainly an agricultural institution, began to spread in Russia as an industrial institution also. The fact that serf owners obtained the right to sell serfs without land, or to move them from landed estates into mines or towns, made it easier for industry in Russia to develop on the basis of unfree labor. Nor were the employers of serfs, in these government enterprises, free to modify or abandon their projects at will. They too were simply in the tsar's service. The economic system rested largely on impressment of both management and labor, not on private profit and wages as in the increasingly capitalistic West. In this way Peter's efforts to force Russia to a European level of material productivity widened the gap between Russia and western Europe.

To oversee and operate this system of tax collecting, recruiting, economic

controls, serf hunting, and repression of internal rebellion Peter created a new administrative system. The old organs of local self-government wasted away. The duma and the national assembly, decadent anyway in that they could not function without disorder, disappeared. In their place Peter put a "senate" dependent on himself, and ten territorial areas called "governments," or *gubernii*—the very words were not Slavic but Latin and showed imitation of the West. The church he ruled through his Procurator of the Holy Synod.[26] At the top of the whole structure was himself, an absolute ruler, tsar, and autocrat of all the Russias. Before his death, dissatisfied with his son, he abolished the rule of hereditary succession to the tsardom, claiming the right for each tsar to name his own successor. Transmission of supreme power was thus put outside the domain of law, and in the following century the accession of tsars and tsarinas was marked by strife, conspiracy, and assassination. The whole system of centralized absolutism, while in form resembling that of the West, notably France, was in fact significantly different, for it lacked legal regularity, was handicapped by the insuperable ignorance of many officials, and was imposed on a turbulent and largely unwilling population. The empire of the Romanovs has been called a state without a people.

Peter, to assure the success of his westernizing program, developed what was called "state service," which had been begun by his predecessors. Virtually all

[26] See p. 239.

landowning and serf-owning aristocrats were required to serve in the army or civil administration. Offices were multiplied to provide places for all. In the state service birth counted for nothing. Peter used men of all classes; Prince Dolgoruky was of the most ancient nobility, Prince Menshikov had been a cook, the tax administrator Kurbatov was an ex-serf, and many others were foreigners of unknown background. Status in Peter's Russia depended not on inherited rank which Peter could not control, but on rank in his state service, civilian grades being equated with military, and all persons in the first eight grades being considered gentry. "History," wrote a Scot serving in Peter's army, "scarcely affords an example where so many people of low birth have been raised to such dignities as in tsar Peter's reign, or where so many of the highest birth and fortune have been leveled to the lowest ranks of life." In this respect especially, Peter's program resembled a true social revolution. It created a new governing element in place of the old, almost what in modern parlance would be called a party, a body of men working zealously for the new system with a personal interest in its preservation. These men, during Peter's lifetime and after his death, were the bulwarks against an anti-Western reaction, the main agents in making Peter's revolution stick. In time the new families became hereditary themselves. The priority of state service over personal position was abandoned a generation after Peter's death. Offices in the army and government were filled by men of property and birth. After Peter's revolution, as after some others, the new upper class became merged with the old.

Revolutionary also, suggesting the great French Revolution or the Russian Revolution of 1917, were Peter's unconcealed contempt for everything reminiscent of the old Russia and his zeal to reeducate his people in the new ways. He required all gentry to put their sons in school. He sent many abroad to study. He simplified the Russian alphabet. He edited the first newspaper to appear in Russia. He ordered the preparation of the first Russian book of etiquette, teaching his subjects not to spit on the floor, scratch themselves, or gnaw bones at dinner, to mix socially with women, take off their hats, converse pleasantly, and look at people while talking. The beard he took as a symbol of Muscovite backwardness; he forbade it in Russia, and himself shaved a number of men at his court. He forced people to attend evening parties to teach them manners. He had no respect for hereditary aristocracy, torturing or executing the highborn as readily as the peasants. As for religion, we are told that he was a pious man and enjoyed singing in church, but he was contemptuous of ecclesiastical dignity, and in one wild revel paraded publicly with drunken companions clothed in religious vestments and mocking the priests. Like most great revolutionists since his time he was aggressively secular.

The Results of Peter's Revolution

Peter's tactics provoked a strong reaction. Some adhered strictly to the old ways, others simply thought that Peter was moving too fast and too indiscriminately toward the new. Many Russians resented the inescapable presence of foreigners, who often looked down on Russians as savages, and who enjoyed special privileges such as the right of free exit from Russia and higher pay for similar employments. One center around which malcontents rallied was the church. Another was Peter's son Alexis, who declared that when he became tsar he would put a stop to the innovations and restore respect for the customs of old Russia. Peter, after some hesitation, finally put his own son to death. He ruled that each tsar should choose his own successor. He would stop at nothing to remake Russia in his own fashion.

Peter died in 1725, proclaimed "the Great" in his own lifetime by his admiring Senate. Few men in all history have exerted so strong an individual influence, which has indirectly become more far-reaching as the stature of Russia itself has grown. Though the years after Peter's death were years of turmoil and vacillation, his revolutionary changes held firm against those who would undo them. It is not simply that he Europeanized Russia and conquered a place on the Baltic; these developments might have come about in any case. It is by the methods he used, his impatient forcing of a new culture on Russia, that he set the future character of his empire. His methods fastened autocracy, serfdom, and bureaucracy more firmly upon the country. Yet he was able to reach only the upper classes. Many of these became more Europeanized than he could dream, habitually speaking French and living spiritually in France or in Italy. But as time went on many upper-class Russians, because of their very knowledge of Europe, became impatient of the stolid immovability of the peasants around them, sensed themselves as strangers in their own country, or were troubled by a guilty feeling that their position rested on the degradation and enslavement of human beings. Russian psychology, always mysterious to the West, could be explained in part by the violent paradoxes set up by rapid Europeanization. As for the peasant masses, they remained outside the system, egregiously exploited, estranged except by force of habit from their rulers and their social superiors, regarded by them as brutes or children, never sharing in any comparable way in their Europeanized civilization. These facts worked themselves out in later times. As for Peter's own time, Russia by his efforts came clearly out of its isolation, its vast bulk was now organized to play a part in international affairs, and its history thenceforward was a part of the history of Europe and increasingly of the world. Russia, like Prussia and the Austrian monarchy, was to be counted among the powers of Europe.

27. *The Partitions of Poland*

The fate of Poland in the eighteenth century reaches beyond the time limits of the present chapter, but it illustrates and brings together many of the strands traced in the preceding pages, so that a few words on it at this point may be useful. Poland in the eighteenth century, if Russia is considered non-European, was still by far the largest European state. It still reached from the Baltic almost to the Black Sea and extended eastward for 800 miles across the north-European plain. But it was the classic example, along with the Holy Roman Empire, of an older political structure which failed to develop modern organs of government.[27] It fell into ever deeper anarchy and confusion. Without army, revenues, or administration, internally divided among parties forever at cross-purposes, with many Poles more willing to bargain with foreigners than to work with each other,

[27] See pp. 217–219, and maps, pp. 212 and 216.

the country was a perpetual theater for diplomatic maneuvering and was finally absorbed by its growing neighbors.

The Polish royal elections in the eighteenth century were as usual the subject of international interference. The election of 1733 precipitated a European war known as the War of the Polish Succession. Two Polish kings in these years were in fact Germans. Stanislas I, a native Pole, was twice dethroned, but since he was supported by France, and was in fact the father of Louis XV's wife, he was set up for his own lifetime as duke of Lorraine. The former duke of Lorraine, by the facile play of the balance of power, became grand duke of Tuscany and the husband of the Habsburg Maria Theresa. After these troubles of the 1730s a reforming movement began to gather strength in Poland. Polish patriots hoped to do away with the *liberum veto* and other elements in the constitution that made government impossible.[28] Their efforts were repeatedly frustrated by foreign influence, notably that of Catherine II, tsarina of Russia (1762-1796), who preferred a Poland in which she could intervene at will. In 1763 she strengthened her hold over the country by obtaining the election of another Russian puppet, a Polish nobleman named Stanislas Poniatowski, her former lover, as king. She declared herself protector of the Polish liberties. It was to the Russian advantage to maintain the existing state of affairs in Poland, which enabled Russian influence to pervade the whole country, rather than to divide the country with neighbors who might exclude Russian influence from their own spheres. The Prussians, however, long awaiting the day when they might join the old duchy of Prussia with Brandenburg-Pomerania in one continuous territory, were more willing to entertain the prospect of a partition of Poland.

The opportunity presented itself in 1772 in connection with a war between Russia and Turkey, which threw the whole situation in eastern Europe into question.[29] The Turkish empire was at last showing unmistakable signs of weakness. Russian victories were so overwhelming that both Austrians and Prussians feared for the balance of power in that part of Europe. The Prussians therefore came forward with a proposal. It was a proposal to prevent an Austro-Russian war and to preserve the balance in eastern Europe by leaving the Ottoman Empire more or less intact, while having all three European powers annex territory from Poland instead. The proposition was accepted by the three parties.

The Russians called off their war with Turkey and withdrew their armies. By the treaty of Kuchuk Kainarji, a village in Romania, the sultan renounced his sovereignty over the Black Sea Tartars, admitted Russian shipping to the Black Sea and the Straits, and recognized the Russian government as the "protector" of Christian interests in Constantinople. The Russians soon used their advantage to absorb the north coast of the Black Sea, and to send Russian naval vessels into the Mediterranean for the first time.

Poland was meanwhile sacrificed. By the first partition, in 1772, its outer territories were cut away. Russia took an eastern slice, around the city of Vitebsk. Austria took a southern slice, the region known as Galicia. Prussia took the Pomerelian borderland in West Prussia. The Prussians thus at last realized their old ambition. Prussia now reached continuously as a solid block from the Elbe

---

[28] See p. 218.
[29] See p. 340.

to the borders of Lithuania.[30] The partition sobered the Poles, who renewed their efforts at a national revival, hoping to create an effective sovereignty which could secure the country against outsiders. But the Polish movement lacked deeper strength, for it was confined mainly to the nobles, who had themselves brought the country to ruin. The mass of the serf population, and the numerous Jews, did not care whether they were governed by Poles, Russians, or Germans.

Nevertheless, in what came to be called the Four Years' Diet, beginning in 1788, a reform party gathered strength. One of its members was King Stanislas Poniatowski himself, who had begun his reign as a protégé of the Russian empress. The reformers produced a new constitution in 1791. It made the Polish kingship hereditary, thus strengthening the executive government, and it reduced the powers of the great magnates while giving political rights to many burghers in the towns. By this time, however, the governments of eastern Europe were afraid of the French Revolution, which they saw as an outbreak of "Jacobinism." Denouncing the Polish reformers as Jacobins, the Russian tsarina said she would "fight Jacobinism and beat it in Poland." In collusion with a few disgruntled Polish noblemen she sent an army into Poland and destroyed the constitution of 1791. In agreement with Prussia she then carried out the Second Partition. In 1794 Thaddeus Kosciuszko led a more revolutionary attempt, which included even a proposed abolition of serfdom. Although it received no aid from the revolutionaries then governing France, it was crushed in the general European counterrevolution when Russian and Prussian armies again invaded Poland, defeated Kosciuszko, and in a Third Partition divided what remained of the country among themselves and Austria.[31] Poland as a political entity ceased to exist.

Many advanced thinkers of the day praised the partitions of Poland as a triumph of enlightened rulers, putting an end to an old nuisance. The three partitioning powers extenuated their conduct on various grounds, and even took pride in it as a diplomatic achievement by which war was prevented between them. What seemed to be robbery was justified by the argument that the gains were equal; this was the diplomatic doctrine of "compensation." It was argued also that the partitions of Poland put an end to an old cause of international rivalry and war, replacing anarchy with solid government in a large area of eastern Europe. It is a fact that Poland had been scarcely more independent before the partitions than after. It is to be noted also, though nationalist arguments were not used at the time, that on national grounds the Poles themselves had no claim to large parts of the old Poland. The regions taken by Russia, in all three partitions, were inhabited overwhelmingly by Byelorussians and Ukrainians, among whom the Poles were mainly a landlord class. Russia, even in the third partition, reached only to the true ethnic border of Poland. But later, after the fall of Napoleon, by general international agreement, the Russian sphere was extended deep into the territory inhabited by Poles.

The partitions of Poland, however extenuated, were nevertheless a great shock to the old system of Europe. Edmund Burke, in England, prophetically saw in the first partition the crumbling of the old international order. His diagnosis was

[30] See map, p. 230, panel 4.
[31] See p. 391.

POLAND SINCE THE EIGHTEENTH CENTURY

The top right panel shows, in simplified form, the ethnic composition of the area included in the great Poland of 1772. In addition to languages shown, Yiddish was spoken by the large scattered Jewish population. Note how the line set in 1795 as the western boundary of Russia persists through later transformations. It reappears as the eastern border of Napoleon's Grand Duchy (pp. 425–427), and of Congress Poland (pp. 447–450). After the First World War the victorious Allies contemplated much this same line as Poland's eastern frontier (the dotted line in the fourth panel, known as the Curzon Line); but the Poles in 1920-1921 conquered territory farther east (p. 752). After the Second World War the Russians pushed the Poles back to the same basic line, but compensated Poland with territory taken from Germany, as far west as the river Oder and its tributary, the Neisse. If readers will compare the position of Warsaw in each panel they will see how Poland has been shoved westward.

a shrewd one. The principle of the balance of power had been historically invoked to preserve the independence of European states, to secure weak or small ones against universal monarchy. It was now used to destroy the independence of a weak but ancient kingdom. Not that Poland was the first to be "partitioned"; the Spanish and Swedish empires had been partitioned, and during the eighteenth century there were attempts to partition Prussia and the Austrian empire also. But Poland was the first to be partitioned without war and the first to disappear totally. That Poland was partitioned without war, a source of great satisfaction to the partitioning powers, was still a very unsettling fact. It was alarming for a huge state to vanish simply by cold diplomatic calculation. It seemed that no established rights were safe even in peacetime. The partitions of Poland showed that in a world where great powers had arisen, controlling modern apparatus of state, it was dangerous not to be strong. They suggested that any area failing to develop a sovereign state capable of keeping out foreign infiltration, and so situated as to be reached by the great powers of Europe, was unlikely to retain its independence. In this way they anticipated, for example, the partitions of Africa a century later, when Africa too, lacking strong governments, was almost totally divided, without war, among half a dozen states of Europe.

Moreover the partitions of Poland, while maintaining the balance in eastern Europe, profoundly changed the balance of Europe as a whole. The disappearance of Poland was a blow to France, which had long used Poland, as it had used Hungary and Turkey, as an outpost of French influence in the East. The three Eastern powers expanded their territory, while France enjoyed henceforth no permanent growth. Eastern Europe bulked larger than ever before in the affairs of Europe. Prussia, Russia, and the Austrian empire became contiguous. They had an interest in common, the repression of Polish resistance to their rule. Polish resistance, dating from before the partitions and continuing after them, was the earliest example of modern revolutionary nationalism in Europe. The independence of Poland, and of other submerged nationalities, became in time a cause much favored in western Europe, while the three great monarchies of eastern Europe were drawn together in common opposition to national liberation; and this fact, plus the fact that the eastern monarchies were primarily landlord states, accentuated the characteristic division of Europe, in the nineteenth century, between a West that inclined to be liberal and an East that inclined to be reactionary. But these ideas anticipate a later part of the story.

In summary, during the eighteenth century, the whole of Eastern Europe north of the Balkans, which is to say north of the Ottoman Empire, had been absorbed by the three monarchies of Russia, Prussia, and Austria. These three empires remained contiguous, except for a few years under Napoleon, covering the whole area until they all collapsed in the First World War. Between the First and Second World Wars Poland and the Baltic states enjoyed twenty years of independence, only to fall subject to the Soviet Union as a consequence of the Second World War. Not until the late twentieth century did Poland reaffirm its national identity, in the 1980s, and the Baltic states regain their independence, in 1991.

VI.
THE STRUGGLE
FOR WEALTH
AND EMPIRE

IN THE PRECEDING chapters we saw how western Europe, and especially England and France, by about the year 1700, came to occupy a position of leadership in Europe as a whole. We have traced the political history of western Europe through the War of the Spanish Succession, terminated in 1713–1714 by the treaties of Utrecht and Rastadt. Affairs of central Europe and Germany have been carried to 1740. In that year a new kingdom of Prussia and a new or renovated Austrian monarchy, each passing into the hands of a new ruler, stood on the eve of a struggle for ascendancy in central Europe. As for eastern Europe, we have observed the Europeanizing and expansion of the Russian empire, and seen how the vast area called Poland ceased to form an independent state.

More important in the long run than these political events, and going on through the seventeenth and eighteenth centuries, was the cumulative increase of all forms of knowledge, to which we turn in the two chapters that follow. Equally important was the growing wealth of Europe, or at least of the Atlantic region north of Spain. The new wealth, in the widest sense, meaning conveniences of every kind, resulted from new technical and scientific knowledge, which in turn it helped to produce; and the two together, more wealth and more knowledge, helped to form one of the most far-reaching ideas of modern times, the idea of progress, which retained its force well into the twentieth century.

The new wealth of Europe was not like the age-old wealth of the gorgeous East, said by Milton to "shower on her kings barbaric pearl and gold." It consisted of gold, to be sure, but even more of bank deposits and facilities for

Chapter Emblem: A Spanish doubloon or gold coin minted in 1790, showing Charles IV as King of Spain and the Indies.

credit, of more and better devices for mining coal, casting iron, and spinning thread, more productive agriculture, better and more comfortable houses, a wider variety of diet on the table, more and improved sailing ships, warehouses, and docks; more books, more newspapers, more medical instruments, more scientific equipment; greater government revenues, larger armies, and more numerous government employees. In the wealthy European countries, and because of the growing wealth, more people were freed from the necessity of toiling for food, clothing, and shelter, and were enabled to devote themselves to all sorts of specialized callings in government, management, finance, war, teaching, writing, inventing, exploring, and researching, and in producing the amenities rather than the barest necessities of life.

28. Elite and Popular Cultures

The accumulation of wealth and knowledge was not evenly distributed among the various social classes.[1] There had always been differences between rich and poor, with many gradations between the extremes, but at the time we are now considering, as the seventeenth century turned into the eighteenth, there came to be a more obvious distinction between elite and popular cultures. The terms are hard to define. The elite culture was not exactly the culture of the rich and well-to-do, nor was the popular culture limited to the general run of the people. The world "elite" suggests a minority within a given range of interests; thus there are elites not only of wealth, but of social position and of power; elites of fashion, of patronage and connoisseurship in the arts, and of artists themselves; elites of education, of special training as in medicine and law, and of discovery and accomplishment in technology and the sciences. In general, persons taking part in an elite culture could share at will in the popular culture, by attending public amusements or simply by talking familiarly with their servants. But the relation was asymmetric. Those born in popular culture could not share in the culture of the elites, at least not without transforming themselves, through education or marriage, which could occur only in exceptional cases.

A main difference was simply one of language. At the popular level people generally used a local form of speech, varying from one place to another, with a distinctive accent, and full of words that had become obsolete elsewhere, or that might not be understood even a few miles away. In the Middle Ages this variety had been overcome by the use of Latin. Since the invention of printing and the rise of national literatures, and with the spreading influence of schools, of which we have seen that many were founded between 1550 and 1650, there came to be standard forms of English, French, Italian, and other languages, employed by all educated persons. Grammar and spelling became regularized. Virtually all printing was in a national language when it was not in Latin. Since only a minority were able to get the necessary education, the mass of the people continued to speak as they did before. Their way of talking was now considered a dialect, a peasant language, or what was called *patois* in French or *Volkssprache* in German. And while it may be true, as some scientific philologists have said, that no form

[1] See pp. 121–123.

of speech is "better" than another, it is also true that facility in the national language was a sign of elite culture until the spread of universal elementary schooling in the nineteenth century. It gave access to at least certain segments of the elite culture, as it continues to do today.

The elite culture was transmitted largely by way of books, although acquired also by word of mouth within favored families and social circles. The popular culture was predominantly oral, although also expressed in cheaply printed almanacs, chapbooks, woodcuts, and broadsides. Since it was so largely oral, and left so few written records, popular culture is difficult for historians to reconstruct, although it made up the daily lives, interests, and activities of the great majority in all countries. It must always be remembered that what we read as history, in this as in most other books, is mostly an account of the work of minorities, either of power-wielders, decision-makers, and innovators whose actions nevertheless affected whole peoples, or of writers and thinkers whose ideas appealed to a limited audience. Persons who were illiterate or barely literate changed their ideas more slowly than the more mobile and more informed members of the elite. Great movements initiated by minorities spread slowly, generation after generation, to wider social classes, so that what was characteristic of popular culture at a given moment, such as a belief in magic, had often been common to all classes a century or two before.

The humanism of the Renaissance, being transmitted so largely through books and the study of Greek and Latin, remained limited to the elite culture. The strength of the Protestant Reformation lay in combining the efforts of highly educated persons, such as Luther and Calvin, with the anger, distress, disillusionment, and hopes of many very ordinary people. The rise of science and the ensuing Enlightenment, to be considered in the two following chapters, were originated by small numbers of experimenters and writers but slowly reshaped the thinking of others. The process of diffusion might be slow and uncertain. Astrology, for example, was in the Middle Ages a branch of scientific inquiry; in the seventeenth century astrologers were still consulted by emperors and kings; then divination by the stars was denounced by both the clergy and secular thinkers as a superstition, and astrology was expelled from astronomy, but horoscopes are still to be found in American and European newspapers in our own time.

The differences of wealth, if not wholly decisive, were of great importance. Culture in the broader or anthropologist's sense of the word includes material circumstances of food, drink, and shelter. In some respects the lot of the poor in the seventeenth century was worse than in the Middle Ages. Less meat was eaten in Europe, because as population grew there was less land available for the raising of livestock. With the growth of a market economy many peasants raised wheat, but ate bread made of rye, barley, or oats, or even looked for acorns and roots in times of famine. The consumption of bread by working people in France in the eighteenth century was about a pound per day per person, because little else except cabbages and beans was eaten on ordinary days; after 1750 the use of white bread became more usual. Meanwhile the rich, or the merely affluent, developed more delicate menus prepared by professional cooks, one of whom is said to have committed suicide when his soufflé fell.

In the towns the poor lived in crowded and unwholesome buildings, and in the country in dark and shabby cabins where stoves only gradually replaced holes in the roof for the escape of smoke. The poor had no glass in their windows, the middle classes had some, and the rich had glass windows and mirrors in profusion. In humble homes the dishes were wooden bowls, slowly replaced by pewter, while china plates began to appear on the tables of the more well-to-do. Table forks, with one for each diner, originating in Italy, were brought to France by Catherine de Medici along with other items of Italian culture, and soon spread among those able to afford them, though Louis XIV still preferred to use his fingers. Silver bowls and pitchers were ancient, but became more elaborate and more often seen in upper-class circles. The poor had no furniture, or only a few benches and a mat to sleep on; the middle classes had chairs and beds; the rich not only had substantial furniture but were becoming more conscious of style. Among persons of adequate income it became usual to have houses with specialized rooms, such as separate bedrooms, and a dining room. The prominent and the fashionable fitted out rooms for social receptions and entertainments, called salons in France, with walls of wood paneling, lighted by chandeliers reflected in mirrors, and provided with sofas and armchairs, which the invention of upholstery made more comfortable. The poor, after dark, huddled on chests or on the floor by a single candle.

In the use of beverages the seventeenth century saw progress, if that is the right word. Coffee and tea, along with sugar and tobacco, all imported from overseas, were exotic rarities in 1600, more widely enjoyed in 1700, and available to all but the very destitute by the time of the French Revolution. Coffee shops developed, and taverns multiplied. Cheap wines became more plentiful in southern Europe, as did beer in the north. The distillation of alcohol had been developed in the Middle Ages, when brandy, a distilled wine, was used as a medicine; by the seventeenth century it was a familiar drink. Whisky and gin also came into use at about this time. The taverns and coffee shops offered a place for neighborly gatherings for the middling and lower sorts of the population, but drunkenness also became more of a social problem, especially for the working classes that could not drink in domestic privacy, and so made themselves visible in the streets, as shown by Hogarth's pictures of "Gin Lane" in London about 1750. Arising from all this poverty and disorganization, especially in the large cities, was an increase in illegitimacy and abandonment of children. It was calculated that in Paris in 1780 there were 7,000 abandoned children for 30,000 births, but many of these infants were brought from the country to be deposited in the foundling hospitals of the city, which were overwhelmed.

There was much that persons of all classes and cultures shared. Most important, in principle, was religion. The refined and the rude, the learned and the untutored, heard the same sermons in church, were baptized, married, and buried by the same sacraments, often by the same priest, and were subject to religious and moral obligations that transcended the boundaries of social class. Such was most likely to be the case in small communities of unmixed religion, or where the lord and lady of the manor attended the same church as the villagers. Where different churches existed in fact, whether or not officially tolerated, religion played less of a role in social cohesion. In England, for example, the Nonconformists, who succeeded the old Puritans after the Stuart Restoration, developed a kind of middle-class culture that was noticeably different from the culture of the Anglican gentry. Rich families in both Protestant and Catholic countries might have their own private chaplains and build chapels of their own. In towns that were big enough for neighborhood diversification some churches became fashionable and others merely popular. In any case some people in the seventeenth century were not very good Christians at all; these would include those in inaccessible rural areas as well as some of the poorest in the larger towns, who were often uprooted and homeless migrants from an overcrowded countryside. Reforming bishops, especially in France, undertook to ameliorate the situation, so that the seventeenth century was a great age of internal missionary work, and it may be that in the following century, as skepticism began to pervade the elite culture, the popular culture was more Christianized than it had been in the past.

Rich and poor were also subject to the same diseases, the same dangers of tainted food and polluted water, and the same smells and filth in noisy streets littered with horse droppings, puddles, and garbage. Not of course equally: in the elite culture people called on the service of doctors, who had been trained in the universities, while ordinary sufferers sought out popular healers, who were often women; and it made a difference whether one rode through the streets in a coach, as the affluent did, or picked one's way on foot with the common people. Congestion was worst in rapidly growing cities, such as London, Paris, Amsterdam, and Naples, where the differences between wealth and poverty were both more extreme and more shockingly visible. There were recurrent fears of shortage of food, as crop failure or local famine struck this or that region, in which case some starved and some ate less, while those able to do so simply paid higher prices. In some towns charitable organizations developed, often on the initiative of upper-class women, to finance and assist religious sisters in relief of the poor. Hunger and the fear of hunger sometimes produced riots, which however had little political significance except insofar as upper-class people tried to make use of them for their own purposes.

It was also in less material aspects that the elite and popular cultures increasingly diverged. The upper strata set a new importance on polite manners, in which the French now set the tone, with much bowing, doffing of hats, and exchange of compliments, beside which the manners of ordinary people now seemed uncouth.[2] The etiquette of princely courts became more formal, the court fools and jesters disappeared, and royalty surrounded itself not with rough retainers but with ladies and gentlemen. About 1600 the plays of Shakespeare were staged in public theaters where all classes mixed and enjoyed the same performance, but in the following century it became usual for the upper classes to have private theaters, of the kind shown on p. 204. People of higher social position took to stylish dancing, which their children had to learn from dancing teachers, while plain people continued to cavort more spontaneously in country dances and jigs. For evening parties, the polite world met in salons to engage in bright conversation, while working people, especially in the country, met in a neighbor's house after the day's labors were over, and there, while the men mended their implements and the women mended the clothes, engaged in local gossip, or listened to storytellers, or sat by while someone read aloud from one of the cheaply printed books that were now widely circulated.

Enough of these books have survived, along with popular almanacs, to make

---

[2] On etiquette see pp. 59–60 and 186–187.

it possible to form some ideas of the mental horizons of the nonliterate and inarticulate classes. They were often written by printers or their employees or by others who were in effect intermediaries between the elite and popular cultures, and who purposely addressed themselves to what they knew of popular interests. The almanacs purveyed astrological observations, advice on the weather, proverbs, and scraps of what had once been science but was now offered as occult wisdom. Other little books undertook to teach the ABCs, or told how to behave in church, how to approach persons of the other sex, how to show respect for superiors, or how to compose a proper letter of love, thanks, or condolence, or have such a letter written by the professional letter writers to whose services illiterate persons resorted. Still others put into print the stories that had long circulated in the oral tradition, fairy tales, saints' lives, or accounts of the doings of outlaws such as Robin Hood. Miracles, prodigies, witches, ogres, angels, and the devil figured prominently in such narratives. It is a curious fact that where educated persons were now schooled in Greek mythology and admired the heroes of ancient Rome, the plain people were still engrossed by tales of medieval chivalry, knights errant, and holy hermits that had once been avidly listened to in baronial halls. Memories of the times of King Arthur and Charlemagne lingered in the popular consciousness. There were many long and complex tales of the exploits of Roland and other paladins who had fought for Christianity against the infidels, all set in a world of faraway adventure without definite location in time or place. Saracens, Moors, Turks, and Muslims in general, along with Jews, were generally seen in such stories as a menace.

Belief in witchcraft and magic was to be found in 1600 in all social classes. The witches in *Macbeth* were perfectly believable to Shakespeare's audience. Learned books were still written on these subjects, and indeed it may be that learned writers, and the judges in law courts, had stirred up more anxiety about witches and magicians than ordinary people would otherwise have felt. By 1700 a great change was evident; witches, magicians, and miscellaneous enchantments were disappearing from the elite culture, but they still figured in the popular mind. Unaffected as yet by either science or doubt, ordinary people inclined to think that there was something true about magic, which they distinguished as good and bad. Good magic unlocked the "secrets" of nature; popular writings on alchemy told of famous sages of the past who knew how to turn base metals into gold; there were special formulas that added to the efficacy of prayer; there were old women who had a secret knowledge of medicinal herbs, in which indeed there might be some pragmatic value, but which was blended with the mysterious and the occult. Bad magic was used to cause harm; it taught the black arts; it gave force to curses; it often involved a compact with the devil; it was what made witches so fearsome. By 1700 such ideas were subsiding. Judges no longer believed that such powers existed, and so would no longer preside at witchcraft trials. The same may be said of belief in prophecies and oracles; in the elite culture only those recorded in the Old Testament retained any credibility, but there was still a popular acceptance of recent prophecies and foretellings of the future.

Popular culture continued to express itself also in fairs and carnivals. For men and women who lived limited lives these were exciting events that occurred only at certain times of the year, and to which people flocked from miles around. At the fairs one could buy things that local shops and wandering peddlers could not supply. There would be puppet shows, jugglers, and acrobats. There were conjurers who refused to admit like modern magicians that they were using merely natural means. A mountebank was someone who mounted a platform (*banco* in Italian) where he sold questionable remedies for various ills, while keeping up a patter of jokes and stories, often accompanied by a clown. Blind singers and traveling musicians entertained the throngs, and for the tougher minded there were cockfights and bear baiting. In such a hubbub itinerant preachers might denounce the vanities of this world, or throw doubt on the wisdom of bishops and lawyers.

Carnival went on for several weeks preceding Lent. The word itself, from the Italian *carne vale,* meant "farewell to meat," from which good Christians were to abstain during the forty-day Lenten fast; in France it climaxed in the Mardi Gras ("fat Tuesday"). It persisted in Protestant countries also. It was a time for big eating and heavy drinking, and for general merrymaking and foolery. Comical processions marched through the streets. Farces were performed, and mock sermons delivered. Young men showed their strength in tugs-of-war, footraces, and a rough-and-tumble kind of football. A common theme was what was called in England "the world turned upside down." Men and women put on each other's clothing. Horses were made to move backward with the rider facing the tail. Little street dramas showed the servant giving orders to the master, the judge sitting in the stocks, the pupil beating the teacher, or the husband holding the baby while the wife clutched a gun. In general, the carnival was a time for defying custom and ridiculing authority. It is hard to know how much such outbursts were expressions of genuine resentments, and how much they were only a form of play. They could, indeed, be both.

In 1600 people of all classes took part in these festive activities. In the following century, as both the Protestant and the Catholic reformations extended their influences, the clergy undertook to purge such public events of what they considered excesses, and with the growth of the state the civil authorities began to frown on them as incitements to subversion. By 1700 the people of elite culture, the wealthy, the fashionable, and the educated, were more inclined to stay away, or attended only as spectators to be amused at the simple pleasures of the common people. In the eighteenth century, as the various elites took to more formal manners and to neoclassicism in literature and the arts, the gulf between the elite and popular cultures widened. The clergy campaigned against necromancy and tried to restrain the faithful in the matter of pilgrimages and veneration of dubious local saints. As the medical profession developed, the popular healers and venders of nostrums were seen as charlatans and quacks. As scientific and other knowledge increased, those who lacked it appeared simply as ignorant. It may be said both that the elites withdrew from the popular culture, and that the people as a whole had not yet been brought into the pale of higher civilization. In any case, class distinctions became sharper than ever. But nothing ever stands still, and before the year 1800 there were persons in the elite culture who were beginning to "rediscover" the people, to collect ballads and fairy tales, and lay a foundation for what in the nineteenth century was called "folklore."[3]

---

[3] See pp. 437–438 and 469–471.

29. The Global Economy of the Eighteenth Century

The opening of the Atlantic in the sixteenth century, it will be recalled, had reoriented Europe. In an age of oceanic communications western Europe became a center from which America, Asia, and Africa could all be reached. A global economy had been created. The first to profit from it had been the Portuguese and Spanish, and they retained their monopoly through most of the sixteenth century, but the decline of the Portuguese and Spanish paved the way for the triumph of the British, the French, and the Dutch. In the eighteenth century the outstanding economic development was the expansion of the global economy and the fact that Europe became incomparably wealthier than any other part of the world.

Commerce and Industry in the Eighteenth Century

The increase of wealth was brought about by the methods of commercial capitalism and handicraft industry. Though the Industrial Revolution in England is usually dated from 1760 or 1780, it was not until the nineteenth century that the use of steam engines and power-driven machinery, and the growth of large factories and great manufacturing cities, brought about the conditions of modern industrialism. The economic system of the eighteenth century, while it contained within itself the seeds of later industrialism, represented the flowering of the older merchant capitalism, domestic industry, and mercantilist government policies which had grown up since the sixteenth century and which have been already described.[4]

Most people in the eighteenth century lived in the country. Agriculture was the greatest single industry and source of wealth. Cities remained small. London and Paris, the largest of Europe, each had a population of 600,000 or 700,000, but the next largest cities did not much exceed 200,000, and in all Europe at the time of the French Revolution (in 1789) there were only fifty cities with as many as 50,000 people. Urbanization, however, was no sign of economic advancement. Spain, Italy, and even the Balkan peninsula, according to an estimate made in the 1780s, each had more large cities (over 50,000) than did Great Britain. Urbanization did not equate with industry because most industry was carried on in the country, by peasants and part-time agricultural workers who worked for the merchant capitalists of the towns. Thus, while it is true to say that most people still lived in the country, it would be false to say that their lives and labors were devoted to agriculture exclusively. One English estimate, made in 1739, held that there were 4,250,000 persons "engaged in manufactures" in the British Isles, a figure that included women and children, and comprised almost half the entire population. These people worked characteristically in their own cottages, employed as wage earners by merchant capitalists under the "domestic" system.[5] Almost half of them, about 1,500,000, were engaged in the weaving and processing of woolens. Others were in the copper, iron, lead, and tin manufactures; others in leather goods; much smaller were the paper, glass, porcelain, silk, and linen trades; and smallest of all, in 1739, was the manufacture of cotton cloth, which

[4] See pp. 114–120.
[5] See p. 117.

accounted for only about 100,000 workers. The list suggests the importance of nonagricultural occupations in the preindustrial age.

England, even with half its population engaged at least part of the time in manufactures, was not yet the unrivaled manufacturing country that it was to become after 1800. England in the eighteenth century produced no more iron than Russia and no more manufactures than France. The population of England was still small; it began to grow rapidly about 1760, but as late as 1800 France was still twice as populous as England and Scotland together. France, though less intensively developed than England, with probably far less than half its people "engaged in manufactures," nevertheless, because of its greater size, remained the chief industrial center of Europe.

Although foreign and colonial trade grew rapidly in the eighteenth century, it is probable that, in both Great Britain and France, the domestic or internal trade was greater in volume and occupied more people. Great Britain, with no internal tariffs, with an insignificant guild system, and with no monopolies allowed within the country except to inventors, was the largest area of internal free trade in Europe. France, or at least Colbert's Five Great Farms,[6] offered a free-trading internal market hardly less great. A great deal of economic activity was therefore domestic, consisting of exchange between town and town or between region and region. The proportions between domestic and international trade cannot be known. But foreign trade was important in that the largest enterprises were active in it, the greatest commercial fortunes were made in it, and the most capital was accumulated from it. And it was the foreign trade that led to international rivalry and war.

The World Economy: The Dutch, British, and French

On the international economic scene a great part was still played by the Dutch. After the Peace of Utrecht the Dutch ceased to be a great political power, but their role in commerce, shipping, and finance remained undiminished, or diminished only relatively by the continuing commercial growth of France and Great Britain. They were still the middlemen and common carriers for other peoples. Their freight rates remained the lowest of Europe. They continued to grow rich on imports from the East Indies. To a large extent also, in the eighteenth century, the Dutch simply lived on their investments. The capital they had accumulated over two hundred years they now lent out to French or British or other entrepreneurs. Dutch capital was to be found in every large commercial venture of Europe and was lent to governments far and wide. A third of the capital of the Bank of England in the mid–eighteenth century belonged to Dutch shareholders. The Bank of Amsterdam remained the chief clearing house and financial center of Europe. Its supremacy ended only with the invasion of Holland by a French Revolutionary army in 1795.

The Atlantic trade routes, leading to America, to Africa, and to Asia, tempted the merchants of many nationalities in Europe. A great many East India companies were established—usually to do business in America as well as the East, for the "Indies" at the beginning of the eighteenth century was still a general term for

[6] See p. 188.

the vast regions overseas. Both the English and the French East India companies were reorganized, with an increased investment of capital, shortly after 1700. A number of others were established—by the Scots, the Swedes, the Danes, the imperial free city of Hamburg, the republic of Venice, Prussia, and the Austrian monarchy. But, with the exception of the Danish company which lasted some sixty years, they all failed after only a few years, either for insufficiency of capital or because they lacked strong diplomatic, military, and naval support. Their failure showed that, in the transocean trade, unassisted business enterprise was not enough. Merchants needed strong national backing to succeed in this sphere. Neither free city, nor small kingdom, nor tiny republic, nor the amorphous Austrian empire provided a firm enough base.

It was the British and French who won out in the commercial rivalry of the eighteenth century. Britain and France were alike in having, besides a high level of industrial production at home, governments organized on a national scale and able to protect and advance, under mercantilist principles, the interests of their merchants in distant countries. For both peoples the eighteenth century—or the three-quarters of a century between the end of the War of the Spanish Succession in 1713 and the beginning of the French Revolution in 1789—was an age of spectacular enrichment and commercial expansion.

Although the trade figures are difficult to arrive at, French foreign and colonial trade may well have grown even more rapidly than the British in the years between the 1720s and the 1780s. In any event, by the 1780s, the two countries were about equal in their total foreign and colonial trade. The British in the 1780s enjoyed proportionately more of the trade with America and Asia, the French more of the trade with the rest of Europe and the Near East. The contest for markets played an important part in the colonial and commercial wars between Britain and France all through the eighteenth century and on into the final and climactic struggle, and British triumph, in the time of Napoleon.

Asia, America, and Africa in the Global Economy

In the expanding global economy of the eighteenth century each continent played its special part. The trade with Asia was subject to an ancient limitation. Asia was almost useless as a market for European manufactures. There was much that Europeans wanted from Asia, but almost nothing that Asians wanted from Europe. The peoples of Chinese, Indian, and Malay culture had elaborate civilizations with which they were content; they lacked the dynamic restlessness of Europeans, and the masses were so impoverished (more so even than in Europe) that they could buy nothing anyway. Europeans found that they could send little to Asia except gold. The drain of gold from Europe to Asia had gone on since ancient times and, accumulating over the centuries, was one source of the fabulous treasures of Oriental princes. To finance the swelling demand for Asian products it was necessary for Europeans constantly to replenish their stocks of gold. The British found an important new supply in Africa along the Gulf of Guinea, where one region (the present Ghana) was long called the Gold Coast. The word "guinea" became the name of a gold coin minted in England from 1663 to 1813 and long remained a fashionable way of saying twenty-one shillings.

What Europeans sought from Asia was still in part spices—pepper and ginger, cinnamon and cloves—now brought in mainly by the Dutch from their East India islands. But they wanted manufactured goods also. Asia was still in some lines superior to Europe in technical skill. It is enough to mention rugs, chinaware, and cotton cloth. The very names by which cotton fabrics are known in English and other European languages reveal the places from which they were thought to come. "Madras" and "calico" refer to the Indian cities of Madras and Calicut, "muslin" to the Arabic city of Mosul. "Gingham" comes from a Malay word meaning "striped"; "chintz" from a Hindustani word meaning "spotted." Most of the Eastern manufactures were increasingly imitated in the eighteenth century in Europe. Axminster and Aubusson carpets competed with Oriental rugs. In 1709 a German named Boettcher discovered a formula for making a vitreous and translucent substance comparable to the porcelain of China; this European "china," made at Sèvres, Dresden, and in England, soon competed successfully with the imported original. Cotton fabrics were never produced in Europe at a price to compete with India until after the introduction of power machinery, which began in England about 1780. Before that date the demand for Indian cotton goods was so heavy that the woolen, linen, and silk interests became alarmed. They could produce nothing like the sheer muslins and bright calico prints which caught the public fancy, and many governments, to protect the jobs and capital involved in the old European textile industries, simply forbade the import of Indian cottons altogether. But it was a time of many laws and little enforcement, the forbidden fabrics continued to come in, and Daniel Defoe observed in 1708 that, despite the laws, cottons were not only sought as clothing by all classes, but "crept into our houses, our closets and bedchambers; curtains, cushions, chairs and at last beds themselves were nothing but calicoes or Indian stuffs." Gradually, in the face of tariff protection for "infant industries" in Europe, and the rapid growth of European cotton manufactures, import of cottons and other manufactures from Asia declined. After about 1770 most of the imports of the British East India Company consisted of tea, which was brought from China.

America in the eighteenth century bulked larger than Asia in the trade of western Europe. The American trade was based mainly on one commodity—sugar. Sugar had long been known in the East, and in the European Middle Ages little bits of it had trickled through to delight the palates of lords and prelates. About 1650 sugar cane was brought in quantities from the East and planted in the West Indies by Europeans. A whole new economic system arose in a few decades. It was based on the "plantation." A plantation was an economic unit consisting of a considerable tract of land, a sizable investment of capital, often owned by absentees in France or England, and a force of impressed labor, supplied by blacks brought from Africa as slaves. Sugar, produced in quantity with cheap labor at low cost, proved to have an inexhaustible market. The eighteenth century was the golden age, economically speaking, of the West Indies. From its own islands alone, during the eighty years from 1713 to 1792, Great Britain imported a total of £162,000,000 worth of goods, almost all sugar; imports from India and China, in the same eighty years, amounted to only £104,000,000. The little islands of Jamaica, Barbados, St. Kitts, and others, as suppliers of Europe, not only dwarfed the whole mainland of British America but the whole mainland of Asia as well. For

France, less well established than Britain on the American mainland and in Asia, the same holds with greater force. The richest of all the sugar colonies, San Domingo, now called Haiti, belonged to France.

The plantation economy, first established in sugar, and later in cotton (after 1800), brought Africa into the foreground. Slaves had been obtained from Black Africa from time immemorial, both by the Roman Empire and by the Muslim world, both of which, however, enslaved blacks and whites indiscriminately. After the European discovery of America, blacks were taken across the Atlantic by the Spanish and Portuguese. Dutch traders landed them in Virginia in 1619, a year before the arrival of the Pilgrim Fathers in Massachusetts. But slavery in the Americas before 1650 may be described as occasional. With the rise of the plantation economy after 1650, and especially after 1700, it became a fundamental economic institution. Slavery now formed the labor supply of a very substantial and heavily capitalized branch of world production. About 610,000 blacks were landed from Africa in the island of Jamaica alone between 1700 and 1786. Total figures are hard to give, but it is certain that, until well after 1800, far more Africans than Europeans made the voyage to the Americas. The transatlantic slave trade in the eighteenth century was conducted mainly by English-speaking interests, principally in England but also in New England, followed as closely as they could manage it by the French. Yearly export of merchandise from Great Britain to Africa, used chiefly in exchange for slaves, increased tenfold between 1713 and 1792. As for merchandise coming into Britain from the British West Indies, virtually all produced by slaves, in 1790 it constituted almost a fourth of all British imports. If we add British imports from the American mainland, including what in 1776 became the United States, the importance of black labor to the British economic system will appear still greater, since a great part of exports from the mainland consisted of agricultural products, such as tobacco and indigo, produced partly by slaves. It can scarcely be denied that the phenomenal rise of British capitalism in the eighteenth century was based to a considerable extent on the enslavement of Africans. The town of Liverpool, an insignificant place on the Irish Sea in 1700, built itself up by the slave trade and the trade in slave-produced wares to a busy transatlantic commercial center, which in turn, as will be seen later, stimulated the "industrial revolution" in Manchester and other neighboring towns.[7]

The west-European merchants, British, French, and Dutch, sold the products of America and Asia to their own peoples and those of central and eastern Europe. Trade with Germany and Italy was fairly stable. With Russia it enormously increased. To cite the British record only, Britain imported fifteen times as much goods from Russia in 1790 as in 1700, and sold the Russians six times as much. The Russian landlords, as they became Europeanized, desired Western manufactures and the colonial products such as sugar, tobacco, and tea which could be purchased only from western Europeans. They had grain, timber, and naval stores to offer in return. Similarly, landlords of Poland and north Germany, in the seventeenth and eighteenth centuries, found themselves increasingly able to move their agricultural products out through the Baltic and hence increasingly

[7] See p. 459.

able to buy the products of western Europe, America, and Asia in return. Landlords of eastern Europe thus had an incentive to make their estates more productive. "Big" agriculture spread, developing in eastern Europe a system not unlike the plantation economy of the New World. It had many effects. It contributed, along with political causes, to reducing the bulk of the east-European population to serfdom. It helped to civilize and refine, in a word to "Europeanize," the upper classes. And it helped to enrich the merchants of western Europe.[8]

The Wealth of Western Europe: Social Consequences

The wealth which accumulated along the Atlantic seaboard of Europe was, in short, by no means produced by the efforts of western Europeans only. All the world contributed to its formation. The natural resources of the Americas, the resources and skills of Asia, the gold and manpower of Africa, all alike went into producing the vastly increased volume of goods moving in world commerce. Europeans directed the movement. They supplied capital; they contributed technical and organizing abilities; and it was the demand of Europeans, at home in Europe and as traders abroad, that set increasing numbers of Indians to spinning cotton, Chinese to raising tea, Malays to gathering spices, and Africans to the tending of sugar cane. A few non-Europeans might benefit in the process— Indian or Chinese merchants "subsidized" by the East Indian companies, African chiefs who captured slaves from neighboring tribes and sold them to Europeans. But the profits of the world economy really went to Europe. The new wealth, over and above what was necessary to keep the far-flung and polyglot labor force in being, and to pay other expenses, piled up in Britain, Holland, and France.

Here it was owned by private persons. It accumulated within the system of private property and as part of the institutions of private enterprise or private capitalism. Governments were dependent on these private owners of property, for governments, in western Europe, had no important sources of revenue except loans and taxes derived from their peoples. When the owners of wealth gave their support, the government was strong and successful, as in England. When they withdrew support, the government collapsed, as it was to collapse in France in the Revolution of 1789.

In a technical sense there were many "capitalists" in western Europe, persons who had a little savings which they used to buy a parcel of land or a loom or entrusted to some other person to invest at interest. And in a general sense the new wealth was widely distributed; the standard of living rose in western Europe in the eighteenth century. Tea, for example, which cost as much as £10 a pound when introduced into England about 1650, was an article of common consumption a hundred years later. But wealth used to produce more wealth, i.e., capital, was owned or controlled in significant amounts by relatively few persons. In the eighteenth century some people became unprecedentedly rich (including some who started quite poor, for it was a time of open opportunity); the great intermediate layers of society became noticeably more comfortable; and the people at the bottom, such as the serfs of eastern Europe, the Irish peasantry, the dispossessed farm workers in England, the poorest peasants and workmen of

[8] See pp. 125–126.

France, were worse off than they had been before. The poor continued to live in hovels. The prosperous created for themselves that pleasant world of the eighteenth century that is still admired, a world of well-ordered Georgian homes, closely cropped lawns and shrubs, furniture by Chippendale or à la Louis XV, coach-and-four, family portraits, high chandeliers, books bound in morocco, and a staff of servants "below stairs."

Families enriched by commerce, and especially the daughters, mixed and intermarried with the old families which owned land. The merchant in England or France no sooner became prosperous than he bought himself a landed estate. In France he might also purchase a government office or patent of nobility. Contrariwise, the landowning gentleman, especially in England, no sooner increased his landed income than he invested the proceeds in commercial enterprise or government bonds. The two forms of property, bourgeois and aristocratic, tended to merge. Until toward the end of the century the various propertied interests worked harmoniously together, and the unpropertied classes, the vast majority, could influence the government only by riot and tumult. On the whole the period, though one of commercial expansion, was an age of considerable social stability in western Europe.

The foregoing might be illustrated from the lives of thousands of men and women. Two examples are enough, one English and one French. They show the working of the world economic system, the rise of the commercial class in western Europe, and the role of that class in the political life of the Western countries.

Thomas Pitt, called "Diamond" Pitt, was born in 1653, the son of a parish clergyman in the Church of England. He went to India in 1674. Here he operated as an "interloper," trading in defiance of the legal monopoly of the East India Company. Returning to England, he was prosecuted by the company and fined £400 but was rich enough to buy the manor of Stratford and with it the borough of Old Sarum, a rotten borough which gave him a seat in the House of Commons without the trouble of an election. He soon returned to India, again as an interloper, where he competed so successfully with the company that it finally took him into its own employment. He traded on his own account, as well as for the company, sent back some new chintzes to England, and defended Madras against the nawab of the Carnatic, buying off the nawab with money. In 1702, though his salary was only £300 a year, he purchased a 410-carat uncut diamond for £20,400. He bought it from an Indian merchant who had himself bought it from an English skipper, who in turn had stolen it from the slave who had found it in the mines and who had concealed it in a wound in his leg. Back in Europe, Pitt had his diamond cut at Amsterdam and sold it in 1717 to the regent of France for £135,000. The regent put it in the French crown; it was appraised at the time of the French Revolution at £480,000. A daughter of "Diamond" Pitt became the Countess of Stanhope, one of his sons the Earl of Londonderry. Another son became father to the William Pitt who guided Britain through the Seven Years' War with France, and who was raised to the peerage as the Earl of Chatham. After this Pitt the city of Pittsburgh was named, so that a fortune gained in the East gave its name to a frontier settlement in the interior of America. Chatham's younger son, the second William Pitt, became prime minister at twenty-four. The younger Pitt guided Britain through another and greater war with France, until his death in 1806 during the high tide of the Napoleonic empire.

Jean Joseph Laborde was born in 1724, of a bourgeois family of southern France. He went to work for an uncle who had a business at Bayonne trading with Spain and the East. From the profits he built up vast plantations and slaveholdings in San Domingo. His ships brought sugar to Europe, and returned with prefabricated building materials, each piece carefully numbered, for his plantations and refineries in the West Indies. He became one of the leading bankers in Paris. His daughter became the Countess de Noailles. He himself received the title of marquis, which he did not use. He bought a number of manors and châteaux near Paris. As a real estate operator he developed that part of Paris, then suburban, now called the Chaussée d'Antin. During the Seven Years' War he was sent by the French government to borrow money in Spain, where he was told that Spain would lend nothing to Louis XV, but would gladly lend him personally 20,000,000 reals. In the War of American Independence he raised 12,000,000 livres in gold for the government, to help pay the French army and navy, thus contributing to the success of the American Revolution. He acted as investment agent for Voltaire, gave 24,000 livres a year to charity, and subscribed 400,000 livres in 1788 toward building new hospitals in Paris. In July 1789 he helped to finance the insurrection which led to the fall of the Bastille and the Revolution. His son, in June 1789, took the Oath of the Tennis Court, swearing to write a constitution for France. He himself was guillotined in 1794. His children turned to scholarship and the arts.

30. *Western Europe after Utrecht, 1713–1740*

The Peace of Utrecht registered the defeat of French ambitions in the wars of Louis XIV. The French move toward "universal monarchy" had been blocked. The European state system had been preserved. Europe was to consist of a number of independent and sovereign states, all legally free and equal, continuously entering or leaving alliances along the principles of the balance of power. More specifically, the peace settlement of 1713–1714 placed the Bourbon Philip V on the Spanish throne but partitioned the Spanish empire.[9] Spain itself, with Spanish America and the Philippines, went to Philip V. Of the remaining Spanish possessions, Belgium, Milan, and Naples-Sicily went to the Austrian Habsburgs, Sardinia ultimately to the Duke of Savoy, Minorca and Gibraltar to Great Britain. Britain likewise took from France Newfoundland, Nova Scotia, and the Hudson Bay region. Great Britain, consolidated during the wars as a combined kingdom of England and Scotland, installed as a naval power in the Mediterranean, winning territory from France and Spain, and receiving trading rights within the hitherto closed domain of Spanish America, emerged as the most dynamic of the Atlantic powers.

Men in authority turned to repairing the damages of war. Spain was somewhat rejuvenated by the French influence under its new Bourbon house. The drift and decadence that had set in under the last Habsburgs were at least halted. The Spanish monarchy was administratively strengthened. Its officials followed the

[9] See pp. 194–197 and maps, pp. 196 and 328.

absolutist government of Louis XIV as a model. The estates of the east-Spanish kingdoms, Aragon and Valencia, ceased to meet, going like the Estates General of France into the limbo of obsolete institutions. They had chosen the losing side in the Spanish civil war that accompanied the War of the Spanish Succession, and their disappearance in the reign of Philip V removed a source of the localism and cross-purposes which afflicted Spain. On the whole the French influence in eighteenth-century Spain was intangible. Nothing was changed in substance, but the old machinery functioned with more precision. Administrators were better trained and took a more constructive attitude toward government work; they became more aware of the world north of the Pyrenees, and recovered confidence in their country's future. They tried also to tighten up the administration of their American empire. More revenue officers and coast guards were introduced in the Caribbean, whose zeal led to repeated clashes with smugglers, mainly British. Friction on the Spanish Main, reinforced by Spanish dislike for British occupation of Gibraltar, kept Spain and Britain in a continual ferment of potential hostility.

The Dutch after Utrecht receded from the political stage, though their alliance was always sought because of the huge shipping and financial resources they controlled. The Swiss also became important in banking and financial circles. The Belgians founded an overseas trading company in 1723 on the authority of their new Austrian ruler; this "Ostend Company" sent out six voyages to China, which were highly profitable, but the commercial jealousy of the Dutch and British obliged the Austrian emperor to withdraw his support, so that the enterprise soon came to an end. The Scots began at about this time to play their remarkable role of energizing business affairs in many countries. Union with England gave them access to the British empire and to the numerous commercial advantages won by the English. John Law, the financial wizard of France, was a Scot, as was William Paterson, one of the chief founders of the Bank of England.

France and Britain after 1713

Our main attention falls on Britain and France. Though one was the victor and the other the vanquished in the wars ended in 1713, and though one stood for absolutism and the other for constitutionalism in government, their development in the years after Utrecht was in some ways surprisingly parallel. In both countries for some years the king was personally ineffective, and in both the various propertied interests therefore gained many advantages. Both enjoyed the commercial expansion described above. Both went through a short period of financial experimentation and frantic speculation in stocks, the bubble bursting in each case in 1720. Each was thereafter governed by a statesman, Cardinal Fleury in France and Robert Walpole in England, whose policy was to keep peace abroad and conciliate all interests at home. Fleury and Walpole held office for about two decades, toward the end of which the two countries again went to war. But the differences are at least as instructive as the parallels.

In France the new king was a child, Louis XV, the great-grandson of Louis XIV, and only five years old when he began to reign in 1715. The government was entrusted to a regent, the Duke of Orleans, an elder cousin of the young king. Orleans, lacking the authority of a monarch, had to admit the aristocracy to a share in power. Most of the nobles had never liked the absolutism of Louis

XIV, and there was much dissatisfaction with absolutism among all classes, because of the ruin and suffering brought by Louis XIV's wars.

The higher nobles, ousted by Louis XIV, now reappeared in the government. For a time Orleans worked through committees of noblemen, roughly corresponding to ministries, a system lauded by its backers as a revival of political freedom; but the committees proved so incompetent that they were soon abandoned. The old parlements of France,[10] and especially the Parlement of Paris, which Louis XIV had reduced to silence, vigorously reasserted themselves after his death. The parlements were primarily law courts, originally composed of bourgeois judges; but Louis XIV and his predecessors, to raise money, had made the judgeships into salable offices, to which they attached titles of nobility to increase the price. Hence in the time of the Regency the judges of the parlements had bought or inherited their seats, and were almost all nobles. Because they had property rights in their offices, they could not be removed by the king. The Regent conceded much influence to the Parlement of Paris, utilizing it to modify the will of Louis XIV. The parlements broadened their position, claiming the right to assent to legislation and taxes, through refusing to enforce what they considered contrary to the unwritten constitution or fundamental laws of France. They managed to exercise this right, off and on, from the days of the Regency until the great Revolution of 1789. The eighteenth century, for France, was a period of absolutism checked and balanced by organized privileged groups. It was an age of aristocratic resurgence, in which the nobles won back many powers of which Louis XIV had tried to deprive them.

In Great Britain the Parliament was very different from the French parlements, and the British aristocracy was more politically competent than the *noblesse* of France. Parliament proved an effective machine for the conduct of public business. The House of Lords was hereditary, with the large exception of the bishops, who were appointed by the government and made up about a quarter of the active members of the upper house. The House of Commons was not at all representative of the country according to modern ideas. Only the wealthy, or those patronized by the wealthy, could sit in it,[11] and they were chosen by diverse and eccentric methods, in counties and towns, almost without regard to the size or wishes of the population. Some boroughs were owned outright, like the Old Sarum of the Pitt family. But through the machinations of bosses, or purchase of seats, all kinds of interests managed to get representatives into the Commons. Some members spoke for the "landed interest," others for the "funded interest" (mainly government creditors), others for the "London interest," the "West India interest," the "East India interest," and others. All politically significant groups could expect to have their desires heeded in Parliament, and all therefore were willing to go through parliamentary channels. Parliament was corrupt, slow, and expensive, but it was effective. For Parliament was not only a roughly representative body; it could also act, having acquired, in practice, a sovereign power of legislation.

Queen Anne, the last reigning Stuart, died in 1714. She was succeeded by George I, Elector of Hanover, as provided for by Parliament in the Act of

---

[10] See pp. 183–184, 187.
[11] See p. 181.

Settlement of 1701.[12] George I was the nearest relative of the Stuarts who was also a Protestant. A heavy middle-aged German who spoke no English, he continued to spend much of his time in Germany, and he brought with him to England a retinue of German ministers and favorites and two ungainly mistresses, dubbed in England the "Elephant and the Maypole." He was never popular in England, where he was regarded as at best a political convenience. He was in no position to play a strong hand in English public life, and during his reign Parliament gained much independence from the crown.

The main problem was still whether the principles of the Revolution of 1688 should be maintained.[13] The agreement of parties which had made that revolution relatively bloodless proved to be temporary. The Whigs, who considered the revolution as their work, long remained a minority made up of a few great land-owning noblemen, wealthy London merchants, lesser business people, and nonconformists in religion. The Whigs generally controlled the House of Lords, but the House of Commons was more uncertain; at the time of the Peace of Utrecht its majority was Tory. We have already noted the significance for English constitutional development of the conflict at that time between the prowar Whig majority in the House of Lords and the Tory majority in Commons, and how the conflict was resolved to help establish the primacy of the House of Commons.[14] After 1714 the two parties tended to dissolve, and the terms "Whig" and "Tory" ceased to have much definite meaning. In general the government, and the Anglican bishops who were close to the government, remained "Whig." Men who were remote from the central government, or suspicious of its activities, formed a kind of country party quite different from the earlier Tories. Gentry and yeomen of the shires and byways were easily aroused against the great noblemen and men of money who led the Whigs. In the established church the lesser clergy were sometimes critical of the Whig bishops. Outside the official church were a group of Anglican clergy who refused the oath of loyalty after 1688 and were called Non-Jurors; they kept alive a shadow church until 1805. In Scotland also, the ancestral home of the Stuarts, many were disaffected with the new regime.

Tories, Non-Jurors, and Scots made up a milieu after 1688 in which what would now be called counterrevolution might develop. Never enthusiastic for the "Whig wars" against France,[15] critical of the mounting national debt which the wars created, distrustful of the business and moneyed interests, they began to look wistfully to the exiled Stuarts. After 1701, when James II died in France, the Stuart claims devolved upon his son, who lived until 1766, scheming time and again to make himself king of England. His partisans were known as Jacobites, from *Jacobus,* the Latin for James; they regarded him as "James III," where others called him the Pretender. The Jacobites felt that if he would give up his Catholic religion, he should be accepted as Britain's rightful king. To strengthen his claims they kept agitating the theory of divine right.

The Whigs could not tolerate a return of the Stuarts. The restoration of "James III" and his divine-right partisans would undo the principles of the Glorious

[12] See p. 179.
[13] See pp. 179-181.
[14] See p. 194.
[15] See pp. 179, 181, 193-196.

Revolution—limited monarchy, constitutionalism, parliamentary supremacy, the rule of law, the toleration of dissenting Protestants, in short all that was summarized and defended in the writings of John Locke.[16] Moreover, those who held stock in the Bank of England or who had lent their money to the government would be ruined, since "James III" would surely repudiate a debt contracted by his foes. The Whigs were bound to support the Hanoverian George I. And George I was bound to look for support in a strange country among the Whigs.

George lacked personal appeal even for his English friends. To his enemies he was ridiculous and repulsive. The successful establishment of his dynasty would ruin the hopes of Tories and Jacobites. In 1715 the Pretender landed in Scotland, gathered followers from the Highlands, and proclaimed a rebellion against George I. Civil war seemed to threaten. But the Jacobite leaders bungled, and many of their followers proved to be undecided. They were willing enough to toast the "king over the water" in protest against the Whigs but not willing in a showdown to see the Stuarts, with all that went with them, again in possession of the crown of England. The Fifteen, as the revolt came to be called, petered out. But thirty years later came the Forty-five. In 1745, during war with France, the Pretender's son, "Bonnie Prince Charlie" or the "Young Pretender," again landed in Scotland and again proclaimed rebellion. This time, though almost no one in England rallied, the uprising was more successful. A Scottish force penetrated to within eighty miles of London and was driven back and crushed with the help of Hanoverian regiments rushed over from Germany. The government set out to destroy Jacobitism in the Highlands. The social system of the Highlands was wiped out; the clans were broken up; McDuffs and McDougals were forcibly reorganized according to modern notions of property and of landlord and tenant.[17]

The Jacobite uprisings confirmed the old reputation of England in the eyes of Europe, namely, as Voltaire said, that its government was as stormy as the seas which surrounded it. To partisans of monarchy on the Continent they illustrated the weaknesses of parliamentary government. But their ignominious collapse actually strengthened the parliamentary regime in England. They left little permanent mark and soon passed into an atmosphere of romantic legend.

The "Bubbles"

Meanwhile, immediately after the Peace of Utrecht, the problem of dealing with a postwar economic situation had to be faced in both England and France. In both countries it meant finding a way to carry the greatly swollen government debt. Organized permanent public debt was new at the time. The possibilities and limitations of large-scale banking, paper money, and credit were not clearly seen. In France there was much amazement at the way in which England and Holland, though smaller and less wealthy than France, had been able to maximize their resources through banking and credit and even to finance the alliance which had eclipsed the Sun King. In addition there was much private demand for both lending and borrowing money. Private persons all over western Europe were looking for enterprises in which to invest their savings. And promoters and

[16] See pp. 178, 311–313.
[17] See pp. 349–350.

organizers, anticipating a profit in this or that line of business, were looking for capital with which to work. Out of this whole situation grew the "South Sea bubble" in England and the "Mississippi bubble" in France. Both bubbles broke in 1720, and both had important long-range effects.

A close tie between government finance and private enterprise was usual at the time, under mercantilist ideas of government guidance of trade. In England, for example, a good deal of the government debt was held by companies organized for that purpose. The government would charter a company, strengthen it with a monopoly in a given line of business, and then receive from the company, after the stockholders had bought up the shares, a large sum of cash as a loan. Much of the British debt, contracted in the wars from 1689 to 1713, was held in this way by the Bank of England, founded in 1694;[18] by the East India Company, reorganized in 1708 in such a way as to provide funds for the government; and by the South Sea Company, founded in 1711. The Bank enjoyed a legal monopoly over certain banking operations in London, the East India Company over trade with the East, the South Sea Company for exploiting the *asiento*[19] and other commercial privileges extorted from Spain. The companies were owned by private investors. Savings drawn from trade and agriculture, put into shares in these companies, became available both for economic reinvestment and for use of the government in defraying the costs of war.

In 1716 the Prince Regent of France was attracted to a Scottish financier, John Law, reputedly by Law's remarkable mathematical system in gambling at cards. Law founded a much needed French central bank. In the next year, 1717, he organized a *Compagnie d'Occident*, popularly called the Mississippi Company, which obtained a monopoly of trade with Louisiana, where it founded New Orleans in 1718. This company, under Law's management, soon absorbed the French East India, China, Senegal, and African companies. It now enjoyed a legal monopoly of all French colonial trade. Law then proposed, and was authorized by the Regent, to assume the entire government debt. The company received from individuals their certificates of royal indebtedness or "bonds," and gave them shares of company stock in return. It proposed to pay dividends on these shares and to extinguish the debt from profits in the colonial trade and from a monopoly over the collection of all indirect taxes in France. The project carried with it a plan for drastic reform of the whole taxation system, to make taxes both more fair to the taxpayer and more lucrative to the government. Shares in the Mississippi Company were gobbled up by the public. There was a frenzy of speculation, a wild fear of not buying soon enough. Quotations rose to 18,000 livres a share. But the company rested only on unrealized projects. Shareholders began to fear for their money. They began to unload. The market broke sharply. Many found their life savings gone. Others lost ancestral estates on which they had borrowed in the hope of getting rich. Those, however, who had owned shares in the company before the rise, and who had resisted the speculative fever, lost nothing by the bursting of inflated prices, and later enjoyed a gilt-edged commercial investment.

Much the same thing happened in England, where it was thought by many that Law was about to provide a panacea for France. The South Sea Company,

[18] See p. 181.
[19] See p. 195.

outbidding the Bank of England, took over a large fraction of the public debt by receiving government "bonds" from their owners in return for shares of its stock. The size and speed of profits to be made in Spanish America were greatly exaggerated, and the market value of South Sea shares rose rapidly for a time, reaching £1,050 for a share of £100 par value. Other schemes abounded in the passion for easy money. Promoters organized mining and textile companies, as well as others of more fanciful or bolder design: a company to bring live fish to market in tanks, an insurance company to insure female chastity, a company "for an undertaking which shall in due time be revealed." Shares in such enterprises were snatched at mounting prices. But in September 1720 the South Sea stockholders began to sell, doubting whether operations would pay dividends commensurate to £1,000 a share. They dragged down the whole unstable structure. As in France, many people found that their savings or their inheritances had disappeared.

Indignation in both countries was extreme. Both governments were implicated in the scandal. John Law fled to Brussels. The Regent was discredited; he resigned in 1723, and French affairs were afterward conducted by Cardinal Fleury. In England there was a change of ministers. Robert Walpole, a country gentleman of Whig persuasion, who had long sat in the Commons, and who had warned against the South Sea scheme from the beginning, became the principal minister to George I.

Britain recovered from the crisis more successfully than France. Law's bank, a useful institution, was dissolved in the reaction against him. France lacked an adequate banking system during the rest of the century. French investors developed a morbid fear of paper securities and a marked preference for putting their savings into land. Commercial capitalism and the growth of credit institutions in France were retarded. In England the same fears were felt. Parliament passed the "Bubble Act," forbidding all companies except those specifically chartered by the government to raise capital by the sale of stock. In both countries the development of joint-stock financing along the lines of the modern corporation was slowed down for over a century. Business enterprises continued to be typically owned by individuals and partnerships, which expanded by reinvestment of their own profits, and so had another reason to keep profits up and wages down. But in England Walpole managed to save the South Sea Company, the East India Company, and the Bank, all of which were temporarily discredited in the eyes of the public. England continued to perfect its financial machinery.

M. BACHELIER, DIRECTOR OF THE LYONS FARMS
by Jean-Baptiste Oudry (French, 1686–1755)

The "farms" of which M. Bachelier was a director were the semiprivate syndicates to which the French monarchy delegated or "farmed" the collection of its indirect taxes. The government received a definite sum in advance from the farmers, who then engaged in the more uncertain but profitable business of actual collection. Tax farmers were generally hated, and many became very rich. Nothing is known of the man in this picture. He may have been one of the wealthy persons who advanced money to the government, or only one of their high-level employees. In any case, he is shown writing at a table as a man of business, but he is not looking at his work; and with his head turned toward the spectator, his huge wig, his lace cuffs, and his left hand politely extended, he typifies the ruling elite at the close of the reign of Louis XIV. Courtesy of the University of Michigan Museum of Art, Ann Arbor.

The credit of the two governments was also shaken by the "bubbles." Much of the French war debt was repudiated in one way or another. Repudiation was in many cases morally justifiable, for many government creditors were unscrupulous war profiteers, but financially it was disastrous, for it discouraged honest people from lending their money to the state. Nor was much accomplished toward reform of the taxes. The nobles continued to evade taxes imposed on them by Louis XIV, John Law's plans for taxation evaporated with the rest of his project, and when in 1726 a finance minister tried to levy a 2 percent tax on all property, the vested interests, led by the Parlement of Paris, annihilated this proposal also. Lacking an adequate revenue, and repudiating its debts, the French monarchy had little credit. The conception of the public or national debt hardly developed in France in the eighteenth century. The debt was considered to be the king's debt, for which no one except a few ministers felt any responsibility. The Bourbon government in fact often borrowed through the church, the Provincial Estates, or the city of Paris, which lenders considered to be better financial risks than the king himself. The government was severely handicapped in its foreign policy and its wars. It could not fully tap the wealth of its own subjects.

In England none of the debt was repudiated. Walpole managed to launch and keep going the system of the sinking fund, by which the government regularly set aside the wherewithal to pay interest and principal on its obligations. The credit of the British government became absolutely firm. The debt was considered a national debt, for which the British people itself assumed the responsibility. Parliamentary government made this development possible. In France no one could tell what the king or his ministers might do, and hence everyone was reluctant to trust them with his money. In England the people who had the money could also, through Parliament, determine the policies of state, decide what the money should be spent for, and levy enough taxes to maintain confidence in the debt. Similarities to France there were; the landowners who controlled the British Parliament, like those who controlled the Parlement of Paris, resisted direct taxation, so that the British government drew two-thirds or more of its revenues from indirect taxes paid by the mass of the population. Yet landowners, even dukes, did pay important amounts of taxes. There were no exemptions by class or rank, as in France. All propertied interests had a stake in the government. The wealth of the country stood behind the national debt. The national credit seemed inexhaustible. This was the supreme trump card of the British in their wars with France from the founding of the Bank of England in 1694 to the fall of Napoleon 120 years later. And it was the political freedom of England that gave it its economic strength.

Fleury in France; Walpole in England

Fleury was seventy-three years old when he took office, and ninety when he left it. He was not one to initiate programs for the distant future. Louis XV, as he came of age, proved to be indolent and selfish. Public affairs drifted, while France grew privately more wealthy, especially the commercial and bourgeois classes. Walpole likewise kept out of controversies. His motto was *quieta non movere*, "let sleeping dogs lie." It was to win over the Tory squires to the Hanoverian and Whig regime that Walpole kept down the land taxes; this policy was successful, and Jacobitism quieted down. Walpole supported the Bank, the trading companies, and the financial interests, and they in turn supported him. It was a time of political calm, in which the lower classes were quiet and the upper classes not quarreling, favorable therefore to the development of parliamentary institutions.

Walpole has been called the first prime minister and the architect of cabinet government, a system in which the ministers, or executives, are also members of the legislative body. He saw to it, by careful rigging, that a majority in the Commons always supported him. He avoided issues on which his majority might be lost. He thus began to acknowledge the principle of cabinet responsibility to a majority in Parliament, which was to become an important characteristic of cabinet government. And by selecting colleagues who agreed with him, and getting rid of those who did not, he advanced the idea of the cabinet as a body of ministers bound to each other and to the prime minister, obligated to follow the same policies and to stand or fall as a group. Thus Parliament was not only a representative or deliberative body like the diets and estates on the Continent, but one that developed an effective executive organ, without which neither representative government nor any government could survive.

To assure peace and quiet in domestic politics the best means was to avoid raising taxes. And the best way to avoid taxes was to avoid war. Fleury and Walpole both tried to keep at peace. They were not in the long run successful. Fleury was drawn into the War of the Polish Succession in 1733. Walpole kept England out of war until 1739. He always had a war party to contend with, and the most bellicose were those interested in the American trade—the slave trade, the sugar plantations, and the illicit sale of goods in the Spanish empire. The British official figures show that while trade with Europe, in the eighteenth century, was always less in war than in peace, trade with America always increased during war, except, indeed, during the War of American Independence.

In the 1730s there were constant complaints of indignities suffered by sturdy Britons on the Spanish Main. The war party produced a Captain Jenkins, who carried with him a small box containing a withered ear, which he said had been cut from his head by the outrageous Spaniards. Testifying in the House of Commons, where he "commended his soul to God and his cause to his country," he stirred up a commotion which led to war. So in 1739, after twenty-five years of peace, England plunged with wild enthusiasm into the War of Jenkins' Ear. "They are ringing the bells now," said Walpole; "they will soon be wringing their hands." The war soon became merged in a conflict involving Europeans and others in all parts of the world.

31. The Great War of the Mid–Eighteenth Century: The Peace of Paris, 1763

The fighting lasted until 1763, with an uneasy interlude between 1748 and 1756. It went by many names. The opening hostilities between England and Spain were called, by the English, the War of Jenkins' Ear. The Prussians spoke of three "Silesian" wars. The struggle on the Continent in the 1740s was often known as the War of the Pragmatic Sanction. British colonials in America called the fighting of the 1740s King George's War, or used the term "French and Indian Wars," for the whole sporadic conflict. Disorganized and nameless struggles at the same time shook the peoples of India. The names finally adopted by history were the War of the Austrian Succession for operations between 1740 and 1748 and the Seven Years' War for those between 1756 and 1763. The two wars were really one. They involved the same two principal issues, the duel of Britain and France for colonies, trade, and sea power, and the duel of Prussia and Austria for territory and military power in central Europe.

Eighteenth-Century Warfare

Warfare at the time was in a kind of classical phase, which strongly affected the development of events. It was somewhat slow, formal, elaborate, and indecisive. The enlisted ranks of armies and navies were filled with men considered economically useless, picked up by recruiting officers among unwary loungers in taverns or on the wharves. All governments protected their productive population, peasants, mechanics, and bourgeois, preferring to keep them at home, at work, and paying taxes. Soldiers were a class apart, enlisted for long terms, paid wages, professional in their outlook, and highly trained. They lived in barracks or great forts, and were dressed in bright uniforms (like the British "redcoats"), which, since camouflage was unnecessary, they wore even in battle. Weapons were not destructive; infantry was predominant and was armed with the smooth-bore musket, to which the bayonet could be attached. In war the troops depended on great supply depots built up beforehand, which were practically immovable with the transportation available, so that armies, at least in central and western Europe, rarely operated more than a few days' march from their bases. Soldiers fought methodically for pay. Generals hesitated to risk their troops, which took years to train and equip, and were very expensive. Strategy took the form not of seeking out the enemy's main force to destroy it in battle, but of maneuvering for advantages of position, applying a cumulative and subtle pressure somewhat as in a game of chess.

There was little national feeling, or feeling of any kind. The Prussian army recruited half or more of its enlisted personnel outside Prussia; the British army was largely made up of Hanoverian or other German regiments; even the French army had German units incorporated in it. Deserters from one side were enlisted by the other. War was between governments, or between the oligarchies and aristocracies which governments represented, not between whole peoples. It was fought for power, prestige, or calculated practical interests, not for ideologies, moral principles, world conquest, national survival, or ways of life. Popular nationalism had developed farthest in England, where "Rule Britannia" and "God Save the King," both breathing a low opinion of foreigners, became popular songs during these mid–eighteenth-century wars.

Civilians were little affected, except in India or the American wilderness where European conditions did not prevail. In Europe, a government aspiring to conquer a neighboring province did not wish to ruin or antagonize it beforehand. The fact that the west-European struggle was largely naval kept it well outside civilian experience. Never had war been so harmless, certainly not in the religious wars of earlier times, or in the national wars initiated later. This was one reason why governments went to war so lightly. On the other hand governments also withdrew from war much more readily than in later times. Their treasuries might be exhausted, their trained soldiers used up; only practical or rational questions were at stake; there was no war hysteria or pressure of mass opinion; the enemy of today might be the ally of tomorrow. Peace was almost as easy to make as war. Peace treaties were negotiated, not imposed. So the eighteenth century saw a series of wars and treaties, more wars, treaties, and rearrangements of alliances, all arising over much the same issues, and with exactly the same powers present at the end as at the beginning.

The War of the Austrian Succession, 1740–1748

The War of the Austrian Succession was started by the king of Prussia. Frederick II, or the "Great," was a young man of twenty-eight when he became king in 1740. His youth had not been happy; he was temperamentally incompatible with his father. His tastes as a prince had run to playing the flute, corresponding with French men of letters, and writing prose and verse in the French language. His father, the sober Frederick William I,[20] thought him frivolous and effeminate, and dealt with him so clumsily that at the age of eighteen he tried to escape from the kingdom. Caught and brought back, he was forced to witness the execution, by his father's order, of the friend and companion who had shared in his attempted flight. Frederick changed as the years passed from a jaunty youth to an aged cynic, equally undeceived by himself, his friends, or his enemies, and seeing no reason to expect much from human nature. Though his greatest reputation was made as a soldier, he retained his literary interests all his life, became a historian of merit, and is perhaps of all modern monarchs the only one who would have a respectable standing if considered only as a writer. An unabashed freethinker, like many others of his day, he considered all religions ridiculous and laughed at the divine right of kings; but he would have no nonsense about the rights of the house of Brandenburg, and he took a solemn view of the majesty of the state.

Frederick, in 1740, lost no time in showing a boldness which his father would have surely dreaded. He decided to conquer Silesia,[21] and on December 16, 1740, he invaded that province, a region adjoining Prussia, lying in the upper valley of the Oder, and belonging to the kingdom of Bohemia and hence to the Danubian empire of the Habsburgs. The Pragmatic Sanction, a general agreement signed by the European powers, including Prussia, had stipulated that all domains of the Austrian Habsburgs should be inherited integrally by the new heiress, Maria Theresa.[22] The issue was between law and force. Frederick in attacking Silesia could invoke nothing better than "reason of state," the welfare and expansion of the state of which he was ruler. But he was not mistaken in the belief that if he did not attack the Austrians someone else soon would.

The Pragmatic Sanction was universally disregarded. All turned against Maria Theresa. Bavaria and Saxony put in claims. Spain, still hoping to revise the Peace

[20] See pp. 233–234.
[21] See map, p. 230, panel 3.
[22] See p. 225–226.

of Utrecht, saw another chance to win back former Spanish holdings in Italy. The decisive intervention was that of France. It was the fate of France to be torn between ambitions on the European continent and ambitions on the sea and beyond the seas. Economic and commercial advantage might dictate concentration on the impending struggle with Britain. But the French nobles were less interested than the British aristocrats in commercial considerations. They were influential because they furnished practically all the army officers and diplomats. They saw in Austria the traditional enemy, in Europe the traditional field of valor, and in Belgium, which now belonged to the Austrians, the traditional object for annexation to France. Cardinal Fleury, much against his will and judgment, found himself forced into war against the Habsburgs.

Maria Theresa was at this time a young woman of twenty-three. She proved to be one of the most capable rulers ever produced by the house of Habsburg. She bore sixteen children, and set a model of conscientious family living at a time of much indifference to such matters among the upper classes. She was as devout and as earnest as Frederick of Prussia was irreligious and seemingly flip. She dominated her husband and her grown sons as she did her kingdoms and her duchies. With a good deal of practical sense, she reconstructed her empire without having any doctrinaire program, and she accomplished more in her methodical way than more brilliant contemporaries with more spectacular projects of reform.

She was pregnant when Frederick invaded Silesia, giving birth to her first son, the future emperor Joseph II, in March 1741. She was preoccupied at the same time by the political crisis. Her dominions were assailed by half a dozen outside powers, and were also quaking within, for her two kingdoms of Hungary and Bohemia (both of which had accepted the Pragmatic Sanction) were slow to see which way their advantage lay. She betook herself to Hungary to be crowned with the crown of St. Stephen—and to rally support. The Hungarians were still in a grumbling frame of mind, as in the days of the Rakoczy rebellion forty years before.[23] She made a carefully arranged and dramatic appearance before them, implored them to defend her, and swore to uphold the liberties of the Hungarian nobles and the separate constitution of the kingdom of Hungary. All Europe told how the beautiful young queen, by raising aloft the infant Joseph at a session of the Hungarian parliament, had thrown the dour Magyars into paroxysms of chivalrous resolve. The story was not quite true, but it is true that she made an eloquent address to the Magyars, and that she took her baby with her and proudly exhibited him. The Hungarian magnates pledged their "blood and life," and delivered 100,000 soldiers.

The war, as it worked out in Europe, was reminiscent of the struggles of the time of Louis XIV, or even of the Thirty Years' War now a century in the past. It was, again, a kind of civil struggle within the Holy Roman Empire, in which a league of German princes banded together against the monarchy of Vienna. This time they included the new kingdom of Prussia. It was, again, a collision of Bourbons and Habsburgs, in which the French pursued their old policy of maintaining division in Germany, by supporting the German princes against the Habsburgs. The basic aim of French policy, according to instructions given by the French foreign office to its ambassador in Vienna in 1725, was to keep the

[23] See pp. 225–226.

Empire divided by the principles of the Peace of Westphalia,[24] preventing the union of German powers into "one and the same body, which would in fact become formidable to all the other powers of Europe." This time the Bourbons had Spain on their side. Maria Theresa was supported only by Britain and Holland, which subsidized her financially, but which had inadequate land forces. The Franco-German-Spanish combination was highly successful. In 1742 Maria Theresa, hard pressed, accepted the proposals of Frederick for a separate peace. She temporarily granted him Silesia, and he temporarily slipped out of the war which he had been the first to enter. The French and Bavarians moved into Bohemia and almost organized a puppet kingdom with the aid of Bohemian nobles. The French obtained the election of their Bavarian satellite as Holy Roman Emperor, Charles VII. In 1745 the French won the battle of Fontenoy in Belgium, the greatest battle of the war; they dominated Belgium, which neither the Dutch nor British were able to defend. In the same year they fomented the Jacobite rebellion in Scotland.

But the situation overseas offset the situation in Europe. It was America that tilted the balance. The French fortress of Louisburg on Cape Breton Island was captured by an expedition of New Englanders in conjunction with the British navy. British warships drove French and Spanish shipping from the seas. The French West Indies were blockaded. The French government, in danger of losing the wealth and taxes drawn from the sugar and slave trades, announced its willingness to negotiate.

Peace was made at Aix-la-Chapelle in 1748. It was based on an Anglo-French agreement in which Maria Theresa was obliged to concur. Britain and France arranged their differences by a return to the *status quo ante bellum*. The British returned Louisburg despite the protests of the Americans and relaxed their stranglehold on the Caribbean. The French returned Madras, which they had captured, and gave up their hold on Belgium. The Atlantic powers recognized Frederick's annexation of Silesia and required Maria Theresa to cede some Italian duchies—Parma and Piacenza—to a Spanish Bourbon. Belgium was returned to Maria Theresa at the especial insistence of Britain and the Dutch. She and her ministers were very dissatisfied. They would infinitely have preferred to lose Belgium and keep Silesia. They were required, in the interest of a European or even intercontinental balance of power, to give up Silesia and to hold Belgium for the benefit of the Dutch against the French.

The war had been more decisive than the few readjustments of the map seemed to show. It proved the weakness of the French position, straddled as it was between Europe and the overseas world. Maintaining a huge army for use in Europe, the French could not, like Britain, concentrate upon the sea. On the other hand, because vulnerable on the sea, they could not hold their gains in Europe or conquer Belgium. The Austrians, though bitter, had reason for satisfaction. The war had been a war to partition the Habsburg empire. The Habsburg empire still stood. Hungary had thrown in its lot with Vienna, a fact of much subsequent importance. Bohemia was won back. In 1745, when Charles VII died, Maria Theresa got her husband elected Holy Roman Emperor, a position for which she could not qualify because she was a woman. But the loss of Silesia

[24] See pp. 145–149.

was momentous. Silesia was as populous as the Dutch Republic, heavily German, and industrially the most advanced region east of the Elbe. Prussia by acquiring it doubled its population and more than doubled its resources. Prussia with Silesia was unquestionably a great power. Since Austria was still a great power there were henceforth two great powers in the vague world known as "Germany," a situation which came to be known as the German dualism. But the transfer of Silesia, which doubled the number of Germans ruled by the king of Prussia, made the Habsburg empire less German, more Slavic and Hungarian, more Danubian and international. Silesia was the keystone of Germany. Frederick was determined to hold it, and Maria Theresa to win it back. A new war was therefore foreseeable in central Europe. As for Britain and France, the peace of Aix-la-Chapelle was clearly only a truce.

The next years passed in a busy diplomacy, leading to what is known as the "reversal of alliances" and Diplomatic Revolution of 1756. The Austrians set themselves to nipping off the growth of Prussia. Maria Theresa's foreign minister, Count Kaunitz, perhaps the most artful diplomat of the century, concluded that the time had come to abandon ideas that were centuries old. The rise of Prussia had revolutionized the balance of power. Kaunitz, reversing traditional policy, proposed an alliance between Austria and France—between the Habsburgs and the Bourbons. He encouraged French aspirations for Belgium in return for French support in the destruction of Prussia. The overtures between Austria and France obliged Britain, Austria's former ally, to reconsider its position in Europe; the British had Hanover to protect, and were favorably impressed by the Prussian army. An alliance of Great Britain and Prussia was concluded in January 1756. Meanwhile Kaunitz consummated his alliance with France. One consequence was to marry the future Louis XVI to one of Maria Theresa's daughters, Marie Antoinette, the "Austrian woman" of Revolutionary fame. The Austrian alliance was never popular in France. Some Frenchmen thought that the ruin of Prussia would only enhance the Austrian control of Germany and so undo the fundamental "Westphalia system." The French progressive thinkers, known as "philosophes," believed Austria to be priest-ridden and backward, and were for ideological reasons admirers of the freethinking Frederick II. Dissatisfaction with its foreign policy was one reason for the growth of a revolutionary attitude toward the Bourbon government.

In any case, when the Seven Years' War broke out in 1756, though it was a continuation of the preceding war in that Prussia fought Austria, and Britain France, the belligerents had all changed partners. Great Britain and Prussia were now allies, as were, more remarkably, the Habsburgs and the Bourbons. In addition, Austria had concluded a treaty with the Russian empire for the annihilation of Prussia.

The Seven Years' War, 1756–1763: In Europe and America

The Seven Years' War began in America. Let us turn, however, to Europe first. Here the war was another war of "partition." As a league of powers had but recently attempted to partition the empire of Maria Theresa, and a generation before had in fact partitioned the empires of Sweden and Spain, so now Austria, Russia, and France set out to partition the newly created kingdom of Prussia.

Their aim was to relegate the Hohenzollerns to the margraviate of Brandenburg. Prussia, even with Silesia, had less than 6,000,000 people; each of its three principal enemies had 20,000,000 or more. But war was less an affair of peoples than of states and standing armies, and the Prussian state and Prussian army were the most efficient in Europe. Frederick fought brilliant campaigns, won victories as at Rossbach in 1757, moved rapidly along interior lines, eluded, surprised, and reattacked the badly coordinated armies opposed to him. He proved himself the great military genius of his day. But genius was scarcely enough. Against three such powers, reinforced by Sweden and the German states, and with no ally except Great Britain (and Hanover) whose aid was almost entirely financial, the kingdom of Prussia by any reasonable estimate had no chance of survival. There were times when Frederick believed all to be lost, yet he went on fighting, and his strength of character in these years of adversity, as much as his ultimate triumph, later made him a hero and symbol for the Germans. His subjects, Junkers and even serfs, advanced in patriotic spirit under pressure. The coalition tended to fall apart. The French lacked enthusiasm; they were fighting Britain, the Austrian alliance was unpopular, and Kaunitz would not plainly promise them Belgium. The Russians found that the more they moved westward the more they alarmed their Austrian allies. Frederick was left to deal only with the implacable Austrians, for whom he was more than a match. By the peace of Hubertusburg in 1763 not only did he lose nothing; he retained Silesia.

For the rest, the Seven Years' War was a phase in the long dispute between France and Great Britain. Its stakes were supremacy in the growing world economy, control of colonies, and command of the sea. The two empires had been left unchanged in 1748 by the peace of Aix-la-Chapelle. Both held possessions in India, in the West Indies, and on the American mainland.[25] In India both British and French possessed only disconnected commercial establishments on the coast, infinitesimal specks on the giant body of India. Both also traded with China at Canton. Both occupied way stations on the route to Asia, the British in St. Helena and Ascension Island in the south Atlantic, the French in the much better islands of Mauritius and Reunion in the Indian Ocean. Frenchmen were active also on the coasts of Madagascar. The greatest way station, the Cape of Good Hope, belonged to the Dutch. In the West Indies the British plantations were mainly in Jamaica, Barbados, and some of the Leeward Islands; the French in San Domingo, Guadeloupe, and Martinique. All were supported by the booming slave trade in Africa.

On the American mainland the French had more territory, the British more people. In the British colonies from Georgia to Nova Scotia lived perhaps two million whites, predominantly English but with strong infusions of Scots-Irish, Dutch, Germans, French, and Swedes. Philadelphia, with some 40,000 people, was as large as any city in England except London. The colonies, in population, bulked about a quarter as large as the mother country. But they were provincial, locally minded, incapable of concerted action. In 1754 the British government called a congress at Albany in New York, hoping that the colonies would assume some collective responsibility for the coming war. The congress adopted an "Albany plan of union" drawn up by Benjamin Franklin, but the colonial

[25] See maps, pp. 196, 284.

legislatures declined to accept it, through fear of losing their separate identity. The colonials were willing, in a politically immature way, to rely on Britain for military action against France.

The French were still in possession of Louisburg on Cape Breton Island, a stronghold begun by Louis XIV, located in the Gulf of St. Lawrence. It was designed for naval domination of the American side of the north Atlantic, and to control access to the St. Lawrence River, the Great Lakes, and the vast region now called the Middle West. Through all this tract of country Frenchmen constantly came and went, but there were sizable French settlements only around New Orleans in the south and Quebec in the north. One source of French strength was that the French were more successful than the British in gaining the support of the Indians. This was probably because the French, being few in numbers, did not threaten to expropriate the Indians from their lands, and also because Catholics at this time were incomparably more active than Protestants in Christian missions among non-European peoples.

Both empires, French and British, were held together by mercantilist regulations framed mainly in the interest of the home countries. In some ways the British empire was more liberal than the French; it allowed local self-government and permitted immigration from all parts of Europe. In other ways the British system was more strict. British subjects, for example, were required by the Navigation Acts to use empire ships and seamen—English, Scottish, or colonial—whereas the French were more free to use the carrying services of other nations. British sugar planters had to ship raw sugar to the home country, there to be refined and sold to Europe, whereas French planters were free to refine their sugar in the islands. The mainland British colonials were forbidden to manufacture ironware and numerous other articles for sale; they were expected to buy such objects from England. Since the British sold little to the West Indies, where the slave population had no income with which to buy, the mainland colonies, though less valued as a source of wealth, were a far more important market for British goods. The colonials, though they had prospered under the restrictive system, were beginning to find much of it irksome at the time of the Seven Years's War, and indeed evaded it when they could.

Fighting was endemic even in the years of peace in Europe. Nova Scotia was a trouble spot. French in population, it had been annexed by Britain at the Peace of Utrecht. Its proximity to Louisburg made it a scene of perpetual agitation. The British government in 1755, foreseeing war with France, bodily removed about 7,000 of its people, who called themselves Acadians, scattering them in small numbers through the other mainland colonies. But the great disputed area was the Alleghenies. British colonials were beginning to feel their way westward through the mountains. French traders, soldiers, and empire builders were moving eastward toward the same mountains from points on the Mississippi and the Great Lakes. In 1749, at the request of Virginia and London capitalists, the British government chartered a land-exploitation company, the Ohio Company, to operate in territory claimed also by the French. The French threw up a fort at the point where the Ohio River is formed by the junction of two smaller rivers—Fort Duquesne, later called Pittsburgh. A force of colonials and British regular troops, under General Braddock, started through the wilderness to dislodge the French.

It was defeated in July 1755, perhaps through its commander's unwillingness to take advice from the colonial officers, of whom one was George Washington.

A year later France and Britain declared war. The British were brilliantly led by William Pitt, subsequently the Earl of Chatham, a man of wide vision and superb confidence. "I know that I can save the country," he said, "and I know that no one else can." He concentrated British effort on the navy and colonies, while subsidizing Frederick of Prussia to fight in Europe, so that England, as he put it, might win an empire on the plains of Germany. Only the enormous credit of the British government made such a policy feasible. In 1758 British forces successfully took Fort Duquesne. Louisburg fell again in the same year. Gaining entry to the St. Lawrence, the British moved upstream to Quebec, and in 1759 a force under General Wolfe, stealthily scaling the heights, appeared by surprise on the Plains of Abraham outside the fortress, forcing the garrison to accept a battle, which the British won. With the fall of Quebec no further French resistance was possible on the American mainland. The British also, with superior naval power, occupied Guadeloupe and Martinique and the French slave stations in Africa.

The Seven Years' War, 1756–1763: In India

Both British and French interests were meanwhile profiting from disturbed conditions in India. As large as Europe without Russia, India was a congested country of impoverished masses, speaking hundreds of languages and following many religions and subreligions, the two greatest being the Hindu and the Muslim. Waves of invasion through the northwest frontier since the Christian year A.D. 1001 had produced a Muslim empire, whose capital was at Delhi and which for a short time held jurisdiction over most of the country. These Muslim emperors were known as Great Moguls. The greatest was Akbar, who ruled from 1556 to 1605, built roads, reformed the taxes, patronized the arts, and attempted to minimize religious differences among his peoples. The Muslim artistic culture flourished for a time after Akbar. One of his successors, Shah Jehan (1628–1658), built the beautiful Taj Mahal near Agra, and at Delhi the delicately carved alabaster palace of the Moguls, in which he placed the Peacock Throne, made of solid gold and studded with gems.

But meanwhile there was restlessness among the Hindus. The Sikhs, who had originated in the fifteenth century as a reform movement in Hinduism, went to war with the Mogul emperor in the seventeenth century. They became one of the most ferociously warlike of Indian peoples. Hindu princes in central India formed a "Mahratta confederacy" against the Muslim emperor at Delhi. Matters were made worse when Aurungzeb, the last significant Mogul emperor (1658–1707), adopted repressive measures against the Hindus. After Aurungzeb, India fell into political dissolution. Many of the modern princely states originated or became autonomous at this time. Hindu princes rebelled against the Mogul. Muslims, beginning as governors or commanders under the Mogul, set up as rulers in their own right. Thus originated Hyderabad, which included the fabulous diamond mines of Golconda, and whose ruler long was called the wealthiest man in the world. Princes and would-be princes fought with each other and with the emperor.

New Muslim invaders also poured across the northwest frontier. In 1739 a Persian force occupied Delhi, slaughtered thirty thousand people and departed with the Peacock Throne. Between 1747 and 1761 came a series of forays from Afghanistan, which again resulted in the looting of Delhi and the massacre of uncounted thousands.

The situation in India resembled, on a larger and more frightful scale, what had happened in Europe in the Holy Roman Empire, where also irreconcilable religious differences (of Catholics and Protestants) had torn the country asunder, ambitious princes and city-states had won a chaotic independence, and foreign armies appeared repeatedly as invaders. India, like central Europe, suffered chronically from war, intrigue, and rival pretensions to territory; and in India, as in the Holy Roman Empire, outsiders and ambitious insiders benefited together.

The half-unknown horrors in the interior had repercussions on the coasts. Here handfuls of Europeans were established in the coastal cities. By the troubles in the interior the Indian authorities along the coasts were reduced, so to speak, to a size with which the Europeans could deal. The Europeans—British and French— were agents of their respective East India companies. The companies built forts, maintained soldiers, coined money, and entered into treaties with surrounding Indian powers, under charter of their home governments, and with no one in India to deny them the exercise of such sovereign rights. Agents of the companies, like Indians themselves, ignored or respected the Mogul emperor as suited their own purpose. They were, at first, only one of the many elements in the flux and reflux of Indian affairs.

Neither the British nor the French government, during the Seven Years' War, had any intention of territorial conquest in India, their policy in this respect differing radically from policy toward America. Nor were the two companies imperialistic. The company directors, in London and Paris, disapproved of fantastic schemes of intervention in Indian politics, insisted that their agents should attend to business only, and resented every penny and every sou not spent to bring in commercial profit. But it took a year or more to exchange messages between Europe and India, and company representatives in India, caught up in the Indian vortex, and overcome by the chance to make personal fortunes or by dreams of empire, acted very much on their own, committing their home offices without compunction. Involvement in Indian affairs was not exactly new. We have seen how "Diamond" Pitt, in 1702, purchased the good will of the nawab of the Carnatic, when the nawab threatened, by military force, to reduce the English traders at Madras to submission.[26] But the first European to exploit the possibilities of the situation was the Frenchman Dupleix. Dupleix felt that the funds sent out by the company in Paris, to finance trade in India, were insufficient. His idea seems to have been not empire-building, but to make the company into a local territorial power, in order that, from taxes and other political revenues, it might have more capital for its commercial operations. In any case, during the years of peace in Europe after 1748, Dupleix found himself with about 2,000 French troops in the Carnatic, the east coast around Madras. He lent them out to neighboring native rulers in return for territorial concessions. The first to drill native Indians by European methods, he was the originator of the "sepoys."

[26] See p. 263.

Following a program of backing claimants to various Indian thrones, he built up a clientele of native rulers under obligation to himself. He was very successful, for a few European troops or sepoys could overcome hordes of purely Indian forces in pitched battle. But he was recalled to France in 1754, after the company became apprehensive of war with Britain and other trouble; and he died in disgrace.

When war came in 1756, British interests in India were advanced chiefly by Robert Clive. He had come out many years before as a clerk for the company but had shown military talents and an ability to comprehend Indian politics. He had maneuvered, with little success, against Dupleix in the Carnatic in the 1740s. In 1756, on hearing the news of war in Europe, he shifted his attention to Bengal, hoping to drive the French from their trading stations there. The French were favored in Bengal by the local Muslim ruler, Suraja Dowla, who proceeded to anticipate Clive's arrival by expelling the British from Calcutta. Capturing the city, he shut up 146 Englishmen in a small room without windows (soon known as the "Black Hole of Calcutta") and kept them there all night, during which most of them died of suffocation. Clive, soon appearing with a small force of British and sepoys, routed Suraja Dowla at the battle of Plassey in 1757. He put his own puppet on the Bengal throne and extorted huge reparations both for the company and for himself. Back in England he was received with mixed feelings, and again, in India, strove to purify the almost incredible corruption of company employees there, men normal enough but demoralized by irresistible chances for easy riches. Finally he committed suicide in 1774.

It was British sea power, more fundamentally than Clive's tactics, that assured the triumph of British over French ambitions in the East. The British government still had no intention of conquest in India, but it could not see its East India Company forced out by agents of the French company in collaboration with Indian princes. Naval forces were therefore dispatched to the Indian Ocean, and they not only allowed Clive to shift from Madras to Calcutta at will, but gradually cut off the French posts in India from Europe and from each other. By the end of the war all the French establishments in India, as in Africa and America, were at the mercy of the British. The French overseas lay prostrate, and France itself was again detached from the overseas world on which much of its economy rested. In 1761 France made an alliance with Spain, which was alarmed for the safety of its own American empire after the British victories at Quebec and in the Caribbean. But the British also defeated Spain.

The Peace Settlement of 1763

The British armed forces had been spectacularly successful. Yet the peace treaty, signed at Paris in February 1763, five days before the Austro-Prussian peace of Hubertusburg, was by no means unfavorable to the defeated. The French Duke of Choiseul was a skillful and single-minded negotiator. The British, Pitt having fallen from office in 1761, were represented by a confused group of parliamentary favorites of the new king, George III. France ceded to Britain all French territory on the North American mainland east of the Mississippi. Canada thereby became British, and the colonials of the Thirteen Colonies were relieved of the French presence beyond the Alleghenies. To Spain, in return for aid in the last days of

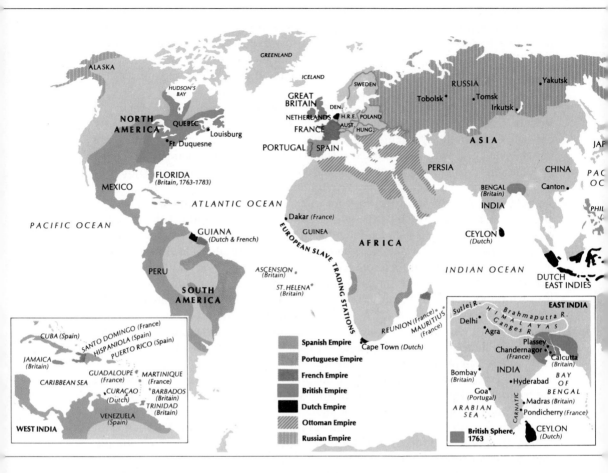

THE WORLD IN 1763

At the Peace of Paris of 1763 the British overseas empire triumphed over the French. The French ceded their holdings on the North American mainland east of the Mississippi to Britain, those west of the Mississippi to Spain. Britain also took Florida from Spain in 1763, but lost it, returning it to Spain in 1783, at the close of the War of American Independence. The French retained their sugar islands in the West Indies and their trading stations in India; they were stopped from empire-building but did not greatly suffer commercially from the Seven Years' War. The British proceeded to build their empire in India. (See also map, p. 328.)

the war, France ceded all holdings west of the Mississippi and at its mouth. France thereby abandoned the North American continent. But these almost empty regions were of minor commercial importance, and the French, in return for surrendering them, retained many economically more valuable establishments elsewhere. In the West Indies the British planters, and in England the powerful "West India interest," feared competition from the French sugar islands, which produced more cheaply, and wanted them left outside the protected economic system of the British empire. France therefore received back Guadeloupe and Martinique, as well as most of its slave stations in Africa. In India, the French remained in possession of their commercial installations—offices, warehouses, and docks—at Pondicherry and other towns. They were forbidden to erect fortifications or pursue political ambitions among Indian princes—a practice which neither the French nor the British government had hitherto much favored in any case.

The treaties of Paris and Hubertusburg, closing the prolonged war of the mid-century, made the year 1763 a memorable turning point. Prussia was to continue in being. The dualism of Germany was to be lasting; Austria and Prussia eyed each other as rivals. Frederick's aggression of 1740 was legalized and even moralized by the heroic defense that had proved necessary to retain the plunder. Frederick himself, from 1763 until his death in 1786, was a man of peace, philosophical and even benign. But the German crucible had boiled, and out of it had come a Prussia harder and more metallic than ever, more disposed, by its escape from annihilation, to glorify its army as the steel framework of its life.

The Anglo-French settlement was far-reaching and rather curious. Although the war was won ovewhelmingly by the British, it resulted in no commercial calamity to the French. French trade with America and the East grew as rapidly after the Seven Years' War as before it, and in 1785 was double what it had been in 1755. For England the war opened up new commercial channels. British trade with America and the East probably tripled between 1755 and 1785.[27] But the outstanding British gains were imperial and strategic. The European balance of power was preserved, the French had been kept out of Belgium, British subjects in North America seemed secure, and Britain had again vindicated its command of the sea. British sea power implied, in turn, that British seaborne commerce was safe in peace or war, while the seaborne commerce for the French, or of any others, depended ultimately on the political requirements of the British. But the French still had a few cards to play, and were to play them in the American and French Revolutions.

For America and India the peace of 1763 was decisive. America north of Mexico was to become part of an English-speaking world. In India the British government was drawn increasingly into a policy of territorial occupation; a British "paramount power" eventually emerged in place of the empire of the Moguls. British political rule in India stimulated British business there, until in the greatest days of British prosperity India was one of the main pillars of the British economic system, and the road to India became in a real sense the lifeline of the British empire. But in 1763 this state of affairs was still in the future and was to be reached by many intermediate steps.

[27] See pp. 259–262.

VII.
THE SCIENTIFIC
VIEW OF
THE WORLD

THE SEVENTEENTH CENTURY has been called the century of genius. One reason is that it was the age when science became "modern." It was the great age of Galileo and Sir Isaac Newton, whose combined lifetimes spanned the century, with Galileo dying and Newton being born in the same year, 1642. When Galileo was young those who probed into the secrets of nature still labored largely in the dark, isolated from one another and from the general public, working oftentimes by methods of trial and error, not altogether clear on what they were trying to do, with their thinking still complicated by ideas not nowadays considered scientific. They had nevertheless accomplished a good deal. Discoveries had been made, and ideas developed, without which the intellectual revolution of the seventeenth century would not have occurred. But in a way all scientific investigators before Galileo seem to be precursors, patient workers destined never to enter into the world toward which they labored. In 1727, when Newton died, all was changed. Scientific men were in continual touch with one another, and science was recognized as one of the principal enterprises of European society. Scientific methods of inquiry had been defined. The store of factual knowledge had become very large. The first modern scientific synthesis, or coherent theory of the physical universe, had been presented by Newton. Scientific knowledge was applied increasingly to navigation, mining, agriculture, and many branches of manufacture. Science and invention were joining hands. Science was accepted as the main force in the advancement of civilization and progress. And science was becoming popularized; many people who were not

Chapter Emblem: A Copernican globe designed by Kepler in 1596 to illustrate movement of the planets about the sun.

themselves scientists "believed" in science and attempted to apply scientific habits of thought to diverse problems of man and society.

The history of science is too great a story to be told in this book, but there are a few ideas about it which even a book of this kind must attempt to make clear. First, science, purely as a form of thought, is one of the supreme achievements of the human mind, and to have a humanistic understanding of man's powers one must sense the importance of science, as of philosophy, literature, or the arts. Second, science has increasingly affected practical affairs, entering into the health, wealth, and happiness of human kind. It has changed the size of populations and the use of raw materials, revolutionized methods of production, transport, business, and war, and so helped to relieve some human problems while aggravating others. This is especially true of modern civilization since the seventeenth century. Third, in the modern world ideas have had a way of passing over from science into other domains of thought. Many people today, for example, in their notions of themselves, their neighbors, or the meaning of life, are influenced by ideas which they believe to be those of Freud or Einstein—they talk of repressions or relativity without necessarily knowing much about them. Ideas derived from biology and from Darwin—such as evolution and the struggle for existence— have likewise spread far and wide. Similarly the scientific revolution of the seventeenth century had repercussions far beyond the realm of pure science. It changed ideas of religion and of God and man. And it helped to spread certain very deep-seated beliefs, such as that the physical universe in which man finds himself is essentially orderly and harmonious, that the human reason is capable of understanding and dealing with it, and that man can conduct his own affairs by methods of peaceable exchange of ideas and rational agreement. Thus was laid a foundation for belief in free and democratic institutions.

The purpose of this chapter is to sketch the rise of modern science in the seventeenth century and the emergence of the scientific view of the world and of human affairs. The chapter that follows will describe the popularization and application of these ideas in the eighteenth century, in the era generally known as the Age of Enlightenment.

32. Prophets of a Scientific Civilization: Bacon and Descartes

Science before the Seventeenth Century

The scientific view became characteristic of European society about the middle of the seventeenth century. There had, indeed, been a few in earlier times who caught glimpses of a whole civilization reared upon science. To us today the most famous of these is Leonardo da Vinci (1452–1519), the universal genius of the Italian Renaissance, who had been artist, engineer, and scientific thinker all in one. Leonardo, by actual dissection of dead bodies, had obtained an accurate knowledge of human anatomy; he had conceived of the circulation of the blood and the movement of the earth about the sun; and he had drawn designs for submarines and airplanes and speculated on the use of parachutes and poison gases. But Leonardo had not published his scientific ideas. He was known almost exclusively as an artist. His work in science remained outside the stream of scientific thought, without influence on its course. It was not even known until the discovery of his private notebooks in recent years. Leonardo thus figures in the history of science as an isolated genius, a man of brilliant insights and audacious theories, which died with their author's death, whereas science depends on a transmission of ideas in which investigators build upon one another's discoveries, test one another's experiments, and fill in the gaps in one another's knowledge.

A century after the death of Leonardo da Vinci educated Europeans were by no means scientifically minded. Among thoughtful persons many currents were stirring. On the one hand there was a great deal of skepticism, a constantly doubting frame of mind, which held that no certain knowledge is possible for human beings at all, that all beliefs are essentially only customs, that some people believe one thing and some another, and that there is no sound way of choosing between them. This attitude was best expressed by the French essayist Montaigne (1533–1592), whose thought distilled itself into an eternal question, *Que sais-je?* "What do I know?" with the always implied answer, "Nothing." Montaigne's philosophy led to a tolerant, humane, and broad-minded outlook; but as a system of thought it was not otherwise very constructive. On the other hand, there was also a tendency to over-believe, arising from the same inability to distinguish between true and false. There was no accepted line between chemistry and alchemy, or between astronomy and astrology; all alike were regarded as ways of penetrating the "secrets" of nature. The sixteenth century had been a great age of charlatans, such as Nostradamus and Paracelsus, some of whom, notably Paracelsus, mixed magic and valid science in a way hardly understandable to us today.[1] As late as the seventeenth century, especially in central Europe where the Thirty Years' War produced chaos and terror, kings and generals kept private astrologers to divine the future. The two centuries from about 1450 to about 1650 were also the period when fear of witches was at its height. The witchcraft panic lasted longest in Germany and central Europe, probably kept alive by the insecurities engendered by the Thirty Years' War. But about twenty persons were hanged as witches in Massachusetts as late as 1692, for the English colonies, as a remote and outlying part of the European world, were among the last to feel some of the waves originating in Europe. It was in Scotland, another outlying region of Europe, that the last known execution for witchcraft took place, in 1722.

It was by no means clear, in the early part of the seventeenth century, which way Europe was going to develop. It might conceivably have fallen into a kind of chaos, as India did at about this time. We have seen that much of Europe was racked by chronic and marauding violence, to which an end was put by the consolidation of the modern state and the conversion of armed bands into organized and disciplined armies. Similarly, in things of the mind, there was no settled order. Doubt went with superstition, indifference with persecution. Science in time provided Europe with a new faith in itself. The rise of science in the

[1] See p. 63.

seventeenth century possibly saved European civilization from petering out in a long postmedieval afterglow, or from wandering off into the diverse paths of a genial skepticism, ineffectual philosophizing, desultory magic, or mad fear of the unknown.

Bacon and Descartes

Two men stand out as prophets of a world reconstructed by science. One was the Englishman Francis Bacon (1561–1626), the other the Frenchman René Descartes (1596–1650). Both published their most influential books between 1620 and 1640. Both addressed themselves to the problem of knowledge. Both asked themselves how it is possible for human beings to know anything with certainty or to have a reliable, truthful, and usable knowledge of the world of nature. Both shared in the doubts of their day. They branded virtually all beliefs of preceding generations (outside religion) as worthless. Both ridiculed the tendency to put faith in ancient books, to cite the writings of Aristotle or others, on questions having to do with the workings of nature. Both attacked earlier methods of seeking knowledge; they rejected the methods of the "schoolmen" or "scholastics," the thinkers in the academic tradition of the universities founded in the Middle Ages. On the whole, medieval philosophy had been rationalistic and deductive.[2] That is, its characteristic procedure was to start with definitions and general propositions and then discover what further knowledge could be logically deduced from the definitions thus accepted. Or it proceeded by affirming the nature of an object to be such-and-such (e.g., that "man is a political animal") and then described how objects of such a nature do or should behave. These methods, which owed much to Aristotle and other ancient codifiers of human thought, had generally ceased to be fruitful in discovery of knowledge of nature. Bacon and Descartes held that the medieval (or Aristotelian) methods were backward. They held that truth is not something that we postulate at the beginning and then explore in all its ramifications, but that it is something which we find at the end, after a long process of investigation, experiment, or intermediate thought.

Bacon and Descartes thus went beyond mere doubt. They offered a constructive program, and though their programs were different, they both became heralds or philosophers of a scientific view. They maintained that there was a true and reliable method of knowledge. And they maintained in addition that once this true method was known and practiced, once the real workings of nature were understood, men would be able to use this knowledge for their own purposes, control nature in their own interests, make undreamed of useful inventions, improve their mechanical arts, and add generally to their wealth and comfort. Bacon and Descartes thus announced the advent of a scientific civilization.

Francis Bacon planned a great work in many volumes, to be known as the *Instauratio Magna* or "Great Renewal," calling for a complete new start in science and civilization. He completed only two parts. One, published in 1620, was the *Novum Organum* or new method of acquiring knowledge. Here he

---

[2] See pp. 39–42.

insisted on *inductive* method. In the inductive method we proceed from the particular to the general, from the concrete to the abstract. For example, in the study of leaves, if we examine millions of actual leaves, of all sizes and shapes, and if we assemble, observe, and compare them with minute scrutiny, we are using an *inductive* method in the sense meant by Bacon; if successful, we may arrive at a knowledge, based on observed facts, of the general nature of a leaf as such. If, on the other hand, we begin with a general idea of what we think all leaves are like, i.e., all leaves have stems, and then proceed to describe an individual leaf on that basis, we are following the *deductive* method; we draw logical implications from what we already know, but we learn no more of the nature of a leaf than what we knew or thought we knew at the beginning. Bacon advised men to put aside all traditional ideas, to rid themselves of prejudices and preconceptions, to look at the world with fresh eyes, to observe and study the innumerable things that are actually perceived by the senses. Thinkers before Bacon used the inductive method, but he formalized it as a method and became a leading philosopher of empiricism. This philosophy, the founding of knowledge on observation and experience, has always proved a useful safeguard against fitting facts into preconceived patterns. It demands that we let the patterns of our thought be shaped by actual facts as we observe them.

The other completed part of Bacon's great work, published in 1623, was called in its English translation *The Advancement of Learning*. Here Bacon developed the same ideas and especially insisted that true knowledge was useful knowledge. In *The New Atlantis* (1627), he portrayed a scientific utopia whose inhabitants enjoyed a perfect society through their knowledge and command of nature. The usefulness of knowledge became the other main element in the Baconian tradition. In this view there was no sharp difference between pure science and applied science or between the work of the purely scientific investigators and that of the mechanics or inventors who in their own way probed into nature and devised instruments or machines for putting natural forces to work. The fact that knowledge could be used for practical purposes became a sign or proof that it was true knowledge. For example, the fact that soldiers could aim their cannon and hit their targets more accurately in the seventeenth century became a proof of the theory of ballistics which had been scientifically worked out. Enthusiastic Baconians believed that knowledge was power. True knowledge could be put to work, if not immediately at least in the long run, after more knowledge was discovered. It was useful to mankind, unlike the "delicate learning" of the misguided scholastics. In this coming together of knowledge and power arose the far-reaching modern idea of progress. And in it arose many modern problems, since the power given by scientific knowledge can be either bad or good.

But Bacon, though a force in redirecting the European mind, never had much influence on the development of actual science. Kept busy as Lord Chancellor of England and in other government duties, he was not even fully abreast of the most advanced scientific thought of his day. Like the public generally of his lifetime, he was undisturbed by the new theories of astronomers who held that the earth moved about the sun. Bacon's greatest weakness was his failure to understand the role of mathematics. Mathematics, dealing with pure abstractions and proceeding deductively from axioms to theorems, was not an empirical or inductive method of thought such as Bacon demanded. Yet science in the seventeenth century went forward most successfully in subjects where mathematics could be applied. Even today the degree to which a subject is truly scientific depends on the degree to which it can be made mathematical. We have pure science where we have formulas and equations, and the scientific method itself is both inductive and deductive.

Descartes was a great mathematician in his own right. He is considered the inventor of coordinate geometry. He showed that by use of coordinates (or graph paper, in simple language) any algebraic formula could be plotted as a curve in space, and contrariwise that any curve in space, however complex, could be converted into algebraic terms and thus dealt with by methods of calculation. And one effect of his general philosophy was to create belief in a vast world of nature that could be reduced to mathematical form.

Descartes set forth his ideas in his *Discourse on Method*, in 1637, and in many more technical writings. He advanced the principle of systematic doubt. He began by trying to doubt everything that could reasonably be doubted, thus sweeping away past ideas and clearing the ground for his own "great renewal," to use Bacon's phrase. He held that he could not doubt his own existence as a thinking and doubting being (*cogito ergo sum,* "I think, therefore I exist"); he then deduced, by systematic reasoning, the existence of God and much else. He arrived at a philosophy of dualism, the famous "Cartesian dualism," which held that God has created two kinds of fundamental reality in the universe. One was "thinking substance"—mind, spirit, consciousness, subjective experience. The other was "extended substance"—everything outside the mind and hence objective. Of everything except the mind itself the most fundamental and universal quality was that it occupied a portion of space, minute or vast. Space itself was conceived as infinite, and everywhere geometric.

This philosophy had profound and long-lasting effects. For one thing, the seemingly most real elements in human experience, color and sound, joy and grief, seemed somehow to be shadowy and unreal, or at least illusive, with no existence outside the mind itself. But all else was quantitative, measurable, reducible to formulas or equations. Over all else, over the whole universe or half-universe of "extended substance," the most powerful instrument available to the human understanding, namely, mathematics, reigned supreme. "Give me motion and extension," said Descartes, "and I will build you the world."

Descartes also, with French genius, expressed the Baconian idea. Instead of the "speculative philosophy of the schools," he wrote in the *Discourse on Method,* one might discover a "practical philosophy by which, understanding the forces and action of fire, water, air, the stars and heavens and all other bodies that surround us, as distinctly as we understand the mechanical arts of our craftsmen, we can use these forces in the same way for all purposes for which they are appropriate, and so make ourselves the masters and possessors of nature. And this is desirable not only for the invention of innumerable devices by which we may enjoy without trouble the fruits of the earth and the conveniences it affords, but mainly also for the preservation of health, which is undoubtedly the principal good and foundation of all other good things in this life."

33. The Road to Newton: The Law of Universal Gravitation

Scientific Advances

Meanwhile actual scientific discovery was advancing on many fronts. It did not advance on all with equal speed. Some of the sciences were, and long remained, dependent mainly on the collection of specimens. Botany was one of these; Europe's knowledge of plants expanded enormously with the explorations overseas, and botanical gardens and herb collections in Europe became far more extensive than ever before, bringing important enlargements in the stock of medicinal drugs. Other sciences drew their impetus from intensive and open-minded observation. The Flemish Vesalius, by a book published in 1543, *The Structure of the Human Body,* renewed and modernized the study of anatomy. Formerly anatomists had generally held that the writings of Galen, dating from the second century A.D., contained an authoritative description of all human muscles and tissues. They had indeed dissected cadavers but had dismissed those not conforming to Galen's description as somehow abnormal or not typical. Vesalius put Galen behind him and based his general description of the human frame on actual bodies as he found them. In physiology also, dealing with the functioning rather than the structure of living bodies, there was considerable progress. Here the method of laboratory experiment could be profitably used. William Harvey, after years of laboratory work, including the vivisection of animals, published in 1628 a book *On the Movement of the Heart and Blood.* Here he set forth the doctrine, confirmed by evidence, of the continual circulation of the blood through arteries and veins. The Italian Malpighi, using the newly invented microscope, confirmed Harvey's findings by the discovery of capillaries in 1661. The Dutch Leeuwenhoek, also by use of the microscope, was the first to see blood corpuscles, spermatozoa, and bacteria, of which he left published drawings.

These sciences, and also chemistry, although work in them went continually on, did not come fully into their own until after 1800. They were long overshadowed by astronomy and physics. Here mathematics could be most fully applied, and mathematics underwent a rapid development in the seventeenth century. Decimals came into use to express fractions, the symbols used in algebra were improved

A SCHOLAR HOLDING A THESIS ON BOTANY
by Willem Moreelse (Dutch, before 1630–1666)
The Netherlands became a great intellectual center in the seventeenth century, with five universities founded during the years of struggle against Spain. The most famous was at Leyden, but the present scholar may be a new doctor of the University of Utrecht, where the little-known painter Willem Moreelse worked. Crowned with laurel, the successful candidate proudly displays his thesis, on which the Latin words announce that "any plant shows the presence of God." The bringing of hitherto unknown plants from the rest of the world to Europe contributed strongly not only to science but to medicine, food supply, and the pleasures of chocolate, tea, and coffee. Courtesy of The Toledo Museum of Art, Gift of Edward Drummond Libbey, 1962.

and standardized, and in 1614 logarithms were invented by the Scot John Napier. Coordinate geometry was mapped out by Descartes, the theory of probabilities developed by Pascal, and calculus invented simultaneously in England by Newton and in Germany by Leibniz. These advances made it more generally possible to think about nature in purely quantitative terms, to measure with greater precision, and to perform complex and laborious computations. Physics and astronomy were remarkably stimulated, and it was in this field that the most astonishing scientific revolution of the seventeenth century took place.

The Scientific Revolution: Copernicus to Galileo

From time immemorial, since the Greek Ptolemy had codified ancient astronomy in the second century A.D.,[3] educated Europeans had held a conception of the cosmos which we call Ptolemaic. The cosmos in this view was a group of concentric spheres, a series of balls within balls each having the same center. The innermost ball was the earth, made up of hard, solid, earthy substance such as people were familiar with underfoot. The other spheres, encompassing the earth in series, were all transparent. They were the "crystalline spheres" made known to us by the poets; their harmony was the "music of the spheres." These spheres all revolved about the earth, each sphere containing, set in it as a jewel, a luminous heavenly body or orb which moved about the earth with the movement of its transparent sphere. Nearest to the earth was the sphere of the moon; then, in turn, the spheres of Mercury and Venus, then the sphere of the sun, then those of the outer planets. Last came the outermost sphere containing all the fixed stars studded in it, all moving majestically about the earth in daily motion, but motionless with respect to each other because held firmly in the same sphere. Beyond the sphere of the fixed stars, in general belief, lay the "empyrean," the home of angels and immortal spirits; but this was not a matter of natural science.

Persons standing on the earth, and looking up into the sky, thus felt themselves to be enclosed by a dome of which their own position was the center. In the blue sky of day they could literally see the crystalline spheres; in the stars at night they could behold the orbs which these spheres carried with them. All revolved about the person, presumably at no very alarming distance. The celestial bodies were commonly supposed to be of different material and quality from the earth. The earth was of heavy dross; the stars and planets and the sun and moon seemed made of pure and gleaming light, or at least of a bright ethereal substance almost as tenuous as the crystal spheres in which they moved. The cosmos was a hierarchy of ascending perfection. The heavens were purer than the earth.

This system corresponded to actual appearances, and except for scientific knowledge would be highly believable today. It was formulated also in rigorous mathematical terms. Ever since the Greeks, and becoming increasingly intricate in the Middle Ages, a complex geometry had grown up to explain the observed motion of the heavenly bodies. The Ptolemaic system was a mathematical system. And it was for purely mathematical reasons that it first came to be reconsidered. There was a marked revival of mathematical interest at the close of the Middle Ages, in the fourteenth and fifteenth centuries, a renewed concentration on the

[3] See p. 13.

philosophical traditions of Pythagoras and Plato. In these philosophies could be found the doctrine that numbers might be the final key to the mysteries of nature. With them went a metaphysical belief that simplicity was more likely to be a sign of truth than complication, and that a simpler mathematical formulation was better than a more complex one.

These ideas motivated Nicholas Copernicus, born in Poland of German and Polish background, who, after study in Italy, wrote his epochal work *On the Revolutions of the Heavenly Orbs*. In this book, published in 1543 after his death, he held the sun to be the center of the solar system and fixed stars, and the earth to be one of the planets revolving in space around it. This view had been entertained by a few isolated thinkers before. Copernicus gave a mathematical demonstration. To him it was a purely mathematical problem. With increasingly detailed knowledge of the actual movement of the heavenly bodies it had become necessary to make the Ptolemaic system more intricate by the addition of new "cycles" and "epicycles," until, as John Milton expressed it later, the cosmos was

> *With Centric and Concentric scribbled o'er,*
> *Cycle and Epicycle, Orb in Orb.*

Copernicus needed fewer such hypothetical constructions to explain the known movements of the heavenly bodies. The heliocentric or sun-centered theory was mathematically a little simpler than the geocentric or earth-centered theory hitherto held.

The Copernican doctrine long remained a hypothesis known only to experts. Most astronomers for a time hesitated to accept it, seeing no need, from the evidence yet produced, of so overwhelming a readjustment of current ideas. Tycho Brahe (1546–1601), the greatest authority on the actual positions and movements of the heavenly bodies in the generations immediately after Copernicus, never accepted the Copernican system in full. But his assistant and follower, John Kepler (1571–1630), not only accepted the Copernican theory but carried it further.

Kepler, a German, was a kind of mathematical mystic, part-time astrologer, and scientific genius. He felt ecstasy at the mysterious harmonies of mathematical forms. He built upon the exact observations of Tycho Brahe. Copernicus had believed the orbits of the planets about the sun to be perfect circles. Tycho showed that this belief did not fit the observable facts. Kepler discovered that the orbits of the planets were ellipses. The ellipse, like the circle, is an abstract mathematical figure with knowable properties. Kepler demonstrated that, as a planet moves in its elliptical path about the sun, the straight line connecting it with the sun sweeps through an area of space proportional to the time taken by the planet's motion; that is, that a planet sweeps equal areas in equal times; or, more simply, that the closer a planet is to the sun in its elliptical orbit, the faster it moves. Kepler further showed that the length of time in which the several planets revolve about the sun varies proportionately with their distance from the sun: the square of the time is proportional to the cube of the distance.

It is not possible for most people to understand the mathematics involved, but it is possible to realize the astounding implications of Kepler's laws of planetary motion. Kepler showed that the actual world of stubborn facts, as observed by Tycho, and the purely rational world of mathematical harmony, as surmised by Copernicus, were not really in any discrepancy with each other; that they really corresponded exactly. Why they should he did not know; it was the mystery of numbers. He digested an overwhelming amount of hitherto unexplained information into a few brief statements. He showed a cosmic mathematical relationship between space and time. And he described the movement of the planets in explicit formulas, which any competent person could verify at will.

The next step was taken by Galileo (1564–1642). So far the question of what the heavenly bodies were made of had hardly been affected. Indeed, they were not thought of as bodies at all, but rather as orbs. Only the sun and moon had any dimension; stars and planets were only points of light; and the theories of Copernicus and Kepler, like those of Ptolemy, might apply to insubstantial luminous objects in motion. In 1609 Galileo built a telescope. Turning it to the sky, he perceived that the moon had a rough and apparently mountainous surface, as if made of the same kind of material as the earth. Seeing clearly the dark part of the moon in its various phases, and noting that in every position it only reflected the light of the sun, he concluded that the moon was not itself a luminous object, another indication that it might be made of earthlike substance. He saw spots on the sun, as if the sun were not pure and perfect. He found that the planets had visible breadth when seen in the telescope, but that the fixed stars remained only points of light, as if incalculably further away. He discovered also that Jupiter had satellites, moons moving around it like the moon around the earth. These discoveries reassured him of the validity of the Copernican theory, which he had in any case already accepted. They suggested also that the heavenly bodies might be of the same substance as the earth, masses of matter moving in space. Contrariwise, it became easier to think of the earth as itself a kind of heavenly body revolving about the sun. The difference between the earth and the heavens was disappearing. This struck a terrifying blow at all earlier philosophy and theology. Some professors were afraid to look through the telescope, and Galileo was condemned and forced to an ostensible recantation by his church.

Moreover, where Kepler had found mathematical laws describing the movement of planets, Galileo found mathematical laws describing the movement of bodies on the earth. Formerly it had been thought that some bodies were by nature heavier than others, and that heavier bodies fell to the ground faster than light ones. Galileo in 1591, according to the story, dropped a ten-pound and a one-pound weight simultaneously from the top of the Leaning Tower of Pisa. The truth of this story has been questioned, but in any case Galileo showed that despite all previous speculation on the subject two bodies of different weights, when allowance was made for differences in air resistance due to differences of size or shape, struck the ground at the same time. His further work in dynamics, or the science of motion of bodies, took many years to accomplish. He had to devise more refined means for measuring small intervals of time, find means of estimating the air resistance, friction, and other impediments which always occur in nature, and conceive of pure or absolute motion, and of force and velocity, in abstract mathematical terms. He made use of a new conception of inertia, in which only *change* in motion, not the origination of motion, had to be explained. This dispensed with the need of an Unmoved Mover felt in the older philosophy.

Of bodies moving on the earth, Galileo discovered that when falling freely they fall with a velocity that increases according to mathematical formula.

The Achievement of Newton: The Promise of Science

It was the supreme achievement of Newton (1642–1727) to bring Kepler and Galileo together, that is, to show that Kepler's laws of planetary motion and Galileo's laws of terrestrial motion were two aspects of the same laws. Galileo's findings, holding that moving bodies move uniformly in a straight line unless deflected by a definite force, made it necessary to explain why the planets, instead of flying off in straight lines, tend to fall toward the sun, the result being their elliptical orbits—and why the moon, similarly, tends to fall toward the earth. Newton seems early to have suspected that the answer would be related to Galileo's laws of falling bodies—that is, that gravity, or the pull of the earth upon objects on earth, might be a form of a universal gravitation, or similar pull, characterizing all bodies in the solar system. Great technical difficulties stood in the way, but finally, after inventing calculus, and using a new measurement of the size of the earth made by a Frenchman and experiments with circular motion made by the Dutch Huyghens on the pendulum, Newton was able to bring his calculations to fruition, and to publish, in 1687, his *Mathematical Principles of Natural Philosophy*.

This stupendous book showed that all motion that could then be timed and measured, whether on the earth or in the solar system, could be described by the same mathematical formulas. All matter moved as if every particle attracted every other particle with a force proportional to the product of the two masses, and inversely proportional to the square of the distance between them. This "force" was universal gravitation. What it was Newton did not pretend to explain. For two hundred years the law stood unshaken, always verified by every new relevant discovery. Only in the last century have its limitations been found; it does not hold good in the infinitesimal world of subatomic structure or in the macrocosm of the whole physical universe as now conceived.

It was in Newton's time that the pursuit of natural knowledge became institutionalized. Organized bodies of men, possessing equipment and funds, were engaged in scientific study, most notably the Royal Society of London, founded in 1662, and the Royal Academy of Sciences in France, founded in 1666. Both originated when earlier and informal groups, usually gentlemen of the landed class, received charters from their governments to pursue scientific interests. Scientific periodicals began to be published. Scientific societies provided the medium for prompt interchange of ideas indispensable to the growth of scientific knowledge. They held meetings, proposed projects for research, and published articles not only on the natural sciences and mathematics, but also on paleography, numismatics, chronology, legal history, and natural law. The work of the learned had not yet yielded to specialization.

In all these activities the promise of science seemed fulfilled. Even in practical affairs conveniences followed, as anticipated by the Baconians. The tides could now be understood and predicted by the gravitational interplay of earth, moon, and sun. Exact mathematical knowledge of the celestial bodies, together with the invention of more accurate timepieces, was of great help to navigation and map-making. Measures of latitude, or of north-south distances on the spherical earth, had been known to the ancient Greeks. But longitude, or east-west distances, could not be measured until the eighteenth century, when it became possible to determine it by use of a chronometer and observation of heavenly bodies at a known time. Merchant ships and naval squadrons could thus operate with more assurance. Places on land could be located and mapped more exactly. Eighteenth-century Europeans were the first human beings to have a fairly accurate idea of the shapes and sizes of continents and oceans. Better local and regional maps of places in Europe also became available.

Or again, mathematical advance, including the development of calculus, which allowed an exact treatment of curves and trajectories, reinforced by technical discoveries in the working of metals, led to an increased use of artillery. Armies in 1750 used twice as many cannon per soldier as in 1650. Naval ordnance also improved. These were items making armed forces more expensive to maintain, requiring governments to increase their taxes, and hence producing constitutional crises. Improved firearms likewise heightened the advantage of armies over insurrectionists or private fighting bands, thus strengthening the sovereignty of the state. They gave Europeans the military advantage over other peoples, in America, India, or elsewhere, on which the world ascendancy of Europe in the European age was built.

The instance of the steam engine may also be cited. Steam power was eventually almost literally to move the world. In 1700 it was a cloud no bigger than a man's hand. Yet it was in sight on the horizon. A Frenchman, Denis Papin, in 1681 invented a device in which steam moved a piston, but it produced so little power that it was used only in cooking. British scientists turned their minds to it. Robert Boyle, discoverer of "Boyle's Law" on the pressure of gases, studied the problem; scientists, mechanics, and instrument makers collaborated. In 1702 Thomas Newcomen, a man without scientific training but associated with scientists, produced the steam engine known thereafter as Newcomen's engine, from which, as will be seen, James Watt developed the steam engine as we know it. Newcomen's engine was primitive according to later ideas. It burned so much fuel that it could be used only in coal mines. But it was used. Not long after 1700 it was widely employed to pump water from the coal pits. It saved labor, cheapened production, and opened hitherto unusable deposits to exploitation. It was the first application of steam to an economic purpose.

No distinction was yet felt between pure and applied science. The modern sense of the word hardly existed; what we call "science" was called natural philosophy or "useful knowledge." Traveling public lecturers in explaining the laws of force and motion showed their application in devices such as pulleys, scales, levers, cogwheels, waterwheels, and pumps. Such lectures were attended, especially in England, by a mixed audience of philosophers, experimenters, inventors, artisans, landed gentlemen who wished to develop their estates, and small businessmen wishing to enlarge their markets. The scientific movement thus opened the way to agricultural and industrial improvements in Great Britain.

The Scientific Revolution and the World of Thought

It was perhaps in the world of thought that the revolution accomplished from Copernicus to Newton was most profound. It has been called the greatest spiritual readjustment that human beings have been required to make. The old heavens were exploded. Humans were no longer the center of creation. The luminaries of the sky no longer shone to light their way or to give them beauty. The sky itself was an illusion, its color a thing in the mind only, for anyone looking upward was really looking only into the darkness of endless space. The old cosmos, comfortably enclosed and ranked in an ascending order of purity, gave way to a new cosmos which seemed to consist of an infinite emptiness through which particles of matter were distributed. Humans were the puny denizens of a material object swinging in space along with other very distant material objects of the same kind. About the physical universe there was nothing especially Christian, nothing that the God portrayed in the Bible would be likely to have made. The gap between Christianity and natural science, always present yet always bridged in the Middle Ages, now opened wider than ever. It was felt with anguish by some in the seventeenth century, notably by the Frenchman Blaise Pascal, a considerable scientist, preeminent mathematician, and deep and troubled Christian believer. He left a record of his state of mind in his *Pensées*, or *Thoughts*, jottings from which he hoped some day to write a great book on the Christian faith. ''I am terrified,'' he said in one of these jottings, ''by the eternal silence of these infinite spaces.''

But on the whole the reaction was more optimistic. Man might be merely a reed, as Pascal said, but Pascal added, ''a thinking reed.'' Man might be no longer the physical center of the world. But it was the human mind that had penetrated the world's laws. The Newtonian system, as it became popularized, a process which took about fifty years, led to a great intellectual complacency. Never had confidence in human powers been so high. As Alexander Pope put it,

> Nature and nature's laws lay hid in night;
> God said, ''Let Newton be,'' and all was light.

Or, according to another epigram on the subject, there was only one universe to discover, and this universe had been discovered by Newton. Everything seemed possible to the human reason. The old feeling of dependency on God lost much of its force, or became something to be discussed by clergymen in church on Sunday. Human beings were not really little creatures, wayfarers in a world that was alien, yearning for the reunion with God that would bring peace. They were creatures of great capacity in their own right, living in a world that was understandable and manageable, and in which they might install themselves with quite adequate comfort. These ideas contributed greatly to the secularizing of European society, pushing religion and churches to the sidelines.

The scientific discoveries also reinforced the old philosophy of natural law. This philosophy, developed by the Greeks and renewed in the Middle Ages, held that the universe is fundamentally orderly, and that there is a natural rightness or justice, universally the same for all people, and knowable by reason. It was very important in political theory, where it stood out against arbitrariness and the mere claims of power. The laws of nature as discovered by science were somewhat different, but they taught the same lesson, namely, the orderliness and minute regularity of the world. It was reassuring to feel that everywhere throughout an infinite space, whether or not yet discovered and probed by man, every particle of matter was quietly attracting every other particle by a force proportionate to the product of the masses and inversely proportional to the square of the distance. The physical universe laid bare by science—orderly, rational, balanced, smoothly running, without strife or rivalry or contention—became a model on which many thinkers, as time went on, hoped to refashion human society. They hoped to make society also fulfill the rule of law.

In some ways it would be possible to exaggerate the impact of pure science. Scientists themselves did not usually apply their scientific ideas to religion and society. Few suffered the spiritual torment of Pascal. Both Descartes and Newton wrote earnest tracts arguing for the truth of certain religious doctrines. Bacon and Harvey were conservative politically, upholders of king against Parliament. The Englishman Joseph Glanvill, in the 1660s, used the Cartesian dualism to demonstrate the probable existence of witches. Descartes, despite his systematic doubt, held that the customs of one's country were to be accepted without question. Natural science, in the pure sense, was not inherently revolutionary or even upsetting. If Europeans in the seventeenth century began to waver in many old beliefs it was not only because of the stimulus of pure science, but also because of an increasing knowledge and study of humanity itself.

34. New Knowledge of Man and Society

Here one of the most potent forces at work was the discovery and exploration of the world overseas. Europe was already becoming part of the world as a whole, and could henceforth understand itself only by comparison with non-European regions. Great reciprocal influences were at work. The influences of European expansion on other parts of the world are easily seen: the Indian societies of America were modified or extinguished, the indigenous societies of Africa were dislocated and many of their members enslaved and transported; in the long run even the ancient societies of Asia were to be undermined. From the beginning the counterinfluence of the rest of the world upon Europe was equally great. It took the form not only of new medicines, new diseases, new foods, new and exotic manufactures brought to Europe, and the growth of material wealth in west-European countries. It affected European thinking also. It undermined the old Europe and its ideas, just as Europe was undermining the old cultures beyond the oceans. Vast new horizons opened before Europeans in the sixteenth and seventeenth centuries. Europeans of this period were the first people to whom it was given to know the globe as a whole, or to realize the variety of the human race and its multifarious manners and customs.

The Current of Skepticism

This realization was very unsettling. The realization of human differences had the effect, in Europe, of breaking what anthropologists call the "cake of custom." A new sense of the relative nature of social institutions developed. It became harder to believe in any absolute rightness of one's own ways. Montaigne, already mentioned, expressed the relativist outlook clearly, and nowhere more clearly than in his famous essay on cannibals. The cannibals, he said humorously, did in fact eat human flesh; that was their custom, and they have their customs as we have ours; they would think some of our ways odd or inhuman; peoples differ, and who are we to judge? Travelers' books spread the same message increasingly through the seventeenth century. As one of them observed (whether or not rightly), in Turkey it was the custom to shave the hair and wear the beard, in Europe to shave the beard and wear the hair; what difference does it really make? That the ways of non-Europeans might be good ways was emphasized by Jesuit missionaries. Writing from the depths of the Mississippi Valley or from China, the Jesuit fathers often dwelt on the natural goodness and mental alertness of the native peoples they encountered, perhaps hoping in this way to gain support in Europe for their missionary labors. Sometimes strange people appeared in Europe itself. In 1684 a delegation of aristocratic Siamese arrived in Paris, followed by another in 1686. The Parisians went through a fad for Siam; they recounted how the king of Siam, when asked by a missionary to turn Christian, replied that divine Providence, had it wished a single religion to prevail in the world, could easily have so arranged it. The Siamese seemed civilized, wise, philosophic; they allowed Christians to preach in their own country, whereas it was well known what would happen to a Siamese missionary who undertook to preach in Paris. China also was seen through an ideal glow. By 1700 there were even professors of Arabic, at Paris, Oxford, and Utrecht, who said that Islam was a religion to be respected, as good for Muslims as Christianity was for Christians.

Thus was created a strong current of skepticism, holding that all beliefs are relative, varying with time and place. Its greatest spokesman at the end of the century was Pierre Bayle (1647–1706). Bayle was influenced by the scientific discoveries also; not exactly that he understood them, for he was an almost purely literary scholar, but he realized that many popular beliefs were without foundation. Between 1680 and 1682 a number of comets were seen. The one of 1682 was studied by a friend of Newton's, Edmund Halley, the first man to predict the return of a comet. He identified the one of 1682 with the one observed in 1302, 1456, 1531, and 1607, and predicted its reappearance in 1757 (it appeared in 1759); it was seen again in 1910 and 1986 and is still called Halley's Comet. In the 1680s people were talking of comets excitedly. Some said that comets emitted poisonous exhalations, others that they were supernatural omens of future events. Bayle, in his *Thoughts on the Comet*, argued at great length that there was no basis for any such beliefs except human credulity. In 1697 he published his *Historical and Critical Dictionary*, a tremendous repository of miscellaneous lore, conveying the message that what is called truth is often mere opinion, that most people are amazingly gullible, that many things firmly believed are really ridiculous, and that it is very foolish to hold too strongly to one's own views.

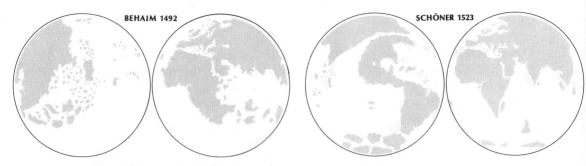

BEHAIM 1492

SCHÖNER 1523

THE GROWTH OF GEOGRAPHICAL KNOWLEDGE

The four maps show the best scientific knowledge at their respective dates. Behaim has no inkling of the existence of America and has filled in the hemisphere opposite to Europe with a mass of islands, representing what he has heard of the East Indies and Japan. He knows pretty well the limits of Africa. Schöner in 1523 fills in America and even distinguishes two American continents. He knows of the Gulf of Mexico but fails to realize the narrowness of the Isthmus of Panama. He knows of the Straits of Magellan (but not Cape Horn) and hopefully fills in a corresponding Northwest Passage in the

Bayle's *Dictionary* remained a reservoir on which skeptical writers continued to draw for generations. Bayle himself, having no firm basis in his own mind for settled judgment, mixed skepticism with an impulse to faith. Born a Protestant, he was converted to Rome, then returned to his Calvinist background. In any case his views made for toleration in religion. For Bayle, as for Montaigne, no opinion was worth burning your neighbor for.

The New Sense of Evidence

But in the study of humankind, as in the study of physical nature, Europeans of the seventeenth century were not generally content with skepticism. They were not possessed by a mere negative and doubting mood, important and salutary as such an attitude was. In the subjects collectively called the humanities, as in pure science, they were looking not for disbelief but for understanding. They wanted new means of telling the true from the false, a new method for arriving at some degree of certainty of conviction. And here, too, a kind of scientific view of the world arose, if that term be understood in a general sense. It took the form of a new sense of evidence. Evidence is that which allows one to believe a thing to be true, or at least truer than something else for which the evidence is weaker. And if to believe without evidence is the sign of primitive or irrational thinking, to require evidence before believing is in a way to be scientific, or at least to trust and use the power of human intelligence.

The new sense of evidence, and of the need of evidence, revealed itself in many ways. One of the clearest was in the law. The English law of evidence, for example, began to take on its modern form at the close of the seventeenth century. Previously the belief had been that the more atrocious the crime the less evidence should be necessary in arriving at a verdict of guilty; this was thought necessary to protect society from the more hideous offenses. From the end of the seventeenth century, in English law, the judge lost his power of discretion in deciding what

north. His conception of the Indian Ocean is quite accurate. To Homan, two centuries later, the size and shapes of oceans and continents are well known, but he believes New Guinea joined to Australia and is frankly ignorant of the northwest coast of North America, representing it by a straight line. The Great Lakes and the interior of North America have become known to Europe. D'Anville in 1761 has no island of Tasmania, does not understand that Alaska is a peninsula, and believes the American polar regions to be impassable by sea. Otherwise his map is indistinguishable from one on the same scale today.

should constitute evidence, and the same rules of evidence were applied in all forms of accusation, the essential question being recognized as always the same— did such-and-such a fact (however outrageous) occur or did it not? After 1650 mere hearsay evidence, long vaguely distrusted, was ruled definitely out of court. After 1696 even persons charged with felony were allowed legal counsel.

The new sense of evidence was probably the main force in putting an end to the delusions of witchcraft. What made witchcraft so credible and so fearsome was that many persons confessed themselves to be witches, admitting to supernatural powers and to evil designs upon their neighbors.[4] Many or most such confessions were extracted under torture. Reformers urged that confessions obtained under torture were not evidence, that people would say anything to escape unbearable pain, so that no quantity of such confessions offered the slightest ground for believing in witches. As for the voluntary confessions, and even the boastings of some people of their diabolical powers, it was noted that such statements often came from half-demented old women, or from persons who would today be called hysterical or psychotic. Witches came to be regarded as self-deluded. Their ideas of themselves were no longer accepted as evidence. But it must be added that, except in England, the use of legal torture lasted on through most of the eighteenth century, in criminal cases in which the judge believed the accused to be guilty.

History and Historical Scholarship

What are called the historical sciences also developed rapidly at this time. History, like the law, depends on the finding and using of evidence. The historian and the judge must answer the same kind of question—did such-and-such a fact really occur? All knowledge of history, so far as it disengages itself from legend and wishful thinking, rests ultimately on pieces of evidence, written records, and

[4] See pp. 51, 255.

other works created in the past and surviving in some form or other in the present. On this mass of material the vast picture of the past is built, and without it people would be ignorant of their own antecedents or would have only folk tales and tribal traditions.

There was much skepticism about history in the seventeenth century. Some said that history was not a form of true knowledge because it was not mathematical. Others said that it was useless because Adam, the perfect man, neither had nor needed any history. Many felt that what passed for history was only a mass of fables. History was distrusted also because historians were often pretentious, claiming to be high-flying men of letters, writing for rhetorical or inspirational appeal or for argumentative reasons, disdaining the hard labor of actual study. History was losing the confidence of thinking people. How was it possible, they asked, to feel even a modicum of certainty about alleged events that had happened long before any living person had been born?

This doubting attitude itself arose from a stricter sense of evidence, or from a realization that there was really no proof for much of what was said about the past. But scholars set to work to assemble what evidence there was. They hoped to create a new history, one that should contain only reliable statements. Europe was littered with old papers and parchments. Abbeys, manor houses, royal archives were full of written documents, many of them of unknown age or unknown origin, often written in a handwriting which people could no longer read. Learned and laborious enthusiasts set to work to explore this accumulation. They added so much to the efforts of their predecessors as virtually to create modern critical scholarship and erudition. The French Benedictine monk Jean Mabillon, in 1681, in his book *On Diplomatics* (referring to ancient charters and "diplomas") established the science of paleography, which deals with the deciphering, reading, dating, and authentication of manuscripts. The Frenchman DuCange in 1678 published a dictionary of medieval Latin which is still used. Others, like the Italian Muratori, spent whole lifetimes exploring archives, collecting, editing, or publishing masses of documents, comparing manuscript copies of the same text and trying to discover what the author had really said, rejecting some as fabrications or forgeries, pronouncing others to be genuine pieces of historical evidence. Others made themselves experts in ancient coins, many of which were far more ancient than the oldest manuscripts; they founded the science of numismatics. Still others, or indeed the same ones, turned to a critical examination of the inscriptions on old buildings and ruins.

Another important but little-known historical "science," namely, chronology, was greatly stimulated also. Chronology deals with the age of the world and with finding a common denominator between the dating systems of various peoples. Probably it is not natural for the human mind to think in terms of dates at all. For simple people it is enough to know that some things happened "long ago." In the seventeenth century the new interest in numbers, evident in physical science, turned also to the human past. Archbishop James Usher, an Anglican prelate of Ireland, after much study of the Bible, announced the date of 4004 B.C. as that of the creation of the world. His chronological system was later printed in the margins of the Authorized Version of the English Bible, and is still adhered to by some fundamentalists as if part of the Bible itself. But Usher's system was not accepted by scholars even in his own time. Geographical knowledge was revealing China and its dynasties to Europe; historical knowledge was beginning to discover ancient Egypt. The Chinese and Egyptian records claimed a greater antiquity for their countries than the Old Testament seemed to allow for the human race. There was much erudite conjecture; one scholar about 1700 counted seventy estimates of the age of the world, ranging as high as 170,000 years, a figure which then seemed fantastic and appalling.

The difficulty was not only in the language of the Old Testament. It was in finding the correspondence between the chronological systems of different peoples. A Chinese system of dating by dynasties might be coherent within itself, but how could it be equated with the European system of dating from the birth of Christ, a date as unknown to the Chinese as the date of Wu Wang was to Europeans? Even European records presented the same difficulty; the Romans counted by consulships, or from the supposed year of the founding of Rome; many medieval documents told only the year of some obscure ruler's reign. Only infinite patience, interminable research, and endless calculation could reduce such a jumble to the simple system of modern textbooks. This is of more importance than may be at first thought. A common system of dating is a great aid to thinking of human history as an interconnected whole. An overall conception of the human race is made easier by the dating of all events according to the Christian era. This itself, it may be pointed out, is an arbitrary and conventional scale, since Christ is now thought to have been born not in A.D. 1, but in 4 B.C.

Common dating was of importance in practical affairs as well as in historical knowledge. Europe was disunited even on the Christian calendar. Protestant and some Orthodox countries followed the old or Julian calendar, Catholic countries the corrected or Gregorian calendar, issued in the sixteenth century under authority of Pope Gregory XIII. The two calendars varied in the seventeenth century by ten days. Only gradually was the Gregorian calendar accepted, by England in 1752, by Russia in 1918. Most other peoples today, in China, India, the Arabic world, and elsewhere, use or recognize the Gregorian calendar. Without a uniform way of specifying days and years it would be less easy to transact international affairs, hold international conferences, make plans, or pay and receive money. This common dating, easily taken for granted, was a consequence of the predominance of Europe in modern times. It is a sign of growing unity in world civilization.

The Questioning of Traditional Beliefs

The historical sciences provided a foundation on which a knowledge of human activities in the past could be built, and the growing geographical knowledge spread a panorama of man's diverse activities and peculiarities in the present. This new knowledge shared with natural science, and probably derived from it, or from philosophers of science like Descartes and Bacon, the view that many traditional ideas were erroneous, but that much could be known by a disciplined use of the human mind. The humanities and the sciences were alike in demanding evidence for belief and in trusting to the power of reason. In their impact on the old certainties of European life, the studies of man exerted possibly a greater direct force than those of nature. Pascal, in his attempt to defend the Christian faith, feared the spirit of Montaigne, the mood of skepticism and denial, which he felt himself, more than he feared the findings of mathematical and physical science. And the movement of historical thought, with its insistence on textual criticism, threw doubt on much of the Christian religion, or at least on the sacred history related in the Bible, which was considered to be part and parcel of religion itself.

In 1678 a French priest, Richard Simon, published a pioneering work in Biblical criticism, his *Critical History of the Old Testament*. Though his book was condemned both by the church and by the government of Louis XIV, Richard Simon always felt himself to be orthodox; Catholic faith, he insisted, depended more on church tradition than on the literal statements of the Bible. He simply applied to the Old Testament the methods of textual criticism which others were applying to secular documents. He concluded that the Old Testament, as known, rested on medieval manuscripts many of which were of unknown or doubtful origin, that monkish copyists had brought in errors and corruptions, and that the books thought to have been written by Moses could not have been written by him, since they contained obvious contradictions and matter clearly inserted after his death. Others went further, questioning not merely the evidence of the Biblical text, but the very possibility of some events that it related. From the scientific idea of the absolute regularity of nature on the one hand, and from a strong sense of human credulity on the other, they denied that miracles had ever occurred and looked upon oracles and prophecies among either the Greeks or the Hebrews with a dubious eye.

The most profoundly disturbing of all thinkers of the time was Baruch Spinoza (1632–1677), the lens grinder of Amsterdam, a Jew who was excommunicated by his own synagogue and who refused a professorship at the University of Heidelberg, craving only the quiet to think in peace. Spinoza drew on both the scientific and humanistic thought of his day. He arrived at a philosophy holding that God had no existence apart from the world, that everything was itself an aspect of God, a philosophy technically called pantheism but considered by many to be really atheistic. He denied the inspiration of the Bible, disbelieved in miracles and the supernatural, rejected all revelation and revealed religion, Jewish or Christian, and held that few if any governments of the day were really just. He taught a pure, stern, and intellectual ethical code, and one which had few consolations for the average person. His name became a byword for impiety and horrendous unbelief. People were literally afraid to read his works, even when they could find them, which was not often because of the censorship. His influence spread slowly, through the mediation of other writers.

More widely read, less abstruse, more reassuring, dwelling on the merits of common sense, were the writings of the Englishman John Locke (1632–1704), who summarized many of the intellectual trends of his lifetime and exerted a strong influence for the following hundred years. He combined practical experience and theoretical interests. Educated in medicine, he kept in touch with the sciences and was acquainted with Newton. He was associated with the great Whig noblemen who were the main authors of the English revolution in 1688. For political reasons he spent several years in the 1680s in the Netherlands, where he became familiar with thought on the Continent. He wrote on many subjects— finance, economics, education, religious policy, political theory, general philosophy—always with an engaging directness and sober air of the sensible man of the world. In his *Letter on Toleration* (1689) he advocated an established church, but with toleration of all except Roman Catholics and atheists; these he held to be dangerous to society, the former because of a foreign allegiance, the latter because they lacked a basis of moral responsibility. In his *Reasonableness of Christianity* he argued that Christianity, rightly considered, is after all a reasonable form of religion; this softened the friction between religion and natural knowledge but tended to shut out the supernatural and merge religious feeling into an unruffled common sense.

Locke's deepest book was his *Essay Concerning the Human Understanding* (1690). Here he faced the great problem of the day, the problem of knowledge; he asked if it was possible to know anything with certainty, and how certain knowledge was arrived at. His answer was that true or certain knowledge is derived from experience—from perceptions of the sense organs and reflection of the mind on these perceptions. Locke at the end of the century thus echoes Bacon at the beginning; they became the two great pillars of empirical philosophy, insisting on experience and observation as the source of truth. Locke denied Descartes' doctrine of innate ideas, or inevitable disposition of the human mind to think in certain ways. He held that the mind at birth is a blank tablet or *tabula rasa,* and that what a person comes to think or believe depends on the environment in which he lives. Locke's environmentalist philosophy became fundamental to liberal and reforming thought in later years. It seemed that false ideas or superstitions were the result of bad environment and bad education. It seemed that the evil in human actions was due to bad social institutions, and that an improvement in human society would improve human behavior. This philosophy, whether or not wholly true in the final analysis, was largely true with respect to many practical conditions. It gave confidence in the possibility of social progress and turned attention to a sphere in which planned and constructive action was possible, namely, the sphere of government, public policy, and legislation. Here we touch on political theory, to which Locke contributed *Two Treatises of Government*. These are discussed below.

35. Political Theory: The School of Natural Law

Political theory can never be strictly scientific. Science deals with what does exist or has existed. It does not tell what ought to exist. To tell what society and government ought to be like, in view of human nature and the capacity to be miserable or contented, is a main purpose of political theory. Political theory is in a sense more practical than science. It is the scientists and scholars who are most content to observe facts as they are. Practical people, and scientists and scholars so far as they have practical interests, must always ask themselves what ought to be done, what policies ought to be adopted, what measures taken, what state of affairs maintained or brought about. Conservatives and radicals, traditionalists and innovators, are alike in this respect. It is impossible in human affairs to escape the word "ought."

But political theory was affected by the scientific view. The Renaissance

Italian, Niccolò Machiavelli (1469–1527), had opened the way in this direction.[5] Machiavelli too had his "ought"; he preferred a republican form of government in which citizens felt a patriotic attachment to their state. But in his book, *The Prince,* he disregarded the question of the best form of government, a favorite question of Christian and scholastic philosophers of the Middle Ages. He separated the study of politics from theology and moral philosophy. He undertook to describe how governments and rulers actually behaved. He observed that successful rulers behaved as if holding or increasing power were their only object, that they regarded all else as means to this end. Princes, said Machiavelli, kept their promises or broke them, they told the truth or distorted or colored it, they sought popularity or ignored it, they advanced public welfare or disrupted it, they conciliated their neighbors or destroyed them, depending merely on which course of action seemed the best means of advancing their political interests. All this was bad, said Machiavelli; but that was not the question, for the question was to find out what rulers really did. Machiavelli, in *The Prince,* chose to be nonmoral in order to be scientific. To most readers he seemed to be simply immoral. Nor was it possible to draw the line between *The Prince* as a scientific description of fact and *The Prince* as a book of maxims of conduct. In telling how successful rulers obtained their successes, Machiavelli also suggested how rulers *ought* to proceed. And though governments did in fact continue to behave for the most part as Machiavelli said, most people refused to admit that they ought to.

Natural Right and Natural Law

Political theory in the seventeenth century did not embrace the cynicism attributed to Machiavelli. Nor did it fall into the skepticism of those who said that the customs of one's country should be passively accepted, or that one form of government was about as good as another. It directly faced the question, What is right? The seventeenth century was the classic age of the philosophy of natural right or of natural law.

The idea of natural law has underlain a good deal of modern democratic development, and its decline in the last century has been closely connected with many of the troubles of recent times. It is not easy to say in what the philosophy of natural law essentially consisted. It held that there is, somehow, in the structure of the world, a law that distinguishes right from wrong. It held that right is "natural," not a mere human invention. This right is not determined, for any country, by its heritage, tradition, or customs, nor yet by its actual laws (called "positive" laws) of the kind that are enforced in the law courts. All these may be unfair or unjust. We detect unfairness or injustice in them by comparing them with natural law as we understand it; thus we have a basis for saying that cannibalism is bad, or that a law requiring forced labor from orphan children is unjust. Nor is natural law, or the real rightness of a thing, determined by the authority of any person or people. No king can make right that which is wrong. No people, by its will as a people, can make just that which is unjust. Right and law, in the ultimate sense, exist outside and above all peoples. They are universal, the same for all. No one can make them up to suit themselves. A good king, or a just people, is a king or people whose actions correspond to the objective standard. But how, if we cannot trust our own positive laws or customs, or our leaders, or even our collective selves, can we know what is naturally right? How do we discover natural law? The answer, in the natural law philosophy, is that we discover it by reason. Man is considered to be a rational animal. And all human beings are assumed to have, at least potentially and when better enlightened, the same powers of reason and understanding—Germans or English, Siamese or Europeans. This view favored a cosmopolitan outlook and made international agreement and general world progress seem realizable goals. As time went on, the premises of this philosophy came to be questioned. By the twentieth century it was widely thought that the human mind was not especially rational but was motivated by drives or urges or instincts, and that human differences were so fundamental that people of different nationalities or classes could never expect to see things in the same way. When this happened the older philosophy of natural law lost its hold on many minds.

In the seventeenth and eighteenth centuries it was generally accepted. Some, carrying over the philosophy of the Middle Ages, thought of natural law as an aspect of the law of God. Others, more secular in spirit, held that the natural law stood of itself. These included even some churchmen; a group of theologians, mainly Jesuits, were condemned by the pope in 1690 for holding that universal right and wrong might exist by reason only, whether God existed or not. The idea of natural law and the faith in human reason went side by side, and both were fundamental in the thought of the time. They were to be found everywhere in Europe, in their religious or their secular form.

On the basis of natural law some thinkers tried to create an international law or "law of nations," to bring order into the maze of sovereign territorial states, great and small, that was developing in Europe. Hugo Grotius, in 1625, published the first great book devoted exclusively to this subject, his *Law of War and Peace*. Samuel Pufendorf followed with his *Law of Nature and of Nations* in 1672. Both held that sovereign states, though bound by no positive law or authority, should work together for the common good, that there was a community of nations as of individuals, and that in the absence of a higher international sovereignty they were all still subordinate to natural reason and justice. Certain concrete doctrines, such as the freedom of the seas or the immunity of ambassadors, were put forward. The principles of international law remained those of natural law. The content came to include specific agreements between governments, certain kinds of admiralty and maritime law, and the terms of treaties such as the treaties of Westphalia, Utrecht, and others. The means of enforcement, to be sure, remained weak or nonexistent in crises.

Hobbes and Locke

In domestic affairs the philosophy of natural law, though it rather favored constitutionalism, was used to justify both constitutional and absolutist governments. Right itself was held to be in the nature of things, beyond human power to change. But forms of government were held to be means to an end. No philosopher at the time thought the state to have an absolute value in itself. The state had to be "justified," made acceptable to the moral consciousness or the reason. There were, indeed, important competing philosophies. On the side of absolutism was the doctrine of the divine right of kings. On the side of constitutionalism were arguments based on heritage or custom, emphasizing the charters, bulls, or compacts of former times and the historic powers of parliaments and estates. But neither the supernatural argument of the divine right of kings, nor the historical argument pointing back to liberties of the Middle Ages, was entirely satisfactory in the scientific atmosphere of the seventeenth century. Neither carried complete conviction to the reason or moral sense of the most acute thinkers. Both were reinforced by arguments of natural law. Two Englishmen stand out above all others in this connection. Absolutism was philosophically justified by Thomas Hobbes, constitutionalism by John Locke.

Hobbes (1588–1679) followed the scientific and mathematical discoveries of his time with more than an amateur interest. In philosophy he held to a materialistic and even atheistic system. In English politics he sided with king against Parliament; he disliked the disorder and violence of the civil war of the 1640s and the unstable conditions of the English republic of the 1650s.[6] He concluded that men have no capacity for self-government. His opinion of human nature was low; he held that people in the "state of nature," or as imagined to exist without government, were quarrelsome and turbulent, forever locked in a war of all against all. In his famous phrase, life in the state of nature was "solitary, poor, nasty, brutish and short." From fear of each other, to obtain order, and enjoy the advantages of law and right, people came to a kind of agreement or "contract" by which they surrendered their freedom of action into the hands of a ruler. It was necessary for this ruler to have unrestricted or absolute power. Only thus could he maintain order. It was intolerably dangerous, according to Hobbes, for anyone to question the actions of government, for such questioning might reopen the way to chaos. Government must in fact be a kind of Leviathan (the monster mentioned in the Bible, Job 41); and it was by the word *Leviathan* that Hobbes entitled his principal book, published in 1651, two years after the execution of King Charles I.

By this book Hobbes became the leading secular exponent of absolutism and one of the principal theorists of the unlimited sovereignty of the state. His influence on later thinkers was very great. He accustomed political theorists to the use of purely natural arguments. He quoted freely from the Bible, but the Bible had no influence on his thought. After Hobbes, all advanced political theorists regarded government as a thing created by human purpose. It was no longer considered, except popularly and except by professional theologians, as part of a divine dispensation of God to man. Hobbes also affected later theorists by his arguments for a sovereign authority, and, more negatively, by obliging them to refute his idea of an unlimited personal sovereign. But he was never a popular writer. In England the cause which he favored was lost. In those continental countries where royal absolutism prevailed his arguments were received with secret gratification, but his irreligion was too dangerous to make public, and the absolutist argument, on the popular level, remained that of the divine right of kings. In any case Hobbes's arguments were in some ways insufficient for real monarchs. Hobbes abhorred struggle and violence. His case for absolutism required absolutism to produce civil peace, individual security,

[6] See pp. 174–176.

and a rule of law. He also held that absolute power depended on, or had at least originated in, a free and rational agreement by which people accepted it. An absolute monarchy that flagrantly violated these conditions could with difficulty be justified even by the doctrines of Hobbes. It is in these respects that Hobbes differs from totalitarian theorists of recent times. For Hobbes, in the final analysis, absolute power was an expedient to promote individual welfare. It was a means necessary to the realization of natural law.

John Locke (1632–1704), as has been seen, also stood in the main current of scientific thought and discovery. But in his political philosophy he carried over many ideas of the Middle Ages, as formulated in the thirteenth century by St. Thomas Aquinas[7] and kept alive in England by successive thinkers of the Anglican church. Medieval philosophy had never favored an absolute power. With Hobbes, Locke shared the idea that good government is an expedient of human purpose, neither provided by divine Providence nor inherited by a national tradition. He held, too, like Hobbes and the whole school of natural law, that government was based on a kind of contract, or rational and conscious agreement upon which authority was based. In contrast to Hobbes, he sided with Parliament against king in the practical struggles of politics. About 1680, in the course of these disputes, he wrote *Two Treatises of Government,* which however were not published until shortly after the parliamentary revolution of 1688–1689.[8]

Locke took a more genial view of human nature than Hobbes. As he showed in his other books, he believed that a moderate religion was a good thing, and above all that people could learn from experience and hence could be educated to an enlightened way of life. These ideas favored a belief in self-government. Locke declared (in contradiction to Hobbes) that people in the "state of nature" were reasonable and well disposed, willing to get along with one another though handicapped by the absence of public authority. They likewise had a moral sense, quite independently of government; and they also possessed by nature certain rights, quite apart from the state. These rights were the rights to life, liberty, and property. Locke threw very heavy emphasis on the right of property, by which he usually meant the possession of land. His philosophy can in fact be regarded as an expression of the landed classes of England in their claims against the king; it should be noted that land ownership in England was more widespread in 1690 than it later became. Individuals in the state of nature are not altogether able, according to Locke, to win general respect for their individual natural rights. They cannot by their own efforts protect what is "proper" to them, i.e., their property. They agree to set up government to enforce observance of the rights of all. Government is thus created by a contract, but the contract is not unconditional, as claimed by Hobbes. It imposes mutual obligations. The people must be reasonable; only rational beings can be politically free. Liberty is not an anarchy of undisciplined will; it is the freedom to act without compulsion by another. Only rational and responsible creatures can exercise true freedom; but adult human beings, according to Locke, are or can be educated to be rational and responsible. They therefore can and should be free. On government, also, certain conditions and obligations are imposed. If a government breaks the

[7] See p. 42.
[8] See pp. 178–181.

contract, if it threatens the natural rights which it is the sole purpose of government to protect, if, for example, it takes away a man's property without his consent, then the governed have a right to reconsider what they have done in creating the government and may even in the last extremity rebel against it. The right to resist government, Locke admits, is very dangerous, but it is less dangerous than its opposite, which would lead to enslavement; and in any case we are talking about reasonable and responsible people.

If Locke's ideas seem familiar, especially to Americans, it is because of the wide popularizing of his philosophy in the century after his death. Nowhere was his influence greater than in the British colonies. The authors of the American Declaration of Independence and of the Constitution of the United States knew the writings of Locke very thoroughly. Some phrases of the Declaration of Independence echo his very language. In Great Britain also, and in France and elsewhere, in the course of time, Locke's influence was immense.

What Locke did was to convert an episode in English history into an event of universal meaning. In England, in 1688, certain great lords, winning the support of the established church, gentry, and merchants, put out one king and brought in another. On the new king they imposed certain obligations—specified in the Bill of Rights of 1689, and all dealing with legal or technical interpretations of the English constitution. The Revolution of 1688 was a very English affair. England in 1688 was still little known to the rest of Europe. The proceedings in England, so far as known, might seem no different from a rebellion of the magnates of Hungary. Locke, in arguing that Parliament had done right to eject James II, put the whole affair on a level of reason, natural right, and human nature. It thus came to have meaning for everyone. At the same time, Locke made the English revolution a sign of progress rather than reaction. The new and modern form of government in 1690 was royal absolutism, with its professional bureaucracy and corps of paid officials. Almost everywhere there was resistance to the kings, led by landed interests and harking back to earlier freedoms. Such resistance seemed to many Europeans to be feudal and medieval. Locke made the form taken by such resistance in England, namely, the Revolution of 1688 against James II, into a modern and forward-looking move. He checked the prestige of absolutism. He gave new prestige to constitutional principles. He carried over, in modified form, many ideas from the scholastic philosophers of the Middle Ages, who had generally maintained that kings had only a relative and restricted power and were responsible to their peoples. To these ideas he added the force of the newer scientific view of the world. He did not rest his case on supernatural or providential arguments. He did not say that constitutional government was the will of God. He said that it rested on experience and observation of human nature, on recognition of certain individual rights and especially the right of property, and on the existence of a purely natural law of reason and justice. He was an almost entirely secular thinker.

One must not claim too much for Locke, or for any writer. England was in fact, in 1688, more modern in many ways than other countries in Europe. The Glorious Revolution was in fact not exactly like uprisings of the landed and propertied classes elsewhere. England in the following century did in fact create a form of parliamentary government that was unique. But facts go together with the theories that give them an understandable meaning. Events in England, as explained by Locke, and as seen in other countries and even in England and its colonies through Locke's eyes, launched into the mainstream of modern history the superb tradition of constitutional government, which has been one of the principal themes in the history of the modern world ever since.

By 1700, at the close of the "century of genius," some beliefs that were to be characteristic of modern times had clearly taken form, notably a faith in science, in human reason, in natural human rights, and in progress. The following period, generally known as the Age of Enlightenment, was to be a time of clarifying and popularizing ideas which the more creative seventeenth century had produced. These ideas were eventually to revolutionize Europe, America, and the world. They were also in subsequent years to be modified, amended, challenged, and even denied. But they are still very much alive today.

VIII.
THE AGE OF
ENLIGHTENMENT

THE EIGHTEENTH CENTURY, or at least the years of that century preceding the French Revolution of 1789, is commonly known as the Age of Enlightenment, and though that name raises more than the usual difficulties, still there is no other that describes so many features of the time so well. People strongly felt that theirs was an enlightened age, and it is from their own evaluation of themselves that our term Age of Enlightenment is derived. Everywhere there was a feeling that Europeans had at last emerged from a long twilight. The past was regarded as a time of barbarism and darkness. The sense of progress was all but universal among the educated classes. It was the belief both of the forward-looking thinkers and writers known as the philosophes and of the forward-looking kings and empresses, the "enlightened despots," together with their ministers and officials.

36. *The Philosophes—And Others*

The Spirit of Progress and Improvement

The spirit of the eighteenth-century Enlightenment was drawn from the scientific and intellectual revolution of the seventeenth century. The Enlightenment carried over and popularized the ideas of Bacon and Descartes, of Bayle and Spinoza,

Chapter Emblem: A French snuffbox showing miniature portraits on tortoise shell of three famous philosophers, Voltaire, Rousseau, and Benjamin Franklin.

and, above all, of Locke and Newton. It carried over the philosophy of natural law and of natural right. Never was there an age so skeptical toward tradition, so confident in the powers of human reason and of science, so firmly convinced of the regularity and harmony of nature, and so deeply imbued with the sense of civilization's advance and progress.

The idea of progress is often said to have been the dominant or characteristic idea of European civilization from the seventeenth century to the twentieth. It is a belief, a kind of nonreligious faith, that the conditions of human life become better as time goes on, that in general each generation is better off than its predecessors and will contribute by its labor to an even better life for generations to come, and that in the long run all mankind will share in the same advance. All the elements of this belief had been present by 1700. It was after 1700, however, that the idea of progress became explicit. In the seventeenth century it had shown itself in a more rudimentary way, in a sporadic dispute, among men of letters in England and France, known as the quarrel of Ancients and Moderns. The Ancients held that the works of the Greeks and Romans had never been surpassed. The Moderns, pointing to science, art, literature, and invention, declared that their own time was the best, that it was natural for people of their time to do better than the ancients because they came later and built upon their predecessors' achievements. The quarrel was never exactly settled, but a great many people in 1700 were Moderns.

Far-reaching also was the faith of the age in the natural faculties of the human mind. Pure skepticism, the negation of reason, was overcome. Nor were the educated, after 1700, likely to be superstitious, terrified by the unknown, or addicted to magic. The witchcraft mania abruptly died. Indeed all sense of the supernatural became dim. "Modern" people not only ceased to fear the devil; they ceased also to fear God. They thought of God less as a Father than as a First Cause of the physical universe. There was less sense of a personal God, or of the inscrutable imminence of divine Providence, or of the human need for saving grace. God was less the God of Love; He was the inconceivably intelligent being who had made the amazing universe now discovered by human reason. The great symbol of the Christian God was the Cross, on which a divine being had suffered in human form. The symbol which occurred to people of scientific view was the Watchmaker. The intricacies of the physical universe were compared to the intricacies of a watch, and it was argued that just as a watch could not exist without a watchmaker, so the universe as discovered by Newton could not exist without a God who created it and set it moving by its mathematical law. It was almighty intelligence that was thought divine.

Of course not everyone was primarily moved by such ideas. The first half of the eighteenth century was in fact also a time of continuing religious fervor. Isaac Watts wrote many hymns that are still familiar in English-speaking churches; the great church music of J. S. Bach was composed mainly in the 1720s; Handel's oratorio, *The Messiah*, was first performed in 1741; and it was at about this time that congregations first sang the *Adeste fideles* ("O Come, All Ye Faithful"), originally Catholic in inspiration but soon adopted by Protestants also. The Lutherans of Germany were stirred by the movement known as Pietism, which stressed the inner experience of ordinary persons as distinct from the doctrines taught and debated in theological faculties. The quest for an "inner light," or illumination of the soul rather than of the reason, was somewhat contrary to the main thrust of the Age of Enlightenment, and a religious urge for improvement of the individual rather than of social institutions was hardly central to the idea of progress, but such ideas were by no means merely conservative, for they were in general highly critical of the existing order.

Within the Church of England John Wesley, while a student at Oxford, joined a group of like-minded young men for prayer and meditation. They engaged in good works to relieve the sufferings of prisoners and the poor, to whom they distributed food and clothing, while also teaching them how to read. Going outside the restrictive system of parishes, Wesley and others took to "itinerant" preaching, often to immense crowds in open fields. Wesley is said to have traveled 250,000 miles within Great Britain over a period of fifty years. He and the similarly inclined George Whitfield preached also in the English American colonies, where they helped to arouse the Great Awakening of the 1740s. Such movements had a kind of democratizing effect in stressing individual worth and spiritual consciousness independently of the established religious authorities. Indeed, the spokesmen for older churches dismissed such movements as "enthusiasm," which was then a word of reproach. By the end of his long life (he died in 1791), Wesley had about half a million followers in what were called Methodist societies. Wesley himself tried to keep them within the Church of England, but separate Methodist churches were already founded in England and the United States.

In a way these expressions of religious feeling reflected differences between the popular and elite cultures such as have already been described. While some of the elite joined in the new movements, it was on the whole those of the least comfortable classes who did so. The official churches, Anglican, Lutheran, Catholic, did not wish to be disturbed by religious revivalism. Bishops were cultivated gentlemen of the age. But the most vehement intellectual leaders pushed all churches aside.

Oddly enough, in this age of reason, there was also a taste for mystification. A Swiss pastor, J. C. Lavater, attracted attention with his supposed science of "physiognomy," by which character could be read in the play of the facial features. An Austrian physician, F. A. Mesmer, created a stir in Paris by arranging seances where people were touched by a wand, or sat in tubs, to receive "animal magnetism" in the hope of curing various ills. His "mesmerism" was an early stage in the discovery of hypnosis, but it is significant that a committee of the Royal Academy of Sciences, after investigation, concluded that Mesmer's own theories to explain these strange phenomena were without foundation. There was a somewhat gullible vogue for popular science in the 1780s, shared in by a few who soon became famous in the Revolution, such as Marat and Brissot. Popular science simply exaggerated the claims of real science for the control of nature by human manipulation.

More in the mainstream was Freemasonry, which took form in England and soon spread to the Continent. The Masons were generally men of typical Enlightenment views, well disposed toward reason, progress, toleration, and humane reforms, and respectful toward God as architect of the universe, but they met secretly in lodges, in an atmosphere of mysterious rituals and occult knowledge. Men of all walks of life, nobles, clergy, and middle classes, belonged to the lodges, which had the effect of bringing persons of different social classes together, somewhat harmlessly for self-improvement and the improvement of others. Masonry, however, aroused suspicion because of its secrecy, and a small deviant offshoot, the Illuminati of south Germany, was considered so dangerous that the Bavarian government suppressed it in 1786. There were later some who insisted that the French Revolution had been caused by a conspiracy of Illuminati, philosophes, and other clandestine plotters, but this idea was never any more than the belief of a few frightened conservatives. The word Illuminati meant "the enlightened ones," but the notion of secrecy was foreign to the Enlightenment, which relied above all else on publicity.

The Philosophes

Philosophe is simply French for philosopher, but to be "philosophical" in the eighteenth century meant to approach any subject in a critical and inquiring spirit. The French word is used in English to denote a group of writers who were not philosophers in the sense of treating ultimate questions of existence. They were men of letters, popularizers, and publicists. Though often learned, they wrote to gain attention, and it was through the philosophes that the ideas of the Enlightenment spread. Formerly authors had generally been gentlemen of leisure, or talented protégés of aristocratic or royal patrons, or professors or clerics supported by the income from religious foundations. In the Age of Enlightenment a great many were freelancers, grub-streeters, or journalists. They wrote for "the publick."

The reading public had greatly expanded. The educated middle class, commercial and professional, was much larger than ever before. Country gentlemen were putting off their rustic habits, and even noblemen wished to keep informed. Newspapers and magazines multiplied, and people who could not read them at home could read them in coffeehouses or in reading rooms organized for that purpose. There was a great demand also for dictionaries, encyclopedias, and surveys of all fields of knowledge. The new readers wanted matters made interesting and clear. They appreciated wit and lightness of touch. From such a public, literature itself greatly benefited. The style of the eighteenth century became admirably fluent, clear, and exact, neither ponderous on the one hand nor frothy on the other. And from writings of this kind the readers benefited also, from the interior of Europe to the America of Benjamin Franklin. The bourgeois middle class was becoming not only educated but thoughtful. But the movement was not a class movement only.

There was another way in which writings of the day were affected by social conditions. They were all written under censorship. The theory of censorship was to protect people from harmful ideas as they were protected from shoddy merchandise or dishonest weights and measures. In England the censorship was so mild as to have little effect. Other countries, such as Spain, had a powerful censorship but few original writers. France, the center of the Enlightenment, had both a complicated censorship and a large reading and writing public. The church, the Parlement of Paris, the royal officials, and the printers' guilds all had a hand in the censoring of books. French censorship, however, was very loosely administered, and after 1750 writers were disturbed by it very little. It cannot be compared to censorship in some countries in the twentieth century. Yet in one way it had an unfavorable effect on French thought and letters. It discouraged writers from addressing themselves, in a common-sense way, to a serious consideration of concrete public questions. Legally forbidden to criticize church or state, they threw their criticisms on an abstract level. Debarred from attacking things in particular, they tended to attack things in general. Or they talked of the customs of the Persians and the Iroquois but not the French. Their works became full of double meanings, sly digs, innuendoes, and jokes, by which authors, if questioned, could declare that they did not mean what all the world knew they did mean. As for readers, they developed a taste for forbidden books, which were always easy enough to obtain through illicit channels.

Paris was the heart of the movement. Here, in the town houses of the well-to-do, there occurred a coming together of literary and social celebrities such as had hardly ever before been seen. It might even happen, though rarely, that a notable philosophe was also wealthy; such was the case of Helvetius, who not only wrote books *On the Mind* and *On Man*, but also gave grand entertainments at which such matters were discussed. Mainly, however, this mingling of people and ideas went on in salons conducted by women who became famous as hostesses. Mme. de Geoffrin, for example, for a period of twenty-five years beginning about 1750, entertained artists and writers at dinner, sometimes helped them financially, and introduced them to persons of influence in high society or in government. She welcomed visiting foreigners also, such as Horace Walpole and David Hume from England, and young Stanislas Poniatowski before he became king of Poland. Since other women held similar salons, philosophes and other writers had frequent opportunity to meet and exchange ideas. Salons of this kind survived the Revolution. In 1795, after the Terror, the widows of two eminent philosophes, Helvetius and Condorcet, opened or reopened their salons in Paris for people of moderate republican or liberal sentiments. Sophie Condorcet became a writer herself and a translator of Adam Smith. Her salon remained a center of liberal opposition during the years of Napoleon. More short-lived was the salon of the even more famous Mme. de Staël, who also wrote widely read books and who, among her many other ideas, deplored the subordination of women to men that the Revolution had done little to change. In these post-Revolutionary salons much of the French liberalism of the nineteenth century was born.

In Paris also, in the mid–eighteenth century, was published the most serious of all philosophe enterprises, the *Encyclopédie*, edited by Denis Diderot in seventeen large volumes and completed over the years 1751 to 1772. It was a great compendium of scientific, technical, and historical knowledge, carrying a strong undertone of criticism of existing society and institutions and epitomizing the skeptical, rational, and scientific spirit of the age. It was not the first encyclopedia, but it was the first to have a distinguished list of contributors or to be conceived as a positive force for social progress. Virtually all the French philosophes contributed—Voltaire, Montesquieu, Rousseau, d'Alembert (who assisted in the editing), Buffon, Turgot, Quesnay, and many others, all sometimes collectively called the Encyclopedists. But although edited in Paris the *Encyclopédie* became very widely known and read. About 25,000 multivolumed sets were sold before the Revolution, about half of them outside of France, since French had become an international language understood by educated persons all over Europe. Within France itself the *Encyclopédie* was read in all parts of the country and in the most influential ranks of society. At Besançon, for example, a city of about 28,000 inhabitants, 137 sets were sold to local residents, of whom 15 were members of the clergy, 53 were of the nobility, and 69 were lawyers, doctors, merchants, government officials, or others of what was called the Third Estate. The privileged groups of whom the Encyclopedists were the most critical, that is, the clergy and the nobility, read it or at least purchased it far out of proportion to their numbers in the population as a whole.

Men and women who considered themselves philosophes, or close to the philosophes in spirit, were found all over Europe. Frederick the Great was an eminent philosophe; not only was he the friend of Voltaire and host to a circle of literary and scientific men at Potsdam, but he himself wrote epigrams, satires, dissertations, and histories, as well as works on military science, and he had a gift of wit, a sharp tongue, and a certain impishness toward the traditional and the pompous. Catherine the Great, empress of Russia, was also a philosophe for much the same reason. Maria Theresa, of Austria, was not a philosophe; she was too religious and too little concerned with general ideas. Her son Joseph, on the other hand, as we shall see, proved to be a philosophe enthroned. In England Bishop Warburton was considered by some of his friends as a philosophe; he held that the Church of England of his day, as a social institution, was exactly what pure reason would have invented. The Scottish skeptical philosopher David Hume counted as a philosophe, as did Edward Gibbon, who shocked the pious by his attacks on Christianity in his famous *Decline and Fall of the Roman Empire*. Dr. Samuel Johnson was not a philosophe; he worried over the supernatural, adhered to the established church, deflated pretentious authors, and even declared that Voltaire and Rousseau were bad men who should be sent "to the plantations." There were also Italian and German philosophes, like the Marquis di Beccaria who sought to humanize the criminal law, or Baron Grimm who sent a literary newsletter from Paris to his many subscribers.

Montesquieu, Voltaire, and Rousseau

Most famous of all philosophes were the French trio, Montesquieu (1689–1755), Voltaire (1694–1778), and Rousseau (1712–1778). They differed vehemently with each other. All were hailed as literary geniuses in their own day. All turned from pure literature to works of political commentary and social analysis. All thought that the existing state of society could be improved.

Montesquieu, twice a baron, was a landed aristocrat, a seigneur or manorial lord of southern France. He inherited from his uncle a seat in the Parlement of Bordeaux and sat actively in that parlement in the days of the Regency.[1] He was part of the noble resurgence which followed the death of Louis XIV and continued on through the eighteenth century. Although he shared many of the ideas in the stream of aristocratic and antiabsolutist thought, he went beyond a mere self-centered class philosophy. In his great work, *The Spirit of Laws,* published in 1748, he developed two principal ideas. One was that forms of government varied according to climate and circumstances, for example, that despotism was suited only to large empires in hot climates, and that democracy would work only in

[1] See pp. 265–266.

small city-states. His other great doctrine, aimed against royal absolutism in France (which he called "despotism"), was the separation and balance of powers. In France he believed that power should be divided between the king and a great many "intermediate bodies"—parlements, provincial estates, organized nobility, chartered towns, and even the church. It was natural for him, a judge in parlement, a provincial and a nobleman, to favor the first three and reasonable for him to recognize the position of the bourgeoisie of the towns; as for the church, he observed that, while he took no stock in its teachings, he thought it useful as an offset to undue centralization of government. He greatly admired the English constitution as he understood it, believing that England carried over, more successfully than any other country, the feudal liberties of the early Middle Ages. He thought that in England the necessary separation and balance of powers was obtained by an ingenious mixture of monarchy, aristocracy, and democracy (king, lords, and commons), and by a separation of the functions of the executive, legislature, and judiciary. This doctrine had a wide influence and was well known to the Americans who in 1787 wrote the Constitution of the United States. Montesquieu's own philosophe friends thought him too conservative and even tried to dissuade him from publishing his ideas. He was, indeed, technically a reactionary, favoring a scheme of things that antedated Louis XIV, and he was unusual among contemporaries in his admiration of the "barbarous" Middle Ages.

Voltaire was born in 1694 into a comfortable bourgeois family and christened François-Marie Arouet; "Voltaire," an invented word, is simply the most famous of all pen names. Until he was over forty he was known only as a smart writer of epigrams, tragedies in verse, and an epic. Thereafter he turned increasingly to philosophical and public questions. His strength throughout lay in the facility of his pen. He is the easiest of all great writers to read. He was always trenchant, logical, and incisive, sometimes scurrilous; mocking and sarcastic when he wished, equally a master of deft irony and of withering ridicule. However serious in his purpose, he achieved it by creating a laugh.

In his youth Voltaire spent eleven months in the Bastille for what was considered to be impertinence to the Regent, who, however, in the next year rewarded him with a pension for one of his dramas. He was again arrested after a fracas with a nobleman, the Chevalier de Rohan. He remained an incorrigible bourgeois, while never deeply objecting to the aristocracy on principle. Through his admirer Mme. de Pompadour (another bourgeois, though the king's favorite) he became a gentleman of the bedchamber and royal historian to Louis XV. These functions he fulfilled *in absentia,* when at all, for Paris and Versailles were too hot for him. He was the personal friend of Frederick the Great, with whom he lived for about two years at Potsdam. The two finally quarreled, for no stage was big enough to hold two such prima donnas for very long. Voltaire made a fortune from his writings, pensions, speculations, and practical business sense. In his later years he purchased a manor at Ferney near the Swiss frontier. Here he became, as he said, the "hotel keeper of Europe," receiving the streams of distinguished admirers, favor hunters, and distressed persons who came to seek him out. He died at Paris in 1778, at the age of eighty-four, by far the most famous man of letters in Europe. His collected writings fill over seventy volumes.

Voltaire was mainly interested in the freedom of thought. Like Montesquieu, he was an admirer of England. He spent three years in that country, where, in 1727, he witnessed the state funeral accorded to Sir Isaac Newton and his burial in Westminster Abbey. Voltaire's *Philosophical Letters on the English* (1733) and *Elements of the Philosophy of Newton* (1738) not only brought England increasingly before the consciousness of the rest of Europe, but also popularized the new scientific ideas—the inductive philosophy of Bacon, the physics of Newton, and the sensationalist psychology of Locke,[2] whose doctrine that all true ideas arose from sense experience undercut the authority of religious belief. What Voltaire mainly admired in England was its religious liberty, its relative freedom of the press, and the high regard paid to men of letters like himself. Political liberty concerned him much less than it did Montesquieu. Louis XIV, a villain for Montesquieu and the neoaristocratic school, was a hero for Voltaire, who wrote a laudatory *Age of Louis XIV* (1751) praising the Sun King for the splendor of art and literature in his reign. Voltaire likewise continued to esteem Frederick the Great, though he quarreled with him personally. Frederick was in fact almost his ideal of the enlightened ruler, a man who sponsored the arts and sciences, recognized no religious authority, and granted toleration to all creeds, welcoming Protestants and Catholics on equal terms if only they would be socially useful.

After about 1740 Voltaire became more definitely the crusader, preaching the cause of religious toleration. He fought to clear the memory of Jean Calas, a Protestant put to death on the charge of murdering a son to prevent his conversion to Rome. He wrote also to exonerate a youth named La Barre, who had been executed for defiling a wayside cross. *Écrasez l'infâme!* became the famous Voltairean war cry—"crush the infamous thing!" The *infâme* for him was bigotry, intolerance, and superstition, and behind these the power of an organized clergy. He assaulted not only the Catholic church but the whole traditional Christian view of the world. He argued for "natural religion" and "natural morality," holding that belief in God and the difference between good and evil arose from reason itself. This doctrine had in fact long been taught by the Catholic church. But Voltaire insisted that no supernatural revelation in addition to reason was desirable or necessary, or rather, that belief in a special supernatural revelation made people intolerant, stupid, and cruel. He was the first to present a purely secular conception of world history. In his *Essai sur les moeurs,* or "Universal History," he began with ancient China and surveyed the great civilizations in turn. Earlier writers of world history had put human events within a Christian framework. Following the Bible, they began with the Creation, proceeded to the Fall, recounted the rise of Israel, and so on. Voltaire put Judeo-Christian history within a sociological framework. He represented Christianity and all other organized religions as social phenomena or mere human opinions. Spinoza had said as much; Voltaire spread these ideas through Europe.

In matters of politics and self-government Voltaire was neither a liberal nor a democrat. His opinion of the human race was about as low as his friend Frederick's. If only a government was enlightened he did not care how powerful it was. By an enlightened government he meant one that fought against sloth and stupidity, kept the clergy in a subordinate place, allowed freedom of thought and religion, and advanced the cause of material and technical progress. He had no

---

[2] See pp. 306–307.

developed political theory, but his ideal for large civilized countries approached that of enlightened or rational despotism. Believing that only a few could be enlightened, he thought that these few, a king and his advisers, should have the power to carry their program against all opposition. To overcome ignorance, habit, credulity, and priestcraft it was necessary for the state to be strong. It may be said that what Voltaire most desired was liberty for the enlightened.

Jean-Jacques Rousseau was very different. Born in Geneva in 1712, he was a Swiss, a Protestant, and almost of lower-class origin. He never felt at ease in France or in Paris society. Neglected as a child, a runaway at sixteen, he lived for years by odd jobs, such as copying music, and not until the age of forty did he have any success as a writer. He was always the little man, the outsider. In addition, his sex life was unsatisfactory; he finally settled down with an uneducated girl named Thérèse Levasseur, and with her mother, who kept interfering with his affairs. By Thérèse he had five children, whom he deposited at an orphanage. He had no social status, no money, and no sense of money, and after he became famous he lived largely by the generosity of his friends. He was pathetically and painfully maladjusted. He came to feel that he could trust no one, that those who tried to befriend him were deriding or betraying him behind his back. He suffered from what would now be termed complexes; possibly he was paranoiac. He talked endlessly of his own virtue and innocence and complained bitterly that he was misunderstood.

But unbalanced though he was, he was possibly the most profound writer of the age and was certainly the most permanently influential. Rousseau felt, from his own experience, that in society as it existed a good person could not be happy. He therefore attacked society, declaring that it was artificial and corrupt. He even attacked reason, calling it a false guide when followed alone. He felt doubts on all the progress which gave satisfaction to his contemporaries. In two "discourses," one on the *Arts and Sciences* (1750), the other on the *Origin of Inequality Among Men* (1753), he argued that civilization was the source of much evil, and that life in a "state of nature," were it only possible, would be much better. As Voltaire said, when Rousseau sent him a copy of his second discourse (Voltaire who relished civilization in every form), it made him "feel like going on all fours." To Rousseau the best traits of human character, such as kindness, unselfishness, honesty, and true understanding, were products of nature. Deep below reason, he sensed the presence of feeling. He delighted in the warmth of sympathy, the quick flash of intuition, the clear message of conscience. He was religious by temperament, for though he believed in no church, no clergy, and no revelation he had a respect for the Bible, a reverent awe toward the cosmos, a love of solitary meditation, and a belief in a God who was not merely a "first cause" but also a God of love and beauty. Rousseau thus made it easier for serious-minded people to slip away from orthodoxy and all forms of churchly discipline. He was feared by the churches as the most dangerous of all "infidels" and was condemned both in Catholic France and at Protestant Geneva.

In general, in most of his books, Rousseau, unlike so many of his contemporaries, gave the impression that impulse is more reliable than considered judgment, spontaneous feeling more to be trusted than critical thought. Mystical insights were for him more truthful than rational or clear ideas. He became the "man of feeling," the "child of nature," the forerunner of the coming age of romanticism, and an important source of all modern emphasis on the nonrational and the subconscious.

In the *Social Contract* (1762) Rousseau seemed to contradict all this. In it he held, somewhat like Hobbes,[3] that the "state of nature" was a brutish condition without law or morality. In other works he had held that the badness of men was due to the evils of society. He now held that good men could be produced only by an improved society. Earlier thinkers, such as John Locke, for example, had thought of the "contract" as an agreement between a ruler and a people. Rousseau thought of it as an agreement among the people themselves. It was a social, not merely a political, contract. Organized civil society, i.e., the community, rested upon it. It was an understanding by which all individuals surrendered their natural liberty to each other, fused their individual wills into a combined General Will, and agreed to accept the rulings of this General Will as final. This General Will was the sovereign; and true sovereign power, rightly understood, was "absolute," "sacred," and "inviolable." Government was secondary; kings, officials, or elected representatives were only delegates of a sovereign people. Rousseau devoted many difficult and abstruse pages to explaining how the *real* General Will could be known. It was not necessarily determined by vote of a majority. "What generalizes the will," he said, "is not the number of voices but the common interest that unites them." He said little of the mechanism of government and had no admiration for parliamentary institutions. He was concerned with something deeper. Maladjusted outsider that he was, he craved a commonwealth in which every person could feel that he or she belonged. He wished a state in which all persons had a sense of membership and participation.

By these ideas Rousseau made himself the prophet of both democracy and nationalism. Indeed, in his *Considerations on Poland,* written at the request of Poles who were fighting against the partitions, Rousseau applied the ideas of the *Social Contract* in more concrete form and became the first systematic theorist of a conscious and calculated nationalism.[4] In writing the *Social Contract* he had in mind a small city-state like his native Geneva. But what he did, in effect, was to generalize and make applicable to large territories the psychology of small city republics—the sense of membership, of community and fellowship, of responsible citizenship and intimate participation in public affairs—in short, of common will. All modern states, democratic or undemocratic, strive to impart this sense of moral solidarity to their peoples. Whereas in democratic states the General Will can in some way be identified with the sovereignty of the people, in dictatorships it becomes possible for individuals (or parties) to arrogate to themselves the right to serve as spokesmen and interpreters of the General Will. Both totalitarians and democrats have regarded Rousseau as one of their prophets.

Rousseau's influence on his contemporaries was spread also by his other writings and especially his novels, *Émile* (1762) and the *Nouvelle Héloïse* (1760). The novels were widely read in all literate classes of society, especially by the women, who made a kind of cult of Jean-Jacques, while he was living and after his death, which occurred in 1778. He was a literary master, able to evoke shades of thought and feeling that few writers had touched before, and by his literary

[3] See p. 310.
[4] See pp. 245–249.

writings he spread in the highest circles a new respect for the common person, a love of common things, an impulse of human pity and compassion, a sense of artifice and superficiality in aristocratic life. Women took to nursing their own babies. Even men spoke of the delicacy of their sentiments. Tears became the fashion. The queen, Marie Antoinette, built herself a village in the gardens at Versailles where she pretended to be a simple milkmaid. In all this there was much that was ridiculous or shallow. Yet it was the wellspring of modern humanitarianism, the force leading to a new sense of human equality. Rousseau estranged the French upper classes from their own mode of life. He made many of them lose faith in their own superiority. That was his main direct contribution to the French Revolution.

Political Economists

In France, somewhat apart from the philosophes, were the Physiocrats, whom their critics called "economists," a word originally thought to be mildly insulting. Many of the Physiocrats, unlike the philosophes, were close to the government as administrators or advisers. Quesnay was physician to Louis XV, Turgot was an experienced official who became minister to Louis XVI, and Dupont de Nemours, an associate of Turgot's, became the founder of the industrial family of the Du Ponts in the United States. Such men concerned themselves with fiscal and tax reform, and with measures to increase the national wealth of France. They opposed guild regulations and price controls as impediments to the production and circulation of goods, and so were the first to use the term laissez faire ("let them do as they see fit") as a principle of economic activity. They favored strong government, however, relying on it to overcome traditional obstructions and to provide inducements for the establishment of new industries.

Economics, or what was long called political economy, arose from these activities of the Physiocrats, from the somewhat similar work of "cameralists" in the German states, and from the collection and analysis of quantitative data, that is, the birth of statistics. A good example of the latter was Sir William Petty's *Political Arithmetic*, published in 1690. Economic thinking flourished especially in Great Britain, where Adam Smith's *Enquiry into the Nature and Causes of the Wealth of Nations* appeared in 1776. By 1800 the *Wealth of Nations* had been translated into every west-European language except Portuguese.

Adam Smith's purpose, like that of the French Physiocrats, was to increase the national wealth by the reduction of barriers that hindered its growth. He undercut the premises of what we have called "the struggle for wealth and empire" in Chapter VI, since he argued that to build up a nation's wealth it was unnecessary to have an empire. He attacked most of the program of mercantilism that had obtained since the sixteenth century, and he expected that Britain's American colonies would soon become independent without loss to British trade. Where others looked to planning by an enlightened government, Adam Smith preferred to limit the functions of government to defense, internal security, and the provision of reasonable laws and fair law courts by which private differences could be adjudicated. For innovation and enterprise he counted more on private persons than on the state. He became the philosopher of the free market, the prophet of free trade. If there was a shortage of a given commodity its price would rise, and so stimulate producers to produce more, while also attracting new persons into that line of production. If there was an excess, if more was produced than purchasers would buy, both capital and labor would withdraw and gradually move into another area where demand was stronger. Demand would increase with lower prices, which depended on lower costs, which in turn depended on the specialization of labor. His most famous example was that of the pin factory of his time, where each of a dozen workers engaged in only one part of the process of manufacture, so that together they produced far more pins than if each man produced whole pins; the price of pins then fell, and more pins could be used by more people. The same principle held in international trade; some countries or climates could produce an article more cheaply than others, so that if each specialized and then exchanged with the others, all would have more. The motivation for all such production and exchange was to be the self-interest of the participants. As he said, we rely for our meat not on the good will of the butcher but on his concern for his own income. To those who might object that this was a system of selfishness Adam Smith would reply (being a professor of moral philosophy at the University of Glasgow) that it was at least realistic, describing how people really behaved, and that it was morally justified since it ultimately produced a maximum both of freedom and of abundance. The mutual interaction of the enlightened self-interest of millions of persons would in the end, as if by an "invisible hand," he said, result in the highest welfare of all. Among problems that Smith minimized, or accepted as lesser evils, were the insecurity of individuals and the dangers of excessive dependency of a whole country on imports of essentials, such as food; and if the visible hand of government continued to regulate the price of bread it was not for economic reasons, but to prevent rioting and obtain social peace.

Main Currents of Enlightenment Thought

It is clear that the currents of thought in France and Europe were divergent and inconsistent. There was a general belief in progress, reason, science, and civilization. Rousseau had his doubts and praised the beauties of character. Montesquieu thought the church useful but did not believe in religion; Rousseau believed in religion but saw no need for any church. Montesquieu was concerned over practical political liberty; Voltaire would surrender political liberty in return for guarantees of intellectual freedom; Rousseau wanted emancipation from the trivialities of society and sought the freedom that consists in merging willingly with nature and with one's fellows. Most philosophes were closest to Voltaire. They were concerned also for equality. It was not a very far-reaching equality, but it meant equality of rights for persons of different religions, a reduction of privileges enjoyed by nobles but not by commoners, more equality of status in law courts and in the payment of taxes, and more opportunity for middle-class persons to rise to positions of honor.

France was the main center of the Enlightenment. French philosophes traveled all over Europe. Frederick II and Catherine II invited French thinkers to their courts. French was the language of the academies of St. Petersburg and Berlin. Frederick wrote his own works in the French language. There was a uniform cosmopolitan culture among the upper classes of Europe, and this culture was predominantly French. But England was important also. Hitherto somewhat on the fringes of the European consciousness, England now moved closer to the center. Montesquieu and Voltaire may be said to have "discovered" England for Europe. Through them the ideas of Bacon, Newton, and Locke, and the whole theory of English liberty and parliamentary government became matters for general discussion and comment. We have seen, too, how Adam Smith's *Wealth of Nations* was soon translated into many languages.

The main agency of progress was thought to be the state. Whether in the form of limited monarchy on the English model favored by Montesquieu, or of an enlightened despotism preferred by Voltaire, or of the ideal republican commonwealth portrayed by Rousseau, the rightly ordered government was considered the best guarantee of social welfare. Even the political economists needed the state to shake people out of the habits of ages, sweep away a mass of local regulation, preserve law and order and the enforcement of contracts, and so assure the existence of a free market. But if they relied on the state, they were not nationalists in any later sense of the word. As "universalists," they believed in the unity of humankind under a natural law of right and reason. In this they carried over the classical and Christian outlook in a secular way. They supposed that all peoples would participate eventually in the same progress. No nation was thought to have a peculiar message. French ideas enjoyed a wide currency, but no one thought of them as peculiarly French, arising from a French "national character." It was simply thought that the French at the time were in the vanguard of civilization. Such was the idea of Condorcet, one of the later philosophes, a leading spokesman of the Enlightenment, who became an active figure in the French Revolution, and also one of its victims, and who in 1794, while in hiding from the guillotine, wrote the great testament to the Enlightenment, his *Sketch of the Progress of the Human Mind*.

37. Enlightened Despotism: France, Austria, Prussia

The Meaning of Enlightened Despotism

Enlightened despotism is hard to define, because it grew out of the earlier absolutism represented by Louis XIV or Peter the Great. Characteristically, the enlightened despots drained marshes, built roads and bridges, codified the laws, repressed provincial autonomy and localism, curtailed the independence of church and nobles, and built up a trained and salaried officialdom. All these things had been done by kings before. The typical enlightened despot differed from his "unenlightened" predecessor mainly in attitude and tempo. He said little of a divine right to his throne. He might even not emphasize his hereditary or dynastic family right. He justified his authority on grounds of usefulness to society, calling himself, as Frederick the Great did, the "first servant of the state."

Enlightened despotism was secular; it claimed no mandate from heaven and recognized no especial responsibility to God or church. The typical enlightened despot consequently favored toleration in religion, and this was an important new emphasis after about 1740; but here again there was precedent in the older absolutism, for the rulers of Prussia had been inclined toward toleration long before Frederick, and even the French Bourbons had recognized a degree of religious liberty for almost a century following the Edict of Nantes.[5] The secular outlook of the enlightened governments is again seen in the common front they adopted against the Jesuits. High papalists and ultramontanes,[6] affirming the authority of a universal church, and at the same time intellectually and in other ways the strongest religious order in the Catholic world, the Jesuits were distasteful to the enlightened monarchs and their civil officials and in the 1760s the order was banned in almost all Catholic countries. In 1773 the pope was persuaded to dissolve the Society of Jesus entirely. The various governments concerned, in France, Austria, Spain, Portugal, and Naples, confiscated the Jesuit property and took over the Jesuit schools. Not until 1814 was the order reconstituted.

Enlightened despotism was also rational and reformist. The typical despot set out to reconstruct his state by the use of reason. Sharing the current view of the past as benighted, he was impatient of custom and of all that was imbedded in custom or claimed as a heritage from the past, such as systems of customary law and the rights and privileges of church, nobles, towns, guilds, provinces, assemblies of estates, or, in France, the judicial bodies called parlements. The complex of such institutions was disparagingly referred to as "feudalism." Monarchs had long struggled against feudalism in this sense, but in the past they had usually compromised. The enlightened despot was less willing to compromise, and herein lay the difference in tempo. The new despot acted abruptly, desiring quicker results.

Enlightened despotism, in short, was an acceleration of the old institution of monarchy, which now put aside the quasi-sacred mantle in which it had clothed itself and undertook to justify itself in the cold light of reason and secular usefulness. In theory even the dynastic claim was awkward, for it rested on inheritance from the past. Under enlightened despotism the idea of the state itself was changing, from the older notion of an estate belonging by a kind of sanctified property right to its ruler, to a newer notion of an abstract and impersonal authority exercised by public officers, of whom the king was simply the highest.

The trend to enlightened despotism after 1740 owed a great deal to writers and philosophes, but it arose also out of a very practical situation, namely, the great war of the mid–eighteenth century.[7] War, in modern history, has usually led to concentration and rationalizing of government power, and the wars of 1740–1748 and 1756–1763 were no exception. Under their impact even governments where the rulers were not considered by philosophes to be enlightened, notably those of Louis XV and Maria Theresa, and even the government of Great Britain, which was certainly not despotic, embarked on programs which all bear features in common. They attempted to augment their revenues, devise new taxes, tax persons or regions hitherto more or less tax-exempt, limit the autonomy of outlying political bodies, and centralize and renovate their respective political systems. The workings of enlightened despotism might be seen in many states,

[5] See pp. 138–140, 189–190.
[6] See p. 91.
[7] See pp. 273–275.

Bourbon Dominions

Habsburg Dominions

Boundary of Holy Roman Empire

SWEDEN

NORWAY

St. Petersb

KINGDOM OF
DENMARK AND NORWAY

Stockholm

SCOTLAND

Riga

Edinburgh

NORTH SEA

BALTIC SEA

Memel

DENMARK

Copenhagen

LITHUAN

IRELAND

GREAT BRITAIN

SCHLESWIG

PRUSSIA

Danzig

EAST
PRUSSIA

Mi

Dublin   Liverpool

ENGLAND

Hamburg

Bremen

Elber R.

Thorn

WALES

UNITED

HANOVER
(Britain)

BRANDENBURG

Warsaw

POLAND

ATLANTIC OCEAN

PROVINCES

Amsterdam

London

Utrecht

Magdeburg

Berlin

AUSTRIAN
NETHERLANDS

CHANNEL I.
(Britain)

CAPE
DE LA HOGUE

Oudenarde

Antwerp

Cologne

Leipzig

SAXONY

SILESIA

Lublin

Rhine R.

MINOR
GERMAN STATES

Dresden

Breslau

Oder R.

Lemberg

Malplaquet

Ramillies

PALATI-
NATE

Frankfurt

Prague

Cracow

Rouen

Reims

Metz

BOHEMIA

POD

Paris

Orléans

Seine R.

Strasbourg

Blenheim

MORAVIA

Munkacz

Quiberon

Loire R.

LORRAINE
(France 1766)

BAVARIA

AUSTRIA

Vistula R.

Tours

Besançon

Munich

Vienna

Pressburg

Budapest

FRANCE

Limoges

Geneva

SWITZERLAND

TYROL

AUSTRIAN MONARCHY

Santiago

Bordeaux

Garonne R.

Lyons

SAVOY

MILAN

VENETIA

KINGDOM
OF HUNGARY

TRANSYLVAN

León

Pamplona

Ebro R.

Toulouse

Rhone R.

Po R.

PAR-
MA

Venice

CROATIA

Save R.

BANAT

Burgos

Turin

Bologna

BOSNIA

Belgrade

WALL

Avignon

Genoa

SERBIA

Danu

PORTUGAL

SPAIN

Marseilles

Toulon

TUSCANY

PAPAL
STATES

DALMATIA
(Venice)

OTTOMAN EMP

CATALONIA

KINGDOM OF SARDINIA

ADRIATIC SEA

MONTENEGRO

Sofia

Lisbon

Tagus R.   Madrid

ARAGON

Barcelona

CORSICA
(Genoa)

Rome

Almanza

BALEARIC I.

MINORCA
(Britain)

Benevento

Bari

ALBANIA

Saloni

Guadalquivir R.

Seville

Granada

MAJORCA
(Spain)

SARDINIA

Naples

NAPLES

IONIAN I.
(Venice)

Cadiz

Tangier

Gibraltar (Britain)

MEDITERRANEAN

Cagliari

KINGDOM
OF THE TWO SICILIES

Palermo

Athens

MOREA

Algiers

SICILY

SEA

MOROCCO
(Independent)

ALGERIA
(Turkish)

Tunis

TUNISIA
(Turkish)

MALTA (Knights of St. John)

0   100   200   300 miles

in Habsburg Tuscany under Leopold, in Bourbon Naples and Spain under Charles III, in Portugal under the minister Pombal, in Denmark under Struensee. But it seems best to consider only the more important countries at some length—France and Austria, Prussia and Russia—and then the rather different, yet not wholly different, course of events in the British empire.

The Failure of Enlightened Despotism in France

It was in France that enlightened despotism had the least success. Louis XV, who had inherited the throne in 1715 and lived until 1774, though by no means stupid, was indifferent to most serious questions, absorbed in the daily rounds at Versailles, disinclined to make trouble for people that he saw personally, and interested in government only by fits and starts. His remark, *après moi le déluge*, whether or not he really said it, sufficiently characterizes his personal attitude to conditions in France. Yet the French government was not unenlightened, and many capable officials carried on its affairs all through the century. These men generally knew what the basic trouble was. All the practical difficulties of the French monarchy could be traced to its methods of raising revenue. It derived some income from the sale of offices and privileges, which had the perverse effect of building up vested interests in the existing system. Of actual taxes the most important was the *taille*, a kind of land tax, generally paid only by peasants. Nobles were exempt from it on principle, and officeholders and bourgeois, for one reason or another, were generally exempt also. In addition, the church, which owned between 5 and 10 percent of the land of the country, insisted that its property was not taxable by the state; it granted to the king a periodic "free gift" which, though sizable, was less than the government might expect from direct taxation. The consequence of the tax exemptions was that, although France itself was wealthy and prosperous, the government was chronically poor, because the social classes which enjoyed most of the wealth and prosperity did not pay taxes corresponding to their incomes. Louis XIV, under pressure of war, had tried to tax everybody alike by creating new levies—the capitation or poll tax and the *dixième* or tenth, both of which were assessed in proportion to income; but these taxes had been widely evaded. A similar effort was made in 1726, but it too had failed. The propertied classes resisted taxation because they thought it degrading. France had succumbed to the appalling principle that to pay direct taxes was the sure mark of inferior status. Nobles, churchmen, and bourgeois also resisted taxation because they were kept out of policymaking functions of government

EUROPE, 1740

Boundaries are as of 1740. There were now three Bourbon monarchies (France, Spain, and the Two Sicilies), while the Austrian monarchy possessed most of what is now Belgium, and in Italy the duchy of Milan and grand duchy of Tuscany, where the Medici family had recently died out. Prussia expanded by acquiring Silesia in the war of the 1740s. The first partition of Poland in 1772 enlarged Prussia, Austria, and Russia (see maps, pp. 222, 230–231, 242–243, 248). France acquired Lorraine in 1766 and Corsica in 1768. Otherwise there were no changes until the Revolutionary-Napoleonic wars of 1792–1814.

and so had no sense of political responsibility or control. There were good historical reasons for this, but the result was financially ruinous.[8]

In the 1740s, under pressure of heavy war costs, a new tax was introduced, the *vingtième* or twentieth, which imposed a 5 percent tax on income from all forms of property—land, manorial rights, commercial investments, and offices such as judgeships—to be paid irrespective of class status, provincial liberties, or previous exemptions of any kind. In practice, the *vingtième* amounted to less than 5 percent and fell only upon land, but it was paid by nobles and bourgeois alike and lasted until the Revolution. During the Seven Years' War the government tried to increase it, without success. A clamor arose from the Parlement of Paris, the eleven provincial parlements, the estates of Brittany, and the church. All these were now stronger than in the days of Louis XIV, and they could now cite Montesquieu to justify their opposition to the crown. The parlements ruled the tax increase to be incompatible with the laws of France, i.e., unconstitutional; and the *pays d'états*, or provinces having assemblies of estates, declared that their historic liberties were being violated. After several years of wrangling, Louis XV decided to push the matter no further.

But after the Seven Years' War, burdened with war debts, the government renewed its determination to win effective central control. It was decided to eliminate the parlements as a political force, and for this purpose, in 1768, Louis XV called to the chancellorship a man named Maupeou, who simply abrogated the old parlements and set up new ones in their place. Maupeou had the sympathy of Voltaire and most of the philosophes. In the "Maupeou parlements" the judges had no property rights in their seats but became salaried officials appointed by the crown with assurances of secure tenure, and they were forbidden to reject government edicts or to pass on their constitutionality, being confined to purely judicial functions. Maupeou likewise proposed to make the laws and judicial procedure more uniform throughout the whole country. Meanwhile, with the old parlements out of the way, another attempt was made to tax the privileged and exempted groups.

But Louis XV died in 1774. His grandson and successor, Louis XVI, though far superior in personal habits to his grandfather, and possessed by a genuine desire to govern well, resembled Louis XV in that he lacked sustained will power and could not bear to offend the people who could get to see him personally. In any case he was only twenty in 1774. The kingdom resounded with outcries against Maupeou and his colleagues as minions of despotism and with demands for the immediate restoration of the old Parlement of Paris and the others. Louis XVI, fearful of beginning his reign as a "despot," therefore recalled the old parlements and abolished those of Maupeou. The abortive Maupeou parlements represented the farthest step taken by enlightened despotism in France. It was arbitrary, high-handed, and despotic for Louis XV to destroy the old parlements, but it was certainly enlightened in the sense then connoted by the word, for the old parlements were strongholds of aristocracy and privilege and had for decades blocked programs of reform.

Louis XVI, in recalling the old parlements in 1774, began his reign by pacifying the privileged classes. At the same time he appointed a reforming ministry. At

[8] See pp. 70, 187–188, 270.

its head was Turgot, a philosophe and Physiocrat and a widely experienced government administrator. Turgot undertook to suppress the guilds, which were privileged municipal monopolies in their several trades. He allowed greater freedom to the internal commerce in grain. He planned to abolish the royal *corvée* (a requirement that certain peasants labor on the roads a few days each year), replacing it by a money tax which would fall on all classes. He began to review the whole system of taxation and was known even to favor the legal toleration of Protestants. The Parlement of Paris, supported by the Provincial Estates and the church, vociferously opposed him, and in 1776 he resigned. Louis XVI, by recalling the parlements, had made reform impossible. In 1778 France again went to war with Britain. The same cycle was repeated: war costs, debt, deficit, new projects of taxation, resistance from the parlements and other semiautonomous bodies. In the 1780s the clash led to revolution.[9]

Austria: The Reforms of Maria Theresa (1740–1780) and of Joseph II (1780–1790)

For Maria Theresa the war of the 1740s proved the extraordinary flimsiness of her empire.[10] Had the Continental allies won a more smashing victory, not only would Silesia have been lost to Prussia, but Belgium would have gone to France, Bohemia and Austria to the elector of Bavaria supported by France, and the emperorship of the Holy Roman Empire, long a source of prestige to the Habsburgs, would have passed permanently in all probability to a Bavarian or other pro-French German prince. Maria Theresa would have become queen of Hungary only. Nor did her subjects show much inclination to remain together under her rule. In Breslau, the capital of Silesia, after the Prussian attack of 1740, the citizens stood so stubbornly by their town liberties that they would not admit her army within their walls. In Bohemia almost half the nobles welcomed the invading Franco-Bavarians. In Hungary Maria Theresa won support but only by confirming the historic Hungarian liberties. The empire was only a loose bundle of territories, without common purpose or common will. The Pragmatic Sanction devised by Charles VI, it should be recalled, had been meant not only to guarantee the Habsburg inheritance against foreign attack, but also to secure the assent of the several parts of the empire to remain united under the dynasty.[11]

The war of the 1740s led to internal consolidation. The reign of Maria Theresa set the course of all later development of the Austrian empire and hence of the many peoples who lived within its borders. She was aided by a notable team of ministers, whose origin illustrated the nonnational character of the Habsburg system. Her most trusted adviser in foreign relations, the astute Kaunitz,[12] was a Moravian; her main assistants in domestic affairs were a Silesian and a Bohemian-Czech. They worked smoothly with the German archduchess-queen and with German officials in Vienna. Their aim was primarily to prevent dissolution of the monarchy by enlarging and guaranteeing the flow of taxes and soldiers.

[9] See pp. 365–369.
[10] See pp. 275–278.
[11] See pp. 225, 275–276
[12] See p. 278.

This involved breaking the local control of territorial nobles in their diets, which corresponded somewhat to the French Provincial Estates. Hungary, profoundly separatist, was let alone. But the Bohemian and Austrian provinces were welded together. The kingdom of Bohemia, in 1749, lost the constitutional charter which it had received in 1627.[13] The several Bohemian and Austrian diets lost their right to consent to taxes. The separate offices, or "chancelleries," by which their affairs had been separately handled at Vienna, were abolished. Formerly local affairs, recruiting, and tax collecting had been dominated by committees of the diets, made up of landed noblemen of the neighborhood, gentlemen amateurs who were often negligent or indifferent, and who, since they served without pay, were impervious to official discipline, reprimand, or coordination. They were replaced by salaried administrators. Bureaucracy took the place of local self-government. Officials (following the form of mercantilist doctrine called "cameralism" in central Europe) planned to augment the economic strength of the empire by increasing production. They checked the local guild monopolies, suppressed brigandage on the roads, and in 1775 produced a tariff union of Bohemia, Moravia, and the Austrian duchies. This region became the largest area of free trade on the European continent, since even France was still divided by internal tariffs. Bohemia, industrially the most advanced part of the empire, benefited substantially; one of its cotton manufacturing plants, at the end of Maria Theresa's reign, employed 4,000 persons.

The great social fact, both in the Habsburg lands and in all eastern Europe, was the serfdom into which the rural masses had progressively fallen during the past 200 years.[14] Serfdom meant that the peasant belonged more to the landlord than to the state. The serf owed labor to the lord, often unspecified in amount or kind. The tendency, so long as the landlords ruled locally through their diets, was for the serf to do six days a week of forced labor on the lord's land. Maria Theresa, from humane motives, and also from a desire to lay hands on the manpower from which her armies were recruited, launched a systematic attack on the institutions of serfdom, which meant also an attack on the landed aristocracy of the empire. With the diets reduced in power, the protests of the nobles were less effective; still, the whole agricultural labor system of her territories was involved, and Maria Theresa proceeded with caution. Laws were passed against abuse of peasants by lords or their overseers. Other laws regularized the labor obligations, requiring that they be publicly registered and usually limiting them to three days a week. The laws were often evaded. But the peasant was to some extent freed from arbitrary exactions of the lord. Maria Theresa accomplished more to alleviate serfdom than any other ruler of the eighteenth century in eastern Europe, with the single exception of her own son, Joseph II.

The great archduchess-queen died in 1780, having reigned for forty years. Her son, who had been co-regent with his mother since 1765, had little patience with her methods. Maria Theresa, though steady enough in aim, had always been content with partial measures. Instead of advertising her purposes by philosophical generalization she disguised or understated them, never carrying matters to the point of arousing an unmanageable reaction or of uniting against her the vested

---

[13] See pp. 142–143, 224.
[14] See pp. 125–126, 210–211, 223–224, 233.

interests that she undermined. She backed and filled, watched and waited. Joseph II would not wait. Though he thought the French philosophes frivolous, and Frederick of Prussia a mere clever cynic, he was himself a pure representative of the Age of Enlightenment, and it is in his brief reign of ten years that the character and the limitations of enlightened despotism can best be seen. He was a solemn, earnest, good man, who sensed the misery and hopelessness of the lowest classes. He believed existing conditions to be bad, and he would not regulate or improve them; he would end them. Right and reason, in his mind, lay with the views which he himself adopted; upholders of the old order were self-seeking or mistaken and to yield to them would be to compromise with evil.

"The state," said Joseph, anticipating the Philosophical Radicals in England, meant "the greatest good for the greatest number." He acted accordingly. His ten years of rule passed in a quick succession of decrees. Maria Theresa had regulated serfdom. Joseph abolished it. His mother had collected taxes from nobles as well as peasants, though not equally. Joseph decreed absolute equality of taxation. He insisted on equal punishment for equal crimes whatever the class status of the offender; an aristocratic army officer, who had stolen 97,000 gulden, was exhibited in the pillory, and Count Podstacky, a forger, was made to sweep the streets of Vienna chained to common convicts. At the same time many legal punishments were made less physically cruel. Joseph granted complete liberty of the press. He ordered toleration of all religions, except for a few popular sects which he thought too ignorant to allow. He granted equal civil rights to the Jews, and equal duties, making Jews liable, for the first time in Europe, to service in the army. He even made Jewish nobles, an amazing phenomenon to those of aristocratic "blood." He clashed openly and rudely with the pope, supporting a movement called Febronianism which urged more national independence from Rome for German Catholic prelates, on the model of the French Gallican liberties. He demanded increased powers in the appointment and supervision of bishops, and he suppressed a good many monasteries, using their property to finance secular hospitals in Vienna, and thus laying the foundations of Viennese excellence as a medical center. He attempted also to develop the empire economically and built up the port of Trieste, where he even established an East India Company, which soon failed for obvious reasons—neither capital nor naval support being forthcoming from central Europe. His attempts to reach the sea commercially through Belgium, like those of his grandfather at the time of the Ostend Company, were blocked by the Dutch and British interests.[15]

To force through his program Joseph had to centralize his state, like earlier rulers, except that he went further. Regional diets and aristocratic self-government fared even worse than under his mother. Where she had always sagaciously let Hungary go its own way, he applied most of his measures to Hungary also—what was right must be right everywhere. His ideal was a perfectly uniform and rational empire, with all irregularities smoothed out as if under a steam roller. He thought it reasonable to have a single language for administration and naturally chose German; this led to a program of Germanizing the Czechs, Poles, Magyars, and others, which in turn aroused their nationalistic resistance. Using the German language, pushing the emperor's program against regional and class opposition,

[15] See p. 225.

was a hard-pressed, constantly growing, and increasingly disciplined body of officials. Bureaucracy became recognizably modern, with training courses, promotion schedules, retirement pensions, efficiency reports, and visits by inspectors. The clergy likewise were employed as mouthpieces of the state to explain new laws to their parishioners and teach due respect for the government. To watch over the whole structure Joseph created a secret police, whose agents, soliciting the confidential aid of spies and informers, reported on the performance of government employees, or on the ideas and actions of nobles, clergy, or others from whom trouble might be expected. The police state, so infamous to the liberal world, was first systematically built up under Joseph as an instrument of enlightenment and reform.

Joseph II, the "revolutionary emperor," anticipated much that was done in France by the Revolution and under Napoleon. He could not abide "feudalism" or "medievalism"; he personally detested the nobility and the church. But few of his reforms proved lasting. He died prematurely in 1790, at the age of forty-nine, disillusioned and broken-hearted. Hungary and the Belgian provinces were in revolution against him. They held that their old constitutional liberties had been outraged—that they were being governed without their consent. In Hungary all the good will won by Maria Theresa seemed to be lost; in Belgium the provinces stood stubbornly by the same medieval privileges, the old *Joyeuse Entrée*, which they had vindicated 200 years before against the king of Spain.[16] Noble landlords throughout the Habsburg empire, having lost their control over labor by the abolition of serfdom, and their caste status by legal and fiscal reforms, naturally were indignant. The church believed itself to be prostituted and despoiled. The peasants were grateful for their new personal liberty but balked at the official attitude of condescending uplift, and often, in real life, sympathized with their priests and their gentlefolk. The officials were unequal to the task demanded of them. There were too few bourgeois in most parts of the empire to staff the civil service, so that many functionaries were members of the landowning nobility which Joseph humiliated; and in any case they frequently found the directives that flowed from Vienna impossible to enforce or even to understand. Joseph was a revolutionist without a party. He failed because he could not be everywhere and do everything himself. His reign demonstrated the limitations of a merely despotic enlightenment. It showed that a legally absolute ruler could not really do as he pleased. It suggested that drastic and abrupt reform could only come with a true revolution, on a wave of public opinion, and under the leadership of men who shared in a coherent body of ideas.

Joseph was succeeded by his brother Leopold, one of the ablest rulers of the century, who for many years as grand duke of Tuscany had given that country the best government known in Italy for generations. Now, in 1790, Leopold was plagued by outcries from his sister, Marie Antoinette, caught in the toils of a real revolution in France.[17] He refused to interfere in French affairs; in any case, he was busy dealing with the uproar left by Joseph. He abrogated most of Joseph's edicts, but he did not yield entirely. The nobles did not win back full powers in their diets. The peasants were not wholly consigned to the old serfdom; Joseph's

[16] See pp. 128–131.
[17] See p. 379.

efforts to provide them with land and to rid them of forced labor had to be given up, but they remained personally free, in law, to migrate, marry, or choose an occupation at will. Leopold died in 1792 and was followed by his son Francis II. Under Francis the aristocratic and clerical reaction gathered strength, terrified by the memory of Joseph II and by the spectacle of revolutionary France, with which Austria went to war soon after Leopold's death.

Prussia under Frederick the Great (1740–1786)

In Prussia, Frederick the Great continued to reign for twenty-three years after the close of the Seven Years' War. "Old Fritz," as he was called, spent the time peaceably, writing memoirs and histories, rehabilitating his shattered country, promoting agriculture and industry, replenishing his treasury, drilling his army, and assimilating his huge conquest of Silesia, and, after 1772, that part of Poland which fell to him in the first partition. Frederick's fame as one of the most eminent of enlightened despots rests, however, not so much on his actual innovations as on his own intellectual gifts, which were considerable, and on the admiring publicity which he received from such literary friends as Voltaire. "My chief occupation," he wrote to Voltaire, "is to fight ignorance and prejudices in this country. . . . I must enlighten my people, cultivate their manners and morals, and make them as happy as human beings can be, or as happy as the means at my disposal permit." He did not conceive that sweeping changes were necessary to happiness in Prussia. The country was docile, for its Lutheran church had long been subordinate to the state, its relatively few burghers were largely dependents of the crown, and the independence of the Junker landlords, as expressed in provincial diets, had been curtailed by Frederick's predecessors.[18] Frederick simplified and codified the many laws of the kingdom and made the law courts cheaper, more expeditious, and more honest. He kept up a wholesome and energetic tone in his civil service. He gave religious freedom, and he decreed, though he did not realize, a modicum of elementary education for all children of all classes. Prussia under Frederick was attractive enough for some 300,000 immigrants to seek it out.

But society remained stratified in a way hardly known in western Europe. Nobles, peasants, and burghers lived side by side in a kind of segregation. Each group paid different taxes and owed different duties to the state, and no person could buy property of the type pertaining to one of the other two groups. Property was legally classified, as well as persons; there was little passing from one group to another. The basic aim of these policies was military, to preserve, by keeping intact their respective forms of property, a distinct peasant class from which to draw soldiers and a distinct aristocratic class from which to draw officers. The peasants, except in the western extremities of the kingdom, were serfs holding patches of land on precarious terms in return for obligations to labor on the estates of the lords. They were likewise considered the lord's "hereditary subjects" and were not free to leave the lord's estate, to marry, or to learn a trade except with his permission. Frederick in his early years considered steps to relieve the burden of serfdom. He did relieve it on his own manors, those

[18] See pp. 232–233.

belonging to the Prussian crown domain, which comprised a quarter of the area of the kingdom. But he did nothing for serfs belonging to the private landlords or Junkers. No king of Prussia could fundamentally antagonize the Junker class which commanded the army. On the other hand, even in Prussia, the existence of a monarchical state was of some advantage for the common person; the serf in Prussia was not so badly off as in adjoining areas—Poland, Livonia, Mecklenburg, or Swedish Pomerania—where the will of the landlords was the law of the land, and which therefore have not inaptly been called Junker republics. In these countries cases came to light in which owners sold their serfs as movable property, or gambled or gave them away, breaking up families in the process, as Russian landlords might do with their serfs or American plantation owners with their slaves. Such abuses were unknown in Prussia.

Frederick's system was centralized not merely at Potsdam but in his own head. He himself attended to all business and made all important decisions. None of his ministers or generals ever achieved an independent reputation. As he said of his army, "no one reasons, everyone executes"—that is, no one reasoned except the king himself. Or again, as Frederick put it, if Newton had had to consult with Descartes he would never have discovered the law of universal gravitation. To have to take account of other people's ideas, or to entrust responsibilities to men less capable than himself, seemed to Frederick wasteful and anarchic. He died in 1786, after ruling forty-six years and having trained no successors. Twenty years later Prussia was all but destroyed by Napoleon.[19] It was not surprising that Napoleon should defeat Prussia, but Europe was amazed, in 1806, to see Prussia collapse totally and abruptly. It was then concluded, in Prussia and elsewhere, that government by a mastermind working in lofty and isolated superiority did not offer a viable form of state under modern conditions.

38. *Enlightened Despotism: Russia*

The Russian empire has long been out of sight in the preceding pages. There are reasons for its absence, for it played no part in the intellectual revolution of the seventeenth century, and its role in the struggle for wealth and empire, which reached a climax in the Seven Years' War, was somewhat incidental. In the Age of Enlightenment the role of Russia was passive. No Russian thinker was known to Europe. But European thinkers were well known in Russia. The French-dominated cosmopolitan culture of the European upper classes spread to the upper classes of Russia. The Russian court and aristocracy took over French as their common conversational language. With French (German was also known, and sometimes English, for the Russian aristocrats were remarkable linguists) all the ideas boiling up in western Europe streamed into Russia. The Enlightenment, if it did not affect Russia profoundly, yet affected it significantly. It continued the westernization so forcibly pushed forward by Peter and carried further the estrangement of the Russian upper classes from their own people and their own native scene.

[19] See p. 421.

Russia after Peter the Great

Peter the Great died in 1725.[20] To secure his revolution he had decreed that each tsar should name his successor, but he himself had named none and had put to death his own son Alexis to prevent social reaction. Peter was succeeded by his wife, a woman of peasant origin, who reigned for two years as Catherine I. Then came the boy Peter II, son of Alexis and grandson of Peter I. Peter II reigned only from 1727 to 1730. He was followed by Anna, 1730–1740; in her reign the old native Russian party tried to surround the tsardom with various constitutional checks. They failed; Anna was followed by Ivan VI, who was tsar for a few months only, during which his mother, a German woman, ran affairs according to the views of the German party in Russia, which was indispensable to the westernization program and was resented by the Russian nativists. A palace revolution in 1741 brought to the throne Peter the Great's daughter, Elizabeth, who managed to hold power until her death twenty-one years later. In her reign the military power of Russia expanded, and she entered into European diplomacy and joined in the Seven Years' War against Prussia, fearing that the continued growth of Prussia would endanger the new Russian position on the Baltic. Her nephew, Peter III, was almost immediately dethroned, and probably assassinated, by a group acting in the name of his young wife, Catherine. The victorious coterie gave it out that Peter III had been almost a half-wit, who at the age of twenty-four still played with paper soldiers. Catherine was proclaimed the Empress Catherine II and is called "the Great." She enjoyed a long reign from 1762 to 1796, during which she acquired a somewhat exaggerated reputation as an enlightened despot.

The names of the tsars and tsarinas between Peter I and Catherine II are of slight importance. But their violent and rapid sequence tells a story. With no principle of succession, dynastic or other, the empire fell into a lawless struggle of parties, in which plots against rulers while living alternated with palace revolutions upon their death. In all the confusion an underlying issue was always how the westernizing program of Peter would turn out. To western Europe Russia still seemed Byzantine and barbaric.

Catherine the Great (1762–1796): Domestic Program

Catherine the Great was a German woman, of a small princely house of the Holy Roman Empire. She had gone to Russia at the age of fifteen to be married. She had immediately cultivated the good will of the Russians, learned the language, and embraced the Orthodox church. Early in her married life, disgusted with her husband, she foresaw the chance of becoming empress herself. She was nothing like her feminine contemporary Maria Theresa, except possibly in having much the same practical sense. Hearty and boisterous, she wore out a long succession of many lovers, mixing them freely with politics and using them in positions of state. When she died at the age of sixty-seven, of a stroke of apoplexy, she was still living with the last of these venturesome paramours. Her intellectual powers were as remarkable as her physical vigor; even after becoming empress she often

---

[20] See pp. 244–245.

got up at five in the morning, lighted her own fire, and turned to her books, making a digest, for example, of Blackstone's *Commentaries on the Laws of England,* published in 1765. She corresponded with Voltaire and invited Diderot, editor of the *Encyclopédie,* to visit her at St. Petersburg, where, she reported, he thumped her so hard on the knee in the energy of his conversation that she had to put a table between them. She bought Diderot's library, allowing him to keep it during his lifetime, and in other ways won renown by her benefactions to the philosophes, whom she probably regarded as useful press agents for Russia. Her gifts to them were substantial, though dwarfed by the £12,000,000 she is estimated to have bestowed on her lovers.

When she first came to power she publicized an intention to make certain enlightened reforms. She summoned a great consultative assembly, called a Legislative Commission, which met in the summer of 1767. From its numerous proposals Catherine obtained a good deal of information on conditions in the country and concluded, from the profuse loyalty exhibited by the deputies, that though a usurper and a foreigner she possessed a strong hold upon Russia. The reforms which she subsequently enacted consisted in a measure of legal codification, restrictions on the use of torture, and a certain support of religious toleration, though she would not allow Old Believers to build their own chapels. Such innovations were enough to raise an admiring chorus from the philosophes, who saw in her, as they saw retrospectively in Peter the Great, the standard-bearer of civilization among a backward people. Like other enlightened despots, Catherine turned assiduously to administrative questions also. Consolidating the machinery of state, she replaced Peter's ten *gubernii* with fifty, each subdivided into districts, and all equipped with appropriate sets of governors and officials.

Whatever ideas Catherine may conceivably have had at first, as a thoughtful and progressive young woman, on the fundamental subject of reforming serfdom in Russia, did not last long after she became empress, and dissolved with the great peasant insurrection of 1773, known as Pugachev's rebellion. The condition of the Russian serfs was deteriorating. Serf owners were increasingly selling them apart from land, breaking up families, using them in mines or manufactures, disciplining and punishing them at will, or exiling them to Siberia. The serf population was restless, worked upon by Old Believers and cherishing distorted popular memories of the mighty hero, Stephen Razin, who a century before had led an uprising against the landlords.[21] Class antagonism, though latent, was profound, nor was it made less when the rough muzhik, in some places, heard the lord and his family talking French so as not to be understood by the servants or saw them wearing European clothes, reading European books, and adopting the manners of a foreign and superior way of life.

In 1773 a Don Cossack, Emelian Pugachev, a former soldier, appeared at the head of an insurrection in the Urals. Following an old Russian custom, he announced himself as the true tsar, Peter III (Catherine's deceased husband), now returned after long travels in Egypt and the Holy Land. He surrounded himself with duplicates of the imperial family, courtiers, and even a secretary of state. He issued an imperial manifesto proclaiming the end of serfdom and of taxes and military conscription. Tens of hundreds of thousands, in the Urals and

[21] See p. 238.

Volga regions, Tartars, Kirghiz, Cossacks, agricultural serfs, servile workers in the Ural mines, fishermen in the rivers and in the Caspian Sea, flocked to Pugachev's banner. The great host surged through eastern Russia, burning and pillaging, killing priests and landlords. The upper classes in Moscow were terrified; 100,000 serfs lived in the city as domestic servants or industrial workers, and their sympathies went out to Pugachev and his horde. Armies were at first unsuccessful. But famine along the Volga in 1774 dispersed the rebels. Pugachev, betrayed by some of his own followers, was brought to Moscow in an iron cage. Catherine forbade the use of torture at his trial, but he was executed by the drawing and quartering of his body, a punishment, it should perhaps be noted, used at the time in western Europe in cases of flagrant treason.

Pugachev's rebellion was the most violent peasant uprising in the history of Russia, and the most formidable mass upheaval in Europe in the century before 1789. Catherine replied to it by repression. She conceded more powers to the landlords. The nobles shook off the last vestiges of the compulsory state service to which Peter had bound them. The peasants were henceforth the only bound or unfree class. As in Prussia, the state came more than ever to rest on an understanding between ruler and gentry, by which the gentry accepted the monarchy, with its laws, officials, army, and foreign policy, and received from it, in return, the assurance of full authority over the rural masses. Government reached down through the aristocracy and the scattered towns, but it stopped short at the manor; there the lord took over and was himself a kind of government in his own person. Under these conditions the number of serfs increased, and the load on each became more heavy. Catherine's reign saw the culmination of Russian serfdom, which now ceased to differ in any important respect from the chattel slavery to which blacks were subject in the Americas. One might read in the Moscow *Gazette* such advertisements as the following: "For sale, two plump coachmen; two girls eighteen and fifteen years, quick at manual work. Two barbers; one, twenty-one, knows how to read and write and play a musical instrument; the other can do ladies' and gentlemen's hair."

Catherine the Great: Foreign Affairs

Territorially Catherine was one of the main builders of Russia. When she became tsarina in 1762 the empire reached to the Pacific and into central Asia, and it touched upon the Gulf of Riga and the Gulf of Finland on the Baltic, but westward from Moscow one could go only 200 miles before reaching Poland, and no one standing on Russian soil could see the waters of the Black Sea.[22] Russia was separated from central Europe by a wide band of loosely organized domains, extending from the Baltic to the Black Sea and the Mediterranean and nominally belonging to the Polish and Turkish states. Poland was an old enemy, which had once threatened Muscovy, and in both Poland and the Ottoman Empire there were many Greek Orthodox Christians with whom Russians felt an ideological tie. In western Europe the disposal of the whole Polish-Turkish tract, which stretched through Asia Minor, Syria, and Palestine into Egypt, came to be called

[22] See map, pp. 242–243.

the Eastern Question. Though the name went out of use after 1900, the question itself has never ceased to exist.

Catherine's supreme plan was to penetrate the entire area, Polish and Turkish alike. In a war with Turkey in 1772 she developed her "Greek project," in which "Greeks," i.e., members of the Greek Orthodox Church, would replace Muslims as the dominant element throughout the Middle East. She defeated the Turks in the war, but was herself checked by the diplomatic pressures of the European balance of power. The result, as has been explained, was the first partition of Poland.[23] The three eastern monarchs began to divide up the territory between them. Frederick took Pomerelia, which he renamed West Prussia; Catherine took parts of Byelorussia; Maria Theresa, Galicia. Frederick digested his portion with relish, realizing an old dream of the Brandenburg house; Catherine swallowed hers with somewhat less appetite, since she had satisfactorily controlled the whole of Poland before; to Maria Theresa the dish was distasteful, and even shocking, but she could not see her neighbors go ahead without her, and she shared in the feast by suppressing her moral scruples. "She wept," said Frederick cynically, "but she kept on taking." Catherine, in 1774, signed a peace treaty with the defeated Turks at Kuchuk Kainarji on the Danube. The sultan ceded his rights over the Tartar principalities on the north coast of the Black Sea, where the Russians soon founded the seaport of Odessa.

Catherine had only delayed, not altered, her plans with respect to Turkey. She decided to neutralize the opposition of Austria. She invited Joseph II to visit her in Russia, and the two sovereigns proceeded together on a tour of her newly won Black Sea provinces. Her favorite of the moment, Potemkin, constructed artificial one-street villages along their way and produced throngs of cheering and happy-looking villagers to greet them, all of which enriched mankind with nothing except the phrase "Potemkin villages" to mean bogus evidence of a nonexistent prosperity. At Kherson the two monarchs passed through a gate marked "The Road to Byzantium." "What I want is Silesia," said Joseph II, but the tsarina induced him to join in a war of conquest against Turkey. This war was interrupted by the French Revolution. Both governments reduced their commitments in the Balkans to await developments in western Europe. It became Catherine's policy to incite Austria and Prussia into a war with revolutionary France, in the name of monarchy and civilization, in order that she might have a free hand in the Polish-Turkish sphere.[24] Meanwhile she contributed to killing off the nationalist and reforming movement among the Poles. In 1793 she arranged with Prussia for the second partition, and in 1795, with both Prussia and Austria, for the third. She was the only ruler who lived to take part in all three partitions of Poland.

Her protestations of enlightenment tempt one to an ironic judgment of her career. Her foreign policy was purely expansionist and unscrupulous, and the net effect of her domestic policy, aside from a few reforms of detail, was to favor the half-Europeanized aristocracy and to extend serfdom among the people. In her defense it may be observed that unscrupulous expansion was the accepted practice of the time, and that, domestically, probably no ruler could have corrected the social evils from which Russia suffered. If there was to be a Russian empire

[23] See pp. 245–249.
[24] See pp. 379–380.

it had to be with the consent of the serf-owning gentry, which was the only politically significant class. As Catherine observed to Diderot on the subject of reforms: "You write only on paper, but I have to write on human skin, which is incomparably more irritable and ticklish." She had reason to know how easily tsars and tsarinas could be unseated and even murdered, and that the danger of overthrow came not from the peasants but from cliques of army officers and landlords.

She remained attuned to the West. She never thought that the peculiar institutions of Russia should become a model for others. She continued to recognize the standards of the Enlightenment at least as standards. In her later years she gave careful attention to her favorite grandson, Alexander, closely supervising his education, which she planned on the Western model. She gave him as a tutor the Swiss philosophe La Harpe, who filled his mind with humane and liberal sentiments on the duties of princes. Trained by Catherine as a kind of ideal ruler, Alexander I was destined to cut a wide circle in the affairs of Europe, to defeat Napoleon Bonaparte, preach peace and freedom, and suffer from the same internal divisions and frustrations by which educated Russians seemed characteristically to be afflicted.

The Limitations of Enlightened Despotism

Enlightened despotism, seen in retrospect, foreshadowed an age of revolution and even signified a preliminary effort to revolutionize society by authoritative action from above. People were told by their own governments that reforms were needed, that many privileges, special liberties, or tax exemptions were bad, that the past was a source of confusion, injustice, or inefficiency in the present. The state rose up as more completely sovereign, whether acting frankly in its own interest or claiming to act in the interest of its people. All old and established rights were brought into question—rights of kingdoms and provinces, orders and classes, legal bodies and corporate groups. Enlightened despotism overrode or exterminated the Society of Jesus, the Parlement of Paris, the autonomy of Bohemia, and the independence of Poland. Customary and common law was pushed aside by authoritative legal codes. Governments, by opposing the special powers of the church and the feudal interests, tended to make all persons into uniform and equal subjects. To this extent enlightened despotism favored equality before the law. But it could go only a certain distance in this direction. The king was after all a hereditary aristocrat himself, and no government can be revolutionary to the point of breaking up its own foundations.

Even before the French Revolution enlightened despotism had run its course. Everywhere the "despots," for reasons of politics if not of principle, had reached a point beyond which they could not go. In France Louis XVI had appeased the privileged classes, in the Austrian empire Joseph's failure to appease them threw them into open revolt, in Prussia and in Russia the brilliant reigns of Frederick and Catherine wound up in an aggravation of landlordism for the mass of the people. Almost everywhere there was an aristocratic and even feudal revival. Religion also was renewing itself in many ways. Many were again saying that kingship was in a sense divine, and a new alliance was forming between "the throne and the altar." The French Revolution, by terrifying the old vested interests, was to accelerate and embitter a reaction which had already begun. Monarchy in Europe, ever since the Middle Ages, had generally been a progressive institution, acting along the line that Europe seemed destined to take, and in any case setting itself against the feudal and ecclesiastical powers. Enlightened despotism was the culmination of the historic institution of monarchy. After the enlightened despots, and after the French Revolution, monarchy became on the whole nostalgic and backward-looking, supported most ardently by the churches and aristocracies that it had once tried to subdue and least of all by those who felt in themselves the surge of the future.

39. New Stirrings: The British Reform Movement

It was not only by monarchs and their ministers, however, that the older privileged, feudal, and ecclesiastical interests were threatened. Beginning about 1760 they were challenged also in more popular quarters. Growing out of the Enlightenment, and out of the failure of governments to cope with grave social and fiscal problems, a new era of revolutionary disturbance was about to open. It was marked above all by the great French Revolution of 1789, but the American Revolution of 1776 was also of international importance. In Great Britain, too, the long-drawn-out movement for parliamentary reform which began in the 1760s was in effect revolutionary in character, though nonviolent, since it questioned the foundations of traditional English government and society. In addition, in the last third of the eighteenth century, there was revolutionary agitation in Switzerland, Belgium, and Holland, in Ireland, Poland, Hungary, Italy, and in lesser degree elsewhere. After 1800 revolutionary ferment was increasingly evident in Germany, Spain, and Latin America. This general wave of revolution may be said not to have ended until after the revolutions of 1848.

Onset of an Age of "Democratic Revolution"

For the whole period the term "Atlantic Revolution" has sometimes been used, since countries on both sides of the Atlantic were affected. It has been called also an age of "Democratic Revolution," since in all the diversity of these upheavals, from the American Revolution to those of 1848, certain principles of the modern democratic society were in one way or another affirmed. In this view, the particular revolutions, attempted revolutions, or basic reform movements are seen as aspects of one great revolutionary wave by which virtually the whole area of Western civilization was transformed. The contrary is also maintained, namely, that each country presented a special case, which is misunderstood if viewed only as part of a vague general international turmoil. Thus the American Revolution, it is argued, was essentially a movement for independence, even essentially conservative in its objectives, and thus entirely different from the French Revolution, in which a thorough renovation of all society and ideas was contemplated; and both were utterly different from what happened in England, where there was no revolution at all. There is truth in both contentions, and it need only be affirmed here that the American revolutionaries, the French Jacobins, the United Irish, the Dutch Patriots, and similar groups elsewhere, though differing from each other, yet shared much in common that can only be characterized as revolutionary and as contributing to a revolutionary age.

It is important to see in what ways the movement that began about 1760 was and was not "democratic." It did not generally demand universal suffrage, though a handful of persons in England did so as early as the 1770s and some of the American states practiced an almost universal male suffrage after 1776, as did the more militant French revolutionaries in 1792. It did not aim at a welfare state, nor question the right of property, though there were signs pointing in these directions in the extreme wing of the French Revolution. It was not especially directed against monarchy as such. The quarrel of the Americans was primarily with the British Parliament, not the king; the French proclaimed a republic by default in 1792, three years after their revolution began; the revolutionary Poles after 1788 tried to strengthen their king's position, not weaken it; and revolutionary groups could come into action where no monarchy existed at all, as in the Dutch provinces before the French Revolution, and the Swiss cantons, the Venetian Republic, or again in Holland, under French influence after 1795. Indeed the first revolutionary outbreak of the period occurred in 1768 at Geneva, a very nonmonarchical small city-republic, ruled by a close-knit circle of hereditary patricians. Royal power, where it existed, became the victim of revolutionaries only where it was used to support various privileged social groups.

The revolutionary movement announced itself everywhere as a demand for "liberty and equality." It favored declarations of rights and explicit written constitutions. It proclaimed the sovereignty of the people, or "nation," and it formulated the idea of national citizenship. In this context the "people" were essentially classless; it was a legal term, the obverse of government, signifying the community over which public authority was exercised and from which government itself was in principle derived. To say that citizens were equal meant originally that there was no difference between noble and common. To say that the people were sovereign meant that neither the king, nor the British Parliament, nor any group of nobles, patricians, regents, or other elite possessed power of government in their own right; that all public officers were removable and exercised a delegated authority within limits defined by the constitution. There must be no "magistrate" above the people, no self-perpetuation or cooptation in office, no rank derived from birth and acknowledged in the law. Social distinctions, as the French said in their Declaration of Rights of 1789, were to be based only "on common utility." Elites of talent or function there might be, but none of birth, privilege, or estate. "Aristocracy" in every form must be shunned. In representative bodies, there could be no special representation for special groups; representatives should be elected by frequent elections, not indeed by universal suffrage, but by a body of voters, however defined, in which each voter should count for one in a system of equal representation. Representation by numbers, with majority rule, replaced the older idea of representation of social classes, privileged towns, or other corporate groups.

In short, everything associated with absolutism, feudalism, or inherited right (except the right of property) was repudiated. Likewise rejected was any connection between religion and citizenship, or civil rights. The Democratic Revolution undermined the special position of the Catholic church in France, the Anglican in England and Ireland, the Dutch Reformed in the United Provinces;

this was also the great period of what has been called Jewish "emancipation." The whole idea that government, or any human authority, was somehow willed by God and protected by religion faded away. A general liberty of opinion on all subjects was countenanced, in the belief that it was necessary to progress. Here again the secularism of the Enlightenment carried on.

On the whole, the Democratic Revolution was a middle-class movement, and indeed the term "bourgeois revolution" was later invented to describe it. Many of its leaders in Europe were in fact nobles who were willing to forgo the historic privileges of nobility; and many of its supporters were of the poorer classes, especially in the great French Revolution. But the middle classes were the great beneficiaries, and it was a kind of middle-class or bourgeois society that emerged. Persons of noble ancestry continued to exist after the storm was over, but the world of noble values was gone; and they either took part in various activities on much the same terms as others or retreated into exclusive drawing rooms to enjoy their aristocratic distinctions in private. The main drive of the working classes was still to come.

The English-Speaking Countries: Parliament and Reform

If the American Revolution was the first act of a larger drama, it must be understood also in connection with the broader British world of which the American colonies formed a part. The British Empire in the middle of the century was decentralized and composite. Thirty-one governments were directly subordinate to Westminster, ranging from the separate kingdom of Ireland through all the crown and charter colonies to the various political establishments maintained in the East by the East India Company. The whole empire, with about 15,000,000 people of all colors in 1750, was less populous than France or the Austrian monarchy. The whole tract of the American mainland from Georgia to Nova Scotia compared in the number of its white population with Ireland or Scotland—or with Brittany or Bohemia—a figure of about 2,000,000 being roughly applicable in each case.

England had its own way of passing through the Age of Enlightenment. There was general contentment with the arrangements that followed the English Revolution of 1688—it has often been remarked that nothing is so conservative as a successful revolution.[25] British thought lacked the asperity of thought on the Continent. The writers who most resembled French philosophes, such as Hume and Gibbon, were innocuously moderate in their political ideas. The prevailing mood was one of complacency, a self-satisfaction in the glories of the British constitution, by which Englishmen enjoyed liberties unknown on the Continent.

In Britain, Parliament was supreme, as in most Continental countries, the monarch. It had the power, as one facetious journalist put it, to do all things except change a man into a woman. The British Parliament was as sovereign as any European ruler, and indeed more so, since less that could be called feudalism remained in England than on the Continent. Nor was there any "despotism" in England, enlightened or otherwise. The young George III, who inherited the throne in 1760, did feel himself to be a "patriot king." He did wish to heighten

[25] See pp. 178–181.

the influence of the crown and to overcome the factionalism of parties.[26] But it was through Parliament that he had to work. He had to descend into the political arena himself, buy up or otherwise control votes in the Commons, grant pensions and favors, and make promises and deals with other parliamentary politicians. What he did in effect was to create a new faction, the "king's friends." This faction was in power during the ministry of Lord North from 1770 to 1782. It is worth noting that all factions were factions of Whigs, that the Tory party was practically defunct, that Britain did not yet have a two-party system, and that the word "Tory," as it came to be used by American revolutionaries, was little more than a term of abuse.

While Parliament was supreme, and constitutional questions apparently settled, there were nevertheless numerous undercurrents of discontent. These were expressed, since the press was freer in England than elsewhere, in many books and pamphlets which were read in the American colonies and helped to form the psychology of the American Revolution. There was, for example, a school of Anglo-Irish Protestant writers, who argued that since Ireland was in any case a separate kingdom, with its own parliament, it ought to be less dependent on the central government at Westminster. The possibility of a similar separate kingdom, remaining within the British Empire, was one of the alternatives considered by Americans before they settled on independence. In England there was the considerable body of Dissenters, or Protestants not accepting the Church of England, who had enjoyed religious toleration since 1689 but continued to labor (until 1828) under various forms of political exclusion. They overlapped with two other amorphous groups, a small number of "commonwealthmen" and a larger and growing number of parliamentary reformers. The commonwealthmen, increasingly eccentric and largely ignored, looked back nostalgically to the Puritan Revolution and the republican era of Oliver Cromwell.[27] They kept alive memories of the Levellers and ideals of equality, well mixed with a pseudo-history of a simple Anglo-Saxon England that had been crushed by the despotism of the Norman Conquest. The commonwealthmen had less influence in England than in the American colonies and especially New England, which had originated in close connection with the Puritan Revolution. The parliamentary reformers were a more diverse and influential group. They were condemned in the eighteenth century to repeated frustration; not until the First Reform Bill of 1832 was anything accomplished.

The very power of Parliament meant that political leaders had to take strong measures to assure its votes. These measures were generally denounced by their critics as "corruption," on the grounds that Parliament, whether or not truly representative, should at least be free. Control of Parliament, and especially of the House of Commons, was assured by various devices, such as patronage or the giving of government jobs (called "places"), or awarding contracts, or having infrequent general elections (every seven years after 1716); or the fact that in many constituencies there were no real elections at all. The distribution of seats in the Commons bore no relation to numbers of inhabitants. A town having the right to send members to Parliament was called a "borough," but no new borough

[26] See pp. 266–268.
[27] See pp. 174–176.

346

was created after 1688 (or until 1832). Thus localities that had been important in the medieval or Tudor periods were represented, but towns that had grown up recently, such as Manchester and Birmingham, were not. A few boroughs were populous and democratic, but many had few inhabitants or none, so that influential "borough mongers" decided who should represent them in Parliament.

The reform movement began in England before the American Revolution, with which it was closely associated. Since complaints were diverse, it attracted people of different kinds. The first agitation centered about John Wilkes. Having attacked the policies of George III, been vindicated when the courts pronounced the arrest of his publisher illegal, and been expelled by a House of Commons dominated by the king's supporters, Wilkes became a hero and was three times reelected to the House, which, however, refused to seat him. In a whirl of protests and public meetings, reams of petitions supported him against the House. His followers in 1769 founded the Supporters of the Bill of Rights, the first of many societies dedicated to parliamentary reform. His case raised the question of whether the House of Commons should be dependent on the electorate and the propriety of mass agitation "out of doors" on political questions. It was in this connection, also, that debates in Parliament for the first time came to be reported in the London press. Parliament stood on the eve of a long transition, by which it was to be converted from a select body meeting in private to a modern representative institution answerable to the public and its constituents. Wilkes himself, in 1776, introduced the first of many reform bills of which none passed for over half a century. Meanwhile Major John Cartwright, called the "father of reform," had begun a long series of pamphlets on the subject; he lived to be eighty-four but not quite long enough to see the Reform Act of 1832. Dissenting intellectuals, such as Richard Price and Joseph Priestley, joined in the movement. Price, a founder of actuarial statistics, announced in 1776 that only 5,723 persons chose half the membership of the House of Commons. Many London merchants favored reform. So did a great many landowners and country gentry, especially in the north of England, led by Christopher Wyvil. These men objected to the fact that four-fifths of the members of the House of Commons sat for the boroughs and

THE HON. MRS. GRAHAM
by Thomas Gainsborough (English, 1727–1788)
This picture and the three following, on pp. 352, 382, and 386, suggest what is meant by the four basic classes of preindustrial society—aristocracy, middle class, urban workers, and peasantry. High social status is very evident in this portrayal of a young gentlewoman, whose title, "The Honorable," is still used in Great Britain for the daughters of viscounts and barons. Wealth is apparent in the brooch, the plumes, the silks, bows and ruffles, and in the pearls which are both worn in strings and sewn on the hat and garments. The meticulous coiffure and complexities of dress suggest the constant attention of lady's maids. The tall stature, delicate hands, refined mouth and haughty expression all reveal high breeding, and the classical colonnade on which the lady so casually rests her arm lends an air of familiarity with magnificent surroundings. Perhaps the aristocrats of the eighteenth century did not often look like this, but this is the way they liked to imagine themselves and to be portrayed for posterity. In Gainsborough, Sir Joshua Reynolds, and Sir Thomas Lawrence, England had an unparalleled group of artists who specialized in painting the upper class. Courtesy of the National Gallery of Scotland.

only one-fifth for the shires or counties. They rightly thought that the boroughs were more easily manipulated by the government; they thought that county elections were more honest; and they initiated in 1780 a movement of county associations to promote change in the electoral system.

The important Whig leaders, who had previously managed Parliament by much the same methods, began to sense "corruption" after control passed to George III and his "friends." Their most eloquent spokesman was Edmund Burke. Other reformers called for more frequent elections, "annual parliaments," a wider and more equal or even universal male suffrage, with dissolution of some boroughs in which no one was really represented. Burke favored none of these things; in fact he came strenuously to oppose them. A founder of philosophical conservatism, he was yet in his way a reformer. He was more concerned that the House of Commons should be independent and responsible than that it should be mathematically representative. He thought that the landowning interest should govern. But he pleaded for a strong sense of party in opposition to royal encroachments, and he argued that members of Parliament should follow their own best judgment of the country's interests, bound neither by the king on the one hand nor by their own constituents on the other. Like other reformers, he objected to "placemen," or jobholders dependent on their ministerial patrons, and he objected to the use made, for political purposes, of a bewildering array of pensions, sinecures, honorific appointments, and ornamental offices, ranks, and titles. In his Economical Reform of 1782 he got many of these abolished.

The reform movement, though ineffectual, remained strong. Even William Pitt, as prime minister in the 1780s, gave it his sponsorship. It took on new strength at the time of the French Revolution, spreading then to more popular levels, as men of the skilled artisan class were aroused by events in France and demanded a more adequate "representation of the people" in England. They then had upper-class support from Charles James Fox and a minority of the Whigs. But conservatism, satisfaction with the British constitution, patriotism engendered by a new round of French wars, and reaction against the French Revolution all raised an impassable barrier. Reform was delayed for another generation.

After the American Revolution, which in a way was a civil struggle within the English-speaking world, the English reformers generally blamed the trouble with America on King George III. This was less than fair, since Parliament on the American question was never dragooned by the king. The most ardent reformers later argued that if Parliament had been truly representative of the British people, the Americans would not have been driven to independence. This seems unlikely. In any case, reformers of various kinds, from Wilkes to Burke, were sympathetic to the complaints of the American colonials after 1763. There was much busy correspondence across the Atlantic. Wilkes was a hero in Boston as well as London. Burke pleaded for conciliation with the colonies in a famous speech of 1775. His very insistence on the powers and dignity of Parliament, however, made it hard for him to find a workable solution; and after the colonies became independent he showed no interest in the political ideas of the new American states. It was the more radical reformers in England, as in Scotland and Ireland, who most consistently favored the Americans, both before and after independence. They of course had no power. On the American side, for a decade before independence, the increasingly discontented colonials, reading English books and pamphlets and reports of speeches, heard George III denounced for despotism and Parliament accused of incorrigible corruption. All this seemed to confirm what Americans had long been reading anyway in the works of English Dissenters or old commonwealthmen, now on the fringes of English society but sure of a receptive audience in the American colonies. The result was to make Americans suspicious of all actions by the British government, to sense tyranny everywhere, to magnify such things as the Stamp Act into a kind of plot against American liberties.

The real drift in England in the eighteenth century, however, despite the chronic criticism of Parliament, was for Parliament to extend its powers in a general centralization of the empire. The British government faced somewhat the same problems as governments on the Continent. All had to deal with the issues raised by the great war of the mid-century, in its two phases of the Austrian Succession and Seven Years' War. Everywhere the solution adopted by governments was to increase their own central power. We have seen how the French government, in attempting to tap new sources of revenue, tried to encroach on the liberties of Brittany and other provinces and to subordinate the bodies which in France were called parlements. We have likewise seen how the Habsburg government, also in an effort to raise more taxes, repressed local self-government in the empire and even abrogated the constitution of Bohemia.[28] The same tendency showed itself in the British system. The revocation of the charter of Bohemia in 1749 had its parallel in the revocation of the charter of Massachusetts in 1774. The disputes of the French king with the estates of Brittany or Languedoc had their parallel in the disputes of the British Parliament with the provincial assemblies of Virginia or New York.

Scotland, Ireland, India

There were also problems nearer home. Scotland proved a source of weakness in the War of the Austrian Succession. The Lowlanders were loyal enough, but the Highlanders revolted with French assistance in the Jacobite rising of 1745, and by invading England threatened to take the British government in the rear as it was locked in the struggle with France.[29] The Highlands had never really been under any government, even under the old Scottish monarchy before the union of 1707 with England. Social organization, in the Highland fastnesses, followed the primitive principle of physical kinship. Men looked to their chiefs, the heads of the clans, to tell them whom and when to fight. The chiefs had hereditary jurisdiction, often including powers of life and death, over their clansmen. A few leaders could throw the whole region to the Stuarts or the French. The British government, after 1745, proceeded to make its sovereignty effective in the Highlands. Troops were quartered there for years. Roads were pushed across the moors and through the glens. Law courts enforced the law of the Scottish Lowlands. Revenue officers collected funds for the treasury of Great Britain. The chiefs lost their old quasi-feudal jurisdiction. The old system of land tenure was broken up. The holding of land from clannish chiefs was ended. The

[28] See pp. 329–331, 331–332.
[29] See p. 268.

clansman swayed by his chief was turned into the subject of the crown of Great Britain. He was turned also, in many cases, into an almost landless "crofter," while some of the chiefs, or their sons, emerged as landed gentlemen of the English type. Fighting Highlanders were incorporated into newly formed Highland regiments of the British army, under the usual discipline imposed by the modern state on its fighting forces. For thirty years the Scots were forbidden to wear the kilt or play the bagpipes.

In Ireland the process of centralization worked itself out more slowly. How Ireland was subjected after the battle of the Boyne has already been described.[30] It was a French army that had landed in Ireland, supported James II and been defeated in 1690. The new English constitutional arrangements, the Hanoverian succession, the Protestant ascendancy, the church and the land settlement in Ireland, together with the prosperity of British commerce, were all secured by the subordination of the smaller island. The native or Catholic Irish remained generally pro-French. The Presbyterian Irish disliked both Frenchmen and popery, but they were alienated from England also; many in fact emigrated to America in the generation before the American Revolution. The island remained quiet in the mid-century wars. When the trouble began between the British Parliament and the American colonies the Presbyterian Irish generally took the American side. They were greatly stirred by the example of American independence. Thousands formed themselves into Volunteer Companies; they wore uniforms, armed, and drilled; they demanded both internal reform of the Irish parliament (which was even less representative than the British) and greater autonomy for the Irish parliament as against the central government at Westminster. Faced with these demands, and fearing a French invasion of Ireland during the War of American Independence, the British government made concessions. It allowed an increase of power to the Irish parliament at Dublin. But from its parliament Catholics were still excluded. In the next war between France and Great Britain, which began in 1793, many Irish felt a warm sympathy for the French Revolution. Catholics and Presbyterians, at last combining, formed a network of United Irish societies throughout the whole island. They sought French aid, and the French barely failed to land a sizable army. Even without French military support, the United Irish rose in 1798 to drive out the English and establish an independent republic. The British, suppressing the rebellion, now turned to centralization. The separate kingdom of Ireland, and the Irish parliament, ceased to exist. The Irish were thereafter represented in the imperial Parliament at Westminster. These provisions were incorporated in the Act of Union of 1801, creating the United Kingdom of Great Britain and Ireland, which lasted until 1922.

British establishments in India also felt the hand of Parliament increasingly upon them. At the close of the Seven Years' War the various British posts in and around Bombay, Madras, and Calcutta were unconnected with each other and subordinate only to the board of directors of the East India Company in London. Company employees interfered at will in the wars and politics of the Indian states and enriched themselves by such means as they could, not excluding graft, trickery, intimidation, rapine, and extortion.[31] In 1773 the ministry of Lord North

[30] See pp. 180–181.
[31] See pp. 282–283.

passed a Regulating Act, of which the main purpose was to regulate, not Indians, but the British subjects in India, whom no Indian government could control. The company was left with its trading activities, but its political activities were brought under parliamentary supervision. The act gathered all the British establishments under a single governor general, set up a new supreme court at Calcutta, and required the company to submit its correspondence on political matters for review by the ministers of His Majesty's Government. Warren Hastings became the first British governor general in India. He was so high-handed with some of the Indian princes, and made so many enemies among jealous Englishmen in Bengal, that he was denounced at home, impeached, and subjected to a trial which dragged on for seven years in the House of Lords. He was finally acquitted. After Clive, he was the main author of British supremacy in India. Meanwhile, in 1784 an India office was created in the British ministry at home. The governor general henceforth ruled the growing British sphere in India almost as an absolute monarch but only as the agent of the ministry and Parliament of Great Britain.

Thus the trend in the British world was to centralization. Despite the flutter of royalism under George III, it was to a centralization of all British territories under authority of the Parliament. What was happening in empire affairs, as in domestic politics in England, was a continuing application of the principles of 1689. The parliamentary sovereignty established in 1689 was now, after the middle of the eighteenth century, being applied to regions where it had heretofore had little effect. And it was against the British Parliament that the Americans primarily rebelled.

40. The American Revolution

Background to the Revolution

The behavior of the Americans in the Seven Years' War left much to be desired.[32] The several colonial legislatures rejected the Albany Plan of Union drafted by Franklin and commended to them by the British officials. During the war it was the British regular army and navy, financed by taxes and loans in Great Britain, that drove the French out of America. The war effort of the Anglo-Americans was desultory at best. After the defeat of the French the colonials had still to reckon with the Indians of the interior, who preferred French rule to that of their new British and British-colonial masters. Many tribes joined in an uprising led by Pontiac, a western chief, and they ravaged as far eastward as the Pennsylvania and Virginia frontiers. Again, the colonials proved unable to deal with a problem vital to their own future, and peace was brought about by officials and army units taking their orders from Great Britain.

The British government tried to make the colonials pay a larger share toward the expenses of the empire. The colonials had hitherto paid only local taxes. They were liable to customs duties, of which the proceeds went in principle to Great Britain; but these duties were levied to enforce the Acts of Trade and Navigation,

[32] See pp. 279–280.

to direct the flow of commerce, not to raise revenue; and they were seldom paid, because the Acts of Trade and Navigation were persistently ignored. American merchants, for example, commonly imported sugar from the French West Indies, contrary to law, and even shipped in return the iron wares which it was against the law for Americans to manufacture for export. The colonial in practice paid only such taxes as were approved by his own local legislature for local purposes. The Americans in effect enjoyed a degree of tax exemption within the empire, and it was against this form of provincial privilege that Parliament began to move.

By the Revenue Act of 1764 (the "Sugar" Act), the British ministry, while reducing and liberalizing the customs duties payable in America, entered upon a program of actual and systematic collection. In the following year the ministry attempted to extend to British subjects in America a tax peaceably accepted by those in Great Britain and commonplace in most of Europe. This imposed on all uses of paper, as in newspapers and commercial and legal documents, the payment of a fee which was certified by the affixing of a stamp. The Stamp Act aroused violent and concerted resistance in the colonies, especially among the businessmen, lawyers, and editors who were the most articulate class. It therefore was repealed in 1766. In 1767 Parliament, clumsily casting about to find a tax acceptable to the Americans, hit upon the "Townshend duties," which taxed colonial imports of paper, paint, lead, and tea. Another outcry went up, and the Townshend duties were repealed, except the one on tea, which was kept as a token of the sovereign power of Parliament to tax all persons in the empire.

The colonials had proved stubborn, the government pliable but lacking in constructive ideas. The Americans argued that Parliament had no authority to tax them because they were not represented in it. The British replied that Parliament represented America as much as it represented Great Britain. If Philadelphia sent no actually elected deputies to the Commons, so this argument ran, neither did Manchester in England, yet both places enjoyed a "virtual representation," since members of the Commons did not in any case merely speak for local constituencies but made themselves responsible for imperial interests as a whole. To this many Americans retorted that if Manchester was not "really" represented it ought to be, which was of course also the belief of the English reformers. Meanwhile the strictly Anglo-American question subsided after the repeal of the Stamp Act and the Townshend program. There had been

MRS. ISAAC SMITH
by John Singleton Copley (American, then English, 1737–1815)

Mrs. Smith may be contrasted with the more aristocratic Mrs. Graham, shown on p. 346. The wife of a Boston merchant, she and her husband both had their portraits painted by Copley in 1769. The picture may be taken to typify, in its portrayal of a middle-aged woman, the bourgeois family background from which came much of the leadership of the American and French revolutions. In general, it was a background of substance, comfort, and hard work. Mrs. Smith's costume and surroundings, though less elegant than Mrs. Graham's, suggest her high station in New England society. Her expression is between the prim and the pleasant. She clearly represents, and expects from others, a settled standard of behavior and decorum. Copley, troubled by the rising revolutionary agitation, left America in 1774 and spent the rest of his long life in England. Courtesy of the Yale University Art Gallery, Gift of Maitland Fuller Griggs.

no clarification of principle on either side. But in practice the Americans had resisted significant taxation, and Parliament had refrained from making any drastic use of its sovereign power.

The calm was shattered in 1773 by an event which proved, to the more dissatisfied Americans, the disadvantages of belonging to a global economic system in which the main policies were made on the other side of the ocean. The East India Company was in difficulties. It had a great surplus of Chinese tea,[33] and in any case it wanted new commercial privileges in return for the political privileges which it was losing by the Regulating Act of 1773. In the past the company had been required to sell its wares at public auction in London; other merchants had handled distribution from that point on. Now, in 1773, Parliament granted the company the exclusive right to sell tea through its own agents in America to American local dealers. Tea was a large item of business in the commercial capitalism of the time. The colonial consumer might pay less for it, but the intermediary American merchant would be shut out. The company's tea was boycotted in all American ports. In Boston, to prevent its forcible landing, a party of disguised men invaded the tea ships and dumped the chests into the harbor. To this act of vandalism the British government replied by measures far out of proportion to the offense. It "closed" the port of Boston, thus threatening the city with economic ruin. It virtually rescinded the charter of Massachusetts, forbidding certain local elections and the holding of town meetings.

And at the same time, in 1774, apparently by coincidence, Parliament enacted the Quebec Act. The wisest piece of British legislation in these troubled years, the Quebec Act provided a government for the newly conquered Canadian French, granting them security in their French civil law and Catholic religion, and laying foundations for the British Empire that was to come. But the act defined the boundaries of Quebec somewhat as the French themselves would have defined them, including in them all territory north of the Ohio River—the present states of Wisconsin, Michigan, Illinois, Indiana, and Ohio. These boundaries were perfectly reasonable, since the few white men in the area were French, and since, in the age before canals or railways, the obvious means of reaching the whole region was by way of the St. Lawrence valley and the Lakes. But to the Americans the Quebec Act was a pro-French and pro-Catholic outrage, and at a time when the powers of juries and assemblies in the old colonies were threatened, it was disquieting that the Quebec Act made no mention of such representative institutions for the new northern province. It was lumped with the closing of an American port and the destruction of the Massachusetts government as one of the "Intolerable Acts" to be resisted.

And indeed the implications of parliamentary sovereignty were now apparent. The meaning of centralized planning and authority was now clear. It was no longer merely an affair of taxation. A government that had to take account of the East India Company, the French Canadians, and the British taxpayers, even if more prudent and enlightened than Lord North's ministry of 1774, could not possibly at the same time have satisfied the Americans of the thirteen seaboard colonies. These Americans, since 1763 no longer afraid of the French empire, were less inclined to forgo their own interests in order to remain in the British.

[33] See p. 260.

British policies had aroused antagonism in the coastal towns and in the backwoods, among wealthy land speculators and poor squatter frontiersmen, among merchants and the workingmen who depended on the business of merchants. The freedom of Americans to determine their own political life was in question. Yet there were few in 1774, or even later, prepared to face the thought of independence.

The War of American Independence

After the "Intolerable Acts" self-authorized groups met in the several colonies and sent delegates to a "continental congress" in Philadelphia. This body adopted a boycott of British goods, to be enforced on unwilling Americans by local organizers of resistance. Fighting began in the next year, 1775, when the British commander at Boston sent a detachment to seize unauthorized stores of weapons at Concord. On the way, at Lexington, in a brush between soldiers and partisans or "minutemen," someone fired the "shot heard round the world." The Second Continental Congress, meeting a few weeks later, proceeded to raise an American army, dispatched an expedition to force Quebec into the revolutionary union, and entered into overtures with Bourbon France.

The Congress was still reluctant to repudiate the tie with Britain. But passions grew fierce in consequence of the fighting. Radicals convinced moderates that the choice now lay between independence and enslavement. It appeared that the French, naturally uninterested in a reconciliation of British subjects, would give help if the avowed aim of American rebels was to dismember the British Empire. In January 1776 Thomas Paine, in his pamphlet *Common Sense*, made his debut as a kind of international revolutionary; he was to figure in the French Revolution and to work for revolution in England. He had come from England less than two years before, and he detested English society for its injustices to men like himself. Eloquent and vitriolic, *Common Sense* identified the independence of the American colonies with the cause of liberty for all mankind. It pitted freedom against tyranny in the person of "the royal brute of Great Britain." It was "repugnant to reason," said Paine, "to suppose that this Continent can long remain subject to any external power. . . . There is something absurd in supposing a Continent to be perpetually governed by an island." *Common Sense* was read everywhere in the colonies, and its slashing arguments unquestionably spread a sense of proud isolation from the Old World. On July 4, 1776, the Congress adopted the Declaration of Independence, by which the United States assumed its separate and equal station among the powers of the earth.

The War of American Independence thereupon turned into another European struggle for empire. For two more years the French government remained ostensibly noninterventionist but meanwhile poured munitions into the colonies through an especially rigged up commercial concern. Nine-tenths of the arms used by the Americans at the battle of Saratoga came from France. After the American victory in this battle the French government concluded, in 1778, that the insurgents were a good political risk, recognized them, signed an alliance with them, and declared war on Great Britain. Spain soon followed, hoping to drive the British from Gibraltar and deciding that its overseas empire was more threatened by a restoration of British supremacy in North America than by the disturbing example of an independent American republic. The Dutch were drawn into hostilities through trading with the Americans by way of the Dutch West Indies. Other powers, Russia, Sweden, Denmark, Prussia, Portugal, and Turkey, irked at British employment of blockade and sea power in time of war, formed an "Armed Neutrality" to protect their commerce from dictation by the British fleet. The French, in a brief revival of their own sea power, landed an expeditionary force of 6,000 men in Rhode Island. Since the Americans suffered from the internal differences inseparable from all revolutions and were in any case still unable to govern themselves to any effect, meeting with the old difficulties in raising both troops and money, it was the participation of regiments of the French army, in conjunction with squadrons of the French fleet, which made possible the defeat of the armed forces of the British Empire and so persuaded the British government to recognize the independence of the United States. By the peace treaty of 1783, though the British were still in possession of New York and Savannah, and though the governments befriending the Americans would just as soon have confined them east of the mountains, the new republic obtained territory as far west as the Mississippi. Canada remained British. It received an English-speaking population by the settlement of over 60,000 refugee Americans who remained loyal to Great Britain.

Significance of the Revolution

The upheaval in America was a revolution as well as a war of independence. The cry for liberty against Great Britain raised echoes within the colonies themselves. The Declaration of Independence was more than an announcement of secession from the empire; it was a justification of rebellion against established authority. Curiously, although the American quarrel had been with the Parliament, the Declaration arraigned no one but the king. One reason was that the Congress, not recognizing the authority of Parliament, could separate from Great Britain only by a denunciation of the British crown; another reason was that the cry of "tyrant" made a more popular and flaming issue. Boldly voicing the natural right philosophy of the age, the Declaration held as "self-evident," i.e., as evident to all reasonable people—that "all men are created equal, that they are endowed by their Creator with certain unalienable rights, that among these are life, liberty, and the pursuit of happiness." These electrifying words leaped inward into America, and outward to the world.

In the new states democratic equality made many advances. It was subject, however, to a great limitation, in that it long really applied only to white males of European origin. It was more than a century before women received the vote. American Indians were few in number, but the black population at the time of the Revolution comprised about a fifth of the whole. It was much larger proportionately than it became later, after mass immigration from Europe raised the proportion of whites. Many American whites of the revolutionary generation were indeed troubled by the institution of slavery. It was abolished outright in Massachusetts, and all states north of Maryland took steps toward its gradual extinction. But to apply the principles of liberty and equality without regard to race was beyond the powers of Americans at the time. In the South, all censuses from 1790 to 1850 showed a third of the population to be slaves. In the North, free blacks found that in fact, and often in law, they were debarred from voting, from adequate schooling, and from the widening opportunities in which white Americans saw the essence of their national life and their superiority to Europe.

For the white majority the Revolution had a democratizing effect in many ways. Lawyers, landowners, and businessmen who led the movement against England needed the support of numbers and to obtain it were willing to make promises and concessions to the lower classes. Or the popular elements, workmen and mechanics, farmers and frontiersmen, often dissidents in religion, extorted concessions by force or threats. There was a good deal of violence, as in all revolutions; the new states confiscated property from the counterrevolutionaries, called Tories, some of whom were in addition tarred and feathered by infuriated mobs. The dissolution of the old colonial governments threw open all political questions. In some states more men became qualified to vote. In some, governors and senators were now popularly elected, in addition to the lower houses of the legislatures as in colonial times. The principle was adopted, still unknown to the parliamentary bodies of Europe, that each member of a legislative assembly should represent about the same number of citizens. Primogeniture and entail, which landed families aspiring to an aristocratic mode of life sometimes favored, went down before the demands of democrats and small property owners. Tithes were done away with, and the established churches, Anglican in the South, Congregationalist in New England, lost their privileged position in varying degree. But the Revolution was not socially as profound as the revolution soon to come in France, or as the revolution in Russia in 1917. Property changed hands, but the law of property was modified only in detail. There had been no such thing in British America as a native nobleman or even a bishop; clergy and aristocracy had been incomparably less ingrained in American than in European society, and the rebellion against them was less devastating in its effect.

The main import of the American Revolution remained political and even constitutional in a strict sense. The American leaders were themselves part of the Age of Enlightenment, sharing fully in its humane and secular spirit. But probably the only non-British thinker by whom they were influenced was Montesquieu, and Montesquieu owed his popularity to his philosophizing upon English institutions. The Americans drew heavily on the writings of John Locke, but their cast of mind went back before Locke to the English Puritan movement of the first half of the seventeenth century. Their thought was formed not only by Locke's ideas of human nature and government, but, as already noted, by the dissenting literature and the neorepublican writings that had never quite died out in England. The realities of life for five generations in America had sharpened the old insistence upon personal liberty and equality. When the dispute with Britain came to a head, the Americans found themselves arguing both for the historic and chartered rights of Englishmen and for the timeless and universal rights of man, both of which were held up as barriers against the inroads of parliamentary sovereignty. The Americans came to believe, more than any other people, that government should possess limited powers and operate only within the terms of a fixed and written constitutional document.

All thirteen of the new states lost no time in providing themselves with written constitutions (in Connecticut and Rhode Island merely the old charters reaffirmed), all of which enshrined virtually the same principles. All followed the thought stated in the great Declaration, that it was to protect "unalienable" rights that governments were instituted among men, and that whenever government became destructive to this end the people had a right to "institute new government" for their safety and happiness. All the constitutions undertook to limit government by a separation of governmental powers. Most appended a bill of rights, stating the natural rights of the citizens and the things which no government might justly do. None of the constitutions were as yet fully democratic; even the most liberal gave some advantage in public affairs to the owners of property.

Federalism, or the allocation of power between central and outlying governments, went along with the idea of written constitutions as a principal offering of the Americans to the world. Like constitutionalism, federalism developed in the atmosphere of protest against a centralized sovereign power. It was a hard idea for Americans to work out, since the new states carried over the old separatism which had so distracted the British. Until 1789 the states remained banded together in the Articles of Confederation. The United States was a union of thirteen independent republics. Disadvantages in this scheme becoming apparent, a constitutional convention met at Philadelphia in 1787 and drew up the constitution which is today the world's oldest written instrument of government still in operation. In it the United States was conceived not merely as a league of states, but as a union in which individuals were citizens of the United States of America for some purposes and of their particular states for others. Persons, not states, composed the federal republic, and the laws of the United States fell not merely on the states but on the people.

The consequences of the American Revolution can hardly be overstated. By overburdening the French treasury the American war became a direct cause of the French Revolution. Beyond that, it ushered in the age of predominantly liberal or democratic revolution which lasted through the European revolutions of 1848. The American doctrine, like most thought in the Age of Enlightenment, was expressed in universal terms of "man" and "nature." All peoples regardless of their own history could apply it to themselves, because, as Alexander Hamilton once put it in his youth, "the sacred rights of man are not to be rummaged for among old parchments or musty records. They are written, as with a sunbeam, in the whole volume of human nature, by the hand of Divinity itself, and can never be erased or obscured by mortal power." The Americans, in freeing themselves, had done what all peoples ought to do.

The revolt in America offered a dramatic judgment on the old colonial system, convincing some, in England and elsewhere, that the empires for which they had long been struggling were hardly worth acquiring, since colonies in time, in the words of Turgot, fell away from the mother country "like ripe fruit." The idea spread, since trade between Britain and America continued to prosper, that one could do business with a country without exerting political influence or control, and this idea became fundamental to the coming movement of economic liberalism and free trade. By coincidence, the book that became the gospel of the free trade movement, Adam Smith's *Wealth of Nations,* was published in England in the year 1776. The American example was pointed to by other peoples wishing to throw off colonial status—first by the Latin Americans, then by the peoples of the older British dominions, and, finally, in the twentieth century, by those of Asia and Africa also. In Europe, the American example encouraged the type of nationalism in which subjugated nations aspire to be free. And at home the

Revolution did much to determine the spirit and method by which the bulk of the North American continent was to be peopled and the attitudes for which the United States, when it became a leading power a century and a half later, was to stand before the world.

More immediately, the American example was not lost on the many Europeans who sojourned in the new states during and after the war. Of these the Marquis de Lafayette was the most famous, but there were many others: Thomas Paine, who returned to Europe in 1787; the future French revolutionist Brissot; the future Polish national leader Kosciusko; the future marshals of Napoleon, Jourdan and Berthier; the future reformer of the Prussian army Gneisenau. Contrariwise various Americans went to Europe, notably the aging Benjamin Franklin, who in the 1780s was incredibly lionized in the fashionable and literary world of Paris.

The establishment of the United States was taken in Europe to prove that many ideas of the Enlightenment were practicable. Rationalists declared that here was a people, free of past errors and superstitions, who showed how enlightened beings could plan their affairs. Rousseauists saw in America the very paradise of natural equality, unspoiled innocence, and patriotic virtue. But nothing so much impressed Europeans, and especially the French, as the spectacle of the Americans meeting in solemn conclave to draft their state constitutions. These, along with the Declaration of Independence, were translated and published in 1778 by a French nobleman, the Duke de la Rochefoucauld. They were endlessly and excitedly discussed. Constitutionalism, federalism, and limited government were not new ideas in Europe. They came out of the Middle Ages and were currently set forth in many quarters, for example, in Hungary, the Holy Roman Empire, and the Parlement of Paris. But in their prevailing form, and even in the philosophy of Montesquieu, they were associated with feudalism and aristocracy. The American Revolution made such ideas progressive. The American influence, added to the force of developments in Europe, made the thought of the later Enlightenment more democratic. The United States replaced England as the model country of advanced thinkers. On the Continent there was less passive trust in the enlightened despotism of the official state. Confidence in self-government was aroused.

The American constitutions seemed a demonstration of the social contract. They offered a picture of men in a "state of nature," having cast off their old government, deliberately sitting down to contrive a new one, weighing and judging each branch of government on its merits, assigning due powers to legislature, executive, and judiciary, declaring that all government was created by the people and in possession of a merely delegated authority, and listing specifically the inalienable rights of men—inalienable in that they could not conceivably be taken away, since men possessed them even if denied them by force. And these rights were the very same rights that many Europeans wanted secured for themselves—freedom of religion, freedom of press, freedom of assembly, freedom from arbitrary arrest at the discretion of officials. And they were the same for all, on the rigorous principle of equality before the law. The American example crystallized and made tangible the ideas that were strongly blowing in Europe, and the American example was one reason why the French, in 1789, began their revolution with a declaration of human rights and with the drafting of a written constitution.

And more deeply still, America became a kind of mirage or ideal vision for

Europe, land of open opportunity and of new beginnings, free from the load of history and of the past, wistfully addressed by Goethe:

> *America, thou hast it better*
> *Than has our Continent, the old one.*

It is evident that this was only part of the picture. The United States, as its later history was to show, bore a heavy load of inherited burdens and unsolved problems, especially racial. But in a general way, until new revolutionary movements set in a century later, America stood as a kind of utopia of the common man, not only for the millions who emigrated to it but for other millions who stayed at home, who often wished that their own countries might become more like it, and many of whom might even agree with Abraham Lincoln in calling it the last best hope of earth.

IX.
THE FRENCH REVOLUTION

IN 1789 FRANCE fell into revolution, and the world has never since been the same. The French Revolution was by far the most momentous upheaval of the whole revolutionary age. It replaced the "old regime" with "modern society," and at its extreme phase it became very radical, so much so that all later revolutionary movements have looked back to it as a predecessor to themselves. At the time, in the age of the Democratic or Atlantic Revolution from the 1760s to 1848, the role of France was decisive. Even the Americans, without French military intervention, would hardly have won such a clear settlement from England or been so free to set up the new states and new constitutions that have just been described. And while revolutionary disturbances in Ireland and Poland, or among the Dutch, Italians, and others, were by no means caused by the French example, it was the presence or absence of French aid that usually determined whatever successes they enjoyed.

The French Revolution, unlike the Russian or Chinese revolutions of the twentieth century, occurred in what was in many ways the most advanced country of the day. France was the center of the intellectual movement of the Enlightenment. French science then led the world. French books were read everywhere, and the newspapers and political journals which became very numerous after 1789 carried a message which hardly needed translation. French

Chapter Emblem: A cockade worn during the French Revolution, with the famous motto, and the fleur-de-lis of the monarchy embellished by the cap of liberty.

was a kind of international spoken language in the educated and aristocratic circles of many countries. France was also, potentially before 1789 and actually after 1793, the most powerful country in Europe. It may have been the wealthiest, though not per capita. With a population of some 24,000,000 the French were the most numerous of all European peoples under a single government. Even Russia was hardly more populous until after the partitions of Poland. The Germans were divided, the subjects of the Habsburgs were of diverse nationalities, and the English and Scots together numbered only 10,000,000. Paris, though smaller than London, was over twice as large as Vienna or Amsterdam. French exports to Europe were larger than those of Great Britain. It is said that half the goldpieces circulating in Europe were French. Europeans in the eighteenth century were in the habit of taking ideas from France; they were therefore, depending on their position, the more excited, encouraged, alarmed, or horrified when revolution broke out in that country.

41. Backgrounds

The Old Regime: The Three Estates

Some remarks have already been made about the Old Regime, as the prerevolutionary society came to be called after it disappeared, and about the failure of enlightened despotism in France to make any fundamental alteration in it.[1] The essential fact about the Old Regime was that it was still legally aristocratic and in some ways feudal. Everyone belonged legally to an "estate" or "order" of society. The First Estate was the clergy, the Second Estate the nobility, and the Third Estate included everyone else—from the wealthiest business and professional classes to the poorest peasantry and city workers. These categories were important in that the individual's legal rights and personal prestige depended on the category to which he or she belonged. Politically, they were obsolescent; not since 1614 had the estates assembled in an Estates General of the whole kingdom, though in some provinces they had continued to meet as provincial bodies. Socially, they were obsolescent also, for the threefold division no longer corresponded to the real distribution of interest, influence, property, or productive activity among the French people.

Conditions in the church and the position of the clergy have been much exaggerated as a cause of the French Revolution. The church in France levied a tithe on all agricultural products, but so did the church in England; the French bishops often played a part in government affairs, but so did bishops in England through the House of Lords. The French bishoprics of 1789 were in reality no wealthier than those of the Church of England were found to be when investigated forty years later. In actual numbers, in the secular atmosphere of the Age of Enlightenment, the clergy, especially the monastic orders, had greatly declined, so that by 1789 there were probably not more than 100,000 Catholic clergy of all types in the entire population. But if the importance of the clergy has often been

---

[1] See pp. 329–331.

overemphasized, still it must be said that the church was deeply involved in the prevailing social system. For one thing, church bodies—bishoprics, abbeys, convents, schools, and other religious foundations—owned between 5 and 10 percent of the land of the country, which meant that collectively the church was the greatest of all landowners. Moreover, the income from church properties, like all income, was divided very unequally, and much of it found its way into the hands of the aristocratic occupants of the higher ecclesiastical offices.

The noble order, which in 1789 comprised about 400,000 persons, including women and children, had enjoyed a great resurgence since the death of Louis XIV in 1715.[2] Distinguished government service, higher church offices, army, parlements, and most other public and semipublic honors were almost monopolized by the nobility in the time of Louis XVI, who, it will be recalled, had mounted the throne in 1774. Repeatedly, through parlements, Provincial Estates, or the assembly of the clergy dominated by the noble bishops, the aristocracy had blocked royal plans for taxation and shown a desire to control the policies of state. At the same time the bourgeoisie, or upper crust of the Third Estate, had never been so influential. The fivefold increase of French foreign trade between 1713 and 1789 suggests the growth of the merchant class and of the legal and governmental classes associated with it. As members of the bourgeoisie became stronger, more widely read, and more self-confident, they resented the distinctions enjoyed by the nobles. Some of these were financial: nobles were exempt on principle from the most important direct tax, the taille, whereas bourgeois obtained exemption with more effort; but so many bourgeois enjoyed tax privileges that purely monetary self-interest was not primary in their psychology. The bourgeois resented the nobleman for his superiority and his arrogance. What had formerly been customary respect was now felt as humiliation. And they felt that they were being shut out from office and honors, and that the nobles were seeking more power in government as a class. The Revolution was the collision of two moving objects, a rising aristocracy and a rising bourgeoisie.

The common people, below the commercial and professional families in the Third Estate, were probably as well off as in most countries. But they were not well off compared with the upper classes. Wage earners had by no means shared in the wave of business prosperity. Between the 1730s and the 1780s the prices of consumers' goods rose about 65 percent, whereas wages rose only 22 percent. Persons dependent on wages were therefore badly pinched, but they were less numerous than today, for in the country there were many small farmers and in the towns many small craftsmen, both of which groups made a living not by wages but by selling the products of their own labor at market prices. Yet in both town and country there was a significant wage-earning or proletarian element, which was to play a decisive part in the Revolution.

The Agrarian System of the Old Regime

Over four-fifths of the people were rural. The agrarian system had developed so that there was no serfdom in France, to be sure, as it was known in eastern

[2] See pp. 265–266.

Europe.[3] The relation of lord and peasant in France was not the relation of master and man. The peasant owed no labor to the lord—except a few token services in some cases. The peasants worked for themselves, either on their own land or on rented land; or they worked as sharecroppers (*métayers*); or hired themselves out to the lord or to another peasant.

The manor, however, still retained certain surviving features of the feudal age. The noble owner of a manor enjoyed "hunting rights," or the privilege of keeping game preserves, and of hunting on his own and the peasants' land. He usually had a monopoly over the village mill, bakeshop, or wine press, for the use of which he collected fees, called *banalités*. He possessed certain vestigial powers of jurisdiction in the manorial court and certain local police powers, from which fees and fines were collected. These seigneurial privileges were of course the survivals of a day when the local manor had been a unit of government, and the noble had performed the functions of government, an age that had long passed with the development of the centralized modern state.

There was another special feature to the property system of the Old Regime. Every owner of a manor (there were some bourgeois and even wealthy peasants who had purchased manors) possessed what was called a right of "eminent property" with respect to all land located in the manorial village. This meant that lesser landowners within the manor "owned" their land in that they could freely buy, sell, lease, and bequeath or inherit it; but they owed to the owner of the manor, in recognition of his "eminent property" rights, certain rents, payable annually, as well as transfer fees that were payable whenever the land changed owners by sale or death. Subject to these "eminent property" rights, landowner-ship was fairly widespread. Peasants directly owned about two-fifths of the soil of the country; bourgeois a little under a fifth. The nobility owned perhaps a little over a fifth, and the church somewhat under a tenth, the remainder being crown lands, wastelands, or commons. Finally, it must be noted that all property rights were subject also to certain "collective" rights, by which villagers might cut firewood or run their pigs in the commons, or pasture cattle on land belonging to other owners after the crops were in, there being usually no fences or enclosures.

All this may seem rather complex, but it is important to realize that property is a changing institution. Even today, in industrialized countries, a high proportion of all property is in land, including natural resources in and below the soil. In the eighteenth century property meant land even more than it does today. Even the bourgeois class, whose wealth was so largely in ships, merchandise, or commercial paper, invested heavily in land, and in France in 1789 enjoyed ownership of almost as much land as the nobility, and of more than the church. The Revolution was to revolutionize the law of property by freeing the private ownership of land from all the indirect encumbrances described—manorial fees, eminent property rights, communal village agricultural practices, and church tithes. It also was to abolish other older forms of property, such as property in public office or in masterships in the guilds, which had become useful mainly to closed and privileged groups. In final effect the Revolution established the institutions of private property in the modern sense and benefited, therefore, most especially the landowning peasants and the bourgeoisie.

---

[3] See pp. 31, 125–126, 210–211.

The peasants not only owned two-fifths of the soil, but occupied almost all of it, working it on their own initiative and risk. That is to say, land owned by the nobility, the church, the bourgeoisie, and the crown was divided up and leased to peasants in small parcels. France was already a country of small farmers. There was no "big agriculture" as in England, eastern Europe, or the plantations of America. The manorial lord performed no economic function. He lived (there were of course exceptions) not by managing an estate and selling his own crops and cattle, but by receiving innumerable dues, quitrents, and fees. During the eighteenth century, in connection with the general aristocratic resurgence, there took place a phenomenon often called the "feudal reaction." Manorial lords, faced with rising living costs and acquiring higher living standards because of the general material progress, collected their dues more rigorously or revived old ones that had fallen into disuse. Leases and sharecropping arrangements also became less favorable to the peasants. The farmers, like the wage earners, were under a steadily increasing pressure. At the same time the peasants resented the "feudal dues" more than ever, because they regarded themselves as in many cases the real owners of the land and the lord as a gentleman of the neighborhood who for no reason enjoyed a special income and a status different from their own. The trouble was that much of the property system no longer bore any relation to real economic usefulness or activity.

The political unity of France, achieved over the centuries by the monarchy, was likewise a fundamental prerequisite, and even a cause, of the Revolution. Whatever social conditions might have existed, they could give rise to nationwide public opinion, nationwide agitation, nationwide policies, and nationwide legislation only in a country already politically unified as a nation. These conditions were lacking in central Europe. In France a French state existed. Reformers did not have to create it but only capture and remodel it. The French in the eighteenth century already had the sense of membership in a political entity called France. The Revolution saw a tremendous stirring of this sense of membership and of fraternity, turning it into a passion of citizenship, civic rights, voting powers, use and application of the state and its sovereignty for the public advantage. At the very outbreak of the Revolution people saluted each other as *citoyen* or *citoyenne* and shouted *vive la nation!*

42. The Revolution and the Reorganization of France

The Financial Crisis

The Revolution was precipitated by a financial collapse of the government. What overloaded the government was by no means the costly magnificence of the court of Versailles. Only 5 percent of public expenditures in 1788 was devoted to the upkeep of the entire royal establishment. What overloaded all governments was war costs, both current upkeep of armies and navies and the burden of public debt, which in all countries was due almost totally to the war costs of the past. In 1788 the French government devoted about a quarter of its annual expenditure to current maintenance of the armed forces and about a half to the payment of its debts. British expenditures showed almost the same distribution. The French debt stood at almost four billion livres. It had been greatly swollen by the War of American Independence. Yet it was only half as great as the national debt of Great Britain, and less than a fifth as heavy per capita. It was less than the debt of the Dutch Republic. It was apparently no greater than the debt left by Louis XIV three-quarters of a century before. At that time the debt had been lightened by repudiation. No responsible French official in the 1780s even considered repudiation, a sure sign of the progress in the interim of the well-to-do classes, who were the main government creditors.

Yet the debt could not be carried, for the simple reason that revenues fell short of necessary expenditures. This in turn was not due to national poverty, but to the tax exemptions and tax evasions of privileged elements, and to complications in the fiscal system, or lack of system, by which much of what taxpayers paid never came into the hands of the treasury. We have already described how the most important tax, the taille, was generally paid only by the peasants—the nobles being exempt by virtue of their class privilege, and office holders and bourgeois obtaining exemption in various ways.[4] The church too insisted that its property was not taxable by the state; and its periodic "free gift" to the king, though substantial, was less than might have been obtained from direct taxation of the church's land. Thus, although the country itself was prosperous, the government treasury was empty. The social classes which enjoyed most of the wealth of the country did not pay taxes corresponding to their income, and, even worse, they resisted taxation as a sign of inferior status.

A long series of responsible persons—Louis XIV himself, John Law, Maupeou, Turgot—had seen the need for taxing the privileged classes. Jacques Necker, a Swiss banker made director of the finances in 1777 by Louis XVI, made moves in the same direction, and, like his predecessors, was dismissed. His successor, Calonne, as the crisis mounted, came to even more revolutionary conclusions. In 1786 he produced a program in which enlightened despotism was tempered by a modest resort to representative institutions. He proposed, in place of the taille, a general tax to fall on all landowners without exemption, a lightening of indirect taxes and abolition of internal tariffs to stimulate economic production, a confiscation of some properties of the church, and the establishment, as a means of interesting the propertied elements in the government, of provincial assemblies in which all landowners, noble, clerical, bourgeois, and peasant, should be represented without regard to estate or order.

This program, if carried out, might have solved the fiscal problem and averted the Revolution. But it struck not only at privileges in taxation—noble, provincial, and others—but at the threefold hierarchic organization of society. Knowing from experience that the Parlement of Paris would never accept it, Calonne in 1787 convened an "assembly of notables," hoping to win its endorsement of his ideas. The notables insisted on concessions in return, for they wished to share in control of the government. A deadlock followed; the king dismissed Calonne and appointed as his successor Loménie de Brienne, the exceedingly worldly-wise archbishop of Toulouse. Brienne tried to push the same program through the Parlement of Paris. The Parlement rejected it, declaring that only the three estates

[4] See pp. 187–188, 329–331.

of the realm, assembled in an Estates General, had authority to consent to new taxes. Brienne and Louis XVI at first refused, believing that the Estates General, if convened, would be dominated by the nobility. Like Maupeou and Louis XV, Brienne and Louis XVI tried to break the parlements, replacing them with a modernized judicial system in which the law courts should have no influence over policy. This led to a veritable revolt of the nobles. All the parlements and Provincial Estates resisted, army officers refused to serve, the intendants hesitated to act, noblemen began to organize political clubs and committees of correspondence. With his government brought to a standstill, and unable to borrow money or collect taxes, Louis XVI on July 5, 1788, promised to call the Estates General for the following May. The various classes were invited to elect representatives and also to draw up lists of their grievances.

From Estates General to National Assembly

Since no Estates General had met in over a century and a half, the king asked all persons to study the subject and make proposals on how such an assembly should be organized under modern conditions. This led to an outburst of public discussion. Hundreds of political pamphlets appeared, many of them demanding that the old system by which the three estates sat in separate chambers, each chamber voting as a unit, be done away with, since under it the chamber of the Third Estate was always outnumbered. But in September 1788 the Parlement of Paris, restored to its functions, ruled that the Estates General should meet and vote as in 1614, in three separate orders.

The nobility, through the Parlement, thus revealed its aim. It had forced the summoning of the Estates General, and in this way the French nobility initiated the Revolution. The Revolution began as another victory in the aristocratic resurgence against the absolutism of the king. The nobles actually had a liberal program: they demanded constitutional government, guarantees of personal liberty for all, freedom of speech and press, freedom from arbitrary arrest and confinement. Many now were even prepared to give up special privileges in taxation; this might have worked itself out in time. But in return they hoped to become the preponderant political element in the state. It was their idea not merely to have the Estates General meet in 1789, but for France to be governed in all the future through the Estates General, a supreme body in three chambers, one for nobles, one for a clergy in which the higher officers were also nobles, and one for the Third Estate.

This was precisely what the Third Estate wished to avoid. Lawyers, bankers, businessmen, government creditors, shopkeepers, artisans, working people, and peasants had no desire to be governed by lords temporal and spiritual. Their hopes of a new era, formed by the philosophy of the Enlightenment, stirred by the revolution in America, rose to the utmost excitement when "good king Louis" called the Estates General. The ruling of the Parlement of Paris in September 1788 came to them as a slap in the face—an unprovoked class insult. The whole Third Estate turned on the nobility with detestation and distrust. The Abbé Sieyès in January 1789 launched his famous pamphlet, *What Is the Third Estate?*, declaring that the nobility was a useless caste which could be abolished without loss, that the Third Estate was the one necessary element of society, that it was identical with the nation, and that the nation was absolutely and unqualifiedly sovereign. Through Sieyès the ideas of Rousseau's *Social Contract* entered the thought of the Revolution. At the same time, even before the Estates General actually met, and not from the books of philosophes so much as from the actual events and conditions, nobles and commoners viewed each other with fear and suspicion. The Third Estate, which had at first supported the nobles against the "despotism" of the king's ministers, now ascribed to them the worst possible motives. Class antagonism poisoned the Revolution at the outset, made peaceful reform impossible, and threw many bourgeois without delay into a radical and destructive mood. And the mutual suspicion between classes, produced by the Old Regime and inflamed by the Revolution, has troubled France ever since.

The Estates General met as planned in May 1789 at Versailles. The Third Estate, most of whose representatives were lawyers, boycotted the organization in three separate chambers. It insisted that deputies of all three orders should sit as a single house and vote as individuals; this procedure would be of advantage to the Third Estate, since the king had granted it as many deputies as the other two orders combined. For six weeks a deadlock was maintained. On June 13 a few priests, leaving the chamber of the First Estate, came over and sat with the Third. They were greeted with jubilation. On June 17 the Third Estate declared itself the "National Assembly." Louis XVI, under pressure from the nobles, closed the hall in which it met. The members found a neighboring indoor tennis court, and there, milling about in a babel of confusion and apprehension, swore and signed the Oath of the Tennis Court on June 20, 1789, affirming that wherever they foregathered the National Assembly was in existence, and that they would not disband until they had drafted a constitution. This was a revolutionary step, for it assumed virtually sovereign power for a body of men who had no legal authority. The king ordered members of the three estates to sit in their separate houses. He now somewhat tardily presented a reforming program of his own, too late to win the confidence of the disaffected, and in any case continuing the organization of French society in legal classes. The self-entitled National Assembly refused to back down. The king faltered, failed to enforce his commands promptly, and allowed the Assembly to remain in being. In the following days, at the end of June, he summoned about 18,000 soldiers to Versailles.

What had happened was that the king of France, in the dispute raging between nobles and commoners, chose the nobles. It was traditional in France for the king to oppose feudalism. For centuries the French monarchy had drawn strength from the bourgeoisie. All through the eighteenth century the royal ministers had carried on the struggle against the privileged interests. Only a year before, Louis XVI had been almost at war with his rebellious aristocracy. In 1789 he failed to assert himself. He lost control over the Estates General, exerted no leadership, offered no program until it was too late, and provided no symbol behind which parties could rally. He failed to make use of the profound loyalty to himself felt by the bourgeoisie and common people, who yearned for nothing so much as a king who would stand up for them, as in days of yore, against an aristocracy of birth and status. He tried instead, at first, to compromise and postpone a crisis; then he found himself in the position of having issued orders which the Third Estate boldly defied; and in this embarrassing predicament he yielded to his wife, Marie Antoinette, to his brothers, and to the court nobles with whom he lived, and who told him that his dignity and authority were outraged and undermined. At the end of June Louis XVI undoubtedly intended to dissolve the Estates General by military force. But what the Third Estate feared was not a return to the old theoretically absolute monarchy. It was a future in which the aristocracy should control the government of the country. There was now no going back; the revolt of the Third Estate had allied Louis XVI with the nobles, and the Third Estate now feared the nobles more than ever, believing with good reason that they now had the king in their hands.

The Lower Classes in Action

The country meanwhile was falling into dissolution. The lower classes, below the bourgeoisie, were out of hand. For them too the convocation of the Estates General had seemed to herald a new era. The grievances of ages, and those which existed equally in other countries than France, rose to the surface. Short-run conditions were bad. The harvest of 1788 had been poor; the price of bread, by July 1789, was higher than at any time since the death of Louis XIV. The year 1789 was also one of depression; the rapid growth of trade since the American war had suddenly halted, so that wages fell and unemployment spread while scarcity drove food prices up. The government, paralyzed at the center, could not take such measures of relief as were customary under the Old Regime. The masses were everywhere restless. Labor trouble broke out; in April a great riot of workers devastated a wallpaper factory in Paris. In the rural districts there was much disorder. Peasants declared that they would pay no more manorial dues and were likewise refusing taxes. In the best of times the countryside was troubled by vagrants, beggars, rough characters, and smugglers who flourished along the many tariff frontiers. Now the business depression reduced the income of honest peasants who engaged in weaving or other domestic industries in their homes; unemployment and indigence spread in the country; people were uprooted; and the result was to raise the number of vagrants to terrifying proportions. It was believed, since nothing was too bad to believe of the aristocrats (though it was not true), that they were secretly recruiting these "brigands" for their own purposes to intimidate the Third Estate. The economic and social crises thus became acutely political.

The towns were afraid of being swamped by beggars and desperadoes. This was true even of Paris, the largest city in Europe except London. The Parisians were also alarmed by the concentration of troops about Versailles. They began to arm in self-defense. All classes of the Third Estate took part. The banker Laborde, whose career was noted in an earlier chapter,[5] and whose son sat in the Assembly at Versailles, was one of many to provide funds. Crowds began to look for weapons in arsenals and public buildings. On July 14 they came to the Bastille, a stronghold built in the Middle Ages to overawe the city, like the Tower of London in England. It was used as a place of detention for persons with enough influence to escape the common jails but was otherwise in normal times considered harmless; in fact there had been talk, some years before, of tearing it down to make room for a public park. Now, in the general turbulence, the governor had placed cannon in the embrasures. The crowd requested him to remove his cannon and to furnish them with arms. He refused. Through a series of misunderstandings, reinforced by the vehemence of a few firebrands, the crowd turned into a mob, which assaulted the fortress, and which, when helped by a handful of trained soldiers and five artillery pieces, persuaded the governor to surrender. The mob, enraged by the death of ninety-eight of its members, streamed in and murdered six soldiers of the garrison in cold blood. The governor was murdered while under escort to the Town Hall. A few other officials met the same fate. Their heads were cut off with knives, stuck on the ends of pikes, and paraded about the city. While all this happened the regular army units on the outskirts of Paris did not stir, their reliability being open to question, and the authorities being in any case unaccustomed to firing on the people.

The capture of the Bastille, though not so intended, had the effect of saving the Assembly at Versailles. The king, not knowing what to do, accepted the new situation in Paris. He recognized a citizens' committee, which had formed there, as the new municipal government. He sent away the troops that he had summoned and commanded the recalcitrants among nobles and clergy to join in the National Assembly. In Paris and other cities a bourgeois or national guard was established to keep order. The Marquis de Lafayette, "the hero of two worlds," received command over the guard in Paris. For insignia he combined the colors of the city of Paris, red and blue, with the white of the house of Bourbon. The French tricolor, emblem of the Revolution, thus originated in a fusion of old and new.

In the rural districts matters went from bad to worse. Vague insecurity rose to the proportions of panic in the Great Fear of 1789, which spread over the country late in July in the wake of travelers, postal couriers, and others. The cry was relayed from point to point that "the brigands were coming," and peasants, armed to protect their homes and crops and gathered together and working upon each other's feelings, often turned their attention to the manor houses, burning them in some cases, and in others simply destroying the manorial archives in which fees and dues were recorded. The Great Fear became part of a general agrarian insurrection, in which peasants, far from being motivated by wild alarms, knew perfectly well what they were doing. They intended to destroy the manorial regime by force.

The Initial Reforms of the National Assembly

The Assembly at Versailles could restore order only by meeting the demands of the peasants. To wipe out all manorial payments would deprive the landed aristocracy of much of its income. Many bourgeois also owned manors. There was therefore much perplexity. A small group of deputies prepared a surprise move in the Assembly, choosing an evening session from which many would be absent. Hence came the "night of August 4." A few liberal noblemen, by prearrangement, arose and surrendered their hunting rights, their *banalités,* their rights in manorial courts, and feudal and seigneurial privileges generally. What was left of serfdom and all personal servitudes was declared ended. Tithes were abolished. Other deputies repudiated the special privileges of their provinces. All personal tax privileges were given up. On the main matter, the dues arising from "eminent property" in the manors, a compromise was adopted. These dues were all abolished, but compensation was to be paid by the peasants to the former owners. The compensation was in most cases never paid. Eventually, in 1793, in the radical phase of the Revolution, the provision for compensation was repealed. In the end French peasant landowners rid themselves of their manorial obligations without cost to themselves. This was in contrast to what later happened in most other countries, where the peasants, when in turn liberated from manorial obligations, either lost part of their land or were burdened with installment payments lasting many years.

In a decree summarizing the resolutions of August 4 the Assembly declared flatly that "feudalism is abolished." With legal privilege replaced by legal equality, it proceeded to map the principles of the new order. On August 26, 1789, it issued the Declaration of the Rights of Man and Citizen.

The Declaration of 1789 was meant to affirm the principles of the new state, which were essentially the rule of law, equal individual citizenship, and collective sovereignty of the people. "Men are born and remain," declared Article I, "free and equal in rights." Man's natural rights were held to be "liberty, property, security, and resistance to oppression." Freedom of thought and religion were guaranteed; no one might be arrested or punished except by process of law; all persons were declared eligible for any public office for which they met the requirements. Liberty was defined as the freedom to do anything not injurious to others, which in turn was to be determined only by law. Law must fall equally upon all persons. Law was the expression of the general will, to be made by all citizens or their representatives. The only sovereign was the nation itself, and all public officials and armed forces acted only in its name. Taxes might be raised only by common consent, all public servants were accountable for their conduct in office, and the powers of government should be separated among different branches. Finally, the state might for public purposes, and under law, confiscate the property of private persons, but only with fair compensation. The Declaration, printed in thousands of leaflets, pamphlets, and books, read aloud in public places, or framed and hung on walls, became the catechism of the Revolution in France. When translated into other languages it soon carried the same message to all of Europe. Thomas Paine's book, *The Rights of Man,* published in 1791 to defend the French Revolution, gave the phrase a powerful impact in English.

The "rights of man" had become a motto or watchword for potentially revolutionary ideas well before 1789. The thinkers of the Enlightenment had used it, and during the American Revolution even Alexander Hamilton had spoken of "the sacred rights of man" with enthusiasm.[6] "Man" in this sense was meant to apply abstractly, regardless of nationality, race, or sex. In French as in English, then as now, the word "man" was used to designate all human beings, and the Declaration of 1789 was not intended to refer to males alone. In German, for example, where a distinction is made between *Mensch* as a human being and *Mann* as an adult male, the "rights of man" was always translated as *Menschenrechte.* Similarly the word "citizen" in its general sense applied to women, as is shown by the frequency of the feminine *citoyenne* during the Revolution, in which a great many women were very active. But when it came to the exercise of particular legal rights the Revolutionaries went no farther than contemporary opinion. Thus they assigned the right to vote and hold office only to men, and in matters of property, family law, and education it was the boys and men who had the advantages. Very few at the time argued for legal equality between the sexes.

One of them, however, was Olympe de Gouges, a woman of some prominence as a writer for the theater, who in 1791 published *The Rights of Woman*. Following the official Declaration in each of its seventeen articles, she applied them to women explicitly in each case, and she asserted also, in addition, the right of women to divorce under certain conditions, to the control of property in marriage, and for equal access with men to higher education and to civilian careers and public employment. Mary Wollstonecraft in England published a similar *Vindication of the Rights of Woman* in 1792. In France some of the secondary figures in the Revolution, and some of the teachers in boys' schools, thought that women should have greater opportunities at least in education. Among the leaders, only Condorcet argued for legal equality of the sexes. Intent on political change, the Revolutionaries thought that politics, government, law, and war were a masculine business, for which only boys and young men needed to be educated or prepared.

Shortly after adoption of the Declaration of the Rights of Man the Revolutionary leadership fell apart. In September 1789 the Assembly began the actual planning of the new government. Some wanted a strong veto power for the king and a legislative body in two houses, as in England. Others, the "patriots," wanted only a delaying veto for the king and a legislative body of one chamber. Here again, it was suspicion of the aristocracy that proved decisive. The "patriots" were afraid that an upper chamber would bring back the nobility as a collective force, and they were afraid to make the king constitutionally strong by giving him a full veto, because they believed him to be in sympathy with the nobles. He was, at the moment, hesitating to accept both the August 4th decrees and the Declaration of Rights. His brother, the Count of Artois, followed by many aristocrats, had already emigrated to foreign parts and, along with these other émigrés, was preparing to agitate against the Revolution with all the governments of Europe. The patriot party would concede nothing, the more conservative party could gain nothing. The debate was interrupted again, as in July, by insurrection and violence. On October 4, a crowd of market women and revolutionary militants, followed by the Paris national guard, took the road from Paris to Versailles. Besieging and invading the château, they obliged Louis XVI to take up his residence in Paris, where he could be watched. The National Assembly also shifted itself to Paris, where it too soon fell under the influence of radical elements in the city. The champions of a one-chamber legislative body and of a suspensive veto for the king won out.

The more conservative revolutionaries, if such they may be called, disillusioned at seeing constitutional questions settled by mobs, began to drop out of the Assembly. Men who on June 20 had bravely sworn the Oath of the Tennis Court now felt that the Revolution was falling into unworthy hands. Some even emigrated, forming a second wave of émigrés that would have nothing to do with the first. So the counterrevolution gathered strength.

But those who wanted still to go forward, and they were many, began to organize in clubs. Most important of all was the Society of Friends of the

Constitution, called the Jacobin club for short, since it met in an old Jacobin monastery in Paris. The dues were at first so high that only substantial bourgeois belonged; they were later lowered but never enough to include persons of the poorest classes, who therefore formed lesser clubs of their own. The most advanced members of the Assembly were Jacobins and used the club as a caucus in which to discuss their policies and lay their plans. They remained a middle-class group even during the later and more radical phase of the Revolution. Mme. Rosalie Jullien, for example, who was as excited a revolutionary as her husband and son, attended a meeting of the Paris Jacobin club on August 5, 1792. Tell your friends in the provinces, she wrote to her husband, that these Jacobins are "the flower of the Paris bourgeoisie, to judge by the fancy jackets they wear. There were also two or three hundred women present, dressed as if for the theater, who made an impression by their proud attitude and forceful speech."

Constitutional Changes

In the two years from October 1789 to September 1791 the National Assembly (or the Constituent Assembly, as it had come to be called because it was preparing a constitution) continued its work of simultaneously governing the country, devising a written constitution, and destroying in detail the institutions of the Old Regime. The old ministries, the old organization of government bureaus, the old taxes, the old property in office, the old titles of nobility, the old parlements, the hundreds of regional systems of law, the old internal tariffs, the old provinces, and the old urban municipalities—all went into the discard. Contemporaries, like Edmund Burke, were appalled at the thoroughness with which Frenchmen seemed determined to eradicate their national institutions. Why, asked Burke, should the French fanatics cut to pieces the living body of Normandy or Provence? The truth is that the provinces, like everything else, were impacted in the whole system of special privilege and unequal rights. All had to disappear if the hope of equal citizenship under national sovereignty was to be attained. In place of the provinces the Constituent divided France into eighty-three equal "departments." In place of the old towns, with their quaint old magistrates, it introduced a uniform municipal organization, all towns henceforth having the same form of government, varying only according to size. All local officials, even prosecuting attorneys and tax collectors, were elected locally. Administratively the country was decentralized in reaction against the bureaucracy of the Old Regime. No one outside Paris now really acted for the central government, and local communities enforced the national legislation, or declined to enforce it, as they chose. This proved ruinous when the war came, and although the "departments" created by the Constituent Assembly still exist, it was long traditional in France after the Revolution, as it was before, to keep local officials under strong control by ministers in Paris.

Under the constitution that was prepared, sometimes called the Constitution of 1791 because it went into effect at that date, the sovereign power of the nation was to be exercised by a unicameral elected assembly, called the Legislative Assembly. The king was given only a suspensive veto power by which legislation desired by the Assembly could be postponed. In general, the executive branch, i.e., king and ministers, was kept weak, partly in reaction against "ministerial despotism," partly from a well-founded distrust of Louis XVI. In June 1791 Louis attempted, in the "flight to Varennes," to escape from the kingdom, join with émigré noblemen, and seek help from foreign powers. He left behind him a written message in which he explicitly repudiated the Revolution. Arrested at Varennes in Lorraine, he was brought back to Paris and forced to accept his status as a constitutional monarch. The attitude of Louis XVI greatly disoriented the Revolution, for it made impossible the creation of a strong executive power and left the country to be ruled by a debating society which under revolutionary conditions contained more than the usual number of hotheads.

Not all this machinery of state was democratic. In the granting of political rights the abstract principles of the great Declaration were seriously modified for practical reasons. Since most people were illiterate it was thought that they could have no reasonable political views. Since the small man was often a domestic servant or shop assistant, it was thought that in politics he would be a mere dependent of his employer. The Constituent therefore distinguished in the new constitution between "active" and "passive" citizens. Both had the same civil rights, but only active citizens had the right to vote. These active citizens chose "electors," on the basis of one elector for every hundred active citizens. The electors convened in the chief town of their new "department," and there chose deputies to the national legislature as well as certain local officials. Males over twenty-five years of age, and well enough off to pay a small direct tax, qualified as "active" citizens; well over half the adult male population could so qualify. Of these, men paying a somewhat higher tax qualified as "electors"; even so, almost half the adult males qualified for this role. In practice, what limited the number of available electors was that, to function as such, a man had to have enough education, interest, and leisure to attend an electoral assembly, at a distance from home, and remain in attendance for several days. In any case, only about 50,000 persons served as electors in 1790–1791 because a proportion of one for every hundred active citizens yielded that figure.

Economic Policies

Economic policies favored the middle rather than the lowest classes. The public debt had precipitated the Revolution, but the revolutionary leaders, even the most extreme Jacobins, never disowned the debt of the Old Regime. The reason is that the bourgeois class, on the whole, were the people to whom the money was owed. To secure the debt, and to pay current expenses of government, since tax collections had become very sporadic, the Constituent Assembly as early as November 1789 resorted to a device by no means new in Europe, though never before used on so extensive a scale. It confiscated all the property of the church. Against this property, it issued negotiable instruments called *assignats*, first regarded as bonds and issued only in large denominations, later regarded as currency and issued in small bills. Holders of *assignats* could use them, or any money, to buy parcels of the former church lands. None of the confiscated land was given away; all was in fact sold, since the interest of the government was fiscal rather than social. The peasants, even when they had the money, could not easily buy land because the lands were sold at distant auctions or in large undivided blocks. The peasants were disgruntled, though they did acquire a good deal of the former church lands through middlemen. Peasant landowners were likewise expected, until 1793, to pay compensation for their old quitrents and many other manorial fees. And the landless peasants were aroused when the government, with its modern ideas, encouraged the dividing up of the village commons and extinction of various collective village rights, in the interest of individual private property.

The revolutionary leadership favored free economic individualism. It had had enough, under the Old Regime, of government regulation over the sale or quality of goods and of privileged companies and other economic monopolies. Reforming economic thought at the time, not only in France but in England, where Adam Smith had published his epoch-making *Wealth of Nations* in 1776, held that organized special interests were bad for society, and that all prices and wages should be determined by free arrangement between the individuals concerned.[7] The more prominent leaders of the French Revolution believed firmly in this freedom from control. The Constituent Assembly abolished the guilds, which were mainly monopolistic organizations of small businessmen or master craftsmen, interested in keeping up prices and averse to new machinery or new methods. There was also, in France, a rather highly organized labor movement. Since the masterships in the guilds were practically hereditary (as a form of property and privilege), the journeymen formed their own associations, or trade unions, called *compagnonnages,* outside the guilds. Many trades were so organized—the carpenters, plasterers, paper workers, hatters, saddlers, cutlers, nail makers, carters, tanners, locksmiths, and glassworkers. Some were organized nationally, some only locally. All these journeymen's unions had been illegal under the Old Regime, but they had flourished nevertheless. They collected dues and maintained officers. They often dealt collectively with the guild masters or other employers, requiring the payment of a stipulated wage or amendment of working conditions. Sometimes they even imposed closed shops. Organized strikes were quite common. The labor troubles of 1789 continued on into the Revolution. Business fell off in the atmosphere of disorder. In 1791 there was another wave of strikes. The Assembly, in the Le Chapelier law of that year, renewed the old prohibitions of the *compagnonnages*. The same law restated the abolition of the guilds and forbade the organization of special economic interests of any kind. All trades, it declared, were free for all to enter. All men, without belonging to any organization, had the right to work at any occupation or business they might choose. All wages were to be settled privately by the workman and his employer. This was not at all what the workingman, at that time or any other, really wanted. Nevertheless the provisions of the Le Chapelier law remained a part of French law for three-quarters of a century. The embryonic trade unions continued to exist secretly, though with more difficulty than under the hit-and-miss law enforcement of the Old Regime.

The Quarrel with the Church

Most fatefully of all, the Constituent Assembly quarreled with the Catholic church. The confiscation of church properties naturally came as a shock to the

[7] See pp. 324–325.

clergy. The village priests, whose support had made possible the revolt of the Third Estate, now found that the very buildings in which they worshiped with their parishioners on Sunday belonged to the "nation." The loss of income-producing properties undercut the religious orders and ruined the schools, in which thousands of boys had received free education before the Revolution. Yet it was not on the question of material wealth that the church and the Revolution came to blows. Members of the Constituent Assembly took the view of the church that the great monarchies had taken before them. The idea of separation of church and state was far from their minds. They regarded the church as a form of public authority and as such subordinate to the sovereign power. They frankly argued that the poor needed religion if they were to respect the property of the more wealthy. In any case, having deprived the church of its own income, they had to provide for its maintenance. For the schools many generous and democratic projects of state-sponsored education were drawn up, though under the troubled conditions of the time little was accomplished. For the clergy the new program was mapped out in the Civil Constitution of the Clergy of 1790.

This document went far toward setting up a French national church. Under its provisions the parish priests and bishops were elected, the latter by the same 50,000 electors who chose other important officials. Protestants, Jews, and agnostics could legally take part in the elections, purely on the ground of citizenship and property qualifications. Archbishoprics were abolished, and all the borders of existing bishoprics were redrawn. The number of dioceses was reduced from over 130 to 83, so that one would be coterminous with each department. Bishops were allowed merely to notify the pope of their elevation; they were forbidden to acknowledge any papal authority on their assumption of office, and no papal letter or decree was to be published or enforced in France except with government permission. All clergy received salaries from the state, the average income of bishops being somewhat reduced, that of parish clergymen being raised. Sinecures, plural holdings, and other abuses by which noble families had been supported by the church were done away with. The Constituent Assembly (independently of the Civil Constitution) also prohibited the taking of religious vows and dissolved all monastic houses.

Some of all this was not in principle alarmingly new, since before the Revolution the civil authority of the king had designated the French bishops and passed on the admission of papal documents into France. French bishops, in the old spirit of the "Gallican liberties," were traditionally jealous of papal power in France.[8] Many were now willing to accept something like the Civil Constitution if allowed to produce it on their own authority. The Assembly refused to concede so much jurisdiction to the Gallican church and applied instead to the pope, hoping to force its plans upon the French clergy by invoking the authority of the Vatican. But the Vatican pronounced the Civil Constitution a wanton usurpation of power over the Catholic church. Unfortunately, the pope also went further, condemning the whole Revolution and all its works. The Constituent Assembly retorted by requiring all French clergy to swear an oath of loyalty to the constitution, including the Civil Constitution of the Clergy. Half took the oath and half refused it, the latter half including all but seven of the bishops. One of the seven willing to

[8] See pp. 52, 70, 87–88, 135, 189.

accept the new arrangements was Talleyrand, soon to be famous as foreign minister of numerous French governments.

There were now two churches in France, one clandestine, the other official, one maintained by voluntary offerings or by funds smuggled in from abroad, the other financed and sponsored by the government. The former, comprising the nonjuring, unsworn or "refractory" clergy, turned violently counterrevolutionary. To protect themselves from the Revolution they insisted, with an emphasis quite new in France, on the universal religious supremacy of the Roman pontiff. They denounced the "constitutional" clergy as schismatics who spurned the pope and as mere careerists willing to hold jobs on the government's terms. The constitutional clergy, those taking the oath and upholding the Civil Constitution, considered themselves to be patriots and defenders of the rights of man; and they insisted that the Gallican church had always enjoyed a degree of liberty from Rome. The Catholic laity were terrified and puzzled. Many were sufficiently attached to the Revolution to prefer the constitutional clergy; but to do so meant to defy the pope, and Catholics who persisted in defying the pope were on the whole those least zealous in their religion. The constitutional clergy therefore stood on shaky foundations. Many of their followers, under stress of the times, eventually turned against Christianity itself.

Good Catholics tended to favor the "refractory" clergy. The outstanding example was the king himself. He personally used the services of refractory priests, and thus gave a new reason for the revolutionaries to distrust him. Whatever chance there was that Louis XVI might go along with the Revolution was exploded, for he concluded that he could do so only by endangering his immortal soul. Former aristocrats also naturally preferred the refractory clergy. They now put aside the Voltairean levities of the Age of Enlightenment, and the "best people" began to exhibit a new piety in religious matters. The peasants, who found little in the Revolution to interest them after their own insurrection of 1789 and the consequent abolition of the manorial regime, also favored the old-fashioned or refractory clergy. Much the same was true of the urban working-class families, where both men and women might shout against priests and yet want to be sure that their marriages were valid and their children properly baptized. The Constituent Assembly, and its successors, were at their wits' end what to do. Sometimes they shut their eyes at the intrigues of refractory clergy; in which case the constitutional clergy then became fearful. Sometimes they hunted out and persecuted the refractories; in that case they only stirred up religious fanaticism.

The Civil Constitution of the Clergy has been called the greatest tactical blunder of the Revolution. Certainly its consequences were unfortunate in the extreme, and they spread to much of Europe. In the nineteenth century the church was to be officially antidemocratic and antiliberal;[9] and democrats and liberals in most cases were to be violently and outspokenly anticlerical. The main beneficiary was the papacy. The French church, which had clung for ages to its Gallican liberties, was thrown by the Revolution into the arms of the pope. Even Napoleon, when he healed the schism a decade later, acknowledged powers in the papacy that had never been acknowledged by the French kings. These were steps in the

[9] See pp. 512–514, 632–634.

process, leading through the proclamation of papal infallibility in 1870,[10] by which the affairs of the modern Catholic church became increasingly centralized at the Vatican.

With the proclamation of the constitution in September 1791, the Constituent Assembly disbanded. Before dissolving, it ruled that none of its members might sit in the forthcoming Legislative Assembly. This body was therefore made up of men who still wished to make their mark in the Revolution. The new regime went into effect in October 1791. It was a constitutional monarchy in which a unicameral Legislative Assembly confronted a king unconverted to the new order. Designed as the permanent solution to France's problems, it was to collapse in ten months, in August 1792, as a result of popular insurrection four months after France became involved in war. A group of Jacobins, known as Girondins, for a time became the left or advanced party of the Revolution and in the Legislative Assembly led France into war.

43. The Revolution and Europe: The War and the "Second" Revolution, 1792

The International Impact of the Revolution

The European governments were long reluctant to become involved with France. They were under considerable pressure. On the one hand, pro-French and pro-revolutionary groups appeared immediately in many quarters. The doctrines of the French Revolution, as of the American, were highly exportable: they took the form of a universal philosophy, proclaiming the rights of man regardless of time or place, race or nation. Moreover, depending on what one was looking for, one might see in the first disturbances in France a revolt of either the nobility, the bourgeoisie, the common people, or the entire nation. In Poland those who were trying to reorganize the country against further partition hailed the French example. The Hungarian landlords pointed to it in their reaction against Joseph II. In England, for a time, those who controlled Parliament complacently believed that the French were attempting to imitate them.

But it was the excluded classes of European society who were most inspired. The hard-pressed Silesian weavers were said to hope that "the French would come." Strikes broke out at Hamburg, and peasants rebelled elsewhere. One English diplomat found that even the Prussian army had "a strong taint of democracy among officers and men." In Belgium, where the privileged elements were already in revolt against the Austrian emperor, a second revolt broke out, inspired by events in France and aimed at the privileged elements. In England the newly developing "radicals," men like Thomas Paine and Dr. Richard Price, who wished a thorough overhauling of Parliament and the established church, entered into correspondence with the Assembly in Paris. Businessmen of importance, including Watt and Boulton, the pioneers of the steam engine, were likewise

---

[10] See p. 634.

pro-French since they had no representation in the House of Commons. The Irish too were excited and presently revolted. Everywhere the young were aroused, the young Hegel in Germany, or in England the young Wordsworth, who later recalled the sense of a new era that had captivated so many spirits in 1789:

> *Bliss was it in that dawn to be alive,*
> *But to be young was very heaven!*

On the other hand the anti-Revolutionary movement gathered strength. Edmund Burke, frightened by the French proclivities of English radicals, published as early as 1790 his *Reflections on the Revolution in France*. For France, he predicted anarchy and dictatorship. For England, he sternly advised the English to accept a slow adaptation of their own English liberties. For all the world, he denounced a political philosophy that rested on abstract principles of right and wrong, declaring that every people must be shaped by its own national circumstances, national history, and national character. He drew an eloquent reply and a defense of France from Thomas Paine in the *Rights of Man*. Burke soon began to preach the necessity of war, urging a kind of ideological struggle against French barbarism and violence. His *Reflections* was translated and widely read. In the long run his book proved an influential work in the history of thought. In the short run it fell on willing ears. The king of Sweden, Gustavus III, offered to lead a monarchist crusade. In Russia old Catherine was appalled; she forbade further translations of her erstwhile friend Voltaire, she called the French "vile riffraff" and "brutish cannibals," and she packed off to Siberia a Russian named Radishchev, who in his *Voyage from St. Petersburg to Moscow* pointed out the evils of serfdom. It is said that Russians were even forbidden to speak of the "revolutions of the heavenly spheres." The terrors were heightened by plaintive messages from Louis XVI and Marie Antoinette, and by the émigrés who kept bursting out of France, led as early as July 1789 by the king's own brother, the Count of Artois. The émigrés, who at first were nobles, settled in various parts of Europe and began using their international aristocratic connections. They preached a kind of holy war. They bemoaned the sad plight of the king, but what they most wanted was to get back their manorial incomes and other rights. Extremists among the émigrés even hinted that Louis XVI himself was a dangerous revolutionary and much preferred his brother, the unyielding Count of Artois.

In short, Europe was soon split by a division that overran all frontiers. The same was true of America also. In the United States the rising party of Jefferson was branded as Jacobin and pro-French, that of Hamilton as aristocratic and pro-British; while in colonial Spanish America ideas of independence were strengthened, and the Venezuelan Miranda became a general in the French army. In all countries of the European world, though least of all in eastern and southern Europe, there were revolutionary or pro-French elements that were feared by their own governments. Russia and Prussia invaded Poland and annulled its constitution of 1791. In all countries, including France, there were implacable enemies of the French Revolution. In all countries were people whose loyalties or sympathies lay abroad. There had been no such situation since the Protestant Reformation, nor was there anything like it again until after the Russian Revolution of the twentieth century.

The Coming of the War, April 1792

Yet the European governments were slow to move. Catherine had no intention of becoming involved in western Europe. She only wished to involve her neighbors. William Pitt, the British prime minister, resisted the war cries of Burke. Son of the Earl of Chatham, prime minister since 1784, chief founder of the new Tory party, Pitt had a reforming program of his own; he had tried and failed to carry a reform of Parliament and was now concentrating on a policy of orderly finance and systematic economy. His program would be ruined by war. He insisted that the domestic affairs of France were of no concern to the British government. The key position was occupied by the Habsburg emperor, Leopold II, brother to the French queen. Leopold at first answered Marie Antoinette's pleas for help by telling her to adjust herself to conditions in France. He resisted the furious demands of the émigrés, whom he understood perfectly, having inherited from Joseph II a fractious aristocracy himself.

Still, the new French government was a disturbing phenomenon. It openly encouraged malcontents all over Europe. It showed a tendency to settle international affairs by unilateral action. For example, it annexed Avignon at the request of local revolutionaries but without the consent of its historic sovereign, the pope. Or again, in Alsace there had been much overlapping jurisdiction between France and Germany ever since the Peace of Westphalia.[11] The Constituent Assembly abolished feudalism and manorial dues in Alsace as elsewhere in France. To German princes who had feudal rights in Alsace the Assembly offered compensation, but it did not ask their consent; and the German princes concerned, deprived by a revolutionary decree of rights guaranteed them by past treaties, appealed to the Holy Roman Emperor to protest the infringement of international understandings. Moreover, after the arrest of Louis XVI at Varennes, after his attempted flight in June 1791, it became impossible to deny that the French king and queen were prisoners of the revolutionaries.

In August Leopold met with the king of Prussia at Pillnitz in Saxony. The resulting Declaration of Pillnitz rested on a famous *if*: Leopold would take military steps to restore order in France if all the other powers would join him. Knowing the attitude of Pitt, he believed that the *if* could never materialize. His aim was mainly to rid himself of the French émigrés. These perversely received the Declaration with delight. They used it as an open threat to their enemies in France, announcing that they would soon return alongside the forces of civilized Europe to punish the guilty and right the wrongs that had been done to them.

In France the upholders of the Revolution were alarmed. They were ignorant of what Leopold really meant and took the dire menaces of the émigrés at their face value. The Declaration of Pillnitz, far from cowing the French, enraged them against all the crowned heads of Europe. It gave a political advantage to the then dominant faction of Jacobins, known to history as the Girondins. These included the philosophe Condorcet, the humanitarian lawyer Brissot, and the civil servant Roland and his more famous wife, Mme. Roland, whose house became a kind of headquarters of the group. They attracted many foreigners also, such as Thomas Paine and the German Anacharsis Cloots, the "representative of the human

---

[11] See maps, pp. 146–147, 188, 328.

race." In December 1791 a deputation of English radicals, led by James Watt, son of the inventor of the steam engine, received a wild ovation at the Paris Jacobin club.

The Girondins became the party of international revolution. They declared that the Revolution could never be secure in France until it spread to the world. In their view, once war had come, the peoples of states at war with France would not support their own governments. There was reason for this belief, since revolutionary elements antedating the French Revolution already existed in both the Dutch and the Austrian Netherlands, and to a lesser degree in parts of Switzerland, Poland, and elsewhere. Some Girondins therefore contemplated a war in which French armies should enter neighboring countries, unite with local revolutionaries, overthrow the established governments, and set up a federation of republics. War was also favored by a very different group, led by Lafayette, which wished to curb the Revolution by holding it at the line of constitutional monarchy. This group mistakenly believed that war might restore the much damaged popularity of Louis XVI, unite the country under the new government, and make it possible to put down the continuing Jacobin agitation. As the war spirit boiled up in France, the Emperor Leopold II died. He was succeeded by Francis II, a man much more inclined than Leopold to yield to the clamors of the old aristocracy. Francis resumed negotiations with Prussia. In France all who dreaded a return of the Old Regime listened more readily to the Girondins. Among the Jacobins as a whole, only a few, generally a handful of radical democrats, opposed the war. On April 20, 1792, without serious opposition, the Assembly declared war on "the king of Hungary and Bohemia," i.e., the Austrian monarchy.

The "Second" Revolution: August 10, 1792

The war intensified the existing unrest and dissatisfaction of the unpropertied classes. Both peasants and urban workers felt that the Constituent and the Legislative Assembly had served the propertied interests and had done little for them. Peasants were dissatisfied at the inadequate measures taken to facilitate land distribution; workers felt especially the pinch of soaring prices, which by 1792 had greatly risen. Gold had been taken out of the country by the émigrés; paper money, the *assignats,* was almost the sole currency, and the future of the government was so uncertain that it steadily lost value. Peasants concealed their food products rather than sell them for depreciating paper. Actual scarcity combined with the falling value of money to drive up the cost of living. The lowest income groups suffered the most. But dissatisfied though they were, when the war began they were threatened with a return of the émigrés and a vindictive restoration of the Old Regime, which at least for the peasants would be the worst of all possible eventualities. The working classes—peasants, artisans, mechanics, shopkeepers, wage workers—rallied to the Revolution but not to the revolutionary government in power. The Legislative Assembly and the constitutional monarchy lacked the confidence of large elements of the population.

In addition, the war at first went very unfavorably for the French. Prussia joined immediately with Austria, and by the summer of 1792 the two powers were on the point of invading France. They issued a proclamation to the French people, the Brunswick Manifesto of July 25, declaring that if any harm befell the French

king and queen the Austro-Prussian forces, upon their arrival in Paris, would exact the most severe retribution from the inhabitants of that city. Such menaces, compounding the military emergency, only played into the hands of the most violent activists. Masses of the French people, roused and guided by bourgeois Jacobin leaders, notably Robespierre, Danton, and the vitriolic journalist Marat, burst out in a passion of patriotic excitement. They turned against the king because he was identified with powers at war with France, and also because, in France itself, those who still supported him were using the monarchy as a defense against the lower classes. Republicanism in France was partly a rather sudden historical accident, in that France was at war under a king who could not be trusted, and partly a kind of lower-class or quasi-proletarian movement, in which, however, many bourgeois revolutionaries shared.

Feeling ran high during the summer of 1792. Recruits streamed into Paris from all quarters on their way to the frontiers. One detachment, from Marseilles, brought with them a new marching song, known ever since as the *Marseillaise,* a fierce call to war upon tyranny. The transient provincials stirred up the agitation in Paris. On August 10, 1792, the working-class quarters of the city rose in revolt, supported by the recruits from Marseilles and elsewhere. They stormed the Tuileries against resistance by the Swiss Guard, many of whom were massacred, and seized and imprisoned the king and the royal family. A revolutionary municipal government, or "Commune," was set up in Paris. Usurping the powers of the Legislative Assembly, it forced the abrogation of the constitution, and the election, by universal male suffrage, of a Constitutional Convention that was to govern France and prepare a new and more democratic constitution. The very word Convention was used in recollection of the American Constitutional Convention in 1787. Meanwhile hysteria, anarchy, and terror reigned in Paris; a handful of insurrectionary volunteers, declaring that they would not fight enemies on the frontiers until they had disposed of enemies in Paris, dragged about 1,100 persons—refractory priests and other counterrevolutionaries—from the prisons of the city and killed them after drumhead trials. These are known as the "September massacres."

For over two and a half years, since October 1789, there had been an abatement of popular violence. Now the coming of the war and the dissatisfaction of the lower classes with the course of events so far had led to new explosions. The

A WOMAN OF THE REVOLUTION
by Jacques-Louis David (French, 1748–1825)
Here is something of what historians mean by the "working class," and it may be compared with the representations of aristocracy and of the middle class already shown (see pp. 346, 352). The coarse garments and untended hair, the colorless lips, the lined forehead, and the evidences of suffering in the eyes—all reveal a life of much labor and few amenities. The woman seems to be observing something with an interest mixed with suspicion, and her air of determination and even of defiance suggests the political-mindedness aroused even in the poorest classes in time of revolution. David painted this portrait in 1795, a year after the Terror in France. He was himself an active revolutionary, a member of the Convention and of the Committee of General Security. It is rare to find portraits of people of this class of society done with so much realism, sympathy, and force. Courtesy of the Musée des Beaux-Arts, Lyon (J. Camponogara).

insurrection of August 10, 1792, the "second" French Revolution, initiated the most advanced phase of the Revolution.

44. The Emergency Republic, 1792–1795: The Terror

The National Convention

The National Convention met on September 20, 1792; it was to sit for three years. It immediately proclaimed the Year One of the French Republic. The disorganized French armies, also on September 20, won a great moral victory in the "cannonade of Valmy," a battle that was hardly more than an artillery duel, but which induced the Prussian commander to give up his march on Paris. The French soon occupied Belgium (the Austrian Netherlands), Savoy (which belonged to the king of Sardinia who had joined with the Austrians), and Mainz and other cities on the German Left Bank of the Rhine. Revolutionary sympathizers in these places appealed for French aid. The National Convention decreed assistance to "all peoples wishing to recover their liberty." It also ordered that French generals, in the occupied areas, should dissolve the old governments, confiscate government and church property, abolish tithes, hunting rights, and seigneurial dues, and set up provisional administrations. Thus revolution spread in the wake of the successful French armies.

The British and Dutch prepared to resist. Pitt, still insisting that the French might have any domestic regime that they chose, declared that Great Britain could not tolerate the French occupation of Belgium. The British and Dutch began conversations with Prussia and Austria, and the French declared war on them on February 1, 1793. Within a few weeks the Republic had annexed Savoy and Nice, as well as Belgium, and had much of the German Rhineland under its military government.[12] Meanwhile, in eastern Europe, while denouncing the rapacity of the French savages, the rulers of Russia and Prussia came to an arrangement of their own, each appropriating a portion of Poland in the second partition in January 1793.[13] The Austrians, excluded from the second partition, became anxious over their interests in eastern Europe. The infant French Republic, now at war with all Europe, was saved by the weakness of the Coalition, for Britain and Holland had no land forces of consequence, and Prussia and Austria were too jealous of each other, and too preoccupied with Poland, to commit the bulk of their armies against France.

In the Convention all the leaders were Jacobins, but the Jacobins were again splitting. The Girondins were no longer the most advanced revolutionary group as they had been in the Legislative Assembly. Beside the Girondins appeared a new group, whose members preferred to sit in the highest seats in the hall, and therefore were dubbed the "Mountain" in the political parlance of the day. The leading Girondins came from the great provincial cities; the leading Montagnards, though mostly of provincial birth, were representatives of the city of Paris and

[12] See map, p. 396.
[13] See pp. 339–340.

owed most of their political strength to the radical and popular elements in that city.

These popular revolutionists, outside the Convention, proudly called themselves "sans-culottes," since they wore the workingman's long trousers, not the knee breeches or *culottes,* of the middle and upper classes. They were the working class of a pre-industrial age, shopkeepers and shop assistants, skilled artisans in various trades, including some who were owners of small manufacturing or handicraft enterprises. For two years their militancy and their activism pressed the Revolution forward. They demanded an equality that should be meaningful for people like themselves, they called for a mighty effort against foreign powers that presumed to intervene in the French Revolution, and they denounced the now deposed king and queen (correctly enough) for collusion with the Austrian enemy. The sans-culottes feared that the Convention might be too moderate. They favored direct democracy in their neighborhood clubs and assemblies, together with a mass rising if necessary against the Convention itself. The Girondins in the Convention began to dismiss these popular militants as anarchists. The group known as the Mountain was more willing to work with them, so long at least as the emergency lasted.

The Convention put Louis XVI on trial for treason in December 1792. On January 15 it unanimously pronounced him guilty, but on the next day, out of 721 deputies present, only 361 voted for immediate execution, a majority of one. Louis XVI died on the guillotine forthwith. The 361 deputies were henceforth branded for life as regicides; never could they allow, in safety to themselves, a restoration of the Bourbon monarchy in France. The other 360 deputies were not similarly compromised; their rivals called them Girondins, "moderatists," counterrevolutionaries. All who still wanted more from the Revolution, or who feared that the slightest wavering would bring the Allies and the émigrés into France, now looked to the Mountain wing of the Jacobins.

Background to the Terror

In April 1793 the most spectacular French general, Dumouriez, who had won the victories in Belgium five months before, defected to Austria. The Allied armies now drove the French from Belgium and again threatened to invade France. Counterrevolutionaries in France exulted. From the revolutionaries went up the cry, "We are betrayed!" Prices continued to rise, the currency fell, food was harder to obtain, and the working classes were increasingly restless. The sans-culottes demanded price controls, currency controls, rationing, legislation against the hoarding of food, and requisitioning to enforce the circulation of goods. They denounced the bourgeoisie as profiteers and exploiters of the people. While the Girondins resisted, the Mountain went along with the sans-culottes, partly from sympathy with their ideas, partly to win mass support for the war, and partly as a maneuver to get rid of the Girondins. On May 31, 1793, the Commune of Paris, under sans-culotte pressure, assembled a host of demonstrators and insurrectionists who invaded the Convention and forced the arrest of the Girondin leaders. Other Girondins fled to the provinces, including Condorcet, who, while

THE GLEANERS
by Jean-François Millet (French, 1814–1875)

Three women of the poorest of the French peasantry are shown here. They may be compared with the women depicted on pp. 346, 352, and 382. Bowed with labor, reaching out with strong, muscular hands, clutching their few stalks of grain, these women are exercising a legal right, "glanage," by which poor people were allowed to glean the fields after the owners had taken in the harvest. Many of the owners were more affluent peasants. Glanage was one of the collective village rights, originally common to France, England, and most of Europe, which tended to disappear with the spread of modern private-property institutions. When the painting was first exhibited in 1857, it reminded one irate critic of the French Revolution. "Behind these three gleaning-women," he said, "against the leaden horizon, we can see silhouetted the pikes, riots and scaffolds of '93." Courtesy of the Louvre (Giraudon).

in hiding, and before his death, found occasion to write his famous book on the *Progress of the Human Mind.*[14]

The Mountain now ruled in the Convention, but the Convention itself ruled very little. Not only were the foreign armies and the émigrés at the gates bent on destroying the Convention as a band of regicides and social incendiaries, but the authority of the Convention was widely repudiated in France itself. In the west, in the Vendée, the peasants had revolted against military conscription; they were worked upon by refractory priests, British agents, and royalist emissaries of the Count of Artois. The great provincial cities, Lyons, Bordeaux, Marseilles, and others, had also rebelled, especially after the fugitive Girondins reached them. These "federalist" rebels demanded a more "federal" or decentralized republic. Like the Vendéans, with whom they had no connection, they objected to the ascendancy of Paris, having been accustomed to more regional independence under the Old Regime. These rebellions became counterrevolutionary, since all sorts of foreigners, royalists, émigrés, and clericals streamed in to assist them.

The Convention had to defend itself against extremists of the Left as well. To the genuine mass action of the sans-culottes were now added the voices of even more excited militants called *enragés.* Various organizers, enthusiasts, agitators, and neighborhood politicians declared that parliamentary methods were useless. Generally they were men outside the Convention—and also women, for women were particularly sensitive to the crisis of food shortage and soaring prices, and an organization of Revolutionary Republican Women caused a brief stir in 1793. All such activists worked through units of local government in Paris and elsewhere, and in thousands of "popular societies" and provincial clubs throughout the whole country. They also formed "revolutionary armies," semimilitary bands that scoured the rural areas for food, searched the barns of peasants, denounced suspects, and preached revolution.

As for the Convention, while it cannot be said ever to have had any commanding leaders, the program it followed for about a year was on the whole that of Maximilien Robespierre, himself a Jacobin but not one to go along forever with popular revolution or anarchy. Robespierre is one of the most argued about and least understood men of modern times. Persons accustomed to stable conditions dismiss him with a shudder as a bloodthirsty fanatic, dictator, and demagogue. Others have considered him an idealist, a visionary, and an ardent patriot whose goals and ideals were at least avowedly democratic. All agree on his personal honesty and integrity and on his revolutionary zeal. He was by origin a lawyer of northern France, educated with the aid of scholarships in Paris. He had been elected in 1789 to sit for the Third Estate in the Estates General, and in the ensuing Constituent Assembly played a minor role, though calling attention to himself by his views against capital punishment and in favor of universal suffrage. During the time of the Legislative Assembly, in 1791–1792, he continued to agitate for democracy and vainly pleaded against the declaration of war. In the Convention, elected in September 1792, he sat for a Paris constituency. He became a prominent member of the Mountain and welcomed the purge of the Girondins. He had always kept free of the bribery and graft in which some others became involved and for this reason was known as the Incorruptible. He was a

---

[14] See p. 326.

great believer in the importance of "virtue." This term had been used in a specialized way among the philosophes: both Montesquieu and Rousseau had held that republics depended upon "virtue," or unselfish public spirit and civic zeal, to which was added, under Rousseauist influence, a somewhat sentimentalized idea of personal uprightness and purity of life. Robespierre was determined, in 1793 and 1794, to bring about a democratic republic made up of good citizens and honest men.

The Program of the Convention, 1793–1794: The Terror

The program of the Convention, which Robespierre helped to form, was to repress anarchy, civil strife, and counterrevolution at home and to win the war by a great national mobilization of the country's people and resources. It would prepare a democratic constitution and initiate legislation for the lower classes, but it would not yield to the Paris Commune and other agencies of direct revolutionary action. To conduct the government, the Convention granted wide powers to a Committee of Public Safety, a group of twelve members of the Convention who were reelected every month. Robespierre was an influential member; others were the youthful St. Just, the partially paralyzed Couthon, and the army officer Carnot, "organizer of victory."

To repress the "counterrevolution," the Convention and the Committee of Public Safety set up what is popularly known as the "Reign of Terror." Revolutionary courts were instituted as an alternative to the lynch law of the September massacres. A Committee of General Security was created as a kind of supreme political police. Designed to protect the Revolutionary Republic from its internal enemies, the Terror struck at those who were in league against the Republic, and at those who were merely suspected of hostile activities. Its victims ranged from Marie Antoinette and other royalists to the former revolutionary colleagues of the Mountain, the Girondin leaders; and before the year 1793–1794 was over, some of the old Jacobins of the Mountain who had helped inaugurate the program also went to the guillotine.

Many thousands of people died in France at the height of the Revolution. Most deaths were in places in open revolt against the Convention, as in the Vendée in western France. Some resulted from acts of private vengeance. But if the Terror is understood to mean the official program of the government, which at one time decreed "terror the order of the day," the number who died in it was not large by the standards of the twentieth century, in which governments have attempted to wipe out whole classes or races. About 40,000 persons perished in the Terror thus defined, and many others were temporarily imprisoned. About 8 percent of the victims of the "official" Terror were nobles, but nobles as a class were not molested unless suspected of political agitation; 14 percent of the victims were classifiable as bourgeois, mainly of the rebellious southern cities; 6 percent were clergy, while no less than 70 percent were of the peasant and laboring classes. A democratic republic, founded on the Declaration of the Rights of Man, was in principle to follow the Terror once the war and the emergency were over, but meanwhile, the Terror was inhuman at best and in some places atrocious, as at Nantes where 2,000 persons were loaded on barges and deliberately drowned.

The Terror left long memories in France of antipathy to the Revolution and to republicanism.

To conduct the government in the midst of the war emergency the Committee of Public Safety operated as a joint dictatorship or war cabinet. It prepared and guided legislation through the Convention. It gained control over the "representatives on mission," who were members of the Convention on duty with the armies and in the insurgent areas of France. It established the *Bulletin des loix,* so that all persons might know what laws they were supposed to enforce or to obey. It centralized the administration, converting the swarm of locally elected officials, left over from the Constituent Assembly, and who were royalists in some places, wild extremists in others, into centrally appointed "national agents" named by the Committee of Public Safety.

To win the war the Committee proclaimed the *levée en masse,* calling on all able-bodied men to rally to the colors. It recruited scientific men to work on armaments and munitions. The most prominent French scientists of the day, including Lagrange and Lamarck, worked for or were protected by the government of the Terror, though one, Lavoisier, "father of modern chemistry," was guillotined in 1794 because he had been involved in tax farming before 1789. For military reasons also the Committee instituted economic controls, which at the same time met the demands of the *enragés* and other working-class spokesmen. The *assignats* ceased to fall during the year of the Terror. Thus the government protected both its own purchasing power and that of the masses. It did so by controlling the export of gold, by confiscating specie and foreign currency from French citizens, to whom it paid assignats in return, and by legislation against hoarding or the withholding of goods from the market. Food and supplies for the armies, and for civilians in the towns, were raised and allocated by a system of requisitions, centralized in a Subsistence Commission under the Committee of Public Safety. A "general maximum" set ceilings for prices and wages. It helped to check inflation during the crisis, but it did not work very well; the Committee believed, on principle, in a free market economy and lacked the technical and administrative machinery to enforce thorough controls. By 1794 it was giving freer rein to private enterprise and to the peasants, in order to encourage production. It tried also to hold down wages and in that respect failed to win the adherence of many working-class leaders.

In June 1793 the Committee produced, and had adopted by the Convention, a republican constitution which provided for universal male suffrage. But the new constitution was suspended indefinitely, and the government was declared "revolutionary until the peace," "revolutionary" meaning extraconstitutional or of an emergency character. In other ways the Committee showed intentions of legislating on behalf of the lower economic classes. The price controls and other economic regulations answered the demands of the sans-culottes. The last of the manorial regime was done away with; the peasants were relieved of having to pay compensation for the obligations that had been abolished at the opening of the Revolution. Purchase of land by the peasants was made somewhat easier. There were even moves, in the Ventôse laws of March 1794, to confiscate the property of suspects (not merely of the church or convicted émigrés), and to give such property gratis to "indigent patriots"; but these laws were drafted in unworkable form, never received much support from the ruling Committee, and came to very little. The Committee busied itself also with social services and measures of public improvement. It issued pamphlets to teach farmers to improve their crops, selected promising youths to receive instruction in useful trades, opened a military school for boys of all classes, even the humblest, and certainly intended to introduce universal elementary education.

It was also at this time, in 1794, that the National Convention decreed the abolition of slavery in the French colonies, meaning chiefly Saint-Domingue, the modern Haiti, the richest of all the sugar islands in the Caribbean. Free blacks had already received civic rights earlier in the Revolution. The black slaves had in fact already liberated themselves in a massive rebellion in 1791. They had produced a leader in Toussaint L'Ouverture, born a slave, who after the French abolished slavery served as a general in the French army against the Spanish and British who had ambitions in Haiti. In the ensuing confusion Toussaint proclaimed an independent Haitian republic. Under pressure of the slave-owning and commercial interests (and the European demand for sugar) the government of Napoleon in 1802 reestablished slavery in the French colonies, captured Toussaint and took him to France, where he died.[15] Unable in any case to defeat the rebellious blacks, most of the French army sent out in this operation perished in Haiti of yellow fever. An unexpected consequence was that Napoleon sold the remaining French possessions on the North American mainland ("Louisiana") to the United States in 1803.

At the climax of the Revolution, in 1793–1794, the Committee of Public Safety was determined to concentrate revolutionary initiative in itself. It had no patience with unauthorized revolutionary violence. With a democratic program of its own, it disapproved of the turbulent democracy of popular clubs and local assemblies. In the fall of 1793 it arrested the leading *enragés*. It also prohibited revolutionary women's organizations at the same time. Extreme revolutionary demands were expressed by Jacques Hébert, a journalist and officer of the Paris Commune. Robespierre called such people "ultra revolutionaries." They were a large and indefinable group and included many members of the Convention. They indiscriminately denounced merchants and bourgeoisie. They were the party of extreme Terror; an Hébertist brought about the drownings at Nantes. Believing all religion to be counterrevolutionary, they launched the movement of Dechristianization. Even a Republican calendar was adopted by the Convention. It was intended to blot out the Christian cycle of Sundays, saints' days, and such holidays as Christmas and Easter. It counted years from the founding of the French Republic, divided each year into new months of thirty days each, and even abolished the week, which it replaced with the ten-day *décade*.[16]

Another form taken by Dechristianization was the cult of reason which sprang up all over France at the end of 1793. In Paris the bishop resigned his office, declaring that he had been deluded; and the Commune put on ceremonies in the cathedral of Notre Dame, in which Reason was impersonated by an actress who was the wife of one of the city officials. But Dechristianization was severely

---

[15] Slavery was not effectively abolished in the French colonies until 1848; see p. 502. On attempts to control the slave trade see pp. 450, 478, and 570.

[16] Though not adopted until October 1793, the revolutionary calendar dated the Year I of the French Republic from September 22, 1792. The names of the months, in order, were Vendémiaire, Brumaire, Frimaire (autumn); Nivôse, Pluviôse, Ventôse (winter); Germinal, Floréal, Prairial (spring); Messidor, Thermidor, Fructidor (summer).

frowned upon by Robespierre. He believed that it would alienate the masses from the Republic and ruin such sympathy as was still felt for the Revolution abroad. The Committee of Public Safety, therefore, ordered the toleration of peaceable Catholics, and in June 1794 Robespierre introduced the cult of the Supreme Being, a deistic natural religion, in which the Republic was declared to recognize the existence of God and the immortality of the soul. Robespierre hoped that both Catholics and agnostic anticlericals could become reconciled on this ground. But Catholics were now beyond reconciliation, and the freethinkers, appealing to the tradition of Voltaire, regarded Robespierre as a reactionary mystery monger and were instrumental in bringing about his fall.

Meanwhile the Committee proceeded relentlessly against the Hébertists, whose main champions it sent to the guillotine in March 1794. The paramilitary "revolutionary armies" were repressed. The extreme Terrorists were recalled from the provinces. The revolutionary Paris Commune was destroyed. Robespierre filled the municipal offices of Paris with his own appointees. This Robespierrist commune disapproved of strikes and tried to hold down wages, on the plea of military necessity; it failed to win over the ex-Hébertists and working-class spokespeople, who became disillusioned with the Revolution and dismissed it as a bourgeois movement. Probably to prevent just such a conclusion, and to avoid the appearance of deviation to the right, Robespierre and the Committee, after liquidating the Hébertists, also liquidated certain right-wing members of the Mountain who were known as Dantonists. Danton and his followers were accused of financial dishonesty and of dealing with counterrevolutionaries; the charges contained some truth but were not the main reason for the executions.

By the spring of 1794 the French Republic possessed an army of 800,000 men, the largest ever raised up to that time by a European power. It was a national army, representing a people in arms, commanded by officers who had been promoted rapidly on grounds of merit, and composed of troops who felt themselves to be citizens fighting for their own cause. Its intense political-mindedness made it the more formidable and contrasted strongly with the indifference of the opposing troops, some of whom were in fact serfs and none of whom had any sense of membership in their own political systems. The Allied governments, each pursuing its own ends, and still distracted by their ambitions in Poland, where the third partition was impending, could not combine their forces against France. In June 1794 the French won the battle of Fleurus in Belgium. The Republican hosts again streamed into the Low Countries; in six months their cavalry rode into Amsterdam on the ice. A revolutionary Batavian Republic soon replaced the old Dutch provinces. The opposite occurred at this time in eastern Europe, where the attempted revolution led by Kosciuszko in Poland was stamped out by Russian and Prussian armies, and Poland was finally merged into the east-European empires.

Military success made the French less willing to put up with the dictatorial rule and economic regimentation of the Terror. Robespierre and the Committee of Public Safety had antagonized all significant parties. The working-class radicals of Paris would no longer support him, and after the death of Danton the National Convention was afraid of its own ruling committee. A group in the Convention obtained the "outlawing" of Robespierre on 9 Thermidor (July 27, 1794); he was guillotined with some of his associates on the following day. Many who turned against Robespierre believed they were pushing the Revolution farther forward, as in destroying the Girondins the year before. Others thought, or said, that they were stopping a dictator and a tyrant. All agreed, to absolve themselves, in heaping all blame upon Robespierre. The idea that Robespierre was an ogre originated more with his former colleagues than with conservatives of the time.

The Thermidorian Reaction

The fall of Robespierre stunned the country, but its effects manifested themselves during the following months as the "Thermidorian reaction." The Terror subsided. The Convention reduced the powers of the Committee of Public Safety, and it closed the Jacobin club. Price control and other regulations were removed. Inflation resumed its course, prices again rose, and the disoriented and leaderless working classes suffered more than ever. Sporadic uprisings broke out, of which the greatest was the insurrection of Prairial in the Year III (May 1795), when a mob all but dispersed the Convention by force. Troops were called to Paris for the first time since 1789. Insurrectionists in the working-class quarters threw up barricades in the streets. The army prevailed without much bloodshed, but the Convention arrested, imprisoned, or deported 10,000 of the insurgents. A few organizers were guillotined, including one militant black. The affair of Prairial gave a foretaste of modern social revolution.

The triumphant element was the bourgeois class which had guided the Revolution since the Constituent Assembly and had not been really unseated even during the Terror. It was not mainly a bourgeoisie of modern capitalists, eager to make a financial profit by developing new factories or machinery.[17] The political victors after Thermidor were "bourgeois" in an older sense, those who had not been noble or aristocratic before 1789 yet had held a secure position under the Old Regime, many of them lawyers or officeholders, and often drawing income from the ownership of land. To them were now added new elements produced by the Revolution itself, parvenus and *nouveaux riches,* who had made money by wartime government contracts, or had profited by inflation or by buying up former church lands at bargain prices. Such people, often joined by former aristocrats, and in reaction against Robespierrist virtue, set a noisy and ostentatious style of living that gave a bad name to the new order. They also unleashed a "white terror" in which many ex-Jacobins were simply murdered.

But the Thermidorians, disreputable though a few of them were, had not lost faith in the Revolution. Democracy they associated with red terror and mob rule, but they still believed in individual legal rights and in a written constitution. Conditions were rather adverse, for the country was still unsettled, and although the Convention made a separate peace with Spain and Prussia, France still remained at war with Great Britain and the Habsburg empire. But the men of the Convention were determined to make another attempt at constitutional government. They set aside the democratic constitution written in 1793 (and never used) and produced the Constitution of the Year III, which went into effect at the end of 1795.

---

[17] On the bourgeoisie and capitalism, see pp. 117–118, 121–123, 257–258, 454.

45. The Constitutional Republic: The Directory, 1795–1799

The Weakness of the Directory

The first formally constituted French Republic, known as the Directory, lasted only four years. Its weakness was that it rested on an extremely narrow social base, and that it presupposed certain military conquests. The new constitution applied not only to France but also to Belgium, which was regarded as incorporated constitutionally into France, though the Habsburgs had not yet ceded these "Austrian Netherlands," nor had the British yielded in their refusal to accept French occupation. The constitution of 1795 thus committed the republic to a program of successful expansion. At the same time it restricted the politically active class. It gave almost all adult males the vote, but voters voted only for "electors," for whom about the same qualifications were set as in the constitution of 1791. Persons chosen as electors were usually men of some means, able to give their time and willing to take part in public life; this in effect meant men of the upper middle class, since the old aristocracy was disaffected. The electors chose all important department officials and also the members of the national Legislative Assembly, which this time was divided into two chambers. The lower chamber was called the Council of Five Hundred, the upper, composed of 250 members, the Council of Ancients—"ancients" being men over forty. The chambers chose the executive, which was called the Directory (whence the whole regime got its name) and was made up of five Directors.

The government was thus constitutionally in the hands of substantial property owners, rural and urban, but its real base was narrower still. In the reaction after Thermidor many people began to consider restoring the monarchy. The Convention, to protect its own members, ruled that two-thirds of the men initially elected to the Council of Five Hundred and Council of Ancients must be ex-members of the Convention. This interference with the freedom of the elections provoked serious disturbances in Paris, instigated by persons called royalists; but the Convention, having now accustomed itself to using the army, instructed a young general who happened to be in Paris, named Bonaparte, to put down the royalist mob. He did so with a "whiff of grapeshot." The constitutional republic thus made itself dependent on military protection at the outset.

The regime had enemies to both right and left. On the right, undisguised royalists agitated in Paris and even in the two councils. Their center was the Clichy Club, and they were in continuous touch with the late king's brother, the Count of Provence, whom they regarded as Louis XVIII (Louis XVI's son, who died in prison, being counted as Louis XVII). Louis XVIII had installed himself at Verona in Italy, where he headed a propaganda agency financed largely by British money. The worst obstacle to the resurgence of royalism in France was Louis XVIII himself. In 1795, on assuming the title, he had issued a Declaration of Verona, in which he announced his intention to restore the Old Regime and punish all involved in the Revolution back to 1789. It has been said, correctly enough in this connection, that the Bourbons "learned nothing and forgot nothing." Had Louis XVIII offered in 1795 what he offered in 1814, it is quite conceivable that his partisans in France might have brought about his restoration and terminated the war. As it was, the bulk of the French adhered not exactly to the republic as set up in 1795, but more negatively to any system that would shut out the Bourbons and privileged nobility, prevent a reimposition of the manorial system, and secure the new landowners, peasant and bourgeois, in the possession of the church properties which they had purchased.

The Left was made up of persons from various levels of society who still favored the more democratic ideas expressed earlier in the Revolution. Some of them thought that the fall of Robespierre had been a great misfortune. A tiny group of extremists formed the Conspiracy of Equals, organized in 1796 by "Gracchus" Babeuf. His intention was to overthrow the Directory and replace it with a dictatorial government which he called "democratic," in which private property would be abolished and equality decreed. For these ideas, and for his activist program, he has been regarded as an interesting precursor to modern communism. The Directory repressed the Conspiracy of Equals without difficulty and guillotined Babeuf and one other. Meanwhile it did nothing to relieve the distress of the lower classes, who showed little inclination to follow Babeuf but did suffer from the ravages of scarcity and inflation.

The Political Crisis of 1797

In March 1797 occurred the first really free election ever held in France under republican auspices. The successful candidates were for the most part constitutional monarchists or at least vaguely royalist. A change of the balance within the Five Hundred and the Ancients, in favor of royalism, seemed to be impending. This was precisely what most of the republicans of 1793, including the regicides, could not endure, even though they had to violate the constitution to prevent it. Nor was it endurable, for other reasons, to General Napoleon Bonaparte.

Bonaparte had been born in 1769 into the minor nobility of Corsica, shortly after the annexation of Corsica to France. He had studied in French military schools and been commissioned in the Bourbon army but would never have reached high rank under the conditions of the Old Regime. In 1793 he was a fervent young Jacobin officer, who had been useful in driving the British from Toulon, and who was consequently made a brigadier general by the government of the Terror. In 1795, as noted, he rendered service to the Convention by breaking up a demonstration of royalists. In 1796 he received command of an army, with which, in two brilliant campaigns, he crossed the Alps and drove the Austrians from north Italy. Like other generals he got out of control of the government in Paris, which was financially too harassed to pay his troops or to supply him. He lived by local requisitions in Italy, became self-supporting and independent, and in fact made the civilian government in Paris dependent on him.

He developed a foreign policy of his own. Many Italians had become dissatisfied with their old governments, so that the arrival of the French republican armies threw north Italy into a turmoil, in which the Venetian cities revolted against Venice, Bologna against the pope, Milan against Austria, and the Piedmontese monarchy was threatened by uprisings of its own subjects. Combining with some of these revolutionaries, while rejecting others, Bonaparte established a "Cisalpine" Republic in the Po valley, modeled on the French system, with Milan as its capital. Where the Directory, on the whole, had originally meant to return Milan to the Austrians in compensation for Austrian recognition of the French conquest of Belgium, Bonaparte insisted that France hold its position in both

Belgium and Italy. He therefore needed expansionist republicans in the government in Paris and was perturbed by the elections of 1797.

The Austrians negotiated with Bonaparte because they had been beaten by him in battle. The British also, in conferences with the French at Lille, discussed peace in 1796 and 1797. The war had gone badly for England; a party of Whigs led by Charles James Fox had always openly disapproved it, and the pro-French and republican radicals were so active that the government suspended habeas corpus in 1794, and thereafter imprisoned political agitators at its discretion. In 1795 an assassin fired on George III, breaking the glass in his carriage. Crops were bad, and bread was scarce and costly. England too suffered from inflation, for Pitt at first financed the war by extensive loans, and a good deal of gold was shipped to the Continent to finance the Allied armies. In February 1797 the Bank of England suspended gold payments to private citizens. Famine threatened, the populace was restless, and there were even mutinies in the fleet. Ireland was in rebellion; the French came close to landing a republican army in it, and it could be supposed that the next attempt might be more successful. The Austrians, Britain's only remaining ally, were routed by Bonaparte, and at the moment the British could subsidize them no further. The British had every reason to make peace. Many were inclined to settle for colonial conquests, regarding the war as a renewal of the eighteenth-century struggle for empire.

Prospects for peace seemed good in the summer of 1797, but, as always, it would be peace upon certain conditions. It was the royalists in France that were the peace party, since a restored king could easily return the conquests of the republic and would in any case abandon the new republics in Holland and the Po valley. The republicans in the French government could make peace with difficulty, if at all. They were constitutionally bound to retain Belgium. They were losing control of their own generals. Nor could the supreme question be evaded: Was peace dear enough to purchase by a return of the Old Regime, such as Louis XVIII had himself promised?

The coup d'état of Fructidor (September 4, 1797) resolved all these many issues. It was the turning point of the constitutional republic and was decisive for all Europe. The Directory asked for help from Bonaparte, who sent one of his generals, Augereau, to Paris. While Augereau stood by with a force of soldiers, the councils annulled most of the elections of the preceding spring. Two Directors were purged; one of them, Lazare Carnot, "organizer of victory" in the Committee of Public Safety, and now in 1797 a strict constitutionalist, was driven into exile. On the whole, it was the old republicans of the Convention who secured themselves in power. Their justification was that they were defending the Revolution, keeping out Louis XVIII and the Old Regime. But to do so they had violated their own constitution and quashed the first free election ever held in a constitutional French republic. And they had become more than ever dependent on the army.

After the coup d'état the "Fructidorian" government broke off negotiations with England. With Austria it signed the treaty of Campo Formio on October 17, 1797, incorporating Bonaparte's ideas. Peace now prevailed on the Continent, since only France and Great Britain remained at war, but it was a peace full of trouble for the future. By the new treaty Austria recognized the French annexation of Belgium (the former Austrian Netherlands), the French right to incorporate the Left Bank of the Rhine, and the French-dominated Cisalpine Republic in

THE FRENCH REPUBLIC AND ITS SATELLITES, 1798–1799

By 1799 the French Republic had annexed Belgium (the Austrian Netherlands) and the small German bishoprics and principalities west of the Rhine, and had created, with the aid of native sympathizers, a string of lesser revolutionary republics in the Dutch Netherlands, Switzerland, and most of Italy. With the treaty of Campo Formio between France and Austria in 1797, the Holy Roman Empire began to disintegrate, for the German princes of the Left Bank of the Rhine, who were dispossessed when their territories went to France, began to be compensated with territory of the church-states of the Holy Roman Empire. These developments were carried further by Napoleon (see map, p. 427).

Italy. In return, Bonaparte allowed the Austrians to annex Venice and most of mainland Venetia. The Venetian possessions in the Ionian Islands, off the coast of Greece, went to France.

In the following months, under French auspices, revolutionary republicanism spread through much of Italy. The old patrician republic of Genoa turned into a Ligurian Republic on the French model. At Rome the pope was deposed from his temporal power and a Roman Republic was established. In southern Italy a Neapolitan Republic, also called Parthenopean, was set up. In Switzerland at the same time, Swiss reformers cooperated with the French to create a new Helvetic Republic.

The Left Bank of the Rhine, in the atomistic Holy Roman Empire, was occupied by a great many German princes who now had to vacate. The treaty of Campo Formio provided that they be compensated by church territories in Germany east of the Rhine, and that France have a hand in the redistribution. The German princes turned greedy eyes on the German bishops and abbots, and the almost one thousand-year-old Holy Empire, hardly more than a solemn form since the Peace of Westphalia, sank to the level of a land rush or real estate speculation, while France became involved in the territorial reconstruction of Germany.

The Coup d'État of 1799: Bonaparte

After Fructidor the idea of maintaining the republic as a free or constitutional government was given up. There were more uprisings, more quashed elections, more purgings both to Left and Right. The Directory became a kind of ineffective dictatorship. It repudiated most of the assignats and the debt but failed to restore financial confidence or stability. Guerrilla activity flared up again in the Vendée and other parts of western France. The religious schism became more acute; the Directory took severe measures toward the refractory clergy.

Meanwhile Bonaparte waited for the situation to ripen. Returning from Italy a conquering hero, he was assigned to command the army in training to invade England. He concluded that invasion was premature and decided to strike indirectly at England, by threatening India in a spectacular invasion of Egypt. In 1798, outwitting the British fleet, he landed a French army at the mouth of the Nile. Egypt was part of the Ottoman Empire, and the French occupation of it alarmed the Russians, who had their own designs on the Near East. The Austrians objected to the French rearrangement of Germany. A year and a half after the treaty of Campo Formio, Austria, Russia, and Great Britain formed an alliance known as the Second Coalition. The French Republic was again involved in a general war. And the war went unfavorably, for in August 1798 the British fleet had cut off the French army in Egypt by winning the battle of the Nile (or Aboukir), and in 1799 Russian forces, under Marshal Suvorov, were operating as far west as Switzerland and north Italy, where the Cisalpine Republic went down in ruin.

General Bonaparte's opportunity had come. He left his army in Egypt and, again slipping through the British fleet, reappeared unexpectedly in France. He found that certain civilian leaders in the Directory were planning a change. They included Sieyès, of whom little had been heard since he wrote *What Is the Third*

Estate? ten years before, but who had sat in the Convention and voted for the death of Louis XVI. Sieyès' formula was now "confidence from below, authority from above"—what he now wanted of the people was acquiescence, and of the government, power to act. This group was looking about for a general, and their choice fell on the sensational young Bonaparte, who was still only thirty. Dictatorship by an army officer was repugnant to most republicans of the Five Hundred and the Ancients. Bonaparte, Sieyès, and their followers resorted to force, executing the coup d'état of Brumaire (November 9, 1799), in which armed soldiers drove the legislators from the chambers. They proclaimed a new form of the republic, which Bonaparte entitled the Consulate. It was headed by three consuls, with Bonaparte as the First Consul.

46. *The Authoritarian Republic: The Consulate,* *1799–1804*

The next chapter takes up the affairs of Europe as a whole in the time of Napoleon Bonaparte, the purpose at present being only to tell how he closed, in a way, the Revolution in France.

It happened that the French Republic, in falling into the hands of a general, fell also to a man of such remarkable talents as are often denominated genius. Bonaparte was a short dark man, of Mediterranean type, who would never have looked impressive in civilian clothing. His manners were rather coarse; he lost his temper, cheated at cards, and pinched people by the ear in a kind of formidable play—he was no "gentleman." A child of the Enlightenment and the Revolution, he was entirely emancipated not only from customary ideas but from moral scruples as well. He regarded the world as a flux to be formed by his own mind. He had an exalted belief in his own destinies, which became more mystical and exaggerated as the years went on. He claimed to follow his "star." His ideas of the good and the beautiful were rather blunt, but he was a man of extraordinary intellectual capacity, which impressed all with whom he came in contact. "Never speak unless you know you are the ablest man in the room," he once advised his stepson, on making him viceroy of Italy, a maxim which, if he followed it himself, still allowed him to do most of the talking. His interests ran to solid subjects, history, law, military science, public administration. His mind was tenacious and perfectly orderly; he once declared that it was like a chest of drawers, which he could open or close at will, forgetting any subject when its drawer was closed and finding it ready with all necessary detail when its drawer was opened. He had all the masterful qualities associated with leadership; he could dazzle and captivate those who had any inclination to follow him at all. Some of the most humane men of the day, including Goethe and Beethoven in Germany, and Lazare Carnot among the former revolutionary leaders, at first looked on him with high approval. He inspired confidence by his crisp speech, rapid decisions, and quick grasp of complex problems when they were newly presented to him. He was, or seemed, just what many Frenchmen were looking for after ten years of upheaval.

Under the Consulate France reverted to a form of enlightened despotism, and Bonaparte may be thought of as the last and most eminent of the enlightened despots. Despotic the new regime undoubtedly was from the start. Self-government through elected bodies was ruthlessly pushed aside. Bonaparte delighted in affirming the sovereignty of the people; but to his mind the people was a sovereign, like Voltaire's God, who somehow created the world but never thereafter interfered in it. He clearly saw that a government's authority was greater when it was held to represent the entire nation. In the weeks after Brumaire he assured himself of a popular mandate by devising a written constitution and submitting it to a general referendum or "plebiscite." The voters could take it—or nothing. They took it by a majority officially reported as 3,011,007 to 1,562.

The new constitution set up a make-believe of parliamentary institutions. It gave universal male suffrage, but the citizens merely chose "notables"; men on the lists of notables were then appointed by the government itself to public position. The notables had no powers of their own. They were merely available for appointment to office. They might sit in a Legislative Body, where they could neither initiate nor discuss legislation, but only mutely reject or enact it. There was also a Tribunate which discussed and deliberated but had no enacting powers. There was a Conservative Senate, which had rights of appointment of notables to office ("patronage" in American terms), and in which numerous storm-tossed regicides found a haven. The main agency in the new government was the Council of State, imitated from the Old Regime; it prepared the significant legislation, often under the presidency of the First Consul himself, who always gave the impression that he understood everything. The First Consul made all the decisions and ran the state. The regime did not openly represent anybody, and that was its strength, for it provoked the less opposition. In any case, the political machinery just described fell rapidly into disuse.

Bonaparte entrenched himself also by promising and obtaining peace. The military problem at the close of 1799, was much simplified by the attitude of the Russians, who in effect withdrew from the war with France. In the Italian theater Bonaparte had to deal only with the Austrians, whom he again defeated, by again crossing the Alps, at the battle of Marengo in June 1800. In February 1801 the Austrians signed the treaty of Lunéville, in which the terms of Campo Formio were confirmed. A year later, in March 1802, peace was made even with Britain.

Peace was made also at home. Bonaparte kept internal order, partly by a secret political police, but more especially through a powerful and centralized administrative machine, in which a "prefect," under direct orders of the minister of the interior, ruled firmly over each of the regional departments created by the Constituent Assembly. The new government put down the guerrillas in the west. Its laws and taxes were imposed on Brittany and the Vendée. Peasants there were no longer terrorized by marauding partisans. A new peace settled down on the factions left by the Revolution. Bonaparte offered a general amnesty and invited back to France, with a few exceptions, exiles of all stripes from the first aristocratic émigrés to the refugees and deportees of the republican coups d'état. Requiring only that they work for him and stop quarreling with each other, he picked reasonable men from all camps. His Second Consul was Cambacérès, a regicide of the Terror, his Third Consul Lebrun, who had been Maupeou's colleague in the days of Louis XV.[18] Fouché emerged as minister of police; he had been an Hébertist and extreme terrorist in 1793 and had done as much as

[18] See pp. 329–331.

any man to bring about the fall of Robespierre. Before 1789 he had been an obscure bourgeois professor of physics. Talleyrand appeared as minister of foreign affairs; he had spent the Terror in safe seclusion in the United States, and his principles, if he had any, were those of constitutional monarchy. Before 1789 he had been a bishop and was of an aristocratic lineage almost unbearably distinguished—no one who had not known the Old Regime, he once said, could realize how pleasant it had been. Men of this sort were now willing, for a few years beginning in 1800, to forget the past and work in common toward the future.

Disturbers of the new order the First Consul ruthlessly put down. Indeed, he concocted alarms to make himself more welcome as a pillar of order. On Christmas Eve, 1800, on the way to the opera, he was nearly killed by a bomb, or "infernal machine," as people then said. It had been laid by royalists, but Bonaparte represented it as the work of Jacobin conspiracy, being most afraid at the moment of some of the old republicans; and over a hundred former Jacobins were again deported. Contrariwise, in 1804, he greatly exaggerated certain royalist plots against him, invaded the independent state of Baden, and there arrested the Duke of Enghien, who was related to the Bourbons. Though he knew Enghien to be innocent, he had him shot. His purpose now was to please the old Jacobins by staining his own hands with Bourbon blood; Fouché and the regicides concluded that they were secure so long as Bonaparte was in power.

The Settlement with the Church; Other Reforms

For all but the most convinced royalists and republicans, reconciliation was made easier by the establishment of peace with the church. Bonaparte himself was a pure eighteenth-century rationalist. He regarded religion as a convenience. He advertised himself as a Muslim in Egypt, as a Catholic in France, and as a freethinker among the professors at the Institute in Paris. But a Catholic revival was in full swing, and he saw its importance. The refractory clergy were the spiritual force animating all forms of counterrevolution. "Fifty émigré bishops, paid by England," he once said, "lead the French clergy today. Their influence must be destroyed. For this we need the authority of the pope." Ignoring the horrified outcries of the old Jacobins, in 1801 he signed a concordat with the Vatican.

Both parties gained from the settlement. The autonomy of the prerevolutionary Gallican church came to an end. The pope received the right to depose French bishops, since before the schism could be healed both constitutional and refractory bishops had to be obliged to resign. The constitutional or pro-revolutionary clergy came under the discipline of the Holy See. Publicity of Catholic worship, in such forms as processions in the streets, was again allowed. Church seminaries were again permitted. But Bonaparte and the heirs of the Revolution gained even more. The pope, by signing the concordat, virtually recognized the Republic. The Vatican agreed to raise no question over the former tithes and the former church lands. The new owners of former church properties thus obtained clear titles. Nor was there any further question of Avignon, an enclave within France, formerly papal, annexed to France in 1791. Nor were the papal negotiators able to undermine religious toleration; all that Bonaparte would concede was a clause that was purely factual, and hence harmless, stating that Catholicism was the religion of the majority of Frenchmen. The clergy, in compensation for loss of their tithes and property, were assured of receiving salaries from the state. But Bonaparte, to dispel the notion of an established church, put Protestant ministers of all denominations on the state payroll also. He thus checkmated the Vatican on important points. At the same time, simply by signing an agreement with Rome, he disarmed the counterrevolution. It could no longer be said that the Republic was godless. Good relations did not, indeed, last very long, for Bonaparte and the papacy were soon at odds. But the terms of the concordat proved lasting.

With peace and order established, the constructive work of the Consulate turned to the fields of law and administration. The First Consul and his advisers combined what they conceived to be the best of the Revolution and of the Old Regime. The modern state took on clearer form. It was the reverse of everything feudal. All public authority was concentrated in paid agents of government, no person was held to be under any legal authority except that of the state, and the authority of government fell on all persons alike. There were no more estates, legal classes, privileges, local liberties, hereditary offices, guilds, or manors. Judges, officials, and army officers received specified salaries. Neither military commissions nor civil offices could be bought and sold. Citizens were to rise in government service purely according to their abilities.

This was the doctine of "careers open to talent"; it was what the bourgeoisie had wanted before the Revolution, and a few persons of quite humble birth profited also. For sons of the old aristocracy, it meant that pedigree was not enough; they must also show individual capacity to obtain employment. Qualification came to depend increasingly on education, and the secondary and higher schools were reorganized in these years, with a view to preparing young men for government service and the learned professions. Scholarships were provided, but it was mainly the upper middle class that benefited. Education, in fact, in France and in Europe generally, came to be an important determinant of social standing, with one system for those who could spend a dozen or more years at school, and another for boys who were to enter the work force at the age of twelve or fourteen.

Another deep demand of the French people, deeper than the demand for the vote, was for more reason, order, and economy in public finance and taxation. The Consulate gave these also. There were no tax exemptions because of birth, status, or special arrangement. Everyone was supposed to pay, so that no disgrace attached to payment, and there was less evasion. In principle these changes had been introduced in 1789; after 1799 they began to work. For the first time in ten years the government really collected the taxes that it levied and so could rationally plan its financial affairs. Order was introduced also into expenditure, and accounting methods were improved. There was no longer a haphazard assortment of different "funds," on which various officials drew independently and confidentially as they needed money, but a concentration of financial management in the treasury; and even in a kind of budget. The revolutionary uncertainties over the value of money were also ended. Because the Directory had shouldered the odium of repudiating the paper money and government debt, the Consulate was able to establish a sound currency and public credit. To assist in government financing, one of the banks of the Old Regime was revived and established as the Bank of France.

Like all enlightened despots, Bonaparte codified the laws, and of all law codes since the Romans the Napoleonic codes are the most famous. To the 300 legal systems of the Old Regime, and the mass of royal ordinances, were now added the thousands of laws enacted but seldom implemented by the revolutionary assemblies. Five codes emerged—the Civil Code (often called simply the Code Napoleon), the codes of civil and of criminal procedure, and the commercial and penal codes. The codes made France legally and judicially uniform. They assured legal equality; all French citizens had the same civil rights. They formulated the new law of property and set forth the law of contracts, debts, leases, stock companies, and similar matters in such a way as to create the legal framework for an economy of private enterprise. They repeated the ban of all previous regimes on organized labor unions and were severe with the individual workingman, his word not being acceptable in court against that of his employer—a significant departure from equality before the law. The criminal code was somewhat freer in giving the government the means to detect crime than in granting the individual the means of defense against legal charges. As for the family, the codes recognized civil marriage and divorce but left the wife with very restricted powers over property, and the father with extensive authority over minor children. The codes reflected much of French life under the Old Regime. They also set the character of France as it has been ever since, socially bourgeois, legally equalitarian, and administratively bureaucratic.

In France, with the Consulate, the Revolution was over. If its highest hopes had not been accomplished, the worst evils of the Old Regime had at least been cured. The beneficiaries of the Revolution felt secure. Even former aristocrats were rallying. The working-class movement, repeatedly frustrated under all the revolutionary regimes, now vanished from the political scene, to reappear as socialism thirty years later. What the Third Estate had most wanted in 1789 was now both codified and enforced, with the exception of parliamentary government, which after ten years of turmoil many people were temporarily willing to forgo. Moreover, in 1802, the French Republic was at peace with the papacy, Great Britain, and all Continental powers. It reached to the Rhine and had dependent republics in Holland and Italy. So popular was the First Consul that in 1802, by another plebiscite, he had himself elected consul for life. A new constitution, in 1804, again ratified by plebiscite, declared that "the government of the republic is entrusted to an emperor." The Consulate became the Empire, and Bonaparte emerged as Napoleon I, Emperor of the French.

But France, no longer revolutionary at home, was revolutionary outside its borders. Napoleon became a terror to the patricians of Europe. They called him the "Jacobin." And the France which he ruled, and used as his arsenal, was an incomparably formidable state. Even before the Revolution it had been the most populous in Europe, perhaps the most wealthy, in the front rank of scientific enterprise and intellectual leadership. Now all the old barriers of privilege, tax exemption, localism, caste exclusiveness, and routine-mindedness had disappeared. The new France could tap the wealth of its citizens and put able men into position without inquiring into their origins. Every private, boasted Napoleon, carried a marshal's baton in his knapsack. The French looked with disdain on their caste-ridden adversaries. The principle of civic equality proved not only to have the appeal of justice, but also to be politically useful, and the resources of France were hurled against Europe with a force which for many years nothing could check.

A REVOLUTIONARY ERA

The years from the American Revolution through the French Revolution and the empire of Napoleon marked a major turning point for both Europe and much of the rest of the world. The old European colonial systems came to an end with the establishment of the United States, the slave revolt in Haiti and independence of that country, the first steps in the creation of the Spanish-American republics, and the separation of Brazil from Portugal. These were also the years of the Industrial Revolution in Great Britain, metaphorically so called, since industrialization was a gradual and sporadic process not always perceptible to contemporaries.

The changes effected by the American and French Revolutions were mainly in new conceptions of liberty and equality, as reflected in constitutions, law, and personal status. The Americans expressed ideas that were well known in Europe, and so had an influence there. In France the Revolution in some ways only accelerated long continuing trends. It "abolished feudalism," but feudalism had been declining for centuries. It consolidated the modern state by professionalizing its civil service, army, law courts, schools, and tax-collecting machinery, but kings had long worked in these directions. It improved the national trading area by overcoming provincial barriers and introducing uniform law codes, as well as uniform weights and measures in the metric system. Monarchies had made similar efforts. In general, a middle class that had been growing for centuries achieved a victory over older vested interests.

But the Revolution was also innovative. Liberty and the possession of rights were not new in Europe, but hitherto they had depended on one's social class or religion, or on agreements between a ruler and a particular group to which one belonged. Now liberty meant liberty for the individual, not for this or that group. Equality meant equality of civil rights irrespective of social class or religion, and in France even of race. Civil rights included freedom from abuse by government, freedom of speech, religion, and association, and the right to own property. Property itself became more "private," i.e., disentangled from the remnants of lordship. Representative government, which had long meant merely consultation with social estates (such as church, nobility, and towns), now meant a system in which individual voters chose legislators and officials by numerical count for limited terms of office. The word "citizen" became a hallmark of the new era. Where formerly it had meant someone sharing in the liberties of a town, it now meant someone participating in the sovereignty of the nation, which protected individual rights. The most famous document of the era was the French Declaration of the Rights of Man and Citizen of 1789, which proclaimed both national sovereignty and what are now called human and civil rights.

At left, above: Lexington green, near Boston, where "the embattled farmers stood, and fired the shot heard round the world." In the picture, local militia meet a detachment of the British army in the first armed clash of the American Revolution in April 1775.

Below: The battle of Fleurus in Belgium in June 1794. This defeat of the Austrians frustrated intervention against the French Revolution by an alliance of European powers. It opened the way for twenty years of French domination of Europe, first by the French Republic, then by the Napoleonic Empire.

The battle of Fleurus also saw the first use of an aircraft in warfare. The balloon, invented in France a few years before, was one of the scientific innovations that the revolutionary government tried to turn to practical use. In the picture an officer observes the battlefield through a telescope as men on the ground hold the balloon in place. Probably the results were disappointing, since balloons were not thereafter used by either side.

COMMON SENSE;

ADDRESSED TO THE

INHABITANTS

OF

AMERICA,

On the following interesting

SUBJECTS.

I. Of the Origin and Design of Government in general, with concise Remarks on the English Constitution.

II. Of Monarchy and Hereditary Succession.

III. Thoughts on the present State of American Affairs.

IV. Of the present Ability of America, with some miscellaneous Reflections.

Man knows no Master save creating HEAVEN,
Or those whom choice and common good ordain.
THOMSON.

PHILADELPHIA;
Printed, and Sold, by R. BELL, in Third-Street.

MDCCLXXVI.

Thomas Paine, author of both books shown here, took part in both the American and French Revolutions and in the movement for reform of Parliament in Great Britain. Born in England, he arrived in Philadelphia in 1774 with recommendations from Benjamin Franklin, and published his Common Sense *anonymously after armed conflict had begun. Widely read, it helped to persuade Americans to fight for complete independence from Britain.*

RIGHTS OF MAN:

BEING AN

ANSWER to Mr. BURKE's ATTACK

ON THE

FRENCH REVOLUTION.

BY

THOMAS PAINE,

SECRETARY FOR FOREIGN AFFAIRS TO CONGRESS IN THE
AMERICAN WAR, AND
AUTHOR OF THE WORK INTITLED " *COMMON SENSE.*"

LONDON:

PRINTED FOR J. S. JORDAN, No. 166, FLEET-STREET.
MDCCXCI.

Paine returned to England, and when Edmund Burke denounced the French Revolution wrote the Rights of Man *in reply. In it he castigated the British political system while defending the first French constitution of 1789–1791. In danger of arrest in England, he fled to France, where he became an honorary citizen and was elected to the National Convention in 1792. By the end of 1792 more than fifty editions of the* Rights of Man *had appeared in London, Philadelphia, Dublin, and elsewhere, and it had been translated into French, German, and Dutch.*

Convoked for the first time in 175 years, the Estates General of France met in a large hall at Versailles in May 1789. The picture shows Louis XVI seated on his throne, with deputies of the clergy seated at his right (the reader's left), those of the nobility, at his left, and those of the Third Estate, facing him at the other end of the hall. The Third Estate, inviting the others to join it, converted itself into a National Assembly, which took an oath to write a new constitution for France.

At right, above: The three men at an anvil are a noble, a cleric, and a commoner hammering out a new constitution together. The idea at the beginning of the Revolution was for the three estates to "fraternize" in the "nation."

Rioting in Paris, prompted by food shortages, was politicized when Louis XVI assembled troops with the obvious intention of dissolving the National Assembly. The result was the capture of the Bastille, which became a symbol of repression. The National Assembly continued to sit for another two years.

tôt tôt tôt
battez chaud
tôt tôt tôt
bon Courage
il faut avoir coeur a l'ouvrage.

Kings fared badly in this revolutionary era, although the main revolutionary thrust was against the "privileged classes"—nobilities, aristocracies, oligarchies, patriciates, hereditary office holders, and the prelates of established churches.

At left, above: Parisians pull down a statue of Louis XIV (1643–1715) three years after the Revolution began. At left, below: a similar incident in New York in 1776, as a statue of King George is pulled down at the beginning of the American Revolution.

With the progress of revolutionary ideas, internal conflict, and foreign war, the French Revolution became more radical and violent. The guillotine, first adopted as a more humane way of inflicting capital punishment, was put to work against enemies of the Revolution. Robespierre himself and four others were denounced as conspirators against liberty. The picture below illustrates their death in July 1794.

The French Revolution (like the American) was financed by paper money. The notes were called assignats *because they were "assigned" to, or secured by, real estate confiscated during the Revolution, mostly from the church. Inflation rose rapidly after price controls were abolished late in 1794, and with the continuing war costs and uncertainty as to the government's future. Even notes of denominations as high as 10,000* livres, *as shown in the picture, became worthless. The* assignats *were abolished in 1796, after which France enjoyed a sound currency for many years.*

Since the paper money could be used to buy land and buildings on advantageous terms, it served as a mechanism by which a large amount of real property passed into individual private ownership. The more prosperous peasants and middle classes in the towns especially benefited.

As the Republic was unable to stabilize itself it was taken over by a young republican general, Napoleon Bonaparte. In his first years in power he consolidated some of the changes made in the first years of the Revolution; then in 1804 he proclaimed himself Emperor. Repeatedly winning battles against the Austrians, Prussians, and Russians, he developed ever more grandiose ideas of imperial greatness. This painting was executed in 1806 by the famous artist Jacques-Louis David, himself an old revolutionary of 1793, as an idealization of the young republican hero who had crossed the Alps in 1800 to win the battle of Marengo.

Napoleon, having defeated all the powers opposed to him and to the French Revolution—except England—conceived of Paris as the capital of a more modern continent of Europe, to be symbolized by evoking the grandeur of ancient Rome. The following pages show architectural monuments to this vision which still remain among the attractions of Paris.

At left: The Vendôme column, modeled on the second-century column of Trajan in Rome. The bas-reliefs were molded from the bronze of cannon captured at the battle of Austerlitz. Figures of soldiers climb along a spiral ascending the column, as in the column of Trajan. A statue of Napoleon was put at the top. It was taken down in 1814, but a later copy replaced it and still stands.

Below: The church of the Madeleine. Construction had begun in 1764, with the intention of building a church, but by 1800 hardly more than the foundations had been laid. Some then talked of using the structure for a utilitarian purpose, such as a stock exchange, but Napoleon decided to turn it into a Temple of Glory, and as such it was completed in 1810. It became a church after Napoleon's fall in 1814.

The Arch of Triumph was designed and building begun in 1806, but it was not completed until 1836. It is a monument to the Republic as well as to the Empire, with the continuous band of bas-reliefs above the curve of the arch representing 172 battles since Valmy in 1792. The mammoth edifice is located in a great open space, the Etoile (the ''star''), first projected by city planners as long ago as Louis XIV. Radiating from this central point are a dozen magnificent avenues, the Champs Elysées to the east and the Avenue de la Grande Armée to the west. The Grand Army was the term used by Napoleon at the height of his power, when his forces included not only French but also Italian, German, and Polish contingents.

The completion of the arch in 1836 signified also the growth of the ''Napoleonic legend,'' when those dissatisfied with the course of events after his fall began to glorify his memory.

X.
NAPOLEONIC
EUROPE

THE REPERCUSSIONS of the French Revolution had been felt throughout Europe since the fall of the Bastille, and even more definitely after the outbreak of war in 1792 and the ensuing victories of the republican armies. They became even more evident after the republican General Bonaparte turned into Napoleon I, Emperor of the French, King of Italy, and Protector of the Confederation of the Rhine. Napoleon came nearer than anyone has ever come to imposing a political unity on the European continent. Of his ascendancy of fifteen years two stories are to be told. One is a story of international relations, reflecting the diverse interests of the contending states of Europe. The other is the story of internal development of the European peoples. The French impact, though based on military success, represented more than mere forcible subjugation. Innovations of a kind made in France by revolution were brought to other countries by administrative decree. There were, for several years, Germans, Italians, Dutchmen, and Poles who worked with the French emperor to introduce the changes that he demanded, and which they themselves often desired. In Prussia it was resistance to Napoleon that gave the incentive to internal reorganization. Whether by collaboration or resistance, Europe was transformed.

It is convenient to think of the fighting from 1792 to 1814 as a "world war," as indeed it was, affecting not only all of Europe but places as remote as Spanish America, where the wars of independence began, or the interior of North America, where the United States purchased Louisiana in 1803 and attempted a conquest

Chapter Emblem: An Italian cameo of 1810, showing the idealized head of Napoleon crowned with laurels as lawgiver and culture hero.

of Canada in 1812. But it is important to realize that this world war was actually a series of wars, most of them quite short, sharp, and distinct. Only Great Britain remained continually at war with France, except for about a year of peace in 1802–1803. Never were the four great powers, Britain, Austria, Russia, and Prussia, simultaneously in the field against France until 1813.

The history of the Napoleonic period would be much simpler if the European governments had fought merely to protect themselves against the aggressive French. Each, however, in its way, was as dynamic and expansive as Napoleon himself. For some generations Great Britain had been building a commercial empire, Russia pushing upon Poland and Turkey, Prussia consolidating its territories and striving for leadership in north Germany. Austria was less aggressive, being somewhat passively preoccupied by the rise of Prussia and Russia, but the Austrians were not without dreams of ascendancy in Germany, the Balkans, and the Adriatic. None of these ambitions ceased during the Napoleonic years. Governments, in pursuit of their own aims, were quite as willing to ally with Napoleon as to fight him. Only gradually, and under repeated provocation, did they conclude that their main interest was to dispose of the French emperor entirely.

47. The Formation of the French Imperial System

The Dissolution of the First and Second Coalitions, 1792–1802

The conflicting purposes of the powers had been apparent from the beginning. Leopold of Austria, in issuing the Declaration of Pillnitz in 1791, had believed a general European coalition against France to be impossible. When war began in 1792, the Austrians and Prussians kept their main forces in eastern Europe, more afraid of each other and of Russia, in the matter of Poland, than of the French revolutionary republic. Indeed, the main accomplishment of the First Coalition was the extermination of the Polish state.[1]

In 1795 the French broke up the coalition. The British withdrew their army from the Continent. The Prussians made a separate peace; the French bought them off by recognizing them as "protectors" of Germany north of the river Main. Spain also made a separate peace in 1795. The world saw the spectacle, outrageous to all ideology or principle, of an alliance between Bourbon Spain and the republic which had guillotined Louis XVI and kept Louis XVIII from his monarchic rights. Spain simply reverted to the eighteenth-century pattern, in allying with France because of hostility to Great Britain, whose possession of Gibraltar, naval influence in the Mediterranean, and attitude toward the Spanish empire were disquieting to the Spanish government. When Austria signed the peace of Campo Formio in 1797 the First Coalition was totally dissipated, only British naval forces remaining engaged with the French.[2]

The Second Coalition of 1799 fared no better. After the British fleet defeated the French at the battle of the Nile, cutting off the French army in Egypt, the

---

[1] See pp. 246–249, 384–385.
[2] See p. 395.

Russians saw their ambitions in the Mediterranean blocked mainly by the British, and withdrew Suvorov's army from western Europe. The acceptance by Austria of the peace of Lunéville in 1801 dissolved the Second Coalition. In 1802 Great Britain signed the peace of Amiens. For the only time between 1792 and 1814 no European power was at war with another—though the British, to be sure, were at war with some Indian princes, the Russians with some peoples in the Caucasus and the French with Toussaint l'Ouverture, the black ex-slave who was attempting to found an independent republic in Haiti.

Peace Interim, 1802–1803

Never had a peace been so advantageous to France as the peace of 1802. But Bonaparte gave it no chance. He used peace as he did war to advance his interests. He dispatched a sizable army to Haiti, ostensibly to win back a rebellious French colony, but with the further thought (since Louisiana had been ceded back by Spain to France in 1800) of reviving the French colonial empire in America. He reorganized the Cisalpine Republic into an "Italian" Republic with himself as president. He reorganized the Helvetic Republic, making himself "mediator" of the Confederation of Switzerland. He reorganized Germany; that is to say, he and his agents closely watched the rearrangement of territory which the Germans themselves had been carrying out since 1797.

By the treaty of Campo Formio,[3] it will be recalled, German princes of the Left Bank of the Rhine, expropriated by the annexation of their dominions to the French Republic, were to receive new territories on the Right Bank. The result was a scramble called by patriotic German historians the "shame of the princes." The German rulers, far from opposing Bonaparte or upholding any national interests, competed desperately for the absorption of German territory, each bribing and fawning upon the French (Talleyrand made over 10,000,000 francs in the process) to win French support against other Germans. The Holy Roman Empire was fatally mauled by the Germans themselves. Most of its ecclesiastical principalities and forty-five out of its fifty-one free cities disappeared, annexed by their larger neighbors. The number of states in the Holy Empire was greatly reduced, especially of the Catholic states, so that it could be foreseen that no Catholic Habsburg would again be elected emperor. Prussia, Bavaria, Württemberg, and Baden consolidated and enlarged themselves. These arrangements were ratified in February 1803 by the diet of the Empire. The enlarged German states now depended on Bonaparte for the maintenance of their new position.

Formation of the Third Coalition in 1805

Britain and France went to war again in 1803. Bonaparte, his communications with America menaced by the British navy, and his army in Haiti decimated by disease and by rebellious blacks, suspended his ideas for re-creating an American empire and sold Louisiana to the United States. Great Britain began to seek allies for a Third Coalition. In May 1804 Napoleon pronounced himself Emperor of the French to assure the hereditary permanency of his system, though he had no son.

[3] See p. 395.

Francis II of Austria, seeing the ruin of the Holy Roman Empire, promulgated the Austrian Empire in August 1804. He thus advanced the long process of integrating the Danubian monarchy. In 1805 Austria signed an alliance with Great Britain. The Third Coalition was completed by the accession of the Russian Tsar Alexander I, who, after Napoleon himself, was to become the most considerable figure on the European stage.

Alexander was the grandson of Catherine the Great, educated by her to be a kind of enlightened despot on the eighteenth-century model.[4] The Swiss tutor of his boyhood, La Harpe, later turned up as a pro-French revolutionary in the Helvetic Republic of 1798. Alexander became tsar in 1801, at the age of twenty-four, through a palace revolution which implicated him in the murder of his father Paul. He still corresponded with La Harpe, and he surrounded himself with a circle of liberal and zealous young men of various nationalities, of whom the most prominent was a Polish youth, Czartoryski. Alexander regarded the still recent partitions of Poland as a crime.[5] He wished to restore the unity of Poland with himself as its constitutional king. In Germany many who had first warmed to the French Revolution, but had been disillusioned, began to hail the new liberal tsar as the protector of Germany and hope of the future. Alexander conceived of himself as a rival to Napoleon in guiding the destinies of Europe in an age of change. Moralistic and self-righteous, he puzzled and disturbed the statesmen of Europe, who generally saw, behind his humane and republican utterances, either an enthroned leader of all the "Jacobins" of Europe or the familiar specter of Russian aggrandizement.

Yet Alexander, more than his contemporaries, formed a conception of international collective security and the indivisibility of peace. He was shocked when Napoleon in 1804, in order to seize the duke of Enghien, rudely violated the sovereignty of Baden.[6] He declared that the issue in Europe was clearly between law and force—between an international society in which the rights of each member were secured by international agreement and organization, and a society in which all trembled before the rule of cynicism and conquest embodied in the French usurper.

Alexander was therefore ready to enter a Third Coalition with Great Britain. Picturing himself as a future arbiter of central Europe, and with secret designs on the Ottoman Empire and the Mediterranean, he signed a treaty with England in April 1805. The British agreed to pay Russia £1,250,000 for each 100,000 soldiers that the Russians raised.

The Third Coalition, 1805–1807: The Peace of Tilsit

Napoleon meanwhile, since the resumption of hostilities in 1803, had been making preparations to invade England. He concentrated large forces on the Channel coast, together with thousands of boats and barges, in which he gave the troops amphibious training in embarkation and debarkation. He reasoned that if his own fleet could divert or cripple the British fleet for a few days he could place enough

---

[4] See p. 341.
[5] See pp. 245–249, 384–385.
[6] See p. 400.

soldiers in the defenseless island to force its capitulation. The British, sensing mortal danger, lined their coasts with lookouts and signal beacons and set to drilling a home guard. Their main defense was twofold: the Austro-Russian armies and the British fleet under Lord Nelson. The Russian and Austrian armies moved westward in the summer of 1805. In August Napoleon relieved the pressure upon England, shifting seven army corps from the Channel to the upper Danube. On October 15 he surrounded an Austrian force of 50,000 men at Ulm in Bavaria, forcing it to surrender without resistance. On October 21 Lord Nelson, off Cape Trafalgar on the Spanish coast, caught and annihilated the main body of the combined fleets of France and Spain.

The battle of Trafalgar established the supremacy of the British navy for over a century—but only on the proviso that Napoleon be prevented from controlling the bulk of Europe, which would furnish an ample base for eventual construction of a greater navy than the British. And to control Europe was precisely what Napoleon proceeded to do. Moving east from Ulm he came upon the Russian and Austrian armies in Moravia, where on December 2 he won the great victory of Austerlitz. The broken Russian army withdrew into Poland, and Austria made peace. By the treaty of Pressburg Napoleon took Venetia from the Austrians, to whom he had given it in 1797, and annexed it to his kingdom of Italy (the former Cisalpine and Italian Republic), which now included a good deal of Italy north of Rome. Venice and Trieste soon resounded with the hammers of shipwrights rebuilding the Napoleonic fleet. In Germany, early in 1806, the French emperor raised Bavaria and Württemberg to the stature of kingdoms and Baden to a grand duchy. The Holy Roman Empire was finally, formally, and irrevocably dissolved. In its place Napoleon began to gather his German client states into a new kind of Germanic federation, the Confederation of the Rhine, of which he made himself the "protector."

Prussia, at peace with France for ten years, had declined to join the Third Coalition. But as Napoleon's program for controlling Germany became clear after Austerlitz the war party in Prussia became irresistible, and the Prussian government, outwitted and distraught, went to war with the French unaided and alone. The French smashed the famous Prussian army at the battles of Jena and Auerstädt in October 1806. The French cavalry galloped all over north Germany unopposed. The Prussian king and his government took refuge in the east, at Königsberg, where the tsar and the re-forming Russian army might protect them. But the terrible Corsican pursued the Russians also. Marching through western Poland and into East Prussia, he met the Russian army first at the sanguinary but indecisive battle of Eylau and then defeated it on June 14, 1807, at Friedland. Alexander I was unwilling to retreat into Russia. He was unsure of his own resources; if the country were invaded there might be a revolt of the nobles or even of the serfs—for people still remembered Pugachev's rebellion.[7] He feared also merely playing the game of the British. He put aside his war aims of 1804 and signified his willingness to negotiate with Napoleon. The Third Coalition had gone the way of the two before it.

The Emperor of the French and the Autocrat of All the Russias met privately on a raft in the Niemen River, not far from the border between Prussia and

[7] See pp. 337–339.

Russia, the very easternmost frontier of civilized Europe, as the triumphant Napoleon gleefully imagined it. The hapless Prussian king, Frederick William III, paced nervously on the bank. Bonaparte turned all his charm upon Alexander, denouncing England as the author of all the troubles of Europe and captivating him by flights of Latin imagination, in which he set before Alexander a boundless destiny as Emperor of the East, intimating that his future lay toward Turkey, Persia, Afghanistan, and India. The result of their conversations was the treaty of Tilsit of July 1807, in many ways the high point of Napoleon's success. The French and Russian empires became allies, mainly against Great Britain. Ostensibly this alliance lasted for five years. Alexander accepted Napoleon as a kind of Emperor of the West. As for Prussia, Napoleon continued to occupy Berlin with his troops, and he took away all Prussian territories west of the Elbe, combining them with others taken from Hanover to make a new kingdom of Westphalia, which became part of his Confederation of the Rhine.

The Continental System and the War in Spain

Hardly had the "peace of the continent" been reestablished, on the foundation of a Franco-Russian alliance, when Napoleon began to have serious trouble. He was bent on subduing the British who, secure in their island, seemed beyond his reach. Since the French naval disaster at Trafalgar, there was no possibility of invading England in the foreseeable future. Napoleon therefore turned to economic warfare. He would fight sea power with land power, using his political control of the Continent to shut out British goods and shipping from all European ports. He would destroy the British trade in exports to Europe, both exports of British products and the profitable British reexport of goods from America and Asia. Thereby, he hoped, he would ruin British commercial firms and cause a violent business depression, marked by overloaded warehouses, unemployment, runs on the banks, a fall of the currency, rising prices, and revolutionary agitation. The British government, which would simultaneously be losing revenues from its customs duties, would thus find itself unable to carry the enormous national debt, or to borrow additional funds from its subjects, or to continue its financial subsidies to the military powers of Europe. At Berlin, in 1806, after the battle of Jena, Napoleon issued the Berlin Decree, forbidding the importation of British goods into any part of Europe allied with or dependent on himself. He thus formally established the Continental System.

To make the Continental System effective Napoleon believed that it must extend to all continental Europe without exception. By the treaty of Tilsit, in 1807, he required both Russia and Prussia to adhere to it. They agreed to exclude all British goods; in fact, in the following months Russia, Prussia, and Austria all declared war on Great Britain. Napoleon then ordered two neutral states, Denmark and Portugal, to adhere. Denmark was an important entrepôt for all central Europe, and the British, fearing Danish compliance, dispatched a fleet to Copenhagen, bombarded the city for four days, and took captive the Danish fleet. The outraged Danes allied with Napoleon and joined the Continental System. Portugal, long a satellite of Britain, refused compliance; Napoleon invaded it. To control the whole European coastline from St. Petersburg around to Trieste he now had only to control the ports of Spain. By a series of deceptions he got both the Bourbon Charles IV and his son Ferdinand to abdicate the Spanish throne. He made his brother Joseph king of Spain in 1808 and reinforced him with a large French army.

He thus involved himself in an entanglement from which he never escaped. The Spanish regarded the Napoleonic soldiers as godless villains who desecrated churches. Fierce guerrillas took the field. Cruelties of one side were answered by atrocities of the other. The British sent an expeditionary force of their small regular army, eventually under the Duke of Wellington, to sustain the Spanish guerrillas; the resulting Peninsular War dragged on for five years. But from the beginning the affair went badly for Napoleon. In July 1808 a French general, for the first time since the Revolution, surrendered an army corps, without fighting, by the capitulation at Baylen. In August another French force surrendered to the British army in Portugal. And these events raised hopes in the rest of Europe. An anti-French movement swept over Germany. It was felt strongly in Austria, where the Habsburg government, undaunted by three defeats, and hoping to lead a general German national resistance, prepared for a fourth time since 1792 to go to war with France.

The Austrian War of Liberation, 1809

Napoleon summoned a general congress which met at Erfurt in Saxony in September 1808. His main purpose was to talk with his ally of a year, Alexander; but he assembled numerous dependent monarchs as well, by whose presence he hoped to overawe the tsar. He even had Talma, the leading actor of the day, play in the theater of Erfurt before "a parterre of kings." Alexander was unimpressed. He was hurt in a sensitive spot because Napoleon, a few months before, had made moves to re-create a Polish state, setting up what was called the Grand Duchy of Warsaw. He had found Napoleon unwilling, despite the grandoise language of Tilsit, really to support his expansion into the Balkans. In addition, Alexander was taken aside by Talleyrand, Napoleon's foreign minister. Talleyrand had concluded that Napoleon was overreaching himself and said so confidentially to the tsar, advising him to wait. Talleyrand thus acted as a traitor, betraying the man whom he ostensibly served, and preparing a safe place for himself in the event of Napoleon's fall; but he acted also as an aristocrat of the prenationalistic Old Regime, seeing his own country as only one part of the whole of Europe, believing a balance among the several parts to be necessary, and holding that peace would be possible only when the exaggerated position of French power should be reduced. For France and Russia, the two strongest states, to combine against all other states was contrary to all principles of the older diplomacy.[8]

Austria proclaimed a war of liberation in April 1809. Napoleon advanced rapidly along the familiar route to Vienna. The German princes, indebted to the French, declined to join in a general German war against him. Alexander stood watchfully on the sidelines. Napoleon won the battle of Wagram in July. In October Austria made peace. The short war of 1809 was over. The Danubian monarchy, by no means as fragile as it seemed, survived a fourth defeat at the hands of the French without internal revolution or disloyalty to the Habsburg

[8] See pp. 162–163.

house. From it, in punishment, Napoleon took considerable portions of its territory. Part of Austrian Poland was used to enlarge Napoleon's Grand Duchy of Warsaw, and parts of Dalmatia, Slovenia, and Croatia, on the south, were erected into a new creation which Napoleon called the Illyrian Provinces.[9]

Napoleon at His Peak, 1809–1811

The next two years saw the Napoleonic empire at its peak. In Austria after the defeat of 1809 the conduct of foreign affairs fell to a man who was to retain it for forty years. His name was Clemens von Metternich. He was a German from west of the Rhine, whose ancestral territories had been annexed to the French Republic, but he had entered the Austrian service and even married the granddaughter of Kaunitz,[10] the old model of diplomatic savoir-faire, of which Metternich now became a model himself. Austria had been repeatedly humiliated and even partitioned by Napoleon, most of all in the treaty of 1809. But Metternich was not a man to conduct diplomacy by grudges. Believing that Russia was the really permanent problem for a state situated in the Danube valley, Metternich thought it wise to renew good relations with France. He was quite willing to go along with Napoleon, whom he knew personally, having been Austrian ambassador to Paris before the short war of 1809.

The French emperor, who in 1809 was exactly forty, was increasingly concerned by the fact that he was childless. He had made an empire which he pronounced hereditary. Yet he had no son. Between him and his wife Josephine whom he had married in youth, and who was six years his senior, there had long since ceased to be affection or even fidelity on either side. He divorced her in 1809, though since she had two children by a first husband she naturally protested that Napoleon's childlessness was not her fault. He intended to marry a younger woman who might bear him offspring. He intended also to make a spectacular marriage, to extort for himself, a self-made Corsican army officer, the highest and most exclusive recognition that aristocratic Europe could bestow. He debated between Habsburgs and Romanovs, between an archduchess and a grand duchess. Tactful inquiries at St. Petersburg concerning the availability of Alexander's sister were tactfully rebuffed; the tsar intimated that his mother would never allow it. The Russian alliance again showed its limitations. Napoleon was thrown into the arms of Metternich—and of Marie Louise, the eighteen-year-old daughter of the Austrian emperor and niece of another "Austrian woman," Marie Antoinette. They were married in 1810. In a year she bore him a son, whom he entitled the King of Rome.

Napoleon assumed ever more pompous airs of imperial majesty. He was now, by marriage, the nephew of Louis XVI. He showed more consideration to French noblemen of the Old Regime—only they, he said, knew really how to serve. He surrounded himself with a newly made hereditary Napoleonic nobility, hoping that the new families, as time went on, would bind their own fortunes to the house of Bonaparte. The marshals became dukes and princes, Talleyrand the Prince of Benevento, and the bourgeois Fouché, an Hébertist of '93, and more

---

[9] See map, p. 427.
[10] See pp. 279, 331.

latterly a police official, was now solemnly addressed as the Duke of Otranto. In foreign affairs also the cycle had been run. With one significant exception all the powers of the successive coalitions were allied with the French, and the Son of the Revolution now gravely referred to the emperor of Austria as "my father."

48. The Grand Empire: Spread of the Revolution

The Organization of the Napoleonic Empire

Territorially Napoleon's influence enjoyed its farthest reach in 1810 and 1811, when it comprehended the entire European mainland except the Balkan peninsula. The Napoleonic domain was in two parts. Its core was the French empire; then came thick layers of dependent states, which together with France comprised the Grand Empire. In addition, to the north and east were the "allied states" under their traditional governments—the three great powers, Prussia, Austria, and Russia, and also Denmark and Sweden. The allied states were at war with Great Britain, though not engaged in positive hostilities; their populations were supposed to do without British goods under the Continental System, but otherwise Napoleon had no direct lawful influence upon their internal affairs.

The French empire, as successor to the French Republic, included Belgium and the Left Bank of the Rhine.[11] In addition, by 1810, it had developed two appendages which on a map looked like tentacles outstretched from it. When he proclaimed France an empire, and turned its dependent republics into kingdoms, Napoleon had set up his brother Louis as king of Holland; but Louis had shown such a tendency to ingratiate himself with the Dutch, and such a willingness to let Dutch businessmen trade secretly with the British, that Napoleon dethroned him and incorporated Holland into the French empire. In his endless war upon British goods he found it useful to exert more direct control over the ports of Bremen, Hamburg, Lübeck, Genoa, and Leghorn; he therefore annexed directly to the French empire the German coast as far as the western Baltic, and the Italian coast far enough to include Rome. Rome he desired for its imperial rather than its commercial value. Harking back to traditions as old as Charlemagne, he considered Rome the second city of his empire and entitled his son the "King of Rome"; and when Pope Pius VII protested, Napoleon took him prisoner and interned him in France. The whole French empire, from Lübeck to Rome, was governed directly by departmental prefects who reported to Paris, and the eighty-three departments of France, created by the Constituent Assembly, had risen in 1810 to a hundred and thirty.

The dependent states, forming with France the Grand Empire, were of different kinds. The Swiss federation remained republican in form. The Illyrian Provinces, which included Trieste and the Dalmatian coast, were administered in their brief two years almost like departments of France. In Poland, since the Russians objected to a revived kingdom of Poland, Napoleon called his creation the Grand Duchy of Warsaw. Among the most important of the dependent states in the

[11] See pp. 384, 393–394, 395–397.

Grand Empire were the German states organized into the Confederation of the Rhine. Too modestly named, the Confederation included all Germany between what the French annexed on the west and what Prussia and Austria retained on the east. It was a league of all the German princes in this region who were regarded as sovereign, and who now numbered only about twenty, the most important being the four newly made kings—of Saxony, Bavaria, Württemberg, and Westphalia. Westphalia was an entirely new and synthetic state, made up of Hanoverian and Prussian territories and of various atoms of the old Germany. Its king was Napoleon's youngest brother Jerome.

For Napoleon used his family as a means of rule. The Corsican clan became the Bonaparte dynasty. His brother Joseph from 1804 to 1808 functioned as king of Naples and after 1808 as king of Spain. Louis Bonaparte was for six years king of Holland, Jerome was king of Westphalia. Sister Caroline became queen of Naples after brother Joseph's transfer to Spain; for Napoleon, running out of brothers (having quarreled with his remaining brother Lucien), gave the throne of Naples to his brother-in-law, Joachim Murat, a madcap cavalry officer who was Caroline's husband. In the "Kingdom of Italy," which in 1810 included Lombardy, Venetia, and most of the former papal states, Napoleon himself retained the title of king, but set up his stepson, Eugene Beauharnais (Josephine's son) as viceroy. "Uncle Joseph," Napoleon's mother's brother, became Cardinal Fesch. The mother of the Bonapartes, Letitia, who had brought up all these children under very different circumstances in Corsica, was suitably installed at the imperial court as Madame Mère. According to legend she kept repeating to herself, "If only it lasts!"; she outlived Napoleon by fifteen years.

Napoleon and the Spread of the Revolution

In all the states of the Grand Empire the same course of events tended to repeat itself. First came the stage of military conquest and occupation by French troops. Then came the establishment of a native satellite government with the support of local persons who were willing to collaborate with the French and who helped in the drafting of a constitution specifying the powers of the new government and

NAPOLEONIC EUROPE, 1810

Napoleon extended the sphere of French power well beyond the republican expansion of 1798–1799. (See map, p. 396.) By 1810 he dominated the whole continent except Portugal and the Balkan peninsula. Russia, Prussia, and Austria had been forced into alliance with him. He made his brothers kings of Spain, Holland, and Westphalia, his brother-in-law king of Naples, and his stepson viceroy of the kingdom of Italy. He gave the title of king to the German rulers of Bavaria, Württemberg, and Saxony, each of which absorbed smaller German states, while becoming members of Napoleon's Confederation of the Rhine. The old Holy Roman Empire disappeared. In Poland Napoleon, supported by Polish nationalists, undid the partitions of the 1790s by setting up the Grand Duchy of Warsaw.

British troops were fighting in Portugal in 1810, and the British fleet controlled all the islands. To counteract British influence Napoleon extended the borders of the French empire to include the kingdom of Holland and the German cities of Bremen, Hamburg, and Lübeck, and to reach along the Italian coast to a point beyond Rome.

Inset map:

0   100   200 miles

Moscow
Borodino
Riga
COURLAND   Vitebsk
Vilna   Smolensk
Kovno   Borisov
Tilsit
gsberg   RUSSIAN EMPIRE
Brest-Litovsk

**Napoleon's Russian Campaign
June to December, 1812**

Main map labels:

FINLAND

St. Petersburg

NORWAY

SWEDEN

ESTONIA

Stockholm

LIVONIA

SCOTLAND

KINGDOM OF DENMARK
AND NORWAY

COURLAND

BALTIC SEA

Edinburgh

Copenhagen

Memel
Tilsit Niemen
Königsberg Friedland Vilna
Eylau

IRELAND

NORTH SEA

DENMARK

GREAT
BRITAIN

SWEDISH
POMERANIA
Danzig

RUSSIA

HELIGOLAND
(Britain)

Lübeck
Hamburg

MECKLEN-
BURG

PRUSSIA

ENGLAND

KINGDOM OF
HOLLAND

Bremen

Berlin

Posen

Warsaw Brest-Litovsk

Amsterdam

Elbe R.

GRAND DUCHY
OF WARSAW

London

K. OF
WESTPHALIA

K. OF
SAXONY

Odel R.

Vistula R.

ANTIC OCEAN

Dover

Rhine R.

Leipzig Dresden

Plymouth

Antwerp
Boulogne Brussels
Cologne

Auerstadt
Erfurt Jena

Breslau

GALICIA

Tarnapol

ENGLISH CHANNEL
CHANNEL I.
(Britain)   Cherbourg

Amiens

BERG

CONFEDERATION
OF THE
RHINE

Prague

Cracow GALICIA

Versailles Paris
Fontainebleau

Valmy

Mainz

BOHEMIA

Austerlitz

Metz

Prague

Nantes Loire R. Orléans

Strasbourg

WÜRTTEM-
BERG

Danube R.

Wagram

Seine R.

BADEN

Ulm

Vienna AUSTRIA

FRENCH EMPIRE

Basel

Munich
Hohenlinden
K. OF BAVARIA

Budapest

Rochefort

SWITZERLAND

AUSTRIA

HUNGARY

Bordeaux

Lyons

SAVOY

Drave R.

La Coruña

Garonne R.

PIEDMONT

LOMBARDY
Milan
Po R.

VENETIA
Trieste
KINGDOM
OF
ITALY

SLOVENIA

ILLYRIAN

GALICIA

Avignon

Genoa

CROATIA Save R.

WALLACHIA

Douro R.

Burgos

Rhone R.

BOSNIA Belgrade

eida

Toulouse

LUCCA
Leghorn

PROVINCES

SERBIA

Danube R.

Ciudad Rodrigo

Saragossa

Marseilles
Toulon

Nice

Florence

DALMATIA

OTTOMAN EMPIRE

R.

Talavera Madrid

ELBA

ADRIATIC SEA

MONTENEGRO

SPAIN Ocaña

Barcelona

CORSICA

Rome

Bari

Salonica

Albuera Guadiana R.

Naples

Taranto

ALBANIA

Baylen

Valencia

MINORCA

Kingdom of
Sardinia

KINGDOM
OF NAPLES

CORFU

Seville

ANDALUSIA

BALEARIC I.
(Spain)

MAJORCA

KINGDOM OF
SARDINIA

MOREA

Gibraltar (Britain)

IVIZA

Cagliari

IONIAN I.
(Britain)

Palermo

OROCCO

Algiers

KINGDOM OF
SICILY

STRAIT OF MESSINA

CERIGO

Legend:

French Empire

Grand Empire

Allied with Napoleon

ALGERIA
(Turkish)

Tunis

TUNISIA
(Turkish)

MALTA (Britain)

MEDITERRANEAN SEA

100   200   300 miles

regularizing its relationships with France. In some areas these two stages had been accomplished under the republican governments before Napoleon came to power. In some regions no more than these two stages really occurred, notably in Spain and the Grand Duchy of Warsaw.

The third stage was one of sweeping internal reform and reorganization, modeled on Bonaparte's program for France and hence derivatively on the French Revolution.[12] Belgium and the German territories west of the Rhine underwent this stage most thoroughly, since they were annexed directly to France for twenty years. Italy, and the main bulk of Germany west of Prussia and Austria, also experienced the third stage.

Napoleon considered himself a great reformer and man of the Enlightenment. He called his system "liberal," and though the word to him meant almost the reverse of what it meant later to liberals, he was possibly the first to use it in a political sense. He believed also in "constitutions"; not that he favored representative assemblies or limited government, but he wanted government to be rationally "constituted," i.e., deliberately mapped out and planned, not merely inherited from the jumble of the past. Man on horseback though he was, he believed firmly in the rule of law. He insisted with the zeal of conviction on transplanting his Civil Code[13] to the dependent states. This code he considered to be based on the very nature of justice and human relationships and to be applicable, therefore, to all countries with no more than minor adaptation. The idea that a country's laws must mirror its peculiar national character and history was foreign to his mind, for he carried over the rationalist and universalist outlook of the Age of Enlightenment. He thought that people everywhere wanted, and deserved, much the same thing. As he wrote to his brother Jerome, on making him king of Westphalia, "the peoples of Germany, as of France, Italy and Spain, want equality and liberal ideas. For some years now I have been managing the affairs of Europe, and I am convinced that the crowing of the privileged classes was everywhere disliked. Be a constitutional king."

The same plan of reform was initiated, with some variation, in all the dependent states from Spain to Poland and from the mouth of the Elbe to the Straits of Messina. The reforms were directed, in a word, against everything feudal. They established the legal equality of individual persons, and gave governments more complete authority over their individual subjects. Legal classes were wiped out, as in France in 1789; the theory of a society made up of "estates of the realm" gave way to the theory of a society made up of 'legally equal individuals. The nobility lost its privileges in taxation, officeholding, and military command. Careers were "opened to talent."

The manorial system, bulwark of the old aristocracy, was virtually liquidated. Lords lost all legal jurisdiction over their peasants; peasants became subjects of the state, personally free to move, migrate, or marry, and able to bring suit in the courts of law. The manorial fees, along with tithes, were generally abolished, as in France in 1789. But whereas in France the peasants escaped from these burdens without having to pay compensation, because they had themselves risen in rebellion in 1789 and because France passed through a radical popular revolution

---

[12] See pp. 370–375, 400–402.
[13] See p. 402.

in 1793, in other parts of the Grand Empire the peasants were committed to payment of indemnities, and the former feudal class continued to receive income from its abolished rights. Only in Belgium and the Rhineland, incorporated into France under the republic, did the manorial regime disappear without compensation as it did in France, leaving a numerous entrenched class of small landowning farmers. East of the Rhine Napoleon had to compromise with the aristocracy which he assailed. In Poland, the only country in the Grand Empire where a thoroughgoing serfdom had prevailed, the peasants received legal freedom during the French occupation; but the Polish landlords remained economically unharmed, since they owned all the land. Napoleon had to conciliate them, for there was no other effective class in Poland to which he could look for support. In general, outside of France, the assault upon feudalism was not socially as revolutionary as it had been in France. The lord was gone, but the landlord remained.

Everywhere in the Grand Empire the church lost its position as a public authority alongside the state. Church courts were abolished or restricted; the Inquisition was outlawed in Spain. Tithes were done away with, church property confiscated, monastic orders dissolved or severely regulated. Toleration became the law; Catholics, Protestants, Jews, and unbelievers received the same civil rights. The state was to be based not on the idea of religious community but on the idea of territorial residence. With the nobility, or on economic matters, Napoleon would compromise; but he would not compromise with the Catholic clergy on the principle of a secular state. Even in Spain he insisted on these fundamentals of his system, a sure indication that he was not actuated by expediency only, since it was largely his religious program that provoked the Spanish populace to rebellion.

Guilds were generally abolished or reduced to empty forms, and the individual's right to work was generally proclaimed. Peasants, gaining legal freedom, might learn and enter any trade as they chose. The old town oligarchies and bourgeois patriciates were broken up. Towns and provinces lost their antique liberties and came under general legislation. Internal tariffs were removed, and free trade within state frontiers was encouraged. Some countries shifted to a decimal system of money; and the heterogeneous weights and measures which had originated in the Middle Ages, and of which the Anglo-American bushels, yards, ounces, and pints are living survivals, yielded to the Cartesian regularities of the metric system. Ancient and diverse legal systems gave way to the Napoleonic codes. Law courts were separated from the administration. Hereditary office and the sale of office were done away with. Officials received salaries large enough to shield them from the temptations of corruption. Kings were put on civil lists, with their personal expenses separated from those of the government. Taxes and finances were modernized. The common tax became a land tax, paid by every landowner; and governments knew how much land each owner really possessed, for they developed systematic registration of property and systematic methods of appraisal and assessment. Tax farming was replaced by direct collection. New methods of accounting and of collecting statistics were introduced.

In general, in all countries of the Grand Empire, some of the main principles of the French Revolution were introduced under Napoleon, with the notable exception that there was no self-government through elected legislative bodies.

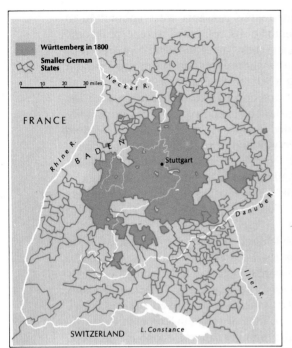

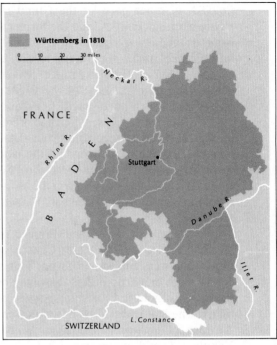

NAPOLEONIC GERMANY

In the panel at the left are shown, by shading, territories of the Duchy of Württemberg in 1800. Note how Württemberg had "islands" of territory unconnected with its main mass, and "holes" or enclaves formed by smaller states enclosed within the mass of Württemberg. Note, too, how Württemberg, itself only fifty miles wide, was surrounded by a mosaic of tiny jurisdictions—free cities, counties, duchies, principalities, abbacies, commanderies, bishoprics, archbishoprics, etc.—all "independent" within the Holy Roman Empire. The right-hand panel shows the Kingdom of Württemberg as consolidated and enlarged in the time of Napoleon. Similar consolidations all over Germany greatly reduced the number of states and added to the efficiency of law and government.

In all countries Napoleon found numerous natives willing to support him, mainly among the commercial and professional men, who were read in the writers of the Enlightenment, often anticlerical, desirous of more equality with the nobility, and eager to break down the old localisms that interfered with trade and with the exchange of ideas. He found supporters also among many progressive nobles and, in the Confederation of the Rhine, among the German rulers. His program appealed to a certain class of people everywhere, and in all parts of the Grand Empire was executed mainly by local persons. Repression went with it, though hardly on a scale to which the twentieth century has become accustomed. There were no vast internment camps, and Fouché's police were engaged more in spying and submitting reports than in the brutalizing of the disaffected. The execution of a single Bavarian bookseller, named Palm, became a famous outrage.

There was, in short, at first, a good deal of pro-Napoleonic feeling in the Grand Empire. The French influence (outside Belgium and the Rhineland) struck deepest in north Italy, where there were no native monarchist traditions, and where the old Italian city-states had produced a strong and often anticlerical burgher class. In south Germany also the French influence was profound. The French system had the least appeal in Spain, where Catholic royalist sentiment produced a kind of counterrevolutionary movement of independence. Nor did it appeal to agrarian eastern Europe, the land of lord and serf. Yet even in Prussia, as will be seen, the state was remodeled along French lines. In Russia, during the Tilsit alliance, Alexander gave his backing to a pro-French reforming minister, Speranski. The Napoleonic influence was pervasive because it carried over the older movement of enlightened despotism and seemed to confer the advantages of the French Revolution without the violence and the disorder. Napoleon, it seemed to Goethe, "was the expression of all that was reasonable, legitimate and European in the revolutionary movement."

But the Napoleonic reforms were also weapons of war. All the dependent states were required by Napoleon to supply him with money and soldiers. Germans, Dutch, Belgians, Italians, Poles, and even Spaniards fought in his armies. In addition, the dependent states defrayed much of the cost of the French army, most of which was stationed outside France. This meant that taxes in France could remain low, to the general satisfaction of the propertied interests that had issued from the Revolution.

49. The Continental System: Britain and Europe

Beyond the tributary states of the Grand Empire lay the countries nominally independent, joined under Napoleon in the Continental System. Napoleon thought of his allies as at best subordinate partners in a common project. The great project was to crush Great Britain, and it was for this purpose that the Continental System had been established. But the crushing of Britain became in Napoleon's mind a means to a further end, the unification and mastery of all of Europe. This in turn, had he achieved it, would doubtless have merely opened the way to further conquests.

At the point where he stood in 1807 or 1810 the unification of continental Europe seemed a not impossible objective. He cast about for an ideology to inspire both his Grand Empire and his allies. He held out the cosmopolitan doctrines of the eighteenth century, spoke endlessly of the enlightenment of the age, urged all peoples to work with him against the medievalism, feudalism, ignorance, and obscurantism by which they were surrounded. And while appealing to the sense of modernity he dwelt also on the grandeur of Roman times. The Roman inspiration reflected itself in the arts of the day. The massive "empire" furniture, the heroic canvases of David, the church of the Madeleine in Paris, resembling a classical temple and converted to a Temple of Glory, the Arch of Triumph in the same city, begun in 1806, all evoked the atmosphere of far-spreading majesty in which Napoleon would have liked the peoples of Europe to live. In addition, to arouse an all-European feeling, Napoleon worked upon the latent hostility to Great Britain. The British, in winning out in the eighteenth-century struggle for wealth and empire, had made themselves disliked in many quarters. There was the natural jealousy felt toward the successful and resentment against the highhandedness by which success had been won and was maintained. Such feelings were present among almost all Europeans. It was believed that the British were really using their sea power to win a larger permanent share of the world's seaborne commerce for themselves. Nor, in truth, was this belief mistaken.

British Blockade and Napoleon's Continental System

The British, in the Revolutionary and Napoleonic wars, when they declared France and its allies in a state of blockade, did not expect either to starve them or to deprive them of necessary materials of war. Western Europe was still self-sufficient in food, and armaments were to a large extent produced locally, from simple materials like iron, copper, and saltpeter. Europe required almost nothing indispensable from overseas. The chief aim of the British blockade was not, therefore, to keep imports out of enemy countries; it was to keep the trade in such imports out of enemy hands. It was to kill off enemy commerce and shipping, in order, in the short run, to weaken the war-making powers of the enemy government by undermining its revenues and its navy, and in the long run to weaken the enemy's position in the markets of the world. Economic warfare was trade warfare. The British were willing enough to have British goods pass through to the enemy either by smuggling or by the mediation of neutrals.

As early as 1793 the French republicans had denounced England as the "modern Carthage," a ruthless mercantile and profit-seeking power which aspired to enslave Europe to its financial and commercial system. With the wars, the British in fact obtained a monopoly over the shipment of overseas commodities into Europe. At the same time, being relatively advanced in the Industrial Revolution, they could produce cotton cloth and certain other articles, by power machinery, more cheaply than other peoples of Europe, and so threatened to monopolize the European market for such manufactured goods. There was much feeling in Europe against the modern Carthage, especially among the bourgeois and commercial classes who were in competition with it. The upper classes were perhaps less hostile, not caring where the goods that they consumed had originated, but aristocracies and governments were susceptible to the argument that Britain was a money power, a "nation of shopkeepers" as Napoleon put it, which fought its wars with pounds sterling instead of blood and was always in search of dupes in Europe.

It was on all these feelings that Napoleon played, reiterating time and again that England was the real enemy of all Europe, and that Europe would never be prosperous or independent until relieved of the incubus of British "monopoly." To prevent the flow of goods into Britain was no more the purpose of the Continental System than to prevent the flow of goods into France was the purpose of the British blockade. The purpose of each was to destroy the enemy's commerce, credit, and public revenues by the destruction of his exports—and also to build up markets for oneself.

To destroy British exports Napoleon prohibited, by the Berlin Decree of 1806, the importation of British goods into the continent of Europe. Counted as British, if of British or British colonial origin, were goods brought to Europe in neutral ships as the property of neutrals. The British, in response, ruled by an "order in council" of November 1807 that neutrals might enter Napoleonic ports only if they first stopped in Great Britain, where the regulations were such as to encourage their loading with British goods. The British thus tried to move their exports into enemy territory through neutral channels, which was precisely what Napoleon intended to prevent. He announced, by the Milan Decree of December 1807, that any neutral vessel that had stopped at a British port, or submitted to search by a British warship at sea, would be confiscated upon its appearance in a Continental harbor.

With all Europe at war, virtually the only trading neutral was the United States, which could now trade with neither England nor Europe except by violating the regulations of one belligerent or the other. It would thus become liable to reprisals, and hence to involvement in war. President Jefferson, to avoid war, attempted a self-imposed policy of commercial isolation, which proved so ruinous to American foreign trade that the United States government took steps to renew trade relations with whichever belligerent first removed its controls over neutral commerce. Napoleon offered to do so, on condition that the United States would defend itself against the enforcement of British controls. At the same time an expansionist party among the western Americans, ambitious to annex Canada, considered that with the British army engaged in Spain the time was ripe to complete the War of Independence by driving Britain from the North American mainland. The result was the Anglo-American War of 1812, which had few results, except to demonstrate the distressing inefficiency of military institutions in the new republic.

But the Continental System was more than a device for destroying the export trade of Great Britain. It was also a scheme—today it would be called a "plan"— for developing the economy of continental Europe, around France as its main center. The Continental System, if successful, would replace the national economies with an integrated economy for the Continent as a whole. It would create the framework for a European civilization. And it would ruin the British sea power and commercial monopoly; for a unified Europe, Napoleon thought, would itself soon take to the sea.

The Failure of the Continental System

But the Continental System failed; it was worse than a failure, for it caused widespread antagonism to the Napoleonic regime. The dream of a united Europe, under French rule, was not sufficiently attractive to inspire the necessary sacrifice—even a sacrifice more of comforts than of necessities. As Napoleon impatiently said, one would suppose that the destinies of Europe turned upon a barrel of sugar. It was true, as he and his propagandists insisted, that Britain monopolized the sale of sugar, tobacco, and other overseas goods, but people preferred to deal clandestinely with the British rather than go without them. The charms of America destroyed the Continental System.

British manufactures were somewhat easier than colonial goods to replace. Raw cotton was brought by land from the Levant through the Balkans, and the cotton manufacturers of France, Saxony, Switzerland, and north Italy were stimulated by the relief from British competition. There was a great expansion of Danish woolens and German hardware. The cultivation of sugar beets, to replace cane sugar, spread in France, central Europe, Holland, and even Russia. Thus infant industries and investments were built up which, after Napoleon's fall, clamored for tariff protection. In general, the European industrial interests were well disposed toward the Continental System.

Yet they could never adequately replace the British in supplying the market. One obstacle was transportation. Much trading between parts of the Continent had always been done by sea; this coastal traffic was now blocked by the British. Land routes were increasingly used, even in the faraway Balkans and Illyrian Provinces, through which raw cotton was brought; and improved roads were built through the Simplon and Mont Cenis passes in the Alps. No less than 17,000 wheeled vehicles crossed the Mont Cenis pass in 1810. But land transport, at best, was no substitute for the sea. Without railroads, introduced some thirty years later, a purely Continental economy was impossible to maintain.

Another obstacle was tariffs. The idea of a Continental tariff union was put forward by some of his subordinates, but Napoleon never adopted it. The dependent states remained insistent on their ostensible sovereignty. Each had widened its trading area by demolishing former internal tariffs, but each kept a tariff against the others. The kingdoms of Italy and Naples enjoyed no free trade with each other nor did the German states of the Confederation of the Rhine. France remained protectionist; and when Napoleon annexed Holland and parts of Italy to France, he kept them outside the French customs. At the same time Napoleon forbade the satellite states to raise high tariffs against France. France was his base, and he meant to favor French industry, which was much crippled by its loss of its Near Eastern and American markets.

Shippers, shipbuilders, and dealers in overseas goods, a powerful element of the older bourgeoisie, were ruined by the Continental System. The French ports were idle and their populations distressed and disgruntled. The same befell all ports of Europe where the blockade was strictly enforced; at Trieste, total annual tonnage fell from 208,000 in 1807 to 60,000 in 1812. Eastern Europe was especially hard hit. In the West there was the stimulus to new manufactures. The East, long dependent on western Europe for manufactured goods, could no longer obtain them from England legally, nor from France, Germany, or Bohemia because of the difficulties of land transport and the British control of the Baltic. Nor could the landowners of Prussia, Poland, and Russia market their produce. The aristocracy of eastern Europe, which was the principal spending and importing class, had additional reason to dislike the French and to sympathize with the British.

As a war measure against Britain the Continental System also failed. British trade with Europe was significantly reduced. But the loss was made up elsewhere because of British control of the sea. Exports to Latin America rose from £300,000 in 1805 to £6,300,000 in 1809. Here again the existence of the overseas world frustrated the Continental System. Despite the System, export of British cotton goods, rising on a continuous tide of the Industrial Revolution, more than doubled in four years from 1805 to 1809. And while part of the increase was due to mere inflation and rising prices, it is estimated that the annual income of the British people more than doubled in the Revolutionary and Napoleonic wars, leaping from £140,000,000 in 1792 to £335,000,000 in 1814.

50. The National Movements: Germany

The Resistance to Napoleon: Nationalism

From the beginning, as far back as 1792, the French met with resistance as well as collaboration in the countries they occupied. There was resentment when the invading armies plundered and requisitioned upon the country, when the newly organized states were required to pay tribute of men and money, when their policies were dictated by French residents or ambassadors, and when the Continental System was used for the especial benefit of French manufacturers. Europeans began to feel that Napoleon was employing them merely as tools against England. And in all countries, including France itself, people grew tired of the peace that was no peace, the wars and rumors of war, the conscription and the taxes, the aloof bureaucratic government from on high, the obviously growing and insatiable appetite of Napoleon for power and self-exaltation. Movements of protest and independence showed themselves even within the Napoleonic structure. We have seen how the dependent states protected themselves by tariffs. Even the emperor's proconsuls tried to root themselves in local opinion, as when Louis Bonaparte, king of Holland, tried to defend Dutch interests against Napoleon's demands, or when Murat, king of Naples, appealed to Italian sentiment to secure his own throne.

Nationalism developed as a movement of resistance against the forcible internationalism of the Napoleonic empire. Since the international system was essentially French, the nationalistic movements were anti-French; and since Napoleon was an autocrat, they were antiautocratic. The nationalism of the period was a mixture of the conservative and the liberal. Some nationalists, predominantly conservative, insisted on the value of their own peculiar institutions, customs, folkways, and historical development, which they feared might be obliterated under the French and Napoleonic system. Others, or indeed the same ones, insisted on more self-determination, more participation in government, more representative institutions, more freedom for the individual against the bureaucratic interference of the state. Both conservatism and liberalism rose up against Napoleon, destroyed him, outlasted him, and shaped the history of the following generations.

Nationalism was thus very complex and appeared in different countries in different ways. In England the profound solidarity of the country exhibited itself; all classes rallied and stood shoulder to shoulder against "Boney"; and ideas of reforming Parliament or tampering with historic English liberties were resolutely put aside. It is possible that the Napoleonic wars helped England through a very difficult social crisis, for the Industrial Revolution was causing dislocation, misery, unemployment, and even revolutionary agitation among a small minority, all of which were eclipsed by the patriotic need of resistance to Bonaparte. In Spain, nationalism took the form of implacable resistance to the French armies that desolated the land. Some Spanish nationalists were liberal; a bourgeois group at Cádiz, rebelling against the French regime, proclaimed the Spanish constitution of 1812, modeled on the French constitution of 1791. But Spanish nationalism drew its greatest strength from sentiments that were counterrevolutionary, aiming to restore the clergy and the Bourbons. In Italy the Napoleonic regime was better liked and national feeling was less anti-French than in Spain. Bourgeois of the Italian cities generally prized the efficiency and enlightenment of French methods, and often shared in the anticlericalism of the French Revolution. The French regime, which lasted in Italy from 1796 to 1814, broke the habit of loyalty to the various duchies, oligarchic republics, papal states, and foreign dynasties by which Italy had long been ruled. Napoleon never unified Italy, but he assembled it into only three parts, and the French influence brought the notion of a politically united Italy within the bounds of reasonable aspiration. With the Poles Napoleon positively encouraged national feeling. He repeatedly told them that they might win a restored and united Poland by faithfully fighting in his cause. A few Polish nationalists, like the aging patriot Kosciuzsko, never trusted Napoleon, and some others, like Czartoryski, looked rather to the Russian tsar for a restoration of the Polish kingdom; but in general the Poles, for their own national reasons, were exceptionally devoted to the emperor of the French and lamented his passing.

The Movement of Thought in Napoleonic Germany

By far the most momentous national movement took place in Germany. The Germans rebelled not only against the Napoleonic rule but against the century-old ascendancy of French civilization. They rebelled not only against the French armies but against the philosophy of the Age of Enlightenment. The years of the French Revolution and Napoleon were for Germany the years of its greatest cultural efflorescence, the years of Beethoven, Goethe, and Schiller, of Herder, Kant, Fichte, Hegel, Schleiermacher, and many others. German ideas fell in with all the ferment of fundamental thinking known as "romanticism," which was everywhere challenging the "dry abstractions" of the Age of Reason and about which more will be said in this and the following chapter. Germany became the most "romantic" of all countries, and German influence spread throughout Europe. In the nineteenth century the Germans came to be widely regarded as intellectual leaders, somewhat as the French had been in the century before. And most of the distinctive features of German thought were somehow connected with nationalism in a broad sense.

Formerly, especially in the century following the Peace of Westphalia, the Germans had been the least nationally minded of all the larger European peoples.[14] They prided themselves on their world citizenship or cosmopolitan outlook. Looking out from the tiny states in which they lived, they were conscious of Europe, conscious of other countries, but hardly conscious of Germany. The Holy Roman Empire was a shadow. The German world had no tangible frontiers; the area of German speech simply faded out into Alsace or the Austrian Netherlands, or into Poland, Bohemia, or the upper Balkans. That "Germany" ever did, thought, or hoped anything never crossed the German mind. The upper classes, becoming contemptuous of much that was German, took over French fashions, dress, etiquette, manners, ideas, and language, regarding them as an international norm of civilized living. Frederick the Great hired French tax collectors and wrote his own books in French.

[14] See pp. 213–217.

About 1780 signs of a change set in. Even Frederick, in his later years, predicted a golden age of German literature, proudly declaring that Germans could do what other nations had done. In 1784 appeared a book by J. G. Herder, called *Ideas on the Philosophy of the History of Mankind*. Herder was an earnest soul, a Protestant pastor and theologian who thought the French somewhat frivolous. He concluded that imitation of foreign ways made people shallow and artificial. He declared that German ways were indeed different from French but not for that reason the less worthy of respect. All true culture or civilization, he held, must arise from native roots. It must arise also from the life of the common people, the *Volk,* not from the cosmopolitan and denatured life of the upper classes.[15] Each people, he thought, meaning by a people a group sharing the same language, had its own attitudes, spirit, or genius. A sound civilization must express a national character or *Volksgeist*. And the character of each people was special to itself. Herder did not believe the nations to be in conflict; quite the contrary, he simply insisted that they were different. He did not believe German culture to be the best; many other peoples, notably the Slavs, later found his ideas applicable to their own needs. His philosophy of history was very different from Voltaire's. Voltaire and the philosophes had expected all peoples to progress along the same path of reason and enlightenment toward the same civilization. Herder thought that all peoples should develop their own genius in their own way, each slowly unfolding with the inevitability of plantlike growth, avoiding sudden change or distortion by outside influence, and all ultimately reflecting, in their endless diversity, the infinite richness of humanity and of God.

The idea of the *Volksgeist* was reinforced from other and non-German sources and soon passed to other countries in the general movement of romantic thought. Like much else in romanticism, it emphasized genius or intuition rather than reason. It stressed the differences rather than the similarity of mankind. It broke down that sense of human similarity which had been characteristic of the Age of Enlightenment,[16] and which revealed itself in French and American doctrines of the rights of man, or again in the law codes of Napoleon. In the past it had been usually thought that what was good was good for all peoples. Good poetry was poetry written according to certain classical principles or "rules" of composition, which were the same for all writers from the Greeks on down. Now, according to Herder and to romantics in all countries, good poetry was poetry that expressed an inner genius, either an individual genius or the genius of a people—there were no more "rules." Good and just laws, according to the older philosophy of natural law, somehow corresponded to a standard of justice that was the same for all men. But now, according to Herder and the romantic school of jurisprudence, good laws were those that reflected local conditions or national idiosyncrasies. Here again there were no "rules," except possibly the rule that each nation should have its own way.

Herder's philosophy set forth a cultural nationalism, without political message. The Germans had long been a nonpolitical people. In the microscopic states of the Holy Roman Empire they had had no significant political questions to think about; in the more sizable ones they had been excluded from public affairs. The

---

[15] On elite and popular cultures see pp. 251–256.
[16] See pp. 325–326.

French Revolution made the Germans acutely conscious of the state. It showed what a people could do with a state, once they took it over and used it for their own purposes. For one thing, the French had raised themselves to the dignity of citizenship; they had become free men, responsible for themselves, taking part in the affairs of their country. For another, because they had a unified state which included all Frenchmen, and one in which a whole nation surged with a new sense of freedom, they were able to rise above all the other peoples of Europe. Many in Germany were beginning to feel humiliation at the paternalism of their governments. The futilities of the Holy Roman Empire, which had made Germany for centuries the battlefield of Europe, now filled them with shame and indignation. They saw with disgust how their German princes, forever squabbling with each other for control over German subjects, disgraced themselves before the French to promote their own interests. The national awakening in Germany, which set in strongly after 1800, was therefore directed not only against Napoleon and the French, but also against the German rulers and many of the half-Frenchified German upper classes. It was democratic in that it stressed the superior virtue of the common people.

Germans became fascinated by the idea of political and national greatness, precisely because they had neither. A great national German state, expressing the deep moral will and distinctive culture of the German people, seemed to them the solution to all their problems. It would give moral dignity to the individual German, solve the vexatious question of the selfish petty princes, protect the deep German *Volksgeist* from violation, and secure the Germans from subjection to outside powers. The nationalist philosophy remained somewhat vague, because in practice there was little that one could do. "Father" Jahn organized a kind of youth movement and became the inventor of what might be termed political gymnastics, having his young men do calisthenics for the Fatherland; he led them on open-air expeditions into the country, where they made fun of aristocrats in French costume; and he taught them to be suspicious of foreigners, Jews, and internationalists, and indeed of everything that might corrupt the purity of the German *Volk*. Most Germans thought him too extreme. Others collected wonderful stories of the rich medieval German past. There was an anonymous anti-French work, *Germany in Its Deep Humiliation,* for selling which the publisher Palm was put to death. Others founded the Moral and Scientific Union, generally known as the *Tugendbund* or league of virtue or manliness, whose members, by developing their own moral character, were to contribute to the future of Germany.

The career of J. G. Fichte illustrates the course of German thought in these years. Fichte was a moral and metaphysical philosopher, a professor at the University of Jena. His doctrine, that the inner spirit of the individual creates its own moral universe, was much admired in many countries. In America, for example, it entered into the transcendental philosophy of Ralph Waldo Emerson. Fichte at first was practically without national feeling. He enthusiastically approved of the French Revolution, as did Jahn and Arndt. In 1793, with the Revolution at its height and many foreign observers turning against it, Fichte published a laudatory tract on the French Republic. He saw it as an emancipation of the human spirit, a step upward in the elevation of human dignity and moral stature. He accepted the idea of the Terror, that of "forcing men to be free"; and he shared Rousseau's conception of the state as the embodiment of the sovereign will of a people. He came to see the state as the means of human salvation. In 1800, in his *Closed Commercial State,* he sketched a kind of totalitarian system in which the state planned and operated the whole economy of the country, shutting itself off from the rest of the world in order that, at home, it might freely develop the character of its own citizens. When the French conquered Germany Fichte became intensely and self-consciously German. He took over the idea of the *Volksgeist:* not only did the individual spirit create its own moral universe, but the spirit of a people created a kind of moral universe as well, manifested in its language, arts, folkways, customs, institutions, and ideas.

At Berlin, in 1808, Fichte delivered a series of *Addresses to the German Nation,* declaring that there was an ineradicable German spirit, a primordial and immutable national character, more noble than that of other peoples (thus going beyond Herder), to be kept pure at all costs from all outside influence, either international or French. The German spirit, he held, had always been profoundly different from that of France and western Europe; it had never yet really been heard from but would be some day. The French army commander then occupying the city thought the lectures too academic to be worth suppression. They had, in fact, few hearers; Fichte was considered a firebrand by most Germans; but they later regarded him as a national hero.

Reforms in Prussia

Politically, in the revolt against the French the main transformations came in Prussia. Prussia after the death of Frederick the Great had fallen into a period of satisfied inertia, such as is likely to follow upon rapid growth or spectacular success. Then in 1806, at Jena-Auerstädt, the kingdom collapsed in a single battle. Its western and most of its Polish territories were taken away. It was relegated by Napoleon to its old holdings east of the Elbe. Even here the French remained in occupation, for Napoleon stationed his Ninth Corps in Berlin. But in the eyes of German nationalists Prussia had a moral advantage. Of all the German states it was the least compromised by collaboration with the French. Toward Prussia, as toward a haven, German patriots therefore made their way. East-Elbian Prussia, formerly the least German of German lands, became the center of an all-German movement for national freedom. The years after Jena contributed to the "Prussianizing" of Germany; but it is to be observed that neither Fichte nor Hegel, Gneisenau nor Scharnhorst, Stein nor Hardenberg, all rebuilders of Prussia, was a native Prussian.

The main problem for Prussia was military, since Napoleon could be overthrown only by military force. And as always in Prussia, the requirements of the army shaped the form taken by the state.[17] The problem was conceived to be one of morale and personnel. The old Prussia of Frederick, which had fallen ingloriously, had been mechanical, arbitrary, soulless. Its people had lacked the sense of membership in the state, and in the army its soldiers had held no hope of promotion and felt no patriotism or spirit. To produce this spirit was the aim of the army reformers, Scharnhorst and Gneisenau. Gneisenau, a Saxon, had served

[17] See pp. 229–234, 335–336.

in one of the British "Hessian" regiments in the War of American Independence, during which he had observed the military value of patriotic feeling in the American soldiers. He was a close observer also of the consequences of the French Revolution, which, he said, had "set in action the national energy of the entire French people, putting the different classes on an equal social and fiscal basis." If Prussia was to strengthen itself against France, or indeed to avoid revolution in the long run in Prussia itself, it must find a means to inspire a similar feeling of equal participation in its own people, and to allow capable individuals to fill important positions in the army and government without regard to their social status.

The reconstruction of the state, prerequisite to the reconstruction of the army, was initiated by Baron Stein and continued by his successor, Hardenberg. Like Metternich, Stein came from western Germany; he had been an imperial knight of the late Holy Roman Empire, who from a bridge near his castle had beheld the domains of no less than eight German princes in one sweep of the eye. Stateless himself, he thought of Germany as a whole; he was long hostile to what he considered the barely civilized Prussia, but finally resorted to it as the hope of the future. Deeply committed to the philosophy of Kant and Fichte, he dwelt on the concepts of duty, service, moral character, and responsibility. He thought that the common people must be awakened to moral life, raised from a brutalized servility to the level of self-determination and membership in the community. This, he believed, required an equality more of duties than of rights.

Under Stein the old caste structure of Prussia became somewhat less rigid. Property became interchangeable between classes; bourgeois were allowed to buy land and serve as officers in the army. The burghers, to develop a sense of citizenship and participation in the state, were given extensive freedom of self-government in the cities; the municipal systems of Prussia, and later of Germany, became a model for much of Europe in the following century. Stein had ideas for parliamentary institutions in Prussia as a whole, thinking they would strengthen the country, but he left office before acting upon them.

His most famous work was the "abolition of serfdom." It was naturally impossible, since the whole reform program was aimed at strengthening Prussia for a war of liberation against the French, to antagonize the Junkers who commanded the army. Stein's ordinance of 1807 abolished serfdom only in that it abolished the "hereditary subjection" of peasants to their manorial lords.[18] It gave peasants the right to move and migrate, marry, and take up trades without the lord's approval. If, however, the peasant remained on the land, he was still subject to all the old services of forced labor in the fields of the lord. Peasants enjoying small tenures of their own continued to be liable for the old dues and fees. By an edict of 1810, a peasant might convert his tenure into private property, getting rid of the manorial obligations, but only on condition that one-third of the land he had held should become the private property of the lord. In the following decades many such conversions took place, of which the result was that the estates of the Junkers grew considerably larger. The reforms in Prussia somewhat reduced the old patriarchial powers of the lords and gave legal status and freedom of movement to the mass of the population, thus laying the foundation for a

[18] See p. 125.

modern state and modern economy. But the peasants tended to become mere hired agricultural laborers; and the position of the Junkers was heightened, not reduced. Prussia avoided the Revolution. Stein himself, because Napoleon feared him, was obliged to go into exile in 1808, but his reforms endured.

51. The Overthrow of Napoleon: The Congress of Vienna

The situation at the close of 1811 may be summarized as follows. Napoleon had the mainland of Europe in his grip. Russia and Turkey were at war on the Danube, but otherwise there was no war except in Spain, where four years of fighting remained inconclusive. The Continental System was working badly. Britain was hurt by it only negatively, in that, without it, British exports to Europe would have risen rapidly in these years. Well launched in the Industrial Revolution, Great Britain was amassing a vast store of national wealth, accumulating the wherewithal to assist European governments financially against Napoleon. The peoples of Europe were increasingly restless, dreaming increasingly of national freedom. In Germany, especially, many awaited the opportunity to rise in a war of independence. But Napoleon could be overthrown only by the destruction of his army, with which neither British wealth nor British sea power, nor the European patriots and nationalists, nor the Prussian nor the Austrian armed forces were able to cope. All eyes turned to Russia. Alexander I had long been dissatisfied with his French alliance. He had obtained from it nothing but the annexation of Finland in 1809. He received no assistance from France in his war with Turkey; he saw Napoleon marry into the Austrian house; he had to tolerate the existence of a French-oriented Poland at his very door. The articulate classes in Russia, namely, the landowners and serf owners, loudly denounced the French alliance and demanded a resumption of open trade relations with England. An international clientele of émigrés and anti-Bonapartists, including Baron Stein, also gradually congregated at St. Petersburg, where they poured into the tsar's ears the welcome message that Europe looked to him for its salvation.

The Russian Campaign and the War of Liberation

On December 31, 1810, Russia formally withdrew from the Continental System. Anglo-Russian commercial relations were resumed. Napoleon resolved to crush the tsar. He concentrated the Grand Army in eastern Germany and Poland, a vast force of 700,000 men, the largest ever assembled up to that time for a single military operation. It was an all-European host. Hardly more than a third was French; another third was German, from German regions annexed to France, from the states of the Confederation of the Rhine, and with token forces from Prussia and Austria; and the remaining third was drawn from all other nationalities of the Grand Empire, including 90,000 Poles. Napoleon at first hoped to meet the Russians in Poland or Prussia. This time, however, they decided to fight on their own ground, and they needed in any case to delay until their forces on the lower Danube could be recalled. In June 1812 Napoleon led the Grand Army into Russia.

He intended a short, sharp war, such as most of his wars had been in the past, and carried with him only three weeks' supplies. But from the beginning everything went wrong. It was Napoleon's principle to force a decisive battle; but the Russian army simply melted away. It was his principle to live on the country, so as to reduce the need for supply trains; but the Russians destroyed as they retreated, and in any case, in Russia, even in the summer, it was hard to find sustenance for so many men and horses. Finally, not far from Moscow, Napoleon was able to join battle with the main Russian force at Borodino. Here again everything miscarried. It was his principle always to outnumber the enemy at the decisive spot; but the Grand Army had left so many detachments along its line of march that at Borodino the Russians outnumbered it. It was Napoleon's principle to concentrate his artillery, but here he scattered it instead, and to throw in his last reserves at the critical moment, but at Borodino, so far from home, he refused the risk of ordering the Old Guard into action. Napoleon won the battle, at a cost of 30,000 men, as against 50,000 lost by the Russians; but the Russian army was able to withdraw in good order.

On September 14, 1812, the French emperor entered Moscow. Almost immediately the city broke into flames. Napoleon found himself camping in a ruin, with troops strewn along a long line all the way back to Poland, and with a hostile army maneuvering near at hand. Baffled, he tried to negotiate with Alexander, who refused all overtures. After five weeks, not knowing what to do, and fearful of remaining isolated in Moscow over the winter, Napoleon ordered a retreat. Prevented by the Russians from taking a more southerly route, the Grand Army retired by the same way it had come. The cold weather set in early and was unusually severe. For a century after 1812 the retreat from Moscow remained the last word in military horror. Men froze and starved, horses slipped and died, vehicles could not be moved, and equipment was abandoned. Discipline broke down toward the end; the army dissolved into a horde of individual fugitives, speaking a babel of languages, harassed by bands of Russian irregulars, picking their way on foot over ice and snow, most of the time in the dark, for the nights are long in these latitudes in December. Of 611,000 who entered Russia 400,000 died of battle casualties, starvation, and exposure, and 100,000 were taken prisoner. The Grand Army no longer existed.

Now at last all the anti-Napoleon forces rushed together. The Russians pushed westward into central Europe. The Prussian and Austrian governments, which in 1812 had half-heartedly supplied troops for the invasion of Russia, switched over in 1813 and joined the tsar. Throughout Germany the patriots, often half-trained boys, marched off in the War of Liberation, though it was the professional armies of the German states that made the difference. Anti-French riots broke out in Italy. In Spain Wellington at last pushed rapidly forward; in June 1813 he crossed the Pyrenees into France. The British government, in three years from 1813 to 1815, poured £32,000,000 as subsidies into Europe, more than half of all the funds granted during the twenty-two years of the wars. An incongruous alliance of British capitalism and east-European agrarian feudalism, of the British navy and the Russian army, of Spanish clericalism and German nationalism, of divine-right monarchies and newly aroused democrats and liberals, combined at last to bring the Man of Destiny to the ground.

Napoleon, who had left his army in Russia in December 1812, and rushed across Europe to Paris, by sleigh and coach, in the remarkable time of thirteen days, raised a new army in France in the early months of 1813. But it was untrained and unsteady, and he himself had lost some of his genius for command. His new army was smashed in October at the battle of Leipzig, known to the Germans as the Battle of the Nations, the greatest battle in number of men engaged ever fought until the twentieth century. The allies drove Napoleon back upon France. But the closer they came to defeating him the more they began to fear and distrust each other.

The Restoration of the Bourbons

The coalition already showed signs of splitting. Should the allies, together or singly, negotiate with Napoleon? How strong should the France of the future be? What should be its new frontiers? What form of government should it have? There was no agreement on these questions. Alexander wanted to dethrone Napoleon and dictate peace in Paris, in dramatic retribution for the destruction of Moscow. He had a scheme for giving the French throne to Bernadotte, a former French marshal, now crown prince of Sweden, who as king of France would depend on Russian support. Metternich preferred to keep Napoleon or his son as French emperor, after clearing the French out of central Europe; for a Bonaparte dynasty in a reduced France would be dependent on Austria. The Prussian counsels were divided. The British declared that the French must get out of Belgium, and that Napoleon must go; they held that the French might then choose their own government but believed a restoration of the Bourbons to be the best solution. The three Continental monarchies had no concern for the Bourbons, and both Alexander and Metternich, if they could make France dependent respectively on themselves, were willing to see it remain strong to the extent of including Belgium. In November 1813 Metternich communicated to Napoleon a proposition known as the "Frankfurt proposals," by which Napoleon would remain French emperor, and France would retain its "natural" frontier on the Rhine. There was a chance of peace on this basis, for the allies could not shake off their old fear of Napoleon, the Prussians could be compensated elsewhere, and among the Russians many of the generals and others were impatient to go home. The British, their diplomatic influence reduced by the fact that they had few troops in Europe, faced the appalling prospect that the Continent would again make peace without them—and a peace in which France should again keep Belgium.

The British foreign minister, Viscount Castlereagh, arrived in person on the Continent in January 1814. He held a number of strong cards. For one thing, Napoleon rejected the Frankfurt proposals. He continued to fight, and the allies therefore continued to ask for British financial aid. Castlereagh skillfully used the promise of British subsidies to win acceptance of the British war aims. In addition, he found a common ground for agreement with Metternich, both Britain and Austria fearing the domination of Europe by Russia. Castlereagh's first great problem was to hold the alliance together, for without Continental allies the British could not defeat France. He succeeded, on March 9, 1814, in getting Russia, Prussia, Austria, and Great Britain to sign the treaty of Chaumont. Each power bound itself for twenty years to a Quadruple Alliance against France, and each agreed to provide 150,000 soldiers to enforce such peace terms as might be arrived at. For the first time since 1792 a solid coalition of the four great powers now existed against France. Three weeks later the allies entered Paris, and on April 4 Napoleon abdicated at Fontainebleau.

He was forced to this step by lack of support in France itself. Twenty years before, in 1793 and 1794, France had fought off the combined powers of Europe—minus Russia. It could not and would not do so in 1814. The country cried for peace. Even the imperial marshals advised the emperor's abdication. But what was to follow him? For over twenty-five years the French had had one regime after another. Now there were some who wished a republic, some who wished the empire under Napoleon's infant son, some who wished a constitutional monarchy, and some even who longed for the Old Regime. Talleyrand stepped into the breach. The "legitimate" king, he said, Louis XVIII, was after all the man who would provoke the least factionalism and opposition. The powers, likewise, had by this time concluded in favor of the Bourbons. A Bourbon king would be peaceable, under no impulse to win back the conquests of the republic and empire. He would also, as the native and rightful king of France, need no foreign support to bolster him up, so that the control of France would not arise as an issue to divide the victorious powers.

So the Bourbon dynasty was restored. Louis XVIII, ignored and disregarded for a whole generation, both by most Frenchmen and by the governments of Europe, returned to the throne of his brother and his fathers. He issued a "constitutional charter," partly at the insistence of the liberal tsar, and partly because, having actually learned from his long exile, he sought the support of influential people in France. The charter of 1814 made no concession to the principle of popular or national sovereignty. It was represented as the gracious gift of a theoretically absolute king. But in practice it granted what most Frenchmen wanted. It promised legal equality, eligibility of all to public office without regard to class, and a parliamentary government in two chambers. It recognized the Napoleonic law codes, the Napoleonic settlement with the church, and the redistribution of property effected during the Revolution. It carried over the abolition of feudalism and privilege, manorialism and tithes. It confined the vote, to be sure, to a very few large landowners; but for the time being, except for a few irreconcilables, France settled down to enjoy the blessings of a chastened revolution—and peace.

The Settlement before the Vienna Congress

It was with the government of the restored Bourbons that the powers, on May 30, 1814, signed a treaty. This document, the "first" Treaty of Paris, confined France to its boundaries of 1792, those obtaining before the wars. The allied statesmen disregarded cries for vengeance and punishment, imposed no indemnity or reparations, and even allowed the works of art gathered from Europe during the wars to remain in Paris. It was not the desire of the victors to handicap the new French government on which they placed their hopes. Napoleon meanwhile was exiled to the island of Elba on the Italian coast.

To deal with other questions, the powers had agreed, before signing the Alliance of Chaumont, to hold an international congress at Vienna after defeating

Napoleon. The recession of the French flood left the future of much of Europe—Belgium, Holland, Germany, Poland, Italy, Spain—fluid and uncertain. There were many other debatable questions also, including the Russian annexation of Finland and ambitions on the Danube, the disintegration of the Spanish American empire, the British occupation of French, Dutch, and Spanish possessions, and the troublesome issue of the freedom of the seas.

Both Russia and Great Britain, before consenting to a general conference, specified certain matters that they would decide for themselves as not susceptible to international consideration. The Russians refused to discuss Turkey and the Balkans; they retained Bessarabia as the prize of their recent war with the Turks. They also kept Finland, as an autonomous constitutional grand duchy, as well as certain recent conquests in the Caucasus almost unknown to Europe, namely Georgia and Azerbaijan. The British refused any discussion of the freedom of the seas. They also barred all colonial and overseas questions. The British government simply announced to Europe which of its colonial and insular conquests it would keep and which it would return. The revolts in Spanish America were left to run their course.

In Europe, the British remained in possession of Malta, the Ionian Islands, and Heligoland. In America, they kept St. Lucia, Trinidad, and Tobago in the West Indies and reasserted their claims to the Pacific Northwest, or Oregon country, to which claims were also made by Russia, Spain, and the United States. Of former French possessions, the British kept the island of Mauritius in the Indian Ocean. Of former Dutch territories, they kept the Cape of Good Hope and Ceylon, but returned the Netherlands Indies. During the Revolutionary and Napoleonic wars in Europe the British had also made extensive conquests in India, bringing much of the Deccan and the upper Ganges valley under their rule. The British emerged, in 1814, as the controlling power in both India and the Indian Ocean.

Indeed, of all the colonial empires founded by Europeans in the sixteenth and seventeenth centuries, and whose rivalry had been a recurring cause of war in the eighteenth, only the British now remained as a growing and dynamic system. The old French, Spanish, and Portuguese empires were reduced to mere scraps of their former selves; the Dutch still held vast establishments in the East Indies, but all the intermediate positions, the Cape, Ceylon, Mauritius, Singapore, were now British. Nor, in 1814, did any people except the British have a significant navy. With Napoleon and the Continental System defeated, with the Industrial Revolution bringing power machinery to the manufacturers of England, with no rival left in the contest for overseas dominion, and with a virtual monopoly of naval power, whose use they studiously kept free from international regulation, the British embarked on their century of world leadership, which may be said to have lasted from 1814 to 1914.

The Congress of Vienna, 1814–1815

The Congress of Vienna assembled in September 1814. Never had such a brilliant gathering been seen. All the states of Europe sent representatives; and many defunct states, such as the formerly sovereign princes and ecclesiastics of the late Holy Roman Empire, sent lobbyists to urge their restoration. But procedure was so arranged that all important matters were decided by the four triumphant Great Powers. Indeed it was at the Congress of Vienna that the terms great and small powers entered clearly into the diplomatic vocabulary. Europe was at peace, a treaty having been signed with the late enemy; France also was represented at the Congress, by none other than Talleyrand, now minister to Louis XVIII. Castlereagh, Metternich, and Alexander spoke for their respective countries; Prussia was represented by Hardenberg. The Prussians hoped, as always, to enlarge the kingdom of Prussia. Alexander was a question mark: he wanted Poland, he wanted constitutional governments in Europe, he wanted some kind of international system of collective security. Castlereagh and Metternich, with support from Talleyrand, were most especially concerned to produce a balance of power on the Continent. Aristocrats of the Old Regime, they applied eighteenth-century diplomatic principles to the existing problem. They by no means desired to restore the territorial boundaries obtaining before the wars. They did desire, as they put it, to restore the "liberties of Europe," meaning the freedom of European states from domination by a single power.[19] The threat of "universal monarchy," a term which diplomats still sometimes used to signify such a system as Napoleon's, was to be offset by an ingenious calculation of forces, a transfer of territory and "souls" from one government to another, in such a way as to distribute and balance political power among a number of free and sovereign states. It was hoped that a proper balance would also produce a lasting peace.

The chief menace to peace, and most likely claimant for the domination of Europe, naturally seemed to be the late troublemaker, France. The Congress of Vienna, without much disagreement, erected a barrier of strong states along the French eastern frontier. The historic Dutch Republic, extinct since 1795, was revived as the kingdom of the Netherlands, with the house of Orange as a hereditary monarchy; to it was added Belgium, the old Austrian Netherlands with which Austria had long been willing to part. It was hoped that the combined Dutch-Belgian kingdom would be strong enough to discourage the perennial French drive into the Low Countries. On the south, the Italian kingdom of Piedmont was restored and strengthened by the incorporation of the defunct republic of Genoa, extinct since 1797. Behind the Netherlands and Piedmont, and further to discourage a renewal of French pressure upon Germany and Italy, two great powers were installed. Almost all the German Left Bank of the Rhine was ceded to Prussia, which was to be, in Castlereagh's words, a kind of "bridge" spanning central Europe, a bulwark against both France in the West and Russia in the East. In Italy, again as a kind of secondary barrier against France, the Austrians were firmly installed. They not only took back Tuscany and the Milanese, which they had held before 1796, but also annexed the extinct republic of Venice. The Austrian empire now included a Lombardo-Venetian kingdom in north Italy, which lasted for almost half a century. In the rest of Italy the Congress recognized the restoration of the pope in the papal states and of former rulers in the smaller duchies; but it did not insist on a restoration of the Bourbons in the kingdom of Naples. There Napoleon's brother-in-law Murat, with support from Metternich, managed for a time to retain his throne. The Bourbons and Braganzas

[19] See pp. 162–163.

restored themselves, respectively, in Spain and Portugal and were recognized by the Congress.

As for Germany, the Congress made no attempt to put together again the Humpty Dumpty of the Holy Roman Empire. The pleas of the former princelings went unheeded. The French and Napoleonic reorganization of Germany was substantially confirmed. The kings of Bavaria, Württemberg, and Saxony kept the royal crowns that Napoleon had bestowed on them. The king of England, George III, was now recognized as king, not "elector," of Hanover. The German states, thirty-nine in number, including Prussia and Austria, were joined in a loose confederation in which the members remained virtually sovereign. The Congress ignored the yearnings of German nationalists for a great unified Fatherland; Metternich especially feared nationalistic agitation; and in any case the nationalists themselves had no practical answer to concrete questions, such as the institutions of government and the frontiers that a united Germany should have. The Congress did declare, somewhat ineffectually, that in each of the German states there should be a representative legislative body.

The Polish-Saxon Question

The question of Poland, reopened by the fall of Napoleon's Grand Duchy of Warsaw, brought the Congress almost to disaster. Alexander still insisted on undoing the crime of the partitions, which to his mind meant reconstituting the Polish kingdom with himself as constitutional king, in a merely personal union with the Russian empire. A similar arrangement was being initiated in the Grand Duchy of Finland, where Alexander reigned as a constitutional grand duke. To reunite Poland required that Austria and Prussia surrender their respective segments of the old Poland, most of which they had in any case lost to Napoleon. The Prussians were willing, with the proviso, which Alexander supported, that Prussia receive instead the whole of the kingdom of Saxony, which was considered available because the king of Saxony had been the last German ruler to abandon Napoleon. The issue presented itself as the Polish-Saxon question, with Russia and Prussia standing together to demand all Poland for Russia, and all Saxony for Prussia.

Such a prospect horrified Metternich. For Prussia to absorb Saxony would raise Prussia prodigiously in the eyes of all Germans, and it would greatly lengthen the common frontier between Prussia and the Austrian Empire. Furthermore, for Alexander to become king of all Poland, and incidentally the protector of an extended Prussia, would incalculably augment the influence of Russia in the affairs of Europe. Metternich found that Castlereagh shared these views. To Castlereagh it seemed that the main problem at Vienna was to restrain Russia. The British had not fought the French emperor only to have Europe fall to the Russian tsar. For months the Polish-Saxon question was debated, Metternich and Castlereagh exploring every device of argument to dissuade the Russo-Prussian combination from its expansionist designs. Finally they accepted the proffered assistance of Talleyrand, who shrewdly used the rift between the victors to bring France back into the diplomatic circle as a power in its own right. On January 3, 1815, Castlereagh, Metternich, and Talleyrand signed a secret treaty, pledging themselves to go to war if necessary against Russia and Prussia. So, in the very

Boundary of the German Confederation

0   100   200 miles

KINGDOM OF NORWAY
AND SWEDEN

FINLAND
(Russia, 1808)

Oslo

Stockholm

St. Petersburg

Reval   Novgorod

BALTIC SEA

Riga

Smolensk

SCOTLAND

Edinburgh

NORTH SEA

Copenhagen
DENMARK

Niemen R.

EAST
PRUSSIA

Danzig

LITHUANIA

UNITED KINGDOM
OF GREAT BRITAIN AND IRELAND

IRELAND   Dublin

ENGLAND

WALES

SCHLESWIG

HELIGOLAND
(Britain)

HOLSTEIN

Hamburg

Elbe R.

P R U S S I A

Vistula R.

Warsaw

KINGDOM OF
POLAND
(1815-1831)

Kiev

UKRA

KINGDOM OF THE
NETHERLANDS

HANOVER

Berlin

London

ENGLISH CHANNEL

BELGIUM
(Ind. 1831)

Cologne

Rhine R.

LUX.

HESSE

SAXON
STATES

SAXONY

Oder R.

Breslau

Cracow

GALICIA

Dniester R.

BESSARABIA
(Russia 1812)

ATLANTIC OCEAN

Rouen

Seine R.

Paris

Metz

LORRAINE

Strasbourg

ALSACE

BADEN

WÜRT-
TEMBERG

BAVARIA

Munich

Prague

AUSTRIA

Vienna

Pressburg

AUSTRIAN EMPIRE

Budapest

HUNGARY

TRANSYLVANIA

MOLDAVIA
(Autonomous 1829)

Loire R.

Tours

FRANCE

Lyons

Berne
SWITZERLAND

TYROL

LOM-
BARDY

VENETIA

Po R.

CROATIA

DALMATIA

Belgrade

WALLACHIA
(Autonomous 1829)

Danube R.

D

Bordeaux

SAVOY

PIEDMONT

Milan

PARMA

MODENA

BOSNIA

SERBIA
(Autonomous
1829)

Sofia

BULGARIA

Constant

Toulouse

Marseilles

Nice

Genoa
LUCCA

TUSCANY

PAPAL
STATES

ELBA

MONTENEGRO

OTTOMA

Burgos

PYRENEES

Ebro R.

Toulon

KINGDOM OF SARDINIA

CORSICA
(France)

Rome

ADRIATIC SEA

Salonica

PORTUGAL

Madrid

Tagus R.

SPAIN

Barcelona

Naples

IONIAN I.
(Britain)

AEGEAN SEA

Lisbon

Valencia

BALEARIC I.
(Spain)

SARDINIA

KINGDOM OF THE
TWO SICILIES

GREECE
(Independent 1829)

Athens

Seville

Cadiz

Gibraltar (Britain)

Palermo

SICILY

CRETE

Algiers

MALTA
(Britain)

MOROCCO

ALGERIA   (France, 1830)

TUNIS
(Turkish)

MEDITERRANEAN SEA

TRIPOLI

TRIPOLI

EUROPE, 1815

Boundaries are those set by the Congress of Vienna in 1815. In general, a system of five "great powers" prevailed over the Napoleonic empire. France was reduced to the borders it had had before the Revolutionary-Napoleonic wars. Prussia was firmly installed on both banks of the Rhine, thus obtaining the part of Germany in which industrialization became important fifty years later. South Germany remained as reorganized under Napoleon. Poland was again partitioned. A larger share of Poland than in 1795 now went to Russia, which also acquired Finland and Bessarabia. The Austrians added Venetia to what they had held before 1796.

The union of the Dutch and Belgian Netherlands lasted only until 1831, when the kingdom of Belgium was established. Otherwise, the boundaries of 1815 lasted until the Italian war of 1859 which led to the unification of Italy.

midst of the peace conference, war again reared its head; and, in the very deliberations of the victors, one party among them allied itself with the vanquished.

No sooner had news of the secret treaty leaked out than Alexander offered to compromise. In his mixed nature he was, among other things, a man of peace, and he agreed to content himself with a reduced Polish kingdom. The Congress therefore created a new Poland (called "Congress Poland," which lasted for fifteen years); Alexander became its king, and he gave it a constitution; it comprised much the same area as Napoleon's Grand Duchy, representing in effect a transfer of this region from French to Russian control. It reached 250 miles farther west into Europe than had the Russian segment of the third partition of 1795. Some Poles still remained in Prussia and some in the Austrian Empire; Poland was not reunited. With the tsar thus content, Prussia too had to back down. It received about two-fifths of Saxony, the rest remaining to the Saxon king. The addition of both Saxon and Rhenish territories brought the Prussian monarchy into the most advanced parts of Germany. The net effect of the peace settlement, and of the Napoleonic wars, in this connection, was to shift the center of gravity of both Russia and Prussia farther west, Russia almost to the Oder, Prussia to the borders of France.[20]

With the solution of the Polish-Saxon question the main work of the Congress was completed. Other incidental matters were taken up. The Congress initiated international regulation of certain rivers. It issued a declaration against the Atlantic slave trade, which, however, remained ineffective, since the Continental powers were unwilling to grant the British navy free powers of search at sea, and the British were unwilling to put naval forces at the disposal of an international body. Committees of the Congress set to work to draft the Final Act. And at this point the whole settlement was brought into jeopardy.

The Hundred Days and Their Aftermath

Napoleon escaped from Elba, landed in France on March 1, 1815, and again proclaimed the empire. In the year since the return of the Bourbons discontent had been spreading in France. Louis XVIII proved to be a sensible man, but a swarm of unreasonable and vindictive émigrés had come back with him. Reaction and a "white terror" were raging through the country. Adherents of the Revolution rallied to the emperor on his dramatic reappearance. Napoleon reached Paris, took over the government and army, and headed for Belgium. He would, if he could, disperse the pompous assemblage at Vienna. To the victors of the year before, and to most of Europe, it seemed that the Revolution was again stirring, that the old horror of toppling thrones and recurring warfare might not after all be ended. The opposing forces met in Belgium at Waterloo, where the Duke of Wellington, commanding an allied force, won a great victory. Napoleon again abdicated, and was again exiled, this time to distant St. Helena in the south Atlantic. A new peace treaty was made with France, the "second" Treaty of Paris. It was more severe than the first, since the French seemed to have shown themselves incorrigible and unrepentant. The

[20] See maps on pp. 230–231, 242–243.

new treaty imposed minor changes of the frontiers, an indemnity of 700,000,000 francs, and an army of occupation.

The effect of the Hundred Days, as the episode following Napoleon's return from Elba is called, was to renew the dread of revolution, war, and aggression. Britain, Russia, Austria, and Prussia, after being almost at war with each other in January, again joined forces to get rid of the apparition from Elba, and in November 1815 they solemnly reconfirmed the Quadruple Alliance of Chaumont, adding a provision that no Bonaparte should ever govern France. They agreed also to hold future congresses to review the political situation and enforce the peace. No change was made in the arrangements agreed to at Vienna, except that Murat, who fought for Napoleon during the Hundred Days, was captured and shot, and an extremely unenlightened Bourbon monarchy was restored in Naples. In addition to the Quadruple Alliance of the Great Powers, bound specifically to enforce or amend the terms of the peace treaty by international action, Alexander devised a vaguer scheme which he called the Holy Alliance. Long attracted to the idea of an international order, appalled by the return of Napoleon, and influenced at the moment by the pietistic Baroness von Krüdener, the tsar proposed, for all monarchs to sign, a statement by which they promised to uphold Christian principles of charity and peace. All signed except the pope, the sultan, and the prince regent of Great Britain. The Holy Alliance, probably sincerely meant by Alexander as a condemnation of violence, and at first not taken seriously by the others who signed it, and who thought it absurd to mix Christianity with politics, soon came to signify, in the minds of liberals, a kind of unholy alliance of monarchies against liberty and progress.

The Peace of Vienna, including generally the Treaty of Vienna itself, the treaties of Paris, and the British and colonial settlement, was the most far-reaching diplomatic agreement between the Peace of Westphalia of 1648 and the Peace of Paris which closed the First World War in 1919. It had its strong points and its weak ones. It produced a minimum of resentment in France; the late enemy accepted the new arrangements. It ended almost two centuries of colonial rivalry; for sixty or seventy years no colonial empire seriously challenged the British. Two other causes of friction in the eighteenth century—the control of Poland and the Austro-Prussian dualism in Germany—were smoothed over for fifty years. With past issues the peace of 1815 dealt rather effectively; with future issues, not unnaturally, it was less successful. The Vienna treaty was not illiberal in its day; it was by no means entirely reactionary, for the Congress showed little desire to restore the state of affairs in existence before the wars. The reaction that gathered strength after 1815 was not written into the treaty itself.

But the treaty gave no satisfaction to nationalists and democrats. It was a disappointment even to many liberals, especially in Germany. The transfer of peoples from government to government, without consultation of their wishes, opened the way under nineteenth-century conditions to a good deal of subsequent trouble. The peacemakers were in fact hostile both to nationalism and to democracy, the potent forces of the coming age; they regarded them, with reason, as leading to revolution and war. The problem to which they addressed themselves was to restore the balance of power, the "liberties of Europe," and to make a lasting peace. In this they were successful. They restored the European state system, or system in which a number of sovereign and independent states existed without fear of conquest or domination. And the peace which they made, though some details broke down in 1830, and others in 1848, on the whole subsisted for half a century; and not for a full century, not until 1914, was there a war in Europe that lasted longer than a few months or in which all the great powers were involved.

XI.
REACTION VERSUS
PROGRESS, 1815–1848

IN THE PERIOD of some thirty years preceding 1815 two "revolutions" had been taking place. One was the upheaval associated with the French Revolution and the Napoleonic empire. At bottom, it was mainly political, having to do with the organization of government, public power and authority, public finance, taxation, administration, law, individual rights, and the legal position of social classes. The other "revolution," a revolution in a more metaphorical sense, was primarily economic, having to do with the production of wealth, the techniques of manufacture, the exploitation of natural resources, the formation of capital, and the distribution of products to consumers. The political and the economic revolutions, in these years, to a surprising degree, went on independently of each other. Until 1815 the political revolution affected mainly the Continent, while the economic revolution was most active in England. The Continent, while renewing itself politically, remained economically less advanced than England. England, transformed economically, remained conservative in other respects. Hence it has been possible, in the preceding chapters, to deal with the French Revolution and its Napoleonic sequel without attending to the Industrial Revolution, as the economic changes then occurring in England are always called.

It may be (the matter is arguable) that the Industrial Revolution was more

Chapter Emblem: A medal commemorating the Congress of Vienna, showing the victorious rulers of Austria, Russia, and Prussia.

important than the French Revolution or any other. In a telescopic view of world history the two biggest changes experienced by the human race in the past ten thousand years may have been the agricultural or Neolithic revolution which ushered in the first civilizations, and the Industrial Revolution which has ushered in the civilization of the nineteenth and twentieth centuries. However that may be, it proves on closer examination that the economic and the political, the Industrial Revolution (or industrialization) and the other institutions of a society, cannot long be kept apart in an attempt at understanding. The Industrial Revolution occurred first in England, becoming evident about 1780, because of certain political characteristics of English society, because access to world markets had been gained by earlier commercial and naval successes, and because English life offered rewards to the individual for a spirit of risk-taking and innovation. Nor can the effects of political and economic revolution, in England or elsewhere, be kept apart for the years after 1815.

With the defeat of Napoleon and signing of the peace treaty at Vienna in 1815, it seemed that the French Revolution was at last over. European conservatism had triumphed; since it frankly opposed the new "French ideas," it can appropriately be called "reaction." But the processes of industrialization, as they accelerated in England and spread to the Continent, worked against the politically conservative settlement. They greatly enlarged both the business and wage-earning classes, and so made it harder for monarchs and landed aristocrats to maintain their control over public power. Industrial development in the nineteenth century was often called "progress," and progress proved stronger than reaction.

Industrial society arose in England, Western Europe, and the United States, in the nineteenth century, within the system known as capitalism. In the twentieth century, since the Russian Revolution, industrial societies have been created in which capitalism has been vehemently rejected. Industrialism and capitalism are therefore by no means the same. Yet all industrial societies use capital, which is defined as wealth that is not consumed but is used to produce more wealth, or future wealth. An automobile is a consumer's good; the automobile factory is the capital. What distinguishes a capitalist from a noncapitalist society is not the existence of capital, but the kinds of people who control it. The distinctions sometimes become blurred. But in one form of society the control of capital is through "private ownership" or institutions of private property, by which capital is owned by individuals or family trusts, or nowadays by foundations, pension funds, or corporations that are in turn owned by shareholders; in any case not by the state. In such societies, though ownership may be widespread, most capital is controlled by relatively few people, responding to market forces. In the other form of society productive capital in principle belongs to the public, and is in effect "owned" and controlled by the state or its agencies; such societies usually call themselves socialist, because the first socialists rejected the principle of private ownership of the means of production, that is, of capital. In these societies the control of capital, or decisions on saving, investment, and production, are also in the hands of relatively few under some form of central plan.

In Europe the institutions of secure private property had been developed since the Middle Ages, and much that happened in the French Revolution was designed to protect property from the demands of the state. Possession of property was held to be the basis of personal independence and political liberty, and the expectation of keeping future profits inspired, in some, a willingness to commit their capital to new and uncertain ventures. It made possible an entrepreneurial spirit. There had been a commercial capitalism in Europe at least since the sixteenth century.[1] Industrialization in Europe was therefore capitalistic. Countries outside the West-European orbit, and industrializing later, faced a different problem. A country in which little capital had accumulated from the trade and agriculture of previous generations, and which had few capital-owners or enterprising individuals, could hardly industrialize by European methods. If it lacked the European background, in which various political, social, legal, and intellectual features were as important as the economic, it would have to achieve industrialization by other methods. This has usually meant that innovation, planning, decision making, control, and even domination would rest with the state.

So in the short run, within a few years, the Industrial Revolution in Western Europe favored the liberal and modernizing principles proclaimed in the French Revolution. In the middle run, or in half a century, it made Europe overwhelmingly more powerful than other parts of the world, leading to a worldwide European ascendancy in the form of imperialism. In the still longer run, by the twentieth century, it provoked a retaliation, in which other countries tried hastily to industrialize in self-protection, or to improve the condition of their peoples, desperately hoping to catch up with the West while loudly denouncing it as imperialistic and capitalistic. Of these newer industrial societies the Soviet Union and the People's Republic of China would be the most prominent.

52. The Industrial Revolution in Britain

On the whole, from the beginning of history until about 1800, the work of the world was done with hand tools. Since then it has been increasingly done by machines. Before about 1800 power was supplied by human or animal muscle, reinforced by levers or pulleys, and supplemented by the force of running water or moving air. Since then power has been supplied by the human manipulation of more recondite forms of energy found in steam, electricity, the combustion of gases, and most recently within the atom. The process of shifting from hand tools to power machinery is what is meant by the Industrial Revolution. Its beginning cannot be dated exactly. It grew gradually out of the technical practices of earlier times. It is still going on, for in some countries industrialization is barely beginning, and even in the most highly developed it is still making advances. But the first country to be profoundly affected by industrialization was Great Britain, where its effects became manifest in the half-century following 1780.

It seems likely, despite the emphasis placed on revolutionary upheavals by historians, that people are habitually quite conservative. Working people do not put off their old way of life, move to strange and overcrowded towns, or enter the deadly rounds of mine and factory except under strong incentive. Well-to-do people, living in comfort on assured incomes, do not risk their wealth in new and untried ventures except for good reason. The shifting to modern machine

[1] See pp. 120–126.

production requires in any country a certain mobility of people and of wealth. Such mobility may be produced by state planning, as in the industrialization of the Soviet Union. In England a high degree of social mobility existed in the eighteenth century in consequence of a long historical development.

The Agricultural Revolution in Britain

The English Revolution of 1688, confirming the ascendancy of Parliament over the king, meant in economic terms the ascendancy of the more well-to-do property-owning classes.[2] Among these the landowners were by far the most important, though they counted the great London merchants among their allies. For a century and a half, from 1688 to 1832, the British government was substantially in the hands of these landowners—the "squirearchy" or "gentlemen of England." The result was a thorough transformation of farming, an Agricultural Revolution without which the Industrial Revolution could not have occurred.

Many landowners, seeking to increase their money incomes, began experimenting with improved methods of cultivation and stock raising. They made more use of fertilizers (mainly animal manure); they introduced new implements (such as the "drill seeder" and "horse-hoe"); they brought in new crops, such as turnips, and a more scientific system of crop rotation; they attempted to breed larger sheep and fatter cattle. An improving landlord, to introduce such changes successfully, needed full control over his land. He saw a mere barrier to progress in the old village system of open fields, common lands, and semicollective methods of cultivation. Improvement also required an investment of capital, which was impossible so long as the soil was tilled by numerous poor and custom-bound small farmers.

The old common rights of the villagers were part of the common law. Only an act of Parliament could modify or extinguish them. It was the great landowners who controlled Parliament, which therefore passed hundreds of "enclosure acts," authorizing the enclosure, by fences, walls, or hedges, of the old common lands and unfenced open fields. Land thus came under a strict regime of private ownership and individual management. At the same time small owners sold out or were excluded in various ways, the more easily since the larger owners had so much local authority as justices of the peace. Ownership of land in England, more than anywhere else in central or western Europe, became concentrated in the hands of a relatively small class of wealthy landlords, who let it out in large blocks to a relatively small class of substantial farmers. This development, though in progress throughout the eighteenth century, reached its height during the Napoleonic wars.

One result was greatly to raise the productivity of land and of farm labor. Fatter cattle yielded more meat, more assiduous cultivation yielded more cereals. The food supply of England was increased, while a smaller percentage of the population was needed to produce it. Labor was thus released for other pursuits. The greater number of the English country people became wage earners, working as hired men for the farmers and landlords, or spinning or weaving in their cottages for merchants in the towns. The English workingman (and woman) was

[2] See p. 181.

dependent on daily wages long before the coming of the factory and the machine. English working people became mobile; they would go where the jobs were, or where the wages were slightly higher. They also became available, in that fewer of them were needed on the land to produce food. Such conditions hardly obtained except in Great Britain. On the Continent agricultural methods were less productive, and the rural workers were more established on the soil, whether by institutions of serfdom as in eastern Europe or by the possession of property or firm leaseholds as in France.[3]

Industrialism in Britain: Incentives and Inventions

Meanwhile, as the Agricultural Revolution ran its course in the eighteenth century and into the nineteenth, the British had conquered a colonial empire, staked out markets all over the Americas and Europe, built up a huge mercantile marine, and won command of the sea. The British merchant could sell more, if only more could be produced. He had the customers, he had the ships, and moreover he could obtain the capital with which to finance new ideas. The profit motive prompted the search for more rapid methods of production. The old English staple export, woolen cloth, could be marketed indefinitely if only more of it could be woven. The possibilities in cotton cloth were enormous. The taste of Europeans for cottons had been already formed by imports from Asia. By hand methods Europeans could not produce cotton in competition with the East. But the market was endless if cotton could be spun, woven, and printed with less labor, i.e., by machines. Capital was available, mobile, and fluid because of the rise of banking, credit, and stock companies. Funds could be shifted from one enterprise to another. Wealthy landowners and merchants could divert some of their profits to industry. If an invention proved a total loss, as sometimes happened, or if it required years of development before producing any income, still the investment could be afforded. Only a country already wealthy from commerce and agriculture could have been the first to initiate the machine age. England was such a country.

These conditions induced a series of successful inventions in the textile industry. In 1733 a man named John Kay invented the fly shuttle, by which only one person instead of two was needed to operate a loom. The resulting increase in the output of weaving set up a strong demand for yarn. This was met in the 1760s by the invention of the spinning jenny, a kind of mechanized spinning wheel. The new shuttles and jennies were first operated by hand and used by domestic workers in their homes. But in 1769 Richard Arkwright patented the water frame, a device for the multiple spinning of many threads. At first it was operated by water power, but in the 1780s Arkwright introduced the steam engine to drive his spinning machinery. Thus requiring a considerable installation of heavy equipment, he gathered his engines, frames, and workers into large and usually dismal buildings, called "mills" by the English, or "factories" in subsequent American usage. Mechanical spinning now for a time overwhelmed the hand weavers with yarn. This led to the development of the power loom, which became economically practicable shortly after 1800. Weaving as well as

---

[3] See pp. 125–126.

spinning was therefore done increasingly in factories. These improvements in the finishing process put a heavy strain on the production of raw cotton. An ingenious Connecticut Yankee, Eli Whitney, while acting as a tutor on a plantation in Georgia, in ten days produced a cotton gin, which by speeding up the removal of seeds greatly increased the output of cotton. The gin soon spread through the American South, where the almost decaying plantation economy was abruptly revived, becoming an adjunct to the Industrial Revolution in England. British imports of raw cotton multiplied fivefold in the thirty years following 1790. In value of manufactures, cotton rose from ninth to first place among British industries in the same years. By 1820 it made up almost half of all British exports.

The steam engine, applied to the cotton mills in the 1780s, had for a century been going through a development of its own.[4] Scientific and technical experiments with steam pressures had been fairly common in the seventeenth century, but what gave the economic impetus to invention was the gradual dwindling away of Europe's primeval stocks of timber. The wood shortage became acute in England about 1700, so that it was more difficult to obtain the charcoal needed in smelting iron, and smelters turned increasingly to coal. Deeper coal shafts could not be sunk until someone devised better methods of pumping out water. About 1702 Thomas Newcomen built the first economically significant steam engine, which was soon widely used to drive pumps in the coal mines. It consumed so much fuel in proportion to power delivered that it could generally be used only in the coal fields themselves. In 1763 James Watt, a technician at the University of Glasgow, began to make improvements on Newcomen's engine. He formed a business partnership with Matthew Boulton. Boulton, originally a manufacturer of toys, buttons, and shoe buckles, provided the funds to finance Watt's rather costly experiments, handmade equipment, and slowly germinating ideas. By the 1780s the firm of Boulton and Watt was eminently successful, manufacturing steam engines both for British use and for the export trade.

At first, until further refinements and greater precision could be obtained in the working of iron, the engines were so cumbersome that they could be used as stationary engines only, as in the new spinning mills of Arkwright and others. Soon after 1800 the steam engine was successfully used to propel river boats, notably on the Hudson in 1807, by Robert Fulton, who employed an imported Boulton and Watt engine. Experiments with steam power for land transportation began at the same time. As it was in the coal fields of England a century before that Newcomen's engine had been put to practical uses, so now it was in the coal fields that Watt's engine first became a "locomotive." Well before 1800 the mines had taken to using "rail ways," on which wagons with flanged wheels, drawn by horses, carried coal to canals or to the sea. In the 1820s steam engines were successfully placed on moving vehicles. The first fully satisfactory locomotive was George Stephenson's *Rocket,* which in 1829, on the newly built Liverpool and Manchester Railway, not only reached an impressive speed of sixteen miles per hour but met other more important tests as well. By the 1840s the era of railroad construction was under way in both Europe and the United States.

The Industrial Revolution in Great Britain in its early phase, down to 1830 or 1840, took place principally in the manufacture of textiles, with accompanying

[4] See p. 298.

developments in the exploitation of iron and coal. The early factories were principally textile factories, and indeed mainly cotton mills; for cotton was an entirely new industry to Europe and hence easily mechanized, whereas the long established woolen trade, in which both employers and workers hesitated to abandon their customary ways, was mechanized more slowly. The suddenness of the change must not be exaggerated. It is often said that the Industrial Revolution was not a revolution at all. As late as the 1830s only a small fraction of the British working people were employed in factories. But the factory and the factory system were even then regarded as the coming mode of production, destined to grow and expand, mighty symbols of the irresistible march of progress.

Some Social Consequences of Industrialism in Britain

The Britain that emerged fundamentally unscathed and in fact strengthened from the wars with Napoleon was no longer the "merrie England" of days of yore. The island was becoming crowded with people, as was the lesser island of Ireland. The combined population of Great Britain and Ireland tripled in the century from 1750 to 1850, rising from about 10 million in 1750 to about 30 million in 1850. The growth was distributed very unevenly. Formerly, in England, most people had lived in the south. But the coal and iron, and hence the steam power, lay in the Midlands and the north. Here whole new cities rose seemingly out of nothing. In 1785 it was estimated that in England and Scotland, outside of London, there were only three cities with more than 50,000 people. Seventy years later, the span of one lifetime, there were thirty-one British cities of this size.

Preeminent among them was Manchester in Lancashire, the first and most famous of industrial cities of modern type. Manchester, before the coming of the cotton mills, was a rather large market town. Though very ancient, it had not been significant enough to be recognized as a borough for representation in Parliament. Locally it was organized as a manor. Not until 1845 did the inhabitants extinguish the manorial rights, buying them out at that time from the last lord, Sir Oswald Mosley, for £200,000 or about 1,000,000 dollars. In population Manchester grew from 25,000 in 1772 to 455,000 in 1851. But until 1835 there was no regular procedure in England for the incorporation of cities. Urban organization was more backward than in Prussia or France. Unless inherited from the Middle Ages, a city had no legal existence. It lacked proper officials and adequate tax-raising and lawmaking powers. It was therefore difficult for Manchester, and the other new factory towns, to deal with problems of rapid urbanization, such as provision of police protection, water and sewers, or the disposal of garbage.

The new urban agglomerations were drab places, blackened with the heavy soot of the early coal age, settling alike on the mills and the workers' quarters, which were dark at best, for the climate of the Midlands is not sunny. Housing for workers was hastily built, closely packed, and always in short supply, as in all rapidly growing communities. Whole families lived in single rooms, and family life tended to disintegrate. A police officer in Glasgow observed that there were whole blocks of tenements in the city, each swarming with a thousand ragged children who had first names only, usually nicknames—like animals, as he put it.

The distressing feature of the new factories was that for the most part they required unskilled labor only. Skilled workers found themselves degraded in

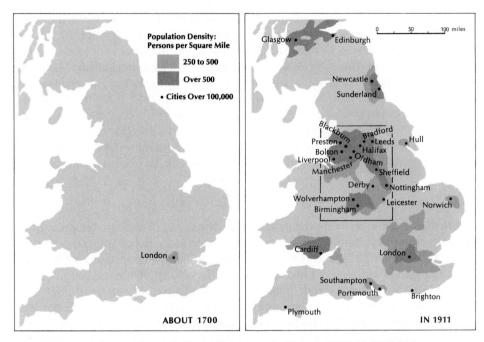

BRITAIN BEFORE AND AFTER THE INDUSTRIAL REVOLUTION
In 1700 England, Scotland, and Wales had only one city with a population of more than 100,000. In 1911 they had nearly thirty. The area within the small rectangle in the right-hand panel, roughly the Midlands, is almost exactly the area of Massachusetts.

status. Hand weavers and spinners, thrown out of work by the new machines, either languished in a misery that was the deepest of that of any class in the Industrial Revolution or else went off to a factory to find a job. The factories paid good wages by the standards for unskilled labor at the time. But these standards were very low, too low to allow a man to support his wife and children. This had generally been true for unskilled labor, in England and elsewhere, under earlier economic systems also. In the new factories the work was so mechanical that children as young as six years old were often preferred. Women, too, worked for less and were often more adept at handling a bobbin.

Hours in the factories were long, fourteen a day or occasionally more; and though such hours were familiar to persons who had worked on farms, or at domestic industry in rural households, they were more tedious and oppressive in the more regimented conditions that were necessary in the mills. Holidays were few, except for the unwelcome leisure of unemployment, which was a common scourge, because the short-run ups and downs of business were very erratic during this period of bewildering expansion. A day without work was a day producing nothing to live on, so that even where the daily wage was relatively attractive the worker's real income was chronically insufficient. Workers in the factories, as in the mines, were almost entirely unorganized. They were a mass of recently assembled humanity without traditions or common ties. Each bargained individually with his employer, who, usually a small businessman himself, facing a ferocious competition with others, often in debt for the equipment in his factory, or determined to save money in order to purchase more, held his "wages bill" to the lowest possible figure that he could manage.

The factory owners, the new "cotton lords," were the first industrial capitalists. They were often self-made men, who owed their position to their own intelligence, persistence, and foresight. They lived in comfort without ostentation or luxury, saving from each year's income to build up their factories and their machines. Hard-working themselves, they thought that landed gentlemen were usually idlers and that the poor tended to be lazy. They were usually honest, in a hard and exacting way; they would make money by any means the law allowed, but not beyond it. They were neither brutal nor knowingly hard-hearted. They gave to charitable and philanthropic causes. They believed that they did "the poor" a favor by furnishing them with work and by seeing to it that they worked diligently and productively. Most of them disapproved of public regulation of their business, though a few, driven by competition to expedients that they did not like, such as the employment of small children, would have accepted some regulation that fell on all competitors equally. It was a cotton magnate, the elder Robert Peel, who in 1802 pushed the first Factory Act through Parliament. This act purported to regulate the conditions in which pauper children were employed in the textile mills, but it was a dead letter from the beginning, since it provided no adequate body of factory inspectors. The English at this time, alone among the leading European peoples, had no class of trained, paid, and professional government administrators; nor did they yet want such a class, preferring self-government and local initiative. To have inspectors for one's affairs smacked of Continental bureaucracy. The fact that the older methods of economic regulation were obsolescent, actually unsuited to the new age, had the effect of discrediting the idea of regulation itself. The new industrialists wanted to be let alone. They considered it unnatural to interfere with business and believed that, if allowed to follow their own judgment, they would assure the future prosperity and progress of the country.

Classical Economics: "Laissez Faire"

The industrialists were strengthened in these beliefs by the emerging science of "political economy." In 1776 Adam Smith published his epochal *Wealth of Nations,* which criticized the older mercantilism, with its regulatory and monopolistic practices, and urged, though with moderation, that certain "natural laws" of production and exchange be allowed to work themselves out.[5] Smith was followed by Thomas R. Malthus, David Ricardo, and the so-called Manchester School. Their doctrine was dubbed (by its opponents) laissez faire and in its elaborated form is still called the classical economics. It held, basically, that there is a world of economic relationships autonomous and separable from government or politics. It is the world of the free market, and is regulated within itself by certain "natural laws," such as the law of supply and demand or the law of diminishing returns. All persons should follow their own enlightened self-interest; each knows his own interest better than anyone else; and the sum total of individual interests will add

[5] See pp. 324–325

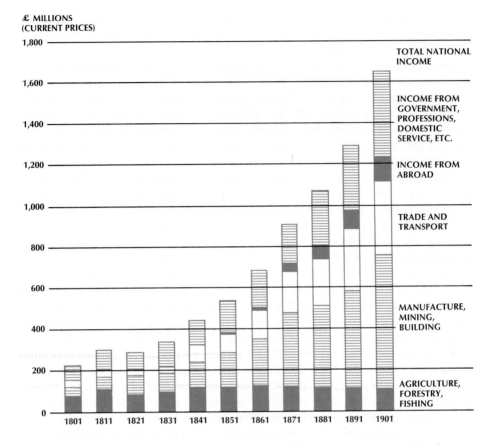

£ MILLIONS
(CURRENT PRICES)

Source: P. Deane and W. A. Cole, *British Economic Growth*
(Cambridge, Eng.: Cambridge University Press, 1962), pp. 166–167.

THE INDUSTRIAL REVOLUTION IN BRITAIN (AS SHOWN BY SOURCES OF INCOME)

Despite uncertainties in such figures several things are apparent. British national income grew about eightfold in the nineteenth century. Incomes derived from agriculture, forestry, and so forth, remained about the same, but sank from one-third to one-sixteenth of all incomes. By 1851 half the national income came from manufacturing, trade, and transportation, and by 1901 three-quarters came from these sources. The category "income from abroad" refers to interest and dividends on loans and investments outside Great Britain, that is, from the export of capital, and this source of income, insignificant in the early years of the century, grew rapidly after the 1850s.

up to the general welfare and liberty of all. Government should do as little as possible; it should confine itself to preserving security of life and property, providing reasonable laws and reliable courts, and so assuring the discharge of private contracts, debts, and obligations. Not only business, but education, charity, and personal matters generally should be left to private initiative. There should be no tariffs; free trade should reign everywhere, for the economic system is worldwide, unaffected by political barriers or national differences. As for workers, according to classical economists before about 1850, they should not expect to make more than a bare minimum living; an "iron law of wages" brings it about that as soon as workers receive more than a subsistence wage they breed more children, who eat up the excess, so that they reduce themselves, and the working class generally, again to a subsistence level. Workers, if discontented, should see the folly of changing the system, for this *is* the system, the natural system—there is no other. Political economy as taught in grim Manchester was not without reason called the "dismal science."

For working people in England the Industrial Revolution was a hard experience. It should be remembered, however, that neither low wages, nor the fourteen-hour day, nor the labor of women and children, nor the ravages of unemployment were anything new. All had existed for centuries, in England and western Europe, as agricultural and commercial capitalism replaced the more self-sufficient economies of the Middle Ages. The factory towns were in some ways better places to live than the rural slums from which many of their people came. Factory routine was psychologically deadening, but the textile mills were in some ways not worse than the domestic sweatshops in which manufacturing processes had previously been carried on. The concentration of working people in city and factory opened the way to improvement in their condition. It made their misery apparent; philanthropic sentiment was gradually aroused among the more fortunate. Gathered in cities, workers obtained more knowledge of the world. Mingling and talking together they developed a sense of solidarity, class interest, and common political aims; and in time they became organized, establishing labor unions by which to obtain a larger share of the national income.

Britain after the fall of Napoleon became the workshop of the world. Though factories using steam power sprang up in France, Belgium, New England, and elsewhere, it was really not until after 1870 that Great Britain faced any industrial competition from abroad. The British had a virtual monopoly in textiles and machine tools. The English Midlands and Scottish Lowlands shipped cotton thread and steam engines to all the world. British capital was exported to all countries, there to call new enterprises into being. London became the world's clearinghouse and financial center. Progressive people in other lands looked to Britain as their model, hoping to learn from its advanced industrial methods, and to imitate its parliamentary political system. Thus more foundations of the nineteenth century were laid.

53. The Advent of the "Isms"

The combined forces of industrialization and of the French Revolution led after 1815 to the proliferation of doctrines and movements of many sorts. These broke out in a general European revolution in 1848. As for the thirty-three years from 1815 to 1848, there is no better way of grasping their long-run meaning than to reflect on the number of still living "isms" that arose at that time.

So far as is known the word "liberalism" first appeared in the English language in 1819, "radicalism" in 1820, "socialism" in 1832, "conservatism" in 1835. The 1830s first saw "individualism," "constitutionalism," "humanitarianism," and "monarchism." "Nationalism" and "communism" date from the 1840s. Not until the 1850s did the English-speaking world use the word "capitalism" (French *capitalisme* is much older); and not until even later had it heard of "Marxism," though the doctrines of Marx grew out of and reflected the troubled times of the 1840s.

The rapid coinage of new "isms" does not in every case mean that the ideas they conveyed were new. Many of them had their origin in the Enlightenment, if not before. Men had loved liberty before talking of liberalism and been conservative without knowing conservatism as such. The appearance of so many "isms" shows rather that people were making their ideas more systematic. To the "philosophy" of the Enlightenment were now added an intense activism and a partisanship generated during the French Revolution. People were being obliged to reconsider and analyze society as a whole. The social sciences were taking form. An "ism" (excluding such words as "hypnotism" or "favoritism") may be defined as the conscious espousal of a doctrine in competition with other doctrines. Without the "isms" created in the thirty-odd years after the peace of Vienna it is impossible to understand or even talk about the history of the world since that event, so that a brief characterization of some of the most important is in order.[6]

Romanticism

One of the "isms" was not political. It was called "romanticism," a word first used in English in the 1840s to describe a movement then half a century old. Romanticism was primarily a theory of literature and the arts. Its great exponents included Wordsworth, Shelley, and Byron in England, Victor Hugo and Chateaubriand in France, Schiller and the Schlegels and many others in Germany. As a theory of art it raised basic questions on the nature of significant truth, on the importance of various human faculties, on the relation of thought and feeling, on the meaning of the past and of time itself. Representing a new way of sensing all human experience, it affected most thinking on social and public questions.

Possibly the most fundamental romantic attitude was a love of the unclassifiable—of moods or impressions, scenes or stories, sights or sounds or things concretely experienced, personal idiosyncrasies or peculiar customs which the intellect could never classify, box up, explain away, or reduce to an abstract generalization. The romantics, characteristically, insisted on the value of feeling as well as of reason. They were aware of the importance of the subconscious. They were likely to suspect a perfectly lucid idea as somehow superficial. They loved the mysterious, the unknown, the half-seen figures on the far horizon. Hence romanticism contributed to a new interest in strange and distant societies and in strange and distant historical epochs. Where the philosophes of the Enlightenment had deplored the Middle Ages as a time of intellectual error, the romantic generation looked back upon them with respect and even nostalgia, finding in them a fascination, a colorfulness, or a spiritual depth which they missed in their own time. The "Gothic," which rationalists thought barbarous, had a strong appeal for romantics. A Gothic Revival set in in the arts, of which one example was the British Parliament buildings, built in the 1830s.

In medieval art and institutions, as in the art and institutions of every age and

[6] For some other "isms" important after 1850, see pp. 519–527.

people, the romantics saw the expression of an inner genius. The idea of original or creative genius was in fact another of the most fundamental romantic beliefs. A genius was a dynamic spirit that no rules could hem in, one that no analysis or classification could ever fully explain. Genius, it was thought, made its own rules and laws. The genius might be that of the individual person, such as the artist, writer, or Napoleon-like mover of the world. It might be the genius or spirit of an age. Or it might be the genius of a people or nation, the *Volksgeist* of Herder, an inherent national character making each people grow in its own distinctive way, which could be known only by a study of its history, and not by ratiocination.[7] Here again romanticism gave a new impetus to study of the past. Politically romantics could be found in all camps, conservative and radical. Let us turn to the more purely political "isms."

Classical Liberalism

The first Liberals, calling themselves by that name (though Napoleon used that word for his own system, as has been seen[8]), arose in Spain among certain opponents of the Napoleonic occupation. The word then passed to France, where it denoted opposition to royalism after the restoration of the Bourbons in 1814. In England many Whigs became increasingly liberal, as did even a few Tories, until the great Liberal party was founded in the 1850s. Nineteenth-century, or "classical," liberalism varied from country to country, but it showed many basic similarities.

Liberals were generally men of the business and professional classes, together with enterprising landowners wishing to improve their estates. They believed in what was modern, enlightened, efficient, reasonable, and fair. They had confidence in man's powers of self-government and self-control. They set a high value on parliamentary or representative government, working through reasonable discussion and legislation, with responsible ministries and an impartial and law-abiding administration. They demanded full publicity for all actions of government, and to assure such publicity they insisted on freedom of the press and free rights of assembly. All these political advantages they thought most likely to be realized under a good constitutional monarchy. Outside of England they favored explicit written constitutions. They were not democrats; they opposed giving every man the vote, fearing the excesses of mob rule or of irrational political action. Only as the nineteenth century progressed did liberals gradually and reluctantly come to accept the idea of universal male suffrage. They subscribed to the doctrines of the rights of man as set forth in the American and French revolutions, but with a clear emphasis on the right of property, and in their economic views they followed the British Manchester School or the French economist J. B. Say. They favored laissez faire, were suspicious of the ability of government to regulate business, wanted to get rid of the guild system where it still existed, and disapproved of attempts on the part of the new industrial laborers to organize unions.

Internationally they advocated freedom of trade, to be accomplished by the

---

[7] See p. 437.
[8] See p. 428.

lowering or abolition of tariffs, so that all countries might exchange their products easily with each other and with industrial England. In this way, they thought, each country would produce what it was most fitted for, and so best increase its wealth and standards of living. From the growth of wealth, production, invention, and scientific progress they believed that the general progress of humanity would ensue. They generally frowned upon the established churches and landed aristocracies as obstacles to advancement. They believed in the spread of tolerance and education. They were also profoundly civilian in attitude, disliking wars, conquerors, army officers, standing armies, and military expenditures. They wanted orderly change by processes of legislation. They shrank before the idea of revolution. Liberals on the Continent were usually admirers of Great Britain.

Radicalism, Republicanism, Socialism

Radicalism, at least as a word, originated in England, where about 1820 the Philosophical Radicals proudly applied the term to themselves. These Radicals in the 1820s included not only the few working-class leaders who were beginning to emerge but also many of the new industrial capitalists, who were still unrepresented in Parliament. They took up where such English "Jacobins" as Thomas Paine had left off a generation earlier, before the long crisis of the French wars had discredited all radicalism as pro-French.[9]

The Philosophical Radicals were a good deal like the French philosophes before the Revolution. They were followers of an elderly sage, Jeremy Bentham, who in prolific writings from 1776 to 1832 undertook to reform the English criminal and civil law, church, Parliament, and constitution. The English Radicals professed to deduce the right form of institutions from the very nature and psychology of man himself. They impatiently waved aside all arguments based on history, usage, or custom. They went to the "roots" of things. ("Radical" is from the Latin word for "root.") They wanted a total reconstruction of laws, courts, prisons, poor relief, municipal organization, rotten boroughs, and fox-hunting clergy. Their demand for the reform of Parliament was vehement and insistent. They detested the Church of England, the peerage, and the squirearchy. Many radicals would just as soon abolish royalty also; not until the long reign of Queen Victoria (1837–1901) did the British monarchy become undeniably popular in all quarters. Above all, radicalism was democratic; it demanded a vote for every adult Englishman. After the Reform Bill of 1832 the industrial capitalists generally turned into liberals, but the working-class leaders remained radical democrats, as will be seen.

On the Continent radicalism was represented by militant republicanism. The years of the First French Republic, which to liberals and conservatives signified horrors associated with the Reign of Terror, were for the republicans years of hope and progress, cut short by forces of reaction. Republicans were a minority even in France; elsewhere, as in Italy and Germany, they were fewer still, though they existed. Mostly the republicans were drawn from intelligentsia such as students and writers, from working-class leaders protesting at social injustice, and from elderly veterans, or the sons and nephews of veterans, to whom the Republic of '93, with its wars and its glory, was a living thing. Because of police

[9] See pp. 379, 394.

repression, republicans often joined together in secret societies. They looked with equanimity on the prospect of further revolutionary upheaval, by which they felt that the cause of liberty, equality, and fraternity would be advanced. Strong believers in political equality, they were democrats demanding universal suffrage. They favored parliamentary government but were much less primarily concerned with its successful operation than were the liberals. Most republicans were bitterly anticlerical. Remembering the internecine struggle between the church and the republic during the French Revolution, and still facing the political activity of the Catholic clergy (for republicanism was most common in Catholic countries), they regarded the Catholic church as the implacable enemy of reason and liberty. Opposed to monarchy of any kind, even to constitutional monarchy, intensely hostile to church and aristocracy, conscious heirs of the great French Revolution, organized in national and international secret societies, not averse to overthrowing existing regimes by force, the more militant republicans were considered by most people, including the liberals, to be little better than anarchists.

Republicanism shaded off into socialism. Socialists generally shared the political attitudes of republicanism but added other views besides. The early socialists, those before the Revolution of 1848, were of many kinds, but all had certain ideas in common. All of them regarded the existing economic system as aimless, chaotic, and outrageously unjust. All thought it improper for owners of wealth to have so much economic power—to give or deny work to the worker, to set wages and hours in their own interests, to guide all the labors of society in the interests of private profit. All therefore questioned the value of private enterprise, favoring some degree of communal ownership of productive assets—banks, factories, machines, land, and transportation. All disliked competition as a governing principle and set forth principles of harmony, coordination, organization, or association instead. All flatly and absolutely rejected the laissez faire of the liberals and the political economists. Where the latter thought mainly of increasing production, without much concern over distribution, the early socialists thought mainly of a fairer or more equal distribution of income among all useful members of society. They believed that beyond the civil and legal equality brought in by the French Revolution a further step toward social and economic equality had yet to be taken.

One of the first socialists was also one of the first cotton lords, Robert Owen (1771–1858) of Manchester and the Scottish Lowlands. Appalled at the condition of the millhands, he created a kind of model community for his own employees, paying high wages, reducing hours, sternly correcting vice and drunkenness, building schools and housing and company stores for the cheap sale of workers' necessities. From such paternalistic capitalism in his early years he passed on to a long lifetime spent in crusading for social reforms, in which he was somewhat handicapped, not only by the opposition of industrialists, but by his unpopular radicalism in matters of religion.

Most of the early socialists were Frenchmen, spurred onward by the sense of an uncompleted revolution. One was a nobleman, the Count de Saint-Simon (1760–1825), who had fought in the War of American Independence, accepted the French Revolution, and in his later years wrote many books on social problems. He and his followers, who called themselves not socialists but Saint-Simonians, were among the first clear exponents of a planned society. They advocated the public ownership of industrial equipment and other capital, with control vested in the hands of great captains of industry or social engineers, who should plan vast projects like the digging of a canal at Suez, and in general coordinate the labor and resources of society to productive ends. Of a different type was Charles Fourier (1772–1837), a somewhat doctrinaire thinker who subjected all known institutions to a sweeping condemnation. His positive program took the form of proposing that society be organized in small units which he termed "phalansteries." Each of these he conceived to contain 1,620 persons, each doing the work suited to his natural inclination. Among the practical French no phalanstery was ever successfully organized. A number were established in the United States, still the land of Europe's utopian dream; the best known, since it was operated by literary people, was the Brook Farm "movement" in Massachusetts, which ran through a troubled existence of five years from 1842 to 1847. Robert Owen also, in 1825, had founded an experimental colony in America, at New Harmony, Indiana, on the then remote and unspoiled banks of the Wabash; it, too, lasted only about five years. Such schemes, presupposing the withdrawal of select spirits to live by themselves, really had little to say on the problems of society as a whole in an industrial age.

Politically the most significant form of antediluvian socialism—before the "deluge" of 1848—was the movement stirring among the working classes of France, a compound of revolutionary republicanism and socialism. The politically minded Paris workers had been republican since 1792. For them the Revolution, in the 1820s, 1830s, 1840s, was not finished but only momentarily interrupted. Reduced to political impotence, discriminated against in their rights in the law courts, obliged to carry identity papers signed by their employers, goaded by the pressures of industrialization as it spread to France, they developed a deep hostility to the owning classes of the bourgeoisie. They found a spokesman in the Paris journalist Louis Blanc, editor of the *Revue de progrès* and author of the *Organization of Work* (1839), one of the most constructive of the early socialist writings. He proposed a system of "social workshops," or state-supported manufacturing centers, in which the workers should labor by and for themselves without the intervention of private capitalists. Of this kind of socialism we shall hear more as the story unfolds.

As for "communism," it was at this time an uncertain synonym for socialism. A small group of German revolutionaries, mainly exiles in France, took the name for themselves in the 1840s. They would have been historically forgotten had they not included Karl Marx and Friedrich Engels among their members. Marx and Engels consciously used the word in 1848 to differentiate their variety of socialism from that of such utopians as Saint-Simon, Fourier, and Owen. But the word "communism" went out of general use after 1848, to be revived after the Russian Revolution of 1917, at which time it received a new meaning.

Nationalism: Western Europe

Nationalism, since it arose so largely in reaction against the international Napoleonic system, has already been discussed in the preceding chapter.[10] It was the most pervasive and the least crystallized of the new "isms." In western

[10] See pp. 435–439.

Europe—Britain, France, or Spain—where national unity already existed, nationalism was not a doctrine so much as a latent state of mind, easily aroused when national interests were questioned, but normally taken for granted. Elsewhere—in Italy, Germany, Poland, the Austrian and Turkish empires—where peoples of the same nationality were politically divided or subject to foreign rule, nationalism was becoming a deliberate and conscious program. It was undoubtedly the example of the West, of Great Britain and France, successful and flourishing because they were unified nations, that stimulated the ambitions of other peoples to become unified nations too. The period after 1815 was in Germany a time of rising agitation over the national question, in Italy of the Risorgimento or "resurgence," in eastern Europe of the Slavic Revival.

The movement was led by intellectuals, who often found it necessary to instill in their compatriots the very idea of nationality itself. They seized upon Herder's conception of the *Volksgeist* or national spirit, each applying it to his own people. Usually they began with a cultural nationalism, holding that each people had a language, history, world view, and culture of its own, which must be preserved and perfected. They then usually passed on to a political nationalism, holding that in order to preserve this national culture, and to assure liberty and justice to its individual members, each nation should create for itself a sovereign state. Governing authorities, they held, should be of the same nationality, i.e., language, as those they governed. All persons of the same nationality, i.e., language, should be encompassed within the same state.

Since such ideas could not be fully realized without the overthrow of every government in Europe east of France, thoroughgoing nationalism was inherently revolutionary. Outspoken nationalists were discountenanced or persecuted by the authorities and consequently formed secret societies in large numbers. The Carbonari, organized in Italy in the time of Napoleon, was the best known. There were many others—the *Veri Italiani,* the Apophasimenes, the Sublime and Perfect Masters, etc. In some regions Masonic lodges might serve the same purpose. In many of the societies nationalism was mixed with liberalism, socialism, or revolutionary republicanism in an as yet undifferentiated way. Members were initiated by a complex ritual intended to impress upon them the dire consequences of betraying the society's secrets. They used special grips and passwords and adopted revolutionary names to conceal their identity and baffle the police. They were usually so organized that the ordinary member knew the identity of only a few others, and never of the higher-ups, so that if arrested he could reveal nothing important. The societies kept busy, circulating forbidden literature and generally maintaining a revolutionary ferment. Conservatives dreaded them, but they were not really dangerous to any government that enjoyed the support of its people.

Best known of the nationalist philosophers in western Europe was the Italian Joseph Mazzini (1805–1872), who spent most of his adult life in exile in France and England. In his youth he joined the Carbonari, but in 1831 he founded a society of his own, called Young Italy, and he edited and smuggled into Italy copies of a journal of the same name. Young Italy was soon imitated by other societies of similar aim, such as Young Germany. In 1834 Mazzini organized a filibustering expedition against the kingdom of Sardinia, hoping that all Italy would rise and join him. Undeterred by its total failure, he continued to organize, to conspire, and to write. For Mazzini nationality and revolution were a holy

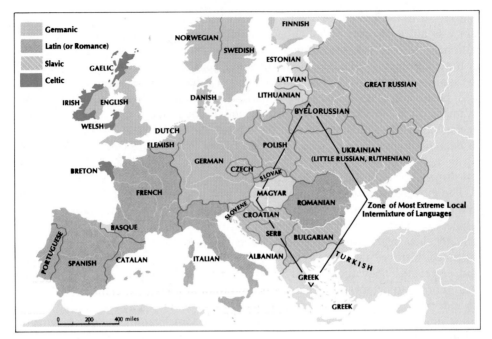

LANGUAGES OF EUROPE

There are three main European language-families—Germanic, Latin, and Slav. It will be seen that they cover most of Europe. Language areas are shown as they were in the first part of the twentieth century, at which time they had not changed much in over five centuries. The map cannot show local complications which have been a leading source of political trouble—such as the overlapping of adjoining languages, bilingual areas, and the existence of small language "pockets," as of Turkish in the Balkans, Greek in Asia Minor, Yiddish in Poland, or German in scattered parts of eastern Europe. In the extreme northwest is the "Celtic fringe," to which the Breton, Welsh, and Gaelic languages were pushed back in the early Middle Ages. For the area within the diamond-shaped zone no map on the present scale can give a realistic idea; the reader must consult an atlas. In any case, during the Second World War and its aftermath, in Eastern Europe many language pockets were wiped out through exchange, transportation, or destruction of peoples. (See maps, pp. 872–873 and 1034.)

cause in which the most generous and humane qualities were to find expression. He was a moral philosopher, as may be judged from the title of his most widely read book, *The Duties of Man*, in which he placed a pure duty to the nation intermediate between duty to family and duty to God.

To the Germans, divided and frustrated, nationality became almost an obsession. It affected everything from folklore to metaphysics. *Grimm's Fairy Tales*, for example, was first published in 1812. It was the work of the two Grimm brothers, founders of the modern science of comparative linguistics, who traveled about Germany to study the popular dialects and in doing so collected the folk tales that for generations had been current among the common people. They hoped in this way to find the ancient, native, indigenous "spirit" of Germany, deep and unspoiled in the bosom of the *Volk*. The same preoccupation with nationhood revealed itself in the philosophy of Hegel (1770–1831), possibly the most stupendous of all nineteenth-century thinkers.

To Hegel, with the spectacle of the Napoleonic years before him, it was evident that for a people to enjoy freedom, order, or dignity it must possess a potent and independent state. The state, for him, became the institutional embodiment of reason and liberty—the "march of God through the world," as he put it, meaning not an expansion in space through vulgar conquest, but a march through time and through the processes of history. Hegel conceived of reality itself as a process, a development having an inner logic and necessary sequence of its own. He thus broke with the more static and mechanical philosophy of the eighteenth century, with its fixed categories of unchangeable right and wrong. He became a philosopher of unfolding change. The pattern of change he held to be the "dialectic," or irresistible tendency of the mind to proceed by the creation of opposites. A given state of affairs (the "thesis") would in this view inevitably produce the conception of an opposite state of affairs (the "antithesis"), which would equally inevitably be followed by a reconciliation and a fusion of the two (the "synthesis"). Thus it could be thought that the very disunity of Germany, by producing the idea of unity, would inevitably bring about the creation of a German state.

The Hegelian dialectic was soon to be appropriated by Karl Marx to new uses, but meanwhile Hegel's philosophy, with other currents in Germany, made the study of history more philosophically meaningful than it had ever been before. History, the study of time process, seemed to be the very key with which to unlock the true significance of the world. Historical studies were stimulated, and the German universities became centers of historical learning, attracting scholars from many countries. Most eminent of the German historians was Leopold von Ranke (1795–1886), founder of the "scientific" school of historical writing. Ranke, too, though intellectually scrupulous to the last degree, owed much of his incentive to his national feeling. His first youthful work was a study of the *Latin and Teutonic Peoples*; and one of his main ideas, throughout his long life, was that Europe owed its unique greatness to the coexistence and interplay of several distinct nations, which had always resisted the attempts of any one nation to control the whole. By the latter Ranke really meant France—the France of Louis XIV and Napoleon. The Germans, said Ranke in 1830, had a mission from God to develop a culture and a political system entirely different from those of the French. They were destined to "create the pure German state corresponding to the genius of the nation." Whether Western constitutional, parliamentary, and individualist principles were suited to the national character of Germany seemed to Ranke very doubtful.

In economics Friedrich List, in his *National System of Political Economy* (1840), held that political economy as taught in England was suited only to England. It was not an abstract truth but a body of ideas developed in a certain historical stage in a certain country. List thus became a founder of the historical or institutional school of economics. The doctrine of free trade, he said, was designed to make England the world's industrial center by keeping other countries in the status of suppliers of raw material and food. But any country, he held, if it was to be civilized and develop its own national culture, must have cities, factories, industries, and capital of its own. It must therefore put up high tariffs (at least temporarily, in theory) for protection. List, it should be remarked, had developed his ideas during a sojourn in the United States, where Henry Clay's "American system" was in fact a national system of political economy.

Nationalism: Eastern Europe

In eastern Europe the Poles and the Magyars had long been active political nationalists, the Poles wishing to undo the partitions and reestablish their Polish state, the Magyars insisting on autonomy of their kingdom of Hungary within the Habsburg empire.[11] But for the most part nationalism in eastern Europe long remained more cultural than political. Centuries of development had tended to submerge the Czechs, Slovaks, Ruthenians, Romanians, Serbs, Croats, Slovenes—and even the Poles and Magyars in lesser degree. Their upper classes spoke German or French and looked to Vienna or to Paris for their ideas. The native languages had remained peasant languages, and the cultures peasant cultures, barely known to civilized Europeans. It seemed that many of these languages would disappear.[12]

But early in the nineteenth century the process began to reverse itself. Patriots began to demand the preservation of their historic cultures. They collected folk tales and ballads; they studied the languages, composing grammars and dictionaries, often for the first time; and they took to writing books in their mother tongues. They urged their own educated classes to give up "foreign" ways. They wrote histories showing the famous exploits of their several peoples in the Middle Ages. A new nationalism stirred the Magyars; in 1837 a national Hungarian theater was established at Budapest. In what was to become Romania a former Transylvanian peasant youth named George Lazar began as early as 1816 to teach at Bucharest. He lectured in Romanian (to the surprise of the upper classes, who preferred Greek), telling how Romania had a distinguished history back to the Roman emperor Trajan. As for the Greeks, they entertained visions of restoring the medieval Greek empire (known to Westerners as the Byzantine Empire) in which persons of Greek language or Greek Orthodox religion should become the predominant people of the Balkans.

The most far-reaching of the east-European movements was the Slavic Revival. The Slavs included the Russians, Poles, Ukrainians, Byelorussians, and Ruthenians; the Czechs and Slovaks; and the South Slavs, consisting of the Slovenes, Croats, Serbs, and Bulgars. All branches of the Slavs began to come to life. In 1814 the Serb Vuk Karajich published a grammar of his native tongue and a collection of *Popular Songs and Epics of the Serbs*; he worked out a Serbian alphabet, translated the New Testament, and declared that the dialect of Ragusa (now Dubrovnik) should become the literary language of all South Slavs. He was opposed by the Serbian clergy, who preferred to have writing confined to Slavonic, a purely learned language, like Latin; but he found much support outside Serbia, including that of the brothers Grimm. The Czechs had always been a more advanced people than the Serbs, but educated Czechs were usually half Germanized. In 1836 the historian Palacky published the first volume of his *History of Bohemia,* designed to give the Czechs a new pride in their national

---

[11] On the Poles, see pp. 245–249, 339–340, 436; on the Magyars, pp. 225, 276, 333.
[12] See p. 251.

past. He first wrote his book in German, the common reading language of educated Czechs. But he soon recast it into Czech, significantly reentitling it a *History of the Czech People*. Among Poles the poet and revolutionary Adam Mickiewicz may be mentioned. Arrested by the Russians in 1823 for membership in a secret society, he was soon allowed by the tsarist government to pass into western Europe. From 1840 to 1844 he taught Slavic languages at the Collège de France, using his lecture platform as a rostrum to deliver eloquent pleas for the liberation of all peoples and overthrow of autocracy. He wrote epic poems on Polish historical themes and continued to be active among the revolutionary Polish exiles settled in France.

Russia itself, which Poles and Czechs regarded as very backward, was slower to develop a pronounced national sense. Under Tsar Alexander I a Western or European orientation prevailed, but in Alexander's last years and after his death the doctrines of Slavophilism began to spread. Russian Slavophilism, or the idea that Russia possessed a way of life of its own, different from and not to be corrupted by that of Europe, was simply the application to Russia of the fundamental idea of the *Volksgeist*. Such views in Russia were at least as old as the opposition to the reforms of Peter the Great.[13] In the nationalistic nineteenth century they crystallized more systematically into an "ism," and they tended to merge into Pan-Slavism, which made substantially the same assertions for the Slavic peoples as a whole. But Pan-Slavism, before 1848, was no more than embryonic.

Other "Isms"

Liberalism, radical republicanism, socialism, and nationalism were after 1815 the political forces driving Europe onward toward a future still unknown. Of other "isms" less need be said. Conservatism, too, remained strong. Politically, on the Continent, conservatism upheld the institutions of absolute monarchy, aristocracy, and church and opposed the constitutional and representative government sought by liberals. As a political philosophy, conservatism built upon the ideas of Edmund Burke, who had held that every people must change its institutions by gradual adaptation, and that no people could suddenly realize in the present any freedoms not already well prepared for in the past.[14] This doctrine lacked appeal for those to whom the past had been a series of misfortunes. Conservatism sometimes passed into nationalism, since it stressed the firmness and continuity of national character. But nationalists at this time were more often liberals or republicans. "Monarchism" was conservative and even reactionary. Gone was the enlightened despotism of the last century, when kings had boldly irritated their nobles and defied their churches. After the thunders of the French Revolution aristocracy and monarchy huddled together, and their new watchword was to maintain "the throne and the altar."

Deeper than other "isms," a feeling shared in varying ways by people of all parties, was the profound current of humanitarianism. It consisted in a heightened sense of the reality of cruelty inflicted upon others. Here the thought of the Age

[13] See pp. 244–245, 337.
[14] See p. 379.

of Enlightenment suffered no reversal. Torture was gone, and even backward governments showed no inclination to restore it. Conditions in prisons, hospitals, insane asylums, and orphanages improved. People began to be moved by the misery of pauper children, chimney sweeps, women in the mines, and black slaves. Russian serf owners and American slave owners began to show psychological signs of moral doubt. To degrade human beings, use them as work animals, torture them, confine them unjustly, hold them as hostages for others, tear apart their families, and punish their relatives were regarded by Europeans as foreign to true civilization, something distant, "Turkish" or "Asiatic," like the castration of eunuchs, the impressment of janissaries, or the burning of widows. The Christian sense of the inviolability of the human person was now again, in a mundane way, beginning to relieve the sufferings of humanity.

54. The Dike and the Flood: Domestic

It is time now to resume the narrative of political events, broken off at the close of the last chapter with the peace settlement of 1814–1815. The governments that defeated Napoleon wanted to assure themselves above all else that the disturbances of the past twenty-five years would not be renewed. In France the restored Bourbon king, Louis XVIII, aspired to keep his throne for himself and his successors. In Great Britain the Tory governing class hoped to preserve the old England that they had so valiantly saved from the clutches of Bonaparte. In Germany, Austria, Italy, and central Europe the chief aim of Metternich, who for another thirty-three years remained the mastermind of these regions, was to maintain a system in which the prestige of the Habsburg dynasty should be supreme. The aims of the tsar, Alexander, were less clear. He was feared by representatives of the other powers as a dreamer, a self-chosen world savior, a man who said he wanted to bring Christianity into politics, a crowned Jacobin, and even a liberal. It became one of Metternich's chief hopes to convert Alexander to conservatism.

The arrangements made by the victorious powers were in some ways moderate, at least when the provocations they had undergone in the late wars are considered. Partly by the tsar's insistence written constitutions existed after 1814 in France and in Russian or "Congress" Poland. Some of the rulers of south German states allowed a measure of representative government. Even the king of Prussia promised a representative assembly for his kingdom, though the promise was not kept. But it was difficult to maintain any kind of stability. The forces of the political right, the privileged classes (or in France the former privileged classes) denounced all signs of liberalism as dangerous concessions to revolution. Those of the political left—liberals, nationalists, republicans—regarded the newly installed regimes as hopelessly reactionary and inadequate. Statesmen were jittery on the subject of revolution, so that they met every sign of agitation with attempts at repression, which though they might drive agitation temporarily underground really only made it worse by creating additional grievances. A vicious circle was set endlessly revolving.

Reaction after 1815: France, Poland

In France Louis XVIII in 1814 granted an amnesty to the regicides of 1793. But the regicides, like all republicans, found the France of 1814 an uncomfortable place to live in, exposed as they were to the unofficial vengeance of counterrevolutionaries, and in 1815 most of them rallied to Napoleon when he returned from Elba. This exasperated the royalist counterrevolutionaries beyond all measure. A brutal "white terror" broke out. Upper-class youths murdered Bonapartists and republicans, Catholic mobs seized and killed Protestants at Marseilles and Toulouse. The Chamber of Deputies chosen in 1815 (by the tiny electorate of 100,000 well-to-do landowners) proved to be more royalist than the king—*plus royaliste que le roi.* The king himself could not control the mounting frenzy of reaction, which he was sensible enough to realize would only infuriate the revolutionary element still further, as in fact happened. In 1820 a fanatical workingman assassinated the king's nephew, the Duke de Berry. Those who said that all partisans of the French Revolution were criminal extremists seemed to be justified. The reaction deepened, until in 1824 Louis XVIII died and was succeeded by his brother Charles X. Not only was Charles X the father of the recently murdered Duke de Berry, but for over thirty years he had been the acknowledged leader of implacable counterrevolution. As the Count of Artois, youngest brother of Louis XVI, he had been among the first to emigrate in 1789. He was the favorite Bourbon among the most obstinate ex-seigneurs, nobles, and churchmen. Regarding himself as hereditary absolute monarch by the grace of God, he had himself crowned at Reims with all the romantic pomp of ages past, and proceeded to stamp out not only revolutionary republicanism but liberalism and constitutionalism as well.

In Poland, it will be recalled, the Vienna settlement created a constitutional kingdom, with Alexander as king, joined in merely personal union with the Russian empire. The new machinery did not work very well. The Polish constitution provided for an elected diet, a very wide suffrage by the standards of the day, the Napoleonic civil code, freedom of press and religion, and exclusive use of the Polish language. But the Poles discovered that Alexander, though favoring liberty, did not like to have anyone disagree with him. They could make little use of their much touted freedom in any actual legislation. The elected diet could not get along with the viceroy, who was a Russian. In Russia the serf-owning aristocracy viewed Alexander's idea of a constitutional kingdom in Poland with a jaundiced eye. They wanted no experimentation with liberty on the very borders of Russia. The Poles themselves played into the hands of their enemies. For the Poles were nationalist at least as much as they were liberal. They were dissatisfied with the boundaries accorded to Congress Poland. They dreamed of the vast kingdom that had existed before the First Partition and so agitated the interminable question of the Eastern Border, laying claim to huge territories in the Ukraine and Byelorussia.[15] At the University of Vilna professors and students began to join secret societies. Some members of these societies were revolutionaries aiming at driving out Alexander, reuniting with Prussian and Austrian Poland, and reconstituting an independent Polish state. It was in the

[15] See map, p. 248.

discovery and breaking up of one such society that Adam Mickiewicz was arrested in 1823. Reaction and repression now struck the University of Vilna.

Reaction after 1815: The German States, Britain

In Germany those who had felt national stirrings during the Wars of Liberation were disillusioned by the peace treaty, which maintained the several German principalities about as Napoleon had left them and purposely united them only in a loose federation, or Bund. National ideas were most common in the numerous universities, where students and professors were more susceptible than most people to the doctrines of an eternal *Volksgeist* and a far-flung *Deutschtum*. National ideas, being a glorification of the German common people, carried with them a kind of democratic opposition to aristocrats, princes, and kings. Students in many of the universities in 1815 formed college clubs, called collectively the *Burschenschaft*, which, as centers of serious political discussion, were to replace the older clubs devoted to drinking and dueling. The *Burschenschaft*, a kind of German youth movement, held a nationwide congress at Wartburg in 1817. Students listened to rousing speeches by patriotic professors, marched about in "Teutonic" costume, and burned a few reactionary books. This undergraduate performance was no immediate threat to any established state, but the nervous governments took alarm. In 1819 a theology student assassinated the German writer Kotzebue, known as an informer in the service of the tsar. The assassin received hundreds of letters of congratulation, and at Nassau the head of the local government barely escaped the same fate at the hands of a pharmacy student.

Metternich now chose to intervene. He had no authority in Germany except in that Austria was a member of the Germanic federation. He regarded all these manifestations of German national spirit, or of any demand for a more solidly unified Germany, as a threat to the favorable position of the Austrian Empire and to the whole balance of Europe. He called a conference of the principal German states at Carlsbad in Bohemia; the frightened conferees adopted certain resolutions, proposed by Metternich, which were soon enacted by the diet of the Bund. These Carlsbad Decrees (1819) dissolved the *Burschenschaft* and the equally nationalistic gymnastic clubs (some of whose members thereupon joined secret societies); and they provided for government officials to be placed in the universities to watch them and for censors to control the contents of books and of the periodical and newspaper press. The Carlsbad Decrees remained in force for many years, and they imposed an effective check on the growth of liberal and nationalist ideas in Germany.

Metternich was unable to persuade the south German rulers to retract the constitutions they had granted. The rulers here, in Bavaria, Württemberg, and elsewhere, found that with representative government they could rally popular support as well as assimilate the numerous new territories that they had obtained from Napoleon. But in general, throughout Germany, after 1820, repression of new or unsettling ideas was the rule. Still more so was this true of the Austrian Empire, which Metternich could more directly control.

Nor did Great Britain escape the dreary rounds of agitation and repression. As elsewhere, radicalism produced reaction, and vice versa. Britain after Waterloo was a country devoted to its old traditions but also afflicted by the most advanced social evils. In 1815, at the close of the wars, the landed classes feared an inrush of imported agricultural products and consequent collapse of farm prices and rentals. The gentry who controlled Parliament enacted a new Corn Law, raising the protective tariff to the point where import of grain became impossible unless prices were very high. Landlords and their farmers benefited, but wage earners found the price of breadstuffs soaring out of reach. At the same time there was a postwar depression in industry. Wages fell and many were thrown out of work. These conditions naturally contributed to the spread of political radicalism, which looked first of all to a drastic reform of the House of Commons, in order that thereafter a radical program of social and economic legislation might be enacted.

A riot broke out in London in December 1816. In the following February the Prince Regent was attacked in his carriage. The goverment suspended habeas corpus and employed *agents provocateurs* to obtain evidence against the agitators. Industrialists of Manchester and the new factory towns, determined to force through the reform of parliamentary representation, took the chance offered by the distress of the working classes to organize mass meetings of protest. At Birmingham a crowd elected a mock member of Parliament. At sprawling Manchester 80,000 people staged an enormous demonstration at St. Peter's Fields in 1819; they demanded universal male suffrage, annual election of the House of Commons, and the repeal of the Corn Laws. Although perfectly orderly they were fired upon by soldiers; 11 persons were killed and about 400 wounded, including 113 women. Radicals called this episode the Peterloo massacre in derisive comparison with the battle of Waterloo. The frightened government thanked the soldiers for their brave upholding of the social order. Parliament rushed through the Six Acts (1819), which outlawed "seditious and blasphemous" literature, put a heavy stamp tax on newspapers, authorized the search of private houses for arms, and rigidly restricted the right of public meeting. A group of revolutionaries thereupon plotted to assassinate the whole cabinet at a dinner; they were caught in Cato Street in London in 1820—whence the name "Cato Street Conspiracy." Five of them were hanged. Meanwhile, for publishing the writings of Thomas Paine, Richard Carlisle spent seven years in prison.

"Our example," wrote the Duke of Wellington to a Continental correspondent in 1819, "will be of value in France and Germany, and it is to be hoped that the world will escape from the general revolution with which we all seem to be threatened."

In summary, reactionary policies entrenched themselves everywhere in the years following the peace. The reaction was due only in part to memories of the French Revolution. It was due even more to the living fear of revolution in the present. This fear, though exaggerated, was no mere hallucination. Sensing the rising flood, the established interests desperately built dikes against it in every country. The same is true of international politics at the time.

55. The Dike and the Flood: International

At the Congress of Vienna the powers agreed to hold meetings in the future to enforce the treaty and take up new issues as they arose. A number of congresses of the Great Powers resulted, which are of significance as an experimental step toward international regulation of the affairs of Europe. The congresses resembled, in a tentative and partial way, the League of Nations that arose after the First World War of 1914–1918, or the United Nations that arose during and after the war of 1939–1945. The powers had also, in 1815, in alarm after the return of Napoleon, subscribed to Alexander I's Holy Alliance, which became the popular term for the collaboration of the European states in the congresses.[16] The Holy Alliance, on the face of it a statement of Christian purpose and international concord, gradually became an alliance for the suppression of revolutionary and even liberal activity, following in that respect the trend of the governments which made it up.

The Congress of Aix-la-Chapelle, 1818

The first general postwar assemblage of the powers took place at the Congress of Aix-la-Chapelle (or Aachen) in 1818. The principal item on the agenda was to withdraw the allied army of occupation from France. The French argued that Louis XVIII would never be popular in France so long as he was supported by a foreign army. The other powers, since they all desired the French to forget the past and accept the Bourbons, withdrew their military forces without disagreement. They arranged also to have private bankers take over the French reparations debt (the 700 million francs imposed by the second Treaty of Paris); the bankers paid the allied governments, and the French in due time paid the bankers. On a few other smaller matters international collective action proved successful.

Tsar Alexander was still the most advanced internationalist of the day. He suggested at Aix-la-Chapelle a kind of permanent European union and even proposed the maintenance of international military forces to safeguard recognized states against changes by violence. Governments if thus reassured against revolution, he argued, would more willingly grant constitutional and liberal reforms. But the others demurred, especially the British foreign minister Lord Castlereagh. The British declared themselves willing to make international commitments against specified contingencies, such as a revival of aggression on the part of France. But they would assume no obligations to act upon indefinite and unforeseeable future events. They reserved the right of independent judgment in foreign policy. Concretely, the congress addressed itself to the problems of the Atlantic slave trade and of the recurring nuisance of the Barbary pirates. It was unanimously agreed that both should be suppressed. To suppress them required naval forces, which only the British possessed in adequate amount, and it meant also that naval captains must be authorized to stop and search vessels at sea. The continental states, always touchy on the subject of British sea power, refused to countenance any such uses of the British fleet. They feared for the freedom of the seas. As for the British, they would not even discuss placing British warships in an international naval pool or putting British squadrons under the authority of an international body. Nothing therefore was done; the slave trade continued, booming illicitly with the endless demand for cotton; and the Barbary pirates were not disposed of until the French occupied and annexed

[16] See p. 451 and map, pp. 448–449.

Algeria some years later. The growth of international institutions was blocked by the separate interests of the sovereign states.

Revolution in Southern Europe: The Congress of Troppau, 1820

Scarcely had the Congress of Aix-la-Chapelle disbanded when revolutionary agitation came to a crisis in southern Europe. It was not that revolutionary or liberal sentiment was stronger here than in the north, in the sense of having more followers, but rather that the governments in question, those of Spain, Naples, and the Ottoman Empire, were inefficient, ignorant, flimsy, and corrupt. Many of the revolutionaries were hardly more than middle-class liberals; indeed, the Spaniards at this time were the first to use the word "liberal" in this modern political sense. Many of them had at first accepted the Napoleonic occupation of Spain as a progressive development, but had then turned against it and proclaimed a new constitution in 1812, modeled on the French revolutionary constitution of 1789–1791.[17] After Napoleon's final defeat they attempted to force the restored Bourbon kings of Spain and Naples to adopt this constitution of 1812.

In 1820 the governments of both Spain and Naples collapsed with remarkable ease before the demonstrations of revolutionaries. The kings of both countries reluctantly took oaths to the Spanish constitution of 1812. But Metternich saw the insurrections as the first symptoms of a revolutionary seizure against which Europe should be quarantined. It was a fact that revolutionary agitation was international, easily leaping across frontiers, because of the operations of secret societies and of political exiles, and because in any case the same ideas had been aroused in all countries by the French Revolution. Metternich considered Italy in particular, since the ejection of Napoleon, to be within the legitimate sphere of influence of the Austrian Empire. He therefore called a meeting of the Great Powers at Troppau, hoping to use the authority of an international congress to put down the revolution in Naples. The governments of Great Britain and France, not eager to play Austria's game, sent only observers to the congress. Metternich's main problem was, as usual, Alexander. What would be the attitude of the liberal tsar, the friend and patron of constitutions, toward the idea of a constitutional monarchy in Naples? At an inn in Troppau Metternich and Alexander met alone, and there held a momentous interview over the teacups. Metternich reviewed the horrors of revolutionism, the unwisdom of granting any concessions lest revolutionaries be encouraged. Alexander was already somewhat disillusioned by the ungrateful feelings of the Poles. He was troubled by rumors of disaffection among officers in his own army. He had always believed that constitutions should be granted by legitimate sovereigns, not extorted from them by revolutionaries, as had happened in Naples. He allowed himself to be persuaded by Metternich. He declared that he had always been wrong, and that Metternich had always been right; and he announced himself ready to follow Metternich's political judgment. The triumph of the Austrian chancellor was complete. The radical tsar now turned reactionary.

Thus fortified, Metternich drew up a document, the protocol of Troppau, for consideration and acceptance by the five Great Powers. It held that all recognized

[17] See pp. 373–374, 435.

European states should be protected by collective international action, in the interests of general peace and stability, from internal changes brought about by force. It was a statement of collective security against revolution. Neither France nor Great Britain accepted it. Castlereagh wrote to Metternich that if Austria felt its interests to be threatened in Naples it should intervene in its own name only. It was not the repression of the Neapolitan revolution that the Tories of 1820 objected to, so much as the principle of a binding international collaboration. Metternich could get only Russia and Prussia to endorse his protocol, in addition to Austria. These three, acting as the Congress of Troppau, authorized Metternich to dispatch an Austrian army into Naples. He did so; the Neapolitan revolutionaries were arrested or put to flight; the incompetent and brutal Ferdinand I was restored as "absolute" king; the demon of revolution was seemingly exorcised. Reaction won out. But the Congress of Troppau, ostensibly a Europe-wide international body, had in effect functioned as an antirevolutionary alliance of Austria, Russia, and Prussia. A gap opened between the three Eastern autocracies and the two Western powers—even when the latter consisted of Tories and Bourbons.

Spain and the Near East: The Congress of Verona, 1822

Thousands of revolutionaries and liberals fled from the terror raging in Italy. Many went to Spain, now dreaded by conservatives as the main seat of revolutionary infection. The Near East also seemed about to ignite in conflagration. Alexander Ypsilanti, a Greek who had spent his adult life in the military service of Russia, in 1821 led a band of armed followers from Russia into Romania (still a part of Turkey), hoping that all Greeks and pro-Greeks in the Turkish empire would join him. He expected Russian support, since the penetration of Turkey by the use of Greek Christians had long been a pet project of Russian foreign policy.[18] The possibility of a Turkish empire converted into a "Greek" empire and dependent on Russia was naturally unpleasant to Metternich. To deal with all these matters an international congress met at Verona in 1822.

Alexander, in shifting from liberal to reactionary views, had not changed his belief in the need for concerted international action. Had pure power politics determined his decisions he would doubtless have favored Ypsilanti's Grecophile revolution. But he stood by the principle of international solidarity against revolutionary violence. He refused to support Ypsilanti, who found less enthusiasm for Greek culture among the Romanians and Balkan peoples than he had expected and was soon defeated by the Turks. As for intervention to repress the uprising in Greece itself, the question did not arise, since the Turkish government proved quite able for a time to handle the matter without assistance.

The question of the revolution in Spain was settled by foreign intervention. The Bourbon regime in France had no taste for a Spain in which revolutionaries, republicans, political exiles, and members of secret societies might be harbored. The French government proposed to the Congress of Verona that it be authorized to dispatch an army across the Pyrenees. The Congress welcomed the offer, and despite many dire predictions of ruin, arising from memories of Napoleon's disaster, a French army of 200,000 men moved into Spain in 1823. The campaign

[18] See p. 340.

proved to be a military promenade through a cheering country. Spanish liberals, constitutionalists, or revolutionaries were a helpless minority. The mass of the people saw the invasion as a deliverance from Masons, Carbonari, and heretics and shouted with satisfaction at the restoration of church and king. Ferdinand VII, unscrupulous and narrow-minded, repudiated his constitutional oath and let the vindictive ecclesiastics, grandees, and hidalgos have their way. The revolutionaries were savagely persecuted, exiled, or jailed.

Latin American Independence

The disturbances in Europe had their repercussions in all parts of America. While Great Britain was engaged against Napoleon, the United States fought its inconclusive War of 1812 against the former mother country, and a few years later, after minor military operations, obtained the cession of Florida from Spain. Latin America was affected more positively. The Portuguese royal family, to escape Napoleon, had taken refuge in its Brazilian empire, but when the dynasty was restored at Lisbon one of its members refused to leave Brazil, which remained as an "empire" independent of Portugal until succeeded by a republican regime in 1889.

Spanish America reached over the enormous area from San Francisco to Buenos Aires. Here, too, the thought of the Enlightenment, the news of the American and French Revolutions, the Napoleonic occupation of Spain, and the restoration in 1814 of the Bourbon Ferdinand VII to the Spanish throne all had their effects. The British had been penetrating Spanish America commercially for over a century, and during the Napoleonic wars they had increased their exports to it twentyfold.[19] There were thus business interests in Spanish America that resisted any return to the old Spanish imperial system of trade controls. More fundamental was the resentment, growing up over several generations, felt by the "creoles" for the "peninsulars," the creoles being the whites of Spanish descent born in America, and the peninsulars those born in Spain who were sent out to occupy the highest offices in the empire. In many places most of the people were native Indians or mestizos of mixed Spanish and Indian origin, often living in depressed conditions and far from the capital cities, so that the movement for independence never took on the widespread popular character that it did in the British colonies that became the United States. It was mainly led by creoles who were active in municipal governments in the towns. At times, as when the revolt was against the Napoleonic government in Spain or against the ephemeral liberal regime in Spain in 1820, the movement for independence recruited some very conservative elements among large landowners and high churchmen. But the important leaders, such as Simón Bolívar and José de San Martín, were men who had spent years in Europe and preferred the new constitutional principles, but were in the end frustrated in their aspirations for their own country. The dissensions that long continued to afflict Spanish America were all present within the independence movement itself.

Because of its vast extent, over six thousand miles interrupted by mountain barriers, there could be less unity in the liberation of Spanish America than had

[19] See p. 435.

been possible, however difficult, in the North American rebellion against England. There could be no Continental Congress such as had met in Philadelphia in 1774. Revolts took place separately within the great vice-royalties: New Spain (Mexico), New Granada (Colombia and Venezuela), Peru (including Ecuador and most of Bolivia and Chile), and La Plata (Argentina, with claims over what are now Uruguay and Paraguay).

The first revolts were against Joseph Bonaparte after Napoleon made him king of Spain in 1808. The rebels proclaimed their loyalty to the deposed Ferdinand VII, who, however, when restored in 1814, refused to make any concessions to American demands, so that revolutionary sentiment turned against him also. There followed a series of disconnected struggles between those fighting for independence (with or without much internal change) and combinations of officials, army officers, landowners, and churchmen who remained loyal to the Spanish crown. Bolívar became the liberator of Venezuela and Colombia, San Martín of Argentina and Chile, and both combined in the liberation of Peru. In Mexico, by way of exception, there was a true mass rising of Indians and mestizos, which was put down by the middle- and upper-class leaders, so that independent Mexico entered upon a long period of chronic turmoil. All Spanish America was troubled by disputes over boundaries, federations formed only to dissolve, and attempted conquests and secessions, so that it was only later in the nineteenth century that the map of South and Central America took form as we know it today.

Let us return to the congress of European powers meeting in Verona in 1822. At the very time when a French army suppressed the revolution in Spain the revolutionaries in Spanish America were declaring their independence. At Verona, the tsar Alexander urged the Congress to mediate between Spain and its colonies. This was a euphemistic way of suggesting military intervention in Spanish America, following the principle of the protocol of Troppau. The British objected. Even the Tory government favored revolutions that might break up the Spanish empire into independent states, with which free trade treaties might be negotiated. Without at least benevolent neutrality from the British fleet no armed force could sail to America. The Spanish Americans therefore maintained their independence, thanks in part to the use made by the British of their sea power on this occasion.

The new republics received strong moral support from the United States also. In December 1823 President James Monroe, in a message to Congress, announced the "Monroe Doctrine." It stated that attempts by European powers to return parts of America to colonial status would be viewed as an unfriendly act by the United States. The British foreign minister George Canning (who had just succeeded Castlereagh) had at first proposed a joint statement by Great Britain and the United States against the East European powers on the Spanish American question. President Monroe, at the advice of his secretary of state John Quincy Adams, decided instead to make a unilateral statement in the form of a message to Congress. They intended to aim their "doctrine" at Great Britain as well as the Continental states, since the British, with their command of the sea, were in fact the only power by which the independence of American states could in practice be threatened. Canning, having no such threats in mind, and concerned more with the Congress of Verona, accepted the line taken by the United States. Indeed, he declared with a flourish that he had "called the New World into existence to redress the balance of the Old." The Monroe Doctrine, at its inception, was a kind of counterblast to the Metternich doctrine of the protocol of Troppau. Where the latter announced the principle of intervention against revolution, the Monroe Doctrine announced that revolutions in America, if they resulted in regimes recognized by the United States, were outside the pale of attention of European powers. In any case the efficacy of the Monroe Doctrine long depended on the tacit cooperation of the British fleet.

Over three hundred years of European colonial empires in America now came to an end, with few exceptions, in the half-century following the United States declaration of independence. One exception was Canada, where membership in the British empire was voluntary, at least for the English-speaking inhabitants, and where both the English and French Canadians resisted threats of annexation by the United States. The other exceptions were in the West Indies, where Haiti was independent, the smaller islands remained British, French, or Dutch, and the large islands of Cuba and Puerto Rico remained Spanish until the Spanish-American War of 1898.

The End of the Congress System

After the Congress of Verona no more such meetings were held. The attempt at a formal international regulation of European affairs was given up. In the broadest retrospect, the congresses failed to make progress toward an international order because, especially after Alexander's conversion to conservatism, they came to stand for nothing except preservation of the status quo. They made no attempt at accommodation with the new forces that were shaping Europe. It was not the policy of the congresses to forestall revolution by demanding that governments institute reforms. They simply repressed or punished all revolutionary agitation. They propped up governments that could not stand on their own feet.

In any case the congresses never succeeded in subordinating the separate interests of the Great Powers. Perhaps Alexander's repudiation of Ypsilanti was a sacrifice of Russian advantage to international principle; but when the Austrian government intervened to crush the revolution in Naples, and when the French government crushed the revolution in Spain, though in both cases they acted with an international mandate, each was really promoting what it conceived to be its own interests. The interest of Great Britain was to pull away from the system entirely. As defined by Castlereagh and by Canning after him, it was to stand aloof from permanent international commitments, to preserve a free exercise of sea power and foreign policy, and to take a benevolent view toward revolution in other countries. Since France eventually pulled away also, the Holy Alliance ceased to be even ostensibly a European system and became no more than a counterrevolutionary league between the three east-European autocracies. With a majority of the five Great Powers highly illiberal, the cause of liberalism in Europe was advanced by the collapse of the international system. At the same time the collapse of the system opened the way to the uncontrolled nationalism of the sovereign states. "Things are getting back to a wholesome state again," wrote George Canning in 1822. "Every nation for itself and God for us all!"

Russia: The Decembrist Revolt, 1825

Alexander I, "the man who defeated Napoleon," the ruler who had led his armies from Moscow to Paris, who had frightened the diplomats by the Russian shadow that he threw over the Continent, and who yet in his way had been the great pillar of constitutional liberalism and international order, died in 1825. His death was the signal for revolution in Russia. Officers of the Russian army, during the campaigns of 1812–1815 in Europe, had become acquainted with many unsettling ideas. Secret socities were formed even in the Russian officer corps; their members held all sorts of conflicting ideas, some wanting a constitutional tsardom in Russia, some demanding a republic, some even dreaming of an emancipation of the serfs. When Alexander died it was for a time uncertain which of his two brothers, Constantine or Nicholas, should succeed him. The restless coteries in the army preferred Constantine, who was thought to be more favorable to innovations in the state. In December 1825 they proclaimed Constantine at St. Petersburg, having their soldiers shout "Constantine and Constitution!" The soldiers, it is said, thought that Constitution was Constantine's wife.

But the fact was that Constantine had already renounced his claims in favor of Nicholas, who was the rightful heir. The uprising, known as the Decembrist revolt, was soon put down. Five of the mutinous officers were hanged; many others were condemned to forced labor or interned in Siberia. The Decembrist revolt was the first manifestation of the modern revolutionary movement in Russia—of a revolutionary movement inspired by an ideological program, as distinguished from the elemental mass upheavals of Pugachev or Stephen Razin. But the immediate effect of the Decembrist revolt was to clamp repression upon Russia more firmly. Nicholas I (1825–1855) maintained an unconditional and despotic autocracy.

Ten years after the defeat of Napoleon the new forces issuing from the French Revolution seemed to be routed, and reaction, repression, and political immobility seemed to prevail everywhere in Europe. The dike—a massive dike—seemed to be containing the flood.

56. The Breakthrough of Liberalism in the West: Revolutions of 1830–1832

The dike broke in 1830, nor in western Europe was the stream thereafter stopped. The seepage, indeed, had already begun. By 1825 Spanish America was independent. The British and the French had pulled away from the congress system. The Greek nationalist movement against the Turks had broken out in the early 1820s.

With the defeat of Ypsilanti in 1821 the Greek nationalists turned somewhat away from the idea of a neo-Greek empire and more toward the idea of independence for Greece proper, the islands and peninsulas where Greek was the predominant language. Tsar Nicholas was more willing than Alexander to assist this movement. The governments of Great Britain and France were not inclined to let Russia stand as the only champion of Balkan peoples. Moreover, liberals in the West thought of the embattled Greeks as ancient Athenians fighting the modern oriental despotism of the Turkish empire.

The result was a joint Anglo-French-Russian naval intervention, which destroyed the Turkish fleet at Navarino Bay in 1827. Russia again, as often in the past, sent armies into the Balkans. A Russo-Turkish war and a great Near Eastern crisis followed, in the course of which the rival powers agreed in 1829 to recognize Greece as an independent kingdom. The Balkan states of Serbia, Wallachia, and Moldavia were also recognized as autonomous principalities within the badly shaken Ottoman Empire.[20] From the same crisis Egypt emerged as an autonomous region under Mehemet Ali. Egypt in time became a center of Arabic nationalism, which cut down Ottoman power in the south just as Balkan nationalism did in the north.

France, 1824–1830: The July Revolution, 1830

It was in 1830, and first of all in France, that the wall of reaction really collapsed. Charles X became king in 1824.[21] In the next year the legislative chambers voted an indemnity, in the form of perpetual annuities totaling 30 million francs a year, to those who as émigrés thirty-odd years before had had their property confiscated by the revolutionary state. Catholic clergy began to take over classrooms in the schools. A law pronounced the death penalty for sacrilege committed in church buildings. But the France of the restored Bourbons was still a free country, and against these apparent efforts to revive the Old Regime a strong opposition developed in the newspapers and in the chambers. In March 1830 the Chamber of Deputies, in which the bankers Laffitte and Casimir-Périer led the "leftist" opposition, passed a vote of no confidence in the government. The king, as was his legal right, dissolved the Chamber and called for new elections. The elections repudiated the king's policies. He replied on July 26, 1830, with four ordinances issued on his own authority. One dissolved the newly elected Chamber before it had ever met; another imposed censorship on the press; the third so amended the suffrage as to reduce the voting power of bankers, merchants, and industrialists and to concentrate it in the hands of the old-fashioned aristocracy; the fourth called for a new election on the new basis.

These July Ordinances produced on the very next day the July Revolution. The upper bourgeois class was of course desperate at being thus brazenly ousted from political life. But it was the republicans—the nucleus of revolutionary workers, students, and intelligentsia in Paris—that actually moved. For three days, from July 27 to 29, barricades were thrown up in the city, behind which a swarming populace defied the army and the police. Most of the army refused to fire. Charles X, in no mood to be made captive by a revolution like his long-dead brother Louis XVI, precipitately abdicated and headed for England.

Some of the leaders wished to proclaim a democratic republic. Working people hoped for better conditions of employment. The political liberals, supported by bankers, industrialists, various journalists, and intellectuals, had other aims. They had been satisfied in general with the constitutional charter of 1814; it was only

---

[20] See maps, pp. 448–449, 660.
[21] See p. 475.

LIBERTY LEADING THE PEOPLE
by Eugène Delacroix (French, 1798–1863)

Delacroix, a founder of the romantic school of painting, painted this picture soon after the July Revolution in Paris in 1830 (see pp. 485–487). It well illustrates the idealistic conception of revolution which prevailed among revolutionaries before 1848, in sharp contrast to the "realistic," "scientific," or "materialistic" conception of revolution that set in after 1848 and was typified by Karl Marx. (See pp. 522–526.) Revolution is shown as a noble and moral act. The figures express determination and courage, but show no sign of hatred or even anger. They are not a class (note how the costume varies from the top hat to the seminude); they are the People, affirming the rights of man. Liberty, holding the tricolor aloft, is a composed and even rational goddess. Romantic though the painter was, he represents the insurgents as realizing an abstract idea—Liberty, or the Republic. It is to this idea that the half-recumbent and presumably wounded figure directs his gaze. Courtesy of the Louvre (Giraudon).

to the policies and personnel of the government that they had objected, and they wished now to continue with constitutional monarchy, somewhat liberalized, and with a king whom they could trust. A solution to the deadlock was found by the elderly Marquis de Lafayette, the aging hero of the American and the French revolutions, who now came forward as symbol of national unity. Lafayette produced the Duke of Orleans on the balcony of the Paris Hôtel de Ville, embraced him before a great concourse of people, and offered him as the answer to France's need. The duke was a collateral relative of the Bourbons; he had also, as a young man, served in the republican army of 1792. The militant republicans accepted him, willing to see what would develop; and the Chamber of Deputies on August 7 offered him the throne, on condition that he observe faithfully the constitutional charter of 1814. He reigned, until 1848, under the title of Louis Philippe.

The regime of Louis Philippe, called the Orléanist, bourgeois, or July Monarchy, was viewed very differently by different groups in France and in Europe. To the other states of Europe and to the clergy and legitimists within France, it seemed shockingly revolutionary. The new king owed his throne to an insurrection, to a bargain made with republicans, and to promises made to a parliament. He called himself not king of France but king of the French, and he flew not the Bourbon lily but the tricolor flag of the Revolution. The latter produced an effect on the established classes not unlike that of the hammer and sickle of a later day. He cultivated a popular manner, wore sober dark clothing (the ancestor of the modern "business suit"), and carried an umbrella. Though in private he worked stubbornly to maintain his royal position, in public he adhered scrupulously to the constitution.

The constitution remained substantially what it had been in 1814. The main political change was one of tone; there would be no more absolutism, with its notion that constitutional guarantees could be abrogated by a reigning prince. Legally the main change was that the Chamber of Peers ceased to be hereditary, to the chagrin of the old nobility, and that the Chamber of Deputies was to be elected by a somewhat enlarged body of voters. Where before 1830 there had been 100,000 voters, there were now about 200,000. The right to vote was still based on the ownership of a considerable quantity of real estate. About one-thirtieth of the adult male population (the top thirtieth in the possession of real property) now elected the Chamber of Deputies. The beneficiaries of the new system were the upper bourgeoisie—the bankers, merchants, and industrialists. The big property owners constituted the *pays légal*, the "legal country," and to them the July Monarchy was the consummation and stopping place of political progress. To others, and especially to the radical democrats, it proved as the years passed to be a disillusionment and an annoyance.

Revolutions of 1830: Belgium, Poland, and Elsewhere

The immediate effect of the three-day Paris revolution of 1830 was to set off a series of similar explosions throughout Europe. These in turn, coming after the collapse of the Bourbons in France, brought the whole peace settlement of 1815 into jeopardy. It will be recalled that the Congress of Vienna had joined Belgium with the Dutch Netherlands to create a strong buffer state against a resurgent France and had also done what it could to prevent direct pressure of Russian power upon central Europe by way of Poland.[22] Both these arrangements were now undone.

The Dutch-Belgian union proved economically beneficial, for Belgian industry complemented the commercial and shipping activity of the Dutch, but politically it worked very poorly, especially since the Dutch king had absolutist and centralizing ideas. The Belgians, though they had never been independent, had always stood stiffly for their local liberties under former Austrian rulers (and Spanish before them); now they did the same against the Dutch. The Catholic Belgians disliked Dutch Protestantism; those Belgians who spoke French (the Walloons) objected to regulations requiring the use of Dutch. About a month after the July Revolution in Paris disturbances broke out in Brussels. The leaders asked only for local Belgian self-government, but when the king took arms against them they went on to proclaim independence. A national assembly met and drafted a constitution.

Nicholas of Russia wished to send troops to stamp out the Belgian uprising. But he could not get his forces safely through Poland. In Poland, too, in 1830, a revolution broke out. The Polish nationalists saw in the fall of the French Bourbons a timely moment for them to strike. They objected also to the appearance of Russian troops bound presumably to suppress freedom in western Europe. One incident led to another, until in January 1831 the Polish diet proclaimed the dethronement of the Polish king (i.e., Nicholas), who thereupon sent in a large army. The Poles, outnumbered and divided among themselves, could put up no successful resistance. They obtained no support from the West. The British government was unsettled by agitation at home. The French government, newly installed under Louis Philippe, had no wish to appear disturbingly revolutionary, and in any case feared the Polish agents who besought its backing as international firebrands and republicans. The Polish revolution was therefore crushed. Congress Poland disappeared; its constitution was abrogated, and it was merged into the Russian empire. Thousands of Poles settled in western Europe, where they became familiar figures in republican circles. In Poland the engines of repression rolled. The tsar's government exiled some thousands to Siberia, began to Russify the Eastern Border, and closed the universities of Warsaw and Vilna. Since meanwhile it was too late for the tsar any longer to contemplate intervention in Belgium, it may be said that the sacrifice of the Poles contributed to the success of the west-European revolution of 1830, as it had to that of the great French Revolution of 1789–1795.[23]

It was true enough, as Nicholas maintained, that an independent Belgium presented great international problems. Belgium for twenty years before 1815 had been part of France. A few Belgians now favored reunion with it, and in France the republican left, which regarded the Vienna treaty as an insult to the French nation, saw an opportunity to win back this first and dearest conquest of the First Republic. In 1831, by a small majority, the Belgian national assembly elected as their king the son of Louis Philippe, who, however, not wishing trouble with the British, forbade his son to accept it. The Belgians thereupon elected Leopold of Saxe-Coburg, a German princeling who had married into the British royal family

[22] See pp. 445–447.
[23] See pp. 384–385 and map on p. 248.

and become a British subject. He was in fact the uncle of a twelve-year-old girl who was to be Queen Victoria. The British negotiated with Talleyrand, sent over by the French government (it was his last public service); and the result was a treaty of 1831 (confirmed in 1839) setting up Belgium as a perpetually neutral state, incapable of forming alliances and guaranteed against invasion by all five of the Great Powers. The aim intended by the Treaty of Vienna, to prevent the annexation of Belgium to France, was thus again realized in a new way. Internally Belgium presently settled down to a stable parliamentary system, somewhat more democratic than the July Monarchy in France but fundamentally offering the same type of bourgeois and liberal rule.

Revolutionary disturbances also took place in 1830 in Germany, Italy, Switzerland, Spain, and Portugal. To trace them in any detail is not necessary. In a word, a greater measure of liberalism was established in Switzerland; Spain entered a long period of tortuous parliamentary development confused by civil wars, which arose from a disputed succession to the throne; and in Italy and Germany the 1830 uprisings were quickly put down, showing only the continuance of a radical dissatisfaction still held in check by the authorities. It was in Great Britain that sweeping changes really came.

Reform in Great Britain

The three-day Paris revolution of 1830 had direct repercussions across the Channel. The quick results following on working-class insurrection gave radical leaders in England the idea that threats of violence might be useful. On the other hand, the ease and speed with which the French bourgeoisie gained the upper hand reassured the British middle classes, who concluded that they might unsparingly embarrass the government without courting a mass upheaval.

The Tory regime in England had in fact already begun to loosen up. A group of younger men came forward in the 1820s in the Tory party, notably George Canning, the foreign minister, and Robert Peel, son of one of the first cotton manufacturers.[24] This group was sensitive to the needs of British business and to the doctrines of liberalism.[25] They reduced tariffs and liberalized the old Navigation Acts, permitting British colonies to trade with countries other than Britain. By repealing certain old statutes, they made it lawful for skilled workers to emigrate from England, taking their skills with them to foreign parts, and for manufacturers to export machinery to foreign countries, even though English industrial secrets would thus be given away. By such measures they advanced the liberal conception of a freely exchanging international system; they moved toward freedom of trade. The Liberal Tories also undermined the legal position of the Church of England, forwarding the conception of a secular state, though such was hardly their purpose. They repealed the old laws (which dated from the seventeenth century) forbidding dissenting Protestants to hold public office except through a legal fiction by which they pretended to be Anglicans. They even allowed the Test Act of 1673 to be repealed and Catholic Emancipation to be adopted. Catholics in

---

[24] See p. 461.
[25] See p. 465.

Great Britain and Ireland received the same rights as others.[26] Capital punishment was abolished for about a hundred offenses. A professional police force was introduced, in place of the old-fashioned and ineffectual local constables. (It is after Robert Peel that London policemen came to be called "bobbies.") The new police were expected to handle protest meetings, angry crowds, or occasional riots without having to call for military assistance.

There were two things that the Liberal Tories could not do. They could not question the Corn Laws, and they could not reform the House of Commons. By the Corn Laws, which set the tariff on imported grain, a tariff raised to new heights in 1815, the gentlemen of England protected their rent rolls; and by the existing structure of the House of Commons they governed the country, expecting the working class and the business interests to look to them as natural leaders.

Never in five hundred years of its history had the Commons been so unrepresentative. No new borough had been created since the Revolution of 1688. The boroughs, or urban centers having the right to elect members of Parliament, were heavily concentrated in southern England. With the Industrial Revolution, population was shifting noticeably to the north. The new factory towns were unrepresented. Of the boroughs, many had decayed over the centuries; some were quite uninhabited, and one was under the waters of the North Sea. In a few boroughs real elections took place, but in some of them it was the town corporation, and in others the owners of certain pieces of real estate, that had the right to name members of Parliament. Each borough was different, carrying over the local liberties of the Middle Ages. Many boroughs were entirely dominated by influential persons called borough-mongers by their critics. As for the rural districts, the "forty-shilling freeholders" chose two members of Parliament for each county, in a convivial assembly much influenced by the gentlefolk. It was estimated about 1820 that less than 500 men, most of them members of the House of Lords, really selected a majority of the House of Commons.

Some two dozen bills to reform the House of Commons had been introduced in the half-century preceding 1830. They had all failed to pass. In 1830, after the Paris revolution, the issue was again raised by the minority party, the Whigs. The Tory prime minister, the Duke of Wellington, the victor of Waterloo and a most extreme conservative, so immoderately defended the existing system that he lost the confidence even of some of his own followers. The existing methods of election in England, he declared, were more perfect than any that human intelligence could contrive at a single stroke. After this outburst a Whig ministry took over the government. It introduced a reform bill. The House of Commons rejected it. The Whig ministry thereupon resigned. The Tories, fearing popular violence, refused to take the responsibility for forming a cabinet. The Whigs resumed office and again introduced their reform bill. This time it passed the Commons but failed in the House of Lords. An angry roar went up over the country. Crowds milled in the London streets, rioters for several days were in control at Bristol, the jail at Derby was sacked, and Nottingham castle burned. Only the passage of the bill, it seemed, could prevent an actual revolution. Using this argument the Whigs got the king to promise to create enough new peers to

[26] See pp. 177–178.

change the majority in the House of Lords.[27] The Lords yielded rather than be swamped, and in April 1832 the bill became law.

The Reform Bill of 1832 was a very English measure. It adapted the English or medieval system rather than following new ideas let loose by the French Revolution. On the Continent, where constitutions existed at all (as in France), the idea was that each representative should represent roughly the same number of voters, and that voters should qualify to vote by a flat uniform qualification, usually the payment of a stated amount of property taxes. The British held to the idea that members of the House of Commons represented boroughs and counties, in general without regard to size of population (with exceptions); in other words, no attempt was made to create equal electoral districts. The qualification for voting was enormously simplified, but it still remained rather complex. The franchise, or right to vote, depended on whether one lived in a borough or in a county. It was defined also very largely in terms of rents, because in England, with the high concentration of landownership in the old landowning class, many important people did not own any land at all.

In a borough, under the new law, a man could vote for a member of Parliament if he occupied premises for which he paid £10 annual rental. In a county (a rural area or a small town not considered a borough), a man could vote if he paid £10 annual rental for land held on a long-term sixty-year lease; but he had to pay as high as £50 rental for land occupied on a shorter-term lease in order to be eligible to vote. If he himself owned the land, he could vote if its annual rental value was £2 a year (the old forty-shilling freehold). Thus the vote was nicely distributed according to evidences of economic substance, reliability, and permanence. The total effect on the size of the electorate was to raise the number of voters in the British Isles from about 500,000 to about 813,000. Some persons actually lost their votes, namely, the poorer elements in the handful of old boroughs which had been fairly democratic, like the borough of Westminster in greater London.

The most important thing was not the increased size of the electorate but its redistribution by region and by class. The Reform Bill reallocated the seats in the House of Commons. Fifty-six of the smallest older boroughs were abolished, their inhabitants thereafter voting as residents of their counties. Thirty other small boroughs kept the right to send only one burgess to Parliament instead of the historic two. The 143 seats thus made available were given to the new industrial towns. Here it was the £10-householders who voted, i.e., the middle classes— factory owners and businessmen and their principal employees; doctors, lawyers, brokers, merchants, and newspaper people; relatives and connections of the well- to-do.

The Reform Bill of 1832 was more sweeping than the Whigs would have favored except for their fear of revolution. It was more conservative than the democratic radicals would have accepted, except for their belief that the suffrage might be widened in the future. Whether Great Britain in 1830 was in danger of any real revolution can never be known. In any case a distressed mass of workers was led by an irate manufacturing interest that was unwilling to tolerate any longer its exclusion from political life. Had these elements consented to general violence a real revolution might have occurred. Yet there was no violent revolution in

<hr>

[27] See p. 194, note 24.

Britain. The reason probably lies first of all in the existence of the historic institution of Parliament, which, erratic though it was before the Reform Bill, provided the means by which social changes could be legally accomplished and continued, in principle, to enjoy universal respect. Conservatives, driven to the wall, would yield; they could allow a revision of the suffrage because they could expect to remain themselves in public life. Radicals, using enough violence to scare the established interest, did not thereafter face a blank wall; they could expect, once the breach was made, to carry some day a further democratization of Parliament and with it their social and economic program by orderly legislation.

Britain after 1832

But the Reform Bill of 1832 was in its way a revolution. The new business interests, created by industrialization, took their place alongside the old aristocracy in the governing elite of the country. The aristocratic Whigs who had carried the Reform Bill gradually merged with formerly radical industrialists and with a few Liberal Tories to form the Liberal party. The main body of the Tories, joined by a few old Whigs and even a few former radicals, gradually turned into the Conservative party. The two parties alternated in power at short intervals from 1832 to the First World War, this being the classic period in Great Britain of the Liberal-Conservative two-party system.

In 1833 slavery was abolished in the British Empire. In 1834 a new Poor Law was adopted. In 1835 the Municipal Corporations Act, second only to the Reform Bill in basic importance, modernized the local government of English cities; it broke up the old local oligarchies and brought in uniform electoral and administrative machinery, enabling city dwellers to grapple more effectively with the problems of urban life. In 1836 the House of Commons allowed the newspapers to report how its members voted—a long step toward publicity of government proceedings was thus taken. Meanwhile an ecclesiastical commission reviewed the affairs of the Church of England; financial and administrative irregularities were corrected, together with the grosser inequalities between the income of upper and lower clergy, all of which had made the church formerly a kind of closed preserve for the landed gentry.

The Tories, thus assaulted in their immemorial strongholds of local government and the established church, carried a counteroffensive into the strongholds of the new liberal manufacturing class, namely, the factories and the mines. Tories

BIG INVESTMENTS
by Honoré Daumier (French, 1808–1879)
The Revolution of 1830, romanticized by Delacroix, was in fact followed by a period of moneymaking and business ferment (as well as genuine economic development) made famous in the novels of Balzac and the graphic art of Daumier. This lithograph of 1837 shows a financier, with bundles of stock certificates piled beside him, offering to sell shares in factories, foundries, breweries, etc., to a skeptical client. Daumier was a satirist and caricaturist of bourgeois society. Where Rembrandt in the seventeenth century could portray businessmen with a high seriousness (as on p. 165), artists since the 1830s have been generally alienated from such subjects. Courtesy of the Bibliothèque Nationale, Paris.

Grand placement d'actions.

Aujourd'hui de bien bonnes actions à placer, M. Desrognures, en voulez-vous ? – C'est selon. Qu'avez-vous en actions ?
– 3000 actions de fonderies. – Affaire fondue ! – 2000 actions des usines – Usé, usé ! – 10,000 action des
... opérations magnifiques – Elle faites les mousser ! – J'en ai du recueil des connaissances – Connu !
... Enfin, combien cela fait-il en bloc ? – Un milliard ou deux, pas plus. – Un milliard... le papier
... cela doit donner cent livres à 4 sous ça vaut 2 francs – Deux milliards posez 2 francs !
...nez-vous mon cher ? ... Mettez au moins 25 francs ! – Pas un liard. – Allons, enlevez. Vous faites
...che et vie. – Farceur, vous ne dites tous les jours la même chose

became champions of the industrial workers. Landed gentlemen, of whom the most famous was Lord Ashley, later seventh Earl of Shaftesbury, took the lead in publicizing the social evils of a rapid and indeed ruthless industrialization. They received some support from a few humanitarian industrialists; indeed, the early legislation tended to follow practices already established by the best or strongest business firms. A Factory Act of 1833 forbade the labor of children less than nine years old in the textile mills. It was the first effective piece of legislation on the subject, for it provided for paid inspectors and procedures for enforcement. An act of 1842 initiated significant regulation in the coal mines; the employment underground of women and girls, and of boys under ten, was forbidden.

The greatest victory of the working classes came in 1847 with the Ten Hours Act, which limited the labor of women and children in all industrial establishments to ten hours a day. Thereafter men commonly worked only ten hours also, since the work of men, women, and young people was too closely coordinated for the men to work alone. The great Liberal John Bright, Quaker and cotton magnate, called the Ten Hours Act "a delusion practiced on the working classes." To regulate the hours of labor was contrary to the accepted principles of laissez faire, economic law, the free market, freedom of trade, and individual liberty for employer and worker. Yet the Ten Hours Act stood, and British industry continued to prosper.

Gathering their strength, the Whig-liberal-radical combination established in 1838 an Anti–Corn Law League. Wage earners objected to the Corn Laws because the tariff on grain imports kept up the price of food. Industrial employers objected to them because, in keeping up food prices, they also kept up wages and cost of production in England, thus working to England's disadvantage in the export trade. Defenders of the Corn Laws argued that protection of agriculture was necessary to maintain the natural aristocracy of the country (most land being owned by peers and gentry, as has been seen), but they also sometimes used more widely framed economic arguments, affirming that Britain should preserve a balanced economy as between industry and farming, and avoid becoming too exclusively dependent on imported food. The issue became a straight contest between the industrialists, acting with working-class support, and the aristocratic and predominantly Tory landowning interest. The Anti–Corn Law League, whose headquarters were at Manchester, operated like a modern political party. It had plenty of money, supplied by large donations from manufacturers and small ones from laboring people. It sent lecturers on tour, agitated in the newspapers, and issued a stream of polemical pamphlets and educational books. It held political teas, torchlight processions, and open-air mass meetings. The pressure proved irresistible and received a final impetus from a famine in Ireland. It was a Tory government, headed by Sir Robert Peel, which in 1846 yielded before so vociferous a demand.

The repeal of the Corn Laws in 1846 stands as a symbol of the change that had come over England. It reaffirmed the revolutionary consequences of the Reform Bill of 1832. Industry was now a governing element in the country. Free trade was henceforth the rule. Great Britain, in return for the export of manufactures, became deliberately dependent on imports for its very life. It was committed henceforth to an international and even worldwide economic system. The first to undergo the Industrial Revolution, possessing mechanical power and methods of mass production, the British could produce yarn and cloth, machine tools and railroad equipment, more efficiently and more cheaply than any other people. In Britain, the workshop of the world, people would pour increasingly into mine, factory, and city, live by selling manufactures, coal, shipping, and financial services to the other peoples of the earth, and obtain raw cotton, rare ores, meat, cereals, and thousands of lesser but still vital necessities from the rest of the earth in exchange. The welfare of Britain depended on the maintenance of a freely exchanging worldwide economic system.

It depended also, more than ever, on British control of the sea, which was rarely mentioned by the civilian-minded Anti–Corn Law League, but which, firmly established in the long duel with Napoleon, was now an assumed postulate of economic discussion. No one understood this better than Lord Palmerston, a flamboyant Anglo-Irish Whig aristocrat, who by risky and audacious moves that alarmed his colleagues and threw Queen Victoria into consternation, came forward as the very British bulldog in defense of Britain's name. For example, in 1850 a Moroccan Jew known as Don Pacifico, who was a British subject, got into trouble in Greece because of certain debts owed to him by the Greek government. Though the claim was not above question, Palmerston unloosed the thunders of the British fleet. He sent a squadron to the Piraeus, the port of Athens, and forbade Greek vessels the use of their own harbor until the matter was settled. On another occasion, in 1856, when Chinese authorities arrested a Chinese ship called the *Arrow*, which, though without due right, was flying the British flag, Palmerston again called on the navy, which proceeded to bombard Canton and precipitated the Second Anglo-Chinese War. In other connections, as a good mid–nineteenth-century liberal, Palmerston favored movements for national independence, including that of the Confederate States of America, expecting them to result in the further extension of free trade.

57. Triumph of the West-European Bourgeoisie

In general, the decades following 1830 may be thought of as a kind of golden age of the West-European bourgeoisie, or what in English would be called the upper middle class. In the older meaning, in French, a *bourgeois* had been someone who was not of the nobility but enjoyed an income from business, or a profession, or the ownership of property.[28] After the French Revolution, and even more after 1830, the word took on new meanings, not all of them consistent. Artists, literary people, and old-line aristocrats might disdain the "bourgeois" as a person of uncultivated tastes, supposedly interested only in making money. From another point of view, shared by social theorists and working-class leaders, the bourgeois was someone who could hire others to work for him, either in his business or recreational activities, or as household servants. In a word, the bourgeois was the employer. In any case, the bourgeoisie and the aristocracy tended to become more alike in the nineteenth century in their daily pursuits and style of life, and to draw income from the possession of income-producing property or capital. The bourgeoisie, formerly identified in contrast to the nobility, was now identified in contrast to the working class, that is, those whose whole income depended on daily labor in shops, offices, farms, or factories.

[28] See pp. 121–123, 353, 393.

The reigning liberal doctrine was the "stake in society" theory; those should govern who have something to lose. In the France of the July Monarchy (1830–1848), only about one adult male in thirty had the vote. In the Britain of the first Reform Bill (1832–1867), one man in eight could vote for a member of the House of Commons. In France only the most well-to-do were enfranchised, in Britain virtually the whole middle class, which, however, long supported members of the aristocracy for the highest public positions. In Britain the continuation of the Tory landed interest in politics somewhat blunted the edge of capitalist and managerial rule, resulting in the passage of significant legislation for the protection of industrial labor. In France the aristocratic landed interest, weaker and less public spirited than in England, lost much of its influence by the Revolution of 1830, and less was done to relieve the condition of labor.

The bourgeois age left its mark on Europe in many ways. For one thing, western Europe continued to accumulate capital and build up its industrial plant. National income was constantly rising, but a relatively small share went to the laboring class, and a relatively large share went to owners of capital. This meant that less was spent on consumers' goods—housing, clothing, food, recreation— and that more was saved and available for reinvestment. New stock companies were constantly formed, and the law of corporations was amended, allowing for the extension of corporate enterprise to new fields. The factory system spread from Britain to the Continent and within Britain from the textile industry to other lines of production. The output of iron, a good index to economic advancement in this phase of industrialism, rose about 300 percent in Great Britain between 1830 and 1848 and about 65 percent in France between 1830 and 1845. (All the German states combined, at the latter date, produced about a tenth as much iron as Great Britain, and less than half as much as France.) Railroad building set in in earnest after 1840. In 1840 Samuel Cunard put four steamships into regular transatlantic service. Much capital was exported; as early as 1839 an American estimated that Europeans (mainly British) owned $200,000,000 worth of stocks in American companies. Such investments financed the purchase of British and other goods and helped to rivet together a world economic system, in which western Europe and especially England took the lead, with other regions remaining in a somewhat subordinate status.

The Frustration and Challenge of Labor

The bourgeois age had the effect also of estranging the world of labor. The state in Britain and France was as near as it has ever been to what Karl Marx was soon to call it—a committee of the bourgeois class. Already in France people spoke worriedly of the *prolétaires,* those at the bottom of society, who had nothing to lose. Republicans in France, radical democrats in Britain, felt cheated and imposed upon in the 1830s and 1840s. They had in each country forced through a virtual revolution by their insurrections and demonstrations and then in each country had been left without the vote. Some lost interest in representative institutions. Excluded from government, they were tempted to seek political ends through extragovernmental, which is to say revolutionary or utopian, channels. Social and economic reforms seemed to the average worker far more important, as a final aim, than mere governmental innovations. Workers were told by respected economists that they could not hope to change the system in their own favor. They were tempted, therefore, to destroy the system, to replace it utterly with some new system conceived mainly in the minds of thinkers. They were told by the Manchester School, and by its equivalent in France, that the income of labor was set by ineluctable natural laws, that it was best and indeed necessary for wages to remain low, and that the way to rise in the world was to get out of the laboring class altogether, by becoming the owner of a profitable business and leaving working people about where they were.[29]

The reigning doctrine emphasized the conception of a labor market. The worker sold labor, the employer bought it. The price of labor, or wage, was to be agreed upon by the two individual parties. The price would naturally fluctuate according to changes in supply and demand. When a great deal of a certain kind of labor was required the wage would go up, until new persons moved into the market offering more labor of this type, with the result that something like the old wage would again be established. When no labor was needed none should be bought, and persons who could not sell labor might then subsist for a time by poor relief.

The new Poor Law of 1834 was especially repugnant to the British working class. It corrected crying evils of the old poor laws that had left millions of people in habitual poverty. But the new law did nothing constructive to relieve productive workers suffering from occasional or cyclical unemployment. The new law followed the stern precepts of the dismal science; its main principle was to safeguard the labor market by making relief more unpleasant than any job. It granted relief only to persons willing to enter a workhouse, or poorhouse; and in these establishments the sexes were segregated and life was in other ways made noticeably less attractive than in the outside world. The workers considered the new law an abomination. They called the workhouses "bastilles." They resented the whole conception of a labor market, in which labor was to be bought and sold (or remain unsold) like any other commodity.

In the long run it would be the increase in productivity that would improve the condition of the workers. Meanwhile the friends of the working class offered two means of escape. One was to improve the position of labor in the market. This led to the formation of labor unions for control of the labor supply and collective bargaining with employers. Such unions, illegal in France, were barely legal in Great Britain after 1825, though it was still illegal in both countries to strike. The other means of escape was to repudiate the whole idea of a market economy and of the capitalist system. It was to conceive of a system in which goods were to be produced for use, not for sale; and in which working people should be compensated according to need, not according to the requirements of an employer. This was the basis of most forms of nineteenth-century socialism.[30]

Socialism and Chartism

Socialism spread rapidly among the working classes after 1830. In France it blended with revolutionary republicanism. There was a revival of interest in the great Revolution and the democratic Republic of 1793. Cheap reprints of the

[29] See pp. 461–463, 466.
[30] See pp. 461–463.

writings of Robespierre began to circulate in the working-class quarters of Paris. Robespierre was now seen as a people's hero. The socialist Louis Blanc, for example, who in 1839 published his *Organization of Work*, recommending the formation of "social workshops," also wrote a long history of the French Revolution, in which he pointed out the equalitarian ideals that had inspired the National Convention in 1793. In Britain, as befitted the different background of the country, socialistic ideas blended in with the movement for further parliamentary reform. This was advanced by the working-class group known as the Chartists, from the People's Charter which they drafted in 1838. Between the British Chartists and the French socialists there was considerable coming and going. One Chartist, the Irish-born journalist Bronterre O'Brien, translated a French book on the "conspiracy of Babeuf" of 1796, which itself was a source and inspiration of the rising socialism of France.[31]

Chartism was far more of a mass movement than the French socialism of the day. Only a few Chartists were clearly socialists in their own minds. But all were anticapitalistic. All could agree that the first step must be to win working-class representation in Parliament. The Charter of 1838 consisted of six points. It demanded (1) the annual election of the House of Commons by (2) universal suffrage for all adult males, through (3) a secret ballot and (4) equal electoral districts; and it called for (5) the abolition of property qualifications for membership in the House of Commons, which perpetuated the old idea that Parliament should be composed of gentlemen of independent income, and urged instead (6) the payment of salaries to the elected members of Parliament, in order that people of small means might serve. A convention composed of delegates sent by labor unions, mass meetings, and radical societies all over the country met in London in 1839. "Convention" was an ominous word, with French revolutionary and even terrorist overtones; some members of this British convention regarded it as the body really representing the people, and favored armed violence and a general strike, while others stood only for moral pressure upon Parliament.

A petition bearing over a million signatures, urging acceptance of the Charter, was submitted to the House of Commons. The violent and revolutionary wing, or "physical force" Chartists, precipitated a wave of riots which were effectively quelled by the authorities. In 1842 the petition was again submitted. This time, according to the best estimate, it was signed by 3,317,702 persons. Since the entire population of Great Britain was about 19 million it is clear that the Charter, whatever the exact number of signatures, commanded the explicit adherence of half the adult males of the country. The House of Commons nevertheless rejected the petition by 287 votes to 49. It was feared, with reason, that political democracy would threaten property rights and the whole economic system as they then existed. The Chartist movement gradually died down in the face of firm opposition by the government and the business classes, and was weakened by mutual fears and disagreements among its own supporters. It had not been entirely fruitless; for without popular agitation and the publicizing of working-class grievances, the Mines Act of 1842 and the Ten Hours Act of 1847 might not have been enacted. These measures in turn alleviated the distress of industrial workers and kept alive a degree of confidence in the future of the economic system. Chartism revived

[31] See p. 394.

briefly in 1848, as will be seen in the next chapter; but in general, in the 1840s, British working people turned from political agitation to the forming and strengthening of labor unions, by which they could deal directly with employers without having to appeal to the government. Not until 1867 was the suffrage extended in Great Britain, and it took about eighty years to realize the full program of the Charter of 1838, except for the annual election of Parliament, for which there soon ceased to be any demand.[32]

It is not easy to summarize the history of Europe between 1815 and 1848. Among all the forces set free by the French and Industrial revolutions—liberalism, conservatism, nationalism, republicanism, democracy, socialism—no stabilization had been achieved. No international system had been created; Europe had rather fallen into two camps, composed of a West in which liberal conceptions moved forward, and an East in which three autocratic monarchies held sway. Western Europe favored the principles of nationality; governments in central and eastern Europe still opposed them. The West was growing collectively richer, more liberal, more bourgeois. Middle-class people in Germany, central Europe, and Italy (as well as in Spain and Portugal) did not enjoy the dignities and emoluments that they enjoyed in Great Britain or France. But the West had not solved its social problem; its whole material civilization rested upon a restless and sorely tried working class. Everywhere there was repression, in varying degree, and everywhere apprehension, more in some places than in others; but there was also hope, confidence in the progress of an industrial and scientific society, and faith in the unfinished program of the rights of man. The result was the general Revolution of 1848.

[32] See pp. 609–613, 778.

XII.
REVOLUTION AND
THE REIMPOSITION
OF ORDER, 1848–1870

FEARS HAUNTING the established classes of Europe for thirty years came true in 1848. Governments collapsed all over the Continent. Remembered horrors appeared again, as in a recurring dream, in much the same sequence as after 1789 only at a much faster rate of speed. Revolutionaries milled in the streets, kings fled, republics were declared, and within four years there was another Napoleon. Soon thereafter came a series of wars.

Never before or since has Europe seen so truly universal an upheaval as in 1848. While the French Revolution of 1789 and the Russian Revolution of 1917 both had immediate international repercussions, in each of these cases a single country took the lead. In 1848 the revolutionary movement broke out spontaneously from native sources from Copenhagen to Palermo and from Paris to Budapest. Contemporaries sometimes attributed the universality of the phenomenon to the machinations of secret societies, and it is true that the faint beginnings of an international revolutionary movement existed before 1848; but the fact is that revolutionary plotters had little influence upon what actually happened, and the nearly simultaneous fall of governments is quite understandable from other causes. Many people in Europe wanted substantially the same things—constitutional government, the independence and unification of national groups, an end to serfdom and manorial restraints where they still existed. With some variation,

Chapter Emblem: A medal showing St. Paul's Church at Frankfurt, then a new building in the neoclassic style, where the German National Assembly met in 1848–1849.

there was a common body of ideas among politically conscious elements of all countries. Some of the powers that the new forces had to combat were themselves international, notably the Catholic church and the far-spreading influence of the Habsburgs, so that resistance to them arose independently in many places. In any case, only the Russian empire and Great Britain escaped the revolutionary contagion of 1848, and the British received a very bad scare.

But the Revolution of 1848, though it shook the whole Continent, lacked basic driving strength. It failed almost as rapidly as it succeeded. Its main consequence, in fact, was to strengthen the more conservative forces that viewed all revolution with alarm. Revolutionary ideals succumbed to military repression. To some extent the governments of the 1850s and 1860s, while hostile to revolution, satisfied some of the aims of 1848, notably in national unification and constitutional government with limited representation, but they did so in a mood of calculated realism, and while reasserting their own authority. The repressed Revolution of 1848 also left a legacy of class fears and class conflict, in which prophets of a new society also became more realistic, as when Karl Marx, branding earlier forms of socialism as "utopian," offered his own views as hard-headed and "scientific."

58. Paris: The Specter of Social Revolution in the West

The July Monarchy in France was a platform of boards built over a volcano. Under it burned the repressed fires of the republicanism put down in 1830, which since 1830 had become steadily more socialistic.[1]

Politics in the July Monarchy became increasingly more unreal. So few interests were represented in the Chamber of Deputies that the most basic issues were seldom debated. Even most of the bourgeois class had no representation. Graft and corruption were more common than they should have been, as economic expansion favored stockjobbing and fraud by business promoters and politicians in combination. A strong movement set in to give the vote to more people instead of to only one man in thirty. Radicals wanted universal suffrage and a republic, but liberals asked only for a broadening of voting rights within the existing constitutional monarchy. The king, Louis Philippe, and his prime minister, Guizot, instead of allying with the latter against the former, resolutely and obtusely opposed any change whatsoever.

The "February" Revolution in France

Reformers, against the king's expressed wishes, planned a great banquet in Paris for February 22, 1848, to be accompanied by demonstrations in the streets. The government on February 21 forbade all such meetings. That night barricades were built in the working-class quarters. These consisted of paving blocks, building stones, or large pieces of furniture thrown together across the narrow streets and intersections of the old city, and constituting a maze within which insurgents prepared to resist the authorities. The government called out the National Guard,

[1] See pp. 485–487, 495–497.

which refused to move. The king now promised electoral reform, but republican firebrands took charge of the semimobilized working-class elements, which held a demonstration outside the house of Guizot. Someone shot at the guards placed around the house; the guards replied, killing twenty persons. The republican organizers put some of the corpses on a torch-lit cart and paraded them through the city, which, armed and barricaded, soon began to swarm in an enormous riot. On February 24 Louis Philippe, like Charles X before him, abdicated and made for England. The February Revolution of 1848, like the July Revolution of 1830, had unseated a monarch in three days.

The constitutional reformers hoped to carry on with Louis Philippe's young grandson as king, but the republicans, now aroused and armed, poured into the Chamber of Deputies and forced the proclamation of the Republic. Republican leaders set up a provisional government of ten men, pending election by all France of a Constituent Assembly. Seven of the ten were "political" republicans, the most notable being the poet Lamartine. Three were "social" republicans, the most notable being Louis Blanc. A huge crowd of workers appeared before the Hôtel de Ville, or city hall, demanding that France adopt the new socialist emblem—the red flag. They were dissuaded by the eloquence of Lamartine, and the tricolor remained the republican standard.

Louis Blanc urged the Provisional Government to push through a bold economic and social program without delay. But since the "social" republicans were in a minority in the Provisional Government (though probably not among Paris republicans generally), Louis Blanc's ideas were very much watered down in the application. He wanted a Ministry of Progress to organize a network of "social workshops," the state-supported and collectivist manufacturing establishments that he had projected in his writings. All that was created was a Labor Commission, with limited powers, and a system of shops significantly entitled "national" rather than "social." The National Workshops, as they are always called in English (though "workshop" suggests something more insignificant than Louis Blanc had in mind), were agreed to by the Provisional Government only as a political concession, and no significant work was ever assigned them, for fear of competition with private enterprise and dislocation of the economic system. Indeed, the man placed in charge of them admitted that his purpose was to prove the fallacies of socialism. Meanwhile the Labor Commission was unable to win public acceptance for the ten-hour day, which the British Parliament had enacted the year before. One action of the Provisional Government, however, had permanent effect, the final abolition of slavery in the French colonies.

The National Workshops became in practice only an extensive project in unemployment relief. Men of all trades, skilled and unskilled, were set to work digging on the roads and fortifications outside of Paris. They were paid two francs a day. The number of legitimate unemployed increased rapidly, for 1847 had been a year of depression and the revolution prevented the return of business confidence. Other needy persons also presented themselves for remuneration, and soon there were too many men for the amount of "work" made available. From 25,000 enrolled in the workshops by the middle of March, the number climbed to 120,000 by mid-June, by which time there were also in Paris another 50,000 whom the bulging workshops could no longer accommodate. In June there were probably almost 200,000 essentially idle but able-bodied men in a city of about a million people.

The Constituent Assembly, elected in April by universal male suffrage throughout France, met on May 4. It immediately replaced the Provisional Government with a temporary executive board of its own. The main body of France, a land of provincial bourgeois and peasant landowners, was not socialist in the least. The new temporary executive board, chosen by the new Constituent Assembly in May, included no "social" republicans. All five of its members, of whom Lamartine was the head, were known as outspoken enemies of Louis Blanc. Blanc and the socialists could no longer expect even the grudging and insincere concessions that they had so far obtained.

The battle lines were now drawn, after only three months of revolution, somewhat as they had been drawn in 1792 after three years.[2] Paris again stood for a degree of revolutionary action in which the rest of the country was not prepared to share. Revolutionary leaders in Paris, in 1848 as in 1792, were unwilling to accept the processes of majority rule or slow parliamentary deliberation. But the crisis in 1848 was more acute than in 1792. A larger proportion of the population were wage earners. Under a system of predominantly merchant capitalism, in which machine industry and factory concentration were only beginning, the workers were tormented by the same evils as the more industrialized working classes of England. Hours were if anything longer, and pay less, in France than in Great Britain; insecurity and unemployment were at least as great; and the feeling that a capitalist economy held no future for the laborer was the same. In addition, where the English worker shrank from the actual violation of Parliament, the French worker saw nothing very sacrilegious in the violation of elected assemblies. Too many regimes in France since 1789, including those preferred by the comfortable classes, had been based on insurrectionary violence for the French workers to feel much compunction over using it for their own ends.

The "June Days" of 1848

On the one hand stood the nationally elected Constituent Assembly. On the other, the National Workshops had mobilized in Paris the most distressed elements of the working class. Tens of thousands had been brought together where they could talk, read journals, listen to speeches, and concert common action. Agitators and organizers naturally made use of the opportunity thus presented to them. Men in the workshops began to feel desperate, to sense that the social republic was slipping from them perhaps forever. On May 15 they attacked the Constituent Assembly, drove its members out of the hall, declared it dissolved, and set up a new provisional government of their own. They announced that a social revolution must follow the purely political revolution of February. But the National Guard, a kind of civilian militia, turned against the insurgents and restored the Constituent Assembly. The Assembly, to root out socialism, prepared to get rid of the National Workshops. It offered those enrolled in them the alternatives of enlistment in the

[2] See pp. 381–384.

army, transfer to provincial workshops, or being put out of Paris by force. The whole laboring class in the city began to resist. The government proclaimed martial law, the civilian executive board resigned, and all power was given to General Cavaignac and the regular army.

There followed the "Bloody June Days"—June 24 to 26, 1848—three days during which a terrifying class war raged in Paris. Over 20,000 men from the workshops took to arms (more would doubtless have done so had not the government continued to pay wages in the workshops during the insurrection), and they were joined by other unnumbered thousands from the working-class districts of the city. Half or more of Paris became a labyrinth of barricades defended by determined men and equally resolute women. Military methods of the time made it possible for civilians to shoot it out openly with soldiers; small arms were the main weapons, and armies had no armored vehicles or even any very devastating artillery. The soldiers found it a difficult operation, even several generals being killed, but after three days the outcome was in doubt no longer. Ten thousand persons had been killed or wounded. Eleven thousand insurgents were taken prisoner. The Assembly, refusing all clemency, decreed their immediate deportation to the colonies.

The June Days sent a shudder throughout France and Europe. Whether the battle in Paris had been a true class struggle, how large a portion of the laboring class had really participated (it was large in any case), how much they had fought for permanent objectives, and how much over the temporary issue of the workshops—all these are secondary questions. It was widely understood that a class war had in fact broken out. Militant workers were confirmed in a hatred and loathing of the bourgeois class, in a belief that capitalism existed in the last analysis by the callous shooting of laboring men in the streets. People above the laboring class were thrown into a panic. They were sure that they had narrowly escaped a ghastly upheaval. The very ground of civilized living seemed to have quaked. After June 1848, wrote a Frenchwoman of the time, society was "a prey to a feeling of terror incomparable to anything since the invasion of Rome by the barbarians."

Nor were the signs in England much more reassuring. There the Chartist agitation was revived by the February Revolution in Paris.[3] "France is a Republic!" cried the Chartist Ernest Jones; the Chartist petition was again circulated and was soon said to have 6 million signatures. Another Chartist convention met, considered by its leaders to be the forerunner of a Constituent Assembly as in France. The violent minority was the most active; it began to gather arms and to drill. The old Duke of Wellington swore in 70,000 special constables to uphold the social order. Clashes occurred at Liverpool and elsewhere; in London the revolutionary committee laid plans for systematic arson and organized men with pickaxes to break up the pavements for barricades. Meanwhile the petition, weighing 584 pounds, was carried in three cabs to the House of Commons, which estimated that it contained "only" 2 million signatures and again summarily rejected it. The revolutionary menace passed. One of the secret organizers in London proved to be a government spy; he revealed the whole plan at the critical moment, and the revolutionary committee was arrested

[3] See pp. 497–499.

on the day set for insurrection. Most Chartists had in any case refused to support the militants, but the truculent minority of radical workers and journalists had a deeper sense of envenomed class consciousness. The word "proletarian" was imported from France. "Every proletarian," wrote the Chartist editor of *Red Revolution*, "who does not see and feel that he belongs to an enslaved and degraded class is a *fool*."

The specter of social revolution thus hung over western Europe in the summer of 1848. Doubtless it was unreal; in all probability there could have been no successful socialist revolution at the time. But the specter was there, and it spread a sinking fear among all who had something to lose. This fear shaped the whole subsequent course of the Second Republic in France and of the revolutionary movements that had by this time begun in other countries as well.

The Emergence of Louis Napoleon Bonaparte

In France, after the June Days, the Constituent Assembly (keeping General Cavaignac as a virtual dictator) set about drafting a republican constitution. It was decided, in view of the disturbances just passed, to create a strong executive power in the hands of a president to be elected by universal male suffrage. It was decided also to have this president elected immediately, even before the rest of the constitution was finished. Four candidates presented themselves: Lamartine, Cavaignac, Ledru-Rollin—and Louis Napoleon Bonaparte. Lamartine stood for a somewhat vaguely moral and idealistic republic, Cavaignac for a republic of disciplined order, Ledru-Rollin for somewhat chastened "social" ideas. What Bonaparte stood for was not so clear. He was, however, elected by an avalanche of votes in December 1848, receiving over 5,400,000, to only 1,500,000 for Cavaignac, 370,000 for Ledru-Rollin, and a mere 18,000 for Lamartine.

Thus entered upon the European stage the second Napoleon. Born in 1808, Louis Napoleon Bonaparte was the nephew of the great Napoleon. His father, Louis Bonaparte, was at the time of his birth the king of Holland. When Napoleon's own son died in 1832 Louis Napoleon assumed the headship of the Bonaparte family. He resolved to restore the glories of the empire. With a handful of followers he tried to seize power at Strasbourg in 1836 and at Boulogne in 1840, leading what the following century would know as *Putsches*. Both failed ridiculously. Sentenced to life imprisonment in the fortress of Ham, he had escaped from it as recently as 1846 by simply walking off the grounds dressed as a stonemason. He expressed advanced social and political ideas, had probably joined the Carbonari in his youth, and had taken part in the Italian revolutionary uprising of 1830. He wrote two books, one called *Napoleonic Ideas*, claiming that his famous uncle had been misunderstood and checkmated by reactionary forces, and one called the *Extinction of Poverty*, a somewhat anticapitalistic tract like so many others of its time. But he was no friend of "anarchists," and in the spring of 1848, while still a refugee in England, he enrolled as one of Wellington's special constables to oppose the Chartist agitation. He soon returned to France. Compromised neither by the June Days nor by their repression, he was supposed to be a friend of the common people and at the same time a believer in order; and his name was Napoleon Bonaparte.

For twenty years a groundswell had been stirring the popular mind. It is known as the Napoleonic Legend. Peasants put up pictures of the emperor in their cottages, fondly imagining that it had been Napoleon who gave them the free ownership of their land. The completion of the Arch of Triumph in 1836 drove home the memory of imperial glories, and in 1840 the remains of the emperor were brought from St. Helena and majestically interred at the Invalides on the banks of the Seine. All this happened in a country where, government being in the hands of a few, most people had no political experience or political sense except what they had gained in revolution. When millions were suddenly, for the first time in their lives, asked to vote for a president in 1848, the name of Bonaparte was the only one they had ever heard of. "How should I not vote for this gentleman," said an old peasant, "I whose nose was frozen at Moscow?"

So Prince Louis Napoleon became president of the republic, by an overwhelming and indubitable popular mandate, in which an army officer was his only even faintly successful rival. He soon saw the way the wind was blowing. The Constituent Assembly dissolved itself in May 1849 and was replaced by the Legislative Assembly provided for in the new constitution. It was a strange assembly for a republic. It may be recalled that in 1797 the first normal election in the First Republic had produced a royalist majority.[4] Now in the Second Republic, under universal male suffrage, the result was the same. Five hundred of the deputies, or two-thirds, were really monarchists, but they were divided into irreconcilable factions—the Legitimists, who favored the line of Charles X, and the Orléanists, who favored that of Louis Philippe. One-third of the deputies called themselves republicans. Of these, in turn, about 180 were socialists of one kind or another; and only about 70 were political or old-fashioned republicans to whom the main issue was the form of government rather than the form of society itself.

The president and the Assembly at first combined to conjure away the specter of socialism, with which republicanism itself was now clearly associated. An abortive insurrection of June 1849 provided the chance. The Assembly, backed by the president, ousted thirty-three socialist deputies, suppressed public meetings, and imposed controls on the press. In 1850 it went so far as to rescind universal male suffrage, taking the vote away from about a third of the electorate—naturally the poorest and hence most socialistic third. The Falloux Law of 1850 put the schools at all levels of the educational system under supervision of the Catholic clergy; for, as M. Falloux said in the Assembly, "lay teachers have made the principles of social revolution popular in the most distant villages," and it was necessary "to rally around religion to strengthen the foundations of society against those who want to divide up property." The French Republic, now actually an antirepublican government, likewise intervened against the revolutionary republic established by Mazzini in the city of Rome. French military forces were sent to Rome to protect the pope; they remained there twenty years.

To the conservatives Bonaparte knew that he was virtually indispensable. They were so sharply divided between two sets of monarchists—Legitimist and Orléanist—that each would accept any antisocialist regime rather than yield to the other. Bonaparte's problem was to win over the radicals. He did so by urging in 1851 the restoration of universal suffrage, which he had himself helped repeal

[4] See p. 394.

in 1850. He now posed as the people's friend, the one man in public life who trusted the common man. He let it be thought that greedy plutocrats controlled the Assembly and hoodwinked France. He put his lieutenants in as ministers of war and of the interior, thus controlling the army, the bureaucracy, and the police. On December 2, 1851, the anniversary of Austerlitz, he sprang his coup d'état. Placards appeared all over Paris. They declared the Assembly dissolved and the vote for every adult Frenchman reinstated. When members of the Assembly tried to meet, they were attacked, dispersed, or arrested by the soldiers. The country did not submit without fighting. One hundred and fifty persons were killed in Paris, and throughout France probably 100,000 were put under arrest. But on December 20 the voters elected Louis Napoleon president for a term of ten years, by a vote officially stated as 7,439,216 to 646,737. A year later the new Bonaparte proclaimed the empire, with himself as Emperor of the French. Remembering Napoleon's son, he called himself Napoleon III.

How the empire functioned will be seen below. Not only the republic was dead. The republic as republicans understood it, an equalitarian, anticlerical regime with socialist or at least antibourgeois tendencies, had been dead since June 1848. Feeble anyway, it was killed by its reputation for radicalism. Liberalism and constitutionalism were dead also. Bourgeois and property-owning monarchists were greater sticklers for constitutional liberalism than were the republicans or the Bonapartists or than town laborers or rural peasants. But the monarchists, hopelessly divided among themselves, were now pushed aside. For the first time since 1815 France ceased to have any significant parliamentary life.

59. *Vienna: The Nationalist Revolution in Central Europe and Italy*

The Austrian Empire in 1848

The Austrian Empire of the Habsburgs, with its capital at Vienna, was in 1848 the most populous European state except Russia. Its peoples, living principally in the three major geographical divisions of the empire, Austria, Bohemia, and Hungary, were of about a dozen recognizably different nationalities or language groups—Germans, Czechs, Magyars, Poles, Ruthenians, Slovaks, Serbs, Croats, Slovenes, Dalmatians, Romanians, and Italians.[5] In some parts of the empire the nationalities lived in solid blocks, but in many regions two or more were interlaced together, the language changing from village to village, or even from house to house, in a way quite unknown in western Europe.

Germans, the leading people, occupied all of Austria proper and considerable parts of Bohemia, and were scattered also in small pockets throughout Hungary. The Czechs occupied Bohemia and the adjoining Moravia. The Magyars were the dominant group in the historic kingdom of Hungary, which contained a mixture of nationalities with a considerable number of Slavic peoples. Two of

---

[5] See maps, pp. 222, 448–449, 470; and pp. 221–223, 275–278, 331–335, 423–425, 447.

the most advanced parts of Italy also belonged to the empire—Venetia, with its capital at Venice, and Lombardy, whose chief city was Milan.

The Czechs, Poles, Ruthenians, Slovaks, Serbs, Croats, Slovenes, and Dalmatians in the empire were all Slavs; i.e., their languages were all related to one another and to the several forms of Russian. Neither the Magyars nor the Romanians were Slavs. The Magyars, as national sentiment grew, prided themselves on the uniqueness of their language in Europe and the Romanians on their linguistic affiliations with the Latin peoples of the West. Romanians, Magyars, and Germans formed a thick belt separating the South Slavs (in later years called Yugoslavs) from those of the north. Germans and Italians within the empire were in continual touch with Germans and Italians outside. The peoples of the empire represented every cultural level known to Europe. Vienna, where the Waltz King Johann Strauss was reigning, recognized no peer except Paris itself. Milan was a great center of trade. Bohemia had long had a textile industry of importance, which was beginning to be mechanized in the 1840s; but 200 miles to the south a Croatian intellectual remarked, about the same time, that the first steam engine he ever saw was in a picture printed on a cotton handkerchief imported from Manchester. In 1848, some denied that any such people as the Ruthenians existed at all. Nor was it clear exactly what groups made up the South Slavs. No such word as Yugoslavia or Czechoslovakia had been invented, and Romania was a term used only by professors.

Thus the empire ruled from Vienna included, according to political frontiers established seventy years later, in 1918, all of Austria, Hungary, and Czechoslovakia, with adjoining portions of Poland, Romania, Yugoslavia, and Italy. But the political authority of Vienna reached far beyond the borders of the empire. Austria since 1815 had been the most influential member of the German confederation, for Prussia in these years was content to look with deference upon the Habsburgs. The influence of Vienna was felt throughout Germany in many ways, as in the enactment and enforcement of the Carlsbad Decrees mentioned in the last chapter.[6] It reached also through the length of Italy. Lombardy and Venetia were part of the Austrian Empire. Tuscany, ostensibly independent, was governed by a Habsburg grand duke. The kingdom of Naples or the Two Sicilies, comprising all Italy south of Rome, was virtually a protectorate of Vienna. The papal states looked politically to Vienna for leadership, at least until 1846, when the College of Cardinals elected a liberal-minded pope, Pius IX—the one contingency upon which Metternich confessed he had failed to reckon. In all Italy there was only one state ruled by a native Italian dynasty and attempting any consistent independence of policy—the kingdom of Sardinia (called also Savoy or Piedmont) tucked away in the northwest corner around Turin. Italy, said Metternich blandly, was only a "geographical expression," a mere regional name. He might have said the same of Poland, or even of Germany, though Germany was tenuously joined in the Bund, or loose confederation, of 1815.

These peoples since the turn of the century had all felt the flutters of the *Volksgeist,* persistent stirrings of a cultural nationalism, and among Germans, Italians, Poles, and Hungarians a good deal of political agitation and liberal reformism had been at work. Metternich, in Vienna, had discouraged such

[6] See pp. 476–477.

manifestations for over thirty years, ominously predicting that if allowed to break out they would produce the *bellum omnium contra omnes*—"the war of all against all." As a prophet he was not wholly mistaken, but if it is the business of statesmanship not merely to prophesy events but to control them it cannot be said that the regime of Metternich was very successful. The whole nationalities question was evaded. The fundamental problem of the century, the bringing of peoples into some kind of mutual and moral relationship with their governments— the problem of which nationalism, liberalism, constitutionalism, and democracy were diverse aspects—remained unconsidered by the responsible authorities of central Europe. All that Metternich offered was the idea that a reigning house, with an official bureaucracy, should rule benevolently over peoples with whom it need have no connection and who need have no connection with each other. They were the ideas of the eighteenth century, dating from before the French Revolution and best suited to an agricultural and localistic society.

The March Days

In March 1848, everything collapsed with incredible swiftness. At that time the diet of Hungary had been sitting for some months, considering constitutional reforms and, as usual, debating further means of keeping German influence out of Hungary. Then came news of the February Revolution in Paris. The radical party in the Hungarian diet was aroused. Its leader, Louis Kossuth, on March 3 made an impassioned speech on the virtues of liberty. This speech was immediately printed in German and read in Vienna, where restlessness was also heightened by the news from Paris. On March 13 workingmen and students rose in insurrection in Vienna, manned barricades, fought off soldiers, and invaded the imperial palace. So flabbergasted and terrified was the government that Metternich, to the amazement of Europe, resigned and fled in disguise to England.

The fall of Metternich proved that the Vienna government was entirely disoriented. Revolution swept through the empire and through all Italy and Germany. On March 15 rioting began in Berlin; the king of Prussia promised a constitution. The lesser German governments collapsed in sequence. On the last day of March a Pre-Parliament met to arrange the calling of an all-German national assembly. In Hungary, aroused by Kossuth's national party, the diet on March 15 enacted the March Laws, by which Hungary assumed a position of complete constitutional separatism within the empire, while still recognizing the Habsburg house. The harassed Emperor Ferdinand a few days later granted substantially the same status to Bohemia. At Milan between March 18 and 22 the populace drove out the Austrian garrison. Venice proclaimed itself an independent republic. Tuscany drove out its grand duke and also set up as a republic. The king of Sardinia,[7] Charles Albert (who, stimulated by the Paris revolution, had granted a constitution to his small country on March 4) declared war on Austria on March 23 and invaded Lombardy-Venetia, hoping to bring that area under the house of

---

[7] "Sardinia" was in the northwest corner of the Italian mainland. See the note on p. 194 for an explanation of how this state, with its capital at Turin and its seaport at Genoa, came to be called after the rather desolate island of Sardinia. Of the king and kingdom we must say "Sardinia"; of the dynasty, "Savoy"; the state was often also called "Piedmont."

Savoy. Italian troops streamed up from Tuscany, from Naples (where revolution had broken out as early as January), and even from the papal states (the new pope being in some sympathy with national and liberal aims) to join in an all-Italian war against the seemingly helpless Austrian government.

Thus in the brief span of these phenomenal March Days the whole structure based on Vienna went to pieces. The Austrian Empire had fallen into its main components, Prussia had yielded to revolutionaries, all Germany was preparing to unify itself, and war raged in Italy. Everywhere constitutions had been wildly promised by stupefied governments, constitutional assemblies were meeting, and independent or autonomous nations struggled into existence. Patriots everywhere demanded liberal government and national freedom—written constitutions, representative assemblies, responsible ministries, a more or less extended suffrage, restrictions upon police action, jury trial, civil liberty, freedom of press and assembly. And where it still existed—in Prussia, Galicia, Bohemia, Hungary—serfdom was declared abolished and the peasant masses became legally free from control by their local lords.

The Turning of the Tide after June

The revolution, as in France, surged forward until the month of June, and then began to ebb. For its steady reflux there are many reasons. The old governments had been only stunned in the March Days, not really broken. They merely awaited the opportunity to take back promises extorted by force. The force originally imposed by the revolutionaries could not be sustained. The revolutionary leaders were not really very strong. Middle-class, bourgeois, property-owning, and commercial interests were nowhere nearly as highly developed as in western Europe. The revolutionary leaders were to a large extent writers, editors, professors, and students, men of ideas rather than spokesmen for large positive interests. In Vienna, Milan, and a few other cities the working class was numerous and socialist ideas fairly common; but the workers were not as literate, organized, politically conscious, or irritated as in Paris or Great Britain. They were strong enough, however, to disquiet the middle classes; and especially after the specter of social revolution rose over western Europe, the middle-class and lower-class revolutionaries began to be afraid of each other. The liberated nationalities also began to disagree. The peasants, once emancipated, had no further interest in revolution. Nor were the peasants at this time conscious of nationality; nationalism was primarily a doctrine of the educated middle classes or of the landowning classes in Poland and Hungary. Since the old internationally minded aristocracy furnished the bulk of officers in the armies, and the peasants the bulk of the soldiers, the armies remained almost immune to nationalist aspirations. This attitude of the armies was decisive.

The tide first turned in Prague. The all-German national assembly met at Frankfurt-on-the-Main in May. Representatives from Bohemia had been invited to come to Frankfurt, since many Germans had always lived in Bohemia, and since Bohemia formed part of the confederation of 1815 as it had of the Holy Roman Empire before it. But the idea of belonging to a national German state, a Germany based on the principle that the inhabitants were Germans (which had not been the principle of the Holy Roman Empire or of the confederation of 1815) did not appeal to the Czechs in Bohemia. They refused to go to the all-German congress at Frankfurt. Instead, they called an all-Slav congress of their own. At Prague, in June 1848, this first Pan-Slav assembly met. Most of the delegates were from the Slav communities within the Austrian Empire, but a few came from the Balkans and non-Austrian Poland. Only one Russian was present, the anarchist revolutionary Michael Bakunin. Slavs generally did not at this time look with favor upon Russia, the oppressor of Poles; nor did the tsarist government, under Nicholas I, think well of Pan-Slavism, seeing in it a subversive popular agitation.

The spirit of the Prague congress was that of the Slavic Revival described in the last chapter;[8] the Czech historian Palacky was in fact one of its most active figures. The congress was profoundly anti-German, since the essence of the Slavic Revival was resistance to Germanization. But it was not profoundly anti-Austrian or anti-Habsburg. A few extremists, indeed, maintained that Slavdom should be the basis of political regeneration, and that the world therefore had no place for an Austrian empire. But the great majority at the Prague congress were Austroslavs. Austroslavism held that the many Slavic peoples, pressed on two sides by the population masses of Russians and Germans, needed the Austrian Empire as a political frame within which to develop their own national life. It demanded that the Slavic peoples be admitted as equals with the other nationalities in the Austrian Empire, enjoying local autonomy and constitutional guarantees.

The Germans of Bohemia, the Sudeten Germans, were of course attracted to the Frankfurt Assembly. They were eager to be included in the unified Germany about to be formed. As the Bohemian Czechs would be a minority in a German Germany, so the Bohemian Germans would be a minority in a Czech Bohemia. There was therefore friction among the mixed people of Bohemia and in Prague, a bilingual city.

Victories of the Counterrevolution, June–December

But the Emperor Ferdinand, and the advisers on whom he chose to rely, would have nothing to do with national movements, since they were also liberal, bristling with restrictions upon the powers of the state. All therefore were to be resisted. The first victory of the old government came at Prague. In that city a Czech insurrection broke out on June 12, at the time when the Slav congress was sitting, and was made worse by local animosities between Czechs and Germans. Windischgrätz, the local army commander, bombarded and subdued the city. The Slav congress dispersed. The Habsburg army was in control.

The next victory of the counterrevolution came in north Italy in the following month. Only Lombardy-Venetia, of all parts of the empire, had declared independence from the Habsburgs during the upheavals of March. The diminutive kingdom of Sardinia had lent support and had declared war on Austria. Italians from all over the peninsula had flocked in to fight; and until after the June Days in Paris it seemed not impossible that republican France might intervene, to befriend fellow revolutionaries, as in 1796. But in France no radical or expansionist revolution succeeded. The Italians were left to themselves. Radetsky, the Austrian

[8] See pp. 468–473.

commander in Italy, overwhelmingly defeated the king of Sardinia at Custozza on July 25. The Sardinian king, Charles Albert, retreated into his own country. Lombardy and Venetia were restored with savage vengeance to the Austrian Empire.

The third victory of the counterrevolution came in September and October. The Hungarian radical party of Louis Kossuth was liberal and even democratic in many of its principles, but it was a Magyar nationalist party above all else. Triumphant in the March Days, it completely shook off the German connection. It moved the capital from Pressburg near the Austrian border to Budapest in the center of Hungary. It changed the official language of Hungary from Latin to Magyar. Less than half the people of Hungary were Magyars, and Magyar is an extremely difficult language, quite alien to the Indo-European tongues of Europe. It soon became clear that one must be a Magyar to benefit from the new liberal constitution, and that the Magyars intended to denationalize and Magyarize all others with whom they shared the country. Slovaks, Romanians, Germans, Serbs, and Croats violently resisted, each group determined to keep its own national identity unimpaired. The Croats, who had enjoyed certain Croatian liberties before the Magyar revolution, took the lead under Count Jellachich, the "ban," or provincial governor, of Croatia. In September Jellachich raised a civil war in Hungary, leading a force of Serbo-Croatians, supported by the whole non-Magyar half of the population. Half of Hungary, alarmed by Magyar nationalism, now looked to the Habsburgs and the empire to protect them. Emperor Ferdinand made Jellachich his military commander against the Magyars. Hungary dissolved into the war of all against all.

At Vienna the more clear-sighted revolutionaries, who had led the March rising, now saw that Jellachich's army, if successful against the Magyars, would soon be turned against them. They therefore rose in a second mass insurrection in October 1848. The emperor fled; never had the Viennese revolution gone so far. But it was already too late. The Austrian military leader Windischgrätz brought his intact forces down from Bohemia. He besieged Vienna for five days and forced its surrender on October 31.

With the recapture of Vienna the upholders of the old order took heart. Counterrevolutionary leaders—large estate holders, Catholic clergy, high-ranking army men—decided to clear the way by getting rid of the Emperor Ferdinand, considering that promises made in March by Ferdinand might be more easily repudiated by his successor. Ferdinand abdicated and on December 2, 1848, was succeeded by Francis Joseph, a boy of eighteen, destined to live until 1916 and to end his reign in a crisis even more shattering than that in which he began it.

Final Outburst and Repression, 1849

For a time in the first part of 1849 the revolution in many places seemed to blaze more fiercely than ever. Republican riots broke out in parts of Germany. In Rome someone assassinated the reforming minister of Pius IX. The pope fled from the city, and a radical Roman Republic was proclaimed under three Triumvirs, one of whom was Mazzini, who hastened from England to take part in the republican upheaval. In north Italy Charles Albert of Sardinia again invaded Lombardy. In

Hungary, after the revived Habsburg authorities repudiated the new Magyar constitution, the Magyars, led by the flaming Kossuth, went on to declare absolute independence. But all these manifestations proved short-lived. German republicanism flickered out. Mazzini and his republicans were driven from Rome, and Pius IX was restored, by intervention of the French army.[9] The Sardinian king was again defeated by an Austrian army on March 23, 1849. In Hungary the Magyars put up a terrific resistance, which the imperial army and the anti-Magyar native irregulars could not overcome. The Habsburg authorities now renewed the procedures of the Holy Alliance. The new Emperor Francis Joseph invited the Tsar Nicholas to intervene. Over a hundred thousand Russian troops poured over the mountains into Hungary, soon defeated the Magyars, and laid the prostrate country at the feet of the court of Vienna. This was in August 1849.

The nationalist upheaval of 1848 in central Europe and Italy was now over. The Habsburg authority had been reasserted over Czech nationalists in Prague, Magyars in Hungary, Italian patriots in north Italy, and liberal revolutionists in Vienna itself. Reaction, or antirevolutionism, became the order of the day. Pius IX, the "liberal pope" of 1846, resumed the papal throne, disillusioned in his liberal ideas. The breach between liberalism and Roman Catholicism, which had opened wide in the first French Revolution, was made a yawning chasm by the revolutionary violence of Mazzini's Roman Republic and by the measures taken to repress it. Pius IX now reiterated the anathemas of his predecessors. He codified them in 1864 in the *Syllabus of Errors*, which warned all Catholics, on the authority of the Vatican, against everything that went under the names of liberalism, progress, and civilization. As for the nationalists in Italy, many were disillusioned with the firecracker methods of romantic republicans and inclined to conclude that Italy would be liberated from Austrian influence only by an old-fashioned war between established powers.

In the Austrian Empire, under Prince Schwarzenberg, the emperor's chief minister, the main policy was now to oppose all forms of popular self-expression, with a sophistication, in view of the events of 1848, that Metternich had never known, and with a candid reliance on military force. Constitutionalism was to be rooted out, as well as all forms of nationalism—Slavism, Magyarism, Italianism, and also Germanism, which would draw the sentiments of Austrian Germans from the Habsburg empire to the great kindred body of the German people. The regime came to be called the Bach system, after Alexander Bach, the minister of the interior. Under it, the government was rigidly centralized. Hungary lost the separate rights it had had before 1848. The ideal was to create a perfectly solid and unitary political system. Bach insisted on maintaining the emancipation of the peasants, which had converted the mass of the people from subjects of their landlords into subjects of the state. He drove through a reform of the legal system and law courts, created a free trading area of the whole empire with only a common external tariff, and subsidized and encouraged the building of highways and railroads. The aim, as in France at the same time under Louis Napoleon, was to make people forget liberty in an overwhelming demonstration of administrative efficiency and material progress. But some, at that time, would not forget. A

[9] See p. 506.

liberal said of the Bach system that it consisted of "a standing army of soldiers, a sitting army of officials, a kneeling army of priests, and a creeping army of informers."

60. Frankfurt and Berlin: The Question of a Liberal Germany

The German States

Meanwhile, from May 1848 to May 1849, the Frankfurt Assembly was sitting at the historic city on the Main. It was attempting to bring a unified German state into being, one which should also be liberal and constitutional, assuring civil rights to its citizens and possessing a government responsive to popular will as manifested in free elections and open parliamentary debate. The failure to produce a democratic Germany was long one of the overshadowing facts of modern times.

The convocation of the Frankfurt Assembly was made possible by the collapse of the existing German governments in the March Days of 1848. These governments, the thirty-nine states recognized after the Congress of Vienna, were the main obstacles in the way of unification. The reigning princes and their ministers enjoyed a heightened political stature from political independence. The German states resisted the surrender of sovereignty to a united Germany just as national states in the next century were to resist the surrender of sovereignty to a United Nations. In another way Germany was a miniature of the political world. It consisted of both great and small powers. Its great powers were Prussia and Austria. Austria was the miscellaneous empire described above. Prussia after 1815 included the Rhineland; the central regions around Berlin; West Prussia and Posen (acquired in the partitions of Poland); and historic East Prussia. The former Polish areas were inhabited by a mixture of Germans and Poles.[10] Neither of these great powers could submit to the other or allow the other to dominate its lesser German neighbors. The small German powers, in turn, upheld their own independence in the balance between the two great ones.

This German "dualism," or polarity between Berlin and Vienna, had been somewhat abated under the common menace of the Napoleonic empire. The whole German question had lain dormant, so far as the governments were concerned, nor did it agitate the old aristocracies. In Prussia the Junkers, the owners of great landed estates east of the Elbe, were singularly indifferent to the all-German dream. Their political feeling was not German but Prussian. They were making a good thing of Prussia for themselves and could expect only to lose by absorption into Germany as a whole, for in Germany west of the Elbe the small peasant holding was the basis of society, and there was no landowning element corresponding to the Junkers. The rest of Germany looked upon Prussia as somewhat uncouth and Eastern; but this feeling, too,

---

[10] See maps, pp. 230–231, 448–449; and see pp. 227–229, 246, 447–450.

had been abated in the time of Napoleon, when patriots from all over Germany enlisted in the Prussian service.[11]

Berlin: Failure of the Revolution in Prussia

Prussia was illiberal but not backward. Frederick William III repeatedly evaded his promise to grant a modern constitution. His successor, Frederick William IV, who inherited the throne in 1840, and from whom much was at first hoped by liberals, proved to be a somewhat cloudy and neomedieval romantic, equally determined not to share his authority with his subjects. At the same time the government, administratively speaking, was efficient, progressive, and fair. The universities and elementary school system surpassed those of western Europe. Literacy was higher than in England or France. The government followed in mercantilist traditions of evoking, planning, and supporting economic life.[12] In 1818 it initiated a tariff union, at first with tiny states (or enclaves) wholly enclosed within Prussia. This tariff union, or *Zollverein,* was extended in the following decades to include almost all Germany.

On March 15, 1848, as noted above, rioting and street fighting broke out in Berlin. For a time it seemed as if the army would master the situation. But the king, Frederick William IV, a man of notions and projects, and erratically conscientious, called off the soldiers and allowed his subjects to elect the first all-Prussian legislative assembly. Thus though the army remained intact, and its Junker officers unconvinced, revolution proceeded superficially on its way. The Prussian Assembly proved surprisingly radical, since it was dominated by anti-Junker lower-class extremists from East Prussia. These men were supporting Polish revolutionaries and exiles who sought the restoration of Polish freedom. Their main belief was that the fortress of reaction was tsarist Russia—that the whole structure of Junkerdom, landlordism, serf-owning, and repression of national freedom depended ultimately on the armed might of the tsarist empire. (The subsequent intervention of Russia in Hungary indicated the truth of this diagnosis.) Prussian radicals, like many elsewhere, hoped to smash the Holy Alliance by raising an all-German or even European revolutionary war against Russia, to precipitate which they supported the claims of the Poles.

Meanwhile the radical-dominated Berlin Assembly granted local self-government to the Poles of West Prussia and Posen. But in those areas Germans and Slavs had long lived side by side. The Germans in Posen refused to respect the authority of Polish officials. Prussian army units stationed in Posen supported the German element. As early as April 1848, a month after the "revolution," the army crushed the new pro-Polish institutions set up in Posen by the Berlin Assembly. It was clear where the only real power lay. By the end of 1848, in Prussia as in Austria, the revolution was over. The king again changed his mind; and the old authorities, acting through the army, were again in control.

[11] See pp. 439–440.
[12] See pp. 119–120, 232, 335–336.

The Frankfurt Assembly

Meanwhile a similar story was enacted on the larger stage of Germany as a whole. The disabling of the old governments left a power vacuum. A self-appointed committee convoked a Pre-Parliament, which in turn arranged for the election of an all-German assembly. Bypassing the existing sovereignties, voters throughout Germany sent delegates to Frankfurt to create a federated superstate. The strength and weakness of the resulting Frankfurt Assembly originated in this manner of its election. The Assembly represented the moral sentiment of people at large, the liberal and national aspirations of many Germans. It stood for an idea. Politically it represented nothing. The delegates had no power to issue orders or expect compliance. Superficially resembling the National Assembly which met in France in 1789, the German National Assembly at Frankfurt was really in a very different position. There was no preexisting national structure for it to work with. There was no all-German army or civil service for the Assembly to take over. The Frankfurt Assembly, having no power of its own, became dependent on the power of the very sovereign states that it was attempting to supersede.

The Assembly met in May 1848. Its members with a handful of exceptions were not at all revolutionary. They were overwhelmingly professional people—professors, judges, lawyers, government administrators, clergy both Protestant and Catholic, and prominent businessmen. They wanted a liberal, self-governing, federally unified, and "democratic" though not equalitarian Germany. Their outlook was earnest, peaceable, and legalistic; they hoped to succeed by persuasion. Violence was abhorrent to them. They wanted no armed conflict with the existing German states. They wanted no war with Russia. They wanted no general international upheaval of the working classes. The example of the June Days in Paris, and the Chartist agitation in Great Britain, coinciding with the early weeks of the Frankfurt Assembly, increased the dread of that body for radicalism and republicanism in Germany. The tragedy of Germany (and hence of Europe) lies in the fact that this German revolution came too late, at a time when social revolutionaries had already begun to declare war on the bourgeoisie, and the bourgeoisie was already afraid of the common man. It is the common man, not the professor or respectable merchant, who in unsettled times actually seizes firearms and rushes to shout revolutionary utterances in the streets. Without lower-class insurrection not even middle-class revolutions have been successful. The combination effected in France between 1789 and 1794, an unwilling and divergent combination of bourgeois and lower-class revolutionaries, was not and could not be effected in Germany in 1848. One form of revolutionary power—controlled popular turbulence—the Germans of the Frankfurt Assembly would not or could not use. Quite the contrary: when radical riots broke out in Frankfurt itself in September 1848 the Assembly undertook to repress them. Having no force of its own, it appealed to the Prussian army. The Prussian army put down the riots, and thereafter the Assembly met under its protection.

But the most troublesome question facing the Frankfurt Assembly was not social but national. What, after all, was this "Germany" which so far existed only in the mind? Where was the line really to be drawn in space? Did Germany include Austria and Bohemia, which belonged to the Bund of 1815 and had in former days belonged to the Holy Roman Empire?[13] Did it include all Prussia, although eastern Prussia had lain outside the Empire and did not now belong to the Bund? On the side toward Denmark, did it include the duchies of Schleswig and Holstein, which belonged to the Danish king, who was therefore himself, as ruler of Holstein, a member of the 1815 confederation? And if, as poets said, the Fatherland existed wherever the German tongue was spoken, what of the German communities in Hungary and Moravia, or along the upper Baltic and in the city of Riga, or in some of the Swiss cantons and the city of Zurich, or for that matter in Holland, which had left the Holy Roman Empire only two hundred years before—not long as time is measured in Europe.

These last and most soaring speculations, though they had already been launched by a few bold spirits, were put out of mind by the men of the Frankfurt Assembly. The other questions remained. The men at Frankfurt, eager to create a real Germany, naturally could not offer one smaller than the shadow Germany that they so much deplored. Most therefore were Great Germans; they thought that the Germany for which they were writing a constitution should include the Austrian lands, except Hungary. This would mean that the federal crown must be offered to the Habsburgs. Others, at first a minority, were Little Germans; they thought that Austria should be excluded, and that the new Germany should comprise the smaller states and the entire kingdom of Prussia. In that case the king of Prussia would become the federal emperor.

The desire of the Frankfurt Assembly to retain non-German peoples in the new Germany, at a time when these peoples also were feeling national ambitions, was another reason for its fatal dependency upon the Austrian and Prussian armies. The Frankfurt Assembly applauded when Windischgrätz broke the Czech revolution. It expressed its satisfaction when Prussian forces put down the Poles in Posen. On this matter the National Assembly at Frankfurt and the Prussian Assembly at Berlin did not agree. The men of Frankfurt, thinking the Prussian revolutionary assembly too radical and pro-Polish, and wanting no war with Russia, in effect supported the Prussian army and the Junkers against the Berlin revolution, without which the Frankfurt Assembly itself could never have existed.

A still clearer case arose over Schleswig-Holstein. These duchies belonged to the Danish king. Schleswig, the northern of the two, had a mixed population of Danes and Germans. The Germans in Schleswig rebelled in March 1848; and the Danes, who also had a constitutional upheaval at the time, proceeded to incorporate Schleswig integrally into their modernized Danish state. When the Frankfurt Assembly met, it found that the Pre-Parliament had already declared an all-German war upon Denmark in defense of fellow Germans in Schleswig. Having no army of its own, the Frankfurt Assembly invited Prussia to fight the war; and the revolutionary Prussian government in Berlin was at first able to persuade the Prussian generals to initiate a campaign. Great Britain and Russia prepared to intervene to keep control of the mouth of the Baltic out of German hands. The Prussian army simply withdrew from the war. Its officers had no desire to antagonize Russia or to advance the interests of nationalist revolutionaries in Germany. The Frankfurt Assembly, humiliated and helpless, was obliged to accept the armistice concluded by the Prussian generals. Radical socionationalistic

[13] See maps, pp. 328, 448–449, 555.

riots broke out against the Junkers, the tsar, and the Frankfurt Assembly; and it was at this time that the Assembly called in Prussian forces for its own protection.

The Failure of the Frankfurt Assembly

By the end of 1848 the debacle was approaching. The nationalists had checkmated each other. Everywhere in central Europe, from Denmark to Naples and from the Rhineland to the Transylvanian forests, the awakening nationalities had failed to respect each other's aspirations, had delighted in each other's defeats, and by quarreling with each other had hastened the return of the old absolutist and nonnational order. At Berlin and at Vienna the counterrevolution, backed by the army, was in the saddle. At this very time, in December, the Frankfurt Assembly at last issued a Declaration of the Rights of the German People. It was a humane and high-minded document, announcing numerous individual rights, civil liberties, and constitutional guarantees, much along the line of the French and American declarations of the eighteenth century, but with one significant difference—the French and Americans spoke of the rights of man, the Germans of the rights of Germans. In April 1849 the Frankfurt Assembly completed its constitution. It was now clear that Austria must be excluded, for the simple reason that the restored Habsburg government refused to come in. The Danubian empire, as already seen, was as profoundly opposed to Germanism as to any other nationalistic movement. The Little Germans in the Assembly therefore had their way. The hereditary headship of a new German empire, a constitutional and federal union of German states minus Austria, was now offered to Frederick William IV, the king of Prussia.

Frederick William was tempted. The Prussian army officers and East-Elbian landlords were not. They had no wish to lose Prussia in Germany. The king himself had his scruples. If he took the proffered crown he would still have to impose himself by force on the lesser states, which the Frankfurt Assembly did not represent and could not bind, and which were in fact still the actual powers in the country. He could also expect trouble with Austria. He did not wish war. Nor was it proper for an heir to the Hohenzollerns to accept a throne circumscribed with constitutional limitations and representing the revolutionary conception of the sovereignty of the people. Declaring that he could not "pick up a crown from the gutter," he turned it down. It would have to be offered freely by his equals, the sovereign princes of Germany.

Thus all the work of the Frankfurt Assembly went for nothing. Most members of the Assembly, having never dreamed of using violence in the first place, concluded that they were beaten and went home. A handful of extremists remained at Frankfurt, promulgated the constitution on their own authority, urged revolutionary outbreaks, and called for elections. Riots broke out in various places. The Prussian army put them down—in Saxony, in Bavaria, in Baden. The same army drove the rump Assembly out of Frankfurt, and that was the end of it.

In summary, Germany in 1848 failed to solve the problem of its unification in a liberal and constitutional way. Liberal nationalism failed, and a less gentle kind of nationalism soon replaced it. The German movement of 1848, like so much else in German history, in the long run contributed to a fateful estrangement between Germany and the West. Thousands of disappointed German liberals and revolutionaries migrated to the United States, which came to know them as the "forty-eighters." They brought to the new country, besides a ripple of revolutionary agitation, a stream of men trained in science, medicine, and music, and of highly skilled craftsmen like silversmiths and engravers.

The Prussian Constitution of 1850

In Prussia itself the ingenious monarch undertook to placate everybody by issuing a constitution of his own, one that should be peculiarly Prussian. It remained in effect from 1850 to 1918. It granted a single parliament for all the miscellaneous regions of Prussia. The parliament met in two chambers. The lower chamber was elected by universal male suffrage, not along the individualist or equalitarian principles of the West, but by a system that in effect divided the population into three estates—the wealthy, the less wealthy, and the general run of the people. Division was made according to payment of taxes. Those few big taxpayers who together contributed a third of the tax returns chose a third of the members of district electoral colleges, which in turn chose deputies to the Prussian lower house. In this way one large property owner had as much voting power as hundreds of working people. Large property in Prussia in 1850 still meant mainly the landed estates of the East-Elbian Junkers, but as time went on it came to include industrial property in the Rhineland also. The Junkers likewise were not harmed by the final liquidation of serfdom. They increased the acreage of their holdings, as after the reforms of Stein;[14] and the former servile agricultural workers turned into free wage earners economically dependent on the great landowners.

For 1850 the Prussian constitution was fairly progressive. If the mass of the people could elect very few deputies under the indirect system described, the mass of the British people, until 1867 or even 1884, could elect no deputies to Parliament at all. But the Prussian constitution remained in force until 1918. By the close of the nineteenth century, with democratic advances making their appearance elsewhere, the electoral system in Prussia, remaining unchanged, came to be reactionary and illiberal, giving the great landowners and industrialists an unusual position of special privilege within the state.

61. The New Toughness of Mind: Realism, Positivism, Marxism

The Revolution of 1848 failed not only in Germany but also in Hungary, in Italy, and in France. The "springtime of peoples," as it was called, was followed by chilling blasts of winter. The dreams of half a century, visions of a humane nationalism, aspirations for liberalism without violence, ideals of a peaceful and democratic republican commonwealth, were all exploded. Everywhere the cry had been for constitutional government, but only in a few small states—Denmark,

[14] See pp. 439–441.

Holland, Belgium, Switzerland, Piedmont—was constitutional liberty more firmly secured by the Revolution of 1848. Everywhere the cry had been for the freedom of nations, to unify national groups or rid them of foreign rule; but nowhere was national liberty more advanced in 1850 than it had been two years before. France obtained universal male suffrage in 1848, and kept it permanently thereafter (except for a brief reversion to a restricted suffrage in 1850–1851); but it did not obtain democracy; it obtained a kind of popular dictatorship under Louis Napoleon Bonaparte. One accomplishment, however, was real enough. The peasantry was emancipated in the German states and the Austrian Empire. Serfdom and manorial restraints were abolished, nor were they reimposed after the failure of the revolution. This was the most fundamental accomplishment of the whole movement. The peasant masses of central Europe were thereafter free to move about, find new jobs, enter a labor market, take part in a money economy, receive and spend wages, migrate to growing cities—or even go to the United States. But the peasants, once freed, showed little concern for constitutional or bourgeois ideas. Peasant emancipation, in fact, strengthened the forces of political counterrevolution.

The most immediate and far-reaching consequence of the 1848 revolutions, or of their failure, was a new toughness of mind. Idealism was discredited. Revolutionaries became less optimistic, conservatives more willing to exercise repression. It was now a point of pride to be realistic, emancipated from illusions, willing to face facts as they were. The future, it was thought, would be determined by present realities rather than by imaginings of what ought to be. Industrialization went forward, with England still far in the lead, but spreading to the Continent and initiating the momentous transformation of Germany. The 1850s were a period of rising prices and wages, thanks in part to the gold rush in California. There was more prosperity than in the 1840s; the propertied classes felt secure, and spokesmen for labor turned from theories of society to the organizing of viable unions, especially in the skilled trades.

Materialism, Realism, Positivism

In basic philosophy the new mental toughness appeared as materialism, holding that everything mental, spiritual, or ideal was an outgrowth of physical or physiological forces. In literature and the arts it was called "realism." Writers and painters broke away from romanticism, which they said colored things out of all relation to the real facts. They attempted to describe and reproduce life as they found it, without intimation of a better or more noble world. More and more people came to trust science, not merely for an understanding of nature, but for insights into the true meaning of man and society. In religion the movement was toward skepticism, renewing the skeptical trend of the eighteenth century, which had been somewhat interrupted during the intervening period of romanticism.[15] It was variously held, not by all but by many, that religion was unscientific and hence not to be taken seriously; or that it was a mere historical growth among peoples in certain stages of development and hence irrelevant to modern

[15] See pp. 314–315, 317–324, 464–465.

civilization; or that one ought to go to church and lead a decent life, without taking the priest or clergyman too seriously, because religion was necessary to preserve the social order against radicalism and anarchy. To this idea the radical counterpart was of course that religion was a bourgeois invention to delude the people.

"Positivism" was another term used to describe the new attitude. It originated with the French philosopher Auguste Comte, who had begun to publish his numerous volumes on *Positive Philosophy* as long ago as 1830 and was still writing in the 1850s. He saw human history as a series of three stages, the theological, the metaphysical, and the scientific. The revolutions in France, he thought, both of 1789 and of 1848, suffered from an excess of metaphysical abstractions, empty words, and unverifiable high-flying principles. Those who worked for the improvement of society must adopt a strictly scientific outlook, and Comte produced an elaborate classification of the sciences, of which the highest would be the science of society, for which he coined the word "sociology." This new science would build upon observation of actual facts to develop broad scientific laws of social progress. Comte himself, and his closest disciples, envisaged a final scientific Religion of Humanity, which, stripped of archaic theological and metaphysical concerns, would serve as the basis for a better world of the future. More generally, however, "positivism" came to mean an insistence on verifiable facts, an avoidance of wishful thinking, a questioning of all assumptions, and a dislike of unprovable generalizations. Positivism in a broad sense, both in its demand for observation of facts and testing of ideas, and in its aspiration to be humanly useful, contributed to the growth of the social sciences as a branch of learning.

In politics the new toughness of mind was called by the Germans *Realpolitik*. This simply meant a "politics of reality." In domestic affairs it meant that people should give up utopian dreams, such as had caused the débacle of 1848, and content themselves with the blessings of an orderly, honest, hard-working government. For radicals it meant that people should stop imagining that the new society would result from goodness or the love of justice, and that social reformers must resort to the methods of politics—power and calculation. In international affairs *Realpolitik* meant that governments should not be guided by ideology, or by any system of "natural" enemies or "natural" allies, or by any desire to defend or promote any particular view of the world; but that they should follow their own practical interests, meet facts and situations as they arose, make any alliances that seemed useful, disregard tastes and scruples, and use any practical means to achieve their ends. The same men who, before 1848, had been not ashamed to express pacifist and cosmopolitan hopes now dismissed such ideas as a little softheaded. War, which governments since the overthrow of Napoleon had successfully tried to prevent, was accepted in the 1850s as an obvious means sometimes necessary to achieve a purpose. It was not especially glorious; it was not an end in itself; it was simply one of the tools of the statesman. *Realpolitik* was by no means confined to Germany, despite its German name and despite the fact that the famous German chancellor Bismarck became its most famous practitioner. Two other tough-minded thinkers, each in his own way, were Karl Marx and Louis Napoleon Bonaparte.

Early Marxism

Karl Marx and Friedrich Engels were among the disappointed revolutionaries of 1848. Marx (1818–1883) was the son of a lawyer in the Prussian Rhineland. He studied law and philosophy at several German universities, received a doctoral degree in 1841, and mixed with young German intellectuals for several years. Engels (1820–1893), the son of a well-to-do German textile manufacturer, was sent as a young man to Manchester in England, where his father owned a factory, to learn the business and then manage it. Marx and Engels met in Paris in 1844. There they began a collaboration in thinking and writing that lasted for forty years.

In 1847 they joined the Communist League, a tiny secret group of revolutionaries, mainly Germans in exile in the more liberal Western Europe. The word "communist" then had only a vague and uncertain meaning, and the League, as Engels later recalled, was at first "not actually much more than the German branch of the French secret societies." It agitated like other societies during the Revolution of 1848, and issued a set of "Demands of the Communist Party in Germany," which urged a unified indivisible German republic, democratic suffrage, universal free education, arming of the people, a progressive income tax, limitations upon inheritance, state ownership of banks, railroads, canals, mines, etc., and a degree of large-scale, scientific, collectivized agriculture. It was such obscurely voiced radicalism that alarmed the Frankfurt Assembly. With the triumph of counterrevolution in Germany the Communist League was crushed.

It was for this League that Marx and Engels wrote their *Communist Manifesto,* which was published in January 1848. But there was as yet no Marxism, and Marxism played no role in the Revolution of 1848. As a historical force Marxism set in during the 1870s. Meanwhile, with the failure of the revolution, Engels returned to his factory at Manchester, and Marx also settled in England, spending the rest of his life in London, where, after long labors in the library of the British Museum, he finally produced his huge work called *Capital,* of which the first volume was published in German in 1867. The final two volumes were edited by Engels and published after Marx's death.

Sources and Content of Marxism

Marxism may be said to have had three sources or to have merged three national streams: German philosophy, French revolutionism, and the British Industrial Revolution. As a student in Germany, and for a while thereafter, Marx mingled with a group known as Young Hegelians, who were actually anti-Hegel in that they expected the course of history to lead to a free and democratic society, instead of to the existing Prussian state as Hegel had maintained. They joined with liberals in resisting the repressive measures that prevailed in Germany after the defeat of Napoleon. Like democrats and republicans, they believed that the promise of the French Revolution had not yet been fulfilled, since social and economic equality should follow the civil and legal equality already won.[16] In keeping with the general movement of romanticism, they hoped for a more

---

[16] See pp. 466–468.

personal emancipation from the trammels of society, government, and religion. In the mid-1840s, elaborating on Hegel, Marx developed the idea of "alienation," a state of mind produced when the human being becomes estranged from the object on which he works, through the historic processes of mechanization, the commercialization of labor, and the ownership of property by others than the workers.

It followed that true freedom was possible only when private property in capital goods was abolished. Some of the writings in which these youthful ideas were worked out in the 1840s were not published until a century later. They then led to a reconsideration of Marxism, in which the early Marx was seen more as a social analyst than as a revolutionary. But they had little impact on the growth of Marxism as a program for revolutionary socialism in the nineteenth century.

Engels, engaged in the Manchester cotton industry, possessed a personal knowledge of the new industrial and factory system in England. He was in touch with some of the most radical Chartists, though he had no confidence in Chartism as a constructive movement. In 1844 he published a revealing book on *The Condition of the Working Classes in England.* He drew from the observation of facts much the same conclusions that Marx drew from philosophical analysis and historical study. The depressed condition of labor was an actual fact.[17] It was a fact that labor received a relatively small portion of the national income, and that much of the product of society was being reinvested in capital goods, which belonged as private property to private persons. Government and parliamentary institutions, also as a matter of fact, were in the hands of the well-to-do in both Great Britain and France. Religion was commonly held to be necessary to keep the lower classes in order. The churches at the time, as a matter of fact, took little interest in problems of the workers. The family, as an institution, was in fact disintegrating among laboring people in the cities, through exploitation of women and children and the overcrowding in inadequate and unsanitary living quarters.

All these facts were seized upon and dramatized in the *Communist Manifesto,* published in January 1848 as a summons to revolution. The outbreak of revolution in France in February, and its rapid spread to other countries, naturally confirmed Marx and Engels in their beliefs. An actual class war that shook Paris in the June Days was taken by them as a manifestation of a universal class struggle, in which the workers or proletariat rose against the owners of capital, the bourgeoisie.

As a call to action, the *Communist Manifesto* was meant to be inflammatory. It went beyond facts to denunciation and exhortation. It said that the worker was deprived of the wealth he had himself created. It called the state a committee of the bourgeoisie for the exploitation of the people. Religion was a drug to keep the worker quietly dreaming upon imaginary heavenly rewards. The worker's family, his wife and children, had been prostituted and brutalized by the bourgeoisie. It seemed to Marx and Engels that the uprooted worker should be loyal to nothing—except his own class. Even country had become meaningless. The proletarian had no country. Workers everywhere had the same problems and faced everywhere the same enemy. Therefore "let the ruling classes tremble at a communist revolution. The proletarians have nothing to lose but their chains.

---

[17] See pp. 459–461, 496–497.

They have a world to win. Workingmen of all countries, unite!'' So closed the *Manifesto*.

But Marx was no mere revolutionary schemer, like the "revolution-makers," as he later scornfully called them. His mature thought was a system for producing revolution, but it showed how revolution would necessarily come by operation of vast and impersonal forces.

It was from English sources that Marx developed much of his economic theory, as expounded at length in *Capital*. From British political economy he adopted the subsistence theory of wages, or Iron Law (which orthodox economists presently abandoned since wages did in fact begin to rise).[18] It held that the average worker could never obtain more than a minimum level of living—of which the corollary, for those who wished to draw it, was that the existing economic system held out no better future for the laboring class as a class. Marx likewise took over from orthodox economists the labor theory of value, holding that the value of any man-made object depended ultimately on the amount of labor put into it—capital being regarded as the stored up labor of former times. Orthodox economists soon discarded the theory that economic value is produced by the input of labor alone. Marx, from the labor theory, developed his doctrine of surplus value. This was very intricate; but "surplus value" meant in effect that workers were being robbed. They received in wages only a fraction of the value of the products which their labor produced. The difference was "expropriated" by the bourgeois capitalists—the private owners of the factories and the machines. And since workers never received in wages the equivalent of what they produced, capitalism was constantly menaced by overproduction, the accumulation of goods that people could not afford to buy. Hence it ran repeatedly into crisis and depressions and was obliged also to be constantly expanding in search of new markets. It was the depression of 1847, according to Marx, that had precipitated the Revolution of 1848; and with every such depression during the rest of his lifetime Marx hoped that the day of the great social revolution was drawing nearer.

What brought all these observations together in a unified and compelling doctrine was the philosophy of dialectical materialism. By dialectic, Marx meant what the German philosopher Hegel had meant,[19] that all things are in movement and in evolution, and that all change comes through the clash of antagonistic elements. The word itself, coming from the Greek, meant originally a way of arriving at a higher conclusion through a series of propositions, as in a logical argument. The implications of the dialectic, for both Hegel and Marx, were that all history, and indeed all reality, is a process of development through time, a single and meaningful unfolding of events, necessary, logical, and deterministic; that every event happens in due sequence for good and sufficient reason (not by chance); and that history could not and cannot happen any differently from the way it has happened and is still happening today. This, it need hardly be said, cannot be demonstrated on any basis of evidence.

Marx differed from Hegel in one vital respect. Whereas Hegel emphasized the primacy of "ideas" in social change, Marx gave emphasis to the primacy of

[18] See pp. 461–463, 623.
[19] See p. 471.

material conditions, or the relations of production, which included technology, inventions, natural resources, and property systems. It is these that create the social world in which people live. It is the relations of production that determine what kind of religions, philosophies, governments, laws, and moral values are accepted. To believe that ideas precede and generate actualities was, according to Marx, the error of Hegel. Hegel had thought, for example, that the mind conceives the idea of freedom, which it then realizes in the Greek city-state, in Christianity, in the French Revolution, and in the kingdom of Prussia. Not at all, according to Marx: the idea of freedom, or any other idea, is generated by the actual economic and social conditions. Conditions are the roots, ideas the trees. Hegel had held the ideas to be the roots and the resulting actual conditions to be the trees. Or as Marx and Engels said, they found Hegel standing on his head and set him on his feet again.

The picture of historical development offered by Marx was somewhat as follows. Material conditions, or the relations of production, give rise to economic classes. Agrarian conditions produce a landholding or feudal class, but with changes in trade routes, money, and productive techniques a new commercial or bourgeois class arises. Each class, feudal and bourgeois, develops an ideology suited to its needs. Prevailing religions, governments, laws, and morals reflect the outlook of these classes. The two classes inevitably clash. Bourgeois revolutions against feudal interests break out—in England in 1642, in France in 1789, in Germany in 1848, though the bourgeois revolution in Germany proved abortive. Meanwhile, as the bourgeois class develops, it inevitably calls another class into being, its dialectical antithesis, the proletariat. The bourgeois is defined as the private owner of capital, the proletarian as the wage worker who possesses nothing but his own hands. The more a country becomes bourgeois, the more it becomes proletarian. The more production is concentrated in factories, the more the revolutionary laboring class is built up. Under competitive conditions the bourgeois tend to devour and absorb each other; ownership of the factories, mines, machines, railroads, etc. (capital) becomes concentrated into very few hands. Others sink into the proletariat. In the end the proletarianized mass simply takes over from the remaining bourgeois. It "expropriates the expropriators," and abolishes the old private property in the means of production. The social revolution is thus accomplished. It is inevitable. A classless society results, because class arises from economic differences which have been done away with. The state and religion, being outgrowths of bourgeois interests, also disappear. For a time, until all vestiges of bourgeois interests have been rooted out, or until the danger of counterrevolution against socialism has been overcome, there will be a "dictatorship of the proletariat." After that the state will "wither away," since there is no longer an exploiting class to require it.

Meanwhile the call is to war. Bourgeois and proletarian are locked in a universal struggle. It is really war, and as in all war all other considerations must be subordinated to it. Periods of social calm are not peace; they are merely interludes between battles. The workers must not be allowed to grow soft or conciliatory, any more than an army should be allowed to forget its primary function of fighting. Workers and labor unions must be kept in a belligerent and revolutionary mood. They must never forget that the employer is their class enemy, and that government, law, morality, and religion are merely so much artillery directed against them. Morals are "bourgeois morals," law is "bourgeois law," government is an instrument of class power, and religion is a form of psychological warfare, a means of providing "opium" for the masses. Workers must not let themselves be fooled; they must learn how to detect the class interest underlying the most exalted institutions and beliefs. In this piece of military intelligence, ferreting out the ways of the enemy, they will be helped by intellectuals especially trained in explaining it to them. Like all fighting forces, the workers need a disciplined solidarity. Individuals must lose themselves in the whole—in their class. It is a betrayal of their class for workers to rise above the proletariat, to "improve themselves," as the bourgeois says. It is dangerous for labor unions merely to obtain better wages or hours by negotiation with employers, for by such little gains the war itself may be forgotten. It is likewise dangerous, and even treasonous, for workers to put faith in democratic machinery or "social legislation," for the state, an engine of repression, can never be made into an instrument of welfare. Law is the will of the stronger (i.e., the stronger class); "right" and "justice" are thin emanations of class interest. We must hold, wrote Marx in 1875, to "the realistic outlook which has cost so much effort to instill into the party, but which has now taken root in it"; and we must not let this outlook be perverted "by means of ideological nonsense about 'right' and other trash common among the democrats and French Socialists."

The Appeal of Marxism: Its Strength and Weaknesses

The original Marxism was a hard doctrine, with both advantages and handicaps in the winning of adherents. One of its advantages was its claim to be scientific. Marx classified earlier and rival forms of socialism[20] as utopian: they rested on moral indignation, and their formula for reforming society was for men to become more just, or for the upper classes to be converted to sympathy for the lower. His own doctrine, Marx insisted, had nothing to do with ethical ideas; it was purely scientific, resting upon the study of actual facts and real processes, and it showed that socialism would be not a miraculous reversal but a historical continuation of what was already taking place. He also considered it utopian and unscientific to describe the future socialist society in any detail. It would be classless, with neither bourgeois nor proletarian; but to lay any specific plans would be idle dreaming. Let the revolution come, and socialism would take care of itself.

Marxism was a strong compound of the scientific, the historical, the metaphysical, and the apocalyptic. But some elements of Marxism stood in the way of its natural propagation. The working people of Europe were not really in the frame of mind of an army in battle. They hesitated to subordinate all else to the distant prospect of a class revolution. They were not exclusively class-people, nor did they behave as such. Enough of religion was still alive in them, and of older natural-law ideas, to inhibit the belief that morality was a class weapon, or right and justice "trash." They had national loyalties to country; they could with difficulty associate themselves emotionally with a world proletariat in an unrelenting struggle against their own neighbors.

[20] See pp. 466–468.

The cure for the revolutionism of 1848 proved in time to be the admission of the laboring classes to a fuller membership in society. Wages generally rose after 1850, labor unions were organized, and by 1870 in the principal European countries the workingman very generally had a vote. Through their unions, workers were often able to get better wages and working conditions by direct pressure upon employers. Having the vote, they gradually formed working-class parties, and as they proceeded to act through the state they had less inclination to destroy it. Marx's word for such maneuvers was "opportunism." Opportunism, the tendency of working people to better themselves by dealing with employers and by obtaining legislation through existing government channels, was the most dangerous of all dangers to the Revolution. For in war people do not negotiate or pass laws; they fight. From Marxism the working class absorbed much, including a watchful hostility to employers and a sense of working-class solidarity; but on the whole, as Marxism spread at the close of the nineteenth century it ceased to be really revolutionary.[21] Had the old Europe not gone to pieces in the twentieth-century wars, and had Marxism not been revived by Lenin and transplanted to Russia, it is probable that Marx's ideas would have been domesticated into the general body of European thought, and that much less would be said about them in this book.

62. Bonapartism: The Second French Empire, 1852–1870

We have seen how Louis Napoleon Bonaparte, elected president of the republic in 1848, in 1852 made himself Emperor of the French with the title of Napoleon III.[22] Those willing to fight for the parliamentary and liberal institutions which he crushed were silenced. He became chief of state on a wave of popular acclaim.

Political Institutions of the Second Empire

Napoleon III, like Napoleon I, came to power because of the fear of radicalism in a discredited republic. Otherwise he bore little resemblance to his famous uncle. He was not a professional soldier or a great organizer. When he became president of the republic at the age of forty he had been an adventurer and a conspirator, but he had also written two books on the "social question," and he undoubtedly felt more concern than Napoleon I for the plight of the working classes. Where Napoleon I had been disdainful of public opinion, his nephew recognized it as an opportunity, not a nuisance. Though journalists and intellectuals generally distrusted him, he drew some of them to his side; he tried to placate the Catholic interests; and he appealed to the masses by giving them the vote (however useless), by promises of prosperity, and by pageantry. He understood perfectly that a single leader exerts more magnetism than an elected assembly. And he knew that a Europe still shuddering over the June Days was hoping desperately for order in France.

---

[21] See pp. 622–625.
[22] See pp. 505–507.

He gloried in modern progress. Toward the changes coming over Europe the monarchs of the old school usually showed an attitude of timidity and doubt if not positive opposition. Napoleon III boldly offered himself as the leader in a brave new world. Like his uncle, he announced that he embodied the sovereignty of the people. He said that he had found a solution to the problem of mass democracy. In all the other great Continental states and in Great Britain, in 1852, universal suffrage was thought to be incompatible with intelligent government and economic prosperity. Napoleon III claimed to put them together. Like Marx and other "realists" after 1848 he held that elected parliamentary bodies, far from representing an abstract "people," only accentuated class divisions within a country. He declared that the regime of the restored Bourbons and the July Monarchy had been dominated by special interests, that the Republic of 1848 had first been violent and anarchic, then fallen into the hands of a distrustful assembly that robbed the laboring man of his vote, and that France would find in the empire the permanent, popular, and modern system for which it had been vainly searching since 1789. He affirmed that he stood above classes and would govern equally in the interests of all. In any case, like many others after 1848, he held that forms of government were less important than economic and social realities.

The political institutions of the Second Empire were therefore authoritarian, modeled on those of the Consulate of the first Bonaparte. There was a Council of State, composed of experts who drafted legislation and advised on technical matters. There was an appointive Senate with few significant functions. There was a Legislative Body elected by universal male suffrage. The elections were carefully managed. The government put up an official candidate for each seat whom all officeholders in the district were required to support. Other candidates might offer themselves for election, but there could be no political meetings of any kind, and if the independent candidate put up posters he had to use a different kind of paper from the official candidate. Few ventured in these circumstances to differ with the government.

The Legislative Body had no independent powers of its own. It could not initiate legislation but only consider what was submitted to it by the emperor. It had no control over the budget, for the emperor was legally free to borrow money as he saw fit. It had no power over the army or the foreign office or the making of war and peace. To publish speeches made in the legislative chamber was against the law. Any five members, by requesting a secret session, could exclude the public from the galleries. Parliamentary life sank toward absolute zero.

To captivate public attention and glorify the Napoleonic name the new emperor set up a sumptuous court at the Tuileries. Balked in the ambition to marry into one of the great dynasties, Napoleon III chose as his empress a young Spanish beauty, Eugénie, who was destined to outlive the empire by fifty years, dying in 1920. It was said to be a love match—a sure sign of popularized royalty. The court life of the empire was brilliant and showy beyond anything known at the time in St. Petersburg or Vienna. The note of pageantry was further struck in the embellishment of the city of Paris. Baron Haussmann, one of the most creative of city planners, gave Paris much of the appearance that it has today. He built roomy railway stations with broad approaches, and he constructed a system of boulevards and public squares offering long vistas ending in fine buildings or monuments, as at the Place de l'Opéra. He also modernized the sewers and the water supply. The building program, like the expensive court, had the additional advantage of stimulating business and employment. And the cutting of wide avenues through the crooked streets and congested old houses would permit easier military operations against insurrectionists entrenched behind barricades, should the events of 1848 ever be repeated.

Economic Developments under the Empire

It was as a great social engineer that Napoleon III preferred to be known. In his youth he had tried to read the riddle of modern industrialism, and now, as emperor, he found some of his main backers in former Saint-Simonians, who called him their "socialist emperor." Saint-Simon, it may be recalled, had been among the first to conceive of a centrally planned industrial system.[23] But the Saint-Simonians of the 1850s shared in the new sense of being realistic, and their most signal triumph was the invention of investment banking, by which they hoped to guide economic growth through the concentration of financial resources. They founded a novel kind of banking institution, the *Crédit Mobilier,* which raised funds by selling its shares to the public, and with the funds thus obtained bought stock in such new industrial enterprises as it wished to develop. A land bank, or *Crédit Foncier,* was likewise established to lend funds to landowners for the improvement of agriculture.

The times were exceedingly favorable for expansion, for the discovery of gold in California in 1849, and in Australia soon afterward, together with the newly organized credit facilities, brought a substantial increase in the European money supply, which had a mildly inflationary effect. The steady rise of prices and all money values encouraged company promotion and investment of capital. Railway mileage, increasing everywhere in the Western world, increased in France from 3,000 to 16,000 kilometers in the 1850s. The demand for rolling stock, iron rails, auxiliary equipment, and building materials for stations and freight houses kept the mines and factories busy. The railway network was rationalized, fifty-five small lines in France being merged into six big regional trunks. Iron steamboats replaced wooden sailing ships. Between 1859 and 1869 a French company built the Suez Canal, which it continued to own for almost a century, though the British government after 1875 was the principal stockholder.

Large corporations made their appearance, in railroads and banking first of all. In 1863 the law granted the right of "limited liability," by which a stockholder could not lose more than the par value of the stock, however insolvent or debt-burdened the corporation might become. This encouraged investment by persons of small means, and by capitalists large and small in enterprises of which they knew very little; thus the wealth and savings of the country were more effectively mobilized and put to work. Stocks and shares became more numerous and diversified. The Stock Exchange boomed. Financiers—those whose business was to handle money, credit, and securities—assumed a new eminence in the capitalistic world. A good many people became very rich, richer perhaps than anyone had ever been in France before.

The emperor aspired also to do something for the working class, within the

[23] See p. 467.

limits of the existing system. The land bank was of some use to the more substantial peasants. Jobs were plentiful and wages good, by the ideas of the day, at least until the temporary depression of 1857. The emperor had a plan, as did some of the Saint-Simonians, for organizing forces of workers in military fashion and setting them to clear and develop uncultivated land. Not much was done in this direction. More was accomplished in the humanitarian relief of suffering. Hospitals and asylums were established, and free medicines were distributed. The outlines of a social-service state began somewhat vaguely to appear. Meanwhile the workers were building up unions. All combinations of workers had been prohibited during the French Revolution, and the Le Chapelier Law of 1791 was deemed to be still in force.[24] Gradually the ambiguous legal position of labor unions was clarified. In 1864 it even became legal for organized workers to go on strike. Large labor units, or unions, and large business units, or corporations, were thus legalized at the same time. Napoleon III hardly did enough for labor to rank as a working-class hero, but he did enough to be suspected as "socialistic" by many middle-class people of the day.

Later authoritarian regimes, bent like the Second Empire on a program of economic development, were usually highly protectionist, unwilling to face open competition with the rest of the world. Napoleon III believed in freedom of international trade. He had a project for a tariff union with Belgium, which some Belgians also supported. Belgium was already well industrialized, and a Franco-Belgian union, especially since Belgium had the coal that France lacked, would have formed a trading area of very great strength. But the plan was blocked by private interests in both countries, and strongly opposed by both Great Britain and the German *Zollverein*. The emperor then turned to an all-around reduction of import duties. Since the repeal of the Corn Laws in 1846 the free traders were in power in England.[25] They were eager to abolish trade barriers between Britain and France. Napoleon III, overriding opposition in his Legislative Body, concluded a free trade treaty with Great Britain in 1860. He set aside 40 million francs of government funds to assist French manufacturers in making adjustments to British competition; but this sum was never spent in full, and it has hence been concluded that French industry was able to compete successfully with the more intensively mechanized industry of Britain. The Anglo-French treaty was accompanied by lesser trade agreements with other countries. It looked, in the 1860s, as if Europe might actually be about to enter the promised land of freedom of trade.

Internal Difficulties and War

But by 1860 the empire was running into trouble. It took a few years to overcome the depression of 1857. By his free trade policy the emperor made enemies among industrialists in certain lines. The Catholics objected to his intervention in Italy.[26] After 1860 opposition mounted. The emperor granted more leeway to the Legislative Body. The 1860s are called the decade of the Liberal Empire—all

[24] See p. 375.
[25] See p. 494.
[26] See p. 547.

such terms being relative. How the empire would have fared had purely internal causes been left free scope we shall never know. Louis Napoleon actually ruined himself by war. His empire evaporated on the battlefield in 1870. But he was at war long before that.

"The empire means peace," he had assured his audiences in 1852: *l'empire, c'est la paix*. But war is after all the supreme pageantry (or was then); France was the strongest country of Europe, and the emperor's name was Napoleon. Less than a year and a half after the proclamation of the empire France was at war with a European state for the first time since Waterloo. The enemy was Russia, and the war was the Crimean War. Napoleon III did not alone instigate the Crimean War. Many forces in Europe after 1848 made for war; but Napoleon III was one of these forces. In 1859 the new Napoleon was fighting in Italy, from 1862 to 1867 in Mexico, and in 1870 in France itself, in a war with Prussia which he could easily have avoided. These wars form part of the story of the following chapter.[27]

It is enough to say here that in 1870 the Second Empire went the way of the First, into the limbo of governments tried and discarded by the French. It had lasted eighteen years, exactly as long as the July Monarchy, and longer than any other regime known in France, up to that time, since the fall of the Bastille. Not until the 1920s and 1930s, when dictators sprouted all over Europe, did the world begin to think that Louis Napoleon had been an omen of the future rather than a bizarre reincarnation of the past.

[27] See pp. 547, 557–558; for Mexico, see p. 651–65.

EARLY INDUSTRIALISM AND SOCIAL CLASSES

Industrialization, as it appeared first in England in the nineteenth century, rested on a combination of coal and iron, of which the steam engine was the most portentous offspring. Steam engines provided power to the textile mills, and when put on wheels they revolutionized transportation. In the factories a new kind of wage-earning working class was assembled. The railway train, powered by steam, running on rails at first made of wood, then of iron, then of steel, carried people and goods at a speed and in a volume never known in the past. It made possible the concentration of population in cities, both gigantic cities such as London, and clusters of smaller cities in which manufacturing processes were carried on. In this urban world, while polite architecture ran through a series of classical, Gothic, Renaissance, and other revivals, more utilitarian structures of a novel kind were built of iron, and then of structural steel. The new habitat provided luxury for a few, comfort for some, and misery for all too many.

Class conflict therefore raged throughout the nineteenth century, but most acutely in the first half. One difficulty was that, though there had long been talk of the progress of science and invention, the actual difficulties of industrialization had been unforeseen. As the first people to undergo the Industrial Revolution, the English had no experience on which to draw. The English imagination dwelt by preference on rural rather than urban themes, especially in the early part of the century, and under the influence of literary romanticism. Government until 1832 was in the hands of a landed aristocracy and country gentry, made conservative in their politics by the French Revolution. Priding themselves on their English liberties, and fearing anything like Continental bureaucracy, the English only gradually endowed their government with adequate powers of regulation, inspection, enforcement, and police.

After 1850 some of the more favorable consequences of modern industry and technology became apparent. While poverty remained chronic, and the working class struggled to better itself, the middle classes grew in numbers and enjoyed new amenities and conveniences. The following pages illustrate the life of social classes in England, and also in France, in this new Age of Iron. The medium here is part of the message, since the nineteenth-century innovations of lithography, photography, and low-cost printing for a wide market are to be observed.

At the left, this piece of popular art (a song-book cover) points up the exciting contrast between new and old. An express train rushes at night, on a high bridge, with the city behind it, through an English countryside illuminated by the moon.

Above: The newly organized London police, in the 1840s, await the arrival of a Chartist procession. Between 1832 and 1848 the Chartists organized mass demonstrations in the vain attempt to democratize the electoral laws and so obtain legislation designed to favor the working classes. The government introduced a more modern and better disciplined police force as a measure of crowd control, and to avoid the kind of chaotic confrontation shown on the following page. The men are in a kind of civilian uniform complete with stovepipe hats.

Upper left: The "Peterloo Massacre" of 1819, as caricatured by Cruikshank. A peaceable crowd in St. Peter's Fields, Manchester, was fired upon and dispersed by the yeomanry, a militia of nonprofessional part-time soldiers, mostly rural people out of sympathy with modern cities.

Lower left: These primitive trains, about 1840, are running on wooden rails with "guidance wheels" at an apparently crazy angle to help keep them on the track.

Above: London, or rather one of its poorer quarters, as seen by the French artist Gustave Doré about 1880. The omnipresent railroad is in the background, while in the foreground the mass housing, with the little yards, or rather pens, evokes the atmosphere of a prison.

Upper left: A workers' meeting in Paris, as seen by the painter Jean Béraud in 1884. The audience is probably hearing some socialist speeches.

Lower left: The future King Edward VII, then Prince of Wales, with his wife, comfortably installed in box seats, observes the new Bessemer steel-making process at Sheffield in 1875.

Above: The Bon Marché department store in Paris about 1880. The new era is evident in the vast expanse, the proliferation of merchandise, and the presence of affluent women, who have come downtown with their children to shop.

539

Buildings of cast iron and glass, appearing about 1850, represented the most significant technical innovation in architecture in centuries. The department store on page 539 was of this kind. At the left, above, is the famous Crystal Palace in Hyde Park, London, built to house the Great Exhibition of 1851. The world's fair, or industrial exposition, was another product of the revolution in transportation.

Lower left: The Café de la Rotonde in Paris about 1860. The new French café was designed to be large, airy, open, cosmopolitan, suitable for ladies, and not necessarily alcoholic.

Above: The Eiffel Tower, built for the Paris exposition of 1889, with elevators to carry visitors to the top 984 feet above the ground, long remained the world's highest structure, and still stands as a symbol of nineteenth-century civilization. It was at first criticized as ungainly and vulgarly colossal. A later generation, accustomed to an architecture of concrete slabs and oblong cages, sees its graceful curves and the delicate tracery of its four immense legs.

541

XIII.
THE CONSOLIDATION OF LARGE NATION-STATES, 1859–1871

O NLY A DOZEN YEARS, from 1859 to 1871, were enough to see the formation of a new German empire, a unified kingdom of Italy, a Dual Monarchy of Austria-Hungary, drastic internal changes in tsarist Russia, the triumph of central authority in the United States, the creation of a united Dominion of Canada, and the modernizing or "Europeanization" of the empire of Japan. All these disparate events reflected profound changes brought in by the railroad, steamship, and telegraph, which made the communication of ideas, exchange of goods, and movement of people over wide areas more frequent and easier than ever before. Politically, all represented the advancing principle of the nation-state.

63. Backgrounds: The Idea of the Nation-State

Before 1860 there were two prominent nation-states—Great Britain and France. Spain, united on the map, was internally so miscellaneous as to belong to a

Chapter Emblem: Medallion to celebrate the Prussian defeat of Austria in 1866, and featuring the King of Prussia, William I, who later became the first German Emperor.

different category. Portugal, Switzerland, the Netherlands, and the Scandinavian countries were nation-states, but small and peripheral. The characteristic political organizations were small states comprising fragments of a nation, such as were strewn across the middle of Europe—Hanover, Baden, Sardinia, Tuscany, or the Two Sicilies—and large sprawling empires made up of all sorts of peoples, distantly ruled from above by dynasties and bureaucracies, such as the Romanov, Habsburg, and Ottoman domains.[1] Except for recent developments in the Americas the same mixture of small nonnational states and of large nonnational empires was to be found in most of the rest of the world.

Since 1860 or 1870 a nation-state system has prevailed. The consolidation of large nations became a model for other peoples large and small. In time, in the following century, other large peoples undertook to establish nation-states in India, Pakistan, Indonesia, Iran, and Nigeria. Small and middle-sized peoples increasingly thought of themselves as nations, entitled to their own sovereignty and independence. Some of these sovereignties that emerged after 1945 comprise fewer people than a large modern city. The idea of the nation-state has served both to bring people together into larger units and to break them apart into smaller ones. In the nineteenth century, outside the disintegrating Ottoman Empire, from which Greece, Serbia, Bulgaria, and Romania became independent, and in which an Arab national movement also began to stir, the national idea served mainly to create larger units in place of small ones. The map of Europe, from 1871 to 1918, was the simplest it has ever been before or since.[2]

About the idea of the nation-state and the movement of nationalism much has been said already in this book. Earlier chapters have described the ferment of national ideas and movements stirred up by the French Revolution and by the Napoleonic domination of Europe, the nationalist agitation and repression of the years after 1815, and the frustration and failure of patriotic aspirations in Germany, Italy, and central Europe in the Revolution of 1848.[3] For many in the nineteenth century, nationalism, the winning of national unity and independence and the creation of the nation-state, became a kind of secular faith.

A nation-state may be thought of as one in which supreme political authority somehow rests upon and represents the will and feeling of its inhabitants. There must be a people, not merely a swarm of human beings. The people must basically will and feel something in common. They must sense that they belong—that they are members of a community, participating somehow in a common life, that the government is their government, and that outsiders are "foreign." The outsiders or foreigners are usually (though not always) those who speak a different language. The nation is usually (though not always) composed of all persons sharing the same speech. A nation may also possess a belief in common descent or racial origin (however mistaken), or a sense of a common history, a common future, a common religion, a common geographical home, or a common external menace. Nations take form in many ways. But all are alike in feeling themselves to be communities, permanent communities in which individual persons, together with

---

[1] See map, pp. 448–449.
[2] See map, pp. 562–563.
[3] See pp. 365, 378–379, 435–441, 468–489, 507–519.

their children and their children's children, are committed to a collective destiny on earth.

In the nineteenth century governments found that they could not effectively rule, or develop the full powers of state, except by enlisting this sense of membership and support among their subjects. The consolidation of large nation-states had two distinguishable phases. Territorially, it meant the union of preexisting smaller states. Morally and psychologically it meant the creation of new ties between government and governed, the admission of new segments of the population to political life, through the creation or extension of liberal and representative institutions. This happened even in Japan and in tsarist Russia. National consolidation in the nineteenth century favored constitutional progress. Although there was considerable variation in the real power of the new political institutions and in the extent of self-government actually realized, parliaments were set up for the new Italy, the new Germany, the new Japan, the new Canada; and the movement in Russia was in the same direction. In Europe, some of the aims which the revolutionists of 1848 had failed to achieve were now realized by the established authorities.

They were realized, however, only in a series of wars. To create an all-German or an all-Italian state, as the revolutions of 1848 had already shown, it was necessary to break the power of Austria, render Russia at least temporarily ineffective, and overthrow or intimidate those German and Italian governments which refused to surrender their sovereignty. In the United States, to maintain national unity as understood by President Lincoln, it was necessary to repress the movement for Southern independence by force of arms. For forty years after 1814 there had been no war between established powers of Europe. Then in 1854 came the Crimean War, in 1859 the Italian War, in 1864 the Danish War, in 1866 the Austro-Prussian War, and in 1870 the Franco-Prussian War. Concurrently the Civil War raged in the United States. After 1871, for forty-three years there was again no war between European powers.

The Crimean War, 1854–1856

Before moving on to the first of the national consolidation movements, the Italian, we must examine the Crimean War which, though seemingly remote and unconnected, helped to make possible the success of the European national movements. Its chief significance in the story of the present chapter is that it seriously weakened both Austria and Russia, the two powers most bent on preserving the peace settlement of 1815 and on preventing national changes. It was also the first war covered by newspaper correspondents, and the first in which women, led by Florence Nightingale, established their position as army nurses.

The pressure of Russia upon Turkey was an old story. Every generation saw its Russo-Turkish war.[4] In the last Russo-Turkish war, to go back no further, that of 1828–1829, the Tsar Nicholas I protected the independence newly won by Greece and annexed the left bank of the mouth of the Danube. Now, in 1853,

---

[4] See pp. 239–240, 339–340, 420, 441, 480, 484–485.

Nicholas again made demands upon the still large but decaying Ottoman Empire, moving in on the two Danubian principalities, Wallachia and Moldavia (later to be known as Romania), with military forces.[5] The dispute this time ostensibly involved the protection of Christians in the Ottoman Empire, including the foreign Christians at Jerusalem and in Palestine. Over these Christians the French also claimed a certain protective jurisdiction. The French had for centuries been the principal Western people in the Near East. They had often furnished money and advisers to the sultan, they carried on a huge volume of trade, they staffed and financed Christian missions, and they were continually talking of building a Suez canal. Napoleon III had especial reason to resent the Tsar Nicholas, who regarded him as a revolutionary adventurer. Napoleon III encouraged the Turkish government to resist Russian claims to protect Christians within Turkey. War between Russia and Turkey broke out late in 1853. In 1854 France joined the side of the Turks, as did Great Britain, whose settled policy was to uphold Turkey and the Near East against penetration by Russia. The two Western powers were soon joined by a small ally, Piedmont, which had no visible interest in the issues in the Near East and entered the war mainly for the purpose of advancing the Italian question.

The British fleet successfully blockaded Russia in both its Baltic and Black Sea outlets. French and British armies invaded Russia itself, landing in the Crimean peninsula, to which all the important fighting was confined. The Austrian Empire had its own reasons not to wish Russia to conquer the Balkans and Constantinople, or to see Britain and France master the situation alone; Austria therefore, though not yet recovered from the upheaval of 1848–1849, mobilized its armed forces at a great effort to itself and occupied Wallachia and Moldavia, which the Russians evacuated under this threat of attack by a new enemy. Tsar Nicholas died in 1855, and his successor Alexander II sued for peace.

A congress of all the great powers made peace at Paris in 1856. By the treaty the powers pledged themselves jointly to maintain the "integrity of the Ottoman Empire." The Russian tide ebbed a little. Russia ceded the left bank of the mouth of the Danube to Moldavia and gave up its claim to the special protection of Christians in the Turkish empire. Moldavia and Wallachia (united as "Romania" in 1858), together with Serbia, were recognized as self-governing principalities under protection of the European powers. It was agreed that Russia should maintain no warships on the Black Sea, and that the Danube should be an international river open to commercial shipping of all nations. At the Congress of Paris all seemed harmonious. There seemed to be such a thing as Europe, undertaking collective obligations, protecting small states, rationally and peaceably conducting its affairs.

But trouble was in the making. Napoleon III needed glory. The Italians wanted some kind of unified Italy. The Prussians, who had done nothing in the Crimean War, and were only tardily invited to the Congress of Paris, feared that their status as a great power might be slipping away. Napoleon III, the Italian nationalists, the Prussians, all stood to gain by change. Change in central Europe and Italy meant a tearing up of the Treaty of Vienna of 1815, long guarded by

[5] See maps, pp. 448–449, 660. The historic Moldavia lay west of the Pruth River; the later Moldavian republic in the Soviet Union, east of that river, was formerly called Bessarabia. After the dissolution of the Soviet Union in 1991, the Moldavian republic was renamed Moldova.

Metternich and unsuccessfully challenged by the revolutionaries of 1848. Now, after the Crimean War, the forces opposing change were very weak. It was the Russian and Austrian empires that had stood firmly for the status quo. But these two powers, which had most seriously attempted to uphold the Vienna settlement, could do so no longer. The first proof came in Italy.

64. Cavour and the Italian War of 1859: The Unification of Italy

Italian Nationalism: The Program of Cavour

In Italy there had long been about a dozen sizable states, together with a few very small ones. Several of them had dissolved in the Italian movements that accompanied the wars of the French Revolution. All had been reorganized, first by Napoleon and then by the Congress of Vienna. In the northwest lay the kingdom of Sardinia, more commonly known as Piedmont. Its royal house of Savoy was the only native Italian dynasty in Italy. East of it lay Lombardy, and east of that, Venetia. Since 1814 Lombardy and Venetia belonged to the Austrian Empire. South of Lombardy, in the northwest corner of the "leg" of the peninsula, was the duchy of Tuscany with its capital at Florence. The smaller duchies of Modena, Parma, and Lucca filled the interstices between Tuscany and the northern states. Across the middle of the peninsula were spread the papal states, the hereditary temporal possession of the Roman See. Further south, comprising half of all Italy, lay the large kingdom of Naples or the Two Sicilies, ruled since 1735 by a branch of the Bourbons. The governments of these states were generally content with their separate independence. But the governments were remote from their peoples.

There was a widespread disgust in Italy with the existing authorities, and a growing desire for a liberal national state in which all Italy might be embodied and which might resurrect the Italian grandeur of ancient times and of the Renaissance. This sentiment, the dream of an Italian Risorgimento, or resurgence, had become very heated at the time of the French Revolution and Napoleon, then had been transformed into a moral purpose by the writings of Mazzini.[6] Mazzini, who had invested the cause of Italian unity with almost a holy character, had seen his hopes for a unified republican Italy elevated for a brief moment and then blasted in the general debacle of 1848. In the stormy events of 1848 the papacy had been frightened off by the radical romantic republicanism of Mazzini, Garibaldi, and other firebrands and could no longer be expected to support the cause of Italian nationalism. And in the same events the kingdom of Sardinia had failed in its vow to oust Austria from the Italian peninsula without the aid of any outside great power.[7]

These lessons were not lost on the prime minister of Piedmont (or Sardinia), which was ruled since 1848 as a constitutional monarchy and was now under

[6] See p. 469.
[7] See pp. 509–514, and p. 194, note 25.

King Victor Emmanuel. This prime minister after 1852 was Camillo di Cavour, one of the shrewdest political tacticians of that or any age. Cavour was a liberal of Western type. He tried to make Piedmont a model of progress, efficiency, and fair government that other Italians would admire. He worked hard to plant constitutional and parliamentary practices in Piedmont. He favored the building of railroads and docks, the improvement of agriculture, and emancipation of trade. He followed a strongly anticlerical policy, cutting down the number of religious holidays, limiting the right of church bodies to own real estate, abolishing the church courts—all without negotiation with the Holy See. A liberal and constitutional monarchist, a wealthy landowner in his own right, he had no sympathy for the revolutionary and republican nationalism of Mazzini. To him it did not seem that Italy would be united by the methods of conspiracy and secret societies, by hortatory literature smuggled in from political exiles, or by the proclamation of idealistic radical republics, as in 1848, which alarmed the most influential people in the country.[8]

Cavour shared in that new toughness of mind described in the last chapter. He embraced a "politics of reality." He did not approve of republicans but was willing to work with them surreptitiously. He did not idealize war but was willing to make war to unify Italy under the house of Savoy. With unruffled calculation he took Piedmont into the Crimean War, sending troops to Russia, in the hope of winning a place at the peace table and raising the Italian question at the Congress of Paris. It was evident to him that against one great power one must pit another, and that the only way to get Austria out of Italy was to use the French army. It became his master plan deliberately to provoke war with Austria, after having assured himself of French military support.

It was not difficult to persuade Napoleon III to collaborate. The Bonapartes looked upon Italy as their ancestral country, and Napoleon III, in his adventurous youth, had traveled in conspiratorial Italian circles and even participated in an Italian insurrection in 1831. Now, as emperor, in his role of apostle of modernity, he entertained a "doctrine of nationalities" which held the consolidation of nations to be a forward step at the existing stage of history. To fight reactionary Austria for the freedom of Italy would also mollify liberal opinion in France, which in other ways Napoleon was engaged in suppressing. The last note in persuasion was furnished by an Italian republican named Orsini, who in 1858, finding the French emperor too slow to make up his mind, attempted to assassinate him with a bomb. Napoleon III reached a secret agreement with Cavour. In April 1859, Cavour tricked Austria into a declaration of war. The French army poured over the Alps.

There were two battles, Magenta and Solferino, both won by the French and Piedmontese. But Napoleon III was now in a quandary. The Prussians began to mobilize on the Rhine, not wishing France to create an Italian sphere of influence for itself. In Italy, with the defeat of the Austrians, revolutionary agitation broke out all over the peninsula, as it had a decade before—and the French emperor was no patron of popular revolution. The revolutionaries overthrew or denounced the existing governments and clamored for annexation to Piedmont. In France, as elsewhere, the Catholics, fearful that the pope's temporal power would be lost, upbraided the emperor for his godless and unnecessary war. The French position was indeed odd, for while the bulk of the French army fought Austria in the north, a detachment of it was still stationed in Rome, sent there in 1849 to protect the pope against Italian republicanism.[9] Napoleon III, in July 1859, at the height of his victories, stupefied Cavour. He made a separate peace with the Austrians.

The Franco-Austrian agreement gave Lombardy to Piedmont but left Venetia within the Austrian Empire. It offered a compromise solution to the Italian question, in the form of a federal union of the existing Italian governments, to be presided over by the pope. This was not what Cavour, or the Piedmontese, or the more fiery Italian patriots wanted. Revolution continued to spread. Tuscany, Modena, Parma, and Romagna drove out their old rulers. They were annexed to Piedmont, after plebiscites or general elections in these regions had shown an overwhelming popular favor for this step. Since Romagna belonged to the papal states the pope excommunicated the organizers of the new Italy. Undeterred, representatives of all north Italy except Venetia met at the Piedmontese capital of Turin in 1860 in the first parliament of the enlarged kingdom. The British government hailed these events with enthusiasm, and Napoleon III also recognized the expanded Piedmontese state, in return for the transfer to France of Nice and Savoy, where plebiscites disclosed enormous majorities for annexation to France.

The Completion of Italian Unity

There were now, in 1860, a north Italian kingdom, the papal states in the middle, and the kingdom of the Two Sicilies still standing in the south. The latter was being undermined by revolutionary agitation, as often in the past.[10] A Piedmontese republican, Giuseppe Garibaldi, brought matters to a head. Somewhat like Lafayette, Garibaldi was a "hero of two worlds," who had fought for the independence of Uruguay, lived in the United States, and been one of the Triumvirs in the short-lived Roman Republic of 1849. He now organized a group of about 1,150 personal followers—"Garibaldi's Thousand," or the Red Shirts— for an armed expedition to the south. Cavour, unable openly to favor such filibustering against a neighboring state, connived at Garibaldi's preparations and departure. Garibaldi landed in Sicily and soon crossed to the mainland. Revolutionists hastened to join him, and the government of the Two Sicilies, backward and corrupt, commanding little loyalty from its population, collapsed before this picturesque intrusion.

[9] See p. 506.
[10] See pp. 479–480, 509–510.

NATION BUILDING, 1859–1867

In eight years from 1859 to 1867 Italy was unified (except for the city of Rome, annexed in 1870), the Habsburg government tried to solve its nationalities problem by creating a Dual Monarchy of Austria-Hungary, the United States affirmed its unity by defeating the Southern secessionist movement, and the Dominion of Canada was formed to include all British North America (with dates shown for accession of provinces) except Newfoundland and Labrador, which were added in 1949. For Germany see the map on p. 555.

UNIFICATION OF ITALY, 1859-1870

PIEDMONT
LOMBARDY
Turin
Milan
VENETIA
Venice
PARMA
MODENA
KINGDOM OF SARDINIA
Florence
TUSCANY
PAPAL STATES
ROME
SARDINIA
NAPLES
SICILY

FORMATION OF DUAL MONARCHY OF AUSTRIA-HUNGARY, 1867

AUSTRIA
Vienna
Budapest
HUNGARY

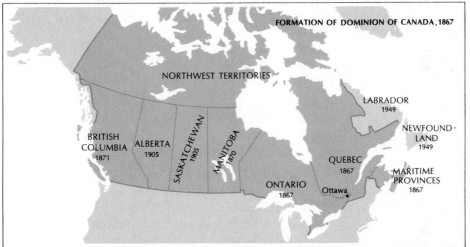

FORMATION OF DOMINION OF CANADA, 1867

NORTHWEST TERRITORIES

LABRADOR
1949

NEWFOUND-
LAND
1949

BRITISH
COLUMBIA
1871
ALBERTA
1905
SASKATCHEWAN
1905
MANITOBA
1870

QUEBEC
1867

MARITIME
PROVINCES
1867

ONTARIO
1867
Ottawa

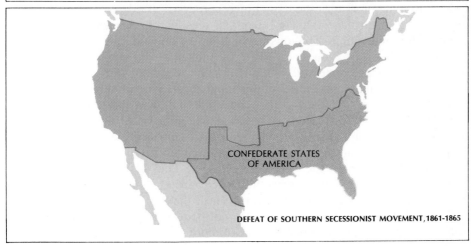

CONFEDERATE STATES
OF AMERICA

DEFEAT OF SOUTHERN SECESSIONIST MOVEMENT, 1861-1865

Garibaldi now prepared to push from Naples up to Rome. Here, of course, he would meet not only the pope but the French army, and the international scandal would reverberate throughout the globe. Cavour decided that so extreme a step must be averted, but that Garibaldi's successes must at the same time be used. Anticipating Garibaldi, a Piedmontese army entered the papal states, carefully avoiding Rome, and proceeded onward into Naples. Garibaldi, though not all his followers, was now ready to accept a monarchy as the best solution to the problem of Italian unification. The chief of the Red Shirts, the one-time foe of kings, consented to ride in an open carriage with Victor Emmanuel through the streets of Naples amid cheering thousands. Plebiscites held in the Two Sicilies showed an almost unanimous willingness to join with Piedmont. In the remainder of the papal states, except for Rome and its environs, plebiscites were held also, with the same result. A parliament representing all Italy except Rome and Venetia met in 1861, and the Kingdom of Italy was formally proclaimed, with Victor Emmanuel II as king "by grace of God and the will of the nation." Venetia was added in 1866, as a prize for Italian aid to Prussia in a war against Austria, and Rome was annexed in 1870 after the withdrawal of French troops in the Franco-Prussian War of 1870.[11]

So Italy was "made," as the phrase of the time expressed it. It had been made by the long high-minded apostolate of Mazzini, the audacity of Garibaldi, the cold policy of Cavour, by war and insurrection, by armed violence endorsed by popular vote.

Persistent Problems after Unification

Very little was settled or ended by unification. Even territorially, the more pronounced nationalists refused to believe that Italian unity was completed. They looked beyond, to regions of mixed population where Italians were numerous or preponderant—to the Trentino, to Trieste, to certain Dalmatian islands, or to Nice and Savoy. They saw in these regions an *Italia irredenta,* "an unredeemed Italy," awaiting in its turn the day of incorporation. "Irredentism" even passed into the English language as a word signifying a vociferous demand, on nationalist grounds, for annexation of regions beyond one's own frontiers.

The occupation of Rome in 1870 by the Italian government opened the rift between church and state still wider. The pope, deprived of territories he had held for a thousand years, renewed his condemnations and chose to remain in lifelong seclusion in the Vatican. His successors followed the same policy until 1929. Hence good Italian patriots were bound to be anticlerical, and good Catholics were bound to look upon the Italian state with unfriendly eyes. The regional differences between northern and southern Italy did not disappear with unification. The north looked upon the agrarian south, the land of priest, landlord, and impoverished peasant, as disgracefully backward. Lawlessness in Sicily and Naples did not disappear with the overthrow of the Bourbons.

The new Italy was parliamentary but not democratic. At first the vote was only given to some 600,000 persons out of more than 20 million. Not until 1913

---

[11] See pp. 556–558, 634–636.

was the suffrage significantly broadened. Meanwhile parliamentary life, confined to a few, was somewhat unrealistic and frequently corrupt. With the mass of the population excluded from the vote, the revolutionary agitation continued unabated after the unification. Garibaldi himself, in the 1860s, made two more attempts to seize Rome by violence. In general, the revolutionary movement shifted from the older republican nationalism to the newer forms of Marxian socialism, anarchism, or syndicalism.

But the dream of ages was realized. Italy was one. The period that seemed so shameful to patriots, the long centuries that had elapsed since the Renaissance, were now terminated in the glories of a successful Risorgimento.

65. Bismarck: The Founding of a German Empire

To play upon the divisions among the Germans, keeping them in rivalry with each other and dependent upon outside powers, had been the policy of France ever since the Reformation and of Russia since it began to take part in the affairs of Europe. The pulverization of the Germanic world was in fact a kind of negative prerequisite to the development of modern history as we know it, for without it the economic and cultural leadership of Europe would hardly have become concentrated along the Atlantic seaboard, or a great military empire have arisen in Russia and spread along the Baltic and into Poland.

Gradually, as we have seen, the Germans became dissatisfied with their position. They became nationalistic.[12] Many German thinkers held that Germany was different from the West, destined some day to work out a peculiarly German way of life and political system of its own. To the Slavs the Germans felt immeasurably superior. German philosophy, as shown most clearly in Hegel, took on a certain characteristic tone. It pronounced individualism to be Western; it skipped lightly over individual liberty; it tended to glorify group loyalties, collectivist principles, and the state. It made a great to-do about History, which in the thought of Hegel, and after him Marx, became a vast force almost independent of human beings. History was said to ordain, require, necessitate, condemn, justify, or excuse. What one did not like could be dismissed as a mere historical phase, opening into a quite different and more attractive future. What one wanted, in the present or future, could be described as historically necessary and bound to come.

The German States after 1848

In 1848 a series of revolutions unseated the several governments of Germany. At the Frankfurt Assembly a group composed essentially of private citizens undertook to organize a united Germany by constitutional methods. They failed because they had no power. Hence after 1848 the Germans began to think in terms of power, developing a somewhat extreme admiration for *die Macht*. The men of Frankfurt failed also, perhaps, because they were insufficiently revolutionary.

[12] See pp. 435–441, 471.

The Germans were a sober, orderly, and respectful people. They were still attached emotionally to their several states. What happened in Italy, a revolutionary extermination of all the old governments except that of Piedmont, could not happen in Germany.[13]

After the failure of the 1848 revolution German nationalists and liberals were confused. By 1850 the old states were restored—Austria and Prussia, the kingdoms of Hanover, Saxony, Bavaria, and Württemberg, together with about thirty other states ranging in size down to the free cities of Hamburg and Frankfurt. The loose confederation of 1815, linking all these states together, was restored also.[14] But within this framework great economic and social changes were occurring. Between 1850 and 1870 the output of both coal and iron in Germany multiplied sixfold. In 1850 Germany produced less iron than France, in 1870 more. Germany was overcoming the economic and social lag which had characterized it for 300 years. A *Zollverein*, formed by Prussia in 1834, included almost all Germany outside of Austria and Bohemia and provided a large measure of economic unity. The German cities were growing, bound together by railroad and telegraph, requiring larger supporting areas on which to live. Industrial capitalists and industrial workers were becoming more numerous. With the advantages of unity more obvious than ever, with the ideals of 1848 badly compromised, with an exaggerated respect for the state and for power, and with a habit of accepting the successful event as the "judgment of history," the Germans were ripe for what happened. They did not unify themselves by their own exertions. They fell into the arms of Prussia.

Prussia in the 1860s: Bismarck

Prussia had always been the smallest and most precarious of the great powers. Ruined by Napoleon, it had risen again. It owed its international influence and internal character to its army. Actually it had fought rather fewer wars than other great powers, but, with its army in being, it had followed a program of expansion by conquest or diplomacy. The taking of Silesia in 1740, of parts of Poland in the 1770s and 1790s, of the Rhineland in 1815 by an international bargain were the highlights of Prussian growth.[15] After 1850 those who controlled the destinies of Prussia were apprehensive. Their state had been shaken by revolution. In the Crimean War and at the Congress of Paris they were hardly more than spectators. Italy was unified without any Prussian saying yes or no. It seemed as if the hard-won and still relatively recent position of Prussia might be waning.

Since 1815 the population of Prussia had grown from 11 to 18 million, but the size of the army had not changed. Merely to enforce existing principles of conscription would therefore almost double the army. But this would require increased financial appropriations. After 1850 Prussia had a parliament.[16] It was a parliament, to be sure, dominated by men of wealth; but some of the wealthy Prussians, notably the capital owners of the Rhineland, were liberals who wished

---

[13] See pp. 469–470.
[14] See pp. 447, 518–519 and map, p. 555.
[15] See maps, pp. 230–231.
[16] See p. 519.

the parliament to have control over government policies. These men did not like professional armies and considered the Prussian Junkers, from whom the officer corps was recruited, as their main rivals in the state. The parliament refused the necessary appropriations. The king at this juncture, in 1862, appointed a new chief minister, Otto von Bismarck.

Bismarck was a Junker from old Brandenburg east of the Elbe. He cultivated the gruff manner of an honest country squire, though he was in fact an accomplished man of the world. Intellectually he was far superior to the rather slow-witted landlord class from which he sprang, and for which he often felt an impatient contempt. He shared in many Junker ideas. He advocated, and even felt, a kind of stout Protestant piety. Although he cared for the world's opinion, it never deterred him in his actions; criticism and denunciation left him untouched. He was in fact obstinate. He was not a nationalist. He did not look upon all Germany as his Fatherland. He was a Prussian. His social affinities, as with the Junkers generally, lay to the East with corresponding landowning elements of the Baltic provinces and Russia.[17] The West, including the bulk of Germany, he neither understood nor trusted; it seemed to him revolutionary, turbulent, free-thinking, materialistic. Parliamentary bodies he considered ignorant and irresponsible as organs of government. Individual liberty seemed to him disorderly selfishness. Liberalism, democracy, socialism were repugnant to him. He preferred to stress duty, service, order, and the fear of God. The idea of forming a new German union developed only gradually in his mind and then as an adjunct to the strengthening of Prussia.

Bismarck thus had his predilections, and even his principles. But no principle bound him, no ideology seemed to him an end in itself. He became the classic practitioner of *Realpolitik*. The time came when the Junkers thought him a traitor to his class, when even the king was afraid of him, when he outraged and then mollified the august house of Habsburg, when he made friends with liberals, democrats, and even socialists, and in turn made enemies of them. First he made wars, then he insisted upon peace. Enmities and alliances were to him only matters of passing convenience. The enemy of today might be the friend of tomorrow. Far from planning out a long train of events, then following it step by step to a grand consummation, he seems to have been practical and opportunistic, taking advantage of situations as they emerged and prepared to act in any one of several directions as events might suggest.

In 1862, as minister president, it was his job, or duty, to outface the liberals in the Prussian parliament. For four years, from 1862 to 1866, Bismarck waged this "constitutional struggle." The parliament refused to vote the proposed taxes. The government collected them anyway. The taxpayers paid them without protest—it was the orderly thing to do, and the collectors represented public authority. The limitations of Prussian liberalism, the docility of the population, the respect for officialdom, the belief that the king and his ministers were wiser than the elected deputies, all clearly revealed themselves in this triumph of military policy over the theory of government by consent. The army was enlarged, reorganized, retrained, and reequipped. Bismarck fended off the showers of abuse from the liberal majority in the chamber. The liberals declared that

[17] See map, p. 212.

the government's policy was flagrantly unconstitutional. The constitution, said Bismarck, could not have been meant to undermine the state. The government, said the liberals, was itself undermining Prussia, for the rest of Germany hoped to find in Prussia, as Italy had found in Piedmont, a model of political freedom. What the Germans admired in Prussia, replied Bismarck coldly, was not its liberalism but its power. He declared that the Prussian boundaries as set in 1815 were unsound, that Prussia must be prepared to seize favorable opportunities for further growth.[18] And he added one of his most memorable utterances: "Not by speeches and majority votes are the great questions of the day decided—that was the great error of 1848 and 1849—but by blood and iron."

Bismarck's Wars: The North German Confederation, 1867

A favorable opportunity was not long in presenting itself. The Schleswig-Holstein question arose again. We have seen how it had arisen in 1848, and how even the mild men of Frankfurt had insisted, to the point of war, upon the incorporation of the two duchies into their German union.[19] Now in 1863 the story was repeated. The Danes, engaged in a process of national consolidation of their own, wished to make Schleswig an integral part of Denmark. The population of Schleswig was part Dane and part German. The diet of the German confederation, unwilling to see Germans thus annexed outright to Denmark, called for an all-German war upon the Danes, just as the revolutionary Frankfurt Assembly had done. Bismarck had no desire to support or strengthen the existing German confederation. He wanted not an all-German war but a Prussian war. To disguise his aims he acted jointly with Austria. In 1864 Prussia and Austria together went to war with Denmark, which they soon defeated. It was Bismarck's intention to annex both Schleswig and Holstein to Prussia, gaining whatever other advantages might present themselves from future trouble with Austria. He arranged a provisional occupation of Schleswig by Prussia, and of Holstein by Austria. Disputes soon arose over rights of passage, the keeping of internal order, and other problems with which occupying forces are commonly afflicted. While pretending to try to regulate these disputes he allowed them to ripen.

He now proceeded to discredit and isolate Austria. The British government was at the time following a policy of nonintervention in the affairs of the Continent. The Russian empire was in no position for action; it was divided internally by a reform program then at its height; it was in a mood of hostility to Austria, because of events of the Crimean War, and well disposed toward Prussia and Bismarck, because Bismarck in 1863 took care to support it against an uprising of the Poles. To win over the new kingdom of Italy Bismarck held out the lure of Venetia. As for France, Napoleon III was embarrassed by domestic discontents and had his army committed to adventures in Mexico. In addition, Bismarck charmed him at a confidential interview at Biarritz, where vague oral intimations of French expansion were exchanged, and the two men seemed to agree to a needed modernization of the map of Europe. To weaken Austria within Germany, Bismarck presented himself as a democrat. He proposed a reform of the German

[18] See maps, pp. 231, 555.
[19] See p. 517.

Legend:

— German Confederation, 1815-1866

Prussia, 1815-1866

Annexed to Prussia, 1866

Joined with Prussia in North German Confederation, 1867

South German States Joined in German Empire, 1871

Alsace-Lorraine, Ceded by France to German Empire, 1871

Austrian Dominions Excluded From German Confederation, 1866, and from German Empire, 1871

Bismarck's German Empire, 1871

0   100   200 miles

THE GERMAN QUESTION, 1815–1871

From 1815 to 1866 there were thirty-nine states in Germany (of which only the largest are shown) joined in the Confederation of 1815. At the Frankfurt Assembly in 1848 (see pp. 516–518) two groups developed: the Great Germans who adhered to the idea of an all-German union, to include the Austrian lands except Hungary; and the Little Germans who were willing to exclude Austria and its empire. Bismarck was a Little German but a Great Prussian. He (1) enlarged Prussia by conquest in 1866, (2) joined Mecklenburg, Saxony, etc., with his enlarged Prussia in a North German Confederation of 1867, (3) combined this in turn with Bavaria, Württemberg, etc., to form the German empire of 1871, (4) conquered Alsace-Lorraine from France, and (5) ejected Austria. The boundaries of Bismarckian Germany remained unchanged until 1918. (See also maps, pp. 230–231, 448–449, 562–563, 728–729.

confederation, recommending that it have a popular chamber elected by universal male suffrage. He calculated that the mass of the German people were wedded neither to the well-to-do capitalistic liberals, nor to the existing government structures of the German states, nor to the house of Habsburg. He would use "democracy" to undermine all established interests that stood in his way.

Meanwhile the occupying powers continued to quarrel over Schleswig-Holstein. Austria finally raised the matter formally in the German federal diet, one of whose functions was to prevent war between its members. Bismarck declared that the diet had no authority, accused the Austrians of aggression, and ordered the Prussian army to enter Holstein. The Austrians called for federal sanctions in the form of an all-German force to be sent against Prussia. The result was that Prussia, in 1866, was at war not only with Austria but with most of the other German states. The Prussian army soon proved its superiority. Trained to an unprecedented precision, equipped with the new needle-gun, by which the infantryman could deliver five rounds a minute, brought into the zone of combat by an imaginative strategy that made use of the new railroads, commanded by the skill of von Moltke, the Prussian army overthrew the Austrians at the battle of Sadowa (or Königgrätz) and defeated the other German states soon thereafter. The Austro-Prussian, or Seven Weeks' War, was amazing in its brevity. Bismarck hastened to make peace before the other European powers could realize what had happened.

Prussia annexed outright, together with Schleswig-Holstein, the whole kingdom of Hanover, the duchies of Nassau and Hesse-Cassel, and the free city of Frankfurt. Here the old governments simply disappeared before the axe of the "red reactionary." The German federal union disappeared likewise. In its place, in 1867, Bismarck organized a North German Confederation, in which the newly enlarged Prussia joined with twenty-one other states, all of which combined it greatly outweighed. The German states south of the river Main—Austria, Bavaria, Baden, Württemberg, and Hesse-Darmstadt—remained outside the new organization, with no kind of union among themselves. Meanwhile the kingdom of Italy annexed Venetia.

For the North German Confederation Bismarck produced a constitution. The new structure, though a federal one, was much stronger than the now defunct Confederation of 1815. The king of Prussia became its hereditary head. Ministers were responsible to him. There was a parliament with two chambers. The upper chamber, as in the United States, represented the states as such, though not equally. The lower chamber, or Reichstag, was deemed to represent the people and was elected by universal male suffrage. Such flirting with democracy seemed madness to both conservative Junker and liberal bourgeois. It was indeed a bold step, for only France at the time illustrated universal suffrage in Europe on a large scale, and in the France of Napoleon III neither old-fashioned conservatives nor genuine liberals could take much satisfaction. As for Great Britain, where voting rights were extended in this same year, 1867, they were still given to less than half the adult male population. Bismarck sensed in the "masses" an ally of strong government against private interests. He negotiated even with the socialists, who had arisen with the industrialization of the past decade, and who, in Germany at this time, were mainly followers of Ferdinand Lassalle. The Lassallean socialists, unlike the Marxian, believed it theoretically possible to improve working-class conditions through the action of existing governments. To the great annoyance of Marx, then in England (his *Capital* first appeared in 1867), the bulk of the German socialists reached an understanding with Bismarck. In return for a democratic suffrage they agreed to accept the North German Confederation. Bismarck, for his part, by making use of democratic and socialist sentiment, won popular approval for his emerging empire.

The Franco-Prussian War

It was clear that the situation was not yet stable. The small south German states were left floating in empty space; they would sooner or later have to gravitate into some orbit or other, whether Austrian, Prussian, or French. In France there were angry criticisms of Napoleon III's foreign policy. French intervention in Mexico had proved a fiasco.[20] A united Italy had been allowed to rise on France's borders. And now, contrary to all principles of French national interest observed by French governments for hundreds of years, a strong and independent power was being allowed to spread over virtually the whole of Germany. Everywhere people began to feel that war was coming between France and Prussia. Bismarck played on the fears of France felt in the south German states. South Germany, though in former times often a willing satellite to France, was now sufficiently nationalistic to consider such subservience to a foreign people disgraceful. To Bismarck it seemed that a war between Prussia and France would frighten the small south German states into a union with Prussia, leaving only Austria outside—which was what he wanted. To Napoleon III, or at least to some of his advisers, it seemed that such a war, if successful, would restore public approval of the Bonapartist empire. In this inflammable situation the responsible persons of neither country worked for peace.

Meanwhile a revolution in Spain had driven the reigning queen into exile, and a Spanish provisional government invited Prince Leopold of Hohenzollern, the king of Prussia's cousin, to be constitutional king of Spain. To entrench the Prussian royal house in Spain would naturally be distasteful to France. Three times the Hohenzollern family refused the Spanish offer. Bismarck, who could not control such family decisions, but who foresaw the possibility of a usable incident, deviously persuaded the Spanish to issue the invitation still a fourth time. On July 2, 1870, Paris heard that Prince Leopold had accepted. The French ambassador to Prussia, Benedetti, at the direction of his government, met the king of Prussia at the bathing resort of Ems, where he formally demanded that Prince Leopold's acceptance be withdrawn. It was withdrawn on July 12. The French seemed to have their way. Bismarck was disappointed.

The French government went still further. It instructed Benedetti to approach the king again at Ems and demand that at no time in the future would any Hohenzollern ever become a candidate for the Spanish throne. The king politely declined any such commitment and telegraphed a full report of the conversation to Bismarck at Berlin. Bismarck, receiving the telegram, which became famous as the "Ems dispatch," saw a new opportunity, as he put it, to wave a red flag before the Gallic bull. He condensed the Ems telegram for publication, so reducing

[20] See pp. 651–652.

and abridging it that it seemed to newspaper readers as if a curt exchange had occurred at Ems, in which the Prussians believed that their king had been insulted, and the French that their ambassador had been snubbed. In both countries the war party demanded satisfaction. On July 19, 1870, on these trivial grounds, and with the ostensible issue of the Spanish throne already settled, the irresponsible and decaying government of Napoleon III declared war on Prussia.

Again the war was short. Again Bismarck had taken care to isolate his enemy in advance. The British generally felt France to be in the wrong. They had been alarmed by French operations in Mexico, which suggested an ambition to re-create a French American empire. The Italians had long been awaiting the chance to seize Rome; they did so in 1870, when the French withdrew their troops from Rome for use against Prussia. The Russians had been awaiting the chance to upset the clause of the Peace of 1856 which forbade them to keep naval vessels in the Black Sea. They did so in 1870.

The War of 1870, like the others of the time, failed to become a general European struggle. Prussia was supported by the south German states. France had no allies. The French army proved to be technically backward compared with the Prussian. War began on July 19; on September 2, after the battle of Sedan, the principal French army surrendered to the Germans. Napoleon III was himself taken prisoner. On September 4 an insurrection in Paris proclaimed the Third Republic. The Prussian and German forces moved into France and laid siege to the capital. Though the French armies dissolved, Paris refused to capitulate. For four months it was surrounded and besieged.

The German Empire, 1871

With their guns encircling Paris, the German rulers or their representatives assembled at Versailles. The château and gardens of Versailles, since Louis XVI's unceremonious departure in October 1789, had been little more than a vacant monument to a society long since dead. Here, in the most sumptuous room of the palace, the resplendent Hall of Mirrors, where the Sun King had once received the deferential approaches of German princes, Bismarck on January 18, 1871, caused the German Empire to be proclaimed. The king of Prussia received the hereditary title of German emperor. The other German rulers (excepting, to be sure, the ruler of Austria, and those whom Bismarck had himself dethroned) accepted his imperial authority. Ten days later the people of Paris, shivering, hungry, and helpless, opened their gates to the enemy. France had no government with which Bismarck could make peace. It was not at all clear what kind of government the country wanted. Bismarck insisted on the election of a Constituent Assembly by universal suffrage. He demanded that France pay the German Empire a war indemnity of five billion gold francs (then an enormous and unprecedented sum) and cede to it the border region of Alsace and most of Lorraine. Though the Alsatians spoke German, most of them felt themselves to be French, having shared in the general history of France since the seventeenth century. There was strong local protest at the transfer to Germany, and the French never reconciled themselves to this cold-blooded amputation of their frontier. The peace dictated by Bismarck was embodied in the treaty of Frankfurt of May 10, 1871. Thereafter, as will be seen, the French Constituent Assembly gradually proceeded to construct the Third Republic.[21]

The consolidation of Germany transformed the face of Europe. It reversed the dictum not only of the Peace of Vienna but even of the Peace of Westphalia.[22] The German Empire, no sooner born, was the strongest state on the continent of Europe. Rapidly industrialized after 1870, it became more potent still. Bismarck, by consummate astuteness, by exploiting the opportunities offered by a Europe in flux and with no more fighting than that involved in a few weeks in three short wars, had brought about what European statesmen of many nationalities had long said should at all costs be prevented. He outwitted everybody in turn, including the Germans. The united all-German state that issued from the nationalist movement was a Germany conquered by Prussia. Prussia, with its annexations of 1866, embraced almost all Germany north of the Main. Within the empire it had about two-thirds of the area. Before such unanswerable success the Prussian liberals capitulated, and the Prussian parliament passed an "indemnity act"; the gist of it was that Bismarck admitted to a certain high-handedness during the constitutional struggle but that the parliament legalized the disputed tax collections *ex post facto,* agreeing to forgive and forget, in view of the victory over Austria and its consequences. Thus liberalism withered away before nationalism.

The German Empire received substantially the constitution of the North German Confederation. It was a federation of monarchies, each based in theory on divine or hereditary right. At the same time, in the Reichstag elected by universal male suffrage, it rested on a kind of mass appeal and was in a sense democratic. Yet the country's ministers were responsible to the emperor and not to the elected chamber. Moreover, it was the rulers who joined the empire, not the peoples. There were no popular plebiscites as in Italy. Each state kept its own laws, government, and constitution. The people of Prussia, for example, remained for Prussian affairs under the rather illiberal constitution of 1850,[23] while in affairs of the Reich, or empire, they enjoyed an equal vote by universal suffrage. The emperor, who was also the king of Prussia, had legal control over the foreign and military policy of the empire. The German Empire in effect served as a mechanism to magnify the role of Prussia, the Prussian army, and the East-Elbian Prussian aristocracy in world affairs.

66. The Dual Monarchy of Austria-Hungary

The Habsburg Empire after 1848

Bismarck united Germany, but he also divided it, for he left about a sixth of the Germans outside his German Empire. These Germans of Austria and Bohemia had now to work out a common future with the dozen other nationalities in the Danubian domain.

The clumsiness of the old Habsburg multinational empire is clear enough, but

[21] See pp. 605–607.
[22] See pp. 145–149, and map, pp. 146–147.
[23] See p. 519.

more impressive is its astonishing capacity to live and to survive. Prussia and France, in the 1740s, had tried unsuccessfully to dismember it. Smashed four different times by the French between 1796 and 1809, it outlived this crisis, and after 1815, under Metternich, it guided the counsels of Europe.[24] Broken up in 1848, restored by the intervention of Russia in 1849, dislocated by its effort at mobilization in 1855, attacked by Napoleon III in 1859 and by Bismarck in 1866, it still continued to hold together and disappeared finally only in 1918 in the cataclysm of the First World War.[25] But the events of the 1850s and 1860s greatly altered its character.

The essential question, in a nationalist age, was how the Habsburg government would react to the problems raised by national self-expression. The nationalities did not wish to destroy the empire. Among the Hungarians after 1848–1849, only a handful of extreme radicals dreamed of a Hungary entirely independent. Most of them desired constitutional autonomy for Hungary but were not prepared to sever the link with Vienna. Slav opinion, at the Slav Congress of Prague in 1848, went basically no further than Austroslavism.[26] The peoples of the empire, while increasingly insistent on certain national rights—such as a degree of local self-government, and schools, law courts, and administration in their own language—felt an underlying need for the large political structure which the empire gave.

By Habsburg, in this period, one means primarily Francis Joseph, who as emperor from 1848 to 1916 reigned even longer than his famous contemporary, Queen Victoria. Francis Joseph, like many others, could never shake off his own tradition. His thoughts turned on his house and on its rights. Buffeted unmercifully by the waves of change, he cordially disliked everything liberal, progressive, or modern. He allied himself with the Catholic hierarchy and the Vatican, which also, for decades after 1848, and for understandable reason, set itself bluntly against compromise with the new age. Personally, Francis Joseph was incapable of enlarged views, ambitious projects, bold decisions, or persevering action. And he lived in a pompous dream world, surrounded in the imperial court by great noblemen, high churchmen, and bespangled personages of the army.

Yet the government was not idle; it was, if anything, too fertile in devising new deals and new dispensations. Various expedients were tried after 1849, but none was tried long enough to see if it would work. For several years the ruling idea was centralization—to govern the empire through the German language and with German efficiency, maintaining the abolition of serfdom as accomplished in 1848 (and which required a strong official control over the landlords if it was to work in practice) and favoring the building of railroads and other apparatus of material progress.[27] This Germanic and bureaucratic centralization was distasteful to the non-German nationalities, and especially to the Magyars. It is important to say Magyars, not Hungarians, because the Magyars composed less than half the very mixed population of Hungary within its then existing borders. Nevertheless the Magyars, as the strongest of the non-German groups, and hence the most able to maintain a political system of their own, felt the Germanic

[24] See pp. 275–278, 394–397, 418–422, 424–425, 474–484.
[25] See pp. 507–514, 545, 548, 554–557, 717–718.
[26] See pp. 510–511.
[27] See p. 514.

influence as most oppressive. In the war of 1859 the Magyars sympathized with the Italians.

The Compromise of 1867

In 1867 a compromise was made, known as the *Ausgleich*. It was essentially a bargain between the Germans of Austria-Bohemia and the Magyars of Hungary. It worked to the common disadvantage of the Slavs. Both Germans and Magyars looked upon the Slavs somewhat as many whites in the United States then looked upon blacks, seeing in them a people who had shown no aptitude for civilization except under tutelage. In fact the word "slave" in many languages (German *Sklave*) had originated from the word "Slav." As Count Beust, the Austrian negotiator, put it in 1867, the idea of the Compromise was that each people, Germans and Magyars, should thereafter govern its own barbarians in its own way.

The Compromise created a Dual Monarchy, of a kind unparalleled in Europe. West of the river Leith was the Empire of Austria, east of it the Kingdom of Hungary. The two were now judged exactly equal. Each had its own constitution and its own parliament, to which in each country the governing ministry was henceforth to be responsible. The administrative language of Austria would be German, of Hungary, Magyar. Neither state might intervene in the other's affairs. The two were joined by the fact that the same Habsburg ruler should always be emperor in Austria and king in Hungary. Yet the union was not personal only; for, though there was no common parliament, delegates of the two parliaments were to meet together alternately in Vienna and Budapest, and there was to be a common ministry for finance, foreign affairs, and war. To this common ministry of Austria-Hungary both Austrians and Hungarians were to be appointed.

In effect, the Compromise treated Austria as a kind of German nation-state and Hungary as a Magyar nation-state. It furnished each with parliamentary and constitutional organs, by which the leading nationality was made to feel a sense of participation in government. But the Germans formed less than half the people of Austria, as did the Magyars of Hungary. Austria included the Slovenes, Czechs, Poles, and Ruthenians (and a few Italians); Hungary the Slovaks, the Croats and Serbs, and the Transylvanians, who were essentially Romanians.[28] All these people felt aggrieved.

---

[28] See maps, pp. 470, 562–563.

EUROPE, 1871

The new features on this map, as compared to the Europe of 1815 (see pp. 448–449), are the existence of a unified German Empire and a unified Kingdom of Italy. The German domain was enlarged by the incorporation of Schleswig (in the neck of the Danish peninsula) and the annexation from France of Alsace and parts of Lorraine, the regions respectively around Strassburg (French Strasbourg) and Metz on the map. From 1871 to 1914 Europe had fewer separate states, fewer land frontiers, and a simpler political geography than at any other time in its history. Except for the voluntary separation of Norway and Sweden in 1905 there were no changes in this period outside the Balkans. (See map, p. 703.)

ARCTIC OCEAN

ICELAND
(Denmark)

NORWAY

LAP

NORWAY
AND
SWEDEN

SWEDEN

SHETLAND I.
(Britain)

Kristiania

Stockholm

GREAT BRITAIN

SCOTLAND

NORTH SEA

BALTIC

Belfast

DENMARK

Copenhagen

IRELAND

Danzig

Dublin

Liverpool

HELIGOLAND
(Britain)

ATLANTIC OCEAN

ENGLAND

Hamburg

Elbe R.

VISTULA

London

NETHERLANDS
Amsterdam

Rhine R.

Bremen

Berlin

Oder R.

English Channel

Brussels

GERMAN EMPIRE

BELGIUM

Cologne

Dresden

Prague

Reims

Seine R.

Paris

LUX.

AUSTRIA

Loire R.

Metz

Strassburg

Munich

Vienna

A

Tours

Budapest

FRANCE

SWITZERLAND

Vienna

H

Bordeaux

Lyons

Milan

Po R.

CROATIA-
SLOVENIA

Bilbao

Rhone R.

Turin

Venice

BOSNIA

Marseilles

ADRIATIC SEA

PORTUGAL

Ebro R.

Madrid

CORSICA
(France)

Rome

Lisbon

Tagus R.

SPAIN

Barcelona

ITALY

Naples

Seville

BALEARIC I.
(Spain)

SARDINIA

Tangier

Gibraltar (Britain)

Algiers

SICILY

Fez

Tunis

MALTA (Brit.)

MEDITERRANEAN

MOROCCO

ALGERIA
(France)

TUNISIA

CAPE

0   100   200   300 miles

WHITE SEA   • Archangel

AND

L.
Ladoga

singfors   • St. Petersburg

tiga

• Orenburg

• Moscow

R   U   S   S   I   A   N   E   M   P   I   R   E

• Vilna

Don R.

Ural R.

Volga R.

Kiev •   Dnieper R.   Astrakhan •

Rostov •

C A S P I A N   S E A

Dniester R.

BESSARABIA   SEA OF
AZOV

Pruth R.   • Odessa   C   A   U   C   A   S   I   A

ROMANIA   CRIMEA
(Autonomous)

RY   DOBRUJA   Sevastopol •   • Baku

Danube R.   BLACK SEA

BULGARIA   • Sinope   • Tabriz

O   • Constantinople   PERSIA

ONIA   O   T   T   O   M   A   N   E   M   P   I   R   E

DARDANELLES   Tigris R.

AEGEAN SEA   • Smyrna   M   E   S   O   P   O   T   A   M   I   A

• Athens   SYRIA   Euphrates R.   Baghdad •

REECE
ependent)

CYPRUS
(Turkish)

CRETE (Turkish)

ARABIA

Both Austria and Hungary, under the Dual Monarchy, were in form constitutional parliamentary states, although the principle of ministerial responsibility was not consistently honored. Neither was democratic. In Austria, after much juggling with voting systems, a true universal male suffrage was instituted in 1907. In Hungary, when the First World War came in 1914, still only a quarter of the adult male population had the vote. Socially, the great reform of 1848, the abolition of serfdom, was not allowed to lead on to upsetting conclusions. The owners of great landed estates, especially in Hungary (but also in parts of the Austrian Empire) remained the unquestionably dominant class. They were surrounded by landless peasants, an agrarian proletariat, composed partly of lower classes of their own nationality, and partly of entire peasant peoples, like the Slovaks and Serbs, who had no educated or wealthy class of their own. National and social questions therefore came together. For some nationalities, and for none more than the Magyars, not only a national but a social and economic ascendancy was at stake. Landlordism became the basic social issue. A landowning class, educated and civilized, faced a peasant mass that was generally ignorant, rude, and left out of the advancing civilization of the day.

67. *Liberalization in Tsarist Russia: Alexander II*

Tsarist Russia after 1856

For Russia also the Crimean War set off a series of changes. The ungainly empire, an "enormous village" as it has been called, stretching from Poland to the Pacific, had proved unable to repel a localized attack by France and Great Britain, into which neither of the Western powers had put anything like its full resources. Alexander II (1855–1881), who became tsar during the war, was no liberal by nature or conviction. But he saw that something drastic must be done. The prestige of western Europe was at its height. There the most successful and even enviable nations were to be found. The reforms in Russia therefore followed, at some distance, the European model.

Imperial Russia was a political organization very difficult to describe. Its own subjects did not know what to make of it. Some, called Westernizers in the mid-nineteenth century, believed Russia destined to become more like Europe. Others, the Slavophiles, believed Russia to be entrusted with a special destiny of its own, which imitation of Europe would only weaken or pervert.

That Russia differed from Europe at least in degree was doubted by nobody. The leading institution was the autocracy of the tsar. This was not exactly the absolutism known in the West. In Russia certain very old European conceptions were missing, such as the idea that spiritual authority is independent of even the mightiest prince or the old feudal idea of reciprocal duties between king and subject.[29] The notion that men have rights, claims for justice at the hands of power, which no one in Europe had ever expressly repudiated, was in Russia a somewhat doctrinaire importation from the West. The tsardom did not rule by

---

[29] See pp. 16–17, 29. On Russia in the sixteenth and seventeenth centuries, see pp. 234–235.

law; it ran the country by ukase, police action, and the army. The tsars, since Peter and before, had built up their state very largely by importing European technical methods and technical experts, often against strong objection by native Russians of all classes, upon whom the new methods were, when necessary, simply forced. More than any state in Europe, the Russian empire was a machine superimposed upon its people without organic connection—bureaucracy pure and simple. But as the contacts with Europe were joined, many Russians acquired European ideas of a kind in which the autocracy was not interested—ideas of liberty and fraternity, of a just and classless society, of individual personality enriched by humane culture and moral freedom. Many people, with such sentiments, found themselves chronically critical of the government and of Russia itself. The government, massive though it seemed, was afraid of such people. Any idea arising outside of official circles seemed pernicious, and the press and the universities were as a rule severely censored.

A second fundamental institution, which had grown up with the tsardom, was legalized bondage or serfdom. The bulk of the population were serfs dependent upon masters. Russian serfdom was more onerous than that found in east-central Europe until 1848.[30] It resembled the slavery of the Americas in that serfs were "owned"; they could be bought and sold and used in other occupations than agriculture. Some serfs worked the soil, rendering unpaid labor service to the gentry. Others could be used by their owners in factories or mines or rented out for such purposes. Others were more independent, working as artisans or mechanics, and even traveling about or residing in the cities, but from their earnings they had to remit certain fees to the lord, or return home when he called them. The owners had a certain paternalistic responsibility for their serfs, and in the villages the gentry constituted a kind of personal local government. The law, as in the American South, did little or nothing to interfere between gentry and servile mass, so that the serf's day-to-day fortunes depended on the personality or economic circumstances of his owner.

By the mid–nineteenth century both conservative and liberal Russians were agreeing that serfdom must some day end. Serfdom was in any case ceasing to be profitable; some two-thirds of all the privately owned serfs (i.e., those not belonging to the tsar or state) were mortgaged as security for loans at the time of Alexander II's accession. Increasingly serfdom was recognized as a bad system of labor relations, making the muzhiks into illiterate and stolid drudges, without incentive, initiative, self-respect, or pride of workmanship, and also very poor soldiers for the army.

Educated Russians, full of Western ideas, were estranged from the government, from the Orthodox church, which was an arm of the tsar, and from the common people of their own country. They felt ill at ease in a mass of ignorance and obscurantism and a pang of guilt at the virtual slavery on which their own position rested. Hence arose, at about the time under discussion, another distinctive feature of Russian life, the "intelligentsia." In Russia it was thought so exciting to be educated, to have ideas, to subscribe to magazines, or engage in critical conversation that the intelligentsia sensed themselves as a class apart. They were made up of students, university graduates, and persons who had a good deal of

---

[30] See pp. 237–238, 337–339.

leisure to read. Such people, while not very free to think, were more free to think than to do almost anything else. The Russian intelligentsia tended to sweeping and all-embracing philosophies. They believed that intellectuals should play a large role in society. They formed an exaggerated idea of the direct influence of thinkers upon the course of historical change. Their characteristic attitude was one of opposition. Some, overwhelmed by the mammoth immobility of the tsardom and of serfdom, turned to revolutionary and even terroristic philosophies. This only made the bureaucrats more anxious and fearful, and the government more fitfully repressive.

The Emancipation Act of 1861 and Other Reforms

Alexander II, on becoming tsar, attempted to enlist the support of the liberals among the intelligentsia. He gave permission to travel outside of Russia, eased the controls on the universities, and allowed the censorship to go relatively unenforced. Newspapers and journals were founded, and those written by Russian revolutionaries abroad, like the *Polar Star* of Alexander Herzen in London, penetrated more freely into the country. The result was a great outburst of public opinion, which was agreed at least on one point, the necessity of emancipating the peasants. This was in principle hardly a party question. Alexander's father, Nicholas I, had been a noted reactionary, who abhorred Western liberalism and is memorable for having organized, as the "Third Section" of his chancellory, a system of secret political police until then unparalleled in Europe for its arbitrary and inquisitorial methods. Yet Nicholas I had taken serious measures to alleviate serfdom. Alexander II, basically conservative on Russian affairs, proceeded to set up a special branch of the government to study the question. The government did not wish to throw the whole labor system and economy of the country into chaos, nor to ruin the gentry class without which it could not govern at all. After many discussions, proposals, and memoranda, an imperial ukase of 1861 declared serfdom abolished and the peasants free.

By this great decree the peasants became legally free in the Western sense. They were henceforth subjects of the government, not subjects of their owners. It was hoped that they would be stirred by a new sense of human dignity. As one enthusiastic official put it shortly after emancipation: "The people are erect and transformed; the look, the walk, the speech, everything is changed." The gentry lost their old quasi-manorial jurisdiction over the villages. They could no longer exact forced and unpaid labor or receive fees arising from servitude.

It is important to realize what the Act of Emancipation did and did not do. Roughly (with great differences from region to region) it allocated about half the cultivated land to the gentry and half to the former serfs. The latter had to pay redemption money for the land they received and for the fees which the gentry lost. The Russian aristocracy was far from weakened; in place of a kind of human property largely mortgaged anyway, they now had clear possession of some half the land, they received the redemption money, and were rid of obligations to the peasants.

The peasants, on the other hand, now owned some half the arable land in their own right—a considerable amount by the standards of almost any European country. They did not, however, possess it according to the principles of private property or independent farming that had become prevalent in Europe. The peasant land, when redeemed, became the collective property of the ancient peasant village assembly, or *mir*. The village, as a unit, was responsible to the government for payment of the redemption and for collection of the necessary sums from its individual members. The village assembly, in default of collection, might require forced labor from the defaulter or a member of his family; and it could prevent peasants from moving away from the village, lest those remaining bear the whole burden of payment. It could (as in the past) assign and reassign certain lands to its members for tillage and otherwise supervise cultivation as a joint concern. To keep the village community intact, the government presently forbade the selling or mortgaging of land to persons outside the village. This tended to preserve the peasant society but also to discourage the investment of outside capital, with which equipment might be purchased, and so to retard agricultural improvement and the growth of wealth. Not all peasants within the village unit were equal. As in France before the Revolution, some had the right to work more land than others. Some were only day laborers. Others had rights of inheritance in the soil (for not all land was subject to reassignment by the commune) or rented additional parcels of land belonging to the gentry. These lands they worked by hiring other peasants for wages. These more substantial peasants, as agricultural entrepreneurs, resembled farmers of the type found in France or the United States. None of the Russian peasants, however, after the emancipation, possessed full individual freedom of action. In their movements and obligations, as in their thoughts, they were restricted by their villages as they had once been restricted by their lords.

Alexander II proceeded to overhaul and westernize the legal system of the country. With the disappearance of the lord's jurisdiction over his peasants a new system of local courts was needed in any case, but the opportunity was taken to reform the courts from bottom to top. The arbitrariness of authority and defenselessness of the subject were the inveterate evils. They were greatly mitigated by the edict of 1864. Trials were made public, and private persons received the right to be represented in court by lawyers of their own choosing. All class distinctions in judicial matters were abolished, although in practice peasants continued to be subject to harsh disadvantages. A clear sequence of lower and higher courts was established. Requirements were laid down for the professional training of judges, who henceforth received stated salaries and were protected from administrative pressure. A system of juries on the English model was introduced.

While thus attempting to establish a rule of law, the tsar also moved in the direction of allowing self-government. He hoped to win over the liberals and to shoulder the upper and middle classes with some degree of public responsibility. He created, again by an edict of 1864, a system of provincial and district councils called zemstvos. Elected by various elements, including the peasants, the zemstvos gradually went into operation and took up matters of education, medical relief, public welfare, food supply, and road maintenance in their localities. Their great value was in developing civic sentiment among those who took part in them. Many liberals urged a representative body for all Russia, a Zemsky Sobor or

Duma, which, however, Alexander II refused to concede. After 1864 his policy became more cautious. A rebellion in Poland in 1863 inclined him to take advice from those who favored repression. He began to mollify the vested interests that had been disgruntled by the reforms and to whittle down some of the concessions already granted. But the essence of the reforms remained unaffected.

Revolutionism in Russia

The autocrat who thus undertook to liberalize Russia barely escaped assassination in 1866, had five shots fired at him in 1873, missed death by half an hour in 1880 when his imperial dining room was dynamited, and in 1881 was to be killed by a bomb. The revolutionaries were not pleased with the reforms, which if successful would merely strengthen the existing order. Dissatisfied intelligentsia in the 1860s began to call themselves "nihilists": they believed in "nothing"—except science—and took a cynical view of the reforming tsar and his zemstvos. The peasants, saddled with heavy redemption payments, remained basically unsatisfied, and intellectuals toured the villages fanning this discontent. Revolutionaries developed a mystic conception of the revolutionary role of the Russian masses. They reminded the peasants of the vast rebellions of Stephen Razin and Pugachev, in which they saw a native Russian revolutionary tradition.[31] Socialists, after the failure of socialism in Europe in the Revolution of 1848, came in many cases to believe, as Alexander Herzen wrote, that the true and natural future of socialism lay in Russia, because of the very weakness of capitalism in Russia and the existence of a kind of collectivism already established in the village assemblies or communes.

More radical than Herzen were the anarchist Bakunin and his disciple Nechaiev. In their *People's Justice* these two called for terrorism not only against tsarist officials but against liberals also. As they wrote in the *Catechism of a Revolutionist*, the true revolutionary "is devoured by one purpose, one thought, one passion— the revolution. . . . He has severed every link with the social order and with the entire civilized world. . . . Everything which promotes the success of the revolution is moral, everything which hinders it is immoral." Terrorism (which is really to say assassination) was rejected by many of the revolutionaries, especially by those who in the 1870s took up the scientific socialism of Karl Marx. To Marx it did not seem that frantic violence would advance an inevitable social process. But other groups, recognizing the inspiration of men like Bakunin and Nechaiev, organized secret terroristic societies. One of these, the People's Will, determined to assassinate the tsar. In an autocratic state, they held, there was no other road to justice and freedom.

Alexander II, alarmed by this underground menace, which of course did not escape the attention of the police, again turned for support to the liberals. The liberals, who were themselves threatened by the revolutionaries, had become estranged from the government by its failure to follow through with the reforms of the early 1860s. Now, in 1880, to rally support, the tsar again relaxed the autocratic system. He abolished the dreaded Third Section or secret police set up by his father, allowed the press to discuss most political subjects freely, and

[31] See pp. 238, 337–339.

encouraged the zemstvos to do the same. Further to associate representatives of the public with the government, he proposed, not exactly a parliament, but two nationally elected commissions to sit with the council of state. He signed the edict to this effect on March 13, 1881, and on the same day was assassinated, not by a demented individual acting wildly and alone, but by the joint efforts of the highly trained members of the People's Will.

Alexander III, upon his father's death, abandoned the project for elected commissions and during his whole reign, from 1881 to 1894, reverted to a program of brutal resistance to liberals and revolutionaries alike. The new regime established by peasant emancipation, judicial reform, and the zemstvos was nevertheless allowed to continue. How Russia finally received a parliament in 1905 is explained below in the chapter on the Russian Revolution. At present it is enough to have seen how even tsarist Russia, under Alexander II, shared in a liberal movement that was then at its height. The abolition of serfdom, putting both aristocrat and peasant more fully on a money economy, opened the way for capitalistic development within the empire. And between the two confining walls of autocracy and revolutionism—equally hard and unyielding—European ideas of law, liberty, and humanity inserted themselves in a tentative way.

68. The United States: The American Civil War

The history of Europe, long interconnected with that of the rest of the world, by the early twentieth century became merged with it entirely. Similarly the development of non-European regions, long a collection of separate stories, was to fuse into a single worldwide theme, to which later chapters of this book are largely devoted. It is no great leap at this point to pass to a treatment of areas overseas (as seen from Europe), some of which underwent in the 1860s the same process of national consolidation, or attempted consolidation, already traced in Italy and Germany, Austria, Hungary, and the Russian empire. In particular, foundations were laid for two new "powers" like those of Europe—the United States of America and the Empire of Japan. The huge Dominion of Canada was also established.

Growth of the United States

As in the time of the American Revolution and Napoleon, the history of the United States in the nineteenth century reflected that of the European world of which it formed a part. The most basic fact, besides territorial expansion, was rapid growth. This was so obvious as to lead a French observer in the 1830s, Alexis de Tocqueville, to make a famous prediction: that within a century the United States would have 100 million people and would, along with Russia, be one of the two leading powers of the world. By 1860, with 31 million, the United States was almost as populous as France and more so than Great Britain.

The growth in numbers was due to a prolific birth rate, but also to the arrival of immigrants, who became prolific in their turn. The immigrants—except for an uncounted, because illegal, importation of slaves—came almost entirely from Europe, and before 1860 almost entirely from Great Britain, Ireland, and Germany.

The immigrants did not desire to surrender their native ways. Some brought skills that the new country greatly needed, but immigration also presented a true social problem, obliging peoples to live together without common tradition. On the whole, it appears that the older Americans accepted the reshaping of their country rather calmly, with anti-foreign movements occasionally surfacing but then quickly subsiding. Few concessions were made. English was the language of the public schools, the police, law courts, local government, and public notices and announcements. Usually the immigrant had to know some English to hold a job. On the other hand no one was exactly forced to become "Americanized"—the new arrivals were free to maintain churches, newspapers, and social gatherings in their own tongues. The fact that the English, Scots, and Irish already spoke English, and that the Germans readily learned it, alleviated the language issue. The immigrants did not constitute minorities in the European sense. They were more than willing to embrace American national attitudes as formed in the eighteenth century—the national traditions of republicanism and self-government, of individual liberty, free enterprise, and unbounded opportunity for self-improvement. The old America impressed itself on the new, being somewhat impressed itself in the process. In this sense a new nationality was being consolidated.

The Estrangement of North and South

But at the same time the nation was falling to pieces. North and South became completely estranged. The Industrial Revolution had contrary effects on the two regions. It turned the South into an economic associate of Great Britain. The South became the world's chief producer of raw cotton for the Lancashire mills. The Southerners, living by the export of a cash crop, and producing virtually no manufactures, wished to purchase manufactured goods as cheaply as possible. Hence they favored free trade, especially with Great Britain. In the North, the Industrial Revolution led to the building of factories. Northern factory owners, usually backed by their workers, demanded protection from the inflow of British goods, with which no other country at the time could easily compete. The North therefore favored a high tariff, which the South declared to be ruinous.

More fundamental was the difference in the status of labor. As the demand for raw cotton reached astronomical magnitudes the South fell more deeply under the hereditary curse of the Americas—the slave and plantation system.[32] In the nineteenth century slavery increasingly revolted the moral conscience of the white man's world. It was abolished in the British colonies in 1833, in the French colonies in 1848, and in the Spanish American republics at different dates in the first half of the century. Similarly, serfdom was abolished in the Habsburg possessions in 1848 and in Russia in 1861. The American South could not, and after about 1830 no longer even wished to shake the system off. The South was the Cotton Kingdom whose "peculiar institution" was unfree labor of blacks. Whites were hurt by the system as well as blacks. Few free men could prosper alongside a mass of subservient and virtually uncompensated labor. The incoming Europeans settled overwhelmingly in the North, the South remaining more purely

[32] See p. 261.

"Anglo-Saxon"—except that in its most densely peopled areas some half of the people were of African descent.

In the movement westward, common in North and South, the pressure in the South came mainly from planters wishing to establish new plantations, in the North from persons hoping to set up small farms and from businessmen bent on founding new towns, building railroads, and creating markets. As once France and Great Britain had fought for control beyond the Alleghenies, so now North and South fought for control beyond the Mississippi. In 1846 the United States made war upon Mexico by methods at which Bismarck would not have blushed. The North widely denounced the war as an act of Southern aggression, but was willing enough to take the ensuing conquests, which comprised the region from Texas to the Pacific. The first new state created in this region, California, prohibited slavery. Since 1820 the United States had held together precariously by the "Missouri Compromise," under which new states, as set up in the West, were admitted to the Union in pairs, one "slave" and one "free," so that a rough equality was maintained in the Senate and in the presidential electoral vote. With the creation of California this balance of power was upset in favor of the North, so that in return, by the "compromise of 1850," the North agreed to enforce the laws on runaway slaves to the satisfaction of the South. But the new strictness toward fugitive slaves ran against mounting sentiment in the North. Attempts to arrest blacks in free states and return them to slavery aroused abolitionist sentiment to a higher pitch. The abolitionists, a branch of the humanitarian movement then sweeping the European world, and somewhat resembling the radical democrats who came forward in Europe in 1848, demanded the immediate and total elimination of slavery, without concession, compromise, or compensation for the property interests of the slave owners. Abolitionists denounced the Union itself as the unholy accomplice in a social abomination.

By 1860 a sense of "sectionalism" had developed in the South not different in principle from the nationalism felt by many peoples in Europe. In their proud insistence on states' rights and constitutional liberties, their aristocratic and warlike codes of ethics, their demand for independence from outside influence and for freedom in ruling their own subject people, the Southern whites suggested nothing in Europe so much as the Magyars of the Austrian Empire. They now wondered whether their way of life could be safely maintained within the Union which they had helped to create. They sensed Northerners as outsiders, unsympathetic, foreign, hostile, and the South as potentially an independent and distinct nation. They were aware that within the Union they were increasingly a minority; for where in 1790 North and South had been approximately equal, by 1860 the North had outrun the South in population, mainly because of the stream of migration from Europe. The incipient nationalism of the South was of the type of small nation struggling against the great empire. In the North, nationalism was a sentiment in favor of maintaining the whole existing territory of the United States. Northerners by 1860, with a few exceptions, refused to admit that any state of the Union could withdraw, or secede, for any reason.

In 1860 the new Republican party elected Abraham Lincoln president. It advanced a program of free Western lands for small farmers, a higher tariff, transcontinental railroad building, and economic and capitalistic development on a national scale. The new party's radical wing, to which Lincoln himself did not belong, was vehemently abolitionist and anti-Southern in sentiment. Southern leaders, after the election of Lincoln, brought about the formal withdrawal of their states from the United States of America and the creation of the Confederate States of America reaching from Virginia to Texas. Lincoln ordered the armed forces to defend the territory of the United States, and the resulting Civil War, or war of Southern independence, lasting for four years and involving battles as great as those of Napoleon, was the most harrowing struggle of the nineteenth century with the exception of the Taiping rebellion in China.[33]

European governments, while never recognizing the Confederacy, were partial to the South. The United States stood for principles still considered revolutionary in Europe, so that, while the European working classes generally favored the North, the upper classes were willing enough to see the North American republic end in collapse and failure. In addition, Great Britain and France saw in the breakup of the United States the same advantages that they had formerly seen in the breakup of the Spanish empire.[34] In the Confederate States the British, and the French to a lesser degree, expected to find another free trade country, supplying western Europe with raw materials and buying its manufactures; in short, they saw not a competitor like the North, but a complementary partner to the industry of the Old World. It was likewise during the American Civil War that a French army sent by Napoleon III invaded Mexico to create a puppet empire under an Austrian archduke.[35] Thus the only serious attempt to ignore the Monroe Doctrine, violate the independence of Latin America, and revive European colonialism in the Americas occurred at the time when the United States was in dissolution.

But the North won the war and the Union was upheld. The Mexicans rid themselves of their unwanted emperor. Tsar Alexander II sold Alaska to the United States. The war ended the idea of the Union as a confederation of member states from which members might withdraw at will. In its place triumphed the idea that the United States was a national state, composed not of member states but of a unitary people irrevocably bound together. This doctrine was written explicitly into the Fourteenth Amendment to the Constitution, which pronounced all Americans to be citizens not only of their several states but of the United States and forbade any state to "deprive any person of life, liberty or property without due process of law"—"due process" to be determined by authority of the national government. The new force of central authority was felt first of all in the South. President Lincoln, using his war powers, issued the Emancipation Proclamation in 1863, abolishing slavery in areas engaged in hostilities against the United States. The Thirteenth Amendment in 1865 abolished slavery everywhere in the country. No compensation was paid to the slave owners, who were therefore ruined. The legal authority of the United States was thus used for an annihilation of individual property rights without parallel (outside of modern communism) in the history of the Western world; for neither the nobility in the French Revolution, nor the Russian serf owners in 1861, nor the slave owners of the West Indies in the nineteenth century, nor the owners of businesses

[33] See p. 674.
[34] See pp. 195, 481–483.
[35] See pp. 651–652.

nationalized by twentieth-century socialists in western Europe had to face such a total and overwhelming loss of property values as the slave owners of the American South.

After the Civil War: Reconstruction; Industrial Growth

The assassination of Lincoln in 1865 by a fanatical Southern patriot strengthened those radical Republicans who said that the South must be drastically reformed. With the old Southern upper class completely ruined, Northerners of many types poured into the defeated country. Some came to represent the federal government, some to dabble in local politics, some to make money, and a great many out of democratic and humanitarian impulses, to teach the distressed ex-slaves the elements of reading and writing or of useful trades. Blacks in the South voted, sat in legislatures, occupied public office. This period, called Reconstruction, may be compared to the most advanced phase of the French Revolution, in that "radical republicans" undertook to press liberty and equality upon a recalcitrant country, under conditions of emergency rule and under the auspices of a highly centralized national government with a mobilized army. The Southern whites strenuously objected, and the Northern radicals discredited themselves and gradually lost their zeal. Reconstruction was abandoned in the 1870s, and, by what Europeans would call a counterrevolution, the Southern whites gradually regained control.

The Northern business interests—financiers, bankers, company promoters, railway builders, manufacturers—expanded greatly with the wartime demand for munitions and military provisioning. They received protection by the Morrill tariff of 1861. In the next year, partly as a war measure, the Union Pacific Railroad was incorporated, and in 1869, at a remote spot in Utah, the last spike was driven in the first railroad to span the American continent. The Homestead Act, providing farms to settlers on easy conditions, and the granting of public lands to certain colleges (ever since called "land-grant colleges"), largely for the promotion of agricultural sciences, encouraged the push of population and civilization into the West. Vast tracts of land were given by the government to subsidize railway building. With the destruction of the Southern slaveholders, who before the war had counterbalanced the rising indusrialists, it was now industry and finance that dominated national politics in the increasingly centralized United States. The Fourteenth Amendment, for many years, was mainly interpreted not to protect the civil rights of individual persons, but the property rights of business corporations against restrictive legislation by the states. The shift of political power from the states to the federal government accompanied and protected the shift of economic enterprise from local businesses to far-flung and continent-embracing corporations. As in France under Napoleon III, there was a good deal of corruption, fraud, speculation, and dishonestly or rapaciously acquired wealth; but industry boomed, the cities grew, and the American mass market was created. On Fifth Avenue in New York, and in other Northern cities, rose the pretentious and gaudy mansions of the excessively rich.

In short, the American Civil War, which might have reduced English-speaking America to a scramble of jealously competing minor republics, resulted instead in the economic and political consolidation of a large nation-state, liberal and democratic in its political principles, and committed enthusiastically to private enterprise in its economic system.

69. The Dominion of Canada, 1867

North of the United States, at the time of the Civil War, lay a number of British provinces unconnected with one another, and each in varying degree dependent on Great Britain. The population had originated in three great streams. One part was French, settled in the St. Lawrence valley since the seventeenth century. A second part was made up of descendants of United Empire Loyalists, old seaboard colonists who, remaining faithful to Britain, had fled from the United States during the American Revolution.[36] They were numerous in the Maritime Provinces and in Upper Canada, as Ontario was then called.[37] A third part consisted of recent immigrants from Great Britain, men and women of the working classes who had left the home country to improve themselves in America.

The French firmly resisted assimilation to the English-speaking world around them. Their statute of freedom was the Quebec Act of 1774, which had been denounced as "intolerable" by the aroused inhabitants of the Thirteen Colonies, but which put the French civil law, French language, and French Catholic church under the protection of the British Crown.[38] The French looked with apprehension upon the stream of immigrants, English-speaking and Protestant, which began to flow into Canada about 1780 and thereafter never stopped. There was constant irritation between the two nationalities.

The British government tried various expedients. In 1791 it created two provinces in the St. Lawrence and Great Lakes region—a Lower Canada to remain French, and an Upper Canada to be English. They received the same form of government as that enjoyed by the Thirteen Colonies before their break from the empire. Each colony, that is, had a locally elected assembly with certain powers of taxation and lawmaking, subject to veto by the British authorities, as represented either by the governor or by the London government itself. For many years there was no objection to these arrangements. The War of 1812, in which the United States embarked on the conquest of Canada, aroused a national sentiment among both French and English in that country, together with a willingness to depend politically upon Great Britain for military security. But the internal political differences continued. In Lower Canada the French feared the English-speaking minority. In Upper Canada the old aristocracy of United Empire Loyalists, who had carved the province from the wilderness, hesitated to share control with the new immigrants from Great Britain. Between the provinces there were grievances also, since Lower Canada stood in the way of Upper Canada's outlet to the sea. In 1837 a superficial rebellion broke out in both provinces. It was put down virtually without bloodshed.

[36] See p. 356.
[37] See map, p. 549.
[38] See p. 354.

Lord Durham's Report

In Great Britain at this time the reforming Whigs were busily renovating many ancient English institutions.[39] Some of them had definite views on the administration of colonies. In general, they held that it was not necessary to control a region politically in order to trade with it. This was an aspect of the free trade doctrine, separating economics from politics, business from power. The Whig reformers were rather indifferent to empire, unconcerned with military, naval, or strategic considerations. A few even thought it natural for colonies, when mature, to drop away entirely from the mother country. Whigs, liberals, and radicals all wished to economize on military expenditure, to relieve British taxpayers by cutting down British garrisons overseas.

After the Canadian insurrection of 1837 the Whig government sent out the Earl of Durham as governor. Durham, one of the framers of the parliamentary Reform Bill of 1832, published his views on Canadian affairs in 1839. Durham's Report was long regarded as one of the classic documents in the rise of the British Commonwealth of Nations. He held that in the long run French separatist feeling in Canada should be extinguished and all Canadians brought to feel a common citizenship and national character. He therefore called for the reuniting of the two Canadas into one province. To consolidate this province he proposed an intensive development of railways and canals. In political matters he urged the granting of virtual self-government for Canada and the introduction of the British system of "responsible government," in which the elected assembly should control the executive ministers in the province, the governor becoming a kind of legal and ceremonial figure like the sovereign in Great Britain.

Most of Durham's Report was accepted immediately. Upper and Lower Canada were combined into one province, with the machinery of self-government, in 1840. The British army was withdrawn. The Canadians undertook to maintain their own military establishment, still regarded as necessary, since the era of the famous undefended frontier between Canada and the United States had not yet dawned. The Webster-Ashburton treaty of 1842 put an end to the long dispute over the Maine border. But as late as 1866 the Canadians had to repel armed invaders from the United States, when several hundred Irish Americans, members of the Fenians, an Irish republican secret society, staged an insurrectionary attempt to detach Canada from the British Empire. Local Canadian forces proved sufficient to meet this threat.

The principle of responsible government was established in the late 1840s, the governors of Canada allowing the elected assembly to adopt policies and appoint or remove ministers as it chose. Responsible government, still confined to internal matters, worked satisfactorily from the beginning. But one feature of the new plan, the union of the two Canadas, began to produce friction as the English-speaking immigration continued. The French were afraid of being outnumbered in their own country. Many Canadians therefore turned to the idea of a federation, in which the French and English areas might each conduct its own local affairs, while remaining joined for larger purposes in a central government.

[39] See pp. 489–495.

Founding of the Dominion of Canada

Federalism in Canada was thus partly a decentralizing idea, aimed at satisfying the French element by a redivision into two provinces, and in part a plan for a new centralization or unification, because it contemplated bringing all the provinces of British North America into union with the St. Lawrence and Great Lakes region, to which alone the term Canada had hitherto been applied. While the people of British North America discussed federation the Civil War was disrupting the United States. In the face of this unpleasant example, the Canadians formed a strong union in which all powers were to rest in the central government except those specifically assigned to the provinces. The federal constitution, drafted in Canada by Canadians, was passed through the British Parliament in 1867 as the British North America Act, which constitutionally established the Dominion of Canada. In 1982 the British North America Act was replaced by new arrangements, which explicitly recognized the sovereign independence of Canada and its power to frame a constitution for itself. By the 1980s, however, the French speakers of Quebec had entered more fully into the modern world, and it was again necessary to recognize a special status for Quebec. The western provinces had also matured. The relationship between the central and provincial governments, along with bilingualism, or the equal recognition of the French and English languages, again became serious problems.

By the legislation of 1867 the new dominion received a common federal parliament, in which a ministry responsible to the majority in parliament governed according to British principles of "responsible," or cabinet, government. The original provinces were Quebec and Ontario, formed from the old Canada, plus the maritime provinces of Nova Scotia, New Brunswick, and Prince Edward Island, which joined the dominion in 1867 on the understanding that a railroad would be built to connect them with Quebec City and Montreal. The old Hudson's Bay Company, founded in 1670, transferred its rights of government over the vast Northwest to the dominion in 1869. From these territories the province of Manitoba was created in 1870 and British Columbia in 1871. To link them solidly with the rest of the dominion the Canadian Pacific Railway was completed in 1885. It made possible the development of the prairies, where the provinces of Saskatchewan and Alberta were added in 1905.

The Dominion of Canada, though at first not large in population, possessed from the beginning a significance beyond the mere number of its people. It was the first example of successful devolution, or granting of political liberty, within one of the European colonial empires. It embodied principles which Edmund Burke and Benjamin Franklin had vainly recommended a century before to keep the Thirteen Colonies loyal to Great Britain. The dominion after 1867 moved forward from independence in internal matters to independence in such external affairs as tariffs, diplomacy, and the decisions of war and peace. It thus pioneered in the development of "dominion status," working out precedents later applied in Australia (1901), New Zealand (1907), the Union of South Africa (1910), and in the 1920s, temporarily, in Ireland. By the middle of the twentieth century the same idea, or what may be called the Canadian idea, was even applied to the worldwide problem of colonialism as it affected non-European peoples, notably in India, Pakistan, Sri Lanka, and the former British colonies in Africa, until all these peoples chose to become republics, though still loosely and voluntarily joined together and to Great Britain in a Commonwealth of Nations.

More immediately, in America, the founding of the dominion, a solid band of self-governing territory stretching from ocean to ocean, stabilized the relations between British North America and the United States. The United States regarded its northern borders as final. The withdrawal of British control from Canadian affairs furthered the United States conception of an American continent entirely free from European political influence.

70. Japan and the West

The Japanese, when they allowed the Westerners to discover them, were a highly civilized people living in a complex society. They had many large cities, they enjoyed the contemplation of natural scenery, they went to the theater, and they read novels. With their stylized manners, their fans and their wooden temples, their lacquer work and their painting on screens, their tiny rice fields and their curious and ineffectual firearms, they seemed to Europeans to be the very acme of everything quaint. This feeling is immortalized in *The Mikado* of Gilbert and Sullivan, first performed in 1885. Not long thereafter the idea of Japanese quaintness, like the idea of the Germans as an impractical people given mainly to music and metaphysics, had to be revised. The Europeans, in "opening" Japan, opened up more than they knew.

In 1853, the American Commodore Perry forced his way with a fleet of naval vessels into Yedo Bay, insisted upon landing, and demanded of the Japanese government, somewhat peremptorily, that it engage in commercial relations with the United States and other Western powers. In the next year the Japanese began to comply, and in 1867 an internal revolution took place, of which the most conspicuous consequence was a rapid westernizing of Japanese life and institutions. But if it looked as if the country had been "opened" by Westerners, actually Japan had exploded from within.

Background: Two Centuries of Isolation, 1640–1854

For over two centuries Japan had followed a program of self-imposed isolation. No Japanese was allowed to leave the islands or even to build a ship large enough to navigate the high seas. No foreigner, except for handfuls of Dutch and Chinese, was allowed to enter. Japan remained a sealed book to the West. The contrary is not quite so true, for the Japanese knew rather more about Europe than Europeans did about Japan. The Japanese policy of seclusion was not merely based upon ignorance. Initially, at least, it was based on experience.

The first Europeans—three Portuguese in a Chinese junk—are thought to have arrived in Japan in 1542. For about a century thereafter there was considerable coming and going. The Japanese showed a strong desire to trade with the foreigners, from whom they obtained clocks and maps, learned about printing and shipbuilding, and took over the use of tobacco and potatoes. Thousands also adopted the Christian religion as preached to them by Spanish and Portuguese Jesuits. Japanese traveled to the Dutch Indies and even to Europe. The Japanese in fact proved more receptive to European ideas than other Asian peoples. But shortly after 1600 the government began to drive Christianity underground; in 1624 it expelled the Spaniards, in 1639 the Portuguese, and in 1640 all Europeans except for a few Dutch merchants who were allowed to remain at Nagasaki under strict control. From 1640 to 1854 these few Dutch at Nagasaki were the only channel of communication with the West.[40]

The reasons for self-seclusion, as for its abandonment later, arose from the course of political events in Japan. The history of Japan showed an odd parallel to that of Europe. In Japan, as in Europe, a period of feudal warfare was followed by a period of government absolutism, during which civil peace was kept by a bureaucracy, an obsolescent warrior class was maintained as a privileged element in society, and a commercial class of native merchants grew wealthier, stronger, and more insistent upon its position.

When the first Europeans arrived, the islands were still torn by the wars and rivalries of the numerous clans into which the Japanese were organized. Gradually one clan, the Tokugawa, gained control, taking over the office of "shogun." The shogun was a kind of military head who governed in the name of the emperor, and the hereditary Tokugawa shogunate, founded in 1603, lasted until 1867. The early Tokugawa shoguns concluded from a good deal of evidence that the Europeans in Japan, both merchants and missionaries, were engaging in feudal or interclan politics and even aspiring to dominate Japan by helping Christian or pro-European Japanese to get into power. The first three Tokugawa shoguns, to establish their own dynasty, to pacify and stabilize the country, and to keep Japan free from European penetration, undertook to exterminate Christianity and adopted the rigid policy of nonintercourse with the rest of the world.

Under the Tokugawa Japan enjoyed peace, a long peace, for the first time in centuries. The Tokugawa shoguns completed the detachment of the emperor from politics, building him up as a divine and legendary being, too august and too remote for the hurly-burly of the world. The emperor remained shut in at Kyoto on a modest allowance furnished by the shoguns. The shoguns established their own court and government at Yedo (later called Tokyo); and as Louis XIV brought nobles to Versailles, or Peter the Great forced his uncouth lords to build town houses in St. Petersburg, so the shoguns required the great feudal chieftains and their men-at-arms to reside at least part of the year in Yedo.

The shoguns administered the country through a kind of military bureaucracy or dictatorship. This formidable instrument of state watched over the great lords (called daimyo), who, however, retained a good deal of feudal authority over their subjects in the regions most distant from Yedo. The great lords and their armed retainers (the samurai), having no further fighting to occupy them, turned into a landed aristocracy which spent a good deal of its time in Yedo and other cities. As a leisure class, they developed new tastes and standards of living and hence needed more income, which they obtained by squeezing the peasants, and which they spent by buying from the merchants.

The merchant class greatly expanded by catering to the government and the gentry. Japan in the seventeenth century passed on to a money economy. Many lords fell seriously into debt to the merchants. Many samurai, like lesser nobles

---

[40] See p. 166.

in France or Poland at the time, were almost ridiculously impoverished, hard-pressed to keep up appearances, with nothing except social status to distinguish them from commoners. The law, as in Europe under the Old Regime, drew a sharp line between classes. Nobles, merchants, and peasants were subject to different taxes and were differently punished for different offenses. What was a crime for a commoner would be excusable for a samurai; or what in a samurai would be a punishable breach of honor would be accepted in a common person. The samurai had the right to carry two swords as a mark of class and could in theory cut down an impudent commoner without arousing further inquiry. In practice the shoguns repressed violence of this kind, but there was much less development of law and justice than in the European monarchies of the Old Regime. Economically the merchants and artisans prospered. By 1723 Yedo was a city with 500,000 people; by 1800 with over 1,000,000, it was larger than London or Paris, and twenty times as large as the largest city in the United States. After 1800 some merchants were able to purchase the rank of samurai for money. The old class lines were beginning to blur.

Though deliberately secluded, the economic and social life of Japan was thus by no means static. The same is true of its intellectual life. Buddhism, the historic religion, lost its hold on many people during the Tokugawa period, so that Japan in its way underwent, like the West, a "secularization" of ideas. As a code of personal conduct there was a new emphasis on Bushido, the "way of the warrior," a kind of nonreligious moral teaching which exalted the samurai virtues of honor and loyalty. With the decline of Buddhism went also a revival of the cult of Shinto, the "way of the gods," the ancient indigenous religion of Japan, which held, among much else, that the emperor was veritably the Son of Heaven. There was much activity in the study and writing of history, arousing, as in Europe, an acute interest in the national past. History, like Shinto, led to a feeling that shoguns were usurpers and that the emperor, obscurely relegated to Kyoto, was the true representative of everything highest and most lasting in the life of Japan.

Meanwhile, through the crack left open at Nagasaki, Western ideas trickled in. The shogun Yoshimune in the mid–eighteenth century permitted the importation of Occidental books, except those relating to Christianity. A few Japanese learned Dutch and began to decipher Dutch books on anatomy, surgery, astronomy, and other subjects. In 1745 a Dutch-Japanese dictionary was completed. For European manufactures also—watches, glassware, velvets, woolens, telescopes, barometers—there came to be an eager demand, satisfied as much as possible by the methodical Dutch. Nor were the Japanese wholly uninformed about politics in the West. While the most assiduous Westerner could learn nothing of the internal affairs of Japan, an educated Japanese could, if he wished, arrive at some idea of the French Revolution, or know who was president of the United States.

The Opening of Japan

When Perry in 1853 made his unwanted visit he therefore had many potential allies within Japan. There were nobles, heavily in debt, unable to draw more income from agriculture, willing to embark upon foreign trade and to exploit their property by introducing new enterprises. There were penurious samurai, with no future in the old system, ready and willing to enter upon new careers as army officers or civil officials. There were merchants hoping to add to their business by dealing in Western goods. There were scholars eager to learn more of Western science and medicine. There were patriots fearful that Japan was becoming defenseless against Western guns. Spiritually the country was already adrift from its moorings, already set toward a course of national self-assertion, restlessly susceptible to hazily understood new ideas. Under such pressures, and from downright fear of a bombardment of Yedo by the Americans, which if it would not subdue Japan would at least ruin the declining prestige of the shogunate, the shogun Iesada in 1854 signed a commercial treaty with the United States. Similar treaties were soon signed with the Europeans.

In the following years were sown the seeds of much later misunderstanding between Japan and the West. The whites in those days—European and American—were somewhat trigger-happy in the discharge of naval ordnance against backward peoples. The Japanese, a proud and elaborately civilized nation, soon found that the whites considered them backward. They found, for example, as soon as they learned more of the West by reading and travel, that the treaties they signed in the 1850s were not treaties between equals as understood in the West. These first treaties provided that Japan should maintain a low tariff on imports and not change it except with the consent of the foreign powers. To give outsiders a voice in determining tariff policy was not the custom among sovereign states of the West. The early treaties also provided for extraterritoriality. This meant that Europeans and Americans residing in Japan were not subject to Japanese law but remained under the jurisdiction of their respective homelands as represented by consular officials. Such extraterritorial provisions had long been established in Turkey and were currently taking root in China.[41] Europeans insisted upon them in countries where European principles of property, debt, or security of life and person did not prevail. At the same time, of course, no civilized state ever permitted a foreign power to exercise jurisdiction within its borders. Extraterritoriality was a mark of inferiority, as the Japanese soon discovered.

A strong antiforeign reaction developed after 1854. It was at first led by certain nobles of the western islands, the lords of Choshu and Satsuma, who had never been fully subordinated to the shogun at Yedo, and who now dreamed of overturning the Tokugawa shogunate and leading a national revival with the emperor as its rallying point. Their first idea was to check Western penetration (as two and a half centuries before) by driving the Westerners out. But in 1862 some Englishmen unintentionally violated a small point of Japanese etiquette. One of them was killed. The British government demanded punishment for the offending Japanese, who were followers of the lord of Satsuma. The shogun proved unable to arrange this, and the British navy thereupon itself sailed up and bombarded the capital of Satsuma. In the same year the lord of Choshu, who commanded the straits of Shimonoseki with some ancient artillery, ordered it to fire on passing vessels. The British, French, Dutch, and United States governments immediately protested, and, when the embarrassed shogun proved unable to discipline Choshu, they dispatched an allied naval force to Shimonoseki. The forts and shipping of Choshu were destroyed, and an indemnity of $3,000,000 was imposed. These incidents were remembered in Japan long after they were

[41] See pp. 220, 675.

forgotten in Europe and the United States. It was likewise remembered that the Western powers, discovering that the shogun was not the supreme ruler of the country, sent a naval expedition to Kyoto itself and required the emperor to confirm the treaties signed by the shogun and to reduce import duties, under threat of naval bombardment.

The Meiji Era (1868–1912): The Westernization of Japan

The lords of Choshu and Satsuma now concluded that the only way to deal with the West was to adopt the military and technical equipment of the West itself. They would save Japan for the Japanese by learning the secrets of the Western power. First they forced the resignation of the shogun, whose prestige had long been undermined anyway, and who had now discredited himself first by signing undesirable treaties with the West and then failing to protect the country from outrage. The last shogun abdicated in 1867. The reformers declared the emperor restored to his full authority. It was their intention to use the plenitude of imperial power to consolidate and fortify Japan for its new position in the world. In 1868 a new emperor inherited the throne; his name was Mutsuhito, but according to Japanese custom a name was given to his reign also, which was called Meiji. The Meiji era (1868–1912) was the great era of the westernization of Japan.

Japan turned into a modern national state. Feudalism was abolished, most of the great lords voluntarily surrendering into the emperor's hands their control over samurai and common people. "We abolish the clans and convert them into prefectures," declared one imperial decree. The legal system was reorganized and equality before the law introduced, in the sense that all persons became subject to the same rules regardless of class. In part with the hope of getting rid of extraterritoriality, the reformers recast the criminal law along Western lines, deleting the bizarre and cruel punishments which Europeans considered barbaric. A new army was established, modeled mainly on the Prussian. The samurai in 1871 lost his historic right to carry two swords; he now served as an army officer, not as the retainer of a clannish chief. A navy, modeled on the British, followed somewhat later. Control of money and currency passed to the central government, and a national currency, with decimal units, was adopted. A national postal service began to function and above all a national school system, which soon brought a high rate of literacy to Japan. Buddhism was discouraged, and the property of Buddhist monasteries was confiscated. Shinto was the cult favored by the government. Shinto gave a religious tincture to national sentiment and led to a renewed veneration of the imperial family. In 1889 a constitution was promulgated. It confirmed the civil liberties then common in the West and provided for a parliament in two chambers, but it stressed also the supreme and "eternal" authority of the emperor, to whom the ministers were legally responsible. In practice, in the new Japan, the emperor never actively governed. He remained aloof, as in the past; and political leaders, never fully responsible to the parliament, tended to govern freely in what they conceived to be the interests of the state.

Industrial and financial modernization went along with and even preceded the political revolution. In 1858 the first steamship was purchased from the Dutch. In 1859 Japan placed its first foreign loan, borrowing 5 million yen by a bond issue floated in England. In 1869 the first telegraph connected Yokohama and Tokyo. The first railroad, between the same two cities, was completed in 1872. In 1870 appeared the first spinning machinery. Foreign trade, almost literally zero in 1854, was valued at $200 million a year by the end of the century. The population rose from 33 million in 1872 to 46 million in 1902. The island empire, like Great Britain, became dependent on exports and imports to sustain its dense population at the level of living to which it aspired.

The westernization of Japan still stands as the most remarkable transformation ever undergone by any people in so short a time. It recalls the westernizing of Russia under Peter over a century before, though conducted somewhat less brutally, more rapidly, and with a wider consent among the population. For Japan, as formerly for Russia, the motive was in large measure defense against Western penetration, together with an admiration for Western statecraft and an ambition to become a "power."[42] What the Japanese wanted from the West was primarily science, technology, and organization. They were content enough with the innermost substance of their culture, their moral ideas, their family life, their arts and amusements, their religious conceptions, though even in these they showed an uncommon adaptability. Essentially it was to protect their internal substance, their Japanese culture, that they took over the external apparatus of Western civilization. This apparatus—science, technology, machinery, arms, political and legal organization—was the part of Western civilization for which other peoples generally felt a need, which they hoped to adopt without losing their own spiritual independence, and which therefore, though sometimes rather scornfully dismissed as materialistic, became the common ground for the interdependent worldwide civilization that emerged at the close of the nineteenth century.

In brief, to conclude a long chapter, the world between 1850 and 1870, revolutionized economically by the railroad and steamship, was revolutionized politically by the formation of large and consolidated nation-states. These states at the time all embodied certain liberal and constitutional principles, or at least the machinery of parliamentary and representative government. But the whole earth had also become an arena in which certain mighty beings, called nations or powers, were to act. The Great Powers in 1871 were Great Britain, Germany, France, Austria-Hungary, and Russia. Britain had produced a daughter nation in Canada. Whether Italy was to be called a Great Power was not yet clear. No one knew what Japan would do. All agreed that the United States would one day play a large role in international politics, but the time was not yet.

[42] See pp. 234–245.

XIV.
EUROPEAN
CIVILIZATION,
1871–1914

HALF A CENTURY elapsed between the period of national consolidation described in the last chapter and the outbreak of the First World War in 1914. In this half-century Europe in many ways reached the climax of the modern phase of its civilization, and also exerted its maximum influence upon peoples outside Europe. The present chapter will attempt a description of European civilization in these years, the next chapter an account of the worldwide ascendancy which Europe enjoyed at this time.

For Europe and the European world the years 1871 to 1914 were marked by hitherto unparalleled material and industrial growth, international peace, domestic stability, the advance of constitutional, representative, and democratic government, and continued faith in science, reason, and progress. But in these very years, in politics, economics, and basic thinking there were forces operating to undermine the liberal premises and tenets of this European civilization. Most of the present chapter will be devoted to the continuing triumphs of liberalism, but the signs of its transformation and wane will be pointed out too.

Chapter Emblem: A painting called The Last of England *dated 1852, by Ford Madox Brown, showing two emigrants looking back from their departing ship.*

71. The "Civilized World"

Materialistic and Nonmaterialistic Ideals

With the extension of the nation-state system Europe was politically more divided than ever. Its unity lay in the sharing by all Europeans of a similar way of life and outlook, which existed also in such "European" countries as the United States, Canada, Australia, and New Zealand. Europe and its offshoots constituted the "civilized world." Other regions—mostly in Asia, Africa, and Latin America— were said to be "backward." (They are today referred to as "developing" or "less developed.") Europeans were extremely conscious and inordinately proud of their civilization in the half-century before 1914. They believed it to be the well-deserved outcome of centuries of progress. Feeling themselves to be the most advanced branch of mankind in the important areas of human endeavor, they assumed that all peoples should respect the same social ideals—that so far as they were unwilling or unable to adopt them they were backward, and that so far as they did adopt them they became civilized in their turn.

These ideals of civilization were in part materialistic. If Europeans considered their civilization to be better in 1900 than in 1800, or better in 1900 than the ways of non-Europeans at the same time, it was because they had a higher standard of living, ate and dressed more adequately, slept in softer beds, and had more satisfactory sanitary facilities. It was because they possessed ocean liners, railroads, and streetcars, and after about 1880 telephones and electric lights. But the ideal of civilization was by no means exclusively materialistic. Knowledge as such, correct or truthful knowledge, was held to be a civilized attainment— scientific knowledge of nature, in place of superstition or demonology; geographical knowledge, by which civilized people were aware of the earth as a whole with its general contours and diverse inhabitants. The ideal was also profoundly moral, derived from Christianity, but now secularized and detached from religion. An Englishman, Isaac Taylor, in his *Ultimate Civilization* published in 1860, defined this moral ideal by listing the contrasting "relics of barbarism" which he thought were due to disappear—"Polygamy, Infanticide, Legalized Prostitution, Capricious Divorce, Sanguinary and Immoral Games, Infliction of Torture, Caste and Slavery." The first four of these had been unknown to the approved customs of Europe at least since the coming of Christianity. Torture went out of use about

TRAIN IN THE SNOW
by Claude Monet (French, 1840–1926)
With the Impressionists, and notably with Claude Monet, some of the conventions of Western painting since the Renaissance began to fade. Emphasis shifted from the representation of objects to the perception of them as experienced through the eye. Solid masses melted into the play of light under a variety of atmospheric conditions. The railway age, which developed rapidly in Monet's youth, furnished many subjects to excite his imagination. In this picture the solid iron of the locomotive merges into the indeterminate grays of a dull day in winter. The chill and the low visibility are conveyed as much as the visual images themselves. Courtesy of the Musée Marmottan, Paris (Giraudon). Permission S.P.A.D.E.M. 1970 by French Reproduction Rights, Inc.

1800, even in the illiberal European states, and legalized caste and slavery in the course of the nineteenth century. But there were few non-European peoples, in 1860, among whom two or three of Taylor's "relics" could not be found.

There are certain other indices, more purely quantitative, worked out by sociologists to show the level of advancement of a given society. One of these is the death rate, or number of persons per thousand of population who die each year. In England, France, and Sweden the "true" death rate (or death rate regardless of the proportion of infants and old people, who are most susceptible to death) is known to have fallen from about 25 (per 1,000 per year) before 1850, to 19 in 1914 and 18 in the 1930s. Indeed, before the Second World War, it stood seemingly stabilized at about 18 in all countries of northwestern Europe, the United States, and the British dominions. Death rates in countries not "modern" run over 40 even in favorable times. A closely related index is infant mortality, which fell rapidly after 1870 in all countries affected by medical science. Thus a woman under civilized conditions had to go through pregnancy and childbirth less often to produce the same number of surviving children. Another index is life expectancy, or the number of years of age which a person has an even chance of attaining. In England life expectancy at birth rose from 40 years in the 1840s to 59 in 1933 and 73 in 1980. In India in 1931 it was less than 27 years. It had risen to about 50 in the 1980s. Still another index is the literacy rate, or proportion of persons above a certain age (such as ten) able to read and write. In northwestern Europe by 1900 the literacy rate approached 100. In some countries it still does not rise very far above zero. A further basic index is the productivity of labor, or amount produced by one worker in a given expenditure of time. This is difficult to compute, especially for earlier periods for which statistical data are lacking. In the 1930s, however, the productivity of a farmer in Denmark was over ten times that of a farmer in Albania. All northwestern Europe was above the European average in this respect with the exception of Ireland, whereas Ireland, Spain, Portugal, Italy, and all eastern Europe were below it.

The essence of civilized living doubtless is in the intangibles, in the way in which people use their minds, and in the attitudes they form toward others or toward the conduct and planning of their own lives. The intangibles, however, are not always agreed upon by persons of different culture or ideology. On the quantitative criteria there is less disagreement; all, with few exceptions, wish to lower the death rate, raise the literacy rate, and increase the productivity of human exertion. Even if we apply quantitative or sociological indices alone, we can say that after 1870 there was in fact, and not merely in the opinion of Europeans, a civilized world of which Europe was the center.

The "Zones" of Civilization

Or rather, a certain region of Europe was the center. For there were really two Europes, an inner zone and an outer. A Frenchman writing in the 1920s, describing the two Europes that had risen since 1870, called the inner zone the "Europe of steam," and bounded it by an imaginary line joining Glasgow, Stockholm, Danzig, Trieste, Florence, and Barcelona. It included not only Great Britain but Belgium, Germany, France, northern Italy, and the western portions of the Austrian Empire. Virtually all heavy European industry was located in this zone. Here the railway network was thickest. Here was concentrated the wealth of Europe, in the form both of a high living standard and of accumulations of capital. Here likewise were almost all the laboratories and all the scientific activity of Europe. Here, in the same zone, lay the strength of constitutional and parliamentary government and of liberal, humanitarian, socialist, and reformist movements of many kinds. In this zone the death rate was low, life expectancy high, conditions of health and sanitation at their best, literacy almost universal, productivity of labor very great. To the same zone, for practical purposes, belonged certain regions of European settlement overseas, especially the northeastern part of the United States.

The "outer zone" included most of Ireland, most of the Iberian and Italian peninsulas, and all Europe east of what was then Germany, Bohemia, and Austria proper. The outer zone was agricultural, though the productivity of agriculture, per farm worker or per acre, was far less than in the inner zone. The people were poorer, more illiterate, and more likely to die young. The wealthy were landlords, often absentees. The zone lived increasingly after 1870 by selling grain, livestock, wool, or lumber to the more industrialized inner zone but was too poor to purchase many manufactured products in return. To obtain capital it borrowed in London or Paris. Its social and political philosophies were characteristically imported from Germany and the West. It borrowed engineers and technicians from the first zone to build its bridges and install its telegraph systems and sent its youth to universities in the first zone to study medicine or other professions. Many areas of European settlement overseas, for example in Latin America and the southern part of the United States, may also be thought of as belonging to this outer zone.

Beyond the European world lay a third zone, the immense reaches of Asia and Africa, all "backward" by the standards of Europe, with the exception of the recently Europeanized Japan, and all destined, with the exception of Japan, to become heavily dependent upon Europe in the half-century after 1870. Much of the world's history since 1870 could be written as the story of relations among these three zones; but it is necessary in all human things to guard against formulas that are too simple.

72. Basic Demography: The Increase of the Europeans

European and World Population Growth since 1650

All continents except Africa gained enormously in population in the three centuries following 1650, but it was Europe that grew the most. There is little doubt that the proportion of Europeans in the world's total, including those of European origin in other continents, reached its maximum for all time between 1850 and the Second World War. Estimates are given in the table on p. 588, beginning with 1650.

The causes of the rise in population after 1650 cannot be positively known. Some of them must obviously have operated in Asia as well as Europe. In Europe the organized sovereign states, as established in the seventeenth century, put an

ESTIMATED POPULATION OF THE WORLD BY CONTINENTAL AREAS*

	Millions					
	1650	1750	1850	1900	1950	1990
Europe	100	150	263	396	532	726
United States and Canada	1	2	26	82	166	278
Australasia-Oceania	2	2	2	6	13	27
Predominantly "European"	103	154	291	484	711	1031
Latin America	12	16	38	74	162	445
Africa	100	106	111	133	217	646
Asia	330	515	822	959	1396	3158
Predominantly "Non-European"	442	637	971	1166	1775	4249
World Total	545	791	1262	1650	2486	5280

	Percentages					
Europe	18.3	19.1	20.8	24.0	21.5	13.8
United States and Canada	.2	.2	2.1	5.0	6.7	5.3
Australasia-Oceania	.4	.2	.2	.3	.5	.5
Predominantly "European"	18.9	19.5	23.1	29.3	28.7	19.6
Latin America	2.2	2.0	3.0	4.5	6.5	8.4
Africa	18.3	13.0	8.8	8.1	8.7	12.2
Asia	60.6	65.0	65.1	58.1	56.1	59.8
Predominantly "Non-European"	81.1	80.0	76.9	70.7	71.3	80.4
World Total	100.0	100.0	100.0	100.0	100.0	100.0

* This table is designed only to show the numbers and proportion of Europeans and persons of European descent in world population over the modern period. It reveals the rapid increase in the proportion of "Europeans" in this sense from 1750 to 1900, and its significant decline in the twentieth century, until by 1990 the proportion is about as it was in 1750. The table is subject to serious reservations. The population of the former Soviet Union is divided between Europe and Asia, but millions of Europeans (i.e., Russians) have long lived in the Asian parts of the former U.S.S.R. It must be remembered also that the population of the United States has always been of both European and African descent, that the Latin American countries differ widely in their racial composition, and that there are over 4 million persons of European origin in South Africa. In short, the table has nothing to do with race, for there are many whites, notably in the Middle East, who are not European, and many nonwhites in the Americas and elsewhere who participate fully in the kind of civilization derived from Europe.

For world population in the twentieth century, see also p. 1062 below. For particular countries, see Appendix III. SOURCE: For 1650 to 1900, A. N. Carr-Sanders, *World Population* (Oxford: Oxford University Press, 1936); for 1750, 1850 and 1900, John D. Durand, "The Modern Expansion of World Population," in *Proceedings of the American Philosophical Society*, vol. 111 (1967); and for 1950 and 1990 the *United Nations Demographic Yearbook* and *World Population Prospects*, published by the United Nations, New York, 1989.

end to a long period of civil wars, stopping the chronic violence and marauding, with the accompanying insecurity of agriculture and family life, which were more deadly than wars fought between governments. Similarly, the Tokugawa kept peace in Japan, and the Manchu or Ch'ing dynasty brought a long period of order in China. The British rule in India and the Dutch in Java, by curbing famine and violence, allowed populations to mount very rapidly. All such factors, which allowed more people to remain alive longer, also favored the stability of families and the birth and raising of children. Death rates could fall and birth rates could rise from similar causes. The great exception to the swelling rise of population was Africa, where the slave trade removed over 10 million people in three or four centuries, and where slave raiding led to the disruption of African cultures. In the Americas the native Indians were devastated by diseases brought from Europe to which at first they had no immunity.

In Europe, sooner than elsewhere, other causes of growth were at work beyond the maintenance of civil peace. They included liberation from certain endemic afflictions, beginning with the subsiding of bubonic plague in the seventeenth century and the use of vaccination against smallpox in the eighteenth. Agricultural improvement produced more food, notably in England about 1750. The improvement of transportation, by road, canal, and railroad, made localized famine a thing of the past, since food could be moved into areas of temporary shortage. With the Industrial Revolution larger populations could subsist in Europe by importing food from overseas. In the cities of Europe and North America, by 1900, the supply of pure drinking water and facilities for the disposal of garbage and sewage were better than in the past.

Hence population grew for several generations more substantially in Europe and its offshoots than elsewhere. Approximate percentages are given in the table. Asia, by these estimates, increased less than threefold between 1650 and 1900, but Europe increased fourfold, and the total number of Europeans, including the descendants of those who migrated to other continents, multiplied fivefold. The ascendancy of European civilization in the two and a half centuries after 1650, was due in some measure to merely demographic growth. But while in 1900 the proportion of "Europeans" in all continents was approaching a third of the human race, after 1900 this proportion began to fall. In the 1990s it could be projected that "Europeans" would constitute only a tenth of the human beings on the planet in the year 2100.

Stabilization of European Population

Stabilization and relative decline of European population followed from a fall in the birth rate. As early as 1830 the birth rate began noticeably to drop in France, with the result that France, long the most populous European state, was surpassed in population by Germany about 1870, by the British Isles about 1895, and by Italy about 1930. France, once thought to be decadent for this reason, was in fact only the leading country in a population cycle through which the European countries seemed to pass. The birth rate, which had fallen below 30 per 1,000 in France in the 1830s, fell to that level in Sweden in the 1880s, in England in the 1890s, and in Germany, Bohemia, and the Netherlands between 1900 and 1910. After the Second World War there was a temporary rise, but by 1990 the birth rate was only 15 per 1,000 or less in Europe and North America, hardly sufficient to maintain existing population levels. In most of the rest of the world, except China, it was still well over 30.

The reduced birth rate is not a mere dry statistical item, nor does it affect populations merely in the mass. It is one of the indices of modern civilization, first appearing in that inner European zone in which the other indices were also highest, and thence spreading outward in a kind of wave. Concretely, a low birth rate in the nineteenth century meant that families averaged from two to four children, where in former times, or today under conditions not "modern," families may be found to consist of ten children or even more. The low birth rate reflects the small family system, than which few things are more fundamental to modern life. The principal means used to hold down the birth rate, or to limit the family, is the practice of contraception. But the true causes, or reasons why parents wish to limit their families, are deeply embedded in the codes of modern society.

Historical demographers have detected a "European family pattern" as far back as the seventeenth century. It was a pattern in which, in comparison to other societies, Europeans married later, and a larger number never married at all. Late marriage shortened the number of years during which a woman bore children, and enabled young people to acquire skills or accumulate savings (as in tools and household goods) before setting up new families. The effect was a less explosive population growth, and less extreme poverty, than occurred in some other parts of the world. Evidence indicating the practice of contraception can be found in the eighteenth century among the upper classes, by study of the number and spacing of their children. The practice seems to have spread to other social classes during the French Revolution. The Code Napoleon then required that inheritances be divided among all sons and daughters. The French peasants, many of them owners of land, began to limit themselves to two or three children, in order that all children (by inheritance, marriage, and dowries) might remain in as high an economic and social position as their parents. It was thus economic security and the possession of a social standard that led to the reduced birth rate in France.

In the great cities of the nineteenth century, in which standards of life for the working classes often collapsed, the effect might at first be a proliferation of offspring. But life in the city, under crowded conditions of housing, also set a premium on the small family. There were many activities in the city that people with many children could only with difficulty enjoy. After about 1880 child labor became much less frequent among the working classes. When children ceased to earn part of the family income parents tended to have fewer of them. About the same time governments in the advanced countries began to require universal compulsory schooling. The number of years spent in education, and hence in economic dependency upon parents, grew longer and longer, until it became common even for young adults to be still engaged in study. Each child represented many years of expense for its parents. The ever rising idea of what it was necessary to do for one's children, and the desire of parents to give them every possible advantage in a competitive world, were probably the most basic causes of voluntary limitation of the family. Hardly less basic was the desire to lighten the burdens upon mothers. The small family system, together with the decline of infant mortality, since they combined to free women from the interminable bearing and tending of infants, probably did more than anything else to improve the position of civilized women.

But the effects of the small family system upon total population became manifest only slowly. More people lived on into the middle and older age groups, and the fall of the birth rate was gradual, so that in all the leading countries total numbers continued to rise, except in France, which hardly grew between 1900 and 1945. The persistent note was one of superabundant increase. In five generations, between 1800 and 1950, some 200 million "Europeans" grew into 700 million. Since productivity increased even more rapidly, the standard of living for most of these "Europeans" rose in spite of the increase of numbers, and there was no general problem of overpopulation.

Growth of Cities and Urban Life

Where did so many people go? Some stayed in the rural areas where most people had always lived. Rural populations in the "inner zone" became more dense, turning to the more intensive agriculture of truck gardening or dairy farming, leaving products like wool and cereal grains to be raised elsewhere and then imported. But it is estimated that of every seven persons added to the western European population only one stayed on the land. Of the other six, one left Europe altogether and five went to the growing cities.[1]

The nineteenth-century city was mostly the child of the railroad, for with the railroads it became possible for the first time to concentrate manufacturing in large towns, to which bulky goods such as foods and fuel could now be moved in great volume. The growth of cities between 1850 and 1914 was phenomenal. In England two-thirds of the people lived in places of 20,000 or less in 1830; in 1914 two-thirds lived in places of 20,000 or more. Germany, the historic land of archaic towns carried over from the Middle Ages, rivaled England after 1870 in modern industrial urbanization. Whereas in 1840 only London and Paris had a million people, the same could be said by 1914 of Berlin, Vienna, St. Petersburg, and Moscow.[2] Some places, like the English Midlands and the Ruhr valley in Germany, became a mass of contiguous smaller cities, vast urban agglomerations divided only by municipal lines.

The great city set the tone of modern society. City life was impersonal and anonymous; people were uprooted, less tied to home or church than in the country. They lacked the country person's feeling of deference for aristocratic families. They lacked the sense of self-help characteristic of older rural communities. It was in the city that the daily newspaper press, which spread rapidly in the wake of the telegraph after 1850, found its most habitual readers. The so-called yellow or sensational press appeared about 1900. Articulate public opinion was formed in the cities, and city people were on the whole disrespectful of tradition, receptive to new ideas, having in many cases deliberately altered their own lives by moving from the country or from smaller towns. That socialism spread among the industrial masses of European cities is hardly surprising. It is less often realized that some of the more blatant nationalism that arose after 1870 was stimulated by city life, for people felt increasingly detached from all institutions except the state. At the same time city life, by its greater facilities for schooling, reading, and discussion, made for a more alert and informed public opinion of an enlightened kind.

[1] See Appendix III for the growth of cities and the map on p. 460 for England.
[2] And, outside Europe, of New York, Chicago, Philadelphia, Rio de Janeiro, Buenos Aires, Calcutta, Tokyo, and Osaka.

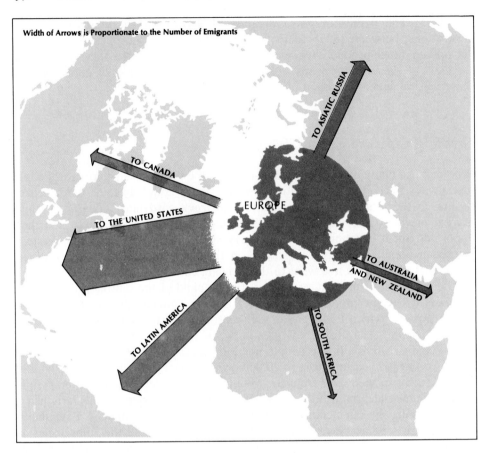

Width of Arrows is Proportionate to the Number of Emigrants

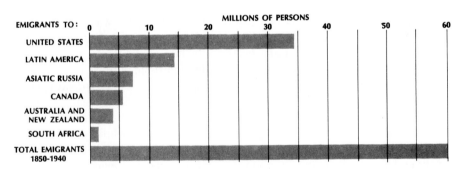

MIGRATION FROM EUROPE, 1850–1940

About 60 million people left Europe in the century preceding the Second World War, distributing themselves as shown in the diagram above. (See figures on p. 593.) About half went to the United States. This huge wave of settlement built up, outside of Europe, populous "European" countries which produced foods and raw materials for Europe and borrowed capital and bought manufactures from Europe, thus helping to support the increasingly dense European population and to build up a worldwide economic system.

Migration from Europe, 1850–1940

During the same period in which cities were growing, almost 60 million people left Europe altogether, of whom possibly a fifth sooner or later returned. The Atlantic Migration—aptly so called, because all crossed the ocean except those who moved from European to Asiatic Russia—towers above all others in magnitude, and possibly also in significance, for it was by this means that earlier colonial offshoots of Europe were transformed into new Europes alongside the old. All parts of Europe contributed, as shown in the table below, which comprises the years from 1850 to 1940. Before 1850 the mass movement had scarcely begun, though at that time over a million immigrants had entered the United States since the close of the Napoleonic wars. After 1940 the character of intercontinental migration was greatly transformed.

It is hard to give satisfactory figures for emigration from Europe. In the statistical sources the English, Scots, Welsh, and Irish are mixed, and until the First World War, that is until 1914, the Poles, Czechs, Yugoslavs, Hungarians, East European Jews, and others were included among emigrants from the Russian, Austro-Hungarian, and German empires. Millions of Jews, Irish, Poles, and many thousands of others are therefore invisible in the figures below, which also include several million Russians who moved from European to Asian parts of what became the Soviet Union. It must be remembered also that some intercontinental migration did not involve Europeans. For a few years after 1850 black slaves were still brought illegally to the United States and Brazil. Workers went from India to the West Indies and South Africa, and many Chinese settled in the United States and southeast Asia. With these reservations, the following table can be presented for the ninety years preceding the Second World War.

EMIGRATION FROM EUROPE, 1850–1940

From:	
British Isles	18,300,000
Italy	10,200,000
Russia	9,000,000
Germany	5,000,000
Spain	4,500,000
Austria-Hungary	4,200,000
Portugal	2,500,000
Sweden	1,200,000
Norway	750,000
Denmark	470,000
Finland	390,000
France	390,000
Switzerland	340,000
Netherlands	210,000
Belgium	150,000
	57,600,000

SOURCE: William Woodruff, *The Impact of Western Man* (New York: St. Martin's Press, 1966), p. 106.

The British and Irish went to the British dominions and the United States. The Italians divided between the United States and Latin America. Spaniards settled overwhelmingly in the Spanish American republics, and the Portuguese in Brazil. The Germans moved overwhelmingly to the United States, though some went to Argentina and Brazil. The new countries received the following influxes of people:

IMMIGRATION INTO VARIOUS COUNTRIES, 1850–1940	
To: United States	32,300,000
Asiatic Russia	7,000,000
Argentina	6,600,000
Brazil	4,700,000
Canada	4,300,000
Australia	2,900,000
New Zealand	650,000
Uruguay	600,000
Cuba	600,000
South Africa	250,000
Mexico	250,000

SOURCE: Woodruff, *Impact*, p. 108.

The extraordinary preponderance of the United States is apparent. At the same time, it is well to rectify the impressions of most Americans on the subject. Almost half the European migration was directed elsewhere than to the United States. Asiatic Russia was second only to the United States in the receipt of new settlers. Germany was by no means a chief source of emigration in this period, especially in proportion to the total national population from which emigrants came. Canada received fewer immigrants than Argentina, and New Zealand was closely followed by Cuba and Uruguay.

The exodus from Europe was due to a remarkable and temporary juxtaposition of causes. One fundamental cause, or precondition, was that before 1914 the new countries welcomed immigration. Hands were wanted to farm the land, build houses, dig in the mines. This was least true of Australia and New Zealand, which preferred to limit themselves to English-speaking settlers, and which also pioneered as social democracies, becoming models, even before 1900, of legislation to protect the working classes. One result was that no inrush of outsiders to compete for jobs at low wages was desired. A similar combination of national preferences and labor protectionism led to laws restricting immigration in the United States in 1921 and 1924. Thereafter immigrants could enter only under quotas, and the quotas were lowest for eastern and southern Europe from which most emigration was then forthcoming.

In Europe there were many conditions propelling emigrants outward. Physically, the steamship made it easier and cheaper to cross the sea, and the railroad helped people to get to the ports as well as to distribute themselves after landing in the new countries. Economically, people in the mass could for the first time afford a long journey. People migrated to improve their material circumstances; but some crests in the wave of emigration coincided with crests in the business cycle in Europe, when jobs in Europe were plentiful and wages at their highest.

Of the opposite case, of actual flight from economic ruin or starvation, the emigration from Ireland after 1846 is the best example. After the revolutions of 1848 a certain number left Europe for political reasons, and, later on, to avoid compulsory military service. The best example of flight from actual persecution is that of the Jews of Russia and Russian Poland, of whom a million and a half moved to the United States in the fifteen years preceding the First World War.

But perhaps most basic in the whole European exodus was the underlying liberalism of the age. Never before (nor since) had people been legally so free to move. Old laws requiring skilled workmen to stay in their own countries were repealed, as in England in 1824.[3] The old semicommunal agricultural villages, with collective rights and obligations, holding the individual to his native group, fell into disuse except in Russia. The disappearance of serfdom allowed the peasant of eastern Europe to change his residence without obtaining a lord's permission.[4] Governments permitted their subjects to emigrate, to take with them their savings of shillings, marks, kronen, or lire, and to change nationality by becoming naturalized in their new homes. The rise of liberty in Europe, as well as the hope of enjoying it in America, made possible the great emigration. For so huge a mass movement the most remarkable fact is that it took place by private initiative and at private expense. Individuals, families, and small local groups (to borrow the metaphor of one authority) detached themselves atom by atom from the mass of Europe, crossed the seas on their own, and reattached themselves atom by atom to the accumulating mass of the New World.

73. The World Economy of the Nineteenth Century

How did the swelling population of Europeans manage to feed itself? How, in fact, did it not merely feed itself but enjoy an incomparably higher standard of living in 1900 than in 1800? By science, industry, transportation, and communications. And by organization—in business, finance, and labor.

The "New Industrial Revolution"

The Industrial Revolution entered upon a new phase. The use of steam power, the growth of the textile and metallurgical industries, and the advent of the railroad had characterized the early part of the century. Now, after 1870, new sources of power were tapped, the already mechanized industries expanded, new industries appeared, and industry spread geographically.

The steam engine itself was refined and improved. By 1914 it still predominated over other power machinery, but electricity with its incomparable advantages came into use. The invention of the internal combustion (or gasoline) engine and the diesel engine gave the world automobiles, airplanes, and submarines in the two decades before 1914; the advent of the automotive and aviation industries made oil one of the most coveted of natural resources. In the new chemical industries industrial research laboratories were replacing the individual inventor.

[3] See p. 489.
[4] See pp. 509–510, 520.

Chemists discovered new fertilizers, and from coal tar alone produced a bewildering array of new products ranging from artificial food flavors to high explosives. With the latter the first great tunnels were built, the Mount Cenis in 1873, the Simplon in 1906—both in the Alps; and great new canals, the Suez in 1869, the Kiel in 1895, the Panama in 1914. Chemistry made possible the production of synthetic fabrics like rayon which revolutionized the textile industry. Electricity transformed all indoor and outdoor lighting. There was a communications revolution too. The telephone appeared in the 1870s. Marconi brought the continents closer together, successfully transmitting wireless signals across the Atlantic in 1901. The moving picture and the radio modestly presented themselves before 1914. Medicine ran a tongue-twisting alphabetical gamut from anesthetics to x-rays; yellow fever was overcome. Vastly improved processes for refining iron ore made possible a great expansion in the production of steel, the key product of the new industrial age; aluminum and other metal alloys were also being produced. Railroad mileage multiplied; the European network, including the Russian, increased from 140,000 miles in 1890 to 213,000 in 1914.

In the new phase of the Industrial Revolution machine industry spread geographically from Britain and Belgium, the only truly industrial countries in 1870, to France, Italy, Russia, Japan, and, most markedly, to Germany and the United States. In Europe industrial production was concentrated in the "inner zone." Three powers alone—Britain, Germany, and France—accounted in 1914 for more than seven-tenths of all European manufactures and produced over four-fifths of all European coal, steel, and machinery. Of the major European powers Germany was now forging ahead. To use steel alone as a criterion, in 1871 Germany was producing annually three-fifths as much steel as Britain; by 1900 it was producing more, and by 1914 it was producing twice as much as Britain— but only half as much as the new industrial giant, the United States. By 1914 American steel output was greater than that of Germany, Britain, and France combined. Britain, the pioneer in mechanization, was being outstripped in both the old world and the new. The three European powers increased their industrial production by about 50 percent in the two decades before 1914, but the United States had a far higher annual growth rate from 1870 to 1913, 4.3 percent as compared to the next leading powers, Germany with 2.9 percent, Britain with 2.2 percent, and France with 1.6 percent.[5] By 1914 the United States had moved ahead of Europe in the mechanization of agriculture, in manufactures, and in coal and steel production, in which it was producing over two-fifths of the world's output. The Americans were pioneering also in assembly-line, conveyor-belt techniques for the mass production of automobiles and all kinds of consumer goods.

Free Trade and the European "Balance of Payments"

It was Britain in the mid–nineteenth century, then the workshop of the world, that had inaugurated the movement toward free trade. It will be recalled that in 1846, by the repeal of the Corn Laws, the British embarked upon a systematic

[5] *The New Cambridge Modern History*, Volume XII, rev. ed. (Cambridge: Cambridge University Press, 1968), p. 40.

CLASSIC LANDSCAPE
by Charles Sheeler (American, 1883–1965)
This landscape depicts the River Rouge plant of the Ford Motor Company in 1931, but it also symbolizes what has been called the Second Industrial Revolution, in which electricity, the internal combustion engine, and the automobile were important, and industry spread beyond its original centers in Britain and Western Europe. The picture is "classic" in its clear delineation, its array of familiar mathematical forms, and the universality of its message. The plant seems rational and precise, but the absence of human beings is to be noted; it is as if the machine had a life of its own and could do without human hands. The sharp shadows suggest bright sunshine, despite the smoke pouring from the tall chimney. When the picture was painted no one was alarmed about atmospheric pollution. Courtesy of Mrs. Edsel B. Ford.

free trade policy, deliberately choosing to become dependent upon overseas imports for their food.[6] France adopted free trade in 1860.[7] Other countries soon followed. It is true that by 1880 there was a movement back to protective tariffs, except in Britain, Holland, and Belgium. But the tariffs were impediments rather than barriers, and until 1914 the characteristic of the economic system was the extreme mobility of goods across political frontiers. Politically, Europe was more than ever nationalistic; but economic activity, under generally liberal conditions in which business was supposed to be free from the political state, remained predominantly international and globe-encircling.

Broadly speaking, the great economic accomplishment of Europe before 1914 was to create a system by which the huge imports used by industrial Europe could be acquired and paid for. All European countries except Russia, Austria-Hungary, and the Balkan states imported more than they exported. It was the British again that had led in this direction. Britain had been a predominantly importing country since the close of the eighteenth century. That is to say, despite the expanding export of cotton manufactures and other products of the Industrial Revolution, Britain consumed more goods from abroad than it sent out. Industrialization and urbanization in the nineteenth century confirmed the same situation. Between 1800 and 1900 the value of British exports multiplied eightfold, but the value of imports into Great Britain multiplied tenfold, and in the decade before 1914 the British had an import surplus of about three-quarters of a billion dollars a year. Great Britain and the industrial countries of Europe together (roughly Europe's "inner zone"), at the beginning of the twentieth century, were drawing in an import surplus, measured in dollars, of almost $2 billion every year (the dollar then representing far more goods than it came to represent later). The imports into Europe's inner zone consisted of raw materials for its industries and of food and amenities for its people.

How were the imports paid for? How did Europe enjoy a favorable "balance of payments" despite an unfavorable balance of trade in commodities? Export of European manufactures paid for some imports, and even most, but not all. It was the so-called invisible exports that made up the difference, that is, shipping and insurance services rendered to foreigners, and interest on money lent out or invested, all bringing in foreign exchange. Shipping and insurance were important. An Argentine merchant in Buenos Aires, to ship hides to Germany, might employ a British vessel; he would pay the freight charges in Argentine pesos, which might be credited to the account of the British shipowner in an Argentine bank; the British shipowner would sell the pesos to someone, in England or elsewhere in Europe, who needed them to buy Argentine meat. The far-flung British merchant marine thus earned a considerable amount of the food and raw materials needed by Britain. To insure themselves against risks of every conceivable kind people all over the world turned to Lloyds of London. With the profits drawn from selling insurance the British could buy what they wished. Governments or business enterprises borrowed money in Europe, mainly in England; the interest payments, putting foreign currencies into European and British hands,

[6] See p. 494.
[7] See p. 530.

constituted another invisible export by which an excess of imports could be financed. But the lending of money to foreigners is only part of a larger phenomenon, the export of capital.

The Export of European Capital

The migration of millions of Europeans had the effect of creating new societies, basically European in character, which both purchased manufactures from Europe and produced the food, wool, cotton, and minerals that Europe needed. It could not have had this effect if Europe had exported people only, especially people of such small means as most emigrants were. Europe also exported the capital necessary to get the new settlers and the new worlds into production.

The export of capital meant that an older and wealthier country, instead of using its whole annual income to raise its own standard of living, or to add to its own capital by expanding or improving its houses, factories, machinery, mines, transportation, etc., diverted some of its income to expanding or improving the houses, factories, machinery, mines, and transportation of foreign countries. It meant that British, French, Dutch, Belgian, Swiss, and eventually German investors in the desire to increase their income bought the stocks of foreign business enterprises and the bonds of foreign businesses and governments; or they organized companies of their own to operate in foreign climes; or their banks granted loans to banks in New York or Tokyo, which then lent the funds to local users. Capital arose in Europe to some extent from the savings of quite small people, especially in France, where peasants and modest bourgeois families were notably thrifty. But most capital accumulated from savings by the well-to-do. The owners of a business concern, for example, instead of spending the concern's income by paying higher wages, took a portion of it in profits or dividends, and instead of spending all this on their own living, reinvested part of it in domestic or foreign enterprises. The gap between rich and poor was thus one cause of the rapid accumulation of capital, though the accumulation of capital, in the nineteenth century, produced in turn a steady rise of living standards for the working classes. In a sense, however, the common people of western Europe, by forgoing the better housing, diet, education, or pleasures that a more democratic or consumer-oriented society might have planned for them, made possible the export of capital and hence the financing and building up of other regions of the world.

The British were the chief exporters of capital, followed at some distance by the French, and at the close of the century by the Germans. As early as the 1840s half the annual increase of wealth in Great Britain was going into foreign investments. By 1914 the British had $20 billion in foreign investments, the French about $8.7 billion, the Germans about $6 billion. A quarter of all the wealth owned by the inhabitants of Great Britain consisted in 1914 of holdings outside the country. Almost a sixth of the French national wealth lay in investments outside of France. All three countries had given hostages to fortune, and fortune proved unkind, for in the First World War the British lost about a quarter of their foreign investments, the French about a third, the Germans all.

These huge sums, pouring out from Europe's inner zone for a century before 1914, at first went mainly to finance the Americas and the less affluent regions of

Europe.[8] No country except Great Britain completely built its railways with its own resources. In the United States the railway system was built very largely with capital obtained from England. In central and eastern Europe British companies often constructed the first railways, then sold out to native operating companies or to governments which subsequently ran them. In the Argentine Republic the British not merely financed and built the railways, but long continued to operate and own them. In addition, up to 1914 the British sold about 75 million tons of coal a year to South America to keep the railways going, not to mention items for replacement and upkeep of equipment. Docks, warehouses, mines, plantations, processing and manufacturing establishments all over the world were similarly built up with capital drawn from Europe. European capital also helped emigrants in the new countries to live in a civilized fashion. In the United States, for example, state and local governments very commonly sold their bonds in Europe, to build roads, pave streets, or construct school systems for the westward-moving population. A few of these American bonds proved a partial or total loss to European investors. On the whole, by 1914, the United States had paid back a good deal of its indebtedness. Even so, in 1914, Americans still owed about $4 billion to Europeans—a sum three times as large as the national debt of the United States at the time.

An International Money System: The Gold Standard

The international economy rested upon an international money system, based in turn upon the almost universal acceptance of the gold standard. England had adopted the gold standard in 1821, when the pound sterling was legally defined as the equivalent of 113 grains of fine gold. Western Europe and the United States adopted an exclusively gold standard in the 1870s. A person holding any "civilized" money—pounds, francs, dollars, marks, etc.—could turn it into gold at will, and a person holding gold could turn it into any money. The currencies were like so many different languages all expressing the same thing. All had substantially the same value, and until 1914 the exchange rates between currencies remained highly stable. It was assumed that no civilized country's currency ever "fell"; such things might happen in Turkey or China, or in the French Revolution, but not in the world of practical men, modern progress, and civilized affairs.

The important currencies were all freely exchangeable. A Frenchman, selling silks to a German, and hence receiving German marks, could turn the marks into francs, pounds sterling, or dollars. That is, he was not obliged to buy from Germany or spend his money in Germany but could use the proceeds of his German sale to buy French, British, or American goods or services as he chose. Trade was multilateral. A country needing imports from another country, such as American cotton, did not have to sell to that country to obtain them; it could sell its own goods anywhere and then import according to its needs.

It was the acceptance of the gold standard, and the fact that all important countries possessed a sufficient share of gold to support their currencies, that

---

[8] The penetration of European capital into Asia and Africa, after about 1890, is considered in the following chapter.

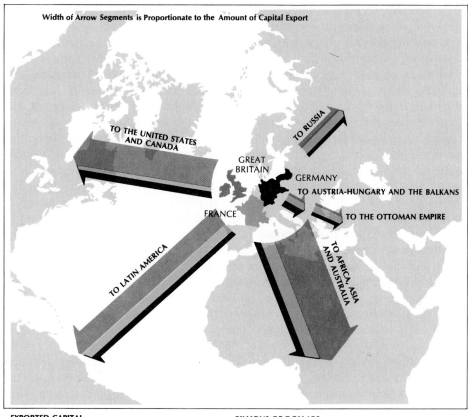

Width of Arrow Segments is Proportionate to the Amount of Capital Export

TO THE UNITED STATES AND CANADA

TO RUSSIA

GREAT BRITAIN

GERMANY

TO AUSTRIA-HUNGARY AND THE BALKANS

FRANCE

TO THE OTTOMAN EMPIRE

TO LATIN AMERICA

TO AFRICA, ASIA AND AUSTRALIA

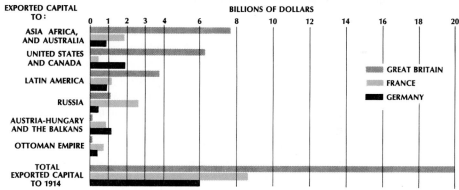

EXPORT OF EUROPEAN CAPITAL TO 1914

In 1914 the British, French, and Germans held upwards of $30 billion in foreign and colonial loans and investments, distributed as shown on the map. Dutch investments, especially in the Netherlands Indies, together with Swiss, Belgian, and Scandinavian holdings, would add several billion dollars more. Proceeds from such investments helped Europeans to pay for the excess of their imports over exports. New and undeveloped countries were built up by capital borrowed from Europe. British capital predominated in the overseas world, while the less advanced regions of eastern Europe and the Near East were financed mainly from Germany and France. Much of the investment shown on this map was lost or expended in the First World War.

made possible so fluid an interchange. At the same time the gold standard had less wholesome effects. It was hard on countries that lacked gold. And it produced a gradual fall of prices, especially between 1870 and 1900, because (until the gold discoveries in South Africa, Australia, and Alaska in the 1890s) the world's production of gold lagged behind the expanding production of industrial and agricultural goods. Persistently declining prices were a hardship to those who habitually worked with borrowed money—many farmers, many businessmen, and debtor nations as a whole. A famous speech of William Jennings Bryan in the United States in 1896, declaring that mankind should not be crucified "upon this cross of gold," expressed a restlessness that was worldwide. But falling prices were an advantage to the wage-earning class, which generally improved its position in these years, and also to the wealthy, the owners and lenders of capital, the bankers and financiers, who so long as prices were falling were repaid in money of more value than that which they had lent.

The center of the global economic and financial system was London. The London banks came forward in consequence of the defeat of Napoleon, the older financial centers in Amsterdam having been ruined in the Revolutionary and Napoleonic wars. It may be recalled also that the victors in 1815 imposed upon France an indemnity of 700 million francs, which in 1818 was taken over by a syndicate of private bankers; the London banks played a leading part in this affair and so developed their connections with many government treasuries.[9] In the Crimean War of 1854–1856, with England at war with Russia, the London banks floated loans for the Russian government—so independent were business and politics at the time. The early adoption of the gold standard in England meant that many people, British and foreign, kept their funds in the form of sterling on deposit in London, where quantities of available capital therefore accumulated.

The banks, too, grew up in the financing of the British export trade, itself borne on the tide of the Industrial Revolution. A small Lancashire manufacturer, for example, might receive an order for a gross of scissors from an unknown merchant in Trieste. He would draw a bill or "sight draft" against the Trieste merchant, and take this bill to a financial institution known as an acceptance house. The acceptance house, which in the course of its business had acquired a microscopic knowledge of the credit of thousands of individuals and firms in all parts of the world, would then "discount" the bill, giving cash to the Lancashire manufacturer and collecting from the Trieste merchant through international banking channels. In this way the bank took a burden off the British manufacturer, and extended short-term credit to foreigners for the purchase of British goods. Many acceptance houses gradually went into the business of long-term foreign lending also. London became the apex of a pyramid which had the world for its base. It was the main center of exchange of currencies, the clearinghouse of the world's debts, the depository from which all the world borrowed, the banker's bank, the insurance agency's resort for reinsurance, as well as the world's shipping center and the headquarters of many international corporations.

[9] See pp. 451, 478.

A World Market: Unity, Competition—and Insecurity

Never had the earth been so unified economically, with each region playing its due role in a global specialization. Western Europe, and in 1870 mainly Great Britain, was the world's industrial workshop. Other parts of the earth supplied its many needs. An English economist marveled in 1866 that Britain now had its granaries in Chicago and Odessa, its forests in Canada and the Baltic, its sheep farms in Australia, and its gold and silver mines in California and Peru, while drinking tea brought from China and coffee from East Indian plantations. The same could have been said of most of Europe's "inner zone" by the time of the First World War.

A true world market had been created. Goods, services, money, capital, people moved back and forth almost without regard to national boundaries. Articles were bought and sold at uniform world prices. Dealers in wheat, for example, followed prices in Minneapolis, Liverpool, Buenos Aires, and Danzig as reported by telegraph and cable from day to day. They bought where it was cheapest, and sold where it was dearest. In this way the world's wheat supply was distributed roughly according to need or ability to pay. The worker of Milan, if the Italian crop was poor and prices high, was fed from another source. On the other hand, the Italian wheat grower would in this case feel the pinch of world competition. The world market, while it organized the world into a unified economic system, at the same time brought distant regions into competition for the first time. The producer—whether businessman, factory employee, farmer, or coffee planter— had no secure outlet for his product, as had generally been true in the past. He was in competition not only with the man across the street or down the road, but with the world.

The creation of an integrated world market, the financing and building up of countries outside of Europe, and the consequent feeding and support of Europe's increasing population were the great triumphs of the nineteenth-century system of unregulated capitalism. The system was intricate, with thousands and even millions of individuals and business firms supplying each other's wants without central planning. But it was extremely precarious, and the position of most people in it was exceedingly vulnerable. Region competed against region, and person against person. A fall of grain prices in the American Middle West, besides ruining a few speculators, might oblige the Prussian or Argentine wheat grower to sell at a price at which he could not live. A factory owner might be driven out of business if his competitor successfully undersold him or if a new commodity made his own product obsolete. The worker, hired only when needed by an employer, faced unemployment when business slackened, or the permanent disappearance of his job by the next labor-saving invention. The system went through cycles of boom and depression, the most notable example of the latter being the long depression that set in about 1873 and lasted to about 1893. It rested on expansion and on credit; but sometimes people could not pay their debts, so that credit collapsed, and sometimes expansion failed to keep pace with expectations, and anticipated profits proved to be losses. To combat the essential insecurity of private capitalism, all manner of devices were resorted to. Governments adopted protective tariffs on the one hand and social insurance and welfare legislation on the other; trade unionism and socialist movements grew; business mergers took place. These and other measures, to which we shall return, signalized the gradual decline in the years after 1880 of nineteenth-century unregulated, laissez-faire capitalism.

Changes in Organization: Big Business

A great change came over capitalism itself about 1880 or 1890. Formerly characterized by a very large number of very small units, small businesses run by individuals, partnerships, or small companies, it was increasingly characterized by large and impersonal corporations. The attractions of the "limited liability" corporation as a form of business organization and as a means of encouraging investment arose from laws, enacted by most countries in the nineteenth century, which limited the individual investor's personal loss in the event of a bankruptcy to the amount of his shares of stock in the enterprise. The corporation, in its modern form appearing first with the railroads, became the usual form of organization for industry and commerce. As machinery grew more complicated only a large pool of capital could finance it. And as corporations grew in size and number, relying on the sale of stock and the issue of bonds, the influence of banking and financial circles was enhanced. Financiers, using not so much their own money as the savings of others, had a new power to create or to extinguish, to stimulate, discourage, or combine corporate enterprises in various industries. Industrial capitalism brought finance capitalism with it.[10]

Corporate organization made it possible to concentrate economic processes under unified management. In retail commerce, large department stores appeared about 1890 in the United States and France. In industry, steel offers a good example. Steel became in any case a big business when heavy blast furnaces were introduced. It was not safe for the steel business, or for the blast furnaces, to rely for iron and coal on independent producers who might sell to whomsoever they pleased. The steel works therefore began to operate mines of their own or to buy out or otherwise reduce coal and iron mines to subsidiary status. Some, to assure their markets, began to produce not merely steel but steel manufactures as well—steel ships, railway equipment, naval and military ordnance. Thus entire processes from mining to finished product became concentrated in a "vertical" integration. By "horizontal" integration concerns at the same level combined with each other to reduce competition and to protect themselves against fluctuations in prices and in markets. Some fixed prices, some agreed to restrict production, some divided up markets among themselves. They were called trusts in the United States, cartels in Europe. They were common in many of the new industries at the close of the century, such as chemicals, aluminum, and oil. In steel such combinations produced the great interests of Krupp in Germany, Schneider-Creusot in France, Vickers-Armstrong in Great Britain. It was in the United States that such big business developed furthest, headed by "captains" of industry and "titans" of finance. Andrew Carnegie, by origin a poor Scottish immigrant boy, produced more steel than all England; in 1901 he sold out to an even more colossal organization, the United States Steel Corporation, formed by the financier J. P. Morgan. It was in the United States, too, that concern over monopoly and

---

[10] See pp. 529–530, 573.

the power of big business in general was felt most strongly; antitrust legislation, beginning with the Sherman Act of 1890, was enacted but never with any substantial effect.

Many of the new combinations were beneficial in making the ups and downs of business less erratic, and so providing more stable prices and more continuous and secure employment. Generally they reduced the costs of production; but whether the savings went into higher profits, higher wages, or lower prices depended on numerous factors. Some trusts were more greedy than others or confronted with only weakly organized or unorganized labor. In any case, for good or ill, decisions rested with management and finance. A new kind of private power had arisen, which its critics like to call "feudal." Since no economic system had ever been so centralized up to that time, never in fact had so few people exercised so much economic power over so many. The middle class, with the rise of great corporations, came typically to consist of salaried employees; the salaried man might spend a lifetime with the same company, and feel toward it, in its disputes with labor or government, a loyalty not unlike that of a lord's retainer in feudal times. The laboring class was less amenable; labor attempted to organize unions capable of dealing with increasingly gigantic employers. It also after about 1880 played an increasingly decisive role in the politics of all advanced nations.

74. The Advance of Democracy: Third French Republic, United Kingdom, German Empire

In the years from 1815 to 1870 European political life had been marked by liberal agitation for constitutional government, representative assemblies, responsible ministries, and guarantees of individual liberties. In the years from 1871 to 1914, even where these liberal objectives were not fully achieved but remained as goals, the most notable political development was the democratic extension of the vote to the working class—the adoption of universal male suffrage, which in turn meant for the first time the creation of mass political parties and the need for political leaders to appeal to a wide electorate. The extension of the suffrage in these years did not take place because of popular agitation as in the days of the Chartists or of the radical reformers in France. Governments for a variety of reasons extended the suffrage on their own. Often democratization took place in a continuing monarchical and aristocratic framework, but almost everywhere by 1914 the machinery at least of democratic self-government was being established. In addition, to counter the growing strength of socialism after 1871, and for humanitarian reasons, governments were also assuming responsibility for the social and economic problems arising from industrialism. The welfare state in its modern form was taking shape.

France: The Establishment of the Third Republic

In France the democratic republic was not easily established, and its troubled early years left deep cleavages within the country. It will be recalled that in

September 1870, when the empire of Napoleon III revealed its helplessness in the Franco-Prussian War, insurrectionaries in Paris, as in 1792 and 1848, again proclaimed the Republic.[11] A provisional government of national defense sought desperately to continue the war, but the cause was hopeless. By January 1871, a bitter siege of Paris came to an end and an armistice was signed. Bismarck, insisting that only a properly constituted government could make peace, permitted the election, by universal male suffrage, of a National Assembly which was to consider his peace terms and draft a constitution for the new French state. When the elections were held in February, it was found, as in 1848 (and, indeed, 1797), that republicanism was so distrusted by the French people as a whole, and most especially in the provinces and rural areas, that a free election brought monarchist elements into power.[12] Republicanism was still thought to be violent—bellicose in its foreign policy, turbulent in its political workings, unfriendly to the church, and socialistic or at least equalitarian in its views of property and private wealth. The new Assembly contained only about 200 republicans out of more than 600 deputies.

But the Paris republicans, who had defended France when Napoleon III failed to do so, who for four months had been besieged, starved, and frozen by the Germans, and who still refused to make peace on the harsh terms imposed by Bismarck and about to be accepted by the Assembly, refused to recognize the latter's authority. A civil war broke out between the National Assembly, now sitting at Versailles, and the city of Paris, where a revolutionary municipal council or "Commune" was set up. Paris, so lately attacked by German soldiers, was now attacked by French.

The Paris Commune, which lasted from March to May 1871, seemed to be another explosion of social revolution. Actually, it was in essence a revival of the Jacobinism of 1793. It was fiercely patriotic and republican, anti-German, opposed to wealthy bourgeois, aristocrats, and clergy, in favor of government controls upon prices, wages, and working conditions, but still not socialist in any sweeping or systematic way. Among its leaders, however, there were a few of the new international revolutionary socialists, who saw in a Jacobin or democratic republic a step toward their new order. Marx in England, and others elsewhere, hopefully read into the Commune the impending doom of the bourgeoisie. This was precisely what more conservative elements feared. To many of the French middle and peasant class, and to people like them all over Europe, it seemed that the "Communards" were wild and savage destroyers of nineteenth-century civilization. The fighting in Paris was atrocious beyond anything known in any preceding French revolution. The Communards, in final desperation, burned a number of public buildings and put to death the archbishop of Paris, whom they held as a hostage. The forces of the National Assembly, when finally triumphant, were determined to root out the inveterate revolutionism of Paris. Some 330,000 persons were denounced, 38,000 arrested, 20,000 put to death, and 7,500 deported to New Caledonia. The Third Republic was born in an atmosphere of class hate and social terror.

The form of government for the new regime still had to be established. The

---

[11] See p. 558.
[12] See pp. 394, 503, 505.

monarchist majority in the Assembly was itself evenly divided between those who favored a restoration of the Bourbon family and those who favored the Orléanist. In the end, even after they were reconciled, the Bourbon candidate alienated everyone by his stiff insistence on a return to the white flag of the Bourbons. The monarchists checkmated each other. Meanwhile, after extended discussion of various constitutional projects, the Assembly adopted in 1875 not a constitution, but certain constitutive laws. By a margin of one vote, a resolution indirectly amounting to the establishment of a republic was passed. The new laws provided for a president, a parliament in two chambers, and a council of ministers, or cabinet, headed by a premier. The Senate was to be elected by a complicated and indirect system of election, the Chamber of Deputies by universal, direct, male suffrage.

Within two years, in 1877, the role of the president, the ministers, and the parliament was further clarified as a result of an unsuccessful attempt by an early president, Marshal MacMahon, to dismiss a premier of whom he did not approve but who had the backing of the Chamber. MacMahon proceeded to dissolve the Chamber and to hold new elections, but the example of Napoleon III's transformation of the Second Republic into an authoritarian regime was still fresh. The elections vindicated the principle of parliamentary primacy and of the responsibility of the premier and his cabinet to the legislature, a responsibility which in France meant generally but not exclusively to the lower house. The true executive in republican France for a long time was to be the premier and his cabinet, themselves held strictly to account by a majority of the legislature. Unfortunately, that majority, in a parliament where a dozen or so parties were represented, was always difficult to form and could be created only by unstable, temporary, shifting party alliances, coalitions, or blocs. No president, and indeed no premier, could henceforth dissolve the Chamber in order to hold new elections and consult the country as could be done in Britain. Actually, under the Third Republic the substantial machinery of state—ministries, prefectures, law courts, police, army, all under highly centralized control—was carried over virtually untouched as in all upheavals since the time of Napoleon I. France in the nineteenth century, so volatile in appearance, in effect underwent less extensive reorganization than any other leading country in Europe.

Troubles of the Third French Republic

Yet the Third Republic was precarious. The government had changed so often since 1789 that all forms of government seemed to be transitory. Questions which in other countries were party questions became in France questions of "regime"— monarchy versus republic. Many people, especially those influenced by the upper classes, the Catholic clergy, and the professional army officers, continued to feel a positive aversion to the republic. On the other hand, the unmerciful and vindictive repression of the Commune made many middle-class people sympathetic to the republicans. Many turned republican simply because no other form of government established itself, or because it was the form of government that divided the country the least. As republicanism took in wider elements of society, it became less revolutionary and less fearsome. In 1879, for the first time, republicans won control of both houses of the government. In the 1880s their radicalism hardly went further than the founding of a democratic and compulsory school system at government expense and the passage of anticlerical legislation intended to curb church influence in education.

For over a quarter of a century, however, republican energies had to be expended in defense of republican institutions in order to ensure the survival of the regime. An initial crisis arose in 1886–1889, when General Boulanger gathered around him an incongruous following that included not only Bonapartists, monarchists, and aristocrats but also extreme radical republicans, who wished a war of revenge against Germany, and workers disgruntled over their general lot. Boulanger became a popular figure and seemed for a moment about to seize power. But the menace collapsed in a comical failure as the general lost heart at the crucial hour and fled into exile. Meanwhile, in the 1880s and 1890s scandals and revelations of corruption in high republican circles provided ammunition for the antirepublicans. Moreover, the hope that unsympathetic French Catholics would rally to the republic, as urged by French prelates and by Pope Leo XIII in 1892, was shattered by the Dreyfus Affair, which in the late 1890s rocked the country and indeed the world.

In 1894 Captain Dreyfus, a Jewish army officer, was found guilty of treason by a military court and deported to Devil's Island. Evidence accumulated showing his innocence and pointing to the guilt of another officer, a Major Esterhazy, an adventurer known to be riddled with gambling debts. But the army refused to reopen the case, unwilling to admit it had erred; a staff officer, Major Henry, even forged documents to confirm Dreyfus' guilt. Meanwhile anti-Semites, royalists, traditionalists, militarists, and most of the "best" people fought the reopening of the case, deeming it unpatriotic to shake the nation's confidence in the army and wishing also to disgrace the republican regime. The partisans of Dreyfus stubbornly upheld him, both because they believed in justice and because they wished to discredit their adversaries. The country was deeply split. Finally, in 1899, Dreyfus was pardoned, and in 1906, fully exonerated. In the aftermath of the affair the left republicans and socialists revenged themselves by blocking the promotions of antirepublican officers and by anticlerical legislation. In 1905, in a series of laic laws, they "separated" church and state, ending the close relationship established under Napoleon's concordat a century earlier.

The Strength and Weakness of the Republic

The Third Republic, when the First World War came in 1914, a test which it was successfully to meet, had lasted over twice as long as any French regime since 1789. Born unwanted and accidentally, though it still had its opponents, it now commanded the loyalty of the overwhelming mass of the French people. What it had done, since 1871, was to domesticate democratic republicanism in Europe. Republicanism, one of the most militant of revolutionary movements down to 1870, had been shown in France to be compatible with order, law, parliamentary government, economic prosperity, and a mutual tolerance between classes, to the extent at least that they no longer butchered each other in the streets. Industrial workers were in many ways less well off than in England or Germany, but there were fewer of them; and for most people France in these years was a pleasant country, full of painters, writers, scholars, and scientists, full of bankers, bourgeois and well-established farmers, a country living comfortably and unhurriedly on the savings of generations, and one in which, in a close-knit family group, the average man could plan securely for his own and his children's future.

But the very comforts and values of bourgeois France were not those that would equip it for leadership in the modern age of technology and industrial power. Though substantial economic progress was made, the country lagged behind Germany in industrial development; the French entrepreneur showed little inclination to take the business risks needed for industrial growth. Politically, the fragmentation of political parties, itself a democratic reflection of a divided public opinion, and the distrust for historic reasons of a strong executive power led to the rise and fall of numerous short-lived ministries—no fewer than fifty in the years between 1871 and 1914. Ministerial instability was to be a chronic symptom of the Third Republic both before and after 1914; continuity of government policy was, however, generally maintained because of stability in certain key ministries and because of the permanent civil service.

French labor remained a steady source of discontent. Although French workers benefited from some labor legislation in the two decades after 1890, they continued to feel frustrated at the failure to establish a "social republic." Socialist representation in the Chamber grew. However, the most important single party of the republic, the Radicals, or Radical Socialists, were in actuality radical republicans—patriotic, anticlerical, spokesmen for the small shopkeepers and the lesser propertied interests; they drew the line at the advanced social legislation that labor expected from them, and on occasion their leaders even took positive steps to prevent unionization and to suppress strikes. Since some of these Radicals had started out as socialists, the distrust of French workers for all politicians and even for political processes was intensified. But the difficulties of the republic went deeper. The political energies of the republican statesmen had gone into liquidating the past, into curbing the political strength of the monarchists, the church, and the army; by the turn of the century, even before these older issues were fully resolved, the republic was compelled to meet the challenge of labor and to face other domestic and international pressures that were to try it sorely. The Third Republic was to weather the crisis of the First World War but not that of the Second.

The British Constitutional Monarchy

The British constitutional monarchy in the half-century before 1914 was the great exemplar of reasonable, orderly, and peaceable self-government through parliamentary methods. For over sixty years, spanning two-thirds of the nineteenth century, Victoria reigned (1837–1901) and gave her name to a distinguished era of material progress, literary accomplishment, and political stability. The two great parties, Liberal and Conservative, the heirs roughly of the Whigs and Tories, took form in the 1850s, the former producing its great leader in William E. Gladstone, the latter, a series of leaders of whom the most colorful was Benjamin Disraeli.

The advance toward an equalitarian political democracy in Britain was more cautious and slower than in France. The Reform Bill of 1832 had granted the vote to about an eighth of the adult male population. The democratic Chartist agitation of the 1830s and 1840s came to nothing.[13] In 1867, in response to continued demand for a wider suffrage, the Second Reform Bill was passed, Conservatives as well as Liberals outdoing one another in an effort to satisfy the country and to win new political strength for their own party. The bill, adopted under Disraeli's Conservative ministry, extended the suffrage from about 1 million eligible voters to about 2 million, or over a third of the adult males in the United Kingdom, reaching down far enough to include most workers in the cities. Disraeli's colleague Lord Derby called it a "leap in the dark." In 1884, under Liberal auspices, the suffrage was again broadened, this time in the rural areas, adding some 2 million additional voters and enfranchising over three-fourths of all adult males in the country. The suffrage still excluded agricultural workers who did not have a fixed residence, servants living with employers, and such people as unmarried grown sons who lived in the homes of their parents. Not until 1918 did Great Britain adopt universal male suffrage, as generally understood; and at that time women over thirty were given the vote too.

Despite the extension of the suffrage, the leadership of the country at the turn of the century was still in the hands of the upper and wealthier classes. Until 1911 the government paid no salaries to members of the House of Commons, who therefore, in both great parties, were usually gentlemen with private incomes, possessing the same family background and education. An attitude of sportsmanship and good feeling was characteristic of British politics. The two parties alternated in power at regular intervals, each indulgent toward the other, carrying over and developing rather than reversing the policies of its predecessor in office. Both parties sought support where they could find it, the Liberals leaning somewhat more on the industrial and commercial interests, the Conservatives on the landed aristocracy; both sought and succeeded in winning their share of the new working-class vote. It was in these years that both parties, when parliamentary reversals occurred, increasingly appealed to the country in general elections; the traditional crown and cabinet basis of British parliamentary government was being transformed into crown, cabinet, and country.

The Liberals were usually the more willing to pioneer, the first of the four

---

[13] See pp. 497–499, 504.

SUNDAY AFTERNOON ON THE ISLAND OF LA GRANDE JATTE
by Georges Seurat (French, 1859–1891)

This picture of sunny calm, painted in 1886, suggests something of the well-being brought to a great many people by the European civilization of the late nineteenth century. Whether boating, or idly fishing, or quietly sitting and watching, or strolling alone or in pairs or in families with their children, the figures seem to live in a peaceable world which a later age of war, speed, and mechanical amusements has made to seem far away. Technically this is one of the most remarkable pictures ever painted. The artist, an impressionist, created it without the use of lines by filling the canvas with thousands of minute dots of the primary colors, which so blur and mix in the eye as to produce the forms and hues of nature. As a result it seems to be a picture of light itself, with an actual shimmer on the water, an astonishing "grassiness" in the grass, with shadows that seem to be real shadows, and distant figures looking really distant as if seen through the intervening air. Courtesy of The Art Institute of Chicago.

ministries of Gladstone being especially notable in this respect. Gladstone in this first ministry (1868–1874) developed the principle of state-supported public education under the Forster Education Act of 1870, introduced the secret ballot, formally legalized labor unions, promoted competitive examinations for civil service posts, reorganized the upper judiciary, eliminated the purchase and sale of commissions in the army (a form of property in office), and by abolishing religious tests enabled persons not members of the Church of England to graduate from Oxford and Cambridge. The Conservative party, less sensitive to pressure from business interests for a laissez-faire policy in economic matters, and continuing the tradition of early Tory reformers, took the initiative in further labor legislation. Under Disraeli's second ministry (1874–1880), the existing acts regulating public sanitation and conditions in mines and factories were extended and codified, safety measures were enacted to protect sailors, and the first attempt to regulate housing conditions for the poorer classes was initiated. But the Liberals, it must be added, protected the workers' interests too. In Gladstone's second ministry (1880–1885) workers were assured of compensation for injuries not of their own responsibility, and in 1892, before the formation of his fourth ministry (1892–1894), Gladstone campaigned to shorten labor hours and to extend employers' liability in accidents.

British Political Changes after 1900

At the turn of the century important changes were discernible on the British political scene. Labor emerged as an independent political force, the Labour party itself being organized shortly after 1900.[14] The rise of labor had a deep impact upon the Liberal party, and indeed upon liberalism itself. With many persons insisting that protective measures be taken to counteract the poor health, low income, and economic insecurity of the British working people, the Liberals abandoned their traditional position of laissez faire and sponsored a policy of government intervention and social legislation in behalf of working people. The Liberals, though they acted in part for humanitarian reasons, were aware that with the emergence of the Labour party workers who customarily had voted for them might readily transfer their allegiance.

In control of the government from 1906 to 1916, with Herbert Asquith as prime minister and David Lloyd George as chancellor of the exchequer during most of this time, the Liberals put through a spectacular program of social welfare. Sickness, accident, old-age, and a degree of unemployment insurance were adopted, and a moderate minimum wage law was enacted. Labor exchanges, or employment bureaus, were set up over the country. Restrictions on strikes and other trade union activities were removed. To meet the costs of the new program as well as of other government expenditures, Lloyd George's budget of 1909 called for progressive income and inheritance taxes: the wealthier the taxpayer, the higher the rate at which he was taxed. He was in effect advancing the then novel idea of using taxation to modify the extremes of wealth and poverty. It was a "war budget," he said, intended "to wage war against poverty." Its fiscal measures were directed primarily at the landed aristocracy, and it aroused great

[14] See pp. 619–621.

opposition, especially in the House of Lords, where the contest over the budget led to a further constitutional curtailment of the power of the upper house. The Parliament Act of 1911 deprived the Lords of all veto power in money matters and of all but a two-year delaying veto on action of the Commons in other legislation. At this time, too, the government voted to pay salaries to members of the House of Commons, making it possible for workers and others without independent incomes to take seats in Parliament. This last measure was adopted to counteract a court ruling, the Osborne Judgment of 1909, that trade unions could not pay the salaries of workers elected to Parliament.

The Liberal party was embracing a program of positive state intervention in social and economic matters that the older liberalism, nurtured on the doctrines of laissez faire and the Manchester School, would not have accepted. With the Liberals actively seeking the support of labor and altering much in their traditional program, the Conservatives in the twentieth century tended to become the party of industry as well as of landed wealth and to replace the Liberals as the champions of economic liberalism and laissez faire. In the next generation, after the First World War, the Conservatives were to remain one of the two major parties of the country; the Liberals were to be far outstripped by the Labour party.

Meanwhile, despite its gains, labor was not pacified. Real wages showed a tendency to fall after 1900, and great coal and railway strikes broke out in 1911 and 1912. The British capacity to survive crises without violence, while still conspicuous, was being strained. An even more serious threat came from Ireland.

The Irish Question

Britain suffered from one of the worst minorities questions in Europe—the Irish question. After 1801 Britain was known as the United Kingdom of Great Britain and Ireland, Ireland having been incorporated into the United Kingdom as a defensive measure against pro-French sympathies in Ireland during the wars of the French Revolution.[15] The Irish representatives who sat in Parliament were generally obstructionist in their tactics. The Irish had many substantial grievances, among which two were conspicuous. The Irish peasant was defenseless against his landlord, far more so, for example, than the French peasant before 1789; and the Irish people, though predominantly Catholic, were obliged to pay tithes to the established Church of Ireland (an Anglican sister church to the Church of England), which also owned a good deal of the land.

Gladstone, in his first ministry, disestablished the Church of Ireland. He also initiated measures to protect the Irish farm tenant. By 1900, under Conservative auspices, Irish tenants were being assisted by the British government to buy out their landlords—often Englishmen or Anglicized and absentee Irishmen. The Irish also wanted home rule, or a parliament of their own. Gladstone, in trying to give it to them in 1886, split his Liberal party, part of which went along with the Conservatives, not wishing political division of the British Isles. Home rule was finally granted to Ireland in 1914. But the Ulstermen, Presbyterians of north Ireland, objected vehemently to inclusion in an autonomous Ireland, in which they would be outnumbered by the Catholics of the south. The latter, however,

---

[15] See pp. 350, 395.

insisted with equal vehemence on the inclusion of Ulster, not wishing a political division of Ireland.

The Ulstermen, backed by British Conservatives, started arming and drilling to resist the act of Parliament that authorized home rule. Great Britain, in 1914, was about to see a civil war on its own doorstep. It suffered from something of the insoluble nationalistic disputes that afflicted Austria-Hungary. During the First World War home rule was suspended, and after considerable violence on both sides Catholic Ireland (Eire) received dominion status in 1922, but eventually dissolved all ties with Britain. Ulster remained in the United Kingdom and was dominated by Protestants, so that its Catholic minority remained discontented. No satisfactory solution has yet been found to the "Irish question."

Bismarck and the German Empire, 1871–1890

The German Empire, as put together by Bismarck in 1871 with William I, king of Prussia, as Kaiser, was a federation of monarchies, a union of twenty-five German states, in which the weight of monarchical Prussia, the Prussian army, and the Prussian landed aristocracy was preponderant. It developed neither the strong constitutionalism of England nor the democratic equality that was characteristic of France. To win popular support for his projects, Bismarck exploited existing democratic and socialist sentiment and provided that members of the Reichstag, the lower chamber, be elected by universal male suffrage.[16] Remaining chancellor of the united empire for some twenty years, from 1871 to 1890, he usually tried to have a majority in the Reichstag on his side, but he recognized no dependence on a majority in principle, holding to the doctrine that it was the emperor and his chancellor who were to govern the country. Moreover, in practice, the legislative powers of the lower house were severely restricted, and the upper chamber, representing the princes and not the people, and favored by the government, tended to be more important. Despite the nature of the empire, the Prussian conservatives, the East-Elbian Junker landlords, were at first by no means enthusiastic over Bismarck's unified Germany.[17] They opposed his democratic concessions and were left horrified when in 1872 he undertook to extinguish what was left of their manorial jurisdiction over their peasants.

Bismarck in the 1870s therefore leaned not on the Conservatives but on the National Liberals. With their aid he put through a number of economic and legal measures designed to consolidate the unity of the new empire. Bismarck's first serious conflict developed with the Catholic church. At the very time that he was bent on subordinating all groups within the state to the sovereign power of the new empire, the church had spoken out. In 1864 in the *Syllabus of Errors,* it denounced the encroachment of all governments on educational and church affairs; in 1870 the new dogma of papal infallibility made it incumbent on Catholics to accept unreservedly the pope's pronouncements in matters of faith and morals.[18] To many, the implication was that the new empire could not count on the

[16] See pp. 556, 559.
[17] See pp. 514, 552–554.
[18] See pp. 632–634.

undivided loyalty of its Catholic citizens. To defend Catholic interests and those of the south German states where Catholicism predominated, Catholic elements had organized the strong Center party, which now upheld the church pronouncements. In 1871 Bismarck launched the so-called *Kulturkampf,* or "battle for modern civilization." The Liberals joined in eagerly. Like nineteenth-century liberals elsewhere (Gladstone's campaign against Anglican privilege and the French laic laws have just been mentioned), they were strongly anticlerical and disapproved of the influence of organized churches in public and private life. Laws were put through imposing restrictions upon Catholic worship and education, the Jesuits were expelled, and many Catholic bishops throughout Germany were arrested or went into exile. But Bismarck gradually concluded that the anti-Catholic legislation was fruitless, that he had overestimated the danger to the state of organized Catholicism, and that he needed the support of the Center party for other parts of his program.

In 1879, with the support of the Center and Conservative parties but to the dismay of many of his erstwhile Liberal allies, Bismarck abandoned free trade and adopted a protective tariff that provided needed revenues for the government and gave satisfaction both to agricultural and industrial interests. Meanwhile, the country's rapid and spectacular industrial expansion had stimulated the growth of the German working class, and to Bismarck's alarm, socialism was spreading.

The German Social Democratic party had been founded in 1875 by a fusion of Marxian socialists and the reformist followers of Ferdinand Lassalle on an essentially moderate program which Marx had denounced. But even a moderate socialism was mistrusted by Bismarck. He shared in the European horror at the recent Paris Commune, he feared socialism as anarchy, and he knew that socialism was in any case republican, and in that alone a potentially revolutionary movement in an empire of monarchies. Two radical attempts on the emperor's life (in neither case by Social Democrats) provided him with all the excuse he needed. In 1878, having already made peace with the Catholics, he set out to eradicate socialism. Antisocialist laws from 1878 to 1890 prohibited socialist meetings and socialist newspapers. For twelve years socialism was driven underground. But repression was not his only weapon; he turned also to another tactic. Bismarck sought to persuade the workers to place their faith in him and the German Empire rather than in Marx and the prophets of socialism. To that end, in the 1880s, he initiated an extensive program of social legislation. Workers were insured by the state against sickness, accident, and incapacity in old age. "Our democratic friends," said Bismarck, "will pipe in vain when the people see princes concerned with their well-being." In social insurance imperial Germany was, from whatever motives, years ahead of more democratic England, France, and the United States.

Bismarck failed to kill socialism. The number of socialists elected to the Reichstag was greater in 1890 than in 1878—for Bismarck's antisocialist campaign, in deference to the then current standards of civilized government, never suppressed the voter's freedom to vote as he chose. It seems, however, that Bismarck by the later 1880s was more apprehensive than ever of social revolution that would destroy his empire and contemplated some kind of coup d'état in which the Reichstag would be throttled. He never reached this point because in 1890, at the age of seventy-five, he was obliged by the new emperor, William II, to retire.

The German Empire after 1890: William II

William I died in 1888 and was succeeded by his son Frederick III who, incurably ill of cancer, died some three months after his accession. Frederick's son, William II, the last king of Prussia and the last German Kaiser, began his reign (1888–1918) as a young man of twenty-nine, full of startling ideas about his personal power and privileges. He was uncomfortable in the presence of an elder statesman who had made the German Empire, who had been his grandfather's aide and adviser, and whom he regarded partly with veneration and partly as an old fogy. William soon quarreled with Bismarck over continuation of the antisocialist laws and over matters of foreign affairs. When Bismarck forbade his ministers to meet with the emperor on policy matters unless he was present, William resolved that he, and not Bismarck, would rule the empire, and in 1890 he ordered Bismarck to resign, "dropping the pilot," in the celebrated phrase. Under the four chancellors who succeeded Bismarck, it was William who dominated policy.

After 1890 Germany embarked upon what was termed a "new course." In foreign affairs this meant a more aggressive and ambitious colonial, naval, and diplomatic policy, as will appear in the next two chapters. In domestic affairs it meant a more conciliatory attitude toward the masses. The antisocialist laws were dropped, and the system of social security legislation was enlarged and codified. But no democratic adjustment seemed possible. William II believed in the divinely ordained prerogatives of the house of Hohenzollern, and the empire still rested on the power of the federated princes, on the Junkers, the army, and the new industrial magnates. But the Social Democrats, the Progressive party, and other democratic forces were growing in strength. They demanded, for Prussia, a reform of the illiberal constitution of 1850,[19] and for the Reich, real control over the federal chancellor by the majority party in the Reichstag. In the election of 1912 the Social Democrats reached a new high by polling four and a quarter million votes, about one-third of the total, and by electing 110 members to the Reichstag, in which they now formed the largest single party; yet they were excluded from the highest posts of government. Even had war not come in 1914, it is clear that the imperial Germany created by Bismarck was moving toward a constitutional crisis in which political democracy would be the issue.

Developments Elsewhere; General Observations

Of political developments in other European states before 1914, something has already been said in the preceding chapter. Italy had become a constitutional monarchy in the 1860s and completed its unification by the forceful seizure of Rome in 1870.[20] Despite parliamentary forms, Italian political life in substance was characterized by unstable majorities and by opportunistic maneuvering and manipulation by moderate liberal political leaders, who maintained themselves in office for long periods of time by shuffling and reshuffling political coalitions. Deputies, in a form of parliamentary politics that was baptized *trasformismo* (or a kind of "crossing over") moved readily from one party group to another—for

---

[19] See p. 519.
[20] See pp. 548–550, 558, 636.

favors granted. Giovanni Giolitti, a shrewd tactician who headed several cabinets, governed in this way with only a few interruptions from 1903 to 1914. The liberal leaders were anticlerical, and the quarrel with the papacy over the seizure of the papal territories remained unsettled. The popes refused to recognize the Italian kingdom and forbade Catholics to participate in its affairs or even to vote in elections. Catholics voted nonetheless and in 1907 bishops in each diocese were permitted to relax the ban, as they increasingly did.

Industry had begun to make an appearance in the northern cities like Milan. More as a matter of expediency than out of any democratic impulse, the government moved to extend the franchise to the working classes. The narrow suffrage of 1861 was broadened, first in 1882, and then in 1912, when the new reform increased the number of eligible voters from 3 to 8 million, or virtually universal male suffrage. Because of illiteracy and political inertia not all of the newly enfranchised hastened to exercise their voting privilege. The social problem remained serious, too, despite some modest labor legislation. Poverty and illiteracy, especially in the agrarian south, were grievous problems and radical unrest appeared in the industrial cities. In 1900 Victor Emmanuel's son and successor Humbert was assassinated. The first manifestations of an antiparliamentary ideology, chauvinistic nationalism, and explosive irrationalism appeared in the writings and political activism of literary men like Gabriele d'Annunzio and Filippo Marinetti, the latter publishing in 1909 the manifesto of a violently nihilistic movement he called "futurism." The machinery of political democracy was established in Italy but there could be no assurance about the direction Italian parliamentary democracy was taking.

In the Dual Monarchy of Austria-Hungary, created by the Compromise of 1867, Austria and Hungary were each in form constitutional parliamentary states.[21] In theory, the Emperor-King Francis Joseph ruled through ministries responsible to the legislature in each state. However, in the important sphere of matters affecting the empire as a whole, such as foreign affairs and military questions, there was little parliamentary restraint on the emperor. Here he had virtually final authority; moreover, in all matters he still had broad powers to govern by decree, which he exercised. As in Germany, the tide of socialism was held back both by repressive laws and by social insurance and benevolent legislation. The most serious problem in the empire remained not socialism but agitation by the various subject nationalities, the Czechs and other Slavic peoples. Political democracy took a different course in Austria than in Hungary. In the former, partly as an effort to placate nationalist sentiment, universal male suffrage was introduced in 1907. In the latter it was bitterly and successfully resisted by the Magyars, who saw in it a weapon that could be employed by the Slavs to contest and destroy their preponderance. Austria itself, despite the democratic suffrage, was ruled very much like the German Empire, with the legislature able to debate and criticize but not control policy.

Of other countries it can be said that the political forms of democracy showed signs of advancing everywhere. Universal male suffrage was adopted in Switzerland in 1874, in Belgium in 1893 (though plural voting was still permitted), in the Netherlands in 1896; and in the next few years in Norway and Sweden

---

[21] See pp. 561–564.

(Norway was peacefully separated in 1905 from Sweden). In southern Europe, besides Italy, universal male suffrage was introduced in Spain, Greece, Bulgaria, Serbia, and after the revolt of 1908, in Turkey. Although both Spain and Portugal were beset by civil wars, constitutional forms were eventually adopted in both countries, universal male suffrage being introduced in Spain in 1890 and a liberal suffrage in Portugal under a republic in 1911. Even tsarist Russia, after the Revolution of 1905, received a Duma, or national parliament, elected on a wide franchise but on an indirect and undemocratic class basis, and with narrow powers.[22] Among states west of the Russian empire, only Hungary and Romania had a highly restricted suffrage on the eve of the First World War. The vote for women progressed more slowly. Women voted before 1914 only in certain western states of the United States, in Australia, New Zealand, Finland, and Norway. Not until after the First World War did female suffrage begin to make significant advances.

The progress of representative and democratic institutions did not mean an end to the rule of monarchs, landed aristocrats, and other minority interests. For one thing, with the exception of France and Switzerland, Europe remained monarchical. Second, despite the growing importance of parliaments, parliamentary control over political life was far from guaranteed; emperors and kings still ruled through their chancellors and prime ministers. Of the major world powers it was mainly in the United States (at least for whites), Britain, and France that democratic and popular control was something of a reality. But the extension of the suffrage, by the relaxation of property qualifications, had a dynamic of its own and was altering the framework of politics everywhere; mass political parties, including socialist parties and confessional, or religious-oriented parties, were replacing the older, narrowly oligarchic political organizations, and support now had to be sought on a wider electoral basis. In almost all Europe, and in many of the outlying areas peopled by European descendants, democracy was advancing, even within the older framework. By 1871, most European nations, with the notable exception of Russia, had already won written constitutions, guarantees of personal freedom, parliamentary and representative institutions, and limitations on absolutism; in the years between 1871 and 1914 the most significant new political factor was the advance of male suffrage.

75. The Advance of Democracy: Socialism and Labor Unions

The artisan and laboring classes had never viewed with much pleasure the rise of capitalism or of "bourgeois" liberalism. They had always been doubtful of free competition, unrestrained private enterprise, the Manchester School, laissez faire, the laws of supply and demand, the free market for goods and labor, the idea of an economy independent of states and governments. These were the ideas of middle-class liberals, not of radical democrats. Popular leaders had opposed them in the French Revolution in 1793. The English Chartists had been outspokenly

[22] See pp. 744–745.

anticapitalistic, and on the Continent the ideas of socialism had been spreading. In 1848 there was a strong movement among the working classes for a "social" republic, and, though the social revolution failed in 1848, the force of it was enough to terrify the possessing classes and shape the philosophy of Karl Marx.[23] With the advent of the ballot, workers pressed for social legislation and used their political power to gain a greater measure of social democracy.

But in addition, before and after obtaining the ballot, working people resorted to other devices for the improvement of their position. Against the owners of capital, who controlled the giving of jobs, there were two principal lines of action. One was to abolish the capitalists, the other to bargain with them. The former led to socialism, the latter to the formation of labor unions. Socialism, in logic, meant the extinction of the private employer as such.[24] Trade unionism, in logic, meant that the workers had every reason to keep their employers prosperously in business in order that bargaining with them might produce more results. The working-class movement thus contained an internal contradiction which was never completely resolved.

Middle-class and educated people who took up the workers' cause, the "intellectuals" of the movement—Karl Marx, Friedrich Engels, Louis Blanc, Ferdinand Lassalle, and thousands of less famous names—tended more to socialism than to unionism. They thought of society as a whole, they saw the economic system as a system, they thought of the future in long-run terms, and their time scale allowed generously for whole historical epochs to come and go. The actual workers, put to work at an early age, barely educated if at all, with the waking hours of their adult lives spent on manual jobs, were inclined to keep their attention more on unionism than on socialism. To earn a shilling more every week beginning next week, to be spared the nervous strain and physical danger of constant exposure to unprotected machinery, to have fifteen minutes more every day for lunch, were likely to seem more tangible and important than far-reaching but distant plans for a reconstructed society. The worker looked on the intellectual as an outsider, however welcome; the intellectual looked on the worker as shortsighted and timid, however much in need of help.

After the failures of 1848 the socialist and trade union movements diverged for a generation. The 1850s, compared with the hungry '40s, were a time of full employment, rising wages, and increasing prosperity for all classes. Workers set to organizing unions, socialist thinkers to perfecting their doctrines.

The Trade Union Movement and Rise of British Labor

Organizations of wage workers, or labor unions in the modern sense (as distinguished from medieval craft guilds), had long maintained a shadowy and sporadic existence, as in the old French journeymen's associations.[25] But they had always been extralegal, frowned upon or actually prohibited by governments. French revolutionaries in the Le Chapelier Act of 1791, British Tories in the Combination Act of 1799, had been as one in forbidding workers to unite. It was

[23] See pp. 495–499, 502–505, 522–526.
[24] See pp. 467–468, 497.
[25] See pp. 374–375, 529–530.

the rise of "bourgeois" liberalism, so insensitive to the worker in most ways, that first gave legal freedom to labor unions. The British unions received a tacit recognition from the Liberal Tories in 1825 and explicit recognition from Gladstone's Liberal ministry in 1871. French unions were recognized by Napoleon III in 1864, then restrained in the reaction caused by the Commune, then fully legalized in 1884. In Germany Bismarck negotiated with labor leaders to find support against the vested interests that stood in his way.

The prosperity of the 1850s favored the formation of unions, for workers can always organize most easily when employers are most in need of their services. The craft union—or union of skilled workers in the same trade, such as carpenters—was at first the typical organization. It was most fully developed in England, where a "new model" unionism was introduced by the Amalgamated Society of Engineers (i.e., machinists) in 1851. It was the policy of the "new model" union officials to take the unions out of politics, to forget the semisocialism of the Chartists, to abandon Robert Owen's grandiose idea of "one big union" for all workers, and to concentrate on advancing the interests of each separate trade. The new leaders proposed to be reasonable with employers, avoid strikes, accumulate union funds, and build up their membership. In this they were very successful; the unions took root; and the two governing parties in England, reassured by the unexpected moderation of working-class spokesmen, combined to give the town worker the vote in 1867.

In the 1880s, and especially with the great London dock strike of 1889, which closed the port of London for the first time since the French Revolution, unions of unskilled workers began to form. Industrial unionism, or the joining in one union of all workers in one industry, such as coal or transportation, regardless of the skill or job of the individual worker, began to take shape at the same time. In some cases the older skilled unionists joined with unskilled laborers who worked beside them. Thus gradually arose, for example, the Transport Workers Union, which half a century later was to give a foreign secretary to the government in the person of Ernest Bevin. By 1900 there were about 2,000,000 union members in Great Britain, compared with only 850,000 in Germany and 250,000 in France.

It was largely because British workers were so far advanced in trade unionism, and so successful in forcing collective bargaining upon their employers, that they were much slower than their Continental counterparts in forming a workers' political party. By the 1880s, when avowed socialists were already sitting in French, Belgian, and German parliaments, the only corresponding persons in Britain were a half-dozen "Lib-Labs," as they were called, laboring men elected on the Liberal ticket. The British Labour party was formed at the turn of the century by the joint efforts of trade union officials and middle-class intellectuals.[26] Where on the Continent the labor unions were often led, and even brought into being, by the socialist political parties, in Britain it was the labor unions that brought into being, and subsequently led, the Labour party. Hence for a long time the Labour party was less socialistic than working-class parties on the Continent. Its origin and rapid growth were due in large measure to a desire to defend the unions as established and respectable institutions. The unions were threatened in their very existence by a ruling of the British courts in 1901, the

[26] See p. 623.

Taff Vale decision, which held a union financially responsible for business losses incurred by an employer during a strike. The shortest and most orderly strike, by exhausting a union's funds, might ruin the union. The year before, steps had been taken to bring together the unions and all other existing labor and socialist organizations into a labor representation committee, in preparation for the elections of 1900; the effort was not very successful and only two of the fifteen labor candidates were returned. But the Taff Vale decision unified all ranks and precipitated the formation of the modern Labour party. In the election of 1906 the new Labour party sent twenty-nine members to Parliament, which thereupon overruled the Taff Vale decision by new legislation. The social legislation put through Parliament by the Liberal party government in the next few years, in good part under pressure from labor, has already been described.[27]

European Socialism after 1850

As for socialism, which had so frightened the middle and upper classes in 1848, it seemed in the 1850s to go into abeyance. Karl Marx, after issuing the *Communist Manifesto* with Engels in 1848, and agitating as a journalist in the German revolution of that year, withdrew to the secure haven offered by England, where, after years of painstaking research, he published the first volume of his *Capital* in 1867. This work, of which the succeeding two volumes were published after his death, gave body, substance, and argument to the principles announced in the *Manifesto*.[28] Marx, during more than thirty years in London, scarcely mixed with the labor leaders then building up the English unions. Hardly known to the English, he associated mainly with political exiles and temporary visitors of numerous nationalities. The first volume of *Capital* was not published in English until 1886.

In 1864 there took place in London the first meeting of the International Working Men's Association, commonly known as the First International. It was sponsored by a heterogeneous group, including the secretary of the British carpenters' union, Robert Applegarth; the aging Italian revolutionary, Mazzini; and Karl Marx. With the union officials absorbed in union business, leadership in the Association gradually passed to Marx, who used it as a means of publicizing the ideas about to appear in his *Capital*. At subsequent annual congresses, at Geneva, Lausanne, Brussels, and Basel, Marx built up his position. He made the Mazzinians unwelcome, and he denounced the German Lassalleans for their willingness to cooperate with Bismarck, arguing that it was not the business of socialists to cooperate with the state but to seize it. His sharpest struggle was with the Russian Bakunin. With his background in tsarist Russia, Bakunin believed the state to be the cause of the common man's afflictions; he was hence an "anarchist," holding that the state should be attacked and abolished. To Marx anarchism was abhorrent; the correct doctrine was that the state—tsarist or bourgeois—was only a product of economic conditions, a tool in the class struggle, a weapon of the propertied interests, so that the true target for revolutionary

[27] See pp. 612–613.
[28] See pp. 523–524.

action must be not the state but the capitalist economic system. Marx drove Bakunin from the International in 1872.

Meanwhile members of the First International watched with great excitement the Paris Commune of 1871, which they hoped might be the opening act of a European working-class upheaval. Members of the International infiltrated the Commune, and the connection between the two, though rather incidental, was one reason why the French provisional government repressed the Commune with such terrified ferocity. But the Commune actually killed the First International. The Commune had been bloody and violent, an armed rebellion against the democratically elected National Assembly of France. Marx praised it as a stage in the international class war. He even saw in it a foretaste of what he was coming to call the "dictatorship of the proletariat." He thus frightened many possible followers away. Certainly British trade unionists, sober and steady men, could have nothing to do with such doings or such doctrines. The First International faded out of existence after 1872.

But in 1875, at the Gotha conference, Marxian and Lassallean socialists effected enough of a union to found the German Social Democratic party, whose growth thereafter, against Bismarck's attempts to stop it, has already been noted. About 1880 socialist parties sprouted up in many countries. In Belgium, highly industrialized, a Belgian Socialist party appeared in 1879. In the industrial regions of France some workers were attracted to Jules Guesde, a self-taught worker, former Communard, and now a rigid Marxist, who held it impossible to emancipate the working class by compromise of any sort; others followed the "possibilist" Dr. Brousse, who thought it possible for workers to arrive at socialism through parliamentary methods; still others supported Jean Jaurès, who eloquently linked social reform to the French revolutionary tradition and the defense of republican institutions. Not until 1905 did the socialist groups in France form a unified Socialist party. In England, in 1881, H. M. Hyndman founded a Social Democratic Federation on the German model and with a Marxist program; it never had more than a handful of members. In 1883 two Russian exiles in Switzerland, Plekhanov and Axelrod, recent converts to Marxism, founded the Russian Social Democratic party, from which the communism of the following century was eventually to be derived. The socialist parties all came together to establish an international league in 1889, known as the Second International, which thereafter met every three years and lasted until 1914.

Revisionist and Revolutionary Socialism, 1880–1914

The new socialist parties of the 1880s were all Marxist in inspiration. Marx died in 1883. Marxism or "scientific socialism," by the force of its social analysis, the mass of Marx's writings over forty years, and an attitude of unyielding hostility to competing socialist doctrines, had become the only widely current form of systematic socialism. Strongest in Germany and France, Marxism was relatively unsuccessful in Italy and Spain, where the working class, less industrialized anyway, more illiterate, unable to place its hopes in the ballot, and habituated to an excitable insurrectionism in the manner of Garibaldi, turned more frequently to the anarchism preached by Bakunin.

Nor was Marxism at all successful in England; workers stood by their trade unions, and middle-class critics of capitalism followed the Fabian Society, established in 1883. The Fabians (so called from the ancient Roman general Fabius Cunctator, the "delayer," or strategist of gradual methods) were very English and very un-Marxist. George Bernard Shaw, H. G. Wells, and Sidney and Beatrice Webb were among early members of the Society. For them socialism was the social and economic counterpart to political democracy, as well as its inevitable outcome. They held that no class conflict was necessary or even existed, that gradual and reasonable and conciliatory measures would in due time bring about a socialist state, and that improvement of local government, or municipal ownership of such things as waterworks and electric lighting, were steps toward this consummation. The Fabians, like the trade union officials, were content with small and immediate satisfactions. They joined with the unions to form the Labour party. At the same time, by patient and detailed researches into economic realities, they provided a mass of practical information on which a legislative program could be based.

The Marxist or Social Democratic parties on the Continent grew very rapidly. Marxism turned into a less revolutionary "parliamentary socialism"—except indeed for the Russian Social Democratic party, since Russia had no parliamentary government. For the growth of socialist parties meant that true workers, and not merely intellectuals, were voting for socialist candidates for the Reichstag, Chamber of Deputies, or whatever the lower house of parliament might be called; and this in turn meant that the psychology and influence of labor unions within the parties were increased. The workers, and their union officials, might in theory consider themselves locked in an enormous struggle with capital; but in practice their aim was to get more for themselves out of their employers' business. They might believe in the internationalism of the workers' interests; but in practice, acting through the parliaments of national states, they would work for orderly legislation benefiting the workers of their own country only—social insurance, factory regulation, minimum wages, or maximum hours. Nor was it possible to deny, by the close of the century, that Marx's anticipations (based initially on conditions of the 1840s) had not come true, at least not yet; the bourgeois was getting richer, but the proletarian was not getting poorer. Real wages—or what the wage earner's income would actually buy, even allowing for the losses due to unemployment—are estimated to have risen about 50 percent in the industrialized countries between 1870 and 1900. The increase was due to the greater productivity of labor through mechanization, the growth of the world economy, the accumulation of capital wealth, and the gradual fall in prices of food and other items that the workers had to buy.

Repeatedly, but in vain, the Second International had to warn its component socialist parties against collaboration with the bourgeoisie. Marxism began in the 1890s to undergo a movement of revisionism, led in France by Jean Jaurès, socialist leader in the Chamber of Deputies, and in Germany by Eduard Bernstein, Social Democratic member of the Reichstag and author in 1898 of *Evolutionary Socialism,* an important tract setting forth the new views. The revisionists held that the class conflict might not be absolutely inevitable, that capitalism might be gradually transformed in the workers' interest, and that now that the workers had not only the vote but a political party of their own, they could obtain their ends through democratic channels, without revolution and without any dictatorship of the proletariat. Most socialists or social democrats followed the revisionists.

This tendency to "opportunism"[29] among Marxists drove the really revolutionary spirits into new directions. Thus there arose revolutionary syndicalism, of which the main intellectual exponent was a Frenchman, Georges Sorel. "Syndicalism" is simply the French word for trade unionism (*syndicat,* a union), and the idea was that the workers' unions might themselves become the supreme authoritative institutions in society, replacing not only property and the market economy, but government itself. The means to this end was to be a stupendous general strike, in which all workers in all industries should simultaneously stop work, thus paralyzing society and forcing acceptance of their will. Syndicalism made most headway where the unions were weakest, as in Italy, Spain, and France, since here the unions had the least to lose and were most in need of sensational doctrines to attract members. Its strongest base was in the French General Confederation of Labor, founded in 1895.

Among orthodox Marxists there was also a revival of Marxist fundamentals in protest against revisionism. In Germany Karl Kautsky arraigned the revisionists as compromisers who betrayed Marxism for petty-bourgeois ends. In 1904 he and other rigorists prevailed upon the Second International to condemn the political behavior of the French socialist Alexandre Millerand who in 1899 had accepted a ministerial post in a French cabinet. Socialists might use parliaments as a forum, the International ruled, but socialists who entered the government itself were unpardonably identifying themselves with the enemy bourgeois state. Not until the First World War did socialists henceforth join the cabinet of any European country. In the Russian Social Democratic party the issue of revisionism came to a head in 1903, at a party congress held in London—for the most prominent Russian Marxists were mainly exiles. Here a group led by Lenin demanded that revisionism be stamped out. Lenin won a majority, at the moment at least, and hence the uncompromising Marxists were called Bolsheviks (from the Russian word for majority), while the revisionist or conciliatory Russian Marxists, those willing to work with bourgeois liberals and democrats, were subsequently known as Mensheviks or the "minority" group.[30] But in 1903 the Russian Marxists were considered very unimportant.

In general, in Europe's "inner zone," by the turn of the century, most people who called themselves Marxists were no longer actively revolutionary. As revolutionary republicanism had quieted down in the Third French Republic, so revolutionary Marxism seemed to have quieted down into the milder doctrines of social democracy. What would have happened except for the coming of war in 1914 cannot be known; possibly social revolutionism would have revived, since real wages no longer generally rose between 1900 and 1914, and considerable restlessness developed in labor circles, punctuated by great strikes. But in 1914 the working class as a whole was in no revolutionary mood. Workers still sought a greater measure of social justice, but the social agitation so feared or hoped for in 1848 had subsided. There seem to have been three principal reasons. Capitalism had worked well enough to raise the workers' living standard above what they

[29] See p. 527.
[30] See p. 739.

could remember of their fathers' or grandfathers'; workers had the vote and so felt that they participated in the state, could expect to benefit from the government, and had little to gain by its overthrow; and third, they had their interests watched over by organized and increasingly powerful unions, by which a larger share in the national income could be demanded and passed on to them.

76. Science, Philosophy, the Arts, and Religion

Faith in the powers of natural science has been characteristic of modern society for over three centuries, but never was there a time when this faith spread to so many people, or was held so firmly, so optimistically, and with so few qualms or mental reservations as in the half-century preceding the First World War. Science lay at the bottom of the whole movement of industrialization; and if science became positively popular after about 1870, in that persons ignorant of science came to look upon it as an oracle, it was because it manifested itself to everybody in the new wonders of daily life. Hardly had the world's more civilized regions digested the railroad, the steamship, and the telegraph when a whole series of new inventions already described[31] had begun to unfold itself. In thirty years following 1875 the number of patents tripled in the United States, quadrupled in Germany, and multiplied in all the civilized countries. The scientific and technical advance was as completely international (though confined mainly to the "inner zone") as any movement the world has ever seen. Never had the rush of scientific invention been so fundamentally useful, so helpful to the constructive labors and serious problems of mankind, and in that sense human.

In more basic scientific thinking important changes set in about 1860 or 1870. Up to that time, generally speaking, the underlying ideas had been those set forth by Isaac Newton almost two centuries before.[32] The law of universal gravitation reigned unquestioned, and with it, hardly less so, the geometry of Euclid and a physics that was basically mechanics. The ultimate nature of the universe was thought to be regular, orderly, predictable, and harmonious; it was also timeless, in that the passage of ages brought no change or development. By the end of the epoch considered here, that is, by 1914, the old conceptions had begun to yield on every side.

The Impact of Evolution

In impact upon general thinking the greatest change came in the new emphasis upon biology and the life sciences. Here the great symbolic date is the publication by Charles Darwin of the *Origin of Species* in 1859. Evolution, after Darwin, became the order of the day. Evolutionary philosophies, holding that the way to understand anything was to understand its development, were not new in 1859. Hegel had introduced the evolutionary conception into metaphysics; and he and Marx, into theories of human society.[33] The idea of progress, taken over from the Age of Enlightenment, was a kind of evolutionary philosophy; and the great

[31] See pp. 595–596
[32] See pp. 297–300.
[33] See pp. 471, 524–525.

activity in historical studies, under romantic and nationalistic auspices, had made people think of human affairs in terms of a time process.[34] In the world of nature, the rise of geology after 1800 had opened the way to evolutionary ideas, and venturesome biologists had allowed themselves to speculate on an evolutionary development of living forms. What Darwin did was to stamp evolution with the seal of science, marshaling the evidence for it and offering an explanation of how it worked. In 1871, in his *Descent of Man,* he applied the same hypotheses to human beings.

By evolution, Darwin meant that species are mutable; that no species is created to remain unchanged once and for all; and that all species of living organisms, plant and animal, microscopic or elephantine in dimensions, living or extinct, have developed by successive small changes from other species that went before them. An important corollary was that all life was interrelated and subject to the same laws. Another corollary was that the whole history of living things on earth, generally held by scientists in Darwin's time to be many millions of years, was a unified history unfolding continuously in a single meaningful process of evolution.

Darwin thought that species changed, not by any intelligent or purposeful activity in the organism, but essentially by a kind of chance. Individual organisms, through the play of heredity, inherited slightly different characteristics, some more useful than others in food getting, fighting, or mating; and the organisms that had the most useful characteristics tended to survive, so that their characteristics were passed on to offspring, until the whole species gradually changed. Certain phrases, not all of them invented by Darwin, summed up the theory. There was a "struggle for existence" resulting in the "survival of the fittest" through "natural selection" of the "most favored races"—races meaning not human races but the strains within a species. The struggle for existence referred to the fact that, in nature, more individuals were born in each species than could live out a normal life span; the "fittest" were those individual specimens of a species having the most useful characteristics, such as fleetness in deer or ferocity in tigers; "natural" selection meant that the fittest survived without purpose in themselves or in a Creator; the "favored races" were the strains within a species having good survival powers.

Darwin's ideas precipitated a great outcry. Scientists rushed to defend and churchmen to attack him. The biologist T. H. Huxley became the chief spokesman for Darwin—"Darwin's bulldog." He debated with, among others, the bishop of Oxford. Darwin was denounced, with less than fairness, for saying that men came from monkeys. It was feared that all grounds of human dignity, morality, and religion would collapse. Darwin himself remained complacent on this score. Under civilized conditions, he said, the social and cooperative virtues were useful characteristics assisting in survival, so that "we may expect that virtuous habits will grow stronger, becoming perhaps fixed by inheritance." Much of the outburst against Darwin was somewhat trivial, nor were those who attacked him generally noted for spiritual insight; yet they were not mistaken in sensing a profound danger.

That Darwinism said nothing of God, Providence, or salvation was not surprising; no science ever did. That evolution did not exactly square with the first chapter of Genesis was disturbing but not fatal; much of the Old Testament

---

[34] See pp. 315, 326, 437, 471–472.

was already regarded as symbolic, at least outside certain fundamentalist circles. Even the idea that man and the animals were of one piece was not ruinous; the animal side of human nature had not escaped the notice of theologians. The novel and upsetting effect of evolutionary biology was to change the conception of nature. Nature was no longer a harmony, it was a scene of struggle, "nature red in tooth and claw." Struggle and elimination of the weak were natural, and as means toward evolutionary development they might even be considered good. There were no fixed species or perfected forms, but only an unending flux. Change was everlasting; and everything seemed merely relative to time, place, and environment. There were no norms of good and bad; a good organism was one that survived where others perished; adaptation replaced virtue; outside of it there was nothing "right." The test was, in short, success; the "fit" were the successful; and here Darwinism merged with that toughness of mind, or *Realpolitik,* which came over Europe at the same time from other causes.[35]

Such at least were the implications if one generalized from science, carrying over scientific findings into human affairs, and the prestige of science was so great that this is precisely what many people wished to do. With the popularization of biological evolution, a school known as Social Darwinists actively applied the ideas of the struggle for existence and survival of the fittest to human society. Social Darwinists were found all over Europe and the United States. Their doctrines were put to various uses, to show that some peoples were naturally superior to others, such as whites to blacks, or Nordics to Latins, or Germans to Slavs (or vice versa), or non-Jews to Jews; or that the upper and middle classes, comfortable and contented, deserved these blessings because they had proved themselves "fitter" than the shiftless poor; or that big business in the nature of things had to take over smaller concerns; or that some states, such as the British or German Empires, were bound to rise, or that war was morally a fine thing, proving the virility and survival value of those who fought.

Genetics, Anthropology, and Psychology

Meanwhile Gregor Mendel (1822–1884), a monk patiently experimenting with the cross-pollination of garden peas in his Augustinian monastery, arrived at an explanation of how heredity operates and how hybridization can take place. Unlike Darwin, his findings, published in 1866, were ignored until 1900, when they were rediscovered and became the basis for the new science of genetics. Mendel's ideas foreshadowed the amazing breakthroughs in the scientific study of heredity and control over genetic materials in the second half of the twentieth century.

Anthropologists studied the physical and cultural characteristics of all branches of mankind. Physical anthropologists became interested in the several human "races," some of which they considered might be "favored" in the Darwinian sense, that is, superior in inheritance and survival value. It was often concluded, even by scientists at the time, that the whites were the most competent race, and among the whites the Nordics, or Germans and Anglo-Saxons. The public became more race conscious than Europeans had ever been before. On the other hand the cultural anthropologists, surveying all manner of primitive or complex

[35] See pp. 520–521.

societies with scientific disinterest, seemed sometimes to teach a more deflating doctrine. Scientifically, it seemed, no culture or society was "better" than any other, all being adaptations to an environment, or merely a matter of custom—of the *mores,* as people said in careful distinction from "morals." The effect was again a kind of relativism or skepticism—a negation of values, a belief that right and wrong were matters of social convention, psychological conditioning, mere opinion, or point of view. We are describing, let it be repeated, not the history of science itself but the effects of science upon European civilization at the time.

The impact of anthropology was felt keenly in religion too. Sir James Frazer (1854–1941) in his multivolumed *The Golden Bough* could demonstrate that some of the most sacred practices, rites, and ideas of Christianity were not unique but could be found among primitive societies, and that, moreover, only the thinnest of lines divided magic from religion. Anthropology, like Darwinian evolution, undermined traditional religious beliefs.

Psychology, as a science of human behavior, led to thoroughly upsetting implications about the very nature of man. It was launched in the 1870s as a natural science by the German physiologist Wilhelm Wundt (1832–1920), who developed various new experimental techniques. The Russian Ivan Pavlov (1849–1936) conducted a famous series of experiments in which he "conditioned" dogs to salivate automatically at the ringing of a bell once they had become accustomed over a period of time to associate the sound with the serving of their food. Pavlov's observations were important. They implied that a great part of animal behavior, and presumably human behavior, could be explained on the basis of conditioned responses. In the case of human beings these are responses which humans make automatically by virtue of their earlier environment and training and not through choice or conscious reasoning.

Most significant of all the developments in the study of human behavior was the work of Sigmund Freud (1856–1939) and those influenced by him. Freud, a Viennese physician, founded psychoanalysis at the turn of the century. He came to believe that certain forms of emotional disturbance like hysteria were traceable to earlier forgotten episodes of patients' lives. After first trying various techniques such as hypnosis, which he soon abandoned, he employed free association, or free recall. If patients could be helped to bring these suppressed experiences into conscious recall, the symptoms of illness would often disappear. From these beginnings Freud and his followers explored the role that the unconscious played in all human behavior, he himself stressing the sexual drive. In one of his most famous books, *The Interpretation of Dreams* (1900), he stressed dreams as a key to understanding the unconscious; elsewhere he related his findings to religion, education, art, and literature. Freud and Freudian ideas had great influence on the social and behavioral sciences, and a good deal of the Freudian vocabulary later entered into everyday language and popular culture. In its deepest significance psychoanalysis, by revealing the wide areas of human behavior outside conscious control, suggested that human beings were not essentially rational creatures at all.

The New Physics

The revolution in biology of the nineteenth century, together with the developments in psychology and anthropology, were soon to be matched and surpassed by the revolution in physics. In the late 1890s physics was on the threshold of a revolutionary transformation. Like Newtonian mechanics in the seventeenth century and Darwinian evolution in the nineteenth, the new physics represented one of the great scientific revolutions of all time. There was no single work comparable to Newton's *Principia* or Darwin's *Origin of Species* unless Albert Einstein's theory of relativity, propounded in a series of scientific papers in 1905 and 1916, might be considered as such. Instead there were a series of discoveries and findings, partly mathematical and then increasingly empirical, that threw new light on the nature of matter and energy. In Newtonian physics the atom, the basic unit of all matter, which the Greeks had hypothesized in ancient times, was like a hard, solid, unstructured billiard ball, permanent and unchanging; and matter and energy were separate and distinct. But a series of discoveries from 1896 on profoundly altered this view. In 1896 the French scientist Antoine Henri Becquerel discovered radioactivity, observing that uranium emitted particles or rays of energy. In the years immediately following, from the observations and discoveries of the French scientists Pierre and Marie Curie and the Englishmen J. J. Thomson and Lord Rutherford, there emerged the notion that atoms were not simple but complex, and, moreover, that various radioactive atoms were by nature unstable, releasing energy as they disintegrated. The German physicist Max Planck demonstrated in 1900 that energy was emitted or absorbed in specific and discrete units or bundles, each called a quantum; moreover, energy was not emitted smoothly and continuously as previously thought, nor was it as distinguishable from matter as once supposed. In 1913, the Danish physicist Niels Bohr postulated an atom consisting of a nucleus of protons surrounded by electrically charged units, called electrons, rotating around the nucleus, each in its orbit, like a minuscule solar system.

With radioactivity scientists were being brought back to the idea long rejected, the favored view of the alchemists, that matter was transmutable; in a way undreamed of even by the alchemists, it was convertible into energy. This the German-born Jewish scientific genius Albert Einstein (1879–1955) expressed in a famous formula $e = mc^2$. From his theory of relativity emerged also the profoundly revolutionary notion that time, space, and motion were not absolute in character but were all relative to the observer and the observer's own movement in space. In later years, in 1929 and in 1954, Einstein brought together into one common set of laws, as Newton formerly had done, a unified field theory, an explanation of gravitation, electromagnetism, and subatomic behavior. Difficult as it was to grasp, and a great deal was still the subject of scientific controversy, it modified much that had been taken for granted since Newton. The Newtonian world was being replaced by a four-dimensional world, a kind of space-time continuum; and in mathematics, non-Euclidean geometries were being developed. It turned out, too, that neither cause and effect nor time and space nor Newton's law of universal gravitation meant very much in the subatomic world nor indeed in the cosmos when objects moved with the speed of light. It was impossible, as the German scientist Werner Heisenberg demonstrated a little later, in 1927, by his principle of uncertainty, or indeterminacy, to ascertain simultaneously both the position and the velocity of the individual electron. On these foundations established before the First World War there developed the new science of nuclear physics and the tapping of the atom's energy. The atom was soon discovered to be even more complex than conceived of before 1914, and its potentialities even greater.

Trends in Philosophy and the Arts

The step from pure science to philosophy is a long one, but one that many were prepared to take. Not only was the faith in science widespread but it was widely held that science was the only means of certain knowledge, and that anything unknowable to science must remain unknowable forever—a doctrine called agnosticism, or the acknowledgment of ignorance. Herbert Spencer (1820–1903) in England and Ernst Haeckel (1834–1919) in Germany were widely read popularizers of agnosticism; both also pictured a universe governed by Darwinian evolution. For Spencer especially, all philosophy could be unified, organized, and coordinated through the doctrine of evolution; this doctrine he applied not only to all living things but to sociology, government, and economics as well. The evolution of society, he felt, was toward the increasing freedom of the individual, the role of governments being merely to maintain freedom and justice; they were not to interfere with natural social and economic processes, not to coddle the weak and unfit. Yet, like Darwin himself, Spencer believed that altruism, charity, and good will as individual ethical virtues were themselves useful and laudable products of evolutionary development.

These latter views were not shared by another of the serious writers of the age, also much influenced by evolutionary ideas, the German philosopher Friedrich Nietzsche (1844–1900). More a philosopher of art than of science, and drawing from many intellectual currents of the century, Nietzsche was an unsystematic and unclear thinker to whom it is easy to do less than justice. It is evident, however, that his opinion of mankind was a low one, and that from a background of evolutionary thinking he developed some kind of doctrine of a Superman, a noble being who, in a final triumph of world history, should issue from, lead, dominate, and dazzle the multitude. Qualities of humility, patience, brotherly helpfulness, hope, and love, in short the specifically Christian virtues, Nietzsche described as a slave morality concocted by the weak to disarm the strong. Qualities of courage, love of danger, intellectual excellence, and beauty of character he considered much better. Such views, for better or worse, were actually a new form of classical paganism. Nietzsche was neither much read nor much respected by his contemporaries, who considered him unbalanced or even insane; but he nevertheless expressed with unshrinking frankness many ideas implied in the outlook of his day.

As in the sciences, so in works of creative imagination—pure literature and the fine arts—the changes at the dawn of the twentieth century ushered in the contemporary age. Some writers, like Zola in France or Ibsen in Scandinavia, turned to the portrayal of social problems, producing a realistic literature dealing with industrial strife, strikes, prostitution, divorce, or insanity. Freudian and other views of psychology slowly made themselves felt in works of fiction; the new novels were often more lifelike than the old even though they added little to one's faith in human nature. The arts followed the intellectual developments of the age, reflecting, as they do today, attitudes of relativism, irrationalism, social determinism, and interest in the subconscious. On the other hand, never had artist and society been so far apart. The painter Gauguin, an extreme case, fled to the South Seas, went primitive, and reveled in the stark violence of tropical colors. Others became absorbed in technicalities or mere capricious self-expression. Art at its extreme fringe became incomprehensible and the average person was deprived of a means (as old as the cave paintings of the Stone Age) of perceiving, seizing, and enjoying the world about him. After the First World War, and on into the present, the same trends of subjectivism in the arts attracted a wider, if still skeptical, audience. People read books without punctuation (or with peculiar punctuation), listened to music called atonal and deliberately composed for effects of discord and dissonance, and studied intently abstract or "nonobjective" paintings and sculpture to which the artists themselves often refused to give titles.

The problem of communication remained serious. The arts suffered from the specialization of the modern world. The artist was not thought of as a collective spokesman or creator of something for common use but as a specialist plying his own trade and pursuing his own concerns. Society itself was divided into busy, self-centered groups, unable to communicate except on superficial matters, and hence in the long run less able to work in common.

The Churches and the Modern Age

Religion, too, was displaced. It was now a long time since almost everyone had looked to religion for guidance. But religion was more threatened after 1860 or 1870 than ever in the past, because never before had science, or philosophies drawing upon science, addressed themselves so directly to the existence of life and of man. Never before had so many of the fundamental premises of traditional religion been questioned or denied. Darwinian evolution had challenged the traditional picture of Creation, and anthropologists had questioned the uniqueness of the most sacred Christian tenets. There developed also the "higher" criticism of the Bible, an effort to apply to the Scriptures the techniques of scholarship long applied to secular documents, to incorporate archeological discoveries, and to reconstruct a naturalistic, historical account of ancient religious times. The movement, going back at least to the seventeenth century,[36] now took on significant proportions and was applied both to the Old Testament and the New. In the case of the Old Testament the patient scrutiny of style and language cast doubt on the validity of certain prophecies; and in the New the inconsistencies of the several Gospel sources were made patent. The German theologian David Friedrich Strauss (1808–1874), one such critical scholar, was the author of a widely discussed *Life of Jesus,* in which many miraculous and supernatural episodes were reverently but firmly explained away as "myth." The sensitive French historian and man of letters Ernest Renan (1823–1892) in a somewhat similar vein wrote on the origins of Christianity and on the life of ancient Israel. The ordinary person's long-established articles of faith were being further undermined. Moreover, the whole tenor of the time, its absorption in material progress, likewise kept people away from church; and the wholesale uprooting, the movement from country to city, often broke religious ties.

[36] See pp. 305–307.

The Protestant churches were less successful than the Catholic in protecting their membership from the disintegrating effects of the age. Church attendance among Protestants became increasingly casual, and the doctrines set forth in sermons seemed increasingly remote. Protestant laymen traditionally trusted their own private judgment and regarded their clergy as their own agents, not as authoritative teachers placed above them. Protestants also had always set special emphasis on the Bible as the source of religious belief; and as doubts accumulated on the literal truth of Biblical narratives there seemed no other source on which to rely.

Protestants tended to divide between modernists and fundamentalists. The fundamentalists, as they were called in the United States, in an effort to defend the literal word of Scripture, were often obliged to deny the most indubitable findings of science. The modernists were willing enough to be scientific and to interpret much of the Bible as allegory, but only with difficulty could they recapture any spirituality or urgent feeling of Christian truth. Most Protestant churches were slow to face the social problems and wholesale injustices produced by the economic system, though a group of "Christian socialists" developed, notably, within the Church of England. And as education and the care of orphans, aged, sick, and insane persons passed to the state, Protestant groups had less to do in the relief of suffering and upbringing of the young. Protestantism, to the regret of many Protestants, became increasingly a customary observance by people whose minds were elsewhere. Not until after the First World War could a strong Protestant revival be discerned, with a reaffirmation of basic doctrines by thinkers like Karl Barth, and a movement on the part of divergent Protestant churches to combine.

The Roman Catholic church proved more resistant to the trends of the age. We have seen how Pope Pius IX (1846–1878), after being driven from Rome by republicans in 1848, gave up his inclinations to liberalism.[37] In 1864, in the

[37] See pp. 512–514.

PAINTING #198 (AUTUMN)

by Vasily Kandinsky (Russian, then in Germany and France, 1866–1944)

What is loosely called modern art dates from the early twentieth century. Where the Impressionists continued to represent objects while losing interest in objective representation, in the next generation many painters gave up the objects themselves, thus launching various nonobjective or "abstract" styles. This *Painting #198* was done in 1914 by Kandinsky, one of the first practitioners of purely abstract painting. Since it is meant to convey color, without reference to physical objects, it does not lend itself to the kind of reproduction here used. Color at this time had a deep and vital meaning for Kandinsky though he later turned to the invention of geometric or linear images as well. For the commonly perceived world of external objects he substituted a universe of his own. "To create a body of artistic work," he said, "is to create a world." Or again, speaking of nature, "it is not enough to see it; we must live it." With such sentiments Kandinsky shared in the antirationalist or vitalistic philosophies of the period. Courtesy of the The Solomon R. Guggenheim Museum. Permission A.D.A.G.P. 1970 by French Reproduction Rights, Inc.

Syllabus of Errors, he denounced as erroneous a long list of widely current ideas, including the faith in rationalism and science, and he vigorously denied that the head of the church "should reconcile and align himself with progress, liberalism, and modern civilization." The *Syllabus* was in form a warning to Catholics, not a matter of dogma incumbent upon them to believe. In dogma, the Immaculate Conception of the Virgin Mary was announced as dogmatic truth in 1854; a century later, in 1950, the bodily assumption of Mary into heaven was proclaimed. Thus the Catholic church reaffirmed in a skeptical age, and against Christian modernists, its faith in the supernatural and miraculous.

Pius IX also convened an ecumenical church council which met at the Vatican in 1870. It was the first such council since the Council of Trent some 300 years before.[38] The Vatican Council proclaimed the dogma of papal infallibility, which holds that the pope, when speaking *ex cathedra* on matters of faith and morals, speaks with a final and supernatural authority that no Catholic may question or reject. The Vatican Council, and the acceptance of papal infallibility by Catholics, was only the climax of centuries of development within the church. In brief, as the world grew more national, Catholicism became more international. As state sovereignty and secularism grew, Catholic clergy looked increasingly to the spiritual powers of Rome for protection against alien forces. Much in the past 300 years had made Catholics distrustful of their own governments or of non-Catholics in their midst—the Protestantism and the state churches of the sixteenth century, the Jansenist movement of the seventeenth, the anticlericalism of enlightened despotism in the eighteenth, the hostility to the church shown by the French Revolution, and by liberalism, republicanism, and socialism in the nineteenth century. By 1870 the net effect was to throw Catholics into the arms of the Holy See. Ultramontanism, the unconditional acceptance of papal jurisdiction, prevailed over the old Gallican and other national tendencies within the church.

---

[38] See pp. 88–90.

COMPOSITION WITH THE ACE OF CLUBS
by Georges Braque (French, 1882–1963)

This painting, of about the same date as the preceding one by Kandinsky, represents a quite different direction in modern art. It is one of the great works of the Cubist movement. Where the Kandinsky painting presents color without line and seeks to express life and feeling, Braque and the Cubists break up the visual world into lines and planes, in a more analytic and intellectual fashion. Objects recede or disappear, not into an impressionist blur nor a burst of color, but into a carefully contrived and almost mathematical pattern. In the new movement, it made sense to "see" things from more than one direction at a time, as the mind conceives them. Perception is not enough; as Braque once wrote, "the senses deform, but the mind forms." In any case, innovative artists after 1900 turned away from the main concerns of Western painting since the Renaissance: realistic representation of persons, places, or objects; natural color; illusionistic three-dimensional volume; a humanly occupied space with perspectives, horizons, location, and distance as seen by the eye from a single fixed viewpoint. Courtesy of the Musée d'Art Moderne, Paris (Service Photographique). Permission A.D.A.G.P. 1970 by French Reproduction Rights, Inc.

In 1870, while the 600 prelates of the Vatican Council were sitting, the new Italian state unceremoniously entered and annexed the city of Rome.[39] The pope's temporal power thus disappeared. It is now widely agreed that with the loss of local temporal interests the spiritual hold of the papacy on Catholics throughout the world has been enhanced. The popes long refused, however, to recognize the loss of Rome; and each pope in turn, from 1870 to 1929, adopted a policy of self-imprisonment in the Vatican grounds. By the Lateran treaty of 1929 the papacy finally recognized the Italian state, and Italy conceded, along with much else, the existence of a Vatican City about a square mile in area, as an independent state not legally within Italy at all. The papacy thus gained that independence from national or secular authority deemed necessary by Catholics to the performance of its role.

Pius IX's successor, Leo XIII (1878–1903), carried on the counteroffensive against irreligion, and instituted a revival of medieval philosophy as represented by Thomas Aquinas.[40] But Leo XIII is chiefly remembered for formulating Catholic social doctrine, especially in the encyclical *Rerum Novarum* ("of modern things") of 1891, to which subsequent pontiffs have adhered, and from which various movements of Catholic socialism are derived. *Rerum Novarum* upheld private property as a natural right, within the limits of justice; but it found fault with capitalism for the poverty, insecurity, and even degradation in which many of the laboring classes were left. It declared that much in socialism was Christian in principle; but it criticized socialism insofar as (like Marxism) it was materialistic and antireligious. The pope therefore recommended that Catholics, if they wished, form socialist parties of their own, and that Catholic workers form labor unions under Catholic auspices. Since the 1830s there had been individual Catholics and Catholic clergy who were socialists, or at least severe critics of the then emerging social order; these were encouraged by the encyclical of 1891, and Catholic (or Christian, as they were often called) socialist parties and labor unions began to appear at the turn of the century. The Roman church thus undertook to free itself from dependency upon capitalism. At the same time it took steps to insure that a future society, if socialist, might be Catholic also.

As for Judaism, the Jews were a small minority, but their condition had always been a kind of barometer reflecting changes in the atmosphere of Europe as a whole. In the nineteenth century the basic trend was toward "emancipation" and "assimilation." Science and secularism had the same dissolving effect upon Orthodox Judaism as upon traditional Christianity. Reform Judaism grew up as the Jewish counterpart to "modernism" in other faiths. Individual Jews increasingly gave up their old distinctive Jewish way of life. In society at large, the prevalence of liberalism allowed them to act as citizens and to enter business or the professions like everybody else. Jews were thus freed from old legal discriminations that had been imposed on them for centuries.

Toward the end of the century two tendencies, counter to assimilation, became evident. One, a cultural and political nationalism, originated with Jews themselves, some of whom feared an assimilation that would lead to a loss of Jewish identity and perhaps even the disappearance of Judaism itself. The other countertendency, or barrier to assimilation, was the rise of anti-Semitism, noticeable in many

[39] See p. 558.
[40] See p. 42.

quarters by 1900. Racist theories, dislike for Jewish competitors in business and the professions, socialist scorn for Jewish capitalists like the Rothschilds, upper-class fears of Jewish revolutionaries and Marxists, together with a growth of ethnic nationalism, which held that France should be purely French and Latin, Germany purely German and Nordic, or Russia purely Russian and Slav, all combined to raise an anti-Semitic hue and cry. In Russia there were actual pogroms, or massacres of Jews. In France the Dreyfus case, dragged out from 1894 to 1906, revealed unsuspected depths of anti-Semitic fury. Many Jews were forced by such hostility into a new sense of Jewish identity. The Hungarian-born Jewish journalist Theodor Herzl was one. Appalled by the turbulence of the Dreyfus affair in civilized France, which he observed firsthand as a reporter for a Vienna newspaper, he founded modern, or political, Zionism when he organized the first international Zionist congress at Basel in 1897. Zionists hoped to establish a Jewish state in Palestine, in which Jews from all the world might find refuge, although there had been no independent Jewish state there since ancient times.

Many Jews, wishing civic assimilation yet despairing of obtaining it, began to sympathize with the Jewish nationalist movement, looking to Zionism and a Jewish renascence as a way to maintain their own dignity. Others insisted that Judaism was a religious faith, not a nationality by itself; that Jews and non-Jews within the same country shared in exactly the same nationality, citizenship, and political and social outlook. Liberals and democrats were of the same opinion. On the integration of Jews into the larger community the traditions of the Enlightenment, the American and French revolutions, the empire of Napoleon I, and the liberalism of the nineteenth century all agreed.

77. *The Waning of Classical Liberalism*

The net effect of the political, economic, and intellectual trends described above was twofold. There was a continued advance of much that was basic to liberalism and at the same time a weakening of the grounds on which liberalism had firmly rested ever since the seventeenth and eighteenth centuries. A third effect might be noted too. Even where the essentials of liberalism persisted, in program and doctrine it underwent important changes; liberalism persisted but the classical type of liberalism was in eclipse.

Classical liberalism, the liberalism in its heyday in the nineteenth century, went back at least as far as John Locke in the seventeenth century and the philosophes of the eighteenth, and found its highest nineteenth-century expression in the writings of men like John Stuart Mill and in the political outlook of men like William Gladstone. Classical liberalism had as its deepest principle the liberty of the individual person.[41] Man, or each specimen of mankind, according to liberals, was or could become a freestanding human being. "Man" meant for them any member of the human race, *homo sapiens,* though in practice, except for a few like Mill, they were thinking of adult males. The very principle of liberalism, however, with its stress on the autonomy of the individual, contributed to the still small but growing movement of women's rights.

[41] See pp. 371, 465–466.

The individual, in this view, was not simply formed by race, class, church, nation, or state but was ultimately independent of all such things. Individuals did not have such and such ideas because they belonged to such and such a group, but were capable of the free use of reason or of thinking things out independently, apart from their own interests, prejudices, or subconscious drives. And, since this was so, people of different interests could reasonably and profitably discuss their differences, make compromises, and reach solutions by peaceable agreement. It was because they thought all persons potentially reasonable that liberals favored education. They opposed all imposition of force upon the individual, from physical torture to mental indoctrination.

In religion, liberals thought each individual should adopt any faith or no faith as he or she chose, and that churches and clergy should play little or no part in public affairs. In politics, they thought that governments should be constitutional and limited in power, with individuals governing themselves through their chosen representatives, with issues presented, discussed, and decided by the use of intelligence, both by the voters in election campaigns and by elected deputies in parliamentary debate. The will of a majority, or larger number of individuals, was taken as decisive, with the understanding that the minority might become a majority in its turn through individual changes of opinion. At first distrustful of democracy, fearing the excesses of popular rule, and eager to limit political power and the suffrage to the propertied classes, in the course of the nineteenth century liberals had accepted the democratic principle of universal male suffrage. In economics, liberals thought of the whole world as peopled by individuals doing business with one another—buying and selling, borrowing and lending, hiring and firing—without interference from governments and without regard to religion or politics, both of which were thought to impose superficial differences upon the underlying uniformity of mankind. The practical consequences of liberalism were toleration, constitutionalism, laissez faire, free trade, and an international or nonnational economic system. It was thought that all peoples would progress to these same ends.

There never was a time, even in one country, when all liberal ideas were simultaneously triumphant. Pure liberalism has never existed except as a doctrine. Advancing in one way, liberalism would be blocked or reversed in another. On the whole, Europe before 1914 was predominantly liberal. But signs of the wane of liberalism set in clearly about 1880; some, like the changing conceptions of human behavior, have already been mentioned.

The Decline of Nineteenth-Century Liberalism: Economic Trends

The free economy produced many hardships. The worker tossed by the ups and downs of a labor market, the producer tossed by those of a world commodity market, alike clamored for protection against exposure. A severe depression in 1873 sent prices and wages into collapse, and the economy did not fully recover until 1893. European farmers, both small French farm owners and big Junker landlords of East Germany, demanded tariff protection: they could not compete with the American Middle West or the steppes of South Russia, both opened up by rail and steamship, and both of which after 1870 poured their cereals at low prices into Europe. The revival of tariffs and decline of free trade, very marked in Europe about 1880, thus began with the protection of agricultural interests. Industry soon demanded the same favors. In Germany the Junkers and the rising Rhineland industrialists joined forces in 1879 to extort a tariff from Bismarck. The French in 1892 adopted a high tariff to shelter both manufacturing and agricultural interests. The United States, rapidly industrializing, also put up protective tariffs beginning in the 1860s, the earliest of all.

The Industrial Revolution was now definitely at work in other countries than Great Britain. There was an increasing resistance to buying manufactures from England, selling only raw materials and foodstuffs in return. Everywhere there was a revival of the arguments of the German economist Friedrich List, who a half-century before, in his *National System of Political Economy* (1840), had branded free trade as a system mainly advantageous to the British and declared that no country could become strong, independent, or even fully civilized if it remained a semi-rustic supplier of unfinished goods.[42] With Germany, the United States, and Japan manufacturing for export, a nationalist competition for world markets set in, contributing also to the drive for colonies and the phenomena of imperialism described in the next chapter. The new imperialism was another sign of the waning of liberalism, which had been largely indifferent to colonies.

In all these respects the division between politics and economics, postulated by liberals, began to fade. A kind of neomercantilism arose, recalling the attempts of governments in the seventeenth and eighteenth centuries to subordinate economic activity to political ends. A better term is economic nationalism, which became noticeable by 1900. Nations struggled to better themselves by tariffs, by trade rivalries, and by internal regulation, without regard to the effect upon other nations. And for the individual worker or businessman also, in purely economic matters, it now made a great difference to what nation he belonged, by what government he was backed, and under what laws he lived.

It was of course to protect themselves against insecurity and abuse as individuals that workers formed labor unions. It was likewise to protect themselves against the uncertainties of uncontrolled markets that business interests began to merge, to concentrate in large corporations, or to form monopolies, trusts, or cartels. The rise of big business and organized labor undermined the theory and practice of individual competition to which classical liberalism had been attached. Organized labor, socialist parties, universal male suffrage, and a sensitivity to social distress all obliged political leaders to intervene increasingly in economic matters. Factory codes became more detailed and better enforced. Social insurance, initiated by Bismarck, spread to other countries. Governments regulated the purity of foods and drugs. The social service state developed, a state assuming responsibility for the social and economic welfare of the mass of its own subjects. The "new" liberalism, that of the Liberals in England of the David Lloyd George era, of the Republican President Theodore Roosevelt and the Democratic President Woodrow Wilson in the United States, accepted the enlarged role of the government in social and economic matters. Both Theodore Roosevelt and Wilson, and others, sought also to reestablish economic competition by government action against monopolies and trusts. The new liberals were generally less well disposed toward business than toward workers and the

[42] See pp. 471–472.

depressed classes; the improvement of the workers' lot would vindicate the old humanitarian concern of liberalism with the dignity and worth of the individual person. The welfare state, remote as it was from the older liberalism, was the direction taken by the new liberals. Others, liberal and otherwise, viewed with concern the growing power of governments and centralized authority and were apprehensive for individual liberties.

Intellectual and Other Currents

Liberalism, both old and new, was undermined also by many developments in the field of thought described earlier in this chapter—Darwinian evolution, the new psychology, trends in philosophy and the arts. Paradoxically, this great age of science found that man was not a rational animal. Darwinian theory implied that man was merely a highly evolved organism whose faculties were merely adaptations to an environment. Psychology seemed to teach that what was called reason was often only rationalization, or a finding of alleged "reasons" to justify material wants or emotional and unconscious needs, and that conscious reflection dominated only a narrow part of human behavior. Ideas themselves were said to be the products of conditioning. There were English ideas or Anglo-Saxon ideas, or bourgeois or progressive or reactionary ideas. In politics, some believed that parties or nations with conflicting interests could never reasonably agree on a program common to both, since neither could ever get beyond the limitations of its own outlook. It became common to dismiss the arguments of an adversary without further thought and without any expectation that thought could overcome difficulties. This insidious "anti-intellectualism" was destructive to liberal principles. If, because of prior conditioning, it was impossible for anyone to change his or her mind, then there was no hope of settling matters by persuasion.

From the view that man was not essentially a rational being, which in itself was only a scientific attempt at a better understanding of human behavior, it was but a short step deliberately to reject reason and to emphasize and cultivate the irrational, to stress the will, intuition, impulse, and emotion, and to place a new value on violence and conflict. A philosophy of "realism," a kind of unrealistic faith in the constructive value of struggle and a tough-minded rejection of ideas and ideals, spread. It was not new. Marxism, since the 1840s, had taught that class war, latent or open, was the motivating power of history. Now Nietzsche rejected the ordinary virtues in favor of courage and daring; and the Social Darwinists glorified the successful and the dominant in all phases of human activity as the "fit" in the perpetual struggle for existence. Other thinkers embraced a frank irrationalism. Georges Sorel, the philosopher of syndicalism, in his *Reflections on Violence* in 1908, declared that violence was good irrespective of the end accomplished (so much did he hate existing society), and that workers should be kept alert in the class war through believing in the "myth" of a future general strike. They should believe in such a strike, with its attendant debacle of bourgeois civilization, even though it was known to be only a "myth." The function of thought, in this philosophy of the social myth, was to keep people agitated and excited and ready for action, not to achieve any correspondence with rational or objective truth. Such ideas passed into the fascism and other activist movements of the twentieth century.

Thus the end of the nineteenth century, the greatest age of peace in Europe's history, abounded in philosophies glorifying struggle. People who had never heard a shot fired in anger solemnly announced that world history moved forward by violence and antagonism. They said not merely that struggle existed (which would have been a purely factual statement) but that struggle was a positive good through which progress was to be accomplished. The popularity of struggle was due not only to the intellectuals but in part to actual historical events. People remembered that before 1871 certain weighty questions had been settled by force, that the movements of social revolution in 1848 and in the Paris Commune of 1871 had been put down by the military, and that the unity of Italy and Germany, as well as of the United States, had been confirmed by war. In addition, after 1871, all continental European states maintained large standing armies, the largest ever maintained until then in time of peace.

In economic and political matters, even in England, the homeland of liberalism, there were numerous signs between 1900 and 1914 that the older liberalism was on the wane. Joseph Chamberlain led a movement to return to tariff protection (to repeal, so to speak, the repeal of the Corn Laws); it failed at the time, but was strong enough to disorient the Conservative party in 1906. The Liberal party abandoned its traditional laissez-faire policy in sponsoring the labor legislation of the years following 1906. The new Labour party required its members in Parliament to vote as directed by the party, thus initiating a system of party solidarity, eventually copied by others, that hardened the lines of opposition, denied that individuals should freely change sides, and hence reduced the practical significance of parliamentary discussion. The Irish nationalists had long used unparliamentary methods; in 1914, when Parliament at last enacted Irish home rule, the anti-Irish and Conservative interests prepared to resist parliamentary action by force. The suffragettes, as women pioneering for female suffrage were called, despairing of ever getting the men to listen to reason, resorted to amazingly "un-English" and unreasonable arguments. They chained themselves to public buildings, smashed the store fronts on Bond Street, threw acid into mailboxes, and broke porcelains in the British Museum. When arrested they went on hunger strikes, threatening self-starvation, to which the police replied by "forcible feeding" through tubes lowered into their stomachs. And in 1911 and 1912 great railway and coal strikes disclosed the sheer power of organized labor.

Still, it is the persistence of liberalism rather than its wane that should be emphasized at the close of a chapter on European civilization in the half-century before 1914. Tariffs existed, but goods still circulated freely in world trade. Nationalism was heightened, but there was nothing like totalitarianism. Racist ideas were in the air, but they had little political importance. Anti-Semitism was sometimes vocal; but all governments except the Russian protected the rights of Jews, and the years from 1848 to 1914 were in fact the great period of Jewish integration into general society. The laissez-faire state was disappearing, but social legislation continued the humanitarian strain that had always been the essence of liberalism. A few advanced revolutionaries preached social catastrophism, but social democrats and working people were overwhelmingly revisionist, loyal to parliamentary procedures and to their existing states. Doctrinaires exalted the grim beauty of war, but all governments down to 1914 tried to prevent war among the great powers. And there was still a supreme faith in progress.

XV.
EUROPE'S WORLD
SUPREMACY

EUROPEAN CIVILIZATION, as described in the last chapter, spread to the whole earth after about 1870. The large nation-states whose consolidation was described in the chapter before last, and which were now equipped with the overwhelming new powers of science and industry, gained empires for themselves throughout the globe. The history of Europe— as of Asia, Africa, and the Americas—became more involved in the history of the world.

For a while the most active of the imperial nation-states were located in Europe, and the forty years preceding the First World War were the years of Europe's world supremacy. With the rise of the United States the term "Western" came into use, signifying European in an expanded sense. The arrival of Japan made the term "Western" inappropriate for some purposes, and later the industrialization of the Soviet Union created similar verbal difficulties, so that by the mid–twentieth century it was customary to speak of "developed" parts of the earth, alongside which others were seen as "developing" or "less developed." There even came to be a "Third World," which had no geographic identity of its own, but which did not wish to be

Chapter Emblem: A medal commemorating the opening of the Suez Canal in 1869.

identified with either the Western or the Soviet form of modern society. All these terms represented efforts to deal with the same basic reality, namely, a bifurcation between modern and traditional societies, rich countries and poor ones, or between the powerful and the weak.

For the first time in human history, by 1900, it was possible to speak of a world civilization. All countries were drawn into a world economy and a world market. The attributes of modernity, where they existed at all, were much the same everywhere—modern science, modern weapons of warfare, machine industry, fast communications, industrial organization, efficient forms of taxation and law enforcement, and of public hygiene, sanitation, and medicine.

But not all peoples participated in this global evolution on equal terms. It was the Europeans (or "Westerners") who reaped the greatest rewards. Under the impact of modernity both tribal societies and massive old civilizations began to come apart. Scientific ideas changed ways of thinking everywhere, as they had done in Europe. In India, China, or Africa the native industries often suffered, and many people found it harder than ever to subsist even at a low level. The building of railways in China, for example, threw boatmen, carters, and innkeepers out of work. In India, the hand spinners and weavers of cotton could not compete in their own villages with the machine-made products of Lancashire. In parts of Africa, native tribes that had lived by owning herds of cattle, moving from place to place to obtain grazing lands, found white farmers or plantation or mine owners occupying their country and were often forced by the white man's law to give up their migratory habits. Peoples of all races began to produce for export—rubber, raw cotton, jute, petroleum, tin, gold—and hence were exposed to the rise and fall of world prices. A depression tended to become a world depression, dragging all down alike.

Imperialism, or the colonialism of the late nineteenth century, may be briefly defined as the government of one people by another. European imperialism proved to be transitory. It was a phase in the worldwide spread of the industrial and scientific civilization which had originated in Europe's "inner zone."[1] That it was not the last phase became clear as the twentieth century unfolded. The subordinated peoples, forcibly introduced to the West by imperialism, came to feel a need for modernizing and industrializing their own countries and for the aid of Western science, skill, and capital; but they wished to get rid of imperialists, govern themselves, and control the conditions under which modernization and borrowing should take place. In opposition to European empires, subject peoples began to assert ideas learned from Europe—ideas of liberty and democracy, and of an anticapitalism that passed easily into socialism. Many such ideas were derived from the French and American revolutions, or from Marxism, or from the whole record of Europe itself.

The present chapter deals only with the imperialist phase of the global transformation. By one of the ironies of history, the imperialist rivalries of the European powers, while representing Europe's world supremacy, also contributed to the disaster of the First World War, and so to the collapse of such supremacy as Europe had enjoyed.

[1] See pp. 160, 586–587.

78. Imperialism: Its Nature and Causes

European civilization had always shown a tendency to expand. In the Middle Ages Latin Christendom spread by conquest and conversion to include the whole area from Spain to Finland. Then came the age of overseas discoveries and the founding of colonial empires, whose struggles filled the seventeenth and eighteenth centuries, and of which the Europeanization of the Americas was the most far-reaching consequence. At the same time European culture spread among the upper classes of Russia. The defeat of Napoleon left only one of the old colonial empires standing in any strength, namely, the British. For sixty years after 1815 there were no significant colonial rivalries. In many circles there was an indifference to overseas empire. Under principles of free trade, it was thought unnecessary to exercise political influence in areas in which one did business. Actually, in these years, the French moved into Algeria, the British strengthened their Indian empire, the Dutch developed Java and the neighboring islands more intensively, and the Western powers "opened" Japan and began to penetrate China. But there was no overt conflict among Europeans, and no systematic program, doctrine, or "ism."

Rather suddenly, about 1870 or 1880, colonial questions came again to the fore. In the short space of two decades, by 1900, the advanced countries partitioned most of the earth among themselves. A world map by 1900 showed their possessions in some nine or ten colors.

The New Imperialism

The new imperialism differed both economically and politically from the colonialism of earlier times. The older empires had been maritime and mercantile. European traders, in India, Java, or Canton, had simply purchased the wares brought to them by local merchants as produced by local methods. They operated on a kind of cash-and-carry basis. European governments had had no territorial ambitions beyond the protection of way stations and trading centers. To these generalizations America had been an exception. It had neither native states which Europeans respected, nor native industries in which Europeans were interested. Europeans therefore developed territorial claims, and invested capital and brought in their own methods of production and management, especially in the then booming sugar islands of the West Indies.[2]

Under the new imperialism Europeans were by no means content simply to purchase what local merchants provided. They wanted goods of a kind or in a quantity that preindustrial handicraft methods could not supply. They moved into the "backward" countries more thoroughly. They invested capital in them, setting up mines, plantations, docks, warehouses, factories, refineries, railroads, river steamships, and banks. They built offices, homes, hotels, clubs, and cool mountain resorts suitable for white men in the tropics. Taking over the productive life of the country, they transformed large elements of the local population into the wage employees of foreign owners and so introduced the class problems of industrial

[2] See pp. 259–262.

Europe in a form accentuated by racial difference. Or they lent money to non-European rulers—the khedive of Egypt, the shah of Persia, the emperor of China—to enable them to hold up their tottering thrones or simply to live with more pleasure and magnificence than they could pay for from their usual revenues. Europeans thus developed a huge financial stake in governments and economic enterprises outside the pale of Western civilization.

To secure these investments, and for other reasons, in contrast to what had happened under the older colonialism, the Europeans now aspired to political and territorial domination. Some areas became outright "colonies," directly governed by white men. Others became "protectorates": here the native chief, sultan, bey, rajah, or prince was maintained and guaranteed against internal upheaval or external conquest. A European "resident" or "commissioner" usually told him what to do. In other regions, as in China or Persia, where no single European state could make good its claims against the others, they arranged to divide the country into "spheres of influence," each European power having advisory privileges and investment and trade opportunities within its own sphere. The sphere of influence was the vaguest of all forms of imperial control; supposedly, it left the country independent.

An enormous differential opened up, about 1875, between the power of European and non-European states. Queen Elizabeth had dealt with the Great Mogul with genuine respect. Even Napoleon had pretended to regard the shah of Persia as an equal. Then came the Industrial Revolution in Europe, iron and steel ships, heavier naval guns, more accurate rifles. Democratic and nationalistic movements produced large and solid European peoples, united in the service of their governments as no "backward" people ever was. Seemingly endless wealth, with modern administration, allowed governments to tax, borrow, and spend almost without limit. The civilized states loomed as enormous power complexes without precedent in the world's history. At the same time it so happened that all the principal non-European empires were in decay. They were receiving a minimum of support from their own subjects. As in the eighteenth century the disintegration of the Mogul empire had enabled the British to take over India,[3] so in the nineteenth century the decrepitude of the sultan of Turkey, the sultan of Zanzibar, the shah of Persia, the emperor of China, and the shogun of Japan made European intervention easy. Only the Japanese were able to revolutionize their government in time to ward off imperialist penetration. Even the Japanese, thanks to early treaties, remained unfree to determine their own tariff policy until after 1900.[4]

So great was the difference in the sheer mechanics of power that usually a mere show of force allowed the whites to impose their will. A garrison of only 75,000 white troops long held India for the British. Numerous sporadic little wars were constantly fought—Afghan wars, Burmese wars, Zulu wars—which passed unnoticed by Europeans in the home country and were no more like true war than the operations of the United States army against the Indians of the western plains. The Spanish-American War of 1898 and the Boer War of 1899 were also wars of colonial type, fought between entirely unequal parties. Often a show of

[3] See pp. 278–281, 350–351.
[4] See pp. 579–581.

naval strength was enough. It was the classic age of the punitive or minatory bombardment. We have seen how the American Commodore Perry threatened to bombard Tokyo in 1854.[5] In 1856 the British consul at Canton, to punish acts of violence against Europeans, called upon the local British admiral to bombard that Chinese city. In 1863 the British bombarded Satsuma, and in 1864 an allied force including Americans bombarded Choshu—precipitating revolution in Japan. Similarly, Alexandria was bombarded in 1882 and Zanzibar in 1896. The usual consequence was that the local ruler signed a treaty, reorganized his government, or accepted a European (usually British) adviser.

Incentives and Motives

Behind the aggressiveness lay many pressures. Europeans could not maintain, for themselves in Europe, the style of life to which they had become accustomed, except by bringing the rest of the world within their orbit. But many other needs felt in Europe drove men into distant and savage places. Catholic and Protestant groups sent growing numbers of missionaries to regions increasingly remote and wild. The missionaries sometimes got into trouble with the local people, and some were even killed. Public opinion in the home countries, soon learning of such events by ocean cable, might clamor for political action to suppress such vestiges of barbarism. Similarly, science required scientific expeditions for geographical exploration, or for botanical, zoological, or mineral discoveries, or for astronomical or meteorological observations. Wealthy persons traveled more, now that travel was so easy; they hunted tigers or elephants, or simply went to see the sights. It seemed only reasonable, at the close of the nineteenth century, that all civilized persons wherever they might choose to go should enjoy the security of life and limb and the orderly procedures that only European supervision could provide.

Economically, European life required material goods, many of which only tropical regions could supply. Even the working classes now drank tea or coffee every day. After the American Civil War Europe relied for its cotton increasingly on Africa and the East. Rubber and petroleum became staple needs. The lowly jute, which grew only in India, was used to make burlap, twine, carpets, and the millions of jute bags employed in commerce. The lordly coconut tree had innumerable common uses, which led to its intensive cultivation in the Dutch Indies. Various parts of it could be eaten, or manufactured into bags, brushes, cables, ropes, sails, or doormats or converted into coconut oil, which in turn went into the making of candles, soap, margarine, and many other products.

Industrial countries also attempted to sell their own products, and one of the reasons given by imperialists, in support of imperialism, was the urgent necessity of finding new markets. The industrialization of Germany, the United States, Japan, and other countries, after about 1870, meant that they competed with each other and with Great Britain for foreign trade.[6] The slowly declining price level after 1873 meant that a business firm had to sell more goods to turn over the same amount of money. Competition was more intense. The advanced countries

---

[5] See pp. 577, 579–581.
[6] See pp. 638–639.

raised tariffs to keep out each other's products. It was therefore argued that each industrial country must develop a colonial empire dependent on itself, an area of "sheltered markets," as the phrase went in England, in which the home country would supply manufactured goods in return for raw materials. The idea was to create a large self-sufficient trading unit, embracing various climates and types of resources, protected if necessary from outside competition by tariffs, guaranteeing a market for all its members and wealth and prosperity for the home country. This phase of imperialism is often called neomercantilism, since it revived in substance the mercantilism of the eighteenth and earlier centuries.[7]

Purely financial considerations also characterized the new imperialism. Money invested in "backward" countries, by the close of the nineteenth century, brought a higher rate of return than if invested in the more civilized ones. For this there were many reasons, including the cheap labor of non-European regions, the heavy and unsatisfied demand for non-European products, and the greater risk of losses in half-unknown areas where European ideas of law and order did not prevail. By 1900 western Europe and the northeastern United States were equipped with their basic industrial apparatus. Their railway networks and first factories were built. Opportunities for investment in these countries became stabilized. At the same time, these countries themselves accumulated capital seeking an outlet. In the mid-century most exported capital was British-owned. By the close of the century more French, German, American, Dutch, Belgian, and Swiss investors were investing or lending outside their own borders. In 1850, most exported capital went to build up Europe, the United States, Canada, Australia, or Argentina—the white man's world. By 1900 more of it was going to the undeveloped regions. This capital was the property of small private savers or of large banking combinations. Investors preferred "civilized" political control over the parts of Asia, Africa, or Latin America in which their railroads, mines, plantations, government loans, or other investments were situated. Hence the profit motive, or desire to invest "surplus" capital, promoted imperialism.

This analysis was put forward by critics like the English socialist J. A. Hobson, who wrote an influential book on imperialism in 1903, and later by Lenin, in his *Imperialism, the Highest Stage of World Capitalism*, written in 1916. They ascribed imperialism primarily to the accumulation of surplus capital and condemned it on socialist grounds. Argued Hobson especially, if more of the national income went to workers as wages, and less of it to capitalists as interest and dividends, or if wealthy people were more heavily taxed and the money used for social welfare, there would be no surplus of capital and no real imperialism. Since the working class, if this were done, would also have more purchasing power, it would be less necessary to look endlessly for new markets outside the country. But the "surplus capital" explanation of imperialism was not entirely convincing. That investors and exporters were instrumental in the rise of imperialism was of course very true. That imperialism arose essentially from the capitalists' pressure to invest abroad was more doubtful. Perhaps even more basic was Europe's need for imports—only by enormous imports could Europe sustain its dense population, complex industry, and high standard of living. It was the demand for such imports—cotton, cocoa, coffee, copper, or copra drawn from the "colonies"—

---

[7] See pp. 119–120, 257–262.

that made investment in the colonies financially profitable. Moreover, non-Europeans themselves often asked for the capital, glad though the European lenders were to lend it at high rates. In 1890 this might mean merely that a shah or sultan wanted to build himself a new palace, but the need of non-Europeans for Western capital was basic, nor was it to decline in later times. Lastly, the imperialism of some countries, notably Russia and Italy, which had little capital and few modern-type capitalists of their own, could not reasonably be attributed to pressure for lucrative foreign investments.

For the British, however, the capitalistic incentive was of great importance. We have seen how the British, in 1914, had $20 billion invested outside of Great Britain, a quarter of all their wealth.[8] About half, or $10 billion, was invested in the British Empire. Only a tenth of French foreign investments was in French colonies. French investment in the colonial world in general, however, including Egypt, Suez, South Africa, and Asia in addition to the French colonies, amounted to about a fifth of all French foreign investments. Only an infinitesimal fraction of German foreign investment in 1914 was in German colonies, which were of slight value. A fifth of German foreign investments, however, was placed in Africa, Asia, and the Ottoman Empire. These sums are enough to suggest the pressures upon the European governments to assert political influence in Africa, Turkey, or China.

In addition, French investors (including small bourgeois and even affluent peasants) had in 1914 a huge stake in the Russian empire. Russia, an imperial power with respect to adjoining countries in the Balkans and Asia, occupied an almost semicolonial status with respect to western Europe. The tsardom in its last twenty years, not unlike the Ottoman sultanate or the Manchu dynasty, was kept going by foreign loans, predominantly French. The French in 1914 had lent over $2 billion to Russia, more than to all colonial regions combined. For these huge outlays the motivation was at least as much political as economic. The French government often urged French banks to buy Russian bonds. The aim was not merely to make a profit for bankers and savers, but to build up and hold together a military ally against Germany.

Politics went along with economics in the whole process of imperialist expansion. National security, both political and economic, was as important an aim as the accumulation of private wealth. So, too, was the growing concern in many quarters over the economic security and welfare of the working classes. The ideas of the British statesman Joseph Chamberlain (1836–1914) illustrated how these motives entered into imperialist thinking.

Chamberlain, father of Neville Chamberlain who was to be prime minister of Britain in the years just prior to the Second World War, began as a Birmingham manufacturer, the type of man who a generation before would have been a staunch free trader and upholder of laissez faire. Discarding the old individualism, he came to believe that the community should and could take better care of its members, and, in particular, that the British community (or empire) could advance the welfare of Britons. As mayor of Birmingham he introduced a kind of municipal socialism, including public ownership of utilities. As colonial secretary from 1895 to 1903, he preached Britain's need for "a great self-sustaining and self-protecting

[8] See p. 599.

empire" in an age of rising international competition—a worldwide British trading area, developed by British capital, which would give a secure source of raw materials and food, markets for exports, and a steady level of profits, wages, and employment.

Chamberlain saw with misgivings the tendencies toward independence in Canada, New Zealand, and the Australian Commonwealth. For these dominions he favored complete self-government, but he hoped that, once assured of virtual independence, they would reknit their ties with each other and with Great Britain. Such a reintegration of the empire he called "imperial federation." Britain and its dominions, in Chamberlain's view, should pool their resources not only for military defense but also for economic well-being. The dominions had already levied tariffs against British manufacturers in order to build up their own. Chamberlain, to favor British exports, urged the dominions to charge a lower duty on British wares than on the same wares coming from foreign countries. In return, he even proposed that Great Britain adopt a protective tariff, so that it might then favor Canadian or Australian goods by imposing on them a lower rate. His plan was to bind the empire together by economic bonds, making it a kind of tariff union, or system of "imperial preference." Since Britain imported mainly meat and cereals from the dominions, Chamberlain was obliged to recommend a tariff even upon these—to "tax the people's food," repudiating the very ark of the covenant of Free Trade upon which the British economy had rested for half a century.[9] The proposal was rejected. Chamberlain died in 1914, his goal unaccomplished. But after the First World War the British Empire, or Commonwealth of Nations, followed closely along the lines he had mapped out.[10]

Whether the economic welfare and security of the European working classes was advanced by imperialism is still debated. It is probable that the worker in western Europe did benefit from imperialism. Socially conservative imperialists were joined in this belief by thinkers of the extreme Left. Marx himself, followed by Lenin, thought that the European worker obtained higher real wages through the inflow of low-priced colonial goods. To Marxists this was unfortunate, for it gave European workers a vested interest in imperialism, made the European proletariat "opportunistic" (i.e., unrevolutionary), and blocked the formation of a true international world proletariat of all races.

Another imperialist argument much heard at the time held that European countries must acquire colonies to which surplus population could migrate without altogether abandoning the native land. It seemed unfortunate, for example, that so many Germans or Italians emigrating to the United States should be lost to the fatherland. This argument was purely specious. No European country after 1870 acquired any colony to which European families in any numbers wished to move. The millions who still left Europe, up to 1914, persisted in heading for the Americas, where in the circumstances no European colony could be founded.[11]

The competitive nature of the European state system introduced other almost exclusively political elements. The European states had to guard their security against each other. They had to keep some kind of balance among themselves,

[9] See pp. 494, 596–599.
[10] See p. 804.
[11] See map, p. 592.

in the overseas world as in Europe. Hence, as in the scramble for Africa, one government often hurriedly annexed territory simply for fear that another might do so first. Or again, colonies came to have an intangible but momentous value in symbolism and prestige. To have colonies was a normal criterion of greatness. It was the sign of having arrived as a Great Power. Britain and France had had colonies for centuries. Therefore the new powers formed in the 1860s—Germany, Italy, Japan, and in a sense the United States—had to have colonies also.

Imperialism as Crusade

Imperialism arose from the commercial, industrial, financial, scientific, political, journalistic, intellectual, religious, and humanitarian impulses of Europe compounded together. It was an outthrust of the whole white man's civilization. It would bring civilization and enlightened living to those who still sat in darkness. Faith in "modern civilization" had become a kind of substitute religion. Imperialism was its crusade.

So the British spoke of the White Man's Burden, the French of their *mission civilisatrice*, the Germans of diffusing *Kultur*, the Americans of the "blessings of Anglo-Saxon protection." Social Darwinism and popular anthropology taught that white races were "fitter" or more gifted than colored.[12] Others argued, more reasonably, that the backwardness of non-Europeans was due to historic and hence temporary causes, but that for a long period in the future the civilized whites must keep a guardianship over their darker protégés. In the psychology of imperialism there was much that was not unworthy. Young men of good family left the pleasant lands of Devonshire or Poitou to spend long and lonely years in hot and savage places, sustained by the thought that they were advancing the work of humanity. It was a good thing to bring clearer ideas of justice to barbaric peoples, to put down slave raiding, torture, and famine, to combat degrading superstitions or fight the diseases of neglect and filth. But these accomplishments, however real, went along all too obviously with self-interest and were expressed with unbearable complacency and gross condescension to the larger part of the human race. As Rudyard Kipling wrote in 1899:

> *Take up the White Man's burden—*
> *Send out the best ye breed—*
> *Go bind your sons to exile,*
> *To serve your captives' need;*
> *To wait in heavy harness,*
> *On fluttered folk and wild—*
> *Your new-caught sullen peoples,*
> *Half devil and half child.*

79. The Americas

After the general considerations above, let us examine each of the earth's great regions in turn, and first the Americas, where we must begin our discussion earlier in the century, before the age of the "new imperialism."

---

[12] See pp. 626–628.

In America the breakup of the Spanish and Portuguese empires in the first quarter of the nineteenth century, during and after the Napoleonic wars, left the vast tract from Colorado to Cape Horn very unsettled. Most of the people were Indian or a mixture of Indian and white *(mestizo)*, with clusters here and there of pure European stock, which the nineteenth-century immigration was greatly to increase.[13] Except in inaccessible spots, the Spanish culture and language predominated. In Brazil the culture was Portuguese, and the country, though independent after 1822, remained a monarchy or "empire" until 1889, when it became a republic. In the former Spanish domains the disappearance of royal control left a large number of flaccid and shifting republics, chronically engaged in border disputes with one another. Fortunately for these republics, at the time of independence in the 1820s, European imperialism was at a low ebb. We have seen how the Congress of Verona considered ways of returning them to Spain but was opposed by Great Britain; and how the United States, in 1823, supplemented the British action by announcing the Monroe Doctrine. But it was by the United States that one of the new republics was first threatened from the outside.

The United States and Mexico

Mexico, on becoming independent of Spain, reached almost to the Mississippi and the Rocky Mountains. Hardly was it independent when land seekers from the United States swarmed over its northeastern borders. They brought with them their slaves, to grow the cotton so voraciously demanded in industrial England. The Mexican Republic did not allow slavery. The newcomers proclaimed their own republic, which they called Texas. Agitation developed for annexation to the United States. Mexico objected, but in 1845 the United States annexed Texas. A war followed, in which Mexico lost to the United States not only Texas but the whole region from Texas to the California coast. As is usual in such affairs, the loser preserved a longer memory than the winner. It soon seemed only natural in the United States to possess these regions; in Mexico many decades had to pass before the wound was healed. Mexico had lost half its territory within the first generation of its independence. It was argued at the time that the United States had far better facilities than Mexico for civilizing the region.

The next threat to Mexico came from Europe. Political leaders in Mexico, at a time of internal disorders, contracted large loans in Europe on exorbitant terms, the European leaders rightly estimating Mexican credit to be highly unsound. When the liberal leader Juárez (a pure-blooded Indian, at least racially "non-European") repudiated the loans, the European bondholders demanded satisfaction from their governments. The United States was paralyzed by the Civil War. Great Britain, France, and Spain, which had never recognized the Monroe Doctrine, in 1861 sent combined military forces to Veracruz. The British proposed seizure of the customs houses in Mexican ports, and appropriation of the customs revenues to pay off the debt (an expedient introduced in China three years before); but the French had more ambitious designs. Unknown both to the British,

[13] See pp. 112–114, 481–483.

who wanted only to collect debts, and to the Spanish, who dreamed of setting up a new Bourbon monarchy in Mexico, the Emperor Napoleon III had a secret project for establishing a French satellite state in Mexico, which French capital and exports might subsequently develop.[14] He planned to create a Mexican empire with the Austrian archduke Maximilian as its figurehead emperor. The British and Spanish disapprovingly withdrew their forces. The French army proceeded into the interior. Maximilian reigned for some years, but Napoleon III gradually concluded that conquest of Mexico was impossible, or too expensive. It further appeared, by 1865, that the United States was not going to collapse after all, as expected and even hoped for by the European governing classes. The United States protested strongly to the French government. The French withdrew, Maximilian was captured and shot, and Juárez and the Mexican liberals came back to power.

United States pressure, before 1870, had thus in turn both despoiled and protected the adjoining part of Latin America. This ambivalent situation became characteristic of the New World. As the United States became a great power the Monroe Doctrine became an effective barrier to European territorial ambitions. Latin America never became subject to imperialism as completely as did Asia and Africa. On the other hand, the United States became the imperialist power feared above all others south of the border. It was the *Yanqui* menace, the Colossus of the North.

In the 1870s in the course of its turbulent politics, both natives of Mexico and foreign residents were obliged to pay forced loans to rival leaders. The State Department at Washington demanded that American citizens be reimbursed by the Mexican government. The double standard characteristic of imperialism— one standard for civilized and one for uncivilized states—became clear in the exchange of notes. The Mexican government, now under Porfirio Díaz, attempted to lay down the principle that "foreigners locating in a country accepted the mode of life of the people . . . and participated not only in the benefits of such residence but also in the adversities. Foreigners should enjoy the same guarantees and the same legal protection as natives, but no more." The Mexicans observed that the United States had never recognized the claims of foreigners for losses sustained in its Civil War. The United States, under President Hayes, held on the other hand that citizens of advanced states, operating in more primitive regions, should continue to enjoy the security of property characteristic of their home countries. When on another occasion the United States sent troops to the border, and the Mexicans objected, the secretary of state remarked on "the volatile and childish character of these people and their incapacity to treat a general question with calmness and without prejudice." Mexico retorted that the United States had "disregarded all the rules of international law and practice of civilized nations and treated the Mexicans as savages, as Kaffirs of Africa."

It was, in fact, a principle of international law in the nineteenth century that civilized states might not intervene in each other's affairs but had the right of intervention in "backward" countries. In the dispute of 1877 the United States classified Mexico as backward, "volatile and childish." What the Mexicans

---

[14] See pp. 529–530.

objected to was being treated like "savages and Kaffirs," and not like a civilized nation. They differed on which of the two standards should apply.

United States Imperialism in the 1890s

The 1890s saw a crescendo of imperialism both in Europe and in the United States. In 1895, in a resounding restatement of the Monroe Doctrine, President Cleveland forbade the British to deal directly with Venezuela in a boundary dispute affecting British Guiana. The British were obliged to accept international arbitration. When, however, the adjacent Colombia faced a revolution in the Isthmus of Panama the United States supported the revolutionaries and, consulting nobody, recognized Panama as an independent republic. Here the United States leased and fortified a Canal Zone, over which it long kept control, and proceeded to build the Panama Canal. Panama became in effect what Europeans would call a protectorate of the United States.

Meanwhile what was left of the old Spanish American empire, confined to Cuba and Puerto Rico, was agitated by revolutionary disturbances looking to independence. Sympathies in the United States lay with the revolutionaries. Every sign of the new imperialism showed itself unmistakably. Americans had $50 million invested in Cuba. They bought the bonds issued by Cuban revolutionaries in New York. Cuban sugar, whose production was interfered with by political troubles, was necessary to the famed American standard of living. An orderly and amenable Cuba was vital to American strategic interests in the Caribbean, in the soon to be built canal, and in the Pacific. The barbarity of the Spanish authorities was deplored as an outrage to modern civilization. The newspapers, especially the new "yellow" press, roused the American public to a fury of moral indignation and imperial self-assertion. The climax came when an American warship, the *Maine*, sank under mysterious circumstances in Havana harbor.

The United States easily won the ensuing war with Spain in 1898. Puerto Rico was annexed outright, as were the Philippine Islands on the other side of the world. Cuba was set up as an independent republic, subject to the Platt Amendment, a series of provisions by which the United States obtained the right to oversee Cuba's relations with foreign powers, and to intervene in Cuba in matters of "life, property, individual liberty" and "Cuban independence." Thus the United States obtained another protectorate in the Caribbean. The right of intervention in Cuba was exercised several times in the following two decades, until the growth of Cuban nationalism and subsiding of American imperialism led to abrogation of the Platt Amendment in 1934. Later, after the Second World War, the Philippines formally received independence in 1946 and Puerto Rico became a self-governing commonwealth in 1952.

It was under President Theodore Roosevelt, the peppery "hero of San Juan hill," that the imperial greatness of the United States was most emphatically trumpeted. He announced in 1904 that weakness or misbehavior "which results in a general loosening of the ties of civilized society may . . . require intervention by some civilized nation," and that the Monroe Doctrine might force the United States "to the exercise of an international police power." In the following year

Santo Domingo fell into such financial disorder that European creditors were alarmed. To forestall any pretext for European intervention, the United States sent a financial administrator to Santo Domingo, reformed the economy of the country, and impounded half the customs receipts to pay its debts. Roosevelt declared—in what came to be known as the "Roosevelt Corollary" to the Monroe Doctrine—that, since the United States would not permit European states to intervene in America to collect debts, it must itself assume the duty of intervention to safeguard the investments of the civilized world. The Monroe Doctrine, initially a negative warning to Europe, now stood with the new corollary as a positive notice of supervision of all America by the United States. A quarter of a century of "dollar diplomacy" followed, in which the United States repeatedly intervened, by military or other means, in the Caribbean and Mexico. But the Roosevelt Corollary, like the Platt Amendment, created so much bad feeling in Latin America that the Washington government finally repudiated it.

The story of the Hawaiian Islands was as typical of the new imperialism as any episode in the history of any of the European empires. Known originally to outsiders as the Sandwich Islands, these spots of land long enjoyed isolation in the vastnesses of the mid-Pacific. The growth of navigation in the nineteenth century introduced them to the world. Sailors, whalers, missionaries, and vendors of rum and cloth filled Honolulu by 1840. The native ruler, confused and helpless in the new situation, almost accepted a British protectorate in 1843 and in 1875 did accept a virtual protectorate by the United States, which guaranteed Hawaiian independence against any third party, obtained trading privileges, and acquired Pearl Harbor as a naval base. American capital and management entered the island. They created huge sugar and pineapple industries, entirely dependent on export to, and investment by, the United States. In 1891, when Queen Liliuokalani came to the throne, she tried to check westernization and Americanization. The American interests, endangered by her nativist policies, overthrew the queen and set up an independent republic, which soon sought annexation to the United States. It was the story of Texas reenacted. For several years the issue hung in the balance because of lingering disapproval in the United States for such strong-arm methods. But with Japan revealing imperial designs in 1895, the rush of the other powers into China, the Spanish-American War, acquisition of the Philippines, and plans for the Panama Canal, the United States "accepted its destiny" in the Pacific, and annexed the Hawaiian Republic by joint resolution of Congress in 1898. Hawaii became a state in the American union in 1959.

80. The Dissolution of the Ottoman Empire

The Ottoman Empire in the 1850s

Of all parts of the non-European world, the Ottoman, or Turkish, Empire was the nearest to Europe, and with it Europeans had for centuries had close relations. It had for long extended from Hungary and the Balkan peninsula to the south Russian steppes and from Algeria to the Persian Gulf. The empire was not at all like a European state. Immense in extent, it was a congeries of religious communities. Most of its people were Muslim, including both orthodox Muslims and such reform sects as Druses and Wahabis; some were Jews who had always lived in the Near East; many were Christian, principally Greek Orthodox and Armenian, who had also always lived there. The Turks were the ruling class and Islam the dominant religion. Only Muslims, for example, could serve in the army; non-Muslims were known as *raya*, the "flock" or "herd"—they paid the taxes. Persons of different religion lived side by side, each under the laws, courts, and customs of his or her own religious group. Religious officials—patriarchs, bishops, rabbis, imams, ulemas—were responsible to the Turkish government for their own people, over whom therefore they had a great deal of authority.[15]

Western Europeans had their own special rights. Roman Catholic clergy, living mainly in Palestine, looked to the pope in religion and to France for a mundane protector. Western merchants enjoyed the regime of the "capitulations," or special rights granted by the Ottoman government in numerous treaties going back to the sixteenth century. By the capitulations Turkey could not levy a tariff of more than 8 percent on imported goods. Europeans were exempt from most taxes. Cases involving two Europeans, civil or criminal, could be settled only in a court held by a European consul under European law. Disputes between a European and an Ottoman subject were settled in Turkish courts, but in the presence of a European observer.

The Ottoman Empire, in short, completely lacked the European idea of nationalism or national unity. The European idea of sovereignty and a uniform law for all its peoples were also absent, as was the idea of the secular state, or of law and citizenship separated from religion. The empire had fallen behind Europe in scientific, mechanical, material, humanitarian, and administrative achievements.

Turkey was the "sick man of Europe," and its long decline constituted the Eastern Question. Since the loss of Hungary in 1699 the Ottoman Empire had entered on a long process of territorial disintegration. That the empire lasted another two centuries was due to the European balance of power.[16] But by the 1850s the empire was falling away at the edges. Russia had advanced in the Crimea and the Caucasus. Serbia was autonomous, Greece independent, and Romania recognized as a self-governing principality. The French occupied Algeria. A native Arab dynasty, the Sauds, of the Wahabi reform sect, ruled over much of Arabia. A former Turkish governor of Egypt, Mehemet Ali, had established his family as hereditary khedives in the Nile valley.[17] Notwithstanding these changes, the Ottoman Empire in the 1850s was still huge. It encompassed not only the Turkish or Anatolian peninsula (including Armenia and territory south of the Caucasus) but also the central portion of the Balkan peninsula from Constantinople to the Adriatic where many Christians of Slavic nationality lived, Tripoli (Libya) in North Africa, and the islands of Crete and Cyprus. Egypt and Arabia, though autonomous, were still under the nominal suzerainty of the sultan.

The Crimean War of 1854–1856 opened a new phase in Ottoman history as in

[15] See pp. 219–221.
[16] See pp. 221–223, 340, 484–485, and map, p. 660.
[17] See p. 485. The Egyptian ruler, as viceroy under the Ottoman Empire, did not adopt the title of "khedive" until 1867; he was called "sultan" from 1914 to 1922; and thereafter "king" until the overthrow of the monarchy in 1952.

that of Europe.[18] We have seen how this war was followed by the consolidation of great nation-states in Europe, and how even the United States, Canada, and Japan consolidated or modernized themselves at the same time. The Turks tried to do the same between 1856 and 1876.

In the Crimean War the Turks were on the winning side, but the war affected them as it affected Russia, the loser. Exposing their military and political weakness, it pointed up the need of organization. The outcome of the war was taken to prove the superiority of the political system of England and France. It was therefore on Western lines that Turkish reformers wished to remodel. It was not merely that they wished to defend themselves against another of the periodic wars with Russia. They wished also to avoid being periodically saved from Russia by the West, a process which if continued could lead only to French or British control of Turkey.

Attempts at Reform and Revival, 1856–1876

In 1856 the Ottoman government issued the Hatt-i Humayun, the most far-reaching Turkish reform edict of the century. Its purpose was to create an Ottoman national citizenship for all persons in the empire. It abolished the civil authority of religious hierarchs. Equality before the law was guaranteed as was eligibility to public office without regard to religion. The army was opened to Christians and Muslims alike and steps were even taken to include both in nonsegregated military units. The edict announced a reform of taxes, security of property for all, abolition of torture, and reform of prisons. It promised to combat the chronic evils of graft, bribery, and extortion by public officials.

For twenty years there were serious efforts to make the reform decree of 1856 a reality. Western and liberal ideas circulated freely. Newspapers were founded. Writers called for a national Turkish revival, threw off the old Persian style in literature, composed histories of the Ottomans, translated Montesquieu and Rousseau. Foreign loans entered the country. Railroads joined the Black Sea and the Danube. Abdul Aziz (1861–1876), the first sultan to travel to Europe, visited Vienna, London, and the great Paris world's fair of 1867. But powerful resistance developed against such radical changes. Also, the best efforts of the Turkish reformers miscarried. There were too few Turks with skill or experience in the work required. Abdul Aziz took to spending his borrowed money somewhat too freely for purposes of the harem. In 1874 the Ottoman government, having recklessly overborrowed, repudiated half its debt.

A new and more determined reforming minister, Midhat Pasha, goaded by opposition and desperate at the weight of inertia, deposed Abdul Aziz in 1876, deposed the latter's nephew three months later, and set up Adbul Hamid II as sultan. The new sultan at first briskly went along with the reform movement, proclaiming a new constitution in 1876. It declared the Ottoman Empire to be indivisible, and promised personal liberty, freedom of conscience, freedom of education and the press, and parliamentary government. The first Turkish parliament met in 1877. Its members earnestly addressed themselves to reform.

[18] See pp. 544–545.

But they reckoned without Abdul Hamid, who in 1877 revealed his true intentions. He got rid of Midhat, packed off the parliament, and threw away the constitution.

Repression after 1876

Abdul Hamid reigned for thirty-three years, from 1876 to 1909. For all this time he lived as a terrified animal, fighting back blindly and ferociously against forces that he could not understand. Once when a consignment of dynamos reached the Turkish customs it was held up by fearful officials, because the contents were declared to make several hundred revolutions per minute. Again, chemistry books for use in the new American college were pronounced seditious, because their chemical symbols might be a secret cipher. The sultan sensed that tampering with the old Ottoman way would lead to ruin. He dreaded any moves to check his own whim or power. He was thrown into a panic by Turkish reformers and westernizers, who became increasingly terroristic in the face of his opposition. Driven away by Abdul Hamid, some tens of thousands of Young Turks, the activists of the reform era before 1876, or their children and successors, lived in exile in Paris, London, or Geneva, plotting their return to Turkey and vengeance upon Abdul the Damned. The sultan was frightened also by agitation among his non-Turkish subjects. Nationalist Armenians, Bulgars, Macedonians, and Cretans defied and taunted the Ottoman authorities, which responded with the Bulgarian massacres of 1876 and the Armenian massacres of 1894. These horrible butcheries of thousands of peasants by Ottoman troops came as a shock to a Europe unused to such violence. Last, and with good reason, Abdul Hamid lived in a creeping fear of the designs of the imperialist European powers upon his dissolving empire.

A thoroughly reformed, consolidated, and modernized Ottoman Empire was the last thing that European governments desired. They might wish for humanitarian reforms in Turkey, for more efficiency and honesty in Turkish government and finance, and even for a Turkish parliamentary system. Such demands were eloquently expressed by liberals like Gladstone in England. But no one wanted what Turkish reformers wanted, a reinvigorated Ottoman Empire that could deal with Europe politically as an equal.

The Russo-Turkish War of 1877–1878: The Congress of Berlin

In Russia, since the time of Catherine II, many had dreamed of installing Russia on the shores of the Bosporus.[19] Constantinople they called Tsarigrad, the Imperial City, which Orthodoxy was to liberate from the infidel. Crusading motives, in a nationalist and imperialist age, reappeared anew in the form of Pan-Slavism.[20] This was now a doctrine preached by leading Russians, including the novelist Dostoevski, the poet Tyutchev, and the publicist Danilevsky. Danilevsky's *Russia and Europe*, published in 1871, predicted a long war between Europe and Russia, to be followed by a grand federation of the East, in which not only Slavs, but Greeks, Hungarians, and parts of Asiatic Turkey would be included under Russian control. This type of Pan-Slavism was favored and patronized by the Russian

[19] See pp. 544–545.
[20] On earlier Pan-Slavism, see pp. 510–511.

government, because it diverted attention from internal and revolutionary troubles. As for the Slav peoples of the Ottoman Empire, they were willing to use Russian Pan-Slavism as a means of combating their Turkish rulers. Insurrection against the Turks broke out in Bosnia in 1875, in Bulgaria in 1876. In 1877 Russia declared war on Turkey. Russia was again on the move against the Ottoman Empire for the sixth time in a hundred years.

The British, who had fought Russia over Turkey in 1854, were prepared to do so again. A number of recent developments added to their apprehension. The Suez Canal was completed in 1869. It was within the territory of the Ottoman Empire. It restored the Near East to its ancient position as a crossroads of world trade. The British also took alarm when Russia, in 1870, in the confusion of the Franco-Prussian War, repudiated a clause in the treaty of 1856 and began to build a fleet on the Black Sea. In 1874 Benjamin Disraeli, a Conservative and an imperialist, became prime minister of Great Britain. By a sudden coup in the following year he was able to buy up, from the almost bankrupt khedive of Egypt, 44 percent of the shares of the Suez Canal Company. In 1876, in a dramatic affirmation of imperial splendor, he had Queen Victoria take the title of empress of India. British commercial and financial interests in India and the Far East were growing, and the Suez Canal, of which the British government was now the principal stockholder, was becoming the "lifeline" of empire. But the Ottoman state, and hence the whole Near East, was now collapsing before the Russians, whose armies advanced rapidly through the Balkans in 1877, reached Constantinople, and forced the Turks to sign a treaty, the treaty of San Stefano. By this treaty Turkey ceded to Russia Batum and Kars on the south side of the Caucasus Mountains, gave full independence to Serbia and Romania, promised reforms in Bosnia, and granted autonomy to a new Bulgarian state, whose boundaries were to be very generously drawn, and which everyone expected to be dominated by Russia. England seethed with a popular clamor for war against Russia. The outcry gave the word "jingoism" to the language:

> We don't want to fight, but by jingo, if we do,
> We've got the men, we've got the ships, we've
>   got the money too.

It now appeared that the weakness of Turkey, its inability to fend off foreigners from its borders, would precipitate at least an Anglo-Russian and possibly a general European war. But war was averted by diplomacy. Bismarck assembled a congress of all the European great powers at Berlin. Once again Europe attempted to assert itself as a unity, to restore life to the much-battered Concert of Europe by dealing collectively with the common problem presented by the Eastern Question. The immediate need was to mediate between the Russians and Turks and to placate the British. To prevent any single power from gaining unequal advantage, and to win the acceptance of all powers for the arrangements agreed to, it was deemed necessary to give something to all, or almost all. The congress in effect initiated a partition of the Ottoman domain. It kept peace in Europe at the expense of Turkey. The European balance now both protected and dismembered Turkey at the same time.

The Russians were persuaded at Berlin to give up the treaty of San Stefano that they had imposed on the Turks, but they still obtained Batum and Kars and won independence for the Serbs and Romanians. Montenegro, too, was recognized as an independent state. They compromised on Bulgaria, which was divided into three zones with varying degrees of autonomy, all still nominally within the Ottoman Empire. Austria-Hungary was authorized by the congress to "occupy and administer" Bosnia (but not annex it) in the interests of civilization and in compensation for the spread of Russian influence in the Balkans. To the British (Disraeli boasted he brought home "peace with honor") the Turks ceded Cyprus, a large island not far from the Suez Canal. The French were told that they might expand from Algeria into Tunisia. To the Italians (who counted least) it was more vaguely hinted that some day, somehow, they might expand across the Adriatic into Albania. As Bismarck put it, "the Italians have such a large appetite and such poor teeth." Germany took nothing. Bismarck said he was the "honest broker," with no interest except in European peace.

The treaty of Berlin in 1878 dispelled the immediate threat of war. But it left many continuing problems for later statesmanship to deal with, problems which, because they were not dealt with successfully, became a principal cause of the First World War thirty-six years later. Neither the Balkan nationalists nor the Russian Pan-Slavs were satisfied. The Turks, both reactionaries like Abdul Hamid and the revolutionary Young Turks in exile, were indignant that peace had been made by further dismemberment of their territory. The demonstrated weakness of Turkey was a constant temptation to all concerned. In the years before 1914 German influence grew. Germans and German capital entered Turkey, projecting, and partially completing, a great Berlin to Bagdad railway to be accompanied by the exploitation of Near Eastern resources. The railroad was all but completed before 1914 despite the protests and representations of the Russians, the French, and particularly the British, who saw in it a direct threat to their empire in India.

Egypt and North Africa

For Egypt, technically autonomous within the Ottoman Empire, the 1850s and 1860s were a time of progress in the Western sense as they had been for the empire as a whole. The Egyptian government modernized its administration, court system, and property law, cooperated with the French in building the Suez Canal, encouraged shipping on the Red Sea, and let British and French interests construct railroads. Between 1861 and 1865, while the American South was unable to export raw cotton, the annual export of Egyptian cotton rose from 60 million to 250 million pounds. Egypt more than Turkey was drawn into the world market, and the khedive more than the sultan became a Western type of man. The khedive Ismail built himself a fine new opera house in Cairo, where, in 1871, two years after the opening of the Suez Canal, Verdi's *Aïda*, written at the khedive's request, was resoundingly performed for the first time.

Such improvements cost a good deal of money, borrowed in England and France. The Egyptian government was soon in financial straits, only temporarily relieved by the sale of Canal shares to Disraeli. By 1879 matters reached the point where Western banking interests forced the abdication of Ismail and his

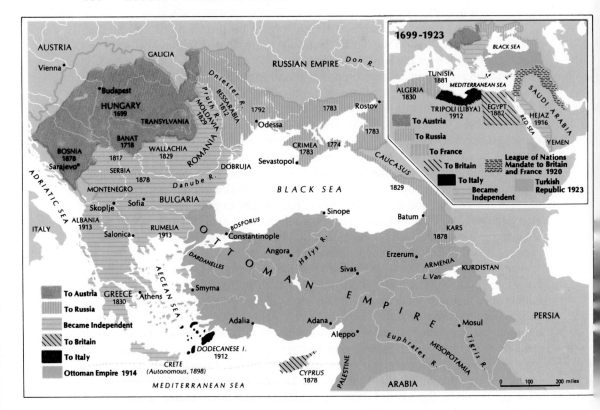

THE DISSOLUTION OF THE OTTOMAN EMPIRE, 1699–1914

Beginning in 1699, with the loss of Hungary to the House of Austria, the Ottoman Empire entered upon a long process of territorial disintegration which lasted for over two hundred years. Dates shown are those at which territories dropped away. In general, regions lost from 1699 to the fall of Napoleon, 1812–1815, were annexed directly by Austria and Russia. European territories lost in the nineteenth century emerged as independent states, owing to the rise of nationalism and the balance among the great European powers. (See maps, p. 703.) In the Arab world, reaching from Algeria to the Persian Gulf, regions lost before the First World War were absorbed into European colonial empires; those lost in the First World War (1918) were at first mostly assigned to France and Britain as mandates, but after the Second World War emerged as independent Arab states, as did the Republic of Israel (see pp. 940–945). During the First World War Britain, France, Italy, Russia, and Greece took steps to partition Turkey proper, but a Turkish nationalist movement blocked these designs and established a Turkish republic (see pp. 661, map, p. 703, 791–792).

replacement by Tewfik, who, with a naïve fascination for the new Western marvels, soon let himself become thoroughly enmeshed by his creditors. This led to nationalistic protests within Egypt, headed by Colonel Arabi. In a pattern repeated in many parts of the colonial world, especially in Manchu China, the nationalists opposed both the foreigners and their own government, charging it with being a mere front for foreign interests. Arabi's movement, an early expression of Arab nationalism, led to riots in Alexandria, where Europeans had to flee aboard British and French shipping in the harbor. A British squadron then unceremoniously bombarded Alexandria. British troops (the French, though invited to take part, refused) disembarked in 1882 at Suez and Alexandria, defeated Arabi, and took Tewfik under their protection. The military intervention of 1882 was said by the British to be temporary, but British troops remained there for a long time, through two world wars and well into the twentieth century, not leaving until 1956.

Egypt became a British protectorate. The British protected the khedive from discontent within his own country, from the claims of the Ottoman Porte, and from the rival attentions of other European powers. The British resident from 1883 to 1907, an exceptionally capable administrator named Evelyn Baring, the first Earl of Cromer, did much to reconstruct the economy of the country, reform its taxation, ease the burdens on the peasants and raise their productivity, while encouraging the growth of raw materials wanted by England and assuring regular payment of interest to British, French, and other holders of Egyptian bonds.

The French strenuously objected when the British stayed on so long in Egypt. It had long been the French who had the greatest investments in the Near East, and Near Easterners who were at all westernized—Egyptian, Syrian, Turkish—overwhelmingly preferred the French language and culture to the English. The French, harboring deep suspicion of British designs in Egypt, compensated themselves by building a North African empire farther west. They developed Algeria, assumed a protectorate over Tunisia, and began to penetrate Morocco. Upon these French advances the British, and soon the Germans, looked with unmitigated disfavor. Rivalry for the spoils of the Ottoman Empire thus created enmity among the Great Powers and constituted a fertile source of the war scares, fears, and diplomatic maneuvers that preceded the First World War. These are related in the following chapter.

The dissolution of the Ottoman Empire became indistinguishable from the whole chronic international crisis before 1914. It is enough to say here, to keep the fate of the Ottoman Empire in focus, that Abdul Hamid's frantic policies came to nothing and that the Young Turks won control of the Ottoman government in 1908. They forced the restoration of the constitution of 1876 and introduced many reforms. In the midst of the revolutionary disturbances of 1908 Bulgaria proclaimed its full independence and Austria annexed Bosnia. In the Turco-Italian War of 1911–1912 Italy took Libya and the Dodecanese Islands from the Turks. In two successive Balkan Wars (1912–1913) Turkey lost nearly all its territory in Europe to Bulgaria, Serbia, Greece, and Albania, the latter becoming an independent state in 1912.[21] Finally, when all Europe became involved in war in 1914, Russia again declared war on Turkey, and the Turks came into the war on the side of Germany, whose political and economic influence in the empire had been steadily growing. During the war, with British aid, the Arabs detached themselves from the empire, becoming eventually independent Arab states. Egypt, too, ended all connections with the empire. In 1923 a Turkish republic was proclaimed. It was confined to Constantinople and the Anatolian peninsula, where

[21] See p. 701, and map, p. 703.

the bulk of the true Turkish people lived. The new republic proceeded to undergo a thorough nationalist and secular revolution.[22]

81. The Partition of Africa

South of Mediterranean Africa lay the Sahara desert, and south of that Black Africa, of which Europeans knew so little that they called it the Dark Continent. Africa is so gigantic that even the part south of the Sahara is almost as large as the whole continent of North America. For centuries Europeans knew only its coasts—the Gold Coast, Ivory Coast, Slave Coast—to which from an inexhaustible interior had come shackled processions of captive slaves, as well as the swelling waters of enormous rivers, like the Nile, Niger, and Congo, whose sources in the dim hinterland were a subject of romantic speculation. The people were black, but diverse both in physique and in culture, and speaking almost a thousand languages. They had learned to work iron as long ago as the third century before Christ, and so only a few centuries later than Europeans. They were adept in many arts, such as bronze sculpture, gold artifacts, weaving, basketry, and the making of ceremonial masks with strikingly symbolic or abstract patterns. Along the northern fringe some had been won to Islam, but mostly they adhered to their traditional religions.

They lived mainly in villages in tribal communities, engaged in agriculture or moving herds of cattle from place to place. But great cities or agglomerations had also arisen, from Timbuktu in the north with its old caravan trade across the Sahara, to the vast complex of buildings at Zimbabwe in the south, which was already in ruins when the Europeans first saw it. There had also been extensive kingdoms whose memory was preserved, in the absence of writing, by specially trained narrators from one generation to the next. But these kingdoms had disappeared or declined. They had been weakened by intertribal wars, or by the slave trade which set Africans against one another to satisfy the demand of outsiders, or by demographic causes that are now hard to trace. Hence Africa, somewhat like the Ottoman Empire and China, met the assault of the Europeans at a time when its powers of resistance were reduced. Before the mid–nineteenth century there were no permanently resident whites south of the Sahara except for a few Arabs who had been on the east coast since the seventh century and the Europeans who had been at the Cape of Good Hope since 1652. In the Union of South Africa, when it was established in 1910, some 1.1 million whites lived along with about 5 million blacks.

The Opening of Africa

Missionaries, explorers, and individual adventurers first opened this world to Europe. The historic pair, Livingstone and Stanley, well illustrate the drift of events. Long before the imperialist age, in 1841, the Scot David Livingstone arrived in southeast Africa as a medical missionary. He gave himself to humanitarian and religious work, with a little occasional trading and much travel and discovery,

[22] See pp. 791–793.

but without political or true economic aims. Exploring the Zambesi River, he was the first white man to look upon the Victoria Falls. Fully at home in inner Africa, safe and on friendly terms with its native people, he was quite content to be let alone. But the hectic forces of modern civilization sought him out. Word spread in Europe and America that Dr. Livingstone was lost. The New York *Herald,* to manufacture news, sent the roving journalist H. M. Stanley to find him, which he did in 1871. Livingstone soon died, deeply honored by the Africans among whom he worked. Stanley was a man of the new era. Seeing vast possibilities in Africa, he went to Europe to solicit backers. In 1878 he found a man with the same ideas, who happened to be a king, Leopold II, king of the Belgians.

Leopold, for all his royalty, was at heart a promoter. China, Formosa, the Philippines, and Morocco had in turn attracted his fancy, but it was the central African basin of the Congo that he decided to develop. Stanley was exactly the man he was looking for, and the two founded at Brussels, with a few financiers, an International Congo Association in 1878. It was a purely private enterprise; the Belgian government and people had nothing to do with it. All Africa inland from the coasts was considered to be, like America in the time of Columbus, a *terra nullius*, without government and claimed by nobody, wide open to the first civilized persons who might arrive. Stanley, returning to the Congo in 1882, in a year or two concluded treaties with over 500 chiefs, who in return for a few trinkets or a few yards of cloth put their marks on the mysterious papers and accepted the blue-and-gold flag of the Association.

Since the Dark Continent was still innocent of internal frontiers, no one could tell how much ground the Association might soon cover by these methods. The German explorer Karl Peters, working inland from Zanzibar, was signing treaties with the chiefs of East Africa. The Frenchman Brazza, departing from the west coast and distributing the tricolor in every village, was claiming on the Congo River itself a territory larger than France. The Portuguese aspired to join their ancient colonies of Angola and Mozambique into a trans-African empire, for which they required a generous portion of the interior. Britain supported Portugal. In every case the home governments in Europe were still hesitant over involvement in an Africa of which they knew nothing. But they were pushed on by small organized minorities of colonizing enthusiasts, and they faced the probability that if they missed the moment it would be too late.

Bismarck, who personally thought African colonies an absurdity, but was sensitive to the new pressures, called another conference at Berlin in 1885, this time to submit the African question to international regulation. Most European states, as well as the United States, attended. The Berlin conference attempted to do two things: to set up the territories of the Congo Association as an international state, under international auspices and restrictions; and to draft an international code governing the way in which European powers wishing to acquire African territory should proceed.

The Congo Free State, which in 1885 took the place of the International Congo Association, was not only an international creation but embodied, in principle, what were to be known after the First World War as international mandates or international trusteeships for "backward" peoples. The Berlin conference specified that the new state should have no connection with any power, including Belgium. It delegated the government to Leopold. It drew the boundaries, making the Congo Free State almost as large as the United States east of the Mississippi, and it added certain specific provisions: the Congo River was internationalized, persons of all nationalities should be free to do business in the Congo state, there should be no tariff levied on imports, and the slave trade should be suppressed. Leopold in 1889 reassembled the signatory powers in a second conference, held at Brussels. The Brussels conference took further steps to root out the slave trade, which remained a stubborn though declining evil, because the Muslim world was several generations behind the Christian in abolishing slavery. The Brussels conference also undertook to protect the rights of the local people, correct certain glaring abuses, and reduce the traffic in liquor and firearms.

This attempt at internationalism failed, because Europe had no international machinery by which the hard daily work of executing general agreements could be carried out. Leopold went his own way in the Congo. His determination to make it commercially profitable led him to unconscionable extremes. Europe and America demanded rubber, and the Congo was at the time one of the world's few sources of supply. The Congo people, among the least advanced in Africa, and afflicted by the disease and enervation of a lowland equatorial climate, could be made to tap enough rubber trees only by inhuman severity and compulsion. The trees themselves were destroyed without thought of replacement. Leopold, by ravaging its resources and virtually enslaving its people, was able to draw from the Congo a princely income to be spent in Brussels, but he could never make the enterprise self-supporting. Consumed with debt, he borrowed another 25 million francs from the kingdom of Belgium, agreeing that Belgium should inherit the Congo on his death if the debt was unpaid. In 1908, the reluctant Belgians thus found themselves heirs to some "tropical gardens" to which they had been consistently indifferent. The Free State became the Belgian Congo, and under Belgian administration the worst excesses of Leopold's regime were removed.

The Berlin conference of 1885 had also laid down, for expansion in Africa, certain rules of the game—a European power with holdings on the coast had prior rights in the hinterland; occupation must not be on paper only, through drawing lines on a map, but must consist in real occupation by administrators or troops; and each power must give proper notice to the others as to what territories it considered its own. A wild scramble for "real occupation" quickly followed. In fifteen years the entire continent was parceled out. The sole exceptions were Ethiopia and, technically, Liberia, founded in 1822 as a colony for emancipated American slaves and virtually a protectorate of the United States.

Everywhere a variant of the same process was repeated. First would appear a handful of white men, bringing their inevitable treaties—sometimes printed forms. To get what they wanted, the Europeans commonly had to ascribe powers to the chief which by the customs of the tribe he did not possess—powers to convey sovereignty, sell land, or grant mining concessions. Thus the Africans were baffled at the outset by foreign legal conceptions. Then the Europeans would build up the position of the chief, since they themselves had no influence over the people. This led to the widespread system of "indirect rule," by which colonial authorities acted through the existing chiefs and tribal forms. There were many things that only the chief could arrange, such as security for isolated Europeans, porter services, or gangs of workmen to build roads or railroads.

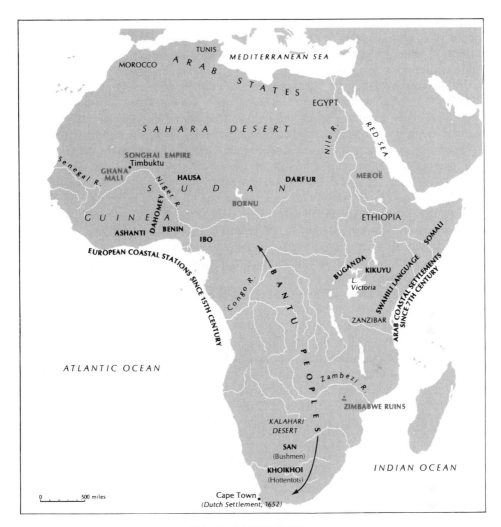

PRECOLONIAL AFRICA: SITES AND PEOPLES

This map is meant to show Africa before penetration by the Europeans in the nineteenth century. It does not refer to any particular date. Names in brown designate ancient or medieval centers, like the Ghana and Mali empires, which no longer existed in modern times. Even the most extensive African kingdoms had indefinite and shifting boundaries which are hard to indicate on a map. The word "Bantu," as in "Bantu peoples," refers to a large group of African languages spoken from points north of the Congo to the southern coast. See also map on p. 667.

Labor was the overwhelming problem. For pure slavery Europeans now had an abhorrence, and they abolished it wherever they could. But the African, so long as he lived in his traditional way, did not react like the free wage earner postulated in civilized business and economics. He had little expectation of individual gain and almost no use for money. He worked rather sporadically according to European ideas; work, continuous and laborious work, was in many

African societies left to the women. The result was that Europeans all over Africa resorted to forced labor. For road building, systems like the French *corvée* before the Revolution reappeared. Or the chief would be required to supply a quota of able-bodied men for a certain length of time, and frequently he did so gladly to raise his own importance in the eyes of the whites. More indirect methods were also used. The colonial government might levy a hut tax or a poll tax, payable only in money, to obtain which the native would have to seek a job. Or the new government, once installed, might allocate so much land to Europeans as private property (another foreign conception) that the local tribe could no longer subsist on the lands that remained to it. Or the whole tribe might be moved to a reservation, like Indians in the United States. In any case, while the women tilled the fields or tended the stock at home, the men would move off to take jobs under the whites for infinitesimal pay. The men then lived in "compounds," away from family and tribal kindred; they became demoralized; and the labor they gave, untrained and unwilling, would scarcely have been tolerated in any more civilized community. In these circumstances everything was done to uproot the Africans, and little was done to benefit them.

Conditions improved with the twentieth century, as traditions of enlightened colonial administration were built up. Colonial officials even came to serve as buffers or protectors of the local peoples against the intruding white man's interest. Throughout, it was part of the ethos of imperialism to put down slavery, tribal warfare, superstition, disease, and illiteracy. Slowly a westernized class of Africans grew—chiefs and the sons of chiefs, Catholic priests and Protestant ministers, warehouse clerks and government employees. Young men from Nigeria or Uganda appeared as students at Oxford, the University of Paris, or universities in the United States. Westernized Africans usually resented both exploitation and paternalism. They showed signs of turning nationalistic, like their counterparts in the Ottoman Empire and Asia. If they wanted westernization, it was at a pace and for a purpose of their own. As the twentieth century progressed, nationalism in Africa grew more vocal and more intense.

Friction and Rivalry between the Powers

Meanwhile, in the fifteen years from 1885 to 1900, the Europeans in Africa came dangerously near to open blows. The Portuguese annexed huge domains in Angola and Mozambique. The Italians took over two barren tracts, Italian Somaliland and Eritrea on the Red Sea. They then moved inland, in quest of more imposing possessions, to conquer Ethiopia and the headwaters of the Nile. Some 80,000 Ethiopians, however, slaughtered and routed 20,000 Italians in pitched battle at Adowa in 1896. It was the first time that Africans successfully defended themselves against the whites, and it discouraged invasion of Ethiopia by the Italians (or other Europeans) for forty years. Italy and Portugal, like the Congo Free State and Spain (which retained a few vestiges of former days), were able to enjoy sizable holdings in Africa because of mutual fears among the principal contenders. The principal contenders were Great Britain, France, and Germany. Each preferred to have territory held by a minor power rather than by one of its significant rivals.

The Germans were latecomers in the colonial race, which Bismarck entered with reluctance. By the 1880s all the usual imperialist arguments were heard in

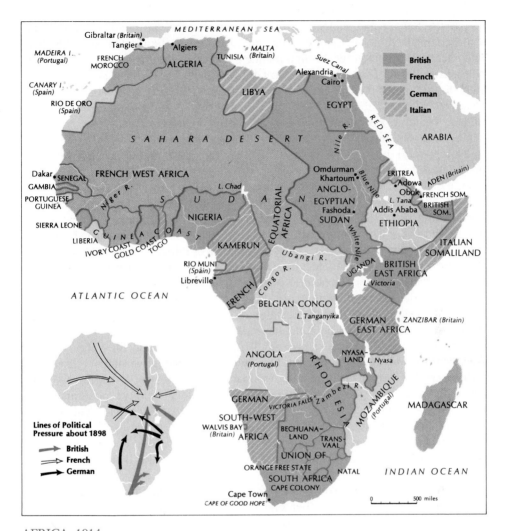

AFRICA, 1914

The map shows the recognized holdings of the Powers in 1914. The inset suggests the directions of political pressure about 1898. These pressures led to the Fashoda crisis in 1898 and the Boer War in 1899. In 1898 the British and German governments held secret discussions on the possible partitioning of the Portuguese colonies, which, however, never came to pass since the British greatly preferred to have the Portuguese colonies remain in the hands of Portugal.

Germany, though most of them, such as the need of new markets, of outlets for emigration, or for the investment of capital, had little or no application in tropical Africa. The Germans established colonies in German East Africa, and in the Cameroons and Togo on the west coast, along with a desert area that came to be called German Southwest Africa. It did not escape the notice of German imperial planners that some day the Congo and the Portuguese colonies might be joined with German East Africa and the Cameroons in a solid German belt across the African heartland. The French controlled most of West Africa, from Algeria across the Sahara and the Sudan to various points on the Guinea coast. They also occupied Obok on the Red Sea, and after the Italian defeat in 1896 their influence in Ethiopia grew. French planners therefore dreamed of a solid French belt across Africa from Dakar to the Gulf of Aden. The French government in 1898 dispatched Captain J. B. Marchand with a small party eastward from Lake Chad, to hoist the tricolor far away on the upper Nile, in the southern part of the Sudan, which no European power as yet "effectively" occupied.

The two presumptive east-and-west belts, German and French, were cut (presumptively) by a north-and-south belt, projected in the British imperial imagination as an "Africa British from the Cape to Cairo." From the Cape of Good Hope Cecil Rhodes pushed northward into what was later called Rhodesia. Kenya and Uganda in the mid continent were already British. In Egypt, a British protectorate since 1882, the British began to support old Egyptian claims to the upper Nile. The first venture proved a disaster, when in 1885 a British officer, "Chinese Gordon," leading an Egyptian force, was killed by aroused Muslims at Khartoum. In the following decade British opinion turned imperialist in earnest. Another British officer, General Kitchener (with a young man named Winston Churchill under his command), again started southward up the Nile and defeated the local Muslims in 1898 at Omdurman. He then pushed on further upstream. At a place called Fashoda he met Marchand.

The ensuing Fashoda crisis brought Britain and France to the verge of war. Already at odds over Egypt and Morocco,[23] the two governments used the encounter at Fashoda to force a showdown. It was a test of strength, not only for their respective plans for all Africa, but for their relative position in all imperialist and international issues. Both at first refused to yield. The British virtually threatened to fight. The French, fearful of their insecurity against Germany in Europe, at last decided not take the risk. They backed down and recalled Marchand from Fashoda. A wave of hatred for the British swept over France.

The British no sooner won this Pyrrhic victory than they became involved in more unpleasantness at the other end of the African continent. In 1890 Cecil Rhodes had become prime minister of the Cape Colony. He was a principal sponsor of the Cape-to-Cairo dream. Two small independent neighboring republics, the Transvaal and the Orange Free State, stood in his way. Their people were Afrikaners—Dutch who had originally settled the Cape in the seventeenth century, then after 1815, when England annexed the Cape of Good Hope, had made the "great trek" to escape from British rule. The Boers, as the English called them, from the Dutch word for "farmer," were simple, obstinate, and old-fashioned. They thought slavery not ungodly and disliked promoters, fortune hunters, foot-loose adventurers, mining-camp people, and other Uitlanders.

The discovery of diamonds and gold in the Transvaal brought the issue to a head. British capital and British people poured in. The Transvaal refused to pass legislation needed by the mining corporations and their employees. In 1895 Rhodes, attempting to precipitate revolution in the Transvaal, sent a party of armed irregulars, under Dr. Jameson, over its borders. This Jameson Raid was a failure, but in Europe a great cry went up against British bullying of a small

23 See p. 661.

inoffensive republic. The German emperor, William II, dispatched a famous telegram to Paul Kruger, president of the Transvaal, congratulating him on his driving off the invaders "without having to call for the support of friendly powers"—i.e., Germany. Three years later, in 1899, the British Empire went to war with the two small republics. The South African War (Boer War) lasted until 1902; the British sent in 300,000 troops, and to combat an elusive and irregular adversary they felt obliged to ravage the country and intern about 120,000 women and children in concentration camps, where about 20,000 died. But once subdued and brought within the British system the two republics were left with their self-governing institutions. In 1910 the Transvaal, Orange Free State, Cape Colony, and Natal were combined to form the Union of South Africa, which received semi-independent status along the lines of the Dominion of Canada.

The Fashoda crisis and the Boer War, coming in rapid succession, revealed to the British the bottomless depths of their unpopularity in Europe. All European governments and peoples were pro-Boer; only the United States, involved at the time in a similar conquest of the Philippines, showed any sympathy for the British. The British, after the Boer War, began to rethink their international position, as will soon be seen.

As in the case of the Ottoman Empire, rivalry between the Great Powers over the spoils of Africa embittered international relations and helped prepare the way for the First World War. The rivalry over Morocco involving France and Germany entered into the general prewar crisis and will be related in the following chapter. As for Africa as a whole, there was little territorial change after the Boer War, although in 1911 Italy took Libya from the Turks. In 1914 the Germans were excluded from their short-lived empire. Had the Germans won the First World War, the map of Africa would probably have been greatly revised, but since they lost it the only change was to assign the German colonies, under international mandate, to the French, British, and Belgians. With this change, and except for Italy's ephemeral conquest of Ethiopia in 1935, the map of Africa remained what the brief years of partition had made it until the spectacular end of the European empires after the Second World War.[24]

82. Imperialism in Asia: The Dutch, the British, and the Russians

The Dutch East Indies and British India

British India and the Dutch East Indies, in the half-century before the First World War, were the world's ideal colonies. They illustrated the kind of empire that all imperialists would have wished to have, and a glance at them suggests the goal toward which imperialism was logically moving.

Whereas all countries of western Europe showed a surplus of imports, receiving more goods from the rest of the world than they sent out, India and Indonesia invariably, year after year and decade after decade, showed a surplus of exports,

[24] See pp. 926–940, and map, p. 927.

sending out far more goods than they took in. This export surplus was the hallmark of the developed colonial area, geared closely into the world market, with low purchasing power for the natives and kept going by foreign investment and management. Both regions, in addition, were so large as to have a good deal of internal business—commerce, insurance, banking, transportation—which never appeared in the statistics for world trade, but which, being dominated by Europeans, added immeasurably to their profits. Both had rich and varied natural resources, tropical in character, so that they never competed with the products of Europe—though India even before 1914 showed tendencies to industrialization. In both regions the people were adept and quick to learn. But they were divided by religion and language, so that, once conquered, they were relatively easy for Europeans to govern. Neither region before the First World War had any self-government at the highest levels. Both were ruled by a civil service, honest and high-minded by its own lights, in which the most illustrious, most influential, and best paying positions were reserved for Europeans. Hence upper-class families in England and the Netherlands valued their empires as fields of opportunity for their sons—somewhat as they had formerly valued an established church. In both India and Indonesia the governments were more or less benevolent despotisms, which, by curbing warfare, plague, and famine, at least allowed the population to grow in numbers. Java, with 5 million people in 1815, had 48 million in 1942. India's population in the same years probably grew from less than 200 million to almost 400 million. Finally, as the last virtue of a perfect colony, no foreign power directly challenged the British in India or the Dutch in their islands.

The Dutch in 1815 occupied little more than the island of Java itself.[25] In the following decades the British moved into Singapore, the Malay peninsula, and north Borneo, and made claims to Sumatra. The French in the 1860s appeared in Indochina. The Germans in the 1880s annexed eastern New Guinea and the Marshall and Solomon islands. Ultimately it was the mutual jealousy of these three that preserved the Dutch position. The Dutch, however, took the initiative themselves. To forestall occupation by other Europeans, and to put down native pirates and find raw materials that the world demanded, the Dutch spread their rule over the whole 3,000-mile extent of the archipelago. They created an empire, in place of the old chain of trading posts concerned only with buying and selling. Revolts were suppressed in 1830, 1849, and 1888; not till the twentieth century was northern Sumatra or the interior of Celebes brought under control. For some decades the Dutch exploited their huge empire by a kind of forced labor, the "culture system," in which the authorities required farmers to deliver, as a kind of tax, stated amounts of stated crops, such as sugar or coffee. After 1870 a freer system was introduced. The Dutch also, as an important matter of policy, favored instruction in the Malay and Javanese languages, not in Dutch. This preserved the native cultures from westernizing disintegration but at the same time meant that Western ideas of nationalism and democracy entered more slowly.

In India, in 1857, the British faced a dangerous rebellion, commonly called the Indian Mutiny, as if it had been a revolt of undisciplined soldiers only. The Indian army, with its sepoys, was the only organization through which Indians could

[25] See p. 166.

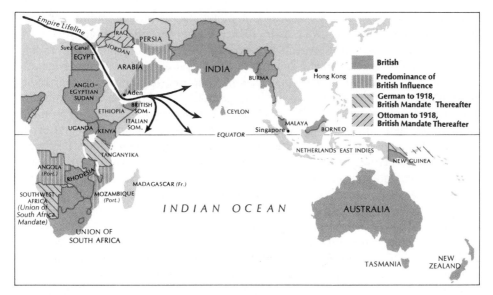

"THE BRITISH LAKE," 1918

This small map shows almost half the surface of the earth. All the most important parts of the British Empire are visible except Canada and the United Kingdom itself. All shores of the Indian Ocean are shown to be British, except for French Madagascar, the politically weak Portuguese, Italian, and Dutch colonies, and the Arabian and Persian coasts, in which British influence was strong. It is easy to see why the Mediterranean and the Suez Canal, leading from Europe into this half-world, were called the lifeline of the British Empire.

exert any collective pressure.[26] The proportion of sepoys in the army was high in 1857 (about five-sixths) because British units had been withdrawn for the Crimean War and for action in China. Many Indians, outside the army, had been restless for decades. Rulers had been conquered and dethroned. Landowners had lost their property and been replaced by new ones more friendly to the British. Religious sentiments were inflamed. The British too obviously regarded Indian beliefs as repulsive; they had outlawed suttee, or widow burning, suppressed the Thugs, a small sect of holy assassins, and one British officer even declared that in ten years the government would abolish caste. The Muslims were agitated by Wahabi fundamentalism. Mysterious propaganda circulated over India. It infiltrated the sepoys, announcing to Muslim soldiers that certain newly issued cartridges were greased with the fat of a pig and to Hindus that the same cartridges were greased with the fat of a cow. Since for Hindus the cow was sacred, and for Muslims to touch pork was profane, much agitation was produced. The sepoys mutinied in the Ganges valley; and with them the other injured interests, including the far-faded Great Mogul and his court, rose against the British.

The British put down the rebellion, aided by the fact that western and southern India took no part in it. But the uprising persuaded the British to a radically new course of policy, pursued basically until the end of the Indian empire almost a

---

[26] On the sepoys see pp. 282–283.

century later. The British East India Company and the Mogul empire were both finally and forever done away with. British authorities ruled directly. But the British concluded that they must rule India with and through the Indians themselves, not against them. This in practice meant a collaboration between the imperial power and the Indian upper classes. The British began to shelter Indian vested interests. They supported the Indian landlords and became more indulgent toward Indian "superstition." Where before 1857, when they conquered an Indian state, they had simply abolished it and incorporated its territories, after the Mutiny they kept the remaining Indian states as protectorates. States existing in 1857, such as Hyderabad and Kashmir and over 200 others, with their galaxy of rajahs and maharajahs, carried on to the end of British rule in 1947. It was largely to provide a fitting summit for this mountain of Indian royalty that Queen Victoria was proclaimed empress of India in 1877.

India had been a considerable manufacturing country by preindustrial standards. Indian merchants had once been important throughout the Indian Ocean, and before 1800 Indian exports to Europe had included many textiles and other finished goods.[27] The native crafts collapsed before modern industrialism reinforced by political power. "India," observed a British expert in 1837, "can never again be a great manufacturing country, but by cultivating her connection with England she may be one of the greatest agricultural countries in the world." Free trade (made possible by military superiority, usually overlooked by the economists) turned Britain into the world's workshop and India into a supplier of raw materials. Indian exports, in the latter part of the nineteenth century, consisted increasingly of raw cotton, tea, jute, oilseeds, indigo, and wheat. The British shipped their manufactures in return. Business in India boomed; India came to have the densest railway network outside of Europe and North America. It is important to note, however, as a commentary on dealing with poor countries, that Britain in 1914 did far more trading with the 6 million people of Australia and New Zealand than with the 315 million impoverished people of India.

The British, in contrast to the Dutch, decided in 1835 to favor instruction in English, not in the native languages. The historian Macaulay, one of the commission to make this recommendation, branded the Indian languages as vehicles of barbarous and unenlightened ideas—a bar to progress. The British also, after the Mutiny, admitted Indians to the civil service and to governors' councils—sparingly indeed, but more than the Dutch in Indonesia. There were also many Indian businessmen. A class of westernized Indians grew up, speaking perfect English, and often educated in England. They demanded more of a role in the affairs of their country. In 1885 the predominantly Hindu Indian National Congress was organized; in 1906, the All-India Muslim League. Muslim separatism, while favored by the British and sometimes even blamed upon them, was natural to India and exploited by some Indian leaders. Nationalism spread. It became increasingly anti-British, and radical nationalism turned also against the Indian princes, capitalists, and businessmen, as accomplices in imperialism, and so took on the color of socialism. In the period of the First World War, under nationalist pressure, the British granted more representation to Indians, especially in provincial affairs, but the movement toward self-rule was never fast enough to overcome the basic anti-British feeling of the Indian peoples.

[27] See pp. 259–262.

Conflict of Russian and British Interests

While no outsider yet threatened the British in India, British statecraft discerned in the northern sky a large cloud which was clearly approaching. The Russian empire had occupied northern Asia since the seventeenth century.[28] About 1850 Russian pressure on inner Asia was resumed. It was a type of imperialism in which neither the demand for markets nor for raw materials, nor for the investment of capital, counted for much. In these matters Russia was itself semicolonial with respect to the West. The Russians had, like the Westerners, a sense of spreading their type of civilization; but Russian expansion was distinctively political in that most of the initiative came from the government. Russia was an icebound empire, craving "warm-water ports." It was a landlocked empire, so that whichever way it turned it moved toward one ocean or another. The ocean was the domain of the Westerners, and in particular the British. In the large picture, Russia pushed by land against the Ottoman Empire, Persia, India, and China, all of which the British (and others) reached by sea. In 1860, on the shores of the Sea of Japan, the Russians founded Vladivostok, the farthest-flung of all Slavic cities, whose name meant Lord of the East. But their advance in the mid-century was mainly in the arid and thinly settled regions of western Asia. The British had already fought two Afghan wars to keep Afghanistan as a no man's land between Russia and India. In 1864 the Russians took Tashkent, in Turkestan. A decade later they touched India itself but were kept away by an Anglo-Russian agreement, which allotted a long tongue of land to Afghanistan and so separated the Indian and Russian empires by twenty miles—the new frontier, in the high Pamirs, on the Roof of the World, was to be sure, scarcely adapted to military operations.

Russian advances in Turkestan, east of the Caspian, increased the pressure on Persia, which had long felt the same pressure west of the Caspian, where cities like Tiflis and Baku, now Russian, had once been Persian. If Tiflis and Turkestan could fall to the Russian empire, there was no reason why Persia should not do so next—except that Persia had a seacoast and so might also be available for occupancy by the British. In 1864 a British company completed the first Persian telegraph as part of the line from Europe to India. Other British investments and interests followed. Oil became important about 1900. In 1890, to bolster the Persian government against Russia, the British granted it a loan—taking the customs in Persian Gulf ports as collateral. In 1900 the Russian government granted the same favor, making its own loan to Persia, and appropriating as security all Persian customs except those of the Gulf. Russian ships appeared in the Persian Gulf in 1900, a demonstration soon countered by a state visit to Persia of the Viceroy of India, Lord Curzon. Clearly Persia was losing control of its own affairs, falling into zones, turning ripe for partition. A Persian nationalist revolution, directed against all foreigners and against the subservient government of the shah, broke out in 1905 and led to the assembly of the first parliament but hardly settled the question of Persian independence. In 1907 the British recognized a Russian "sphere of influence" in northern Persia, the Russians a British sphere in the south.[29]

---

[28] See pp. 235–236.
[29] See pp. 673–674, 698, and map, pp. 676–677.

Imperial ambitions had deepened the hostility between Great Britain and Russia, with disputes over Persia and the Indian borderlands adding fuel to the quarrel they had long waged over the Ottoman Empire. We have seen how the struggle for Africa had at the same time estranged Britain from France and indeed from all Europe.

83. Imperialism in Asia: China and the West

China before Western Penetration

But the biggest bone of imperialist contention was offered by China. On this bone every Great Power without exception tried to bite. The Manchu, or Ch'ing, dynasty (1644–1912) held a suzerainty over the whole area affected by Chinese civilization, from the mouth of the Amur River (as far north as Labrador) to Burma and Indochina (as far south as Panama), and from the ocean westward into Mongolia and Tibet. In the old Chinese view China was the Middle Kingdom, the civilized center of the world surrounded by less enlightened peoples. The Europeans were outlandish barbarians. A few had trickled through to China since the European Middle Ages. But the Chinese people persistently wanted nothing to do with them.

China was moving into an upheaval of its own even before Western influence became of any importance. For 2,000 years the country had seen dynasties come and go in a kind of cycle. The Manchu dynasty in the nineteenth century was clearly nearing its end. It was failing to preserve order or to curb extortion. About 1800 a White Lotus Society revolted and was suppressed. In 1813 a Heavenly Reason Society attempted to seize Peking. In the 1850s a Muslim rebellion set up a temporary independent state in the southwest. Greatest of all the upheavals was the Taiping Rebellion of 1850, in which as many as 20 million people, approximately the population of Great Britain at the time, are thought to have perished. Except that some fragmentary Christian ideas, obtained from missionaries, were expressed by some of the Taipings, the rebellion was due entirely to Chinese causes. The rebels attacked the Manchus, who had come from Manchuria two centuries before, as corrupt foreigners ruling over China. Their grievances were poverty, extortion, rack-renting, and absentee landlords. The Taipings at first set up a state in south China, and their armies were at first disciplined, but the fighting lasted so long that both the Taiping leaders and the Manchu commanders sent against them got out of control, and much of the country sank into chronic banditry and disorder. It was in this period that China's war lords, men controlling armed forces but obeying no government, appeared. The Manchus managed to put down organized Taiping resistance after fourteen years, with some European assistance, led by the British General Gordon, the "Chinese Gordon" who later died at Khartoum. But it is clear that Chinese social confusion, agrarianism, and nationalism (the latter at first only anti-Manchu) antedated the impact of European imperialism.

Into this distracted China the Europeans began to penetrate about 1840. It became their policy to extort concessions from the Manchu empire but at the same time to defend the Manchu empire against internal opposition, as was shown by the exploits of Gordon. This was because they needed some kind of government in China with which they could make treaties, legalizing their claims and binding upon the whole country.

The Opening of China to the West

The modern phase of Chinese relations with the West was inauspiciously opened by the Opium War of 1839–1841. We have already observed how, though Europeans wanted Chinese products, the Chinese had no interest in buying European products in return. Trade therefore was difficult, and the British East India Company had for decades solved the problem of getting Chinese tea for Europe by shipping Indian-grown opium in return, since opium was one available commodity for which a Chinese demand existed.[30] When the Chinese government attempted to control the inflow of opium the British government went to war. Fifteen years later, in 1857, Britain and France combined in a second war upon China to force the Chinese to receive their diplomats and deal with their traders. The Chinese proving contumacious, 17,000 French and British soldiers entered Peking and deliberately burned the emperor's very extensive Summer Palace, an appalling act of vandalism from which soldiers brought back so much loot—vases, tapestries, porcelain, enamels, jades, wood carvings—as to set a fashion in Europe and America for Chinese art.

From the first of these wars arose the treaty of Nanking (1842), from the second the treaties of Tientsin (1857), whose terms were soon duplicated in still other treaties signed by China with other European powers and with the United States. The resulting complex of interlocking agreements imposed certain restrictions on China, or conferred certain rights upon foreigners, which came to be known as the "treaty system." To the British in 1842 the Chinese ceded the island of Hong Kong outright, and somewhat later granted adjoining territories on a long lease. They opened over a dozen cities, including Shanghai and Canton, to Europeans as "treaty ports." In these cities Europeans were allowed to make settlements of their own, immune to all Chinese law. Europeans traveling in the Chinese empire remained subject only to their own governments, and European and American gunboats began to police the Yangtse River. The Chinese likewise paid large war indemnities, though it was they themselves who suffered most of the damages. They agreed to levy no import duty over 5 percent and so became a free trade market for European products. To administer and collect the customs a staff of European experts was introduced. Money from the customs, collected

[30] See pp. 260, 354.

IMPERIALISM IN ASIA, 1840–1914

Boundaries and possessions are as of 1914. During these years the British and Dutch filled out their holdings in India and the East Indies, in each case moving outward from establishments founded long before. The Russians, who had long occupied Siberia, pressed southward in Central Asia, founded Vladivostok in 1860, and penetrated Manchuria at the close of the century. The French built an empire in Indochina, while the United States acquired the Philippines, and the Germans, as latecomers, were confined to miscellaneous parts of the western Pacific. The Japanese won control of Korea and replaced the Russians as the chief outside influence in Manchuria. Meanwhile all obtained special rights and concessions in China. A bid for such concessions by Italy was refused.

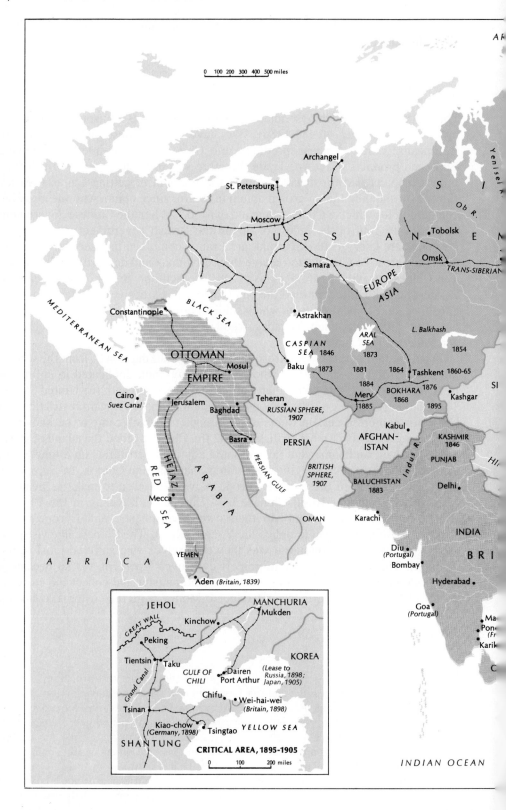

0 100 200 300 400 500 miles

Archangel

St. Petersburg

Moscow

R U S S I A N

Tobolsk

S I

Yenisei R.

Ob R.

Samara

Omsk

TRANS-SIBERIAN

EUROPE

ASIA

Astrakhan

ARAL
SEA
1873

L. Balkhash

1854

Constantinople

BLACK SEA

CASPIAN
SEA 1846

MEDITERRANEAN SEA

Baku   1873

1881

1864 Tashkent 1860-65

1884

1876

SI

OTTOMAN

Mosul

EMPIRE

Cairo
Suez Canal

Jerusalem

Teheran

RUSSIAN SPHERE,
1907

Merv
1885

BOKHARA
1868

1895

Kashgar

Baghdad

Basra

PERSIA

Kabul

AFGHAN-
ISTAN

KASHMIR
1846

RED

HEJAZ

A R A B I A

PERSIAN GULF

BRITISH
SPHERE,
1907

BALUCHISTAN
1883

PUNJAB

Delhi

Indus R.

HI

Mecca

SEA

OMAN

Karachi

INDIA

BR I

Diu
(Portugal)

Bombay

Hyderabad

A F R I C A

YEMEN

Aden *(Britain, 1839)*

Goa
(Portugal)

Ma
Pon
(Fr
Karik

C

Critical Area inset:

JEHOL

MANCHURIA
Mukden

GREAT WALL

Kinchow

Peking

KOREA

Tientsin Taku

GULF OF
CHILI

Dairen
Port Arthur

(Lease to
Russia, 1898;
Japan, 1905)

Grand Canal

Chifu

Wei-hai-wei
(Britain, 1898)

Tsinan

Kiao-chow
(Germany, 1898) Tsingtao

YELLOW SEA

SHANTUNG

CRITICAL AREA, 1895-1905

0   100   200 miles

INDIAN OCEAN

ALASKA
(Purchased by U.S.A. from Russia, 1867)

BERING SEA

ALEUTIAN I. (U.S.A., 1867)

KAMCHATKA

Lena R.

Yakutsk

R I A

SEA OF OKHOTSK

SAKHALIN

KURILE I. (Japan, 1875)

AMUR PROVINCE 1858

KARAFUTO (Japan, 1905)

Baikal   Chita   *Amur R.*   Khabarovsk

Irkutsk   *MANCHURIA*   MARITIME PROVINCE *(Russia, 1868)*

R E

Urga   Harbin   Vladivostok 1860

JAPANESE EMPIRE

ER MONGOLIA   Mukden   *SEA OF JAPAN*

us, 1912 Russian Sphere)   *INNER MONGOLIA*   JEHOL   KOREA *(Japan, 1905, 1910)*   Tokyo

Peking   Port Arthur *(Japan, 1905)*

Tientsin   Kiao-chow *(Germany, 1898)*

PACIFIC OCEAN

Huang Ho   Shanghai *(Britain, 1842)*

Nanking

C H I N A   Hankow   Ningpo 1842   *EAST CHINA SEA*

Chungking   *Yangtse R.*   Foochow   *RYUKYU I.*

Amoy   *FORMOSA (Japan, 1895)*   *MARIANA I. (Germany, 1899)*

Canton   *PESCADORES (Japan, 1895)*

YÜNNAN   KWANGSI *(French Sphere)*   Hong Kong *(Britain, 1842)*   *GUAM (U.S.A., 1898)*

Maçao *(Portugal, 1557)*

Kwang-chow *(Lease to France, 1898)*

URMA , 1852, 1885)   Hanoi   *HAINAN*   Manila   PHILIPPINE I. *(U.S.A., 1898, 1899)*   *CAROLINE I. (Germany, 1899)*

A 1852   *ANNAM*   FRENCH INDOCHINA 1884, 1907   *YAP*

on   SIAM   *Mekong R.*

1826   *SOUTH CHINA SEA*   *PALAU I.*

Bangkok   Saigon

BRITISH NORTH BORNEO 1888   *NEW GUINEA*

KAISER WILHEMSLAND *(Germany, 1884)*

SARAWAK 1888

MALAY STATES *(Britain, 1800, 1824)*   *BORNEO*   *CELEBES*

SUMATRA   Singapore *(Britain, 1819)*   *D U T C H   E A S T   I N D I E S*

(Portugal, 1859)

Batavia   *TIMOR*   Darwin

JAVA   AUSTRALIA

with a new efficiency, on a swelling volume of imports, went in part to the British and French in payment of the indemnities, but part remained with the Manchu government, which, as noted, the Europeans had no desire to overthrow.

Annexations and Concessions

While China was thus permeated at the center like an aging cheese, by extraterritorial and other insidious privileges for Europeans, whole slabs of it were cut away at the outer rim. The Russians moved down the Amur River, established their Maritime Province, and founded Vladivostok in 1860. The Japanese, now sufficiently westernized to behave like Europeans in such matters, in 1876 recognized the independence of Korea. The British annexed Burma in 1886. The French in 1883 assumed a protectorate over Annam despite Chinese protests; they soon combined five areas—Annam, Cochin China, Tonkin, Laos, and Cambodia—into French Indochina. (The first three were known also as Vietnam, a word not familiar in the West until after the Second World War.) These outlying territories had never, it is true, been integral parts of China proper; but it was with China that they had had their most important political and cultural relations and to the Chinese emperor that they had paid tribute.

Japan, whose modernization has been described already, lost little time in developing an imperialistic urge.[31] An expansionist party already looked to the Chinese mainland and to the south. Japanese imperialism first revealed itself to the rest of the world in 1894, when Japan went to war with China over disputes in Korea. The Japanese soon won, equipped as they were with modern weapons, training, and organization. They obliged the Chinese to sign the treaty of Shimonoseki in 1895, by which China ceded Formosa and the Liaotung peninsula to Japan and recognized Korea as an independent state. The Liaotung was a tongue of land reaching down from Manchuria to the sea; at its tip was Port Arthur. Manchuria was the northeastern part of China itself.

This sudden Japanese triumph precipitated a crisis in the Far East. No one had realized how strong Japan had become. All were astounded that a people

---

[31] See pp. 581–582.

NORTHEAST CHINA AND ADJOINING REGIONS

This area has long been one of the world's trouble zones. Note how Vladivostok is shut off from the ocean by the Japanese islands and Korea, and almost shut off from the mass of Russia by the intervening bulk of Manchuria. Manchuria, which began to be industrialized about 1900, became an object of dispute among China, to which it belonged historically, the Russian empire, to which it had strategic value and offered an access to the open ocean, and the Japanese empire, which found in it an outlet for commercial and military expansion and a buffer against Russia. Manchuria was dominated by the Russians from 1898 to 1905, by the Japanese from 1905 to 1945, and again by the Russians from 1945 to 1950, when they handed over their concessions and privileges to the Chinese Communist government. Korea was dominated by Japan after its victories over China in 1895 and over Russia in 1905. After World War II, Korea was promised independence but was divided at the 38th parallel into a Russian occupation zone and an American zone. After the Korean War (1950–1953, see pp. 879–883) the country remained divided at roughly the same parallel with a Communist regime in the north and a Western-sponsored regime in the south.

who were not "European," i.e., white, should show such aptitude for modern war and diplomacy. It was to be supposed that Japan had designs on Manchuria.

Now it so happened that Russia, not long before, in 1891, had begun to build the Trans-Siberian Railway, whose eastern terminus was to be Vladivostok, the "Lord of the East." Manchuria extended northward in a great hump between central Siberia and Vladivostok. The Russians, whether or not they ever dominated Manchuria themselves, could not allow its domination by another Great Power. It happened also that Germany was at this time looking for a chance to enter the

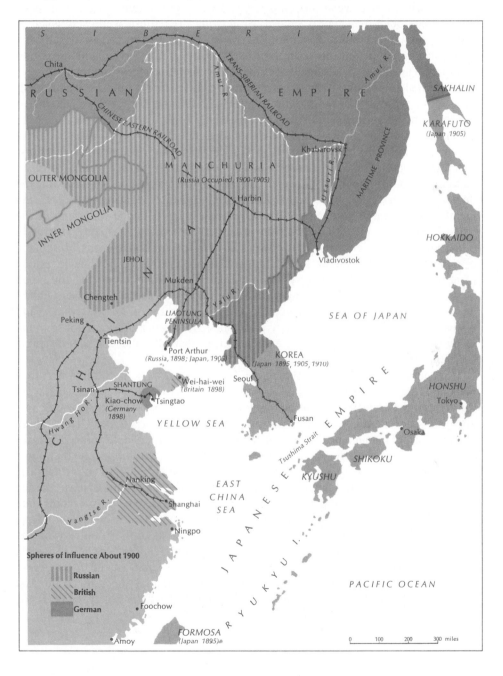

Spheres of Influence About 1900

Russian

British

German

Far Eastern arena, and that France had formed an alliance with Russia, whose good will it was eager to retain.[32]

Russia, Germany, and France therefore registered an immediate joint demurrer with the Tokyo Foreign Office. They demanded that Japan give up the Liaotung peninsula. The Japanese hesitated; they were indignant, but they yielded. The Liaotung went back to China.

In China many alert people were humiliated at the defeat by the Japanese whom they had despised. The Chinese government, at last facing the inevitable, began madly to plan westernization. Huge loans were obtained from Europe—the customs being pawned as security, following the pattern well established in Turkey, Persia, and Santo Domingo. But the European powers did not wish China to become consolidated too soon. Nor had they forgotten the sudden apparition of Japan. The result was a frantic scramble for further concessions in 1898.

It seemed in 1898 as if the Chinese empire in its turn would be partitioned. The Germans extorted a ninety-nine-year lease on Kiaochow Bay, plus exclusive rights in the Shantung peninsula. The Russians took a lease on the Liaotung peninsula from which they had just excluded Japan; they thus obtained Port Arthur and rights to build railroads in Manchuria to interlock with their Trans-Siberian system. The French took Kwangchow and the British Wei-hai-wei, in addition to confirming their sphere of influence in the Yangtse valley. The Italians demanded a share but were refused. The United States, fearing that all China might soon be parceled out into exclusive spheres, announced its policy of the Open Door. The idea of the Open Door was that China should remain territorially intact and independent, and that powers having special concessions or spheres of influence should maintain the 5 percent Chinese tariff and allow businessmen of all nations to trade without discrimination. The British supported the Open Door, as a means of discouraging actual annexations by Japan or Russia, which, as the only Great Powers adjacent to China, were the only ones that could dispatch real armies into its territory. The Open Door was a program not so much of leaving China to the Chinese, as of assuring that all outsiders should find it literally "open."

If readers will imagine what the United States would be like if foreign warships patrolled the Mississippi as far as St. Louis, if foreigners came and went throughout the country without being under its laws, if New York, New Orleans, and other cities contained foreign settlements outside its jurisdiction, but in which all banking and management were concentrated, if foreigners determined the tariff policy, collected the proceeds, and remitted much of the money to their own governments, if the western part of the city of Washington had been burned (the Summer Palace), Long Island and California annexed to distant empires (Hong Kong and Indochina), and all New England were coveted by two immediate neighbors (Manchuria), if the national authorities were half in collusion with these foreigners and half victimized by them, and if large areas of the country were the prey to bandits, guerrillas, and revolutionary secret societies conspiring against the helpless government and occasionally murdering some of the foreigners— then they can understand how observant Chinese felt at the end of the last century, and why the term "imperialism" came to be held by so many of the world's peoples in abomination.

---

[32] See pp. 696–698.

One Chinese secret society, its name somewhat literally translated as the Order of Literary Patriotic Harmonious Fists, and so dubbed the Boxers by the amused Westerners, broke out in insurrection in 1899. The Boxers pulled up railway tracks, fell upon Chinese Christians, besieged the foreign legations, and killed about 300 foreigners. The European powers, joined by Japan and the United States, sent a combined international force against the insurgents, who were put down. The victors imposed still more severe controls on the Chinese government and inflicted an indemnity of $330 million. Of this the United States received $24 million, of which, in 1924, it canceled the balance that was still due. On the other hand, as a consequence of the Boxer Rebellion, the Manchu officials strove desperately to strengthen themselves by westernization, while at the same time the revolutionary movement in China, aiming at expulsion of Manchus and foreigners alike, spread rapidly throughout the country, especially in the south, under the leadership of Sun Yat-sen.

84. The Russo-Japanese War and Its Consequences

Meanwhile Russia and Japan opposed each other's intrigues in Manchuria and Korea. The Japanese felt a need for supplying their new factories with raw materials and markets on the Asian mainland, for employment for their newly westernized army and navy, and for recognized status as a Great Power in the Western sense. The Russian government needed an atmosphere of crisis and expansion to stifle criticism of tsarism at home; it could not abide the presence of a strong power directly on its East Asian frontier; it could use Manchuria and Korea to strengthen the exposed outpost of Vladivostok, which was somewhat squeezed against the sea and landlocked by Japanese waters. The Russians had obtained a concession from China to build the Chinese Eastern Railway to Vladivostok across the heart of Manchuria. A railway, in Manchuria, implied special zones, railway guards, mining and timber rights, and other auxiliary activities. The Japanese saw the fruits of their successful war of 1895 against China greedily enjoyed by their rival. In 1902 Japan signed a military alliance with Great Britain. We have seen how the British were alarmed by their diplomatic isolation after Fashoda and the Boer War, and how for many years, in the Far East, the Middle East, and the Near East, they had been expecting to have trouble with Russia. The Anglo-Japanese military alliance lasted twenty years.

War broke out in 1904, undeclared, by Japanese naval attack on Russian installations at Port Arthur. Both sides sent large armies into Manchuria. The battle of Mukden, in the number of men engaged, which was 624,000, was the largest battle that human experience had thus far witnessed. Military observers were present from all countries, anxiously trying to learn what the next war in Europe would be like. The Russians sent their Baltic fleet around three continents to the Far East, but to the world's amazement the Russian fleet was met and destroyed at Tsushima Strait by the new and untested navy of Japan. Russian communications by sea were thereby broken, and since the Trans-Siberian Railway was unfinished, and since the Japanese also won the battle of Mukden, Russia was beaten.

At this point the president of the United States, Theodore Roosevelt, stepped upon the scene. With an outpost in the Philippines and growing interest in China, it was to the American advantage to have neither side win too overwhelming a victory in the Far East. The most imperially minded of all American presidents offered his mediation, and plenipotentiaries of the two powers met at Portsmouth, New Hampshire. By the treaty of Portsmouth, in 1905, Japan recovered from Russia what it had won and lost in 1895, namely, Port Arthur and the Liaotung peninsula, a preferred position in Manchuria, which remained nominally Chinese, and a protectorate in Korea, which remained nominally independent, although a few years later in 1910, it was annexed by Japan. Japan also received from Russia the southern half of the island of Sakhalin. Much of what Russia lost to Japan in 1905 was regained forty years later at the end of the Second World War.[33]

The Russo-Japanese War was the first war between Great Powers since 1870. It was the first war fought under conditions of developed industrialism. It was the first actual war between westernized powers to be caused by competition in the exploitation of undeveloped countries. Most significant of all (except for the Ethiopian rout of the Italians), it was the first time that a nonwhite people had defeated a white people in modern times. Asians had shown that they could learn and play, in less than half a century, the game of the Europeans.

The Japanese victory set off long chains of repercussions in at least three different directions. For one thing, the Russian government, frustrated in its foreign policy in East Asia, shifted its attention back to Europe, where it resumed an active role in the affairs of the Balkans. This contributed to a series of international crises in Europe, of which the result was the First World War. Second, the tsarist government was so weakened by the war, both in prestige and in actual military strength, and opinion in Russia was so disgusted at the clumsiness and incompetency with which the war had been handled, that the various underground movements were able to come to the surface, producing the Revolution of 1905. This in turn was a prelude to the great Russian Revolution twelve years later, of which Soviet communism was the outcome. Third, news of Japan's victory over Russia electrified those who heard of it throughout the non-European world. The fact that Japan was itself an imperialist power was overlooked in the excited realization that the Japanese were not white. Only half a century ago the Japanese, too, had been "backward"—defenseless, bombarded, and bulldozed by the Europeans. The moral was clear. Everywhere leaders of subjugated peoples concluded, from the Japanese precedent, that they must bring Western science and industry to their own countries, but that they must do it, as the Japanese had done, by getting rid of control by the Europeans, supervising the process of modernization themselves, and preserving their own native national character. Nationalist revolutions began in Persia in 1905, in Turkey in 1908, in China in 1911. In India and Indonesia many were stirred by the Japanese achievement. In the face of rising agitation, the British admitted an Indian to the Viceroy's executive Council in 1909, and in 1916 the Dutch created a People's Council, to include Indonesian members, in the Indies. The self-assertion of Asians was to grow in intensity after the First World War.

The Japanese victory and Russian defeat can therefore be seen as steps in three mighty developments: the First World War, the Russian Revolution, and the Revolt of Asia. These three together put an end to Europe's world supremacy and almost to European civilization; or at least they so transmuted them as to make the world of the twentieth century far different from that of the nineteenth.

[33] See p. 864.

THE BRITISH IN INDIA

The British presence in India, reaching over three centuries, spanned the whole period from the early trading empires to the latest phases of European imperialism. In the seventeenth century the Indian subcontinent was held together by a Muslim empire whose ruler was known in Europe as the Great Mogul. His revenues, in 1605, were some twenty times greater than those of the King of England. The Europeans were for a long time only handfuls of foreigners operating out of small coastal stations. After 1700 the Mogul authority fell to pieces, leaving a disorganized situation in which the British emerged as the supreme power throughout the country.

India in the nineteenth century represented, in its full form, the European imperialism that by 1900 reached throughout Asia and Africa. Parts of it were ruled by the British directly, parts through the rajahs and maharajahs of Indian states. British power prevented internal warfare and subordinated the conflicts between Hindus and Muslims. Peace generally prevailed except for the great Mutiny, or rebellion, of 1857, which was quickly suppressed. The British introduced their own ideas of law, government, civil service, and education. With food production increased by irrigation and famine relieved by transport of provisions by railroad, population grew very rapidly.

The British invested a great deal of capital in India, in railroads, coal mines, and tea plantations. There was also much development of Indian capital, especially in the new jute, cotton, and steel industries. As the railroad opened the interior to the cheaper products of Lancashire, the old handicraft and village industries were destroyed, to be symbolically revived by Gandhi and his spinning wheel in the 1920s, and in fact replaced by an extensive development of modern manufactures. India moved into the twentieth century as a land of extreme contrasts, of endless villages interrupted by teeming cities, with staggering problems of poverty and over population, yet also as an important industrial country with a heavy involvement in world trade.

The British, throughout their rule in India, lived very much to themselves, occasionally mixing with the Indian upper classes but avoiding intimate or even equal relationships. For many Indians, nevertheless, English became a second language, used both for contacts with the Western world and as a common medium among themselves. A modern Indian upper class, largely English-speaking, grew up with the development of business, government, and the professions. It ultimately took the lead in the national movement against foreign rule. But historic divisions within the country, between Hindu and Muslim, dating back to the Mogul empire and before, brought it about that upon the British withdrawal, in 1947, what had formerly been known as India became the separate states of India and Pakistan. Later Bangladesh was formed by secession from Pakistan.

The gorgeous East, as Milton called it, had been fabled in Europe for its riches since ancient times. Above, right, we see the weighing of the Great Mogul on his birthday, upon which he was to receive an equal weight in gold and jewels. The picture is from an English geography of 1782. As the French Encyclopédie put it at about this time: "The most solemn day of the year was when the emperor was weighed in golden balances in the presence of the people; on that day he received over 50 millions in presents."

At the left is the English factory at Surat, near Bombay, in the early seventeenth century. A "factory" was only a trading center where the agents, or factors, of the East India Company stored their goods.

Calcutta, now the largest city in India, is far from being one of the oldest. It was founded by the English East India Company in 1690, and acquired many Western-style buildings in the two following centuries. At the left above is the Old Court House; at the right the early nineteenth-century Government House, with a large British lion astride the neoclassic gate. At the left an English lady is carried in a palanquin, and in both pictures important persons ride by in carriages, surveyed at a distance by some of the plain people of India, one of them with a bullock cart. The two cultures never really merged.

Darjeeling, in the mountains 300 miles north of Calcutta, grew up after 1840 as a cool retreat for Britons in refuge from the Indian heat. At the left is the "big loop" of the Darjeeling Railway, a substantial feat of engineering, by which the imperial rulers were able to make the journey more comfortably. The clouds probably obscure a view of the Himalayas for which Darjeeling is famous.

687

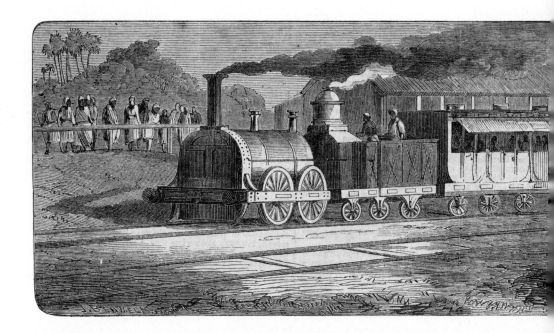

The railroad also had a transforming impact on India as a whole. By carrying goods it brought the interior into the world market, breaking up old native industries while creating new ones, and by transporting persons it drew together the members of diverse religions, castes, and linguistic groups. A passenger train of 1863 appears above. In its crowded coaches Indians who in former times would have kept scrupulously apart, for fear of pollution, had to rub elbows together, and on long journeys even eat together and breathe the same tainted air. Such proximity, together with the increasing adoption of English, produced a new basis for Indian unity which in the end was to make the British position untenable.

At the right, before the track is laid, a team of elephants hauls the first locomotive into Indore in Central India.

Above left: Queen Victoria is proclaimed Empress of India at Bombay in 1877. The neo-Gothic canopy, built for the occasion, under which an effigy of the queen is enthroned, seems incongruous in the circumstances. It reminds us, together with the more permanent church in the background, that the British maintained their own ways with supreme confidence, making few concessions to the alien culture over which they presided.

In the nineteenth century the traveling Englishwoman became legendary for her indomitability. At the right, two of them go on a jungle picnic. The pith helmets of their escorts, and the bearer carrying the refreshments on his head, may be taken as symbols of the heyday of empire.

691

*The two scenes depicted in the drawings above represent the administration of justice,
with a British magistrate at the right, and an Indian magistrate at the left. They seem
much alike, and their purpose may be to show how under British rule the Indian judicial
system was brought up to British standards of legal procedure.*

*Many Indians received a thoroughly English education. At the far right is Jawaharlal
Nehru at Harrow about 1905. Nehru, born in 1889 of Brahmin parents, his father a wealthy
lawyer, was educated at home by English tutors, then sent to Harrow and Cambridge. He
joined Gandhi in the independence movement in the 1920s, and served as first prime
minister of independent India from 1947 until his death in 1964. British India dug its own
grave, or prepared its own successors.*

XVI.
THE FIRST
WORLD WAR

SOMEWHERE BEFORE 1914 Europe went off its course. Europeans believed themselves to be heading for a kind of high plateau, full of a benign progress and more abundant civilization, in which the benefits of modern science and invention would be more widely diffused, and even competitive struggle worked out somehow for the best. Instead, Europe stumbled in 1914 into disaster. It is not easy to see exactly where Europe went astray, at what point, that is, the First World War became inevitable, or (since the human mind does not know what is truly inevitable) so overwhelmingly probable that only the most Olympian statesmanship could have avoided it.

85. The International Anarchy

After 1870 Europe lived in a repressed fear of itself. The great questions of the mid-century had been settled by force. The German Empire was only the strongest and most obvious of the new structures which armed power had reared. Never had the European states maintained such huge armies in peacetime as at the beginning of the twentieth century. One, two, or even three years of compulsory military service for all young men became the rule. In 1914 each of the Continental

Chapter Emblem: A German medal to celebrate the sinking of the Lusitania in 1915, showing the Cunard Line as a skeleton selling tickets, under an inscription, "Business First."

Great Powers had not only a huge standing army but millions of trained reserves among the civilian population. Few people wanted war; all but a few sensational writers preferred peace in Europe, but many took it for granted that war would come some day. In the last years before 1914 the idea that war was bound to break out sooner or later probably made some statesmen, in some countries, more willing to unleash it.

Rival Alliances: Triple Alliance versus Triple Entente

Political diagnosticians, from Richelieu to Metternich, had long thought that an effective union of Germany would revolutionize the relationships of Europe's peoples. After 1870 their anticipations were more than confirmed. Once united (or almost united), the Germans entered upon their industrial revolution. Manufacturing, finance, shipping, population grew phenomenally. In steel, for example, of which Germany in 1865 produced less than France, by 1900 Germany produced more than France and Great Britain combined. Germans felt that they needed and deserved a "place in the sun," by which they vaguely meant some kind of acknowledged supremacy like that of the British. Neither the British nor the French, the leaders of modern Europe since the seventeenth century, could share wholeheartedly in such German aspirations. The French had the chronic grievance of Alsace and Lorraine, annexed to Germany in 1871. The British as the years passed saw German salesmen appear in their foreign markets, selling goods often at lower prices and by what seemed ungentlemanly methods; they saw Germans turn up as colonial rivals in Africa, the Near East, and the Far East; and they watched other European states gravitate into the Berlin orbit, looking to the mighty German Empire as a friend and protector to secure or advance their interests.

Bismarck after 1871 feared that in another European war his new German Empire might be torn to pieces. He therefore followed, until his retirement in 1890, a policy of peace. We have seen him as the "honest broker" at the Berlin Congress of 1878, helping to adjudicate the Eastern Question, and again offering the facilities of Berlin in 1885 to regulate African affairs.[1] To isolate France, divert it from Europe, and keep it embroiled with Britain, he looked with satisfaction on French colonial expansion. He took no chances, however; in 1879 he formed a military alliance with Austria-Hungary, to which Italy was added in 1882. Thus was formed the Triple Alliance, which lasted until the First World War. Its terms were, briefly, that if any member became involved in war with two or more powers its allies should come to its aid by force of arms. To be on the safe side, Bismarck signed a "reinsurance" treaty with Russia also; since Russia and Austria were enemies (because of the Balkans), to be allied to both at the same time took considerable diplomatic finesse. After Bismarck's retirement his system proved too intricate, or too lacking in candor, for his successors to manage. The Russo-German agreement lapsed. The French, faced by the Triple Alliance, soon seized the opportunity to form their own alliance with Russia, the Franco-Russian Alliance signed in 1894. In its time this was regarded as politically almost impossible. The French Republic stood for everything radical, the Russian

[1] See pp. 658, 663–664.

empire for everything reactionary and autocratic. But ideology was thrown to the winds, French capital poured into Russia, and the tsar bared his head to the *Marseillaise*.

The Continent was thus divided by 1894 into two opposed camps, the German-Austrian-Italian against the Franco-Russian. For a time it seemed that this rigid division might soften. Germany, France, and Russia cooperated in the Far Eastern crisis of 1895.[2] All were anti-British at the time of Fashoda and the Boer War. The Kaiser, William II, outlined tempting pictures of a Continental league against the global hegemony of England and her empire.

Much depended on what the British would do. They had long prided themselves on a "splendid isolation," going their own way, disdaining the kind of dependency that alliance with others always brings. Fashoda and the Boer War came as a shock. British relations with France and Russia were very bad. Some in England, including Joseph Chamberlain, therefore thought that a better understanding with Germany was to be sought. Arguments of race, in this race-conscious age, made Englishmen and Germans feel akin.[3] But politically it was hard to cooperate. The Kaiser's Kruger Telegram of 1896 was a studied insult.[4] Then in 1898 the Germans decided to build a navy.

A new kind of "race" now entered the picture, the naval competition between Germany and Great Britain. British sea power for two centuries had been all too successful. The American Admiral Mahan, teaching at the Naval War College, and taking his examples largely from British history, argued that sea power had been the foundation of Britain's greatness, and that in the long run sea power must always choke off and ruin a power operating on the land. Nowhere were Mahan's books read with more interest than in Germany. The German naval program, mounting rapidly after 1898, in a few years became a source of concern to the British, and by 1912 was felt as a positive menace. The Germans insisted that they must have a navy to protect their colonies, secure their foreign trade, and "for the general purposes of their greatness." The British held with equal resolution that England, as a densely populated industrial island, dependent even for food upon imports, must at all costs control the sea in both peace and war. They adhered stubbornly to their traditional policy of maintaining a navy as large as the next two combined. The naval race led both sides to enormous and increasing expenditures. In the British it produced a sense of profound insecurity, driving them as the years passed ever more inescapably into the arms of Russia and France.

Slowly and cautiously the British emerged from their diplomatic isolation. In 1902 they formed a military alliance with Japan against their common enemy, Russia.[5] The decisive break came in 1904, from which may be dated the immediate series of crises issuing in the World War ten years later.

In 1904 the British and French governments agreed to forget Fashoda and the

---

[2] See pp. 679–680.
[3] The will of Cecil Rhodes, who died in 1902, illustrates this point. Rhodes left most of his fortune (£6 million) to establish scholarships at Oxford to be awarded to students in the United States, as an Anglo-Saxon country, the British dominions and colonies, and Germany. The German Rhodes Scholarships were suspended from 1914 to 1930 and again after 1938. The same feeling that Germans were racially akin was common in the United States also; a prominent example of this viewpoint was President Theodore Roosevelt.
[4] See p. 669.
[5] See p. 681.

accumulated bad feeling of the preceding twenty-five years. The French recognized the British occupation of Egypt, and the British recognized the French penetration of Morocco. They also cleared up a few lesser colonial differences and agreed to support each other against protests by third parties. There was no specific alliance; neither side said what it would do in the event of war; it was only a close understanding, an *entente cordiale*. The French immediately tried to reconcile their new friend to their ally, Russia. After defeat by Japan the Russians proved amenable. The British, increasingly uncertain of German aims, proved likewise willing. In 1907 Britain and Russia, the inveterate adversaries, settled their differences in an Anglo-Russian Convention. In Persia, the British recognized a Russian sphere of influence in the north, the Russians a British sphere in the south and east. By 1907 England, France, and Russia were acting together. The older Triple Alliance faced a newer Triple Entente, the latter somewhat the looser, since the British refused to make any formal military commitments.

The Crises in Morocco and the Balkans

The Germans, who already felt encircled by the alliance of France and Russia, naturally watched with concern the drift of England into the Franco-Russian camp. The Entente Cordiale was barely concluded when the German government decided to test it, to find out how strong it really was, or how far the British would really go in support of France. The French, now enjoying British backing, were taking over more police powers, concessions, and loans in Morocco. In March 1905 William II disembarked from a German warship at Tangier, where he made a startling speech in favor of Moroccan independence. To diplomats everywhere this carefully staged performance was a signal: Germany was attempting not primarily to keep France out of Morocco, nor even to reserve Morocco for itself, but to break up the new understanding between France and England. The Germans demanded and obtained an international conference at Algeciras (at which the United States was represented), but the conference, which met in 1906, supported the French claims in Morocco, only Austria voting with Germany. The German government had thus created an incident and been rebuffed. The British, disturbed by German diplomatic tactics, stood by the

ANGLO-GERMAN INDUSTRIAL COMPETITION, 1898 AND 1913

This diagram really shows two things: first, the huge increase in world trade in the last fifteen years before the First World War, shared in by all countries; and second, the fact that German exports grew more rapidly than British. The exports of both countries together, as shown on the diagram, multiplied no less than threefold in these fifteen years. The increase, while due in small part to a slight rise of prices, was mainly due to a real increase in volume of business. If the reader will compare the shaded bands within the large arrows he will see that, for the countries shown, British exports about doubled, but those of Germany multiplied many times. In 1913 total German exports about equaled the British, but German exports to the United States and Russia greatly exceeded the British. Note how the Germans even gained in exports to British India, where the liberalism of British policy freely admitted competitive goods. In merchant marine, though the Germans doubled their tonnage, the British continued to enjoy an overwhelming lead.

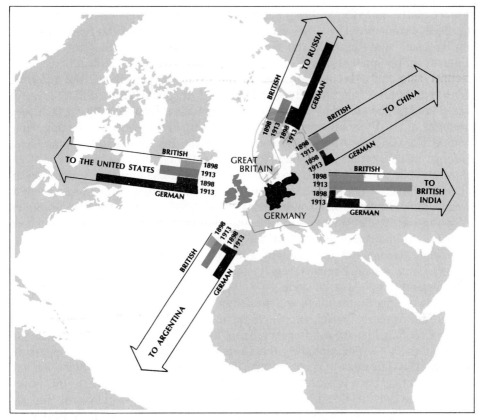

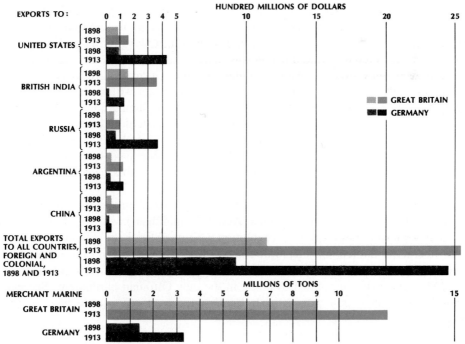

French all the more firmly. French and British army and naval officers now began to discuss common plans. Distrust of Germany also inclined the British to bury the hatchet with Russia in the next year. The German attempt to break the Entente simply made it more solid.

In 1911 came a second Morocco crisis. A German gunboat, the *Panther*, arrived at Agadir "to protect German interests." It soon developed that the move was a holdup; the Germans offered to make no further trouble in Morocco if they could have the French Congo. The crisis passed, the Germans obtaining some trifling accessions in Africa. But a member of the British cabinet, David Lloyd George, made a rather inflammatory speech on the German menace.

Meanwhile a series of crises rocked the Balkans. The Ottoman Empire, in an advanced state of dissolution, still held a band of territory from Constantinople westward to the Adriatic.[6] South of this band lay an independent Greece. North of it, on the Black Sea side, lay an autonomous Bulgaria and an independent Romania. In the center and west of the peninsula, north of the Turkish belt, was the small, landlocked independent kingdom of Serbia, adjoined by Bosnia-Herzegovina, which belonged legally to Turkey but had been "occupied and administered" by Austria since 1878. Within the Austro-Hungarian Empire, adjoining Bosnia on the north and west, lay Croatia and Slovenia.

Serbs, Bosnians, Croats, and Slovenes all spoke basically the same language, Serbo-Croatian, the main difference being that Serbs and Bosnians wrote with the eastern or Cyrillic alphabet, the Croats and Slovenes with the western or Roman. The difference reflected deep differences in religion. The Slovenes and Croats had long been Roman Catholic, and hence affiliated with Western Europe; the Serbs and many Bosnians were Eastern Orthodox and so closer to Russia; and there were also, especially in Bosnia, large numbers of Slavs who were Muslims, converted during the Ottoman domination. With the Slavic Revival, which emphasized language, many of these peoples came to feel that they were really one people, for which they took the name South Slavs, or Yugoslavs. After the Dual Monarchy was formed in 1867, as we have seen, the Slavs of the Habsburg empire were kept subordinate to the German Austrians and the Hungarian Magyars.[7] By 1900 radical Slav nationalists within the empire had concluded that the Dual Monarchy would never grant them equal status, that it must be broken up, and that all South Slavs should form an independent state of their own. Concretely, this meant that an element of the Austro-Hungarian population, namely, the Croatian and Slovenian nationalists, wished to get out of the empire and join with Serbia across the border. Serbia became the center of South Slav agitation.

This brew was brought to a boil in 1908 by two events. First, the Young Turks, whose long agitation against Abdul Hamid has been noted, managed in that year to carry through a revolution.[8] They obliged the sultan to restore the liberal parliamentary constitution of 1876. They showed, too, that they meant to stop the dissolution of the Ottoman Empire, by taking steps to have delegates from Bulgaria and Bosnia sit in the new Ottoman parliament. Second, Russia, its foreign policy in the Far East ruined by the Japanese war, turned

[6] See maps, pp. 470, 660, and 703, and see also map, p. 1034.
[7] See p. 561.
[8] See p. 657.

actively to the Balkan and Turkish scene. Russia, as always, wanted control at Constantinople. Austria wanted full annexation of Bosnia, the better to discourage Pan-Yugoslav ideas. But if the young Turks really modernized and strengthened the Ottoman Empire, Austria would never get Bosnia nor the Russians Constantinople.

The Russian and Austrian foreign ministers, Isvolsky and Aehrenthal, at a conference at Buchlau in 1908 came to a secret agreement. They would call an international conference, at which Russia would favor Austrian annexation of Bosnia, and Austria would support the opening of the Straits to Russian warships. Austria, without waiting for a conference, proclaimed the annexation of Bosnia without more ado. This infuriated the Serbs, who had marked Bosnia for their own. Meanwhile, that same year, the Bulgarians and the Cretans broke finally with the Ottoman Empire, Bulgaria becoming fully independent, Crete uniting with Greece. Isvolsky was never able to realize his plans for Constantinople. His partners in the Triple Entente, Britain and France, refused to back him; the British in particular were evasive on plans for opening the Straits to the Russian fleet. The projected international conference was never called. In Russia itself public opinion knew nothing of Isvolsky's secret deal. The known fact in Russia was that the Serbs, the little Slav brothers of Russia, had their toes rudely stepped on by the Austrians by the annexation of Bosnia.

This "first Balkan crisis" presently passed. The Russians, weakened by the Japanese war and by recent revolution,[9] accepted the Austrian *fait accompli*. Russia protested but backed down. Austrian influence in the Balkans seemed to be growing. And South Slav nationalism was frustrated and inflamed.

In 1911 Italy declared war on Turkey, from which it soon conquered Tripoli and the Dodecanese Islands. With the Ottomans thus embarrassed, Bulgaria, Serbia, and Greece joined forces in their own war against Turkey, hoping to annex certain Balkan territories to which they believed they had a right. Turkey was soon defeated, but the Bulgarians claimed more of Macedonia than the Serbs would yield, so that the first Balkan war of 1912 was followed in 1913 by a second, in which Serbia, Greece, Romania, and Turkey turned upon and defeated Bulgaria. Albania also, a mountainous region on the Adriatic, mainly Muslim, and known as the wildest place in all Europe, was the subject of angry discord. The Serbs occupied part of it in the two Balkan wars, but the Greeks also claimed a part, and it had also on several occasions been vaguely promised to Italy.[10] Russia supported the Serbian claim. Austria was determined to shut off the Serbs from access to the sea, which they would obtain by annexation of Albanian territory. An agreement of the great powers, to keep the peace, conjured up an independent kingdom of Albania. This confirmed the Austrian policy, kept Serbia from the sea, and aroused vehement outcries in both Serbia and Russia. But Russia again backed down. Serbian expansionism was again frustrated and inflamed.

The third Balkan crisis proved to be the fatal one. It was fatal because two others had gone before it, leaving feelings of exasperation in Austria, desperation in Serbia, and humiliation in Russia.

[9] See pp. 681–682, 741–744.
[10] See pp. 658–659.

The Sarajevo Crisis and the Outbreak of War

On June 28, 1914, a young Bosnian revolutionary, a member of the Serbian secret society called "Union or Death," and commonly known as the Black Hand, acting with the knowledge of certain Serbian officials, assassinated the heir to the Habsburg empire, the Archduke Francis Ferdinand, in the streets of Sarajevo, the Bosnian capital, in the Austrian Empire. The world was shocked at this terrorist outrage and at first sympathized with the protests of the Austrian government. Francis Ferdinand, who would soon have become emperor, was known to favor some kind of transformation of Austria-Hungary, in which a more equal place might be given to the Slavs; but the reformer who makes a system work is the most dangerous of all enemies to the implacable revolutionary, and it is perhaps for this reason that the archduke was killed by the Black Hand.

The Austrian government was determined to make an end to the South Slav separatism that was gnawing its empire to pieces. It decided to crush the independence of Serbia, the nucleus of South Slav agitation, though not to annex it, since there were now thought to be too many Slavs within the empire already. The Austrian government consulted the German to see how far it might go with the support of its ally. The Germans, issuing their famous "blank check," encouraged the Austrians to be firm. The Austrians, thus reassured, dispatched a drastic ultimatum to Serbia, demanding among other things that Austrian officials be permitted to collaborate in investigating and punishing the perpetrators of the assassination. The Serbs counted on Russian support, even to the point of war, judging that Russia could not again yield in a Balkan crisis, for the third time in six years, without losing its influence in the Balkans altogether. The Russians in turn counted on France; and France, terrified at the possibility of being some day caught alone in a war with Germany, and determined to keep Russia as an ally at any cost, in effect gave a blank check to Russia. The Serbs rejected the critical item in the Austrian ultimatum as an infringement on Serbian sovereignty, and Austria thereupon declared war upon Serbia. Russia prepared to defend Serbia and hence to fight Austria. Expecting that Austria would be joined by Germany, Russia rashly mobilized its army on the German as well as the Austrian frontier. Since the power which first mobilized had all the advantages of a rapid offensive, the German government demanded an end to the Russian mobilization on its border and, receiving no answer, declared war on Russia on August 1, 1914. Convinced that France would in any case enter the war on the side of Russia, Germany also declared war on France on August 3.

The German decisions were posited on a reckless hope that Great Britain might not enter the war at all. England was bound by no formal military alliance. Even the French did not know for certain, as late as August 3, whether the British would join them in war. The British clung to scraps of their old proud isolation; they hesitated to make a final choice of sides; and as the foreign secretary, Sir Edward Grey, repeatedly explained, in England only Parliament could declare war, so that the foreign office could make no binding promise of war in advance. It has often been said that, had the German government known as a positive fact that England would fight, the war might not have come. Hence the evasiveness of British policy is made a contributing cause of the war. In reality, the probability that England would fight was so great that to underestimate it, as the Germans

THE BALKANS, 1878 AND 1914

The Ottoman Empire, under the blows of Austria and Russia, had been receding from Europe since 1699 (see map, p. 660). The Congress of Berlin of 1878 undertook to stabilize the situation by recognizing Romania, Serbia, and Montenegro as independent monarchies, and northern Bulgaria as an autonomous principality within the Ottoman Empire. The ambitions of these new states (and of Greece, independent since 1829), together with the discontents of all non-Turkish peoples remaining under Ottoman rule, led to successive altercations culminating in the Balkan wars of 1912–1913. Albania then became independent, and Serbia, Bulgaria, and Greece contiguous. Austrian and Russian pressures meanwhile continued; in 1908 Austria annexed Bosnia, where the South Slav population was related to the Serbs. In Bosnia, at Sarajevo, six years later, the assassination of an Austrian archduke by a South Slav patriot precipitated the First World War.

did, was an act of supreme folly. The British were deeply committed to France, especially through naval agreements. As the German High Seas Fleet grew, the British had been obliged to concentrate naval forces in the North Sea. They had therefore had to withdraw forces from the Mediterranean. In 1914, by agreement with France, the French fleet was concentrated in the Mediterranean, watching over British interests, while the British fleet attended to French interests in the north. The French Channel coast was therefore open to German naval attack, unless the British defended it. Sir Edward Grey accepted this moral obligation, but what swept the British public was the invasion of Belgium. The German plan to crush France quickly was such that it could succeed only by crossing Belgium. When the Belgians protested, the Germans invaded anyway, violating the treaty of 1839 which had guaranteed Belgian neutrality.[11] England declared war on Germany on August 4.

[11] See pp. 488–489.

The mere narration of successive crises does not explain why the chief nations of Europe became locked in combat over the murder of an imperial personage within a few days. Among more obvious general causes, the alliance system may be singled out. Europe was divided into two camps. Every incident tended to become a test of strength between the two. A given incident, such as German intervention in Morocco, or the assassination of Francis Ferdinand, could not be settled on its own merits, merely by the parties concerned; however it was dealt with, one of the two camps was deemed to have lost or gained and hence to have lost or gained in influence in other incidents, of perhaps greater purport, that would arise in the future. Each power felt that it must stand by its allies whatever the specific issue. This was because all lived in the fear of war, of some nameless future war in which allies would be necessary. The Germans complained of being "encircled" by France and Russia. They dreaded the day when they might have to face a war on two fronts. Willing to accept even a European-wide war to break their threatened "encirclement" by the Entente powers, they were obliged to hold to their one ally, Austria-Hungary, which was in turn able to sell its support at its own price. The French dreaded a coming conflict with Germany, which in forty years had far surpassed France in population and industrial strength; they were obliged to cling to their ally Russia, which therefore could oblige the French to yield to Russian wishes. As for Russia and Austria, they were both tottering empires. Especially after 1900, the tsarist regime suffered from endemic revolutionism, and the Habsburg empire from chronic nationalistic agitation. Authorities in both empires became desperate. Like the Serbs, they had little to lose and were therefore reckless. It was Russia that drew France and hence England into war in 1914, and Austria that drew in Germany. Seen in this light, the tragedy of 1914 is that the most backward or politically bankrupt parts of Europe, through the alliance system, dragged the more advanced parts automatically into ruin.

The German Empire, too, faced an internal crisis. The Social Democrats became the largest party in the Reichstag in 1912.[12] Their sentiments for the most part were antimilitarist and antiwar. But the German imperial government recognized no responsibility to a majority in the chamber. Policy was determined by men of the old unreconstructed upper class, in which army and navy interests, now reinforced by the new business interests, were very strong; and even moderates and liberals shared in the ambition to make Germany a world power, the equal of any. The perplexities the ruling groups faced at home, the feeling that their position was being undermined by the Social Democrats, may have made them less unwilling to view war as a way out. And while it is not true that Germany started the war, as its enemies in 1914 popularly believed, it must be granted that its policies had for some years been rather peremptory, arrogant, devious, and obstinate. In a broad sense, the emergence of a consolidated industrial Germany after 1870, making its bid for world-power status relatively late, was a distant and basic cause of the war.

The alliance system was only a symptom of deeper trouble. In a word, the world had an international economy but a national polity. Economically, each European people now required habitual contact with the world as a whole. Each people was to that extent dependent, and insecure. Industrial countries were

[12] See pp. 616–617.

WORLD WAR I

Land fighting in the First World War was mainly confined to the areas shown by the darker horizontal shading. The huge battles on the Western Front, which in expenditure of manpower exceeded those of the Second World War in the West, for four years swayed back and forth over the small area indicated, less than a hundred miles wide.

especially vulnerable, relying as they did on import of raw materials and food, and on export of goods, services, or capital in return. There was, however, no world state to police the worldwide system, assuring participation in the world economy to all nations under all conditions. Each nation had to take care of itself.

Hence came much of the drive for imperialism, in which each Great Power tried to stake out part of the world system for itself. And hence also came the quest for allies and for binding alliances. The alliances, in a world that was in the strict sense anarchic (and seemed likely to remain so), were a means by which each nation attempted to bolster up its security; to assure that it would not be cut off, conquered, or subjected to another's will; to obtain some hope of success in the competitive struggle for use of the world's goods.

86. *The Armed Stalemate*

The First World War lasted over four years, from 1914 to the end of 1918, the United States entering with effective result in the last year. Germany and its allies were called the Central Powers, while the Entente governments were termed the Allies. The war was appalling in its human costs; on the Western Front, more men were used and killed in the First World War than in the Second.

At first a short war, as in 1870, was universally expected. The German General Staff had its plans ready for a two-front struggle against France and Russia. The disadvantage of fighting on two fronts was offset by the possession of good rail lines, which allowed the rapid shuttling of troops from one front to the other. The German war plan, known as the Schlieffen Plan, rested upon this fact. The idea was first to defeat France by the rapid wheeling motion of a tremendous army through Belgium and then to turn at more leisure against Russia, whose great size and less developed railways would make its deployment much slower.

The War on Land, 1914–1916

On August 3, 1914, the Germans launched 78 infantry divisions in the West. They were opposed by 72 French divisions, 5 British, and 6 Belgian. The Germans swept irresistibly forward. The Schlieffen Plan seemed to be moving like clockwork. The civilian authorities made plans for the conquest and annexation of large parts of Europe. Then a hitch occurred: the Russians were fulfilling the terms of their alliance; the 10 billion francs invested by Frenchmen in Russia now paid their most significant dividend. The Russians pushed two armies into Germany, penetrating into East Prussia. Moltke withdrew forces from the German right wing in France, on August 26, for service in the east. The Germans moved on, but their striking arm was weakened, and their lines of communication were already overextended. Joffre, the French commander, regrouping his forces, with strong support from the relatively small British contingent, and at exactly the right moment, ordered a counterattack. The ensuing battle of the Marne, fought from September 5 to 12, changed the whole character of the war. The Germans were obliged to retreat. The hope of felling France at a single blow was ended. Each side now tried to outflank and destroy the other until the battle lines extended to the sea. The Germans failed to win control of the Channel ports; French and British communications remained uninterrupted. For these reverses the great victories meanwhile won by the Germans in the east, though of gigantic proportions (the battles of Tannenberg and the Masurian Lakes, at which 225,000 Russians were captured), were in the long run small consolation.

In the West the war of movement now settled into a war of position. The armies on the Western Front became almost immobile. The units of horse cavalry—the uhlans, hussars, and lancers that had pranced off to war in high spirits—disappeared from the field. Since aviation was barely beginning, and motor transport was still new (the armies had trucks, but no self-propelled guns, and no tanks until very late in the war), the basic soldier more than ever was the man on foot. The most deadly new weapon was the machine gun, which made it impossible for foot soldiers to advance across open fields without overwhelming artillery preparation. The result was a long stalemate of war in the trenches in which the indispensable infantry sought protection.

In 1915 the Germans and Austro-Hungarians put their main effort into an attempt to knock out Russia. They pressed far into the tsarist empire. The Russian losses were enormous—2 million killed, wounded, or captured in 1915 alone. But at the end of the year the Russian army was still fighting. Meanwhile the British and French, hoping to open up communications with Russia, launched a naval attack on Turkey, aiming at Constantinople by way of the Dardanelles. They poured 450,000 men into the narrow peninsula of Gallipoli, of whom 145,000 were killed or wounded. After almost a year the enterprise was given up as a failure.

In 1916 both sides turned again to northern France in an attempt to break the deadlock. The Allies planned a great offensive along the river Somme, while the Germans prepared one in the neighborhood of Verdun. The Germans attacked Verdun in February. The French commander, Joffre, put in General Pétain to defend it but resisted committing his main reserves, holding them for the coming offensive on the Somme. Pétain and his troops, held to minimum numbers, thus had to take the full weight of the German army. The battle of Verdun lasted six months, it drew the horrified admiration of the world, and it became a legend of determined resistance (''they shall not pass''), until the Germans finally abandoned the attack because they sustained almost as many casualties as the French—330,000 to 350,000—so that their purpose was baffled. While the inferno still raged at Verdun the Allies opened their offensive on the Somme in July. They brought up unheard of amounts of artillery, and the newly raised British army was present in force. The idea was to break through the German line simply by stupendous pressure; on both sides, Allied and German, the art of generalship had sunk to an all-time low. Despite a weeklong artillery bombardment the British lost 60,000 men on the first day of the attack. In a week they had advanced only a mile along a six-mile front. In a month they had advanced only two miles and a half. The battle of the Somme, lasting from July to October, cost the Germans about 500,000 men, the British 400,000, and the French 200,000. Nothing of any value had been gained. It was, indeed, at the Somme that the British first used the tank, an armored vehicle with caterpillar tracks that could crash through barbed wire, lunge over trenches, and smash into machine gun nests; but the tanks were introduced in such small numbers, and with such skepticism on the part of many commanders, that they had no effect on the battle.

The War at Sea

With land armies thus helpless, both sides looked to the sea. The long preponderance of British sea power, and the more recent Anglo-German naval race, would now be tested. The British, with French aid, imposed a strict naval blockade. International law at the time placed goods headed for a country at war into two classes. One class was called "contraband"; it included munitions and certain specified raw materials which might be used in the manufacture of military equipment. The other class, including foodstuffs and raw cotton, was defined as "noncontraband." A country was supposed, by international law, to be able to import noncontraband goods even in wartime. These terms of wartime law had been set forth as recently as 1909 at an international conference held in London. The purpose was to make it impossible for a sea power (that is, the British) to starve out an enemy in wartime, or even to interfere with normal civilian production. The jealousy of Continental Europe for British sea power was an old story.

Such law, if observed, would make the blockade of Germany entirely ineffective, and the Allies did not observe it. To starve out the enemy and ruin his economy was precisely their purpose. Economic warfare took its place alongside armed attack as a military weapon, as in the days of Napoleon.[13] The Allies announced a new international law. The distinction between contraband and noncontraband was gradually abolished. The British navy (aided by the French) proceeded to stop all goods of whatever character destined for Germany or its allies. Neutrals, among whom the Americans, Dutch, and Scandinavians were the ones mainly affected, were not allowed to make for German ports at all.

The United States protested vehemently against these regulations. It defended the rights of neutrals. It reasserted the distinction between contraband and noncontraband, claimed the right to trade with other neutrals, and upheld the "freedom of the seas." Much mutual bad feeling resulted between the American and British governments in 1915 and 1916. But when the United States entered the war it adopted the Allied position, and its navy joined in enforcing exactly the same regulations. International law was in fact changed. In the Second World War the very words "contraband" and "freedom of the seas" were never heard.

The Germans countered with an attempt to blockade England. A few isolated German cruisers were able for some time to destroy British shipping in the several oceans of the world. But the Germans relied mainly on the submarine, against which the British naval power at first seemed helpless. The submarine was an unrefined weapon; a submarine commander could not always tell what kind of ship he was attacking, nor could he remove passengers, confiscate cargo, escort the vessel, or indeed do much except sink it. Citing British abuses of international law in justification, the German government in February 1915 declared the waters surrounding the British Isles to be a war zone, in which Allied vessels would be torpedoed and neutral vessels would be in grave danger. Three months later the liner *Lusitania* was torpedoed off the Irish coast. About 1,200 persons were drowned, of whom 118 were American citizens. The *Lusitania* was a British ship; it carried munitions of war manufactured in the United States for Allied use; and

[13] See pp. 431–434.

the Germans had published ominous warnings in the New York papers that Americans should not take passage upon it. Americans then believed that they should be able to sail safely, on peaceable errands, on the ship of a belligerent power in wartime. The loss of life shocked the country. President Wilson informed the Germans that another such act would be considered "deliberately unfriendly." The Germans, to avoid trouble, refrained for two years from making full use of their submarines. For two years the Allied use of the sea was only partly impeded.

Allied access to the sea was confirmed by the one great naval engagement of the war, the battle of Jutland. The German admirals became restless at seeing their newly built navy skulking behind minefields on the German shores, yet they could not presume to challenge the superior British Grand Fleet, posted watchfully at Scapa Flow. They hoped, however, to decoy smaller formations of British ships, destroy them one by one, and perhaps eventually obtain enough of a naval balance in the North Sea to loosen the British blockade, by which Germany was slowly being strangled. They were themselves, however, trapped into a major engagement in which the British Grand Fleet of 151 ships took them by surprise. After a few hours of furious combat the Germans were able to withdraw into mined waters. They had lost less tonnage and fewer men than the British. They had proved themselves to be dangerously proficient in naval combat. But they had failed to undermine the British preponderance at sea.

Diplomatic Maneuvers and Secret Agreements

With no military solution in sight, both sides looked about for new allies. The Ottoman Empire, fearing Russia, had joined Germany and Austria-Hungary as early as October 1914. Bulgaria, being anti-Serb, had done the same in 1915.

The leading new prospect was Italy, which, though formally a member of the Triple Alliance, had long ago drifted away from it. Both sides solicited the Italian government, which bargained imperturbably with both. The Italian public was divided. Both Catholic and socialist leaders recommended staying at peace, but extreme nationalists saw a chance to obtain their *irredenta*, the border regions in which Italians lived, but which had not been incorporated in the time of Cavour.[14] The Italian government cast its lot with the Allies in the secret treaty of London of 1915. It was agreed that if the Allies won the war Italy would receive (from Austria) the Trentino, the south Tyrol, Istria and the city of Trieste, and some of the Dalmatian Islands. If Britain and France took over Germany's African colonies, Italy should receive territorial increases in Libya and Somaliland. The treaty of London, in short, carried on the most brazen prewar practices of territorial expansionism. It must be remembered that the Allies were desperate. Italy, thus bought, and probably against the will of most Italians, opened up a front against Austria-Hungary in May 1915.

The Allies likewise made plans for a final partition of the Ottoman Empire, which still reached from Constantinople through the Middle East into Arabia and modern Iraq. Britain and France were so dependent on Russia that they gave up their age-old opposition to Russian domination of the Straits. By a secret treaty of 1915 they agreed that, upon an Allied victory, Russia might proceed to the

[14] See p. 550.

annexation of Constantinople, along with the whole Bosporus, the Sea of Marmara, and the Dardanelles. By another agreement Mesopotamia was to go to Britain, Syria and southeastern Asia Minor to France, small portions to Italy, and Kurdistan and Armenia to Russia.[15]

Each side tampered with minorities and discontented groups living within the domains of the other. The Germans promised an independent Poland, to embarrass Russia. They stirred up local nationalism in the Ukraine. They raised up a pro-German Flemish movement in Belgium. They persuaded the Ottoman sultan, as caliph, to proclaim a holy war in North Africa, hoping that irate Muslims would drive the British from Egypt and the French from Algeria. This had no success. German agents worked in Ireland, and one Irish nationalist, Sir Roger Casement, landed in Ireland from a German submarine, precipitating the Easter Rebellion of 1916, which was suppressed by the British.

To Americans the most amazing of similar activities was the famous Zimmermann telegram. In 1916 an American military force had crossed the Mexican border in pursuit of bandits, against protests by the Mexican government. Relations between the United States and Germany were also deteriorating. In January 1917 the German state secretary for foreign affairs, Arthur Zimmermann, dispatched a telegram to the German minister at Mexico City, telling him what to say to the Mexican president. He was to say that if the United States went to war with Germany, Germany would form an alliance with Mexico and if possible Japan, enabling Mexico to get back its "lost territories." These latter referred to the region conquered by the United States from Mexico in the 1840s—Texas, New Mexico, and Arizona (California was not mentioned by Zimmermann, who was no doubt somewhat vague on the exact history and location of these Alsace-Lorraines of America). Zimmermann's telegram was intercepted and decoded by the British, and passed on by them to Washington. Printed in the newspapers, it shocked public opinion in the United States.

The Allies were more successful in appealing to nationalist discontent, for the obvious reason that the most active national minorities were within the lands of their enemies. They were able to promise restoration of Alsace-Lorraine to France without difficulty. They promised independence to the Poles, though with some difficulty as long as the Russian monarchy stood. It was easier for them to favor national independence for Czechs, Slovaks, and Yugoslavs, since an Allied victory would dissolve the Austro-Hungarian empire.

Within the Ottoman Empire the British aroused Arab hopes for independence. The British Colonel T. E. Lawrence led an insurrection in the Hejaz against the Turks; and the emir Hussein of Hejaz, with British support, in 1916 took the title of king of the Arabs, with a kingdom reaching from the Red Sea to the Persian Gulf. Zionists saw in the impending Ottoman collapse the opportunity to realize their dream for Palestine.[16] Since Palestine was peopled by Arabs (and had been for over 1,000 years) the Zionist program conflicted with British plans to sponsor Arab nationalism. Nevertheless, in the Balfour note of 1917, the British government promised support for the idea of a "Jewish homeland" in Palestine. For the Armenians these years were especially disastrous. They were a Christian

---

[15] See map on p. 660.
[16] See p. 637, and for Israel, pp. 941–945 below.

people living in the eastern part of the Anatolian peninsula where it abuts on Russia, and like other peoples in the Ottoman Empire, including the Turks themselves, they had developed aspirations for a national state of their own, which conflicted with the plans of Turkish reformers to Turkify the empire. It was only twenty years since such clashes had produced the Armenian massacres of 1894 which had horrified Europe. Now in 1915 the Turkish government, as the Russian army threatened its eastern frontier, ordered the deportation of Armenians from the war zone as potential sympathizers with Russia and the Western Allies. Supposedly they were to be resettled in Syria and Palestine. In fact, in the atmosphere of military crisis, political hatred, bureaucratic contempt, and wartime scarcities hundreds of thousands of Armenians perished. It is a fact also that virtually no Armenians remained within what became the Turkish republic a few years later. The surviving Armenians became another of the world's scattered peoples, with no state of their own, except for a small Armenian republic, briefly independent after 1918, then part of the Soviet Union for seventy years, and independent again after 1991.

Meanwhile during the war the British and French easily moved into the German colonies in Africa. The British foreign secretary, Sir Edward Grey, revealed to Colonel House, President Wilson's personal emissary, that the Allies did not intend that Germany should ever get its colonies back.

In China, too, the third important area of imperialist competition, the war accelerated the tendencies of preceding years. The Japanese saw their own opportunity in the self-slaughter of the Europeans. Japan had also been allied to Britain since 1902. In August 1914 Japan declared war on Germany. It soon overran the German concessions in China and the German islands in the Pacific, the Marshalls and Carolines. In January 1915 Japan presented its Twenty-One Demands on China, a secret ultimatum most of which the Chinese were obliged to accept. Japan thereby proceeded to turn Manchuria and north China into an exclusive protectorate.

As for the Germans, their war aims were even more expansionist, and more menacing to existing boundaries in Europe itself. Early in September 1914, when a quick victory seemed within their grasp, Bethmann-Hollweg, who remained chancellor until the summer of 1917, drew up a list of German war aims which stayed unaltered until the end of hostilities. The plans called for an enlarged German Empire dominating all central Europe, and annexations or satellites in both western and eastern Europe. In the east, Lithuania and other parts of the Baltic coast were to become German dependencies, large sections of Poland were to be directly annexed, and the remainder joined with Austrian Galicia to form a German-dominated Polish state. In the west, Belgium was to become a German dependency to provide more direct access to the Atlantic, and French Lorraine with its rich iron ore was to be added to the already German parts of Alsace-Lorraine. Colonial adjustments, including the acquisition of most of central Africa from coast to coast, were also projected. The political map of Europe and of colonial Africa would thus be transformed.

All these developments, especially the Allied negotiations, whether accomplished facts or secret agreements, affecting Europe, Asia, or Africa, became very troublesome later at the peace conference. They continued some of the most unsettling tendencies of European politics before the war. It does not appear that the Allies, until driven by Woodrow Wilson, gave any thought to means of controlling anarchic nationalism or of preventing war in the future. As president of the United States, Wilson for a long time could see little to choose between the warring alliances, though his personal sympathies were with England and France. In 1916 he attempted to mediate, entering into confidential discussions with both sides; but both still hoped to win on their own terms, so that negotiation was fruitless. Wilson judged that most Americans wished to remain uninvolved, and in November 1916 he was reelected to a second term, on the popular cry, "he kept us out of war." Wilson urged a true neutrality of thought and feeling, or a settlement, as he said, that should be a "peace without victory."

As of the end of 1916, it is hard to see how the First World War would have turned out, had not two new sets of forces been brought in.

87. The Collapse of Russia and the Intervention of the United States

The Withdrawal of Russia: Revolution and the Treaty of Brest-Litovsk

The first victim of the First World War, among governments, was the Russian empire. As the Russo-Japanese War had led to the Revolution of 1905 in Russia, so the more ruinous conflict in Europe led to the far greater Revolution of 1917. The story of the Russian Revolution is told in the following chapter. It is enough to say here that war offered a test that the tsarist government could not meet. Bungling, dishonest, and secretive, incapable of supplying the materiel required for modern fighting, driving hordes of peasants into battle in some cases even without rifles, losing men by the millions yet offering no goal to inspire sacrifice, the tsarist regime lost the loyalty of all elements of its people. In March 1917 the troops in St. Petersburg mutinied, while strikes and riots desolated the city. The Duma, or Russian parliament, used the occasion to press its demands for reform. On March 15 Nicholas II abdicated. A Provisional Government took over, made up of liberal noblemen and middle-class leaders, generally democrats and constitutionalists, with at first only one socialist. The Provisional Government remained in office from March to November 1917. Its members, who shared in the liberalism of western Europe, believed that a liberal and parliamentary regime could not succeed in Russia unless the German Empire were defeated. They took steps, therefore, to prosecute the war with a new vigor. In July 1917 an offensive was opened in Galicia, but the demoralized Russian armies again collapsed.

The mass of the Russian people were wearied of a war in which they were asked to suffer so much for so little. Nor did the Russian peasant or workingman feel any enthusiasm for the westernized intellectuals and professional men who manned the Provisional Government. The ordinary Russian, so far as he had any politics, was drawn to one or another of numerous forms of socialism, Marxist and non-Marxist. The Russian Marxist party, the Social Democrats, was divided between Menshevik and Bolshevik factions, the latter being the more extreme. The Bolshevik leaders had for some time lived as exiles in western Europe. Their principal spokesman, V. I. Lenin, with a few others, had spent the war years in Switzerland. In April 1917 the German government offered safe passage to Lenin through Germany to Russia. A railway car full of Bolsheviks, carefully "sealed" to prevent infection of Germany, was thus hauled by a German train to the frontier, whence it passed on to St. Petersburg, or Petrograd, as the city was renamed during the war. The aim of the Germans in this affair, as in the sending of Roger Casement to Ireland in a submarine, was of course to use a kind of psychological warfare against the enemy's home front. It was to promote rebellion against the Provisional Government and thus at last to eliminate Russia.

The position of the Provisional Government became rapidly more untenable, from many causes, until by November 1917 the situation was so confused that Lenin and the Bolsheviks were able to seize power. The Bolsheviks stood for peace with Germany, partly to win popular favor in Russia, and partly because they regarded the war impartially, as a struggle between capitalist and imperialist powers which should be left to exhaust and destroy each other for the benefit of socialism. On December 3, 1917, a peace conference opened between the Bolsheviks and the Germans at Brest-Litovsk. Meanwhile the peoples within the western border of the old Russia—Poles, Ukrainians, Bessarabians, Estonians, Latvians, Finns—with German backing, proclaimed their national independence. The Bolsheviks, since they would not or could not fight, were obliged to sign with Germany a treaty to which they vehemently objected, the treaty of Brest-Litovsk of March 3, 1918. By this treaty they acknowledged the "independence," or at least the loss to Russia, of Poland, the Ukraine, Finland, and the Baltic provinces.

For the Germans the treaty of Brest-Litovsk represented their maximum success during the First World War; it accomplished some of the war aims formulated at the beginning of hostilities. Not only had they neutralized Russia; they also now dominated eastern Europe through puppets placed at the head of the new independent states. They relieved the effects of the naval blockade by drawing considerable quantities of foodstuffs from the Ukraine, though less than they expected. A certain number of German troops remained in the East to preserve the new arrangements. But it was no longer a two-front war. Masses of the German army were shifted from east to west. The High Command, under Hindenburg and Ludendorff since August 1916, prepared to concentrate for a last blow in France to end the war in 1918.

The year 1918 was essentially a race to see whether American aid could reach Europe soon enough, in sufficient amount, to offset the added strength which Germany drew from the collapse of Russia. In March of that year the Germans, beginning with gas attacks and a bombardment by 6,000 artillery pieces, opened a formidable offensive before which the French and British both recoiled. On May 30, 1918, the Germans again stood at the Marne, thirty-seven miles from Paris. At this time there were only two American divisions in action, though the United States had been at war over a year. At this point in the story there are therefore two open questions: how the United States entered the war, and the length of time required for the build-up of its forces overseas.

The United States and the War

We have seen how President Wilson clung persistently to neutrality. The American people were divided. Many had been born in Europe or were the children of immigrants. Those of Irish origin were anti-British; those of German origin were often sympathetic to Germany. On the other hand, since the time of the Spanish-American and Boer Wars, a noticeable current of friendliness to the English had been running, more than ever before in American history. The sale of war materials to the Allies, and the purchase of the bonds of Allied governments, had given certain limited though influential circles a material interest in an Allied victory. The idealism of the country was on the side of England and France, so far as it was not isolationist. An Allied victory would clearly advance the cause of democracy, freedom, and progress far more than a victory of the German Empire. On the other hand, England and France were suspected of somewhat impure motives, and they were allied with the Russian autocracy, the reactionary and brutal tsardom.

The fall of tsarism made a great impression. Democratic and progressive men now came forward even in Russia. No one had ever heard of Lenin or foresaw the Bolshevik Revolution. It seemed in the spring of 1917 that Russia was struggling along the path that England, France, and America had already taken. An ideological barrier had dropped away, and the demand for American intervention to safeguard democracy became more insistent.

The Germans gave up the attempt to keep the United States out. Constricted ever more tightly by the blockade, and failing to get a decision on land, the German government and High Command listened more readily to the submarine experts, who declared that if given a free hand they could force British surrender in six months. It was the chief example in the First World War of the claim that one branch of the service could win the war alone. Civilian and diplomatic members of the government objected, fearing the consequences of war with the United States. They were overruled; it was a good example of the way in which, in Germany, the army and navy had taken the highest policy into their hands. Unrestricted submarine warfare was to be resumed on February 1, 1917. It was foreseen that the United States would declare war, but the German High Command believed that this would make no immediate difference. They estimated in 1917 (correctly) that between the time when the United States entered a European war and the time when it could take part with its own army about a year must intervene. Meanwhile, the planners said, in six months they could force Britain to accept defeat.

On January 31, 1917, the Germans notified Wilson of the resumption of unrestricted submarine attacks. They announced that they would sink on sight all merchant vessels found in a zone around the British Isles or in the Mediterranean. Wilson broke off diplomatic relations and ordered the arming of American freighters. Meanwhile, the publication of the Zimmermann telegram convinced many Americans of German aggressiveness. German secret agents also had been at work in America, fomenting strikes and causing explosions in factories engaged in the manufacture of munitions for the Allies. In February and March several American ships were sunk. Americans regarded all these activities as an interference with their rights as neutrals. Wilson at last concluded that Germany was a menace. Having made his decision, Wilson saw a clear-cut issue between right and wrong, and he obtained a rousing declaration of war from Congress, on April 6, 1917. The United States went to war "to make the world safe for democracy."

At first the German campaign realized and even exceeded the predictions of its sponsors. In February 1917 the Germans sank 540,000 tons of shipping, in March 578,000 tons, in April, as the days grew longer, 874,000 tons. Something akin to terror, with difficulty concealed from the public, seized on the government in London. Britain was reduced to a mere six-weeks' reserve of food. Gradually countermeasures were developed—mine barrages, hydrophones, depth charges, airplane reconnaissance, and most of all the convoy. It was found that a hundred or more freighters together, though all had to steam at the pace of the slowest, could be protected by a sufficient concentration of warships to keep submarines away. The United States navy, which, unlike the army, was of considerable size and ready for combat, supplied enough additional force to the Allies to make convoying and other antisubmarine measures highly effective. By the end of 1917 the submarine was no more than a nuisance. For the Germans the great plan produced the anticipated penalty without the reward—its net result was only to add America to their enemies.

On the Western Front in 1917, while the Americans desperately got themselves ready for the war they had entered, the French and British continued to hold the line. The French, finding in General Nivelle a commander who still believed in the breakthrough, launched an offensive so unsuccessful and so bloody that mutiny spread through the French army. Pétain then replaced Nivelle and restored discipline to the exhausted and disillusioned soldiers, but he had no thought of further attack. "I am waiting for the Americans and the tanks," he said. The British then assumed the main burden. For three months late in 1917 they fought the dismal battle of Passchendaele. They advanced five miles, near Ypres, at a cost of 400,000 men. At the very end of 1917 the British surprised the Germans with a raid by 380 tanks, which penetrated deep into the German lines, but were obliged to withdraw, since no reserve of fresh infantry was at hand to exploit their success. Meanwhile the Austro-Hungarians, strongly reinforced by German troops, overwhelmed the Italians at the disastrous battle of Caporetto. The Central Powers streamed into northern Italy, but the Italians, with British and French reinforcements, were able to hold the line. The net effect of the campaigns of 1917, and of the repulse of the submarine at the same time, was to reemphasize the stalemate in Europe, incline the weary Allies to await the Americans, and give the Americans what they most needed—time.

The Americans made good use of the time given them. Conscription, democratically entitled selective service, was adopted immediately after the declaration of war. The United States army, whose professionals in 1916 numbered only 130,000, performed the mammoth feat of turning over 3.5 million civilians into soldiers. With the navy, the United States came to have over 4 million in its armed services (which may be compared with over 12 million in the Second World War). Aid flowed to the Allies. To the loans already made through private bankers were added some $10 billion lent by the American government itself. The Allies used the money mainly to buy food and munitions in the United States. American farms and factories, which had already prospered by selling to the Allies during the period of neutrality, now broke all records for production. Civilian industry was converted to war uses; radiator factories turned out guns, and piano factories airplane wings. Every possible means was employed to build up ocean shipping, without which neither American supplies nor American armies could reach the theater of war. Available shipping was increased from 1 million to 10 million tons. Civilian consumption was drastically cut. Eight thousand tons of steel were saved in the manufacture of women's corsets, and 75,000 tons of tin in the making of children's toy wagons. Every week people observed meatless Tuesday, and sugar was rationed. Daylight-saving time, invented in Europe during the war, was introduced to save coal. By such means the United States made enormous stocks available for its Allies as well as itself, though for some items, notably airplanes and artillery ammunition, the American armies, when they reached France, drew heavily on British and French manufactures.

The Final Phase of the War

The Germans, as we have seen, victorious in the East, opened a great final offensive in the West in the spring of 1918, hoping to force a decision before American participation turned the balance forever. To oppose it, a unity of command was at last achieved, for the first time, when a French general, Ferdinand Foch, was made commander in chief of all Allied forces in France, with the national commanders subordinate to him, including Pershing for the Americans. In June the Germans first made contact with American troops in significant force, meeting the Second Division at Château-Thierry. The German position was so favorable that civilians in the German government thought it opportune to make a last effort at a compromise peace. The military, headed by Hindenburg and Ludendorff, successfully blocked any such attempts; they preferred to gamble on one final throw. The German armies reached their farthest advance on July 15 along the Marne. There were now nine American divisions in the Allied line. Foch used them to spearhead his counterattack on July 18. The badly overstrained Germans began to falter. Over 250,000 American troops were now landing in France every month. The final Allied offensive which opened in September, with American troops in the Argonne occupying an eastern sector, proved more than the Germans could withstand. The German High Command notified its government that it could not win the war. The German foreign office made peace overtures to President Wilson. An armistice was arranged, and on November 11, 1918, firing ceased on the Western Front.

Since Germany's allies had surrendered during the preceding weeks, the war, or at least the shooting war in western Europe, was now over. The horror it brought to individual lives cannot be told by statistics, which drily report that almost 10 million men had been killed, and 20 million wounded. Each of the European Great Powers (except Italy) lost from 1 million to 2 million in killed alone. The United States, with some 330,000 casualties of all types (of whom 115,000 died) lost in the entire war fewer men than the main combatants had lost in such a single battle as Verdun or Passchendaele.[17] American assistance was

---

[17] Of the 115,000 American deaths only 50,000 represented men killed in battle, the remainder representing mainly deaths by disease. The great influenza epidemic of 1918, which brought death to over 20 million people, civilians and military alike, in all parts of the world, probably accounted for 25,000 deaths in the American army.

decisive in the defeat of Germany. But it came so late, when the others had been struggling for so long, that the mere beginnings of it were enough to turn the scale. On the date of the armistice there were 2 million American soldiers in France, and another 1 million were on the way. But the American army had really been in combat only four months. During the whole year 1918, out of every hundred artillery shells that were fired by the three armies, the French fired 51, the British 43, and the Americans only 6.

88. The Collapse of the Austrian and German Empires

The war proved fatal to the German and Austro-Hungarian empires, as to the Russian. The subject Habsburg nationalities, or the "national councils" representing them in the Western capitals, obtained recognition from the Allies, and in October 1918 declared their independence. The last Austrian emperor, Charles I, abdicated on November 12, and on the next day Austria was proclaimed a republic, as was Hungary in the following week. Before any peace conference could convene, the new states of Czechoslovakia, Yugoslavia, an enlarged Romania, a republican Hungary, and a miniature republican Austria were in existence by their own action.

The German Empire stood solid until the closing weeks. Liberals, democrats, and socialists had lately begun to press for peace and democratization. Yet it was the High Command itself that precipitated the debacle. In the last years of the war dictatorial powers had become concentrated in the hands of General Ludendorff, and in September 1918 only he and his closest military associates realized that the German cause was hopeless.On September 29, at supreme headquarters at Spa in Belgium, Ludendorff informed the Kaiser that Germany must ask for peace. He urged that a new government be formed at Berlin, reflecting the majority in the Reichstag, on democratic parliamentary principles.

In calling for immediate peace negotiations, he seems to have had two ideas in mind. First, he might win time to regroup his armies and prepare a new offensive. Or if collapse became unavoidable, then the civilian or democratic elements in Germany would be the ones to sue for peace.

The liberal Prince Max of Baden was found to head a cabinet in which even socialists were included. In October various reforms were enacted, the Bismarckian system was ended, and Germany became a liberal constitutional monarchy. For Ludendorff the changes were not fast enough. What was happening was essentially simple. The German military caste, at the moment of Germany's crisis, was more eager to save the army than to save the empire. The army must never admit surrender; that was an affair for small men in business suits. Emperor, High Command, officers, and aristocrats were unloading frantically upon civilians.

President Wilson unwittingly played into their hands. Speaking now as the chief of the Allied coalition, the one to whom peace overtures were first made, he insisted that the German government must become more democratic. It may be recalled how Bismarck, after defeating France in 1871, demanded a general election in France before making peace.[18] Wilson, unlike Bismarck, really believed

---

[18] See pp. 559, 605.

in democracy; but in a practical way his position was the same. He wanted to be sure that he was dealing with the German people itself, not with a discredited elite. He wanted it to be the real Germany that applied for and accepted the Allied terms. In Germany, as realization of the military disaster spread, many people began to regard the Kaiser as an obstacle to peace. Or they felt that Germany would obtain better terms if it appeared before the Allies as a republic. Even the officer corps, to halt the fighting before the army disintegrated, began to talk of abdication. Sailors mutinied at Kiel on November 3, and councils of workers and soldiers were formed in various cities. The socialists threatened to withdraw from the newly formed cabinet (i.e., go into opposition and end the representative nature of the new government) unless William II abdicated. A general strike, led by minority socialists and syndicalists, began on November 9. "Abdication," Prince Max told the emperor, "is a dreadful thing, but a government without the socialists would be a worse danger for the country." William II abdicated on November 9, and slipped across the frontier into Holland, where despite cries to try him as a "war criminal" he lived quietly until his death in 1941. Germany was proclaimed a republic on the same day. Two days later the war stopped.

The fall of the empire in Germany, with the consequent adoption of the republic, did not arise from any basic discontent, deep revolutionary action, or change of sentiment in the German people. It was an episode of the war. The republic (soon called the Weimar Republic) arose because the victorious enemy demanded it, because the German people craved peace, because they wished to avoid forcible revolution, and because the old German military class, to save its face and its future strength, wished at least temporarily to be excused. When the war ended, the German army was still in France, its discipline and organization still apparently unimpaired. No hostile shot had been fired on German soil. It was said later, by some, that the army had not been defeated, that it had been "stabbed in the back" by a dissolving civilian home front. This was untrue; it was the panic-stricken Ludendorff who first cried for "democracy." But the circumstances in which the German republic originated made its later history, and hence all later history, very troubled.

89. The Economic and Social Impact of the War

Effects on Capitalism: Government-Regulated Economies

European society was forced by the First World War into many basic changes that were to prove more lasting than the war itself. First of all, the war profoundly affected capitalism as previously known. Essential to the older capitalism (or economic liberalism, or free private enterprise) had been the idea that government should leave business alone, or at the most regulate certain general conditions under which businessmen went about their affairs. Before 1914 governments had increasingly come into the economic field. They had put up tariffs, protected national industries, sought for markets or raw materials by imperialist expansion, or passed protective social legislation to benefit the wage-earning classes. During the war all belligerent governments controlled the economic system far more minutely. Indeed, the idea of the "planned economy" was first applied in the First World War. For the first time (with such rare and archaic precedents as the French dictatorship of 1793)[19] the state attempted to direct all the wealth, resources, and moral purpose of society to a single end.

Since no one had expected a long war, no one had made any plans for industrial mobilization. Everything had to be improvised. By 1916 each government had set up a system of boards, bureaus, councils, and commissions to coordinate its war effort. The aim was to see that all manpower was effectively utilized, and that all natural resources within the country, and all that could possibly be imported, were employed where they would do the most good. In the stress of war free competition was found to be wasteful and undirected private enterprise too uncertain and too slow. The profit motive came into disrepute. Those who exploited shortages to make big profits were stigmatized as "profiteers." Production for civilian use, or for mere luxury purposes, was cut to a minimum. Businessmen were not allowed to set up or close down factories as they chose. It was impossible to start a new business without government approval, because the flotation of stocks and bonds was controlled, and raw materials were made available only as the government wished. It was equally impossible to shut down a business engaged in war production; if a factory was inefficient or unprofitable the government kept it going anyway, making up the losses, so that in some cases management came to expect government support. Here too the tests of competition and profitableness were abandoned. The new goal was coordination or "rationalization" of production in the interests of the country as a whole. Labor was discouraged from protesting against hours or wage rates, and the big unions generally agreed to refrain from strikes. For the upper and middle classes it became embarrassing to show their comforts too openly. It was patriotic to eat meagerly and to wear old clothes. War gave a new impetus even to the idea of economic equality, if only to enlist rich and poor alike in a common cause.

Military conscription was the first step in the allocation of manpower. Draft boards told some men to report to the army, granting exemptions to others to work safely in war industries. Given the casualty rates at the front, state determination over individual life could hardly go farther. With the insatiable need for troops, drawing in men originally exempted or at first rejected as physically inadequate, great numbers of women poured into factories and offices, and in Britain even into newly organized women's branches of the armed forces. Women took over many jobs which it had been thought only men could do. Women did not remain in the labor force after the war in such large numbers, most making way for the returning veterans, but the wartime experience in this and the Second World War was part of the process by which the labor force in all countries was enlarged, women's place in society revolutionized, and the lives and outlook of millions of individual women turned outward from the home. It was a process that would be intensified during the Second World War and in the years that followed. During the war governments did not directly force men or women to drop one job and take another. There was no systematic labor conscription except in Germany. But by influencing wage scales, granting draft

[19] See pp. 388–390.

exemptions, forcing some industries to expand and others to contract or stand still, and propagandizing the idea that work in an arms factory was patriotic, the state shifted vast numbers of workers to war production. Impressed or "slave" labor was not used in the First World War nor were prisoners of war obliged to give labor service, though there were some abuses of these rules of international law by the Germans, who were possibly the least scrupulous and certainly the most hard pressed.

Governments controlled all foreign trade. It was intolerable to let private citizens ship off the country's resources at their own whim. It was equally intolerable to let them use up foreign exchange by importing unneeded goods, or to drive up prices of necessities by competing with one another. Foreign trade became a state monopoly, in which private firms operated under strict licenses and quotas. The greatest of the exporting countries was the United States, whose annual exports rose from $2 billion to $6 billion between 1914 and 1918. The endless demand for American farm and factory products naturally drove up prices, which, however, were fixed by law in 1917, for the most important items.

As for the European Allies, which even before the war had exported less than they imported, and were now exporting as little as possible, they could make purchases in the United States only by enormous loans from the American government. British and French citizens, under pressure from their own governments, sold off their American stocks and bonds, which were bought up by Americans.[20] The former owners received pounds sterling or francs from their own governments, which in return took and spent the dollars paid by the new American owners. In this way the United States ceased to be a debtor country (owing some $4 billion to Europeans in 1914), and became the world's leading creditor country, to which by 1919 Europeans owed about $10 billion.

The Allies controlled the sea, but they never had enough shipping to meet rising demands, especially with German submarines taking a steady though fluctuating toll. Each government set up a shipping board, to expand shipbuilding at any cost and to assign available shipping space to whatever purposes—troop movements, rubber imports, foodstuffs—the government considered most urgent in view of overall plans. Control and allocation eventually became international under the Interallied Shipping Council, of which the United States was a member after entering the war. In England and France, where all manufactures depended on imports, government control of shipping and hence of imports was itself enough to give control over the whole economy.

Germany, denied access to the sea and also to Russia and western Europe, was obliged to adopt unprecedented measures of self-sufficiency. The oil of Romania and grain of the Ukraine, which became available late in the war, were poor substitutes for the world trade on which Germany had formerly depended. The Germans went with less food than other belligerents. Their government controls became more thorough and more efficient, producing what they called "war socialism." In Walter Rathenau they found a man with the necessary ideas. He was a Jewish industrialist, son of the head of the German electrical trust. One of the first to foresee a long war, he launched a program for the mobilization of raw materials. Early in the war it seemed that Germany might be soon defeated by

[20] See pp. 599–600.

lack of nitrogen, necessary to make explosives. Rathenau sweepingly requisitioned every conceivable natural source, including the very manure from the farmers' barnyards, until German chemists succeeded in extracting nitrogen from the air. The German chemical industry developed many other substitute products, such as synthetic rubber. German production was organized into War Companies, one for each line of industry, with private business firms working under close government supervision.

The other belligerent governments also replaced competition between individual firms and factories with coordination. "Consortiums" of industrialists in France allocated raw materials and government orders within each industry. The War Industries Board did the same in the United States. In Britain, similar methods became so efficient that by 1918, for example, the country produced every two weeks as many shells as in the whole first year of the war and turned out seventy times as much heavy artillery.

Inflation, Industrial Changes, Control of Ideas

No government, even by heavy taxes, could raise all the funds it needed except by printing paper money, selling huge bond issues, or obliging banks to grant it credit. The result, given heavy demand and acute shortages, was rapid inflation of prices. Prices and wages were regulated but were never again so low as before 1914. The hardest hit by this development were those whose money income could not easily be raised—people living on "safe" investments, those drawing annual salaries, professional people, government employees. These classes had been one of the most stabilizing influences in Europe before the war. Everywhere the war threatened their status, prestige, and standard of living. The huge national debts meant higher taxes for years to come. The debt was most serious when it was owed to a foreign country. During the war the Continental Allies borrowed from Britain, and they and the British both borrowed from the United States. They thereby mortgaged their future. To pay the debt, they were bound for years to export more than they imported—or, roughly, to produce more than they consumed. It may be recalled that in 1914 every advanced European country habitually imported more than it exported.[21] That fact, basic to the European standard of life, was now threatened with reversal.

Moreover, with Europe torn by war for four years, the rest of the world speeded up its own industrialization. The productive capacity of the United States increased immensely. The Japanese began to sell in China, in India, in South America the cotton textiles and other civilian goods which these countries for the time being could not obtain from Europe. Argentina and Brazil, unable to get locomotive parts or mining machinery from England, began to manufacture them themselves. In India the Tata family, a group of wealthy Parsees controlling $250 million of native Indian capital, developed numerous manufacturing enterprises, one of which became the largest iron and steel works in the British Empire. With Germany entirely out of the world market, with Britain and France producing desperately for themselves, and with the world's shipping commandeered for war uses, the position of western Europe as the world's workshop was undermined.

[21] See p. 598.

After the war Europe had new competitors. The economic foundations of the nineteenth century had slipped away. The age of European supremacy was in its twilight.

All the belligerent governments during the war attempted to control ideas as they did economic production. Freedom of thought, respected everywhere in Europe for half a century, was discarded. Propaganda and censorship became more effective than any government, however despotic, had ever been able to devise. No one was allowed to sow doubt by raising any basic questions.

It must be remembered that the facts of the prewar crises, as related above, were then largely unknown. People were trapped in a nightmare whose causes they could not comprehend. Each side wildly charged the other with having started the war from pure malevolence. The long attrition, the fruitless fighting, the unchanging battle lines, the appalling casualties were a severe ordeal to morale. Civilians, deprived of their usual liberties, working harder, eating dull food, seeing no victory, had to be kept emotionally at a high pitch. Placards, posters, diplomatic white papers, schoolbooks, public lectures, solemn editorials, and slanted news reports conveyed the message. The new universal literacy, the mass press, the new moving pictures, proved to be ideal media for the direction of popular thinking. Intellectuals and professors advanced complicated reasons, usually historical, for loathing and crushing the enemy. In allied countries the Kaiser was portrayed as a demon, with glaring eyes and abnormally bristling mustaches, bent on the mad project of conquest of the world. In Germany people were taught to dread the day when Cossacks and Senegalese should rape German women and to hate England as the inveterate enemy which inhumanly starved little children with its blockade. Each side convinced itself that all right was on its side and all wrong, wickedness, and barbarity on the other. An inflamed opinion helped to sustain men and women in such a fearsome struggle. But when it came time to make peace the rooted convictions, fixed ideas, profound aversions, hates, and fears became an obstacle to political judgment.

90. The Peace of Paris, 1919

The late ally, Russia, was in the hands of the Bolsheviks, ostracized like a leper colony, and taking no part in international relations. The late German and Austro-Hungarian empires were already defunct, and more or less revolutionary regimes struggled to establish themselves in their places. New republics already existed along the Baltic coast, in Poland, and in the Danube basin but without effective governments or acknowledged frontiers. Europe east of France and Italy was in a state approaching chaos, with revolution on the Russian style threatening. Western Europe was wrenched out of all resemblance to its former self. The Allied blockade of Germany continued. In these circumstances the victors assembled in Paris, in the bleak winter of 1919, to reconstruct the world. During 1919 they signed five treaties, all named after Paris suburbs—St.-Germain with Austria, Trianon with Hungary, Neuilly with Bulgaria, Sèvres with Turkey (1920), and most especially, with Germany the Treaty of Versailles.

The world looked with awe and expectation to one man—the president of the United States. Wilson occupied a lone eminence, enjoyed a universal prestige.

Victors, vanquished, and neutrals admitted that American interve
decided the conflict. Everywhere people who had been long tried, co.
bereaved, were stirred by Wilson's thrilling language in favor of a higher cau.
of a great concert of right in which peace would be forever secure and the world
itself at last free. Wilson reached Europe in January 1919, visiting several Allied
capitals. He was wildly acclaimed, and almost mobbed, greeted as the man who
would lead civilization out of its wasteland.

The Fourteen Points and the Treaty of Versailles

Wilson's views were well known. He had stated them in January 1918 in his
Fourteen Points—principles upon which, after victory, peace was to be established. The Fourteen Points demanded an end to secret treaties and secret
diplomacy (or in Wilsonian language, "open covenants openly arrived at");
freedom of the seas "alike in peace and in war"; removal of barriers and
inequalities in international trade; reduction of armaments by all powers; colonial
readjustments; evacuation of occupied territory; self-determination of nationalities
and a redrawing of European boundaries along national lines; and, last but not
least, an international political organization to prevent war. On the whole, Wilson
stood for the fruition of the democratic, liberal, progressive, and nationalistic
movements of the century past, for the ideals of the Enlightenment, the French
Revolution, and of 1848. As Wilson saw it, and as many believed, the World War
should end in a new type of treaty. There was thought to be something sinister
about peace conferences of the past, for example, the Congress of Vienna of
1815.[22] The old diplomacy was blamed for leading to war. Lenin in his own way
and for his own purposes was saying this in Russia too. It was felt that treaties
had too long been wrongly based on a politics of power, or on unprincipled deals
and bargains made without regard to the people concerned. Democracy having
defeated the Central Powers, people hoped that a new settlement, made in a
democratic age, might be reached by general agreement in an atmosphere of
mutual confidence. There was a real sense of a new era.

Wilson had had some difficulty, however, in persuading the Allied governments
to accept his Fourteen Points. The French demanded a guarantee of German
payment for war damages. The British vetoed the freedom of the seas "in peace
and war"; it was naval rivalry that had estranged them from Germany, and they
had fought the war to preserve British command of the sea. But with these two
reservations the Allies expressed their willingness to follow Wilson's lead. The
Germans who asked for the armistice believed that peace would be made along
the lines of the Fourteen Points with only the two modifications described. The
socialists and democrats now trying to rule Germany thought also that, having
overthrown the Kaiser and the war lords, they would be treated by the victors
with some moderation, and that a new democratic Germany would reemerge into
the place in the world which they considered to be due it.

Twenty-seven nations assembled at Paris in January 1919, but the full or
plenary sessions were unimportant. Matters were decided by conferences among
the Big Four—Wilson himself, Lloyd George for England, Clemenceau for France,

---

[22] See pp. 444–450.

Orlando for Italy. The conjunction of personalities was not a happy one. Wilson was sternly and stubbornly righteous; Lloyd George, a fiery and changeable Welshman; Clemenceau, an aged patriot, the "tiger of France," who had been not exactly young in the War of 1870 (he was born in 1841); Orlando, a passing phenomenon of Italian politics. None of them was especially equipped for the task in hand. Clemenceau was a pronounced nationalist, Lloyd George had always been concerned with domestic reforms, Orlando was by training a professor like Wilson, and Wilson, a former college president, lacked concrete knowledge or intimate feeling for peoples other than his own. However, they democratically represented the governments and peoples of their respective countries, and thus spoke with an authority denied to professional diplomats of the old school.

Wilson first fought a hard battle for a League of Nations, a permanent international body in which all nations, without sacrificing their sovereignty, should meet together to discuss and settle disputes, each promising not to resort to war. Few European statesmen had any confidence in such a League. But they yielded to Wilson, and the covenant of the League of Nations was written into the treaty with Germany. In return, Wilson had to make concessions to Lloyd George, Clemenceau, Orlando, and the Japanese. He was thus obliged to compromise the idealism of the Fourteen Points. Probably compromise and bargaining would have been necessary anyway, for such general principles as national self-determination and colonial readjustment invariably led to differences of opinion in concrete cases. Wilson allowed himself to believe that, if a League of Nations were established and operating, faults in the treaty could later be corrected at leisure by international discussion.

A special kind of disagreement arose over the covenant of the League. Wilson wished to include a clause endorsing religious freedom. The Japanese insisted that it be broadened to condemn racial discrimination as well. The Americans and British were opposed for fear that an international authority might interfere with their immigration practices. In the end both proposals were abandoned.

The great demand of the French at the peace conference was for security against Germany. On this subject the French were almost rabid. The war in the West had been fought almost entirely on their soil. To trim Germany down more nearly to French size, they proposed that the part of Germany west of the Rhine be set up as an independent state under Allied auspices. Wilson and Lloyd George objected, sagely observing that the resulting German resentment would only lead to another war. The French yielded, but only on condition that they obtain their security in another way, namely, by a promise from both Britain and the United States to join them immediately if they were again attacked by the Germans. An Anglo-French-American guarantee treaty, with these provisions, was in fact signed at Paris. France obtained control over the Saar coal mines for fifteen years; during that time, a League commission would administer the Saar territory and in 1935 a plebiscite would be held. Lorraine and Alsace were returned to France. German fortifications and troops were banned from a wide belt in the Rhineland. Allied troops would occupy the Rhineland for fifteen years to assure German compliance with the treaty.

In the east the Allies wished to set up strong buffer states against Bolshevism in Russia. Sympathies with Poland ran very high. Those parts of the former German Empire that were inhabited by Poles, or by mixed populations of Poles and Germans—Posen and West Prussia—were assigned to the new Polish state. This gave Poland a corridor to the sea, but at the same time cut off the bulk of Germany from East Prussia.[23] Danzig, an old German town, became a free city, belonging to no country. Memel also was internationalized; it was soon seized by Lithuania. Upper Silesia, a rich mining country, went to Poland after a disputed plebiscite. In Austria and among the Sudeten Germans of Bohemia, now that there was no longer a Habsburg empire (whose existence had blocked an all-German union in 1848 and in the time of Bismarck),[24] a feeling developed for annexation to the new German republic. But the feeling was unorganized, and in any case the Allies naturally refused to make Germany bigger than it had been in 1914. Austria remained a dwarf republic, and Vienna a former imperial capital cut off from its empire—a head severed from its body, and scarcely more capable of sustaining life. The Bohemian Germans became disgruntled citizens of Czechoslovakia.

Germany lost all its colonies. Wilson and the South African General Smuts, to preserve the principle of internationalism against any imputation of raw conquest, saw to it that the colonies were actually awarded to the League of Nations. The League, in turn, under "mandates," assigned them to various powers for administration. In this way France and Great Britain divided the best of the African colonies; the Belgian Congo received a slight enlargement; and the Union of South Africa took over German Southwest Africa. In the colonial world, Italy got nothing. Japan received the mandate for the German Pacific islands north of the equator, Australia for German New Guinea and the Solomon Islands, New Zealand for German Samoa. The Japanese claimed rights over the German concessions in China. The Chinese at the Paris conference tried to get all special concessions and extraterritorial rights in China abolished.[25] No one listened to such proposals. By a compromise, Japan received about half the former German rights. The Japanese were dissatisfied. The Chinese walked out of the conference.

The Allies took over the German fleet, but the German crews, rather than surrender it, solemnly scuttled it at Scapa Flow. The German army was limited to 100,000. Since the Allies forbade conscription, or the annual training of successive groups of young civilians, the army became exclusively professional, the officer class retained political influence in it, and the means used by the Allies to demilitarize Germany served if anything the contrary purpose. The treaty forbade Germany to have any heavy artillery, aviation, or submarines. Wilson saw his plan for universal disarmament applied to Germany alone.

The French, even before the armistice, had stipulated that Germany must pay for war damages. The other Allies made the same demand. Wilson, at the conference, was stupefied at the size of the bills presented. The Belgians suggested, for their own share, a sum larger than the entire wealth of all Belgium according to officially published Belgian statistics. The French and British proposed to charge Germany with the entire expenses, including war pensions, incurred by them during the war. Wilson observed that "total" reparation, while not strictly unjust, was absolutely impossible, and even Clemenceau noted that

[23] See maps, p. 248, panel 4, and 728–729.
[24] See pp. 514–518, 551–557.
[25] See pp. 675–680.

"to ask for over a trillion francs would lead to nothing practical." The insistence on enormous reparations was in fact largely emotional. No one knew or considered how Germany would pay, though all dimly realized that such sums could only be made up by German exports, which would then compete with the Allies' own economic interests. The Germans, to avoid worse, even offered to repair physical damages in Belgium and France, but were brusquely refused on the ground that the Belgians and French would thereby lose jobs and business. No total at all was set for reparations in the treaty; it was made clear that the sum would be very large, but it was left for a future commission to determine. The Allies, maddened by the war, and themselves loaded with fantastic debts to the United States, had no desire in the matter of reparations to listen to economic reason and regarded the reparations as simply another means of righting a wrong and of putting off the dangers of a German revival. As a first payment on the reparations account the treaty required Germany to surrender most of its merchant marine, make coal deliveries, and give up all property owned by German private citizens abroad. This last proviso ended Germany's prewar career as an exporter of capital.

It was with the specific purpose of justifying the reparations that the famous "war guilt" clause was written into the treaty. By this clause Germany explicitly "accepted the responsibility" for all loss and damage resulting from the war "imposed upon them (the Allies) by the aggression of Germany and her allies." The Germans themselves felt no such responsibility as they were now obliged formally to accept. They considered their honor as a people to be impugned. The "war guilt" clause gave a ready opening to agitators in Germany and made even moderate Germans regard the treaty as something to be escaped from as a matter of self-respect.

The Treaty of Versailles was completed in three months. The absence of the Russians, the decision not to give the Germans a hearing, and the willingness of Wilson to make concessions in return for obtaining the League of Nations, made it possible to dispose of intricate matters with considerable facility. The Germans, when presented with the completed document in May 1919, refused to sign. The Allies threatened a renewal of hostilities. A government crisis ensued in Berlin. No German wished to damn himself, his party, or his principles, in German eyes, by putting his name to a document which all Germans regarded as outrageous. A combination drawn from the Social Democratic and Catholic parties finally consented to shoulder the hateful burden. Two abashed and virtually unknown representatives appeared at the Hall of Mirrors at Versailles, and signed the treaty for Germany in the presence of a large concourse of Allied dignitaries.

The other treaties drafted by the Paris conference, in conjunction with the Versailles treaty, laid out a new map for eastern Europe and registered the recession of the Russian, Austrian, and Turkish empires. Seven new independent states now existed: Finland, Estonia, Latvia, Lithuania, Poland, Czechoslovakia, and Yugoslavia. Romania was enlarged by adding areas formerly Hungarian and Russian; Greece was enlarged at the expense of Turkey. Austria and Hungary were now small states, and there was no connection between them. The Ottoman Empire presently disappeared: Turkey emerged as a republic confined to Constantinople and Asia Minor, Syria and Lebanon went to France as mandates of the League of Nations, Palestine and Iraq to Great Britain on the same basis.[26] The belt of states from Finland to Romania was regarded as a *cordon sanitaire* (sanitary zone) to prevent the infection of Europe by communism. The creation of Yugoslavia (or the Kingdom of the Serbs, Croats, and Slovenes, as it was called until 1929), although dominated by the Serbs and under the Serbian monarchy, seemed to fulfill the aims of the South Slav movement which had set off the fatal crisis of 1914. The fact, however, that Italy received Trieste and some of the Dalmatian Islands (in keeping with the secret treaty of 1915) left the more ambitious Yugoslavs discontented.

Significance of the Paris Peace Settlement

The most general principle of the Paris settlement was to recognize the right of national self-determination, at least in Europe. Each people or nation, as defined by language, was in principle set up with its own sovereign and independent national state. Nationalism triumphed in the belief that it went along naturally with liberalism and democracy. It must be added that the peacemakers at Paris had little choice in this matter, for the new states had already declared their independence. Since in eastern Europe the nationalities were in many places intermixed, and since the peacemakers did not contemplate the actual movement and exchange of populations to sort them out, each new state found alien minorities living within its borders or could claim that people of its own kind still lived in neighboring states under foreign rule. There were Hungarians in Czechoslovakia, Ruthenians in Poland, Poles in Lithuania, Bulgars in Romania— to cite only a few examples. Hence minority problems and irredentism troubled eastern Europe, as they had before 1914. Eventually it was the complaint of Germans in Czechoslovakia that they were an oppressed minority, together with the irredentist demand of Germany to join these outlying Germans to the Fatherland, that produced the Munich crisis preceding the Second World War.[27]

The Treaty of Versailles was designed to put an end to the German menace.

---

[26] The secret treaty of 1915 (p. 709) promising the Straits to Russia lapsed with the Revolution, neither the Bolsheviks nor the Allies recognizing an agreement made with the tsarist government.
[27] See pp. 840–842.

EUROPE, 1923

The map shows European boundaries between the two World Wars, after the Peace of Versailles and certain other agreements. Comparison with the language map (p. 470) will suggest how the principle of nationality was recognized. Germany returned Alsace-Lorraine to France and lost the region around Danzig (the "Polish corridor") to Poland— essentially the area taken by Prussia in the First Partition of 1772 (see map, p. 230.) In place of the Austro-Hungarian empire we find the "succession states," Austria, Hungary, Czechoslovakia, Yugoslavia, and Romania. Austria-Hungary also lost Trieste and some of the Dalmatian Islands to Italy. Poland regained its independence, and Finland and the three Baltic states, Estonia, Latvia, and Lithuania, emerged from the tsarist empire. Most of Ireland became a "free state" in the British Commonwealth of Nations, only Ulster remaining in the United Kingdom.

These boundaries lasted until 1938, when, as the Second World War approached, the Germans annexed Austria and the Sudeten part of Czechoslovakia.

Areas Lost by Germany

Areas Lost by Russia

Areas Lost by Ottoman Empire

Austria and Hungary plus areas lost by
Austro-Hungarian Empire

CAPE

Murmansk

Archangel

AND

L. Onega

Sverdlovsk

L. Ladoga

elsinki   Leningrad   Volgoda

eval

ONIA

iga   Moscow   Orenburg

VIA   Samara

S O V I E T   U N I O N

ANIA   Saratov

aunas

Vilna   BYELO-
RUSSIAN   KAZAK S.S.R.
S.S.R.

ND   Tsaritsyn

Brest-
Litovsk   Astrakhan

Kiev   UKRAINIAN S.S.R.

Dniester R.   CASPIAN SEA

ICIA

BUKO
VINA   BESSARABIA   CAUCASIA

NSYLVANIA   CRIMEA   GEORGIAN S.S.R.   Baku

ROMANIA   Sevastopol   Tiflis

DOBRUJA   BLACK SEA   Batum   AZERBAIJAN
S.S.R.
Bucharest   Danube R.   ARMENIAN S.S.R.

Sofia

BULGARIA   Tabriz

(Turkey) Istanbul

Ankara   IRAN

T U R K E Y   Mosul

ECE   Tigris R.

Smyrna   SYRIA AND   Baghdad
LEBANON   Euphrates R.

Athens   IRAQ

DODECANESE I   CYPRUS
(Italy)   (Britain)
LEBANON

CRETE (Greece)

PALESTINE   TRANS-
JORDAN   SAUDI ARABIA

It was not a successful treaty. The wisdom of it has been discussed without end, but a few comments can safely be made. For practical purposes, with respect to Germany, the treaty was either too severe or too lenient. It was too severe to conciliate and not severe enough to destroy. Possibly the victors should have dealt more moderately with the new German republic, which professed their own ideals, as the monarchical victors over Napoleon, in 1814, had dealt moderately with the France of the restored Bourbons, regarding it as a regime akin to their own. As it was, the Allies imposed upon the German Republic about the same terms that they might have imposed upon the German Empire. They innocently played the game of Ludendorff and the German reactionaries; it was the Social Democrats and liberals who bore the ''shame'' of Versailles. The Germans from the beginning showed no real intention to live up to the treaty. On the other hand, the treaty was not sufficiently disabling to Germany to destroy its economic and political strength. Even the degree of severity that it incorporated soon proved to be more than the Allies were willing to enforce. The treaty makers at Paris in 1919, working hastily and still in the heat of war, under pressure from press and propaganda in their own countries, drafted a set of terms which the test of time showed that they themselves did not in the long run wish to impose. As the years passed, many people in Allied countries declared various provisions of the Versailles treaty to be unfair or unworkable. The loss of faith by the Allies in their own treaty only made easier the task of those German agitators who demanded its repudiation. The door was opened for Adolf Hitler.

Even at the beginning the Allies showed doubts. Lloyd George, in the last weeks before the signing, tardily called for certain amendments, though in vain; for in 1919 British opinion shifted somewhat from fear of Germany to the fear of Bolshevism, and already the idea of using Germany as a bulwark against communism was expressed. The Italians disliked the whole settlement from the beginning; they observed that the spoils of Africa and the Near East went only to France and Great Britain. The Chinese were also dissatisfied. The Russians, when they reentered the international arena some years later, found a situation that they did not like and had had no part in making. They objected to being faced with a *cordon sanitaire* from Finland to Romania and soon remembered that most of this territory had once belonged to the Russian empire.

The United States never ratified the Treaty of Versailles at all. A wave of isolationism and disgust with Europe spread over the country; and this feeling, together with some rational criticism of the terms, and a good deal of party politics, caused the Senate to repudiate Wilson's work. The Senate likewise refused to make any advance promises of military intervention in a future war between Germany and France, and hence also declined to ratify the Anglo-French-American guarantee treaty on which Wilson had persuaded Clemenceau to rely. The French considered themselves duped, deprived both of the Rhineland and of the Anglo-American guarantee. They raised more anguished cries over their insecurity. This led them to try to hold Germany down while it was still weak, in turn raising many further complications.

The League of Nations was established at Geneva. Its mere existence marked a great step beyond the international anarchy before 1914. Wilson's vision did not die. But the United States never joined; Germany was not admitted until 1926, or Russia until 1934. The League could handle and dispatch only such business as the Great Powers were willing to allow. It was associated with a west-European ascendancy that no longer corresponded to the facts of the world situation. Its covenant was part of the Versailles treaty, and many people in many countries, on both sides in the late war, saw in it, not so much a system for international adjudication, as a means for maintaining a new status quo in favor of Britain and France.

The First World War dealt a last blow to the ancient institutions of monarchy and aristocratic feudalism. Thrones toppled in Turkey, in Russia, in Austria-Hungary, in the German Empire and the individual German states; and with the kings went the courtly retainers and all the social preeminence and special advantage of the old landed aristocracies. The war was indeed a victory for democracy, though a bitter one. It carried further a process as old as the French and American revolutions. But for the basic problems of modern civilization, industrialism and nationalism, economic security and international stability, it gave no answer.

XVII.
THE RUSSIAN
REVOLUTION
AND THE
SOVIET UNION

No LESS POWERFUL than the First World War as a force shaping the twentieth century has been the revolution in Russia, of which the decisive step was the seizure of power by the Bolshevik party in November 1917. The Russian Revolution of 1917 can be compared in its magnitude only with the French Revolution of 1789. Both originated in deep-lying and distant causes, and both made their repercussions felt in many countries for many years. The present chapter will set forth the revolutionary process in Russia over half a century. We shall begin with the old regime before 1900, pass through the two revolutions of 1905 and 1917, and survey the Union of Soviet Socialist Republics down to 1939, at which time a new order had been consolidated under Joseph Stalin, a form of "planned economy" realized, and the last of the original revolutionaries, or Old Bolsheviks, either silenced or put to death.

The comparison of the Russian Revolution to the French is enlightening in many ways. Both were movements of liberation, the one against "feudalism" and "despotism," the other against "capitalism" and "imperialism." Neither was a strictly national movement dealing with merely domestic troubles; both addressed their message to all the world. Both attracted followers in all countries. Both aroused a strong reaction on the part of those whose view of life was endangered. And both showed the same pattern of revolutionary politics: a

Chapter Emblem: One of a series of bronze medals issued by the Leningrad mint in honor of Lenin and the Russian Revolution of 1917.

relative unity of opinion so long as the problem was to overthrow the old regime, followed by disunity and conflict over the founding of the new, so that one set of revolutionaries eliminated others, until a small, organized, and determined minority (Jacobin democrats in 1793, Bolshevik communists in 1918) suppressed all opposition in order to defend or advance the revolutionary cause; and in short order (within a matter of months in France, years in Russia), many of the most intensely revolutionary leaders were themselves suppressed or liquidated.

The differences are equally deserving of notice. Relatively speaking, or compared in general civilization with other European countries, Russia in 1900 was in the rear, and France in 1780 in many ways in the lead. The main strength of the French Revolution lay in the middle classes, who soon managed to prevail over more extreme pressures. In the Russian Revolution middle-class people were also active, especially at first, but they proved unable to cope with mass discontents, and succumbed to a more radical party which appealed to workers and peasants. In France, so to speak, the revolution just "happened," in that ordinary people from many walks of life unexpectedly found themselves in a revolutionary situation, and even the Jacobin dictatorship was improvised by individuals who had spent their lives thinking of other things. In Russia professional revolutionaries worked for the revolution long in advance, and the dictatorship of the Bolsheviks realized the plans and preparations of twenty years. In France the revolution was followed by a reaction in which émigrés returned, dispossessed classes reappeared in politics, and even the Bourbons were restored. The French Revolution was followed by a century of uneasy compromise. The Russian Revolution effectively wiped out its opposition; few émigrés returned; no Romanovs regained their throne. The Russian Revolution was in this sense more immediately successful. But in the long run the differences reemerged. By the 1990s the ideas proclaimed in Russia in 1917 were in ruins, while those proclaimed in France in 1789 were widely accepted, such as representative constitutional government, with equal civil rights under national sovereignty and legal safeguards for persons and property.

The repercussions of the Russian Revolution were the more far-reaching because of the very ambivalence of Russia itself. Since the days of Peter the Great and before, it had always faced toward both Europe and Asia. It was European, yet it was also outside Europe, and even opposed to it. If about 1900 it was the least developed of the major European countries, it was at the same time the most developed, industrialized, or modernized part of the non-European world. Its revolution could win sympathy on the left in Europe because it reinforced the old European socialist objections to capitalism. It aroused the interests of submerged peoples in other continents because it also denounced imperialism (i.e., the possession of colonies by Europeans), affirming that imperialism was merely the "highest stage" of capitalism, and that both must be overthrown together. The Soviet Union, once established, came to occupy an intermediate position between the West and the colonial world (or what later came to be called the Third World). In the West it could long be feared or admired as the last word in social revolution. In the colonial, or formerly colonial, world it suggested new beginnings, a new way to become modern without being capitalistic or European, a step in a worldwide rebellion against European supremacy. The Russian Revolution thus not only produced communism and hence fascism in Europe, but added strength to the revolt of Asia, as explained in the following chapters.

Although professional revolutionaries worked for revolution in Russia, they did not "cause" it. Lenin and the Bolsheviks did not bring about the Russian Revolution. They captured it after it had begun. They boarded the ship in midstream. The Russian Revolution, like all great revolutions, originated in a totality of previous history and in the prolonged dissatisfaction of many kinds of people.

91. Backgrounds

Russia after 1881: Reaction and Progress

We have seen in earlier chapters how the tsarist autocracy arose, how it ruled as a machine superimposed upon its subjects, how the upper class became westernized while the masses sank further into serfdom, and how an intelligentsia developed, divorced both from the work of government and the activities of the people.[1] It has been explained in Chapter XIII how Alexander II freed the serfs in 1861 and created provincial and district councils or zemstvos, elected mainly by landowners, which attended to such matters as roads, schools, and hospitals.[2]

In 1881 Alexander II was assassinated by members of the People's Will. His son, Alexander III (1881–1894), tried to stamp out revolutionism and to silence even peaceable criticism of the government. Revolutionaries and terrorists were driven into exile. The People's Will as an organized group became extinct. Jews were subjected to pogroms, by far the worst of any (until then) in modern times. For the first time the empire adopted a program of systematic Russification. Poles, Ukrainians, Lithuanians, the peoples of the Caucasus, the scattered German communities, the Muslim groups in central Asia, all faced the prospect of forcible assimilation to the Great Russian culture. The philosopher and chief official of this movement was Pobiedonostsev, procurator of the Holy Synod, or layman head, under the tsar, of the Russian Orthodox Church. Pobiedonostsev saw in the West something alien and doomed. Drawing on such old enemies of the French Revolution as Edmund Burke, he attacked Western rationalism and liberalism in his writings, declared that Slavs had a peculiar national character of their own, and dreamed of turning Holy Russia into a kind of churchly community, in which a disciplined clergy should protect the faithful from the insidious influence of the West.

This is not, however what happened. In the closing decades of the nineteenth century Russia became more than ever before a part of European civilization. Almost overnight it presented Europe with great works of literature and music that Europeans could appreciate. The Russian novel became known throughout the Western world. All could read the novels of Tolstoy (1828–1910) without a

---

[1] See pp. 234–245, 336–342, 564–569.
[2] See p. 567.

feeling of strangeness; and if the characters of Turgenev (1818–1883) and of Dostoevski (1821–1881) behaved more queerly, the authors themselves were obviously within the great European cultural family. The melodies of Tchaikovsky (1840–1893) and of Rimsky-Korsakov (1844–1908) became very familiar throughout Europe and America; if they sometimes seemed hauntingly wild, distant, or sad, they still betrayed no more than the usual amount of national idiosyncrasy. Russians also contributed to the sciences, notably chemistry. They were considered to be especially talented in the more abstruse intellectual exercises, such as higher mathematics, physics, or chess.

Russia also, from the 1880s, began to pass through the Industrial Revolution and take its place as an integral part of the world economic system. European capital entered the country, financing railways, mines, and factories (as well as government and the army) until by 1914 Europeans had about the same amount invested in Russia as in the United States, some four billion dollars in each case.[3] In 1897, under the reforming ministry of Count Witte, Russia adopted the gold standard, making its currency readily convertible with all others. In the quarter-century between 1888 and 1913 the Russian railway mileage more than doubled, the miles of telegraph wires multiplied fivefold, the number of post offices trebled, and the number of letters carried by the mails multiplied seven times. Although still industrially undeveloped by Western standards, without, for example, any machine tool industry or chemical plants, Russia was industrializing rapidly. Exports rose in value from 400 million rubles in 1880 to 1.6 billion in 1913. Imports, though smaller, grew more rapidly, quintupling in the same period. They consisted of such items as tea and coffee and of the machines and industrial goods made in western Europe. For a long time after the Revolution, the Soviet Union conducted less foreign trade than did the Russian empire on the eve of the First World War. The Soviet regime, to keep control over its own economic system, tried to depend as little as possible on outside markets and sources of supply.

Industrialization, in Russia as in all countries, brought an increase both of the business and of the wage-earning classes, or, in socialist terminology, of the bourgeoisie and of the proletariat. Though growing, they were still not numerous by standards of the West. Factory workers, laboring for eleven or more hours a day, for low wages under hard conditions, were in somewhat the same position as in England or France before 1850.[4] Unions were illegal, and strikes prohibited. Nevertheless, great strikes in the 1890s called attention to the misery of the new industrial workers. There was one distinctive feature to the Russian proletariat. Russian industry was heavily concentrated; half of Russia's industrial workers were employed in factories employing over 500 persons. It was easier for workers under such circumstances to be organized economically and at the proper time to be mobilized politically. As for the Russian business and capitalist class, it was relatively the weaker because of several features in the situation. Ownership of much of Russia's new industrial plant was in foreign hands. Much was owned by the tsarist government itself; Russia already had the largest state-operated economic system in the world. Moreover, in Russia (unlike the United States at

---

[3] See pp. 599–600, 648.
[4] See pp. 459–461, 492–499, 501–505.

the time) the government itself was a heavy borrower from Europe; hence it was less dependent financially on its own people and more able to maintain an absolutist regime.

Nevertheless, the rising business and professional classes, reinforced by enterprising landowners, were strong enough to form a liberal segment of public opinion, which emerged in 1905 as the Constitutional Democratic party (or "Cadets"). Many of those who were active in the provincial zemstvos also became Constitutional Democrats. They were liberals, progressives, or constitutionalists in the Western sense, thinking less about the troubles of factory workers and peasants than about the need for a nationally elected parliament to control the policies of state.

Russia remained predominantly agricultural. Its huge exports were mainly farm and forest products. The peasants formed four-fifths of the population. Free from their former lords since 1861, they lived in their village communes or *mirs*.[5] In most communes much of the land was divided and redivided among peasant households by agreement of the village community, nor could anyone leave without communal permission. The peasants still carried a considerable burden. Until 1906 they paid redemption money arising from the Emancipation of 1861, and even after that other forms of onerous payments. They also paid high taxes, for the government defrayed the interest on its foreign loans from taxes raised at home. The constantly rising export of cereals (also used to pay off debts contracted by Russia in the West) tended to keep food from the farmer's table; many peasants raised the best wheat for sale and ate black bread themselves. The farm population, in short (as in other countries in similar stages of their development), bore a considerable share of the costs of industrialization.

Under such pressures, and because of their crude methods of cultivation, the peasants were forever demanding more land. "Land hunger" was felt both by individual families and by the *mirs*. The Emancipation had turned over roughly half the land to peasant ownership, individual and collective; and in the following half-century the peasants added to their share by buying from nonpeasant owners. The *mirs* were by no means obsolescent. They were in fact flourishing; they acquired far more land by purchase than did individual buyers, and perhaps half or more of the peasants valued communal security above the uncertain pleasures of private property. The exceptions were the minority of more enterprising and wealthier peasants, later called the kulaks. Such a one was Leon Trotsky's father, who, a hard-working, plain, and illiterate man, owned or leased the equivalent of a square mile of land, employed scores of field hands at harvest time, and permanently maintained a large domestic staff. That such a "big farmer" could afford so many employees suggests the poverty in which the bulk of the peasants lived. Not all of the well-to-do peasants were as affluent as Trotsky's father, but the big farmers stood out conspicuously from the mass, by whom they were not liked.

The Emergence of Revolutionary Parties

The peasants were the ancient source of revolutionary disturbance in Russia. Fables about Pugachev and Stephen Razin circulated in peasant legend.[6] After

[5] See pp. 566–567.
[6] See pp. 238, 338–339.

the Emancipation the peasants continued to believe that they had some kind of rights in *all* the land of former estates on which they had formerly been serfs— not merely in the portion that had been allotted to peasant possession. They demanded (and obtained) credit from the government to buy from the big landowners or former masters. Their land hunger could not be appeased. They remained jealous of the landed aristocrat's very existence. In Russia, as elsewhere in Europe, and unlike the United States, the rural population was divided into two sharply distinct classes, on the one hand the peasants of all types, who worked the soil, and on the other the gentry who resided upon it. The two never intermarried. They differed not merely economically but in speech, dress, and manners, and even in the looks of their faces and hands. But in the last three decades of the nineteenth century the Russian peasants were notably quiet, insurrectionism seemingly having subsided.

The other traditional source of revolutionary disturbance lay among the intelligentsia.[7] In the conditions in which the Russian empire had grown up, many of the best and purest spirits were attracted to violence. Revolutionary intelligentsia (as distinguished from those who were simply liberal or progressive) yearned for a catastrophic overthrow of the tsardom. Since the days of the Decembrists[8] they had formed secret organizations, comprising a few hundreds or thousands of members, engaged in outwitting the tsarist police, by whom they were bafflingly interpenetrated. At a Bolshevik party congress held in 1913, out of twenty-two delegates present, no less than five, unknown to the others, were government spies.

The revolutionary intelligentsia, since there was normally little that they could do, spent their time in vehement discussion and interminable refinement of doctrine. By 1890 the terrorism and nihilism of the 1870s were somewhat passé. The great question was where these willing officers of a revolutionary movement could find an army. Disputation turned upon such topics as whether the peasants or the new factory workers were the true revolutionary class, whether the peasants were potentially proletarian or incurably petty bourgeois, whether Russia was bound to experience the same historical process as the West, or whether it was different; and, specifically, whether Russia had to go through capitalism or might simply skip the capitalist stage in reaching the socialist society.

Most of the revolutionary intelligentsia were "populists." Some had once belonged to the now broken People's Will. Some continued to approve of terrorism and assassination as morally necessary in an autocratic country. They generally had a mystical faith in the vast inchoate might of the Russian people, and since most Russians were peasants, the populists were interested in peasant problems and peasant welfare. They believed that a great native revolutionary tradition existed in Russia, of which the peasant rebellion of Pugachev, in 1773, was the chief example.[9] The populists admired the Russian communal village or *mir*, in which they saw the European socialist idea of a "commune" represented. They read and respected Marx and Engels (indeed, a populist first translated the *Communist Manifesto* into Russian); but they did not believe that an urban

[7] See pp. 565–566.
[8] See p. 484.
[9] See pp. 338–339.

proletariat was the only true revolutionary class. They did not believe that capitalism, by creating such a proletariat, had inevitably and logically to precede socialism. They said that, in Russia, the horrors of capitalism could be skipped. They addressed themselves to the plight of the farmer and the evils of landlordism, favored strengthening the *mir* and equalizing the shares of all peasants in it, and, since they did not have to wait for the prior triumph of capitalism in Russia, they thought that revolution might come quite soon. This populist sentiment crystallized in the founding in 1901 of the Social Revolutionary party.

Two populists, Plekhanov and Axelrod, fleeing to Switzerland in the 1870s, there became converted to Marxism. In 1883 they founded in exile the organization from which the Russian Social Democratic or Marxist party was to grow. A few Marxists began to declare themselves (though not publicly) in Russia itself. When the youthful Lenin met his future wife Krupskaya in 1894, she already belonged to a circle of argumentative Marxists. The fact that the peasants in the 1890s were disappointingly quiescent, while machine industry, factory labor, and strikes were developing rapidly, turned many of the revolutionary intelligentsia, though only a minority, from populism to Marxism. To Plekhanov and Axelrod were added, as young leaders, Vladimir Ilyich Lenin (1870–1924), Leon Trotsky (1879–1940), Joseph V. Stalin (1879–1953), and others.

Of these it was Lenin who, after Marx, was to be claimed by communism as a father. Lenin was a short almost rotund man, with a bounding quickness and intense, penetrating gaze. High cheekbones and somewhat slanting eyes showed an Asiatic strain on the paternal side; Russian friends at first said that he looked "like a Kalmuck." His hair receded in early youth, leaving a massive forehead, behind which a restless mind was inexhaustibly at work. Even in his twenties he was called the Old One. He was of upper-middle-class origin, son of an inspector of schools who rose in the civilian bureaucracy to a rank equivalent to major general. His boyhood was comfortable and even happy, until the age of seventeen, when his elder brother, a student at St. Petersburg, became somewhat incidentally involved in a plot to assassinate Alexander III, for which he was put to death by order of the tsar himself. Because of the blot on the family record it became impossible for Lenin to continue with his law studies. He soon joined the ranks of professional revolutionaries, having no other occupation and living precariously from the party funds, which came mainly from the donations of well-to-do sympathizers.

Arrested as a revolutionary, he spent three years of exile in Siberia. Here the tsarist government treated educated political prisoners with an indulgence not later shown by the Soviet regime. Lenin and most of the others lived in cottages of their own or boarded with local residents. No labor was required of them. They borrowed books from Europe; met and visited with one another; debated, played chess, went hunting, meditated, and wrote. They chafed, however, at being cut off from the mainstream of Russian political life back home. Lenin, his term over, proceeded in 1900 to western Europe, where except for short secret trips to Russia he remained until 1917. His intellectual vigor, irresistible drive, and shrewdness as a tactician soon made him a force in the party. Genius has been called the faculty for everlasting concentration upon one thing. Lenin, said his one-time close associate Axelrod, "for twenty-four hours of the day is taken up with the revolution, has no thoughts but thoughts of revolution, and even in his sleep dreams of nothing but revolution.''

In 1898 the Marxists in Russia, spurred on by émigrés, founded the Social Democratic Labor party. They were not more revolutionary than the larger group of Social Revolutionaries. They simply had a different conception of the revolution. First of all, as good Marxists, they were more inclined to see the revolution as an international movement, part of the dialectical process of world history in which all countries were involved. Russia for them was no different from other countries except that it was less advanced. They expected the world revolution to break out first in western Europe. They particularly admired the German Social Democratic party, the largest and most flourishing of all the parties that acknowledged the fatherhood of Marx.[10]

If the Social Democrats were more oriented to Europe than the Social Revolutionaries, it was because so many of their spokesmen lived there in exile. They tended to think that Russia must develop capitalism, an industrialist proletariat, and the modern form of class struggle before there could be any revolution. Seeing in the urban proletariat the true revolutionary class, they looked upon all peasantry with suspicion, ridiculed the *mir*, and abhorred the Social Revolutionaries. Like Marx himself, the Russian Marxists disapproved of sporadic terrorism and assassination. For this reason, and because their doctrine seemed somewhat academic and their revolution rather conditional and far in the future, the Marxists were for a time actually favored by the tsarist police, who regarded them as less dangerous than the Social Revolutionaries.

Split in the Social Democrats: Bolsheviks and Mensheviks

The Russian Marxists held a second party congress in Brussels and London in 1903, attended by émigrés like Lenin and delegates from the underground in Russia, and by Social Democrats and members of lesser organizations. The purpose of the congress was to unify all Russian Marxism, but in fact it split it forever. The two resulting factions called themselves Bolshevik, or majority, and Menshevik, or minority. Lenin was the main author of the split and hence the founder of Bolshevism. Although he obtained his majority after one participating organization, the Jewish Bund, had seceded in indignation, and by calling for surprise votes on tactical issues, and although after 1903 it was usually the Mensheviks who had the majority, Lenin clung proudly and stubbornly to the term Bolshevism, with its favorable connotation of a majority in his support. For a number of years after 1903 the Social Democrats remained at least formally a single Marxist party, but they were irreconcilably divided into two wings. In 1912 the Bolshevik wing organized itself as a separate party.

Bolshevism, or Leninism, originally differed from Menshevism mainly on matters of organization and tactics. Russian Marxists referred to each other as "hards" and "softs." The "hards" were attracted to Lenin, the "softs" repelled by him. Lenin believed that the party should be a small revolutionary elite, a hard core of reliable and zealous workers. Those who wished a larger and more

[10] See pp. 615–616, 622–623.

open party, with membership for mere sympathizers, became Mensheviks. Lenin insisted upon a strongly centralized party, without autonomy for national or other component groups. He demanded strong authority at the top, by which the central committee would determine the doctrine (or "party line") and control personnel at all levels of the organization. The Mensheviks favored a greater degree of influence by the membership as a whole. Lenin thought that the party would strengthen itself by purges, expelling all who developed deviations of opinion. The Mensheviks favored covering up or bridging over all but the most fundamental disagreements. The Mensheviks came to recommend cooperation with liberals, progressives, and bourgeois democrats. Lenin regarded such cooperation as purely tactical and temporary, never concealing that in the end the Bolsheviks must impose their views through a dictatorship of the proletariat. The Mensheviks, in short, came to resemble the Marxists of western Europe, so far as that was possible under Russian conditions.[11] Lenin stood for the rigid reaffirmation of Marxian fundamentals—dialectical materialism and irreconcilable class struggle.

If we ask what Leninism added to the original Marxism,[12] the answer is not easy to find. Lenin accepted Marx's governing ideas: that capitalism exploited the workers, that it necessarily produced and preceded socialism, that history was logically predetermined, that class struggle was the law of society, that existing forms of religion, government, philosophy, and morals were weapons of the ruling class. He did, however, develop and transform into a first-rank element of Marxism certain theories of "imperialism" and of the "uneven development of capitalism" that had been propounded in only general terms by Marx and Engels. In the Marxist-Leninist view, "imperialism" was exclusively a product of monopoly capitalism, that is, capitalism in its big business, "highest," and "final" stage, which develops differently and at different times in each country. Monopoly capitalism is bent on exporting surplus capital and investing it in underdeveloped areas for greater profits.[13] The unceasing drive for colonies and markets in a world already almost completely partitioned leads inevitably to international "imperialist" wars for the "redistribution" of colonies, as well as to intensified national colonial struggles for independence; both provide new revolutionary opportunities for the proletariat.

In other respects, Lenin roundly denounced all who attempted to "add" anything to the fundamental principles of Marx. Nothing infuriated him so much as revisionist efforts to tone down the class struggle, or hints that Marxism might in the last analysis perhaps find room for some kind of religion. As he wrote in 1908: "From the philosophy of Marxism, cast of one piece of steel, it is impossible to expunge a single basic premise, a single essential part, without deviating from objective truth, without falling into the arms of bourgeois-reactionary falsehood." Lenin was a convert. He discovered Marxism; he did not invent it. He found in it a theory of revolution which he accepted without reservation as scientific and on which he was more outspokenly dogmatic even than Marx himself. His powers of mind, which were very great, were spent in demonstrating how the unfolding events of the twentieth century confirmed the analysis of the master.

But it was by his powers of will that Lenin was most distinguished, and if

[11] See pp. 622–623.
[12] See pp. 522–526.
[13] See pp. 647–648.

Leninism contributed little to Marxism as a theory it contributed a great deal to it as a movement. Lenin was an activist. He was the supreme agitator, a field commander in the class war, who could dash off a polemical pamphlet, dominate a party congress, or address throngs of workingmen with equal ease. Beside him, Marx and Engels seem almost to be mere recluses or sociologists. Marx and Engels had preferred to believe that the dictatorship of the proletariat, when it came, would represent the wishes of the great majority in a society in which most people had become proletarians. Lenin more frankly foresaw the possibility that the proletarian dictatorship might represent the conscious wishes of a small vanguard and might have to impose itself on great masses by an unshrinking use of force.

Above all, Lenin developed Marx's idea of the role of the party. He drew on the rich experience of pre-Marxist revolutionaries in Russia—the mysterious use of false names, invisible ink, secret ciphers, forged passports, and hidden rendezvous—the whole conspiratorial wonderland which, when it existed to a lesser degree in the West before 1848, drew Marx's scorn and laughter. Lenin's conception of the party was basically Marx's, reinforced by his own experience as a Russian. The party was an organization in which intellectuals provided leadership and understanding for workers, who could not see for themselves. For trade unionism, concerned only with the day-to-day demands of workers, Lenin had even less patience than Marx. "The unconscious growth of the labor movement," he wrote, "takes the form of trade unionism, and trade unionism signifies the mental enslavement of the workers to the bourgeoisie." The task of intellectuals in the party, the elite, or experts, was to make the trade unions and the workers class-conscious and hence revolutionary. Armed with "objective" knowledge, known to be correct, the party leadership naturally could not listen to the subjective opinions of others—the passing ideas of laborers, of peasants, of mistaken party subordinates, or of other parties pretending to know more than Marx himself. The idea that intellectuals supply the brains and workers the brawn, that an elite leads while the toilers meekly follow, is understandable enough in view of the Russian background, which had created on the one hand a painfully self-conscious intelligentsia, and on the other a repressed working class and peasantry deprived of all opportunity for political experience of their own. It was one of the most distinctive traits of Leninism and one of the most foreign to the democratic movement of the West.

Leninism accomplished the marriage of Russian revolutionary traditions with the Western doctrine of Marxism. It was an improbable marriage, whose momentous offspring was to be communism. But at the time, when Bolshevism first appeared in 1903, it had little or no effect. A real revolution broke out in Russia in 1905. It took the revolutionary émigrés almost entirely by surprise.

92. The Revolution of 1905

Background and Revolutionary Events

The almost simultaneous founding at the turn of the century of the Constitutional Democratic, Social Revolutionary, and Social Democratic parties was clearly a sign of mounting discontent. None of these was as yet a party in the Western sense, organized to get candidates elected to office, for there were no elections in Russia above the provincial zemstvo level. All three parties were propaganda agencies, made up of leaders without followers, intellectuals who followed various lines of thought. All, even those who became Constitutional Democrats, were watched by the police and obliged to do most of their work underground. At the same time, after 1900, there were signs of growing popular unrest. Peasants were trespassing on lands of the gentry and even rising in local insurrections against landlords and tax collectors. Factory workers sporadically refused to work. But with these popular movements none of the new parties had formed any solid links.

The government refused to make concessions of any kind. The tsar, Nicholas II, who had mounted the throne in 1894, was a man of narrow outlook. To the Little Father all criticism seemed merely childish. Tutored in his youth by Pobiedonostsev,[14] he regarded all ideas questioning autocracy, Orthodoxy, and Great Russian nationalism as un-Russian. That persons in the government should be controlled by interests outside the government—the mildest liberalism or most orderly democracy—seemed to the tsar, the tsarina, and the leading officials to be a monstrous aberration. Autocracy, for them, was the best and only, as it was the God-given, form of government for Russia.

The chief minister, Plehve, and the circles at court, hoped that a short successful war with Japan would create more attachment to the government. The war went so badly that its effect was the reverse.[15] Critics of the regime (except for the handful of the most internationalist Marxists) were sufficiently patriotic to be ashamed at the ease with which Russia was defeated by an upstart and Asian power. As after the Crimean War, there was a general feeling that the government had exposed its incompetence to all the world. Liberals believed that its secret methods, its immunity to criticism or control, had made it sluggish, torpid, obstinate, and inefficient, unable either to win a war or to lead the economic modernization that was taking place in Russia. But there was little that the liberals could do.

The police had recently allowed a priest, Father Gapon, to go among the St. Petersburg factory workers and organize them, hoping thus to counter the propaganda of revolutionaries. Father Gapon took up their grievances in all seriousness. They believed, as simple peasants only recently transplanted to the city, that if only they could reach the ear of the Little Father, the august being high above all hard capitalists and stony officials, he would hear their complaints with shocked surprise and rectify the evils that afflicted Russia. They drew up a petition, asking for an eight-hour day, a minimum daily wage of one ruble (fifty cents), a repudiation of bungling bureaucrats, and a democratically elected Constituent Assembly to introduce representative government into the empire Unarmed, peaceable, respectful, singing "God save the Tsar," a crowd of 200,000—men, women, and children—gathered before the tsar's Winter Palace one Sunday in January 1905. But the tsar was not in the city, and his officials

---

[14] See p. 734.
[15] See pp. 681–682.

were afraid. Troops marched up and shot down the demonstrators in cold blood, killing several hundred.

"Bloody Sunday" in St. Petersburg snapped the moral bond upon which all stable government rests. The horrified workers saw that the tsar was not their friend. The autocracy stood revealed as the force behind the hated officials, the tax collectors, the landlords, and the owners of the industrial plants. A wave of political strikes broke out. Social Democrats (more Mensheviks than Bolsheviks) appeared from the underground or from exile to give revolutionary direction to these movements. Councils or "soviets" of workers were formed in Moscow and St. Petersburg. The peasants, too, in many parts of the country spontaneously began to erupt, overrunning the lands of the gentry, burning manor houses and doing violence to their owners. Social revolutionaries naturally tried to take this movement in charge. The liberal Constitutional Democrats, professors, engineers, business people, lawyers, leaders in the provincial zemstvos founded forty years before, tried also to seize leadership or at least use the crisis to force the government's hand. All agreed on one demand—that there should be more democratic representation in the government.

The tsar yielded grudgingly and as little as possible. In March 1905 he promised to call to office men "enjoying the confidence of the nation." In August (after the ruinous battle of Tsushima) he agreed to call a kind of Estates General, for which peasants, landowners, and city people should vote as separate classes. Still the revolution raged unchecked. The St. Petersburg Soviet, or workers' council, led mainly by Mensheviks (Lenin had not yet reached Russia), declared a great general strike in October. Railroads stopped, banks closed, newspapers ceased to appear, and even lawyers refused to go to their offices. The strike spread to other cities and to the peasants. With the government paralyzed, the tsar issued his October Manifesto. It promised a constitution, civil liberties, and a Duma to be elected by all classes alike, with powers to enact laws and control the administration.

The tsar and his advisers intended to divide the opposition by releasing the October Manifesto, and in this they succeeded. The Constitutional Democrats, with a Duma promised, allowed themselves to hope that social problems could henceforth be dealt with by parliamentary methods. Liberals were now afraid of revolutionaries, industrialists feared the strength shown by labor in the general strike, and landowners demanded a restoration of order among the peasants. Aroused peasants and workers were not yet satisfied: the former still wanted more land and less taxation, the latter a shorter working day and a living wage. The several branches of revolutionary intellectuals worked upon the continuing popular agitation, hoping to carry matters forward until the tsarist monarchy was abolished and a socialist republic established with themselves at its head. They believed also (and correctly) that the October Manifesto was in any case a deception, which the tsar would refuse to adhere to as soon as revolutionary pressure was removed. The soviets continued to seethe, local strikes went on, and there were mutinies among soldiers at Kronstadt and sailors in the Black Sea fleet.

But the government was able to maintain itself. With the middle-class liberals now inactive or demanding order, the authorities arrested the members of the St.

Petersburg Soviet. Peace was hastily made with Japan, and reliable troop units were recalled from the Far East. The revolutionary leaders fled back to Europe, or again went underground, or were caught and sent to prison or to Siberia; executions were carried out in the countryside.

The Results of 1905: The Duma

The chief apparent result of the Revolution of 1905 was to make Russia, at least ostensibly, into a parliamentary type of state, like the rest of Europe. The promised Duma was convoked. For ten years, from 1906 to 1916, Russia had at least the superficial attributes of a semiconstitutional monarchy.

But Nicholas II soon showed that he did not intend to yield much. He drew the teeth of the new Duma before the creature could even be born, by announcing in advance, in 1906, that it would have no power over foreign policy, the budget, or government personnel. His attitude toward constitutional monarchy continued until 1917 to be entirely negative; the one thing that tsarism would not allow was any real participation in government by the public. Within this "public" the two extreme fringes were equally impervious to liberal constitutionalism. On the right, stubborn upholders of pure autocracy and the Orthodox church organized the Black Hundreds, terrorizing the peasantry and urging them to boycott the Duma. On the left, in 1906, the Social Revolutionaries and both the Bolshevik and Menshevik wings of the Social Democrats likewise refused to recognize the Duma, urged workers to boycott it, and refused to put up any candidates for election.

The short-lived first Duma was elected in 1906 by a system of indirect and unequal voting, in which peasants and workers voted as separate classes, and with proportionately far less representation than was granted to the landlords. In the absence of socialist candidates, workers and peasants voted for all sorts of people, including the liberal Constitutional Democrats (the "Cadets"), who obtained a sweeping majority. The Cadets, when the Duma met, found themselves still fighting for the bare principle of constitutional government. They demanded true universal male suffrage and the responsibility of ministers to a parliamentary majority. The tsar's response was to dismiss the Duma after two months. The Cadets fled to Viborg in autonomous Finland, which the tsarist police generally let alone. It is significant that these constitutional liberals and democrats, in council at Viborg, again appealed for a general strike and nonpayment of taxes— that is, for mass revolution. But real revolutions are not easy to start, and nothing happened.

A second Duma was elected in 1907, with the government trying to control the elections through suppression of party meetings and newspapers, but since Social Revolutionaries and Mensheviks now consented to take part, some eighty-three socialists were elected. The Cadets, becoming fearful of the revolutionary left, concluded that constitutional progress must be gradual and showed a willingness to cooperate with the government. But the Duma came to an abrupt end when the government denounced and arrested some fifty socialists as revolutionaries bent only on destruction. A third Duma, elected after an electoral change that gave increased representation to the landed propertied class and guaranteed a conservative majority, managed to hold several sessions between

1907 and 1912, as did a fourth Duma from 1912 to 1916. The deputies, by following the lead of the government, by addressing themselves only to concrete issues, by losing themselves in committee work, and by avoiding the basic question of where supreme power lay, kept precariously alive a modicum of parliamentary institutions in the tsarist empire.

The Stolypin Reforms

Some officials believed that the way to checkmate the revolutionaries, and strengthen the hold of the monarchy, was for the government, while keeping all controls in its own hands, to attract the support of reasonable and moderate people by a program of reforms. One of these was Peter Stolypin, whom the tsar retained as his principal minister from 1906 to 1911. It was Stolypin who dissolved the first two Dumas. But it was not his policy merely to stand still. His aim was to build up the propertied classes as friends of the state. He believed, perhaps rightly, that a state actively supported by widespread private property had little to fear from doctrinaire intellectuals, conspirators, and émigrés. He therefore favored and broadened the powers of the provincial zemstvos, in which the larger landowners took part in administering local affairs. For the peasantry he put through legislation more sweeping than any since the Emancipation.

Seeing in the *mir* the source of communal agrarian restlessness, Stolypin hoped to replace this ancient institution with a regime of private individual property. He abolished what was left of the redemption payments for which the *mirs* had been collectively responsible.[16] He allowed each peasant to sell his share of the communal rights and to leave the commune at will. He authorized peasants to buy land freely from the communes, from each other, or from the gentry. He thus favored the rise of the class of "big farmers," the later kulaks, who obtained control of large tracts, worked them with hired help, and produced cash crops for the market. At the same time, by allowing peasants to sell out and leave the *mir* (it would generally be the worst farmers or most improvident persons who did so), he hastened the formation of a migratory wage-earning class, which would either seek work from the big farmers or go off to take jobs in the city. The creation of a mobile labor force, and of a food supply raised by big farmers for the market, would thus advance the industrialization of Russia.

The Stolypin policy was successful. Between 1907 and 1916, 6.2 million families out of 16 million who were eligible applied for legal separation from the *mir*. There was no mistaking the trend toward individual property and independent farming. But the results of the Stolypin program must not be exaggerated. The *mir* was far from broken. A vast majority of peasants were still involved in the old system of common rights and communal restrictions. The land shortage was still acute in the agricultural areas where yields were highest. Land hunger and poverty continued in the countryside. There were kulaks, to be sure, to be resented and envied, but the largest landed proprietors were still the gentry. About 30,000 landlords owned nearly 200 million acres of land, and another 200 million acres made up other large landed estates.

Stolypin was not left long to carry on his program. The tsar gave him only an

---

[16] See pp. 566–567.

unwilling support. Reactionary circles disliked his tampering ways and his Western orientation. Social Revolutionaries naturally cried out against dissolution of the communes. Even Marxists, who should in theory have applauded the advance of capitalism in Russia, feared that Stolypin's reforms might do away with agrarian discontent. "I do not expect to live to see the revolution," said Lenin in these years. Stolypin was shot dead while attending the theater in Kiev, in the presence of the tsar and tsarina, in 1911. The assassin, a member of the terrorist wing of the Social Revolutionaries, is thought also to have been a secret agent of the reactionary tsarist police. It may be added that Stolypin's predecessor, Plehve, and about a dozen other high officials within the past few years had similarly died at the hands of assassins.

But all in all, violent and half barbaric though it still was, the Russian empire on the eve of the First World War was moving in a Western direction. Its industries were growing, its railways expanding, its exports almost half as great in value as those of the United States. It had a parliament, if not a parliamentary government. Private property and individualist capitalism were spreading to new layers of the people. There was a guarded freedom of the press, illustrated, for example, by the legal and open establishment of the Bolshevik party paper, *Pravda*, in St. Petersburg in 1912. It is not possible to say how far this development might have gone, for it was menaced on both the right and the left by obstinate and obscurantist reactionaries upholding the absolute tsardom and by revolutionaries whom nothing but the end of tsardom and wholesale transformation of society could appease. But both extremes were discouraged. The desperation of extreme reactionaries in the government, the feeling that they might in any case soon lose their position, perhaps made them the more willing to precipitate a European war by armed support of Serbian nationalists. As for the revolutionary parties, and especially the Bolsheviks, they were losing in membership on the eve of the war, their leaders lived year after year in exile, dreaming of the great days of 1905 which stubbornly failed to repeat themselves and sometimes pessimistically admitting, as Lenin did, that there might be no revolution in their time.

93. The Revolution of 1917

End of the Tsardom: The Revolution of March 1917

War again put the tsarist regime to a test that it could not meet. In this war, more total than any had ever been, willing cooperation between government and people was indispensable to success. This essential prerequisite the tsarist empire did not have. National minorities, Poles, Ukrainians, the peoples of the Caucasus, Jews, and others, were disaffected. As for the socialists, who in every other European parliament voted for funds to finance the war, the dozen otherwise disunited socialists in the Duma refused to do so and were promptly jailed.[17] The ordinary worker and peasant marched off with the army, but without the sense

[17] See p. 772.

of personal conviction felt by common people in Germany and the West. More decisive was the attitude of the middle class. Because they patriotically wished Russia to win, the glaring mismanagement of the government was the more intolerable to them. The disasters with which the war opened in 1914, at Tannenberg and the Masurian Lakes, were followed by the advance of the Central Powers into Russia in 1915, at the cost of 2 million Russian soldiers killed, wounded, or captured.[18]

At the war's outbreak middle-class people, as in all countries, offered their assistance to the government.[19] The provincial zemstvos formed a union of all zemstvos in the empire to facilitate the mobilization of agriculture and industry. Business groups at Petrograd (as St. Petersburg was briefly renamed) formed a Commercial and Industrial Committee to get the factories into maximum production. The government distrusted these signs of public activity arising outside official circles. On the other hand, organized in this way, middle-class people became conscious of their own strength and more critical of the bureaucracy. Rumors spread that some officials in the war ministry itself were pro-German, reactionaries who feared the liberalism of England and France, with which Russia was allied.

Life at court was bizarre even for Russia. The tsarina Alexandra, German by origin, looked upon all Russians outside her own circle with contempt, incited her husband to play the proud and pitiless autocrat, and took advice from a self-appointed holy man, the mysterious Rasputin. She was convinced that Rasputin possessed supernatural and prophetic powers, because he had apparently cured her young son, the tsarevitch, of hemophilia. Rasputin, by his influence over her, had a voice in appointments to high office. All who wished an audience with the imperial pair had to go through him. Patriotic and enlightened persons of all classes vainly protested. In these circumstances, and given the military defeats, the union of zemstvos and other such war-born bodies complained not merely of faults of administration but of fundamental conditions in the state. The government responded by holding them at arm's length. The tsarist regime, caught in a total war, was afraid of the help offered by its own people.

During the war, in September 1915, the Duma was suspended. It was known that reactionaries—inspired by the tsarina, Rasputin, and other sinister forces—expected that a victory in the war would make it possible to kill liberalism and constitutionalism in Russia. The war thus revived all the basic political issues that had been latent since the Revolution of 1905. The union of zemstvos demanded the assembly of the Duma. The Duma reassembled in November 1916 and, conservative though it had always been, expressed loud indignation at the way affairs were conducted. Among all elements of the population, dissatisfaction with the course of the war and with the government's ineptitude mounted. In December Rasputin was assassinated by nobles at the court. The tsar began to consider repression and again adjourned the Duma. Machine guns were issued to the police. Members of the Duma, and of the new extragovernmental bodies, concluded that the situation could be saved only by force. It is when moderate persons, normally concerned with their own business, come to such conclusions

---

[18] See p. 707.
[19] See pp. 718–721.

that revolution becomes a political possibility. The shift of moderates and liberals, their need of a coup d'état to save themselves from reactionaries, likewise raised the long failing prospects of the minority of professional revolutionaries.

Again it was the workers of Petrograd who precipitated the crisis. Food had become scarce, as in all the belligerent countries. But the tsarist administration was too clumsy and too demoralized by graft to institute the controls that had become usual elsewhere, such as maximum prices and ration cards. It was the poorest who felt the food shortage most keenly. On March 8, 1917, food riots broke out, which soon developed, doubtless with the help of revolutionary intellectuals, into political insurrection. Crowds shouted, "Down with the tsar!" Troops within the city refused to fire on the insurgents; mutiny and insubordination spread from unit to unit. Within a few days a Soviet of Workers' and Soldiers' Deputies, on the model of 1905, had been organized in Petrograd.

Middle-class leaders, with the government now helpless, demanded dismissal of the ministry and formation of a new one commanding the confidence of a majority of the Duma. The tsar retaliated by disbanding the Duma. The Duma set up an executive committee to take charge until the situation clarified. There were now two new authorities in the city: one, the Duma committee, essentially moderate, constitutionalist, and relatively legal; the other, the Petrograd Soviet, representing revolutionary forces arising by spontaneous upsurge from below. The Petrograd Soviet (or workers' "council") was to play in 1917 a role like that of the Paris Commune of 1792, constantly pushing the supposedly higher and more nationwide authority to the left. The Soviet became the public auditorium and administrative center of the working-class upheaval. Since it was generally socialist in its outlook, all the factions of doctrinaire socialists—Social Revolutionaries, Mensheviks, Bolsheviks—tried to win it over and utilize it for their own ends.

The Duma committee, under pressure from the Petrograd Soviet, on March 14 set up a Provisional Government under Prince Lvov. The Duma liberals, as a concession to the Soviet, admitted one socialist to the new government, Alexander Kerensky, a moderate, legal-minded Social Revolutionary, and they furthermore consented to demand the abdication of Nicholas II. The tsar was then at the front. He tried to return to his palace near Petrograd, but the imperial train was stopped and turned back by troops. The army, fatefully, was taking the side of the Revolution. The very generals in the field, unable to vouch for the loyalty of their men, advised abdication. Nicholas yielded; his brother the grand duke declined to succeed him; and on March 17, 1917, Russia became a republic.

The Bolshevik Revolution: November 1917

The Provisional Government, following the best precedents of European revolutions, called for elections by universal male suffrage to a Constituent Assembly, which was to meet late in the year and prepare a constitution for the new regime. It tried also to continue the war against Germany. In July an offensive was mounted but the demoralized armies were quickly routed. Pending final decision by the Constituent Assembly, the Provisional Government promised wholesale redistribution of land to the peasants but took no action. Meanwhile, the peasants, driven by the old land hunger, were already overrunning the rural districts, burning and looting. At the front the armies melted away; many high officers refused to serve the republic, and masses of peasant soldiers simply turned their backs and went home, unwilling to be absent while land was being handed out. The Petrograd Soviet, opposing the Provisional Government, called for speedy termination of the war. Fearing reactionary officers, it issued on March 14 its Order No. 1, entrusting command within the army to committees elected by both officers and soldiers. Discipline collapsed.

The Revolution was thus already well advanced when Lenin and the other Bolsheviks arrived in Petrograd in the middle of April.[20] They immediately took sides with the Petrograd Soviet against the Provisional Government, and with similar soviets that had sprung up in other parts of the country. In July an armed uprising of soldiers and sailors, which the Bolshevik central committee disapproved of as premature, was put down. The Bolsheviks were blamed, and Lenin had to flee to Finland. But as a bid for popular support the Provisional Government named the socialist Kerensky as its head in place of Prince Lvov in an uneasy coalition of moderate socialists and liberals. Kerensky's middle position was next threatened from the right. The newly appointed military commander, General Kornilov, dispatched a force of cavalry to restore order. Not only conservatives but liberals wished him success in the hope that he would suppress the soviets. Kornilov's movement was defeated, but with the aid of the Bolsheviks, who rallied with other socialists, and of revolutionary-minded soldiers in the city who offered armed resistance. Radicals denounced liberals as accomplices in Kornilov's attempt at counterrevolution, and both camps blamed Kerensky for having allowed the plot to be hatched under his government. Both liberals and moderate socialists abandoned Kerensky, and he had to form a government of uncertain political support. Meanwhile the food shortage worsened, with transport disarranged and the farm population in turmoil, so that workers in the city listened more willingly to the most extreme speakers.

The Bolsheviks adapted their program to what the most aroused elements in a revolutionary people seemed to want. Lenin concentrated on four points: first, immediate peace with the Central Powers; second, redistribution of land to the peasants; third, transfer of factories, mines, and other industrial plants from the capitalists to committees of workers in each plant; and, fourth, recognition of the soviets as the supreme power instead of the Provisional Government. Lenin, though a rigid dogmatist on abstract questions, was a flexible and bold tactician and his program in 1917 was dictated more by the immediate situation in Russia than by considerations of theoretical Marxism. What was needed was to win over soldiers, peasants, and workers by promising them "peace, land, and bread." With this program, and by infiltration and parliamentary stratagems, as well as by their accuracy as political prophets—predicting the Kornilov counterrevolution and "unmasking" the trend of middle-way liberals to support it—the Bolsheviks won a majority in the Petrograd Soviet and in soviets all over the country.

Lenin thereupon raised the cry, "All power to the Soviets!" to crush Kerensky and forestall the coming Constituent Assembly. Kerensky, to broaden the base on which he stood, and unable to wait for the Constituent Assembly, convoked a kind of preparliament representing all parties, labor unions, and zemstvos.

[20] See pp. 713, 737–741.

Lenin and the Bolsheviks boycotted his preparliament. Instead they called an all-Russian Congress of Soviets.

Lenin now judged that the hour had come for the seizure of power. The Bolsheviks themselves were divided, many like Zinoviev and Kamenev opposing the move, but Lenin was backed by Trotsky, Stalin, and a majority of the party Central Committee. Troops garrisoned in Petrograd voted to support the soviets, which the Bolsheviks now controlled. On the night of November 6–7, 1917, the Bolsheviks took over telephone exchanges, railway stations, and electric power plants in the city. A warship turned its guns on the Winter Palace, where Kerensky's government sat. The latter could find almost no one to defend it. The hastily assembled Congress of Soviets pronounced the Provisional Government defunct and named in its place a Council of People's Commissars, of which Lenin became the head. Trotsky was named commissar for foreign affairs, Stalin commissar for nationalities. Kerensky fled, eventually arriving in the United States, where he lived until 1970.

At the Congress of Soviets Lenin introduced two resolutions. One called upon the belligerent governments to negotiate a "just democratic peace," without annexations and without indemnities; the second "abolished all landlord property" immediately and without compensation. Although determined to establish a proletarian dictatorship, the Bolsheviks knew the importance of the Russian peasants. The millions of acres belonging to the large estates that were now expropriated provided a base of support for the new regime without which it could hardly have survived.

Thus was accomplished the Bolshevik or November Revolution.[21] But the long awaited Constituent Assembly remained to be dealt with. It met in January 1918. Thirty-six million persons had voted for it. Of these, 9 million had voted for Bolshevik deputies, showing that the Bolshevik program, launched less than a year before by a small band of émigrés, had a widespread mass appeal. But almost 21 million had voted for Kerensky's party, the agrarian, populist, peasant-oriented Social Revolutionaries. However, said Lenin, "to hand over power to the Constituent Assembly would again be compromising with the malignant bourgeoisie." The Assembly was broken up on the second day of its sessions; armed sailors dispatched by the people's commissars simply surrounded it. The dissolution of the Constituent Assembly was a frank repudiation of majority rule in favor of "class rule"—to be exercised for the proletariat by the Bolsheviks. The dictatorship of the proletariat was now established. Two months later, in March 1918, the Bolsheviks renamed themselves the Communist party.

The New Regime: The Civil War, 1918–1922

In these same months, the Communists, or Bolsheviks, signed the peace of Brest-Litovsk with Germany, surrendering to Germany control over the Baltic provinces, Poland, and the Ukraine.[22] The conquests of two centuries were thus abandoned; not since the days of Peter the Great had the Russian frontier been so far from

[21] Also known as the October Revolution, since according to the Julian calendar, used in Russia until 1918, the events described took place in October.
[22] See p. 713.

central Europe. To Lenin it made no difference. He was convinced that the events that he had just mastered in Russia were the prelude to a general upheaval; that the war, still raging in the west, would bring all Europe to the inevitable proletarian or Marxist revolution; that Imperial Germany was therefore doomed; and that Poles, Ukrainians, and others would soon emerge, like the Germans themselves, as free socialist peoples. In any case, it was largely by promising peace that Lenin had won enough backing to overthrow Kerensky, who on this deep popular demand had delayed too long, waiting for England and France to release Russia from its treaty obligations as an ally. But real peace did not come, for the country sank immediately into civil war.

Not only old tsarist reactionaries, and not only liberals, bourgeois, zemstvo members, and Constitutional Democrats, but all types of anti-Leninist socialists as well, Mensheviks and Social Revolutionaries, scattered in all directions to organize resistance against the regime of soviets and people's commissars, and they obtained aid from the Western Allies. Both sides competed for the support of the peasants.

As for the new regime, the oldest of its institutions was the party, founded as a wing of the Social Democrats in 1903; the next oldest were the soviets, dating from 1905 and 1917; and then came the Council of People's Commissars set up on the day of the coup d'état. The first institution founded under the new order was a political police, an Extraordinary All-Russian Commission of Struggle Against Counterrevolution, Speculation, and Sabotage, commonly known from its Russian initials as the Cheka and in later years, without basic change of methods or purpose, under such successive names as the OGPU, the NKVD, the MVD, and the KGB. It was established on December 7, 1917. In January 1918 the Red Army was founded, with Leon Trotsky as war commissar and virtually its creator. In July a constitution was promulgated.

In social policy the Bolsheviks at first adopted no long-range plans, contenting themselves with a mixture of principle and expediency known as "war communism." They nationalized some of the largest industrial enterprises but left the bulk under the control of workers' committees. The pressing problem was to find food, which had ceased to move through any normal channels. The peasants, very much as in the French Revolution under similar conditions—worthless money, insecure property titles, unruly hired hands, armed marauding, and a doubtful future—were producing less food than usual, consuming it themselves, or hoarding it on their own farms. The response of the government and city workers was also much as in 1793. The new government levied requisitions, required the peasants to make stated "deliveries," and invited labor unions to send armed detachments into the country to procure food by force. Since it was naturally the big farmers who had the surplus, they came into disrepute as starvers of the people. Class war broke out, rabid, ferocious, and elemental, between farmers who feared that their very subsistence as well as their property would be taken away, and city people, often supported by hungry agricultural laborers, who were driven to desperation by famine. Many peasants, especially the larger farmers, therefore rallied to anti-Bolshevik political leaders.

Centers of resistance developed on every side. In the Don valley a small force assembled under Generals Kornilov and Denikin, with many army officers, gentry landowners, and expropriated business people taking part in it. The Social

Revolutionaries gathered followers on the middle Volga. In the spring of 1918 Georgia, Armenia, and Azerbaijan in the Caucasus, all proclaimed their independence. At Omsk a disaffected group proclaimed the independence of Siberia. As a military organization the most significant was a force of some 45,000 Czechs, who had deserted or been captured from the Austro-Hungarian armies and had then been organized as a Czech Legion to fight on the side of Russia and the Allies. After the November Revolution and the peace of Brest-Litovsk, these Czechs decided to leave Russia by way of the Trans-Siberian Railroad, return to Europe by sea, and resume fighting on the Western Front. When Bolshevik officials undertook to disarm them they allied with the Social Revolutionaries on the Volga.

The Allied governments believed that Bolshevism was a temporary madness that with a little effort could be stopped. They wished above all to bring Russia back into the war against Germany. So long as the war in Europe lasted, they could not reach Russia by the Black or Baltic Sea. A small Allied force took Murmansk and Archangel in the north. But for Allied military intervention the best opening was in the Far East, through Vladivostok. The Japanese, who had declined military aid to their Allies in any other theater, received this proposal with enthusiasm, seeing in the ruin of the Russian empire a rare opportunity to develop their sphere of influence in East Asia. It was agreed that an interallied military force should land at Vladivostok, cross Siberia, join with the Czechs, break up Bolshevism, and fall upon the Germans in eastern Europe. For this ambitious scheme Britain and France could supply no soldiers, engaged as they were on the Western Front; the force turned out to be American and Japanese, or rather almost purely Japanese, since Japan contributed 72,000 men and the United States only 8,000. They landed at Vladivostok in August 1918.

The civil war lasted until 1920, or even later in some places. It became a confused melee in which the Bolsheviks struggled against Russian opponents, independence-minded nationalities, and foreign intervention. The Red Army fought in the Ukraine first against the Germans, and then against the French, who occupied Odessa as soon as the war ended in Europe. It reconquered the Ukraine, Armenia, Georgia, and Azerbaijan, which had declared their independence; put to flight a hundred thousand "Whites," as the counterrevolutionaries were called, under Wrangel in the south; and fought off Admiral Kolchak, who in Siberia proclaimed himself ruler of all Russia. In 1920, the Bolsheviks carried on a war with the new republic of Poland, which was scarcely organized when it set out to recover the huge Ukrainian and Byelorussian territories that had been Polish before 1772.[23] British, French, and American troops remained at Archangel until the end of 1919, the Japanese at Vladivostok until the end of 1922.

But the anti-Bolshevik forces could never unite. The anti-Communist Russians represented every hue of the political spectrum from unregenerate tsarists to left-wing Social Revolutionaries. Many of the rightist anti-Bolsheviks openly antagonized the peasants by proceeding to restore expropriated landed estates in areas they occupied; many engaged in vindictive reprisals in a kind of "white terror." The Allies themselves could not agree; the French sent troops to the

---

[23] See map, p. 248.

Ukraine and gave aid to the Poles, but the British and Americans wanted to be rid of all military entanglements as soon as the armistice with Germany was signed. Leon Trotsky, on the other hand, forged in the crucible of the civil wars the hard and solid metal of the Red Army, recruiting it, organizing it, restoring its discipline, equipping it as best he could, assigning political commissars to watch it, and assuring that trustworthy officers occupied its high command. The Bolsheviks could denounce the foreign intervention and appeal to national patriotism; and they could win peasant support by the distribution of land. By 1922 the Bolsheviks, or Communists, had established themselves up to the frontiers of the former tsarist empire in every direction except on the European side. There the band of Baltic states—Finland, Estonia, Latvia, and Lithuania—remained independent; Romania had acquired Bessarabia, the new Romanian frontier reaching now almost to Odessa; and Poland, as a result of the war of 1920, retained a frontier farther east than the Allies themselves had intended. Russia had lost thousands of square miles of territory and buffer areas acquired over the centuries by the tsars.[24] They remained lost until the Second World War. But peace was won and the regime stood.

It was during these civil wars that the Red Terror broke out in Russia. Like the famous Terror in France in 1793, it was in part a response to civil and foreign war. Before the Bolshevik Terror, the old Jacobin Terror paled. They differed as the cruelty and violence endemic in the old Russia differed from the more humane or law-abiding habits of western Europe. Thousands were shot merely as hostages (a practice unknown to Europe for some centuries); and other thousands without even the summary formalities of revolutionary tribunals. The Cheka was the most formidable political police that had yet appeared. The Bolshevik Terror was aimed at the physical extermination of all who opposed the new regime. A bourgeois class background would go far to confirm the guilt of the person charged with conspiring against the Soviet state. As a chief of the Cheka said: "The first questions you should put to the accused person are, To what class does he belong, what is his origin, what was his education, and what is his profession? These should determine the fate of the accused. This is the essence of the Red Terror." But a working-class background for a man or a woman made little difference. In 1918 a young woman named Fanny Kaplan shot at Lenin and wounded him. She deposed that she had favored the Constituent Assembly, that her parents had emigrated to America in 1911, that she had six working-class brothers and sisters; and she admitted that she had intended to kill Lenin. She was of course executed, as were others in Petrograd. When the sailors at Kronstadt, who were among the first adherents of the Bolsheviks, rose in 1921, objecting to domination of the soviets by the party (threatening a kind of leftist renewal of the revolution, like the Hébertists who had opposed Robespierre), they were branded as petty-bourgeois and shot down by the thousands. The Terror struck at the revolutionists themselves quite as much as it did the bourgeoisie; it was to continue to do so long after the Revolution was secure.

The Terror succeeded in its purpose. Together with the victories of the Red Army, it established the new regime. Those "bourgeois" who survived took on the protective coloration of "toilers." No bourgeois as such presumed to take

[24] See p. 726 and map on pp. 728–729.

part in the politics of Russia. Mensheviks and other socialists fleeing to Europe told appalling stories of the human toll taken by Lenin. Horrified European socialists repudiated communism as an atrocious, Byzantine, Asiatic perversion of Marxism. But, at whatever cost, Lenin and his followers were now able to start building the socialist society as they understood it.

94. The Union of Soviet Socialist Republics

Government: The Nationalities and Federalism

With the end of the civil wars and foreign intervention, and with the termination of the war with Poland, it became possible in 1922 to establish the Union of Soviet Socialist Republics. Its first members were four in number: The Russian Soviet Federated Socialist Republic (which extended to Siberia and the Pacific), the Ukrainian Soviet Socialist Republic, the Byelorussian (or White Russian, i.e., ethnic White Russian) Soviet Socialist Republic, and the Transcaucasian Soviet Federated Socialist Republic (which united the reconquered Caucasus republics of Georgia, Armenia, and Azerbaijan).[25] In the new Union, which geographically replaced the old Russian empire, the name Russia was not officially used. The

[25] The original Russian and Transcaucasian federated republics were subsequently reorganized to create additional republics so that there were eleven in number. Out of the Transcaucasian republic emerged the Georgian, Armenian, and Azerbaijan Soviet Socialist Republics; out of the Russian S.F.S.R. were created five republics in central Asia: the Uzbek, Turkmen, Tadzhik, Kazakh, and Kirghiz S.S.R.'s. After the outbreak of the Second World War the U.S.S.R. occupied and sovietized adjoining territory and created five additional soviet republics (one of them, the Karelo-Finnish, lost that status in 1956). For the fifteen soviet republics the population figures for 1940 and 1989 were as follows:

	1940	1989
Russian S.F.S.R.	109,000,000	147,000,000
Ukrainian S.S.R.	40,000,000	51,700,000
Byelorussian (White Russian) S.S.R.	10,000,000	10,200,000
Armenian S.S.R.	1,250,000	3,300,000
Georgian S.S.R.	3,500,000	5,500,000
Azerbaijan S.S.R.	3,200,000	7,000,000
Uzbek S.S.R.	6,300,000	19,900,000
Turkmen S.S.R.	1,200,000	3,500,000
Tadzhik S.S.R.	1,500,000	5,100,000
Kazakh S.S.R.	6,100,000	16,500,000
Kirghiz S.S.R.	1,500,000	4,300,000
ADDED IN 1940:		
Karelo-Finnish S.S.R.	500,000	——
Moldavian S.S.R.	2,500,000	4,300,000
Lithuanian S.S.R.	2,900,000	3,700,000
Latvian S.S.R.	2,000,000	2,700,000
Estonian S.S.R.	1,100,000	1,600,000
TOTAL U.S.S.R.	192,550,000	286,300,000

It will be seen that the Russian and the other two Slavic republics (the Ukrainian and the Byelorussian) grew in half a century by scarcely one-third, while the others (except the three Baltic republics) more than doubled in population. Although the Russians remained by far the most numerous, the trend was toward more rapid growth for the Asian (and Islamic) population. See also below, p. 1016.

guiding conception was a blend of the national and the international: to recognize nationality by granting autonomy to national groups, while holding these groups together in a higher union and allowing new groups to enter regardless of historic frontiers. In 1922 the expectation of world revolution was still alive. The constitution, formally adopted in 1924, pronounced the founding of the U.S.S.R. to be "a decisive step by way of uniting the workers of all countries into one World Soviet Socialist Republic." It made the Union, in principle, fluid and expansible, declared that any member republic might secede (none did so until 1991) and that newly formed soviet socialist republics might join (none ever did voluntarily). When after the outbreak of the Second World War the U.S.S.R. occupied contiguous territories (once part of the tsarist empire)—the three Baltic states, Estonia, Latvia, and Lithuania, after two decades of independence; Bessarabia, detached from Romania; and Karelia, taken from Finland after the Russo-Finnish War—these territories were added to the U.S.S.R. in 1940 as soviet socialist republics. Bessarabia became the Moldavian S.S.R., and Karelia temporarily, from 1940 to 1956, had the status of a Karelo-Finnish S.S.R.

The federal principle in the U.S.S.R. was designed to answer the problem of nationalism. The tsardom, in its last decades, had tried to deal with this problem by systematic Russification. The nationalities had resisted, and nationalist discontent had been one of the forces fatally weakening the empire. Nationalism, or the demand that national groups should have their own political sovereignty, had not only broken up the Austro-Hungarian empire but "Balkanized" central and eastern Europe. This might have happened after 1917 in Russia except for the fact that the Red Army during the civil wars occupied large parts of the tsarist empire which had broken away and declared their independence. As it turned out, in 1922 the U.S.S.R. occupied a sixth of the world's land area and was adjoined on the west by a Europe which in one twenty-seventh of the world's land surface contained twenty-seven independent states.

A hundred languages were spoken in the Soviet Union, and fifty distinct nationalities were recognized within its borders. Many of these were extremely small, splinter groups or isolated communities left by the ebb and flow of humanity in inner Asia over thousands of years. All recognized nationalities received a cultural autonomy, or the right to use their own language, have their own schools, wear their own dress, and follow their own folkways without interference. Indeed, the Soviet authorities favored the growth of cultural nationalism. Some fifty languages were reduced to writing for the first time, and the new regime encouraged the singing of national songs, performance of dances, and collection of folklore. Administratively the nationalities were put on various levels, with varying degrees of separate identity according to their size and importance. The most important were the soviet republics themselves. Within the soviet republics were autonomous republics, autonomous regions, and cultural districts, all having some representation in the upper legislative house, the Soviet of Nationalities, created by the constitution of 1936. But in practice the Russian S.F.S.R., with over half the population and three-fourths of the territory of the Union, predominated over the others. When to the Russian were added the Ukrainian and the Byelorussian republics, the overwhelmingly Russian and Slavic character of the Union was marked. Moreover all political and economic rights were severely limited by the concentration of authority in the hands of the central government. There was little substance in the formal claim that each constituent republic was sovereign and had the right to conduct its own foreign affairs (like the British Dominions), on the basis of which the Soviets demanded sixteen (and received three) votes in the assembly of the United Nations when that body was formed in 1945. During the Second World War there was evidence that separatism had not wholly died down, remaining especially alive in the Ukraine, and several autonomous areas were officially dissolved for separatist acitivites or even for collusion with the German invaders. By the late 1980s there were openly voiced discontents and secessionist pressures in every one of the fifteen constituent republics. It became impossible for the Soviets to prevent the disintegration of the multinational state that they had inherited from the tsars.

Government: State and Party

Government in the Union, and in each component republic, followed a pattern worked out during the Revolution and written into the constitutions of 1924 and 1936. In theory, a principle of parallelism was adopted. On the one hand was the state; on the other, paralleling the state but technically not part of it, was the party. But the close interlocking relationship between the two made the parallelism virtually meaningless.

On the side of the state, the distinctive institution was the council or soviet. Here elections took place, and authority proceeded from the bottom upward to the top. Under the constitution of 1924 only "toilers" had the right to vote. Surviving bourgeois, private traders, "persons using the labor of others to make a profit," as well as priests, were excluded from the suffrage. An indirect system of elections prevailed. In each village and town the voters chose a local soviet; the local soviet elected delegates to a provincial soviet, which in turn sent delegates to a soviet of the republic; the soviets of these republics sent delegates to a Union-wide Congress of Soviets, the supreme law-enacting body of the country. Soviets at all levels chose executive officials; the Congress of Soviets chose the Council of People's Commissars, or ministry.

In the constitution of 1936 a more direct democratic procedure was introduced. Voters henceforth directly elected members of the higher soviets, a secret ballot was adopted, and no class was any longer denied the vote. A bicameral parliament was created, a Supreme Soviet, with an upper chamber, the Soviet of Nationalities, and a lower chamber, the Soviet of the Union, in which there was one representative for every 300,000 persons. On the state side, as set forth in the constitution of 1936, the government embodied many seemingly democratic features.

Yet alongside the state, at all levels and in all localities, was the party. Only one party was allowed, the Communist, though nonparty members might be elected to the soviets or to other official positions. In the party, authority began at the top and proceeded downward. At its apex stood the Central Committee, whose membership varied from about seventy in the 1930s to more than double that in later years. Within the Central Committee a powerful Politburo,[26] or political bureau, of about a dozen members dominated discussions of policy and personnel. An even more powerful general secretary, the office that Stalin virtually fashioned, dominated the entire structure and apparatus with authority over appointments and assignments at all levels. Although a party congress was held every few years, and issues debated, ultimately the congress simply registered policies already laid out by the higher bodies. Thus power and authority flowed downward and outward, as in an army, or as in a highly centralized government agency or large private corporation in the West, except that the party was not subject to any outside control. Discipline was likewise enforced in ways not used in liberal countries, the fearsome machinery of the secret police being available for use against party members as well as those outside.

The number of party members, men and women, which could not have been more than 70,000 at the time of the Revolution, rose to about 2 million by 1930, 3 million by 1940, and to 19 million in the late 1980s. The Leninist ideal of a highly disciplined party, made up of faithful and zealous workers who willingly carried out orders, the ideal on which the Bolsheviks had separated from the Mensheviks in 1903, continued to characterize the communist party in the Soviet Union. Old Bolsheviks, those who had been members in the lean years before 1917, long continued to occupy the seats in the Politburo and other important party positions. A party of 2 million members, though small in contrast to the population of the U.S.S.R., still represented an enormous growth for the party itself, in which for each old member (who had joined before 1917) there were thousands of new ones. To preserve party unity under the new conditions strict uniformity was enforced. Members intensively studied the principles of Marxism-Leninism, embraced dialectical materialism as a philosophy and even a kind of religion, learned to take orders without question or compunction and to give authoritative leadership to the mass of nonparty members among whom they worked. The base of the party structure consisted of small nuclei or cells. In each factory, in each mine, in each office, in each class at the universities and technical schools, in each labor union, in each at least of the larger villages, one, two, or a dozen of the local people (factory workers, miners, office workers, students, etc., as the case might be) belonged to the party and imparted party views and party momentum to the whole.

The function of the party, in Marxist terms, was to carry out the dictatorship of the proletariat. It was to lead the people as a whole to the realization of socialism and, in day-to-day affairs, to coordinate the ponderous mechanism of government and make it work. Party members were present at all levels of the government. Throughout the whole structure, the party decided what the state should do.

The party in the U.S.S.R., by the 1930s, functioned as a tightly knit, highly disciplined leadership group. Those who joined it were willing to work hard, devote themselves to party matters day and night, absorb and communicate the party policy (or "line"), go where they were sent, attend meetings, speak up, perceive and explain the significance of small passing events for the Soviet Union or the world revolution, and master intricate technical details of farming,

---

[26] For a few years, from 1952 to 1966, it was called the Presidium.

THE UNION OF SOVIET SOCIALIST REPUBLICS, 1922–1991

The U.S.S.R. was over 5,000 miles long and covered one-sixth of the land area of the globe, including 42 percent of Europe and 43 percent of Asia, though the conventional distinction between Europe and Asia was not officially recognized in the Soviet Union. It was the only state that immediately adjoined so many important political regions — Europe in the west, the Middle East in the south, China along a long frontier, Japan across a narrow sea, and the United States on the side toward Alaska and the Aleutian

Islands. The Union had fifteen member republics, of which the Russian was by far the largest. Most of it lay farther north than Lake Superior, but around Tashkent, in the latitude of New York and Chicago, cotton and citrus fruits have been grown by irrigation. The diversion of rivers for this purpose, however, has led to the spread of deserts and the gradual drying up of the Aral Sea.

manufacturing, or the care of machinery, so that others would look to them willingly for advice. The party was a specially trained elite whose members were in constant touch with each other. It was the thin stream of lifeblood which, by circulating through all the diverse tissues of the U.S.S.R.—the multitudinous republics, soviets, bureaus, army, industrial, and other enterprises owned under socialism by the state—kept the whole complex body unified, organic, functioning, and alive.

If the party was a leadership group, the corollary was that more than ninety-five out of a hundred persons were condemned to be followers, and while it is perhaps true (as apologists for the system have said) that under any system true leadership is exercised by a tiny fraction of people, the difference between Communist and non-Communist in the U.S.S.R. became a clear matter of social status. As the years passed, many Communists in the U.S.S.R. were less the revolutionary firebrand type than the successful and efficient man or woman in any social system. They represented the satisfied, not the dissatisfied. They enjoyed material privileges, such as access to the best jobs, better housing, special food coupons, automobiles, or priorities on trains. They developed a bourgeois concern for the advantages of their own children. They became a new vested interest. Within the party, members had to be not so much leaders as followers. A homogeneous and monolithic organization had to present a solid front to the far more numerous but unorganized outsiders. Within the party, from time to time, a great deal of difference of opinion and open discussion was tolerated (indeed, since there was only one party all political questions were intraparty disputes), but in the end the entire membership had to conform. The party favored a certain fertility of mind in inventing ways to get things done, but it did not favor, and in fact repressed, originality, boldness, risk-taking, or freedom of thought or action. The dangers of stagnation in such a system became apparent within the Soviet Union itself in later times.

The New Economic Policy, 1921–1927

By 1920 "war communism," as we have seen, had hopelessly antagonized the peasants, who, it was estimated, were cultivating only 62 percent as much land as in 1914.[27] This fact, together with a severe drought and the breakdown of transportation, produced a great famine. Millions of people died. The ravages of eight years, of the World War, the Revolution, the civil wars, the Terror, had left the country in ruins, its productive facilities thrown back by decades as compared with 1914. The rising of the Kronstadt sailors in 1921 revealed profound disillusionment in the revolutionary ranks themselves. Lenin concluded that socialization had advanced too fast. He openly advocated a compromise with capitalism, a strategic retreat. The New Economic Policy, or NEP, adopted in 1921, lasted until 1927. Most of the decade of the 1920s saw a relaxation of tempo (and of terror) for most people in the U.S.S.R.

Under the NEP, while the state controlled the "commanding heights" of the economy, maintaining state ownership of the basic productive industries, it allowed a great deal of private trading for private profit. The basic problem was

[27] See pp. 750–752.

to restore trade between town and country. The peasants would produce nothing beyond the needs of their own subsistence unless they could exchange their surplus for city-made wares such as clothing or tools. The city people had to be fed from the country if they were to turn out factory products or even continue to live in the city. Under the NEP, peasants were allowed to sell their farm products freely. Middlemen were allowed to buy and sell farm products and manufactured articles at will, to whom they pleased, at market prices, and at a profit to themselves. The NEP therefore favored the big individualist farmer or kulak. Indeed, rural changes initiated before 1914 were still at work;[28] peasant families consolidated millions of acres as private property in 1922, 1923, and 1924. Correspondingly, other peasants became "proletarians," wage-earning hired hands. The NEP also favored the sprouting of a new-rich commercial class, neobourgeois who ate expensive dinners in the restaurants of Moscow, and whose very existence seemed to explode the dream of a classless society. Under the NEP the worst damages of war and revolution were repaired. But there was no real progress, for in 1928 Russia was producing only about as much grain, raw cotton, cattle, coal, and oil as in 1913, and far less than it presumably would have produced (given the rate of growth before 1913) had there been no revolution.

Stalin and Trotsky

Lenin died in 1924 prematurely at the age of fifty-four after a series of paralyzing strokes that left him incapacitated in the last two years of his life. His embalmed remains were put permanently on view in the Kremlin; Petrograd was renamed Leningrad; a leader cult was built up around his name and image. The party presented him as a deified equal of Marx himself, and it became necessary for all schools of communist thought to claim unflinching fidelity to the Leninist tradition. Actually, in his own lifetime, the Old Bolsheviks had never regarded Lenin as infallible. They had often differed with him and with each other. As he lay dying, and after his death, his old companions and contemporaries, carrying on the feuding habits of the émigré days, fought with each other for control of the party in Lenin's name. They disputed over Lenin's intentions. Had he secretly thought of the NEP as a permanent policy, as Bukharin maintained? If not, how would he have modified it, and, most especially, how soon? Quietly, behind the scenes, as general secretary of the party, without much attention to broader problems, a hitherto relatively modest member named Joseph Stalin, whom Lenin had warned against, was drawing all the strings of party control into his own hands. More openly and vociferously Leon Trotsky, who as war commissar in the critical years had been only less conspicuous than Lenin himself, raised the basic issues of the whole nature and future of the movement.

Trotsky, in 1925 and 1926, inveighed against the lassitude that had descended upon socialism.[29] The NEP with its tolerance of bourgeois and kulaks excited his contempt. He developed his doctrine of "permanent revolution," an incessant

<hr>

[28] See pp. 745–746.

[29] For communists, though not for socialists, the terms "communism" and "socialism" were almost interchangeable, since Russian Communists regarded their own system as true socialism and all other socialism as opportunistic, reactionary, or false. Communism was also defined, in the U.S.S.R., as a future state of society toward which socialism, i.e., Soviet socialism, is the intermediate stage.

drive for proletarian objectives on all fronts in all parts of the world. He stood forth as the exponent of world revolution, which many in the party were beginning to discard in favor of first building socialism in one country. He denounced the tendency to bureaucratic ossification in the party and urged a new movement of the masses to give it life. He called for more forceful development of industry and for the collectivization of agriculture, which had figured in Communist manifestos ever since 1848.[30] Above all, he demanded immediate adoption of an overall plan, a central control and operation of the whole economic life of the country.

Trotsky failed to carry the party with him. He was charged with leftist deviationism, machinations against the Central Committee, and inciting to public discussion of issues outside the party. Stalin wove his web. At a party congress in 1927, 95 percent of the delegates dutifully voted for Stalin and the Central Committee and fewer than 5 percent for Trotsky. Trotsky was first exiled to Siberia, then banished from the U.S.S.R.; he lived first in Turkey, then France, then Mexico, writing and propagandizing for the "permanent revolution," stigmatizing developments in the U.S.S.R. as "Stalinism," a monstrous betrayal of Marxism-Leninism, organizing an underground against Stalin as he had done in former days against the tsar. He was murdered in Mexico in 1940 under mysterious circumstances, presumably by a Soviet agent or sympathizer. Not until the late 1980s was anyone in the U.S.S.R. permitted to talk or write about him and his contributions to the Revolution.

95. Stalin: The Five-Year Plans and the Purges

Economic Planning

Hardly had Trotsky been expelled when Stalin and the party appropriated certain fragments of his program. In 1928 the party launched the First Five-Year Plan, aimed at rapid industrialization and the collectivization of agriculture. "Planning," or the central planning of a country's whole economic life by government officials, was to become the distinctive feature of Soviet economics and the one that, for a time, was to have the greatest influence on the rest of the world.

In retrospect, it seems strange that the Communists waited ten years before adopting a plan. The truth seems to be that the Bolsheviks had only confused ideas of what to do after their seizure of power. Marxism for the most part gave only general hints. Marxism was primarily an analysis of existing or bourgeois society. It was also a theory of class war. But to portray any details of a future society, or specify what should be done after the class war had been won by the proletariat, was according to Marx and Engels sheer utopian fantasy. The bourgeoisie, to be sure, would be destroyed; there would be "social ownership of the means of production," and no "exploitation of man by man"; everyone would work, and there would be neither leisure class nor unemployment. This was not much to go on in the operation of a modern industrial system.

[30] See pp. 522–523.

One great constructive idea had been mapped out, most clearly by Engels. *Within* each private enterprise, Engels had observed, harmony and order reigned; it was only *between* private enterprises that capitalism was chaotic. In the individual factory, he noted, the various departments did not compete with each other; the shipping department did not purchase from the production department at prices fluctuating according to daily changes in supply and demand; the output of all departments was planned and coordinated by management. In a larger way, the great capitalist mergers and trusts, controlling many factories, prevented blind competition between them, assigned specific quotas to each, anticipated, coordinated, and stabilized the work of each plant and each person by an overall policy. With the growth of large corporate enterprise, observed Engels, the area of economic life under free competition was constantly reduced, and the area brought under rational planning was constantly enlarged. The obvious next step, according to Engels and other socialists, was to treat *all* the economic life of a country as a single factory with many departments, or a single enormous monopoly with many members, under one unified, far-seeing management.

During the First World War the governments of belligerent countries had in fact adopted such centralized controls.[31] They had done so not because they were socialistic, but because in time of war people were willing to subordinate their usual liberties to a single overwhelming and undisputed social purpose—victory. The "planned society" therefore made its first actual (though incomplete) appearance in the First World War. It was partly from socialist doctrine as exemplified by Engels, partly from experience of the war, and in even larger measure from the irresistible pressure to meet the continuing chronic problems of the country by raising its productive level that Stalin and the party in Russia gradually developed the idea of a plan. The war experience was especially valuable for the lessons it gave on technical questions of economic planning, such as the kind of bureaus to set up, the kind of forecasts to make, and the kind of statistics to collect.

In the U.S.S.R. it was decided to plan for five years into the future, beginning with 1928. The aim of the plan was to strengthen and enrich the country, make it militarily and industrially self-sufficient, lay the groundwork for a true workers' society, and overcome the Russian reputation for backwardness. As Stalin said in a speech in 1929: "We are becoming a country of metal, a country of automobiles, a country of tractors. And when we have put the U.S.S.R. in a motor car and the *muzhik* in a tractor . . . we shall see which countries may then be 'classified' as backward and which as advanced."

The First Five-Year Plan was declared fulfilled in 1932, and a Second Five-Year Plan was launched, lasting until 1937. The Third, inaugurated in 1938, was interrupted by the war with Germany in 1941. New plans were introduced after 1945.[32]

The First Five-Year Plan (like its successors) listed the economic goals to be achieved. It was administered by an agency called the Gosplan. Within the frame of general policy set by the party, the Gosplan determined how much of every article the country should produce, how much of the national effort should go

[31] See pp. 718–721.
[32] See pp. 906–908.

into the formation of capital, and how much into producing articles for daily consumption, what wages all classes of workers should receive, and at what prices all goods should be exchanged. Because all decisions were made at the top, it was as much a command economy as a planned economy. At the bottom level, in the individual factory, the local management drew up its "requirements," or estimates of what it would need, in raw material, machinery, trained workers, plant facilities, and fuel, if it was to deliver the planned quantity of its product at a stated date. These estimates were passed up the planning ladder (or, thousands of such estimates up thousands of ladders) until they reached the Gosplan, which, balancing them against each other and against other needs as seen at the top, determined how much steel, coal, etc., should be produced, and in what qualities and grades; how many workers should be trained in technical schools and in what particular skills; how many machines should be manufactured and how many spare parts; how many new freight cars should be constructed and which lines of railway track needed repair; and how, where, when, and to whom the steel, coal, technicians, machines, and rolling stock should be made available. The plan, in short, undertook to control, by conscious management, the flow of resources and work force which under free capitalism was regulated by shifts in demand and supply, and through changes in prices, wage levels, profits, interest rates, or rent.

The system was exceedingly intricate. It was not easy to have the right number of ball bearings, for example, arrive at the right place at the right time, in exact correspondence to the amounts of other materials or to the number of workers waiting to use them. Sometimes there was overproduction, sometimes underproduction. The plan was often amended as it was applied in action. Countless reports, checkups, and exchanges of information were necessary. A huge class of bureaucrats came into existence to handle the paperwork. The plan achieved some of its goals, exceeded a few, and failed in some. The criterion for fulfillment was almost always quantitative.

The primary objective of the First Five-Year Plan was to build up the heavy industry, or capital wealth, of the U.S.S.R. The aim was to industrialize without the use of foreign loans.[33] Russia in 1928 was still chiefly an agricultural country. The world offered hardly any case of a country shifting from agriculture to industry without borrowing capital from abroad. Britain, the original home of the Industrial Revolution, was the best example, although even there, in the eighteenth century, a great deal of capital invested in England was owned by the Dutch. An agricultural country could industrialize from its own resources only by drawing upon agriculture itself. An agricultural revolution had been prerequisite to an industrial revolution in England.[34] By enclosure of land, the squeezing out of small independent farmers, and the introduction of scientific cultivation, under the auspices of a growing class of wealthy landowners, England had both increased its production of food and released many of the rural population to find employment

---

[33] The Bolsheviks had repudiated the entire debt of the tsarist empire. Their credit in capitalist countries was therefore not good, so that, in addition to fearing dependence upon foreign lenders, they were in any case for a long time unable to borrow large sums.

[34] See pp. 456–457.

in industry. The First Five-Year Plan called for a similar agricultural revolution in Russia, without benefit to landlords and under the auspices of the state.

The Collectivization of Agriculture

The plan, as originally conceived, called for the collectivization of only one-fifth of the farm population, but Stalin suddenly revised the plan in the winter of 1929 to include the immediate collectivization of the greater part of the peasantry. The plan set up collective farms, averaging a few thousand acres apiece, which were considered to be the property not of the state but of the peasants collectively who resided on them. (A few state-operated collective farms were also established, as models for the others.) Individual peasants were to pool their privately owned fields and livestock in these collectives. Those peasants who possessed fields or stock in considerable amount, the prosperous peasants or kulaks, resisted surrendering them to the new collectives. The kulaks were therefore liquidated as a class. Zealous detachments of Communists from the cities used violence; poor peasants turned upon rich ones; hundreds of thousands of kulaks and their families were killed and many more transported to labor camps in remote parts of the Soviet Union. The trend that had gone on since Stolypin and indeed since the Emancipation, building up a class of property-owning, labor-hiring, and ''bourgeois'' peasants, was now abruptly reversed. Collectivization was intended to convert the peasantry into a class more nearly resembling the proletariat of Marxian doctrine, a class of people who as individuals owned no capital and employed no labor, and so would better fit into a proletarian, or socialist, state. The year 1929, not 1917, was the great revolutionary year for most people in Russia.

Collectivization was accomplished at the cost of village class war in which the most capable farmers perished, and at the cost also of a wholesale destruction of livestock. The big farmers slaughtered their horses, cattle, pigs, and poultry rather than give them up. Even middling and small farmers did the same, caring nothing about animals that were no longer their own. The ruinous loss of animals was the worst unforeseen calamity of the First Five-Year Plan. The agricultural disorders led to a deadly famine in southeast Russia in 1932 that cost millions of lives. Despite the famine Stalin refused to cut back on cereal and other food exports because they were needed to pay for industrial imports under the Five-Year Plan.

By introducing thousand-acre units in place of very small ones, collectivization made it possible to apply capital to the soil. Formerly the average peasant had been far too poor to buy a tractor and his fields too tiny and dispersed for him to use one, so that only a few rare kulaks had employed any machinery. In the course of the First Five-Year Plan hundreds of Machine Tractor Stations were organized throughout the country. Each, in its region, maintained a force of tractors, harvesting combines, expert agronomists, etc., which were dispatched from one collective farm to another by local arrangement. The application of capital was intended to increase the output per peasant. It was also much easier administratively for higher authorities to control the agricultural surplus (products not consumed by the village itself) from a single collective farm than from numerous small and unorganized peasants. Each collective was assigned a quota.

Members of the collective could sell in a free market any products they raised beyond this quota; but meanwhile the government knew the quantity of agricultural produce it could count on, either to feed the cities and other regions that did not produce their own food, or for export in the world market to pay for imports of machinery from the West. By 1939 all but a negligible fraction of the peasantry was collectivized. But collectivization failed to increase agricultural output, and agriculture remained a troubled sector of the economy. Collectivization made possible, however, the success of industrialization by augmenting the supply of industrial workers. Since the villages needed less labor, 20 million people moved from country to city between the years 1926 and 1939 and were available for jobs in the new industries.

It was the peasants who bore the burden of collectivization. Not only had they been subjected to violence and expropriation, but the new collectives threw the peasants back into something like the *mir*, condemning them to the rounds of communal living, robbing them of the chance to make any decisions of their own. The incentive to improve the land they worked, and to pass on those improvements to their heirs, was gone. By obliging peasants to make "deliveries" below market prices, it even revived some features of the type of serfdom and forced labor that had prevailed a century before over most of eastern Europe.[35] On the other hand, although the collectives varied widely in their degree of prosperity, it is probable that by 1939 a great many of the rural people were better housed and better fed than they had been before the Revolution. But millions had not survived the ordeal of collectivization, and the whole experience undermined the morale of those who had.

The Growth of Industry

While the agricultural base was being revolutionized, industrialization went rapidly forward. At first there was considerable dependence on the capitalist countries. Engineers and other technicians from western Europe and the United States took service in the Soviet Union. Much machinery was imported. But the worldwide depression that set in about 1931, bringing a catastrophic fall of agricultural prices, made foreign-made machines more costly in terms of the cereals that were the chief Soviet export. The international situation also deteriorated. While the U.S.S.R. always considered the whole outside world hostile to it, both Japan and Germany in the 1930s showed overt hostility. From the beginning the Five-Year Plans had as one of their objectives the military self-sufficiency of the country. The Second Five-Year Plan, launched in 1933, though in some ways less ambitious than the first, showed an even greater determination to cut down imports and achieve national self-sufficiency, especially in the heavy industry basic to war production.

No ten years in the history of any Western country ever showed such a rate of industrial growth as the decade of the first two plans in the Soviet Union. In Great Britain industrialization had been gradual; in Germany and the United States it had been more rapid, and in each country there had been decades in which output of coal or iron doubled; but in the U.S.S.R., from 1928 to 1938,

[35] See pp. 509–510, 566–567.

production of iron and steel expanded four times and that of coal three and a half times. In 1938 the U.S.S.R. was the world's largest producer of farm tractors and railway locomotives. Four-fifths of all its industrial output came from plants built in the preceding ten years. Two plants alone, at the new cities of Magnitogorsk in the Urals and Stalinsk 1,000 miles farther east, produced as much iron and steel as the whole Russian empire in 1914. In 1939 the U.S.S.R., as measured by purely quantitative standards, was surpassed in gross industrial output only by the United States and Germany.

The plans called for a marked development of industry east of the Urals, and so brought a modernization of life for the first time to inner Asia, in a way comparable only to the movement of machine industry into the once underdeveloped Great Lakes region of the American Middle West. Pittsburghs, Clevelands, and Detroits rose in the old Turkestan (now divided into the five Asian Soviet socialist republics) and in Siberia. Copper mines were opened in the Urals and around Lake Balkhash, lead mines in eastern Asia and in the Altai Mountains. New grain-producing regions were developed in Siberia and in the Kazakh S.S.R., whence grain was shipped westward to Russia proper, or southward to the Uzbek S.S.R., which was devoted mainly to cotton. Tashkent, the Uzbek capital, formerly a remote town of bazaars and caravans, grew to be a city of over half a million, a center of cotton culture, copper mining, and electrical industries, connected with the north by the newly built Turksib Railway. The Kuznetsk basin, in the south, 2,000 miles inland from every ocean, was found to possess coal deposits of high grade. Kuznetsk coal and the iron ores of the Urals became complementary, though separated by a thousand miles, somewhat like Pennsylvania coal and Minnesota iron in the United States. The opening of all these new areas, requiring the movement of food to the Uzbek S.S.R. in exchange for cotton, or of Ural iron to the new Kuznetsk cities, demanded a revolution in transportation. The railroads in 1938 carried five times as much freight as in 1913.

These astounding developments were enough to change the relative economic strength of the world's peoples with respect to one another. It was significant that inner Asia was for the first time turning industrial. It was significant, too, that although the U.S.S.R. had less foreign trade than had the Russian empire, it carried on more trade than the old Russia with its Asian neighbors, with which it formed new and close connections. In part because of these developments in Asia, the Russia that went to war with Germany in 1941 proved to be a different antagonist from the Russia of 1914. Industrialization in the Urals and in Asia enabled the U.S.S.R. (with a good deal of Allied assistance) to survive the German occupation and destruction of the older industrial areas in the Don valley. The new "socialist fatherland" proved able to absorb terrible losses and strike back. A great deal of the increased industrial output had gone to equip and modernize the Red Army.

At the same time, the degree of industrialization of the U.S.S.R. can easily be exaggerated. It was phenomenal because it started from so little. Qualitatively, by Western criteria, standards of production were low. Many of the hastily constructed new plants were shoddy and suffered from rapid depreciation. In efficiency, as shown by output per worker employed, the U.S.S.R. continued to lag behind the West. In intensity of modernization, as shown by output of certain items in proportion to the whole population, it also lagged. Per capita of its huge population, in 1937, the U.S.S.R. produced less coal, electricity, cottons, woolens, leather shoes, or soap than did the United States, Britain, Germany, France, or even Japan, and less iron and steel than any of them except Japan. Production of paper is revealing because paper is used in so many "civilized" activities— in books, newspapers, magazines, schools, correspondence, placards, maps, pictures, charts, business and government records, and household articles and amenities. Where the United States about 1937 produced 103 pounds of paper per person, Germany and Great Britain each 92, France 51, and Japan 17, the U.S.S.R. produced only 11.

Social Costs and Social Effects of the Plans

Industrialization in Russia demanded a huge and continuing sacrifice on the part of the people. It was not merely that kulaks lost their lives, or that millions of others, whose exact numbers have never been known, were found to be enemies of the system and sent off to correctional labor camps. All were required to accept a program of austerity and self-denial, going without the better food, housing, and other consumers' goods that might have been produced, in order that the capital wealth and heavy industry of the country might be built up. As much as a third of the national income was reinvested in industry every year— twice as much as in the England of 1914, though probably not more than in the England of 1840. The plan required hard work and low wages. People were told to look to the future, to the time when, the basic industries having been built, better housing, better food, better clothing, and more leisure would follow. Morale was sustained by propaganda. One of the chief functions of party members was to explain why sacrifices were necessary. In the late 1930s life began to ease; food rationing was abolished in 1935, and a few more products of light industry, such as dishes and fountain pens, began to appear in Soviet retail stores. Living standards were at least up to those of 1927 with prospects brighter for raising them. But the need for war preparations, as the world again approached chaos, again drove back the vision of the Promised Land.

Socialism, as realized in the plans, did away with some of the evils of unrestrained free enterprise. There was no acknowledged unemployment. There was no cycle of boom and depression. There was less misuse of women and children than in the early days of industrialism in the West. There was a minimum below which no one was supposed to fall. On the other hand, there was no economic equality. Marxism, indeed, had never seen complete equality of income as a principal objective. While there was no handful of very rich people, as in the West (where the income of the very rich usually came from inherited property), the differences in income were nevertheless great. High government officials, managers, engineers, and favored artists and intellectuals received the highest rewards. People with large incomes, by buying government bonds or accumulating personal possessions, could build up precarious little fortunes for themselves and their children. They could not, however, under socialism, own any industrial capital, i.e., buy shares of stock or other equities. There was, of course, no stock exchange.

Competition persisted. In 1935 a miner named Stakhanov greatly increased his

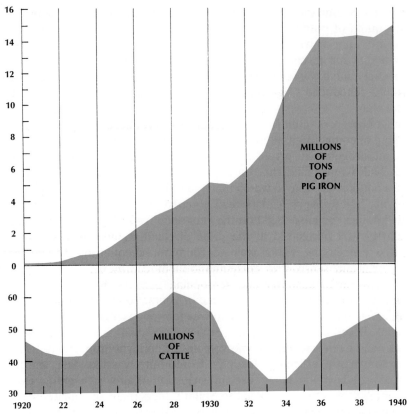

Source: B. R. Mitchell, *European Historical Statistics* (New York: Columbia University Press, 1975), pp. 316, 396.

PIG IRON AND CATTLE IN THE SOVIET UNION, 1920–1940

If pig iron is taken as a measure of industrial activity and number of cattle as a similar indication for agriculture, the chart reveals clearly what happened in the twenty years after the Revolution—an enormous build-up of heavy industry at the expense of food supplies. Iron mines and forges, in the disorganization of the Revolution and civil war, were producing almost nothing in 1920. By the late 1920s, output of pig iron regained the pre-Revolutionary level, but the great upsurge came with the Second Five-Year Plan. By 1940 Russia produced more pig iron than Germany, and far more than Britain or France. Numbers of cattle grew in the 1920s, but fell catastrophically during the collectivization of agriculture after 1929, and by 1940 hardly exceeded the figure for 1920.

daily output of coal by devising improvements in his methods of work. He also greatly increased his wages, since Soviet workers were paid at piece rates. His example proved contagious; workers all over the country began to break records of all kinds. The government publicized their achievements, called them Stakhanovites and "labor heroes," and pronounced the movement to be "a new and higher stage of socialist competition." In labor circles in the United States such straining to increase output would be called a speed-up, and piecework wages had long been anathema to the organized labor of all countries. Nor was management free from competitive pressure. A factory manager who failed to show the net income (or "profit") upon which the plan counted, or who failed to meet his quota of output, might lose not only his job but his social status—or even his life. Poor management was often construed as sabotage. Insufficient use of the workers and resources allocated to a factory was considered a betrayal of Soviet society and a waste of the property of the nation. The press, not otherwise free, freely denounced whole industries or individual executives for failures to meet the plan.

Foreign observers often found the distinctive feature of the new system to lie in this kind of competition or emulation, or in a feeling that everybody was busily toiling and struggling to create a socialist fatherland. Workers in the 1930s, it seemed, had a real belief that the new industrial wonders were their own. It became a national pastime to watch the mounting statistics, the fulfilling of quotas or "targets." Newspaper readers read no comic strips; they read eagerly about the latest doings (or misdoings) on the economic front.

Solidarity was purchased at the price of totalitarianism.[36] The government supervised everything. There was no room for skepticism, independence of thought, or any criticism that weakened the will to achieve. As in tsarist times, no one could leave the country without special permission, which was given far more rarely than before 1914. There was, of course, only one party. There were no free labor unions, no free press, no freedom of association, and at best only an irritable tolerance for religion. Soviet Jews had many complaints. Art, literature, and even science became vehicles of political propoganda. Dialectical materialism was the official philosophy. Conformity was the ideal, and the very passion for solidarity made for fear and suspicion of all who might go astray. As for the number of people sacrificed to Stalin's Juggernaut—liquidated bourgeois, liquidated peasants, purged party members, disaffected persons sentenced to long terms in labor camps—a precise figure is difficult to arrive at, but it certainly reached many millions over the years, which many suspected at the time, and which a later generation of Soviet leaders confirmed.

The Purge Trials of the 1930s

In 1936 socialism was judged to have proved so successful that a new constitution for the U.S.S.R. was proclaimed. It enumerated, as rights of Soviet citizens, not merely the usual civil liberties of Western democracy but the rights to steady employment, rest, leisure, economic security, and a comfortable old age. All forms of racism were condemned. It reorganized the Soviet republics and granted equal and direct universal suffrage, as explained above.[37] The constitution of 1936 was favorably commented upon in the West, where it was hoped that the Russian Revolution, like former revolutions, had at last turned into more peaceable and quiet channels. It was nonetheless apparent that the Communist party remained the sole governing group in the country, that Stalin was tightening his dictatorship, and that the party was racked by internal troubles.

It was natural that the rapid changes of the 1930s should provide divergences of opinion among the party leaders. Because open disagreement with Stalin's

[36] On totalitarianism, see pp. 828–832.
[37] See p. 756.

policies was not possible, many may have turned to conspiracy. A moderate group, led by Bukharin, had urged more gradual methods in collectivizing the peasants and greater latitude for small private business, as in the days of the NEP. On the left, the mastermind was the exiled Trotsky. Whether there were conspiracies or not, Stalin acted preemptorily. As early as 1933 the party underwent a drastic purge, in which a third of its members were expelled. Even the faithful were appalled at Stalin's growing ruthlessness. Serge Kirov, an old friend and revolutionary companion of Stalin since 1909, head of the Leningrad party apparatus, and member of the Politburo since 1930, showed signs of leading the disaffected. In 1934 he was assassinated in his office, very probably by a police agent of Stalin's. Stalin used the assassination to strike out at his opponents, imagined or real, by a revival of terror, immediately executing over a hundred persons, and launching the extraordinary purges of the next four years.

A series of sensational trials took place. In 1936 sixteen Old Bolsheviks were brought to trial. Some, like Zinoviev and Kamenev, had been expelled from the party in 1927 for supporting Trotsky and subsequently, after the proper recantations, had been readmitted. Now they were charged with the murder of Kirov, with plotting the murder of Stalin, and with having organized, in 1932, under Trotsky's inspiration, a secret group to disorganize and terrorize the Central Committee. To the amazement of the world, all the accused made full confession to the charges in open court. All blamed themselves as unworthy and erring reprobates. All were put to death. In 1937, after similar trials, seventeen other Old Bolsheviks met the same fate or received long prison sentences. In 1938 Bukharin and others, denounced as "rightists," were charged with wanting to restore bourgeois capitalism and were executed. The same confessions and self-accusations followed in almost every case, with no other verifiable evidence adduced. How these confessions were obtained in open court from hardened revolutionaries apparently in full possession of their faculties and bearing no sign of physical harm mystified the outside world. Only later did it become clear that psychological torture had broken the will of those accused, and that threats against their families (or promises to spare them) had played a part.

In addition to these public trials there were other arrests, private inquisitions, and executions. In 1937, in a secret court martial, Marshal Tukhachevski and seven other top generals were accused of Trotskyism and conspiring with the Germans and Japanese, and were summarily shot. The purges embraced the highest levels of the party, government, military, intellectual, and scientific circles, and reached down to the lesser echelons as well. In later years the KGB itself disclosed that in the years 1930–1953 (the year of Stalin's death) 3,778,334 persons had been tried and sentenced for "counterrevolutionary" activity and crimes against the state, most of them in the Great Terror of 1934–1938, and that 786,098 were executed; unknown others died in prison camps. The innocence of many of Stalin's victims was officially confirmed and their reputations posthumously restored.

By these purges Stalin's dictatorship was reinforced. It may be that a real danger of renewed revolution was averted. Had the tsarist government dealt as summarily with Bolsheviks as Bolsheviks dealt with one another there could have been no November Revolution. Above all, Stalin rid himself by the purges of all possible rivals for his own position. He disposed of the embarrassment of having colleagues about him who could remember the old days, who could quote Lenin as a former friend, or belittle the reality of 1937 by recalling the dreams of 1917. After 1938 there were virtually no Old Bolsheviks left. The aging but still explosive professional revolutionaries were now dead. A younger group, products of the new order, practical, constructive, impatient of "agitators," and acquiescing in Stalin's dictatorship, were operating what was now an established system.

96. The International Impact of Communism, 1919–1939

Socialism and the First World War

Marxism had always been international in its outlook. To Marx, and the early Marxists, existing states (like other institutions) owed their character to the class struggle. They were no more than committees of the bourgeoisie to govern the proletariat, destined to be dismantled and pass away in the course of inevitable historic processes. After Marx's death, as Marxist parties grew in numbers, and as states of western Europe became more democratic, most people who called themselves Marxists accepted the national state, seeing in it a means by which the workers' lot could be gradually improved. This view was part of the movement of "revisionism," or what more rigorous Marxists called "opportunism."[38] In the First World War national loyalty proved its strength. The socialist parties in the Reichstag, the French Chamber, and other parliamentary bodies voted for war credits without hesitation. Socialist workers reported for mobilization like everyone else. In Germany socialists said that the reactionary Russian tsardom must be resisted; in France, that the Germans menaced the entire French nation. In general, all political parties, including the socialists, declared a moratorium on party politics during the war.

Small minorities of socialists in every country, however, refused to accept the war. Marxian socialism had long taught that workers of all nations were bound by the supreme loyalty of class, that their real enemies were the capitalists of their own countries, that international wars were capitalist and "imperialist" quarrels, and that class struggle was the only kind of warfare that the proletarian should accept. These socialists denounced the action of the socialist majorities as a sellout to capitalism and imperialism. They met in international conferences with each other and with socialists from the neutral countries. Active among them were Lenin and other Russian Social Democrats then in Switzerland. "The only task for socialists," wrote Lenin in 1914, "is to convert the war of peoples into a civil war." The minority or antiwar socialists met at the small Swiss town of Zimmerwald in 1915, where they drew up a "Zimmerwald program," calling for immediate peace without annexations or indemnities. This had no effect on most socialists in the belligerent countries. The Zimmerwald group itself soon began to split. Most Zimmerwalders regarded peace, or the repudiation of the

---

[38] See pp. 526–527, 622–625.

war, as their aim. But a "Zimmerwald Left" began to develop, inspired mainly by Lenin and the Russian émigrés. This faction made its aim not peace but revolution. It hoped that the war would go on until it caused social revolution in the belligerent countries.

Then in April 1917, with the German imperial government arranging their trip and wishing them *bon voyage*, Lenin and the other Bolsheviks went back to Russia and accomplished the November Revolution. Lenin, until his death in 1924, believed that the Russian Revolution was only a local phase of a world revolution—of *the* revolution of strict Marxian doctrine. Russia, for him, was the theater of currently most active operations in the international class war. Because he expected proletarian upheaval in Germany, Poland, the Danube valley, and the Baltic regions, he accepted without compunction the treaty of Brest-Litovsk. He took no pride in Russia; he was no patriot or "social-chauvinist," to use his own term. In the founding of the U.S.S.R. in 1922 he saw a nucleus around which other and greater soviet republics of any nationality might coalesce. "Soviet republics in countries with a higher degree of civilization," he wrote, "whose proletariat has greater social weight and influence, have every prospect of outstripping Russia as soon as they start upon the road of proletarian dictatorship."

The First World War was in fact followed by attempted revolutions in Germany and eastern Europe. With the German and Austro-Hungarian empires wrecked, socialists and liberals of all descriptions strove to establish new regimes. Among socialists the old differences persisted, between socialists or social democrats favoring gradual, nonviolent, and parliamentary methods, and a more extreme group which saw in postwar disintegration a chance to realize the international proletarian revolution. The first group looked upon the Bolshevik Revolution with horror. The second looked upon it with admiration. The first group included not only trade union officials and practical socialist politicians, but such prewar giants of Marxian exegesis as Karl Kautsky and Eduard Bernstein. Even Kautsky, who had upheld pure Marxism against the revisionism of Bernstein, could not stomach the methods of Lenin. The mass of European socialists, with their fiercest leaders removed, were to remain characterized by relative moderation. Marxist in principle, they were in fact more than ever wedded to gradual, peaceable, and parliamentary methods.

In the second group, the sifted residue of uncompromising Leninist neo-Marxists, who accepted the Bolshevik Revolution, were Karl Liebknecht and Rosa Luxemburg. Organizing the Spartacist movement[39] in Germany, they attempted, in January 1919, to overthrow the majority socialist government in Germany, as Lenin had overthrown the Provisional Government in Russia in November 1917. In the second group also was Béla Kun, who had turned Bolshevik during a sojourn in Russia, and who set up and maintained a soviet regime in Hungary for several months in 1919.

Lenin and the Bolsheviks, though absorbed in their own revolution, gave all possible aid to the fringe of left socialists of Europe. They sent large sums of money to Germany, to Sweden, to Italy. When the Bolshevik Radek was arrested in Berlin he was said to have a plan for proletarian revolution in all central Europe

[39] See p. 783 and note 11.

in his possession. The party considered sending Russian troops to Hungary to support Béla Kun. But the chief instrument of world revolution, created in March 1919, was the Third or Communist International.

The Founding of the Third International

The Second International, which since its foundation in 1889 had met every two or three years until 1914, held its first postwar meeting at Berne in 1919.[40] It represented socialist parties and labor organizations of all countries. The Berne meeting was stormy, for a small minority vehemently demanded "revolution as in Russia, socialization of property as in Russia, application of Marxism as in Russia." Overruled at Berne, they repaired to Moscow and there founded a new International in conjunction with the Russian Communist party, and with Lenin and the Russians dominating it completely. It was Lenin's hope, by founding a new International of his own, to discredit moderate socialism and to claim for the Communists the true line of succession from the First International of Karl Marx. The First International, he declared, had laid the foundations for proletarian struggle, the Second had broadened it, the Third "took over the work of the Second International, cut off its opportunistic, social-chauvinist, bourgeois and petty-bourgeois rubbish, and began to carry into effect the dictatorship of the proletariat."

The first congress of the Third International in 1919 was somewhat haphazard, but at the second, in 1920, the extreme left parties of thirty-seven countries were represented. The Russian party was supposedly only one component. Actually, it supplied most of the personnel and most of the funds; the Bolshevik Zinoviev was its first president, remaining in this office until his disgrace as a Trotskyist in 1927. The Third or Communist International—the Comintern—was in part a spontaneous rallying of Marxists from all countries who accepted the Bolshevik Revolution as the true fruition of Marxism and so were willing to follow the Russian lead; but, even more, it was the creation and weapon of the Bolsheviks themselves, by which to discredit and isolate the moderate socialists and bring about world revolution. Of all enemies the Communists hated the socialists most, reserving for them even choicer epithets than they bestowed upon capitalists and imperialists, because Communists and socialists were competing for the same thing, the leadership of the world's working class.

Parties adhering to the Comintern were obliged to drop the old name "socialist" and call themselves Communist. They were obliged to accept strong international centralization. Where the Second International had been a loose federation, and its congresses hardly more than forums, the Third International put strong powers in the hands of its Executive Committee, whose orders the Communist parties of all countries had to obey. Since there was a kind of interlocking directorate by which members of the Central Committee of the party in Russia sat also as members of the Executive Committee of the Third International, the top Communists in Russia had, in the Comintern, an "apparatus" by which they could produce desired effects in many countries—the use of party members to

[40] See pp. 622–624.

penetrate labor unions, foment strikes, propagandize ideas, or interfere in elections.

The second congress of the International, in 1920, endorsed a program of Twenty-One Points, written by Lenin. These included the requirements that each national party must call itself Communist, repudiate "reformist" socialism, propagandize labor unions and get Communists into the important union offices, infiltrate the army, impose an iron discipline upon members, require submission to the orders of the international Executive, use both legal channels and secret underground methods, and expel promptly any member not hewing to the party line. Making no pretense of respect for parliamentary democracy, the second congress ruled that "the only question can be that of utilizing bourgeois state institutions for their own destruction." As for the labor movement, Lenin wrote that "the struggle against the Gomperses, the Jouhaux, the Hendersons[41] . . . who represent an *absolutely similar* social and political type as our Mensheviks . . . must be waged without mercy to the end." The Comintern was not an assemblage of humanitarians engaged in welfare work; it was a weapon for revolution, organized by revolutionaries who knew what revolution was.

For several years the U.S.S.R., using the Comintern or more conventional diplomatic channels, promoted world revolution as best it could. Communists from many countries went to Russia for indoctrination. Native-born or Russian agents proceeded to the Dutch Indies, to China, to Europe, to America. Until 1927 the Chinese revolutionists welcomed assistance from Moscow; the Russian Borodin became an adviser in their affairs. In 1924, in England, publication of the "Zinoviev letter," in which, at least allegedly, the Comintern urged British workers to provoke revolution, led to a great electoral victory for the Conservative party. The Bolshevik menace, real and imagined, produced everywhere a strong reaction. It was basic to the rise of fascism described in the following chapters.

In 1927, with the suppression of Trotskyism and world revolutionism in Russia, and with the concentration under Stalin on a program of building socialism in one country, the Comintern moderated its activities. In 1935, as fascist dictators became noisily bellicose and threatened the Soviet Union, the U.S.S.R. through the Comintern instructed all Communist parties, each in its own country, to enter into coalitions with socialists and advanced liberals in what were called "popular fronts," to combat fascism and reaction and so support the national defense of their own countries. During the Second World War (in 1943), as a gesture of good will to Great Britain and the United States, the U.S.S.R. abolished the Comintern entirely. It reappeared for a few years from 1947 to 1956 under a new name, the Communist Information Bureau or Cominform, and was then disbanded.[42]

It was not through the Comintern that the U.S.S.R. exerted its greatest influence on the world in the years after 1917. It exerted its influence by the massive fact of its very existence. By 1939 it was clear that a new type of economic system had appeared. Before 1917 no one in Europe or Asia had thought

---

[41] Samuel Gompers (1850–1924), began as a cigar maker, president of the American Federation of Labor, 1886–1924; Léon Jouhaux (1879–1954), began as a factory worker, secretary general of the French General Confederation of Labor, 1909–1947, resigned in 1947 to found a new labor organization in opposition to communism; Arthur Henderson (1863–1935), began as an iron-molder's apprentice, chairman of the Parliamentary Labour Party, 1908–1910, 1914–1917, Member of Parliament, 1903–1931, Secretary of State for Foreign Affairs, 1929–1931.

[42] For the U.S.S.R. and for international communism after 1945, see pp. 903–918, 978–992, and 1012–1037.

that anything was to be learned from Russia. Twenty years later even critics of the U.S.S.R. feared that it might represent the wave of the future. Its sheer power was soon demonstrated in the Second World War. Marxism was no longer merely a theory; there was an actual society, embracing a sixth of the globe, which called itself Marxist.

In every country those who were most critical of capitalist institutions compared them unfavorably to those of the Soviet Union. Most of those who in the 1930s hoped to profit from the Soviet experience were not actually communist. Some believed that something like Soviet results might be obtained without the use of Soviet methods, which were dismissed as typically Russian, a deplorable heritage from the Byzantine Empire and the tsars. With the appearance of Communism and Communist parties, socialism and socialist ideas seemed in contrast to be middling and respectable. Everywhere in the 1930s the idea of "planning" began to find favor. Workers obtained more security against the fluctuations of capitalism. The so-called backward peoples, especially in Asia, were particularly impressed by the achievement of the U.S.S.R., which had shown how a traditional society could modernize without falling under the influence of foreign capital or foreign guidance.

For a long time the Communist party in the Soviet Union presented itself as the leader of world revolution and tried to exert control over Communist parties in all other countries. This became increasingly difficult. Over the years the U.S.S.R. pursued diplomatic and military policies, and engaged in acts of aggression and territorial expansion, such as the tsarist state might have done. By the late 1980s the U.S.S.R. was no longer an innovative, or some would say, a viable society. Its economic system was in a shambles; the component republics demanded autonomy or independence. The revelation from within the Soviet Union itself of the persecution and deaths of millions of innocent victims, along with the restiveness of its own nationalities, undermined its role as leader of oppressed peoples elsewhere. European Communist parties proclaimed their independence from Moscow and a new form of communism emerged in the People's Republic of China. Yet all Communist parties, including the Chinese, derived from Marxism and from the Russian Revolution of 1917, once hailed as the first great victory over capitalism and imperialism.

XVIII.
THE
APPARENT
VICTORY OF
DEMOCRACY

W E HAVE FOLLOWED events in the Soviet Union to about the year 1939 but have left the story of Europe and the rest of the world at the signing of the peace treaties of 1919. We must deal now with the period of just twenty years that elapsed betweeen the formal close of the First World War in 1919 and the outbreak of the Second World War in 1939. In these twenty years the world made a dizzy passage from confidence to disillusionment and from hope to fear. It went through a few years of superficial prosperity, abruptly followed by unparalleled economic disaster. For a time, in the 1920s, democracy seemed to be advancing almost everywhere; then, in the 1930s, dictatorship began to spread. Let us first examine the apparent triumphs of democracy in the 1920s, turn next to the devastating worldwide effects of the Great Depression that began in 1929, and then, in the following chapter, trace the painful decade of the 1930s.

97. The Advance of Democracy after 1919

The first years following the war were troubled. Even the victors faced serious difficulties in reconversion from war to peace. Veterans demobilized from the huge armies found themselves unemployed and psychologically restless. Farms and factories geared to maximum production during the war faced a sudden disappearance of markets. They produced more than could now be sold, so that the war was followed by a sharp postwar depression, which, however, had run its course by 1922. Basically, the economic position even of the victors was

Chapter Emblem: A medal struck in honor of the Peace of Versailles, 1919.

seriously damaged, for the war had disjointed the world of 1914, in which industrial western Europe had lived by exchange with eastern Europe and with overseas countries.

Gains of Democracy and Social Democracy

The war, President Wilson had said, was fought to make the world safe for democracy. Political democracy now made advances everywhere. The new states that emerged from the war all adopted written constitutions and universal suffrage. Democracy made advances even in countries that had long been in large measure democratic. Great Britain dropped the last barriers to universal male suffrage in 1918. The most conspicuous innovation was the growing enfranchisement of women. In 1918 female suffrage with certain restrictions was adopted in Great Britain; in 1928 the restrictions were dropped and the vote was granted on an equal basis with men. In 1920, through an amendment to the constitution, female suffrage became general in the United States. Women voted also in Germany and in most of the new states of Europe. In the Soviet Union women received the vote on an equal basis with men after the Revolution in 1917.

In most European countries the successors of the old prewar socialists gained in strength. With the left wings of the old socialists generally seceding, calling themselves Communists, and affiliated with each other and with Moscow in the Communist International, the European socialists or social democrats were preponderantly a party of peaceable or revisionist Marxism, entirely willing to carry on the class conflict by parliamentary and legislative methods. Labor unions, with new self-confidence gained from the role they had played in the war, grew in membership, prestige, and importance.

Social legislation which before the war would have seemed radical was now enacted in many places. An eight-hour legal working day became common, and government-sponsored insurance programs against sickness, accident, and old age were either adopted or extended; an act of 1930, in France, insured almost 10 million workers. An air of progressive democracy pervaded Europe and the European world. The social service, or welfare, state, already under way in the late nineteenth century, was becoming more firmly established.

Only in Italy in the early postwar years, of the states that might have been expected to continue their prewar democratic gains, did democracy receive a sharp setback. Italy had been a parliamentary state since 1861 and had introduced a democratic suffrage in the elections of 1913. In 1919 the Italians held their second elections under universal male suffrage. But Italian democracy soon abruptly ended. In 1922 an agitator named Benito Mussolini, leading a movement which he called Fascism (thereby adding a new word to the world's political vocabulary), killed off the Italian parliament and founded his Fascist regime.[1] Lenin had already founded the first single-party state; Mussolini became the first of the dictators of postwar Europe outside the Soviet Union. Fascist Italy, in the 1920s, was the chief exception in what seemed to be a rising tide of democracy.

[1] See pp. 550–551, 818–822.

The New States of Central and East-Central Europe

In central and east-central Europe—in Germany, in the territory of the former Austro-Hungarian empire, and in the western fringe of former tsarist Russia— new states and new governments struggled to establish themselves. The new states included, besides republican Germany, the four successor states to the Habsburg empire—Austria, Hungary, Czechoslovakia, and Yugoslavia; and the five states that had broken away from the Russian empire—Poland, Finland, Estonia, Latvia, and Lithuania.[2] The other small states in eastern Europe, Romania, Bulgaria, Greece, and Albania, had already been independent before 1914; their boundaries underwent some modification and their governments considerable reorganization after the war. Turkey, the successor to the Ottoman Empire, is considered elsewhere.[3]

The new states were to a large extent accidents of the war. Nowhere, except possibly in Poland, did they represent a deeply felt, long-maturing, or widespread revolutionary sentiment. Only an infinitesimal number of Germans in 1914 would have voted for a republic. Even among the nationalities of Austria-Hungary in 1914 few persons would have chosen the complete breakup of the Habsburg empire. The republicans, moderate socialists, agrarians, or nationalists who now found themselves in power had to improvise governments for which there had been little preparation. They had to contend with reactionaries, monarchists, and members of the old aristocracy. They had also to deal with the real revolutionaries, who, inspired by Lenin's success, hoped to bring about the dictatorship of the proletariat. A communist revolt broke out in Germany in 1919 but was quickly suppressed; soviet regimes were actually set up but soon crushed in Hungary and in the German state of Bavaria; and as late as 1923 there was a communist uprising in the German state of Saxony.

The new states all embodied the principle of national self-determination, which held that each nationality should enjoy political sovereignty—one nation, one government. But people in this region were and always had been locally intermixed.[4] Each of the new states therefore included minority nationalities; for, with the exception of an exchange of populations between Greece and Turkey, arranged in 1923, there was no thought of the actual physical removal of "alien" groups. Poland, Czechoslovakia, and Yugoslavia were the most composite of the new states. Poland and Czechoslovakia each had many disaffected Germans. In Czechoslovakia the Slovaks resented Czech domination and in Yugoslavia Croatian and other separatist movements developed.

Nevertheless, despite economic and nationalist troubles, the new states and governments attempted at the outset to make themselves democratic. Except for the German republic they were all relatively small. All the newly created states were republics except Yugoslavia, which was under the older Serbian dynasty. Hungary started out in 1918 as a republic, but the attempt of Béla Kun to found a Hungarian Soviet Republic in 1919 brought back the counterrevolutionaries who restored the Habsburg monarchy in principle, though they were prevented by foreign pressure from restoring the king in person. Hungary emerged in 1920

[2] See map, pp. 728–729.
[3] See pp. 791–793.
[4] See maps, pp. 470 and 1034.

as a monarchy with a perennially vacant throne, under a kind of dictatorship exercised by Admiral Horthy. All smaller states of Europe, including Hungary, possessed at least the external apparatus of democracy until the 1930s; that is, they had constitutions, parliaments, elections, and a diversity of political parties. If civil liberty was sometimes violated, the right to civil liberty was not denied; and if the elections were sometimes rigged, they were at least in principle supposed to be free.

Economic Problems of Eastern Europe; Land Reform

Eastern Europe for centuries had been an agrarian region of large landed estates, which supported on the one hand a wealthy landowning aristocracy of almost feudal outlook, and on the other an impoverished mass of agricultural workers with little or no property of their own. The landed aristocracy had been the chief support of the Austro-Hungarian empire and an important pillar of the old order in the tsarist empire and in eastern Prussia. The mass of the rural population, through all this region, had been free from serfdom, or released from subjection to manorial landlords, only since the middle of the preceding century.[5] The middle class of business and professional men was small except in Austria and Bohemia, the western portion of Czechoslovakia. In general, the whole region was conscious of lagging behind western Europe, not only in industry, factories, railroads, and great cities, but also in literacy, schooling, reading habits, health, death rates, length of life, and material standard of living.[6]

The new states set out to modernize themselves, generally on the model of the West. They introduced democratic and constitutional ideas. They put up protective tariffs, behind which they tried to develop factories and industries of their own. But the new national boundaries created difficulties. Where Europe in 1913 had had 6,000 miles of frontiers, after the war it had almost 10,000, and all the increase was in eastern Europe. Goods circulated much less easily. Protected industries in the old agricultural regions produced inefficiently and at high cost. Old and

[5] See pp. 513, 520, and map, p. 212.
[6] See pp. 586–587.

AUTOUR d'ELLE
by Marc Chagall (Russian, then French, 1887–1984)

Where some painters departed from the Western tradition by cultivating pure abstraction or geometrized patterns (see pp. 630–635, 1049–1051), others did so by evoking unconscious or dreamlike mental phenomena. This picture was painted by Chagall in France in 1945 in memory of his wife. The houses in the center represent the Russian city of Smolensk, where they had been married thirty years before. The surrounding faces and figures are individually quite distinct, but they float disconnectedly like the vivid images in a dream, without location in space or time, or any rational relationship to each other. Past and present, memory and perception, fantastic and real objects flow together in a kind of free play of the unconscious mind. These qualities characterized surrealism, of which Chagall in his younger days had been a forerunner. Courtesy of the Musée d'Art Moderne, Paris (Service Photographique). Permission A.D.A.G.P. 1970 by French Reproduction Rights, Inc.

established industries, in Austria, Czechoslovakia, and western Poland, cut off by the new frontiers and new tariffs from their former markets, fell upon hard times. The working class of Vienna lived in misery, because Vienna, a city of 2 million persons, formerly the capital of an empire of 50 million, was now the capital of a republic of 6 million. In Czechoslovakia the German minority living in the Sudetenland complained that in hard times the German businesspeople and workers, because of government policies, always suffered more than their Czech counterparts. Economically, the carving up of eastern Europe into a dozen independent states was self-defeating.

The greatest of reforms undertaken by the new east-European states was the reform of landownership. Although it far from solved basic economic problems in the area, it did have substantial effect on the pattern of land distribution. The whole traditional agrarian base of society was overturned. The work of the revolutions of 1848, which, in the Habsburg lands, had liberated the peasants but left them landless, was now carried a step further. The example of the Russian Revolution gave a powerful stimulus, for in Russia in 1917 peasants had driven off landlords, and communists won a hearing among discontented and propertyless peasants from Finland to the Balkans. Not until 1929, it should be recalled, did the Soviet Union embark on the collectivization of agriculture; until then, communism appeared to favor the small individual farmer. But it may be said with equal truth that the model for agrarian reform lay in the West, especially in France, the historic land of the small peasant proprietor.

Land reform worked out differently in different countries. In the Baltic states the big properties belonged almost entirely to German families, the "Baltic barons," descendants of the medieval Teutonic Knights.[7] In Estonia, Latvia, and Lithuania the nationalist dislike for Germans made it easier to liquidate landlords. Small farms here became the rule. In Czechoslovakia over half the arable land was transferred from large to small owners; here again, the fact that many great landowners had been German, in some cases since the days of the Thirty Years' War,[8] made the operation more palatable, though it inflamed the German minority in Bohemia. In Romania and Yugoslavia the breakup of large estates, though considerable, was less thorough. In Finland, Bulgaria, and Greece the issue hardly arose, since small landownership was already common. Land reform had least success in Poland and Hungary, where the landed magnates were exceptionally strong and well rooted.

After the land reforms, political parties of peasants or small landholders became the chief democratic force within the various states on the western border of Russia. Often they inclined to socialism, especially since capitalism was associated in their minds with foreign investors and outsiders. On the other hand, the great landowners, the former aristocrats of the prewar empires, whether already expropriated or merely threatened with expropriation, were confirmed in a reactionary outlook. The land reforms did not solve basic economic problems. The new small farms were very small, frequently no more than ten acres. The peasant owners lacked capital, agricultural skill, and knowledge of the market. Farm productivity did not rise. In place of old differences between landlord and

---

[7] See p. 79 and map, p. 44.
[8] See pp. 141–142, 224.

tenant there developed new differences between the more comfortable peasants and the proletarian hired hands. The continuance of relative poverty, the obstinacy of reactionary upper classes, the new stresses and strains among the peasants themselves, the economic distortions produced by numerous tariff walls, and the lack of any sustained tradition of self-government all helped to frustrate the democratic experiments launched in the 1920s.

98. The German Republic and the Spirit of Locarno

The keystone of Europe was Germany. Germany, too, had its revolution in 1918. But it was a revolution without revolutionaries, a negative revolution caused more by the disappearance of the old than by any vehement arrival of the new. The emperor and the High Command of the army, in the last weeks of the war, had bowed out of the picture, leaving it to others to face defeat and humiliation.[9] For a time, after November 1918, the men in charge of affairs were mainly Social Democrats. The Social Democrats were Marxists, but their Marxism was the tamed, toned down, and revisionist Marxism that had prevailed for twenty years before the advent of Lenin. They were trade union officials and party managers. They could look back, in 1918, on decades spent in developing labor organizations and building up the Social Democratic party, which in 1912 had become the largest single party in the Reichstag.[10] Now, in 1918, they were a cautious and prudent group, essentially conservative, more anxious to preserve what they had already achieved than to launch audacious new social experiments. Before 1917 the Social Democrats considered themselves well to the left. But the Bolshevik Revolution in Russia, and the emergence of a pro-Bolshevik or communist element in Germany, put the Social Democrats in the middle. The middle is an awkward spot, especially in disturbed times; the Communists regarded the Social Democrats as reactionaries, despicable traitors to the working-class movement; whereas the true reactionaries, recruited from old monarchists, army officers, Junker landowners, and big business groups, saw in social democracy, or professed to see in it, a dangerous flirtation with Bolshevism.

The middle group in Germany, the Social Democrats reinforced by the Catholic Center party and others, was more afraid of the left than of the right. They were appalled, in 1918 and 1919, by the stories brought out of Russia, not merely by fugitive bourgeois or tsarist aristocrats, but by refugee Social Democrats, Mensheviks, and anti-Leninist Bolsheviks, many of whom the socialists had long known and trusted in the Second International. In January 1919 the Spartacists,[11] led by Karl Liebknecht and Rosa Luxemburg, attempted to bring about a proletarian revolution in Germany, like that in Russia. Lenin and the Russian Bolsheviks aided them. For a time, there seemed to be a possibility that Germany might go communist, that the Spartacists might succeed in imposing a dictatorship of the proletariat. But the Social Democratic Provisional Government crushed the Spartacist uprising, turning for that purpose to demobilized army officers and

[9] See pp. 717–718.
[10] See pp. 615–616, 622–625.
[11] So named from Spartacus, a Roman slave who led a slave revolt in south Italy in 72 B.C.

volunteer vigilantes recruited from the disbanding army. The Spartacist leaders Liebknecht and Luxemburg were arrested and shot while in police custody. The events of "Spartacus Week" widened a chasm between Social Democrats and Communists, not bridged even in Hitler's concentration camps.

Shortly after, elections were held for a National Constituent Assembly. No single party received a majority, but the Social Democrats were the leading party. A coalition of Social Democrats, Center party, and liberal democrats dominated the Assembly. After several months of deliberations at the city of Weimar, in July 1919, a constitution was adopted establishing a democratic republic. The Weimar Republic (as the regime in Germany from 1919 to the advent of Hitler in 1933 is called) was soon threatened ominously from the right. In 1920 a group of disaffected army officers staged a *Putsch*, or armed revolt, put the republican government to flight, and attempted to place a puppet of their own, one Dr. Kapp, at the head of the state. The Berlin workers, by turning off public utilities, stopped the Kapp *Putsch* and saved the republic. But the Weimar government never took sufficiently firm measures to put down private armed bands led by reactionary or outspokenly antidemocratic agitators. One of these was soon to be Adolf Hitler, who as early as 1923 staged an abortive revolt in Munich.[12] Nor, being democratic and liberal, did it ever deny the rights of election to the Reichstag, and of free speech in the Reichstag and in public, either to communists or to antidemocratic reactionaries.

The Weimar Republic was in principle highly democratic. The constitution embodied all the devices then favored by the most advanced democrats, not only universal suffrage, including the vote for women, but proportional representation and the initiative, referendum, and recall. But except for the legal eight-hour day and a few other such safeguards to the workers' welfare (and traditional demands of organized labor) the republic of which the Social Democrats were the main architects in its formative years was remote from anything socialistic. No industries were nationalized. No property changed hands. No land laws or agrarian reforms were undertaken, as in the new states of eastern Europe; the East-Elbian Junkers remained untouched in their landed estates. There was almost no confiscation even of the property of the former kaiser and other ruling dynasties of Bismarck's federal empire. The very statues of emperors, kings, princes, and grand dukes were left standing in the streets and squares. Officials, civil servants, police agents, professors, schoolteachers of old imperial Germany remained at their respective duties. The army, though limited by the Versailles treaty to 100,000 men, remained the old army in miniature, with all its essential organs intact, and lacking only in mass. The soldiers were peasant youths enlisted for long terms and soon formed to German and Prussian military traditions. In the officer corps the old professional and aristocratic influences remained strong.

Never had there been a revolution so mild, so reasonable, so tolerant. There was no terror, no fanaticism, no stirring faith, no expropriation, no émigrés. There had in truth been no revolution at all, in the sense in which England, France, the United States, Russia, and other countries, either recently or in the more distant past, had experienced revolutions.

---

[12] See p. 824.

The German Democracy and Versailles

The supreme question, for Europe and the world, was how Germany would adjust to the postwar conditions. How would the Germans accept the new internal regime of democracy? How would they accept the new German frontiers and other provisions of the Treaty of Versailles? These two questions were unfortunately interconnected. The Weimar Republic and the Treaty of Versailles were both products of the defeat of Germany in the war. There were many in Germany who favored democracy, notably the numerous Social Democrats, and many more possibly could have been won over to it, given time and favorable conditions. But no one, not even the Social Democrats, accepted the Treaty of Versailles or the new German frontiers as either just or final. If "democracy" in Germany meant the perpetual acceptance of the treaty without amendment, or if it meant economic distress or hardship which could either reasonably or unreasonably be explained as consequences of the treaty, then "democracy" would lose such appeal as it had for the Germans.

The German republicans, we have seen, protested against the Versailles treaty before signing, and signed only under pressure.[13] The Allies continued the wartime naval blockade after the armistice; this confirmed, in German eyes, the argument that the Treaty of Versailles was a *Diktat*, a dictated peace, Carthaginian, ruthless, and vengeful. The "war guilt" clause, while it perhaps on the one hand satisfied a peculiar Anglo-American sense of morality, on the other hand offended a peculiar German sense of honor. Neither the reparations demanded of them, nor the new frontiers, were accepted by the Germans as settled. Reparations they regarded as a perpetual mortgage on their future. They generally expected, some day, to revise their eastern frontier, recover at least the Polish corridor, and merge with German-speaking Austria.

The French lived in terror of the day when Germany would recover. Their plans for their own security, and for the collective security of Europe against a German revival, had been disappointed. They had been unable to detach the Rhineland from Germany. The United States Senate had refused to ratify the treaty, signed at Paris by Wilson, by which the United States was to guarantee France against German invasion in the future.[14] Both Britain and the United States showed a tendency to isolation, to pull away from the Continent, to get back to "normalcy," to work mainly for a restored trade in which a strong Germany would be a large customer. The League of Nations, of which the United States was not a member, and in which every member nation had a veto, offered little assurance of safety to a people so placed as the French. The French began to form alliances, against a potentially resurgent Germany, with Poland, Czechoslovakia, and other east-European states. They insisted also on German payment of reparations. The amount of reparations, left unstated in the treaty, was fixed by a Reparations Commission in 1921 at 132 billion gold marks. This sum, the equivalent of $35 billion, was soon pronounced by various Western economists to be more than Germany could possibly contrive to pay.

[13] See p. 726.
[14] See pp. 723–724, 730.

The Weimar government in these circumstances looked to the Soviet Union, which had been no party to the Versailles treaty and claimed no reparations. The Soviet government meanwhile, concluding from the failure of proletarian revolution in Germany and Hungary that the time was not ripe for the sovietizing of Europe, prepared to enter into normal diplomatic relations with established governments. Germany and the Soviet Union, despite ideological repugnance, thus signed the treaty of Rapallo in 1922. In the following years the Soviet Union obtained needed manufactures from Germany, and German factories and workers were kept busy by orders from the Soviets. The German army dispatched officers and technicians to give instruction to the Red Army. Obliged by the Treaty of Versailles to restrict its activities, the German army was in fact able, through its work in Russia, and through a number of subterfuges at home, to maintain a high standard of training, planning, technical knowledge, and familiarity with new weapons and equipment. The good understanding between Germany and Russia naturally caused apprehension in the West.

Reparations, the Great Inflation of 1923, Recovery

The French, blocked in the attempt to collect reparations, and assisted by the Belgians, in 1923 sent units of the French army to occupy the industrial sites of the Ruhr valley. The Germans responded by general strikes and passive resistance. To sustain the workers the Weimar government paid them benefits, grinding paper money off the printing presses for this purpose. Germany, like other belligerent countries, had suffered from inflation during and after the war; neither the imperial government nor the Weimar statesmen had been willing to impose heavier taxes to offset it. But what now swept Germany was different from ordinary inflation. It was of catastrophic and utterly ruinous proportions. Paper money became literally worthless. By the end of 1923 it took over 4 trillion paper marks to equal a dollar.

This inflation brought far more of a social revolution than the fall of the Hohenzollern empire had ever done. Debtors paid off debts in worthless money. Creditors received baskets full of meaningless paper. Salaries even when raised lagged behind the soaring cost of living. Annuities, pensions, proceeds of insurance policies, savings accounts in the banks, income from bonds and mortgages—every form of revenue which had been arranged for at some time in the past, and which often represented the economy, foresight, and personal planning of many years—now turned to nothing. The middle class was pauperized and demoralized. Middle-class people were now materially in much the position of workers and proletarians. Their whole view of life, however, made it impossible for them to identify themselves with the laboring class or to accept its Marxist or socialist ideologies. They had lost faith in society itself, in the future, in the old burgher codes of self-reliance and rational planning of their own lives in an understandable world. A kind of moral void was created, with nothing for them to believe in, hope for, or respect.

The inflation, however, by wiping out all outstanding indebtedness within the country, made it possible, once the losses were written off and accepted, to start up economic production afresh. The United States was persuaded to play a reluctant role. The United States, in these years, demanded payment of the huge war debts owed to it by the Allies.[15] The Allies—Britain, France, Belgium—insisted that they could not pay debts to the United States unless they collected reparations from Germany. In 1924 the Dawes Plan, named for the American Charles G. Dawes, was instituted in Germany to assure the flow of reparations. By the Dawes Plan the French evacuated the Ruhr, the reparations payments were cut down, and arrangements made for the German republic to borrow abroad. A good deal of American private capital was invested in Germany in the following years, both in German government bonds and in German industrial enterprises. Gradually, so at least it seemed, Germany was put on its feet. For four or five years the Weimar Republic even enjoyed a bustling prosperity, and there was a good deal of new construction in roads, housing, factories, and ocean liners. But the prosperity rested in good measure on foreign loans, and the Great Depression that began in 1929 reopened all the old questions.

The Spirit of Locarno

These years of economic prosperity were years also of relative international calm. No issue, in truth, was dealt with fundamentally. The universal German hatred for the Treaty of Versailles elicited no concessions from the Allies. Conceivably, had the Allies been willing at this time to amend the treaty by international agreement, they might have taken wind from the sails of nationalistic rabble-rousers in Germany and so spared themselves much later grief. It may be, however, that no possible concession would have sufficed. The great problem was to prevent a German overthrow of the treaty structure by violence, especially in eastern Europe where the Germans regarded the new frontiers as basically subject to reconsideration. After the Ruhr incident, and adoption of the Dawes Plan, a group of moderate and peace-loving men shaped the foreign policy of the principal countries—Gustav Stresemann in Germany, Édouard Herriot and Aristide Briand in France, Ramsay MacDonald in England.

The charter of the League of Nations provided for international sanctions against potential aggressors. Like the system of congresses after the Peace of Vienna, the League was supposed to assure peaceable compliance with the peace treaties, or their modification without resort to force.[16] No one expected the League, by any authority of its own, to prevent war between Great Powers, but the League achieved various minor pacifications in the 1920s, and in any case its headquarters at Geneva offered a convenient meeting place in which statesmen could talk.

As a further assurance against war, in 1925 at Locarno, the European powers signed a number of treaties. These marked the highest point in international good will reached between the two World Wars. Germany signed a treaty with France and Belgium guaranteeing their respective frontiers unconditionally. It signed arbitration treaties with Poland and Czechoslovakia—not guaranteeing these frontiers as they stood, but undertaking to attempt changes in them only by international discussion, agreement, or arbitration. France signed treaties with Poland and Czechoslovakia promising military aid if they were attacked by

[15] See pp. 721–722, 725–726.
[16] See pp. 477–481, 482.

Germany. France thus fortified its policy of balancing German power in the East by its own diplomatic alliances and by supporting the Little Entente, as the alliance of Czechoslovakia, Yugoslavia, and Romania was called. Great Britain "guaranteed"—i.e., promised military aid in the event of violation—the frontiers of Belgium and France against Germany. It did not give an equivalent guarantee with respect to Czechoslovakia or Poland. The British took the view that their own security would be threatened by German expansion westward, but not by German expansion to the east. It was on the borders of Czechoslovakia and Poland, fourteen years later, that the Second World War began. Had Britain gone along with France in 1925 in guaranteeing these two countries, then stuck to the guarantee, the Second World War might possibly have been prevented. On the other hand, no war ever depends on any single decision; it is the accumulation of many decisions that matters.

In 1925 people talked with relief of the "spirit of Locarno." In 1928 international harmony was again strengthened when the French foreign minister Briand and the United States Secretary of State Frank B. Kellogg arranged for the Pact of Paris. Ultimately signed by sixty-five nations, it condemned recourse to war for the solution of international controversies. Although no measures of enforcement were provided and a number of reservations were added before certain countries signed, the Pact solemnly affirmed the will of the nations to renounce war as an instrument of national policy.

In the mid-1920s the outlook was indeed full of hope. At Locarno, Germany had of its own volition (and not by the *Diktat* of Versailles) accepted its borders both east and west, to the extent of abjuring violence and unilateral action even in the east. In 1926 Germany joined the League of Nations. Germany was a going concern as a democratic republic. Democracy seemed to work, as well as could be expected, in most of the new states of eastern Europe, and Communist Russia itself had halted its postwar revolutionary offensive. The world was again prosperous, or seemed to be so. World production was at or above the prewar level. In 1925 the world's production of raw materials, it was estimated, was 17 percent greater than in 1913. World trade, by 1929, measured in hard money— gold—had almost doubled since 1913. The war and the postwar troubles were remembered as a nightmare escaped from. It seemed that, after all, the world had been made safe for democracy.

But complacency was shattered by the great world depression, by the growth of a malignant nationalism in Germany, due in part to the depression, and by the assertion of a new militancy in Japan, which also was not unrelated to the depression. But let us turn first to the postwar years in Asia.

99. The Revolt of Asia

Resentments in Asia

The peoples of Asia had never been satisfied with the position in which the great European expansion of the nineteenth century had placed them.[17] Increasingly

---

[17] See pp. 642–650, 669–681.

they condemned everything associated with "imperialism." In this respect there was little difference between countries actually governed by Europeans as parts of European empires in the nineteenth century, such as British India, the Netherlands Indies, French Indochina (or the American Philippines), and countries that remained nominally independent under their own government, such as China, Persia, and the Ottoman Empire. In the former, as political consciousness awakened, there was objection to the monopoly of Europeans in the important offices of government. In the latter, there was objection to the special rights and privileges enjoyed by Europeans, the widespread impounding of customs revenues to pay foreign debts, the capitulations in Turkey, the extraterritorial rights in China, the spheres of influence in Persia which divided the country between British and Russians.

By imperialism, in either case, aroused Asians meant a system whereby the affairs of their own country were conducted, its resources exploited, its people employed, for the benefit of foreigners, Europeans, or white people. They meant the system of absentee capitalism, by which the plantations, docks, or factories before their eyes, and on which they themselves labored, were the property of owners thousands of miles away whose main interest in them was a regular flow of profits. They meant the constant threat that an alien civilization would disintegrate and eat away their own ancient cultures. They meant the nuisance of having to speak a European language, or the calamity of having to fight in wars originated by Europeans. And they meant the airs of superiority assumed by whites, the race consciousness exhibited by all Westerners, though perhaps most of all the British and Americans, the color line that was everywhere drawn, the attitudes varying between contempt and condescension, the relation of native "boy" and European "sahib." Imperialism to them signified the gentlemen's clubs in Calcutta to which no Indian was ever admitted, the hotels in Shanghai from which Chinese were carefully kept out, the park benches in various cities on which no "native" could ever sit. In deeper psychology, as well as in economics and in politics, the revolt of self-conscious Asians was a rebellion against social inferiority and humiliation.

The revolt against the West was generally ambivalent or two-sided. It was a revolt against Western supremacy, but at the same time, in most cases, those who revolted meant to learn from and imitate the West, in order that, by taking over Western science, industry, organization, and other sources of Western power, they might preserve their own identity and emerge as the West's equals.

The crisis in Asia had broken out with the Russo-Japanese War, when an Asian people, in 1905, defeated a great European power for the first time.[18] In 1906 revolution began in Persia, leading to the assembly of the first majlis, or parliament. In 1908 the Young Turks staged a successful revolution in Constantinople and summoned a parliamentary assembly to represent all regions then in the Ottoman Empire. In 1911 the revolutionists in China, led by Sun Yat-sen, overthrew the Manchu dynasty and proclaimed the Chinese Republic. In each case the rebels charged their old monarchs—shah, sultan, emperor—with subservience to Western imperialists. In each case they summoned national assemblies on the prevailing democratic model of Europe, and they proposed to revive, modernize, and

[18] See pp. 681–682.

westernize their countries to the degree necessary to avoid domination by the West.

First World War and Russian Revolution

In the First World War almost all the Asian peoples were somehow involved. The Ottoman Empire, allied with Germany, immediately repudiated all the capitulations, or special legal rights of Europeans. Persia attempted to remain neutral and to get rid of the partition made in 1907 between British and Russian spheres, but it became a battleground of British, Russian, and Turkish forces. China, which joined the Allies, attempted at the peace conference to have the extraterritorial rights in China abolished. We have seen how this request of the Chinese Republic was refused, and how the Allies, instead, transferred many of the prewar German concessions to the Japanese.[19] The dependent regions of Asia, the Dutch, French, and British possessions, were stimulated economically by the war.[20] The Netherlands Indies, though remaining neutral, increased its output of foodstuffs, oil, and raw materials. India developed its steel industry and textile manufactures and contributed over a million soldiers, combat and service troops, to the British cause. All the dependent regions were stirred by Woodrow Wilson's call to make the world safe for democracy.

The home governments made concessions. They were naturally afraid to go too far; they insisted that their subject peoples were not yet capable of self-government. They had huge investments at stake, and the whole world economy depended on the continuing flow of raw materials from tropical and subtropical countries. But they did compromise. In 1916 the Dutch created a legislative assembly to advise the governor general of the Indies; half its members were Indonesians. In 1917 the British agreed to a measure of self-government in India; an Indian legislative assembly was set up with 140 members, of whom 100 were elected, and in the provinces of British India the number of elected representatives and of local Indian officials was increased. The French in 1922 provided for a somewhat similar assembly in Indochina. Thus all three imperial powers, at about the same time, began to experiment with consultative bodies whose membership was partly elective, partly appointive, and partly non-European, partly European. The United States introduced an elected assembly in the Philippine Islands in 1916.

The Russian Revolution added a new stimulus to unrest in Asia. The Bolsheviks denounced not only capitalism but also imperialism. In Marxist-Leninist ideology imperialism was an aspect of capitalism.[21] Colonial peoples also tended to identify the two, not so much for Marxist reasons as because modern capitalism was a foreign or "imperialist" phenomenon in colonial countries, where the ownership and the management of large enterprises were both foreign. Nationalism in Asia, the movement for independence or for more equality with the West, thus easily shaded off into socialism and the denunciation of capitalistic exploitation. The Bolsheviks were quick to see the advantages for themselves in this situation. As

---

[19] See p. 725.
[20] See p. 721.
[21] See p. 740.

it became clear that the world revolution, as expected by Lenin, would not soon come to pass in Europe, the Russian communists turned to Asia as the theater in which world capitalism might be attacked by a great flanking movement. In September 1920 a "congress of oppressed Eastern peoples" assembled at Baku, on the coast of the Caspian Sea. Zinoviev, head of the Communist International, called for war upon "the wild beasts of British capitalism." Not much was accomplished at the conference. But a few extremists from Asian countries in the following years sojourned in Moscow, and a few communists dispatched from Moscow stirred up the discontents which existed, quite without Russian instigation, all over Asia.

The postwar situation in Asia was thus extremely fluid. People who were not communists hailed communism as a liberating force. Anti-Westerners declared that their countries must westernize. Nationalism overshadowed all other isms. In the Indian National Congress rich Indian capitalists consorted with socialist leaders, with whom they were held together in relative harmony so long as the common enemy was the British.

The Turkish Revolution: Kemal Atatürk

The most immediately successful of the revolutionary movements was the one in Turkey. The Young Turks at first, in 1908, had meant to prevent the further dissolution of the Ottoman Empire.[22] This proved to be impossible. In the Balkan wars of 1912–1913 the Ottoman power was almost totally excluded from the Balkan peninsula. In the World War, in which the Turks were on the losing side, the Arabs with a great deal of British assistance broke away. After the war, in 1921, the Greeks invaded the Anatolian peninsula. They dreamed of a Great Greece embracing both sides of the Aegean. Europeans still regarded Turkey as the sick man of Europe, the Ottoman state as doomed to extinction, and the Turkish people as barbarous and incompetent. The Allies had agreed in 1915 to partition Turkey; and after the war the Western powers favored the Greek invasion. Italian and French forces occupied parts of Anatolia, and Italians, French, and British undertook to take Constantinople from Turkish rule, though its disposition remained uncertain. (It had been promised to Russia in 1915, before the Bolshevik Revolution.[23]) In these circumstances a powerful army officer named Mustapha Kemal rallied Turkish national resistance. Within two years, and with aid from the Soviet Union, the Turks drove the Greeks and the Western Allies away. They affirmed their hold on the Anatolian peninsula, and on both shores of the Straits, including Constantinople, which was renamed Istanbul.[24]

The Nationalists, under the energetic drive of Mustapha Kemal, now put through a sweeping revolution. They abolished the sultanate and the caliphate, since the sultan had somewhat compromised himself with foreigners, and was also, as caliph or commander of the faithful, a religious functionary for all Islam and hence a conservative influence. The Turkish Republic was promulgated in 1923.

[22] See p. 657, and maps, pp. 660, 703.
[23] See pp. 709–710.
[24] See map, p. 660.

Where the Ottoman Empire had been a composite organization made up of diverse religious communities, among which the Muslims were the ruling group, the Turkish Republic was conceived as a national state in which the "people," i.e., the Turkish people, were sovereign. Universal suffrage was introduced, along with a parliament, a ministry, and a president with strong powers. Non-Turks in Asia Minor now became "foreign" in a way they had not been before. We have seen the fate of the Armenians during the First World War.[25] The other large non-Turkish and Christian people were the Greeks. After the war about 1.4 million Greeks either fled or were officially transported from Asia Minor to Greece, and, in exchange, some 400,000 Turks residing in northern Greece were transported to Turkey. The exchange of populations caused great hardship, it uprooted most of the Greek element that had lived in Asia Minor since 1000 B.C., and it overwhelmed the impoverished Greek kingdom by obliging it suddenly to absorb a mass of destitute refugees, who were a quarter as numerous as the population of Greece itself. But it enabled the Turkish Republic to acquire a relatively homogeneous population, ending minority disputes between Greece and Turkey until Cyprus posed new problems after the Second World War.

For the first time in any Muslim country the spheres of government and religion were sharply distinguished. The Turkish Republic affirmed the total separation of church and state. It declared religion to be a private belief, and it tolerated all religions. Government was reorganized on secular and nonreligious principles stemming from the French Revolution. The law of the Koran was thrust aside. The new law was modeled on the Swiss Code, the most recently codified European legislation, itself derived from the Code Napoleon.

Mustapha Kemal urged women to put aside the veil, to come out of the harem, to vote, and to occupy public office. He made polygamy a crime. Men he required by law to discard the fez. He fought against the fez as Peter the Great had fought against the beard, and for the same reason, seeing in it the symbol of conservative and backward habits. The hat, "headgear of civilization," correspondingly became the symbol of progress. The people shifted to Western dress. The Western alphabet became mandatory; literate Turks had to learn to read again, and illiteracy was reduced. The Western calendar and the metric system were adopted. Turks were required to assume hereditary family surnames, like Westerners; Kemal himself took the name Atatürk, or Great Turk. The capital was moved from Istanbul to Ankara. The republic put up a high tariff. In 1933 it adopted a five-year plan for economic development. The Turks, having shaken off foreign influence, were determined not to become again dependent on Western capital or capitalism. The five-year plan provided for mines, railroads, and factories, mainly under government ownership. At the same time, while willing to accept Russian aid against the Western powers, the republic had no patience with communism, which it suppressed. The Turks wanted a modern Turkey—by and for the Turks.

Persia experienced a similar revolution, somewhat less drastic. In 1921 Reza Khan, an army officer, overthrew the older ruling dynasty and in 1925 became shah. The old concessions, capitulations, and spheres were done away with, and the Persian government renegotiated its oil contracts, asserting more control over

---

[25] See pp. 710–711. On the multinational character of the Ottoman Empire see pp. 219–220 and 654–656.

foreign corporations and receiving a larger return from them in taxes and royalties. In 1935, to emphasize its break with the past, Persia took the name of Iran.

The National Movement in India: Gandhi and Nehru

India at the close of the First World War was on the verge of revolution against British rule.[26] Discontented Indians looked for leadership to Mohandas K. Gandhi, the Mahatma, or Holy One, who in the following decades, though hardly typical of modern Asia, attained a worldwide eminence as the champion of subjected peoples. Gandhi had been educated in England in the 1890s and had practiced law in South Africa, where he became aware of racial discrimination as a worldwide problem. In India, after 1919, he led a movement for self-government, for economic and spiritual independence from Great Britain, and for greater tolerance within India itself both between Hindus and Muslims and between upper-caste Hindus and the depressed outcastes and untouchables. The weapons he favored were those of the spirit only; he preached nonviolence, passive resistance, civil disobedience, and the boycott. He took to self-imposed fasts and hunger strikes to cope with his British jailers and later with the Indians themselves. He and his most loyal followers, as the troubles mounted, refused to be elected or take part in the partially representative institutions that the British cautiously introduced and also boycotted the British economic position in India, by refusing to buy or use goods imported from England. The latter touched the British in a sensitive spot. Before the World War half of all exports of British cotton cloth had gone to India. By 1932 this proportion fell to a quarter. Gandhi turned against all industrialism, even the mechanized industry that was growing up in India itself. He put aside Western costume, took to using a spinning wheel and living on goat's milk, urged Indian peasants to revive their old handicrafts, and appeared on solemn occasions clad in no more than a homespun loincloth. By the high level of his principles Gandhi made himself an inspiration to many groups that differed on more mundane matters. Even in the West he was regarded as one of the great religious teachers of all time.

India was very much divided within, and the British maintained that because of these divisions the ending of British rule would precipitate anarchy. There were Hindus and Muslims, between whom clashes and terrorist outrages were chronic. (Gandhi was himself murdered in 1948 by an anti-Muslim Hindu fanatic.) There were the hundreds of oriental potentates of the native states. There were Indian capitalists, like the Tata family, and growing masses of proletarians produced by Indian industrialization.[27] There were the higher castes and the outcastes, and there were hundreds of millions of peasants living in a poverty unimaginable in the West. In politics, there were those who demanded full independence, boycotted the British, and spent years in jail, as did Gandhi and his more practical-minded but devoted follower, Jawaharlal Nehru; and there were the moderates who believed that they might best advance the welfare of India by accepting government office, cooperating with the British, and working for dominion status within the British Empire. Marxism exerted a strong appeal,

---

[26] See pp. 669–672, 682.
[27] See p. 721.

not indeed on the spiritual and pacific Gandhi, but on Nehru and even many of the less radical leaders. In the 1920s the Soviet Union stood in their eyes for the overthrow of imperialism; in the 1930s it pointed the way by its adoption of five-year plans. For a people wishing to raise itself by its own bootstraps, to move from poverty to industrial strength and higher living standards without loss of time, and without dependence on foreign capital and capitalism, the Soviet Union with its economic planning seemed to offer a more appropriate model and more practical lessons than the rich democracies of the West, with their centuries of gradual progress behind them.

The twenty years between world wars were years of repeated disturbance, of rioting and repression, of sporadic violence despite the exhortations of Gandhi, of conferences and round tables, reforms and promises of reform, with a drift in the 1930s toward more participation of Indians in the affairs of the Indian empire. Independence was not won until after the Second World War; with it took place a partition of the Indian subcontinent into two new nations, a predominantly Hindu India and a predominantly Muslim Pakistan.[28]

In the Netherlands Indies, where the nationalist movement was less developed than in India,[29] the interwar years were more quiet. A serious rebellion, in which communists took part, broke out in 1922 but was suppressed by the Dutch. The peoples of the archipelago were almost as diverse as those of India. Only the Dutch empire had brought them politically together. Opposition to the Dutch gave them a common program. In 1937 the legislative council petitioned for the grant of dominion status. But not until after the Second World War and the failure of a military effort to repress the nationalists did the Dutch concede independence.

The Chinese Revolution: The Three People's Principles

The Chinese Revolution had opened in 1911 with the overthrow of the Manchu dynasty, which itself had belatedly begun to introduce westernizing reforms. The Chinese Republic was proclaimed, but the first immediate result was the establishment in Peking of a military dictatorship exercised by General Yüan Shih-kai, who had been a close adviser to the Manchus and who, until his death in 1916, never ceased to cast covetous eyes on the now empty imperial throne itself. In the south the veteran revolutionary Dr. Sun Yat-sen reorganized the Kuomintang (National People's, or Nationalist party), successor to the prerevolutionary network of underground societies of which he had been the chief architect.[30] Sun, elected the first president of the republic by a revolutionary provisional assembly, resigned within a few months in favor of General Yüan, who he mistakenly believed would unite the country under a parliamentary regime. Subsequently, in the confusion that followed the struggle for power in Peking after Yüan's death in 1916, Sun was proclaimed president of a rival government in the south at Canton, which exercised a nominal power over the

[28] See pp. 920–923.
[29] See pp. 669–670.
[30] For the change in spelling of Chinese names after 1979, see p. 916, note 43.

southern provinces. Not until 1928 could any government have any basis for claiming actual rule over China—and even then, there were important exceptions. For most of these years the country was virtually in the hands of contending war lords, each of whom pocketed the customary taxes in his own locality, maintained his own army, and recognized no superior authority.

It was Sun Yat-sen who best expressed the ideas of the Chinese Revolution. Born in 1867 and educated under American influence in the Hawaiian Islands, he had received a medical degree at Hong Kong, had traveled extensively about the world, studied Western ideas, lectured to Chinese audiences in America, collected money for his conspiracies against the Manchus, and had returned from Europe to take part in the revolution. Shortly before his death in 1925 Sun gathered the lectures which he had been expounding for years into a book, *The Three People's Principles*. The book sheds much light on the revolt of China, and of all Asia, against the supremacy of the West.

The three people's principles, according to Sun Yat-sen, were democracy, nationalism, and livelihood. Livelihood meant social welfare and economic reform—a more equitable distribution of wealth and land, a gradual end to poverty and unjust economic exploitation. By nationalism Dr. Sun meant that the Chinese who had always lived mainly in the clan and family had now to learn the importance of the nation and the state. They were in fact a great nation, he thought, the world's most cultured, and had once prevailed from the mouth of the Amur to the East Indies. But they had never been cohesive. The Chinese had been "a sheet of loose sand"; they must now "break down individual liberty and become pressed together into an unyielding body like the firm rock which is formed by the addition of cement to sand."

By democracy Sun Yat-sen meant the sovereignty of the people. Like Rousseau, he gave little attention to voting, elections, or parliamentary processes. He believed that while the people were sovereign, the able should govern. Government should be conducted by experts, a principle he criticized the West for neglecting. Dr. Sun felt a warm sympathy for Lenin. Yet he was by no means a doctrinaire Marxist. Marxism he thought inapplicable to China, arguing that the Chinese must take Marxism as they took all other Western ideas, avoiding slavish imitation, using, adapting, amending, rejecting as they saw fit. China had no native capitalism in any Marxist or Western sense. The "capitalists" in China, he said, were owners of land, especially in the cities, such as Shanghai, where the coming of Westerners had raised land values to dizzy heights. Hence if China could get rid of imperialism it would take a long step toward getting rid of capitalism also; it could begin to equalize landowning and confiscate unearned rents. Since China, he observed, had no true capitalists the state itself must undertake capitalist and industrial development. This would require loans of foreign capital and the services of foreign managers and technicians, adding another reason why the Chinese state, to maintain control, must be strong.

With Sun Yat-sen, in short, democracy easily shaded off into a theory of benevolent and constructive dictatorship. Marxism, communism, socialism, "livelihood," the planned society, welfare economics, and antiforeign and anti-imperialist sentiment were all mixed together—in some ways as the ideas of the Chinese Communists would later be.

The first aim of Sun Yat-sen and of the revolutionists in China was to shake off the "treaty system" that had bound China to outside interests since 1842.[31] In this respect the Paris peace conference had been disappointing; the Chinese not only failed to obtain the abolition of Western privileges and extraterritorial rights but could not block the retention by Japan of many of the former German concessions that the Japanese had taken over during the war.[32] Widespread student and worker demonstrations directed against the Western powers took place on May 4, 1919. The May Fourth movement heightened the antiforeign consciousness.

As the Western powers proved obdurate, Sun and the Kuomintang turned to Russia. They declared the Russian and Chinese revolutions to be two aspects of the same worldwide movement of liberation. The Chinese Communist party, organized in 1921, became allied with the Kuomintang in 1923. The latter accepted Russian communist advisers, notably the veteran revolutionist Borodin, whom Sun Yat-sen had known years before in the United States.[33] The Soviet Union, following its strategy of outflanking world capitalism by penetrating Asia, sent military equipment, army instructors, and party organizers into China. It also surrendered the Russian concessions and extraterritorial rights acquired in China by the tsars. The Chinese policy of friendliness to Russia began to produce the hoped for effects; the British, to draw China from Russia, gave up a few of their lesser concessions at Hankow and other cities.

China: Nationalists and Communists

The Kuomintang, its armies reorganized and strengthened, now displayed a fresh vitality and after 1924 launched a military and political offensive, planned by the ever active Russian advisers, supported by the Chinese Communists, and headed by Chiang Kaï-shek, who succeeded to the leadership of the Kuomintang upon Sun's death in 1925. Chiang's main objectives were to compel the independent war lords and the regime still holding office in Peking to accept the authority of a single Nationalist government. By the end of 1928 Chiang's armies had swept northward, occupied Peking, and transferred the seat of government to Nanking. Chiang now exercised at least nominal control over most of China, although effective control was still limited by the recalcitrance of many provincial war lords. The outside powers, acknowledging the accomplishments of the Kuomintang, extended diplomatic recognition to the Nanking government and conceded its right to organize and run the country's tariff and customs affairs. They also partially surrendered their extraterritorial privileges and pledged to abolish them completely in the near future.

In 1927, while a measure of national unity was being forged in the country, an open break occurred between the Kuomintang and its left wing. In the course of the northern military campaign, and particularly in the seizure of Nanking, popular disturbance and excesses, including the killing of a number of foreigners, had

---

[31] See pp. 678–681.
[32] See p. 725.
[33] See p. 775.

taken place, allegedly fomented by the Communists. These radical disturbances frightened and alienated the wealthier and more conservative element in the Kuomintang and so jeopardized Chiang's chief source of financial assistance for his government and army. Chiang himself, also, had never apparently considered the alliance with either the Communists or the Russians as anything more than one of convenience. Chiang took decisive action, purging Communists and Russian advisers from the Kuomintang, and executing many. Borodin and others fled to Moscow, and a Communist-led uprising in Canton was forcefully suppressed. A number of armed Communist groups fled to the safety of the mountain regions in the south and joined other guerrilla contingents. In that way the Chinese Red Army was formed; among its leaders were Mao Tse-tung, a former librarian, teacher, newspaper editor, and union organizer, who had been one of the founding members of the party, and Chu Teh, who had held high rank in the Kuomintang armies.

Chiang, with the renewed financial and moral support of the Kuomintang bankers, resumed the northern offensive whose success by 1928 has been described. But the original revolutionary impulse of the Kuomintang was now very much dissipated. Made up of men who feared social upheaval and who often regarded their own maintenance in power as their chief problem, it exercised a kind of one-party dictatorship over most of China under Chiang's leadership. Chiang himself recognized mounting popular dissatisfaction with the reluctance or inability of the Kuomintang to initiate reforms, but he was still busy consolidating the regime and after 1931 he had to contend with Japanese aggression. During these years he conceived a deadly hatred for Communists and those who actively agitated for revolutionary reform.

The Communists, operating now in southeast China, fed on popular discontent and drew support from the poor peasantry by a systematic policy of expropriation and distribution of large landed estates as well as by intensive propaganda. They succeeded in fighting off Chiang's armies and even in winning over part of his troops. Organizing a network of local soviets, in 1931 they proclaimed a Chinese Soviet Republic in the southeast. When the Nationalist armies succeeded in dislodging them, the Communists, under Mao's leadership, undertook in 1934–1935 an amazing 6,000-mile march over near-insuperable terrain to north-central Yenan, closer, it was said, to Soviet supply lines. About 90,000 began the Long March, of which only half survived. They entrenched themselves again, fought off the Nationalist armies, and built up a strong popular following among the rural masses. With the Japanese invasion of north China well under way they abandoned their revolutionary offensive and pressed Chiang to end the civil war and to create a united front against the Japanese aggressor. Chiang reluctantly consented, so that by 1937 an alliance was formed between the Kuomintang and the Communists; the Chinese Red Army was placed under Nationalist control; a united China would face the Japanese. But the uneasy alliance between Kuomintang and Communists was not to last even until the defeat of Japan in the Second World War. Kuomintang and Communists would soon engage in a deadly struggle for power.[34]

[34] See pp. 914–918.

Japan: Militarism and Aggression

The Nationalist movement in China caused apprehension in Japan, whose rise as a modern power has already been traced.[35] The Japanese, at least since the Sino-Japanese War of 1895, had looked upon the huge disintegrating area of China as a field for expansion of their own interests, in this scarcely differing from Europeans, except that they were closer to the scene. During the World War they had presented their Twenty-One Demands on China, taken over the German concessions in Shantung, and sent troops into eastern Siberia.[36] During the war the industrialization of Japan proceeded apace; Japan captured many markets while the Europeans were locked in the struggle; and after the war the Japanese remained one of the chief suppliers of textiles for the rest of Asia. The Japanese could produce at lower prices than the Europeans, prices at which the penniless masses of Asia were more able to buy. Densely packed in their mountainous islands, they sustained their standard of living by importing raw materials and selling manufactures. But the Chinese Nationalists hoped to erect a protective tariff; it was for this reason, among others, that they denounced the treaty system, which for almost a century had bound China to international free trade. The Chinese, like the Turks, hoped to industrialize and westernize their own country behind a high tariff wall, which would shut out Japanese manufactures as well as others.

During the 1920s the civilian, liberal, Western-oriented element in Japan remained in control of the government. In 1925 universal male suffrage was adopted. It was still the fashion in Europe and America to view the Japanese with sympathetic approval, as the most progressive of all non-Europeans, the one Asian people who had ably learned to play its part in the advancing worldwide civilization. But there was another facet to Japan. The constitution of 1889 and parliamentary operations were but a façade that concealed political realities. Only in Japan of all modern countries did a constitutional law prescribe that the war and navy ministers must be active generals or admirals. The diet itself had sharply restricted powers. Ministers governed in the name of the supreme and sacred authority of the emperor, to whom they were alone responsible. Economically, the government's sponsorship of industrial growth had resulted in a tremendous concentration of economic power in the hands of four family trusts known collectively as the Zaibatsu. The business interests and the civilian political leaders all looked to an expanding empire and growing markets, but the most restless group in Japan drew its strength from the nationalist revival which, even before the "opening" of Japan in 1854, had cultivated Shinto, emperor worship, and the way of the warrior as a new and modern way of life.[37] This element was recruited in large part from the old clansmen and samurai, whom the "abolition of feudalism" had uprooted from their accustomed ways, and who in many cases found no outlet for their energies in the new regime. Many of these men now served as officers in the army. Often they regarded the West as decadent. They dreamed of the day when Japan would dominate all East Asia.

[35] See pp. 577–582.
[36] See pp. 711, 725, 752.
[37] See pp. 579, 581.

About 1927 this group began to hold ministries in the Japanese government and to turn Japanese policy into increasingly aggressive and militaristic attitudes toward China. In 1931 Japanese army units stationed in southern Manchuria (where the Japanese had been since defeat of the Russians in 1905), alleging the mysterious murder of a Japanese officer at Mukden, seized Chinese arsenals and spread northward over all Manchuria. In 1932, charging the Chinese with economic warfare against Japan (Chinese boycotts were in fact damaging the Japanese export trade), the Japanese landed 70,000 troops at Shanghai. They soon withdrew, preferring to concentrate at this stage on the occupation of the northern part of China. They declared Manchuria to be an independent state under an emperor they themselves selected (the last Chinese emperor, the "boy-emperor" Pu Yi, deposed in 1911), and renamed the state Manchukuo.

After the Manchurian invasion the Chinese appealed to the League of Nations. The League sent a commission of inquiry, which, under Lord Lytton, found Japan at fault for disturbing the peace. Japan defiantly withdrew from the League. The small powers in the League generally cried for military sanctions, but the Great Powers, knowing that they would be the ones to bear the burden of military intervention against Japan, and in any case inclined to see no threat to their own immediate security, refused to take any stronger measures, so that, in effect, the Japanese remained in occupation of Manchuria and northeast China. With the Japanese conquest of Manchuria one tributary of the coming torrent had begun to flow. But the world at this time was also stunned by economic depression. Each government was preoccupied with its own internal social problems.

100. The Great Depression: Collapse of the World Economy

The capitalist economic system was a delicate and interlocking mechanism, in which any disturbance was rapidly transmitted with accelerating impact through all the parts.[38] For many basic commodities prices were determined by the free play of supply and demand in a worldwide market. There was much regional division of labor; large areas lived by producing a few specialized articles for sale to the world as a whole. A great deal of production, both local and international, especially in the 1920s, was financed by credit, which is to say by promises of repayment in the future. The system rested upon mutual confidence and mutual exchange—on the belief of the lender, creditor, or investor that he would get his money back, on the belief of the borrower that he could pay his debts, on the ability of farms and factories to market their products at prices high enough to bring a net return, so that farmers and factory people might purchase the output of other factories and farms, and so on round and round in countless circles of mutual interdependence, and throughout the world as a whole.

The Prosperity of the 1920s and Its Weaknesses

The five years after 1924 were a period of prosperity, in that there was a good deal of international trade, building, and development of new industries. The

---

[38] See pp. 595–604, 718–722.

automobile, for example, still an oddity in 1914, became an article of mass production after the war; and its widespread use increased the demand for oil, steel, rubber, and electrical equipment, caused the building or rebuilding of tens of thousands of miles of roads, and created whole new secondary occupations for thousands as truckdrivers, garage mechanics, or filling-station attendants. Similarly the mass popularity of radios and moving pictures had repercussions in all directions. The ensuing expansion was most phenomenal in the United States, but almost all countries enjoyed it in greater or lesser degree. "Prosperity" became a mystic term, and some thought that it would last indefinitely, that the secret of human plenty and of progress had been found, and that science and invention were at last realizing the hopes of ages.

But there were weaknesses in this prosperity, various imperfections in this or that gear or valve of the mechanism, flaws which, under stress, were to bring the whole intricate structure to a halt. The expansion was largely financed by credit, or borrowing. Laboring people received less than a balanced share; wages lagged behind profits and dividends, so that mass purchasing power, even when inflated by installment buying (another form of credit), could not absorb the vast output that it was technically possible to produce. And throughout the world the whole decade of the 1920s was a time of chronic agricultural depression, so that farmers could neither pay their debts nor purchase manufactures to the degree required for the smooth functioning of the system.

Military operations in the First World War had reduced wheat fields under cultivation in Europe by a fifth. The world price of wheat went up, and farmers in the United States, Canada, and elsewhere increased their acreage. Often, to acquire land at high prices, they assumed mortgages which in later years they were unable to repay. After the war Europe restored its own wheat production, and eastern Europe reentered the world market. Agriculture was increasingly mechanized. Where, in the nineteenth century, one man could cut ten times as much grain with a single horse-drawn reaper as with a scythe, and where, before 1914, he could cut fifty times as much with a combined reaper and binder, he could again increase his output fivefold after the war, by using a tractor-drawn harvester-thresher combine. At the same time dry farming opened up new land, and agronomic science increased the yield per acre. The result of all these numerous developments was a superabundant output of wheat. But the demand for wheat was what economists call "inelastic." By and large, within the area of the Western world, people already ate as much bread as they wanted and would buy no more; and the undernourished masses of Asia, who in pure theory could have consumed the excess, could not pay even low costs of production or transportation. The world price of wheat fell incredibly. In 1930 a bushel of wheat, in terms of gold, sold for the lowest price in four hundred years.

Wheat growers in all continents were faced with ruin. Growers of many other crops faced the same dismal prospect. Cotton and corn, coffee and cocoa all collapsed. Brazilian and African planters were caught by overproduction and falling prices. In Java, where not only had the acreage in sugar been extended, but the unit yield of sugar from the cane had multiplied ten times under scientific cultivation over the past century, the bottom dropped out of prices in the world market. There were indeed other and more profitable forms of agricultural production—for example, in oranges and eggs, of which world consumption was steadily growing. But the coffee planter could not shift to eggs, nor the Iowa farmer to oranges. Not to mention the requirements of climate, the ordinary farmer or peasant lacked the capital, the special knowledge, or the access to refrigerated transportation that these newer branches of agriculture demanded. For the one thing that the average farmer or peasant knew how to do—grow wheat and other cereals—the new wonderful world of science and machinery had too little place.

The acute phase of the Great Depression, which began in 1929, was made worse by this chronic background of agricultural distress, since there was no reserve of purchasing power on the farms. The farmer's plight became even worse when the city people, struck by depression in industry, cut down their expenditures for food. Agricultural depression, rather than industrial depression, was at the bottom of widespread troubles in the interwar years throughout eastern Europe and the colonial world.

The Crash of 1929 and the Spread of Economic Crisis

The depression, in the strict sense, began as a stock market and financial crisis. Prices of stocks had been pushed upward by years of continuing expansion and high dividends. At the beginning of 1929 prices on the European stock exchanges began to weaken. But the real crisis, or turning point, came with the crash on the New York Stock Exchange in October 1929. Here values had been driven to fantastic heights by excessive speculation. Not only professional speculators, but quite ordinary people, in the United States, as an easy way to make a good deal of money, bought stock with borrowed funds. Sometimes, trading on "margin," they "owned" five or ten times as much stock as the amount of their own money put into it; the rest they borrowed from brokers, and the brokers borrowed from banks, the purchased stock in each case serving as collateral. With money so easy to obtain, people pushed up stock prices by bidding against each other and enjoyed huge fortunes on paper; but if prices fell, even a little, the hapless owners would be obliged to sell their stock to pay off the money they had borrowed. Hence the weakening of values on the New York Stock Exchange set off uncontrollable tidal waves of selling, which drove stock prices down irresistibly and disastrously. In a month stock values dropped by 40 percent, and in three years, from 1929 to 1932, the average value of fifty industrial stocks traded on the New York Stock Exchange dropped from 252 to 61. In these same three years 5,000 American banks closed their doors.

The crisis passed from finance to industry, and from the United States to the rest of the world. The export of American capital came to an end. Americans not only ceased to invest in Europe but sold the foreign securities that they had. This pulled the foundations from under the postwar revival of Germany and hence indirectly of much of Europe. Americans, their incomes falling, ceased to buy foreign goods; from Belgium to Borneo people saw their American markets slip away, and prices tumbled. In 1931 the failure of a leading Vienna bank, the *Creditanstalt*, sent a wave of shivers, bankruptcies, and business calamities over Europe. Everywhere business firms and private people could not collect what was owed them, or even draw on money that they thought they had in the bank. They could not buy, and so the factories could not sell. Factories slowed down

or closed entirely. Between 1929 and 1932, the latter year representing the depth
of the depression, world production is estimated to have declined by 38 percent,
and the world's international trade fell by two-thirds. In the United States the
national income fell from $85 billion to $37 billion.

Unemployment, a chronic disease ever since the war, assumed the proportion
of pestilence. In 1932 there were 30 million unemployed persons statistically
reported in the world; and this figure did not include the further millions who
could find work only for a few hours in the week, or the masses in Asia or Africa
for whom no statistics were to be had. The worker's wages were gone, the
farmer's income now touched bottom; and the decline of mass purchasing power
forced more idleness of machinery and more unemployment. People in the prime
of life spent years out of work. Young people could not find jobs or establish
themselves in an occupation. Skills and talents of older people grew rusty.
Millions were reduced to living, and supporting their families, on the pittances of
charity, doles, or relief. Great modern cities saw an outburst of sidewalk art, in
which, at busy street corners, jobless able-bodied men drew pictures on the
pavement with colored chalk, in the hope of attracting a few sixpence or dimes.
People were crushed in spirit by a feeling of uselessness; months and years of
fruitless job hunting left them demoralized, bored, discouraged, embittered,
frustrated, and resentful. Never had there been such waste, not merely of
machinery which now stood still, but of the trained and disciplined labor force
on which all modern societies were built. And people chronically out of work
naturally turned to new and disturbing political ideas.

Reactions to the Crisis

Optimists at the time, of whom President Herbert Hoover in the United States
was one, declared that this depression, though a severe one, was basically only
another periodic low point in the business cycle, or alternation of expansion and
contraction, which had ebbed and flowed in the Western world for over a century.
Prosperity, they blithely said, was "just around the corner." Others felt that the
crisis represented the breakdown of the whole system of capitalism and free
private enterprise. These people, in many cases, looked for signs of the future in
the planned economy then being introduced in the U.S.S.R. There was something
in both views. After 1932, in part for purely cyclical reasons—because the
depression cut down indebtedness and reduced the costs of doing business—it
again became possible to produce and sell. World steel production, for example,
which had stood at 121 million tons in 1929, and then collapsed to 50 million in
1932, by 1936 again reached 122 million. To a considerable degree, to be sure,
revival was due to rearmament. On the other hand, the Great Depression did put
an end to the old economic system in the old sense. Even if such a stricken
economy had internal powers of full recuperation after a few years, people would
not stand for such terrifying insecurity in their personal lives. The horrors of
mass unemployment were long remembered.

All governments took steps to provide work and incomes for their people. All,
in one way or another, strove to free themselves from dependency on the
uncertainties of the world market. The interlocking world economy collapsed
both from the depression itself and from the measures adopted to cure it. The

most marked economic consequence of the depression was a strong movement toward economic nationalism—toward greater self-sufficiency within the sphere which each government could hope to control.

The internationalism of money, the gold standard, and the free convertibility of currencies one into the other were gradually abandoned. Countries specializing in agricultural exports were among the first to be pinched. Agricultural prices were so low that even a large quantity of exports failed to produce enough foreign currency to pay for needed imports; hence the exporting country's currency fell in value. The currencies of Argentina, Uruguay, Chile, Australia, and New Zealand all depreciated in 1929 and 1930. Then came the turn of the industrial countries. England, as the depression went on, could not sell enough exports to pay for imports. It had to pay for imports in part by sending gold out of the country; thus the gold reserve supporting the pound sterling declined, and people who had pounds sterling began to convert their pounds into dollars or other currencies for which they thought the gold basis was more secure. This was known, in the poetic language of economics, as the "flight from the pound." In 1931 Great Britain went off the gold standard, which is to say that it devalued the pound. But after Britain devalued, some twenty-odd other countries, to protect their own exports and their own industries, did the same. Hence somewhat the same relative position reappeared. Even the United States, which possessed most of the world's gold supply, abjured the gold standard and devalued the dollar in 1934. The purpose was mainly to help American farmers, for with dollars cheaper in terms of foreign currencies, foreigners could afford to buy more American agricultural products. But it became harder for foreigners to sell to the United States.

Hence the depression, adding its effects to those of the World War and postwar inflation, led to chaos in the international monetary exchanges. Governments manipulated their currencies to uphold their sagging exports. Or they imposed exchange controls: they required that foreigners from whom their own people purchased, and to whom they thus gave their own currency, should use this currency to buy from them in return. Trade, which had been multilateral, became increasingly bilateral. That is, where a Brazilian importer of steel, for example, had formerly bought steel wherever he wished, at such price or of such quality as he preferred, he now had to obtain steel, often regardless of price or precise quality, from a country to which Brazil had sold enough of its own products to make payment possible. Sometimes, notably in the relations between Germany and east-European countries in the 1930s, bilateralism degenerated into actual barter. The Germans would exchange a certain number of cameras with Yugoslavia in return for a certain number of pigs. In such cases the very conception of a market disappeared.

Currency control was one means of keeping one's own factories from idleness, by holding or capturing export markets in time of depression. Another way of keeping one's own factories going (or farms, or mines, or quarries) was to shut out competitive imports by the old device of protective tariffs. The United States, hit by depression in 1929, enacted the unprecedentedly high Hawley-Smoot tariff in 1930. Other countries, equally or more distressed, now could sell less to America and hence buy less American goods. Other countries likewise raised their own tariffs, in the desperate hope of reserving national markets for their own people. Even Great Britain, citadel of free trade in the nineteenth century, turned to protectionism. It also revived and adopted Joseph Chamberlain's old idea of an imperial tariff union, when in 1932, by the Ottawa agreements, Britain and the British dominions adopted a policy of having lower tariffs against one another than against the world outside.[39]

Even tariffs were not always enough. Quotas or quantitative restrictions were adopted in many states. By this system a government said in effect not merely that goods brought into the country must pay a high tariff duty, but that above a certain amount no goods could be brought in at all. Increasingly both importers and exporters worked under government licenses, in order that a country's entire foreign trade could be centrally planned and managed. Such methods approached those of the Soviet Union, which asserted a government monopoly of all foreign trade, exported only in order to finance imports, and determined, without the bother of tariffs, the exact quantity of imported commodities that it would take.

Thus the world economy disintegrated into fiercely competing national economic systems. In the oceanic wreckage of the Great Depression, each state tried to create an island of economic security for its own people. Some efforts were made to break down the rising barriers. An International Monetary and Economic Conference, meeting in London in 1933, attempted to open the clogged channels of world trade; it ended in failure, as did attempts to stablilize the exchange rates of various currencies. Soon thereafter, the wartime Allies defaulted on their debt payments to the United States.[40] Legislation in Congress then denied them the right to float bonds, or obtain new loans, in the American securities market. American actions thus reinforced economic nationalism. The era that had opened with Woodrow Wilson's dream of international economic cooperation was ending with an unprecedented intensification of economic rivalry and national self-centeredness; it was only one of the promises of the postwar world to be blasted by the Great Depression.

[39] See p. 649.
[40] See pp. 720, 725–726, 786–787.

XIX.
DEMOCRACY
AND
DICTATORSHIP

IN THE 1920s, people in a general way believed that the twentieth century was realizing all those goals summed up in the idea of progress; in the 1930s, they began to fear that "progress" was a phantom, to speak the word self-consciously with mental quotation marks, and to be content if only they could prevent a relapse into positive barbarization and a new world war.

The Great Depression ushered in the nightmare of the 1930s. Everywhere the demand was for security. Each nation tried to live economically, so far as possible, within itself. Each regulated, controlled, guided, planned, and tried to rescue its own economic system, attempting to be as little influenced as possible by the unpredictable behavior of other countries, or by the free rise and fall of prices in an uncontrolled world market. Within each country the same search for security encouraged the advancement of the welfare state and social democracy. Where democratic institutions were strong and resilient, governments took steps to protect individuals against the ravages of unemployment and destitution, and to help guard against future catastrophes. On the other hand, where democratic governments were not well established or taken for granted, which was the case in many countries after the First World War, dictatorship spread alarmingly in the 1930s with the coming of the depression. Democracy was said to be suited only to wealthy or prosperous countries. Unemployed people generally cared far more for economic help, or for promises of economic help, than for any theory of how persons wielding public power should be selected. The cry was for a leader, someone who would act, make decisions, assume responsibilities, get results, inspire confidence, and restore national pride. The Great Depression

Chapter Emblem: A postage stamp featuring Hitler and Mussolini, and reading "Two Peoples, One War," for use in Italian East Africa about 1940.

opened the way for unscrupulous and ambitious political adventurers, for dictators like Adolf Hitler in Germany, whose solution to all problems, economic, political, and international, it turned out, was war.

101. The United States: Depression and New Deal

Profound changes took place in the United States, where the stock market crash of 1929 had precipitated the great economic collapse. In 1932 national income had dropped to less than half of what it had been in 1929; 12 million to 14 million were unemployed. The Republican President Herbert Hoover, elected in 1928 at the floodtide of prosperity, was identified in the public mind with the hard times. Hoover viewed with disfavor any large-scale government intervention, convinced that the business cycle that had brought the depression would in turn bring prosperity, and that once business confidence was restored recovery would begin. His administration did act, proposing for the world economy a one-year suspension of payments on all intergovernmental debts and at home giving financial assistance to banks and railroads, expanding credit facilities, and helping to save the mortgages of some farmers and small home owners. But Hoover would not go further; he opposed immediate direct federal relief to the jobless; veterans seeking payment of their wartime bonuses to tide them over the bad times were ejected from Washington; unemployment, business failures, and farm foreclosures continued. In the election of 1932 the millions of unemployed workers, disheartened urban lower middle classes, and distressed farmers swept the Republican administration from office and elected the first Democratic president since Woodrow Wilson. The new president was Franklin Delano Roosevelt. The combination of recovery, relief, and reform legislation that he inaugurated is known as the New Deal.

The new president embarked on a program of improvisation and experimentation, but with such dispatch and vigor as to generate at once an electric enthusiasm. Within a short time an impressive array of legislation was put through Congress. The program of assistance to farmers, small home owners, and industry initiated under the Hoover administration was expanded so that it was no longer recognizable.

THE ASSEMBLY LINE
by Diego Rivera (Mexican, 1886–1957)
Not all twentieth-century artists have been attracted to pure abstraction or exploration of the unconscious. Among others, social activists and revolutionaries have continued to engage in narrative painting and realistic representation. Diego Rivera was one of the great painters of the Mexican Revolution. Regarded as the greatest living muralist and known also for his Marxist opinions, he was commissioned in 1931 by The Detroit Institute of Arts to decorate the walls of a large new hall. The fragment reproduced here shows part of the assembly line in an automobile plant, with workers of various races working speedily and as a team, while "bourgeois" visitors in the background somewhat stupidly watch and marvel. It was the machine age that Rivera meant to portray, rendering it with a mixture of realism and artistic heightening, and a sense of automatism, movement, and power. Courtesy of The Detroit Institute of Arts.

The government provided financial assistance for the relief of the unemployed and sponsored a broad public works program to absorb the jobless, first by loans to the states for the construction of housing, roads, bridges, and schools, later by a direct federal works program. To meet the financial crisis, the banks were temporarily closed and then reopened under stricter supervision. The dollar was taken off the gold standard and devalued, principally to help the farmers compete in foreign markets. In agriculture the government gave subsidies to farmers who agreed to curtail farm production, even subsidizing the destruction of crops and livestock, so that ruinous surpluses which had been one cause of the agricultural distress might be eliminated. It was a paradox, to be sure, for the government to reduce acreage and destroy agricultural products while city populations were in want. But the administration was endeavoring not only to cope with the immediate situation but to meet the deep-seated agricultural crisis that antedated the depression. Subsequently, farmers received subsidies for devoting part of their land to soil-conserving crops. A Civilian Conservation Corps promoted conservation and reforestation, and relieved unemployment by giving jobs to almost 3 million young people. For industry a National Recovery Administration (the NRA) for a time encouraged business firms to set up voluntary "codes of fair competition," which helped to regulate prices and production.

All these measures were designed to set the ailing capitalist system on its feet again by creating purchasing power and stimulating industrial activity. The major innovation was government spending, or "deficit financing." Although never following any consistent economic philosophy, the New Deal policies indirectly reflected the theories of the British economist John Maynard Keynes. In his earlier writings and in his most famous book, *The General Theory of Employment, Interest, and Money*, published in 1936, he argued that if private investment funds were idle, government funds must be employed to encourage economic activity and to increase purchasing power until such time as private funds flowed again. In order to get money into circulation and to "prime the pump" of industrial production, the government undertook a huge borrowing and spending program. Unorthodox as "deficit financing" was, it seemed to many at the time the only direct and rapid method of preventing economic collapse in a capitalist system. In all these recovery and reform activities the federal government assumed a role that it had hitherto played only in wartime. Alphabetical agencies proliferated; the federal payroll grew; the government debt more than doubled between 1932 and 1940.

From the beginning, some longer-range reform measures were adopted in addition to the recovery measures. To prevent overspeculation and the recurrence of a crash such as that of 1929, a Securities and Exchange Commission was created to regulate the issuance of stock and to supervise the operations of the stock exchange. Bank deposits were guaranteed by federal insurance so that depositors would not lose their lifetime savings. A Tennessee Valley Authority served as a pilot program in flood control, regional economic development, and cheap public power production.

After 1935 the focus shifted to regulation and reform. Sound economic recovery had not been achieved; there were still at least 5 million persons who could not find jobs in private industry. Businessmen who at first had been responsive to the government's leadership now resisted the government's regulation of finance and industry. The Supreme Court declared the NRA and other New Deal measures unconstitutional.

The major New Deal reforms after 1935 were designed to improve the condition of labor and to moderate economic insecurity. A broad national Social Security Act in 1935 provided for unemployment, old-age, and disability insurance. Here the United States was a latecomer. Germany, Britain, and other European countries had had such legislation since before the First World War. A Fair Labor Standards Act established forty hours as a maximum normal workweek and set a minimum hourly wage; child labor was abolished. A third measure, the National Labor Relations (or Wagner) Act, virtually transformed the American industrial scene. For the first time the federal government and the law were solidly aligned on the side of the unions. The new act guaranteed the right of workers to set up and bargain through unions of their choice, outlawed company unions, and prohibited employers from interfering with union organizing or discriminating against union members. Under its aegis the older American Federation of Labor (AFL) was revitalized and a new vigorous Congress of Industrial Organizations (CIO) came into being, which organized workers on an industrywide basis and reached down to unskilled workers in such industries as automobile, steel, textile, maritime, and rubber. Millions never before organized, including women and black workers, became part of powerful labor unions with expanding treasuries. Total union membership rose from about 4 million in 1929 to 9 million by 1940. Militant and conscious of its new strength but hardly touched by revolutionary ideology, American labor chose not to create a third party but to operate within the traditional two-party system.

Other reforms included a tax revision bill, which arranged for steeply graduated income taxes, levies on corporate profits, and the plugging of various corporate tax-evasion loopholes. The New Deal later tried also to reverse the trend toward the concentration of economic power, which it had itself stimulated under the NRA, by an investigation into monopoly and monopoly practices, and a trust-busting campaign. A program of slum clearance and low-cost housing made a start toward providing adequate housing. Aid was given to the tenant farmer and the sharecropper. All this was undertaken to help those whom the president described in 1937 as "one-third of a nation ill-nourished, ill-clad, ill-housed." If the New Deal did not feed, clothe, and house them, or strike at the deeper roots of American poverty, urban decay, and racial discrimination, as many later argued, it at least demonstrated that the national community cared, and it showed the enormous potential for government action along all those fronts.

Government spending and renewed confidence in the soundness of the country's institutions created a slow, gradual, and partial recovery. In mid-1937, however, a recession occurred, i.e., business activity slid backward, when government spending slowed down; the recession did not end until 1938 when government spending was resumed. National income reached $71 billion by 1939, double what it had been at the depth of the depression but still short of 1929. Despite substantial progress, business activity did not regain the high-water mark of June 1929. Resistance from the business community itself may have played a part. The rising public debt, antibusiness pronouncements by the government, heavier corporate and income taxes, and the many concessions to labor undoubtedly frightened off business investments and led to what was called a "sit-down strike" of capital. Some claimed that wage rates had risen too sharply, adding to production costs and therefore discouraging business expansion. The New Deal did much to help economic recovery, but it did not end the depression. Complete recovery, the elimination of unemployment, the full use (and expansion) of the nation's productive capacity had to wait upon the huge war expenditures, by which Depression spending was to be dwarfed. By 1938 or so the New Deal was over; the administration turned its attention from domestic reform to the gathering storm in Europe and the Far East.

The changes were substantial under what some called the "Roosevelt Revolution." Enlarging the role of the federal government as no previous administration had done, the New Deal transformed the noninterventionist state into a social service or welfare state. The government imposed controls on business, entered business itself (as in the TVA), used its powers to redistribute wealth, and introduced a broad social security system. Labor's power and political influence grew. The responsibility of public authority for the social and economic welfare of the people was clearly established. When the Republican party later returned to power, it opposed in principle the further growth of the welfare state and the expanding role of the federal government, but it retained the New Deal reforms, a tacit admission that the New Deal had not intended to destroy capitalism but to revive it.

The New Deal, however, engendered violent feelings, which lingered on. Roosevelt, himself of patrician and well-to-do background, denounced the "economic royalists"; in turn he was called a "traitor to his class." When the Supreme Court declared New Deal measures unconstitutional, he made plans to reorganize and enlarge the court, which aroused more political hostility. Despite vociferous opposition, in the election of 1936 Roosevelt won all but two states, and he was subsequently reelected in 1940 and 1944 (during the wartime emergency, to be sure, and with increasingly smaller majorities) for an unprecedented third and fourth term. A constitutional amendment, adopted in 1951, limited a president to two terms.

Roosevelt's opponents, at the time and later, argued that the New Deal had created an enormous regulatory bureaucracy, expensive and cumbersome, a threat to the freedom and self-reliance of the citizenry. But others contended that despite its waste and inconsistencies, unorthodox financial policies, enlargement of the executive power, and expansion of the bureaucracy, it represented a bold and humanitarian way of meeting the great crisis; it preserved and reaffirmed American faith in its democratic system—at a time when democracy was succumbing elsewhere.

102. Trials and Adjustments of Democracy in Britain and France

British Politics: The 1920s and the Depression

Britain, like the United States, even in the troubles of the depression, remained firmly attached to representative institutions and democratic principles. The Great

Depression aggravated and intensified Britain's older economic difficulties. More dependent on overseas markets than any other people, the British until 1914 had managed to hold their lead, exporting industrial products and capital, selling insurance and other services, and importing foodstuffs. But in the years before 1914 the British were increasingly losing their markets because of the emergence of other economically aggressive industrial nations, the growth of tariff barriers, the development of indigenous textile and other industries in India and elsewhere in the East, the competition of new textile products with British cottons and woolens, and the substitution of new sources of fuel for British coal. The losses were accelerated by the economic disruption of the First World War, the disappearance of many overseas investments, and the postwar disorganization and impoverishment of markets. The rise in tariffs after the war and the customs barriers raised in the new small states of Europe also hurt British exports. After 1918 Britain lived in a world no longer dependent on, or eager for, its manufactures. Britain's very historical primacy as the pioneer industrial country was also a handicap. Both labor and management had become adjusted to older conditions, and the more recently industrialized countries had less antiquated techniques and machinery.

The net result of all this was that in the interwar years, even in times of relative prosperity for the rest of the world, Britain was in depression and suffered severely from unemployment. The unemployment insurance adopted in 1911 was called heavily into play. By 1921 over 2 million unemployed were receiving benefit payments, contemptuously called the "dole" by those who disliked it. Unemployment insurance, an expanded old-age pension system, medical aid, government-subsidized housing, and other social welfare measures helped to relieve economic distress and to prevent any drastic decline in the living standards of British workers. The welfare state was well under way in Britain before the Labour party took office after the Second World War.

The labor unions made a strenuous effort to retain wage gains and other concessions won in wartime. Industry, hard-pressed itself, resisted. This situation reached a climax in 1926 in the coal-mining industry, which was in a particularly bad plight; government subsidies had not helped and even conservative investigators had recommended some form of amalgamation and public management. A strike by the coal miners led to a "general strike" supported by the other British unions; about half of the 6 million organized workers in Britain left their jobs as a token of sympathy and solidarity. But the government declared a state of emergency and made use of army and navy personnel and middle-class volunteers to take over essential services. The strike ended in failure, and even in a setback for the trade unions, which were put under stricter control by the Trades Disputes Act of 1927, a measure that declared all general or sympathy strikes illegal and even forbade the unions from raising money for political purposes.

After the election of 1922, the Labour party displaced the Liberal party as the second of the two great parties of the country and faced the Conservatives as the official opposition.[1] The Labour party could more consistently and more actively champion both labor legislation and bolder measures to deal with Britain's troubled economic state. The Labour party, moreover, which had been no more

[1] See pp. 612–613, 619–621, 640–641.

than a loose federation of trade union and socialist organizations before the war, tightened its organizational structure and, bridging the gap between the trade unionists and the socialists, committed itself in 1918 to a program of socialism. But it was a program of gradualist, democratic socialism operating through customary British parliamentary procedures and hence able to gain the good will of large sections of the middle classes.

Twice, in 1924 and in 1929, Labour governed the country with Ramsay MacDonald as prime minister, in each case as a coalition government. In 1924 Labour proved its moderation. It did no more than extend unemployment relief and inaugurate housing and public works projects; indeed it acted firmly in the face of strikes that broke out. But it aroused opposition when it gave diplomatic recognition to the Soviet Union and pledged a loan to the Soviets for the purchase of British goods. Meanwhile newspapers published the so-called Red (or Zinoviev) letter purporting to be secret instructions for British Labour groups from the head of the Communist International urging preparations for a Communist uprising in Britain.[2] The document's authenticity has never been established, but the Conservatives successfully exploited it and won the election of 1924.

In the election of May 1929, however, Labour's representation almost doubled, and the Conservative representation dropped proportionately. MacDonald again became prime minister. Thus the Wall Street crash and the worldwide depression came while the Labour party government was in office. The effects of the depression were quickly felt. Unemployment, which had hovered about the 1 million mark in 1929, soon approached the 3 million figure. The government expended large sums to supplement the unemployment insurance payments. Gold flowed out of the country, tax receipts declined, the public debt grew. Alarmed by the mounting deficit, MacDonald made plans to introduce a severe retrenchment policy, even to the extent of reducing the "dole" payments. The Labour party was outraged; some of the Labour ministers in his cabinet refused to support him. He was read out of the party, along with those ministers who had gone along with him. MacDonald thereupon formed an all-party coalition cabinet known as the National government, which in an election of 1931 won an overwhelming victory, but it was the Conservative members of the coalition who took a majority of the seats in Parliament.

The new government represented an effort to maintain national unity in the face of economic emergency. Not a single seat in Parliament in the next election in 1931 went to either the Communists or to a British Fascist party organized by Sir Oswald Mosley; in 1935 the Communists won one seat.

The National government coped with the depression chiefly along retrenchment lines, under Ramsay MacDonald from 1931 to 1935, Stanley Baldwin to 1937, and Neville Chamberlain after 1937. In addition to retrenchment and budget balancing, the government encouraged industry to reorganize and rationalize production by providing low-interest loans. Mainly, the government concentrated on the kind of economic nationalist measures that have already been described.[3] As in the United States, despite some recovery from the depths of the depression, none of the steps taken brought full recovery or full employment. Unemployment persisted

[2] See p. 775.
[3] See pp. 802–804.

until military conscription and an expanded armament program absorbed the jobless. The Labour party, partially recovering its strength in the election of 1935, denounced the timid expedients of the Conservatives, whom it held responsible for the apathy and gloom gripping the country.

Britain and the Commonwealth: Imperial Relations

To the older British Empire—India, the crown colonies, protectorates, and spheres of influence—the postwar settlement added a number of League of Nations mandates. British rule in its various forms extended to almost 500 million people, a fourth of the earth's population and land surface. It was principally in Ireland, Egypt, India, and Palestine that the British faced complex imperial problems after the First World War. In Palestine, where the British exercised a League of Nations mandate, Arabs and Jews fought with each other and with Britain. In Egypt, in 1922, Britain, although retaining the right to station some troops there, formally ended the protectorate it had established forty years earlier; but many questions, especially the status of the Sudan, remained unresolved. In India the agitation for national independence, as we have seen, grew more intense. In these areas nothing resembling a solution was arrived at until after the Second World War. In Ireland the independence movement managed to establish a separate republic.

The Irish question had disoriented English politics for forty years.[4] Irish home rule, authorized by Parliament in 1914, was deferred for the duration of the war. Irish nationalists, during the war, accepted German support and rose in rebellion in 1916. After the war, in 1919 and 1920, the Irish Nationalist or Sinn Fein party fought a small but savage war of independence against the British forces known as "Black and Tans." The British blocked independence, but in 1922 recognized the Irish Free State, granting it dominion status. The Protestant majority in Ulster, the northern counties where Presbyterians of Scottish origin had lived for three centuries, preferred to remain outside the Free State and continued to be part of the United Kingdom of Great Britain and Northern Ireland, to the vehement dissatisfaction of the Irish republicans. In 1937 a new constitution for the Irish Free State affirmed the full sovereignty of Ireland (or Eire, as it was called for the next twelve years), the country remaining, however, in the British Commonwealth of Nations. Politics remained unsettled, for the Irish agitated for the annexation of Ulster, conducted tariff wars with a Britain from which they were now cut off, strove to revive Gaelic in place of the English language, and fell into disputes in which Irish moderates were pitted against Irish extremists, the latter perpetrating an occasional assassination, or other outrage, to further their cause. The last formal ties with the British Commonwealth were severed in 1949, when the Republic of Ireland was proclaimed. The Irish continued to claim jurisdiction over Ulster and to support the cause of the Irish Catholic minority there.

As for the dominions, the political status of these areas of white settlement overseas was now more clearly defined than ever before. The dominions—Canada, Australia, New Zealand, and the Union of South Africa—had long pursued their own policies, even levying tariffs against British goods. They had

[4] See pp. 613–614, 641, 710; for developments after 1945, see p. 889.

all joined loyally with Great Britain in the First World War, but all were stirred by a nationalism of their own and desired their independence to be regularized and promulgated to the world. An imperial conference of 1926 defined "dominion status," which was corroborated by the Statute of Westminster of 1931. The dominions became legally equal with each other and with Great Britain. No act passed by the British Parliament could apply to a dominion save by the dominion's own consent. Despite independent policies in economic matters and even in foreign affairs, the bonds between the dominions and Britain were firm; the support of the dominions in the Second World War was to be vital in Britain's survival. After the war the Commonwealth became a larger and even more flexible institution.

France: The 1920s and the Coming of the Depression

When the depression came to France, agitation of fascist type made more headway than in Britain or the United States. Earlier, in the 1920s, France was preoccupied with recovery from the physical destruction of the war, the instability of public finances, and the fear of a resurgent Germany. Immediately after 1919, and for most of the 1920s, the government was run by coalitions of parties of the conservative right, i.e., parties supported by business and financial interests, well disposed toward the army and church, and interested in economy and stability in domestic affairs. For about two years, from 1924 to 1926, the Radical Socialists were in control; this party of the moderate left, whose leader was Edouard Herriot, served as spokesman for the lower classes, the small businessmen and farmers; it advocated progressive social legislation so long as increased taxes were not necessary. Despite its name, a carryover from an earlier era, it was firmly committed to private enterprise and private property; it was staunch in its defense of individual liberties and was fervently anticlerical; sometimes, it seemed, its anticlericalism was a substitute for any more positive program.

Although the Radical Socialists cooperated in parliamentary elections with the Socialists, the other major party of the left, the two parties differed too profoundly on economic policies to preserve stable coalitions. In the 1920s the Socialists, led by Léon Blum, were still recovering from the secession of the more orthodox Marxists who had formed a French Communist party. Both left and right in France shaded off into antidemocratic groups that were hostile to the parliamentary republic. These included the Communists on the left, who sat in parliament and took part in elections; and on the extreme right, royalists of the *Action Française* and other antirepublican organizations, which operated principally outside the Chamber as militant and noisy pressure groups.

The outstanding figure of the moderate conservative right was Raymond Poincaré; it was he who sent troops into the Ruhr in 1923, when the Germans failed to pay reparations; and it was he who now "saved" the franc. The reparations question was extremely important for French finances. The country had undertaken a large-scale reconstruction program to repair the wartime devastation of northern and eastern France, and had counted upon the defeated enemy to pay. When German reparations were not paid as anticipated, the public debt mounted, a balanced budget became impossible, and the franc declined precipitously. The huge war expenditures, heavy loss of foreign investments, notably in Russia, and an outmoded taxation program which invited widespread evasion added to French difficulties. After 1926, when the financial crisis reached a climax, a "national union" ministry under Poincaré inaugurated new taxes, tightened tax collection somewhat, cut down drastically on government expenditures in order to balance the budget, and eventually stabilized the franc—at about one-fifth of its prewar value. The internal debt was thus in effect largely repudiated, to the despair of many bondholders, but the threat of a runaway inflation, like that of the Weimar Republic, was avoided. From 1926 to 1929 the country prospered. New factories, replacing those destroyed in the war, were modern and up to date. The index of industrial production rose; tourists flocked in. As in many other countries, workers did not share proportionately in the prosperity of the 1920s. The unions received a sharp setback when, immediately following the war, a series of strikes of major proportions ended in failure; the unions were also divided between a Communist and non-Communist national confederation; collective bargaining in the country was virtually unknown. The workers were not mollified by a social insurance program adopted by a reluctant parliament, which went into effect in 1930.

The Great Depression came later to France and was less severe than in the United States or Germany. Trade declined. Unemployment and part-time employment increased; at the worst period, in 1935, close to 1 million workers were unemployed; perhaps half of those employed worked part-time. Industrial production, which in 1930 was 40 percent above the prewar level, sank by 1932 back to the 1913 figure. The government displayed the usual pattern of unstable, shifting, short-lived ministries; in 1933 five ministries rapidly succeeded one another (there were some forty all told in the twenty interwar years). The cabinets formed after 1932 followed a policy of retrenchment and economy, and clung to the gold standard. Meanwhile, in Germany Adolf Hitler had become chancellor in 1933; France's domestic difficulties were intensified by mounting international tension.

Depression Ferment and the Popular Front

In the uneasy years of the depression, the latent hostility to the republic came to the surface. Fascist-type "leagues" appeared in open imitation of Italian and German fascist organizations, many obtaining funds from wealthy industrialists; the older *Action Française* and right-wing veterans' associations like Colonel de le Rocque's *Croix de Feu* were also active. The same elements that had been antirepublican, antidemocratic, or monarchist since the French Revolution and which had rallied behind Boulanger and denounced Dreyfus[5] now grew more strident in their attacks on the parliamentary republic.

In 1934 it seemed for a moment that the opportunity awaited by the antirepublican elements had come. A political and financial scandal of the kind familiar in prewar French public life shook the country. A financial manipulator and adventurer with excellent political connections, Stavisky by name, induced the municipal authorities at Bayonne to launch a flotation of worthless bonds. Faced with exposure, he fled and apparently committed suicide; the sensationalist press

[5] See pp. 607–608.

encouraged the rumor that he had been shot by the police to prevent the implication of high-ranking politicians. A clamor went up accusing the government of involvement in the financial scandal. Where elsewhere such an affair would have called only for turning the incumbents out of office, in France it supplied ammunition for those who demanded the end of the republic itself, which was equated with corruption and venality.

The agitation reached a climax in the riots of February 1934. A mob of fascist tendency assembled in the Place de la Concorde, threatened the Chamber, and battled with the police; several were killed and hundreds injured. French liberals and democrats, organized labor, and socialists were outraged by the threat to the republic. The Communists, hostile to the fascist groups, were unfriendly to the government too, but soon, guided by the Comintern, they sensed the danger to the Soviet Union in the event of a French fascist triumph and joined with the antifascists. As elsewhere, in the 1930s the Communists emerged from their sectarian revolutionary isolation, became intensely patriotic, and widened their prestige, influence, and appeal. An impressive labor-sponsored general strike was held a week after the riots. Shortly thereafter, liberals, socialists, and communists drew together in a political coalition that came to be known as the Popular Front, of the kind that was being organized, or advocated, in many countries in the 1930s. It campaigned on a pledge to defend the republic against fascism, to take measures against the depression, and to introduce labor reforms. In the spring of 1936 it won a decisive victory at the polls. The French Socialists for the first time in their history became the leading party in the Chamber; their chief, Léon Blum, long a spokesman for democratic and reformist socialism, became premier of a coalition cabinet of Socialists and Radical Socialists; the Communists, who had increased their representation in the Chamber from 10 to 72 seats, did not join the cabinet but pledged their support.

The Popular Front and After

Blum's Popular Front ministry, although it lasted little more than a year, put through a program of far-reaching legislation. In part, this was due to the Popular Front election program, in part to unforeseen events, for the tremendous enthusiasm generated by the victory led to a spontaneous nationwide wave of "sit-down strikes," which did not subside until Blum pledged a number of immediate reforms.

Parliament in short order passed laws providing for a forty-hour week, vacations with pay, and a collective bargaining law. As in the case of the Wagner Act in the United States, the encouragement given to collective bargaining led to the nationwide signing of collective contracts for the first time in the country's history and to enormous growth in trade union membership, from about 1 million to 5 million in a year's time. Labor's strength grew also when the Communist and non-Communist labor confederations reunited. Other legislation was important too. Steps were taken to nationalize the armaments and aviation industry; the fascist armed leagues were, at least in theory, dissolved; the Bank of France was reorganized and placed under government control to break the power of the "two hundred families." Machinery was established for the arbitration of labor disputes. Aid was given to farmers through price fixing and government purchases of wheat.

As in the United States all these measures aimed at both recovery and reform; Blum spoke openly of his program as a "French New Deal." But French conservatives, and the quasi-fascists to their right, cried revolution; they uttered dark predictions that a French Lenin would follow Blum. They did not conceal their sullen resentment at what had come to pass: the fate of Catholic France in the hands of a leftist, a Socialist, and a Jew. Even salvation by a warrior from outside the country, one who had demonstrated his anti-Bolshevism, would be preferable. They envied the protection given to established interests by Mussolini, and there were those who even muttered "better Hitler than Léon Blum."

The Popular Front reforms, long overdue though they were, came to France at a time when the sands were rapidly running out. While France had a forty-hour week, German arms plants were operating at full capacity. In the shadow of Nazi remilitarization a rearmament program had to be undertaken at the very same time as reform; even moderates argued that the country could not afford both. Opposition from many quarters hindered success. French employers balked at cooperating in the new reforms and tried to pass on rising production costs to the consumer. Labor was disgruntled at the price rises that canceled out its wage gains. Both employers and labor applied the forty-hour week in such a manner that plants were shut down for two days a week instead of operating in shifts, as the law had intended. Nothing could check the flight of gold from the country. Industrial production hardly rose; even in 1938, when it had shown substantial recovery in other countries, it was only 5 percent higher in France than at the depth of the depression. In July 1936 the Spanish Civil War had broken out. The Communists attacked the Blum government for refusing aid to the hard-pressed Spanish Popular Front government across the Pyrenees; Blum, following the lead of Britain and fearing involvement, resisted. In 1937, after a year in office, the Blum government was overthrown by the Senate, which refused to grant it emergency financial powers. The Popular Front coalition rapidly disintegrated. By mid-1938 the Radical Socialists had abandoned their allies on the left, and under Edouard Daladier formed a conservative ministry, whose attention was increasingly occupied by the international crisis. Little remained of the Popular Front, or indeed of the strength of labor, which declined rapidly and exhausted itself further by an unsuccessful general strike in 1938 in protest against nullification of the forty-hour week. For the French worker, 1936 had gone the way of other "great years"; the comfortable classes had been thrown into panic by the social turmoil; internal division and class hatreds had grown sharper. Yet the French democracy, the Third Republic itself, had been successfully preserved and its domestic enemies repulsed, at least for a time.

Western Europe and the Depression

Britain and France, and indeed all western Europe, Europe's "inner zone," never fully recovered from the Great Depression before the Second World War came. When economic expansion later resumed after the war, the interwar years seemed like a deep trough in Europe's economic history. Western Europe barely maintained its old inherited equipment in the depression and was unable to utilize even its existing machinery to capacity. Moreover, as the events of 1929 had clearly shown, Europe's economic dependence on the United States was pronounced, and the U.S.S.R. was becoming an industrial giant. The economic destiny of Europeans in the 1930s was very much in doubt.

There were other signs of decline. The birth rate in western Europe in the 1930s declined to its lowest recorded levels as young people postponed marriage and married people limited the size of their families because of economic and psychological stresses. Birth rates did not run significantly higher than death rates, the population stagnating and growing older. There was a scarcity of men of middle age because of the casualties of the First World War. Politically neither British nor French democratic political leaders were able to cope successfully with the economic dilemmas of the depression era. Nor could the Socialists, who found neither Marxian economics nor class struggle ideas helpful but failed to renew or reinvigorate their own doctrines in any significant way.

103. Italian Fascism

Though they shade into each other imperceptibly, it is possible to distinguish dictatorship from totalitarianism. Dictatorship, an old phenomenon in history, has commonly been regarded as a mere expedient, designed for emergencies and believed to be temporary; at most, it is a theory of government. Totalitarianism, as it arose after the First World War, was not merely a theory of government but a theory of life and of human nature. It claimed to be no expedient but a permanent form of society and civilization, and so far as it appealed to emergency for justification, it regarded life itself as an everlasting emergency. Let us first review the pertinent events in Italy and Germany and then return to the idea of totalitarianism.

The belief widely held in the 1920s that democracy was generally advancing was not deeply disturbed by the failure of Russia or Turkey or China to develop effective parliaments or liberal institutions. These were backward countries, in the throes of revolution; some day, when conditions quieted down, it could be supposed, they would move forward to democracy as known in the West. The first jarring exception to the apparent victory of democracy was furnished by Italy, a country that was an integral part of civilized Europe, one that since 1861 had accepted parliamentary liberalism, but where, in 1922, Benito Mussolini seized control of the government and proclaimed *Fascismo*.

Mussolini, born in 1883, the son of a blacksmith, was a fiery and pugnacious character, who before the war had followed the career of professional revolutionary, left-wing socialist, and radical journalist. He had read and digested such works as Sorel's *Reflections on Violence* and Nietzsche's writings.[6] During the war he turned intensely nationalist, clamored for intervention on the side of the Allies, and demanded the conquest from Austria of *Italia irredenta*, the "unredeemed" Italian lands to the north and across the Adriatic. In the war he rose to the rank of corporal. In March 1919 he organized, mainly from demobilized and restless ex-soldiers, his first fighting band, or *fascio di combattimento*. *Fascio* meant a bunch or bundle, as of sticks; it called to mind the Latin *fasces*, or

[6] See pp. 630, 640.

bundle of rods, carried by the lictors in ancient Rome as a symbol of state power—for Mussolini loved to conjure up ancient glories.

In 1919 Italian glories were dim. Italy had entered the war on the side of the Allies quite frankly for territorial and colonial spoils; the secret treaty of London in 1915 promised the Italians certain Austrian lands and a share in German and Turkish possessions. During the war Italian arms did not especially shine; Italian troops were routed at Caporetto in 1917. Yet Italy lost over 600,000 lives in the war, and the Italian delegates came to the peace conference confident that their sacrifices would be recognized and their territorial aspirations satisfied. They were rapidly disappointed. Wilson refused to honor the provisions of the London secret treaty and other demands of the Italians. Britain and France displayed no eagerness to side with Italy. The Italians received some of the Austrian territories promised to them, but they were given no part of the former German or Turkish possessions as mandates.

After the war Italy, like other countries, suffered from the burden of wartime debt and from acute postwar depression and unemployment. Social unrest spread. In the countryside land seizures took place, not in any significant proportions but enough to spread concern among landowners; tenant farmers refused to pay rents; peasants burned crops and destroyed livestock. In the cities great strikes broke out in heavy industry and in transportation. Some of the strikes turned into sit-down strikes, the workers refusing to leave the plants; demands were raised even for worker control of the factories. Moderate socialist and labor leaders disavowed all such extremism, but left-wing socialists who, as elsewhere, had turned communist and joined the Third International, fanned the existing discontents. Meanwhile, armed bands of young men, most prominent of whom were the Blackshirts or Fascists, brawled with Communists and ordinary workers in the streets. By the late summer of 1920 the strikes and the agrarian unrest had subsided, although violence in the streets persisted.

During the months of turmoil the government refrained from any bold action. The Italian parliamentary system in the prewar years had never functioned impressively nor commanded widespread esteem; now respect for parliament and the weak, shifting, coalition ministries sank even lower. In 1919 the first postwar election was held, under a law that added proportional representation to the universal male suffrage introduced in 1913. The Socialists and a new Catholic Popular, or Christian Socialist, party made an impressive showing. In 1921, in the wake of the postwar disturbances, new elections were held. Liberals and democrats, moderate socialists, and the Catholic Popular party were all returned in large numbers. Mussolini's Fascist movement won 35 of the 500-odd seats. Despite this less than impressive showing (the best ever made by the Fascists in a free election), the Fascist ranks were swelling, in the backwash, as it were, of the postwar unrest.

Mussolini and the Fascists at first went along with the radical tide; they did not disapprove the factory seizures; they inveighed against plutocracy and war profiteers and called for a high levy on capital and profits. But Mussolini, never one to sacrifice opportunity for principles or doctrine, soon came forward with his Fascists as the upholders of national law and order, and hence property; he now pledged battle "against the forces dissolving victory and nation." Although the social agitation subsided, burning itself out on its own, and there had never been any real threat of a Soviet-style revolution, the propertied classes had gone through a great fright; they found comfort in the Fascist movement and were willing to lend it financial support. Patriots and nationalists of all classes rallied to it, as well as the lower middle class, pinched by economic inflation and, as elsewhere, unable to find protection or solace in labor unions or socialist movements. The black-shirted upholders of national order proceeded methodically to administer beatings (and doses of castor oil) to Communists and alleged Communists, to Socialists and Christian Socialists, and to ordinary persons who did not support them; nor did they refrain from arson and murder. Vigilante squadrons, the *squadristi*, broke up strikes, demolished labor union headquarters, and drove from office duly elected Socialist and Communist mayors and town officials. Mussolini reinforced his claim as paladin of law, authority, and order by declaring his loyalty to king and church; a few years earlier he had been a rabid republican and anticlerical.

In October 1922 the "March on Rome" took place. The Blackshirts mobilized for a threatened coup and began to converge from various directions on the capital; Mussolini remained at a safe distance in Milan. The liberal-democratic coalition cabinet had viewed the events of the past two years with disapproval but at the same time with satisfaction that the Blackshirts were serving a useful national purpose by suppressing troublemakers on the left. Now they made belated but ineffectual gestures to save the situation by an effort to have martial law declared; the king refused to approve. The cabinet resigned and Mussolini was named premier. It was all quite legal, or almost so. Indeed Italy was still in form a constitutional and parliamentary government. Mussolini headed only a coalition ministry and received from parliament no more than a year's grant of full emergency powers to restore order and introduce reforms.

But soon it was clear in whose hands power rested. Before the expiration of his emergency powers Mussolini forced through parliament a law providing that any party securing the largest number of votes in an election should automatically receive two-thirds of the seats in the legislature. This was Mussolini's solution to the instability of coalitions and blocs in parliamentary governments like those of Italy and France (and indeed of most other Continental democracies), where a single party hardly ever enjoyed a majority. The two-thirds law was not even necessary. In the 1924 elections, although seven opposition slates appeared, the Fascists, aided by government control of the electoral machinery and the use of *squadristi*, received well over three-fifths of the total vote.

After the elections of 1924 the highly respected Socialist deputy Matteotti publicly exposed hundreds of cases of armed Fascist violence, and of fraud and chicanery. He was murdered by Fascists. There was widespread indignation in the country, and the press clamored for Mussolini's resignation. The opposition parties even seceded from the Chamber, wanting to have nothing to do with such a government. Mussolini, not directly involved in the assassination, expressed a willingness to punish the perpetrators, but he eventually took full responsibility, and moved to consolidate his dictatorship. Within a few years he reduced the Italian parliament to a nonentity, put the press under censorship, destroyed the labor unions, deprived labor of the right to strike, and abolished all political parties except the Fascist party.

Fascism in the 1920s was an innovation which the rest of the world was slow to understand. In his more flamboyant moments Mussolini strutted, stuck out his jaw, and glared ferociously; he jumped through flaming hoops to show his virility and had his chief subordinates do likewise; to the outside world this seemed an odd way of demonstrating fitness for public office. He denounced democracy as historically outmoded and declared that it accentuated class struggle, split people into countless minority parties, and led to selfishness, futility, evasion, and empty talk. In place of democracy he preached the need of vigorous action, under a strong leader; he himself took the title of Leader, or *Duce*. He denounced liberalism, free trade, laissez faire, and capitalism, along with Marxism, materialism, socialism, and class consciousness, which he said were the evil offspring of liberal and capitalistic society. In their place he preached national solidarity and state management of economic affairs, under the same Leader's farseeing and audacious vision. And in fact Mussolini seemed to bring a kind of efficiency; as the saying went, he at least made the trains run on time.

Mussolini introduced, at least in theory, the syndical, or corporative state. This had been discussed in both left- and right-wing circles for many years. Left-wing syndicalism, especially before the First World War, looked to revolutionary labor unions to expropriate the owners of industry and then to assume the direction of political and economic life. A more conservative syndicalism was endorsed and encouraged by the Catholic church, with which, as has been noted in a previous chapter, Mussolini made his peace with the signing of the Lateran accord in 1929.[7] The conservative type looked nostalgically toward a revival of the medieval guilds, or "corporations," in which master and journeymen, employer and employees, had labored side by side in a supposedly golden age of social peace.

The Fascist corporative system really resembled neither, because in it the hand of the state was writ large, something that none of the older corporative doctrines had anticipated. It went through a number of complicated stages, but as it finally emerged in the 1930s, it provided for the division of all economic life into twenty-two major areas, for each of which a "corporation" was established. In each corporation representatives of the Fascist-organized labor groups, the employers, and the government determined working conditions, wages, prices, and industrial policies; and in a national council these representatives were supposed jointly to devise plans for Italy's economic self-sufficiency. In each case the role of government was decisive and the whole structure was under the jurisdiction of the minister of corporations. As a final step, these corporative economic chambers were integrated into the government proper so that in 1938 the old Chamber of Deputies was superseded by a Chamber of Fasces and Corporations representing the corporations and the Fascist party, its members selected by the government and not subject to popular ratification.

None of this was democratic, but this was an improvement over democracy, the Fascists asserted. A legislature in an advanced economic society, they said, should be an economic parliament; it should represent not political parties and geographical constituencies but economic occupations. Organization along such lines would do away with the anarchy and class conflict engendered by free capitalism, which only sap the strength of the national state. Real authority in

[7] See p. 636.

any event rested with the government—the Head of the Government, who settled most matters by decree. In point of fact, social unrest and class conflict were "ended," not by the corporative system as such, but by the prohibition of strikes and lockouts and the abolition of independent labor unions. The corporative system represented the most extreme form of state control over economic life within a framework of private enterprise and a relatively capitalistic economy, that is, one in which ownership continued to rest in private hands. It was the Fascist answer to Western-style democracy and to Soviet proletarian dictatorship. Fascism, said Mussolini, is the "dictatorship of the state over many classes cooperating."

When the depression struck, none of Italy's economic controls availed very much. Mussolini was eager to lay upon the world depression the blame for Italy's continuing economic ills. He turned to a vigorous program of public works and to increasing economic self-sufficiency. A "battle of wheat" was launched to increase food production; progress was made in reclaiming swamp areas in central Italy and in developing hydroelectric power as a substitute for the coal that Italy lacked. Throughout the Fascist era no fundamental reform took place in the position of the peasants. The existing structure of society, which in Italy meant social extremes of wealth and poverty, remained unaltered. Fascism failed to provide either the economic security or the material well-being for which it had demanded the sacrifice of individual freedom. But it undeniably substituted a widespread psychological exhilaration, a feeling that Italy was undergoing a heroic national revival; and after 1935 to support that feeling Mussolini turned increasingly to military and imperialist adventures.

Fascism came to be regarded in other countries as a possible alternative to democratic or parliamentary government, as an actual corrective to troubles whose reality no one could deny. All communists hated it, and so did all socialists, labor leaders, moderate leftists, and idealistic liberals. Wealthier or established people, because of fear of Bolshevism, made more allowances in its favor. In east-European countries, often highly nationalistic, or influenced by disgruntled landowners, or simply unused to settling questions by majority vote, Fascism made a considerable appeal. In the Latin countries, in Spain, Portugal, and France, Mussolini's corporative state found champions and admirers. Sometimes, in Europe and elsewhere, intellectuals spun refined, sophisticated theories about the new order of discipline and authority, forgetting how Mussolini himself with unusual candor had written, "Fascism was not the nursling of a doctrine worked out beforehand with detailed elaboration; it was born of the need for action."

104. Totalitarianism: Germany's Third Reich

The Rise of Adolf Hitler

It was in Germany that Mussolini found his aptest pupil. Born in Austria in 1889, Adolf Hitler did little before the war. He was not an intellectual, like the prewar journalist Mussolini. He was never a socialist, but he fell into a restless and somewhat ignorant type of radicalism. Son of an Austrian customs official, he lost his father at fourteen and his mother a few years later. He dropped out of high school at sixteen and at nineteen came to the great metropolis of Vienna as an art student but was never accepted into the academy to which he sought admission. When the small inheritance left by his parents ran out and a government grant for orphan students ended, he drifted into various menial jobs, occasionally selling a few of his postcard and poster paintings but mainly eking out a marginal existence with hardly any friends, money, or livelihood. The young Hitler did not like what he saw in Vienna: neither the trappings of the Habsburg court, nor the noblemen of eastern Europe who rode by in their carriages, nor the mixed nationalities of the Danubian empire, nor the Vienna worker's attachment to international Marxism, nor above all the Jews, who thanks to a century of liberal influences had become assimilated into the German culture and now occupied many distinguished positions in business, law, medicine, and journalism in the city. He became exceedingly race conscious, like many others in many countries at the time;[8] the youthful Hitler took a special satisfaction in thinking of himself as a pure German of the good old German stock. He became violently anti-Semitic, and he also disliked aristocracy, capitalism, socialism, cosmopolitanism, internationalism, and "hybridization."

His aversion to Austria led him in 1913 to move to Munich, capital of the South German state of Bavaria. Once again he drifted without livelihood except by occasionally selling a few of his watercolors. When the war broke out, he volunteered for the German army. He was a good soldier, serving as a dispatch runner to the front line, and at one point was the victim of a gas attack that temporarily blinded him and injured his vocal cords. Although he rose in rank only to the rough equivalent of corporal, he received important military decorations for his services. For Hitler, as for Mussolini and others, the war was a thrilling, noble, and liberating experience. The average individual, in modern society, led a pretty dull existence. Peace, for many, was a drab routine from which war was an exciting emancipation. Human atoms, floating in an impersonal and unfriendly world, they were stirred by the nationalism which the war aroused into a sense of belonging to, believing in, fighting for something greater than themselves, but which was yet their own. When peace returned, they felt a moral letdown.

When the war ended, Hitler remained for a time on active duty and was transferred to Munich. Bavaria in 1919 was a principal focus of the Communist offensive in central Europe; a Bavarian Soviet Republic even existed for about three weeks until crushed by the federal government in Berlin. The Communist threat made Bavaria a busy center for anticommunist, antisocialist, antirepublican, and antidemocratic agitation of all kinds, and the seat of a disgruntled illiberalism. It swarmed with secret societies and paramilitary organizations led by discontented army officers or others who fitted with difficulty into the new Weimar democracy. Hitler, working with the army's political instruction program which had been created to combat socialist and democratic propaganda among the demobilized veterans and workers and to keep alive a patriotic and military spirit, joined at the army's behest a tiny party called the German Workers' party and soon became its leader. Early in 1920 he proclaimed its 25-point program, the party now calling itself the National Socialist German Workers' party. Thus were born the Nazis,

[8] See pp. 627–628, 636–637, 650, 697, 788–790.

so called from the German way of pronouncing the first two syllables of *National*. Now demobilized, Hitler was fully launched on a career of radical politics.

In earlier pages we have noted the beginnings of the Weimar Republic and the burdens it was compelled to bear from the start—the Versailles peace, reparations, the catastrophic inflation of 1923.[9] Something has been said also of the failure of the republicans to inaugurate the kind of deep social changes that might have democratized the political and social structure of German society and thereby strengthened republican forces. For five years after the war, violence remained sporadic in Germany. Communist agitation continued; but more dangerous, because they attracted more sympathy among the Germans, were the maneuvers of monarchist and antirepublican organizations, which maintained armed bands and threatened uprisings like the Kapp *Putsch* of 1920.[10] (One such private "army" was the Brownshirts or Storm Troopers maintained by the Nazis.) Such bands even resorted to assassination. Thus Walter Rathenau was murdered in 1922; he had organized German production during the war, and in 1922 he was foreign minister, but he had democratic and internationalist inclinations—and was a Jew. Another victim was Matthias Erzberger, a leading moderate politician of the Catholic Center party—he had helped "betray" the army by signing the armistice.

In 1923, when reparations payments were not forthcoming, the French army occupied the Ruhr. A clamor of national indignation swept over Germany. Hitler and the National Socialists, who since 1919 had obtained a considerable following, denounced the Weimar government for shameful submission to the French. They judged the moment opportune for seizing power, and at the end of 1923, in imitation of Mussolini's march on Rome the year before, the Brownshirts staged the "beer hall *Putsch*" in Munich. Hitler jumped on the platform, fired a revolver at the ceiling, and shouted that the "national revolution has broken out." But the police suppressed the disturbance, and Hitler was sentenced to five years in prison. He was released in less than a year; the Weimar democracy dealt mildly with its enemies. In prison he wrote his book, *Mein Kampf (My Struggle)*, a turbid stream of personal recollection, racism, nationalism, collectivism, theories of history, Jew baiting, and political comment. *Mein Kampf* sold widely. The book and the publicity that had accompanied the five-week trial converted Hitler into a political figure of national prominence. The former soldier was not alone in his ideas; no less a person than General Ludendorff, who had distinguished himself in the war,[11] and after the war became one of the most grotesquely unbalanced of the old officer class, gave his warm support to Hitler and even took part in the beer hall *Putsch*.

Beginning in 1924, with the French out of the Ruhr, reparations adjusted, a new and stable currency adopted, and loans from foreign countries, mainly the United States, Germany began to enjoy an amazing economic revival. National Socialism lost its appeal; the party lost members, Hitler was regarded as a charlatan and his followers as a lunatic fringe. All seemed quiet. Then came the Great Depression in 1929. Adolf Hitler, who might have faded out of history, was

[9] See pp. 717–718, 783–787.
[10] See p. 784.
[11] See p. 717.

made by the circumstances attending the depression in Germany into a figure of Napoleonic proportions.

No country suffered more than Germany from the worldwide economic collapse. Foreign loans abruptly ceased or were recalled. Factories ground to a halt. There were 6 million unemployed. The middle class had not really recovered from the great inflation of 1923;[12] when struck again, after so brief a respite, they lost all faith in the economic system and in its future. The Communist vote steadily mounted; the great middling masses, who saw in communism their own death warrant, and who are extremely numerous in any highly developed society, looked about desperately for someone to save them from Bolshevism. The depression also stirred up the universal German loathing for the Treaty of Versailles. Many Germans explained the ruin of Germany by the postwar treatment it had received from the Allies—the constriction of its frontiers, the loss of its colonies, markets, shipping, and foreign investments, the colossal demand for reparations, the occupation of the Ruhr, the inflation, and much else.

Any people in such a trap would have been bewildered and resentful. But the way out chosen by the Germans was perhaps a product of deeper attitudes formed by German experience in the past centuries. Democracy—the agreement to obtain and accept majority verdicts, to discuss and compromise, to adjust conflicting interests without wholly satisfying or wholly crushing either side—was hard enough to maintain in any country in a true crisis. In Germany democracy was itself an innovation, which had yet to prove its value, which could easily be called un-German, an artificial and imported doctrine, or even a foreign system foisted upon Germany by the victors in the late war.

Hitler inflamed all such feelings by his propaganda. He denounced the Treaty of Versailles as a national humiliation. He denounced the Weimar democracy for producing class struggle, division, weakness, and wordy futility. He called for "true" democracy in a vast and vital stirring of the people, or *Volk*, behind a Leader who was a man of action. He declared that Germans, pure Germans, must rely only on themselves. He inveighed against Marxists, Bolsheviks, communists, and socialists, throwing them all together in a deliberate beclouding of the issues; but he claimed to favor the right kind of socialism for the little man, i.e., the doctrine of the National Socialist German Workers' party. He ranted against unearned incomes, war profits, the power of the great trusts and chain stores, land speculators, interest slavery, and unfair taxes. Above all, he denounced the Jews. Jews, like others, were found in all political camps. To the left, Jewish capitalists were anathema. To the right, Jewish revolutionaries were a horror. In anti-Semitism Hitler found a lowest common denominator upon which to appeal to all parties and classes. At the same time the Jews were a small minority (only 600,000 in all Germany), so that in an age of mass politics it was safe enough to attack them.

In the election of 1930 the Nazis won 107 seats in the Reichstag; in 1928 they had won only 12; their popular vote went up from 800,000 to 6.5 million. The Communist representation rose from 54 to 77. By July 1932 the Nazis more than doubled their popular vote, won 230 seats, and were now by far the largest single party though because of the multiplicity of parties they fell well short of a majority.

[12] See pp. 786–787.

In another election, in November 1932, the Nazis, though still well out in front, showed some loss of strength, losing 2 million votes, and dropping to 196 seats. The Communist vote had risen progressively to a peak of 100 in November 1932.

After the relative setback of November 1932 Hitler feared that his movement was passing. But certain conservative, nationalist, and antirepublican elements— old aristocrats, Junker landowners, army officers, Rhineland steel magnates, and other industrialists—had conceived the idea that Hitler could be useful to them. From such sources, which supported other reactionary causes as well, came a portion of Nazi funds. This influential group, mainly from the small Nationalist party, imagined that they would be able to control Hitler and hence control the wave of mass discontent of which in such large measure he had made himself the leader; they were little disturbed by his anticapitalist program.

After Bruening's resignation in June 1932, Franz von Papen headed a Nationalist cabinet with the backing of the influential army leader General Kurt von Schleicher. In December 1932 Schleicher forced Papen's downfall and succeeded him. When he, too, was compelled to resign a month later, both men, intriguing separately, prevailed upon President Hindenburg to name Hitler chancellor of a coalition cabinet. On January 30, 1933, by entirely legal means, Adolf Hitler became chancellor of the German Republic; other positions in the new cabinet were occupied by the Nationalists, with whom the Nazis were to share power. But to share power was not their aim. Hitler called for another election. A week before election day the Reichstag building caught fire. The Nazis, without any real evidence, blamed it on the Communists. They frightened the population with a Red scare, suspended freedom of speech and press, and set loose the Brownshirts to bully the voters. Even so, in the election, the Nazis won only 44 percent of the vote; with their Nationalist allies, they had 52 percent. Hitler, trumpeting a national emergency, was voted dictatorial powers by a pliant Reichstag from which the Communist deputies had been excluded. The Nazi revolution now began.

The Nazi State

Hitler called his new order the Third Reich. He declared that, following on the First Reich, or Holy Roman Empire, and the Second Reich, or empire founded by Bismarck, the Third Reich carried on the process of true German history, of which, he said, it was the organic outgrowth and natural culmination. The Third Reich, he prophesied, would last a thousand years.

Like Mussolini, Hitler took the title of Leader, or, in German, the *Führer*. He claimed to represent the absolute sovereignty of the German people. Jews were considered un-German. Democracy, parliamentarianism, and liberalism were stigmatized as "Western" and together with communism labeled as "Jewish." The new "racial science" classified Jews as non-Aryans[13] and included as Jewish anyone who had one Jewish grandparent. Almost at once Jews were driven from public office, the civil service, teaching, and other professions. The Nuremberg laws of 1935 deprived Jews of all citizenship rights and forbade intermarriage or even sexual relations between Jews and non-Jews. On November 9, 1938,

[13] See note, p. 11.

Kristallnacht, the "night of broken glass," the anti-Semitism of Nazi Germany turned to fierce violence. When a seventeen-year-old Polish-Jewish student, distraught by the mistreatment of his parents, shot and killed a German diplomatic official in the German Embassy in Paris, Nazi storm troopers in a savage orgy of vandalism, looting, and incendiarism smashed Jewish shops, businesses, and synagogues in German cities, beat up thousands of Jews, and rounded up 30,000 to be sent to concentration camps. Party and government leaders moved in to control the storm troopers and to use anti-Semitism for their own purposes. The government levied a billion-mark fine on the Jewish community for provoking the assault and collected the insurance payments for the shattered glass and other property damage. Jews who in the wake of these events belatedly tried to flee the country discovered that neither they nor their families could readily find places of refuge; the doors in Europe and the United States were for the most part closed to them. The events of 1938 in Germany still resembled an older-style pogrom, but they foreshadowed the state-organized systematic destruction, in the Holocaust, of six million East European (and German) Jews in the grisly death camps.[14]

The new totalitarian order was thought of as absolutely solid, or monolithic, like one huge single slab of rock in which no particle had any separate structure. Germany ceased to be federal; all the old states such as Prussia and Bavaria were abolished. All political parties except the National Socialists were destroyed. The Nazi party was itself violently purged on the night of June 30, 1934, when many of the old Brownshirt leaders, those who represented the more social revolutionary wing of the movement, were accused of plotting against Hitler and were summarily shot. A secret political police, the Gestapo (*Geheime Staatspolizei*), together with People's Courts, and a system of permanent concentration camps in which thousands were detained without trial or sentence, suppressed all ideas at variance with the Leader's. Law itself was defined as the will of the German people operating in the interests of the Nazi state. Churches, both Protestant and Catholic, were "coordinated" with the new regime; their clergy were forbidden to criticize its activities, international religious ties were discouraged, and efforts were made to keep children out of religious schools. The government encouraged anti-Christian pagan movements, in worship of the old Teutonic gods, but nothing was sponsored so much as worship of Nazism and its *Führer*. A Nazi Youth Movement, and schools and universities, indoctrinated the rising generation in the new concepts. The total, all-encompassing repression thwarted the efforts of a few dedicated Germans to develop a broad resistance movement.

Labor unions also were "coordinated"; they were replaced by a National Labor Front. Strikes were forbidden. Under the "leadership principle" employers were set up as small-scale *Führers* in their factories and industries and given extensive control, subject to close government supervision. An extensive public works program was launched, reforestation and swamp drainage projects were organized, housing and superhighways were built. A vast rearmament program absorbed the unemployed and within a short time unemployment disappeared. Even under Nazi statistics labor's share in the national income was reduced, but workers had jobs; and an organization called Strength Through Joy attended to

[14] See p. 859 and map, p. 858.

the needs of people with small incomes, providing entertainment, vacations, and travel for many who could never otherwise afford them.

The government assumed increasing controls over industry, while leaving ownership in private hands. In 1936 it adopted a Four-Year Plan of economic development. All countries after the Great Depression tended to economic nationalism, but Nazi Germany set up the goal of autarchy and self-sufficiency—absolute independence from foreign trade. German chemists developed artificial rubber, plastics, synthetic textiles, and many other substitute products to enable the country to do without raw materials imported from overseas. Germany took advantage of its position as the chief market on which east Europeans were dependent. Mixing political threats with ordinary business, the Nazis bartered for Polish wheat, Hungarian lumber, or Romanian oil, often giving in return such articles as it was convenient for Germany to dispose of, rather than those that the east Europeans wanted.

For Europe as a whole one of the basic economic problems, especially after the World War, was that while the Continent was economically a unit dependent on exchange between diverse regions, politically it was cut to pieces by tariff restrictions, currency differences, and hothouse industries artificially nurtured by nationalist ambition. The Nazis claimed to have a solution for this problem in a network of bilateral trade agreements assuring all neighboring peoples an outlet for their products. But it was a solution in which Germans were to be the most industrial, most advanced, most powerful, and most wealthy, and other Europeans relegated to permanently inferior status. And what could not be accomplished under trade agreements and economic penetration could be accomplished by conquest and war. Within a few years after 1933, although the regime had its share of bureaucratic confusion and personal rivalries, the Nazi revolution had turned Germany into a huge disciplined war machine, its internal foes liquidated or silenced, its mesmerized masses roaring their approval in giant demonstrations, ready to follow the Führer in storming new Valkyrian heights. "Today Germany," went an ominous phrase, "tomorrow the whole world."

Totalitarianism: Some Origins and Consequences

Totalitarianism was a many-sided thing. It had appeared first with the Bolshevik Revolution, for in the denial of individual liberty the Soviet regime did not differ from the most extreme anti-Soviet totalitarianism as manifested in Germany. (Although Mussolini was the first to use the term "totalitarian," and advance it as an ideology, the Fascist regime that he established was probably not sufficiently all-encompassing to merit that term.) There were at first important differences in principle. Theoretically, the proletarian dictatorship was temporary; it did not glorify the individual Leader-Hero; and it was not nationalistic, for it rested on a principle of worldwide class struggle in all nations alike. It adopted a democratic-sounding constitution and paid at least lip service to individual rights. Its constitution officially condemned racism, and it did not deliberately and consciously cultivate an ethics of war and violence. But as time passed, Soviet totalitarianism became harder to distinguish from others. The Soviet dictatorship and one-party state seemed as permanent as any political system; the hollowness of the constitution and the guarantee of individual rights became more apparent; a cult developed around the person of Stalin; and the emphasis became more nationalistic, falling less on the workers of the world and more on the glories of the Soviet Fatherland.

Totalitarianism, as distinct from mere dictatorship, though it appeared rather suddenly after the First World War, was no historic freak. It was an outgrowth of a good deal of development in the past. The state was an institution that had continuously acquired new powers ever since the Middle Ages; step by step, since feudal times, it had assumed jurisdiction over law courts and men at arms, imposed taxes, regulated churches, guided economic policy, operated school systems, and devised schemes of public welfare. The First World War had continued and advanced the process.[15] The twentieth-century totalitarian state, mammoth and monolithic, claiming an absolute domination over every department of life, now carried this old development of state sovereignty to a new extreme. For centuries, for example, the state had clashed with the church. The twentieth-century dictators did the same. In addition, however, they were in most cases not merely anticlerical but explicitly anti-Christian, offering, or rather imposing, a "total" philosophy of life.

This new philosophy drew heavily upon a historic nationalism which it greatly exaggerated. It derived in part from the organic theory of society, which held that society (or the nation or state) was a kind of living organism within which the individual person was but a single cell. Individuals, in this theory, had no independent existence; they received life itself, and all their ideas, from the society, people, nation, or culture into which they were born and by which they were nurtured. In Marxism, the absolute subordination of individuals to their class came to much the same thing. Individuals were a microscopic cell, meaningless outside the social body. They were but clay to be molded by the imprint of their groups. It made little sense, given such theories, to speak of the individual's "reason" or "freedom," or to allow individuals to have their own opinions (which were formed for them by environment), or to count up individual opinions to obtain a merely numerical majority. Valid ideas were those of the group as a whole, of the people or nation (or, in Marxism, the class) as a solid block. Even science was a product of specific societies; there was a "Nazi science" which was bound to differ in its conclusions from democratic bourgeois, Western, or "Jewish" science; and for the Soviets there was a Soviet science, consistent with dialectical materialism, and better equipped to see the truth than the decadent bourgeois, capitalistic, or "fascist" science of the non-Soviet world. All art, too—music, painting, poetry, fiction, architecture, sculpture—was good art insofar as it expressed the society or nationality in which it appeared.

The avowed philosophy of totalitarian regimes (like much modern thought) was subjective. Whether an idea was held to be true depended on whose idea it was. Ideas of truth, or beauty, or right were not supposed to correspond to any outer or objective reality; they had only to correspond to the inner nature, interests, or point of view of the people, nation, society, or class that entertained such ideas. The older concepts of reason, natural law, natural right, and the

---

[15] See pp. 718–722.

ultimate alikeness of all mankind, or of a common path of all mankind in one course of progress, disappeared.[16]

The totalitarian regimes did not simply declare, as a dry finding of social science, that peoples' ideas were shaped by environment. They set about shaping them actively. Propaganda became a principal branch of government. Propaganda was hardly new, but in the past, and still in the democratic countries, it had been a piecemeal affair, urging the public to accept this or that political party, or to buy this or that brand of coffee. Now, like all else, it became "total." Propaganda was monopolized by the state, and it demanded faith in a whole view of life and in every detail of this coordinated whole. Formerly the control of books and newpapers had been mainly negative; under Napoleon or Metternich, for example, censors had forbidden statements on particular subjects, events, or persons. Now, in totalitarian countries, control of the press became frighteningly positive. The government manufactured thought. It manipulated opinion. It rewrote history. Writers were required to present whole ideologies, and books, newspapers, magazines, and the radio diffused an endless and overwhelming cloud of words. Loudspeakers blared in the streets, gigantic blown-up photographs of the Leader looked down in public places. The propaganda experts were sometimes fanatics, but often they were cynics like Dr. Goebbels in Germany, too intelligent to be duped by the rubbish with which they duped their country.

The very idea of truth evaporated. No norm of human utterance remained except political expediency—the wishes and self-interest of those in power. No one could learn anything except what the government wanted people to know. No one could escape the omnipresent official doctrine, the insidious penetration of the very recesses of the mind by ideas planted by outsiders for their own purposes. People came to accept, and even to believe, the most extravagant statements when they were endlessly repeated, year after year. Barred from all independent sources of information, having no means by which any official allegation could be tested, the peoples of totalitarian countries became increasingly in fact, and not merely in sociological theory, incapable of the use of reason.

Racism, more characteristic of Nazi Germany than of totalitarianism in general, was a further exaggeration, or degradation, of older ideas of nationalism and national solidarity. It defined the nation in a tribal sense, as a biological entity, a group of persons possessing the same physical ancestry and the same or similar physical characteristics. Anti-Semitism was the most venomous form of racism in Europe. While a latent hostility to Jews had always been present in the Christian world, modern anti-Semitism had little to do with Christianity. It arose in part from the fact that, in the nineteenth century, with the general removal of religious disabilities, the Jews entered into general society and many of them achieved positions of prominence, and especially so in Germany, so that from the point of view of any individual non-Jew they could be represented as dangerous competitors in business or the professions. But most of all, anti-Semitism was inflamed by propagandists who wished people to feel their supposed racial purity more keenly or to forget the deeper problems of society, including poverty, unemployment, and economic inequities.

For totalitarianism was an escape from the realities of class conflict. It was a

[16] See pp. 308–309, 312, 315, 325–327, 371–372, 473–474, 584, 637.

way of pretending that differences between rich and poor were of minor importance. Typically, a totalitarian regime came into power by stirring up class fears, then remained in power, and represented itself as indispensable, by declaring that it had settled the class problem. Thus Mussolini, Hitler, and certain lesser dictators, before seizing office, pointed alarmingly to the dark menace of Bolshevism; and, once in power, declared that all classes stood shoulder to shoulder in slablike solidarity behind the Leader. Nor were events in Russia (or in China after the Second World War) altogether different. The Bolsheviks in 1917, armed with the ideas of Karl Marx, aroused the workers against capitalists, landlords, middle-class people, and rich peasants; then, once in power and after extensive liquidations, they declared that the classless society had arrived, that no true social classes any longer existed, and that all citizens stood solidly behind a regime from which, they said, all good citizens benefited equally. Only the democracies admitted that they suffered from internal class problems, from maladjustments between rich and poor or between favored and unfavored groups in society.

The dictatorships blamed their troubles on forces outside the country. They accused dissatisfied persons of conspiring with foreigners or refugees—with being the tools of Trotskyism, imperialism, or international Jewry. Or they talked of the struggle between rich nations and poor nations, the "have" and the "have not" countries, and thus transformed the problem of poverty into an international struggle. In the distinction between "have" and "have not" countries there was, of course, more than a grain of truth; in more old-fashioned language some countries (in fact the European democracies, as well as the United States and the British dominions of the 1930s) had "progressed" farther than others. It is probable that any propaganda is more effective if partly true. But when the totalitarians blamed their troubles on other countries and transformed the conflict between "have" and "have not" into a struggle between nations, they gave the impression that war might be a solution for social ills.

Violence, the acceptance and even glorification of violence, was indeed the characteristic most clearly distinguishing the totalitarian from the democratic systems. We have seen how a cult of violence, or belief that struggle was beneficial, had arisen before the First World War.[17] The war itself habituated people to violence and direct action. Lenin and his followers showed how a small group could seize the helm of state under revolutionary or chaotic conditions. Mussolini in 1922 taught the same lesson, with further refinements; for the Italy in which he seized power was not at war, and it was merely the threat or possibility of revolution, not revolution itself, that provided him with his opportunity. In the 1920s, for the first time since the seventeenth century, some of the most civilized parts of Europe, in time of peace, saw private armies marching about the country, bands of uniformed and organized ruffians, Blackshirts or Brownshirts, who manhandled, abused, and even killed law-abiding citizens with inpunity. Nor would anyone in the 1920s have believed that, by the 1930s, Europe would see the reintroduction of torture.

The very ethics of totalitarianism was violent and neopagan. It borrowed from Nietzsche and other prewar theoreticians, who, safe and civilized, had declared

---

[17] See pp. 640–641.

that men should live dangerously, avoid the flabby weakness of too much thought, throw themselves with red-blooded vigor into a life of action. The new regimes all instituted youth movements. They appealed to a kind of juvenile idealism, in which young people believed that by joining some kind of squad, donning some kind of uniform, and getting into the fresh air they contributed to a great moral resurgence of their country. Young men were taught to value their bodies but not their minds, to be tough and hard, and to regard mass gymnastics as patriotic demonstrations. Young women were taught to breed large families without complaint, to be content in the kitchen, and to look with awe upon their virile mates. The body cult flourished while the mind decayed. Especially in National Socialism the ideal was to turn the German people into a race of splendid animals, pink-cheeked, Nordic, and upstanding. Contrariwise, euthanasia was adopted for the insane and was proposed for the aged. Later, in the Second World War, when the Nazis overran eastern Europe, they committed Jews to the gas chambers, destroying some 6 million human beings by the most scientific methods. Animals were animals; one bred the kind one wanted and killed the kind one did not.

The Spread of Dictatorship

The trend toward dictatorship spread in Europe in the 1930s. By 1938 only ten out of twenty-seven European countries remained democratic, in the sense that different political parties honestly competed for office and that citizens within generous limits thought and acted as they pleased. They were Great Britain and France; Holland, Belgium, and Switzerland; Czechoslovakia and Finland; and the three Scandinavian countries.

The promise of the early 1920s that constitutional and democratic government would flourish was thwarted. The weakness or absence of a parliamentary or democratic tradition, low education and literacy standards, the hostility of reactionary elements, the fear of Bolshevism, and the dissatisfaction of existing national minorities, all coupled with the economic strains resulting from the Great Depression, contributed to the collapse of the new representative institutions. Apart from the avowedly totalitarian or fascist regimes of Germany and Italy, the new dictatorships and authoritarian systems generally rested on a combination of personal and military power, but several reflected or absorbed some of the ideological features of a generic fascism. In Portugal, Salazar inaugurated a clerical-corporative dictatorship in 1932 that lasted for over four decades. In Austria, Dollfuss fused various right-wing political and military elements into a clerical-fascist "Christian" dictatorship which violently suppressed the Socialists and sought in vain to counter the German threat. In Spain General Franco came to power (after a bloody civil war to be described). In many respects the dictatorships of Latin America under a diversity of caudillos and military juntas, in both origin and character, resembled the European military dictatorships.

The authoritarian regimes were alike in repressing individual liberties, banning opposition parties, and abolishing or nullifying parliamentary institutions. Many borrowed features of fascism, establishing a corporative state, outlawing independent labor organizations, and forbidding strikes; many, like Hungary, Romania, and Poland, instituted anti-Semitic legislation. None went so far in the total coordination of all political, economic, intellectual, and biological activities in a revolutionary mass-based dictatorship as did Hitler's Third Reich.

The acceptance and glorification of violence, it has been noted, was the feature most clearly distinguishing the totalitarian from the democratic systems. War in the Nazi and Fascist ethics was a noble thing, and the love of peace a sign of decadence. (The Soviet regime by its own theory regarded war with non-Soviet powers as inevitable some day, but did not preach it as a positive moral good.) The exaltation of war and struggle, the need for maintaining national solidarity, the habit of blaming foreign countries for social troubles, together with the considerable armaments programs on which the dictatorships embarked, plus the personal ambition and egotistical mania of individual dictators, made the decade of the 1930s a time not only of domestic reaction but of recurrent international crises, of which the last, in 1939, led to war.

XX.
THE
SECOND
WORLD WAR

PEACE IN THE ABSTRACT, the peace that is the mere absence of war, does not exist in international relations. Peace is never found apart from certain conditions; it means peaceable acceptance of given conditions, or peaceable and orderly transformation of conditions by negotiation and agreement. The conditions, in the 1930s, were basically those laid down by the Paris peace conference of 1919—the states recognized, the frontiers drawn, the terms agreed to, at the close of the First World War. In the 1930s neither Germany, Italy, Japan, nor the U.S.S.R. was content with these conditions; they were "revisionist" or dissatisfied powers; and the first three were willing to undertake war itself to make a change. Great Britain, France, and the United States were satisfied powers, expecting no benefit from change in the conditions; but on the other hand they had lost faith in the conditions and were unwilling to risk war for the sake of upholding them. They had made a treaty in 1919 which a dozen years later they were unwilling to enforce. They stood idly by, as long as they could, while the dissatisfied powers tore to pieces the states recognized, the frontiers drawn, and the terms agreed to at the Peace of Paris. From the Japanese invasion of Manchuria in 1931 to the outbreak of European war in 1939, force was used by those who wished to upset international order, but never by those who wished to maintain it.

Chapter Emblem: A pocket watch stopped when the atomic bomb was dropped on Hiroshima, Japan, in 1945.

834

105. *The Weakness of the Democracies: Again to War*

The Pacifism and Disunity of the West

While dictators stormed, the Western democracies were swayed by a profound pacifism, which may be defined as an insistence on peace regardless of consequences. Many people now believed, especially in England and the United States, that the First World War had been a mistake, that little or nothing had been gained by it, that they had been deluded by wartime propaganda, that wars were really started by armaments manufacturers, that Germany had not really caused the war of 1914, that the Treaty of Versailles was too hard on the Germans, that vigorous peoples like the Germans or Italians needed room for expansion, that democracy was after all not suited to all nations, that it took two to make a quarrel, and that there need be no war if one side resolutely refused to be provoked—a whole system of pacific and tolerant ideas in which there was perhaps the usual mixture of truth and misunderstanding.

The pacifism of the West had other roots, most evident in France. About 1.4 million Frenchmen had died in World War I; half of all French males between the ages of 20 and 32 in 1914 had been killed. To the French it was inconceivable that such a holocaust should be repeated. French strategy was therefore defensive and sparing of manpower. If war came, the French expected to fight it mainly in the elaborate fortifications, called the Maginot Line, which they built on their eastern frontier facing Germany, from the Swiss to the Belgian border; to its north the Ardennes forest was to be a barrier to any invader. During the depression France was torn by internal class conflict and by fascist and quasi-fascist agitation.[1] Many French of the right, historically unsympathetic to the republic and seeing, or claiming to see, in such movements as the Popular Front the threat of social revolution, did not conceal their admiration for Mussolini or even for Hitler. Abandoning their traditional role as ardent nationalists, they would do nothing to oppose the dictators. On the other hand, many on the left looked with sympathy upon the Soviet Union. France was ideologically too divided in the 1930s to possess any firm foreign policy, and all elements took false comfort from the supposed impregnability of the French Chinese Wall.

A similar situation, in lesser degree, prevailed in Great Britain and the United States. The loss and bloodshed of the First World War were remembered. It was well known that another world war would be even more horrible; there was an unspeakable dread of the bombing of cities. Typical of the time was a resolution adopted by students at Oxford in 1933 that they would never take up arms for their country under any conditions; peace movements appeared among American college students too. The pull between left and right was felt in England and America. In the 1930s, when any international action seemed to favor either the U.S.S.R. on the one hand, or Hitler and Mussolini on the other, it was hard to establish any foreign policy on a firm basis of national unity. In Britain some members of the upper classes were overtly sympathetic to the fascist dictators,

[1] See pp. 815–817.

or saw in them a bulwark against communism. The government itself tried to be noncommittal; it believed that some means of satisfying or appeasing the more legitimate demands of the dictators might be found. Neville Chamberlain, prime minister after 1937, became the principal architect of the appeasement policy.

The United States government, despite President Roosevelt's repeated denunciation of the aggressors, followed in practice a policy of rigid isolation. Neutrality legislation, enacted by a strong isolationist bloc in Congress in the years 1935 to 1937, forbade loans, export of munitions, and use of American shipping facilities to any belligerent once the president had recognized a state of war in a given area. Many believed that the United States had been drawn into the First World War by such economic involvement. From this American neutrality legislation the aggressors of the 1930s derived great benefit, but not the victims of aggression.

As for the rulers of the U.S.S.R., they were revisionist and dissatisfied in that they did not accept the new frontiers of eastern Europe nor the territorial losses incurred by Russia in the First World War. They resented the *cordon sanitaire* created in 1919 against the spread of Bolshevism, the ring of small states on their borders from Finland to Romania, which were almost without exception vehemently anti-Soviet. They had no fondness for the international status quo nor had they abandoned their long-range revolutionary objectives. But, as Communists and as Russians, they were obsessed by fear of attack and invasion. Their Marxist doctrine taught the inherent hostility of the entire capitalist world; the intervention of the Western Allies in the Revolution and civil wars confirmed their Marxist theory. And long before the Bolshevik Revolution, in the days of Napoleon and earlier, the fertile Russian plains had tempted ambitious conquerors. Resentful and suspicious of the outside world, in the 1930s the men in the Kremlin were alarmed primarily by Germany. Hitler, in *Mein Kampf* and elsewhere, had declared that he meant to obliterate Bolshevism and subordinate large stretches of eastern Europe to Germany.

The Soviets became interested in collective security, in international action against aggression. In 1934 they joined the League of Nations. They instructed Communist parties to work with socialists and liberals in popular fronts.[2] They offered assistance in checking fascist aggressors, signing mutual assistance pacts with France and Czechoslovakia in 1935. But many people fled from the Soviet embrace with a shudder. They distrusted Soviet motives, or they were convinced that the purges and trials of the 1930s had left the Soviets weak and undependable as allies, or they felt that the fascist dictators might be diverted eastward against the Soviets and so spare the Western democracies. Here again, though the Soviet Union was ostensibly willing, no effective coaliton against aggression could be formed.

The March of Nazi and Fascist Aggression

Adolf Hitler perceived these weaknesses with uncanny genius. Determined to wreck the whole treaty system, which most Germans, to be sure, found humiliating, he employed tactics of gradual encroachment that played on the hopes and fears of the democratic peoples. He inspired in them alternating tremors

[2] See p. 775.

of apprehension and sighs of relief. He would rage and rant, arouse the fear of war, take just a little, declare that it was all he wanted, let the former Allies naïvely hope that he was now satisfied and that peace was secure; then rage again, take a little more, and proceed through the same cycle.

Each year he precipitated some kind of emergency, and each time the French and British saw no alternative except to let him have his way. In 1933, soon after seizing power, he took Germany out of the League and out of the Disarmament Conference then taking place. He successfully wooed Poland, long France's ally, and in 1934 the two countries signed a nonaggression treaty. That same year the Nazis of Austria attempted a *Putsch*, assassinated the Austrian chancellor, Dollfuss, and demanded the union of Austria with Germany. The Western powers did nothing. It was Mussolini who acted. Not desiring to see Germany installed at the Brenner Pass, he mobilized large Italian forces on the frontier, discouraged Hitler from intervening openly in Austria, and so preserved the independence of Austria for four more years. In January 1935 a plebiscite was conducted in the Saar by the League of Nations as stipulated under the Versailles treaty. Amidst intense Nazi agitation, the Saar voted for reunion with the Reich. Two months later, in March 1935, Hitler dramatically repudiated those clauses in the Versailles treaty intended to keep Germany disarmed; he now openly built up the German armed forces. France, England, and Italy protested such arbitrary and one-sided denunciation of an international treaty but did nothing about it. Indeed, Great Britain entered into a naval agreement with Germany, to the consternation of the French.

On March 7, 1936, using as his justification the new Franco-Soviet pact, Hitler repudiated the Locarno agreements[3] and reoccupied the Rhineland; i.e., he sent German troops into the German territory west of the Rhine, which by the Treaty of Versailles was supposed to be a demilitarized zone. There was talk in the French government of action, and at this time Hitler might have been checked, for German military strength was still weak and the German army was prepared to withdraw, or at least consult, at signs of resistance. But the French government was divided and unwilling to act without Britain; and the British would not risk war to keep German troops from occupying German soil. The next year, 1937, was a quiet one, but Nazi agitation flared up in Danzig, which the Treaty of Versailles had set up as a free city. In March 1938 German forces moved into Austria, and the union of Austria and Germany, the *Anschluss*, was at last consummated. In September 1938 came the turn of Czechoslovakia and the Munich crisis. To understand it we must first pick up other threads in the story.

Mussolini, too, had his ambitions and required sensational foreign triumphs to magnetize the Italian people. Since 1919 the Italians had been dissatisfied with the peace arrangements. They had received nothing of the former Turkish territories and German colonies that had been liberally parceled out, as mandates, to Great Britain, France, Belgium, Japan, South Africa, Australia, and New Zealand.[4] They had never forgotten the humiliating defeat of Italian forces by Abyssinia at Adowa in 1896.[5] Ethiopia, as Abyssinia was now called, remained

[3] See p. 788.
[4] See p. 725.
[5] See p. 666.

the only part of black Africa (with the exception of Liberia) that was still independent.

In 1935 Italy went to war with Ethiopia. The League of Nations, of which Ethiopia was a member, pronounced the Italian action an unwarranted aggression and imposed sanctions on Italy, by which members of the League were to refrain from selling Italy either arms or raw materials—oil was excepted. The British even gathered large naval forces in the Mediterranean in a show of strength. In France, however, there was considerable sympathy for Mussolini in important quarters, and in England there was the fear that if sanctions became too effective, by refusal of oil or by closure of the Suez Canal, Italy might be provoked into a general war. Mussolini was thus able to defeat Ethiopia in 1936 and to combine it with Italian Somaliland and Eritrea in an Italian East African empire. The Ethiopian Emperor Haile Selassie made futile pleas for further action at Geneva. The League of Nations again failed, as in the case of the occupation of Manchuria by Japan, to provide machinery for disciplinary action against a wayward Great Power.[6]

The Spanish Civil War, 1936–1939

Hardly had the Ethiopian crisis been disposed of, to the entire satisfaction of the aggressor, when an even more serious crisis broke out in Spain. In 1931, after a decade of political disturbance, a rather mild revolution had driven out Alfonso XIII, of the Bourbon family, and brought about the establishment of a democratic Spanish Republic. Old hostilities within the country came to a head. The new republican government undertook a program of social and economic reform. To combat the old entrenched power of the church, anticlerical legislation was enacted: church and state were separated, the Jesuit order dissolved and its property confiscated, and the schools removed from clerical control. The old movement for Catalan independence was somewhat mollified by the grant of considerable local autonomy. To placate the peasantry the government began to break up some of the larger landed estates and to redistribute the land. The government's program was never pushed vigorously enough to satisfy extremist elements, who manifested their dissatisfaction in strikes and uprisings, particularly in industrial Barcelona, the Catalan capital, and the mining areas of the Asturias, but it was radical enough to antagonize the great property owners and the churchmen. After 1933 the government fell into the hands of rightist and conservative parties, who ruled through ineffective and unpopular ministries. An insurrection of the miners in the Asturias was put down with much brutality. Agitation for Catalan independence was repressed.

In February 1936 new elections were held. All groups of the left—republicans, socialists, syndicalists, anarchists, communists—joined in a Popular Front against monarchists, clericals, army officers, other adherents of the old regime, and Falangists, or Spanish fascists. The left won a victory at the polls, and pressed forward with a reform program. In July 1936, a group of military men led an insurrection against the republican government; General Francisco Franco emerged as leader. The parties of the left united in resistance and the whole

---

[6] See p. 799.

country fell into civil war. It was the most devastating war in all Spanish history; over 600,000 human beings lost their lives, and it was accompanied by extreme cruelties on both sides. For nearly three years the republican or loyalist forces held their own before finally succumbing to the insurgents led by Franco, who in March 1939 established an authoritarian, fascist-type rule over the exhausted country.

Spain provided a rehearsal for the greater struggle soon to come. The republican government could legitimately have looked forward to the purchase of arms abroad to suppress the rebellion, but Britain and France were resolved not to let the war expand into a general conflict. They forbade the shipment of war materials to the republican government; even the French Popular Front government put obstacles in the way of aid to the hard-pressed Spanish Popular Front. The United States extended its neutrality legislation to cover civil wars and placed an embargo on the export of arms to Spain. At British and French instigation twenty-seven nations, including all the major European powers, agreed not to intervene or take sides. But the nonintervention policy proved a fiasco. Germany, Italy, and the Soviet Union intervened anyway. The former two supported Franco and denounced the republicans as the tools of Bolshevism, while the U.S.S.R. supported the republic, reinforced the growing strength of the Spanish Communists, and stigmatized the rebels under Franco as the agents of international fascism. Germans, Italians, and Russians sent military equipment to Spain, testing their tanks and planes in battle. The fascist bombings of Guernica, Madrid, and Barcelona horrified the democratic world. The Germans and Italians sent troops (the Italians over 50,000); the Soviets if only for geographical reasons did not send troops but sent technicians and political advisers. Thousands of volunteers of leftist or liberal sympathy, from the United States and Europe, went to Spain to serve with the republican forces. Spain became the battlefield of contending ideologies. The Spanish Civil War split the world into fascist and antifascist camps.

As in the case of Ethiopia, the war in Spain helped bring Germany and Italy together. Mussolini had at first, like others, feared the revival of a militant Germany. He had outfaced Hitler when the latter threatened to absorb Austria in 1934. The Ethiopian war, Italian ambitions in Africa, and a clamorous Italian demand for ascendancy in the Mediterranean, the *mare nostrum* of the ancient Romans, estranged Italy from France and Britain. In 1936, soon after the outbreak of the Spanish Civil War, Mussolini and Hitler came to an understanding, which they called the Rome-Berlin Axis—the diplomatic axis around which they hoped the world might turn. That year Japan signed with Germany an Anti-Comintern Pact, soon ratified by Italy too; ostensibly an agreement to oppose communism, it was actually the foundation for a diplomatic alliance. Each, thus furnished with allies, was able to push its demands with more success. In 1938 Mussolini accepted what he had denied to Hitler in 1934—the German absorption of Austria.

Meanwhile, in 1937, Japan, using as a pretext the firing upon Japanese troops at the Marco Polo Bridge near Peking, launched a brutal full-scale invasion of China and within a short time controlled most of the country. The Chinese could fight on only from the hinterland. The League again ineffectually condemned Japan. The United States refrained from applying its neutrality legislation since no war was officially declared. This made possible the extension of loans to

China, the victim of aggression, but also made possible the purchase by the Japanese of vitally needed scrap iron, steel, oil, and machinery from American industry. The Japanese profited from the tensions in the Western world, which in 1938 were rapidly mounting.

The Munich Crisis: Climax of Appeasement

By annexing Austria in March 1938 Hitler added about 6 million Germans to the Reich. Another 3 million Germans lived in Czechoslovakia.[7] All those who were adults in 1938 had been born under the Habsburg empire. They had never, since 1918, been content with their new position as a minority in a Slavic state and had long complained about various forms of subtle discrimination. There were Polish, Ruthenian, and Hungarian minorities also, and since even the Slovaks had a strong sense of separate identity, there was in actuality no preponderant national majority of any kind. The fact that Czechoslovakia had one of the most enlightened minorities policies in Europe, enjoyed the highest living standard east of Germany, and was the only country in central Europe in 1938 that was still democratic only demonstrated the difficulty of maintaining a multinational state even under the most favorable of conditions.

Czechoslovakia was strategically the keystone of Europe. It had a firm alliance with France, which had repeatedly guaranteed to defend it against German attack, and an alliance with the Soviet Union, which was contingent on the functioning of the French alliance. With Romania and Yugoslavia it formed the Little Entente, upon which France relied to maintain the existing boundaries in that part of Europe. It had a well-trained army, important munitions industries, and strong fortifications against Germany, which, however, were located in precisely the Sudeten border area where the population was almost all German. When Hitler annexed Austria—since Vienna is further east than Prague—he enclosed Czechoslovakia in a vise. From the German point of view it could now be said that Bohemia-Moravia, which was almost a third German anyway, formed a bulge protruding into the German Reich.

The Sudeten Germans of Czechoslovakia, whether Nazis or not, fell under the influence of agitators whose aim was less to relieve their grievances than to promote National Socialism. Hitler fomented their demands for union with Germany. In May 1938 rumors of an imminent German invasion caused the Czechs to mobilize; Russia, France, and England issued warnings. Hitler, not actually intending to invade at that time, was forced to issue assurances but was nevertheless determined to smash the Czechs in the autumn. France and England were appalled by their narrow escape from war. The French were nervous and acquiesced in the leadership of Britain, which in the following months strove to avoid any firm stand that might precipitate war. The Czechs, under pressure from Britain and France, accepted British mediation on the Sudeten issue and in the summer of 1938 offered wide concessions to the Sudeten Germans amounting to regional autonomy, but this was not enough to satisfy Hitler, who loudly proclaimed that the plight of the Germans in Czechoslovakia was intolerable and must be corrected. The Soviets urged a firm stand, but the Western powers had

[7] See pp. 725, 727–730, 779–783, and maps, pp. 470 and 728–729.

little confidence in Soviet military strength and, given the Soviet geographical situation, their ability to render assistance to Czechoslovakia; moreover, they feared that firmness might mean war. They could not be sure whether Hitler was bluffing. He might, if opposed, back down; but it seemed equally likely, or indeed more so, that he was entirely willing to fight. The Western powers discounted intelligence reports of a military-civilian plot to unseat Hitler if, in the event of Western resistance, war broke out over Czechoslovakia.

As the crisis grew in September 1938, the British prime minister, Neville Chamberlain, who had never flown in his life before, flew to Germany twice to sound out Hitler on his terms. The second time Hitler raised his demands so that even the British and French could not accept them. Mobilization began; war seemed imminent. Suddenly, in the midst of the unbearable tension, Hitler invited Chamberlain and Edouard Daladier, the French premier, to a four-power conference at Munich, to be attended by his ally, Mussolini. The Soviet Union and Czechoslovakia itself were excluded. At Munich Chamberlain and Daladier accepted Hitler's terms and then put enormous pressure on the Czech government to yield—to sign its own death warrant. France, urged on by England in an appeasement course that it was only too willing to follow, repudiated its treaty obligation to protect Czechoslovakia, ignored the Soviets who reaffirmed their willingness to aid the Czechs if the French acted, and abandoned its whole system of a Little Entente in the East. The Munich agreement permitted Germany to annex the adjoining fringe of Bohemia in which the majority of the people were Germans. This fringe contained the mountainous approaches and the fortifications, so that its loss left Czechoslovakia militarily defenseless. After promises to guarantee the integrity of what remained of Czechoslovakia, the conference disbanded. Chamberlain and Daladier were welcomed home with cheers. Chamberlain reported that he had brought "peace in our time." Again the democracies sighed with relief, hoped that Hitler had made his last demand, and told themselves that, with wise concessions, there need be no war.

The Munich crisis, with its death sentence to Czechoslovakia, revealed the helpless weakness into which the Western democracies had fallen by 1938. It may be that there was, in fact, little that the French and British could do, at Munich, to save Czechoslovakia. Their countries lagged behind Germany in military preparedness. They were impressed by the might of the German army and air force. Bolder leaders than Daladier and Chamberlain, knowing the state of their own armed forces, would have declined to risk a quarrel. They loved peace and would buy it at a high price, not daring to believe that they were dealing with a blackmailer whose price would always be raised. They suffered, too, from another moral uncertainty; by the very principle of national self-determination, accepted by the victors after the First World War, Germany could argue that it had a right to all that it had hitherto demanded. Hitler, in sending German troops into the German Rhineland, in annexing Austria, stirring up Danzig, incorporating the Bohemian Germans, had only asserted the right of the German people to have a sovereign German state. Moreover, if Hitler could be diverted eastward, enmeshed in a war with Russia, then communism and fascism might destroy each other—so one might hope. Possibly it was one of Hitler's motives, in the Munich crisis, to isolate Russia from the West and the West from Russia. If so, he succeeded well enough.

In the weeks following Munich the international commission set up to arrange the new boundaries worked further injustices on Czechoslovakia, dispensing even with the plebiscites which had been agreed to for disputed areas. Meanwhile the Poles and Hungarians brought forth their demands on the hapless Czechs. The Poles seized the Teschen district; and Hungary, under a German and Italian award, took 7,500 square miles of Slovakia. France and Britain were not consulted and did not seriously protest.

End of Appeasement

The final disillusionment came in March 1939. Hitler marched into Bohemia-Moravia, the really Czech part of Czechoslovakia, which he transformed into a German protectorate. Exploiting Slovak nationalism, he declared Slovakia "independent." Czechoslovakia, merely trimmed down at Munich, now disappeared from the map. Having promised to take only a bite, Hitler swallowed the whole. He then seized Memel from Lithuania and raised demands for Danzig and the Polish Corridor. A horrible realization now spread in France and Britain. It was clear that Hitler's most solemn guarantees were worthless, that his designs were not limited to Germans, but reached out to all eastern Europe and beyond, that he was essentially insatiable, that he could not be appeased. In April 1939 his partner in aggression, Mussolini, took over Albania.

The Western powers now began to make preparations for a military stand. Britain, changing its East European policy at the eleventh hour, gave a guarantee to Poland, and followed that with guarantees to Romania and Greece. That spring and summer the British tried to form an anti-German alliance with the U.S.S.R. But Poland and the Baltic states were unwilling to allow Soviet armies within their borders, even for the purpose of defending themselves against the Germans. The Anglo-French negotiators refused to put pressure on them. Since the Poles, in 1920, had conquered more territory than the Allies had meant them to have,[8] pushing their eastern border well into Byelorussia, almost to Minsk, the Anglo-French scruples seemed to the Soviets unnecessarily delicate. They did not wish the Germans to launch an attack on them from a point as far east as Minsk. They may have thought also that what the French and British really wanted was for the Soviet Union to take the brunt of the Nazi attack. They considered it an affront that the British sent lesser officials as negotiators to Moscow when the prime minister himself had three times flown personally to deal with Hitler. Having quietly undertaken negotiations earlier that spring, the Soviets, on August 23, 1939, openly signed a treaty of nonaggression and friendship with Hitlerite Germany. In a protocol kept secret at the time, it was agreed that in any future territorial rearrangement the Soviet Union and Germany would divide Poland between them, that the Soviet Union would enjoy a preponderant influence in the Baltic states and have its claim to Bessarabia, lost to Romania in 1918, recognized. In return the Soviets pledged to stay out of any war between Germany and Poland, or between Germany and the Western democracies.

The Nazi-Soviet Pact stupefied the world. Communism and Nazism, supposed to be ideological opposites, had come together. A generation more versed in

[8] See pp. 752–753, and map, p. 248.

ideology than in power politics was dumbfounded. The pact was recognized as the signal for war; all last minute negotiations failed. The Germans invaded Poland on September 1. On September 3 Great Britain and France declared war on Germany. The second European war in a generation, soon to be a world war, began.

106. The Years of Axis Triumph

Nazi Europe, 1939–1940: Poland and the Fall of France

The Second World War opened with an assault on Poland. German forces totaling over 1 million men, spearheaded by armored divisions and supported by the massed air power of the *Luftwaffe*, rapidly overran western Poland and subdued the ill-equipped Polish armies. The outcome of the campaign, a spectacular example of *Blitzkrieg*, or lightning warfare, was clear within the first few days; organized resistance ended within a month. The Germans set about to integrate their Polish conquest into the Reich.

Simultaneously, the Soviet Union, acting under the secret clauses of the Nazi-Soviet Pact, moved into the eastern half of Poland two weeks after the German invasion; the territory occupied was roughly equivalent to that lost to Poland in 1920. The Soviets proceeded also to establish fortified bases in the Baltic states—Estonia, Latvia, and Lithuania. Finland resisted Soviet demands. It refused to cede border territories sought by the Russians or to yield military rights within their country. The Soviets insisted; Leningrad, the second major city of the U.S.S.R., lay only twenty miles from the Finnish frontier. When negotiations foundered, the Soviets attacked in November 1939. Finnish resistance was valiant and at first effective, but the small country was no match for the U.S.S.R. Western democratic sympathies were with the Finns; the British and French sent equipment and supplies and planned an expeditionary force. The Soviet Union was expelled from the League of Nations for the act of aggression—the only power ever to be expelled. By March 1940 the fighting was over. Finland had to yield somewhat more territory to the U.S.S.R. than originally demanded but retained its independence.

Meanwhile all was deceptively quiet in the West. The pattern of 1914, when the Germans reached the Marne in the first month of hostilities, failed to repeat itself. The French sat behind their Maginot Line; the British had few troops; the Germans did not stir from behind their Siegfried Line, or West Wall, in the Rhineland. Hardly any air action took place. It was called the "phony war." The Western democracies rejected Hitler's peace overtures after the conquest of Poland but clung to their peacetime outlook. The hope still lingered that somehow a real clash might even yet be averted. During this same strange winter, a cold and bitter one, the Germans put their forces through special training, whose purpose became apparent in the spring.

On April 9, 1940, the Germans suddenly attacked and overran Norway, ostensibly because the British were laying mines in Norwegian waters in an endeavor to cut off German sources of Swedish iron ore. Denmark, too, was overrun, and an Allied expeditionary force with inadequate air strength had to withdraw. Then on May 10, the Germans delivered their main blow, striking at the Netherlands, Belgium, Luxembourg, and France itself. Nothing could stand against the German armored divisions and dive bombers. The Nazi use of massed tanks, though already demonstrated in Poland, took the French and British by surprise. Strategically, the Allies expected the main advance to be in central Belgium, as in 1914, and indeed as in the original German plan, which had been altered only a few months earlier. Hence the French and British sent into Belgium the best-equipped troops they had. But the Germans delivered their main armored thrust, seven divisions, through Luxembourg and the Ardennes forest, long considered by the French General Staff impassable to tanks. In France, skirting the northwestern end of the Maginot Line, which had never been extended to the sea, the German armored divisions crossed the Meuse, drove deep into northern France against confused and ineffective resistance and, racing westward toward the Channel ports, cut off the Allied armies in Belgium. The Dutch, fearful of further air attack on their crowded cities, capitulated. The Belgian king sued for an armistice, and a large part of the French armies surrendered. The British fell back upon Dunkirk and could hope only to salvage their broken forces before the trap closed completely. Fortunately Hitler had halted the advance of his overextended armored divisions. In the week ending June 4 an epic evacuation of over 330,000 British and French troops was successfully executed from the beaches of Dunkirk, under air cover, with the help of all kinds of British vessels, manned in part by civilian volunteers, even though the precious equipment of the shattered army was all but totally abandoned.

In June the German forces drove relentlessly southward. Paris itself was occupied on June 13, Verdun two days later; by June 22 France sued for peace and an armistice was signed.

France, obsessed by a defensive military psychology at the outset of the war, its armies unprepared for mechanized warfare, its government divided, its people split into hostile and suspicious factions, had fallen into the hands of an openly defeatist group of leaders. The fall of France left the world aghast. Everyone knew that France was no longer its former self, but it had still been considered a Great Power, and its collapse in one month seemed inconceivable. Some French, fleeing to England, established a Free French movement under General Charles de Gaulle; others formed a resistance movement in France. The British made the bitter decision to destroy a part of the French fleet anchored in the Algerian harbor of Oran to prevent its falling into enemy hands.

France itself under the terms of the armistice was occupied in its northern two-thirds by the Germans. The Third Republic, its capital now at Vichy in the unoccupied southern third, was transformed by vote of a confused and stunned parliament into an authoritarian regime headed by the eighty-four-year-old Marshal Pétain and the cynical and unscrupulous Pierre Laval. The republic was dead; the very slogan *Liberty, Equality, Fraternity* was banned from official use. Pétain, Laval, and others, claiming that they were acting to shield France from further suffering, proceeded to collaborate with the Nazis and to integrate Vichy France into the "new order" in Europe.[9] The French people had hard choices to make.

[9] See maps, pp. 850–851 and 893.

Some chose to cooperate with the collaborators and the victorious Germans; others chose in a variety of ways to resist; most went about their daily lives waiting out the trying times until the fortunes of war might change.

Mussolini attacked France in June 1940, as soon as it was clear that Hitler had defeated it. Shortly thereafter, he invaded Greece and moved against the British in Africa. The *Duce* tied his own destinies, for good or ill, to those of the *Führer*. Since the Germans were emphatically the senior partner in this combination, since they were on good terms with Franco in Spain, and since the U.S.S.R. was benevolently neutral, they now dominated the European continent. History seemed to repeat itself, in the distant and unreal way in which it ever repeats. The Germans controlled almost exactly the same geographical area as Napoleon. Organizing a new "continental system," they made plans to govern, exploit, and coordinate the resources, industry, and labor of Europe. Not having planned for a long war, and only belatedly mobilizing their resources for a sustained military effort, they intensified the exploitation of their conquered subjects. They impressed millions, prisoners of war or civilians, as slave labor, to work under close control in the German war industries. They garrisoned Europe with their soldiers, creating what they called *Festung Europa*, the Fortress of Europe. In every country they found sympathizers, collaborators, or "quislings"—the prototype was Vidkun Quisling, who had organized a Norwegian Fascist party in 1933 and was Norwegian premier from 1942 to 1945. Once Hitler was at war with the Soviet Union, some Europeans joined Hitler in the crusade against Bolshevism; 500,000 non-Germans fought in the divisions of the Waffen SS.

The Battle of Britain and American Aid

In 1940, as in 1807, only Great Britain remained at war with the conqueror of Europe. After Dunkirk the British awaited the worst, momentarily expecting invasion. Winston Churchill, who replaced Chamberlain as prime minister in May 1940 during the military debacle, rose to the summit of leadership in adversity. To Parliament and the British people he promised nothing but "blood, toil, tears, and sweat." He pledged implacable war against "a monstrous tyranny, never surpassed in the dark, lamentable catalogue of human crime." To the American democracy across the Atlantic he appealed "Give us the tools, and we will finish the job." The United States began to respond.

Since 1939, and even before, the American government had been anything but neutral. Opinion was excitedly divided. One group, called isolationist, opposed involvement in the European war, believing that Europe was hopeless, or that the United States could not save it, or that the Germans would win anyway before America could act, or that Hitler, even if victorious in Europe, constituted no danger to the United States. Another group, the interventionists, urged immediate aid to the Allies, believing that Hitler was a menace, that fascism must be destroyed, or that the Nazis, if they subjugated all Europe, would soon tamper with the Latin American republics. President Roosevelt was an interventionist, convinced that American security was endangered; he tried to unite national opinion by declaring that the United States might openly assist the Allies without itself fighting, by using "measures short of war."

The neutrality legislation of the mid-1930s was amended in November 1939, when the ban on the sale of arms was repealed. Roosevelt described Britain as "the spearhead of resistance to world conquest"; the United States was to be "the great arsenal of democracy." Both were fighting for a world, he said, in which the Four Freedoms were to be secure—freedom of speech, freedom of worship, freedom from want, and freedom from fear. In June 1940, immediately after Dunkirk, the United States sent a small initial shipment of arms to Britain. A few months later the United States gave the British fifty overage destroyers in return for the right to maintain American bases in Newfoundland, the Bermudas, and the British Caribbean islands. In 1941 it adopted Lend-Lease, a policy of providing arms, raw materials, and food to powers at war with the Axis. At the same time, in 1940 and 1941, the United States introduced conscription, built up its army and air force, and projected a two-ocean navy. Plans for joint hemisphere defense were developed with the Latin American republics. To protect its shipping it secured bases in Greenland and Iceland and convoyed Allied shipping as far as Iceland. In October 1941 German submarines sank an American destroyer. It is likely that the Germans, as in 1917, would have eventually provoked war with the United States to stop the flow of aid to their enemies even had war not come from another quarter.

After the fall of France, the Germans stood poised for an invasion of Britain. But they had not calculated on such rapid and easy successes in Europe, they had no immediately practical plan for an invasion, and they needed to win control of the air before a sea invasion could take place. Moreover, there was always the hope, in Hitler's mind at least, that the British might sue for peace, or even become an ally of Germany. The air assault on Britain began that summer and reached its climax in the autumn of 1940. Never until then had any bombing been so severe. But the Germans were unable to win control over the air in the battle of Britain. Gradually the British Royal Air Force fought off the bombers with more success; new radar devices helped detect the approach of enemy planes, as did a remarkable British intelligence operation called Ultra, by which the British (with the help of the Poles) early in the war broke the code of an important German communications device, called Enigma, used for military conversations at the highest level. This crucial intelligence operation was not revealed until many years after the war's end. Although Coventry was wiped out, the life and industry of other cities badly disrupted, and thousands of people killed, 20,000 in London alone, still the productive activity of the country carried on. Nor, contrary to the predictions of air power theorists, did the bombings break the morale of the civilian population.

In the winter of 1940–1941 the Germans began to shift their weight to the east. Hitler set aside the planned invasion of Britain, for which he seems never to have had much enthusiasm anyway. He had already decided, like Napoleon before him, that before committing his resources to an invasion of England he must dispose of the U.S.S.R., a project much closer to his heart.

The Nazi Invasion of Russia: The Russian Front, 1941–1942

The Nazi-Soviet Pact of 1939 which had precipitated the war, like the alliance between Napoleon and Alexander I, was never a warm or harmonious understanding. Both parties probably entered it mainly to gain time. The Soviets gained space as well, pushing their borders westward. Stalin, incredibly, seems to have convinced himself that he could remain uninvolved in the war going on. But he and the Nazis soon began to dispute over eastern Europe. The Soviets, with the Nazis preoccupied by the war, hoped to win complete control over the Baltic and to gain influence in the Balkans as well. They had already occupied eastern Poland and the three Baltic states and won territory from Finland. In June 1940, to the chagrin of the Germans, they quietly sovietized and converted the three Baltic states into member republics of the U.S.S.R. The old German landowning class, the famous "Baltic barons," who had lived there for centuries, were uprooted and were returned to German soil. At the same time, the Soviets seized from Romania the Bessarabian province that they had lost in the First World War and incorporated it, too, as a Soviet republic. The Russians were expanding toward the Balkans, another area of historic Russian interest, and seemed bent on winning control over eastern Europe.

This the Germans viewed with dismay. They wished to reserve eastern Europe for themselves as a counterpart to industrial Germany. Hitler moved to bring the Balkans under German control. By early 1941 he blackmailed or, by territorial concessions, cajoled Romania, Bulgaria, and Hungary into joining the Axis; they became Axis lesser partners and were occupied by German troops; Yugoslavia also was occupied despite resistance by the army and population. Greece, too, was subjugated, the Germans coming to the rescue of Mussolini's hard-pressed troops. Hitler thus barred Soviet expansion in the Balkans and made the Balkan states part of the Nazi new order. The Balkan campaigns delayed his plans, but now, to crush the Soviets, and to gain the wheat harvests of the Ukraine and the oil wells of the Caucasus, the core of the Eurasian "heartland," Hitler struck, and on June 22, 1941, invaded the U.S.S.R. Stalin, ignoring warnings he had received, was caught completely by surprise and momentarily seemed incapable of mounting any kind of defense.

The German army threw 3 million men into Russia along a vast 2,000-mile front. The Russians gave way. One swift moving battle melted into another. By the autumn of 1941 the Germans had overrun Byelorussia and most of the Ukraine. In the north, Leningrad was in a state of siege; in the south, the Germans had entered the Crimean peninsula and were besieging Sebastopol. And toward the center of the vast front, the Germans stood, exhausted, but apparently victorious, within twenty-five miles of Moscow. But the overconfident German forces had not calculated on the stubbornness of Soviet resistance as Stalin recovered from his initial shock, replaced some of his military commanders, and rallied the country to the defense of the Russian motherland. Nor were the Germans prepared to fight in an early and extraordinarily bitter Russian winter, which suddenly descended upon them. A counteroffensive, launched by the Red Army that winter, saved Moscow. Hitler, disgusted and impatient with his subordinates, took over direct command of military operations; he shifted the main attack to the south and began a great offensive in the summer of 1942 directed toward the oil fields of the Caucasus. Sebastopol soon fell; the siege of Stalingrad began. After the failure to take Moscow, Hitler, aware now that the war would not be brief, took steps to mobilize the German economy on a full wartime basis. Germany had been ready for war in 1939 as no other major power had been, but without preparation in depth for a protracted conflict. In the early months of 1942 Hitler found in Albert Speer an organizing genius who, despite all kinds of obstacles from party leaders and government functionaries, coordinated labor and resources in the next two years and tripled armaments production.

1942, the Year of Dismay: Russia, North Africa, the Pacific

A year after the invasion, in the fateful summer of 1942, the German line reached from beleaguered Leningrad in the north, past the western outskirts of Moscow, past Stalingrad on the Volga southward to the Caucasus Mountains; the Germans were within a hundred miles of the Caspian Sea. But the Russians had traded space for time. Though the industrial Don basin and the food-producing Ukraine were overrun, the deliveries of Caucasus oil rendered hazardous and uncertain, the Russians continued to fight; industries were shifted to the new Ural and Siberian cities; and neither the Soviet economy nor the Soviet government was yet struck in a vital spot. A "scorched earth" policy, in which the retreating Russians destroyed crops and livestock, and guerrilla units wrecked industrial and transportation facilities, guaranteed that Russian resources would not fall into the hands of the advancing conqueror.

Simultaneously, late in 1942 the Axis also moved forward in North Africa. Here the desert campaigns started in September 1940 with an Italian eastward offensive from Libya, which succeeded in crossing over into Egypt. The stakes were high—control over Suez and the Mediterranean. At the height of the battle of Britain, Churchill made the decision to send troops and supplies, much needed at home, to North Africa. A British counteroffensive against vastly superior numbers swept the Italians out of Egypt and by early 1941 the British moved deep into Libya. Shortly thereafter the British overran Ethiopia and ended Mussolini's short-lived East African empire. But in North Africa fortunes were fickle. A German elite force, the Afrika Korps under General Rommel, in the spring of 1941 attacked in Libya and drove the British back to the Egyptian frontier. A few months later, once more on the offensive, the British advanced into Libya. Again fortunes shifted. By mid-1942 Rommel had repulsed the British and penetrated Egypt. The British took up a stand at El Alamein, seventy miles from Alexandria, their backs to the Suez Canal. Here they held the Germans.

But it seemed in 1942 that the Axis armies, breaking through the Soviet Caucasus and across the isthmus of Suez in North Africa, might enclose the whole Mediterranean and Middle East in a gigantic vise, and even, moving farther east, make contact with their allies the Japanese, who were at this time penetrating into the Indian Ocean. For the Pacific situation in the latter half of 1941 had also exploded. It was Japan that finally drew the United States into war.

The Japanese, in 1941, had conducted a war against China for ten years. With the war raging in Europe, Japanese expansionists saw a propitious moment to assert themselves throughout east Asia. In 1940 they cemented their alliance with Germany and Italy in a new three-power pact; the following year they concluded a neutrality treaty with the Soviet Union. From the Vichy French the Japanese obtained a number of military bases and other concessions in Indochina. The United States belatedly placed an embargo on the export of such materials as scrap iron and steel to Japan. Hesitating to precipitate any all-out drive of the Japanese toward the Dutch East Indies and elsewhere, the United States still sought some definition of Japanese ambitions in southeast Asia. The new Japanese prime minister, General Hideki Tojo, a staunch champion of the Axis, publicly proclaimed that the influence of Britain and the United States was to be totally eliminated from Asia, but he agreed to send representatives to Washington for negotiations.

At the very time that the Japanese representatives in Washington were carrying on conversations with the Americans, on December 7, 1941, without warning, the Japanese launched a heavy air raid on the American naval base at Pearl Harbor in Hawaii and began to invade the Philippines. Simultaneously, they launched attacks on Guam, Midway, Hong Kong, and Malaya. The Americans were caught off guard at Pearl Harbor; close to 2,500 were killed, the fleet was crippled, and the temporary disablement of the American naval forces allowed the Japanese to roam at will in the western Pacific. The United States and Great Britain declared war on Japan on December 8. Three days later Germany and Italy declared war on the United States, as did the Axis puppet states.

The Japanese, working overland through Malaya, two months later captured Singapore, a British naval base long famous for its supposed impregnability, the veritable Gibraltar of the East. The sinking by air of the British battleship *Prince of Wales*, a feat often pronounced by naval experts to be impossible, added to the general consternation. In 1942 the Japanese conquered the Philippines, Malaya, and the Netherlands Indies. They invaded New Guinea and threatened Australia; they moved into the Aleutians. They streamed into the Indian Ocean, occupied Burma, and seemed about to invade India. Everywhere they found ready collaborators among enemies of European imperialism. They held up the idea of a Greater East Asia Co-Prosperity Sphere under Japanese leadership, in which the one clear element was that the European whites should be ejected. Meanwhile, as noted, the Germans stood at the Caucasus and almost at the Nile. And in the Atlantic, even to the shores of the United States and the American republics, German submarines were sinking Allied ships at a disastrous rate. The Mediterranean was unusable. For the Soviet-Western alliance, 1942 was the year of dismay. Despite Allied naval and air victories in the Pacific, the late summer and autumn of 1942 was the worst period of the war. Few realized, wrote the United States Chief of Staff General George C. Marshall some years later, how "close to complete domination of the world" were Germany and Japan and "how thin the thread of Allied survival had been stretched." That Germany and Japan had no plans to concert their strategy and operations was no small factor in the eventual Allied victory.

EUROPE, 1942

The map shows Europe at the height of Axis military successes during World War II, just before the Soviet victory at Stalingrad and the Western invasion of North Africa. Austria, the Sudetenland, Bohemia-Moravia, Poland, and Alsace-Lorraine were all joined to Hitler's Reich. The Atlantic Coast from southern France to northern Norway was under German military occupation, as was much of Russia almost to the Caspian Sea. Southern Europe from Vichy France to Romania was also occupied or allied. See also the map on pp. 856–857.

ARCTIC OCEAN

ICELAND

Reykjavik

Narvi

Hitler's "Empire"

Allied With Germany

Occupied by the Axis

At War Against the Axis

NORWAY

SWED

Relations between the Axis and Vichy France were governed by the Armistice of June 1940, but Germany occupied the whole of France in November 1942.

FAEROE I.
(Denmark)

SHETLAND I.
(Britain)

Bergen

0   100   200   300 miles

ORKNEY I.

Oslo

Stock

NORTHERN
IRELAND

NORTH
SEA

DENMARK

Copenhagen

ATLANTIC OCEAN

EIRE

UNITED
KINGDOM

Hamburg

Coventry

NETHERLANDS

Elbe R.

London

Rotterdam

Berlin

ENGLISH CHANNEL   Dunkirk

Essen   GERMANY   Bres

BELGIUM   Cologne

Brest

Sedan   LUX.   Nuremburg   SUDETEN-
LAND   BOHEMIA

Paris

Rhine R.   M

Munich   Vienn

FRANCE

SWITZERLAND   AUSTRIA

Vichy

Bordeaux

Toulon

ADRIATIC

Bilbao

PORTUGAL

Madrid

CORSICA
(Vichy France)

ITALY

Lisbon

SPAIN

Barcelona

Rome

Anzio

C

Cass

SARDINIA
(Italy)

Salerno   T

Cadiz

BALEARIC I.
(Spain)

Gibraltar (Britain)

Tangier

Palermo

SPANISH
MOROCCO   Oran

Algiers

Bizerte   SICILY

Casablanca

MEDITERRA   MAL

MOROCCO
(Vichy France)

ALGERIA
(Vichy France)

TUNISIA
(Vichy France)

MEDITERRAN

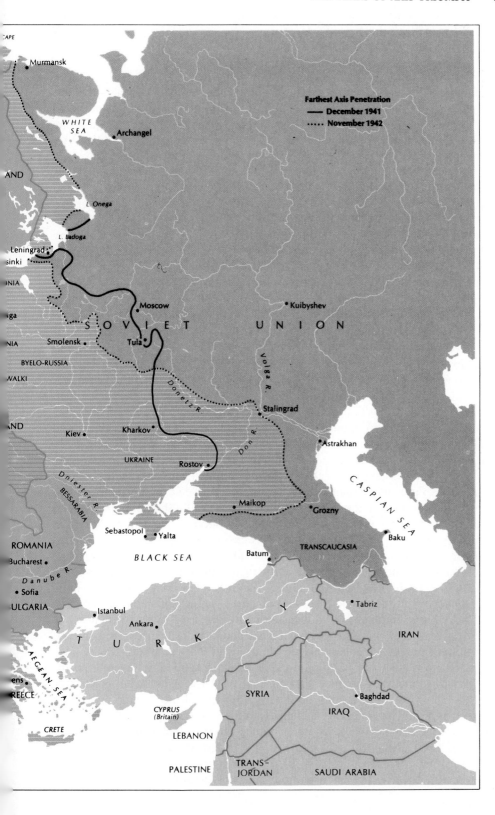

Farthest Axis Penetration
——— December 1941
·········· November 1942

CAPE

Murmansk

WHITE SEA

Archangel

AND

L. Onega

L. Ladoga

Leningrad

sinki

NIA

ga

Moscow

Kuibyshev

S O V I E T   U N I O N

NIA

Smolensk

Tula

BYELO-RUSSIA

Volga R.

WALKI

Donetz R.

Stalingrad

AND

Kiev

Kharkov

Don R.

Astrakhan

UKRAINE

Rostov

CASPIAN SEA

Dniester R.

BESSARABIA

Maikop

Grozny

ROMANIA

Sebastopol

Yalta

Baku

Bucharest

BLACK SEA

Batum

TRANSCAUCASIA

Danube R.

Sofia

BULGARIA

Istanbul

Tabriz

Ankara

T   U   R   K   E   Y

IRAN

AEGEAN SEA

ens

REECE

SYRIA

Baghdad

CRETE

CYPRUS
(Britain)

IRAQ

LEBANON

PALESTINE

TRANS-
JORDAN

SAUDI ARABIA

107. *The Western–Soviet Victory*

Plans and Preparations, 1942–1943

By January 1942 twenty-six nations, including the three Great Powers—Britain, the United States, and the U.S.S.R.—and representing every continent, were aligned against the Axis, a combination to which President Roosevelt gave the name the United Nations. Each pledged to use all its resources to defeat the Axis and never to make a separate peace. The Grand Alliance against the Axis aggressors, which could not be created in the 1930s, had at last been consummated.

The two Atlantic democracies, the United States and Great Britain, pooled their resources under a Combined Chiefs of Staff. Never had any two sovereign states formed so intimate a coalition. In contrast with the First World War an overall strategy was in effect from an early date. It was decided that Germany was the main enemy, against which it was necessary to concentrate first. For the time being the Pacific war was relegated to the background. Australia became the chief base for operations against the Japanese. The American navy and air force soon brought Japanese southward expansion to a halt and frustrated Japanese efforts to cut off supply lines to Australia; naval and air victories were won in the spring of 1942 in the battle of the Coral Sea and at Midway, the only relief to the overall gloom of that period. In the summer American forces landed at Guadalcanal in the Solomon Islands. A long ordeal of "island hopping" began.

In Europe the first point of concentration was an air bombardment of Germany. The Soviet Union, dissatisfied, called for a true "second front," an immediate invasion by ground forces that would relieve the pressure of the German divisions that were devastating their country. Suspicious of the West as ever, they regarded the failure to establish a second front as new evidence of anti-Soviet feeling.

But neither the United States nor Britain, in 1942, was ready to undertake land action by a direct assault on *Festung Europa*. Although in the Second World War, as in the First, more than two years elapsed between the outbreak of war in Europe and the intervention of the United States, and although in the second war American military preparations began much sooner, the United States in 1942 was still involved in the cumbersome processes of mobilization, converting industry to the production of war materials for itself and its Allies, imposing controls on its economy to prevent a runaway inflation, and giving military training to its profoundly civilian-minded people, of whom over 12 million eventually served in the armed forces—over three times as many as in the First World War. Large numbers of women, as in Britain, and more so than in the First World War, took wartime jobs in defense and other industries. (In contrast, almost to the end, Nazi ideology placed obstacles in the way of utilizing women in German factories.) In any case, for a year after the United States entered the war, German submarines enjoyed enough control of the Atlantic to make large shipments of troops too risky. In effect, they blockaded the American army in the United States. The American and British navies gradually won the battle of the Atlantic; the submarine menace was reduced to tolerable proportions by the first part of 1943. The Americans and British decided to begin the assault upon Germany, from Great Britain as a base, with a massive and prolonged air bombardment. Because precision bombardment of factories and other military targets proved difficult either by day or by night, the air assaults became area bombings; German cities were bombed mercilessly and civilians were the largest casualties. In Hamburg in 1943 fires raged on and destroyed most of the city after several days of incessant bombing. Since not everything could be shipped across the Atlantic at the same time, and since the United States and Britain were engaged in war with Japan as well, land invasion had to be deferred until 1944. The embattled Russians questioned whether the Western Allies ever really meant to face the German army at all.

The Turning of the Tide, 1942–1943: Stalingrad, North Africa, Sicily

Meanwhile, at the end of 1942 the tide had begun to turn. In November an Anglo-American force under the command of General Dwight D. Eisenhower effected a surprise invasion of Algeria and Morocco in an amphibious operation of unprecedented proportions. The Allies, failing to win the cooperation of the French in North Africa as they had hoped to do, turned to the Vichy French political leader Admiral Darlan in a calculated act of expediency that brought protest in many quarters. Darlan assisted the Allies in assuming control but was soon assassinated. In the competition that developed in the succeeding months for leadership of the French liberation committee, newly established in Algiers, General de Gaulle, though virtually ignored by President Roosevelt, easily pushed aside all rivals and moved forward with plans for France's revival.

On the Continent, after the North African landings, the Germans took over control of unoccupied France as well; they were frustrated, however, in the effort to seize the remainder of the French fleet when French crews scuttled their ships at Toulon. In North Africa the invading forces fought their way eastward into Tunisia. Meanwhile British forces under General Montgomery, having held the Germans at El Alamein in June 1942, had already launched their third (and final) counteroffensive in October, even before the invasion; they now pushed the Germans westward from Egypt until a large German force was crushed between the two Allied armies and destroyed in Tunisia. By May 1943 Africa was cleared of Axis forces. Mussolini's dream of an African empire had been thwarted; the Mediterranean was open; the threat to Egypt and the Suez Canal was ended.

At the same time it became clear, in the winter of 1942–1943, that the Germans had suffered a catastrophic reversal in the Soviet Union in the titanic battle of Stalingrad. In August 1942 massive German forces, an army of over a quarter million, began an all-out assault on Stalingrad, the vital key to all transport on the lower Volga; by September they had penetrated the city itself. Stalin ordered his namesake city held at all costs; Russian soldiery and the civilian population took a desperate stand. Hitler, still gambling on one big victory, was as obstinate in ordering the city taken. After weeks of fighting the Germans occupied most of the city when suddenly a great Red Army counterattack, led by General Zhukov, trapped the German army, and took a terrible toll; fewer than 100,000 were left to surrender in February 1943. The Soviets followed up their victory with a new counteroffensive, a great westward drive that regained for them what they had initially lost in the first year of the war. After Stalingrad, despite some setbacks, the Soviet Union was on the offensive for the remainder of the war. Stalingrad (or Volgograd as it was later renamed) was a turning point not only in the history of the war but in the history of central and eastern Europe as well.

American equipment meanwhile all through 1943 arrived in the Soviet Union in prodigious quantities. The terms of Lend-Lease were liberally extended to the Soviets; a stream of American vehicles, clothing, food, and supplies of all kinds made its way laboriously to the U.S.S.R. through the Arctic Ocean and through the Persian Gulf. Machinery and equipment were sent for the Soviet arms plants, which were themselves tremendously increasing their output. Anglo-American bombing meanwhile was cutting into German airplane production at home. The Allied contribution to the Soviet war effort was indispensable, but Russian human losses were tremendous. The Soviet Union lost more men in the battle of Stalingrad than the United States lost in combat during the entire war in all theaters combined.

With contemporary American successes in the Solomon Islands at the end of 1942 and the slow throttling of German submarines in the Atlantic, the beginning of the year 1943 brought new hope for the Allies in all quarters. In a spectacular campaign in July–August 1943, the British, Canadians, and Americans conquered the island of Sicily. Mussolini fell; the twenty-one-year-old Fascist regime came to an end. Mussolini set up an "Italian Social Republic" in the north, but it was no more than a German puppet government. (Some months later, in April 1945, the *Duce*, as he attempted to flee the country, was seized, shot, and strung up like a slaughtered pig by anti-Fascist Italians.) When the new Italian government under Marshal Badoglio, in August 1943, tried to make peace, the German army occupied Italy. The Allies, having crossed to the Italian mainland from Sicily, attacked from the south. In October the Badoglio government declared war on Germany, and Italy was recognized by the Allies as a "cobelligerent." But the Germans stubbornly blocked the advance of the Allies to Rome despite new Allied landings and beachheads. The Italian campaign turned into a long and disheartening stalemate because the Western Allies, concentrating troops in Britain for the approaching cross-Channel invasion, could never spare enough for the Italian front.

The Allied Offensive, 1944–1945: Europe and the Pacific

Festung Europa, especially along its western approaches, the coasts of Holland, Belgium, and France, bristled with every kind of fortification that German scientific and military ingenuity could devise. A seaborne attack upon Europe was an operation of wholly unprecedented kind. It differed from the earlier amphibious attacks on Algeria, Sicily, or the Pacific islands in that the defender in Europe, in the very part of Europe where the road and railway network was thickest, could immediately rush overwhelming reserves to the spot attacked— except insofar as feinting tactics kept him uncertain, air power destroyed his transport, or the Russians held the bulk of his forces in the East. Precise and elaborate plans had been worked out. Ten thousand aircraft were to provide aerial protection, scores of warships were to bombard the coast, 4,000 ships were to carry the invading troops and their supplies across the Channel, artificial harbors were to be created where none existed.

The invasion of Europe began before dawn on June 6, 1944. The spot selected was the coast of Normandy directly across the Channel from England; false intelligence reports, planted by the Allies, led the Germans to expect the main thrust at Calais. An unparalleled combination of forces, British, Canadian, and American, land, sea, and air, backed up by huge accumulations of supplies and troops assembled in Great Britain, and the whole under the unified command of General Eisenhower, assaulted the French coast, established a beachhead, and maintained a front. The Allies poured in their strength, over 130,000 men the first day, 1 million within a month. The Germans were at first thrown back more easily than had been expected. By August Paris was liberated, by September the Allies crossed the frontier of Germany itself. In France, Italy, and Belgium the Resistance movements, which had grown up in secret during the years of German occupation, came into the open and drove out Germans and pro-German collaborators. In Germany itself no widespread or deeply rooted Resistance movement ever developed, but a small group of Germans, military and civilian, formed an underground. On July 20, 1944, after the failure of earlier efforts, it attempted to assassinate Hitler by exploding a bomb at his military headquarters in East Prussia; Hitler was only injured and took a fearsome revenge on the conspirators.

In August, in another amphibious operation, the Allies landed on the French Mediterranean coast and swept up from southern France to join the Allied forces advancing against stiffening resistance. At one point, momentarily, the Allied offensive suffered a serious reversal. A sudden German drive under Hitler's direct personal orders in December 1944, unleashed under radio silence to thwart Allied intelligence, was launched against thinly held American lines on the Belgian sector in the Ardennes, created a "bulge" in the advancing armies, and caused heavy losses and confusion. But the Allies rallied, and Hitler used up his armored reserves in the effort. Neither the Ardennes counteroffensive nor the new destructive weapons rained on Britain, jet-propelled flying bombs and rockets, opening up the missile age, availed the Germans. All this time the American and British kept up their massive air bombardments, killing over 50,000 civilians in the fire-bombing of Dresden in February 1945. On the ground they pushed on and smashed through the heavily fortified Siegfried Line. The last natural obstacle, the Rhine, was crossed when in March 1945 American forces by a stroke of luck discovered an undestroyed bridge at Remagen; they poured troops over it and established a bridgehead—the first troops to cross the Rhine in combat since the armies of Napoleon. The main crossing, under the British, subsequently took place farther to the north. Soon the Allies were accepting wholesale surrenders in the Ruhr valley.

Meanwhile in 1944 the Russian armies swept the Germans from the Ukraine, Byelorussia, the Baltic states, and eastern Poland. By August they reached the suburbs of Warsaw. The Polish underground rose against the Germans but the Soviets, determined that Poland not be liberated by noncommunist Polish leadership, refused to permit aid to the rising, and it was crushed, with a heavy loss of Polish lives. The Polish martyrdom was severe. Earlier, the mass graves of 12,000 Polish army officers were found in the Katyn Forest, the evidence indicating, despite Soviet denials, that they were the victims of the retreating Russian armies after the German invasion began. The Russians, their lines overextended, and checked for several months by German strength in Poland, pushed southward into Romania and Bulgaria; both countries changed sides and

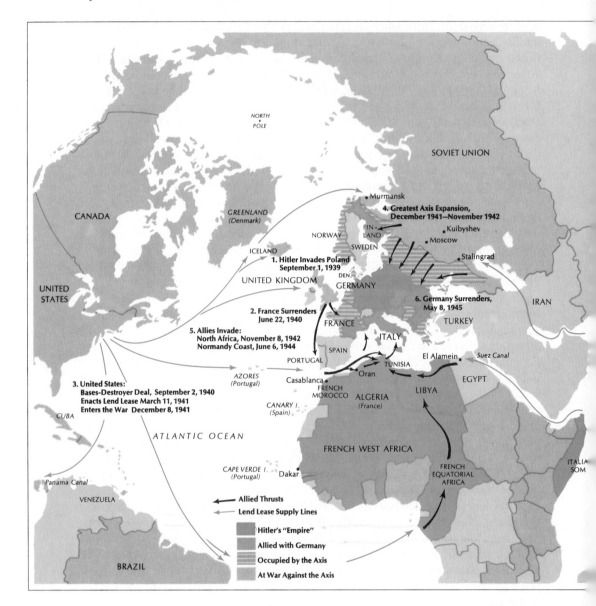

WORLD WAR II

These two maps show the global character of the war and the central position of the United States with respect to the European and Pacific theaters. The numbered legends summarize the successive stages of the war in both the Eastern and Western hemispheres. In 1942, with the Germans reaching as far east as Egypt and Stalingrad, and the Japanese as far west as Burma, the great danger to the Soviet-Western alliance was that these two might join forces, dominate southern Asia, control the oil resources of the Persian Gulf, and stop the flow of Western supplies to the Soviet Union from this direction. The almost

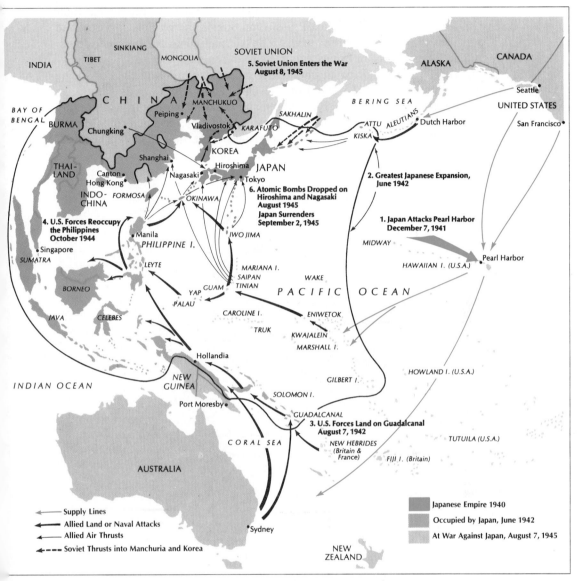

simultaneous Soviet-Western successes, late in 1942, at Stalingrad and El Alamein, and in the invasion of Morocco-Algeria and of Guadalcanal, proved to be the turning point of the war. In 1943 the German submarine campaign in the Atlantic was defeated, so that American troops and supplies could move more freely to Europe. The invasion of Normandy in June 1944, with continuing Soviet pressure from the east, brought about German surrender in May 1945. Meanwhile, in the Pacific, American occupation of the islands and reoccupation of the Philippines prepared the way for the surrender of Japan, consummated by two atomic bombs in August 1945.

declared war against Germany. Early in 1945 the Soviets, reopening their offensive, forced their way into East Prussia and Silesia and by February reached the Oder, forty miles from Berlin, where Zhukov paused to regroup his forces. In March and April Russian forces occupied Budapest and Vienna.

The final drive on Germany began. Hitler moved troops from the collapsing western front to reinforce the stand on the Oder and to protect his capital. In April the Americans reached the Elbe, about sixty miles from Berlin, with hardly any obstacles before them; but here they halted, by decision of General Eisenhower. The Americans, whose supply lines were already overextended,

THE HOLOCAUST

The map shows what the Nazis called their Final Solution, that is, their program of destroying the Jews and Judaism. Before the Second World War most European Jews lived in Poland and the adjoining parts of the Soviet Union which the Germans occupied during the war, so that most of the deaths occurred in these areas. The map shows both the number killed in each country and the percentage of its Jewish population that were victims of this deliberate genocide. The numbers add up to about 6 million men, women, and children, or an estimated two-thirds of the Jewish population of Europe as a whole. Although word of this annihilation policy reached the outside world through the Vatican and other sources, the Allied leaders at first disbelieved the reports, and then, giving priority to their military objectives, did nothing to stop the systematic slaughter.

wanted a clear line of demarcation from the Russians; they also believed it necessary to divert forces southward against a possible German last stand in the Alps. But mainly the decision was made as a gesture of good will toward the Russians, who were to be permitted to take Berlin as compensation for the heavy sacrifice in the common cause, and to preserve the Western-Soviet coalition until final victory. Similarly, the American troops that moved southward were held back from taking Prague and the Soviets were permitted to take the Czech capital too. At the end of the war the Soviets were in control of all the major capitals of central and eastern Europe.

The Western Allies and the Soviets offered no terms to Hitler, nor to any Germans. They demanded unconditional surrender, and the Germans fought on in the very streets of Berlin. On the last day of April Hitler perished by his own hand in the ruins of his capital after denouncing some of his closest party subordinates as traitors. Admiral Doenitz, designated by Hitler as his successor, went through the formalities of surrender on May 8, 1945. Since fighting had already ceased on the Italian front a few days earlier, the war in Europe was over.

Meanwhile a generation reared to mistrust the fabricated atrocity tales of the First World War painfully, and belatedly, became aware of the real German horrors of the Second—hostages rounded up and shot in reprisal for resistance; whole villages like Lidice in Czechoslovakia or Oradour-sur-Glane in France razed to the ground and their inhabitants slain or deported; concentration camps like Dachau and Buchenwald, where the prisoners were given minimal rations and worked to death, and where Allied troops found only pitifully emaciated survivors; above all, the mass death camps with gas chambers and crematory ovens at Auschwitz (where at its peak 12,000 victims a day were gassed to death), Treblinka, Belzéc, Sobibor, and others, where "inferior" peoples could be systematically liquidated. In the areas of Nazi domination in Eastern Europe, the Nazis first used special mobile units to gas "undesirables," but as the war went on they transported millions of men, women, and children in cattle cars to these mass death camps where they were put to death. By far the largest proportion killed were almost 6 million Jews, but Poles, Russians, other Slavic peoples, Gypsies, and others were slain as well. For the Jews in what came to be known as the Holocaust, the annihilation policy, decided upon at a high-level Nazi meeting at Wannsee in January 1942, was to be the "Final Solution" to the "Jewish problem" which Hitler had agitated, with maniacal fury, for so many years. Genocide, the planned, systematic effort to destroy a whole people, was the greatest of the Nazi sins against humanity.

In the Pacific, against Japan, operations had dragged on for three years, hampered by the strategic decision to concentrate against Germany first. Slowly, from points in the Solomon Islands, the easternmost fringe of the Indonesian archipelago, American forces, at first very small, worked their way in a northwest-erly direction toward faraway Japan. They had to fight in turn for Guadalcanal, for New Guinea, for the reconquest of the Philippines. They had to fight for the Japanese islands and atolls in the mid-Pacific (taken by Japan from the Germans after the First World War and converted into powerful naval bases), the Gilbert Islands, the Marshalls, the Carolines, the Marianas. In October 1944 they won a great naval victory at the battle of Leyte Gulf. Finally, in one of the war's greatest and final battles, they won the island of Okinawa, only 300 miles from Japan itself. Okinawa was captured just as the Germans collapsed in Europe. From the new Allied bases that had been won, from Saipan, from Iwo Jima, from Okinawa, and from aircraft carriers a heavy bombing offensive was launched against Japan, such as had devastated Germany in the preceding two years, shattering Japanese industry, destroying the remnants of the Japanese navy, and compelling the Japanese government to give serious thought to suing for peace. The Allied leaders refused to believe that Japanese defenses were ready to crumble or that the Japanese were ready to negotiate. The American army prepared to shift combat troops from the European theater to the Far East. The stage was being set for a full-scale invasion of Japan itself.

Then, on August 6, 1945, an American aircraft dropped an atomic bomb, built in the United States in utmost secrecy by European refugee and American scientists, on the city of Hiroshima, with a population of 200,000 people. The city was destroyed in this single explosion, and 78,000 lives were lost; thousands of others were injured or suffered the long-term effects of radiation. Two days later, the Soviet Union, which had pledged to enter the conflict in the East within three months after the surrender of Germany, declared war on Japan and invaded Manchuria. On August 9 a second atomic bomb struck Nagasaki and killed tens of thousands more. The Japanese made peace at once. On September 2, 1945, the formal surrender was signed. The emperor was permitted to remain as head of state, but Japan was placed under a United States army of occupation.

The Second World War of the twentieth century was over, the greatest conflict in human history. The same cold impersonal statistics that had recorded 10 million killed in the First World War reported 15 million military deaths and (unlike the First World War) twice as many civilian fatalities. Soviet military deaths were estimated at over 6 million (and total deaths at 20 million), German at 3.5 million, Chinese at 2.2 million, Japanese at 1.3 million, Polish at 700,000. British and Commonwealth losses were over 400,000, American about 300,000, French about 200,000. Over 25 million suffered battle wounds. The military death figures would have been higher except that one of every two of those wounded was saved by new sulfa and penicillin drugs and blood plasma transfusions. None of these statistics could be more than approximate, and no one could estimate the complete toll of human lives lost from Allied and Axis bombings, Nazi mass slayings of Jews in the Holocaust and of others, Nazi and Soviet deportation policies, and postwar famines and epidemics. Some estimates place the total at 60 million men, women, and children, but at such figures the human mind retreats and human sensitivities are dulled.

108. The Foundations of the Peace

Whereas the First World War had been concluded by a peace conference a few months after the close of hostilities, the Second World War ended in no such clear-cut settlement. Nothing like the Treaty of Versailles of 1919 followed the defeat of Germany in 1945. The terms of peace, as they gradually developed, left no such single symbol of humiliation as the Versailles treaty had represented.

THE SURVIVOR
by George Grosz (German, then American, 1893–1959)

George Grosz, born in Germany, came to the United States in 1932 to avoid the Nazis. He painted this powerful picture in 1945 at the close of the Second World War. It suggests what is meant by the collapse of civilization. The hideous figure crawling out of the wreckage, according to the artist's own explanation, is insane with fear. He is starving, filthy, abandoned, and alone. In his teeth he desperately clasps a knife, which he will use to fight another terrified survivor, should he meet one, or to hunt for and cut up food. Note the symbolism of a broken swastika in the arrangement of the man's body and the debris. The picture is of course meant to be repulsive, to show the depths to which humanity can be degraded, and so shock people into constructive action. Courtesy of Mrs. Marc J. Sandler.

The peace terms emerged episodically, at first during a series of conferences among the Allied nations during the war, and then in a series of de facto arrangements in the years after 1945.

The foundations of a peaceable postwar world were being laid, it was thought, at a number of meetings where the strategy of the war itself was being planned. In August 1941 Roosevelt and Churchill met at sea off the coast of Newfoundland and drew up the Atlantic Charter. There were meetings in 1943 at Casablanca, at Cairo, and at Teheran (close enough to the Soviet Union for Stalin to participate); and in the final phase of the war, in February 1945, at Yalta, and in July 1945, at Potsdam, in the environs of shattered Berlin.

The Atlantic Charter, issued jointly by Roosevelt and Churchill at their first meeting, resembled in spirit the Fourteen Points of Woodrow Wilson. It pledged that sovereign rights and self-government would be restored to all who had been forcibly deprived of them, that all nations would have equal access to world trade and world resources, that all peoples would work together to achieve improved living standards and economic security. The postwar peace, it promised, would assure people of all lands freedom from fear and want, and end force and aggression in international affairs. Here, and in the Four Freedoms enunciated by President Roosevelt, the ideological basis of the peace was proclaimed. At the 1943 conferences, and through other consultations, the Allies endeavored to concert their military plans. At Casablanca, in January 1943, they resolved to accept nothing less than the "unconditional surrender" of the Axis powers. This vague formula, adopted somewhat cavalierly at American initiative, and without much thought to possible political implications, was intended mainly to prevent a recurrence of anything like the ambiguity surrounding the armistice of 1918.[10] Though much criticized in later years (and not fully applied in the case of Japan), it is doubtful whether the decision had any bearing on the outcome of events. German resistance was stubbornly prolonged because of Hitler's fierce obstinacy and the loyalty of the German military, not because the Allies did not offer suitable peace terms.

At Teheran, in December 1943, Roosevelt and Churchill met with Stalin for the first of two wartime meetings. They discussed the postwar occupation and demilitarization of Germany, laid plans for a postwar international organization, and debated strategy for winning the war. Throughout the war Roosevelt, unwilling to disturb the unity of the Western-Soviet coalition in the global struggle in which America was engaged, followed a policy of postponing controversial territorial and political decisions until victory was assured. Churchill was more apprehensive. Steeped in traditional balance-of-power politics, he sensed that without prior diplomatic bargaining and political arrangements, the victory over the Nazis would leave Russia dominant over all central and eastern Europe. At Teheran he proposed operations in the Mediterranean and an invasion through the Balkans, for political reasons but mainly out of concern for the casualties that a cross-Channel invasion would involve. But Roosevelt persuaded him otherwise. It was agreed that a landing in France would take place in the spring of 1944; thus the major second front that Stalin had been promised would finally be opened. Stalin pledged that he would launch a simultaneous offensive on the eastern front.

[10] See p. 723.

The strategy that would win the war in the next eighteen months was decided upon at Teheran, but that strategy, without political agreements, all but guaranteed the Soviet domination of eastern Europe. Later, in October 1944, as the Russian armies advanced westward, Churchill visited Stalin and sketched out a demarcation of spheres of influence for the Western powers and the Soviets in the Balkan states (a Soviet preponderance in Romania and Bulgaria, a Western preponderance in Greece, and an even division of influence in Hungary and Yugoslavia). Soviet control over the Baltic states had virtually been conceded by the British earlier. But Roosevelt would not agree to any such arrangement, which he considered old-fashioned and a dangerous revival of the worst features of pre-1914 diplomacy.

Soon, however, political decisions had to be made. The two conferences that arrived at the most important political decisions were the meetings at Yalta and at Potsdam in 1945. The Yalta meeting in February 1945 took place when the Allies were close to final victory—closer, events disclosed, than anyone at the time realized. The three Allied statesmen met at an old tsarist Crimean summer resort on the Black Sea, toasted their common triumphs, and, as at Teheran, took the measure of each other. Roosevelt thought of himself as a mediator between Churchill and Stalin where European issues were involved. He took pains to avoid giving Stalin the impression that he and Churchill were in any sense united against him; in point of fact, Roosevelt was suspicious of Churchill's devotion to empire and colonial ties, which he considered anachronistic for the postwar world. Despite differences, the Big Three reached agreements, at least formally, on Poland and eastern Europe, the future of Germany, the war in the Far East, and the projected postwar international organization, the United Nations.

The discussion of Poland and eastern Europe raised the most serious difficulties. Stalin's armies, having driven the Nazi forces to within forty miles of Berlin, were in control of Poland and almost all eastern and central Europe. The Russians remembered these areas as anti-Soviet, and Poland particularly as the perpetrator of aggression against Soviet territory in 1920, and as the ancient corridor of attack upon Russia. Stalin had already taken steps to establish a "friendly" government in Poland, i.e., a government subservient to the Soviets. Neither Roosevelt nor Churchill had fought the war against the Nazis to leave the Soviet Union the undisputed master of central and eastern Europe and in a position to impose a totalitarian political system on all this vast area. At Yalta, Roosevelt and Churchill extracted from Stalin a number of promises for the areas he controlled. In accordance with the Atlantic Charter, the liberated states were to be permitted provisional governments "broadly representative of all democratic elements in the population," i.e., not consisting merely, as in the case of the provisional government of Poland already established, of authorities subservient to the Soviets. They pressed Stalin to pledge also the "earliest possible establishment through free elections of governments responsive to the will of the people." The pledge was a verbal concession that cost the Soviet leader little; he rejected the suggestion of international supervision over the elections. The Declaration on Liberated Europe, promising sovereign rights of self-determination, provided a false sense of agreement.

A number of territorial changes were also accepted, pending final settlement at a postwar peace conference. It was agreed that the Russian-Polish, or eastern, boundary of Poland should be set roughly at the so-called Curzon line, the frontier contemplated by the Allies in 1919 before the Poles conquered territory to their east. The Poles were to be compensated, in the north and west, at the expense of Germany.[11] On this and on other matters relating to Germany there was a large area of accord; the three were united in their hatred of German Nazism and militarism. Germany was to be disarmed and divided into four occupation zones under the administration of the Big Three powers and France—the latter at the insistence of Churchill. There was vague talk, at Yalta and earlier, of dismembering Germany, of undoing the work of Bismarck, but the difficulties of such an undertaking were understood and the proposal was eventually discarded. Also discarded, as impracticable, was the Morgenthau plan, seriously considered as late as 1944, which was designed to transform industrial Germany back into an eighteenth-century pastoral and agricultural economy. The Americans and British rejected as excessive the Soviet proposals for reparations, a sum of $20 billion to be paid in kind, half to the Soviets. It was agreed, however, that reparations would go to those countries that had borne the main burdens of the war and suffered the heaviest losses. The Soviet Union was to receive half of whatever total sum was set.

To the satisfaction of everyone, the participants agreed on plans for a postwar international organization, to be called the United Nations. Roosevelt believed it essential to win the Soviets over to the idea of an international organization. He was convinced that the Great Powers, cooperating within the framework of the United Nations, and acting as international police, could preserve the future peace and security of the world. No less than Stalin or Churchill, he emphasized the importance of the Great Powers in the new organization, although he accepted a dignified role for the smaller nations as well. All agreed that each of the Great Powers, the permanent members of the new organization's Security Council, would have a veto power on important decisions. The Soviets pressed for sixteen votes in the General Assembly of the new organization, arguing that their constitution gave sovereign rights to each of their constituent republics and that the British dominions would each have a seat. In the interests of harmony, at Churchill's behest, they were given three seats.

Critical agreements were reached on East Asia. Here political and military decisions were inextricably linked. The Soviets had remained neutral in the Pacific war despite their historic interests in the Far East. Given the magnitude of the war effort on the European front, no one had pressed them to enter the Pacific war earlier. It was agreed to wait at least until the Germans were on the verge of defeat. At Yalta, Stalin agreed to enter the war against Japan, but Soviet "public opinion," he averred, would demand compensation. The U.S.S.R. would enter the war against Japan "two to three months" after Germany had surrendered. In return, the Soviets were to have restored to them territories and rights that tsarist Russia had lost to Japan forty years before in the Russo-Japanese war of 1904–1905,[12] with the addition of the Kurile Islands, which had never been Russian before. The concessions were the price to be paid for Soviet assistance against

[11] See maps, pp. 248 and 893.
[12] See pp. 681–682 and map, p. 679.

the Japanese, considered indispensable for the final defeat of Japan. What really exasperated so many in later years was that the Soviet Union's entry into the war, as pledged, was not of any military consequence; it came two days after the Hiroshima bomb had been dropped and at a time when the Japanese were in a desperate state, near collapse and surrender, even without the dropping of the atomic bomb. The concessions in the Far East need not have been made. Even without the Yalta agreement, nothing perhaps except outright force could have deterred Stalin from moving into Manchuria after the Japanese collapse (and thereby contributing to the eventual Chinese Communist victory over the Chinese Nationalists), or indeed from controlling central and eastern Europe as he wished. The Yalta agreement, however, lent an aura of respectability to Soviet expansion.

Roosevelt made concessions at Yalta because he believed he needed Soviet support in the last phase of the war against Japan and because he wished to preserve the Western-Soviet coalition until final victory was guaranteed. He believed also that wartime cooperation would produce postwar harmony. Churchill, less sanguine about the future and about "diplomacy by friendship," would have preferred a franker definition of spheres of influence. Such ideas were ruled out as the thinking of a bygone era. Yet the spirit of the Atlantic Charter, so closely identified with the American president, the pledge of sovereign self-determination of all peoples, was already being contravened.

At Potsdam, in July 1945, after the German collapse, the Big Three met again. A new American president, Harry S Truman, represented the United States; President Roosevelt had died in April, on the eve of final victory. Churchill, in the midst of the conference, was replaced by a new British prime minister, Clement Attlee, after the Labour party's victory at the polls. Stalin still represented the Soviet Union. By now, disagreements between the Western Allies and the Soviets had deepened, not only over Soviet control in Poland, eastern Europe, and the Balkans, but over German reparations and other matters. Yet the Western leaders were still prepared to make concessions in the hope of establishing harmonious relations. Agreements were announced on the postwar treatment of Germany, on German disarmament, demilitarization, "denazification," and the punishment of war criminals. It was agreed that each power might take reparations in kind from its occupation zone and that the Russians would get substantial additional deliveries from the Western zones so that the original $10 billion Soviet demand was virtually met.

Pending the final peace treaty, German territory east of the Oder-Neisse rivers was committed to Polish administration. The details of this decision had earlier been postponed; the Polish-German boundary was now set at the western Neisse, even further west than originally envisaged. Poland thus extended its territorial boundaries about a hundred miles westward as compensation for Russian westward expansion at Polish expense. German East Prussia was divided between the Soviet Union in the north and Poland in the south. Königsberg, founded by the Teutonic Knights, for centuries the ducal seat of Prussian dukes and the coronation city of Prussian kings, became the Russian city of Kaliningrad. The ancient German cities of Stettin and Breslau became the Polish cities of Szczecin and Wroclaw. Danzig became Gdansk. The de facto administration of these areas hardened into permanent rule. The transfer of the German population in these eastern areas was supposed to be effected in an orderly and humane fashion; but millions of Germans were driven from their homes or fled within a few months. For them (and for the Germans who were expelled from Czechoslovakia) it was the final consummation of the war that Hitler had unleashed.

The Potsdam participants agreed that peace treaties would be signed as soon as possible with the former German satellite states; the task of preparing them was entrusted to a council of foreign ministers representing the United States, Britain, France, the Soviet Union, and China. In the months that followed, the widening chasm between the Soviets and the West manifested itself in stormy meetings in London, Paris, and New York, as well as in a peace conference held in Paris in 1946, at which were represented the twenty-one states that had contributed substantial military forces to the defeat of the Axis powers. In February 1947, treaties were signed with Italy, Romania, Hungary, Bulgaria, and Finland. All these states paid reparations and agreed to certain territorial adjustments. In 1951 a peace treaty was signed with Japan, but not by the Soviets, who made their own peace in 1956. The years went by but no final peace treaty was signed with Germany, a Germany divided into two. For the wartime Western-Soviet coalition had fallen apart, shattering the dreams and aspirations of those who had fought the Second World War to a resounding triumph over one kind of aggression and totalitarianism, and then found themselves confronted with a new age of crisis.

XXI.
THE POSTWAR ERA:
THE AGE OF THE
SUPERPOWERS

A CATACLYSM, according to Webster's dictionary, is "any violent change involving sudden and extensive alterations of the earth's surface; hence, any upheaval, especially a social or political one." A cataclysm in nature, as we may imagine it, is a time when volcanoes erupt, earthquakes rumble, old mountain systems are broken down, new peaks and ranges thrust themselves upward, the very coastlines assume new shapes, living creatures flee from destruction, old forms of life become extinct, and new forms of life, at first unnoticed, enter upon careers in which they are later to flourish.

The human world has been in the grip of such a cataclysm since 1914. The First World War, the collapse of the old European dynasties, the Russian Revolution, the Great Depression, the Nazi dictatorship, the Second World War, the nuclear bomb, the rise of Communist China, the end of the European colonial empires, the power and collapse of the Soviet Union—all are part of the changes that have altered the coastlines of modern human society, and for which "cataclysm" is not too strong a word.

It is difficult to do justice to the complexities of contemporary history and to keep current with the onrushing events of our own times. The chapters that follow can only sketch the most memorable developments of the postwar era and the years that have followed.

Chapter Emblem: The United Nations emblem, showing a wreath enclosing the earth as seen from above the North Pole.

109. The Cold War: The Opening Decade, 1945–1955

Certain problems that had confronted mankind for over a century became even more complex and more urgent in the second half of the twentieth century. Three can be singled out: science, the organization of industrial society, and national sovereignty.

The atomic bomb dramatized the problem of science. The world shuddered at the instantaneous destruction of Hiroshima. The postwar contest to produce more sophisticated nuclear weapons spurred the realization that a third world war would be unimaginably more awful, and even unthinkable. Human beings possessed the means to annihilate not only civilization but even human existence on the planet, a thought especially shocking to a world that set one of its highest values on scientific progress.

The problem of science was not new. Science, and its partner, invention, had for a long time transformed both industry and war. It had conquered many of the dread plagues and diseases of the world. People had long known that science could be applied either constructively or destructively. It was the magnitude of destructive possibilities that now made thoughtful people worry over the problem. The accumulation of scientific knowledge, instead of heightening the quality of human life, took on the ghastly distortions of a nightmare. Scientists themselves, after the first atomic explosion, affirmed the need for a moral regeneration. They insisted that science was neutral, free from blame for the horrors of Hiroshima and Nagasaki, that the trouble lay not with science but the uses to which scientific knowledge was put.

The problem of organizing industrial society was also unresolved. There were in theory two opposite social poles. At one, best represented by the U.S.S.R., all capital was owned by the state and supplied to workers as needed, and all interchange was carefully planned by public authorities in advance. At the other pole, best demonstrated by the United States, capital was owned by private persons, who chose the channels of investment and hence determined the availability of jobs, and interchange took place through the mechanism of the market. Neither the "socialist" nor the "capitalist" system was pure in practice, and mixed economies became the rule in many countries. The chief drawback in the Soviet system was its lack of freedom, in the American its lack of economic stability. Over the years Americans expended a good deal more effort trying to correct the lack of security than the Soviets did to correct the lack of freedom.

Another question hinged on the unity and diversity of the modern world. Was the modern world really "one world," or was it not? It was one world in the sense that there was a close-knit, interdependent economy, that political events and environmental changes affected the whole globe, and that world cultures and religions interacted as never before. But it was far from homogeneous. All admired the steam turbine and stood in awe of nuclear fission, but beyond the material level schemes of values diverged. No people wished to be subordinated to another, or to an international body, or to lose its way of life in a uniform world civilization. Here lay the root of the problem of national independence and of its corollary, world organization.

After the Second World War, as after the First, an international organization was set up to prevent war in the future.[1] A conference of all anti-Axis powers, held at San Francisco in 1945, established the United Nations and drew up its Charter. The new organization was designed to maintain international peace and security and encourage cooperation in solving international social, economic, and cultural problems. Of its numerous agencies, two were central. The General Assembly was a deliberative body in which all member states, however small, were considered equal. The Security Council, whose primary responsibility was to preserve peace, consisted of fifteen members: the five Great Powers, who were permanent members, and ten rotating members chosen by the Assembly for two-year terms. Apart from the two superpowers, the United States and the U.S.S.R., it was not easy to define the Great Powers in 1945, but the permanent seats were assigned to the United States, the Soviet Union, Great Britain, France, and China.[2]

Each permanent member had a veto power. Thus the Security Council could act on important matters only if the Great Powers were unanimous. Although widely criticized, the veto was considered necessary. In major crises the agreement of the Great Powers would be needed to maintain world peace. The U.S.S.R. demanded the veto most frankly (and used it most freely), but the United States, too, would not have joined without this safeguard. Many remembered that the old League was weak because the United States had never joined, and the Soviet Union had been admitted only belatedly. In the following years even small countries refused to abide by judgments of the United Nations. No nation, large or small, was willing to forgo its independence or submerge itself in a world state with authority to put down violence, as any national state could do within its own borders.

The United Nations had fifty-one original members. Its headquarters was located in New York. The Charter provided for the admission of new members, including the former Axis countries and their satellites, and also wartime neutrals, so that it could be truly international. From 1947 to 1955 a few additional states were admitted; in 1955 sixteen additional nations; and in the next two decades, after decolonization, the organization expanded to over three times its original number. In 1948 it adopted a Declaration of Universal Rights, but left unanswered the means of implementing it.

The United Nations failed to fulfill the role projected for it in the postwar era. The Security Council was powerless to intervene in matters affecting relations between the United States and the U.S.S.R. The United Nations remained one of the few arenas where the Americans and Soviets could meet and debate, but it could not prevent the two superpowers from drifting further and further apart. On the other hand the UN from the beginning helped mediate regional disputes and played a role in peacekeeping missions. The office of the secretary general grew in importance. With the expansion of the UN to include the nations of the Third World—a term devised to describe the "developing" countries, mostly former colonial countries, not directly aligned with either the Western or Soviet camp—the General Assembly became

---

[1] See pp. 724, 730–731, 864.

[2] Nationalist China (the Republic of China, or Taiwan) occupied the seat until 1971, even though the People's Republic of China (Communist China) governed the Chinese mainland after 1949.

a forum for debate in which the developing nations, critical of the wealthier West, gave voice to their social and economic grievances.

The Cold War: Origins and Nature

The Second World War, in effect, left only two Great Powers still standing in any strength, the United States and the Soviet Union. The United States emerged physically unscathed from the war, its economy stronger than ever before. Although it quickly demobilized, it alone possessed the atomic bomb. The Soviet Union had been devastated by the war, in which over 20 million of its population had perished, but it was still a formidable military power, with 4 million soldiers under arms and in control of populations and territories in central and eastern Europe well beyond its pre-1939 boundaries. It became common to speak of the two as superpowers—continental land giants, possessing enormous resources, overshadowing all other states, including the powers of Western Europe long dominant in the modern centuries. The characteristic of a two-state system is that each power knows in advance who its only dangerous enemy can be. In such a situation a diplomatic equilibrium is more difficult. Measures taken by either power for its security are seen as aggression or as provocations to the other, and each exaggerates the other's strength. After the war the United States and the U.S.S.R. fell into this unhappy dual relationship. It was compounded by deep-seated ideological tensions between capitalist democracy and Marxist-Leninist communism dating back to the Bolshevik Revolution of 1917. A diplomatic and ideological clash of interests set in that came to be known as the "Cold War," so called because the antagonisms and rivalries, intense though they were, fell short of open or direct hostilities between the two powers.

It was not possible for anyone (even in the U.S.S.R.) to know what Stalin, who dictated all decisions, or his lieutenants in the Kremlin really believed or intended at the end of the Second World War. Probably, as Marxist-Leninists, they considered a clash between the U.S.S.R. and the Western capitalist powers as inevitable at some point in the future. Probably they were disturbed by the economic strength of American capitalism, which sought free markets in Eastern Europe and elsewhere, and by the American monopoly of the atomic bomb. Undoubtedly they saw an opportunity to consolidate their hold over the territories gained during the war (or regained, since some of these had been lost at the end of the First World War[3]), and to create a favorable outer buffer zone for Soviet national security. Undoubtedly they also saw in the aftermath of the Second World War, as of the First, an opportunity to promote the international Marxist revolution (even if Stalin was wary about Communist movements, as in Yugoslavia or China, over which he did not have full control). Whether the Soviets were acting to protect their national security, fulfill old Russian territorial ambitions, or promote communism on a world scale, President Truman and his advisers, and a great majority of the American people, became convinced that the Soviets were bent not only on consolidating their grip on Eastern Europe but were embarking on a worldwide Communist offensive, which it was the responsibility of the United States, as the only power in the West able to act effectively, to

---

[3] See pp. 713, 727, and map, pp. 728–729.

contain. Before long the Americans came to ascribe almost all unrest on the globe to initiatives launched by the Kremlin.

In Europe, at the close of hostilities, Soviet armies occupied Eastern Europe and Germany as far west as the Elbe River. American, British, and French armies held the remainder of Germany, most of Austria, and all of Italy.[4] During the war, the power, or powers, liberating an area exercised political authority. In that way in the sweep of the Red Army the Soviets came to control much of Central and Eastern Europe; 100 million people passed under Soviet domination. On the other hand, the United States excluded the Soviets from any active role in its occupation of Italy (and, in Asia, of Japan). For the Soviets, occupation meant full control over the political, economic, and social institutions of a country and the right to shape them in the Soviet image. The Western powers, on the other hand, had hoped for pluralist and democratic societies, open to Western trade and influence. During the war the Americans and British had conceded Soviet predominance in Eastern Europe, but they now resented the transformation of Poland and other East European countries into Soviet-dominated Communist states, even if for Stalin it was the only way to guarantee "friendly regimes" on his borders. From Potsdam on, Truman denounced the Soviets for violating their pledge of free elections for the East-European states and for failing to cooperate in the joint occupation of Germany. To the Americans Soviet consolidation of control over Eastern Europe seemed like the first step in a plan for unlimited expansion in Europe and elsewhere, not unlike the Nazi and Fascist aggression of the 1930s, to which Truman, resolved not to repeat the lessons of appeasement, frequently compared it. Stalin may have been more a Russian nationalist than an ideologue committed to worldwide Communist revolution, but his stubbornness, paranoia about Western capitalist encirclement, and lack of concern for world public opinion, made it difficult for the West to deal with him or to distinguish between what might have been legitimate Soviet security needs and expansionist missionary zeal. In time Americans, too, became obsessed with a missionary zeal of their own.

Soviet actions fed the belief that Stalin's ambitions transcended Eastern Europe. In Asia, as agreed at Yalta, the Soviets had declared war on Japan in August 1945, after the end of the war in Europe, and moved into Manchuria, where they were well positioned to help the Chinese Communists. In Korea, once the Japanese were defeated, the Soviets by agreement occupied the northern part of the country down to the thirty-eighth parallel, but also took steps to consolidate their occupation zone into a Communist government. The Americans, British, and Soviets had jointly occupied Iran during the war to forestall a Nazi takeover. The Soviets refused to evacuate their troops at the stipulated time, pressed for oil concessions (such as the British and the Americans enjoyed), and lent aid to separatists in the north. The Soviets also pressed for a trusteeship over the former Italian colonies in North Africa on the southern coast of the Mediterranean, within easy reach of the Suez Canal, and they massed troops on the Turkish border, pressing for joint control over the Black Sea straits in order to guarantee naval access to the Mediterranean through the Dardanelles—an old tsarist goal. The British, as the guardians of the Mediterranean and Middle East, attempted

---

[4] See pp. 855–859, 864–866.

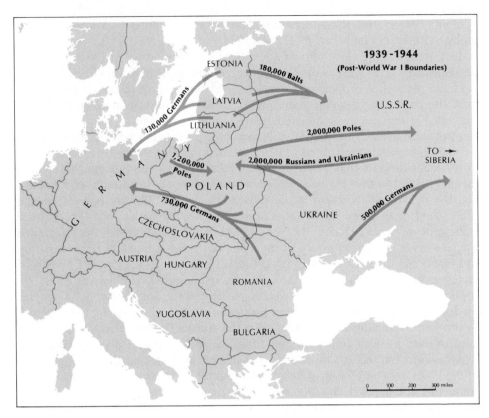

DEPORTATION AND RESETTLEMENT, 1939–1950

The age-old distribution of nationalities in Central and Eastern Europe was radically transformed between 1939 and 1950. Not only were about 6 million Jews put to death, with over 300,000 of the survivors emigrating to Israel by 1950, but millions of Germans, Poles, and others were forcibly uprooted.

The first stage, shown in the left-hand panel, began with the Nazi-Soviet Pact of 1939, after which the Germans occupied western Poland, while the Russians annexed eastern Poland and the three Baltic republics. Western Poland received Poles expelled from Germany, while in eastern Poland about 2 million Poles were deported to Siberia, being replaced by about the same number of Russians and Ukrainians. Many Estonians, Latvians, and Lithuanians were moved to other parts of the Soviet Union. Germans who had lived in Eastern Europe for centuries were displaced. Thousands "returned" to Germany from the Baltic republics and from places in Romania and elsewhere where they had long formed German enclaves. The "Volga Germans", Tatars, and others in south Russia were sent to Siberia.

to bolster the Turkish defenses. In Greece, in a bitter civil war which raged from 1946 to 1949, Communist guerrilla forces, which emerged from the Resistance and enjoyed wide popular support, battled the British-supported royalist, or nationalist, army. Stalin, as if recognizing his wartime commitment to Churchill that Greece should lie in the Western sphere of influence, lent little aid, but Tito's independent Communist regime in Yugoslavia helped the Communist guerrillas. The Communist pressures on Turkey, Greece, and Iran aroused deep concerns

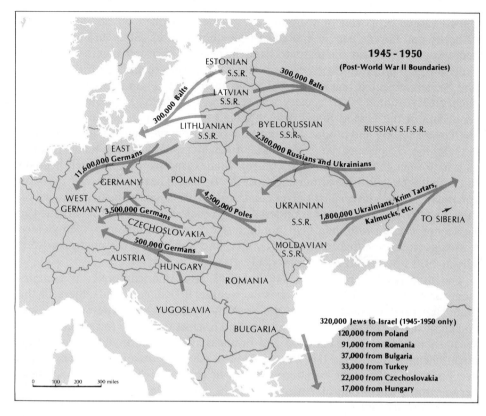

A second stage (right-hand panel) came with the Soviet victory and the collapse of Hitler's Reich. The German-Polish frontier was now moved westward to the Oder River. Millions of Germans from east of the Oder, along with more millions from the Sudeten regions of Czechoslovakia and a continuing stream from Hungary and Romania, were thrown back into what remained of Germany, most of them fleeing to the Western zone, but some to what was the Soviet zone in 1945. Poles streamed into what had been Germany east of the Oder; others came into Poland from the Ukraine. Russians moved into what had been eastern Poland and the Baltic states. Ukrainians and various non-Russian minorities were sent to Siberia. Some Balts escaped to the West (including the United States); others were redistributed to various places in the Soviet Union.

There was a considerable resettlement also of Hungarians, Slovaks, and Finns. The most conspicuous changes, however, in addition to the virtual disappearance of East European Jewry, were the expulsion of the Germans from Eastern Europe and a westward movement of Poles and Russians. (Source: *Westermanns Atlas zur Weltgeschichte.*)

in the West about Soviet strategic designs on the eastern Mediterranean and on the precious oil reserves of the Middle East.

One of the casualties of the tense atmosphere was a plan for international supervision of atomic weapons. The United States knew that it was only a matter of time before the Soviets (and other nations) could build the atomic bomb, since the scientific basis for it was known. At the moment the British alone shared the secret. Under the Baruch Plan introduced into the United Nations in 1946, the

United States proposed that atomic energy be controlled by an international authority and that its use be limited to peaceful purposes. Such an international body would have had the right to send inspectors into any country to check violations and enforce sanctions, not subject to a veto in the Security Council. The Soviets objected and would not forgo their veto. The idea that foreigners might freely examine their society was repugnant to them. They questioned the good faith of the United States, which would not destroy its atomic bombs (or halt further testing and production) until the proposed international authority was in operation. To be sure, large segments of American public opinion also favored national rather than international control. Some Americans were even hesitant to continue the wartime partnership with the British. They, in turn, fearful of an American relapse into isolationism, undertook to become a nuclear power on their own. The Baruch Plan foundered on mutual suspicion and mistrust. The Soviets proceeded with their own atomic research and technology, which yielded results even sooner than expected: by 1949 the Soviets were a nuclear power. The nuclear armaments race, universally dreaded, began.

The atmosphere hardened in 1946 and 1947. The American policy of containment, as formulated by Dean Acheson, George F. Kennan, and others in the State Department, postulated that the Russians would expand wherever a power vacuum existed. Because the Soviets had no precise timetable for conquest, the West should show both patience and firmness; with time Soviet society itself might change. Meanwhile the West needed to maintain its military strength and use economic and other counterpressures to resist the Soviets. Containment became the cornerstone of American policy, but it came to be interpreted in more rigorously military terms than some of its proponents had intended and it was accompanied by a tendency to blame all global restlessness on a monolithic Soviet-controlled communism. Meanwhile Churchill, even before the Soviets had fully completed the transformation of Eastern Europe into Communist satellites, made an eloquent speech in March 1946 in which he described the "iron curtain" that had descended separating Eastern and Western Europe—"from Stettin in the Baltic to Trieste in the Adriatic." That spring the United States turned down a long-pending Soviet request for a reconstruction loan, Lend-Lease having ended with the war, and also cut off reparations deliveries to the Soviets from the American occupation zone of Germany.

In 1947 Great Britain, forced to reassess its priorities because of financial difficulties, and to cut back on its commitments in the Mediterranean, informed Washington that it could no longer aid the anti-Communist forces in Greece or support Turkey in its resistance to Soviet pressures. The United States quickly moved to fill the vacuum. Truman not only agreed to provide the necessary assistance in the Mediterranean but formulated in March 1947 in the Truman Doctrine a broad national policy to contain communism everywhere—"to assist free peoples who are resisting attempted subjugation by armed minorities or by outside pressures." The Truman Doctrine committed the United States to unprecedented global responsibilities. Some advisers believed that the policy was too broad, that American national interests were not clearly enough defined, and that the United States was committing itself to a global enterprise that could overstrain its resources. The Marshall Plan, designed to hasten European economic recovery and hence check Communist expansion, as we shall see, was also announced that spring.[5]

The American national security state began to take shape. A National Security Council was created in 1947 to advise the president on security matters and a Central Intelligence Agency to coordinate the gathering of intelligence. The CIA soon received authorization to conduct covert operations as well. The authority of the executive branch to conduct foreign policy grew. In 1948, the United States adopted its first peacetime military draft.

The Soviets meanwhile denounced the American capitalist and imperialist "warmongers." With the United States arming Greece and Turkey, American carriers able to sail the length of the Mediterranean or lie off the coast of Murmansk, American air bases established in the Middle East, the Americans in occupation of Japan, Okinawa, and South Korea, and the Americans possessing the atomic bomb, the Soviets felt threatened and encircled. Soviet suspicions, dating from Western intervention in the Russian Revolution and civil war in 1918, their exclusion from the Munich Pact, the delay in opening up a second front in the Second World War, the cessation of Lend-Lease at the end of the war, the rejection of the postwar loan, and other sources of friction, became inflamed.[6] In 1947 the Soviets, in order to exert closer control over all Communist parties, reestablished the old Communist International, or Comintern, abandoned in 1943 as a gesture of wartime cooperation and goodwill, renaming it the Communist Information Bureau, or Cominform. In 1947 the Soviets replaced coalition governments in central and eastern Europe, in which the Communists had shared power, with regimes completely dominated by Communist parties. In Czechoslovakia, where President Benes's democratic coalition was seen by many as a possible bridge between East and West, the Czech Communist party, faced with defeat in a forthcoming election, seized power in February 1948. A grave crisis next arose over Berlin.

Germany: The Berlin Blockade and the Airlift of 1948–1949

The key to the rebuilding of Europe, and the strongest area of Soviet-Western contention, was Germany, divided by agreement into four zones and occupied by the wartime Allies. The Ruhr, in the Western zone, was still Europe's industrial heartland. During the war the Allies had agreed to joint Allied policies for a defeated Germany, even though each of the four powers was to occupy a separate zone. Berlin also was divided into four separate Allied sectors, but with joint administration for the city as a whole. All had agreed that Germany should pay reparations, both in capital equipment and current production, especially to the Soviet Union, which had suffered most from German military power, and that limits should be placed on German productive capacity.

At the war's end the Americans quickly came to favor the economic reconstruction of Germany as necessary for European recovery and for the

[5] See pp. 883–884.
[6] See pp. 752, 840–842, 852–853.

reduction of European dependence on American financial aid. The Soviets, on the other hand, were determined to use German resources to repair the devastation in the Soviet Union. They removed large amounts of food and machinery, stripping entire plants in their eastern zone. The refusal of the Western Allies to permit the dismantling of factories in their zones and their insistence that the Soviets take their share of current production only from the Soviet zone fueled strong Soviet resentment. By May 1946 joint administration of occupied Germany had all but broken down. Early in 1947 the United States and Britain united their two zones (which they called "Bizonia"); the French, overcoming their initial reluctance to see a revived Germany, soon merged their zone as well. The Western powers encouraged the reconstruction of governments in the individual states and the naming of delegates to a constituent assembly to set up a federal republic. The Soviets, in their zone, took steps to establish a Communist-dominated government. Two Germanys were emerging.

In June 1948 the Western powers, recognizing the need for drastic currency reform to speed West German economic revival, suddenly revoked the old worthless currency and at a one-to-ten ratio issued a new German mark, the Deutsche mark. The Soviets, who had not been consulted, objected to this as a violation of the wartime agreement to treat Germany as a single economic unit and in retaliation cut off all road and rail access to Berlin, which lay one hundred miles deep within the Soviet zone. The blockade was a sharp challenge and test of will. If the West abandoned Berlin, it could lose authority in all Europe, and open the way for Soviet westward expansion. Aware that they could not resort to military measures against the much stronger Soviet ground forces, the Allies responded to the blockade with a massive air lift. For close to a year, American and Western aircraft flew in thousands of tons of food and other supplies to the occupation forces and to the 3 million inhabitants of West Berlin. The Soviets harassed the planes but avoided direct confrontation, and finally, in May 1949, lifted the blockade.

Each side proceeded with the formation of a German government. The Federal Republic of Germany, its capital in Bonn, came into existence in September 1949; the German Democratic Republic, its capital in the eastern sector of Berlin, one month later. There were now two Germanys.[7] The division of Europe had further hardened.

The Atlantic Alliance

In 1948 Britain, France, Belgium, the Netherlands, and Luxembourg had formed a West European Union for collective self-defense. In 1949 the United States took the lead in creating a larger military alliance and collective security system. The United States, Canada, and ten European nations met in Washington, signed the Atlantic Pact, and agreed to military arrangements for the joint defense of Western Europe. It was a military alliance of unlimited duration and broad scope: "an armed attack against one or more" was to be considered "an attack against all." By it the United States formally committed itself to the security of Western

[7] See map, p. 893.

Europe and agreed to supply funds and equipment for European rearmament. It was the first military alliance of its kind in American history.

Out of the treaty developed the North Atlantic Treaty Organization (NATO) with a network of military arrangements and chain of command under an American general. Because West Germany remained the most vulnerable target for Soviet aggression, large numbers of American troops (eventually over 300,000) were stationed there as the nucleus of the NATO armed forces. With overwhelming Soviet superiority in ground forces, the NATO defense strategy was based not on ground troops alone but on American air power, which would provide a nuclear umbrella for Western Europe as well. The treaty was a solemn affirmation of American determination not to abandon the Continent. In later years the West Europeans became restive with American leadership, or alternatively feared an American decoupling from Europe, but NATO remained Western Europe's shield against Soviet aggression. The Truman Doctrine, the Marshall Plan, and the Atlantic alliance were the three prongs of the American and Western response to a potential Soviet bid for global supremacy, of which Western Europe would be the principal prize.

Meanwhile the West European countries were making impressive economic progress and cooperating with each other in economic and other ways. In a few short years after the devastating war Western Europe had reconstructed itself politically, recovered economically, and was rearming. The Soviets could not be expected to view the revival and growing unity of Western Europe with equanimity. American financial and military assistance to Western Europe, the Atlantic alliance, the containment policy, all defensive in Western eyes, were hostile acts from the Soviet perspective. The Soviet Union drew its six satellite or client states, variously styled people's republics or people's democracies, closer to it. It formalized economic ties by creating in 1949 a Council for Mutual Economic Aid (or Comecon), and a few years later consummated the existing network of military alliances in the Warsaw Pact of 1955. The Soviets augmented their existing armor and air power and continued their nuclear research.

By 1949 Stalin's postwar expansion effort seemed contained and Truman could claim success for his policies. The Soviets had dropped their demands on Turkey and departed from Iran. Quasi-insurrectionary strikes launched by Communist parties in Western Europe had failed, as did a Communist bid for power in Italy in the elections of 1948, in which the Vatican and the United States strongly supported the anti-Communist camp. Marshal Tito in 1948 successfully defied the Cominform and Yugoslavia went its separate Communist way. In Greece the American- and British-backed Greek royalists triumphed in 1949 against the Communist guerrillas. The Soviet blockade of Berlin had failed to drive the West from the city.

The rivalry over Europe ended in stalemate. The Soviet threat to Western Europe diminished. The continent remained divided into a Western and Eastern Europe (the term Central Europe tended to drop from use), Germany into two Germanys, Berlin into West and East Berlin. After the failure of the Soviet blockade of Berlin, there was no further overt conflict in Europe. Despite renewed threats to Berlin, each side recognized the strength and security concerns of the other. But any thoughts that the world might settle into peace, no matter how uneasy, were shattered in June 1950. The Western-Soviet struggle shifted to Asia.

The Revival of Japan

In Asia events also moved rapidly in the early postwar years. In China the Chinese Communists triumphed over the Nationalists and proclaimed the People's Republic of China in 1949. In Japan the United States used its military occupation from 1945 to 1952 to foster parliamentary institutions and revive the Japanese economy.

Rejecting Soviet demands for a share in the occupation of Japan, the United States, with British and French approval, lodged full authority in General Douglas MacArthur, the supreme commander of the occupation forces. In large part in response to Cold War tensions the American occupation encouraged economic revival and political reconstruction, and the Japanese, in the wake of their disastrous defeat, cooperated fully. A new constitution in 1946 ended divine-right rule, transferred sovereignty from the emperor to the people, established machinery for parliamentary government, gave women the vote, and encouraged local self-government. The constitution forever renounced war and the threat or use of force as a means of settling international disputes; the small Japanese armed forces were restricted to defense purposes. Although trials of Japanese war criminals were held, there were no extensive purges. The Japanese paid reparations to Asian nations that had been the victims of Japanese conquest, but they made no open admission of the brutality that had accompanied these conquests.

Efforts at social and economic reform under the occupation were less sweeping than originally planned. The large family holdings in heavy industry and banking were dissolved, but within a short time new forms of economic concentration replaced them. Labor unions were reinstituted but their powers were curtailed. The occupation inaugurated a program of land redistribution, with a limit on large landholdings, but many peasants lacked the means to purchase the land offered them. Although a moderate socialist party emerged, and militant activists in later years frequently demonstrated their discontent, political control remained in the hands of conservatives drawn from the upper social classes. By the end of the occupation the Liberal Democratic party, a conservative political grouping, dominated the government.

The conservative-led political consensus that emerged had a strong commitment to economic recovery and growth. Like Western Europe, Japan, too, rose from the ashes. In 1945 it had been prostrate, a fourth of its housing destroyed, agricultural and industrial output reduced to half its prewar level, its shipping and financial reserves gone. Under the occupation and with American help the economy revived and expanded; by 1954 its gross national product reached prewar levels. Labor self-discipline and social patterns of deference and loyalty kept industrial unrest to a minimum. Close cooperation between government and business encouraged savings, investment, research, and economic growth. The very need to rebuild the economy from the bottom up proved to be an advantage. Beginning in the early 1950s the economy grew at an amazing rate of nearly 10 percent each year, manufacturing output at 14 percent a year. Despite the forced repatriation of millions of Japanese from Manchuria, Korea, and other parts of Asia, and the addition of large numbers of rural workers to the labor force, Japan still had a labor shortage. The response to it was an intense level of automation. Japan became a pioneer in advanced high technology and came to depend on technology and productivity to sustain its growth. Its consumer products soon entered the world economy; its exports came to rival those of the Americans and the Europeans. Because a large military establishment was forbidden, expenditures that might have gone into the military, as in the past, were now plowed into investment. By the 1950s Japan was once again a major economic power, a bastion of social stability, and a major new element in the global economy. For the Soviets the revival of Japan under American auspices, which they saw as a counterweight to Soviet influence, and as a bulwark against revolution in Asia, was still another threat.

Containment in Asia: The Korean War

In June 1950 the Korean War broke out. The Western Allies and the Soviet Union had agreed that Korea, once an object of imperialist rivalry between Japan and tsarist Russia, but under Japanese rule since 1910, would become free and independent after Japan's defeat. At the war's end the United States, for reasons of military expediency, proposed that Soviet troops temporarily occupy the northern part of the country down to the thirty-eighth parallel and United States troops the southern half. But postwar negotiations on the unification of the country foundered. The U.S.S.R. established a satellite government in its occupation zone under the Communist leader Kim Il Sung and built up North Korean military strength. The United States developed its own client state in the south and lent economic and military assistance. In 1947 a UN commission sought to sponsor nationwide elections, but the Soviet Union would not permit supervision of elections in the north. The elections in the south in May 1948 resulted in the presidency of Syngman Rhee, who, despite superficial forms of democracy, governed repressively. Anticommunism in Asia and elsewhere did not necessarily equate with democratic government. After the elections the United States withdrew its occupation forces but continued military and economic support. The Soviet Union also removed its occupation forces but left behind a well-trained and well-equipped North Korean army. Despite the original intention, there were now two Koreas.

By 1950 the situation in East Asia, as we have seen, had altered dramatically. First, Japan had revived. The United States through its postwar occupation had created a stable Japan, friendly to the West, and with a prospering economy. Second, the Chinese Communists, with only limited and grudging Soviet support, had triumphed over the Nationalists in the long civil war, and in October 1949 had proclaimed the Chinese People's Republic. Although relations between the Chinese Communists and the Soviets were neither warm nor cordial, the two countries, out of mutual concern over the revival of Japan and the deepening American influence in East Asia, drew together in a mutual defense pact in February 1950. The U.S.S.R. campaigned to have the People's Republic of China replace Nationalist China in the United Nations. When the effort failed, the Soviets in protest boycotted the Security Council meetings.

Although border skirmishes between North and South Korea had been frequent, the full-scale North Korean invasion of the south came as a surprise. To the West it was an open act of military aggression, the first clear-cut act of military aggression of the Cold War. Because of the boldness of their initiative and their superior forces, the North Koreans expected a quick victory. They gambled that the United States would not intervene and that the outside world would lodge no more than a moral protest. Only a few months earlier the American Secretary of State Dean Acheson, although one of the architects of containment, had somewhat narrowly defined the defense perimeter vital to American interests in East Asia as including Japan and the Philippines but had failed to include South Korea, perhaps omitting it because it was so clearly known to be an American client state.

The precise inspiration for the invasion remained unclear. North Korea, concerned over South Korea's avowed ambition to unite the country on pro-Western terms, may have taken the initiative on its own. The invasion seems to have surprised the Soviets who, as noted, were boycotting the Security Council at the time and hence unable to exercise their veto when the Americans persuaded the Security Council to condemn the invasion and authorize military countermeasures. The Chinese, recovering from their civil war, barely established in power, and still facing a challenge from the Nationalists in Taiwan, could scarcely have helped initiate it. Although Stalin may not have incited the North Korean attack, the sweeping initial North Korean successes offered the Soviets an opportunity to profit from the fast-moving events and to check the growing American influence in Japan and East Asia. The Soviets quietly furnished military aid to North Korea and denounced the United States for intervening in Asian affairs—on the very doorsteps of the U.S.S.R. and of the People's Republic of China.

For the American government, and for most Americans, it was difficult to believe that the attack had not been engineered in Moscow, or that the North Koreans were capable of independent action. The assumption was that the Soviets, probing in Asia for weak spots, as they had elsewhere, had found one and now must be halted. Korea, like Berlin, became another test of American and Western will. Truman, already concerned about the "loss of China" (the formula used at the time for the Chinese Communist victory) saw it as a test, as he said, of the "free world's commitment to liberty." The attack challenged the entire system of collective security and containment constructed to stem the tide of Soviet communism. The Soviets had passed "beyond the use of subversion" to "armed invasion and war." Korea, he said, would be "the Greece of the Far East." The Americans quickly prevailed on the Security Council to condemn North Korea as an aggressor and to take military action. Without asking for an American declaration of war because it was a "police action," Truman ordered American combat troops to Korea and called for air strikes above the thirty-eighth parallel. General MacArthur, the wartime hero of the Pacific, who had successfully presided over the occupation of Japan, was named commander of the UN forces.

In the early fighting that summer the American-led United Nations forces were driven south and forced to retreat to the very water's edge, but in September MacArthur made a remarkable amphibious landing on the western side of the peninsula, drove the North Koreans back above the thirty-eighth parallel, and rapidly moved north toward the Yalu River, the boundary between Korea and the Manchurian province of the People's Republic of China. In late October, Chinese soldiers suddenly appeared in large numbers and drove back the advancing

UN armies. Within two weeks Chinese troops drove the UN forces back below the thirty-eighth parallel. It was an entirely new war. The People's Republic of China was committed. The European allies, gratified at first by the American show of determination, grew worried that the war could escalate into a global, possibly nuclear, conflict.

Meanwhile the battle lines seesawed. MacArthur forced the Chinese and North Korean troops to retreat, again crossed the thirty-eighth parallel, and demanded unconditional surrender. He proposed to blockade the Chinese coast, bomb Chinese cities, encourage the Chinese Nationalists to attack the Chinese mainland, and even seal off Korea from Manchuria by a field of radioactive waste. Truman, however, recognized that MacArthur's actions could lead to full-scale war with China, Soviet intervention, and even world war, and without the full support of the European allies. When the general publicly flouted his authority, he relieved him of his command and replaced him.

In July 1951 a cease-fire agreement brought large-scale fighting to a halt, but armistice negotiations dragged on, deadlocked over the repatriation of North Korean prisoners who did not wish to return home. In July 1953 under General Eisenhower's presidency, an armistice was signed, the line of partition drawn roughly where the fighting had begun three years earlier, at the thirty-eighth parallel, with provision for a demilitarized buffer zone. The partition hardened into a long-term division. North Korea became a Communist state and a full-fledged ally of the Soviet Union. South Korea, unable to achieve political democracy under Syngman Rhee or his successors, nonetheless developed a dynamic capitalist economy, far outstripping North Korea in economic strength. In later years pressures emerged for the reunification of the country or at the least for closer relations between the two regimes. Militants blamed the artificial division of their country on the Cold War and on the superpowers, and on the Americans more than anyone else. Four decades later, over 40,000 American troops remained stationed in South Korea.

The United States spent over $15 billion on the war. Because it could not supply all its military needs on its own, the war vastly stimulated the economic growth of Western Europe and Japan, and also quickened the pressures for German rearmament. Fifteen countries supported the United States and participated in the fighting, but it was largely an American military operation, the United States furnishing half the ground forces and close to all the naval and air power. The Americans suffered over 34,000 battle deaths in the undeclared war, three-fifths as many as in the First World War; the American wounded were estimated at over 100,000. The South Koreans suffered over 1 million casualties in dead, wounded, and missing, the North Koreans and the Chinese an equal number. The Soviets had fought by proxy.

In American eyes a flagrant act of aggression had been checked. In Western Europe, despite the anxiety over MacArthur's recklessness, the show of American firmness was reassuring. As seen in the Communist world, however, and indeed in many of the nonaligned countries in Asia like India or Indonesia, the great capitalist power, the United States, had been prevented from reasserting Western imperialist supremacy in the East. In its efforts to create regional security pacts in Asia, the United States found little enthusiasm among the larger non-Communist Asian powers, who disliked communism but also distrusted the West. Although the United States had been the least involved of all the Great Powers in nineteenth-century territorial imperialism in Asia, its new leadership of the Western world made it a symbol of Western oppression, buttressed by the suspicion that its free-world rhetoric masked the drive to open world markets for American capitalism—an image assiduously cultivated by the Soviets and, even more aggressively, by the Chinese Communists.

On the other hand, the success in checking the North Korean act of aggression by force of arms reinforced the American belief that military strength and decisiveness could check Communist expansion anywhere; containment would be global. The Korean War inaugurated an era of deep American involvement in Asia and served as prelude to an even longer and more costly conflict, the war in Vietnam in the following decade.[8] In late 1952 the United States successfully tested its first thermonuclear or hydrogen bomb, hundreds of times more powerful than the atomic bomb used at Hiroshima; the Soviets shortly thereafter, in 1953, did the same.

The Korean War had its repercussions in Europe. Even though there were still misgivings in France and in other parts of Europe over a revival of German military strength, the Americans pressed for West German rearmament. When a French proposal for a European Defense Community (with a "European" army, in which the Germans would serve as "European" soldiers) failed to pass the French legislature in 1954, West Germany was authorized to create an army of its own under the overall command of NATO. Concern over a resurgent German militarism by now was receding. The West German constitution guaranteed civilian control over the military; a strong antimilitarist movement had emerged in the country itself. By agreement, however, Germany was prohibited from manufacturing nuclear weapons or materials for chemical or biological warfare. In 1955 the Federal Republic of Germany became a full member of NATO.

The Korean War hastened a peace treaty with Japan. In the peace treaty signed in 1951 in San Francisco by fifty nations, but without Soviet participation, no general reparations were exacted, but individual countries were to work out their own reparations agreements. In a separate security pact the United States retained military rights in Japan and occupied nearby islands, where, it was agreed, the United States would remain as long as necessary for peace and security. A year later the American occupation of Japan itself formally ended. The Soviets made no move to return the Kurile Islands, which they had occupied at the end of the Second World War. The United States meanwhile signed security pacts with Australia, New Zealand, and the Philippines and tightened its global commitments.

The decades that followed the troubled international relations of the early Cold War brought new confrontations and crises—over Berlin, Cuba, Vietnam, the Middle East, Afghanistan, to name only the most important—and above all, a mounting nuclear arms race between the two superpowers and the stockpiling of the most formidable weaponry ever assembled. But before continuing with the Cold War, we must examine in this and the following chapter many other developments of these years—the remarkable economic recovery and political reconstruction of Western Europe, the reshaping of the

[8] See pp. 984–990.

global economy, the world of the Communist countries, and the emergence of new nations from the old Western colonial empires. Let us turn first to Western Europe.

110. *Western Europe: Economic Reconstruction*

The Second World War left Europe in a worse state of disorder than the First. Physical destruction was incomparably greater. The war had ruined one of the world's chief industrial areas and brought its economic system to collapse. Even when the worst local devastation was repaired, suffering and distress persisted. With problems of transportation and exchange unresolved, Western Europe was cut off from the areas with which it had carried on trade. It had long lived on imports, for which it could no longer pay. During the war the West Europeans, and especially the British, had used up their overseas investments and lost a good share of the shipping services they had once provided. Overseas countries had built up their own industries and needed those of Europe less, and the United States had taken over markets once in European hands.

At the same time, Western Europe was not to be written off. Its population exceeded that of either of the superpowers; and even in ruins, despite the wartime strategic bombing, it still possessed one of the world's leading industrial plants and the skills needed to rehabilitate and run it. The Europeans did not wish to be rescued by either of the superpowers. Most rejected communism as a form of slavery. Yet dependence on the benefactions of the United States they feared as a gamble. Memories of the stock-market crash of 1929, the economic collapse of Europe after the withdrawal of American capital, and the Great Depression bred skepticism about dependence on American capitalism. But between the two superpowers the Soviets had more to gain by chaos in Western Europe, and the United States more to gain by its rebuilding.

The Marshall Plan and European Recovery

For the non-Communist world, the single most important factor in the early postwar years was the productivity of the American economic system. The American economy had expanded enormously during the war. At the war's end the United States accounted for two-thirds of the world's industrial production and held two-thirds of the world's gold. Its gross national product was two and a half times higher than in 1939, its exports three times greater, and despite predictions about postwar economic collapse, its economy continued to grow rapidly.

When Lend-Lease ended after the war, the United States sent billions of dollars worth of goods to Western Europe to relieve distress and made loans to individual states, especially to Britain. The Europeans quickly set about to salvage their industrial plant, less severely devastated, it turned out, than originally thought, and to rebuild their economies. Within two years, by 1947, the nations of Western Europe were approaching their prewar levels of production. But American aid was still desperately needed to continue the purchase of food, fuel, raw materials, and industrial parts essential to full economic recovery and expansion. By the spring of 1947 recovery appeared at risk. The poorest harvest in a century was feared. With Cold War tensions mounting, Communist parties in France and Italy, which had earlier cooperated in postwar reconstruction, began launching strikes. Even if the Soviet Union was not actively promoting revolutionism in Western Europe, understanding perhaps that the West would not tolerate overt revolution there, the Americans were concerned about European stability. American economic aid so far had been improvised and piecemeal. But in June 1947, on the basis of confidential American reports of continuing distress and threats to stability, Secretary of State George C. Marshall used the occasion of his Harvard commencement address to invite the Europeans to cooperate in drawing up blueprints for a broad program of reconstruction, for which the United States would provide the financial support. The plan, formulated in humanitarian terms, was "directed not against country or doctrine, but against hunger, poverty, desperation, and chaos." To reinforce its nonpolitical character, the United States extended the invitation to all European governments, including the Soviet Union and the East European states. The Soviet Union, as some of the plan's sponsors may have suspected, rejected the proposal and summarily withdrew from the initial planning conference in Paris. It forbade the participation of its East European satellites, some of which had evinced interest, recognizing that involvement would subject their economies to outside scrutiny and perhaps draw them into the Western economic orbit. It denounced the plan as "a new venture in American imperialism."

The West-European countries responded with alacrity. Under the Marshall Plan, or European Recovery Program, as it was enacted by Congress, American aid was coordinated with each country's needs and with joint European priorities in order to maximize the benefits. The Office for European Economic Cooperation (OEEC) in Paris, with which the Americans worked closely, identified projects, coordinated the planning, and allocated the funds.

The Marshall Plan had a profound psychological and economic effect on the European economies and the results exceeded the boldest anticipations of its American sponsors. The West Europeans utilized their technical and managerial skills to improve transportation facilities, modernize their infrastructure, and vastly expand their productive capacity. They reduced trade barriers among themselves and facilitated trade by setting up a payments union. Hard currency, now available for needed imports, reduced financial pressures and the need for further austerity. The Marshall Plan accelerated the recovery already under way, made recovery smoother than it would have been, and encouraged the economic cooperation of the European countries with each other. The United States used its economic resources to help revive its competitors, but the program also served American interests by restoring a world market, of which the United States would be one of the chief beneficiaries. By creating markets for American exports, it helped fuel the postwar economic boom in the United States. The Americans thus satisfied their humanitarian impulse, served their economic needs, and reduced the drift of Europeans into the Communist camp. At the same time the Marshall Plan sharpened the division between the Soviet bloc and the West.

Economic Growth in Western Europe

For West Germany the currency reform of 1948, which precipitated the Berlin blockade, ignited an amazing economic revival and expansion, the *Wirtschafts-wunder*, or "economic miracle." Marshall Plan funds were at first administered by the Western occupation authorities, but once the Federal Republic of Germany was established, it joined the other European nations in the Office of European Economic Cooperation. Like the other European countries, West Germany benefited from the Korean War and the demand for goods that the Americans could not satisfy. By 1950 West Germany exceeded prewar German production levels before embarking on a spectacular economic boom. By 1958 it was the leading industrial country of Western Europe. Not only West Germany but France, Italy, and other West European countries experienced an "economic miracle" also. For two and a half decades, from 1948 to 1974 (when a worldwide recession set in), the Western European economies grew at unprecedented and uninterrupted rates of growth. The West Europeans basked in prosperity and rising living standards. Europeans would later speak of the "silver fifties" and the "golden sixties," the French (counting from 1944) of the "thirty glorious years." Although Britain's economy, burdened by older industries and the loss of overseas markets, lagged behind, it too grew faster than at any time in the interwar years. Japan, as earlier noted, from the 1950s on also embarked on a phenomenal economic expansion.

The prosperity of Western Europe derived from a competitive free-market and private-enterprise economy, but it was accompanied everywhere by extensive economic planning, systematic government intervention, and a network of social services to help cope with the instability of competitive capitalism and the business cycle. No one anywhere wished to repeat the hard times and suffering of the Great Depression. Keynes's theories, first formulated in the 1930s but without many adherents at that time,[9] took hold in the postwar era and dominated government policy in the 1950s and 1960s even when conservative governments were in control. Governments kept their economies under close surveillance and used their fiscal and monetary powers to promote investment, production, and employment and to control inflation. They took "countercyclical" measures, that is, at signs of decline in the business cycle they increased government expenditures in order to keep demand high. Full employment was accepted as a goal. Improved statistical techniques and economic forecasting, although scarcely precision instruments, made economic planning and "fine tuning" feasible. Planning took the form of guidance and direction, not coercion, and differed markedly from the rigid, detailed, and doctrinaire centralized planning of the Soviet bloc.

In Britain, France, and Italy (less so in West Germany, which had lived through heavy state control under the Nazis), the postwar governments also nationalized a number of the key sectors of the economy to bring them under government control. But even in these mixed economies, the private capitalist sector represented the major share of economic activity. In all Western Europe economic growth became a central objective, virtually an obsession. Governments and

[9] See pp. 799–804 and 808.

people came to expect growth rates far exceeding those of the past. It was as if Western Europe was catching up, compensating for the lost time of the interwar years and the Second World War, and for the economic stagnation of a generation.

When the sustained economic growth of the next two decades led to a labor shortage, West Germany and other countries invited foreign workers to join their labor force. Turks, Greeks, Yugoslavs, Spaniards, Portuguese, and Italians from southern Italy were invited in as "guest workers." Four and a half million arrived in the Federal Republic of Germany alone, over half of them Turks, who did not return home but formed large unassimilated enclaves, following their Muslim faith, in West Berlin and other cities. After the collapse of the European empires, immigrants from the former European colonies in Asia, Africa, and the Caribbean also arrived in Western Europe in large numbers. From the 1950s on a steady stream of immigrants came to Britain from India, Pakistan, the West Indies, and Africa. France drew large numbers from its former North African colonies, especially Algeria. The Netherlands became home for many Indonesians. Political refugees also arrived in Europe from Vietnam and other parts of Asia. The new Europeans were often of different cultures, religion, racial composition, or skin color. Mosques became a not uncommon sight in European cities. The influx of guest workers and immigrants by the millions created difficulties later in less affluent times. The presence of the new Europeans led to friction, often overtly racial, testing the flexibility and tolerance of a European society becoming increasingly multiethnic and multicultural.

With a postwar baby boom and an influx of at least 13 million immigrants and refugees the population of Western Europe grew by 25 percent between 1945 and 1970. But by the 1960s the birth rate of the West Europeans leveled off and the West European population began to decline.

In these same postwar years the contemporary welfare state grew, going well beyond its pre-1914 origins or its expansion in the interwar years. The postwar governments gave a high priority to social objectives, to what the French Resistance charter had called "a more just social order": the right to a suitable job, government compensation in the event of unemployment or disability, social security in old age, free or subsidized health care, and the redistribution of wealth and income through progressive taxation. The protection of the contemporary welfare state was intended to be universal, not confined, as in earlier times, to the poor and disadvantaged. Its social objectives could be achieved in the 1950s and 1960s because of a salutary interplay of government, management, and labor; all shared in the consensus about investment and growth. Only later, from the late 1970s on, did the argument gather strength that all these entitlements had become excessive, and an impediment to economic growth.

111. Western Europe: Political Reconstruction

Western Europe also faced overwhelming challenges of political reconstruction at the end of the war. Britain was economically exhausted and in the process of liquidating its empire. France, recovering from the collapse of 1940, the occupation, and the divisiveness of collaboration, faced colonial wars. Italy had to renew its political life after two decades of fascism. Germany, after the Nazi rout, was divided and under military occupation. Nevertheless political reconstruction went forward. Britain resumed its role as the world's oldest parliamentary democracy; France and Italy adopted new constitutions; out of the Western zone of occupied Germany the Federal Republic of Germany emerged in 1949.

The smaller states of Western Europe also resumed democratic processes. Only Spain and Portugal remained under their prewar dictatorships until those regimes also came to an end in the mid-1970s. The memories of dictatorship receded. The suffrage was broadened. Women finally received the vote in France and Italy immediately after the war, in Switzerland in 1971. In a suffrage reform that went almost unnoticed, the legal voting age in most countries was quietly reduced to eighteen in the 1970s.

In the early postwar years a renovating spirit swept Western Europe. The memories of 1914–1918, the economic dislocations of the 1920s, the miseries of the Great Depression of the 1930s, the sacrifices of the Second World War, haunted everyone. The wartime Resistance movements, demanding an end to the aggressive nationalism and militarism that cost Europe so much travail, called for a federal union of Europe to prevent future wars. The Resistance proclamations emphasized economic and social rights as well as political freedom. Liberal democracy was important but not sufficient; postwar governments were asked to provide protection against the insecurities of old age, disability, unemployment, ill health.

The earliest elections confirmed the strength of the new spirit, but before long politics reverted to older ways. The welfare state idea persisted, as did the impulse for an integrated Europe, but politics became more pragmatic and less ideological. Socialists, following the Scandinavian model, became social-democratic reformists, accepting capitalism but insisting that they could manage capitalist economies more effectively than liberals, centrists, or conservatives. In France and Italy the presence of large Communist parties, with strong attachments to the Soviet Union in the early postwar years, complicated matters. In West Germany, Italy, and France, the Christian Democrats, drawing inspiration from religious and ethical precepts, played a key role in shaping the new regimes. They accepted the welfare state but backed away from the egalitarianism of the socialists and, over time, became increasingly representative of conservative and business interests.

Great Britain: Labour and Conservative

In Great Britain, the first elections in ten years unseated Winston Churchill and the Conservative-led wartime coalition and voted in a Labour government in July 1945. For the first time in its history Labour had a majority of its own.[10] Governing from 1945 to 1951, with Clement Attlee as prime minister, it set the course of British life for years to come. It was a Labour government that accepted the liquidation of the British empire in India.

Once the center of high capitalism, Britain became the world's chief exemplar

[10] See pp. 619–621, 811–812.

of parliamentary socialism and the modern welfare state. On the premise that the country's basic industries could not be left to the unplanned anarchy of capitalism and unregulated competition, the Labour government nationalized the Bank of England, the coal mines, electricity and gas, iron and steel, and other parts of the economy. Because four-fifths of industry remained in private hands, what emerged was a mixed economy. At the same time Labour greatly expanded and revamped the social insurance program inherited from the Liberal reforms of 1906–1914.[11] All parties had committed themselves during the war to an extension of these welfare services. The Beveridge Report of 1942 had sketched a program to guarantee "full employment in a free society" and social security for all "from the cradle to the grave." Labour now extended insurance coverage for unemployment, old age, and other contingencies, inaugurated a comprehensive national health service, and sharply increased income and inheritance taxes.

In the elections of 1951 Labour lost its majority in Parliament. The Conservatives returned to office and governed uninterruptedly for the next thirteen years under a succession of prime ministers, but after 1964 the two parties alternated in office.[12] The shifting electoral fortunes stemmed from division within the country over the welfare state introduced by Labour, dissatisfaction with the performance of the economy, and frustration at Britain's diminished global status.

During their years in office, the Conservatives restored some nationalized industries to private control and modified the national health insurance program, but did little else to dismantle the welfare state. Both parties recognized, however, that the social reforms of the welfare state could be absorbed only if the economy prospered. But the country faced nagging economic problems. After the Second World War Britain was much weaker than after the First.[13] The liquidation of its investments to pay for the war, the loss of export markets, and its reduced income from shipping and other services adversely affected its balance of payments, and undermined the pound. With American financial aid, an intensified export drive, an austerity program that reduced imports, and curtailment of military and imperial commitments, the British economy and trade position improved and the country experienced a modest prosperity. But the British failed to rebuild their obsolescent capital equipment and infrastructure as effectively as their West European neighbors across the Channel.

British industry was outstripped even in its own domestic market. Its economy grew more slowly than that of Western Europe and Japan. When out of power, Labour argued that the Conservatives lacked economic dynamism and were responsible for the lagging economy. But Labour in office did no better and was forced to devalue the pound and extend austerity measures. When inflation set in during the late 1960s, and intensified in the 1970s, the trade unions demanded wage increases to match rising prices. Strikes and prolonged work stoppages troubled the economy and divided British society. Until the late 1970s, when a

---

[11] See pp. 612–613.

[12] The prime ministers in the years 1945–1990 were: Clement R. Attlee (Labour), 1945–1951; Sir Winston Churchill (Conservative), 1951–1955; Sir Anthony Eden (Conservative), 1955–1957; Harold MacMillan (Conservative), 1957–1963; Sir Alec Frederick Douglas-Home (Conservative), 1963–1964; Harold Wilson (Labour), 1964–1970; Edward Heath (Conservative), 1970–1974; Harold Wilson (Labour), 1974–1976; James Callaghan (Labour), 1976–1979; and Margaret Thatcher (Conservative), 1979–1990.

[13] See pp. 810–811.

new era raised fresh hopes,[14] the question was whether Labour or the Conservatives could better manage British decline, not how they could overcome it.

Meanwhile troubles in Northern Ireland persisted. After the partition in 1922, the six counties of Northern Ireland, predominantly Protestant, had remained part of the United Kingdom. The Catholic minority, about one-third the population, protested militantly that they were victims of political and economic discrimination, and pressed for annexation to the Republic of Ireland. Open violence broke out in 1969, inflamed by the Irish Republican Army on the one hand and Protestant extremists on the other. In the years that followed, over 2,500 persons lost their lives, and no compromise was in sight.

The French Republic: Fourth and Fifth

After the liberation of France General Charles de Gaulle, the very incarnation of the Resistance, became provisional president. Because no one wished to return to the Third Republic after its ignominious collapse in 1940, nor to the stalemate society of the interwar years, elections were held for a Constituent Assembly. With the parties of the right discredited by their role in Vichy, the left emerged enhanced in strength and prestige. The Communists, the Socialists, and the Popular Republic Movement (or MRP), a Catholic progressive party akin to Christian Democrats elsewhere on the Continent, formed the provisional government. The left parties pressed for a systematic purge of collaborators, despite the difficulties in determining levels of guilt. The purge, which had begun as soon as the army reached French soil, initially took the form of angry drumhead trials and executions. Gradually, the process was brought under more orderly judicial procedures. Even so, the trials of Pétain and Laval were impassioned showpieces. The debate over collaborationism continued to divide the country in later decades.

The Fourth Republic in its machinery of government differed in only a few details from the Third.[15] Once again the presidency was only ceremonial and the premier and cabinet were responsible to an all-powerful legislature. De Gaulle made no secret of his dislike for the constitution being prepared in 1946, the return of party rivalries, and the domination of the legislature, all of which interfered with his vision of a strong France ready to resume a leadership role in world affairs. He resigned in protest in December 1946. The three parties continued their tripartite coalition under Socialist leadership until the Communists, reflecting the heightened tensions of the Cold War, fomented a series of strikes and were expelled from the cabinet in May 1947.

Parliamentary division and ministerial instability grew more serious. The Socialists and the MRP formed unstable coalitions with each other and with the reviving smaller parties. Periodically de Gaulle returned to the political scene, heading a movement called the "Rally of the French People," which he described as "above parties." Except for the brief reform ministry of Pierre Mendès-France in 1954–1955, governmental ineffectiveness in the midst of domestic and foreign crises filled the public with cynicism, hostility, and indifference.

Yet despite its record of political instability—25 cabinets succeeding one

[14] See pp. 995–998.
[15] See pp. 605–609, 814–817.

another from 1946 to 1958—the Fourth Republic enacted a significant body of legislation. The provisional government nationalized several key industries. As in Britain, a mixed economy emerged. The existing social security legislation was expanded. A farsighted economic plan, drawn up by Jean Monnet, who later played a large role in the creation of the European Economic Community,[16] enlarged and modernized the country's economic base and paved the way for industrial expansion. A flexible form of economic planning, inspired by Monnet, in which government, management, and labor played mutually reinforcing roles, became an accepted part of French economic life. By 1952 production levels were one and a half times those of 1938, and industrial output was growing at an annual rate of over 5 percent. From 1946 to 1966 production tripled whereas in the half-century from 1889 to 1940 it had merely doubled. Meanwhile Monnet and the MRP premier, Robert Schuman, took the lead in promoting European economic integration in the 1950s and in tightening ties with the other West-European countries. The country also displayed a demographic vitality for a time that confounded earlier pessimists.[17]

What finally brought down the Fourth Republic was the strain of trying to preserve the old French colonial empire. France alone, of all the major powers, was almost continuously at war for close to fifteen years. It could envy the lot of the losers in the Second World War, Germany, Italy, and Japan, with no restless colonies to subdue. France fought relentlessly to preserve its empire. The constitution of 1946 provided representation in Paris for the colonies, but the limited reforms did not satisfy nationalists pressing for independence. From 1946 to 1954 the French forces unsuccessfully fought in Indochina until they finally had to withdraw. Within a matter of months, the Algerian war broke out. That war drained the resources, morale, and self-esteem of the French even more.[18] The *colons*, as the European settlers in Algeria were called, and army leaders adamantly opposed French withdrawal and staged an insurrectionary coup in Algiers in May 1958. When civil war threatened, the country turned to the one man it believed could save the situation—Charles de Gaulle, then living quietly in self-imposed retirement. The army leaders, the settlers in Algeria, and the parties of the right were convinced, given his solicitude for the army and French national pride, that he would keep Algeria French. De Gaulle accepted the summons. In June 1958 the National Assembly invested him as premier, giving him emergency powers for six months and the authority to prepare a new constitution.

In that way the Fifth Republic was born. In the autumn of 1958 the new constitution was overwhelmingly accepted in a popular referendum, and de Gaulle was elected president. The presidency, as de Gaulle had long urged, became the fulcrum of power in the Fifth Republic. The president was the final authority in foreign affairs and national defense. The president named the prime minister (as the premier was now called), and had the right to dissolve the National Assembly, call for new elections, submit important questions to popular referendums, and

---

[16] See pp. 900–902.
[17] See pp. 589–591, 818.
[18] See pp. 924–928, 933–934.

assume emergency powers, all of which de Gaulle did in his eleven years in office. Political instability disappeared; in the first eleven years of the Fifth Republic there were only three cabinets.

De Gaulle settled the Algerian crisis in his own way. Sensitive to the revolution sweeping the colonial world, he step by step evolved a policy of independence for Algeria, which the country approved in a referendum in July 1962. Even earlier he granted independence to all of the French colonies in sub-Saharan Africa. With peace, governmental stability, and economic prosperity, the French reconciled themselves to the loss of empire and took pride in their heightened importance on the world scene under de Gaulle. France became the world's fifth industrial power in the 1960s, behind only the United States, the U.S.S.R., West Germany, and Japan. In 1960 France became the fourth nation, along with the United States, the U.S.S.R., and Britain, to develop a nuclear capacity. De Gaulle even created an independent nuclear strike force. France also became Western Europe's largest producer of nuclear energy for peacetime energy needs.

After the settlement of the Algerian crisis, de Gaulle built a kind of plebiscitary democracy by direct appeals to the electorate. Although civil liberties were preserved and free speech and free elections maintained, the old democratic ferment disappeared. The older political parties were paralyzed or impotent; skilled technicians ran the affairs of state; and de Gaulle, an uncrowned republican monarch, presided as arbiter over the nation's destinies.

The nation grew restless. A reorganized Socialist party took the lead in uniting the left and reaching out to the middle classes. The country also became impatient with de Gaulle's extravagant posturing in world affairs. Suddenly, in May 1968, grievances in the overcrowded universities sparked a revolt that led to demonstrations by hundreds of thousands of students and then brought 10 million workers out on strike, paralyzing the economy and threatening the regime itself. De Gaulle survived the revolt but only after assuring himself of army support. Holding out the threat of communism and chaos, he won an overwhelming majority for his party in new elections. The country seemed to forget the outburst. Educational changes were introduced, but the economic disruption of the spring hurt the economy. In 1969 de Gaulle chose to make a referendum on a series of constitutional and regional reforms a vote of confidence in himself. When it lost by a small margin, he resigned and retired to his country estate, where he died a year later, an august, heroic, austere, and always controversial figure, whose exploits in war and peace assured him a lasting place in France's history. The stability of the Fifth Republic was one of his greatest accomplishments.

The Federal Republic of Germany

To communicate to the German people and to the entire world the enormity of the Nazi crimes, the four wartime Allies convened an international trial in 1945–1946 at Nuremberg. Hitler, Himmler, and Goebbels were already dead, but twenty-two other Nazi leaders and the major Nazi organizations were indicted for crimes against peace, i.e., plotting and waging a war of aggression; war crimes, which were defined as violations of the accepted laws and conventions of warfare;

and crimes against humanity, i.e., acts of mass murder and genocide. The evidence of evil deeds, massive and incontrovertible, was set down for posterity in many volumes of recorded testimony. Despite the high moral purpose of the trials and an honest effort to establish fair judicial procedures for the accused, some critics at the time and later questioned their appropriateness, especially the decision to try the leaders of a defeated sovereign nation for planning and waging war, and to indict an agency like the General Staff. Some questioned the propriety of the Soviet Union, which had itself contributed to the outbreak of the war, shared in the partition of Poland, and incorporated the Baltic states into its borders, sitting in judgment on the Nazis. Others dismissed the trials as victors' justice. Yet the Nuremberg trials contributed in their way to reinforcing international standards of civilized behavior. The court condemned twelve of the defendants to execution and eleven were hanged, Goering escaping execution by taking poison in his prison cell. Seven received prison terms of varying length, including life sentences; three were acquitted. The last of the Nuremberg prisoners, Rudolf Hess, serving a life sentence, died in Spandau prison in 1987.

On a lesser scale a "denazification" program, carried out by the four occupation authorities, each in its own way, and later by German courts under Allied supervision, produced mixed results. Because so many technically trained and professional Germans had been members of Nazi organizations, it became difficult to exclude them from public life if the normal processes of government were to resume. Some individuals guilty of the more heinous crimes associated with the Third Reich and who had fled the country were still being apprehended and tried many decades after the war's end, by the Germans themselves or in French or Israeli courts.

Divided Germany (and divided Berlin) became a central arena of the Cold War. There was no intention initially of keeping Germany divided, but the sharp differences between the Western powers and the Soviets led to the creation of two German states. The German Democratic Republic became a Communist state, one of the most dependable client states of the Soviet Union. The Federal

GERMANY AND ITS BORDERS, 1919–1990

The upper panel shows the boundaries established after the Treaty of Versailles. Note the free city of Danzig and the Polish Corridor; for these and other areas lost in the First World War see also the map on pp. 728–729. In the middle panel we see the borders at the height of the Second World War in 1942. The Reich proper had then annexed (1) Luxembourg, (2) Alsace and Lorraine from France, (3) Carniola from Yugoslavia, (4) Austria, (5) the Sudeten regions and a Bohemian-Moravian protectorate from Czechoslovakia, (6) the free city of Danzig, and (7) Poland, which was renamed the "General Government." Beyond the borders of the Reich, the Germans occupied France, Belgium, the Netherlands, Denmark, and Norway, and in Eastern Europe had set up controls over the former Baltic states, Byelorussia, and the Ukraine. The lower panel shows Germany after Hitler's defeat. East Prussia has been divided between Poland and the U.S.S.R., and Poland reaches westward almost to Berlin. A communist East Germany (the German Democratic Republic) and a democratic West Germany (the Federal Republic of Germany) grew out of the zones occupied respectively by the Soviets and the West. After the fall of the Communist regime the two Germanys were reunited in 1990.

THE WEIMAR REPUBLIC

HITLER'S
GROSSDEUTSCHES REICH

GERMANY DIVIDED

Republic of Germany became a prosperous parliamentary democracy, fully integrated into the Western political, economic, and military structure.

The German *Wirtschaftswunder*, or "economic miracle," has already been mentioned. By 1950 industrial production surpassed the level of all prewar Germany and within a few years the Federal Republic of Germany with its dynamic export economy became the leading industrial country of Western Europe. The chaos and ruin of 1945, when Hitler's total defeat brought the collapse of organized government, the loss of territory, and widespread suffering, were all but forgotten.

The West German government, even while shaping overall economic policies, encouraged private industry and a capitalist, competitive economy, but also provided broad social services so that it was accurate to refer to a "social market economy." The guaranteed benefits came to exceed those of most other major industrial Western countries. The Federal Republic also pioneered in bringing labor and capital together; a "codetermination" law gave workers seats on the boards of directors of larger firms. The labor unions accepted a role as social partners in the expanding economy, moderating their wage demands to avoid aggravating inflationary pressures.

With the support of the Western occupying powers, which had first encouraged the establishment of independent governments in each state (or *Land*) in West Germany, a constitutional convention representing the ten German states met in 1948–1949 in the quiet Rhineland city of Bonn, which became the federal capital, wrote a Basic Law (or *Grundgesetz*), and officially established the Federal Republic of Germany. The Basic Law, designedly not called a constitution, was to be temporary, valid only until at some future date the two parts of Germany could be reunited. An extensive bill of rights was one of the most prominent features of the Basic Law. Power was decentralized under a federal system, with considerable authority delegated to the states. The founders deliberately set out to avoid the weaknesses of the Weimar Republic.[19] The president, elected indirectly and not by popular vote, was a ceremonial figure with limited political power; a president of stature could, however, as the years revealed, exercise considerable moral authority. The head of government, or real executive, was the chancellor, responsible, along with the cabinet, to the majority in the popularly elected lower house, the Bundestag. To avoid instability, a chancellor could be overthrown only when a new majority was ready with an immediate replacement. Proportional representation guaranteed that each party would be apportioned seats equivalent to its share of the popular vote, but to prevent splinter parties and political fragmentation, a party received seats in the legislature only if it won at least 5 percent of the national vote. The Christian Democratic Union and the Social Democrats emerged as the chief parties and shared between them a large proportion of the popular vote. The Free Democrats, a liberal centrist party, were for a long time the only small party in the legislature and formed coalitions, when necessary, with one or the other of the two major parties.

The Christian Democratic Union (CDU) governed uninterruptedly for twenty years, from 1949 to 1969. In reaction to the Nazi barbarism, it sought to

---

[19] See pp. 785–786, 824.

infuse politics with a moral idealism and ethical purpose. Not a confessional party, it appealed to both Protestants and Catholics, almost equally represented in West Germany, and received strong support from the business community and large segments of the middle classes. The dominating figure in the party and government in the early years was the Christian Democratic leader, Konrad Adenauer, who had begun his career in the pre-1914 imperial era. A patriarchal, strong-willed personality, his ambition was to regain for Germany a position of dignity and international respect. He became chancellor in 1949 at the age of seventy-three (with only a slim majority) and governed for fourteen years. Opponents criticized *der Alte* ("the old man") for creating a "chancellor's democracy," but he provided the resolute leadership, stability, and continuity that made possible the remarkable economic expansion of the early 1950s and the regaining of West German sovereignty. His economics minister, Ludwig Erhard, succeeded him as chancellor in 1963. Elections held every four years confirmed the Christian Democrats as the leading party. Adenauer successfully integrated the Federal Republic of Germany into the emerging political, economic, and military structures of Western Europe. He strengthened ties with France, cooperated in the movement for European economic integration, and won the support and confidence of the United States and the other Western powers. The major opposition party, the Social Democrats, heirs to the Social Democratic party founded in the 1870s,[20] criticized him for his close identification with the United States and the West, and for ignoring the issue of national reunification. Dropping its Marxist ideology at a key party congress in 1959, it broadened its appeal to the middle classes and younger voters.

In 1965 the Social Democrats, who by now had softened their neutralist stand in foreign affairs, joined the Christian Democrats and the Free Democrats in a "grand coalition." Willy Brandt, for many years the popular Social Democratic mayor of West Berlin, as foreign minister launched his "Eastern policy," or *Ostpolitik*, a policy which without abandoning ties to the West encouraged building bridges to the Soviet Union and Eastern Europe, including East Germany. In 1969, he received the support of the Free Democrats and became chancellor of a new coalition, ending the twenty-year rule of the Christian Democrats. Brandt negotiated important treaties with the Soviet Union and Poland in 1970, formally conceding the German frontier at the Oder-Neisse boundary. His government officially recognized the German Democratic Republic, and promoted closer economic ties with it and Eastern Europe. A spy scandal cut short his chancellorship in 1974 and his Social Democratic colleague Helmut Schmidt took over.

Within a decade after the disastrous military defeat that had left a shattered and divided country, West Germany was a major economic and political power, a coveted ally of the West in the Cold War, an equal member of the North Atlantic Treaty Organization. In time a new generation appeared that felt little responsibility for the crimes of the Nazis. Inflammatory issues faded, material progress seemed triumphant over ideology, and democracy seemed assured. Reunification with East Germany remained unlikely, only a remote possibility.

[20] See pp. 615–616.

The Italian Republic

During the bitter struggle to oust the German armies from the Italian peninsula after the fall of Mussolini in 1943, the Italian political parties, repressed for over two decades, sprang to life. All supported the provisional governments in the task of postwar reconstruction and committed themselves to social and moral renewal. In 1946, even though the king had abdicated in favor of his son, the country voted by a narrow margin to abolish the Savoy monarchy, never very distinguished, and now tarnished by its cooperation with the Fascist regime.[21] A constitution for the new Italian Republic established a ceremonial presidency, cabinet government, and legislative supremacy. Proportional representation guaranteed equitable representation for all political parties, large and small; the electorate voted for party lists, not for individuals.

The Christian Democrats became the dominant party. More than a successor to the old Catholic Popular party,[22] it appealed to all classes and sectors of Italian society, successfully blending support for democratic political principles, a moderately regulated free-enterprise economy, and the labor tenets of social Catholicism. Although the party maintained its independence of the Church, it remained close to the hierarchy. In Alcide De Gasperi, who had survived the Fascist years as a librarian in the Vatican, it found an effective leader. For seven formative years from 1946 to 1953 he presided over a series of coalition governments, which made possible postwar economic reconstruction and expansion. In the Cold War he kept Italy firmly in the Western camp. The Communist party successfully publicized its role in the Resistance, capitalized on the cooperation of the country's elites with Fascism, and exploited existing grievances to become the second leading party in the country, which it long remained. As in France, the Communists at first held seats in the cabinet and cooperated in economic reconstruction. But when they fomented politically inspired strikes in 1947, De Gasperi dismissed them from his ministry. In 1948, as noted earlier, the United States, intervening openly for the first time in its history to influence a European election, threw its weight behind the Christian Democrats to thwart the Communist campaign. The Christian Democrats for the first and only time won an absolute majority in the legislature. The Communists, despite their continuing parliamentary strength and support from a third to a fourth of the electorate, remained excluded from the cabinet.

After De Gasperi's disappearance from the political scene in 1953, the Christian Democrats continued to govern under a succession of short-lived coalition cabinets formed with small centrist parties, but the average life of a cabinet was seven months. Although it was difficult for the party to form stable parliamentary coalitions or durable ministries, it clung to power. Over the years the Christian Democrats became faction-ridden and less interested in reform than in patronage. Abandoning their initial idealism, they catered to propertied and conservative interests, and many in the party profited from these connections. In the early 1960s the Socialists, who had by now dissociated themselves from the Communists, for a time became part of the governing coalition, but this "opening to the left" by

[21] See pp. 818–822.
[22] See p. 819.

the Christian Democrats did not alter political rigidities. Although prospering economically, the country grew impatient with the uninterrupted tenure of the Christian Democrats.

The Communists gained further strength in the 1960s. They weakened their ties with Moscow, renounced such tenets of Marxist-Leninist orthodoxy as the dictatorship of the proletariat, and tempered their assault on religion. Architects of what came to be known as "Eurocommunism," they declared that each nation, without deferring to Moscow, must find its own way to a new society through parliamentary democracy and national consensus. The Italian Communists condemned the Soviet military intervention in Eastern Europe and elsewhere (soon to be described) and, ironically, accepted Italian membership in NATO. The strongest Communist party in the Western world, the Italian party counted 1.8 million members at its peak in the mid-1970s, winning the support of 35 percent of the electorate, controlling a powerful labor union confederation, and governing in many major cities, including Rome, with Communist mayors and municipal councils. But when it pressed for seats in the national government, the Christian Democrats rejected the proposal. With the emergence of a revived Socialist party on the national and municipal levels, Communist strength later eroded.

The unstable political scene did not interfere with unprecedented economic growth and prosperity. The industrial triangle of Genoa, Milan, and Turin in northern Italy provided the nucleus for recovery and expansion. A prosperous mixed economy emerged. By 1949 industrial production reached 1939 levels. From 1953 on, Italy's rate of industrial growth rivaled that of West Germany and France. Only the underdeveloped south remained an unresolved trouble area, even in times of advancing prosperity. Italy was transformed from the primarily agricultural country it had been before the Second World War into one of the world's leading industrial nations.

In the late 1960s the economic scene clouded. Italian products became less competitive, a trade deficit developed, inflation set in, and the lira weakened. Because austerity measures were required, the government retrenched on social services. In the autumn of 1969 labor discontent burst out in a wave of strikes that subsided only after substantial wage increases, which further accelerated inflation and ushered in a period of economic uncertainties in the 1970s.[23]

Despite one-party domination, cabinet instability, and periodic social turbulence (a former prime minister was kidnapped and murdered in 1978), the Italian republic in these postwar decades seemed to show flexibility and resilience, an ability to absorb a large Communist party into its parliamentary democracy, and a commitment to honor civil rights and individual freedoms. Fascism seemed forgotten, like a bad dream of the interwar years, a hiatus in history. An economic revolution had elevated living standards for most, if not all, Italians.

112. Reshaping the Global Economy

Even before the close of hostilities the United States, with British support, had developed a bold initiative to reshape the postwar world economy. Determined

---

[23] See pp. 995–998 and 1037–1039.

to avoid the economic nationalism, trade restrictions, and currency instability of the interwar years, the planners hoped to restore the free flow of multilateral trade and the stable currencies of the pre-1914 era.[24] In 1944 the United States convened an international conference of forty-four nations at Bretton Woods in New Hampshire. The participants pledged to reduce trade barriers and work for stable currencies in the postwar world.

The first effort after the war to establish a formal international trade organization to oversee world commerce foundered. Attempts to curtail or abolish preferential systems, trade restrictions, and protectionism met with resistance. Even Britain refused to end its "imperial preferences" arrangements. But an alternative strategy proved more successful. The United States had earlier negotiated trade agreements with a number of countries to reduce tariffs on a reciprocal basis, each agreement including a "most-favored nation" clause whereby a concession to one country was extended to all. These piecemeal arrangements led in 1947 to a broader commitment, the General Agreement on Tariffs and Trade (GATT), subscribed to by twenty-three nations initially, which became the foundation of postwar global commerce. GATT laid down rules to prevent discrimination in international trade, set up administrative procedures for handling complaints, and provided a framework for continuing negotiations. Lengthy bargaining sessions, or "rounds," designed to lower tariffs and remove nontariff barriers, became a prominent feature of the economic landscape. By 1990 ninety-seven countries were participating. GATT was only a partial substitute for a formal international trade organization, but it contributed to the vast expansion of world trade in the 1950s and 1960s. Even when more competitive trade rivalries threatened a revival of protectionism it kept alive the need for negotiation and compromise.

The "world economy" in the postwar years meant the world's non-Communist or free-market economies. The strategic centers were North America and Western Europe, soon joined by Japan, which doubled its share of world trade between 1951 and 1960 and continued to increase its share. Integrated into this world economy were Latin America, Asia, the Middle East, Australasia, and Africa, so that it was truly an economy of global dimensions. The Soviet Union played no part in any of the postwar trade negotiations and restricted its commerce principally to the East European bloc, tying the satellites closely to it. Not until the late 1960s did the Soviet Union and the East European countries develop significant trade and financial relations with the West; not until the late 1980s did they seek full integration into the global economy.

Currency Stability: Toward the "Gold-Dollar" Standard

If the liberalization of trade was the first goal of the wartime Bretton Woods conference, the second objective was stabilization of the world's currencies. The chaos of the interwar years when nation after nation abandoned the gold standard and competed in currency devaluations to gain trade advantages haunted

---

[24] For the "global economy" of the nineteenth century, see pp. 595–605 and 643, and for its changing character after 1914, see pp. 718–722 and 799–804. For a "global economy" in the eighteenth century, see also pp. 257–264. The theme is also noted at the beginning of this book; see pp. 9–10.

everyone.[25] The Bretton Woods conference sought to restore the equivalent of the pre-1914 gold standard, which under British leadership had provided fixed exchange rates and the ready convertibility of all currencies into gold (or into British pounds sterling, then considered the equivalent of gold itself). Currency stabilization, however, turned out to be more difficult than anticipated. The plan for sterling to serve as a reserve currency alongside the dollar proved impossible because of British financial weakness. Britain, the world's second largest creditor nation in 1939, became one of the world's largest debtor nations after the war, its currency in chronic difficulties. Meanwhile huge American trade and dollar surpluses made it impossible for nations with dollar shortages to convert their currencies at fixed exchange rates into dollars (the dollar having been set at $35 per ounce of gold). Not until the end of 1958, by which time Western Europe and Japan had expanded their trade and doubled their dollar reserves, was convertibility possible. For about a dozen years thereafter, until 1971, each major currency had a par value in gold and in dollars. For that same short time the American dollar, like the British pound before 1914, was accepted as the equivalent of gold itself. But the postwar economic scene changed rapidly; the era of the "gold-dollar standard," as we shall see, proved short-lived.

Meanwhile two agencies projected at Bretton Woods and established after the war helped in international financial settlements. The International Monetary Fund (IMF) provided loans for temporary balance of payments difficulties to help reduce the need for currency devaluations. The International Bank for Reconstruction and Development (or World Bank) made long-term loans to governments for economic development or guaranteed the loans made by private bankers. Both agencies played a larger role in later years than in the immediate postwar era. Both were located in Washington, their major funding provided by the United States. The economic center of gravity for the West, like the political and the military, lay on the American side of the Atlantic.

European Integration: The Common Market and the European Community

As Western Europe expanded economically, it also drew closer together. There had long been proposals for a European federation, but it was the wartime Resistance movements that reinforced the idea that Europe's future lay in unity. The Cold War, the Marshall Plan, and cooperative European recovery efforts further promoted the desire for unity. A number of European leaders pressed for the creation of a "United States of Europe." In 1948 delegates representing the parliaments of ten countries met in Strasbourg to establish a Council of Europe with the hope that it might become a legislative body for a federated Europe. The British, interested in cooperation but not integration, opposed any form of supranational authority. Although the Council of Europe grew in membership over the years and continued to support the idea of federation, it never became an important political force.

European integration took a different path. In 1948 the three small countries,

---

[25] See pp. 802–804.

Belgium, the Netherlands, and Luxembourg, created a customs union, called Benelux, which provided the benefits of a sizable free trade area. At the same time Jean Monnet, a visionary but intensely practical French economist and administrator, at an early date recognized that the first steps to unity had to be along economic lines. Political leaders like Schuman in France, Paul-Henri Spaak in Belgium, Adenauer in West Germany, and De Gasperi in Italy responded warmly to proposals for economic integration. In 1952, under a plan designed by Monnet, six West European countries, France, West Germany, Italy, and the three Benelux nations, placed their coal and steel industries under a form of supranational authority, establishing the European Coal and Steel Community (ECSC) with headquarters in Luxembourg. Initially the plan was designed to allay anxiety about the revival of German heavy industry and guarantee access for all to the coal and steel resources of the Ruhr, but it went much further. The participating nations not only agreed to eliminate import duties and quotas on coal and steel but placed production under a common High Authority with extensive decision-making powers. A council of ministers represented the six governments, but the High Authority carried out major administrative functions.

Monnet was the first president of the ECSC, which in the years that followed integrated West European heavy industry, modernized production, provided new kinds of institutional machinery for cooperation among the member states, and paved the way for additional economic integration that would extend beyond a single sector of the West European economy. In a momentous second step, the same six nations, on March 25, 1957, signed the Treaty of Rome, creating a large free trade area or customs union, the European Economic Community (EEC) or Common Market, its headquarters in Brussels, with the explicit goal of moving toward full economic and even political integration. The treaty called for the elimination of tariff barriers among the six nations, the development of a common tariff with respect to the outside world, the harmonization of social and economic policies, and the free movement of capital and labor. The last provision made it possible for migrant, or "guest" workers to move back and forth without impediment to meet the labor needs of the expanding economies. Under a second treaty the six countries also agreed to coordinate their nonmilitary atomic research and technology in a European Atomic Community (Euratom). The European Economic Community (and Euratom) took over much of the institutional machinery of the ECSC.

The European Economic Community, or Common Market, in operation in 1958, embracing six nations and 175 million people, quickly became one of the thriving economic aggregates of the expanding world economy. By 1968, even earlier than anticipated, the last internal tariff was dropped and trade among the six nations grew at a rate double that of trade with outside countries. The EEC represented the six nations in negotiations with GATT. Its influence spread to the former European colonies, with which it worked out preferential trade arrangements. A value-added tax imposed by each member-country at the point of production eliminated the need for indirect taxes; a portion of that tax and of the external tariffs gave the Community independent revenues. Through the Common Market, Western Europe set about to recapture a key role in the new configuration of global affairs; without it, Europe would be dwarfed by the superpowers. It helped absorb a revived West Germany into Europe and ended the internecine rivalries that had exhausted the Continent in the first half of the twentieth century.

In 1967 the three "communities," the European Coal and Steel Community, the European Economic Community, and Euratom consolidated themselves into what was designated the European Community. The three high commissions became the European Commission and the common assemblies became the European Parliament, meeting in Strasbourg. Walter Hallstein, the West German president of the European Commission, described himself as "the first European prime minister." The members of the European Parliament took seats by party affiliation and not by nation. In 1979, for the first time, they were not chosen by their respective governments but were elected by a European-wide electorate. The European Parliament enjoyed only limited legislative authority, but it kept alive the idea of unity. Final decision making still rested with the council of ministers representing each of the member nations, whose decisions on fundamental matters had to be unanimous.

At the beginning Great Britain refrained from joining the Common Market. Britain's economic ties to the Commonwealth, its dependence on low-priced food imports, and its unwillingness to accept any supranational authority persuaded both the Labour and Conservative parties to refrain from joining. As an alternative, Britain helped create in 1960 a more limited customs union of seven states, a European Free Trade Association (EFTA), in which Norway, Sweden, Denmark, Austria, Switzerland, and Portugal joined with Britain in reducing tariff barriers but which had no larger ambitions for economic or political integration. For a time EFTA seemed to be a rival to the Common Market, but the sense of competition between them eased and trade between the two trading blocs grew. Britain, its own economy lagging behind that of the West Europeans, eventually sought membership in the Common Market in 1963, but its request was twice vetoed by President de Gaulle, who was wary of Britain's special relationship with the United States and saw Britain as a rival to his own country for leadership on the Continent. Not until after he passed from the political scene in 1969 was Britain admitted and the Community enlarged.[26]

If the years 1958–1968 showed remarkable gains in economic integration, the advance toward political unity was slower. De Gaulle understood the contribution of the Common Market to the prosperity of Western Europe as well as the importance of a strong Western Europe as a counterpoise to the two "hegemonic superpowers," but he firmly opposed political or supranational authority for the Community. Europe had to be a Europe of sovereign states, a *"Europe des patries."* The council of ministers retained its importance. The more dedicated Europeanists were disappointed. Yet the supranational economic and political machinery of the Community, the day-to-day cooperation of the European civil servants or bureaucrats (inevitably called "Eurocrats") in Luxembourg, Brussels, and Strasbourg, and the close consultation on common interests were favorable signs for unity, even apart from the military and defense ties that brought the Western Europeans together in NATO. French-German friendship, cemented by de Gaulle and Adenauer, and reinforced by their successors, remained the linchpin of cooperation within the Community. The likelihood of political union, a "United

[26] See p. 1000.

States of Europe'' remained remote. The Europeans showed no haste to surrender their national sovereignty and independence, but the European Community created a strong sense of common destiny, a shared faith in democratic institutions and market economies, and a concern for human rights and social needs. The European Community not only contributed immeasurably to the economic and political strength of Western Europe but helped restore it to a larger role in world affairs.

Western Europe once again played a central role in the world's economy, accounting in the 1960s for one-fourth of all imports and one-fifth of all exports; for a time its exports equalled those of the United States and Japan combined. One-third of the largest multinational corporations, that is, corporations which set up subsidiaries outside their own country for manufacturing or sales, were European. London, Frankfurt, and Paris again became important financial centers. In 1971 West European steel production surpassed that of the United States. European (and Japanese) automobiles cut sharply into American domestic and foreign markets. Self-sufficient in food, Western Europe became the world's largest exporter of dairy products, even though 10 million people left the farms for the cities in the 1950s and 1960s. The Federal Republic of Germany enjoyed a gross national product second only to that of the United States and the U.S.S.R., even though it had only one-fourth the population of each; it accounted for one-third of the Common Market gross national product. Although the United States still led Western Europe in per capita income, the gap was narrowing. Western Europe and Japan were whittling away at the American economic lead in production and trade and bringing to a close the era of the dollar's supremacy.

End of the Gold-Dollar Standard, 1971

New trading patterns created new monetary problems. The growth of the West European economies, especially that of West Germany, and of the Japanese economy led to an explosive expansion in the 1960s of West European and Japanese exports, which competed successfully in the American domestic market and in markets throughout the world. Because American exports no longer exceeded its imports, the American trade balance shifted unfavorably. By 1970 the American trade deficit with Western Europe rose to over $10 billion a year. Continuing American military expenditures abroad as well as corporate investment in Western Europe and in the developing countries accelerated the outflow of American capital. Not only the balance of trade but the total balance of payments shifted unfavorably. The United States spent more abroad than it earned abroad. The postwar dollar shortage in other countries gave way to a ''dollar glut.'' Western Europe accumulated large dollar reserves (or ''Euro-dollars''), some $50 billion by 1971; oil-rich Arab states held ''petrodollars.'' The number of dollars held abroad exceeded American gold reserves.

The shift in the American economic position undermined confidence in a dollar which many now viewed as overvalued. The Americans argued that they had faithfully kept the dollar pegged to its gold value to preserve international stability. De Gaulle, ever resentful of American political and economic hegemony, demanded an end to the gold-dollar standard and a return to gold itself. In 1965 France, claiming its right under the existing system, redeemed hundreds of millions of its dollar holdings for gold. Even though other central banks in Europe and Japan did not follow suit, private investors speculated against the dollar. American gold and foreign currency reserves dropped precipitously. The image of the dollar as an unassailable citadel of strength in the postwar era faded.

In 1971 President Nixon unilaterally suspended gold convertibility and devalued the dollar; a second devaluation followed in 1973. The monetary system projected at Bretton Woods came to an end. The world monetary system entered a new era. Despite many proposals, there was no formal reform of the system. Instead, on a day-to-day basis, and with mixed success, the world's major currencies were allowed to "float," that is, to fluctuate daily against each other and against the dollar. Gold itself fluctuated freely and official gold prices were abolished. Although the American dollar remained the world's principal reserve currency, the West German mark and the Japanese yen took their place beside the dollar as key currencies. The new arrangements more accurately reflected the redistribution of economic power.

The breakdown of the postwar monetary arrangements did not affect the world's currencies as seriously as might have been expected. Currencies did not collapse because they were no longer exchangeable for gold, but fluctuations in the major currencies remained unsettling. Private speculators could outwit the central banks and run up spectacular overnight profits. The West European countries established a European Monetary System in 1979, with an exchange rate mechanism to keep currency variations within narrower limits, but it too developed problems. The world continued to grope its way toward new monetary arrangements, relying mainly on close international consultation and rapid exchange of information. The major nations were trying to manage exchange rates but still had much to learn. Some looked to a modified Bretton Woods system, with predictable if not fixed exchange rates; others to a strengthened International Monetary Fund, or other international agency. In the interdependent global economy everyone knew that cooperation and partnership were essential.

113. The Communist World: The U.S.S.R. and Eastern Europe

Stalinism in the Postwar Years

In March 1953 Russia's twentieth-century Peter the Great died. Stalin had a massive impact during his close to thirty years in power. He was responsible for industrialization, the rallying of the country in the Great Patriotic War, the expansion of the nation's borders, the consolidation of Communist regimes in Eastern Europe, and the emergence of the Soviet Union as a nuclear superpower.[27] But the human costs of the Stalinist transformation of the country were staggering. Millions fell victim to his forced collectivization of the countryside and the ensuing famine, and additional millions to his purges. Western and Soviet scholars alike have estimated the total figure of Stalin's victims at least as high as 20 million.

[27] See pp. 762–772, 855–858, 870–875, 882.

Because the civil war and war communism earlier, under Lenin, also cost millions of lives, the Bolshevik Revolution must be counted among the costliest experiments in social engineering in all history.

The Stalinist terror continued during the war. Entire ethnic groups like the Crimean Tatars and the Volga Germans, suspected of collaboration with the Nazis, were forcibly moved east to Siberia. Mass deportations took place from the three Baltic republics formally annexed in 1940.[28] At the war's end, returning Soviet soldiers who had been prisoners of war and civilian deportees forced to work for the Nazis in Europe were sent off to labor camps because their exposure to the West made them suspect. The network of forced labor camps grew in size. Ideological restrictions tightened. Stalin's personal suspicions, growing sharper with the passage of the years, filled even his closest associates with dismay. The unbridled authority of the NKVD (later the KGB), the secret political police that did Stalin's bidding, continued in power, gaining ascendancy over the party itself. In later years, in a freer atmosphere, the country debated whether Stalin's dictatorship represented a logical outgrowth of the Bolshevik Revolution itself and of many of Lenin's policies, or was an aberration.

Controls over intellectual life in the postwar years took on a vehemently nationalistic and xenophobic tone; deviations from Stalin's "line" in economics, music, genetics, history, and linguistics were forbidden. An officially inspired anti-Semitism, thinly disguised as anti-Zionism, emerged; Jewish intellectuals were accused of being "rootless cosmopolitans." Party purges and massive arrests continued into the last years of Stalin's life. The political police meanwhile fabricated conspiracies to justify the terror. In the fictitious "doctors' plot," officially announced in early 1953, a score of Jewish doctors were arrested for plotting to poison Stalin and other Kremlin leaders; one month after Stalin died, his successors withdrew the charges and freed the imprisoned doctors.

Khrushchev: The Abortive Effort at Reform

After Stalin's death the party leaders were resolved to exercise collective control, determined that no single leader should again dominate party and government. To thwart a coup by Lavrenti Beria, who had headed the secret police since 1939, the new leaders quickly arrested and executed him. In the struggle for power, authority gradually shifted to Nikita S. Khrushchev. Outwardly jovial and ebullient, Khrushchev was a tough and hardened realist who had enforced Stalin's purges in the Ukraine as provincial secretary and had been a member of the Central Committee since 1934 and of the Politburo since 1939. But he was shrewd enough to recognize the need for change.

In part to win allies against conservatives in the party who were opposed to change, Khrushchev encouraged a greater measure of cultural and intellectual freedom—a "thaw." He put restraints on the still formidable powers of the political police. He surprised many with his attack on Stalin himself. In a speech to the twentieth party congress in 1956, he officially revealed or corroborated the "crimes of the Stalin era," making partial but nonetheless startling disclosures of the Stalinist terror and confirming the worst speculations of Western critics

---

[28] See map, pp. 872–873.

over the years. Stalin had been personally responsible for the purges and executions of the 1930s and millions of victims had been innocent of the charges against them; his most intimate colleagues had lived in fear for their lives. Khrushchev also revealed Stalin's initial loss of nerve and ineptitude at the time of the German invasion in June 1941.

The attack on Stalin undermined faith in a regime which had permitted these evils. Khrushchev's speech immediately unloosed a reaction in the East European satellites. Open rebellion broke out in Hungary. The other party leaders were uneasy at Khrushchev's liberalizing reforms; his flamboyant personality made them also fear a new "cult of personality."

The "thaw" was never systematic or thorough. In 1958 Boris Pasternak was forbidden to accept the Nobel Prize in literature because his novel, *Dr. Zhivago*, by stressing individual freedom, implicitly condemned the oppressiveness of Soviet society. But in 1962 Alexander Solzhenitsyn was permitted to publish his *One Day in the Life of Ivan Denisovich*, a depiction of human suffering in the world of the forced labor camps. Khrushchev continued his de-Stalinization campaign. Cities named in Stalin's honor were renamed; Stalingrad, the most famous, became Volgograd. Stalin's body was removed from the mausoleum on Red Square, where it lay next to Lenin's, and buried outside the Kremlin Wall.

For the economy Khrushchev pressed decentralization. He attempted to loosen tight central economic controls by creating regional economic councils. He offered factory managers greater autonomy and incentives for efficiency and profitability. Meanwhile the country successfully tested the hydrogen bomb, launched Sputnik, and built its first intercontinental ballistic missiles. The Soviet economy was said to be second only to that of the United States in gross national product. Within a decade, Khrushchev boasted in the 1960s, the Soviet economy would surpass the American. The stress on heavy industry and on military expenditures meant, of course, continuing privation for the ordinary citizen and the emphasis on quantitative production concealed deep flaws in the system as a whole.

Khrushchev's most ambitious effort lay in agriculture, the weakest sector of the economy ever since Stalin's forced collectivization. He sought to bring under cultivation the "virgin lands" of Soviet Central Asia, in Kazakhstan and elsewhere, but crop failures thwarted the experiment. His reforms did little to alter the bureaucratized system of collective and state farms inherited from Stalin or inspire the collective farmers to increase their crops. For the party itself he unsuccessfully sought fixed terms of office for important party posts. Few of his reforms were acceptable to the government and party bureaucrats, the *apparatchki*, who saw their privileged positions threatened and who mustered opposition to his "hare-brained" schemes.

Khrushchev pursued an erratic and truculent foreign policy. Proclaiming that war was not inevitable with the United States and other capitalist countries, he spoke of "peaceful coexistence," and relations for a time improved, as we shall see. But in 1960 he scuttled a summit meeting with Allied leaders and in 1962 overreached himself in the Cuban missile crisis.[29] He also clashed openly with Communist China. His boastfulness and recklessness, his retreat in Cuba, the failure of his agricultural and other economic policies, his attempt to tamper with

[29] See p. 984.

the party itself led to his downfall. In 1964 he was ousted from all of his offices. He lived quietly in Moscow until his death in 1971. In the post-Stalin era, a reformer did not necessarily have to fear for his life, but there were clear limits to the reforms the party and bureaucracy would tolerate.

The Brezhnev Era

In replacing Khruschev in 1964, the party again attempted unsuccesssfully to separate the top government and party posts and to stress collective leadership. Leonid I. Brezhnev, who became party secretary, soon eclipsed all other colleagues. A tough-minded, colorless, and dour political personality, Brezhnev dominated the party and government for close to eighteen years. He repressed dissent at home and in Eastern Europe. The "thaw," incomplete as it was, ended. Physically incapacitated at the close of his tenure but still clinging to power, Brezhnev died in office in 1982. During his rule, he increased the country's military and naval strength but he also renewed efforts at détente with the West. The superficial stability of the Brezhnev years concealed social tensions and serious economic failures.

Yet the Brezhnev years began with a promise of reform. The party reversed some of Khruschev's policies but moved forward with others. While phasing out his regional economic councils, it tried to provide incentives for higher productivity in industry and agriculture. But the reforms, never far-reaching, aroused the opposition of the ever wary party and government bureaucracy, and were abandoned within a relatively short time.

A Troubled Economy and Society

Centralized planning for the economy, inaugurated by Stalin in 1928,[30] resumed after the war under the Fourth Five Year Plan (1946–1950) and subsequent plans. Wartime devastation was repaired and the economy grew impressively, even if not as rapidly as outsiders at the time were given to believe. Gross national product increased at a respectable annual rate. By the 1970s the Soviet Union was the world's leading producer of coal, steel, pig iron, cement, cotton, natural gas, and oil. It built defense industries and pioneered in space technology, and was one of the two nuclear superpowers of the world. Whereas in 1950 Soviet gross national product was only 30 percent of the American, in 1975 it was 60 percent. The Soviet Union appeared to be developing into a modern industrial society; many hoped that industrialization would lead it toward a more democratic society as well. But there were deep flaws in the system.

Rigid controls, concentration of expenditures and skills on heavy industry and armaments, and overall planning that virtually ignored consumer needs, all features of the Soviet economy since the 1930s, prevented any real advance in living standards. Conditions improved, to be sure, after 1950, and Soviet citizens enjoyed job security and a network of social services. Per capita consumption tripled; people were better clothed and ate a more varied diet; more refrigerators, more washing machines, and television sets were available in the 1970s than

[30] See pp. 762–770.

before. But consumer products were of shoddy quality; many items, including food, remained scarce; store shelves were empty; people spent long hours waiting in queues. Urban housing needs remained especially urgent. The intense demand for consumer goods encouraged a thriving black market and an underground economy.

All these problems were openly acknowledged, but efforts to remedy the situation would have required loosening party and governmental controls. Many years after the Revolution, despite industrialization and military strength that made it one of the world's two military superpowers, the Soviet citizen could purchase only two-fifths the goods and services that an American could, and living standards were below those of several of the satellite states in Eastern Europe.

The U.S.S.R. lagged in newer industrial technology. After the war it had restored its old factories, coal mines, steel mills, shipyards, and railroad network, but with the older technology of the 1930s. It was this obsolescent economy that expanded after the war at a time when the West, Japan, and other parts of East Asia were turning to computers, electronics, and automation. Only in military and space technology could the Soviets still marshal talents and resources for impressive projects. Otherwise central planning stifled initiative and entrepreneurship. From the late 1960s on, the U.S.S.R. encouraged foreign capital and Western industrial technology, but after 1974 the socialist countries, too, were caught up in the global economic recession. At the outset of the 1980s the Soviet economic growth rate dropped to 2 percent, then virtually to zero. The infrastructure fell into decay. The Soviet Union ranked as a formidable military and nuclear superpower but not as a modern industrial society. Official production targets were met at the sacrifice of quality. Support for improved technology, efficient management, and productivity, all spurred in open market economies by competition, lagged.

Agriculture persisted as the weakest part of the economy. Despite large investments in the 1970s, double those of the previous decade, and the creation of an artificial fertilizer industry, output did not increase. The much vaunted mechanization of the collective farms proved to be an illusion. Farm machinery was often poorly utilized and spare parts were unavailable. Poor roads made it difficult to transport farm products to markets or to processing plants. Meanwhile, in the 1970s, 15 million farm workers left the farms for the cities in search of better opportunities. Because the government decided to increase meat production, grain needs for livestock tripled between 1960 and 1980, adding further to the strain on agriculture. There were poor harvests as well. By 1980 domestic production of grain had fallen so far below government targets that for the next six years the government ceased publishing production figures. What began in the 1960s as the need to import grain intermittently became a permanent practice after 1972, with the United States one of the chief suppliers. The imports consumed foreign exchange that might otherwise have been available to purchase industrial machinery.

The Brezhnev regime refused to face the flawed economy realistically. Bribery, embezzlement of state funds, and corruption became widespread. For the average citizen life remained bleak. There was a sharp increase in drunkenness and absenteeism. Economic tinkering alone could not reverse the trend, but the entrenched party and government bureaucracy, the *nomenklatura,* the dignitaries in the party and government named to their posts by the party, rejected any reforms that might reduce their authority. An aging party and government elite controlled the country. From 1966 to 1985 three-fourths of the party's Central Committee were regularly and dutifully reelected. From 1975 on, when Brezhnev suffered a stroke, a small clique around him made the important decisions. When he became further incapitated in the next few years, the same sycophantic circle continued to project the image of the strong leader, shielding him, inflating his merits, showering him with decorations and medals, and building up a cult of adulation.

On the cultural front, a hard line prevailed. De-Stalinization ended. The regime clamped down on dissidents who, encouraged by the earlier relaxation of controls, pressed for greater freedom. Yet in spite of repression, the dissident movement grew. Never large in numbers, the dissidents represented the scientific and cultural leaders of the country—the intelligentsia. Underground journals appeared; privately-printed manuscripts (called *samizdat*) circulated secretly; scientists and other intellectuals signed open petitions of protest. Some fled abroad and others were expelled from the country. Solzhenitsyn was exiled for allowing the publication abroad of his book, *The Gulag Archipelago,* which described the network of forced labor camps in even more brutal detail than his earlier work. The nuclear physicist, Andrei Sakharov, for speaking up against the return to Stalinism, was removed from his work in Moscow and banished from the capital. Soviet Jews, chafing at the restrictions on their cultural and religious freedom, attempted to emigrate, and in the peak year 1979 over 50,000 left the country; but the rules soon changed, and in the early 1980s emigration was sharply reduced. The Brezhnev coterie also kept an iron grip on the East European satellites, as we shall see, and in 1979 the Soviets sent troops into Afghanistan to prop up a faltering Marxist regime, involving the country in what became a nine-year military misadventure.[31]

At great cost to an already strained economy, the Brezhnev regime directed vast expenditures into a defense program designed to achieve parity with the United States in strategic arms and to build a modern navy. The United States in turn responded with its own build-up and the arms race escalated. In other ways the regime made efforts to relax tensions with the West. The Soviets joined in the European Economic and Security Conference at Helsinki in 1975 and signed the Helsinki accords, pledging peace, cooperation, and respect for human rights. Strategic arms limitation talks with the United States resulted in the signing of a treaty in 1979. But the brief period of détente soon ended and in the early 1980s the Cold War entered a more intense phase.[32]

When Brezhnev died in 1982, the cult of Brezhnev disappeared overnight. There had been little enthusiasm for him or for the small circle that surrounded him. The Brezhnev years, it was widely acknowledged, had led to stagnation, an unwillingness to address the growing problems of the economy, repression in Eastern Europe, and an unpopular war in Afghanistan. Although the country no

[31] See pp. 1002–1003.
[32] See pp. 1005–1006.

longer had the Stalinist terror to fear, repression and abuse of authority continued in the party-dominated police state.

Brezhnev's Successors: Andropov and Chernenko

In choosing Yuri V. Andropov as Brezhnev's immediate successor in 1982, the party leadership conceded the need for change. Although Andropov had headed the state security police for fifteen years, he had curbed some of its arbitrary powers. As head of the KGB, he had been in a unique position to appreciate the true state of Soviet society and the economy. He brought economists and other specialists to Moscow to assist him. Publicly he inveighed against the corruption of party and government officials, dismissed some of the old guard, and pledged incentives and rewards for farm and factory workers. Andropov might have changed matters, but for a good part of his brief fifteen-month tenure he was incapacitated by illness and died in office. The Politburo, determined to avoid further change, chose as his successor Konstantin U. Chernenko, who had been a close associate of Brezhnev. Ironically, he, too, was aging and ill at the time of his selection. He took no new initiatives. The party and country seemed to be marking time while economic problems worsened, the war dragged on in Afghanistan, and the arms race continued. By the end of 1984 Chernenko, terminally ill, made no further public appearances and died in March 1985. His successor was to open a new era in Soviet history.[33]

Eastern Europe: The Decades of Dictatorship

Although nothing like the Russian Revolution of 1917[34] erupted in Europe after the Second World War, communism made dramatic advances in Central and Eastern Europe, not through popular revolution but through the Red Army's military presence and the support given to local Communist leaders. The revolutionary flare-ups in Europe after the First World War had flickered out,[35] but with the Second World War eleven European states and 100 million Europeans fell under Communist-style governments. The areas considered in 1919 to be a protective buffer against Bolshevism were now under Communist domination. An "iron curtain," as Churchill said, had descended, roughly along the old Elbe-Trieste line, sharpening the centuries-old divergencies in the development of Western and Eastern Europe.[36]

In 1939, even before the U.S.S.R. was at war, the three Baltic states Estonia, Latvia, and Lithuania came under Soviet control under the terms of the Nazi-Soviet pact, and in 1940 they were incorporated into the U.S.S.R. as Soviet socialist republics. Later in the sweep of military operations during the last months of the war Poland, Hungary, Romania, Bulgaria, and Czechoslovakia fell into the orbit of Soviet influence. In all these states, which the West came to

[33] See pp. 1025–1033.
[34] See pp. 722, 746–754.
[35] See p. 779.
[36] See pp. 125–126, 210–249, 586–587, 781–783, and map, p. 212.

call satellites, Communist-dominated coalition governments took control. East Germany, initially part of the joint Allied occupation of Germany, was shaped into a sixth Soviet satellite as the German Democratic Republic. Yugoslavia and Albania, liberated by their own partisan leaders rather than by the Red Army, were governed by Communist regimes but with looser ties to the Soviet Union and soon broke with the Soviets. Despite its defeat in the Soviet-Finnish War in 1940, Finland escaped Communist domination. Accepting its wartime territorial losses, it maintained its independence by a cautious neutrality in foreign policy and a discreetly correct relationship with the Soviets. Austria, after a decade of joint occupation by the four Allied powers, gained independence as a neutral state in 1955.

Consolidation of Communist Control

The Soviets consolidated control in Eastern Europe in stages. In Poland, Bulgaria, Romania, and Hungary, Soviet military occupation made it possible for local Communist leaders, many trained in Moscow and returning from exile, to dominate left coalition governments. In Bulgaria, Communist domination was complete from the beginning. In the case of Poland, Western pressure at Yalta and Potsdam forced the Soviets to give representation to the government-in-exile in London; the leader of the agrarian party returned to Poland to serve for a time as deputy premier. In the early coalition governments, the Communists shared power but held the key ministries of interior, propaganda, and justice, and controlled the police, the army, and the courts. Individuals alleged to have been "fascist" or to have collaborated with the Nazis were barred from public life and from voting; the loose definition of "fascist" and "reactionary" barred many who were only anti-Communist. In the first elections, in Poland and elsewhere, purges and disfranchisement made a mockery of Stalin's pledge at Yalta to hold free and unfettered elections in Eastern Europe. Protests by the United States and Great Britain only hardened the Soviet position.

The new regimes confiscated and redistributed large estates and put uncultivated land to use, so that 3 million peasant families acquired about 6 million acres of land; the agrarian reforms were the final blow to the landed aristocracy that had once ruled in Eastern Europe.[37] They also nationalized the economy. As they struggled with postwar reconstruction, the new regimes, as noted earlier, lent a sympathetic ear to the American invitation in 1947 to accept Marshall Plan aid. But Stalin was not disposed to permit the East European countries to drift into the Western economic orbit, nor did he view favorably the growing pressure for free elections in which the Communists could lose their hold. After the summer of 1947, wherever non-Communists were still strong, the Communists ousted their political rivals and banned or reduced to impotence all other political parties. In Czechoslovakia, as we have seen, the coalition government lasted longer than elsewhere but fell victim to a Communist coup in February 1948.

With the Communists in control, the leaders of the opposition political parties were forced into flight, imprisoned, or in other ways silenced. The new regimes, most notably in Poland and Hungary, clashed also with the Catholic Church;

[37] See pp. 781–783.

high-ranking prelates were denounced, brought to public trial and imprisoned, and church property confiscated. The Communist leaders themselves soon became Stalin's victims. From 1949 to 1953, reflecting the repression in the Soviet Union in Stalin's last years, purges, arrests, trials, confessions, and executions occurred in the highest ranks of each party. Leaders were accused of nationalist deviations and of conspiring with Tito, the independent-minded Communist leader of Yugoslavia.

After the consolidation of Communist power in the new "people's democracies" steps were taken to collectivize agriculture, with uneven results. In Bulgaria, the most docile of the satellites, over half the arable land was collectivized, but in Hungary only about a third. In Poland, where resistance was strongest, collectivization was halted after a short time, and most of the land remained in private possession. The collectivization process delayed the postwar recovery of Eastern Europe. Agriculture in the people's republics, as in the Soviet Union, remained the weakest part of the economy. Peasants diligently cultivated the land permitted them individually but worked reluctantly on the large collectives.

Under Soviet-style centrally planned economies and five-year plans, the East European countries industrialized. Poland and Hungary, agricultural before the war, became industrial states; Czechoslovakia and East Germany, already industrial, expanded their manufacturing base. But as a result of the emphasis on heavy industry to the neglect of consumer goods, and pressures to complement the economy of the Soviet Union, industrialization brought only slow improvement in East European living standards.

The Soviets formalized their economic relationship with East Europe through the Council for Mutual Economic Assistance (COMECON), established in 1949 in reaction to the integration of Western Europe accompanying the Marshall Plan, but it never worked as cooperation among equals. The Soviets provided low-cost raw materials and oil and offered a large market for East European goods, regardless of their quality, but much of the economic cooperation principally benefited the Soviet Union. The Warsaw Pact, signed in 1955, brought the six East European countries together into a mutual defense alliance. Large numbers of Soviet troops remained stationed in Eastern Europe, mainly in East Germany.

In the early postwar years, Yugoslavia, freed from the Nazis largely by its own partisan armies, made a remarkable show of resistance to the Soviets. The Yugoslav Communist leader, Marshal Tito, loosened centralized controls over the economy, abandoned the collectivization of agriculture, pursued an independent foreign policy, and openly defied Moscow. The Soviet leadership denounced him but after Stalin's death sought to woo him back to the fold. The first major Communist figure to declare his independence of Moscow, Tito established a model that other Communist leaders and parties would later follow.

Ferment and Repression in East Germany,
Poland, and Hungary, 1953–1956

The changes in the Soviet Union after Stalin's death directly affected the Soviet satellites. The East Europeans chafed at land collectivization, forced industrialization, austere living standards, subservience to the Soviet Union, and harsh rule by Stalinist-type leaders who remained in power for years after Stalin's death. An initial outburst, riots in East Berlin in June 1953, was quickly suppressed. The ferment rose to the surface after Khrushchev denounced the brutal character of the Stalin dictatorship and, in an attempt to win back Yugoslavia, made the official concession that "different roads to socialism" were possible. That concession and his "de-Stalinization" speech in 1956 opened a Pandora's box; destroying Stalin's infallibility destroyed Soviet infallibility as well.

In 1956, open revolt broke out in Poland and Hungary, led by the East European Communist party leaders themselves. In Poland, where national sentiment and religious attachments ran deep, pressures for internal freedom and for independence from Moscow led to riots and demonstrations. The unrest brought to power the Communist leader Wladyslaw Gomulka, who had at one time been discredited and even imprisoned for his nationalist deviationism. Gomulka relaxed political and economic controls, halted collectivization of the farms, improved relations with the Catholic church, and took steps to loosen the bonds to Moscow. The country as a whole saw him as an alternative to direct Soviet control. Khrushchev threatened military action, but then backed down. For a few years, Gomulka curbed police terror and created a freer atmosphere, but the reform era was short-lived.[38]

In Hungary, in 1956, events took a tragic turn. When news of Gomulka's success in Poland reached Budapest, demonstrations broke out; young rioters even toppled a statue of Stalin. The reform-minded Communist leader Imre Nagy, who had earlier been driven from the premiership in 1955 for his efforts at liberalization, returned to power. His reform program and release of political prisoners ignited pressures for democratization, parliamentary government, and the severance of ties to Moscow. The Soviets took alarm. They forced the party leadership to remove Nagy from power and to replace him with János Kádár, a leader more subservient to Moscow, who accepted Soviet intervention. Khrushchev dispatched troops, tanks, and artillery to suppress the "counterrevolution," as the Soviets termed it, and forcefully reestablished Communist rule. Severe reprisals followed. Nagy himself was imprisoned, then tried and hanged, and his body thrown into a mass grave. In the wake of the repression, 200,000 Hungarians fled into exile, mainly to the United States, more than at any time since the crushing of the European revolutions of 1848–1849.[39] The Soviet tanks in Budapest destroyed any remaining illusions about the benevolence and liberalism of Stalin's successors and shook the Communist faithful in Western Europe and elsewhere.

The 1960s: The "Prague Spring"

Despite the failure of the Hungarian uprising, the longing for liberalization and independence refused to be suppressed. In Hungary, once the regime was preserved, even Kádár, who remained in power for the next three decades, created a freer cultural and intellectual atmosphere and loosened economic controls. In Poland the church retained a powerful hold on the population, an

---

[38] See pp. 990 and 1018–1021.
[39] See pp. 512–513, 519.

unofficial culture flourished, and agitation grew in the cities and countryside. In Romania, Nicolae Ceausescu took over as party leader in 1964 and ruled through a harsh personal dictatorship, but the Romanian leader asserted his independence of the Soviets in foreign affairs and resisted pressures for tighter economic integration into the Soviet economy.

In Czechoslovakia in the 1960s the internal reforms went furthest and posed the most direct challenge to the Soviets. The reform movement climaxed in 1968 when Alexander Dubcek, who spoke openly of "communism with a human face," emerged as party and government leader. Dubcek curbed police repression, permitted freedom of the press, democratized the government, and legalized non-Communist political organizations. Compatriots and outsiders alike hailed the "Prague spring." For Brezhnev, who had displaced Khrushchev in 1964, and the Soviet leadership, such far-reaching reforms represented a threat to the Soviet grip on Eastern Europe. In August 1968 they ended the "Prague spring." Brezhnev dispatched 250,000 troops, including token Polish, Hungarian, Bulgarian, and East German contingents to crush the incipient revolution. The hapless revolutionists, stunned and infuriated, were forced to restore Communist party control, remove Dubcek, reimpose censorship, and curb democratization. Reprisals followed and the new leadership imposed severe dictatorial controls. Once again the Soviets had crushed a "counterrevolution." The Soviets served notice that under the "Brezhnev Doctrine" (as it came to be called) they reserved the right to intervene if a socialist regime was threatened anywhere. They served notice also of the limits to which they would tolerate freedom and independence in central and eastern Europe. The events in Prague in 1968, even more than the suppression of the 1956 Hungarian uprising, alienated the Communist faithful in many parts of the world.

In the Era of Détente

By the 1960s, despite the continuing political repression, an agrarian Eastern Europe was being shaped into an urban, industrial society. Consumer goods were scarce but in greater supply, and in the case of East Germany, Czechoslovakia, and Hungary, more abundant than in the Soviet Union itself. Hungary pioneered in introducing elements of a market economy and in encouraging a consumer society—"goulash communism," it was called. The German Democratic Republic, although small in population, with no more than 17 million people, emerged as one of the world's leading industrial powers. Poland's economy grew, in spite of many strains and scarcities. In the 1960s and early 1970s, the satellites all enjoyed moderate rates of economic growth, but mainly in the old-line industries. In the 1970s, the East European countries sought and obtained private investment capital and advanced technology from the West, linking themselves to the world economy. All of the states, including the Soviet Union, traded with countries outside the Soviet sphere, borrowed capital, and encouraged tourism. The value of trade between the Soviet bloc and the outside world increased fourfold. But the East European states, especially Poland, became heavily indebted to the West and the prospects of a continuing expansion of trade faded with the onset of the world economic slowdown in 1974.[40] Export markets shrank and the East Europeans found it difficult to meet even the interest payments on their debts. From the mid-1970s on, Eastern Europe, like the Soviet Union, entered a period of retrenchment, economic stagnation, and deteriorating living conditions.

114. The Communist World: The People's Republic of China

The Civil War

The proclamation in October 1949 of the People's Republic of China by the Chinese Communists, the final episode in the long civil war between the Nationalists and the Communists, was among the most momentous of events shaping the postwar world.

The civil war had gone on intermittently since 1927.[41] An uneasy alliance, formed in 1937 to fight the Japanese, barely survived the war years. The People's Liberation (or Red) Army, although nominally under the command of Chiang Kai-shek and the Kuomintang, waged its own guerrilla warfare against the Japanese. The Nationalists, cut off by the Japanese from the urban centers of eastern China, suffered from chaotic economic conditions and uncontrolled inflation. Chiang's regime became increasingly corrupt, authoritarian, and repressive.

The victory over Japan in 1945 set the stage for renewed civil war. Nationalist troops, with United States aid, returned to eastern China. The Communists, moving out from their guerrilla bases, poured into the northern provinces and made contact with the Russians in Manchuria. They rejected the demand that they surrender the northern provinces, disband their army, and accept Nationalist political control. An American-sponsored truce temporarily halted hostilities, but when the U.S.S.R. withdrew from Manchuria in the spring of 1946 (after removing Manchurian industrial assets as reparations), Nationalists and Communists clashed over control of the border province. The Communists, for their part, were quite willing to plunge the country into civil war to achieve their ends; the Nationalists were bent on repressing all opposition, even non-Communist.

In the fighting from 1946 to 1949, the Nationalists, despite substantial financial and material support from the United States, lost ground steadily. By the autumn of 1949 the Communists had routed the Kuomintang armies. Chiang withdrew his shattered forces to the island of Taiwan (and to the lesser islands of Matsu and Quemoy) where he established a small but soon prospering Republic of China; until 1971 it continued to occupy the seat set aside for China in the United Nations.

---

[40] See p. 994.
[41] See pp. 796–797.

The New Regime

For the next twenty-seven years, until his death in 1976, Mao Zedong, as uncontested head of the party, guided the destinies of the new state, officially named the People's Republic of China. For the first time since the Revolution of 1911, and indeed for generations before that, a unified central government controlled China, able to direct and mobilize the most populous nation in the world. Although the Chinese Communists were a small hardened group of successful Marxist-Leninist revolutionaries, they were not completely alien to the Chinese cultural tradition. They continued a long pattern of imperial bureaucratic government that stretched back three to four thousand years. Moreover, they articulated a widespread hostility to Western imperialism, which had all but carved their country to pieces in the nineteenth century,[42] and they inherited an ancient tradition of Chinese preeminence in the East Asian world. With traditional ways of life disrupted by decades of revolution, civil struggle, and the war against Japan, the Communists provided a surrogate for older Confucian values and set China on a modern path.

The Chinese Communists leaned heavily on Soviet experience. The party controlled each level of government and manipulated all organs of information and indoctrination. In the first few years, revolutionary excesses were committed and by Mao's own estimate, some 700,000 "counterrevolutionaries" lost their lives and countless others were sent to labor camps. In 1956, in a burst of enthusiasm for greater diversity and toleration, Mao proclaimed: "let a hundred flowers bloom, let a hundred schools of thought contend." But as soon as critics came forward, he quickly instituted a new period of repression that sent thousands, labeled "rightists," to forced labor camps.

The new regime mobilized the nation in order to rebuild the war-devastated economy and to transform the country into an industrial power. It nationalized the economy; eliminating the old landlord class in the countryside, it established agricultural cooperatives as a preliminary to collectivization. The country's initial Five-Year Plan, launched in 1953, concentrated on heavy industry and, with Soviet economic and technical assistance, recorded considerable success. Not all targets were reached, especially not in agriculture. The same floods and droughts that had troubled China for centuries refused to obey government decrees.

Impatient with the slow progress, Mao launched a radical plan in 1957, heralded as the "Great Leap Forward," designed to speed up economic change and quickly transform the country's industry and agriculture. The existing cooperatives were amalgamated into larger and more comprehensive collectivized units, or "people's communes." Planned as self-sufficient entities, tightly organized in military fashion in a hierarchy of production brigades, the communes became responsible for the mechanization of the farms along with the development of local rural industry. Communal kitchens, nurseries, and boarding schools left women freer to work on an equal basis in the fields and factories.

The "Great Leap Forward" turned into a disaster. Despite the image Mao had cultivated as the champion of the peasantry, he met immediate resistance from

---

[42] See pp. 674–681.

the countryside. The persistent opposition of the peasants and crop failures in the next two years brought a disastrous famine, which took millions of lives. The government retreated. Moderates came forward within the party to curb Mao's excessive zeal. Although the land remained collectivized, the more rigid and utopian aspects of the communal experiment were suspended. Farmers were even permitted to sell or barter a portion of their crops.

In contrast the industrial sector continued to grow. In the years before the Communist regime, annual steel production had never reached 1 million tons; by 1960 it exceeded 18 million. By 1960 China ranked among the top ten powers in the world in industrial output and had created an industrial base for further expansion. The government also marshaled the country's scientific and technological talents and successfully tested an atomic bomb in 1964 and a hydrogen bomb in 1967, and orbited space satellites in the 1970s.

The regime transformed life in many ways. Road, rail, and air transport physically unified the country. Impressive strides were made in public sanitation and public health, which received a high national priority. Labor gangs systematically drained and filled snail-infested canals, curbing the spread of diseases like schistosomiasis. The government made progress in overcoming illiteracy. It reformed and simplified the written Chinese language, and moved toward a single spoken tongue. It also adopted a new transliteration system for Chinese names spelled in the Roman alphabet.[43] Women, encouraged to reject traditional virtues of obedience and deference, received legal equality with men and could count on new opportunities. Old abuses like child marriage and concubinage were outlawed. More profoundly than the Russian, the Chinese Revolution refashioned the habits and ethos of a gigantic population, reaching remote villages and hamlets untouched for centuries. Within a generation an agrarian, semifeudal country was developing into a modern industrial society.

Suddenly, beginning in 1966, the country was convulsed by the Cultural Revolution, unleashed by Mao himself and his close associates. Fearful that the Revolution would not survive him, and that its purity was endangered, he called for a purge of the highest ranks of government and party, and for the removal of all those who had allegedly succumbed to bureaucratic routine or lacked the zeal to push on with the social revolution. He mobilized millions of students and other young people as Red Guards, or armed shock troops, to press the Maoist revolutionary cause. Converging on Beijing and other cities, they denounced bourgeois ways, attacked the vestiges of Western imperialist culture, and brutally harassed and humiliated government and party officials as well as cultural and educational leaders. When fanatical mobs threatened to tear the country apart, army leaders intervened with Mao and received his authorization to restore order.

The revolutionary turbulence continued, even if not at the same peak. Because Mao proclaimed the virtues of the land, white collar workers, students, professors, and party officials were forcibly sent off to the countryside to labor in the fields. The economy and the entire educational system broke down. By the time the

---

[43] The Pinyin (or phonetic) system, which more closely approximates Mandarin Chinese pronunciation, replaced the older Wade-Giles spelling in 1979. Mao Tse-tung is rendered as Mao Zedong, Peking as Beijing, Kuomintang as Kuomindang, Chou En-lai as Zhou Enlai, Teng Hsiao-p'ing as Deng Xiaoping, etc. For some older names like Sun Yat-sen or Chiang Kai-shek the original spellings are often retained; the older spellings for all names have been retained throughout the earlier pages of this book.

worst of the disturbances were over in 1969, hundreds of thousands of lives had been lost. Three million persons had been sent to labor camps or to work in the fields. Thousands of high-ranking officials in the government and party, including two-thirds of the party's central committee, had been purged. The impact of the Cultural Revolution lingered on and an authoritarian pall settled over the country.

The pragmatic and moderate Zhou Enlai, who had faithfully served Mao for many years as premier and foreign minister, and who might have been his successor, died early in 1976. A few months later, Mao died, long ailing and in his eighties. The Great Helmsman was widely mourned as the towering father of the Revolution for over half a century, and as one of the giant figures in the history of China. He had forged a revolutionary party and a revolutionary army, led the Long March,[44] fought the Japanese, defeated the Nationalists, and presided over a revolution that had unified, revitalized, and modernized the country. His theoretical teachings on the struggle against imperialism and on the vanguard role of the peasantry, and his practical successes in guerrilla warfare, influenced revolutionaries all over the world. His most famous precept, that "political power grows out of the barrel of a gun," reinforced revolutionary zeal everywhere. His homilies, published in a little red book called *The Living Thoughts of Chairman Mao*, were widely quoted and assiduously studied. Mao's revolution had brought equality for the peasants, technological progress, unity, and pride. But his radical experiments and the uncontrolled violence he had unleashed were costly. His successors tempered their praise for Mao, lauding his monumental achievements as a revolutionary leader, but criticizing him for his "grave blunders."

Foreign Affairs

The emergence of China as a second major Communist power undermined the ideological leadership of the Soviet Union. Although the Soviets had not always wholeheartedly supported the Chinese Communists in their civil war with the Kuomindang, once the Communist regime was established the U.S.S.R. surrendered to China the concessions it had acquired in Manchuria under the Yalta agreement.[45] For a time relations remained cool but correct, although Mao always resented being treated as a junior partner. In the 1950s the Chinese received military aid, capital loans, and technical assistance from the Soviets. The Korean War, in which Chinese troops fought the Americans as alien intruders who threatened their very borders, drew them close for a time to the Soviet Union. Western observers were convinced that a monolithic world communist movement existed. The Chinese Communists meanwhile bitterly resented American support for the regime in Taiwan and the continuing American effort to bar the People's Republic of China from the United Nations.

Although professing peace, China itself pursued an aggressive foreign policy. In 1950, pressing old Chinese claims of suzerainty and in the guise of liberating the country from clerical, i.e., Buddhist, despotism, China occupied Tibet and forcibly maintained its rule there over the years. Monasteries were closed; the Dalai Lama, the country's ruler was forced into exile; and large numbers of

[44] See p. 797.
[45] See p. 864.

Chinese arrived as settlers. In 1962 China clashed also with India, formerly one of its staunchest champions, in border disputes along India's northeastern frontier.

In the 1960s relations with the Soviet Union became strained. The two states hurled polemics at each other in their rivalry for ideological leadership and for control of the lands of inner Asia into which Russia had expanded in the age of the tsars. Mao accused Khrushchev of pusillanimous behavior in the Cuban missile crisis of 1962. In 1972 the two countries clashed in armed conflict along the Ussuri River over border territory that divided Manchuria and Russia's maritime provinces, and they continued to confront one another with large armies in other border areas. While both countries supported North Vietnam in the Vietnam War, after the war China opposed the Soviet-backed intervention by Vietnam in Cambodia. Not until the 1980s was there a rapprochement and a promise of troop reductions along their borders.

With time relations with the United States improved. In 1971, when American objections were withdrawn, the People's Republic of China finally replaced Nationalist China in the United Nations and took a permanent seat on the Security Council. The following year the American president, Richard Nixon, paid a dramatic visit to China and was welcomed by Mao. Diplomatic channels opened up and relations were normalized. The Chinese People's Republic, despite domestic problems, was emerging as one of the great potential centers of global power. And in 1976 it was about to embark on an impressive new era of modernization under Mao's successor.

XXII.
EMPIRES INTO
NATIONS: THE
DEVELOPING
WORLD

OF ALL THE GREAT POLITICAL CHANGES in the history of the modern world, affecting hundreds of millions of people, nothing was more revolutionary, more dramatic, or more unexpected than the end of the European overseas colonial empires. In 1945 the British, the French, the Dutch, the Belgians, and the Portuguese still governed large parts of the world's population, but within thirty years each of these colonial empires disappeared. Europe's world supremacy came to an end.

Wartime ideology during the Second World War had reinforced nationalist agitation for independence and freedom. It was difficult to wage war in the name of self-determination and democracy, often with the colonial countries as allies, without encouraging the idea of freedom among subject peoples. After the war the Europeans learned that they could rule only at prohibitive military cost, and in embarrassing contradiction to their professed ideals of self-government. In some instances the colonial powers, bowing to agitation for independence, liquidated their colonial holdings without armed struggle, as in the British withdrawal from the Indian subcontinent in 1947. In others the European powers withdrew only after protracted bloody wars, as in the case of the Dutch in Indonesia, the French in Indochina and Algeria, and the Portuguese in Angola and Mozambique. The United States also played a part in the transformation; it gave independence to the Philippines, granted Puerto Rico commonwealth status, took in Alaska and Hawaii as equal members of the federal union, and surrendered its privileges in the Panama Canal Zone.

Chapter Emblem: The official symbol for the World Population Year, 1974.

The end of the colonial empires and the emergence of dozens of new nations must count among the most far-reaching consequences of the two World Wars, and especially of the Second. But many of the new nations were nations only in a limited sense. They were sovereign territorial entities, with definite boundaries, internationally recognized, and with seats in the United Nations, but many of them lacked the internal coherence and shared experience of nations in the older sense of the word.[1] Nor did nationhood for the most part bring democracy, civil rights, or the rule of law.

The colonial experience had also left these regions of the world underdeveloped economically. They had learned to depend on the industrial nations for technology, capital, and manufactures, while they in turn furnished the industrial countries with raw materials, foodstuffs, minerals, oil, and other primary commodities. It was an uneven exchange that left the underdeveloped world at a disadvantage compared with the economically advanced nations. After independence, the new nations, aided by the outside world, undertook economic modernization programs—against many obstacles and with mixed results. The winning of political independence in Asia and Africa, the mixed record of self-government after independence, the effort to share in the earth's advanced technology and financial riches, and the struggle to reconcile older cultural values with modernization, all in the context of rapid population growth and international tensions, contributed to the drama of the developing world in the years after 1945. The Latin American nations, despite their more than a century of political independence by 1945, shared in many of the same experiences. Like the newer nations elsewhere, they were still making their way to constitutional government, social stability, and industrial development.

In the years after the Second World War the term "Third World" came to describe the less economically advanced, or developing, nations of Asia, Africa, the Middle East, and Latin America. The term was coined originally to distinguish the "developing world" from the two "industrial worlds"—the American-led bloc of nations and the Soviet-led Communist bloc. The term "Third World" carried the additional political meaning of nonalignment, signifying the intention of many of the formerly colonial nations to remain uncommitted in the Cold War. Although its political meaning has been eroded by the disintegration and collapse of Soviet communism, the term in its economic sense has retained its usefulness. It seems destined to survive as a synonym for the developing world.

115. End of the European Empires in Asia

End of the British Empire

The end in 1947 of British rule in India, the largest and most populous of all colonial areas ruled by Europeans, was epoch-making. The Indian National Congress, founded in 1885, grew in strength in the interwar years under the political and moral leadership of Gandhi and Nehru. The Congress party leaders, educated and affluent, demanded independence but also wished to avoid social

[1] See pp. 543–544.

revolution in the giant country. Along with the British-trained Indian civil service, they were well prepared to carry on the functions of an independent state.[2]

During the Second World War India supported the British, but at the same time Gandhi, Nehru, and the Congress party stepped up a "quit India" campaign. To retain Indian support in the war effort and to counter Japanese anti-Western propaganda, the British pledged independence. But the Muslim League, also founded before the First World War, claimed to speak, under Muhammad Ali Jinnah's leadership, for millions of Muslims unwilling to live in an India dominated by the Hindus and the Congress party. The Muslims insisted on their own national state, rooted in Islam. The Congress leadership pressed for a unified, secular India, with freedom of worship for all religions.

To end the impasse the British decided to partition the subcontinent. In 1947 they granted independence, as dominions, to two states: India, predominantly Hindu, with a population at that time of 350 million, which in 1950 formally became the Republic of India, and Pakistan, mainly Muslim, with a population of 75 million, which came to call itself the Islamic Republic of Pakistan. Because of the Muslim demographic concentration in the old empire, Pakistan was established in two disconnected parts, West and East Pakistan, separated by a thousand miles of Indian territory. About 60 million Muslims were left in India, which helped keep India a multireligious, secular state, as Gandhi and Nehru had desired.

Independence brought with it terrible communal riots between the Hindu and Muslim communities costing an estimated 1 million lives; 12 million Hindus and Muslims were caught up in mass expulsions and turbulent migrations. Gandhi was himself assassinated in 1948 by a Hindu fanatic, who resented his appeals for reconciliation. Only after the uglier features of the communal warfare subsided could the tasks of governing begin.

Nehru, who governed India as prime minister from 1947 until his death in 1964, set the country firmly on the course of parliamentary democracy, even though the Congress party remained the dominant political organization. The new government wrestled with the country's enormous problems of poverty, overpopulation, and linguistic, ethnic, and religious diversity. Nehru believed that economic planning and government controls were necessary for an underdeveloped country like India with its vast and heterogeneous population, and he laid the foundations for a moderate flexible socialism along with a mixed economy. A modern industrial India took shape, and by the 1970s it came to be ranked as the eighth largest industrial nation of the world. In 1974 India demonstrated its scientific and technological prowess when it developed a nuclear bomb. With extensive government assistance, agricultural production rose, so that by the late 1970s the country was exporting grain and other agricultural products; between 1965 and 1983 its wheat harvest tripled. When economic growth slowed down in the 1980s, later governments, abandoning the socialist emphasis, moved toward a market economy and encouraged private investment.

The country maintained its democratic course except for a brief lapse in 1975–1977, when the prime minister, Nehru's daughter, Indira Gandhi (her name by marriage—she was unrelated to the founder of Indian nationalism) proclaimed

[2] See pp. 669–672, 793–794.

emergency rule and suspended constitutional government. She was driven from office by an aroused opposition. Returning as prime minister in 1980, she governed constitutionally until assassinated four years later by Sikh soldiers of her own bodyguard, who resented the government's repression of Sikh secessionism in the Punjab. Her second son, Rajiv Gandhi, governed for the next five years. But after 1989 the fortunes of the long-entrenched Congress party were in decline. A strong fundamentalist Hindu party emerged to challenge the secular-minded Congress party, itself divided, and Hindu extremists increasingly turned to violence against the country's large Muslim population.

India remained a land of contradictions. Rising consumer standards for some classes barely affected nine-tenths of the population. Village India remained impoverished, illiteracy continued high, and the caste system persisted. The cities were congested and slum-ridden. Population more than doubled in the first forty years after independence and threatened to outstrip economic advances. Demographers predicted that India, with over 900 million people in the mid-1990s and an annual growth rate of over 2 percent, could overtake China as the world's most populous nation. Sporadic government efforts to promote birth control proved relatively ineffective.

India set an example of constitutional government and parliamentary democracy in the postcolonial era. But rising ethnic and religious tensions, graver in the early 1990s than at any time since independence, threatened to undermine its democracy and destroy the dream of a secular and pluralist India. In foreign affairs Nehru's policy of neutralism and nonalignment in the Cold War, which he articulated at the 1955 Bandung conference of emergent Asian and African nations, found a responsive chord in many parts of the Third World. Although Nehru initially championed the People's Republic of China and its right to pursue its own path of social development, he opposed the Chinese occupation of Tibet in 1950. Moreover, open fighting broke out between India and China in 1962 over border disputes. India twice went to war with Pakistan over the border territory of Kashmir, which remained in dispute even in later years. India also intervened with troops in Sri Lanka (as Ceylon came to be called in 1972) to mediate ethnic violence in its small island neighbor to the south, which in 1948 had also received independence from Britain.

In Pakistan the independence leader, Jinnah, died shortly after independence, and his successor was assassinated. Despite efforts to establish a parliamentary democracy, the country succumbed to military dictatorship within a decade. Authoritarian governments pressed forward with agricultural reform and industrialization, and an industrial Pakistan also took shape. Its awkward territorial arrangement did not last. In East Pakistan, carved out of the old state of Bengal, more than half the population lived in a crowded area one-sixth the size of West Pakistan, where the federal capital was located. In 1971 political and social resentments exploded into secession and civil war. When the leaders of East Pakistan proclaimed a new state of Bangladesh (or "Bengali nation"), the Pakistani government dispatched a large army to suppress the rebellion and killed hundreds of thousands in the unequal civil war. The secession would have failed except that India massively intervened, quickly defeated the Pakistani army, and compelled the recognition of Bangladesh. It was one of the few secessionist movements that succeeded in the postcolonial world. The Indian subcontinent was now divided into three large nations. Bangladesh remained impoverished, one of the poorest and most densely populated nations in the world, with a rapidly growing population of over 110 million in the 1990s, subject not only to natural disasters like floods, drought, and famine but also to political violence, assassinations, and military coups.

Civilian rule was restored in Pakistan after the war over Bangladesh, but in 1977 the military took power and imprisoned and executed the president, Ali Bhutto. Not until 1988 were democratic elections held. Benazir Bhutto, the Western-educated daughter of the former president, returned from exile, won the election, and became the first woman to become prime minister of an Islamic nation, with the high promise of liberalization and modernization. Fundamentalist and military pressures brought her downfall within two years, but she regained the office after new elections in 1993. Instability continued. Pakistan's quarrel with India over largely Muslim Kashmir and over other issues was especially disturbing because of Pakistan's intention to develop a nuclear capacity to match India's.

Burma became independent in 1948 and followed a course of its own; in 1989 it renamed itself Myanmar. From the outset the military exercised a parallel power with the authorities established by the democratic constitution. The country embarked on a "Burmese road to socialism," nationalizing industry and agriculture and cutting itself off from the outside world. The result was stagnation, poverty, and continued civil war. In the late 1980s a democratic movement swept the country and tried to end the "constitutional dictatorship," but the military retained control.

To the south, in the Malayan peninsula, independence was delayed for a decade because of ethnic tensions and a Chinese-led Communist insurgency that the British stubbornly fought for years. In 1957 Britain granted independence to Malaya, which shortly thereafter joined with Singapore and other small former British dependencies to form the Federation of Malaysia. Singapore withdrew in 1965 to become a small thriving island nation on its own. Malaysia, despite ethnic antagonisms, also developed a prospering economy.

The British empire in Asia was gone, but most of its former members in Asia (as well as in Africa, the Caribbean, and the Pacific), even after becoming independent, retained a voluntary association with Britain and each other in a new Commonwealth of Nations. The adherence of the newly independent states made the Commonwealth an even more flexible institution than in the past.[3] It grew into an association of fifty independent communities that accepted the British sovereign as symbolic head of the Commonwealth and agreed to consult, though not necessarily act in concert, on matters of common concern. Although the new members of the Commonwealth lacked the ties that bound Australians, New Zealanders, and Canadians to Britain in the old "white" Commonwealth, the new Commonwealth helped to transmit Western technology, political institutions, and economic aid to parts of the world as far flung as the British empire had once been, and promoted Western and non-Western interaction. Not all the

---

[3] See pp. 813–814.

former members of the British empire joined. Burma from the beginning chose to remain outside, and as the years went by the Commonwealth lost Ireland in 1949 and South Africa in 1969.

The Dutch Empire: Indonesia

Another great empire in the East, the Netherlands Indies,[4] also came to an end, although not without bloodshed. As elsewhere in Asia, the Japanese during the war exploited anti-Western sentiment and even found nationalist leaders to use as collaborators in their occupation, but at the same time a broad resistance movement emerged in which the Communists played a major role. Once the Japanese were ousted at the war's end, and before the Dutch could return, the Indonesian nationalist leader Sukarno (Indonesians use only their family name in public life) proclaimed the country's independence. When the Dutch returned, they fought the nationalist movement for four years, until in 1949 they ceded independence.

Sukarno, who retained power over the next two decades, governed dictatorially under a policy variously called "guided democracy" and "Indonesian socialism." For a time he managed to control the large Indonesian Communist party, which, backed by the People's Republic of China, grew in numbers and influence and in 1965 attempted a coup. An army leader, General Suharto, suppressed the rebellion, ousted Sukarno, and permitted the slaughter by Islamic fundamentalists of thousands of Communists and others accused of leftist sympathies. Suharto retained power over the years under a system of controlled elections, moved the country closer to the West, encouraged foreign investment, and promoted economic modernization with considerable success. But his brutal annexation in 1976 of the formerly Portuguese eastern half of the island of Timor, which cost thousands of lives, evoked sharp criticism.

In Indonesia, as elsewhere in the developing countries, population growth imposed continuing pressure on the economy. In the first four decades after independence the population of Indonesia doubled to an estimated 190 million, making it the fourth most populous country in the world (behind only China, India, and the United States). Indonesia, Malaysia, Singapore, Taiwan, South Korea, and other parts of Asia made striking economic advances, but they lagged in encouraging democratic political institutions. There was no absolute repression, but no genuine democracy either. Under more or less authoritarian regimes, the ruler or dominant ruling group co-opted all political parties under the umbrella of national unity, and discouraged militant opposition or open dissent.

End of the French Colonial Empire: Indochina

The French colonial empire also fell apart, not, however, without a struggle. The first of France's postwar colonial wars was fought over Indochina. When France offered autonomy to the states of Indochina at the end of the Second World War within a continuing French federation, Cambodia and Laos accepted, but Vietnam (as Cochin-China, Tonkin, and Annam had jointly come to be called) demanded

---

[4] See pp. 669–670.

full independence. Open warfare broke out in 1946. French armies and Communist-led Vietnamese forces fought each other for seven and a half years.

The Communist leader Ho Chi Minh, who headed the independence movement in Vietnam, had spent many earlier years in London, in Paris (where he helped found the French Communist party in 1920), and in Moscow. He returned to Vietnam in 1941, organized a Vietnamese independence movement (called the Viet Minh), and mobilized guerrilla armies to fight the Japanese. At the war's end he proclaimed the independence of Vietnam, with Hanoi as its capital. The French, willing to concede autonomy but not independence, tried at first to reassert control by using an ineffectual former emperor of Annam as a puppet. When negotiations failed and fighting began at the end of 1946, Ho turned his armies against the French. Because the Communists led the independence movement, the French could claim that they were fighting to stem the tide of world communism, not to preserve nineteenth-century colonial privileges. Yet communism here, as often in Asia, was linked to nationalism, anticolonialism and anti-Westernism, and genuine popular discontent.

The United States, anticolonial but ready to champion anti-Communist causes in the Cold War, aided the French financially but refrained from open military intervention. The war drained French morale and resources. In the spring of 1954 an international conference met in Geneva to arrange, among other matters, a settlement in Indochina. At the very time that the conference met, the French army, after a long, costly siege, suffered a severe defeat at the battle of Dien Bien Phu. The conference, with French acquiescence, recognized the independence of Vietnam, as well as of Cambodia and Laos. The colonial empire in French Indochina came to an end. Vietnam was provisionally partitioned at the seventeenth parallel into a northern and southern sector until elections could be held for the entire country. Neither Ho nor the Western-backed regime in the south was satisfied with this decision, and the settlement of 1954 was short-lived. A civil war of increasing intensity broke out, in which the United States from the early 1960s on became deeply involved. That story is recounted elsewhere.[5]

The Americans and the Philippines

The Americans, too, shared in the liquidation of colonial empires in Asia. The United States, which had granted self-governing commonwealth status to the Philippines in 1934 as a first step, granted full independence in 1946. The Philippines retained close economic and military ties with the United States. A succession of repressive goverments did little to help the lot of the impoverished peasants, curb the power of the landholding elite, or suppress political disorder. For over twenty years Ferdinand Marcos, elected president in 1965, governed virtually as a dictator, with American acquiescence. The assassination in 1983 of an opposition leader, Benigno Aquino, sparked a widespread opposition movement, which in 1986 forced Marcos into exile. His successor, Corazón Aquino, widow of the martyred opposition leader, faced continuing pressures from the right and left but restored democracy and civil rights, and slowly inaugurated land and other reforms, setting an example for those who followed her.

[5] See pp. 984–990.

116. *The African Revolution*

Africa is a large continent, considerably larger than North and Central America combined. With an estimated population of 280 million in 1950 and 800 million in the mid-1990s, it has one of the fastest growing populations in the world. North Africa, stretching from Morocco to Egypt, Muslim and Arab, belongs also to the Mediterranean world and, even more, to the Islamic Middle East in ethnic composition, culture, geography, and history. To the south, below the Sahara Desert, is black Africa, where Islam, Christianity, and various traditional African animist faiths are found. An ethnographic and linguistic map of black Africa would reveal hundreds of different ethnic concentrations and over 50 major (and hundreds of minor) languages; and a large number of Africans, since the colonial era, also speak English or French. In some areas there has been substantial settlement by Europeans, most notably at the southern end of the continent.

Politically, in 1945, and even in 1950, the map of Africa was scarcely different from what it had been in 1914 in the sense that all of Africa was European-governed with the three exceptions of Egypt, Liberia, and Ethiopia (which had regained its independence from Italy during the war).[6] By the early 1960s, however, there were 35 independent states, and most of Africa was either independent or close to achieving independence. In 1993, with the addition of Eritrea, there were 53 independent states. They made up close to a third of the membership of the United Nations. The new states differed from the older European nations in many ways. Because African geographical boundaries had been drawn, often arbitrarily, by the European colonial powers, the new states contained within their borders diverse ethnic and linguistic groups, many antagonistic to each other, and related peoples were often distributed over two or more of the new countries. The African states had less of a unified national heritage than older nations in Europe and elsewhere. Once the African states obtained independence, they rapidly assumed the full panoply of national sovereignty but faced the need to weld their disparate peoples into nationhood.

French North Africa: The French-Algerian War

The decision by the wartime Allies in 1951 to grant independence to the former Italian colony of Libya, along with agitation for the British to end the vestiges of their control in Egypt, galvanized all of French North Africa into action. Arab nationalist leaders in Morocco, Tunisia, and Algeria—the Maghreb, as these Arab states of northwest Africa are called—mounted a vigorous campaign for independence. Morocco and Tunisia were not outright colonies but protectorates under their traditional rulers, the Moroccan sultan and the Tunisian bey.[7] After the failure of various concessions and maneuvers, the French in 1956 granted independence to the two countries. The Moroccan sultan became king, with the trappings of a constitutional monarchy, but the monarchy supervised both spiritual and temporal life and allowed little dissent or dilution of its authoritarian powers.

[6] See pp. 662–669, 813, 837, 853.
[7] See pp. 661, 698–700.

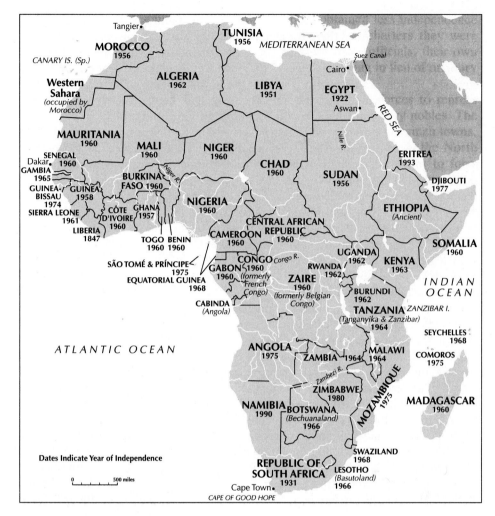

Tangier•

MOROCCO
1956

CANARY IS. (Sp.)

TUNISIA
1956   *MEDITERRANEAN SEA*

Suez Canal

Cairo•

Western Sahara
(occupied by Morocco)

ALGERIA
1962

LIBYA
1951

EGYPT
1922

Aswan•

RED SEA

Nile R.

MAURITANIA
1960

MALI
1960

NIGER
1960

CHAD
1960

SUDAN
1956

ERITREA
1993

DJIBOUTI
1977

SENEGAL
Dakar.• 1960
GAMBIA
1965

BURKINA FASO 1960

Niger R.

ETHIOPIA
(Ancient)

GUINEA-BISSAU
1974
GUINEA
1958
SIERRA LEONE
1961
LIBERIA
1847

CÔTE
D'IVOIRE
1960
GHANA
1957

NIGERIA
1960

SOMALIA
1960

TOGO BENIN
1960   1960

CENTRAL AFRICAN REPUBLIC
1960

CAMEROON
1960

UGANDA
1962

KENYA
1963

SÃO TOMÉ & PRÍNCIPE
1975

CONGO Congo R.
1960
(formerly French Congo)

GABON
1960

RWANDA 1962

ZAIRE
1960
(formerly Belgian Congo)

BURUNDI
1962

INDIAN OCEAN

EQUATORIAL GUINEA
1968

CABINDA
(Angola)

TANZANIA ZANZIBAR I.
(Tanganyika & Zanzibar)
1964

ATLANTIC OCEAN

ANGOLA
1975

ZAMBIA 1964

MALAWI
1964

SEYCHELLES
1968

COMOROS
1975

Zambezi R.

ZIMBABWE
1980

MOZAMBIQUE
1975

MADAGASCAR
1960

NAMIBIA
1990

BOTSWANA
(Bechuanaland)
1966

SWAZILAND
1968

Dates Indicate Year of Independence

0 ———— 500 miles

REPUBLIC OF SOUTH AFRICA
Cape Town•
CAPE OF GOOD HOPE

LESOTHO
(Basutoland)
1931   1966

CONTEMPORARY AFRICA

This map should be compared with those for Precolonial Africa (p. 665) and for Africa in 1914 at the height of European colonialism (p. 667). The first of the new sub-Saharan states was Ghana, the former British Gold Coast, which became independent in 1957 and took its name from a medieval African kingdom that had been located further north. The following decades saw the independence of numerous republics in black Africa in place of the French, British, Belgian, and Portuguese colonial empires.

Tunisia became a republic and was governed by its first president under a one-party regime for thirty years. In both countries modernization and pressures for liberalization continued, often against counterpressures from Muslim tradition-alists.

Algeria, a French colony since the 1830s, the French considered an integral part of France. It was represented in the French legislature like any constituency of metropolitan France, except that the vote for its representatives was heavily weighted in favor of the European settlers and to the disadvantage of the Arab majority. Of the 9 million inhabitants, at least 1 million were French and Italian settlers, or *colons*, mostly French who, like the family of the French writer Albert Camus, had lived there for generations. Because the Europeans controlled the economy and owned most of the land and industry, they feared for their political and economic privileges if Algeria were cut loose from France and governed by an Arab majority smarting from years of unequal treatment. At a moment when France and the French army had barely recovered from the disastrous rout in Indochina, revolt broke out in the autumn of 1954.

The French-Algerian war lasted seven and a half years, involving 500,000 French troops at its peak. The Algerian Liberation Front received aid and support from Egypt and other Arab states. Torture and cruelty became common on both sides; the violence spread to Paris as extremist Algerians attacked moderates. The French were confronted with a choice of losing Algeria or continuing to bear the military, financial, and moral strain of a divisive colonial war. In the midst of a cabinet crisis in Paris, an insurrection in Algiers in May 1958, led by die-hard settlers and army leaders, brought General Charles de Gaulle to power;[8] the army leaders were convinced that he would press on with the war. But de Gaulle soon spoke of autonomy and self-determination for the Algerians once a truce had been arranged, and in 1961 he won the backing of the French electorate for full independence. Army leaders rebelled, and some of his closest former associates helped form a secret army of terrorists, who bombed and killed, and even attempted his assassination. Nevertheless, in 1962 French rule ended.

After independence there was a mass exodus of Europeans from Algeria, but most of the French and Algerians were grateful that de Gaulle had ended the ordeal. The French accepted the loss of Algeria, and of other parts of their empire, and with a prospering economy turned their attention to other matters. For Algeria the French provided technical assistance in the joint development of Algerian oil and natural gas resources. Despite oil revenues, the economy ran into difficulties, and debt and unemployment mounted. Over 2 million Algerians migrated in search of jobs, mainly to France. The presence of large numbers of Algerians in Paris and other French cities created friction. But the bitterness of the long struggle for independence, which had cost well over 100,000 lives, faded.

Algeria came to be governed by a military-dominated one-party secular regime. In an effort to cement ties with other Arab states, it allowed Islamic fundamentalists to teach and grow in political influence. When the regime, in response to popular pressures, finally permitted elections in 1991, a fundamentalist Islamic party won. The military rejected the results and took steps to control the increasingly militant movement. Here, as elsewhere in the Muslim world, Islamic traditionalists were challenging secular regimes.

End of British Rule: West Africa

In North Africa, as in Asia, nationalist agitation for independence, already under way in the interwar years,[9] might have been expected. In Africa south of the Sahara the movement for liberation was never as far advanced, and the pace of

---

[8] See p. 890.
[9] For Asia see pp. 788–799.

independence after the Second World War was unexpectedly rapid. Here black populations lived in colonial empires carved out by the Europeans either in the colonial age that had opened in the fifteeenth century or in the brief decade and a half after 1885 of European imperialist competition.[10]

Independence movements, barely in existence earlier, made their presence felt. The British first resisted the mounting nationalist pressures, imprisoning or exiling nationalist leaders, but then yielded. Compelled earlier to dissolve their Indian empire, and to cut military and imperial commitments, they gave way in Africa too. They first provided broader African representation in the colonial legislative assemblies, then granted autonomy and independence to the colonies as dominions, and in short order the dominions became independent republics.

The Gold Coast (Ghana) became the first British colony to achieve independence. The British initially resisted a militant civil disobedience movement led by the British- and American-educated Kwame Nkrumah. When they conceded self-government, they freed the imprisoned Nkrumah, and he became prime minister. In 1957 the British granted the colony dominion status, and in 1960 it became an independent republic. Nkrumah was elected president. With independence, the country shed a name identified with centuries of imperialist exploitation and called itself Ghana, recalling an African kingdom somewhat to the north, which had flourished from the sixth to the eleventh centuries. The immensely popular Nkrumah gathered extensive power into his own hands, banned opposition parties, and governed for close to ten years as a dictator. In Africa (and in Asia) the charismatic nationalist leaders who led the struggles for independence often turned into personal dictators once independence was won, and the party of the independence movement often became the sole legal party. In 1966 Nkrumah's arbitrary rule, unbridled public and private extravagances, and cult of personality led to his overthrow by military leaders; a series of other coups followed. Military dictatorships continued to govern the country.

Nkrumah introduced, and his successors continued, "African socialism," placing the economy under rigorous state control. In these new forms of socialism in Asia, Africa, and the Middle East, the state ran the economy, but the ruling elites accumulated power and wealth, and the bureaucracy expanded. There was little of the egalitarianism promised by earlier socialism. Once prosperous with abundant natural resources, the world's largest producer of cocoa and the source of a tenth of the world's gold, the Ghanaian economy declined in the years after independence and the country became heavily dependent on foreign loans. In the mid-1980s, as elsewhere, the emphasis on state socialism waned. The government sold many state enterprises to private investors, and encouraged a profit incentive in industry and agriculture. With financial assistance from the World Bank and with market-oriented reforms, economic growth slowly resumed, but there was little change in the authoritarian political system.

Nigeria, the largest British-governed territory in Africa, became the most populous country in postcolonial Africa. Its 1990 census showed a population close to 90 million, growing at over 3 percent annually. It encompassed over 200 ethnic groups, the largest of which were the Hausa and Fulani in the north and the Yoruba and Ibo in the south. As pressures for independence mounted, 15 of

[10] See pp. 107–114, 662–669.

the larger ethnic groups at one point sought independence as individual sovereign states. The British granted dominion status to Nigeria as a whole in 1960, and in 1963 it became a republic. To cope with the ethnic diversity, the constitution established three large geographical regions and 21 federal states. The Nigerian republic, with democratic machinery, a federal structure, multiple political parties, and guarantees of civil rights offered a democratic model for the rest of the continent in the 1960s.

But the northern region dominated the country, regional and ethnic dissatisfactions erupted, and military coups thwarted the experiment in constitutional democracy. The educated and skilled Ibos, economically advanced and politically ambitious, saw themselves excluded from an appropriate national role. The Ibos themselves initiated a military coup in 1966, but a Hausa-led military takeover almost immediately followed and became the signal for a widespread slaughter of Ibos. Large numbers fled to the east, where in 1967 they proclaimed an independent state of Biafra. A terrible civil war and blockade to end the secession lasted two and a half years, from 1967 to 1970, and resulted in a million deaths, many from starvation. After the war, the federal government followed a policy of reconciliation, reintegrated the Ibos into national life, and sought, with some success, to overcome regional and religious differences.

The Nigerian military leaders at first helped restore constitutional government, but in the face of continuing political instability and economic difficulties, they reimposed military control. When presidential elections were eventually permitted in 1993, the ruling general nullified the results. The nationwide protests that followed signaled the widespread desire in the country for civilian and constitutional government.

For a time, in the 1970s, Nigeria had a booming economy, based on its large oil resources, discovered and exploited in the 1950s, which made it the world's sixth largest oil producer. People flocked to the urban areas from the countryside and from neighboring states like Ghana to take part in the boom. Lagos, the Nigerian capital, quadrupled in size. But in the mid-1980s, when the world market experienced an oil glut, petroleum prices plummeted. The oil wealth had not stimulated broader economic development; the country became dependent on food imports and suffered from inflation and debt.

End of British Rule: East Africa

In East Africa, especially in Kenya, the independence movement encountered greater obstacles. In Kenya a minority of white settlers, who owned the rich plantation areas, stubbornly resisted the independence movement headed by Jomo Kenyatta. The nationalists responded in the 1950s with violence, acts of terrorism, and the armed revolt of a terrorist organization, the Mau Mau. Kenyatta was imprisoned and then exiled. But pressures for independence grew. After a decade of rising tension, the British brought Kenyatta back from exile, and in 1963 granted Kenya independence. Most of the British planters left the country. Until his death in 1978 Kenyatta dominated the country's political life. Despite a facade of parliamentary government, he permitted only one legal party and imprisoned ethnic and political opponents. His successor continued to govern on into the 1990s under the same kind of authoritarian one-party regime, rejecting pressures for liberalization.

In 1961 the British granted independence to Tanganyika, where they exercised a UN trusteeship over what had been, in 1914, the major part of German East Africa, and to Zanzibar, a British island protectorate since 1890. The two states united in 1964 to form Tanzania.

Here, too, the nationalist leader dominated the government after independence. Julius Nyerere allowed only one party, and relinquished power to a successor only after twenty-five years in office. By promoting literacy and establishing Swahili as the official language of public life, he helped unite the country's ethnic and linguistic groups more effectively than elsewhere on the continent. His economic policies were less successful. Also a champion of "African socialism," he nationalized much of the economy, including agriculture. He drew close to the Soviet Union and to China, and for a time Tanzania served as a bridgehead for Chinese Communist influence on the continent. In the mid-1980s with new leadership emerging, the government denationalized many state industries, sought to end overly rigid planning and controls, and restored collective farms to family cultivation, but the country remained a one-party state.

Uganda, a third state in East Africa, which Winston Churchill once described as the "pearl of Africa," had a promising beginning in 1962 as a parliamentary republic. Within a few years it became the sad scene for two decades of continuing turmoil and butchery. At independence, Buganda and other traditional kingdoms were incorporated into the new nation-state, with autonomy under a federal system. In 1966 the prime minister, Milton Obote, took over as dictator and in a push for instant nationhood summarily abolished Buganda and the other old kingdoms as obstacles to national unity. After five years of disorder during which Obote promoted his fellow northerners to leading positions, a flamboyant, ruthless soldier, Idi Amin, rose from the ranks, seized power, and for the next eight years brutalized the country, shocking Africa and the world with executions, massacres, and torture in which he personally participated. Over 250,000 lost their lives; whole ethnic groups were singled out for destruction. A once prosperous agricultural economy with thriving coffee, tea, and cotton exports, lay in ruins. Professionals and intellectuals fled. Some 60,000 Asians, mostly Indian, who had been deeply involved in the country's commerce and industry, were expelled. When in 1979 Amin seemed likely to invade Tanzania over disputed border territory, a Tanzanian army with the backing of other African states, in an action unprecedented in postcolonial Africa, invaded Uganda, overthrew the dictator, and oversaw elections in which Obote returned to power.

Once the Tanzanian army withdrew, Obote crushed internal opposition with a repression reminiscent of his predecessor; additional tens of thousands lost their lives or fled into exile, and authority collapsed. Even when five years later a military coup overthrew Obote, chaos continued. In 1986, a new military leader, Yoweri Museveni, moved to end what he deplored as the "massive hemorrhage" of Ugandan lives, set about to restore constitutional government, and with international assistance took the first steps to rehabilitate the devastated country. Economic production in Uganda in 1989 was one-fifth what it had been at the time of independence, but a measure of political stability and internal security made economic growth once again possible. Uganda still faced a grim future, including the epidemic spread of AIDS, which from the mid-1980s on, even more than in other parts of Africa, was ravaging the country.

Southern Africa

In southern Africa the British peacefully transferred power in the early 1960s to black majority governments in Zambia (formerly Northern Rhodesia), Malawi, and Botswana. But elsewhere in this part of the continent a white colonial minority held out against yielding or even sharing power.

In Southern Rhodesia the British government in London tried to negotiate political rights for the black majority before granting independence, but the small self-assertive white community resisted, and in 1965 proclaimed independence from Britain. After fifteen years of escalating guerrilla warfare and international pressure, including economic sanctions, the recalcitrant white leaders yielded, and in 1980 Southern Rhodesia became the state of Zimbabwe, with a black majority government. The independence leader Robert Mugabe, combining the posts of president and prime minister, virtually created a one-party state within a few years.

In the extreme south of the continent, in what had become the Union of South Africa in 1910,[11] the situation long remained tense. Here the whites, though a minority, were far more numerous than elsewhere in Africa south of the Sahara, and had lived there for a much longer time. About half the whites, the Afrikaners, were mainly descendants of Dutch Calvinist immigrants from as far back as the founding of Cape Town in 1652; the other half represented immigration from Great Britain since the 1820s. The two halves did not easily mix. The Afrikaners, during their long isolation from Europe, developed a new language of their own, Afrikaans, derived mainly from Dutch, and they retained unpleasant memories of British expansion, especially of the "Boer" war and the concentration camps of 1899–1902. In the late 1980s in a population of just over 40 million, about 6 million whites lived uneasily with 30 million blacks, 3 million mixed peoples (or "coloureds"), and 1 million Asians; both the latter groups were also classified as nonwhites. The whites were numerous enough to constitute an established outpost of European civilization and to develop the most advanced economy of the continent, but they were greatly outnumbered, and many feared losing their dominant status.

In 1948 the Afrikaner-controlled Nationalist party came to power for the first time. To segregate the races and to ensure a white-dominated society it legislated a sweeping policy of "apartheid" (the Afrikaans word for separation). The new laws excluded blacks completely from political life and imposed blatant forms of discrimination in housing, transportation, land ownership, and employment. Between 1950 and 1980 well over 1 million nonwhites were forced to leave white areas of residence in the cities and to relocate. Permits to blacks for urban jobs were granted only as industry required workers. Under a program of "separate development," the government also established four of a projected ten autonomous homelands ("bantustans") for various black ethnic groups, but they met with little favor. The land was poor and movement to the rest of the country was

[11] See pp. 668–669.

strictly regulated. The practises of apartheid and the laws enforcing it were internationally condemned. Finding itself increasingly isolated from the rest of the world, the South African government in 1961 broke all official ties with Britain and the Commonwealth, and proclaimed itself the Republic of South Africa.

Opponents of the restrictive laws, black and white, encountered police brutality, torture, preventive detention, and long prison sentences. Nelson Mandela, the black leader of the African National Congress, was sentenced to life imprisonment. The black leadership of the African National Congress grew more militant and turned to armed struggle, strikes, riots, and demonstrations which the regime forcefully suppressed. There were tragic clashes at Sharpeville in 1960 and at Soweto in 1976, among others. By the 1970s increasing numbers of whites were protesting apartheid. The United Nations imposed sanctions. The United States, which had gone through its own civil rights movement in the 1960s to overcome the legacy of slavery and racism, and had its own black heroes like Martin Luther King, Jr., joined in the economic sanctions and encouraged business corporations to withdraw or withhold investments.

By the 1980s the political and economic pressures began to have an impact on the regime. A more enlightened wing of the Nationalist party made efforts at moderation. But initial reforms aroused opposition from Afrikaner diehards, and repression continued. In 1989 President F.W. de Klerk, anxious to defuse the explosive situation, and seeing the deterioration of the economy, accelerated the reform program. Nelson Mandela was freed in 1991 after 27 years in prison. In 1991 the apartheid laws were repealed. A year later the white electorate voted in a referendum to end white minority rule. In Mandela's words, the "countdown to democracy" had begun. In 1994 the first democratic nonracial elections brought Mandela and the African National Congress to power, with provisions for a government of national unity in a period of transition. After its long travail, and with enormous challenges still to overcome, South Africa at last had the opportunity to create a nonracial democratic political system.

The white-dominated South African government had also refused over the years to surrender the League mandate that it had exercised since 1919 over what had once been German Southwest Africa. The black leadership there sought independence as the new state of Namibia, but a long guerrilla war had to be fought before Namibia's independence was officially recognized in 1990.

The French Sub-Saharan Empire

The French, largely as a consequence of the bloody war in Algeria, dissolved their vast colonial empire in sub-Saharan Africa peacefully. After the Second World War they had hoped that a French-educated and assimilated African elite would maintain its ties to France in a loosely organized French Union. They gave the African colonies representation in the French parliament and promised self-governing institutions. But control remained centralized in Paris and by the mid-1950s the African colonies, inspired by nationalist movements elsewhere, pressed for independence. De Gaulle, still facing the Algerian crisis, recognized the inexorable pressure for independence and offered the black sub-Saharan colonies their freedom. By 1960 all fifteen colonies had chosen independence.

Many, however, retained close ties with France for economic aid and cultural cooperation. France remained a strong presence among the francophone nations[12] (and indeed the strongest presence of all the Western countries on the African continent), training the armies of the new states, lending financial assistance, and taking a leading role in economic development. On almost a dozen occasions after 1960 the French intervened with military forces, small in number but mobile and well-equipped. In 1979 they helped overthrow a brutal dictator who had seized power in the Central African Republic in 1966 and proclaimed himself emperor. In Chad, they intervened when rebels in the north backed by Libya threatened to overthrow the government. The French organized the African Financial Community, helped stabilize the African currency, and became the largest donor of aid to the continent. While some African leaders criticized the French presence as neocolonialism, others welcomed it and viewed it more as a partnership than an intrusion. As elsewhere in Africa, the promise of democratic government in the former French colonies turned for the most part into civilian or military dictatorships, with varying degrees of repression. Senegal stood out as a rare exception.

The Belgian Congo: Zaire

The Belgian Congo was a byword for European imperialist exploitation in the late nineteenth century.[13] The most abusive features were remedied before 1914, but political control remained concentrated in Brussels and little was done to prepare the large colony (it was eighty times the size of Belgium) for self-government. Agitation for independence intensified when the French Congo and other French African colonies won their freedom. Faced with pressure for independence, the Belgian government, which had once proposed a transition period of thirty years, decided against gradualism and in 1960 announced its withdrawal in six months' time. The two leading nationalist leaders, Joseph Kasavubu and Patrice Lumumba, were at odds with one another, innumerable ethnic and regional antagonisms created obstacles, and no one was prepared to carry out the responsibilities of government. The army mutinied, the soldiers turning against their European officers; violence broke out against those European whites who had not fled; and the copper-producing province of Shaba (then called Katanga) seceded, under the leadership of a third nationalist leader, Moise Tshombe, supported by Belgian copper interests. Belgian paratroopers, hastily flown back, and a United Nations international military force attempted to restore order and depose Tshombe. When the leftist leader Lumumba was assassinated in 1961, the troubled situation became even more dangerous because of a

---

[12] The francophone, or French-speaking, sub-Saharan African states in 1960 were Benin (until 1975 called Dahomey), Cameroon, Central African Republic, Chad, Republic of Congo, Gabon, Guinea, Ivory Coast, Madagascar (or Malagasy Republic), Mali, Mauritania, Niger, Senegal, Togo, and Burkina Faso (until 1984 Upper Volta). Comoros became independent in 1975, and Djibouti in 1977. Morocco, Algeria, and Tunisia, in North Africa, are also part of francophone Africa, as are Zaire, once the Belgian Congo, and Burundi and Rwanda.
[13] See pp. 662–664.

threatened Soviet-Western confrontation. The Soviet Union charged the Europeans and their American supporters with deliberately creating the chaos so that the Europeans might return, and threatened intervention to defend the new state.

Two and a half years later, in 1963, the Shaba secession ended. But the government, with Belgian and American help, continued to battle leftist rebels. In 1965, Colonel Joseph Désiré Mobutu ended the anarchy with a personal dictatorship. He nationalized the large mining enterprises and most of the rest of the economy. To symbolize the new era, he Africanized all geographical and personal names. Because Christian names were dropped, he called himself Mobutu Sese Seko. In 1971 the Belgian Congo became Zaire, as did the famous river. Leopoldville, the capital, and Stanleyville, the second largest city, both carrying names reminiscent of European imperialism, became Kinshasa and Kisangani; Lake Albert became Lake Mobutu.

Zaire, the third largest country in size in Africa (second only to Sudan and Algeria), its cities widely separated and with poor, overgrown roads, had vast copper, diamond, cobalt, and other mineral resources, but its potential riches remained underdeveloped. Food had to be imported, the country fell heavily into debt, and corruption became an open scandal under Mobutu's repressive regime.

Belgium had governed the Congo directly, but it had also administered, under a League mandate and United Nations trusteeship, two small territories, part of German East Africa before 1914. In 1962 they became the independent states of Rwanda and Burundi. Long-standing tensions in each state between the traditionally dominant Tutsi minority and the resentful Hutu majority led to fierce power struggles and internecine warfare over the years. Hundreds of thousands lost their lives, most tragically in a mind-numbing outburst of mass killings in Rwanda in 1994.

End of the Portuguese Colonial Empire

Of all the colonial powers Portugal, itself under an authoritarian dictatorship until 1974, clung longest to its colonies, symbols of grandeur from the days of Vasco da Gama's explorations and the early age of European expansion.[14] To retain Angola, on the southwestern African coast, and Mozambique, on the southeastern, both at one time flourishing centers of the slave trade and under Portuguese rule for over 400 years, the Portuguese dictatorship stubbornly fought a colonial revolt which broke out in 1961 and lasted thirteen years. In the course of the fighting disaffected officers and soldiers in the Portuguese army, radicalized by the prolonged colonial war, turned against the regime and overthrew it in 1974 in a bloodless coup. The following year Portugal granted independence to Angola, Mozambique, and its smaller African colonies. Hundreds of thousands of Portuguese fled, many to South Africa.

In Angola independence touched off a struggle for power by competing nationalist groups in which outside powers intervened, the Sovet Union and Cuba on the one side, the United States and South Africa on the other. The Soviet bloc provided weapons and advisers to a Marxist faction. Fidel Castro, who, as

[14] See pp. 107–109.

we shall see, projected himself as a Marxist-Leninist defender of oppressed colonial peoples everywhere, dispatched 50,000 troops. The leftist group, which won out, proclaimed a "people's republic" in 1976 and consolidated power, but rebel groups with the support of the United States and South Africa continued the struggle. The war dragged on for years, ruined the country, and cost hundreds of thousands of lives. Not until 1991 did all the outside powers withdraw. The arduous task of economic reconstruction began and UN-supervised elections were held in 1993.

Mozambique, exhausted by the decade of guerrilla war against Portugal, also established a "people's republic." The government was engaged for the next sixteen years in a continuing civil war with a militant rightist group. The war against Portugal, the rightist insurgency, and drought and famine cost over half a million lives in the small country and displaced one and a half million others. In the early 1990s both Angola and Mozambique abandoned Marxism, loosened economic controls, and turned to the West for desperately needed economic assistance.

Ethiopia, Eritrea, Somalia, and Sudan

Ethiopia, Eritrea, and Somalia, on the Horn of Africa—the easternmost part of the continent—had all been part of Italy's short-lived East African empire. Ethiopia, conquered by Mussolini in 1936, was the last European colonial annexation in Africa. Once the Italian armies were routed in Africa in 1941, early in the Second World War, Haile Selassie returned as emperor.[15] Somalia, initially under a postwar UN trusteeship, won independence in 1960. Eritrea, considered a part of Ethiopia, was unsuccessful in its bid for independence. When in 1962 Ethiopia formally annexed it, Eritrea launched an armed rebellion that continued for the next three decades, until its independence was recognized in 1993.

In Ethiopia a Soviet-backed military coup in 1974 deposed Haile Selassie as emperor, established a Marxist and vehemently anti-Western regime, nationalized much of the economy, and transformed the country into a client-state of the Soviet Union. In Somalia an army coup also brought a Soviet-backed military dictatorship to power. But when Somalia in 1977 invaded Ethiopia, laying claim to a region where many Somalis lived, the Soviets chose to support Ethiopia. Soviet military aid (and 17,000 Cuban troops airlifted from Angola) assured Ethiopia's victory. Somalia shifted its allegiance to the West.

In 1984 Ethiopia proclaimed itself a "people's democratic republic," established an authoritarian state socialism with one legal party, the "Workers' Party of Ethiopia," and drew even closer to the Soviets. Eventually the Soviets lost interest in supporting Ethiopia in its war against the Eritrean secessionists, and Ethiopia also turned to the West. All this time the entire region suffered from extended drought and famine.

The Horn of Africa was no longer entangled in Cold War rivalries after 1985, but political instability continued. In both Ethiopia and Somalia the overthrow in 1991 of their long-time military dictatorships, each armed by outside powers during the Cold War, created new problems. Ethiopia's new regime finally

---

[15] See pp. 837–838, 853.

recognized the sovereignty of Eritrea. In Somalia the overthrow of a military dictator who had been in power for twenty-one years plunged the country into civil war and anarchy when clan-based guerrilla forces fought each other, preventing even international shipments of food and medical supplies from reaching the population. At American initiative, multinational military forces intervened under UN auspices in 1992 to relieve the distress and restore order. The humanitarian and peacemaking task proved more formidable than anticipated, and the United States withdrew its troops in frustration fifteen months later.

Sudan, on the very eve of independence in 1956, when joint Anglo-Egyptian rule ended, fell into deadly civil war. The black population in the south, Christians or followers of traditional African animist faiths, rose in rebellion against the Arab government in the north, which was bent on imposing Islamic law on the entire country. After the government put down the rebellion, which lasted seventeen years and cost over a million and a half lives, it granted a measure of autonomy to the south. But its recurrent efforts in later years to extend Islamic law by force provoked renewed violence and resistance in the 1990s.

The casualties of the wars, famine, and drought from which Ethiopia, Somalia, Eritrea, and Sudan suffered in the postwar years numbered in the millions, and the turmoil displaced a human flood of some 2 million refugees.

Liberia: Civil War

Civil war also devastated Liberia, the only country in Africa that had not formed part of a European colonial empire. Founded in the early nineteenth century in West Africa as a home for freed American ex-slaves, it became an independent republic in 1847. The black American settlers and their descendants, although never more than a small percentage of the population, dominated the country's business and political life. After years of relative stability, Liberia fell victim to the postcolonial ferment in Africa. In 1980 an army sergeant, alleging misrule and corruption on the part of the ruling settler group, staged a bloody coup and held power for the next ten years. His overthrow by a former aide in 1989 precipitated a brutal three-and-a-half-year civil war in which tens of thousands of lives were lost, civilians massacred, and half the population left homeless. In 1993 Nigeria and other West African nations intervened militarily to restore peace. The African nations seemed to be abandoning their earlier principle of nonintervention in other African states. The international community appeared powerless to control the turmoil or even to provide basic humanitarian aid.

The African Revolution

For Africa one age came to a close after the Second World War and a new era opened. Only a map of contemporary Africa can communicate the vast political transformation that had occurred.[16] The unfinished item on the political agenda, the extension of democratic rights to the black majority in South Africa, was resolved with the momentous transfer of power in 1994.

[16] See map, p. 927.

Independence provided a deep source of self-esteem. The word *uhuru,* or freedom, rang through the continent in the heady days of decolonization. Léopold Sédar Senghor, the poet-president of the formerly French colony of Senegal, gave voice to the idea of *négritude*, a powerful, far-reaching black self-consciousness, a pride in ancient cultural roots and modern achievements, which struck a responsive chord in Americans of African descent, whose ancestors had been brought in chains from some of the very lands, like Senegal, that were now modern sovereign states. Black Africa exulted when the Nigerian playwright, poet, and novelist Wole Soyinka, who blended Yoruba and Western traditions in his writings, received the Nobel Prize for literature in 1986.

The African revolution brought an end to Western colonialism and ushered in a new era of independence and national sovereignty, but it did not bring democratic government, civil and human rights, the resolution of ethnic and regional antagonisms, or a meaningful improvement in the quality of human lives. Ethnic hatreds, civil wars, regional conflict, and brutal internal repression, took a toll in the millions. Africans killed Africans in the years of independence, mainly in civil wars within the borders of the new states. Ethnic loyalties still transcended national loyalty. Natural disasters and old and new diseases added to the death toll. African refugees made up one-third of the world's millions of refugees in the mid-1990s.

Most of the new states began their political careers after independence with constitutions, elected parliaments, independent judiciaries, and formal guarantees of civil liberties. But under the pressure of ethnic conflict, economic burdens, and political instability, the machinery of constitutional government quickly became submerged under dictatorship, generally military. In country after country, generals, admirals, colonels, majors, captains, even a flight lieutenant in Ghana and a master sergeant in Liberia, pushed aside the civilian rulers. The warrior caste became the new rulers, often a law unto themselves, tyrannizing the population. Nigeria, alone, which at least made sporadic efforts to preserve constitutional government and a federal system for its multi-ethnic state, counted six military coups in the years from 1966 to 1985. At the very outset, charismatic independence leaders, like Nkrumah in Ghana, Kenyatta in Kenya, and Nyerere in Tanzania, transformed themselves into virtual dictators under varying degrees of authoritarianism; some became "presidents for life." Of over 150 African heads of state in the first three decades of independence, only six voluntarily relinquished their offices. In Zambia and Ivory Coast, leaders like Kenneth Kaunda and Félix Houphouët-Boigny governed under a milder authoritarianism, but mainly the dictatorships, military, or civilian with military backing, were repressive and tyrannical. There were only a few examples of free elections, multiparty systems, political pluralism, and freedom from censorship.

Some African leaders argued that strong central governments were needed, not multiparty democratic systems, to counter the separatist ethnic and regional forces, cope with economic underdevelopment, and provide the cohesiveness for national unity. Others considered democracy an alien concept, an importation from the West, difficult to nurture in societies with high illiteracy, a small middle class, and different cultural patterns, including a political tradition of lifetime tenure for tribal chieftains and of government by consensus. Many Africans rejected such arguments and maintained that, like other peoples of the world, they should choose and control their rulers, and one day would do so. In earlier years the West, too, had experienced turbulent periods of nation-building, had looked to absolute and hereditary monarchy as a source of stability, and had contributed its share of bloodshed and warfare to history. In the 1990s Africans could point to the sharp rise of ethnic tensions in Europe that brought the violent breakup of Yugoslavia and hastened the dissolution of the Soviet Union.

Many of the African states for a time were professedly Marxist. They spoke of "African socialism" and styled their regimes "people's democratic republics." In Mozambique the main avenues were named for Lenin and Mao Zedong; the flag of the People's Republic of the Congo (formerly the French Congo) displayed a hammer and sickle. They turned away from free enterprise, which they identified with the profit-making, exploitation, and racial humiliation of Western colonialism. They looked to government to oversee the new economies to guarantee rapid development; they nationalized their foreign and domestic enterprises and they collectivized agriculture. Public ownership, they believed, would better promote the welfare of the people and provide the promise of a more egalitarian society. In the years of the Cold War many of these countries received technical and material assistance from the U.S.S.R., the Soviet bloc, and the People's Republic of China. But rigid state control and overly centralized planning (as in the Communist countries themselves) led to economic stagnation. Widespread corruption took an additional economic toll. At the close of the 1980s many African governments began to encourage the private profit sector, and some regimes were becoming more flexible politically, permitting dissent, opposition parties, and contested elections. Democracy and economic progress, however, were still far from assured.

Africa had the highest population growth rate of any continent, many sub-Saharan countries growing annually at well over 3 percent. At that rate Africa's population could double by the year 2010. It was common for African women on an average to bear six or seven children during their lifetime whereas the worldwide average was three to four. Fertility was highly prized: children provided security in case of disability and in old age. Yet explosive population growth led to excessive pressures on the natural environment and frustrated efforts at economic improvement. Natural disasters such as drought and famine, exacerbated by such practices as overgrazing, and the disastrous spread of AIDS in Africa could check population expansion, but at the price of unconscionable human suffering. Rational control over population growth was the more desirable alternative.

The catalogue of disaster and suffering in the first generation of independence was grim: civil war, ethnic slaughter, regional wars, drought, floods, and famine; the frustration of democratic hopes, the emergence of brutalizing dictatorships and military tyrannies; economic stagnation; disease and malnutrition; a flood of refugees from wars, persecution, and natural catastrophes; a population growing faster than food production; and a crushing accumulation of external debt. In the early 1990s Africa had the slowest economic growth of any part of the world. Once self-sufficient in food, after 1964 it became a net importer of food. In any list of the world's poorest nations, Mozambique, Mali, Niger, Chad, Ethiopia, and other African countries were at or close to the bottom. Meanwhile African expenditures on arms exceeded the international assistance received for economic development. The African revolution had far to go before the quality of life could improve. Yet in spite of the painfully slow progress, Africans felt a sense of control over their own destiny. They did not necessarily wish to be recast in the Western democratic image, or follow Western models of economic development; they knew that material progress did not by itself make for a humane society. Nonetheless economic growth was prerequisite to survival and to the improvement of human life, as were political and social stability, and peace.

117. Ferment in the Middle East

In the Islamic, or Muslim, world, Arab and non-Arab, the older age of imperialism also ended, and a powerful new sense of identity swept through it. The huge wealth pouring in from oil resources strengthened pressures for modernization but also reinforced Islamic pride in its cultural and religious heritage. The Islamic world was determined to share in Western material advances on its own terms. Meanwhile religious and cultural barriers slowed the pace of modernization. An elitist organization of society, opposition to full equality for women, and widespread illiteracy presented powerful obstacles. The pace of transformation was uneven, and the more than forty Islamic countries differed vastly from each other, but everywhere older life styles were undermined by new wealth, industry, modern forms of urbanization, and Western technology and culture at the same time that Islamic self-consciousness intensified.

The principal non-Arab Muslim states were Pakistan, Bangladesh, Indonesia, Malaysia, Iran, Afghanistan, and Turkey.[17] The Arab states stretched from the Atlantic coast of North Africa to the Persian Gulf, from Morocco to Iraq. Millions of Muslims, Arab and non-Arab, also lived in India, the republics of the former Soviet Union, Africa, and increasingly in recent times in Western Europe and the United States. In the Middle East, Arab and non-Arab, lay an important part of the world's petroleum reserves on which the economic activity of the industrial world depended. The region became one of the world's most troubled areas.

The Arab states emerged from the Ottoman Empire during and after the First World War to become British and French League of Nations mandates.[18] Egypt became nominally independent in 1922 and Iraq in 1932, although the British retained treaty rights in each until after 1945. Syria, Lebanon, Jordan, Saudi Arabia, and Yemen became independent during or after the Second World War, when the British and French ended their mandates. In 1945 the seven states formed an Arab League. Libya, independent in 1951, soon became a member. In the decades that followed, newly independent Arab states in Africa, like Algeria, and in the Arabian peninsula, like Kuwait, joined so that it grew to have twenty-two members. The unity of the Arab world was more superficial than real; divisive rivalries persisted. The pan-Arabism advocated by Egypt's Colonel Nasser in the 1950s and Libya's Colonel Qaddafi in the 1980s failed to rally much

---

[17] Several of these countries are discussed in other pages. See pp. 921–924, and see below, pp. 948–953, 1002. Of all the Muslim countries, Turkey was distinctive in that state and religion had been separate since the secularizing reforms of Kemal Atatürk; see pp. 791–793.

[18] See pp. 661, 710, 725, 813, and maps, pp. 660 and 941.

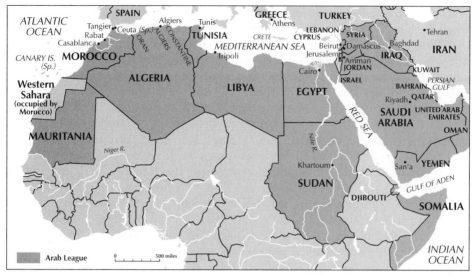

THE ARAB WORLD

The Arabic language zone is one of the most extensive in the world, reaching from the Atlantic Ocean to the Persian Gulf. In 1945 the Arab states formed a League, which came to have twenty-two members, including the Palestine Liberation Organization. The League proved to be rather loose, with much disagreement among its members, except for their attitude toward an Israeli state in the midst of an otherwise predominantly Arab world.

support. What united Arabs after the Second World War was a common opposition to the state of Israel, which itself emerged as a new state in 1948.

The Arab opposition to Israel largely reflected anti-Westernism. From the beginning the Arab states viewed Israel as a Western-backed intrusion into their land. The result was a series of continuing tensions that brought wider international forces into play and made the Middle East one of the most unsettled and most turbulent parts of the world.

The Emergence of Israel

Zionism, the commitment to establish (or reestablish) a Jewish homeland developed in the late nineteenth century in response to European anti-Semitism. Before 1914 a small number of Jewish pioneers from Eastern Europe made their way to Palestine, then part of the Ottoman Empire. During the First World War the British, by the Balfour Declaration of 1917, voiced support for a Jewish homeland in Palestine[19] but in other ways supported emergent Arab nationalism. After the demise of the Ottoman Empire, the British received a League of Nations mandate for Palestine. From 1919 on Jewish settlers arrived in larger numbers, and in the 1930s, after the triumph of Nazism in Germany, immigration swelled. To placate the Arabs, who opposed the influx and all proposals for partition, the British placed a limit on Jewish immigration.

[19] See pp. 636–637, 710.

The whole question poignantly reemerged at the end of the Second World War when the homeless survivors of the Nazi Holocaust, which had all but wiped out the European Jews, sought out Palestine as a place of refuge and were turned away by the British in deference to Arab protests. The Arabs objected to the surrender, or partition, of land that they considered theirs because of Europe's persecution of the Jews. Britain, failing to work out a compromise, terminated its mandate and turned the matter over to the United Nations. In 1947 the UN divided Palestine into a Jewish and an Arab zone, and placed the city of Jerusalem under international control. The Arab states rejected the partition. In May 1948 the Zionist leaders, who had made preparations for independence and could count on strong American support, proclaimed the Republic of Israel. Syria, Lebanon, Jordan, Egypt, and Iraq refused to recognize the new state and went to war. The Arab armies invaded, but the Israelis (as the citizens of the new republic called themselves) won. At the cease-fire in 1949 Israel increased its original territory by about half and established its capital in West Jerusalem. But Jordan during the war annexed central Palestine, including the West Bank of the Jordan River, and assumed control of East Jerusalem, from which it barred Jewish worshipers. Tensions remained high.

The Arab states, unwilling to negotiate peace or recognize the existence of Israel, refused to absorb the half-million Palestinian refugees who had fled. To many Arabs Israel was a new form of Western expansion into the Middle East. The Israelis, on the other hand, saw themselves as creating a Jewish homeland so that persecuted Jews would never again be without a refuge. Jewish immigrants from anywhere in the diaspora were automatically entitled to citizenship. The Israelis also saw themselves as building a bridgehead for Western scientific, technological, and democratic advances in an economically underdeveloped area where democracy had made little headway.

In the decades after independence Israel under a parliamentary government succeeded in building a modern, Western-style, urban, industrial, and democratic society with a large role for labor unions and cooperatives and extensive social services, in keeping with the socialist ideals of the founders of Zionism. The Israelis produced and exported not only foodstuffs and other consumer goods but high-technology products and military hardware. Through ingeniously engineered irrigation schemes, they reclaimed vast stretches of the Negev desert, where they grew citrus fruits and other crops. For close to three decades, they enjoyed one of the world's highest economic growth rates. In later years Israel received many immigrants with widely disparate backgrounds, from Asia, the Middle East, Africa, and from the Soviet Union before and after its dissolution. The economy began to falter because of heavy defense burdens, and also because of large social service expenditures insisted on by the powerful labor interests. Although Israel was a secular state, orthodox religious leaders (as in many of the Muslim countries) exercised influence out of proportion to their numbers and insisted on Sabbatarian rules and on clerical authority in such matters as marriage and divorce. At great financial strain, the Israelis developed powerful modern military forces and air power, on which they depended for survival. Four more Arab-Israeli wars were fought after 1948–1949: with Egypt over the Suez Canal crisis in 1956, the Six-Day War in 1967, the Yom Kippur War in 1973, and the war in Lebanon in 1982. The Middle East became a theater of the Cold War as well.

The United States supported Israel. The U.S.S.R., which had originally supported Israel, reversed itself and for many years backed and armed the Arab states, a change that caused concern to the United States, which was determined to prevent the expansion of Soviet influence in the Middle East.

The Arab-Israeli Wars after Independence

At first Egypt took the lead in the *jehad*, or holy war, against Israel. In 1956 the Egyptian leader Colonel Nasser announced that the Suez Canal would be nationalized and placed under Egyptian control. The British, the French (resentful of Arab support to the Algerian rebels), and the Israelis retaliated with military intervention. The Soviet Union backed Nasser, as did the emergent states of Asia and Africa, which looked upon Egypt as resisting an old-fashioned imperialist invasion. When the United States refused to support the military action, Britain, France, and Israel to their chagrin were compelled to withdraw. The Egyptians agreed to operate the canal on an impartial basis, but continued to bar Israeli shipping. Meanwhile the Syrians mounted border raids.

In 1967 Egypt moved to close the Gulf of Aqaba, which threatened to strangle the Israeli economy, and Israel retaliated in a preemptive strike. In six days of hostilities, the Israelis defeated the Egyptian, Syrian, and Jordanian armies, captured vast amounts of equipment, mostly of Soviet origin, and occupied extensive territories. Israel took over the West Bank of the Jordan River and East Jerusalem from Jordan, the Golan Heights from Syria, and the Sinai peninsula and the Gaza Strip from Egypt. It now governed a territory four times its original size; over one million additional Arabs came under Israeli rule. The Arab states, smarting under the humiliating defeat, refused to sign a peace treaty and still refused even to recognize Israel's existence.

After the 1967 war, Nasser's successor Anwar al-Sadat projected himself as leader of the Arab crusade against Israel. In October 1973 Egyptian forces surprised the Israelis by attacking on the Jewish holy day Yom Kippur, establishing a bridgehead on the Sinai Peninsula. Syria simultaneously attacked in the north. Recovering from the surprise attack, Israel first defeated the Syrian army, then crossed the Suez Canal and trapped the Egyptian forces.

With the Israelis near victory and in control of additional Arab territory, the Arab countries supporting Egypt and Syria dramatically introduced a new strategic weapon, an embargo on oil shipments. They sought to pressure the United States and Western Europe into demanding Israeli withdrawal from all Arab territories occupied since 1967, including the newly conquered ones. Although the embargo was lifted a few months later, early in 1974, the oil-producing nations had meanwhile quadrupled the price of oil. The embargo and the rise in oil prices had consequences far beyond the conflict in the Middle East.[20] The war ended with an American-mediated settlement. Israel withdrew its forces from the west bank of the Suez Canal, but continued to occupy most of the Sinai Peninsula. The Arab states, Syria in the lead, rejected any settlement and pressed for Israeli withdrawal from all occupied Arab territories. In 1975 the Arab states persuaded the UN General Assembly, in which the former colonial states of Asia and Africa

[20] See pp. 992–993.

now held a majority, to adopt a resolution condemning Zionism as a form of racism—even though Zionism had originated as a defense against anti-Semitism, and Israel as a response to the Nazi Holocaust. The resolution was repealed in 1992.

Unless a settlement were reached, new and even deadlier conflicts could explode. To be agreed upon was the disposition of the territories occupied by Israel since 1967, the demand of the Palestinian Arabs for an independent national state, and the recognition and guarantee of Israel's legitimacy and security. Sadat, recognizing the impasse, broke the united Arab front against Israel. In 1979, with the United States acting as mediator, the two hitherto implacable foes, Egypt and Israel, signed a peace treaty under which Israel agreed to withdraw from the Sinai Peninsula, retaining only the Gaza Strip, and was guaranteed the free use of the Suez Canal. Outraged, the other Arab states expelled Egypt from the Arab League. Sadat himself was later assassinated by Islamic extremists in his own army. Syria, Libya, and Iraq took the lead in rejecting any wider settlement.

The Palestinian Arabs added a highly volatile element. They grew increasingly militant, conducting guerrilla warfare against Israel and engaging in violent terrorist activities in many parts of the world to call attention to their cause. In 1964, under the leadership of Yasir Arafat, they organized the Palestine Liberation Organization (PLO), which became a full member of the Arab League and received official recognition from many quarters as a government-in-exile for the Palestinian Arabs. Refusing to recognize the legitimacy of Israel, the PLO professed to speak for all Palestinians, not only the 1.5 million under Israeli rule but also those who had taken refuge in other countries. It demanded the evacuation of all territories occupied by Israel since 1967 and called for the establishment of a Palestinian state on the West Bank of the Jordan River and the Gaza Strip.

Israel itself became more intransigent. In 1977 a conservative, nationalist party, the Likud, founded in 1973 by orthodox religious groups, replaced the

ISRAEL AND ADJOINING REGIONS

"Palestine" is the term by which Europeans long designated a small region of mixed, but predominantly Arab, population, which belonged to the Ottoman Empire until the First World War. European Jews, with the Zionist movement, began to migrate to it in the nineteenth century. In 1922 the League of Nations mandated it to the British, who tried to restrict Jewish immigration in an attempt to satisfy the Arabs. After the death of millions of Jews during the Second World War the Zionist idea of an independent Jewish state won increasing numbers of adherents. In 1947 the United Nations proposed a partition between Jewish and Arab states, with Jerusalem as a separate zone. The Arabs rejected the plan, and in the Arab-Israeli war of 1948 the Israelis won recognition of wider boundaries than those first proposed. The Arab states still refused recognition of Israel. In the Six-Day War of 1967 the Israelis occupied additional territory as shown in the lower left-hand panel. In 1973, in the Yom Kippur War, Egypt and Syria attacked Israel, but Israel defeated them and continued to occupy the Sinai Peninsula and other territories, although Egypt was allowed to regain the east bank of the Suez Canal. Under the peace treaty negotiated between Israel and Egypt in 1979, Israel returned the Sinai to Egypt but retained the small area known as the Gaza Strip. In 1993 Israel agreed to take the first steps toward self-government for the Palestinians in selected areas of the occupied territories.

Labor party, which had governed since independence. Even though the conservative leader Menachem Begin signed the peace treaty with Egypt, the new leadership encouraged Israelis to make permanent settlements in the occupied West Bank of the Jordan River (for which Begin even used the old Biblical names of Judea and Samaria) and the Gaza Strip, and rejected negotiations with the Palestinian Arabs. In 1980 the government unified the Israeli capital by formally annexing East Jerusalem, which it had occupied since 1967. It also reacted aggressively to a new threat from within Lebanon, its northern neighbor.

Turmoil in Lebanon

In 1975 a long-simmering civil war broke out in Lebanon that brought bloodshed, turmoil, and anarchy. The Muslims, who had grown to become a majority of the Christian and Muslim population, took up the cause of the Palestinian Arabs. When the Christian-dominated government attempted to suppress activist Muslim groups, a civil war erupted, which quickly became complicated by outside intervention. The Palestine Liberation Organization, expelled from Syria for fomenting unrest, settled in Beirut and systematically organized guerrilla incursions into Israel. Muslim armed forces of various Islamic sects fought the Lebanese army and the Christian militia, as well as each other. In the chaos in Beirut and elsewhere, the authority of the government collapsed. Syria intervened to restore peace, but with little success. Israel, to counter the repeated PLO guerrilla raids, crossed the Lebanese border and set up a buffer area in southern Lebanon. But the raids did not end. In 1982 the Israelis launched a full-scale invasion, reached Beirut, and forced the ouster of the PLO forces.

Lebanon's travail did not end, nor did the Israeli intervention halt new guerrilla raids. Continuing civil war among warring militias reduced Beirut to shambles. Syria, Iran, and Iraq armed and trained extremist militants, who kidnapped and held hostage American and European civilians. A multinational peacekeeping force in 1983 failed to restore order and withdrew after terrorist bomb explosions killed American and French soldiers. Syria's 40,000 troops soon controlled almost three-fourths of the country's territory.

In 1988 Christians and Muslims in Lebanon, in the hope of restoring peace, agreed to provide greater representation for the Muslims, but the fighting continued. Israel was still threatened by the unsettled conditions in Lebanon and by the threat of Syrian expansion. Many, even within the Arab world, feared the territorial ambitions and aspirations for pan-Arab leadership of the Syrian ruler, Hafaz al-Assad, who had governed his own country dictatorially since 1971, was an implacable foe of Israel, and had spoken openly of "a greater Syria." The worst of the civil war, which had cost 150,000 casualties in the small country of three and a half million, seemed over by the early 1990s, but Syrian occupation forces remained and Israel refused to withdraw from the security zone it had established in southern Lebanon, where sporadic warfare continued. Hostilities would probably end only within the context of a more general peace between Israel and its Arab neighbors.

Israel, the Occupied Territories, and Peace Negotiations

Over 1.5 million Palestinian Arabs lived in the West Bank and Gaza Strip, occupied by Israel since the 1967 war. At the end of 1987 nationalist agitation by young Palestinians flared up into what became a sustained uprising—the *intifada*, as it was called in Arabic. The Israeli military met the stone-throwing, firebombing, and civil disobedience with armed repression that cost hundreds of lives. The suppression of the rebellion divided Israel politically, hurt its economy, and threatened to undermine its democracy. The PLO exploited the popular explosion to press for recognition of an independent Palestinian state. The Israelis, although willing to consider elections in the occupied territories, adamantly rejected a role for the PLO.

With the waning of the Cold War, the Arab states recognized in the late 1980s that they could no longer count on Soviet support. The United States continued to encourage negotiations. Any genuine settlement would have to revolve around the formula "territory for peace": Israel to give up some or all of the territory occupied since 1967 in return for Arab recognition of Israel's legitimacy and existence. The status of the Palestinians would have to be resolved in favor of some form of self-government. Israel's insecurity, despite American support, lay rooted in the fact that its small population lived in a hostile Middle East. Many Israelis had no desire to govern large numbers of Arabs but feared that surrender of the occupied territories would open the path to the destruction of their state. The possibilities of peace negotiations with the Arabs revived when the Labor party, with Yitzak Rabin as prime minister, replaced the governing conservative and orthodox religious coalition in 1992.

Official negotiations continued, but it was secret talks carried on between Israelis and Palestinians in Norway outside all regular diplomatic channels that led to an extraordinary agreement in 1993, climaxed in a ceremonial signing in Washington. Israel recognized the Palestine Liberation Organization as representative of the Palestinian people and agreed to the first steps for Palestinian self-government in the occupied territories, beginning with the town of Jericho on the West Bank of the Jordan River and with the Gaza Strip. The PLO in turn recognized Israel's legitimate existence as a sovereign state and agreed to abjure acts of violence, preparing the way for an end to the turmoil in the occupied territories. Many details of the fragile agreement remained to be settled. Intransigent elements on both sides could derail it, and tragic violence continued, including the killing in a mosque in 1994 of a number of Muslims at prayer by a crazed Israeli settler. Yet despite obstacles, the larger issue of Arab-Israeli relations seemed open to a more general peace settlement in which several Arab states could be expected to join.

Libya

Libya, in North Africa, added to the explosiveness in the Middle East. Once part of the Ottoman Empire, Libya had been annexed by Italy in 1912. But after the Second World War, by decision of the United Nations in 1951, it became an independent state. The discovery of oil in 1958 transformed the country of only 4 million into a leading petroleum producer. In 1969 Colonel Qaddafi ousted the existing monarchy and established a dictatorship that blended Islamic orthodoxy, Arab nationalism, and a self-styled state socialism. Using his country's oil wealth for political purposes, he projected himself as a spokesman for pan-Arabism and aspired to a large role in African affairs as well.

Libya became headquarters for terrorist activities on behalf of the Palestinians— bomb explosions in European airports, the hijacking of commercial airliners and ships, and the taking of hostages. Matters reached such a pass that in 1986, in retaliation for such activities, the United States sent aircraft to bomb military installations in Tripoli. Libya remained one of the most vehemently anti-Western of the Arab states.

Revolution in Iran

Where change occurred rapidly in the Middle East, in Arab and non-Arab countries, traditionalists resented modernization. They especially opposed secularism and the disruption of older religious and cultural institutions as a Western subversion of their society. Yet few were prepared for the fierce anti-Westernism of the fundamentalist Islamic revolution that erupted in 1979, not in an Arab state but in Iran, where the language was not Arabic but Persian. Iran was a Shiite state—nine-tenths of the Islamic world adhered to the Sunni branch of Islam[21]—but Shiite revolutionary leaders in Iran sought to foment fundamentalist revivalism everywhere in the Muslim world.

Over the centuries Persia (it was renamed Iran in 1935) had a long history of foreign domination. At the opening of the twentieth century, like the Ottoman Empire, it was too weak to resist foreign control. Britain and tsarist Russia, coveting its newly discovered oil resources, partitioned it into spheres of influence.[22] After the First World War the British made an effort to consolidate control, but in 1921 an army officer Reza Khan seized power, made himself hereditary ruler, or shah, in 1925, and embarked on a program of modernization, abolishing extraterritorial rights for foreigners and curtailing the powers of the *mullahs*, the Islamic clergy. During the Second World War, when his machinations brought him uncomfortably close to the Axis, the British and Russians occupied the country and in 1941 forced him to abdicate in favor of his son.

After the war, American influence became paramount and the young shah, Muhammad Reza, identified with the West. When a reform prime minister, Muhammad Mossadegh, and an assertive parliament moved to nationalize the oil industry in the early 1950s, the shah, with American and British support, blocked the effort. In the 1960s, with oil wealth, he embarked upon an extensive development program, broke up estates controlled by the clergy and feudal landowners, sent students in large numbers to study abroad, and with American aid reorganized the armed forces. At the same time he presided over a repressive, authoritarian regime, crushing opposition from traditionalist clerical leaders, moderates, and leftists alike. The United States, pleased with the economic and military modernization of its anti-Soviet ally in a strategic part of the world, ignored the swelling tides of resentment within the country. In 1978 opposition forces coalesced. Strikes and riots broke out. The shah invoked martial law, but he was forced to flee in January 1979.

In February the aged leader of the religious community, Ayatollah Ruhollah Khomeini, returned from Paris. For fifteen years the ayatollah (the highest rank in the Shiite religious hierarchy) had lived in exile, denouncing the shah's pro-Western and anticlerical regime. Within a matter of days he assumed leadership of the revolution and proclaimed an "Islamic republic." His Revolutionary Guards quickly defeated the shah's troops. Supreme control rested with the

---

[21] The schism originated in an armed struggle over the succession to Muhammad after the prophet's death in 632, in which the Shiite faction supported Ali, Muhammad's son-in-law, and the Sunni favored another line of succession. The schism became permanent. There are also differences in doctrine and ritual between the two branches. The Shiite form of Islam became the state religion in Persia (Iran) in the sixteenth century; there are important Shiite communities in Iraq and elsewhere.

[22] See p. 698.

ayatollah and his council of religious associates, appointed to guarantee the fidelity of the new regime to Islam and to assure control of the revolution through a network of mosques throughout the land. The revolutionary authorities restored traditional Islamic ways of life. Women were ordered to wear veils and head scarves or the traditional long black dress, the *chador*. All Western music was banned from radio and television; the Islamic prohibition on alcohol was strictly enforced. Islamic law, interpreted by the clerics, took precedence over secular law. Revolutionary justice, in the form of drumhead trials and public execution for religious, moral, or political offenses, took the lives of thousands. The ayatollah's theocracy pushed aside the Westernized leaders, even those who had welcomed the overthrow of the shah. The first president was forced to flee into exile, the foreign minister executed. Industry was nationalized, and tight state control imposed over the economy. In the chaos, oil production and revenues fell. Militants, among them university students, were aroused to frenzied heights by the ayatollah's fervid denunciations of the West.

The anti-Western fury turned against the United States, excoriated as "the great Satan." When in the autumn of 1979 the United States admitted the exiled and ailing shah to its shores, Revolutionary Guards and student militants seized the American Embassy in Teheran in retaliation, and held fifty American hostages for close to fifteen months, demanding the return of the shah and his wealth to Iran. The failure of an ill-conceived rescue mission added to the American humiliation.

The War between Iran and Iraq

Iran made no secret of its desire to establish its leadership in the Muslim world, non-Arab and Arab, and to project its theocracy as a model for others. In 1980 war broke out with Iraq, its Arab neighbor to the west. The ayatollah had denounced Iraq both for persecuting its large Shiite community and for abandoning Islamic principles. Iraq, also rich in oil, was a nationalistic Arab state under an authoritarian, military-backed secular regime headed by Saddam Hussein, who for many years had ruled the country ruthlessly, suppressing all dissent and summarily executing political opponents. He led the Arab Baath Socialist party, a component of a pan-Arab movement dedicated to Arab revival—the word "Baath" means "renaissance." (A rival branch of the movement ruled in Syria.) As part of the regime's program of state socialism, it had nationalized oil production and used the revenues to modernize the economy and the military. But ideology was less important to Hussein than the consolidation of political power at home and the use of military power for nationalist ends abroad.

The war itself erupted over a long-smoldering border dispute between the two states over a waterway that served as a vital outlet for Iraq to the Persian Gulf. Once awarded to Iraq by an international commission, it had since fallen under Iran's control. Iraq, seizing an opportunity to exploit the revolutionary turmoil in Iran, and gambling on a quick victory, bombed Iranian oil fields in 1980, invaded Iran, and occupied the disputed territory. Iran rallied after the initial invasion, expelled the Iraqi forces from its borders in 1982, and pushed deep into Iraq, hoping to overthrow Hussein and his hated regime. When Iraq stiffened its defenses, Iran dispatched assault waves of young conscripts, many scarcely in their teens, with small gains at huge human costs. In one of the rare instances in the years since the First World War, poison gas was used on the battlefield by both sides. Iraq used it as well against its Kurdish minority, accused of collaborating with Iran. Both sides rained missiles on each other's cities.

As the war dragged on, it assumed a larger international dimension. The land war became a tanker war in the Persian Gulf, involving Saudi Arabia, Kuwait, and other Arab Gulf states dependent on trade with the West and unsympathetic to Iran's Shiite fundamentalism. Both Iran and Iraq attacked neutral shipping in the Persian Gulf to prevent arms deliveries. When the attacks threatened the

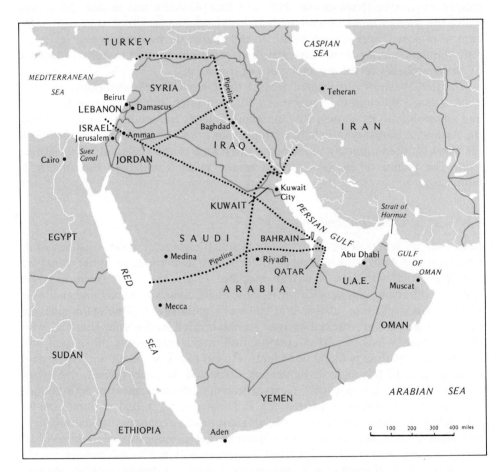

THE PERSIAN GULF AND THE MIDDLE EAST

The industrialized world of Europe, Japan, and North America is heavily dependent on oil imported from this region. The Third World, except where oil is produced locally, is also vulnerable. The oil is exported both by sea from the Persian Gulf and by pipeline to the Red Sea and Mediterranean, from which it must be transported by sea to the consuming countries to provide heating oil, motor fuel, and electric light and power. To protect the flow of this vital commodity the consuming countries sent naval forces to the Gulf during the Iran-Iraq war of 1980–1988 and resorted to full-scale military intervention in 1991. See pp. 943, 951–952, 1057–1058.

flow of oil, the United States stepped up its naval presence, with support from the British and French. The Western presence kept oil shipments flowing and reinforced the continuing strategic objective of preserving Western influence in the Gulf.

By 1987 it was clear that the Iranian counteroffensive had failed. In August 1988 Iran accepted a cease-fire. The war had gone on for eight years, and cost hundreds of thousands of lives. At the end of the war the Iranian economy was in chaos, its armed forces exhausted and depleted. The ayatollah's appeal for a holy war had gone unheeded by other Muslim states and had alienated the Arab Gulf states. But the ayatollah retained a dedicated following in Iran and still sought to assert his authority in the Islamic world. His call to the faithful for the assassination of a writer, Salman Rushdie, for blaspheming the founder of Islam in a novel published in the West shocked the international community. After Khomeini's death in 1989 more moderate and pragmatic elements sought to reestablish the country's ties to the outside world and to undertake economic reconstruction. The stringent dress and behavior codes were relaxed somewhat. But power remained divided between political leaders, many of them Western-educated, and the clerics, who had a strong following in parliament and country, and sought to reimpose the Islamic orthodoxy of the revolutionary decade. The Iranian revolution raised the larger question whether traditional Islamic values, rigidly enforced, could accommodate secularism, modernization, democracy, and a pluralist society. The events in Iran unsettled the entire Islamic world as well as the West.

Iraq, for its part, emerged from the war with battle-seasoned armed forces but without real victory and with a troubled economy. Saddam Hussein was resolved to recoup his country's economic fortunes. Unable to persuade the other oil-producing states, particularly Kuwait, to curb production and raise oil prices, he denounced his small Arab neighbor to the south, pressed vague territorial claims (going back to the Ottoman Empire and the British protectorate), and in August 1990 invaded and annexed the emirate. Many feared that he might move next against Saudi Arabia, expand his influence over the Persian Gulf, and acquire a stranglehold over much of the world's oil resources.

The United States took the lead in winning support from the international community, including several of the Arab nations, and from the UN Security Council for economic sanctions against Iraq and military measures if necessary. Over the next few months the United States pursued a massive build-up of its armed forces in the deserts of Saudi Arabia, with the support of a multinational coalition. When Iraq refused to leave Kuwait, the Americans and their allies unleashed a crushing air attack and followed with a ground assault, which quickly forced Iraq's withdrawal from Kuwait, but failed to dislodge Hussein from power.

In defiance of the cease-fire terms, Iraq repeatedly challenged the UN-imposed ban on the manufacture of nuclear and other weapons of mass destruction and obstructed international inspection. How to maintain stability in this vital area of the Middle East with its many rivalries and competing interests remained a critical concern for the states of the Persian Gulf, the Arab nations, Israel, and the international community.[23] As eager as many were to see Hussein dislodged

[23] See map, p. 950, and pp. 1004, 1057–1058.

from power, it was apparent that his removal would create a new power vacuum in the region and generate further instability.

118. *Changing Latin America*

Unlike the new nations that emerged after the Second World War in Asia and Africa, most of the Latin American nations had been in existence in 1945 for well over a century. Yet the legacy of colonialism had left the region, like other parts of the Third World, with unbalanced economic development, heavily dependent on the outside world, and burdened with a host of unresolved political, social, and economic problems.[24] During the Cold War some Latin American nations, suspicious of "Yankee imperialism," joined with other formerly colonial countries in the bloc of neutralist, nonaligned states.

A large region of over 7 million square miles stretching from the Rio Grande to the southern tip of Argentina and Chile, the collective term Latin America includes Mexico, Central America, South America, and the islands of the Caribbean. It is mainly Spanish in language and culture, but Portuguese is the language in Brazil, the continent's largest and most populous country. English and French are spoken in some islands of the Caribbean, and a variant of French in Haiti. There are many indigenous Indian languages and dialects, but they are everywhere submerged in the majority cultures.

It is a region of great racial diversity and mixture, and each part of the region reflects that diversity in its own way. Argentina, because of the flood of immigration in the nineteenth century, is overwhelmingly European in composition, but in Bolivia over half the population is of indigenous Indian origin, although European whites and people of mixed European and Indian ancestry, the *mestizos*, dominate. In Brazil, where the slave trade and slavery once flourished, there are European whites, indigenous Indians, blacks, and mainly an amalgam of mixed peoples; half the population is wholly or in part of West African ancestry. With high growth rates, the population of Latin America tripled after 1945, increasing from 160 million in 1950 to over 470 million in the mid-1990s. Of the ten most populous cities in the world Latin America could claim four: Mexico City, São Paulo and Rio de Janeiro in Brazil, and Buenos Aires in Argentina.

The Colonial Experience and the Wars for Independence

The three centuries of colonial rule after the Spanish *conquista* left an ineradicable mark. Wherever the Spanish found large, highly advanced, indigenous Indian populations, as in Mexico and in the area then known as Peru, they incorporated them into their colonial system and imposed upon them the hierarchical and authoritarian social structure of the home country. To encourage settlement and occupation, the crown granted (or "entrusted") large estates to Spanish nobles sent out to the New World. The Roman Catholic church, also the recipient of large land grants, systematically carried out its holy mission to convert the infidels in the name of Catholic Spain. The indigenous Indian population were put to

---

[24] See pp. 112–114, 195–196, 481–482.

work on the large estates with modest protection provided by the crown and church, but they labored also in underground gold and silver mines, where working conditions were more difficult to control. The initial encounter with the Europeans led in many places to demographic disaster. In the first generation the diseases brought by the Europeans (to which the Europeans themselves had developed immunity) decimated the indigenous populations. In the lowland areas, as in coastal Brazil settled by the Portuguese, coastal Colombia, and throughout the Caribbean, the Europeans imported black slave laborers from Africa, eventually in the millions, to work on the sugar plantations. Slavery was nominally abolished in most areas by the 1850s, but in Brazil not until 1888; more or less disguised forms of servitude, like peonage, persisted. Indians and enslaved blacks were at the bottom rung of colonial society.

The wealth of the colonies flowed out from the landed estates, plantations, and silver mines to the mother country, and Spain in turn provided for the shipment (or transshipment from other European countries) of needed finished goods, even though over the years the English succeeded in making many inroads into the Spanish monopoly. Spain did not nurture a commercial class either at home or in the colonies, but ranching and mining became large-scale colonial operations, and a variety of related commercial enterprises sprang up. The proud status-oriented nobles in Spain disdained commercial, banking, and business activities, as did the creole (or American-born Spanish) elite that emerged in the New World. The church was tightly integrated into the colonial system; it employed hundreds of thousands of laborers on its extensive holdings and in 1800, toward the end of the colonial period, owned one-half the productive land.

As the years passed, the American-born creole elite grew wealthy but chafed at control by Europe. They found an opportunity to break away when Napoleon occupied Spain and Portugal and displaced the two royal houses. Although touched by Enlightenment and French Revolutionary ideas about the "rights of man," the creole leaders were also frightened by the popular violence of the French Revolution. They intended to control their own revolution and protect their positions of privilege and landed wealth. From 1808 to 1826 they fought and won a series of bitterly contested wars for independence, except that in Brazil members of the Portuguese royal family led the country peacefully into independence. The wars for independence became a narrowly based and controlled political struggle among the privileged that scarcely improved the status of the lower classes who fought the battles, or prepared the way for a more mobile society. Independence, in effect, permitted the local elites to wield political power commensurate with their wealth.

To integrate their indigenous populations many of the new nations pressured them to give up their old customs and cultures and even to sell off their communal property, often to the profit of the creole landowners. From the wars for independence and from the subsequent conflicts among the new republics there emerged a large military establishment, a powerful military class, and a succession of caudillos, or military dictators.

With the Spanish and Portuguese gone, dependency on the outside world took a new turn. It was the British, the pioneers in the Industrial Revolution, who moved even more actively than ever before into the Latin American market. The new republics debated whether to adopt tariffs to protect their existing infant industries, but the question was settled by the creole landowners, who wanted low-priced manufactured imports. The flood of British manufactured goods met with little resistance or competition. British capital also financed the infrastructure—the docks, the roads, and eventually the railroads—to support the expanding trade. Economic penetration by Great Britain (and not long thereafter by the United States) represented a new form of colonialism (or neocolonialism), an economic colonialism that required no acquisition of territory. In the late nineteenth century European and American investments and a flood of European immigration further tied Latin America to the industrial world.[25]

The Colossus to the North

The ambivalent role played by the United States in the first half of the nineteenth century as both "protector and despoiler" of Latin America has been sketched in an earlier chapter.[26] Independence had left the region politically fragmented and unstable, and the republics became mired in civil wars or in wars with each other. European political control might have been reimposed except for the Monroe Doctrine and British support for the United States in opposing any Continental interference with the independence of the new states. As the century unfolded, the United States also made clear that in cases of civil disorder in the Western Hemisphere the Europeans would not be permitted to intervene to restore stability, protect investments, or collect debts, as they were accustomed to elsewhere in the non-European world during the high tide of imperialism. And in what came to be known as the corollary to the Monroe Doctrine, President Theodore Roosevelt announced in 1904 that the United States alone would assume the responsibility of intervention for such purposes. For the next quarter of a century the United States followed a policy of active armed intervention, or "dollar diplomacy," mainly in Central America and the Caribbean, until modifying, without completely abandoning, it in the mid-1930s.

By the opening years of the twentieth century the United States had begun to rival the British as the dominant trading partner of the region, exporting manufactures and purchasing a good share of its primary agricultural and mineral products. After the First World War it also gradually displaced Britain as the leading source of loans and capital investment in Latin America. Centers of manufacturing emerged, but the region remained industrially underdeveloped, in part because its impoverished masses provided inadequate demand for industries to expand. Meanwhile the prices of the region's commodities seemed increasingly hostage to the world's markets.

Economic Growth and Its Problems

Latin America suffered heavily when commodity prices plummeted in the dismal years of the Great Depression and foreign investment also dried up. But the economic crisis encouraged the Latin Americans to look to their own resources and to attempt to industrialize, as Brazil did under the populist dictator Getulio

[25] See pp. 594, 601.
[26] See pp. 650–654.

Vargas in the years 1930 to 1945. When during the Second World War the region was cut off from traditional sources of consumer goods, industrialization received a further stimulus. Practical necessity produced a policy that came to be known as "import substitution."

But neither the Great Depression nor the Second World War did more than modify dependence on the outside world or lessen the need to export agricultural products. Only after 1945 did the economic structure of the region undergo significant transformation. Latin America benefited from the increased demand for its raw materials and agricultural products in the 1950s and from an influx of foreign investment, and shared in the world postwar economic boom. The Alliance for Progress, sponsored by the United States in the early 1960s, signalized United States commitment to the economic development of the region, even though Latin Americans repeatedly complained of being slighted in favor of other parts of the developing world. In the three decades from 1945 to 1975, Latin American economies grew steadily at impressive rates; steel production multiplied 20 times, electrical energy, metals, and machinery 10 times.

Mexico, Argentina, Brazil, and Chile, despite many internal problems, could justifiably be classified among the newly industrialized countries of the world. The years of dependency were ending. Latin Americans manufactured in larger volume than ever before their own steel, textiles, petrochemicals, processed foods, cement, and motor vehicles, and no longer relied on foreign imports only for their industrial needs. American and European multinational corporations further stimulated economic progress. But much of this industrialization developed within a network of protective tariffs, subsidies, and state-controlled enterprises, and the region had only begun to incorporate the advanced technology of modern industry. Low mass purchasing power continued to impede growth.

To support economic development the major Latin American governments had borrowed heavily from Western (mainly American) banks and international lending agencies in the 1970s, and became the most heavily indebted nations in the world. The region's foreign debt added up to hundreds of billions of dollars, and for many countries foreign debt nearly quadrupled. By the 1980s the failure to meet payments on these debts posed a financial threat to the rest of the world. The international crisis receded when the foreign banks and creditor agencies took steps to "recycle" the debt and ease interest payments. The austerity measures imposed by the lending agencies, however, threatened to reduce already depressed living standards. Even in better times many of the Latin American governments, because they did not manage their public finances on a sound basis or levy appropriate taxes, failed to fund desperately needed schools, hospitals, roads, and public health facilities. They assigned a low priority to such needs and allowed large military establishments and bureaucracies to consume much of their resources. Driven by development ambitions and burdened with bloated budgets, many countries had simply printed paper money, thereby debasing the currency and promoting spiraling price rises. In the 1980s, several countries allowed a staggering "quadruple-digit" hyperinflation to develop—inflation rates of over 1,000 percent.

Difficulties were compounded because the prices of agricultural commodities had risen sharply in the inflationary spiral that began in 1973 and then fallen in the 1980s when the commodities boom ended. Economic growth in Latin America slowed to below 1 percent, or even at times turned negative. As in Africa, in many ways the 1980s were a "lost decade." Real income dropped sharply in many countries. In 1989 production per capita was lower than in 1980. But after receding to a low point in 1989, growth gradually resumed. The Latin American countries encouraged freer market economies. Sounder public finances brought inflation under control, and with renewed confidence, foreign capital, American, European, and Japanese, once again became available.

One of the region's fundamental problems, however, seemed intractable. As elsewhere in the developing world, where death rates declined dramatically after 1945, population growth surged. In Latin America it was even more difficult to cope with rising growth rates because of the Catholic church's prohibition of artificial birth control (circumvented or ignored by many, to be sure). The population, growing in many years at 3 percent annually, tripled between 1950 and the early 1990s, and the increase all but canceled economic and social gains for the masses of people. On the positive side, there was evidence that growth appeared to be stabilizing in the more industrialized Latin American countries.

The region remained overwhelmed by the acute needs of its depressed classes, urban and rural. Over the years landless rural workers fled the impoverished countryside, settling in the slums of the congested and polluted cities. Land and wealth were tightly held by a privileged upper-class minority, which kept many of its assets safely abroad. Extremes of wealth and poverty were the norm. Estimates in the mid-1990s indicated that about 180 million people, or about 40 percent of the population of Latin America, lived below the poverty line. Countries like Haiti and Honduras ranked among the poorest in the world. Bolivia, whose mineral wealth had once enriched the Incas and the Spanish, had the lowest per capita income of all the South American republics. Beginning in the 1960s, many Roman Catholic priests and nuns, touched by the plight of their compatriots, preaching "liberation theology" or the "church of the poor", threw themselves into efforts to improve the lot of the impoverished, even at times at risk to their own lives.

In Mexico, one of the most developed countries, a large proportion of its 90 million people lived at subsistence levels, and wealth remained highly concentrated. Yet Mexico could look back upon a generation of social revolution in the early twentieth century beginning in 1910, during which the power of the church and the military was curbed and a land redistribution program initiated. In the 1930s agrarian reform continued under the government of Lázaro Cárdenas, who reached out to the working classes, peasants, and Indian masses in various ways. When he expropriated foreign-owned oil fields, he added to his popularity but discouraged outside investment. By 1945 the country was in more conservative hands. The dominant political organization, the Institutional Revolutionary Party, heir to the Revolution of 1910, was revolutionary in name only. Opposition parties existed, but a small business elite kept tight rein over the country, and protected its own interests, promoting modernization but slighting social needs. Here, as elsewhere in the hemisphere, the human cost of social neglect was malnutrition, disease, high infant mortality, limited schooling, illiteracy, and lower life expectancy for all but the elite. The country's leaders contended that these social problems would be resolved by economic progress; excessive investment in social welfare might even impede economic growth. The armed revolt in 1994 of an Indian-led peasant movement in the poor southern state of Chiapas dramatized Mexico's ongoing social problems.

End of Yankee Imperialism?

Did the second half of the twentieth century change relationships with the economic colossus to the north? The United States in its "good neighbor" policy in the 1930s took an important positive step, in principle, toward surrendering its interventionist prerogatives. The interventions before 1933 in Mexico, Nicaragua, Panama, Cuba, the Dominican Republic, and Haiti were part of the historical record. But American marines and troops continued to land on Latin American shores even after 1945, especially in Central America and the Caribbean—in Guatemala in 1954, the Dominican Republic in 1965–1966, Grenada in 1983, and Panama in 1989. As a gesture of good will after the Second World War, the United States promoted the establishment in 1948 of the Organization of American States (or OAS). In the OAS 35 nations of the Western Hemisphere, including the United States and Canada, joined together to provide a mechanism for settling disputes among the republics and to curtail all other outside intervention. The OAS achieved a few practical results and provided a more dignified alternative than United States interventionism.

Among the signs of change in the Western Hemisphere was a growing sense of economic interdependence. The United States needed a stable and prospering Latin America for its own hard-pressed export economy. Together with Canada, it took steps to create a trade bloc with Mexico, working out in the early 1990s a North American Free Trade Agreement which over a period of time would eliminate all trade barriers among the three countries. Nevertheless, the Latin Americans remained wary of their neighbor to the north. For hostility to "Yankee imperialism" to diminish, the United States, it seemed, would have to accept a larger role for the OAS in the affairs of the hemisphere, demonstrate its ongoing commitment to the economic development of the region, and give a higher priority to Latin America in its foreign-aid programs. Meanwhile large numbers of immigrants from Mexico and other parts of Latin America were changing the ethnic composition of the United States itself.

The Political Record

Politically, the Latin American record in the twentieth century was a history of ephemeral constitutional regimes and repressive military dictatorships, civil wars and social revolution, ethnic tensions and labor unrest, coups and countercoups, and agitation directed against foreign, notably American, interests. There were also episodes of broad-based populist dictatorships with wide mass support, as in Brazil under Vargas, mentioned earlier, and in Argentina under Juan Perón from 1946 to 1955 (with *peronismo* exerting an influence on into later years). Disheartening cycles of attempted reform and repression recurred. Central America reflected even greater volatility. Instability troubled the area in the 1980s, intensified by American anti-Communist commitment in the Cold War and by American military support for rightist forces in Nicaragua and El Salvador.

When leftist regimes were overthrown in Latin America, frequently with

United States help, as in Guatemala in 1954, Brazil in 1964, Chile and Uruguay in 1973, Argentina in 1976, and El Salvador in 1980, harsh repression often followed. Political opponents simply "disappeared"—imprisoned, tortured, and often executed, as the later record showed. One such example was Chile. A left coalition elected in 1970, committed to land reform and the nationalization of American-owned copper mines, was toppled in a bloody coup three years later by a military junta encouraged by the United States. The country's president, Salvador Allende, and thousands of his supporters lost their lives, and brutal repression followed under a military regime headed by General Augusto Pinochet. The worst excesses ended after a few years, but constitutional government was not restored until 1990, when a new reform era opened. The Pinochet era left bitter memories and a divided country despite a substantial record of economic growth. In Chile, as in Argentina, Brazil, and elsewhere, military regimes in power promoted industrialization but tended to neglect social issues.

The most sweeping attempt at social revolution in the second half of the twentieth century occurred in Cuba, which had experienced recurrent periods of dictatorship and reform. In 1933 it fell under a heavy-handed dictatorship. In 1959 Fidel Castro and a small band of guerrillas returning from exile gathered enough strength to overthrow the well-entrenched dictatorship. Castro pledged to institute land reform and end economic dependence on the United States. When the new government confiscated United States corporate investments and large American landholdings, the United States retaliated with a trade embargo. Friction mounted. Castro, not initially a Moscow-oriented Communist, moved completely into the Soviet orbit, and the United States sponsored an unsuccessful attempt to overthrow him. Later tensions, in the context of the Cold War, as we shall see, brought the world in 1962 to the brink of nuclear war.[27]

Cuba became the only professedly Marxist state in the Western Hemisphere. Castro championed anti-imperialism worldwide, aided leftist movements in Bolivia and in Central America, and sent troops across the Atlantic to support anticolonial guerrilla armies in Africa. At home he created an advanced network of social services, promoted public health and literacy, and improved life for the rural masses, but economic chaos and totalitarian coercion overshadowed these achievements. He ignored all pledges of democracy and became increasingly dependent on the Soviet bloc for economic aid, receiving favorable terms for the export of sugar and the import of oil. Castro, first secretary of the Cuban Communist party, the only party permitted, ruled as a dictator. Political opponents fled into exile or were imprisoned. His militarized regime and global adventurism cost him support among the reform-minded in Latin America and elsewhere. When Soviet communism collapsed in 1989–1991, Castro, who by then had been in power for over 30 years, lost the economic subsidies on which he depended and became an isolated figure. The economy deteriorated. It was difficult to remember that *fidelismo* had once represented a threat to the United States, and an opening wedge to communism in the Western Hemisphere.

As the twentieth century drew to a close, Latin America was still a diverse region economically and politically, and in the midst of rapid flux. Many

---

[27] See below, p. 984.

Latin American countries in the early 1990s were moving toward constitutional government, trying to soften ideological conflict, and working to loosen state controls over their economies. They were hampered by a worldwide economic slowdown and by their own inflation, debt, and population growth, all of which made it difficult to cope with fundamental social ills. The constitutional democracies emerging (or reemerging) were fragile. Military insurrections could still break out in the early 1990s in Argentina and in Venezuela. The president of Peru, beset by a powerful extremist guerrilla movement, the Maoist-inspired Shining Path, which claimed to represent the oppressed Indian masses, suspended the constitution and imposed emergency rule. In Haiti the military were thwarting the attempt to establish democracy. In Central America the military were again bidding for power. In Colombia drug trafficking disrupted orderly government. In Mexico not only the peasant insurrection in Chiapas early in 1994 but the assassination of the leading candidate in the scheduled presidential election gave reasons for concern. Even if a larger measure of political stability could be achieved, and regional economic modernization furthered, Latin Americans would still have to cope with widespread poverty and deep-seated social inequities, many of them the legacy of their history. But political stability and economic development would make it possible to position such issues higher on the political agenda.

119. The Developing World

The End of Empire

At the beginning of the twentieth century, or even in 1945, the sweeping nature and extent of the colonial revolution was unanticipated. At best the colonial world was expected to evolve slowly toward self-government. The rapid and complete dissolution of the colonial empires was astounding. The age of imperialism, to be sure, had been accompanied by exploitation, brutality, and degradation, and it left a permanent scar on subject peoples all over the globe. Yet it was also the instrument whereby many of the scientific, material, intellectual, and humanitarian achievements of the West spread to the rest of the world. The West no longer dominated these areas politically, but the culture, technology, and institutions that had been nurtured in the West remained important. Industry, science, secularization, social mobility, and the idea of individual freedom affected remote parts of the world. The new values and institutions created dislocations and tensions, transforming the landscape of the non-Western world. In some instances, as in the Islamic revolution in Iran, and rising fundamentalist pressures in Algeria, Egypt, and elsewhere, resentments at the Western intrusion were evident, but mostly there was hope that some amalgam could be forged of modernization, secularism, and traditional values.

In few parts of the formerly colonial world did Western-style democracy prevail along with independence. Not until the 1980s did pressures for political and economic liberalization begin to gather in the former colonial world—in parts of Asia, Africa, and the Middle East, as well as in Latin America. For the most part neither by their own efforts nor by internationally assisted development programs were levels of agricultural and industrial production raised significantly, illiteracy and disease overcome, and living standards elevated. Independence, the end of imperialism, brought a new sense of dignity but did not automatically bring freedom, self-government, human rights, and the improvement of the human condition.

The Third World: The Developing Countries

After the Second World War the United States took the lead in promoting the economic and social advancement of the developing countries, assisting them with money and technical aid. Other industrial countries, once recovered from the war, committed small but significant shares of their annual gross national product to development assistance. International agencies emerged to provide additional funding and expertise. With Western science and technology available and with economic planning by their governments, the developing countries looked forward to modernization, economic growth, and social progress. Central planning, nationalized economies, and government controls held the attraction of accomplishing these ends more rapidly than private capitalism. Nehru's moderate socialism and economic planning in India was one model. Others turned to the Soviet or Chinese examples and received development assistance from those sources. A few, in Asia, followed the Japanese example and developed export economies, with striking success.

In the postwar decades the international community financed projects for improving agriculture, building industry, and combatting disease and illiteracy. The 1960s were known as the "development decade." President Kennedy spoke of raising the "banner of hope" for the poor and hungry. Dams and wells, irrigation schemes, hydroelectric projects, factories and processing mills, and education at all levels were all part of the program. Industrialization was expected to end or reduce dependence on imports. In agriculture a "Green Revolution," involving the extensive use of chemical fertilizers, new high-yield hybrids, and modern planting and harvesting techniques, would enable farmers to increase productivity. The initial results of development were gratifying. Many of the developing countries experienced significant progress, achieving targets of 5 to 6 percent growth annually; per capita income rose; infant mortality rates fell. It seemed possible to speak of a revolution of rising expectations.

But advances were slow and many of the developing states found little change in their relative position. Despite measurable progress, they did not share proportionately in the industrial world's spectacular postwar economic expansion, in the course of which per capita income in the wealthiest nations had tripled. The gap between richer and poorer nations widened, rather than narrowed. Using the United Nations and other organizations as a forum for their economic grievances, the developing nations in the late 1960s argued for a reshaping of the international economy—a "New International Economic Order"—to give them greater access to the investment funds, capital goods, and technology of the West and to shift international financing from Western-dominated agencies like the World Bank. They resented also the multinational corporations, which while introducing Western capital and technology, kept economic decision making in private hands in their own countries. In the tensions of the Cold War the

RICH COUNTRIES AND POOR COUNTRIES*

	Gross National Product per Capita		
	1970	1980	1990
Japan	$1,950	$ 9,870	$25,890
United States	4,950	12,000	21,700
European Community	2,360	9,760	16,500
Kuwait	3,350	17,790	—
Saudi Arabia	560	10,400	7,060
Latin America and Caribbean	590	1,920	2,140
China	130	300	370
India	110	240	350
Sub-Saharan Africa	150	560	340

* The table shows the extreme difference between high-income and low-income countries over a period of twenty years, from data assembled and analyzed by the World Bank and converted into United States dollars, with adjustments for inflation so far as is possible. The extraordinary growth of Japan is apparent, as is the rapid rise of two oil-producing states in the Persian Gulf. The poverty of the "south," the southern parts of the continents, is also clear. Economic well-being in sub-Saharan Africa has declined.

The figures are averages, and like all averages must be approached with caution. As averages per inhabitant they tell nothing about differences of income within each area. The average for the European Community is lowered by membership of relatively poor countries such as Greece, Portugal, and Ireland. It is low for China and India partly because of their enormous populations, and high for Kuwait because its population is very small. The absence of a 1990 figure for Kuwait is due to Iraq's invasion of Kuwait that year.

A new method of reporting statistics such as these was being adopted in the early 1990s. If a country's output is measured in terms of its "purchasing power parity" (i.e., the purchasing power of its currency at home rather than its currency's value on international exchanges), the statistics above would be quite different. For example, China's gross national product per capita in the early 1990s would be $2,040 by one estimate, $1,450 by another; and India's, $1,150. Comparable figures for earlier years are not yet available. Hence for comparison with 1970 and 1980 the figures are given as in the table above.

SOURCE: The World Bank, *World Tables, 1992*. Johns Hopkins University Press, Baltimore, 1993.

developing countries formed a bloc of nonaligned states, which grew from twenty-five in 1961 to over one hundred in the 1980s—"nonaligned" but always more critical of the wealthier West than of the Soviet Union. Since the former colonial world was situated mainly in the southern parts of the two hemispheres, the confrontation also assumed the configuration of a "north-south" contest.

In the recession that began in 1974[28] the developing countries experienced not only a decline in international trade but a shrinkage of international assistance funds. In the 1980s, they staggered under heavy debts incurred during the optimistic years of expanding world trade and rising commodity prices. Some oil-producing countries, to cite one example, had overcommitted themselves to the rise in oil prices. Third World debt, principally to private commercial banks, soared, one-third of it owed by the Latin American countries, Brazil, Mexico, Venezuela, and Argentina.

After four decades of the development experience, both the developing countries and the industrial countries were reassessing the mixed results. Despite advances in some countries, per capita income in the poorest countries had scarcely risen. Almost everywhere the agricultural sector had received a lower

[28] See pp. 993–995.

priority than the industrial. Agricultural production, even when it increased, often failed to keep up with explosive population growth. To earn foreign exchange, governments had encouraged export crops and neglected food production for their own people—an agricultural economy was thought to be a sign of inferiority. The developing countries were anxious to build their own industries and end dependence on others, but their products were often not competitive either at home or in the world market. Much of the economic aid and capital investment was channeled to industrial projects in the capitals or other large cities, sometimes to nonproductive and extravagant showpieces; little went to help the rural poor, who sank into ever deepening poverty. Millions meanwhile had fled the countryside for the presumed attractions of city life, only to face joblessness, live in congested shantytowns and slums, and breathe polluted air. Many industrial projects were undertaken at enormous cost to the environment.

In the rush for development, government control frequently led to clumsy bureaucracies and often to extravagance and corruption (not entirely unknown in private-enterprise economies either). In many instances governments used development funds to boost prestige and pride, rather than to improve the lives of their people. In frustration the developing countries increasingly looked to the West, to Japan, and to the newly industrialized countries of the Pacific Rim for models.

Changing Worlds and Continuing Problems

In the 1980s economic growth even regressed. Forty-three developing countries finished the decade with lower per capita real income. The percentage of the world's population living in poverty, slowly declining in earlier decades, rose again. Because of population growth, the numbers of the impoverished were far larger than before. An estimated 1.2 billion human beings, almost one-fourth the world's population, lived in poverty, in sub-Saharan Africa, Asia, Latin America, and the Middle East. Hundreds of millions suffered from tropical diseases and malnutrition.

The developing countries, of course, were far from homogeneous. The People's Republic of China (generally not included at all as part of the Third World) continued to industrialize and modernize in its own way. The "little tigers" in East Asia built powerful export economies and raised living standards (in South Korea per capita income rose in the years 1970 to 1990 from $270 to $5,400). Indonesia, Malaysia, and Thailand in Asia, and Argentina, Brazil, Chile, and Mexico in Latin America all were industrializing and modernizing. India, despite its enormous population problems, industrialized and also turned into an exporter of grain. The oil-rich states of the Middle East and elsewhere had the potential to turn their national wealth into the further modernization of their economies and societies. All these nations (the list is incomplete and growing) were leaving the Third World behind and forming an intermediate category of their own as newly industrialized countries (or NICs, as they came to be called).

It was not by accident that the countries with the most success in development had moved forward within a framework of market economies. Yet the debate continued over the role of government in stimulating economic development. Even in the successful market economies, governments had played a supporting role. But in many of the poorer developing countries the overriding presence of the state, government ownership and controls, bureaucratic interference, and imprudent fiscal policies had choked off growth and progress. Meanwhile at the very bottom of the economic scale—among the "least developed" countries— were a number of sub-Saharan African states, Bangladesh in South Asia, and Haiti and other states in the Western Hemisphere. Together they formed a kind of "Fourth World," an impoverished group of hundreds of millions of people.

Life expectancy and infant survival rates were rising in the developing world but in no way approaching those prevalent in the industrial countries. In parts of sub-Saharan Africa, of every 1,000 infants, over 170 still died before reaching their first birthday. In Malawi in 1990 life expectancy at birth was 48, in Kenya it was 59—higher figures, to be sure, than for the European or American middle or upper classes only a century ago, but no match for the life expectancy at birth of well over 75 in industrially advanced countries. Sadly, the spread of AIDS in sub-Saharan Africa and elsewhere in the developing world threatened to interfere with the rising trends in life expectancy and infant survival.

The distribution of wealth—a problem in the wealthier countries as well—was particularly acute in the nations where there were fewer goods and services to distribute, and where they were often distributed with gross inequity between an elite cultivating Western standards of luxury and the impoverished masses. Despite the success stories of the newly industrialized countries, the rising expectations and hopeful visions of the early postwar decades were turning into ever-deeper frustrations for many of the world's peoples. In point of fact there was no Third World. There were still only two worlds, one relatively rich, one poor.

THE MODERN WORLD IN VARIED SETTINGS

Evidences of modernity have spread by the late twentieth century to all parts of the world. Among them are airplanes and oil derricks, computer technology and carbonated soft drinks, such as may be seen in different continents in the following pages.

There is a new global uniformity in certain aspects of civilization. It is no longer a matter of Westernization, as used to be said of what happened in Japan and Russia, nor of the Americanization of the world that has sometimes been pointed to with alarm. It is a process in which Europeans and Americans have been instrumental, but which arises from the effects of modern science, engineering, medicine, transportation, television, and almost instantaneous communications. It seems that human beings of all cultures and races may develop an aptitude to pursue these activities, and that they have wants that such activities can supply.

But as modern civilization becomes more widespread it must adapt to a variety of traditional cultural settings, which must in turn adapt to it. Cultures interpenetrate each other. Older ones are eroded not only in Asia and Africa but in the West itself, where practices that have characterized Europe at least since the Renaissance—in painting, sculpture, architecture, literature, religion, personal values, child rearing, and family life—have increasingly been called into question. Some may resist modernization by reaffirming their own identity, and so may feel a new attachment to their own background, especially in religion. Accepting the interdependence of a world civilization, they strive not only for political but for cultural and spiritual independence.

To operate an airline, or any other appurtenance of modern civilization, requires a high degree of accuracy, division of labor, and the synchronization of the efforts of many persons who must perform certain actions at a given time. These in turn presuppose the objectivity of knowledge and rationality of behavior, and an acceptance of discipline, foresight, organization, and management. But these very qualities generate their opposite. It is a paradox that new philosophies of subjectivity and irrationalism, revolts against form, and demands for free self-expression have also been thought of as signs of modernity in the twentieth century. Organization restricts liberty, yet is necessary to modern life. It is not easy to adapt to the social environment created to improve the human condition. The paradox is as old as Rousseau, yet is felt increasingly every day.

The office of International Business Machines seems in strange company alongside the mosque in Istanbul, Turkey, but it would seem no more so alongside a Gothic church in Europe. Here there is the additional juxtaposition of East and West.

Nigeria, the most populous state in black Africa, has become one of the most important producers and exporters of crude oil. Here is an oil derrick in the swampy area of the delta of the Niger River. As other countries become dependent on Nigeria for energy, so Nigeria becomes vulnerable to fluctuations in the demand for oil.

The older centers of industrial production in Europe, North America, and Japan all feel the pressure from newer competitors. Here Brazilian workers assemble a Volkswagen in São Paulo.

Right: Pope John Paul II upholds the traditional values of Roman Catholic Christianity by using the most advanced technology in his frequent travels. He is shown here arriving in Warsaw.

Below: At Jiddah on the Red Sea, now a city with high-rise apartments, automobiles, and parking problems, a group of Muslims engage in one of the daily prayers prescribed by Islam. They may be on their way to Mecca, only a few miles away.

The assumptions underlying Western art since the Renaissance have perhaps been abandoned most fully in sculpture. The statue which celebrated a great individual or an allegorical figure from the fifteenth century through the nineteenth has become even more rare than the realistic portrait painting; it might even be thought ludicrous today.

Henry Moore, at the left, born in England in 1898, was one of the leading sculptors of the twentieth century. He is shown in a room with his collection of plaster maquettes, the working models for the finished products over his long career. As early as 1920, breaking with European traditions of sculpture, he became interested in the art of pre-Columbian America, black Africa, and archaic or preclassical Greece. The models on these shelves reveal influences of this kind. In the quest for a new accent, for boldness of line or emphatic abstraction, the modern and the primitive come together.

971

Above: Ayatollah Khomeini's revolution in Iran brought out violent anti-Western demonstrations. Depicted here is a group of Iranian women, wearing the chador to assert their traditional Islamic values, which they mean to enforce with these modern and imported weapons.

Left: One effect of modern medicine and public hygiene has been a huge growth of population. At New Delhi in India a large sign, promoting a government campaign for family planning, poses a question: Do you want joy and comfort with two children, or destitution with four?

Above: Life goes on as this Chinese boy enjoys a Western beverage while sitting on the Great Wall of China. Most of the present wall dates from the seventeenth century, but some parts were built two thousand years ago to protect Chinese culture from the barbarians of that day.

   Right: Two youths work on a computer problem at Ibadan University in Nigeria. Their costumes reflect their own time and place, but the young man at the right shows a concentration and perplexity that are universal. The multiplication of universities, with their attendant problems, is a sign of modernization in all countries.

Some modern improvements have been introduced sooner in Japan than in Europe or America. Here a super-express passes Mount Fuji on the way from Tokyo to Osaka. Initiated in 1964, these trains achieved a speed of over 150 miles an hour. Since then, very high-speed trains with a special roadbed have been built also in France.

Right: These apartments in the South Bronx in New York City, built at the beginning of the present century, have proved less durable than most human constructions. The decay is not in the masonry of the buildings but in economic and social conditions.

Below: This pyramid at Giza, near Cairo, was built about 2500 B.C., some two thousand years before the introduction of the camel into Egypt and more than four thousand before the motor car. It will outlast "modern times."

XXIII.
A WORLD
ENDANGERED:
THE COLD WAR

BY THE LATE 1950s the immediate postwar era had slipped into the past. Western Europe and Japan had rebuilt themselves with American aid.Western Europe had grown closer together economically in the European Community and had buried many of its old antagonisms. Regions of the world that formerly belonged to European colonial empires, and China as well, were asserting their independence. The global economy grew increasingly interdependent and the vicissitudes of economic expansion and contraction were felt worldwide. Older distinctions became blurred. The emergence of Japan made it impossible to identify industrial and financial might with the West. The Soviet bloc traded with and borrowed from the West.

Yet the Cold War continued to manifest itself in an escalating nuclear arms race and in the confrontation of the two superpowers in many parts of the globe, each attempting to prevent the other from gaining the ascendancy. The stockpiling of nuclear arms and the development of sophisticated long-range delivery systems led to the accumulation of unparalleled destructive power. It was of some consolation to know that the nuclear missiles were built for deterrence and not for use, and it turned out that a new kind of balance of power emerged that preserved the peace. The world nonetheless lived in the shadow of nuclear catastrophe in these years.

As time passed, the phenomenon of "bipolarity," or the predominance of the United States and the Soviet Union, might have given way to new global configurations. But while the charged atmosphere lasted, despite periods of détente, the world had to learn to live with repeated crises. No one could foresee how or when the Cold War would end.

Chapter Emblem: The symbol of the twelve-member European Community in 1986.

120. Confrontation and Détente, 1955–1975

The Soviet leaders who succeeded Stalin after 1953 seemed at times more conciliatory, and willing to acknowledge the need for arms control and cooperation in the nuclear age. An alternative of peaceful coexistence and competing world systems promised to open up and there were even recognizable periods of détente, or formal relaxation of tensions. But dangerous confrontations recurred, the nuclear arms build-up assumed unprecedented forms and dimensions, and relations seesawed over the next several decades between conciliation and crisis.

By 1955 the Cold War had stabilized. In Asia the Korean War was over. In Europe the North Atlantic Treaty Organization, strengthened by the West German armed forces, faced the Warsaw Pact nations. The iron curtain still divided Europe, but the threat of direct military confrontation receded. The Western powers and the Soviet Union were able to agree in 1955 on a treaty with Austria, ending the joint Allied occupation and leaving Austria independent and neutral. Nikita S. Khrushchev had emerged as the dominant Soviet leader. Sharp-tongued, volatile, boastful, he announced that the Soviets would abandon their revolutionary principles only "when shrimp learn to whistle" and pledged that the Soviets would "bury" Western capitalism. At the same time he rejected the inevitability of war and emphasized the "possibility and necessity of peaceful coexistence." President Eisenhower, in office from 1953 to 1961, continued the American policy of containment and the American military build-up. Eisenhower's secretary of state, John Foster Dulles, who saw the Cold War in almost apocalyptic terms as a Manichean contest between good and evil, at one point urged a "rollback" of Soviet power. Despite his rhetoric, and despite active American military support for anti-Communist forces in Central America, Asia, and elsewhere, American policy remained limited to containment. NATO meanwhile adopted a policy of "massive retaliation," that is, a resort to nuclear arms were it to be necessary in the event of Soviet aggression.

In 1955 Eisenhower, along with the British and French, met at Geneva with Soviet leaders in a friendlier atmosphere than any since the Second World War. Although no agreements were reached, the American president could speak of "a new spirit of conciliation and cooperation." But tensions mounted over Berlin. The Soviets, incensed that East Germans were fleeing in large numbers to West Berlin and then to West Germany, demanded that the Western powers end their occupation of West Berlin, but backed down when Eisenhower forcefully rejected the ultimatum. In 1959 Khrushchev visited President Eisenhower at his weekend retreat in Camp David, spoke of peaceful coexistence, and even of mutual disarmament. At a second summit conference in Paris, the superpowers seemed to recognize their common interests in preserving stability and peace. But by then Khrushchev, under attack at home, and from Mao in China, for being too conciliatory toward the West, produced evidence, irrefutable to be sure, of American reconnaissance flights over Soviet territory and broke up the conference. By the summer of 1960 the "spirit of Geneva" and the "spirit of Camp David" had faded. When Khrushchev spoke before the United Nations, he boasted of Soviet arms production and denounced the United States. Crises over Berlin and elsewhere were far from settled.

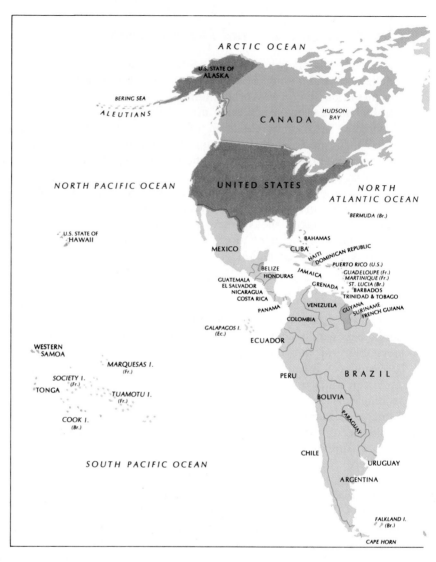

The United States, unwavering in its resolve to maintain its defense of Western Europe, accepted Soviet hegemony east of the iron curtain. As we have seen, the Americans protested but did not intervene when in 1953 the Soviets put down antigovernment riots in East Berlin, or when in 1956 the Soviets exerted pressure on Poland to curb its reform movement, or when the Soviets, even more dramatically, sent troops and tanks that year to crush the Hungarian revolt, or later, in 1968, the Czech revolt. The United States offered little more than moral

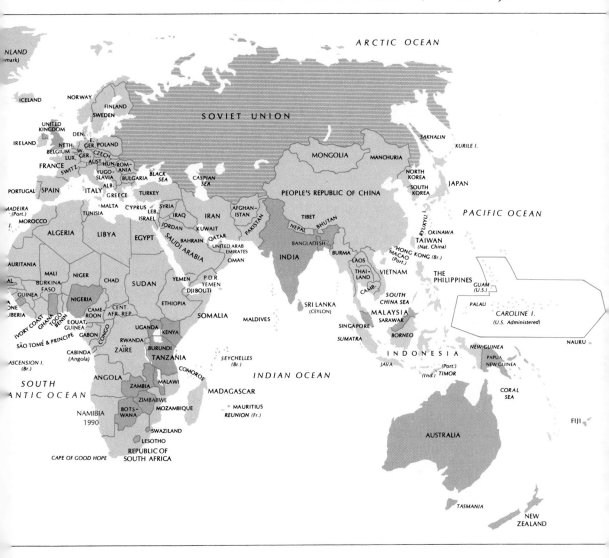

THE WORLD ABOUT 1970

On a small political map of the world about 1970 the most readily visible changes, as compared to a map of the world before the Second World War, are the breakup of the European colonial empires in Asia and Africa, the emergence of several new states in Asia and of some fifty independent republics in Africa, the peripheral expansion of the Soviet Union, and the emergence of the People's Republic of China.

encouragement.[1] At the same time one part of the world after another was being brought into the American strategic defense system. In the Suez crisis (which broke out simultaneously with the troubles in Hungary) the United States deterred Britain, France, and Israel from pressing military action against Egypt,[2] at least

---

[1] See pp. 912–913.
[2] See p. 943.

in part because it might have encouraged Soviet intervention on the other side. The three countries were frustrated, but the Soviets were kept out. The "Eisenhower Doctrine," which asserted American primacy in the defense of the Middle East, pledged assistance to any government in that region requiring protection against "international Communism." Under that policy, Eisenhower dispatched marines to Jordan and Lebanon in 1958 when their pro-Western governments were threatened. In the Western Hemisphere the United States rallied the Latin American republics to resist domination or control of any American state by the "international Communist movement." American foreign policy in the Cold War remained firmly based on the premise that all unrest was Soviet-inspired.

The nuclear arms race continued. In October 1957 the Soviets, to the world's astonishment, demonstrated their prowess in the new era of rocket technology when they successfully launched *Sputnik*, the first artificial satellite to orbit in outer space. A few months later the United States launched its own space satellite, *Explorer I*. The space age had opened. The military implications of space rocketry quickly became apparent. The same principles of propulsion could launch armed missiles over long distances. In 1958 the Soviets developed the first intercontinental ballistic missile (or ICBM, as it came to be called), capable of delivering nuclear warheads to North America and elsewhere thousands of miles away. The United States developed its own intercontinental ballistic missiles and proceeded to build an arsenal of nuclear weapons far larger than that of the Soviets. A new kind of arms race, based on "mutual deterrence," emerged; it was useless to speak of "massive retaliation." An uneasiness spread in Western Europe that the United States might not so readily defend it once American cities were vulnerable to nuclear destruction. Charles de Gaulle, the French president, gave voice to these and other misgivings in the 1960s and called for a more independent role for the West Europeans. Rejecting the rigid patterns of the Cold War and viewing postwar international affairs more as a struggle between Great Powers than as a conflict of ideologies, he called for a return to a more traditional recognition of spheres of national interest and for a reunification of Europe— "from the Atlantic to the Urals." He declined to follow the American lead in foreign policy in Europe or elsewhere. Although he kept France in the Atlantic alliance, in a gesture of independence he withdrew France from the integrated NATO military command in 1966 and pressured NATO into moving its headquarters from French soil. His aspirations for a leadership role for France created uneasiness among Europeans, but he nevertheless articulated a widespread European discontent with American hegemony in world affairs.

The Kennedy Years, 1961–1963

The gravest direct Soviet-American confrontation came during the Kennedy presidency. President Kennedy heightened the rhetoric of the Cold War. The country "had to pay any price, bear any burden, meet any hardship, support any friend or oppose any foe in order to assure the success and survival of liberty." He accused his Republican predecessor of allowing the Soviets to move ahead in the missile race and took steps to close the "missile gap." Alarmed by Soviet successes in space, he pledged that the Americans would reach the moon before the end of the decade, and encouraged large expenditures on space exploration. The defense budget increased, as did missile production. Under the policy of "flexible response," the United States and its NATO allies were prepared to meet aggression with conventional weapons before resorting to nuclear arms. At the same time Kennedy increased foreign aid to the developing countries and sponsored the Peace Corps, which took young Americans to Latin America, Asia, and Africa to aid in social and economic development programs designed to improve life and reduce the attractions of communism. For Latin America, which resented the large sums that had gone to Europe, he organized the Alliance for Progress to encourage investment and growth, but economic development remained slow there, for the most part, and democracy difficult to achieve.

In Cuba, as we have seen, Kennedy inherited an explosive situation. Many in the United States and elsewhere initially regarded Castro as a progessive revolutionary favorably disposed to democracy and committed to much-needed change in a country where a dictatorship supported by American business interests had long kept the population impoverished. But Castro was no simple reformer. He inaugurated a sweeping agrarian program, expropriated large American corporate holdings, and imprisoned or executed political opponents. Thousands of Cubans fled to the United States, mostly to Miami. Although he had originally kept his movement aloof from the Cuban Communist party, he now openly joined ranks with the Communists. When Eisenhower, alarmed by Castro's leftist regime and the threat of communism in the Western Hemisphere, imposed a strict embargo on imports from Cuba, Castro moved closer to the Soviet Union. Within a short time, four-fifths of Cuban trade was with the Soviet Union and Eastern Europe. The United States broke off diplomatic relations, and the CIA secretly trained a small group of Cuban refugees for an armed invasion of the island, confident that the invaders could easily topple the Castro regime.

Kennedy inherited the plans for the invasion and, without seriously reassessing the Castro threat, resolved to go forward with them and end the Communist menace ninety miles from the American mainland. The invasion at the Bay of Pigs in April 1961, without adequate air protection, turned into a fiasco; most of the 1,500 invaders were captured. Castro inflated his revolutionary rhetoric, openly projected himself as a Marxist-Leninist, reaffirmed the country's ties as a client state of the Soviet Union, and championed the cause of international revolution throughout Latin America and elsewhere. The United States tightened its embargo.

At a meeting with Kennedy in Vienna that year, the Soviet leader delivered a new ultimatum for the powers to leave Berlin. Kennedy, smarting over the Bay of Pigs defeat, reaffirmed the Western resolve to remain in Berlin, asked Congress to expand the military forces, inaugurated a civil defense program, and made plans for fall-out shelters in the event of nuclear war. The Atlantic alliance backed him. The immediate crisis passed. But in the summer of 1961 the Soviets, still bent on checking the exodus from East Berlin (over 3 million East Germans had already fled), constructed the Berlin Wall, a twenty-eight-mile rampart of concrete and barbed wire, with armed sentry stations. The Wall stood as a grim physical reminder of the Cold War; hundreds of East Germans who braved the barrier met their deaths. The Soviet Union also ended a three-year moratorium on nuclear testing; both countries resumed tests, both underground and in the atmosphere.

The Cuban Missile Crisis of 1962

The most dangerous Western-Soviet confrontration did not occur in Berlin, but in Cuba, where in the fall of 1962 Khrushchev showed an unanticipated recklessness. Announcing his intention to defend Cuba against a second American invasion (plans for which existed), he dispatched Soviet soldiers and technicians to the island to construct missile sites that would have brought the American mainland within easy target range. For the United States to allow this Soviet intrusion on America's own doorstep was unthinkable; moreover, it could inalterably change the nuclear balance between the two superpowers. During thirteen tense days in October President Kennedy and his advisers resolved not to take any hasty military action but to stand firm, fully aware that the showdown could lead to nuclear war. Kennedy imposed a blockade (or "quarantine") of the island, forbidding further deliveries of arms and supplies. The launching of any nuclear missile from Cuba, he made clear, would lead to a "full retaliatory response upon the Soviet Union." At the height of the emergency American planes carrying nuclear bombs were airborne. Although he blustered that the blockade was illegal, the Soviet leader backed down; on October 24 two Soviet ships and their submarine escort turned back. In one note Khrushchev agreed to remove the missile sites in return for an American pledge not to invade Cuba. In a second note, more aggressive in tone, he demanded the removal of American missile sites in Turkey. Kennedy replied only to the first message, but privately let it be known that the United States would eventually remove its missiles in Turkey. By October 28, the most ominous crisis of the Cold War, an eyeball-to-eyeball confrontation that brought the superpowers to the brink of nuclear war, was over.

Khrushchev had lost face; he was weakened still further at home, and in 1964 he was ousted from power. China, which was assuming the role of spokesman for the Third World, ridiculed his capitulation. Even though tensions once again eased, and the Soviets would never again show such recklessness, the Cuban crisis had a direct effect on the arms race. Both the Soviet Union and the United States moved to expand their nuclear arsenals, and the Soviets under Khrushchev's successors were determined to achieve nuclear parity.

The United States and the Vietnam War

The resolve to contain Communist expansion entangled the United States in deepening hostilities in Southeast Asia. In Vietnam, as we have seen, the Communist leader Ho Chi Minh had led the Viet Minh, the Vietnamese independence movement in which Communists and non-Communists fought side by side, in the struggle against the Japanese in the Second World War and against the French in the war for independence from 1946 to 1954. After France acknowledged its military defeat, an international conference at Geneva in 1954 formally recognized the independence of Vietnam, Laos, and Cambodia, all part of former

French Indochina.[3] But in Vietnam Communists and anti-Communist nationalists confronted each other. In the north Ho had consolidated his Communist regime, the Democratic Republic of Vietnam, which he had proclaimed at the end of the Second World War, its capital in Hanoi. A Western-backed regime under a former emperor with ties to the French Union, governed in the south, its capital in Saigon. Neither regime wanted a divided country, and the Geneva conference had not wished to hand the country over to Communist rule. As a compromise, the conference provisionally partitioned Vietnam at the seventeenth parallel until general elections for a unified country could be held in 1956. In the interval the armies of the rival regimes were to withdraw behind the stipulated boundary, across which there was to be free movement of peoples. In the months that followed, close to one million Vietnamese fled southward. In South Vietnam a referendum in 1955 ended all ties with the French Union and established an independent republic under Ngo Dinh Diem as president.

Diem, knowing that the Communists had acquired a large popular following in the wars against the Japanese and French, refused to participate in the elections scheduled for 1956. Ho denounced the unilateral action as illegal. Hostilities, already underway, quickly mounted. Guerrilla soldiers, the Viet Cong (or Vietnamese Communists), who had stayed behind when the main army withdrew under the Geneva agreement, set about to undermine the South Vietnamese government. A civilian arm, the National Liberation Front, was soon set up as a projected civil authority. Skilled in insurgent warfare, the Viet Cong won popular support by distributing land to the peasants and by denouncing South Vietnam as a puppet of the West. The guerrilla units before long were being reinforced by regular army units from North Vietnam infiltrating the south through Laos. Ho Chi Minh, while never sacrificing his political independence, received generous aid for his regime and for the revolutionaries in the south from the U.S.S.R. and from the People's Republic of China. South Vietnam, hard pressed despite technical advice and assistance from the United States, appealed for more and more American aid.

The United States, from President Eisenhower on, saw a need to fill the vacuum created by the French withdrawal and to check Communist expansion in Indochina. In order to prevent the other states in Southeast Asia from toppling one by one—"like a tumbling row of dominoes," in Eisenhower's phrase, Eisenhower sent some limited aid and military advisers, but Kennedy further bolstered the Diem regime with additional military advisers, financial backing, and arms. The United States acted on the premise that the war was not a civil war among the Vietnamese but a war between two independent states, one anti-Communist and therefore to be supported, and the other Communist, receiving aid and support from the Soviet Union. Vietnam was simply part of the global struggle between communism and democracy. In time the Saigon regime's authoritarian practices, ineptitude, corruption, and acts of coercion against its large Buddhist population became increasingly embarrassing to its American sponsors.

American involvement deepened and spanned the administration of five presidents, from Eisenhower to Gerald Ford. Under Eisenhower a few hundred

---

[3] See pp. 924–925.

military advisers were present, and military and economic aid began; as early as 1959 two military advisers were killed in an attack north of Saigon. In 1961, under Kennedy, additional military advisers and American support troops arrived; a year later 4,000 military personnel were on hand, and the first battle deaths were reported. The Kennedy administration, through the CIA, intervened directly in South Vietnamese politics; the Americans first propped up and then in 1963 helped to overthrow the increasingly repressive government of Diem, in the course of which Diem and his brother were murdered.

VIETNAM AND ITS NEIGHBORS

French Indochina, for about sixty years before World War II, comprised the old Asian territories of Cambodia, Laos, and Vietnam, though the French called northern Vietnam Tonkin and southern Vietnam Annam. Shaken by Japanese invasion in World War II, the French proved unable after a long struggle to resist the Vietnamese movement for independence that drew strength also from Communist affiliations. When the French withdrew in 1954, an international agreement (the Geneva Accords) provided for partition of Vietnam until unity could be restored. Since the north was now Communist, the United States undertook to strengthen South Vietnam by favoring reforms and by measures of economic and military assistance. This involvement grew in the 1960s into a large-scale though undeclared war, in which the United States intervened with over half a million troops. Hostilities ended in 1975 with Communist regimes established in Vietnam, Laos, and Cambodia.

After Kennedy's tragic assassination in November 1963, and the succession of Lyndon B. Johnson to the presidency, American intervention to achieve a military victory in Vietnam gained momentum. In 1964, on the alleged ground that North Vietnamese torpedo boats in the Gulf of Tonkin had attacked United States destroyers, Johnson ordered immediate air strikes against North Vietnam and secured support for a joint congressional resolution empowering him to take "all necessary measures" to defend the United States and its ally. The Gulf of Tonkin resolution was the only explicit congressional sanction for the deepening American involvement. After 1965 heavy air raids on supply bases in the north and on Communist-controlled areas in the south became an almost daily occurrence. American bombers attacked as far north as Hanoi. To root out the elusive Viet Cong in the countryside, American soldiers conducted "search and destroy" missions among the villagers, and American planes dropped incendiary materials and chemicals, burning whole villages, defoliating hundreds of thousands of acres of land, and turning the survivors into homeless refugees. The bombing raids, the commitment of American ground troops, and the casualties mounted. In 1966 there were close to 200,000 American troops in Vietnam; by 1969 at the maximum there were close to 550,000. Military forces, besides the South Vietnamese army, participated from Thailand, the Philippines, Australia, and New Zealand, but it was an American war. In the massive bombings from 1965 to 1968 more tons of explosives were dropped than against all the Axis powers in the Second World War, but at no point were nuclear weapons used.

The large-scale American military intervention was unable to overcome the persistence of the North Vietnamese, aided by the Soviet Union, which never directly intervened with combat troops but lent assistance of other kinds. Exaggerated military reports to Washington about the "pacification" of the countryside and about the number of enemy casualties (or "body counts") were confounded by the Communists' Tet, or New Year's, offensive at the opening of 1968, which although unsuccessful, shook American complacency about the outcome of the war. To many it was clear that a negotiated settlement would be necessary.

America's allies in Western Europe were critical of the deepening American involvement. De Gaulle, a moralizer when it suited his purposes, called it "detestable" for "a great nation to ravage a small one." At home the war became a root cause of disorders and protests on college campuses and in the cities. A wide array of public opinion turned against the war. Some opponents raised larger issues. They questioned whether the United States, despite its enormous strength, should assume the responsibility, or even had the capability, to police the world against Communist aggression; whether the American presence in Vietnam was an unwanted foreign presence reminiscent of Western intrusion in the age of imperialism; whether the South Vietnamese regime could be stabilized and democratized to make the sacrifices worthwhile; and whether the air raids and continued hostilities might not end in the utter destruction of the hapless country. Critics with a knowledge of Asian history argued that the Vietnamese had a long record of independence and that even a Vietnam united under the Communists would not lead to subordination to the Soviets, or to China, with which Vietnam historically had had many differences.

The need to win the war became an obsession with President Johnson. Like his predecessors, he was convinced that it was in America's vital interest to contain communism in Southeast Asia; otherwise the Communists would be "in Hawaii and next they will be in San Francisco." Like his predecessors, he too, refused to repeat the lessons of appeasement of the 1930s. Above all, he could not see himself presiding over the first war lost by the United States. But with victory remote, and with resentment against the war rising, he decided not to seek reelection in 1968 and announced a halt to the bombing in the north so that peace negotiations could go forward. By November 1968 all bombing ceased— for a time. The Hanoi government and the National Liberation Front opened preliminary peace talks in Paris with the United States and South Vietnam even though the fighting went on. Johnson's successor, President Nixon, pledged an early end to the war, promised to shift to South Vietnam the major responsibility for its own defense, and began to withdraw troops. Yet the United States in the next three years in some ways became even more deeply involved. In response to stalemated peace talks in Paris and continuing Communist advances, Nixon ordered the resumption of heavy air attacks and widened the war by an "incursion" into Cambodia to cut off North Vietnamese supply lines. The war spread to Laos as well.

Demonstrations mounted in the United States at the widening of the unpopular war. At the end of 1972 North Vietnam was subjected to even heavier bombing. Meanwhile Nixon's national security adviser and later secretary of state, Henry Kissinger, encouraged the bombings and military pressure but at the same time held secret talks with the North Vietnamese representatives and finally brought about a cease-fire agreement in January 1973. The agreement ended direct military involvement for the United States and concluded the longest war—like the Korean, an undeclared one—the country had ever fought. Over eight years elapsed from the arrival of the first Marine contingent in 1965 to the withdrawal of the last troops at the end of March 1973, or twelve years, if the involvement is dated from 1961.

Even though American troops were withdrawn, hostilities between North Vietnam and South Vietnam continued as each sought additional territory before a final settlement was reached. Both sides violated the cease-fire, and fighting resumed on a major scale in 1973. Although the administration remained committed to the defense of South Vietnam, Congress refused additional expenditures for military aid. Corruption and demoralization in South Vietnam grew worse; army desertions mounted. Nevertheless, the end came as a surprise. At the close of 1974, the North Vietnamese captured key cities in the southern provinces. The government of South Vietnam lost heart and ordered withdrawal to the coast; a planned retreat degenerated into rout. The North Vietnamese, with complete victory in their grasp, poured thousands of troops south across the demilitarized zone. Swarms of refugees fleeing south added to the confusion. By April 1975 North Vietnam's armies controlled three-fourths of South Vietnam, and Saigon fell.

North Vietnamese troops entered Saigon, and renamed the capital Ho Chi Minh City in honor of the Communist leader who had died in 1969. After over thirty years of almost continuous fighting, against the Japanese, the French, and in the civil war between north and south in which the United States had massively intervened, peace had finally come, and with it total Communist victory. Reunification and reorganization of the country along Communist lines proceeded quickly. The new regime launched a "political reeducation" campaign, nationalized property, and forcibly moved large numbers of the population from the cities to the countryside. Thousands, mostly ethnic Chinese, tried to flee in makeshift, overcrowded boats, many perishing in the attempt or discovering that the countries which they reached would not offer them a haven. The term "boat people" for the unfortunate refugees became part of the world's political lexicon.

In the wake of North Vietnam's victory, Cambodia and Laos also fell under Communist control. Thirty years after the end of the Second World War, all that had once been French Indochina was in Communist hands, and a reunified Vietnam emerged as an important military power in Southeast Asia.

The Vietnam War was costly; 1.3 million Vietnamese died in the fighting. For the United States the war was a searing experience. Battle and battle-related deaths (from wounds, etc.) exceeded 58,000, higher than in the Korean War.[4] From 1960 to 1975 the hostilities cost the United States over $140 billion. The impact of these expenditures was heightened by the failure to place taxes on a wartime basis, contributing to inflationary pressures. The political and moral costs were enormous. The war also created a mistrust of presidential power—of an "imperial presidency." Congress adopted legislation in 1973 intended to curb and control presidential initiatives that could lead to future episodes like Vietnam. The deadly bombings, the reports of enemy casualties, the gruesome war scenes visible in the first war reported in detail on television, the revelation of atrocities and war crimes committed by American troops (as at My Lai in 1968, first covered up and then made the subject of a public inquiry and trial), the disclosure of widespread drug use among American soldiers, the sensitivity of veterans that their sacrifices in the unpopular war were unappreciated, were all deeply disturbing. America's giant industrial and military power had failed to bring

[4] Department of Defense estimates show:

	Battle Deaths	Other Deaths	Total Deaths
World War I (1917–1918)	53,402	63,114	116,516
World War II (1941–1945)	291,557	113,842	405,399
Korean War (1950–1953)	33,629	20,617	54,246
Vietnam War (1965–1973)	47,382	10,753	58,135

victory. Technological superiority in armaments and air power proved inadequate against an enemy skilled in insurgent warfare and imbued with a revolutionary zeal.

The travail of Southeast Asia did not end. During the Vietnam War the North Vietnamese had infiltrated border areas of Cambodia and helped arm Communist insurgents, the Khmer Rouge, who, after five years of civil war, overthrew the government in 1975. The ruthless Pol Pot, the leader of the Cambodian Communists, subjected Cambodia (or Kampuchea, as it was renamed) to brutal dictatorship and grisly terror; an unknown number, perhaps 2 to 3 million, died in the small country from 1975 to 1978 as a result of mass executions, forced labor, and famine.

But the Khmer Rouge turned out to be more pro-Chinese than suited the Vietnamese. In 1979 Vietnam, backing a dissident group of Communist rebels, and invading with large numbers of troops, overthrew the Pol Pot regime. In retaliation, China invaded the border provinces of Vietnam, but soon withdrew. The Soviet Union throughout these events supported Vietnam. International pressure for the withdrawal of Vietnam from Cambodia was without effect until in the late 1980s the Soviets themselves encouraged the withdrawal, but instability persisted. Ancient rivalries between China and Vietnam, and between Vietnam and Cambodia, and tensions between the Soviet Union and China prolonged the agonies of Southeast Asia. There was no monolithic communism in this part of the globe.

Brezhnev in the 1970s: Détente, the Helsinki Conference of 1975

After Khrushchev's fall from power in 1964 the more phlegmatic Leonid I. Brezhnev emerged as the dominant Soviet leader and headed both party and state for the next eighteen years, building the country's military and naval strength with a reckless disregard for the costs to the economy. Brezhnev avoided direct confrontation and saw political and economic advantages in a relaxation of tensions and arms negotiations. The open rift with China made détente with the West even more important. No direct confrontation even approximating the Cuban missile crisis occurred. On the other hand, the two superpowers vied with each other for influence in the Middle East, Africa, and other strategic areas of the world and the Soviets consolidated their hold on Eastern Europe. Brezhnev told his compatriots that détente did not "in the slightest abolish, nor can it alter, the laws of the class struggle," and he defined détente as "a way to create more favorable conditions" for advancing the Communist cause.

The Soviet grip on Eastern Europe grew tighter. When, in 1968, liberalizing reforms in Czechoslovakia threatened the one-party state, Brezhnev, as we have seen, ruthlessly crushed the "Prague spring." In what came to be known as the "Brezhnev Doctrine" the Soviets proclaimed the right to intervene in the name of "proletarian internationalism" in any socialist country to protect socialism against "internal or external forces" and prevent the "restoration of a capitalist regime." It was a kind of mirror image of the Truman Doctrine. Czechoslovakia returned to a tight dictatorship ruled by party bosses with close ties to Moscow. The United States did no more than protest the armed intervention in Czechoslovakia; once again it would not challenge Soviet control behind the iron curtain. But the invasion of Czechoslovakia undermined Soviet leadership among Western Communist parties, which openly denounced the brutal intervention.

Although the war in Vietnam continued, President Nixon, taking office in 1969, introduced greater flexibility into the American policy of containment and pursued a policy of more systematic détente. Under Kissinger's influence he came to believe, not unlike de Gaulle, that in foreign policy national self-interest for any country counted more than ideology. The United States would be unable to curb Soviet expansionism altogether but it could offer economic concessions and other inducements for cooperation and peace. Under the Nixon-Kissinger policy the United States linked Western technology, trade, and investment to Soviet cooperation in international affairs and to a softening of Soviet policies at home and in its client states in Eastern Europe. The economic inducements were important because the Soviet Union's economic difficulties were aggravated by its growing arms burden. Khrushchev's earlier boast of surpassing the West economically had proved hollow. The Soviets badly needed Western technology, Western investment credits, and because of its persistent agricultural crises, Western grain. In the new atmosphere American and Western European private bankers made large loans to the East European nations, which benefited even more than the Soviets from détente. The two Germanys moved closer together in economic relations, recognized each other diplomatically, and were admitted to the United Nations in 1973 as two separate sovereign states.

The Nixon-Kissinger policies developed out of a reassessment of global realities. Unlike the bipolar situation in 1945 when there were only two superpowers, there were now five existing or emergent power centers: the United States, the U.S.S.R., Western Europe, Japan, and the People's Republic of China. In addition, the developing countries, despite their heterogeneity, had emerged as an important presence. The world's most populous nation, China, even if still isolated and in the throes of its Maoist Cultural Revolution, required special attention. The United States moved to normalize relations. In 1971 the United States supported the entry of the People's Republic of China into the United Nations and the transfer to it of the permanent seat on the Security Council occupied by Taiwan. Nixon, who had built his domestic political career on anticommunism, visited Mao in Beijing in 1972 and then initiated diplomatic and economic relations.

The American opening to China increased pressure on the Soviets to pursue détente. At the same time the Soviet arms build-up under Brezhnev meant that the Soviets were approaching nuclear parity. Both sides were interested in negotiating arms limitations. The Strategic Arms Limitation (or SALT) talks begun under President Johnson were resumed. In 1972 Nixon and the Soviet leaders reaffirmed the goal of "peaceful coexistence" and signed the SALT I treaty. Each nation agreed to reduce its antimissile defense system to make it possible to work toward equality in offensive weapons. They agreed also to hold stipulated offensive weapons to a fixed ceiling for a period of five years. The treaty did not halt the arms race, but it reduced fears on both sides of a preemptive strike, and promised continued negotiations. After Nixon resigned from the presidency in 1974 following the Watergate scandal, détente continued under President Ford, his successor and former vice president.

Détente offered an opportunity to settle or phase out some unresolved issues of the Second World War. In 1975, in what resembled a peace conference for Europe, three decades after the Second World War had ended, thirty-five nations—the sixteen members of NATO, the seven Warsaw Pact states, and twelve European countries not formally members of either alliance—met at Helsinki in a Conference on Security and Cooperation in Europe, and pledged themselves to work for permanent peace in Europe, economic and cultural cooperation, and the protection of human rights. The Helsinki accords, although not a formal treaty, ratified the de facto European territorial boundaries set up after the Second World War, including the Oder-Neisse boundary between East Germany and Poland. For the surveillance of human rights "Helsinki watch committees" were established. The U.S.S.R. considered the commitment to human rights a small price to pay in exchange for the economic and other benefits of détente. It expected to keep strict limits on dissent within its own country and in the East European states. It failed to see how much Helsinki would encourage dissenters to defy repression. The Helsinki conference was the high point of détente in the 1970s; not long thereafter Soviet-Western relations took another downward turn. But before we examine it, we must turn to the changes in the world's economy, to which the Soviet Union and the Eastern bloc were more closely tied than ever before.

121. The Global Economy

Interdependence is a form of dependency, and the expansion of the global economy after the Second World War made each country vulnerable to events in distant places. In 1974, after two and a half decades of spectacular growth,[5] the Western economic boom wound down abruptly. Signs of economic slowdown and inflationary pressures were already visible in the late 1960s and a recession might have occurred in any event, but it was the oil embargo growing out of the third Arab-Israeli War in the autumn of 1973 that precipitated the crisis.[6]

Oil had replaced coal as a major source of energy in Europe by the 1960s. Readily available at low prices, the oil came primarily from the vast reserves of the Middle East and was transported easily and economically by tanker through the Persian Gulf and Suez Canal. The major international oil companies, mostly American, controlled prices and production, and the oil was paid for in dollars. The Western economies as well as the Japanese had come to depend on cheap oil. In 1960, fourteen of the oil-exporting countries in the Middle East, Africa, and Latin America formed the Organization of Petroleum Exporting Countries (or OPEC) to curb the monopoly concessions enjoyed by foreign companies and to assume a larger share of authority over production and prices. Within OPEC the Arab states of the Middle East were the most assertive. The oil issue turned intensely political in October 1973 when in the course of the Yom Kippur War the Arab oil-producing states embargoed the shipment of oil to states accused of supporting Israel. That winter the OPEC cartel cut back production and quadrupled oil prices. Panic spread in Western Europe and Japan, and in the United States,

---

[5] See pp. 885–886.
[6] See p. 943.

which needed foreign oil to supplement its domestic resources. Never had an essential commodity risen in price so rapidly; the entire global industrial complex seemed vulnerable. The oil shortage and the price escalation, coming on the heels of the international monetary difficulties of 1971–1973 described earlier, sharply increased balance of payment deficits for all oil-importing countries, undermined currencies, and accelerated an inflationary spiral already under way. Not only did the oil crisis interrupt the spectacular growth of the West European economies, it also revealed the weaknesses in European unity. Apprehensive over their oil supplies, some European states scrambled to negotiate individual agreements with the Arab states.

The immediate panic caused by the oil embargo passed, but prices remained at a higher level than ever before. Later in the decade, in 1979, a second oil crisis occurred when Iran, in the midst of its revolution, halted oil exports and the OPEC cartel again doubled prices. In the 1980s the Iran-Iraq War once more cut off oil supplies and threatened the free movement of tankers through the Persian Gulf, prompting the United States and other Western countries to take naval action. On balance, the oil cartel proved less cohesive and intimidating than originally feared. Additional energy resources also became available. After the discovery of oil in the North Sea, Britain and Norway became exporters of oil. The Netherlands and other countries turned to natural gas, France to nuclear energy. Many countries initiated energy conservation measures. When prices declined in the 1980s as a result of falling demand, oil-producing countries like Nigeria and Mexico found themselves deeply in debt because they had geared their economies to the sale of high-priced oil. The decline in oil revenues led to restlessness in the Arab states. The Persian Gulf crisis precipitated by Iraq's invasion of Kuwait in August 1990, and the American and international response, demonstrated the critical role that oil still played in international affairs.

The Recession: Stagnation and Inflation

The recession that began in 1974 was the most severe since the 1930s, although it never approximated the depths of the Great Depression.[7] What set it apart from previous economic declines was the accompanying inflation, triggered by the oil crisis, which raced on in major industrial countries at double-digit annual figures.

In some European countries the annual rate of inflation rose to over 20 percent; it reached 27 percent in Britain in 1975. For a time economic growth ground to a standstill in Western Europe. By the late 1970s the recession was worldwide. Bankruptcies shook several countries; production declined; economic growth halted or slowed. In the twenty-four non-Communist industrial countries the number of jobless was estimated at 15 million in 1975 and over 32 million in 1983. Over 10 percent of the American and West European labor force was unemployed. American factories operated at only two-thirds their capacity. Unemployment once more became the bane of industrial capitalism.

The economic troubles were somewhat cushioned for the unemployed in

---

[7] See pp. 799–804.

industrial countries. Labor unions were still strong, although declining in member-ship and influence, and welfare benefits more advanced than they had been in the 1930s. Unemployed automobile workers in Essen, Turin, or Detroit could count on severance pay, trade union benefits, and government unemployment compensation far beyond the welfare payments and dole of earlier generations. These benefits reduced some of the human suffering and also limited the decline in consumer purchasing power. The recession aggravated the problem of "structural unemployment." Because of automation, high technology, and the dwindling importance of older, less efficient sectors (like coal mining, shipbuilding, textiles, and other so-called "smokestack" industries), many workers would never return to their old jobs or use their old skills again. Even after prosperity returned, some cities in the United States and England remained depressed and blighted.

The combination of stagnation and inflation (dubbed "stagflation" by journal-ists) created unprecedented problems for governments attempting to cope with the recession. Keynesian theory,[8] which had gained a wide following after 1945, called for government spending and deficit financing in slow times to buoy demand and keep employment stable. With inflation rampant, such measures became questionable. The dilemma centered on whether curbing inflation or reducing unemployment should claim the highest priority. Efforts to fight inflation by tight money and high interest rates would discourage investment, aggravate the business slowdown, and swell the ranks of the unemployed. Government spending to prime the pump or lower interest rates to facilitate private borrowing could feed inflation. With the American economy also troubled, the Western industrial countries looked to West Germany and its powerful economy and trade surplus to take the lead in expanding investment and production. West Germany, however, mindful of the hyperinflation of the 1920s,[9] set its highest priority on controlling inflation; it kept interest rates high and rejected expansionist policies. Other countries followed the same policies. By the early 1980s inflation was brought under control in the United States and in Western Europe, but with levels of unemployment unheard of in the early postwar decades.

Tight control over the amount of money in circulation and high interest rates were the tools used to control inflation. Faith in Keynesianism, and even in government spending for social purposes, the hallmark of twentieth-century progressive liberalism and the welfare state, was seriously shaken. From 1950 to the mid-1970s the percentage of gross national product expended on social measures in the industrial countries had more than doubled. The leader of the British Conservative party, Margaret Thatcher, who became prime minister in 1979, led the campaign against the welfare state and was joined by Ronald Reagan, the American Republican president from 1981 to 1989. They challenged it as costly, wasteful, paternalistic, and bureaucratic, and as undermining individual responsibility and initiative. Nationalized industries, where they ex-isted, came under attack. Spending for social measures was curbed (but heavy expenditures maintained for national defense); private enterprise was encouraged by tax reductions, deregulation, and other profit incentives. Restraints were

[8] See pp. 808 and 885.
[9] See pp. 786–787.

placed on strikes and on union efforts to interfere with technological innovation. Economic growth was seen as dependent on stimulating production, the "supply" side of the market, rather than consumption, the "demand" side. The results would then "trickle down" for everyone's benefit, with a safety net in place for the truly disadvantaged.

The return of prosperity in the 1980s reinforced faith in the free-market economy, despite uneasiness about the continuing vicissitudes of the business cycle. The conservative position appeared to be confirmed by a worldwide movement toward market economies and away from centralized planning, which in its rigidly Marxist form in the Soviet Union and Eastern Europe had manifestly failed. The defenders of the welfare state, however, continued to stress the importance of supplementing market economies with direct action by governments to meet individual and social needs. The welfare, or interventionist, state seemed destined to survive, even if in modified form.

Economic and Political Change in Western Europe

Britain was especially hard hit by the recession. Of all the industrial nations, it suffered the highest rate of inflation. Unemployment climbed, and the pound dropped to the lowest point in its history. To avert collapse, the country depended on foreign loans. The trade unions refused to accept the sacrifices that even their own Labour party believed necessary, and their disruptive strikes in coal and transportation weakened and exasperated the country. Radical factions in the Labour party pressed for increased nationalization of industry, and for a foreign policy of nonalignment in the Cold War. Alienated by the confusion and collapse of moral authority, which they blamed on Labour, in office since 1974,[10] the voters in 1979 turned to the Conservatives. Margaret Thatcher, the first woman prime minister in any major Western country, headed a government resolved to change matters. She immediately and decisively cut government expenditures, reduced imports, and resisted trade union wage demands. The focus shifted to investment, productivity, and economic growth. Inflation was curbed, but unemployment rose. The Thatcher government in its early years seemed headed for trouble until Argentina invaded the Falkland (or Malvina) Islands off the coast of South America in 1982. The prime minister stirred old patriotic and imperial memories when she dispatched a small armada 8,000 miles and thwarted the attempted takeover. The Conservatives won a sweeping parliamentary majority in 1983.

For a time in the 1980s the Thatcher policies were successful. She curtailed the power of the unions, returned to private enterprise over one-third of the nationalized industries, and made easy credit available for business and for home buyers. Britain could point to the highest economic growth rate of all the European countries, rising productivity, low inflation, a stronger pound, a higher standard of living for most people, widened home ownership, and buoyant self-confidence. Unemployment, however, remained high; fiscal retrenchment hurt education, especially the universities; and pockets of deep depression persisted,

[10] See p. 888, note 12.

especially in the north of England and in Scotland and Wales where traditional industries like coal mining and shipbuilding were in difficulties. The south and southeast enjoyed a bustling prosperity, especially in the high-technology industries around London and Cambridge. London reinforced its position as a world fianncial center and the United Kingdom became once again a leading creditor nation. Decades of economic decline and demoralization seemed to have been reversed. The opposition was disunited and in disarray. In the elections of 1987, Labour's popular vote dropped to its lowest point in decades, and union membership declined. But when economic growth slowed after the stimulus of privatization and deregulation wore off, Thatcher introduced a number of fiscal measures that brought to a head an accumulation of resentments and led to her fall from leadership of the Conservative party in 1990. Thatcher's successor as prime minister, John Major, had to cope with a new recession that set in after 1990, a weakened pound, and persistent unemployment. Labour, meanwhile, under new leadership, continued to challenge the Conservatives, arguing that the Thatcher era had favored the rich and created a less equitable society.

In France, politics in the 1980s initially veered left. The austerity program adopted in the 1970s by the conservative parties to combat inflation was unpopular, and the government's aloofness, elitism, and seeming unconcern with social issues under de Gaulle's successors helped the Socialist-led opposition grow in strength. In 1981 François Mitterrand achieved the goal he had set for himself and the Socialist party. A moderate Socialist, whose socialism owed more to liberal idealism than to Marxism, he revitalized the Socialist party, persuaded it to drop its class-struggle rhetoric, relegated the Communists to a subordinate place on the left, and successfully reached out to many who chafed at the social insensitivities of the Gaullists and conservatives. Not only did he win the presidency, but his Socialist party triumphantly gained an unprecedented absolute majority in the National Assembly.

Inspired in part by the Popular Front reforms of 1936 and by those of the early postwar years, he at once introduced labor reforms, reducing the work week and adding a fifth week of annual paid vacations. Following up on the nationalizations of 1945, he nationalized the remaining large banks as well as several leading industrial corporations. One of the few European leaders still faithful to Keynesian precepts, Mitterrand expected government pump priming and labor reforms to raise purchasing power, stimulate the economy, and thus absorb the costs of the expanded welfare state. But increased labor costs reduced French competitiveness abroad, and private investment also dried up. The consequences were slow economic growth, trade deficits, inflation, unemployment, and a weakening franc. Within two years Mitterrand abruptly changed course. He halted further nationalization and other reforms, insisted on retrenchment and austerity to cope with inflation, and placed the new emphasis on modernization. Cutting off subsidies to decaying industries, he shifted government support to high technology. The new policies encouraged economic growth but contributed little to reducing unemployment. His Socialist followers were disenchanted and frustrated. Others in the country, however, were relieved to see him concentrate on the nation's economy rather than on sectarian politics.

In assuming the leadership of the left, Mitterrand had isolated the Communists and dramatically reduced their electoral strength. Without a dynamic Communist competitor, the French Socialists could act more like Socialists and Social Democrats elsewhere, campaigning for moderate reform, counting on middle-class support, and content to help manage capitalist economies. Pressed by renewed economic problems, however, the party could not hold onto its popular following. It lost its parliamentary majority in 1986 and Mitterrand was forced to govern with a conservative prime minister ("cohabitation" the French called it). In 1988 Mitterrand was reelected president and the Socialists regained a small plurality. Economic and political dissatisfaction, high levels of unemployment, scandals involving Socialist ministers, and inroads by environmental and other groups led to a decisive rout of the Socialists in 1993 and the return of a large conservative majority.

Socialists holding office in Western Europe in the 1980s, as distinct from the French Socialists in the initial phase of the Mitterrand experiment, consistently encouraged modernization, market economies, and economic growth. Moderation and pragmatism overshadowed, if they did not entirely replace, older ideologies. Helmut Schmidt, the Social Democratic chancellor in West Germany, was the leading exemplar. In Italy, Bettino Craxi and a Socialist coalition in 1983 ended the long tenure of the Christian Democrats, who with small centrist parties had formed 40 consecutive cabinets since 1945. The Italian Socialists governed for an unprecedented four years, but were barely distinguishable in policies and practices from the long entrenched Christian Democratic establishment. Government, state-owned enterprises, private business, politicians, and political parties remained closely linked. In Spain the immensely popular Socialist party leader, Felipe Gonzalez, in 1982 headed the first left government since the Spanish Civil War,[11] and governed on into the mid-1990s. In Portugal, after the revolutionary turbulence of 1974, a Socialist and a Social Democratic party competed with each other, but on moderate platforms. Greece, still recovering from the end of "the regime of the colonels" in 1974, took a somewhat different turn when Andreas Papandreou headed a Socialist government from 1981 to 1989. His attempts at radical reform, which brought severe inflationary pressures, and his personality and personal scandals divided the country; he was returned nonetheless to office in 1994.

In West Germany the Social Democratic government of Helmut Schmidt moved to control inflation, its chief concern, through policies of retrenchment and fiscal conservatism, but industrial slowdown brought unemployment to a country which for years had known only labor scarcity. Even after recovery, unemployment persisted at about 8 percent. The doors once open to guest workers closed; bonuses were offered to those who would return home; extremist groups (as in Britain and France) alarmingly exploited antiforeign sentiment. The Christian Democrats, regaining the support of the Free Democrats, returned to office in 1982 with Helmut Kohl as chancellor. Economic growth resumed, although at more modest rates, and the mark maintained itself as one of the world's strongest currencies. The German Federal Republic remained the most productive nation in Western Europe, accounting for a third of the combined output of the European Community. But excessive labor costs, resulting from high wages and generous social benefits, burdened the economy and reduced its

[11] See pp. 838–839.

competitiveness in world markets. Meanwhile the prospects for reunification of the two Germanys in the 1980s seemed remote—Germany would remain "one nation and two states," in Willy Brandt's phrase. The transformation of Eastern Europe in 1989 upset many predictions, as we shall see.

The American Economy

The United States recovered from the post-1974 recession sooner than the Europeans. The American economy suffered business slowdown and high inflation from 1974 to 1982, but once inflation was brought under control it embarked on an extended period of expansion over the next eight years. In the 1980s unemployment even dropped below the "acceptable" figure of 6 percent and the labor force grew, although many of the newly employed were in lower-paid service industries. The American recovery helped to promote world recovery.

The economic primacy of the United States accentuated some of its own economic problems. The oil crisis of the 1970s had reinforced the strength of the dollar and, with recovery, the dollar rose steadily in value from 1981 to 1985. Meanwhile American exports faced strong competition from Western Europe and Japan, and from the newly industrialized small states in the Pacific like Singapore, South Korea, Taiwan, and Hong Kong, where labor costs were low and newer highly mechanized and automated plants provided a competitive edge. The strong dollar made it even more difficult for the United States to sell abroad and aggravated its already heavy trade deficit. With the cooperation of other major industrial countries, the United States brought down the high value of the dollar in 1985. Over the next three years the dollar lost almost 50 percent of its value in relation to foreign currencies, declining to its lowest level since 1945. Japanese, West Europeans, Canadians, Arabs, and others seized the opportunity to buy into American corporations, banks, brokerage houses, and real estate. By the late 1980s foreign holdings of American assets totaled $1 trillion. The Japanese economy reached such giant dimensions that corporations like the Fujita Bank and the Toyota Corporation were valued at five to ten times the market value of the largest American companies. The Nomura Securities Corporation of Tokyo became the largest brokerage firm in the world. Not one of the world's ten largest banks was American. From 1985 on, for the first time since 1914, the United States was a debtor nation. Foreign interests owned more assets in the United States than Americans owned abroad, which meant a steady outflow of interest, dividends, and rents. Even when American exports expanded, imports did not decline and the trade balance remained unfavorable. The annual budget deficit mounted and the national debt soared; from less than $1 trillion in 1981 it climbed to well over $4 trillion in the 1990s. Foreign capital financed the American debt and profited from the interest on loans.

There was concern in the United States, even in prosperous times, over the weakness in exports, the balance-of-payments deficits, the burden of defense expenditures, the foreign acquisition of American assets, and the fluctuations of the dollar. Some analysts pointed to inadequate savings and investment, a relative decline in productivity, a lag in industrial research and development, and shortcomings in American education for an increasingly competitive world. In spite of its problems, the American economy was still the largest in the world;

in the early 1990s its gross domestic product exceeded $5 trillion, far ahead of Japan and Germany. But it had shown a relative decline in growth in relation to the other major industrial nations. Between 1970 and 1990 American economic output dropped from five times that of Japan to less than twice as much; the gap between American and German output also shrank. Deep pockets of poverty and racial tensions persisted within the country. It was debated whether the United States, still the premier political, economic, and military power, might lose its primacy because of economic weaknesses—as Spain, France, and Britain had in the modern centuries. The prospects that opened up in the late 1980s of an end to the Cold War, and of a measure of relief from the burden of arms expenditures, brought some reassurances. In the recession that began in 1990 the United States recovered faster than other countries; its productivity and economic competitiveness surprised many. But the continuing demands of unavoidable international responsibilities could further erode its economic leadership.

The Financial World

The world's stock exchanges and financial markets were centered in New York City. Deregulation in the 1980s brought with it a sharp increase in financial acquisitions, mergers, and takeovers. Computerized trading, considered superior to human judgment, contributed to market volatility, as did new forms of trading in "options" and "futures." As in the 1920s, the lines between speculation and investment (in the banking world as well) became blurred. In October 1987, a tremor ran through the United States and world markets when stocks on the New York Stock Exchange declined sharply, losing close to one-fourth their value and conjuring up memories of the October 1929 crash and the ensuing Great Depression.[12] The market recovered and the 1987 crash did not, as feared, have serious repercussions on the American and world economy. The episode made clear the interdependence of the world's financial markets. The reverberations of the 1987 shock in New York were felt instantly in London, Frankfurt, Tokyo, Hong Kong, Singapore, Taipei, Sydney, and elsewhere. The financial markets, like the currency markets, were decentralized but more interwoven than ever before. With telecommunications and other advanced technology, even if New York remained the center, a single financial market operated around the world and around the clock, sensitive to changes anywhere.

The sense of mutual interdependence in the global economy came to be widely shared. The United States, Western Europe, and Japan recognized that the prosperity of each depended on the smooth functioning of the world economy. The heads of state of the seven largest industrial powers with market economies (the "Group of Seven"—the United States, Britain, France, the Federal Republic of Germany, Italy, Canada, and Japan) met from the 1970s on in annual economic summits to consult on the state of the economy. The leading central banks made efforts to stabilize interest and exchange rates. The Organization for Economic Cooperation and Development (OECD) brought together the twenty-four leading industrial nations of the world, and GATT continued its "rounds" of negotiations to reduce tariffs. The integration of the Soviet Union and Eastern Europe into

[12] See pp. 799–804.

the world economy, initiated in the 1970s in the first period of détente, and the vast changes in that part of the world after 1985, provided new opportunities for international cooperation. The developing Third World nations, however, remained on the periphery, their heavy debt and slow economic growth intensifying their dependence on the industrial world.

The Enlarged European Community: Problems and Opportunities

After de Gaulle's passing from the political scene in 1969, the way opened for enlarging the six-nation European Community (the EC).[13] In 1973 Britain, Denmark, and Ireland were admitted; the six became nine. In the next decade, with the admission of Greece in 1981 and Spain and Portugal in 1986, the nine became twelve.

The EC expanded just as the economic crisis struck in 1973. The diversity in membership in the midst of economic instability added tensions. Britain opposed additional supranational authority for the Community, or even closer economic integration. A large food importer, Britain objected also to the common agricultural policy agreed upon in 1968, whereby countries like France and Italy received large subsidies for their farmers, whose products were withheld from the open market and stored at great expense in order to keep prices artificially high. The British complained of paying a disproportionate share of the EC budget without receiving commensurate benefits. The admission of the less industrially advanced southern Mediterranean states introduced serious regional differences. Despite the original promise and accomplishments of the Community as a whole, the free trading area was still far from complete. Countries still placed quotas on agricultural imports; France kept out Italian wines. Burdensome administrative regulations at the borders persisted.

Except for a limited circle of Europeanists, the enthusiasm for political unification had dimmed. With enlargement and greater diversity, the Community became even more intergovernmental and less supranational. It was the national governments themselves that had to cope with the economic slowdown and monetary instability. In 1973 the government leaders began meeting on a regular basis, the presidency rotating among the member states. The first elections to the European Parliament in 1979 were more symbolic than substantial, and the Parliament's influence as a legislature failed to grow significantly. While the more ambitious dream of a United States of Europe went unrealized, the Community, for all its problems, remained an important and vibrant institution.

Toward a "Single Europe": the European Union

Even during the prosperous 1960s, the European economy did not maintain its growth in all areas. The world itself had entered a new phase of the Industrial Revolution, in which automation and other forms of advanced or high technology dominated production. Progress was no longer measured in coal and steel or in ships and textiles but in nuclear reactors, microelectronics, telecommunications, computers, robotics, and space technology. In the "postindustrial" age data

[13] See pp. 900–902.

processing, information storage and retrieval, and more and more sophisticated communications capabilities were the keys to competitive success. More workers were employed in the service sectors than in the older basic industries. The service, or tertiary, sector grew faster than agriculture or industry. In the new technology, the Europeans found themselves outdistanced by the Americans and the Japanese. American multinational corporations controlled most of the high-technology industries in Europe—before the Japanese arrived to compete. Trade competition from Japan and the new industrial countries of the Pacific Rim increased. The post-1974 recession hit Europe hard and made it more difficult to promote research and development. Western Europe lagged behind other parts of the world. Unemployment persisted. On into the 1980s journalists spoke of "Eurosclerosis" and "Europessimism."

New approaches were advanced to reinvigorate the European Community. Although internal tariffs had disappeared, nontariff obstacles still impeded the flow of trade. Nationally dictated, and therefore varying, standards of production and quality prevailed. In 1987, by the Single European Act, the twelve member-nations laid plans to create a "single Europe." They agreed to establish common production standards, eliminate paperwork at border crossings, remove impediments to the flow of capital, seek uniformity in tax rates, recognize each other's professional and commercial licensing, work toward a unified currency and central banking system, honor a common charter of labor rights, and create a truly integrated "single Europe," a "Europe without borders"—much of it to be accomplished by the close of 1992. A common defense and a common foreign policy were envisaged for the future, and a unified European currency and central banking system projected for the end of the 1990s. The arrangements were confirmed in a Treaty of European Union, signed at Maastricht in the Netherlands at the close of 1991 by the twelve governments of the EC. The treaty required unanimous approval by either the parliaments or electorates of the member states. Opponents in several countries raised objections to the loss of national control in so many areas, but the treaty was ratified in 1993. The European Community became the European Union; additional states were expected to join. The "single market" as a unified trading bloc came into existence at the end of 1992, but the protracted debate over the ratification of the treaty made clear that Western Europe was not ready for the more visionary aspects of unification.

The European Union already represented a domestic market of 345 million people (a third larger than that of the United States), and was the largest trading bloc in the global economy, accounting for 40 percent of all international trade. If it succeeded in achieving true integration, it could enlarge investment, develop high technology, increase productivity, end the lagging rate of growth, and reduce unemployment, still distressingly high. It could compete with the Americans, the Japanese, and the dynamic Pacific Rim countries.

For the world as a whole, there was always the danger of a return to global protectionism. The advanced industrial nations might divide into large regional trading blocs—a North American or Western Hemisphere bloc led by the United States, a Japanese-led Pacific bloc, the European Union, and possibly others. New competitive barriers could block the free trade that had contributed so much to prosperity. The world's economic interdependence needed to be respected universally if world commerce was to flourish.

122. The Cold War Rekindled

Under President Jimmy Carter, who took office in 1977, détente took a downward turn. More than any American president since Woodrow Wilson, Carter sought to infuse American foreign policy with moral idealism; human rights, he said, must be "the soul of our foreign policy." Détente with the Soviet Union was more closely linked than before to respect for human rights; economic aid would be forthcoming only if the Soviets permitted freedom to dissenters, the right of emigration for Soviet Jews and others, and an end to the coercion of Poland. The Soviets did not take kindly to these public pressures. Both sides meanwhile reinforced their military and nuclear strength.

Carter, however, encouraged the strategic arms talks and after tortuous negotiations, a SALT II treaty was signed in January 1979. Both countries agreed to parity in strategic, or long-range, nuclear missiles. Although the number of missiles remained high and nothing prevented the development of new sophisticated weapons, the agreement might have been another breakthrough in achieving a balance of strategic power. But before it could be ratified by the Senate, the Soviet Union, brandishing the "Brezhnev Doctrine,"[14] moved troops later that year into the neighboring state of Afghanistan in order to bolster a weak pro-Soviet leftist regime. It was the first Soviet military intervention of this kind outside Eastern Europe.

Condemning the act as invasion and aggression, Carter denounced it as a new phase of expansion by the Soviets threatening the entire Middle East—"a stepping stone in their possible control over much of the world's oil supplies." He warned that "an attempt by any outside force to gain control of the Persian Gulf region will be regarded as an assault on the vital interests of the United States" and would be repulsed "by any means necessary, including military force." He withdrew the SALT II treaty from the Senate, embargoed sales of grain and high technology to the Soviets, approved aid to the Afghan insurgents in rebellion against the leftist government, sent arms to Pakistan for the use of the rebels, increased the military budget, and set up procedures at home for a renewal of the draft.

The Soviet invasion of Afghanistan, Carter informed the U.S.S.R., was the most serious threat to world peace since 1945. The European allies were taken aback. Some argued that the Afghanistan episode was a regional matter, that the Soviet Union was acting to prevent instability on its borders, and that détente should continue. Unwilling to disturb commercial relations with the Soviets and Eastern Europe, they refused to support the economic embargo which, among other consequences, would have interfered with the completion of a Soviet natural gas pipeline to Western Europe. Afghanistan turned out to be the U.S.S.R.'s Vietnam; 100,000 troops fought for over eight and a half years before withdrawing ignominiously in 1989. Like the Americans in Vietnam, the Soviets were unable to use their overwhelming military power to defeat the Muslim guerrillas who, armed with American weapons, fought fiercely and stubbornly from their mountain strongholds.

At the very time of the Soviet intervention in Afghanistan the United States

---

[14] See pp. 912–913, 990.

itself became preoccupied with the Iran hostage crisis.[15] The crisis was a heavy blow to American prestige. To add to Carter's humiliation, the hostages were freed on the day of the inauguration of his Republican successor, Ronald Reagan, as president in January 1981.

The Reagan Years: From Revived Cold War to New Détente

There was no doubt of the new president's commitment to a hard line in the Cold War. The Soviet Union, Reagan asserted, represented "the forces of evil in the modern world" and was "an evil empire" with "dark purposes." After the humiliation of the hostage crisis, he pledged to restore America's lost prestige. During the 1970s, the Soviet Union, despite the strain on its economy, had built up its military strength, modernized its conventional fighting forces, created a powerful navy, and achieved nuclear parity. Although there was evidence that the United States had kept up in the arms race, Reagan was convinced that the United States had fallen behind. He substantially increased defense appropriations, sponsored the largest peacetime military spending in the nation's history, and took a confrontational stand against communism everywhere. In Afghanistan, he stepped up arms shipments to the Muslim guerrillas and to Pakistan, which was backing the rebels. Against the Communist government in Poland he applied economic sanctions when, under pressure from the Soviets, it imposed martial law in 1981 in an effort to suppress the Solidarity trade union movement.[16] He reinforced the embargo on the sale of high technology to the Soviets and to Eastern Europe; the embargo on grain sales was dropped because of opposition from American farmers.

In Central America and the Caribbean, Reagan accused the Soviets of using Castro's Cuba and the leftist Sandinista regime in Nicaragua as proxies to spread communism in the Western Hemisphere. The United States armed anti-Communist opponents of the regime in Nicaragua and reinforced anti-Communist regimes in neighboring states to the point where congressional critics feared that events in Central America could lead to a new Vietnam. In 1983 American forces invaded the small Caribbean island of Grenada to overthrow a leftist government that was permitting the Cubans to build an airport of possible military use.

Even more than his predecessors, Reagan and his advisers supported repressive authoritarian regimes so long as they were anti-Communist on the theory that one day such regimes might be liberalized, whereas Communist governments would transform their societies in an irreversible way. Critics argued that the revolutionary movements in Latin America and elsewhere sprang not from the Cold War but from old systems of privilege and exploitation, and they opposed military solutions and support to repressive regimes as inappropriate responses.

In Libya, the administration demonstrated the American capacity for unilateral military action when it bombed military installations in Tripoli in retaliation for what it was convinced were Libyan-sponsored terrorist activities.[17] Some European allies, alarmed by the president's belligerency, opposed the operation and

[15] See p. 949.
[16] See pp. 1019–1020.
[17] See p. 947.

refused to permit air passage to the American bombers. In Lebanon, in the throes of its confused and bloody civil war,[18] the United States organized a multinational peacekeeping force. The American fleet bombarded the Lebanon coast in 1982 and landed marines; in retaliation, terrorists blew up the American Embassy and the American and French command centers, killing American marines and French soldiers. The peacekeeping force withdrew shortly thereafter.

In the war between Iran and Iraq that broke out in 1980,[19] in the course of which attacks by both belligerents on tankers in the Persian Gulf threatened the flow of oil from the Arab Gulf states, the United States escorted a selected number of tankers under the protection of the American flag; there were some armed clashes and loss of lives, but the oil deliveries went through. The United States was intent on asserting American leadership in world affairs and on keeping the Soviets, insofar as possible, out of the Middle East.

Nuclear Arms Control

No nuclear weapons were used in any conflict in the years after 1945, yet over every crisis hung the ultimate threat of a nuclear clash. We have seen how the earliest negotiations on nuclear disarmament, at a time when the United States alone possessed the atomic bomb, were broken off in 1947, how in 1949 the Soviets successfully tested their first atomic bomb, ending the American monopoly, and how the United States in 1952 and the Soviet Union shortly thereafter developed the hydrogen or thermonuclear bomb, which by its chain reaction had vastly more destructive capacity than the mere 20,000 tons of TNT of the Hiroshima bomb.[20] By the 1960s both superpowers were building strategic long-range missiles, i.e., intercontinental ballistic missiles, capable of delivering their nuclear warheads accurately and swiftly thousands of miles away to targets in each other's homeland; they could be launched from land (from stationary or mobile sites), from sea (from ships or submarines), or from bombers in the air. The world had entered a new age of military technology. Guided missiles were the key strategic weapons of the modern age. Because of their immense destructive power, the nuclear weapons could not be used without unleashing unspeakable damage. Nuclear arms were built not for use but for deterrence.

Because nuclear testing threatened to poison the earth's atmosphere, and perhaps even damage the genetic endowment of present and future generations, controls were imperative. In 1963, despite Cold War tensions, the United States and the U.S.S.R. initiated a partial test-ban treaty, which banned testing in the atmosphere, water, and outer space, and permitted only underground testing. Concern over the spread of nuclear weapons prompted the two superpowers to propose a nonproliferation treaty, which was endorsed by the UN General Assembly in 1968, and eventually signed by over 130 states. It lacked binding force and was ignored by countries bent on developing nuclear power. France in 1960 followed Britain in becoming a fourth major nuclear power; China in 1964 became a fifth, India in 1974 a sixth. By the mid-1990s the list of countries that

[18] See p. 946.
[19] See pp. 949–952.
[20] See p. 860.

had achieved or were on the threshold of achieving a nuclear capacity included Israel, Pakistan, Iran, Iraq, and North Korea, and perhaps others. In contrast, South Africa in 1989 abandoned its nuclear weapons program and dismantled the nuclear bombs it had built. That terrorist organizations might divert nuclear materials for their political purposes remained an ever-present danger.

So long as the peaceful use of nuclear energy was encouraged, it was difficult to prevent proliferation. Nations purchasing nuclear power plants from industrial countries, ostensibly for peaceful purposes, could reprocess the plutonium from the spent fuel and build nuclear bombs, as India did. The search for alternative energy sources in the 1970s to replace oil stimulated many nations to build nuclear power plants that could easily be diverted to nonpeaceful purposes. Accidents at nuclear power plants at Three Mile Island, Pennsylvania, in 1979 and at Chernobyl in the Soviet Union in 1986 did not deter the building of nuclear power plants but underscored the need for safer construction. From Chernobyl, radioactive materials in the atmosphere traveled as far as Western Europe.

From the 1960s on debate continued in the United States about the "missile gap," about the comparative numbers of the American and Soviet missile systems deployed on land and sea and in the air, and about the vulnerability to attack of the American land-based systems. By the 1970s, with the Soviet missile build-up after the Cuban crisis of 1962, the two superpowers had achieved a rough parity. Although both recognized superiority as a self-defeating goal, nothing restrained them from adding more and more strategic arms. Strategists on each side supported the build-up. Using advanced computer programs, they calculated the potential casualties in a nuclear exchange between the superpowers in millions of deaths (or "megadeaths") and evaluated the effects of deterrents and counterdeterrents, and of "first strikes" and "counterstrikes" on each nation's ability to wage and survive nuclear war. The balance of power was spoken of as a "balance of terror;" experts referred to "mutually assured destruction" (the acronym for which, ironically, was MAD). Deterrence was the accepted formula.

Each side amassed huge stockpiles of arms, capable of destroying each other many times over, in what was described as "overkill." The two countries were also under continuing pressure to modernize their systems competitively—at exorbitant cost. When the Soviets developed defense systems, that is, antiballistic missiles, which undermined deterrence, the American response was to build its own defense systems and more powerful offensive weapons—like the MIRV (a "multiple independently targeted reentry vehicle"), a delivery system carrying up to ten nuclear warheads, each independently guided to separate targets, each warhead many times more powerful than the Hiroshima bomb. The Russians developed their own multiwarhead systems—all leading to an even higher level of armaments and greater uncertainty. Each side had satellite reconnaissance systems, but for a time neither could determine the number of warheads on the other side and hence know with accuracy the other's capability. After the first SALT treaty, signed in 1972,[21] each side developed new weapons outside the classes that were limited. The United States developed cruise missiles, designed to fly low to the ground and hence protected from defense systems; the Soviets, supersonic bombers. SALT II, signed in 1979 but (as we have seen) not ratified,

[21] See p. 991.

produced tentative agreement on equality in the total number of strategic long-range weapons. But protracted discussions continued. Each side had its triad of land-based, sea-based, and air-launched missiles.

At the close of the 1980s each superpower possessed about 25,000 nuclear weapons, of which 11,000 on each side were strategic, i.e., long-range, or intercontinental. Together the two arsenals exceeded 500,000 megatons (millions of tons) of explosive power, dwarfing the total explosive power used in all previous wars. If only a small number of these nuclear arms reached their targets, the two countries could destroy each other's major cities and countryside and kill millions in the attack and in the radioactive effects, which would spread to neighboring areas. In the "nuclear winter" that might follow, some feared for human survival. There was always the dread possibility also of accident, miscalculation, or failure of communication. So deliberately suspended over the human race was the nuclear sword of Damocles that a direct communication link, or "hot line," was installed between the Kremlin and the White House in 1963, soon after the Cuban missile crisis, and in the following decades modernized and improved. It was designed to prevent the accidental outbreak of a nuclear war because of political misunderstanding, human error, or mechanical slipup; direct communication between the tribal chieftains was necessary in the nuclear age. No more than a twenty-minute warning might be available.

The debate over security in the Cold War went beyond that of the defense strategists. Many pointed to the danger, the paradox, and even the immorality of building vast nuclear arsenals to prevent nuclear war; some (in the West) even urged unilateral disarmament. Others argued that without a high level of armaments a nation could be subject to nuclear blackmail. They maintained that the nuclear balance between the two opposing camps, and the principle of deterrence, had protected the peace. Everyone, to be sure, recognized the need to reduce the political tensions and insecurity that fed the arms competition. Yet in the rekindled Cold War tensions of the early 1980s there seemed to be no solution to the impasse. Reluctantly, the world had to reconcile itself to the existing "balance of terror," except for piecemeal negotiations on arms limitations. The unexpected changes in the Soviet Union and the end of the Cold War brought unprecedented opportunities for nuclear arms reduction. But the altered situation raised different dangers, left proliferation a continuing threat, and called for reassessments of global security.

123. China after Mao

After Mao died in 1976 moderates and radicals competed for leadership.[22] Mao's widow Jiang Qing, one of the firebrands of the Cultural Revolution, together with a small group of Maoist radicals, sought to win control and purge the moderates, but the attempt failed and she and her three associates—"the gang of four", they were called—were arrested and imprisoned. From behind the scenes Deng Xiaoping, the leader of the moderates, emerged by 1977 to become the most powerful figure in the country. Deng was a veteran party leader who had fallen

[22] See p. 917.

out of favor with Mao in 1956–1957, was purged and humiliated in 1967 during the Cultural Revolution for having taken the "capitalist road," and purged for a third time in 1976 by the Maoists. To counteract the Maoist cult of personality Deng declined over the years to accept the leading post in either government or party, but instead placed his protégés in top positions.

Deng's Reforms

By late 1978 Deng won the party over to a sweeping reform program, designed to curb the radical and utopian phases of the Revolution, deemphasize Marxist ideology and class struggle, and focus on economic growth. The moderates proposed "modernization" in agriculture, industry, science and technology, and defense. Deng thoroughly transformed the central economic planning, nationalized industry, and collectivized agriculture inherited from Mao—and indirectly from the Soviets. Because the country was still "in the primary stage of socialism," he sanctioned capitalist practices, encouraging private enterprise, production for profit, and a competitive marketplace at first in limited areas in the country, and then more extensively. For state-owned industries he demanded profitability and accountability. The new system would be "a marriage," he said, "between a planned and a market economy." Dismantling the collectivized farms and communes, which had proved disastrous for agriculture, he restored the land to individual farmers and their families to cultivate. He opened the country to foreign investment, welcoming Western science, technology, and management techniques. Although heavy industry was not neglected, a new emphasis was placed on consumer goods; factories that once manufactured military hardware now produced refrigerators, washing machines, bicycles, and motorcycles.

Deng's "socialist market economy" transformed the country. Its most striking success was in the countryside. Farmers sold a significant portion of their product on the open market. Within a decade output doubled; food became available for the cities, and even for export. In other parts of the economy retail outlets, repair shops, and other small businesses were in private hands. Special economic enclaves were established along the southern coast to encourage foreign enterprise, much of it from Hong Kong. Foreign capital flowed in; a stock exchange was introduced. The results were impressive. Gross domestic product, which had never risen by more than 2 or 3 percent annually under Mao, grew at an average 9 percent annually in the 1980s and then at even higher rates. By some calculations China's economic output was the third largest in the world.[23] Many of the new entrepreneurs (and even some farmers) became wealthy. The big cities took on aspects of a consumer society. Temporary joblessness was tempered by a state network of social services—an "iron rice bowl." The country enjoyed an unprecedented rise in living standards. The People's Liberation Army was reduced in size, but modernized and made more professional, and the government

---

[23] As indicated earlier, international agencies have begun to report national gross domestic product, or economic output, on the basis of the purchasing power of a country's currency at home rather than on its international exchange value. By that measure China's economic output in the mid-1990s was ranked third in the world by the International Monetary Fund and the World Bank, behind only the United States and Japan, and ahead of Germany. By the same measure China's per capita income, though still low because of its enormous population, would be between four to five-and-a-half times higher than the $370 or so of older estimates. See table and caption, p. 961.

bureacracy trimmed down. State-owned industries still accounted for a major share of production, but the growing private sector, flourishing in the coastal regions, represented the most vigorous part of the economy.

Even if China remained a one-party state, a "people's democratic dictatorship" in the official phrase, and individual human rights frequently violated, a more open and relaxed cultural and intellectual atmosphere prevailed. People tuned in on radio and television programs from the outside world. Students traveled and studied abroad. Many Western books (including this one, in its 1978 edition) were translated into Chinese. At no time since the Communist triumph in 1949 were the people as free to absorb ideas from the outside world. Foreign tourists visited in large numbers to see the new China. What earlier patriots and reformers like Sun Yat-sen had dreamed of, and Mao had failed to achieve because of his revolutionary excesses, Deng seemed to be accomplishing. Ideology was taking a back seat to material advance, to the idea of a "rich and strong China."

Deng wished to provide an orderly succession. He dislodged veterans of the older generation (many, like him, survivors of the Long March[24]) who clung to older Maoist ways, resisted Western political and economic ideas, and tried to block reform. The old guard retained a network of influence, but younger leaders emerged. The country deferred to Deng as a central authority figure, but he seemingly used his vast powers without presumption or arrogance.

As the decade progressed, it became clear that Deng's reform program, for all its accomplishments, had serious imperfections. The rapid economic growth fueled inflation (a 20 to 30 percent annual rate in the late 1980s). The emphasis on rising levels of consumption strained resources. In the effort to decentralize, the provincial governments won greater independence and a larger control over revenues. Despite its avowals, the government did not liquidate its unprofitable state-owned industries, one-fifth of which operated at a loss. An erratic system of price controls encouraged a black market. Even agricultural production slowed down. The consumer society bred extravagance, conspicuous consumption, and wastefulness. Corruption, always endemic in China, became widespread because government and party leaders were closely tied to business enterprises, government and private. The idealistic voiced dissatisfaction with growing inequalities and inequities in the socialist society. In response to these cumulative problems Deng in 1988 called for retrenchment and a pause in further reform.

With time and vigilance the economic difficulties in the transitional economy might have been overcome. What interrupted Deng's memorable decade of reform was the refusal to permit political reform and democratization to accompany the economic changes. Deng and others in the party believed that the country, for all its advances, was unprepared for democracy, which would only breed chaos and confusion, as it had in the Cultural Revolution, and interfere with the order and stability needed for economic growth and modernization. Further, nothing could be permitted to weaken the stewardship of the party, the heir to the old imperial dynasties, over the country's destiny. Yet in the freer atmosphere that Deng had encouraged, many of the country's intellectual leaders, and younger people destined to be its future leaders, pressed for a loosening of the party's political controls, a freer press, and the right to criticize the widespread corruption

[24] See p. 797.

and other shortcomings of the system. The beginnings of political liberalization in socialist societies in the Soviet Union and in Eastern Europe and democratic advances elsewhere in the world reinforced the restlessness in China. When at the end of 1986, Hu Yaobang, general secretary of the party and at the time the 82-year-old Deng's designated successor, encouraged the belief that greater political freedom might be permitted, students took to the streets to show their support. When Hu vacillated in suppressing the demonstrations, the party summarily replaced him.

The "Democracy Movement"

Two years later the democratic ferment came to a head. Hu's death in April 1989 set off a series of student demonstrations in the huge central square in Beijing called Tiananmen, or Gate of Heavenly Peace. The demonstrators demanded democratization. Students from other parts of the country arrived to join what came to be called the "democracy movement" and ordinary citizens lent their support. The demonstrations mounted in intensity. At one point a mock statue of the Goddess of Liberty (its name and Phrygian cap recalling both the American and French Revolutions) appeared. For seven weeks the demonstrators brought the capital and other parts of the country to a standstill. At the height of the ferment as many as a million people may have been massed in and around Tiananmen Square.

For a time the party seemed likely to accede to some demands. Zhao Ziyang, who had succeeded Hu as party leader, pressed for conciliation. But Deng, who took the side of the hard-liners, would not tolerate a recurrence of anarchy and turmoil nor permit the continuing embarrassment and humiliation of the party and government. The government imposed martial law. Although their numbers had somewhat declined, the students refused to abandon the square. In the predawn hours of June 4, the army moved in with tanks, trucks, and armored cars and opened fire, with hundreds of victims. Perhaps no government could have tolerated such defiance of law and order and loss of prestige, but even modest concessions, patience, or the exhaustion of the demonstrators might have brought the demonstrations to a peaceful end. The army and the Deng regime now had the people's blood on their hands. Deng's enormous popularity at once plummeted.

In the repressive atmosphere that followed, Deng and the party attributed the "counterrevolutionary" rebellion to a "Western-inspired conspiracy." For his conciliatory stance Zhao was dismissed from his posts. The new party and government leaders, echoing Deng, alleged that counterrevolutionaries "had attempted to install capitalism in China and make it dependent on certain foreign countries." While the nation still urgently needed Western technology and foreign investment, and wished to continue with its "socialist market economy," the party would henceforth supervise the private sector closely, reinforce Marxist ideology and political education, and determine the pace and timetable of change. Thousands remained political prisoners, and the government resisted, and resented, all international pressures for their release.

Forty years after its founding in 1949 the People's Republic of China could look back upon a quarter-century of revolutionary transformation and turmoil under Mao, a brief interlude before Deng, and a decade under Deng of economic progress, stability, openness to the West, and a freer intellectual atmosphere—until the yearning for greater freedom led to the massive demonstrations in the spring of 1989 and their repression. In the euphoria of the Deng years, many forgot the intense suspicion of the West that Deng shared with Mao, derived from the years when a weak China had lain open to exploitation.[25]

In the distant past Confucian scholars, trained to enter the emperor's service, accepted the right of the emperor to rule autocratically but reserved the right to criticize harsh or incompetent rule. A ruler governed not by force alone, but by moral example, virtue, and rectitude—or risked losing the "mandate of Heaven." The democracy movement brought into question the right of the party to rule in the old way, especially when authoritarianism was itself in decline in other parts of the world. The democracy movement demonstrated how deeply liberal values— or "bourgeois liberalism," as it was denounced—had penetrated China and how powerful were the pressures for political change. Continuing economic modernization, even under authoritarian control, could still lead to political liberalization. Fortunes were fickle in China, as Deng's own career demonstrated; Zhao or other moderates might reemerge. After the passing of Deng and his aged contemporaries, a new generation was preparing to come to power.

Population Growth

On a less dramatic front (beneath the surface of mere "events," as some historians would say), the pressure of the expanding population on the economy remained serious. Not irrelevantly, the character for "population" in the Chinese language depicts a mouth. Of all the larger developing countries China was the most successful in coping with population growth. Through a system involving central direction and local control, a one-child-per-family rule, massive education programs, social pressures, and outright coercion, the birth rate declined significantly, which had an impact on global demography as well. In the years of relative prosperity under Deng the government found it more difficult to enforce the one-child rule because affluent families, both in the cities and countryside, were willing to risk large fines for having more than one child. Nor were contraceptive devices always the most modern or most efficient. Yet on balance the program was the most effective in the world, and nowhere was the effort more needed.

In 1982 the Chinese population, one-fifth the world's total, passed the billion mark and in the mid-1990s the population, close to 1.2 billion, was growing at the rate of 15 million annually. The need to feed, clothe, and house this immense population at rising consumption levels continued to make enormous demands on the economy, no matter how modernized, and on the country's natural resources. China in the mid-1990s was a regional superpower, and a nuclear power, with a rapidly growing economy and rising living standards, but it was still under a tight authoritarian and Marxist regime—in sharp contrast to changes elsewhere.

XXIV.
A WORLD
TRANSFORMED

A SERIES OF extraordinary events in Central and Eastern Europe culminating in 1989 has sometimes been called the Revolution of 1989, as if the great French Revolution of 1789 were being reenacted in its bicentennial year. The old regimes in Central and Eastern Europe collapsed and were replaced with virtually no violence. In an even more epochal event in 1991, the Communist regime of the Soviet Union, in power for over seven decades, ended, and the U.S.S.R. disintegrated into Russia and its other component republics. In a strict sense there was no actual "revolution" in 1989–91, and indeed it was a source of wonder and satisfaction that such sweeping change could occur without armed struggle. The older regimes disappeared less by explosion than by "implosion"— by a bursting or breakup from within. The "revolution" could remain peaceful because it faced no strong internal resistance or threat of foreign intervention. Yet the upheavals were revolutionary in that they demolished existing authority and brought abrupt and radical change. They reasserted ideals that were revolutionary when proclaimed in America in 1776, in France in 1789, throughout Europe in 1848, and in the West in 1919 and 1945. What were now called human rights were the old "Rights of Man"; democracy meant representative and constitutional government and contested elections; and freedom meant guarantees against repression by one's own government and oppressive foreign rule.

Chapter Emblem: The earth as seen from a satellite 22,300 miles away, transmitting a photograph to a station in North Carolina.

With the Revolution of 1989 Central and Eastern Europe could rejoin the West. With the collapse of the U.S.S.R. one of the two superpowers that had dominated international affairs disappeared. The Cold War, as the world had known it since 1945, ended. A new era opened, with new challenges. But neither the transformation of Central and Eastern Europe nor of the Soviet Union could have taken place as they did without the changes in the U.S.S.R. that began in 1985.

124. The Crisis in the Soviet Union

The world was astonished in the mid-1980s to see some of the basic structures of Soviet communism, as developed since the Russian Revolution of 1917, begin to come apart. It is not easy to explain how someone as seemingly unorthodox as Mikhail S. Gorbachev could have risen to supreme power from within the Soviet system except that the country was in dire straits and the party leadership itself desperate. As a young man Gorbachev studied law in Moscow and took additional training at the agricultural institute in Stavropol, his home city in southwestern Russia. After working as an agricultural researcher, he received a full-time party assignment in the region and came to the attention of Yuri V. Andropov (soon to be the party general secretary) and other party leaders in Moscow. His appointment to the party secretariat in Moscow in 1978, with special responsibility for agriculture, afforded him a privileged view of the country's deep economic troubles. In 1980 he became a member of the Politburo, and by 1984 he was not only directing the party secretariat but was being groomed by Andropov for top party leadership. After the frustrating experience of an incapacitated Brezhnev clinging to power and of Andropov and Chernenko, his two successors, dying in office at a time when the country was mired in difficulties,[1] the Politburo in March 1985 seems to have decided that it was time for change. At 54, Gorbachev was by far its youngest member. Gromyko, too closely identified with the Stalin years to be chosen general secretary himself, ultimately endorsed Gorbachev and is said to have reassured those with doubts: "He has a nice smile but he has iron teeth."

Gorbachev at once demonstrated a dynamism and vigor absent from the leadership for years. His first task was to convince the party and country of the need for fundamental economic restructuring if economic stagnation was to be overcome—*perestroika* he called it. By *perestroika* he meant a drastic modification of the centrally planned command economy inherited from Stalin and carried forward with only minor changes since. However well the older system had served the industrialization of the country, the test of the Second World War, and postwar reconstruction, it was ill-suited for the contemporary industrial world, which demanded advanced technology and new skills. Industry and agriculture urgently needed independence in order to release creative energies, provide incentives for productivity, raise quality levels, and satisfy consumer needs. Gorbachev's proposed remedies were decentralization, self-management for industry and agriculture, an end to the rigidities imposed by the *apparat,* or party and government bureaucracy, and incentives for productivity. He moved

[1] See p. 909.

cautiously, believing that exhortation and a sense of urgency would bring results, but his appeals and initial moderate reforms quickly clashed with the vested interests of the entrenched bureaucrats.

For his economic restructuring to succeed, Gorbachev needed the support of the country, which he hoped to win through political change. Thus his call for *glasnost,* or "openness," which he closely linked to economic reform. By *glasnost* he meant the right to voice the need for change, the freedom to criticize the existing system, the willingness even to reexamine past mistakes and wrongdoings. Even if *glasnost* originally had a more limited objective, it took on a dynamic of its own. It led to a totally unprecedented liberalization of Soviet society, a freer press, and an end to the decades of totalitarian control over political, cultural, and intellectual life. The ferment choked off after Khrushchev's "thaw" was reborn. The press, publications, theater, and political discourse opened up as at no time before. Books and plays written in the 1960s or earlier but not permitted publication or performance made their appearance, including Pasternak's *Dr. Zhivago* (and eventually even Solzhenitsyn's *Gulag Archipelago*). Gorbachev permitted the physicist Sakharov, a leading dissenter and committed opponent of the regime, to return to Moscow from exile and take an active part in political life. Soviet Jews, who at one point had been refused permission to leave the country, were permitted to emigrate in larger numbers. The atmosphere changed profoundly. People were freer and less fearful. The legal codes were revised to encompass civil liberties, allow freedom of expression, and reduce police abuses. The KGB itself came under public and legislative scrutiny. Gorbachev even spoke of freedom of conscience and tolerance for religion, negotiating a rapprochement with the Orthodox church. He also endorsed freedom for the arts, stifled by years of uniformity and conformity.

In 1987, on the occasion of the seventieth anniversary of the Bolshevik Revolution, Gorbachev spoke openly of "Stalin's enormous and unforgivable crimes." The courts rehabilitated Stalin's political opponents and victims; leaders like Bukharin, Zinoviev, and Kamenev were restored to their places in history.[2] A monument to Stalin's victims was planned, while the press openly discussed their total number, clearly in the tens of millions. New history textbooks were prepared, as well as a revised history of the party. Gorbachev told the country that there should be "no forgotten names or blanks in history or literature."

Despite his wide-ranging strictures, Gorbachev did not challenge the role of the Communist party as the directing agent of Soviet society, but he was clearly introducing changes that would curb its monopoly on power. Remembering how Khrushchev had been dislodged after only a few years,[3] he set out to mobilize a wide popular base for himself. Reform could not be imposed from above. The people, he said, needed more than a "good tsar." Constitutional reforms in 1988 created a new national legislature; multicandidate elections were to replace the older one-party slate of nominees. What began as a technocratic vision of a more efficient economy was setting the country on the way to a sweeping transformation of Soviet life and society.

In the freer atmosphere the government released information suppressed for

[2] See pp. 770–772.
[3] See pp. 905–906, 984.

years, even of nuclear accidents before Chernobyl. At sessions of party meetings and of the new legislature the public heard for the first time outspoken critiques of Soviet society: descriptions of poverty, corruption, crime, alcoholism, and drugs; of shortcomings in medicine, health, and housing; of environmental decay. Tens of millions, perhaps one-fifth the population, lived in poverty. Despite its once much-praised health care system, the country ranked fiftieth internationally in infant mortality, with an average in 1985 of 26 deaths per 1,000 births. (In the United States, by no means a shining example itself, the rate was 10.6 per 1,000.) The Soviet Union was the only industrial country in which life expectancy was regressing; it ranked thirty-second. Because of inadequate housing, there was intense pressure to limit families, but since modern contraceptive measures were unavailable, abortion was the common procedure; one and a half abortions were performed for every live birth. Also disclosed were statistics on the poor grain harvests, as well as the drain on the budget resulting from defense costs and the subsidization of inefficient state enterprises.

Gorbachev came to recognize that the country's economic problems were more intractable than he had thought, but he persisted with his gradualist reform program. For the first time since Lenin's NEP, when Lenin had liberalized the economy in the early 1920s,[4] individuals were encouraged to start up businesses on their own or form cooperatives, and even hire workers. Private enterprise and state industries were one day to be integrated into a market-based economy, linked to the outside world. Foreign capital for trade and investment and joint ventures with foreign firms were welcomed. Soviet managers were encouraged to travel abroad to learn advanced (sometimes elementary) business and accounting practices. But there were limits to these reforms. Many remained paper decrees only and the party officials and government bureaucrats helped checkmate others. Little privatization took place; the cooperatives, lacking support from the party authorities, fell into the hands of profiteers. The older economic system remained virtually unchanged. Gorbachev shrank from moving more rapidly to a market-oriented competitive economy. His concerns about painful short-term dislocations and political unrest reinforced his commitment to preserve rather than abandon the older system.

Gorbachev's reforms in agriculture fell far short of what was needed. Accepting the existing structure of state and collective farms, he did little more than allow them greater managerial autonomy. Yet nearly half the country's 50,000 state and collective farms showed a loss, and required large subsidies. Production did not rise. Belatedly, he launched a more extensive agrarian policy. Farmers and farm families would be permitted to work with state and collective farms on a share-crop basis, or farm their own land. They could lease land for their lifetime and even bequeath this right to their children. But the state remained the legal owner of the land—not as in China, where Deng had at the very beginning of his reforms dismantled the collective farms, returned the land outright to the farmers, and reaped the benefit in increased production. Despite Gorbachev's encouragement to small independent farming, little more than 1 percent of the land shifted to private hands. The Stalinist system of collectivized agriculture remained intact.

[4] See pp. 760–761.

But the constitutional and political changes initiated in 1988–1989 significantly loosened the monopoly grip of the party. The new legislature differed from the older Supreme Soviet, which had been elected on the basis of a single slate and met only to rubber-stamp legislation prepared for it. In March 1989 openly contested and multicandidate elections were held, the first since 1917.[5] On the other hand well over half the seats were reserved for the party and various state-sponsored "social associations." Voters elected a Congress of People's Deputies, with 2,250 seats, which in turn chose a smaller standing legislative body, with 542 members, to meet more frequently. Both bodies were empowered to initiate legislation and freely debate issues. Regional and local elections, and elections in the constituent republics were also held throughout the country. In 1990, under another constitutional reform, the Congress of People's Deputies created a presidency with broad executive powers modeled on the American and French examples. The Congress elected Gorbachev president.

Gorbachev had brought about stunning political changes, unprecedented in the years since the Revolution. If the initial impulse of *perestroika* was only to restructure and revitalize the economy, his reforms developed a momentum of their own and democratic values were becoming ends in their own right. Western political leaders in the Great Depression had sought to save capitalism by reforming it. Gorbachev was bent on saving the Communist system by reform. Meanwhile his friendly attitude toward the West and his acceptance of the end of Communist rule in Central and Eastern Europe, as we shall see, showed his flexibility.

Yet the country remained divided, disoriented, dissatisfied. It was torn between the old guard who resisted the Gorbachev changes and a growing group of democratic reformers in the central legislature—many of them intellectuals, scholars, and scientists (like Sakharov)—and in the parliaments of the restless component republics, who believed that Gorbachev had not gone far enough in either political or economic matters. As time went by, praise for his policies gave way to trenchant criticism—for the continuing dismal economic record, for his indecisive, sometimes contradictory, steps in building a market economy, for his reluctance to revamp the collectivized agricultural system, for the repression of ethnic unrest, for rejecting the demands of the constituent republics that they be given greater freedom from central control, and for the role still exercised by the party.

The relaxing of totalitarian controls had released long suppressed ethnic tensions in the country. Azerbaijan and Armenia fought over a disputed enclave within Azerbaijan where the majority of the inhabitants were Armenian; violence flared in Georgia and elsewhere. Every one of the fifteen federated constituent republics of the Soviet Union began to raise demands for sovereignty, self-government, and an end to central control in all spheres, political and economic. Secessionist pressures and demands for independence understandably went furthest in the three Baltic republics, forcibly incorporated into the U.S.S.R. in 1940. Latvia, Lithuania, and Estonia remembered their twenty years of independence between the two world wars, and how they had fallen victim to

---

[5] They were the first since the election in November 1917 of the Constituent Assembly that Lenin subsequently disbanded; see pp. 748–750.

NATIONALITIES IN THE SOVIET UNION ABOUT 1990

		Percentage within Each Republic of		
Member Republics	Population	Major Nationality	Russians	Others
Slavic				
RSFSR	147,000,000	82%	—	18% — of about 30 nationalities
Ukraine	51,700,000	73	22%	5 — mainly Byelorussians
Byelorussia	10,200,000	78	13	9 — mainly Poles, Ukrainians
Baltic				
Lithuania	3,700,000	80	9	11 — mainly Poles
Latvia	2,700,000	52	34	14 — mainly Ukrainians
Estonia	1,600,000	62	30	8 — mainly Ukrainians
Moldavian	4,300,000	64	13	23 — mainly Ukrainians
Caucasian				
Georgia	5,500,000	70	6	24 — mainly Armenians, Azerbaijanis
Armenia	3,300,000	93	2	5 — mainly Kurds, Azerbaijanis
Azerbaijan	7,000,000	83	6	11 — mainly Armenians
Central Asian				
Uzbek	19,900,000	71	8	21 — mainly Tadzhiks, Kazakhs
Kazakh	16,500,000	40	38	22 — mainly Ukrainians
Tadzhik	5,100,000	62	8	30 — mainly Uzbeks
Kirghiz	4,300,000	52	22	26 — mainly Uzbeks, Ukrainians
Turkmen	3,500,000	72	10	18 — mainly Uzbeks, Kazakhs
Total U.S.S.R.	286,300,000			

NATIONALITIES IN THE SOVIET UNION ABOUT 1990

The Soviet Union consisted of fifteen national republics before its dissolution in 1991. Since an individual's nationality was officially recorded in the U.S.S.R. census, each of its republics was known to have a mixed population. The term "Major Nationality" in the table means the nationality from which the republic took its name.

Many nationalities are quite dispersed. Each republic, with independence, could lose many valuable workers by emigration, expulsion, or ethnic conflict. The Russians in particular are spread throughout the area of the former Soviet Union in many key positions. About half the population within the old Soviet boundaries is Russian, and two-thirds is Slavic. All the nationalities have had an interest in independence, either because they are historically rooted where they have been for centuries, as in Ukraine and the Baltic and Caucasian republics, or because of their Islamic religion in Azerbaijan and Central Asia. More rapid growth of the Muslim population in Central Asia has been reducing the proportion of Russians in these areas.

The U.S.S.R. was a pluralistic society, but not in the same sense as the United States. The mixed ethnicity of the United States has arisen from immigration since colonial times, in which the former slave trade must be included, while in the former U.S.S.R. it arose mainly from conquest and annexation. This generalization must be qualified by the fact that for centuries there has been much migration within the borders of the former U.S.S.R. and that the United States has also engaged in conquest and annexation, as in the case of the American Indians and the annexations from Mexico in the 1840s. The great difference is that in the United States the ethnic groups in the past have tended generally to merge into an English-language mainstream, while they strongly resisted Russification under both the tsarist empire and the Soviet Union.

For population changes since 1940 see p. 754.

Source: Soviet Census of 1989; Office of Population Research, Princeton University.

the Nazi-Soviet pact of 1939, and how one-third of their population had been killed, deported, or driven into exile in the war and postwar years. In the freer atmosphere they were able to denounce Soviet control and demand independence. For his part Gorbachev was willing to create a federation council to advise on matters relating to all of the republics but not go beyond that.

Gorbachev and the West

As the new era evolved, Communist ideology and the view of world affairs that had helped to create and prolong the Cold War were also transformed. Gorbachev repudiated ideological struggle. He cited the progress of science and technology as requiring "a different road to the future." In an interdependent globe besieged by nuclear, ecological, and economic dangers, the highest concern must be "universal human interests" and the "universal human idea." Since Marx and Lenin had taught their followers to reject "universal" ideals as a smoke screen for class rule and oppression, the turnabout was startling.

Gorbachev demolished the image of the Soviet Union as a military threat and promoter of world revolution. He became a familiar and popular figure in Western capitals as a negotiator, diplomat, statesman, and often Western-style politician. He followed his conciliatory words with deeds, removing troops and weapons from Eastern Europe, negotiating nuclear arms reduction agreements with the United States, ending the war in Afghanistan, and helping to resolve Cold War regional conflicts in Namibia, Angola, Cambodia, and elsewhere. And he accepted, even encouraged, reforms in Eastern Europe, probably not foreseeing how far they would go and how quickly they would end all Soviet control over the region. He spoke up for human rights, paid tribute to the standards embodied in the Helsinki accords, and called for a "common European home" for Western and Eastern Europe. The Cold War of the post-1945 years, which had been brought on, or intensified, by Soviet revolutionary ideology and expansionism—which in turn had led to the American containment policy and countercrusade—gave promise of ending. For Gorbachev, détente and arms reduction were essential to relieve the intolerable military burden on the Soviet economy; détente went hand in hand with domestic reform. From their low point in the early 1980s Soviet–United States relations abruptly changed after 1985. A new and more genuine spirit of détente emerged, holding out higher expectations for peace and disarmament than at any time since 1945.

Early in the Reagan administration, in 1981, during the Brezhnev era, discussions resumed on strategic arms limitations (now called START), but in an atmosphere of mistrust, suspicion, and continuing arms build-up. Especially disturbing was the deployment in Eastern Europe in the late 1970s of new Soviet intermediate-range nuclear missiles capable of reaching targets within a radius of 600 to 1,500 miles. Together with its European allies the United States made plans to reinforce existing defenses in Western Europe with equally modern American missiles, while simultaneously pressing the Soviets to reduce or remove theirs. The construction of the American missile sites touched off popular protest demonstrations in Western Europe, but the West European governments remained firm in their support. In Reagan's first term of office he did not meet with the incapacitated Brezhnev or with either of the two ailing Soviet leaders who in quick succession followed him. But in 1985, after the emergence of Gorbachev, who was himself anxious to reduce the strain on the troubled Soviet economy, the possibilities for arms limitation opened up. Unlike his predecessors, Gorbachev seemed to view détente not as an alternate way of pursuing revolutionary goals but as essential to avoid catastrophe in the nuclear age. For his part, Reagan, confident that the United States had rebuilt its own military strength, held four summit meetings with Gorbachev over the next two and a half years, with impressive results.

At their third meeting, in Washington, in December 1987, the two presidents, in a remarkable breakthrough, consented to remove the intermediate-range missiles each had installed in Europe. Gorbachev agreed also to reduce the number of short-range nuclear missiles. The Soviets were willing to destroy over four times as many missiles as the United States. Even more unprecedented was the willingness to permit the United States to verify the destruction of the weapons—the on-site verification which had long been a stumbling block to arms reduction. Finally, the two leaders agreed to continue negotiations on the reduction of strategic, or long-range, nuclear weapons.

In summit meetings in Washington and in Moscow, the two presidents had closer contact with each other's people than ever before. Gorbachev mingled with throngs in crowded Washington streets. Reagan, in Moscow, in the shadow of Lenin's tomb, spoke openly about the Soviet repression of dissidents, the refusal to permit Jews to emigrate, religious repression, and the war in Afghanistan. Gorbachev in turn committed his country to the withdrawal of Soviet troops from Afghanistan—a "bleeding wound" he called it. The Soviets were eager to cut their commitments and abandon their adversarial stance all over the globe. Meanwhile Gorbachev lent encouragement to the vast changes taking place in Eastern Europe. In 1990 Gorbachev and President George Bush, Reagan's successor, could jointly hail the end of the Cold War. In 1991 they signed a strategic arms treaty pledging each nation to scale down by about a third its arsenal of long-range nuclear missiles.

125. The Collapse of Communism in Central and Eastern Europe

In the mid-1980s Central and Eastern Europe remained under Stalinist-type party bosses, some in office for over thirty years, impervious to pressure for reform.[6] But cracks and fissures had begun to appear even before Gorbachev's reforms in the Soviet Union. The years of détente had already opened up the East European states to Western loans and investments and to closer contacts with the West. Dissidents called for a recognition of the human rights guaranteed by the Helsinki accords, to which the Soviet Union and the East European bloc had subscribed. They wrote about ending their party-state dictatorships and the restoration one day of a "civil society," in which people could live their lives free from the dictates of the state.

As in the Soviet Union itself, East Europeans discussed the shortcomings of

[6] See pp. 909–914.

their centrally planned economies. Excessive centralization and bureaucratic control stifled initiative and productivity, and large subsidies went to maintain inefficient state-run monopolies unchallenged by competition. The older plants and the infrastructure of the countries were decaying, the environment deteriorating. A scarcity of investment capital interfered with the growth of new industries. Only in Hungary were decentralizing reforms and tentative steps toward a market economy being tried. Since the 1970s the East European economies had stagnated. In East Germany, the showcase for achievements under central planning, economic growth had slowed and consumer goods were scarce. Even if state-run planned economies were to continue, many argued for greater latitude for market competition, incentives for entrepreneurs and workers, and encouragement of joint ventures with the outside capitalist world.

The East European countries also had to cope with the billions of dollars of debt incurred to Western banks in the 1970s, of which Poland owed close to half. To pay the interest alone on these huge sums and simultaneously control inflation demanded austerity and reduced living standards.

Poland: The Solidarity Movement

In the 1970s and 1980s demands for economic reform and political liberalization surfaced almost everywhere, but nowhere so forcefully as in Poland. Gomulka, who governed Poland for fourteen years after 1956, had disappointed the reformers.[7] He used troops to put down strikes, persecuted church leaders, and in 1968 permitted an anti-Semitic campaign against the small number of Jews still living in Poland. In 1970, after riots over food prices, the party replaced him with the reform-minded Edmund Gierek, who embarked on an ambitious economic development program, financed by heavy borrowing from the West. The initial results were promising, but to meet its debt obligations, the country had to expand exports at the expense of domestic consumption. The shrinkage of Western markets, heavy interest burdens, and the inefficient central planning system itself caused economic conditions steadily to deteriorate.

In 1980 the rise in food prices led to widespread strikes, which began in the Lenin shipyards in Gdansk and spread rapidly. The freer atmosphere under Gierek made it possible for workers to organize trade unions outside the official structure and to create an aggressive independent trade union federation called Solidarity, the first of its kind in any Communist country. It found a militant leader and national symbol of protest in Lech Walesa. When the swelling movement demanded legal authorization, the government yielded. Before long Solidarity claimed a national membership of 10 million industrial and agricultural workers. With church backing, its leaders called for free elections and a role for Solidarity in the central government. The Soviets, still in the Brezhnev era, once again saw a socialist regime threatened. They put heavy pressure on the Polish government and party to curb Solidarity, oust Gierek, and install the steely General Jaruzelski as party head and premier. When strikes and demonstrations continued, raising the possibility of Soviet military intervention, Jaruzelski in

[7] See p. 912.

1981 imposed martial law, imprisoned Walesa and other labor leaders, and banned Solidarity.

But once the power of Solidarity was curbed and the Soviet threat of intervention minimized, Jaruzelski himself took a different tack. To placate the sullen labor force he released Walesa and other labor leaders, lifted martial law, and initiated a reform program of his own. International pressure also contributed to liberalization. John Paul II, the first Polish pope to head the Roman Catholic church, inspired huge demonstrations for freedom during his visits to Poland. Lech Walesa was honored with a Nobel Peace Prize in 1983. The United States had imposed economic sanctions against Poland when martial law was declared.

Although Solidarity remained outlawed, Jaruzelski's economic measures, modeled on the Hungarian reforms, provided some opportunities for private enterprise and incentives for economic productivity. But his efforts failed to improve the economy, satisfy popular restiveness, or mollify widespread resentment at the dictatorship. Labor militancy, economic discontent, the church, and pressure by intellectual leaders reinforced nationwide resistance. Gorbachev's liberalizing reforms in the Soviet Union after 1985 lent further encouragement to reform. His example and the sense that the Soviets would not intervene to check liberalization in Eastern Europe—that the "Brezhnev Doctrine" was dead—encouraged the movement for reform within the Polish party itself.

In 1989 General Jaruzelski and the party leadership promised contested parliamentary elections, in which Solidarity and other groups were free to put forward candidates, although the Communist party was to be guaranteed a fixed number of seats. The government also restored freedom of worship and legalized the status of the church. In 1989 the first open elections in Poland in over forty years gave Solidarity a landslide victory in all the contested seats. A coalition cabinet was formed in which the Communists were a minority; before long a Solidarity leader was prime minister. The Communist party, eager to discard the past, took steps to transform itself into a Western-type socialist party, but its members drifted away. The party-state dictatorship ended without bloodshed. The dike in Eastern Europe was breached. The new coalition government moved to restructure the economy all at once along free-market lines. Economic hardships followed, sharp differences emerged between Lech Walesa and his one-time political allies, and former Communists returned to the political scene. But Poland was in charge of its own destiny.

Hungary: Reform into Revolution

In Hungary the attempt at reform in 1956, initiated by the Communist party leadership itself, had been brusquely interrupted when the Soviets intervened with troops and tanks to suppress the "counterrevolution." Imre Nagy, the party leader, and other leaders of the revolt were hanged.[8] For the next thirty-two years, the hard-line János Kádár ran the country. But even under Kádár the party, without relinquishing its monopoly on political control, moved away from the rigidities of a centrally planned command economy, encouraged a degree of private enterprise, turned to the West for capital investment, and relaxed its hold

[8] See p. 912.

on the country. For a time the economy expanded and standards of living rose, but the limited reforms accomplished no fundamental change. The economy stagnated in the early 1980s. After 1985, in the wake of Gorbachev's reforms in the Soviet Union, many modeled on the Hungarian example itself, a new impetus for action surfaced in the country and party.

In 1988 the party, eager to encourage change and still maintain power, eased Kádár out of office. The new leadership opened the way to opposition parties and multiparty elections, and began to dismantle the older party-state apparatus, including the security police. To expunge the past it dissolved the party, reconstituting it along socialist and social democratic lines. A wide range of independent political groups came forward. Reform, initiated by the party itself, had turned into revolution, and without bloodshed. The new leaders reclaimed the 1956 uprising as a progressive movement and formally condemned those who had invited Soviet intervention. Nagy's body was exhumed from a mass grave and given a hero's reburial. Whatever the problems ahead, the country had swept aside the humiliation of 1956, reasserted its national independence, restored self-government and civic freedom, and opened the way to a market-oriented economy and a pluralist democracy.

The developments in Hungary precipitated even more dramatic events. The new Hungary, looking westward, symbolically demolished a portion of the barbed-wire barrier on its Austrian border. A few months later, in September 1989, when large numbers of East Germans vacationing in Hungary sought to emigrate to the West, Hungary opened its border with Austria and allowed the Germans to exit. For the first time since 1961 East Germans found a way to leave their country. Hungary opened a floodgate for even more sweeping changes in Eastern Europe.

The German Democratic Republic: A "Gentle" Revolution

Given Gorbachev's positive attitude toward reform, it was understandable that the pace of change in Eastern Europe would accelerate, but neither he nor anyone else could have anticipated its full dimensions. In the spring of 1989 there still appeared to be little chance for a Communist sharing of power, let alone a revolutionary transformation, in the four hard-line dictatorships, the German Democratic Republic, Czechoslovakia, Bulgaria, and Romania.

In the German Democratic Republic Erich Honecker, in power since 1961, stubbornly held the line against reform. Although the country boasted the strongest economy and highest per capita income in Eastern Europe, its citizens enjoyed far fewer amenities than the West Germans. The Berlin Wall built in 1961 barred their exodus to the West. Even though Honecker after 1970 agreed to the closer economic and political relations with West Germany initiated by Willy Brandt's *Ostpolitik,* he remained adamant against relaxing controls at home. But the East Germans excitedly watched the Gorbachev changes and the rush of events in Poland and then in Hungary. When in the autumn of 1989 Hungary opened the way for them to leave, thousands seized the opportunity. Honecker, gambling that if given freedom to travel his compatriots might choose not to emigrate, eased traveling restrictions. But the trickle soon became a flood. The East Germans, many of them skilled workers and professionals, fled the repression and drabness of the German Democratic Republic for the Federal Republic of Germany, where as Germans they were entitled by law to receive citizenship and assistance in finding homes and jobs. By the end of 1989, 350,000 of East Germany's population of 17 million had left, and many more emigrated in the early months of 1990.

When demonstrations against the East German government mounted, Gorbachev made clear that Honecker could not expect the Soviet troops stationed in East Germany to save the regime, and he even warned against the use of force to prevent reform. In Leipzig, over 100,000 demonstrators, assembling in churches, marched in solemn procession with lighted candles, calling for the resignation of party and government leaders and for an end to the police state. The party forced Honecker to resign.

The new leadership pleaded for an end of the flight to the West, promised elections, and confirmed the right of free and unrestricted travel. On November 9, 1989, the government opened up the hated symbol of confinement itself, the Berlin Wall. East Berliners could cross over freely to West Berlin, make purchases, and return home. But the exodus to West Germany continued. By now even the freedom of movement, the end of censorship, parliamentary supervision over the state security police, and the pledge of free elections did not suffice. With the public disclosure of abuses, corruption, and luxurious living by Honecker and the party elite while ordinary people had suffered over the years the entire party structure came crashing down. The Politburo and Central Committee resigned. Honecker and other leaders were arrested on charges of corruption and embezzlement, and younger reformers assumed control. Delegates from a wide variety of opposition groups, exultant over their "gentle" revolution and the collapse of the dictatorship, met with reform-minded representatives of the former Communist party to oversee the transition to a new constitutional regime, still envisaged by many as a socialist society.

Once the German Democratic Republic was no longer Communist, however, pressure for reunification began to build, especially in West Germany, at the initiative of Helmut Kohl, the Christian Democratic chancellor. For many of the wartime Allies the prospect of a reunified Germany of close to 80 million people, possessing one of the world's most powerful economies, stirred grim ghosts of the past. The "German question" resurfaced.[9] The entire postwar settlement stood at issue. Since no final peace treaty had ever been signed, reunification required the approval of the four major Allied powers of the Second World War. There was hesitation, especially in France and Britain, but it was difficult, as the Americans argued, to deny the German people the right of self-determination 45 years after the end of the war. Moreover, the Federal Republic of Germany had demonstrated its commitment to democracy. There was confidence that a reunified Germany could integrate East Germany and remain part of democratic Western Europe and the European Community. Despite the unspeakable crimes of the Nazi era, it seemed unreasonable to insist upon unalterable traits of national character, or blame the Nazi atrocities on the generations that followed.

Reunification moved forward swiftly. The four Allied powers, including the U.S.S.R., gave their approval and relinquished their occupation rights. Germany

---

[9] See pp. 516–518, 551–559, and maps, pp. 555 and 893.

confirmed the earlier cession of territories in the east to the U.S.S.R. and Poland and pledged the inviolability of the German-Polish border.[10] The two German states merged their economies and the West German mark became the common currency. On October 3, 1990, the two states formally united to become an enlarged Federal Republic of Germany, its capital once again, at some point in the future, to be in Berlin. In the first nationwide elections, Chancellor Kohl and his Christian Democrats, who played a key role in the reunification, won a sweeping victory. The postelection exhilaration was soon tempered by the gigantic problems of modernizing and absorbing the thoroughly decayed East German economy.

Czechoslovakia: " '89 Is '68 Upside Down"

Revolution erupted also in Czechoslovakia in 1989. The hard-liners who had taken over after Soviet and Warsaw Pact military forces had ruthlessly crushed the "Prague spring" in 1968,[11] disapproved of Gorbachev's reforms in the Soviet Union and stifled dissent at home. But the dissidents quietly grew in numbers and influence. Charter '77, an organization of intellectuals formed after the Helsinki accords, became a rallying point for the struggle against the dictatorship. The country followed with intense interest the disintegration of Communist power in Poland, Hungary, and East Germany. When demonstrations broke out in the autumn of 1989, the government responded by arresting the dissident leaders. In October, thousands of demonstrators gathering in Wenceslas Square in Prague called for the release of the imprisoned dissidents—and for the resignation of the government. The reform movement gained additional momentum when the Soviet Union and other Warsaw Pact nations voted to express regret for the military invasion of 1968. The opposition coalesced in a loose coalition, which looked for leadership and inspiration to the dissident playwright Vaclav Havel, an outspoken opponent of the regime, who over the years had suffered imprisonment for his views.

The demonstrations grew in intensity. When 350,000 demonstrators in Prague on November 24 furiously demanded an end to the party-state dictatorship, and a general strike threatened to bring the country to a standstill, the government and party leaders all at once resigned. Alexander Dubcek, the hero of 1968, dramatically appeared on a balcony alongside a new reform-minded Communist prime minister, who appointed opposition leaders to his cabinet, pledged a free press and free elections, dissolved the secret police, and abolished the compulsory teaching of Marxism-Leninism in the universities. The party's forty-one year monopoly on power ended. Havel became provisional president. In the new cabinet the Communists were a minority. Gorbachev took steps to withdraw the 75,000 Soviet troops stationed in the country since 1968. Someone exultantly observed: " '89 is '68 upside down." The people had wrested control without bloodshed—in a "velvet" revolution—and liberated the country.

Of all the nations in the Eastern bloc Czechoslovakia had the strongest democratic tradition. Despite ethnic tensions from the beginning, and resentment

---

[10] See pp. 863, 992, and maps, pp. 248 and 872–873.
[11] See pp. 913, 990–991.

at Czech domination, it had experienced genuine parliamentary democracy in the interwar years and was the last of the East European states to succumb to Communist dictatorship after the Second World War.[12] Even though its economy was one of the strongest of the Eastern bloc, it lagged far behind the West and required large infusions of capital to modernize and replace its older technology. It, too, moved toward a market-oriented economy and a pluralist democracy— the "civil society" that Havel, soon elected president of the republic, and others had sought.

But within three years of its newly acquired freedom, the country came apart when Slovak political leaders pressed for an independent Slovakia, which some had wanted since 1918. No referendum was held, but a negotiated settlement arranged for the peaceful division of the country in January 1993 into the Czech Republic and Slovakia—two independent and sovereign nations.

Bulgaria and Romania

Even Bulgaria, the most docile of the Soviet client states, fell to the revolutionary contagion. Mass demonstrations in Sofia demanded an end to the dictatorship, and pressure from within the party forced the resignation of the party chief who had run the country since 1954. His foreign minister took over, pledged parliamentary elections, economic reforms, and an end to the party's monopoly on power. New political groups emerged, fragmented yet strong enough to press for a variety of reforms.

The revolution in Bulgaria was essentially a palace coup within the party, but it, too, arose in response to deep mass resentments. In a country that had known little freedom even in the pre-Communist years, the question was whether the reform-minded former Communists who, like others elsewhere, renamed themselves Socialists, could work together with the opposition to create a parliamentary democracy.

Everywhere the end of the Communist dictatorships in Central and Eastern Europe had come without bloodshed. But in Romania events took a violent turn. At first it seemed as though the revolution would not reach Bucharest. Since 1965, for twenty-four years, the dictator Nicolae Ceausescu had held firm control over party and government, ruling with the help of his wife and family, and building a cult of personality around himself. He remained isolated in a rigid autocracy with a large private security force, favored over the regular army. His ambition was to transform a backward agrarian society into a modern industrial society regardless of the human cost. For his modernization program he borrowed heavily from the West, but to remain independent of the outside world he insisted that the country regularly pay the interest on its foreign debt despite the sacrifices this meant for an already suffering population. All dissent, even grumbling, was kept under tight surveillance and control. What was distinctive about Ceausescu was his early break from Moscow and his independent position in foreign and military affairs. Unlike the other members of the Warsaw Pact, he supported Israel in the Arab-Israeli wars and refused to join in the invasion of Czechoslovakia in 1968. Because of his independent foreign policy he had received favorable

---

[12] See pp. 779–783, 840–842, 875.

treatment from the West despite revulsion at his harsh tyranny and unconcealed megalomania.

Throughout the revolutionary autumn of 1989 Ceausescu ignored the upheavals in Central and Eastern Europe. But in December protest riots broke out in Timisoara, a key provincial capital. When the military refused to fire on the demonstrators, the dictator's security forces took over, killing hundreds, and word of the brutality spread. The security forces next attempted to suppress demonstrators in Bucharest, but angry crowds forced the dictator to flee the capital.

For days a battle raged between the security forces and regular army units supporting the revolutionists until the security forces were routed. Ceausescu and his wife were apprehended in the provinces, given a hasty military trial, and executed by a firing squad. A National Salvation Front, consisting of former officials of the Ceausescu regime and emergent opposition leaders, came forward to take control, restore order, and dismantle the police state. Although former Communists dominated the new regime, and the strength of the democratic forces remained unclear, the party's authority had been abolished and the most repressive dictatorship of the Eastern bloc had come to an ignominious end.

The Revolutions of 1989 in Central and Eastern Europe

Except in Romania, the revolution was carried out for the most part by placards and candles, not by rifles. Solidarity's early struggle in Poland and Gorbachev's liberalization in the Soviet Union made it possible for revolutionary changes in Central and Eastern Europe to take place as they did. With a suddenness in the autumn of 1989 that took even the closest observers by surprise, smoldering resentments came to a head all at once. Gorbachev, committed to curtailing economic and military obligations for the sake of the Soviet economy, accepted the end of the Communist regimes imposed by Stalin forty years earlier in the wake of the Second World War. The groundwork for change had been prepared by the close economic ties and contacts with the West during the years of détente, the Helsinki accords, the stubborn challenge of Solidarity, and the unwavering courage of the dissidents. But it was Gorbachev's clear signal that the Soviets would not intervene outside their own borders that made the stupendous chain of events possible, toppling one regime after another. The dramatic flight of the East Germans symbolized the desire of all Eastern Europe to escape from behind the iron curtain. The revolutionists, armed only with a moral cause, would have found it difficult to prevail if any of their own governments had chosen to use the full power of the army and police. The repression at Tiananmen Square in China in June 1989[13] might have been repeated in Eastern Europe. But the ruling elites, without Soviet support to bolster them, yielded; they simply lacked the will to govern under what was for them, too, an alien system.

126. The Collapse of Communism in the Soviet Union

Before the stunning developments in Eastern Europe could be fully absorbed by amazed outsiders an even more epochal event occurred. An all but bloodless

---

[13] See p. 1009.

revolution brought the collapse of communism in 1991 in the very epicenter of world communism, undoing the Russian Revolution of 1917 and ending three-quarters of a century of Communist party rule. The U.S.S.R. itself, heir to the one-time tsarist empire, dissolved into its component republics. Russia reemerged.

How did this collapse of a seemingly impregnable regime with a heavy apparatus of military and police security occur? We have already seen how Gorbachev in the years after 1985 opened up Soviet society as never before in order to revitalize the system, but how he avoided the more decisive measures that might have ended the hegemony of the Communist party, established a competitive free market, and allowed genuine self-government for the component republics of the U.S.S.R. Gorbachev vacillated between the reformers and the hard-line conservatives. A superb political tactician—no one could have brought the party and the system as far as he had—he nonetheless gave the impression that he did not know where he was taking the country or how thorough a transformation he would permit. The old guard became further embittered when they witnessed the loss of Soviet control over Eastern Europe. Meanwhile the economy worsened, and by 1990 production was in steep decline. Gorbachev tried plan after plan, but the economic structure remained virtually unchanged. In addition, not only the Baltic republics, as might have been expected, but the Russian republic (the R.S.F.S.R.) and all of the other component republics of the U.S.S.R. were pressing for "sovereignty"—self-government and control over their political and economic fortunes.

The "Creeping Coup d'État"

In the autumn of 1990 Gorbachev again was maneuvering, turning now for support to the hard-liners. He replaced reform-minded ministers, including his own prime minister, and other key officials with old-guard appointees openly unsympathetic to his reform program. He summarily abandoned an important "500-Day" economic plan that would have freed prices and moved more swiftly to a market economy; it would, in addition, have curtailed the military budget and given broad economic powers to the republics. It also became clear that he intended to use military force against the secessionist Baltic republics, which in the spring of 1990 had proclaimed their independence. Edward Shevardnadze, his foreign minister and closest political associate, resigned, with ambiguous but pessimistic allusions to the future of democratic reform in the country. In January 1991 Soviet troops used military force against demonstrators in Lithuania, with a loss of lives, and there was anxiety about where the military might move next.

The democratic reformers who had supported the Gorbachev reform program grew alarmed at the turn of events. Some spoke of "six wasted years of reform communism," and of a "creeping coup d'état." They had concluded that the country's economic problems could not be resolved short of demolishing the entire central planning structure, and also that each republic must be allowed to work out its own destiny. To the reformers Gorbachev seemed a barrier to further change, and he in turn grew increasingly hostile to them.

The democratic reformers turned to a political figure who on the surface seemed an unlikely choice as their leader. Boris N. Yeltsin was blunt and outspoken, not by any definition an intellectual, and in striking contrast to the suave, smooth, and worldly Gorbachev. But Yeltsin knew the party well, and all its secrets. He had been party boss in Moscow and a member of the Politburo. When in 1987 he had openly attacked the privileges, perquisites, and downright incompetence of the party, he was dismissed from his posts, vilified in the press, and sent off into the political wilderness. Humiliated by Gorbachev and the party, he had found allies among the democratic reformers, who saw in him a populist figure around whom they could rally public support. They helped polish his rough edges, undertook his political reeducation, and converted him into an opposition leader of stature.

Elected to the all-Soviet legislature in March 1989, he played a key role in the opposition. With the encouragement of his political allies, however, he turned to a new, and seemingly unpromising, power base, the Russian legislature, i.e., the legislature of the Russian constituent republic. Elected to it in 1990, he became chairman and used his position to step up his attacks on Gorbachev and the party. Then, benefiting from a Gorbachev concession permitting the constituent republics to choose their presidents in direct popular elections, he was elected in June 1991 president of the Russian republic in an overwhelming victory over his Communist opponents—the first president to be elected by popular vote in Russian history. It was a distinction that Gorbachev, elected president of the U.S.S.R. by the Soviet legislature, itself chosen on only a partially democratic basis, could not claim. (It was at the time of Yeltsin's election that the voters in Russia's second largest city, in another repudiation of communism, chose to change the name of Leningrad back to St. Petersburg, as it had been called before 1914.) From his new position of strength Yeltsin pressed for immediate independence for the three Baltic states and for self-government for Russia and the other Soviet constituent republics.

Gorbachev, intent above all else on keeping the country and the union intact, began negotiations with the presidents of the republics. He agreed to surrender more and more autonomy to the republics, including substantial control over economic and financial resources that Moscow had always tightly guarded. The three Baltic republics, insisting on full independence, refused to participate in the negotiations, as did Georgia, embroiled in its own internal turmoil. But in August the Russian republic and ten other constituent republics agreed to sign Gorbachev's "union treaty."

The Bungled August Coup

For the old-guard hard-liners the treaty was the final straw—the end of the union as originally created by Lenin in 1922 after the Bolshevik Revolution of 1917 and the ensuing civil wars. Despite lip service to the sovereignty of the republics and the federal structure set forth in the Soviet constitution, the Soviet Union was from the beginning, and increasingly under Stalin, a Russian-dominated centralized state, the successor to the empire of the tsars. To abandon the union was more than many of the old guard could tolerate. The day before the treaty was to be signed, a small coterie of eight hard-liners acted to seize power. They included high-ranking party and state functionaries, among them, the head of the KGB and the commander of the Soviet land forces. All key figures were Gorbachev appointees. Three, including the chief of Gorbachev's personal cabinet, arrived at Gorbachev's summer home in the Crimea, where he was vacationing, possibly hoping to win him to their side. When he refused to cooperate or yield to pressure, they proclaimed a Committee of State Emergency, headed by the country's vice president, to replace him.

The *putschists* expected the coup to be a simple operation. Resistance in the country, they were convinced, could be overcome by a simple show of military strength. But they miscalculated, underestimating the new political forces alive in the country. Gorbachev disavowed the plotters. In Moscow Yeltsin rallied the Russian legislature in defense of Gorbachev, warned that anyone supporting the coup would be subject to grave criminal charges, and appealed for popular support against any military show of force. But the assault never came. At least one KGB unit disobeyed orders to attack; other tank units advanced only half-heartedly. There was some sporadic street fighting, and three civilian deaths. The coup failed, over in four days. The plotters turned out to be feckless and irresolute bunglers. The Central Committee of the party did not speak out during these events, but its silence seemed to sanction the coup.

Gorbachev, his ordeal over, returned to Moscow. He had demonstrated that he was not the prisoner of the old guard. Because of the party's complicity in the affair, he resigned as general secretary. Yet he still failed to comprehend how far matters had gone. He believed it sufficient only to replace the traitors and "return to the business of reform." Once again he defended "socialism" as "the choice made in 1917" and stressed the need to preserve the unity of the U.S.S.R., so that the country not fall apart. Or as he pleaded, with some distortion of the historical record of the tsarist empire, not to undo "a thousand years of common history."

Yeltsin acted immediately and decisively on an entirely different agenda. As president of the Russian republic, he issued a series of decrees, describing the Communist party as "not a political party but an unlawful apparatus that took over the Soviet state" and denouncing it as "one of the principal villains" in the attempted coup. Suspending its activities throughout the Russian republic, he transferred to the state the party's vast property, along with its files and archives. The Soviet Congress of People's Deputies soon validated the decrees for the entire country before voting itself out of existence. In all this Gorbachev acquiesced. In many ways what happened in the aftermath of the failed coup was the culmination of the Gorbachev six-year reform era. But the ending of the party-state regime, at Yeltsin's hands, was the revolution.

All that remained of the earlier framework was a federation council consisting of the presidents of the constituent republics, over which Gorbachev continued to preside. One of its first acts was to recognize the independence of the three Baltic republics. For the country as a whole Gorbachev still hoped to salvage his older idea, a "union of sovereign states," which, while granting self-government to the republics, would retain a central authority. But the republics would have none of the union and pressed for full independence; hostility toward central authority had intensified after the bungled coup. The very party leaders, as in the Ukrainian S.S.R., who had themselves suppressed separatist movements in the not distant past, had by now taken over the leadership of nationalist independence movements.

The Ukrainian S.S.R. proclaimed itself an independent Ukraine (no longer *the*

Ukraine) immediately after the August coup. In December, Yeltsin announced that Russia would not stay in the union without Ukraine. Thereupon the three Slavic states—Russia, Ukraine, and Belarus (the new name for Byelorussia), the states that had originally created the Soviet Union in December 1922—dissolved it. Gorbachev resigned as president. Yeltsin at once preempted his office in the Kremlin.

The other republics of the Soviet Union also agreed to its dissolution. A loose organization called the Commonwealth of Independent States (CIS) consisting of Russia and ten other republics came into existence.[14] The Baltic states had already gone their separate ways. Georgia, still in turmoil, did not join until a few years later. The U.S.S.R., for close to seven decades the world's largest multinational state, stretching over one-sixth the earth's surface and eleven time zones, with close to 300 million people, one of the world's two superpowers for over forty years after the Second World War, simply disappeared from the map. Russia, still the world's largest nation in area, and itself a mixture of many peoples, succeeded to the Soviet Union's permanent seat on the UN Security Council.[15]

Gorbachev returned to private life, declaring "the main task" of his life to have been accomplished. He has to be counted as one of the great reformers in history. His tragedy was that he undermined communism but failed to build a new system in its place. He had unleashed powerful winds of change that ultimately he could not direct or control. He drastically altered a totalitarian system yet refused to recognize that the demolition of the entire structure was necessary. He was not "the last Leninist," as he has been called; Lenin would have disavowed him for not being ruthless enough. Nor was he sufficiently Machiavellian in his treatment of friends and foes. Eventually he became a danger to the old order and an impediment to the new. Yeltsin, who took undisguised satisfaction in the fall of his once all-powerful rival, said of him: "We, like the world, respect him for what he did, especially in the first years of *perestroika* beginning with 1985 and 1986." After that, he said, the "errors" began. But it was not yet time to render final judgment. For the vast lands and peoples that had once been the Soviet Union, and for Russia and Yeltsin himself in 1991, the future held many uncertainties, a future in which the entire world had an enormous stake.

127. After Communism

Marxist-Leninist ideology as the undergirding for one-party dictatorship still persisted in the early 1990s in the People's Republic of China, the world's most

---

[14] The eleven republics affiliating themselves with the Commonwealth of Independent States, created December 25, 1991, as successor to the U.S.S.R. in order of population (with their capitals in parentheses) were as follows: Russian Federation (Moscow), Ukraine (Kiev), Uzbekistan (Tashkent), Kazakhstan (Alma-Ata), Belarus (Minsk), Azerbaijan (Baku), Tajikistan (Dushanbe), Moldova (Chisinau), Kyrgyzstan (Bishkek), Turkmenistan (Ashkhabad), and Armenia (Yerevan). The names adopted at the time of independence sometimes differ slightly from earlier names or represent variant spellings. Georgia (Tbilisi) did not join until 1994. For population figures for each republic, as reported in the Soviet census of 1989, see p. 754, note 25, and for the distribution of nationalities within each republic, see the table and caption, p. 1016.

[15] See p. 869.

populous country, and in the smaller states of North Korea, Vietnam, and Cuba. Albania, the last of the Communist regimes in Europe, and the most impoverished, threw off Communist rule in 1991. In Western Europe, most notably in France, Italy, Spain, and Portugal, once strong Communist parties reexamined their beliefs, generally abandoned the party name, and adapted to changed circumstances. Marxism, born in the mid–nineteenth century in response to the instability and inequities of industrial capitalism, could survive as a scholarly and analytical tool, but it seemed destined to limited appeal as a political philosophy or program of action, at least in the distorted form given it by Lenin and the Russian Revolution of 1917. Proletarian internationalism likewise lost much of its appeal because it had resulted in an ill-concealed Soviet hegemony.

The revolutions of the late twentieth century in the Soviet Union and in Central and Eastern Europe heralded the triumph of the political processes and rights inherent in the historic liberalism of the West. The democratic reformers sought free elections, an end to the Communist party's monopoly of power, political and civil rights, and human dignity. Their people had too long been the pawns of omnipotent party-state regimes—totalitarianism was not too strong a word[16]— which had self-righteously demanded sacrifice and subservience in the name of an ultimate utopia. The reformers objected to the centrally planned bureaucratic command economies, which had deprived everyone of decent living standards. They envied the immeasurably more prosperous economies of the United States, Western Europe, and elsewhere, even if they, too, had their problems. The official formula that all citizens enjoyed the rights and privileges of an egalitarian "socialist" society had only concealed political repression, economic stagnation, and social immobility. For many the public revelation of the privileges and luxuries enjoyed by the party elite proved the final shock.

The revolutionary changes made possible, but did not guarantee, democratic and pluralist societies, in which the citizens themselves through responsible government could work out their political and economic destinies. The growth of democracy and market economies was not easily forced. If democratic governments failed to take root, new authoritarian political parties and repressive governments could reemerge, even if not in the name of Marxism-Leninism. The revolutionary changes also released many ugly currents, ominous for the future— anti-Semitism, xenophobia, violent nationalism, irredentism, among them. Such unsavory forces are easily mobilized when discontented people seek scapegoats for their frustrations.

Russia, the other former Soviet republics, and the countries of Central and Eastern Europe entered a period of painful transition. In principle, they were transforming their political systems into representative democracies and their centrally planned economies into competitive market economies. But there were many obstacles. Bureaucrats and managers of the old order were still in control, often under new labels. Despite infusions of international aid, the new regimes struggled to take the necessary first steps.

The market economy could take many forms. The state had always played a large role in Central and Eastern Europe. It was unlikely that the new regimes would turn to any laissez-faire model of private enterprise. Governments would

[16] See pp. 828–832.

remain actively engaged and try to ensure a protective network of social services. As for socialism, marginal as it was in American life, democratic socialism still had a lingering appeal in Europe. The Soviet experience had tarnished, even poisoned, the image of socialism, but its egalitarian message retained an attraction when linked to respect for democracy and individual rights, as propounded by British Labour and other European Socialist and Social Democratic parties. Meanwhile all countries with capitalist market economies and democratic political systems, in the West and elsewhere, were being challenged to create societies that could overcome economic instability, individual insecurity, unemployment, and gross social and economic injustices in their own worlds. Democracies and market economies were means toward desired ends, not final goals in themselves.

Russia after 1991

By the close of 1991 the Russian flag had replaced the Soviet hammer and sickle over the Kremlin. Reemergent Russia, with almost twice the land area of the United States and a population of 150 million, even if in desperate economic straits, was still a Great Power. Officially, Russia was the Russian Federation, with 21 federated republics and 67 additional regional units. The most pressing international concern was the nuclear weaponry of the former U.S.S.R. Although the bulk of the nuclear missiles were located on Russian soil, there were also nuclear weapons in Ukraine, Kazakhstan, and Belarus. Yeltsin worked out an initial agreement with the other former Soviet republics whereby Russia alone was to be a nuclear power, but that agreement hinged on preserving harmonious relations with them, especially with Ukraine. Nationalists in the Ukrainian parliament later opposed the surrender of the weapons, but the United States mediated a new agreement under which the three republics consented to dismantle their weapons in return for generous financial reimbursement and other commitments. Russia for its part broadened the agreement reached earlier with the United States on reducing strategic nuclear weapons.[17]

The new Russia, like the old Soviet Union, also faced serious secessionist threats. Several of its republics, many of which had their own constitutions, flags, and anthems, were demanding independence, and many of the regions were pressing for the status of republics. Meanwhile 25 million Russians who had for a long time made their home in other parts of the former Soviet Union were now viewed in those places as foreigners and in some instances treated with hostility. Violence and civil war also persisted or flared up in several of the former Soviet republics. In Tajikistan, where some of the worst fighting occurred, Muslim insurgents, dislodged from power by old-guard Russians, received assistance from Muslim guerrilla units across the border in Afghanistan. Georgia was the scene of continuing civil war.

In domestic affairs Yeltsin faced many of the same economic problems as Gorbachev. In making the transition to a market economy, he met little success. Production declined, inflation soared, the ruble fell in value, and standards of living sank. Life at times seemed more trying for the average citizen than before the collapse of communism. The separate republics and regional and local

[17] See p. 1018.

governments tended to ignore Moscow, even holding back tax collections. The erosion of authority contributed to widening corruption and crime throughout the country. A political struggle with the old-guard legislature added to Yeltsin's difficulties. The Russian Congress of People's Deputies had been elected in 1989 in open and contested elections but at a time when many of the candidates were still part of the old party apparatus. Some never forgave Yeltsin for agreeing to the dissolution of the Soviet Union.

The economy and finances remained in deep disorder. After temporizing at first, Yeltsin turned to a Western-oriented economist as his key adviser and economics minister. In the belief that a swift transition to a market economy would be the least painful course, the government moved ahead with a program of "economic shock therapy." From late 1991, a flood of decrees deregulated prices, ended or cut subsidies to state-owned industries and collective farms, and moved forward with privatization. Deregulation and fiscal restraint were the order of the day. By the spring of 1992, however, the freeing of prices and the reduction in government spending brought a serious decline in living standards for most Russians, while privatization had enriched others.

The economic program served to intensify Yeltsin's power struggle with the Congress of People's Deputies. The majority, led by the Russian vice president and by the chairman of the Congress, rejected the program and attacked the "elite theorists" who had allowed prices to rise and made life difficult for ordinary citizens. All this time Yeltsin could not prevent the Central Bank from continuing to print money, and the value of the ruble kept declining. By the spring of 1992 the program was in retreat. At the end of the year the hard-liners in the legislature forced Yeltsin's economic minister, who was also acting prime minister, to resign. The new prime minister, although a centrist and a pragmatist, was formerly a Soviet bureaucrat, the director of the Soviet natural gas industry, who did not conceal his lack of sympathy for the radical reformers and their policies.

In the spring of 1993 Yeltsin, increasingly frustrated, appealed to the country to support a new constitution that would provide for "a strong presidential republic." The deadlock continued. In September Yeltsin, in an even more dramatic move, issued a decree dissolving the legislature. He called for new elections and for a referendum at the same time to approve his new constitution. The lawmakers denounced the dissolution as a coup d'état and defying the decree, refused to leave the parliament building. Over the next several days demonstrators converged on the building, many of them armed militant members of extremist hard-line groups. The Congress leaders urged them to seize the Moscow town hall and the central television center. Army units turned back the insurrectionists, but in the clashes people were killed.

As the days went by and the legislators continued their occupation, Yeltsin felt bound to act. On October 4, without any new ultimatum, tanks surrounding the building fired and set it ablaze. The legislators were evacuated and the leaders arrested. An estimated 140 were dead, many more injured. Blood had been shed in the October Days in the first mass violence in Russia in the post-Soviet era. Fear and confusion followed, but Yeltsin acted to defuse the crisis. He announced that elections would be held as planned and that simultaneously the voters would be asked to endorse the new constitution. Opinions divided over the events. Some argued that Yeltsin's decree of dissolution was illegal and unconstitutional under the existing constitution (as the Constitutional Court ruled), others that in the context of the times it represented only "a revolutionary violation" of the constitution. Even though Yeltsin had been provoked by the obstructionism of the legislators and their call for armed insurrection, he had set what could be an ominous precedent. In point of fact, both sides shared in the blame. The October Days of 1993 demonstrated that Russia was still living through an ongoing revolution.

In the referendum in December the new constitution was approved. It unconditionally guaranteed the sanctity of individual rights in contrast to Soviet-era constitutions that had subordinated all such rights to the paramount interests of the party. It gave broad political authority to the president, who could dissolve the legislature and make key appointments, and it confirmed the federal structure of the country. A popularly elected lower house, the State Duma, the name deliberately chosen because of its pre-Soviet roots, replaced the Congress.[18]

The elections, on the other hand, proved a setback for the reformers, who had underestimated popular discontent. The leading reform party did less well than expected. The reformed, legally recognized, Communist party and its political allies won a share of the seats. But the most stunning result was the emergence as the top popular vote winner of an ultranationalist, Vladimir Zhirinovsky by name, who in inflammatory rhetoric spoke openly of reuniting the old Russian empire, and reviving Russia's military might. If his right-wing party were to unite with the reorganized Communist party and its affiliates, a coalition of ultranationalists and former Communists could dominate the legislature and continue to obstruct change. The prospect raised images of Weimar Germany in the pre-Hitler days.

In a stinging rebuke to Yeltsin, the new Duma, as one of its first acts, voted amnesty to the legislative leaders arrested in October—and to the hard-line old-guard plotters against Gorbachev in the failed coup of August 1991. The prime minister, who continued in office, dropped the remaining reformers from the cabinet and pointedly announced an end to "the period of market romanticism." Economic reforms were shelved. Credits were again available to state-owned industries. Wage, price, and profit controls were reimposed. The focus was to be on production, jobs, and incomes, and on social services, regardless of the country's financial condition and the concerns about inflation. Yeltsin himself as president now possessed greatly expanded executive powers but waning actual authority, and was showing the physical and emotional strain of the turbulent events. Erratic and impulsive as he was, the question was whether he possessed the political skills to control events.

The Resurgence of Nationalism: the Breakup of Yugoslavia

Of all the explosive issues that confronted Europe after the downfall of communism, nationalism proved the most intractable. When boundaries were redrawn after the upheavals of the Second World War, sizable minorities still remained within the borders of many states, as the accompanying map shows. National ambitions, suppressed (or permitted only cultural expression) during the decades

---

[18] See pp. 744–745.

of Communist rule, quickly resurfaced in Central and Eastern Europe. Czechoslovakia, as we have seen, divided peacefully in 1993 in response to Slovak pressures. But in Yugoslavia centuries-old national and religious tensions, kept in check under previous regimes, tore the state apart.

The entire large area of the Balkan peninsula in southeastern Europe, including the once powerful medieval kingdom of Serbia, had been conquered by the Ottoman Turks in the fourteenth century and brought under Muslim rule; some parts of the area were gradually reconquered by the Habsburgs. When the Ottoman Empire decayed in the nineteenth century, Serbia, after 500 years of Muslim rule, regained its status as an independent kingdom. In the late nineteenth century it found a patron in tsarist Russia, with which it shared its Eastern

NATIONALITIES IN CENTRAL AND EASTERN EUROPE

Boundaries and names are essentially as they were from the end of the Second World War until 1990–1991. Ethnic differences in these countries made democratization and economic renewal difficult and even threatened their existence as viable states. Poland and Hungary are the most homogeneous, but there are many Hungarians in three countries bordering on Hungary. Yugoslavia and Czechoslovakia have disintegrated into their component parts. In what was Yugoslavia, Serbs, Croats, and Slovenes were inextricably intermixed; about 2 million Slavic-speaking Muslims have also long lived in Bosnia-Herzegovina; and there are many Albanians, not Slavs and mostly Muslim, in Kosovo and in Macedonia. In Bulgaria there are about 1 million Turks from the days of the Ottoman Empire. The word "Moldavia," which once meant northern Romania, was appropriated in 1940 by the U.S.S.R. for Bessarabia, which became the Moldavian Soviet Socialist Republic (since 1991, independent Moldova), where most people speak Romanian. A small number of Jews in these countries have survived the Holocaust. There are many Gypsies, also victims of Nazi persecution, most numerously in Romania. For the shifting boundaries and movements of people that have resulted in this ethnic diversity, see maps on pp. 248, 470, 660, 728–729, 872–873, and the front end papers.

Orthodox Christianity. With Russian encouragement, the Serbs agitated for an enlarged South Slav (or "Yugoslav") state for all people speaking the Serbo-Croatian language, which included themselves and the Croats, Slovenes, and Bosnians then living in the Austro-Hungarian empire. That agitation, because it became entangled with the pre-1914 alliance systems of the great powers, led to the First World War. The assassination at Sarajevo of the heir to the Austrian throne kindled the great conflagration in 1914.[19]

At the collapse of the Habsburg empire in 1918, Serbia, together with like-minded South Slav nationalists, proclaimed the Kingdom of the Serbs, Croats, and Slovenes under the Serbian monarchy, which Bosnia-Herzegovina also joined. There were ethnic, religious, and historical differences, and populations were mixed throughout the new kingdom. In religion the Serbs were Eastern Orthodox Christians, the Croats and Slovenes were Roman Catholic, and in Bosnia-Herzegovina there were many Slavs who had converted to Islam during the long Ottoman domination. But the differences, it was thought, could be submerged in the new state, which in 1929 was officially renamed Yugoslavia.

Yugoslavia was overrun and occupied by Nazi Germany during the Second World War and Croatia for a time was governed as a separate Nazi puppet state. The Yugoslavs forcefully resisted the Nazis but also fought a bitter civil war among themselves, between royalists and Communists led by Marshal Tito. The country emerged under a Communist regime headed by Tito, who in 1946 created a federal Yugoslav republic with six component "republics": Serbia, Croatia, Slovenia, Bosnia-Herzegovina, Montenegro, and Macedonia; there were two "autonomous provinces" as well. Although himself a Croat, Tito suppressed Croatian and other separatist movements as counterrevolutionary but allowed the component republics various forms of autonomy. In Bosnia-Herzegovina he recognized the Bosnian Muslims as a distinct "national" group, on an equal

---

[19] For the earlier history of both Serbia and Yugoslavia, see pp. 46, 472, 654–659, 700–701, 726–727, 779. For the Sarajevo crisis and Serbia's role in precipitating the First World War, see p. 702.

standing with the Bosnian Serbs and Bosnian Croats. Although the Serbs and Croats together comprised over half the population of Bosnia, the Muslims, as the largest single "national" group, came to dominate the government. After Tito's death in 1980, separatist movements at once emerged. His successors, struggling with many other problems, including a failing economy, tried various solutions, among them a rotating federal presidency, but none worked satisfactorily. When revolutionary changes transformed Central and Eastern Europe in the late 1980s, Yugoslavia's Communist reformers loosened the regime's authoritarian grip, and the separatist pressures exploded.

Here, as elsewhere in Eastern Europe and in the former Soviet Union, one-time Communist leaders, seeing power slip away because of the collapse of Communist regimes, placed themselves at the head of nationalist crusades. The Serbian one-time party leader, Slobodan Milosevič, made clear from the late 1980s on his intention to rally Serbs in every one of the Yugoslav republics to his pan-Serb cause. Alarmed by Serb militancy, Croatia and Slovenia held referendums and in 1991 proclaimed themselves independent states. They received immediate recognition from the international community, which was persuaded by Germany that prompt recognition would forestall Serbian aggression. Bosnia-Herzegovina, at the behest of its Muslim-dominated government but over the opposition of its Serb and Croat populations, soon followed suit. The secession of the three states and their immediate international recognition infuriated Serbia.

War broke out in mid-1991 when Serbian armed forces proceeded to carve out enclaves in the many areas where Serbian minorities lived, claiming the need to protect fellow Serbs. Serbian guerrilla forces, supported by the Serb-controlled central Yugoslav army, took up arms against Croatia and Slovenia, and seized territory in each. After several months of fighting, in which 25,000 lives were lost, a cease-fire was arranged. But the worst violence occurred when both Serbs and Croats attempted to create enclaves for themselves in Bosnia-Herzegovina. For years the mixed population, despite ethnic and religious differences, had lived peacefully side by side. In the war that ensued, which included a protracted siege of Sarajevo and other cities, terrible atrocities occurred on all sides. But it was Serbian military units and armed forces that were principally responsible for brutalizing the Muslim population and for acts of cruelty not seen for a generation in Europe. The savage deeds, shamelessly labeled "ethnic cleansing," included wholesale civilian slaughter, pillage, and mass rape. A shocked world could scarcely believe such events were occurring in civilized Europe in the closing decade of the twentieth century. Religion and national fervor made for a toxic brew.

The international community could not agree on steps to confront the situation. Armed contingents of the UN were unable even to deliver humanitarian relief. The Security Council imposed economic sanctions against the rump state of "Yugoslavia," consisting now of only Serbia and its historic ally, Montenegro; embargoed the shipment of arms (which mainly hurt the Muslims); and made plans for war crimes trials. But the fighting and atrocities continued. Given the historical complexity of the Balkans and the memories of earlier ferocious conflicts, neither the European powers, which might have been expected to take the lead, nor the United States would intervene at any early stage with any meaningful show of force. Much later, in 1994, to end the brutal siege of Sarajevo the UN, the United States, and NATO mediated a cease-fire and committed themselves to air strikes if it were violated. For Bosnia-Herzegovina a diplomatic settlement was being negotiated whereby Croats and Muslims agreed to create a Croat-Muslim federation in what remained to them of Bosnia after the Serb conquests. Any larger diplomatic settlement had to depend on the Serbs, who occupied two-thirds of Bosnia and a fourth of Croatia, with every intention of retaining them. On the other hand, the Russians were now using their influence with the Serbs to bring them to the conference table. Notwithstanding the enormous differences to be resolved, there was some hope that the fighting might end, or taper off. By 1994 200,000 were dead or missing, mostly in the fighting in Bosnia-Herzegovina since 1991; there were about 4.4 million displaced persons. Even with some kind of negotiated settlement, grave complications were still likely in the Balkans because of ethnic and religious tensions, ties to the outside world, and the residue of hatred and mistrust.

Western Europe and Japan after the Cold War: Economic and Political Uncertainties

It was generally expected that the nations of Central and Eastern Europe would suffer in the wrenching transition to market economies and parliamentary democracies. What was unanticipated was the heavy burden of economic and political troubles that Western Europe found itself confronting in the 1990s. Buoyant and self-confident for many years because of its continuing prosperity since the 1950s, it was jolted first by the sharp 1973 oil price increase and the subsequent recession marked by inflation and economic stagnation. In the mid-1980s, the European democracies once again experienced five years of economic expansion, although with lower growth rates than in the past, and with discomfiting levels of high unemployment. Soon thereafter, in 1990, a new economic downturn affected the United States, then Western Europe and other parts of the world, and for the first time, Japan. The American economy showed signs of revival late in 1992. In Western Europe, and especially in Germany, the recession evolved into a serious economic setback.

As in earlier years, the West Europeans found themselves following the lead of Germany, the situation there complicated this time by the reunification with East Germany. The German Bundesbank, mandated to combat inflation as the highest priority regardless of other economic needs, kept interest rates high. The unexpectedly steep costs of absorbing East Germany's decayed economy and the decision to convert the East German mark on an equal basis with the West German currency, made inflation a genuine threat. But tight money also choked off credit and investment, delaying economic recovery for Germany and for its European neighbors as well. Other European countries could not lower their own interest rates without weakening their currencies against the mark and encouraging currency speculation. The European Monetary System, set up in 1979 to keep European exchange fluctuations within a narrow range,[20] was unable to meet the recurrent monetary crises. Italy and Britain (the latter had joined the system only belatedly) withdrew in the fall of 1992 and devalued their currencies. By the summer of 1993, intense speculative pressures on the franc and other currencies

[20] See p. 903.

led to a restructuring of the exchange system to permit much wider fluctuation than originally envisaged. French-German relations and other ties within the European Union became strained. The whole concept of West European political and economic unity was set back, and the recession aggravated by the currency unrest.

Despite recovery in the 1980s, many West Europeans remained unemployed. In the new economic slowdown unemployment rose to postwar highs. For the twelve members of the European Union unemployment approached 19 million, or more than 12 percent of the work force. (In the United States the comparable figure in the early 1990s was six to seven percent; in Japan, 2.5 percent.) If the seven West European countries not members of the European Union were included, the total number was 23 million. Worldwide, extensive unemployment was reported; urban joblessness in parts of the developing world ran as high as 30 percent. Long-term unemployment became a recognized phenomenon, as well as the disconcerting corollary that many workers would never again be employed at their old skills. Young people especially were hurt by the shrinkage of job prospects.

The Europeans slowly came to realize what had only been suspected in the earlier recession, that the problem of unemployment was not temporary, limited to the business cycle, but was deep-seated and structural. High labor costs that included generous postwar welfare-state benefits for unemployment, disability, retirement, paid vacations (all considerably more extensive than in the United States or Japan or, of course, the developing countries) were undercutting Western Europe's ability to compete globally. Many corporations, like their American counterparts, began to restructure, cutting employment rolls sharply, and introducing other economies. Multinational corporations shifted manufacturing operations to areas like Southeast Asia or to Eastern Europe where labor costs and benefits were lower. For the first time in postwar history the West European nations took steps to roll back the welfare state as it had evolved by consensus since the end of the Second World War.[21] The dream of full employment in a free society and of guaranteed security against the recurrent instabilities of industrial capitalism suddenly clouded.

Western Europe: Political Crises and Discontents

The economic downturn had its counterpart in political malaise and discontent. There was widespread dissatisfaction with the governing political parties and political leaders, especially of the center, all of which were judged to have held office too long and to be unable to provide any fresh vision for the future. Shocking revelations of scandal and corruption also came to light, involving the Christian Democratic and Socialist parties in several major countries.

Nowhere did dissatisfaction with the political system reach the proportions that it did in Italy. For years the Christian Democrats, dominating the political scene, had formed one government after another, usually in coalition with other smaller centrist parties. In the 1980s the Socialists (who had long abandoned any commitment to socialism) headed a coalition cabinet which in its four-year tenure outlasted all previous cabinets. All of the governing parties kept a tight grip on

[21] See pp. 885–886.

power and patronage and maintained close ties to the state-owned enterprises in Italy's mixed economy and to the world of private business. The country's second leading vote-getter, the Italian Communist party, was deliberately excluded from government at the national level and had to satisfy itself with numerous mayoralties and other municipal posts. Even though it had declared its independence from Moscow, it was still viewed with suspicion in the Cold War years. In 1989 it renamed itself the Democratic Party of the Left. It was largely because the governing parties projected themselves as Italy's defenders against communism that they could maintain their long political ascendancy shielded from scrutiny or criticism. Despite cabinet instability, mounting budgetary deficits, and the grip of organized crime on parts of the country, the Italian Republic had prospered economically. In the mid-1980s it surpassed Britain in per capita gross economic output.

Irrefutable evidence surfaced in the early 1990s of widespread corruption in government and business circles. Official investigations begun in 1992 revealed that public officials up to the highest levels had long received bribes, kickbacks, and payoffs from business corporations, generally in connection with government contracts; there was evidence also of illegal payments to the political parties themselves. Former prime ministers and cabinet ministers and past and present parliamentary deputies from both the Christian Democratic and Socialist parties as well as top business executives were implicated, the numbers running into the thousands. So tainted was the Christian Democratic party that it renamed itself the Popular party, reverting to the name of the Roman Catholic center party of the early 1920s.

The electorate, inured over the years to lesser corruption, was finally aroused and in 1993 approved a new electoral system designed to curb the power of the political parties, solidify closer ties of the deputies with the electorate, and make possible more stable political alignments. Abandoning proportional representation, it substituted for three-fourths of the parliamentary seats direct balloting for candidates in each district. In the first elections under the new system, in 1994, three new, or virtually new, parties of the right swept close to three-fifths of the seats, the former Communist party and its allies won a third, and the centrist parties were routed. But the three major parties of the right inspired little confidence and made up an uneasy coalition. It consisted of a new populist party, Forza Italia, headed by a powerful business magnate who among his many enterprises owned half of Italy's television industry, which he successfully exploited during the election campaign; a separatist Northern League party, which favored either outright secession of the wealthier northern region or at least some form of federalist structure; and the neo-fascist National Alliance which, demonstrating that the ghosts of the past had not been laid to rest, looked back with nostalgia to Mussolini and the Fascist era.[22] The new government inherited a host of serious problems: large public deficits, economic slowdown, unemployment, and rising social tensions. The older governing parties were swept away by the new regime, to be sure, but it was questionable whether the political leaders and parties chosen to succeed them could provide stability and democracy, or serve as models of civic probity.

[22] See pp. 818–822, 837–838, 854.

Europe's Immigrants and Refugees

The influx of large numbers of immigrants and refugees was altering the nature of European societies.[23] Many immigrants had arrived as "guest workers" in the 1960s, coming mainly from southern Europe and Turkey, and principally to Germany, at a time of labor shortages in expanding economies. Others had emigrated from the former European colonial dependencies in Asia, North Africa, sub-Saharan Africa, and the Caribbean, fleeing poverty, and generally filling low-paid or less desirable jobs. When the Cold War ended and Communist barriers came down, thousands fled Eastern Europe, and additional refugees later streamed in from war-torn Yugoslavia. In the twelve years from 1980 to 1992, 15 million immigrants arrived to make their home in Western Europe. Some sought political asylum, but mainly they came in search of wider economic opportunities than could be found in their own impoverished countries.

The surges of immigration changed the ethnic composition of the West European population. In Germany the Turkish workers settled in as permanent residents and reared their children as Muslims. In France in a population of 57 million in the mid-1990s, 4 million, or 7 percent, were foreign-born, mainly Arabs from North Africa but also Vietnamese from Southeast Asia. In Britain, with a population of 56 million, about 2½ million residents could be counted as "ethnic minorities," mainly from South Asia, Africa, and the Caribbean. Because so many of the newer immigrants were non-European and differed from the Europeans in religion, race, or skin color, tensions assumed an ethnic and racial dimension.

The hostility which had manifested itself earlier flared up more seriously in the troubled economic times of the 1990s. There were physical assaults on Turks in Germany and firebombings and acts of violence elsewhere. Allegations of crime and wrongdoing by the immigrants fueled intolerance. Neo-Nazis in Germany, "skinheads" in Britain (who dated from the 1950s), neo-fascists in Italy, and followers in France of Jean-Marie Le Pen's National Front agitated the immigrant issue, or took vigilante action. Governments adopted laws and strategies to reduce or eliminate further immigration. Germany in 1993 repealed a constitutional provision going back to the Basic Law of 1949 that had offered asylum to "all persecuted on political grounds;" it became virtually impossible to distinguish between political and economic refugees. France moved toward a policy of "near-zero" immigration and abandoned a tradition going back to the Revolution of unconditionally granting citizenship to anyone born on French soil. With unemployment and troubled economies, the tensions became even more potentially explosive; the atmosphere fed prejudices of all kinds, including anti-Semitism. But Western Europe was only one outpost of a global crisis of refugees and migrants on the move.

Western Europe seemed enveloped in gloom and pessimism in the mid-1990s unprecedented in the postwar years and was groping for solutions to its pressing problems. The end of the Cold War had not automatically ushered in an era of peace, prosperity, and harmony. The vision nurtured since the 1950s of a unified

[23] See p. 886.

democratic Western Europe built on economic prosperity and widely shared benefits for all social classes seemed to be receding. The influx of immigrants and refugees was further testing its social fabric. Unemployment, especially for the young, marred the economic scene. In the euphoria following the collapse of communism, few anticipated the resurgence of the kind of nationalism that exploded in the Balkans. In the Yugoslav crisis Western Europe, for all its announced commitment to democratic institutions, and its military strength, feared the entanglements of intervention so much that it refrained from decisive action. The political scene was filled with uncertainties. Conservative and centrist political leaders offered little guidance for the future; the left seemed in disarray, the "socialist alternative" all but gone. On the other hand, many retained confidence that Western Europe, buffeted as it was by its troubles, could return to its goal of building a united Europe, reaching out to Eastern Europe as well, and resume once again, along with others, a central role in the world's economy and in international affairs.

Japan in the 1990s

The 1990s were an economic and political watershed for Japan also. The Japanese economy had expanded almost uninterruptedly since its postwar recovery. In the 1980s capital investment in industry, and especially in high technology, at times grew at twice the rate of American and West European investment. But in the summer of 1991, a year after the world slowdown began, it sank into a deep and stubborn recession. The downturn signaled a problem that was more than a business cycle swing. Japan's export economy was faltering. While over the years it exported freely, at the same time it had sharply restricted imports, and other nations finally rebelled. New low-cost competition was invading its markets. The country was also paying the price for years of excessive speculation worldwide in real estate and on financial exchanges; some, perhaps prematurely, spoke of a "bubble economy." Adding to the prospect of slow recovery, Japan also was forced to deal with irresistible pressures for social and structural changes that would enable larger numbers of its population to benefit from the country's productivity and wealth, and enjoy higher levels of consumption.

In the midst of its economic troubles a political crisis, unprecedented in the years since the Second World War, shook the country as cumulative evidence mounted, here too, of nationwide bribery and corruption involving the country's political and business leaders. On the heels of the revelations, the Liberal Democratic party, which had dominated political life and had been the architect of the country's prosperity and stability since the 1950s, lost its parliamentary majority and fell from office in 1993. New faces and new parties emerged to replace the old guard, even though the country's strong bureaucracy seemed to remain entrenched. The transformed atmosphere stimulated a reexamination of the past and aroused hopes for a new start, a more democratic future, and a more flexible society, which would make possible closer ties to its Asian neighbors and the West.

128. Intellectual and Social Currents

Although much of twentieth-century culture had its origins in the years 1871 to 1914,[24] science, philosophy, the arts, and religion crossed new frontiers or took new directions in the course of the century. Even to single out a few of these developments will suggest the vast changes of the contemporary era.

The Advance of Science and Technology

Science and technology expanded rapidly in the half-century before the First World War, but the pace quickened in the following years. Scientific discovery advanced more rapidly in the years after 1919 than in all previous human history. For one thing, more scientists were at work. At the opening of the twentieth century, about 15,000 scientists were exploring scientific problems; in the latter half of the century, over a half-million scientists were engaged in research, more than in all previous centuries combined. Over 85 percent of all scientists who had ever lived were at work in our own age.

The average person experienced the triumphs of science most dramatically in medicine and public health. Nothing in previous medical discovery could equal the contributions of sulfa drugs, antibiotics, cortisone, and other substances used to combat formerly crippling or deadly diseases, including pneumonia and tuberculosis; hormones, adrenalin, and insulin were also available to promote health or relieve suffering. Vaccines combated a number of dread diseases, including, after 1955, poliomyelitis; by 1975 smallpox had been eradicated worldwide. Remarkable accomplishments in surgery included the transplanting of vital organs. Apart from the advances in medical science, people benefited from modern technology in ways too familiar to need recounting. For entertainment, radio and the motion picture were available and, after the Second World War, television. Washing machines, freezers, frozen foods, and microwave ovens lightened household duties. After 1947 airplanes could fly faster than the speed of sound; giant aircraft could traverse huge distances in a few hours; tourist travel to distant parts of the earth became commonplace. A world of computers, electronics, robotics, rocketry, and space technology opened, and a new industrial age based on nuclear power was emerging.

It was a shattering experience when the fatal disease AIDS (Acquired Immunity Deficiency Syndrome) appeared in the early 1980s and threatened to assume global epidemic proportions. The first case was reported in the United States in mid-1981, but the disease seems to have originated earlier and elsewhere. Although statistics were difficult to track, it was estimated that millions were infected globally. While many were confident that medical science would devise a vaccine or other method of treatment or prevention, and that education about sexual practices and intravenous drug use and a system of protected blood supplies would help check its spread, uncertainty and anguish increased as time went by without a cure.

[24] See pp. 625–637.

Nuclear Physics

In pure, or theoretical, science the transformation of physics in the twentieth century could be compared only to the scientific revolution of the sixteenth and seventeenth centuries. Early in the twentieth century scientists had discovered the natural radioactivity of certain elements, physicists like Max Planck and Albert Einstein had developed quantum physics and relativity theory, and Einstein had propounded his now famous theory for the conversion of mass into energy.[25] After 1919 a series of discoveries led to a deeper understanding of the atom. The cyclotron, developed in 1932 at Cambridge University, made it possible to penetrate or "bombard" the nucleus of the atom at high speed. The nucleus, scientists learned, consisted not only of protons but of other particles like neutrons as well. In 1938 the German chemist Otto Hahn discovered that when he bombarded the atomic nucleus of the heavy radioactive element uranium with neutrons it became unstable and split into two, which meant that energy trapped within the atom could be released. Other scientists, including Lise Meitner, a German-Jewish scientist who had been forced to flee Nazi Germany, further expanded upon these findings. In 1939 Nils Bohr, a Danish physicist, brought word of these developments to American scientists.

The implications of this breakthrough in theoretical science were clear. If the atoms in a large amount of uranium were split in a chain reaction, enormous amounts of energy would be released. In the troubled atmosphere of 1939 the possibility arose of its use for military purposes. When the war came, scientists in the United States, including Einstein, who had fled the Nazis in 1934, prevailed upon the American government to explore its military use before the Germans succeeded in doing so. In 1942 American and British scientists and European refugee scientists like the Italian Enrico Fermi brought about the first sustained nuclear chain reaction. This in turn led to the secret preparation of the atomic bomb at Los Alamos, its testing at Alamagordo in the New Mexican desert in July 1945, and its use by the United States against Japan at Hiroshima and Nagasaki in August 1945. The bomb tested at Alamagordo and the bombs dropped on Japan heralded the atomic age.

After the war even more staggering technical developments followed. The hydrogen or thermonuclear bomb was built independently by the Americans and by the Soviets in 1952–1953; it involved nuclear fusion, or the joining together of hydrogen and other light elements at great heat, using the atomic or fission bomb as a detonator with a stupendous chain reaction. Such thermonuclear fusion is responsible for the energy of the sun itself.

The first use of nuclear energy was for military purposes, but it held constructive peacetime potential; a tiny grain of uranium (or plutonium, another radioactive element) could produce power equal to almost 3 tons of coal. In the early 1990s over 15 percent of the world's electricity was generated by nuclear power plants; in a country like France over 65 percent. At the same time the awesome explosive powers unleashed by the scientists and the dangers of radioactivity were alarming. Accidents in nuclear power plants threatened the surrounding population and environs with the release of radioactive gases; nor could nuclear meltdowns be

---

[25] See pp. 294–298, 628–630.

ruled out. Popular opposition to the building of nuclear power plants grew, as did concern over their proper design.

In military affairs a true nuclear clash of arms could mean apocalypse. Scientists who had prepared the first atomic bomb believed it to be so awesome a weapon as to make its future use unthinkable and in that way bar future major wars. In part they were correct; a balance of terror emerged so that over the years since August 1945 no nuclear weapon has been used in warfare. But nuclear bombs became part of the world's arsenal, an ever-present threat to human life and to the planet itself. The nuclear powers possessed missiles and warheads in the thousands, representing an accumulation of explosive power unparalleled in history.

In later years scientists used linear accelerators like the cyclotron and even more powerful colliders and supercolliders as atom smashers to explore the nature of the atom and the behavior of its subatomic particles. Building upon the work of Einstein and others, the theoretical physicists searched for an overarching theory that would explain the interrelationship of gravity, electromagnetism, and nuclear force, all of which were to be found in the subatomic world and in the cosmos as a whole.

Implications of Science and Technology

As in the case of nuclear physics, science in the contemporary age was closely allied with technology and the organized effort to exploit new scientific findings. Government and industry subsidized most scientific research. Laboratory equipment was expensive, and complex investigation required large-scale collaborative efforts; the solitary scientific investigator (and inventor) was disappearing. The subsidization of research for national purposes raised fears that scientific discoveries might serve political and not human goals.

Science had always affected the way people thought about themselves and their universe. The Copernican revolution had removed the earth from its central position in the scheme of things; Darwinian evolution had demonstrated that *Homo sapiens* was biologically a species that had evolved and survived.[26] The philosophical implications of twentieth-century physics were only vaguely understood, yet they reinforced theories of relativism in all spheres. Ironically, at the very time that the average person was awed by the capabilities of science, scientists themselves recognized that they had no magic key to the nature of things. Generally they claimed no more than the ability to determine, or guess at, relationships, which in the world of the atom (as in the cosmos itself) were mysterious and uncertain.

Some thoughtful persons questioned scientific and technological advance and asked whether modern technology had grown beyond human control. Ecologists pointed to the wastage and spoliation of natural resources and the threat to the environment. In another way the life-preserving features of medicine and public health could result in overpopulation and in perhaps unmanageable pressure upon the limited resources of the globe. The techniques developed to save or prolong human life also raised ethical and legal issues, including new definitions of life

[26] See pp. 294–295, 626.

and death, and the rights in such matters of patients, families, hospitals, and physicians. Questions arose over test-tube fertilization and other forms of artificial conception made possible in the late 1970s. Those who condemned modern technology extolled the virtues of a prescientific and preindustrial age; others called for sharper awareness of present and future dangers. No longer was the advance of science and technology equated with the idea of progress.

Meanwhile, in the quest to understand nature the old divisions between the sciences broke down and new sciences appeared. Biochemistry, cell and molecular biology, biophysics, astrophysics, geophysics, and other subdisciplines arose, and all made intensive use of mathematics. In biology genetics made striking advances. While physicists discovered new atomic particles, biochemists isolated the organic substance found in the genes and chromosomes of all living cells, the chemical carriers of all hereditary characteristics. When scientists deciphered the genetic "code" and synthesized the basic substance of heredity (DNA), it became possible by splicing genes to alter the characteristics of plant and animal species, with staggering implications. Biotechnologists could revolutionize food production by genetically engineering new varieties of crops. Medical scientists could hope to conquer inherited diseases.

The other life sciences and social sciences also grew in importance. Psychological exploration of human behavior, as well as the treatment of mental and emotional disorders through psychiatry and psychoanalysis, expanded rapidly. Freud, who had first developed his theories of psychoanalysis before 1914, became more widely known in the 1920s.[27] His emphasis on the human sex drive and sexual repression was much modified. Many students of human behavior argued that his contributions were not universally or scientifically valid but reflected the values of pre-1914, middle-class, male-dominated Viennese society. New schools emerged with different interpretations and techniques, but the search, initiated by Freud, for the unconscious sources of individual and collective human conduct remained a hallmark of contemporary thought and culture.

Anthropologists and other social scientists increasingly stressed the relativism of all culture. They denied notions of cultural superiority or hierarchies of cultural values, or even that there were objective criteria of historical progress. If Western society, they noted, made notable progress in science and technology, other cultures accomplished more in self-discipline, individual integrity, and human happiness. The very adjective "primitive," as opposed to "civilized," tended to disappear, and a new cultural humanism emerged that recognized and esteemed values distinct from the Western tradition.

Space Exploration

Among the most dramatic developments in science and technology in the second half of the twentieth century was space exploration. In the 1950s the Soviets and the Americans competed with each other as part of the Cold War; each made important advances in rocket research. Even before 1914 the significance of rocketry had been grasped by pioneers in aerodynamics, and toward the end of

[27] See p. 628.

the Second World War the Germans first used rockets in warfare.[28] Both the U.S. and the U.S.S.R now mastered multistage rocket launching. The Soviets opened the space age when in 1957 they launched *Sputnik*, the world's first artificial satellite; in 1961 they sent the first human in orbital flight around the earth. In 1961 and 1962 the Americans sent their own astronauts into space. In the 1960s both countries launched unmanned automated spaceships to probe and explore the moon and then the planets of the solar system and their satellites. Early in the 1960s President Kennedy pledged that Americans would land on the moon before the end of the decade. In 1969 three American astronauts, as planned in Project Apollo, made the quarter-million-mile journey to the moon while millions over the globe watched on television. In the next three years the Americans made five additional trips to the moon. Automated robot spaceships were launched in the 1960s on long journeys to explore the planets of the solar system. The American spaceships approached or orbited the planets and soft-landed instrument packages, which over a period of years sent back a rich harvest of data, providing more knowledge than ever before possessed about the nature and origins of the planets, and about the earth itself. The later space probes explored the more distant planets. *Voyager 2,* launched in 1977, traveling close to 4.5 billion miles over twelve years' time, reached the outermost planets before flying into interstellar space. In 1990 the United States placed in orbit a powerful space telescope, capable of seeing light years away into distant galaxies.

The Soviets also conducted impressive space probes, to the moon, to Mars, and to Halley's Comet, whose behavior had been predicted in the seventeenth century,[29] and which once again returned close enough for observation in 1986. The Soviets also built a permanent space station and set records in testing human endurance in weightless space.

As time went on, Cold War rivalries played less of a role in space exploration, but military objectives were never completely absent. The U.S. and the U.S.S.R., and later other countries, launched spy satellites for reconnaissance and informa-tion-gathering. The United States initiated research in the 1980s into an enormously costly strategic defense initiative that would deploy laser-like weapons in outer space (hence called ''star wars'') to thwart nuclear missile attacks, but abandoned the project by 1990.

In the 1980s space enterprise showed promise of international cooperation, and was no longer confined to the military superpowers. France, China, Japan, and other countries became spacefaring nations, planning and launching satellites and space probes of their own. The European Space Agency carried out its own operations. A multinational human expedition to Mars sometime in the twenty-first century was discussed. After the Cold War the Americans and the Russians began to cooperate in space. On the other hand, the need for human expeditions came under serious scrutiny. Dismayed by a number of serious accidents and impressed by the accomplishments of the robot spaceships, some critics contended that unmanned space flights could accomplish more, at less cost, and at less risk to human life. Others objected to the enormous expense of space exploration when acute social needs remained unfulfilled. But its champions defended it as

[28] See p. 855.
[29] See p. 301.

part of the continuing human effort to cross new frontiers, expand horizons, and explore the unknown. The twentieth century may be remembered, apart from the destructiveness of its wars, as the century in which humans first set foot on the moon and with robot spaceships, devised and guided by human intelligence, began to explore the universe.

Philosophy: Existentialism in the Postwar Years

A loosely organized body of ideas called "existentialism" grappled in the early postwar years with the human predicament. The existentialists formed no one school of thought and held no coherent body of principles. There were Christian and atheist existentialists. Yet all held some beliefs and attitudes in common. All reflected a troubled civilization, a world disturbed by war and oppression, a civilization of material progress and moral uncertainty in which the individual could be crushed by the very triumphs of science and technology.

Existentialist thought owed a debt to Pascal, Nietzsche, and others who had underscored the tragic element in human existence and the limitations on the power of human reason.[30] More directly it owed a debt to Søren Kierkegaard, the nineteenth-century Danish religious philosopher. But it was French writers, and especially Jean-Paul Sartre, who after the Second World War developed existentialist thought in literature and philosophy in a form that for a time gave it a wide popular following. In a hostile world, the existentialists contended, human beings had to make choices and commitments on their own. They were "condemned to be free," and were alone responsible for their choices. The authentic existentialist could not be contemplative only but had to be committed to belief and action, even though aware that human action could not change the world. Albert Camus, influenced by the existentialists, drew upon the myth of Sisyphus, who was condemned to roll his stone uphill even though it rolled back down again, his very humanity growing out of courage and perseverance at a hopeless and absurd task. Existentialism emphasized the anguish of human existence, the frailty of human reason, the fragility of human institutions, and the need to reassert and redefine human freedom. Although its popular following waned, and Sartre himself was dislodged from his earlier lofty eminence, existentialism never completely disappeared from contemporary thought in philosophy or religion.

Philosophy: Logic and Language; Literary Criticism; History

Professional philosophy in the twentieth century seemed to contribute less to an understanding of contemporary problems than in the past. Always concerned with the origins and nature of knowledge, it had also shared an interest in metaphysics and ethics. In the twentieth century it became highly analytical. In the formal study of logic, symbolic logic substituted mathematical symbols for language. On the eve of the First World War Bertrand Russell and Alfred North Whitehead explored logic and mathematics in their monumental *Principia Mathematica*. In the 1920s an influential group of philosophers and mathematicians

---

[30] See pp. 299, 630.

in Vienna, among them Ludwig Wittgenstein, sought to introduce the methodology and precision of mathematics into the study of philosophy as a whole, in what they called logical positivism. They rejected the ambiguities of language used in traditional speculation on morals and values, turning away from the nondemonstrable—i.e., "God, death, what is higher," in Wittgenstein's phrase. The Vienna group disintegrated in the 1930s, but logical positivism remained influential. Most professional philosophers continued to emphasize scientific rigor and linguistic analysis. A smaller number, responsive to contemporary ethical concerns, devoted themselves to unresolved human and social dilemmas.

New studies in philosophy, linguistic analysis, and semiotics (i.e., the study of signs and symbols in communication) drew attention to the wide gap between language and reality. Philosophers also challenged many of the dualisms taken for granted in Western thought. In literary studies "deconstruction" theory emerged to offer new methods of analysis and criticism. Its proponents asked the reader to analyze, or "deconstruct," a given body of writing (a "text," which could be any cultural object as well) with no regard for previous interpretations, the historical setting, or the life of the author, but to link it to all related "texts." No single valid meaning was to be attached to any individual work. Deconstruction made it possible, its proponents claimed, to reveal the class, racial, ethnocentric, or sexual assumptions hidden in the language of a work. It also contested older rigid hierarchical standards of literary quality, blurred distinctions between elite and popular culture, made less of a dichotomy between fact and fiction (and other dualisms), and broadened the existing canon of writings studied in literature, history, law, religion, and other disciplines.

The work of the critic was said to be as much a creative enterprise as literary or artistic creation itself. Propounded originally in the 1960s in broad philosophical terms by the French philosopher Jacques Derrida, and developed further by other writers and scholars of various disciplines and nationalities, deconstruction won its largest following in the United States. Its opponents viewed it as abandoning traditional literary history and undermining the values and standards that had long held a place in literary studies.

The writing of history also underwent a profound change. A group of French historical scholars (called the *Annales* school, from a journal with which they were associated) gained wide influence after the Second World War. They focused on long-term elements in historical change such as population, economy, climate, and natural resources, relegated politics to a lesser role, and avoided the traditional narrative of "events." They studied also the lives of ordinary people in the past and tried to reconstruct the collective outlook of social classes. The newer social history in France, England, and the United States also paid special attention to the inarticulate and illiterate, and to all those with strong oral traditions, such as the American slaves in the antebellum south, the English working classes, and the peoples of Africa, reconstructing their culture and lives despite understandably scarce sources. Another new emphasis simultaneously opened up on the historical study of women from antiquity to the present, leading, among other results, to the reassessment of some historical eras. A variety of themes were also newly explored historically: marriage, divorce, the family, childhood, sexuality, even insanity and death through the ages. For their part, many traditional historians, who had not been wholly insensitive to these concerns, deepened their own narratives under the influence of the newer history.

The Creative Arts

The revolution against older traditions in the creative arts assumed new dimensions. Ever since the Renaissance visual artists had followed certain norms of representation and space perspective. But much of twentieth-century art prided itself on being nonobjective; it rejected the idea of imitating or reconstructing nature, or mirroring it with realism or photographic fidelity. The artistic revolution inaugurated before 1914[31] accelerated in the interwar years and after 1945. It seemed to mirror the political turbulence of the times and the disillusionment with rationalism and optimism. It reflected the influence of Freudian and other schools of psychology and the emphasis on the unconscious and irrational, as well as the relativity of the new physics and its uncertainties about the nature of matter, space, and time.

Artists continued the pre-1914 experimentation in color, form, and use of materials, but went well beyond, seeing the world around them in new ways. The Spanish artist Pablo Picasso systematically distorted and deformed in order to convey his image of human and nonhuman figures. Some artists expressed themselves through geometric form; others left reality behind and worked out of their own subconscious. The results were fascinating but frequently baffling. After the Second World War, the United States took over from Europe the leadership role in the visual arts. American artists built upon earlier improvisation and automatic painting in which the subconscious was said to dictate the artist's work. Additional, even broader, experimentation continued.

Contemporary art resulted in original and striking expressions of form and color, but the conscious subjectivism widened still further the gap between artist and public. The artist, painter, and sculptor (and the poet, musician, playwright, and novelist, who were also rejecting the older conventions) were conveying their own vision of the world, not an objective reality that could easily be understood by others. Perhaps the greatest innovation was that the public, baffled as it was by much of contemporary art, came to accept the avant-garde as normal, even if on occasion it rebelled against it. Democratic societies accepted the need for artistic experimentation and innovation, which had been frowned upon or banned as degenerate or socially dangerous in totalitarian societies like Nazi Germany or the Soviet Union. Representational art, of course, never completely disappeared anywhere, and many artists reaffirmed it, contributing to a growing pluralism in contemporary art.

The focus on subjectivism and the unconscious was reflected in literature too. The reconstruction of lost time and the unfolding of the individual's innermost experience through a stream of consciousness and flood of memories appeared first in the work of Marcel Proust and James Joyce before and shortly after the First World War. After 1945, not only writers but cinematographers experimented with probing the unconscious in evocative but mystifying ways. All of this was

[31] See illustrations, with captions, on pp. 632–635, 780, 861, 1051, 1060.

in contrast to the entertainment provided through the mass media, especially movies and television, and hardly touched the average citizen.

Sometime in the early 1970s the phenomenon of postmodernism emerged in architecture, literature, and other art forms. In all areas the postmoderns borrowed from the past and mixed the old and new to suit their tastes. Unlike modernists from the late nineteenth century on, the postmodernists did not reject the commercialization and materialism of contemporary culture but embraced it and incorporated it in new ways, often with humor. The American architect Robert Venturi and his collaborators wrote a book called *Learning from Las Vegas* (1972). Composers introduced street noises (and silences) into their music. Repetition, as in the commercial world of packaging, marketing, and television advertising, was adopted as technique. The artist Andy Warhol painted serial pictures in that manner of Coca-Cola bottles and of the film star Marilyn Monroe. In fiction the postmoderns mingled actual events and fantasy. A play by Harold Pinter, Samuel Beckett, or Eugène Ionesco was very different from a play by Shakespeare, Molière, Ibsen, or Shaw. The postmoderns also rejected traditional ideas of structure, seeing no need in literature or art for a beginning, a middle, and an end. Postmodernism was both a phase of the modernist rebellion against traditionalism and a sequel to it with new messages.

Religion in the Modern World

Religion was in flux in the modern world. With the continuing inroads of secularism, the challenges of science, and the post-1945 advances of communism in Eastern Europe, China, and elsewhere, organized religion encountered many obstacles. But the churches survived Marxist regimes and despite setbacks they retained their vitality. Statistics on religious affiliation are never exact, but some figures in the closing decade of the twentieth century were clear. Islam, with over 950 million adherents, was the fastest growing faith; it made large inroads in postcolonial Africa. In Asia, in addition to over 600 million Muslims, there were 715 million Hindus and 310 million Buddhists. Christianity, if all branches are added together, remained the largest religion, counting 1.7 billion adherents, of which more than half were Roman Catholic, a fourth Protestant, and a fourth Eastern Orthodox.

The ecumenical movement in Christianity, the organized effort to unite the many branches of Protestantism, and eventually all Christianity, which began in the nineteenth century, made headway after the Second World War. A World Council of Churches was founded in 1948. When in the 1960s the Roman Catholic

TWINNED COLUMN
by Antoine Pevsner (Russian, then French, 1886–1962)

Antoine Pevsner, like Kandinsky and Chagall (see pp. 633 and 780), left his native Russia after the Soviet regime began to disapprove of "modern" art. The picture here shows one of his sculptures, a bronze piece about forty inches high, constructed in 1947. The symmetry and the column recall the classical tradition, but the work also conveys the scientific and technological interests of the twentieth century. Pevsner's sculptural space is not the familiar medium in which human beings live and move, but a more abstract space, known to mathematics, quite apart from man's peculiarities of size and physical senses. Courtesy of the Solomon R. Guggenheim Museum.

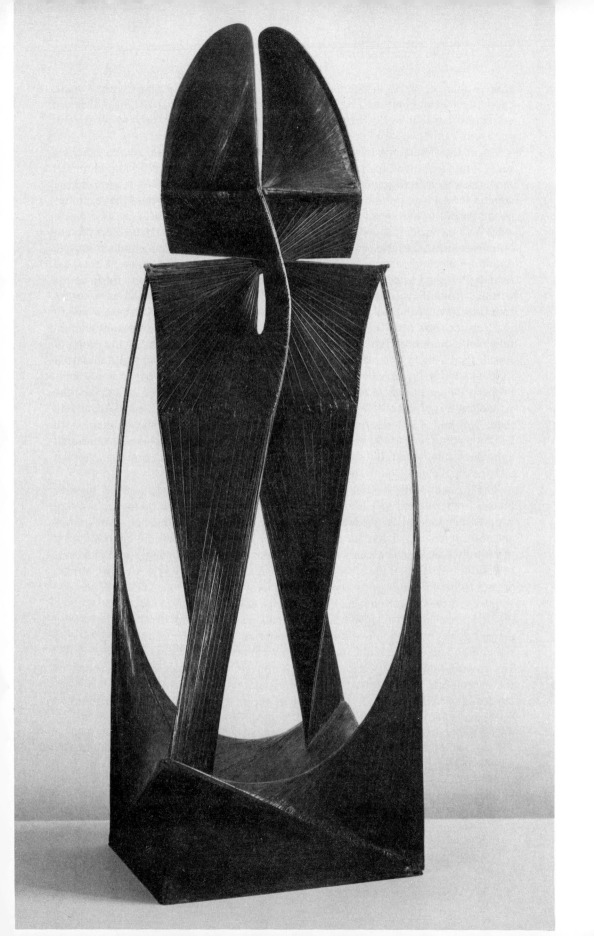

church abandoned its insistence on a privileged position in Christianity, it too encouraged ecumenicism. The Christian churches moved toward a closer dialogue with non-Christian world faiths as well. In Judaism, the older trend to secularism persisted, but more striking was the vitality of all its branches.

As in the nineteenth century, tensions between modernism (in its religious sense) and fundamentalism continued.[32] For the most part the Protestant churches reconciled their traditional teachings with science and scholarship, minimized the supernatural and dogmatic aspects of their faith, and sought to adapt the teachings of the gospel to the social needs of the contemporary world. But the two world wars and the troubled century dealt a blow to modernism and to the inherent optimism of the social gospel. In the 1920s, not only did fundamentalism revive, but an intellectual reaction set in among Protestant theologians that emphasized revealed religion and elements of faith. The Swiss theologian Karl Barth in his writings from 1919 to the 1960s endeavored to lead Protestantism back to the root principles of the Reformation. There was much interest in Kierkegaard who, like Luther, had resolved his own deep anguish by a personal commitment to religious experience. After the Second World War, as a result of the work of Barth, Paul Tillich, and others, a powerful movement in Protestantism reasserted its dependence on revealed religion and denied that human reason could ever properly judge divine revelation. Some church writers, unable to explain the wrenching experience of the war and the Holocaust, spoke of "post-Auschwitz theology" and of "God's removal from history." Evangelical Protestantism, with its literal adherence to the gospel, spellbinding preachers, and revivalist emotional appeal also flourished, but Protestantism generally accepted religious scholarship and the challenge of modernism.

The Roman Catholic church was passing through one of its great historic phases in the second half of the century. Although the church no longer actively suppressed modernism, the Vatican reaffirmed dogmatic training in the seminaries and the catechism for the laity. In 1950 Pius XII, who headed the church during the war and for fourteen years thereafter, proclaimed the Assumption, the literal, or bodily, taking-up of the Virgin Mary into heaven, the only new Roman Catholic dogma to be promulgated in the twentieth century.

Pius XII was succeeded in 1959 by John XXIII. Although elected at the age of 77, and reigning for only four and a half years until his death in 1963, John proved to be one of the most innovative popes of modern times, working to bring the church and its teachings into greater harmony with the contemporary world. His powerful encyclicals gave a global emphasis to the older social teachings of the church and called upon the wealthier nations to share their resources with the less favored. *Pacem in Terris* (1963), the first encyclical ever addressed to Catholics and non-Catholics alike, appealed for peace and human rights. A champion of ecumenicism, he opened dialogues with other faiths. In 1962, against the advice of his own theologians, he convened the Second Vatican Council, the first such council since 1870, and as it turned out, the most important since the sixteenth-century Council of Trent.[33] Vatican II reshaped contemporary Catholicism.

[32] See pp. 631–636.
[33] See pp. 88–90, 634.

John did not live to see the Council's labors completed. His successor, Paul VI, shared John's social concerns and encouraged ecumenism, but he was more conservative in other ways. The Council completed its work in 1965. Accepting the principle of religious pluralism, it abandoned the older insistence on a Catholic monopoly on religious truth. It affirmed the principle of collegiality, which had gone into eclipse in the modern centuries, the view that the pope must share his authority with the prelates of the church, thus strengthening the authority of the national churches on substantive matters. It revised the liturgy and various church practices. The Mass, henceforth, would be said in vernacular tongues instead of in Latin—the practice since the eighth century. The Council relaxed restrictions on dress for priests and nuns. It gave the laity a larger role in religious practices. In one historic declaration, the Council explicitly absolved the Jewish people from the charge of deicide that had inflamed anti-Semitism over the ages. John XXIII's goal—the revitalization and updating of church teachings and practices—was amply fulfilled by the Council. There were limitations, to be sure. Celibacy for the clergy remained unmodified; nor was the ordination of women as priests sanctioned. Paul VI, meanwhile, upheld papal supremacy and took a firm conservative stance on moral issues, especially against birth control.

After Paul VI's death in 1978 (and when a successor died after only 34 days in office), John Paul II, the archbishop of Cracow, became the new head of the church, the first Polish pope ever elected, and the first non-Italian pontiff in over 450 years. Robust, earthy, energetic, versatile in languages, and with a keen sense of pageantry and papal majesty, he became a widely admired but controversial pope. Not only did he encourage the Christian ecumenical movement, he reached out to non-Christians as well, traveling widely in Asia and Africa. With the Soviet Union and the countries of Eastern Europe he entered into diplomatic negotiations to improve the status of the church and contributed much to the revolutionary transformation of his own country and Eastern Europe in the 1980s.

Although on global, social, and economic issues John Paul held progressive views, in matters of church doctrine and governance he favored orthodoxy and papal supremacy, and a narrow interpretation of sexual morality, disappointing many. He appointed conservative archbishops and bishops, silenced dissenting theologians, and curbed the growing assertiveness of national churches. In Latin America he put an end to "liberation theology." He would not countenance marriage for the clergy, the ordination of women as priests (an innovation accepted by the Church of England in 1994), rights of divorce (or of remarriage for the divorced), or homosexuality. His authoritarian stance on controversial issues engendered protest against the "new Roman centralism," the failure to modernize the church more thoroughly, and the unwillingness to respect the spirit of shared authority promised by the Council. His defenders argued that in upholding tradition, he was restoring a balance upset by overly rapid change in the church.

Judaism, the third important faith of the Western world, was haunted in the years after 1945 by the traumatic experience of the Holocaust.[34] Of the world's 18 million Jews, one-third lived in the United States. Jews everywhere, and

---

[34] See p. 859 and map, p. 858.

especially in the United States, and not only Zionists, lent moral and financial support to the state of Israel, although many were troubled by Israeli militancy and intransigence, especially in its occupied territories, and by the role in domestic politics of ultraorthodox religious groups that refused to accept a secular state. Anti-Zionism, not only in the Arab world but elsewhere as well, at times served as a thin screen for anti-Semitism. In the former Soviet Union, Jews insistent on practising their faith had met harassment and persecution and, when permitted, they emigrated in large numbers. The collapse of communism reignited older currents of anti-Semitism in Eastern Europe.

The major non-Western religions, Islam, Hinduism, and Buddhism, also made efforts to adjust millennia-old doctrines to the secular tendencies of the contemporary age, but in some instances adamantly refused. Eastern religions attracted adherents in the West: Islam among African-Americans, Buddhist meditative teachings and practices among students, intellectuals, and others. The large numbers of African and Asian immigrants to Western Europe, and of Asian immigrants to the United States, brought their religious faiths with them.

The latter part of the twentieth century saw the rise and spread of militant fundamentalism, especially in the Islamic world, and its rejection of the secularism of the modern world. Nowhere did popular frenzy and the adulation of a religious leader reach such heights as in Iran,[35] but Muslim activists were also at work in Egypt, Algeria, and elsewhere seeking to subvert secular regimes, impose theocracies, and use state power to enforce religious views. In several states militant regimes attempted to impose Koranic law on non-believers.

The fundamentalists demanded an unswerving adherence to sacred texts regardless of changing times and circumstances, an identification of religion with political and moral values, a strict moral code extending to diet, dress, and the relationship of the sexes, all interpreted and enforced by messianic religious leaders who mobilized mass followings to accomplish these ends. Muslim fundamentalism had a counterpart in an extremist Hindu movement in India, which unleashed violence against the Muslims in the country and threatened the secular state.

Fundamentalism could be found in evangelical Christian sects and in extremist Orthodox Jewish quarters as well. It easily bred intolerance and separatism, and ran counter to the blending of cultures in the contemporary world. In the West the separation of political and religious authority had become so widely accepted that it became difficult to grasp the strength and appeal of the new religious ferment.

Activism: The Youth Rebellion of the 1960s

In the second half of the twentieth century young people seemed to acquire a collective identity that historically youth did not possess earlier. It was possible to speak of a youth market, a youth culture, youth movements. In part the phenomenon was demographic in origin, the result of the extraordinary number of births in the decade and a half after the Second World War—the "baby boom." A large cohort grew up in a rapidly changing world.

[35] See pp. 948–951.

In the 1960s a youth activism made a startling appearance, marked by a widespread student rebellion. A generation came to college age and attended institutions of higher learning in larger numbers than ever before. It was a generation that knew nothing firsthand of the turbulence of the 1930s or the Second World War. Young people grew up in an era of global change and scientific breakthrough, to which their elders were no certain guides. They took for granted the scientific, technological, and other accomplishments of their world and concentrated on its deficiencies—the flagrant contradictions of wealth and poverty within and among nations, racial injustice, discrimination, colonialism, the impersonal quality of mechanized society and bureaucratized institutions (including colleges and universities), the violence that destroyed human beings in continuing wars, and always the threat of nuclear destruction. The rebelliousness extended beyond the traditional generation gap; it was directed at all established society.

The revolt burst forth in the late 1960s in widely separate parts of the world. The Cultural Revolution in China,[36] although in an entirely different context, was not unrelated, and indirectly inspired it. At the peak of the movement in 1967–1968 students demonstrated and rioted on campuses and battled police all over the world; American, Canadian, Mexican, West German, French, Italian, and Spanish universities were heavily involved. France was at the center of the storm. Demonstrations there reached near-revolutionary dimensions in the spring of 1968 and threatened to overthrow the regime when 10 million workers also went out on strike, partly in sympathy and partly for their own grievances. But the militancy of the students alienated many, and the government restored order. Such initial grievances as inadequate physical facilities in the overcrowded universities and impersonal and remote instruction were almost forgotten in the upheavals in France and elsewhere. Some of the earliest and largest demonstrations took place in the United States, sparked by the struggle for civil rights for American blacks and heightened by resistance to American involvement in the unpopular Vietnam War. The assassinations in 1968 of the dedicated black leader of the civil rights movement, Martin Luther King, Jr., and of Robert Kennedy, brother of the slain president, fueled further anger in the ranks of the young.

The rebelling students made heroes of the sworn foes of the established order: Fidel Castro and his martyred lieutenant Che Guevara, Ho Chi Minh, Mao Zedong, militant American black leaders like Malcolm X, the heralds of the colonial revolution such as Frantz Fanon (the West Indian author of *The Wretched of the Earth*), and others. They read the neo-Marxist philosopher Herbert Marcuse, who warned that the very tolerance of bourgeois society was a trap to prevent true protest against injustice; they learned from him that the industrial working class, co-opted by the existing system, was no longer a revolutionary force. A "New Left" dismissed older revolutionaries in the Soviet Union as stodgy bureaucrats and affirmed that revolutionary leadership would come from Maoist China and the Third World. They attacked materialism, affluence, and conformity, and the power structure of contemporary society. Many believed in confrontation and action for the sake of action, recalling an older anarchism and nihilism. They called on each other to destroy in order to purify.

[36] See pp. 916–917.

The rebellion in its mass phase faded by the early 1970s. In the United States it helped bring the Vietnam War to an end. Only a small number of extremists continued a kind of urban guerrilla war through underground terrorist organizations. Mostly, the rebels of 1968 moved on to places in established society. While many people shuddered at the attack on traditional institutions and orderly processes, others were shaken out of their complacency about social and racial inequities. Efforts were made to reform university administration and to provide more adequate teaching facilities. The youth movement, even after it subsided, had a continuing effect on all age groups in loosening older standards of language, dress, and sexual mores.

The Women's Liberation Movement

The feminist, or women's liberation, movement was another, but more enduring, manifestation of contemporary social ferment. From the time of the French Revolution a few thinkers in France and England had raised the question of equal rights for women.[37] The modern movement had its origin in the United States in the mid–nineteenth century when Elizabeth Cady Stanton and a small group of associates in 1848 proclaimed a declaration of independence for women, demanding the right to vote, equal compensation for work, legal equality, and expanded educational opportunities. The movement spread abroad. In Britain, later in the century, it was taken up by the suffragettes. The right to vote was won in a few American states and in a few smaller countries before the First World War, in many more nations after 1918, and in almost all other countries after 1945.[38] But other objectives went unrealized.

The militant contemporary phase began in the United States in the mid-1960s, a sequel to the civil rights movement on behalf of the American black population. The women's liberation movement, inspired by Simone de Beauvoir's *The Second Sex,* published in France in 1949, and Betty Friedan's *The Feminine Mystique,* which appeared in the United States in 1963, contended that women, half or more of the human race, had been and continued to be oppressed by a male-dominated society and that they were not permitted access to positions of authority, leadership, and power. Although the more blatant forms of legal discrimination, in such matters as property rights for example, had been or were being removed, feminists demanded an end to all barriers to equality.

The campaign for equal rights called upon a different agenda in the poorer, less developed countries, where women generally had to overcome centuries-old neglect, abject repression, abuse, and disregard of the most elementary human rights. The United Nations from the time of its founding had committed itself to equal political, economic, and educational rights for women. But in Africa, Asia, and Latin America adult illiteracy rates were still significantly higher for women and were declining more slowly. In these areas, where a majority of the world's women lived, equal opportunities for women, especially in education, could become one of the most effective means of accelerating social advances for the

---

[37] See p. 372.
[38] See pp. 617–618, 641, 778, 887.

entire population. Discrimination was not confined to capitalist societies. Despite Communist promises, the advance to equality, or even to equality of opportunity, in the former Soviet Union and in the People's Republic of China was disappointing.

Some women, more so than in the past, when authority resided only with reigning women sovereigns, held positions of the highest authority in their countries at various times in the years after 1945. Among them were Indira Gandhi in India, Golda Meir in Israel, Margaret Thatcher in Britain, Corazón Aquino in the Philippines, Benazir Bhutto in Pakistan, and a growing list of other women presidents or prime ministers in such widely differing countries as Sri Lanka, Portugal, Norway, Iceland, Nicaragua, Ireland, Bangladesh, France, Poland, Turkey, and Canada.

Meanwhile the development of advanced contraceptive technology, especially the birth control pill in the early 1960s, and legalized abortion provided a new biological freedom for women. Changing social patterns tolerating sexual freedom and new forms of relationships also contributed to social liberation. In the last decades of the twentieth century women were filling a higher share of places in higher education and in professional schools than ever before. As more women became part of the labor force at all levels, the demand arose not only for equal compensation for equal work, still far from realized, but also for better pay for skilled jobs that were poorly compensated because they had been traditionally filled by women. Although there were disagreements in and outside the women's liberation movement on the methods and tempo of change, wide agreement existed on the need to utilize fully all of society's human resources in every part of the globe. If that could be accomplished, it would count among the most memorable of the revolutionary changes of the contemporary era.

129. A New Era

The Gorbachev years and the collapse of the Soviet Union itself in 1991 transformed the foundations on which international relations had rested for over four decades. A new shape of world affairs, whose outlines were only roughly apparent, was emerging. It was clear that the end of the Cold War had not brought peace to the world.

The International Scene

The United States, as the strongest political, economic, and military power, the sole superpower, was still called upon to exercise the leading role in international affairs, even if in concert with its European allies, the other major powers, and the United Nations. At times it took initiatives that made it difficult to distinguish between American unilateralism and international action. The Security Council in 1990 condemned Iraq's agression against Kuwait, but it was the United States that assembled a formidable multinational military force, including over a half-million American troops, and in 1991 forced the withdrawal from Kuwait and enforced the terms of the cease-fire.[39] When the collapse of central authority in Somalia made the humanitarian deliveries of food and medical supplies by the United Nations impossible without military protection, the United States in 1992 organized what was to be a brief military intervention, which other nations joined. The crisis in the former Yugoslav republics sorely tested Europe, the United States, and the United Nations. The Security Council imposed economic sanctions on Serbia, provided humanitarian aid to besieged cities in Bosnia, and laid plans for war crimes trials. Without military backing by the European powers or the United States, however, the United Nations actions were ineffective.

The United States was torn between exercising the leadership to which it had grown accustomed in the Cold War years and the need to focus on domestic affairs, economic competitiveness, and urgent social needs. It no longer had the resources to act as the world's policeman but could not easily abdicate its leadership role and responsibilities. President Clinton, elected in 1992 on a program emphasizing domestic and economic themes, inherited unresolved foreign policy issues in Iraq, Somalia, Bosnia, Haiti, and elsewhere, and Arab-Israeli tensions in the Middle East.

Clinton inherited also the instability of the post–Cold War international order. The disintegration of the U.S.S.R. ended the nuclear balance of power that had resulted from the rivalry of the two superpowers and their defense strategy of mutual deterrence. At the dissolution of the U.S.S.R. the successor republics agreed that Russia alone would be a nuclear power, but much rested on the willingness of the three republics with nuclear arms to surrender or dismantle their weaponry. Despite initial obstacles, the dismantling proceeded. The United States and Russia confirmed and broadened their commitment to the mutual reduction of long-range nuclear arms, and negotiations continued on scaling down existing stockpiles of strategic nuclear missiles and banning multiple warheads. In a symbolic gesture both countries agreed in 1994 to retarget their missiles so they were no longer aimed at each other's cities and military objectives, or in the Russian case at those of the Western allies. Although the missiles could easily be retargeted, the step was reassuring to a tense world.

Globally, the threat of nuclear proliferation persisted. That North Korea, Iraq, and other states were developing a nuclear capacity gave grave concern; North Korea's capability especially alarmed South Korea, Japan, and the People's Republic of China. The issue of nonproliferation remained high on the international agenda. The world had to live with nuclear arms; the genie could not be put back into the bottle.

The dissolution of the Soviet Union left a vast part of the world politically and economically unstable. Russia itself was economically bankrupt, struggling internally to create a viable constitutional and political order, and confronted by secessionist threats. Yet it was still a major power and not ready to abandon aspirations to a central role in world affairs. After an initial period of relative passivity, Russia again began to assert itself. When Russia objected to the admission of the former Warsaw Pact nations to NATO, the United States worked out a compromise whereby the East European states could participate in joint

---

[39] See pp. 951–952.

military activities but not yet receive full membership. That Russia itself might wish to join NATO was another sign of a world transformed. Russia also made clear that it expected to exercise its hegemony in the troubled former Soviet republics, as in Georgia, where it had already intervened with military forces. The suggestion that it aspired again to a sphere of influence in Eastern Europe, reinforced by the appearance of an ultranationalist party in domestic Russian politics, alarmed Russia's neighbors and others. Russia also insisted on conventional armed forces larger than originally agreed upon, for its many new borders. In the Bosnian crisis, refusing to abandon its historical interests in the Balkans, it rejected unilateral action by NATO but made a positive contribution by exerting influence on the Serbs to bring them to the negotiating table.

The winding down of the Cold War after 1985 in the Gorbachev era had already opened up new opportunities for the United Nations and the Security Council. It created a climate of cooperation for the five permanent members of the Council—the United States, Britain, France, the People's Republic of China, and the then Soviet Union—enabling the Council to return to the peacekeeping functions intended for it by the Charter.[40] The Council had played only a marginal role during the Cold War, powerless to act in the great crises, largely because of the Soviet Union's use of its veto. The need for international action, however, had scarcely diminished. While Europe as a whole had known an uneasy peace since 1945 (until the violent breakup of Yugoslavia), in those same years tens of millions had died in wars and civil strife in Asia, Africa, the Middle East, and Latin America. The explosion of virulent nationalism after the end of the Cold War posed new challenges to the Council. The pressure for humanitarian assistance and for intervention in Somalia, Bosnia, and elsewhere complicated its mission, which was originally intended to preserve peace among the sovereign states, not internally within states. But it accepted the new responsibilities, and its peacekeeping functions grew in scope and magnitude once the Cold War ended. Supporters of its expanding role even urged early intervention to prevent conflicts from escalating. They called also for rapid deployment forces, a "standby army," with contingents drawn from the member states, as once envisaged. But many governments and private citizens were apprehensive about surrendering authority to the Council, or to the United Nations secretary-general, and about losing control over their own military and foreign policy.

The original roster of five permanent members—the victors in the Second World War—had changed only in 1971 when the People's Republic of China replaced Nationalist China and in 1991 when Russia succeeded to the seat of the dissolved U.S.S.R. But the political and economic reordering of the world spurred repeated proposals that Germany and Japan be given permanent seats (without veto power), so that they might exercise international responsibilities commensurate with their economic resources and not be vulnerable to criticism for their "checkbook diplomacy." There were lingering historical grounds for opposition, and Germany and Japan would have to amend their constitutions to participate in military peacekeeping activities, yet it seemed only a matter of time before they and perhaps other nations might serve as permanent members.

---

[40] See p. 869.

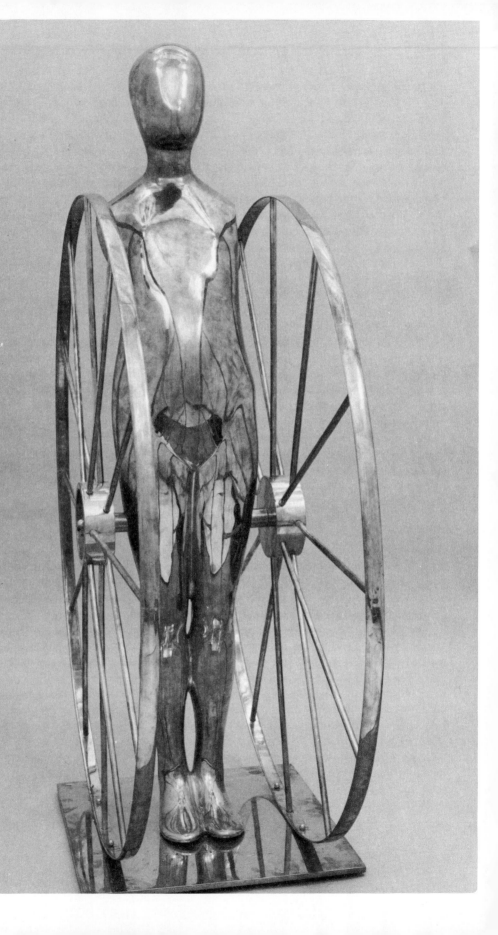

The United Nations counted 51 members at its inception in 1945. It grew dramatically from the 1960s on with the admission of the independent states emerging from the former European colonial empires. By the mid-1990s, after the breakup of the U.S.S.R., Yugoslavia, and Czechoslovakia (which together accounted for about 20 new states) and the addition of a few more former colonies, it counted over 180 members and could be expected to add more. Macedonia, once part of Yugoslavia, became the 184th member in 1993. When small colonies achieved independence, as in the case of the Caribbean or Pacific island dependencies, many of these new states had populations no larger than those of a small American or European city. St. Kitts and Nevis, a former British colony in the Caribbean, admitted to the UN in 1983, had 40,000 people. Andorra, long jointly ruled by France and Spain, a new member in 1993, had 56,000. The eighty or so smallest members of the UN represented less than 10 percent of the earth's population.

It was in the General Assembly that the new states mainly exercised their authority. Regardless of size, each member deliberated and voted in full equality with larger nations. Over the years the General Assembly served as a forum for the developing nations to discuss their grievances against the industrial world. Many of the social and economic issues raised were significant, many politically inspired. Several of the UN's smaller agencies, part of a growing international bureaucracy, played positive roles in dealing with population, health, and social welfare issues. After the Cold War, the developing nations showed signs of tempering their anti-Westernism, but they continued to insist that their enormous needs be recognized and not diverted by other priorities.

Debate went on in the United Nations and elsewhere over the interpretation of human rights. The Universal Declaration of Human Rights, adopted by the UN in 1948, had focused on political and civil rights, emphasizing such rights as protection from arbitrary arrest or imprisonment, or torture. Over the years pressure mounted to broaden this largely political definition to include economic rights, meaning social and economic human needs within each country and the right to development assistance internationally. The debate sharpened because it had become the practice of the United States and other industrial nations to withhold development assistance from repressive regimes. In the 1990s a number of developing states proclaimed an "absolute" right to development assistance and rejected the linkage to political freedom. They further contended that the political and civil rights generally described as "universal" were really "Western" and should be modified to fit the culture, history, religions, and phases of

WHEEL MAN
by Ernest Trova (American, 1927–   )
Shown here is a somewhat dehumanized, life-size bronze figure of a human being of no particular sex, age, race, culture, or environment. Compressed between the two wheels, it seems to present humanity as the victim of its own complicated inventions. The wheels also symbolize the blind ups and downs of fortune. The date 1965 is inscribed on the base, and the whole sad assemblage seems to say that human history and civilization have not exactly turned out as was once more hopefully expected. Ernest Trova, though widely exhibited internationally, is an American sculptor living in St. Louis. Courtesy of the Solomon R. Guggenheim Museum, John V. Powers Fund.

development of other parts of the world. Equality for women, for example, could have different meaning in an Islamic country, as could the rights of children in traditional patriarchal societies. But many in the international community, including non-Westerners, continued to maintain that human rights, no matter how difficult to define, of Western origin or not, represented a common core of values to protect the individual against the state. Respect for cultural pluralism, they argued, should not serve as a cover for repression or discrimination. The inclusion of human needs in the definition of human rights, however, won adherents.

Even as the UN assumed a larger role, it was still far from an emergent world government. Its goals were those formulated in 1945: to prevent the scourge of war, advance human rights, promote equality, protect the independence of nations, encourage social progress, raise living standards, and work for peace and security. But the world's nations, large and small, were not ready to subordinate their national interests to any international organization. And national-ism itself emerged in the new era as a powerful force beyond most reasonable expectations. The United States and the other major powers still bore the principal responsibility for peacekeeping and peacemaking in a troubled globe. Without their armed power, the United Nations was powerless. The world was still fumbling its way toward an international community of sovereign states, unsure of how to secure peace, security, and justice for the world's peoples.

The major countries were beset with economic, social, and political difficulties in the mid-1990s. Western Europe was suffering from economic slowdown, political challenges, and social dilemmas, as was Japan in its way. In Eastern Europe the transition to market economies and democracy had caused so much pain and discontent that electorates were voting former Communists back into parliamentary majorities or, as in Russia, lending support to revanchist expansionist ultranationalists. China was barely recovered from the ferment of 1989, still facing dissidence, but it could be expected to make its not inconsiderable weight felt in world affairs. Meanwhile the world's trouble spots grew in number. Whether the latest eruptions would occur in the Middle East, Africa, the Balkans, Asia, or as yet unidentified places was a matter of conjecture. The international community could hope only to keep conflict and tensions within bounds, overcome old antagonisms, and nourish the soil in which international cooperation might grow.

The Population Explosion, Environment, the Future of Humanity

Of all the nonpolitical developments in the second half of the twentieth century one of the most spectacular was the rapid growth of the world's population. After 1950, as a result of medical discoveries, improved health and sanitation measures, and more efficient food production and distribution, death rates declined dramati-cally, but without a counterbalancing drop in birth rates. The number of human beings grew so rapidly, and at so fast a rate, that demographers spoke of a population explosion. It took the world several millions of years to reach the 1 billion mark, sometime about 1830. At the opening of the twentieth century the global population was just over 1.5 billion and in 1950, when the takeoff began, 2.5 billion. By 1960, the figure was 3 billion; fifteen years later, 4 billion; and

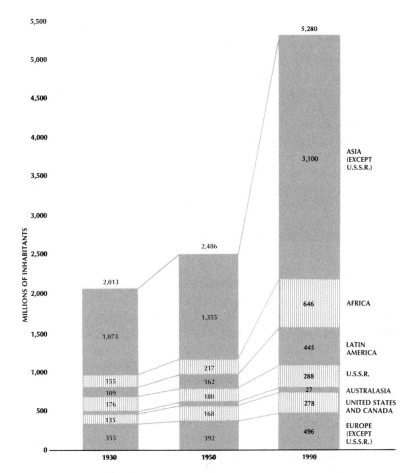

THE POPULATION EXPLOSION

In the late 1980s the world's population passed the 5 billion mark. It had doubled in less than half a century, and more than doubled in Asia, Africa, and Latin America. It was projected to exceed 6 billion before the year 2000. Growth was most rapid in the poorer countries, where it contributed to chronic social unrest and political instability. The wealthier or "developed" part of the world, including Japan and other parts of East Asia, had a slower growth rate, but in 1990 it comprised only about a quarter of the world's population.

Comparison may be made with the table on page 588, where the categories are somewhat different, being designed to show the rise and decline in the proportion of "Europeans" in the global total. But the table shows no doubling of world population in any half-century from 1650 to 1950, so that the recent increase is truly an "explosion." Such a rate of increase cannot continue indefinitely; the question is whether it can be slowed down before the earth's resources are overstrained.

Source: *United Nations Demographic Yearbook.*

only twelve years later, in 1987, 5 billion. The total was projected to reach 6 billion in 1997, in no more than ten years. The time required to add a billion people to the world's population was growing strikingly shorter. The annual growth rate, close to 2 percent, meant the addition of 90 million people each year. Demographers pushed well into the twenty-first century the time and estimated figure at which stabilization might be achieved and they debated the maximum numbers that the earth's resources could sustain.

The impact of falling death rates on population growth was demonstrated in India, where the death rate in 1990 was half the 1950 figure, and the population rose from 350 million in 1950 to an estimated 900 million. Adding 16 million people annually, India's population could exceed 1 billion by the end of the twentieth century. If China maintained its slower growth rate, India could surpass it as the world's most populous nation. China and India together accounted for two-fifths of the global population.

The population increase in the second half of the twentieth century was largely a phenomenon of the developing world in Asia, Africa, the Middle East, and Latin America, where three-fourths of the world's population lived, and where birth rates were highest. In North America and in Europe natural increase was low. Industrialization, urban life, and social pressures for smaller families had begun to slow long-term birth rates ever since the late nineteenth century.[41] Measured against the dramatic rise in global figures, the population of Europe and North America translated into a shrinking share of world population. In the developing countries, and especially in sub-Saharan Africa where the population was increasing at 3 percent annually, population growth threatened to cancel economic advances. No ready solution was in sight. Contraceptive technology, which made many advances, was not always available. Several of the world's major religions continued to ban artificial birth control, numerous societies restricted educational and vocational opportunities for women, and traditional patterns of life in many parts of the world, especially the poorest, encouraged large families for sustenance and support.

As grave a threat as global population growth posed for the world's resources, the planet faced other potential dangers. From 1950 to 1990 world industrial production grew fivefold, burning coal, oil, and natural gas, and consuming a variety of synthetic chemicals, all of which emitted heat-trapping gases into the atmosphere. Some scientists and aroused citizens believed that these emissions were eroding the protective ozone layer that shields the earth from excessive solar heat and radiation, and could produce a warming of the earth's climate and other serious consequences. The ongoing debate, though still inconclusive, prompted governments and industry to introduce regulatory measures.

Industrial pollution also caused the acid rain that laid waste to forests, lakes, and rivers. Severe environmental damage in the former U.S.S.R. and Soviet-bloc nations confirmed that pollution was not confined to any single economic system; economic planners there had pressed development with no regard for the ecological consequences. Developing nations also paid little attention to their environment. Under the pressure of expanding population and rapid urbanization, they permitted the slashing and burning of tropical forests for ranching, other

---

[41] See pp. 589–591.

commercial purposes, and resettlement. Arable acreage declined; pasture land turned into desert. In the four decades from 1950 to 1990, the world lost one-fifth its topsoil and one-fifth its tropical rain forests. Nowhere was this more striking than in Latin America and Africa. The partial loss of the Amazon Forest in Brazil dramatized the extent of the damage.

From the 1980s, a newly sensitized world began to speak of sustainable growth rates, growth that could be maintained without the destruction of humanity's natural habitat. Alternative forms of energy, some as old as the sun and the wind, others new, like nuclear energy (although expensive and still dangerous in some respects), were proposed. As awareness of ecological dangers grew, grass-roots environmental organizations multiplied, and in several countries turned into ''Green'' political parties. Many nations pledged measures to counter the threat of environmental deterioration, but opposition from vested economic interests and conflicts with plans for economic growth slowed their adoption.

Population growth and the threat to the environment added to the world's concerns as it approached the twenty-first century. The problems were many—the social implications of science and technology, the independence of nations, the rivalry among nations, and the quest within nations for freedom, dignity, and economic well-being. All were aspects of one overriding problem. How could human beings in each generation, regardless of sex, color, creed, religion, or nationality—beings said by some to be made in the image of God, by others to have a natural right to liberty and happiness, by still others to have the freedom to create meaning in a meaningless universe—live out their lives in peace, fulfill their destiny, and pass on their heritage to future generations?

These concluding chapters began with the image of a cataclysm. The analogy is still pertinent. A cataclysm, as already observed, is not a time of downfall only. Mountains crumble, but others are thrust up. Lands vanish, but others rise from the sea. So it is with the political and social cataclysm of our times. Old landmarks are worn down. Empires pass away; new nations arise in their place. Subjugated peoples regain independence. Rigid ideologies are undermined. The ascendancy of Europe, the West, and the white race closes; they learn to negotiate with others, not rule them. Everywhere there is a fluidity in social relationships. Women and minorities struggle for equal places in society. But social justice and peace remain elusive goals. The gap between rich and poor among nations, and often within nations, is not easily overcome. Diseases beyond immediate control, natural catastrophes, and armed conflict exact their toll. Resurgent nationalism feeds intolerance and hatred. Never has war been so potentially destructive, and the menace of a nuclear war that would blight much of civilization wanes but does not disappear. Uncontrolled economic development threatens the environment, and population growth presses on natural resources. New forms of intervention are needed to sustain the earth's billions. But there is a growing global recognition of all these concerns. To close this long history on a note of placidity would indeed be inappropriate, but so, too, would it be to close it on a note of doom.

APPENDIXES, BIBLIOGRAPHY, AND INDEX

APPENDIX I: CHRONOLOGICAL TABLES

TABLE ONE: TO 1517

EUROPE AS A WHOLE: POLITICAL AND SOCIAL	EUROPE AS A WHOLE: THOUGHT AND LETTERS	BRITISH ISLES
	500–300 B.C. Classical Greek civilization: Plato, Aristotle	
146 B.C. Greeks conquered by Roman Republic		
31 B.C. Roman Empire		
306–337 Emperor Constantine: toleration of Christianity	1st century B.C.–1st century A.D. Classical Roman civilization: Cicero, Vergil	43–410 Roman Empire in Britain
5th century: Germanic invasions	426 Saint Augustine's *City of God*	
476 Roman Empire in West ends		596 Conversion of Anglo-Saxons
7th century: spread of Islam		
800 Coronation of Charlemagne		871–899 Alfred the Great
9th century: Norse and Magyar invasions		
1054 Schism of West and East: Roman Catholic church and Orthodox Eastern church	1033–1109 Anselm	1066 Norman conquest
1073–1085 Pope Gregory VII	1079–1142 Abelard	
1095–1099 First Crusade	12th century: coming of Arabic and Greek science	12th century: development of the monarchy in England
12th century: rise of towns		
1147–1221 Crusades: Second–Fifth	12th–13th century: universities, scholasticism	
1198–1216 Pope Innocent III		
	1215 Fourth Lateran Council	1215 Magna Carta
13th century: rise of parliaments	1267–1273 Thomas Aquinas' *Summa Theologica*	
1294–1303 Pope Boniface VIII		1295 Model Parliament

WESTERN EUROPE	CENTRAL EUROPE	EASTERN EUROPE
		6th–4th centuries B.C. Greek city-states
		356–323 B.C. Alexander the Great
		4th–1st centuries B.C. Hellenistic Age
31 B.C.–476 Roman Empire	31 B.C.–476 Roman Empire in western and southern Germany	31 B.C.–1453 Roman Empire in East
		330 Constantinople founded (formerly Byzantium)
496 Conversion of Franks		395–1453 Eastern Roman (Byzantine) Empire
	568 Founding of Venice	
711 Muslims in Spain		
732 Muslim defeat at Tours		
768–814 Charlemagne	768–814 Charlemagne	
987–1792 Capetian monarchy in France	*962–1806 Holy Roman Empire*	
		10th century: conversion of Swedes, Poles, Hungarians to Rome; Russians to Constantinople
	1056–1106 Emperor Henry IV	
		1001–1918 Kingdom of Hungary
	1075–1122 Investiture struggle	1054 Schism of East and West: Orthodox Eastern church
12th century: development of the monarchy in France		
		12th century: Teutonic Knights in Prussia
1208 Albigensian Crusade	13th century: failure of the Empire to organize Germany and Italy	
		13th century: conversion of East Baltic peoples to Rome
1309–1378 Babylonian Captivity: papacy in Avignon		
		1236 Tartars in Russia
	1356 Golden Bull	
		1389 Turks in Balkan Peninsula

EUROPE AS A WHOLE: POLITICAL AND SOCIAL	EUROPE AS A WHOLE: THOUGHT AND LETTERS	BRITISH ISLES
1348–1350 Black Death	1328–1384 John Wycliffe	1337–1453 Hundred Years' War
1378–1417 Schism of the West: papacy in Rome and Avignon		
1414–1418 Council of Constance	1415 Death of John Huss	1381 Wat Tyler's rebellion
1453 Roman Empire in East ends	15th century: Italian Renaissance	1455–1485 Wars of the Roses
	1452–1519 Leonardo da Vinci	
	1454–1455 Printing; Gutenberg Bible	
1492 Columbus reaches America	1466–1536 Erasmus	*1485–1603 The Tudors*
1498 Portuguese reach India	1513 Machiavelli's *The Prince*	1485–1509 Henry VII
1517 Protestant Reformation begins	1517 Luther's 95 Theses	1509–1547 Henry VIII

TABLE TWO: 1517–1618

EUROPE AS A WHOLE: POLITICAL AND SOCIAL	EUROPE AS A WHOLE: THOUGHT AND LETTERS	BRITISH ISLES
1517 Protestant Reformation begins	1517 Luther's 95 Theses	1509–1547 Henry VIII
1519–1648 Habsburg supremacy		
1519–1556 Charles V		
1519–1522 Magellan circumnavigates globe		1521 Henry VIII's *Defense of Seven Sacraments*
1529 Turks besiege Vienna	1530 Loyola's *Spiritual Exercises*	
1531 First stock exchange at Antwerp	1534 Luther's German Bible	1534 Act of Supremacy
	1536 Calvin's *Institutes of the Christian Religion*	1536–1539 Dissolution of monasteries
		1539 Six Articles
1540 Founding of Jesuits	1543 Copernicus' *Revolutions of Heavenly Orbs* and Vesalius' *Structure of the Human Body*	
1541–1564 Calvin at Geneva		1547–1553 Edward VI
1545–1563 Council of Trent	1550–1650 Golden age of Spanish literature	1553–1558 Mary I
1555 Peace of Augsburg		
1556–1598 Philip II of Spain		1558–1603 Elizabeth I
		1559 Knox and the Reformation in Scotland
	1561–1626 Francis Bacon	

WESTERN EUROPE	CENTRAL EUROPE	EASTERN EUROPE
1337–1453 Hundred Years' War		
1378–1417 Schism in church: papacy in Rome and Avignon		
	1420–1431 Hussite Wars	
1412–1431 Joan of Arc		
	1438–1918 Habsburg emperors	
		1453 Turks take Constantinople; end of Byzantine Empire
1461–1489 Louis XI of France		
1479–1516 Ferdinand and Isabella of Spain		
1494 French invasion of Italy		1480 Ivan the Great ends Tartar control over Russia
1515–1547 Francis I of France	1519–1556 Charles V	

WESTERN EUROPE	CENTRAL EUROPE	EASTERN EUROPE
1515–1547 Francis I of France	1519–1556 Charles V Emperor	
1516 Concordat of Bologna		
		1520–1566 Suleiman the Magnificent
	1521 Luther banned	
	1526 Charles V at war with Turks	1526 Turks occupy Hungary
	1529 Turks besiege Vienna	
		1533–1584 Ivan the Terrible, first Tsar of Russia
1536 Franco-Turkish alliance against Charles V		1535 First French capitulations in Turkey
1547–1559 Henry II of France	1546–1547 Schmalkaldic War	
		1553 English in White Sea
1556–1598 Philip II of Spain	1555 Peace of Augsburg	
	1556–1564 Ferdinand I	
1559–1589 Weakness of monarchy in France		
1562–1598 Wars of Religion in France		

EUROPE AS A WHOLE: POLITICAL AND SOCIAL	EUROPE AS A WHOLE: THOUGHT AND LETTERS	BRITISH ISLES
		1563 The 39 Articles
	1564–1642 Galileo	
	1564–1616 Shakespeare	
		1569 Norfolk's rebellion
1571 Defeat of Turks at Lepanto		
	1576 Bodin's *Republic*	
	1580 Montaigne's *Essays*	1577 Alliance with Nether- lands
	1582 Gregorian calendar	
1588 Spanish Armada		1588 Spanish Armada
	1596–1650 Descartes	
		1603–1714 The Stuarts
		1603–1625 James I
1607 English found Virginia		
1608 French found Quebec		
1609 Spanish found Santa Fé		
1612 Dutch found New York	1611 King James' Bible	

TABLE THREE: 1618–1714

EUROPE AS A WHOLE: POLITICAL AND SOCIAL	EUROPE AS A WHOLE: THOUGHT AND LETTERS	BRITISH ISLES
	1561–1626 Francis Bacon	*1603–1714 The Stuarts*
	1564–1642 Galileo	1603–1625 James I
	1596–1650 Descartes	
1618–1648 Thirty Years' War		
17th century: English, French, Dutch in America; Dutch in South Africa and Indonesia	1623–1662 Pascal	1625–1649 Charles I
	17th century: flowering of English, French, and Dutch literature	
1619 First African slaves in Virginia	1625 Grotius' *Law of War and Peace*	1637 Ship money case
		1640–1660 Long Parliament
	1642–1727 Isaac Newton	1642–1648 Puritan Revolution and Civil War
1648 Peace of Westphalia		1649 Execution of Charles I
		1649–1658 Rule of Cromwell
		1649–1653 Commonwealth
1650 World population estimate: 500 million		1653–1660 Protectorate
	1660s Beginnings of scientific societies	1660 Restoration
1661–1715 Age of Louis XIV		1660–1685 Charles II
		1670s Rise of Whigs and Tories
		1673 Test Act

WESTERN EUROPE	CENTRAL EUROPE	EASTERN EUROPE
	1564–1576 Maximilian II	
1566 Netherlands revolt begins		
1572 Massacre of St. Bartholomew		1571 Defeat of Turks at Lepanto
1574–1589 Henry III of France	1576–1612 Rudolf II	1574 Turks take Tunis
1589–1792 Bourbons in France		
1589–1610 Henry IV of France		1604–1613 Russia: Time of Troubles
1598 Edict of Nantes		
	1608 Protestant Union	
	1609 Catholic League	
1610–1643 Louis XIII of France	1612–1619 Matthias	*1613–1917 Romanovs in Russia*
	1618 Thirty Years' War begins	1613–1645 Michael Romanov, Tsar

WESTERN EUROPE	CENTRAL EUROPE	EASTERN EUROPE
1610–1643 Louis XIII of France	1618–1648 Thirty Years' War	*1613–1917 Romanovs in Russia*
	1619 Emperor Ferdinand II	1613–1645 Tsar Michael Romanov
	1620 Battle of White Mountain	
1624–1642 Richelieu		17th century: spread of serfdom in Russia and Eastern Europe
1629 Peace of Alais	1629 Edict of Restitution	
1635 France in Thirty Years' War		
1642–1661 Mazarin	1640–1688 Frederick William, Great Elector of Brandenburg	
1643–1715 Louis XIV of France		
1648 Peace of Westphalia	1648 Peace of Westphalia	
1652–1674 Three Anglo-Dutch Wars		
1659 Peace of Pyrenees	17th and 18th centuries: decline in German states	
1665–1700 Charles II of Spain		1667 Russian church reforms: Old Believers
1667–1668 Louis XIV's War of Devolution		1670 Revolt of Stephen Razin in Russia
1672–1678 Louis XIV's Dutch war		
		1682–1725 Peter the Great

EUROPE AS A WHOLE: POLITICAL AND SOCIAL	EUROPE AS A WHOLE: THOUGHT AND LETTERS	BRITISH ISLES
1683 Turks threaten Vienna		
		1685–1688 James II
	1687 Newton's *Principia*	
		1688 "Glorious Revolution"
1689–1697 War of League of Augsburg		1688–1702 William and Mary
	1690 Locke's *Treatises on Government; Human Understanding*	
	1697 Bayle's *Dictionary*	
1701–1714 War of Spanish Succession		1702–1714 Anne
		1707 Union of England and Scotland: United Kingdom of Great Britain
1713–1714 Treaties of Utrecht and Rastadt		

TABLE FOUR: 1714–1815

EUROPE AS A WHOLE: POLITICAL AND SOCIAL	EUROPE AS A WHOLE: THOUGHT AND LETTERS	BRITISH ISLES
1713–1714 Treaties of Utrecht and Rastadt	18th century: Age of Enlightenment	
		1714–1837 Hanoverians
		1714–1727 George I
		1720 South Sea Bubble
		1721 Walpole's ministry
1740–1789 Enlightened despotism in Europe	1740–1789 Enlightenment at its peak	1727–1760 George II
		1739 War of Jenkins' Ear
1740–1763 British-French colonial wars: America, India	1740–1760 Voltaire at his height	
1740–1748 War of Austrian Succession	1748 Montesquieu's *Spirit of Laws*	1745 Jacobite Rebellion
1750 World population estimate: 700 million		
1756 Diplomatic Revolution	1751–1768 French *Encyclopedia*	
		1760–1820 George III
1756–1763 Seven Years' War	1761 Rousseau's *Social Contract*	
1763 Treaties of Paris and Hubertusburg: British supremacy in Canada and India		1769 Watt's steam engine
		1769 Arkwright's waterframe

WESTERN EUROPE	CENTRAL EUROPE	EASTERN EUROPE
	1683 Turks threaten Vienna	1683 Turks threaten Vienna
1685 Revocation of Edict of Nantes		1683–1718 Habsburg victories over Turks
1689–1697 War of League of Augsburg	1697–1733 Augustus of Saxony King of Poland	1697–1718 Charles XII of Sweden
		1699 Austro-Turkish Peace of Karlowitz
1700–1931 Bourbons in Spain 1700–1746 Philip V of Spain 1701–1714 War of Spanish Succession	*1701–1918 Hohenzollern kings in Prussia* 1701–1713 Frederick I of Prussia	
		1709 Battle of Poltava

WESTERN EUROPE	CENTRAL EUROPE	EASTERN EUROPE
	1711–1740 Charles VI of Austria	1682–1725 Peter the Great
1715–1774 Louis XV of France 1715–1723 Regency in France 1720 Mississippi Bubble	1713–1740 Frederick William I of Prussia 1713–1740 Austria: Pragmatic Sanction	
		1721 Russo-Swedish Treaty of Nystadt
18th century: culmination of "Old Regime" in France	1740–1786 Frederick II of Prussia 1740–1780 Maria Theresa of Austria 1740–1745 Silesian Wars	1733–1738 War of Polish Succession 1739 Austro-Turkish Peace of Belgrade
	1756 Habsburg-Bourbon Alliance 1756–1763 Seven Years' War	
		1762–1796 Catherine II of Russia 1768–1774 Russo-Turkish War

EUROPE AS A WHOLE: POLITICAL AND SOCIAL	EUROPE AS A WHOLE: THOUGHT AND LETTERS	BRITISH ISLES
1776 American Declaration of Independence 1776–1783 War of American Independence	1776 Adam Smith's *Wealth of Nations*	1776 American Revolution
1789 French Revolution begins	1784 Herder's *Philosophy of History of Mankind* 1790 Burke's *Reflections on the French Revolution* 1790s Spread of French revolutionary ideas Beginnings of romanticism	1782–1806 Ministries of William Pitt the Younger
1792–1815 Revolutionary and Napoleonic wars		
1792–1797 War of First Coalition 1798–1801 War of Second Coalition		1793–1814 War with France 1798 Rebellion of Ireland 1801 Union of Great Britain and Ireland 1802–1803 Peace of Amiens
1803–1805 War of Third Coalition 1804–1814 "Grand Empire" 1806–1812 Continental System	1804–1811 Napoleonic codes	
1809–1811 Napoleon at height 1812 Invasion of Russia, and retreat 1812 U.S.–British War 1813 Battle of Leipzig 1814–1815 Congress of Vienna 1815 Waterloo		1808–1814 Peninsular War in Spain 1814 Alliance of Chaumont

TABLE FIVE: 1815–1871*

WORLD AS A WHOLE	EUROPE AS A WHOLE	BRITISH ISLES
		1760–1820 George III 1760–1830 Beginnings of modern industry
1806–1825 Latin American countries win independence	1814–1815 Congress of Vienna 1814–1848 Influence of Metternich	1807 British slave trade ended 1815 Corn Laws: higher taxes on grain imports
	1818 Congress of Aix-la-Chapelle	
	1820 Congress of Troppau 1822 Congress of Verona	1819 Repression: Peterloo massacre, Six Acts

* Note change in column headings.

WESTERN EUROPE	CENTRAL EUROPE	EASTERN EUROPE
		1772 First Partition of Poland
		1773–1774 Pugachev Rebellion
1774–1793 Louis XVI of France		1774 Russo-Turkish Treaty of Kuchuk Kainarji
1778 French-American Alliance	1780–1790 Joseph II of Austria	
1789 French Revolution begins	1780s Cultural revival of Germany	1787–1792 Russo-Turkish War
1792 First French Republic established		1793 Second Partition of Poland
		1795 Third Partition of Poland
1793–1794 The Terror	1797 Treaty of Campo Formio	
1795–1799 Directory		1796–1801 Paul I of Russia
1799 Bonaparte's coup	1798–1814 French predominance	
1799–1804 Consulate		1801–1825 Alexander I of Russia
1804–1814 Napoleon I: The Empire		
1807 Peace of Tilsit	1806 End of Holy Roman Empire	1806–1812 Russo-Turkish War
	1806 Confederation of the Rhine	1807 Franco-Russian Alliance
		1812 Napoleon's invasion of Russia
1814 Restoration of Bourbons	1813–1814 German War of Liberation: Leipzig	
1815 Hundred Days; Waterloo		

WESTERN EUROPE	CENTRAL EUROPE	EASTERN EUROPE
		1801–1825 Alexander I of Russia
1814–1830 Restoration: Bourbons in France	1814–1848 Influence of Metternich	
1814–1824 Louis XVIII of France		
	1819 Carlsbad Decrees	

WORLD AS A WHOLE	EUROPE AS A WHOLE	BRITISH ISLES
1823 Monroe Doctrine		
	1830 Revolutions	
		1832 First Reform Bill
1839–1842 First Anglo-Chinese (Opium) War		1833 Slavery abolished
		1837–1901 Victoria: the Victorian Age
		1838–1848 Chartism
		1842 Mines Act
1842–1858 "Treaty System" established in China		1846 Repeal of Corn Laws
		1847 Ten Hours Act
	1848 Revolutions; Marx and Engels' *Communist Manifesto*	
1850 World population estimate: 1.2 billion		1850–1873 Golden age of British capitalism: free trade
1850–1864 Taiping Rebellion in China		
1854–1868 Japan opened to West	1854–1856 Crimean War	
1857–1858 Indian Mutiny: Sepoy Rebellion		
1859 Darwin's *Origin of Species*	1859 Austro-Italian War	
1860 Russians found Vladivostok		
1861–1865 American Civil War		
1863–1867 French in Mexico		
	1864–1876 First International	
	1866 Austro-Prussian War	
1867 Dominion of Canada	1867 Marx's *Capital*	1867 Extension of suffrage
1868 Meiji Restoration in Japan		1868–1874 Gladstone's first ministry
1870 Vatican Council I	1870–1871 Franco-Prussian War	
	1871–1918 German Empire	

TABLE SIX: 1871–1919

WORLD AS A WHOLE	EUROPE AS A WHOLE	BRITISH ISLES
1871 Darwin's *Descent of Man*		
		1874–1880 Disraeli's ministry
	1878 Congress of Berlin	
	1879 Dual Alliance: Germany, Austria	

WESTERN EUROPE	CENTRAL EUROPE	EASTERN EUROPE
1824–1830 Charles X of France		
		1825 Decembrist revolt in Russia
1830 Revolution in France and Belgium	1830 Revolutionary flurries	1825–1855 Nicholas I of Russia
		1828–1829 Russo-Turkish War
1830–1848 July Monarchy in France: Louis Philippe		1829 Independence of Greece
		1830 Revolution in Poland fails
1848 Revolution: Second French Republic	1848 Revolution: Frankfurt Assembly	
1852 Napoleon III: Second French Empire	1848–1916 Francis Joseph of Austria	
		1853 Russo-Turkish War
		1854–1856 Crimean War
		1855–1881 Alexander II of Russia
		1858 Formation of Romania
	1859–1870 Unification of Italy	
1860 Free trade with England		
1860–1870 Liberal empire		1861 Emancipation of Russian serfs
	1862–1871 Bismarck: minister in Prussia	
	1866–1871 Unification of Germany	
	1867 Dual Monarchy in Austria-Hungary	
1870–1871 Franco-Prussian War; fall of Napoleon III		
1870–1940 Third Republic in France	*1871–1918 Hohenzollerns in Germany*	1870s Populism and Nihilism in Russia

WESTERN EUROPE	CENTRAL EUROPE	EASTERN EUROPE
1870–1940 Third Republic in France	1871–1918 German Empire	
1871 Paris Commune	1871–1890 Bismarck chancellor	1877 Russo-Turkish War
		1878 Autonomy of Bulgaria; independence of Serbia

WORLD AS A WHOLE	EUROPE AS A WHOLE	BRITISH ISLES
1880–1914 Height of imperialism	1880s Socialist parties founded: revisionism 1882 Triple Alliance: Germany, Austria, Italy	1880–1886 Gladstone's ministries
1883–1893 French in Indochina		
1885 Berlin Conference on Africa		1884 Extension of suffrage
1885–1898 Partition of Africa		
	1889 Second International	1892–1894 Gladstone's fourth ministry
1893 New Zealand: vote to women		
1894 Sino-Japanese War	1894 Franco-Russian Alliance	
1895–1898 Western imperialism in China		
1898 Spanish-American War		
1899–1902 Boer War		1899–1902 Boer War
1900 Freud's *Interpretation of Dreams*		1900–1906 Labour party formed
1900 World population estimate: 1.6 billion		
1902 Anglo-Japanese Alliance		
1902 Australia: vote to women		
		1903–1914 Women's suffrage movement
1904–1905 Russo-Japanese War	1904 Anglo-French Entente	
1905 Einstein's relativity theory	1905 Morocco crisis	
		1906–1911 Liberal party: social legislation, parliamentary reform
1907 Anglo-Russian division of Persia	1907 Triple Entente: Britain, France, Russia	
	1908 Bosnian crisis	
1910 Mexican Revolution		
1911 Chinese Revolution	1911 Agadir crisis	
	1912–1913 Balkan crises	
1914 Assassination of Francis Ferdinand		1914 Ulster crisis
1914–1918 First World War	1914–1918 First World War	1914–1918 First World War
		1916 Battle of Jutland
		1916–1922 Irish troubles
1917 United States enters war		
1917 Russian Revolution		
1919 Peace of Paris	1919 Peace of Paris	

TABLE SEVEN: 1919–1945

WORLD AS A WHOLE	EUROPE AS A WHOLE	BRITISH ISLES
		1918 Limited suffrage for women
1919 Peace of Paris	1919 Peace of Paris	
	1919 Parliamentary regimes in new states	
1920 U.S.: vote to women		

WESTERN EUROPE	CENTRAL EUROPE	EASTERN EUROPE
		1881 Assassination of Alexander II
	1888–1918 William II of Germany	
1894–1906 Dreyfus affair in France		1894–1917 Nicholas II, Tsar
1901–1905 Laic laws: separation of church and state in France	1898–1914 German naval race with England	
	1900ff. Growth of democracy: male suffrage in Austria 1907, etc.	
1900 Growth of democracy: male suffrage in Netherlands 1896, vote to women in Norway 1913		
		1903 Russian Social Democrats: Bolshevik-Menshevik split
		1904–1905 Russo-Japanese War
		1905 Revolution in Russia
		1906 Finland: vote to women
		1908 Bosnian crisis
		1908 Young Turk Revolution
		1912–1913 Balkan Wars
1914 Battle of Marne	1914 Assassination of Francis Ferdinand	1914 Battle of Tannenberg
1916 Verdun and the Somme		1917 Russia: fall of tsardom; Bolshevik Revolution
1918 Armistice	1918 Fall of German, Austro-Hungarian, and Ottoman empires	

WESTERN EUROPE	CENTRAL EUROPE	EASTERN EUROPE
		1918–1920 Russian Civil War
1919 Paris Peace Conference	1919 Treaty of Versailles	1919–1923 Greek-Turkish War
	1919–1933 Weimar Republic	
		1920–1943 Third International

WORLD AS A WHOLE	EUROPE AS A WHOLE	BRITISH ISLES
1922–1929 Prosperity decade	1922–1943 Fascism in Italy: Mussolini	1922 Irish Free State; British Northern Ireland
	1923 Turkish Republic	
	1923 Ruhr crisis	
		1924 First Labour government
	1925 Locarno Pact	
		1926 General Strike
		1926 Statute of Westminster: independence of Dominions
		1928 Full suffrage for women
1929 Stock market crash; Great Depression begins		1929–1931 Second Labour Government: MacDonald resignation
1930 World population estimate: 2 billion	1930s Great Depression	
1931–1932 Manchurian crisis	1930s Decline of democracy: rise of dictators	1931–1940 National Government
1931–1945 Japanese in China		1931 Britain leaves gold standard
		1932 Britain adopts tariffs; imperial preferences
1933–1945 F. D. Roosevelt's presidency	1933–1945 Hitler in Germany; Third Reich 12yrs .	
1933 Failure of World Economic Conference	1933–1938 Germany rearms, remilitarizes Rhineland, annexes Austria	
1935–1936 Ethiopian crisis		
1936–1939 Spanish Civil War	1936–1938 Popular Fronts: France, Spain	1936 Keynes' *General Theory of Employment, Interest, and Money*
	1936–1939 Spanish Civil War	1936 Edward VIII abdicates; George VI
	1937 Rome-Berlin-Tokyo Axis	
1938 Munich crisis	1938 Munich crisis	1938 Chamberlain: Munich Conference
1939–1945 Second World War	1939 Nazi-Soviet Pact	
	1939–1945 Second World War	1939–1945 Britain at war
1940–1942 Axis victories	1940–1945 German domination of Europe: racist policies: concentration camps, the Holocaust 5yrs .	1940 Churchill replaces Chamberlain
		1940 Battle of Britain
1941 Atlantic Charter		
1941 U.S.S.R., U.S. enter war		
1944–1945 Allies liberate Europe, Asia		
1945 Yalta and Potsdam conferences		
1945 U.S. drops atomic bombs: Hiroshima, Nagasaki		
1945 United Nations established	1945 Death of Hitler and of Mussolini	1945 Labour election victory

WESTERN EUROPE	CENTRAL EUROPE	EASTERN EUROPE
		1920–1921 Russo-Polish War
	1922–1943 Fascism in Italy: Mussolini	1921–1928 NEP in Russia
		1922 U.S.S.R. established
		1922 Russo-German treaty of Rapallo
	1923 French occupy Ruhr	
	1923 German currency crisis	
	1924 Dawes Plan	
		1924 Death of Lenin
		1924–1953 Stalin in power
		1927 Expulsion of Trotsky
1928–1974 Dictatorship in Portugal: Salazar		1928–1933 First Five-Year Plan; collectivization of agriculture
1930s Great Depression	1930s Great Depression	
1931 Spanish Republic		
1934 Stavisky riots in Paris	1933–1945 Germany: Third Reich, Hitler	1934 U.S.S.R. joins League of Nations
1936–1939 Spanish Civil War	1934 First Austrian crisis	
1936–1937 Popular Front government in France	1936 Germany remilitarizes Rhineland	1936 New Soviet constitution
		1936–1938 Soviet purges and trials
	1938 Germany annexes Austria	
	1938 Munich: Sudeten territory to Germany	
1939 Spain: Franco dictatorship established	1939 Germany annexes Czechoslovakia	1939 Nazi-Soviet Pact
1940 Fall of France	1939 Nazi-Soviet Pact	1939 Germany invades Poland
	1940–1944 Germany dominates Europe	1939–1940 Russo-Finnish War
1940–1944 German occupation of Western Europe		1939–1940 Soviets absorb Baltic states
		1941 Germany invades Russia
		1942–1943 Battle of Stalingrad
	1943 Allies invade Italy; fall of Mussolini	1943–1945 Russian offensives
1944–1945 Allies liberate Western Europe	1944–1945 Allied and Russian offensives	

TABLE EIGHT: 1945–1959*

WORLD AS A WHOLE	ASIA	AFRICA
1945 United Nations established: 51 members 1945 Death of Roosevelt 1945 Cold War begins	1945 Arab League formed: 7 states	1945 Colonial empires continue; only four independent African states
	1945–1946 Occupation of Japan; new constitution	
1945–1953 U.S.: Truman presidency		
	1946–1954 French war in Indochina	
1947 Truman Doctrine; Marshall Plan 1947 General Agreement on Tariffs and Trade (GATT) 1947–1949 End of British and Dutch empires in Asia 1948 UN: Declaration of Human Rights 1949 U.S.S.R. tests atomic bomb 1949 Communist triumph in China: People's Republic of China 1949 North Atlantic Treaty Organization (NATO) 1950 World population estimate: 2.5 billion; beginning of population explosion 1950–1953 Korean War	1947 India and Pakistan independent 1947–1964 India: Nehru prime minister 1948 Assassination of Gandhi 1948 Burma independent 1948 Israel established 1948 First Arab-Israeli War 1949 People's Republic of China established: Mao Zedong 1949 Dutch leave Indonesia 1950–1953 Korean War 1950s Japan: regains sovereignty; economic expansion 1950 China occupies Tibet	1948 South Africa: Nationalist party enforces apartheid
1951 Japanese peace treaty		1951 Libya independent
1952 U.S. tests hydrogen bomb		1952 Egypt: monarchy ousted; Nasser
1953 U.S.S.R. tests hydrogen bomb 1953 Genetics: DNA double-helix structure discovered 1953–1961 U.S.: Eisenhower presidency	1954 French leave Indochina; Vietnam partitioned: North and South Vietnam	1954–1962 French-Algerian War

* Note change in column headings.

WESTERN EUROPE	CENTRAL EUROPE	EASTERN EUROPE
1945–1946 Cold War: Europe divided	1945 Allied occupation of Germany: four zones	1945–1948 Communist satellites established
1945–1946 Woman suffrage in France, Italy, Belgium, etc.	1945 Italian elections: Christian Democratic coalitions begin	1946–1950 Soviet Fourth Five-Year Plan
1945–1951 Britain: Labour Government		
1945–1958 Fourth French Republic	1946 Italy: monarchy ends; Italian Republic	
1946 France: Monnet Plan	1946 Nuremberg trials	
	1946–1953 Italy: De Gasperi premier	
	1947 Peace treaties with Italy, Hungary, etc.	1947–1956 Cominform
1948–1952 Marshall Plan: European Recovery Plan	1948–1949 Berlin blockade and airlift	1948 Communist takeover in Czechoslovakia
	1948 Italian elections: Communist setback	1948–1955 Yugoslavia splits with U.S.S.R.: Tito
1949 Council of Europe	1949 German Federal Republic (West Germany); German Democratic Republic (East Germany)	1949 Council of Mutual Economic Assistance
1949 North Atlantic Treaty Organization (NATO)		
1950s West European economic expansion	1949–1963 West Germany: Adenauer chancellor; economic expansion	1949 U.S.S.R. tests atomic bomb
1951 European Coal and Steel Community (ECSC)		1951–1955 Soviet Fifth Five-Year Plan
1951–1964 British Conservatives in office		
1952 Britain: Elizabeth II succeeds George VI	1952 Allied occupation of West Germany ends	
1952 Britain tests atomic bomb		
	1953 East Berlin uprising	1953 Death of Stalin
		1953 Soviets test hydrogen bomb
		1953–1955 Malenkov premier; emergence of Khrushchev
1954 West German rearmament		
1954 French defeat in Indochina; war in Algeria begins		

WORLD AS A WHOLE	ASIA	AFRICA
	1955 Bandung Afro-Asian conference	
1956 Suez Canal crisis	1956 Suez crisis: second Arab-Israeli War	1956 Suez crisis: Britain, France, Israel vs. Egypt
		1956 Morocco, Tunisia independent
		1956–1972 Sudan independent: civil war
1957 U.S.S.R. launches space satellite: Sputnik		1957 Gold Coast (Ghana) gains independence: Nkrumah presidency, dictatorship
1957–1962 End of British, French, Belgian colonial empires in Africa		1957–1962 British colonies gain independence: Ghana, Nigeria, Kenya, Uganda, etc.
1958–1963 Pope John XXIII: reforms in Catholic church	1958–1960 China: Great Leap Forward; famine	1958 French colonies win self-government; French Community formed
	1958–1961 Syria, Egypt form United Arab Republic; union dissolved	1958–1961 Egypt and Syria form short-lived United Arab Republic
1959 Cuban revolution: Castro		

TABLE NINE: 1960–1975

WORLD AS A WHOLE	ASIA	AFRICA
1960 World population estimate: 3 billion		
1960–1962 Belgian Congo: civil war		1960–1962 Belgians leave Congo (Zaire): civil war
1960s U.S., U.S.S.R.: nuclear arms build-up	1960s North–South Vietnam War	1960 French colonies fully independent: Gabon, Senegal, Mali, etc.
1960s U.S.: civil rights movement; women's liberation movement		
1961–1973 U.S. involvement in Vietnam War		
1961–1963 U.S.: Kennedy presidency		
1961 U.S.S.R. and U.S. space flights; Soviets launch first man in space		1961 South Africa leaves Commonwealth: white minority government
		1961–1975 Portuguese colonies: war for independence
1962 U.S.–Soviet Cuban missile crisis	1962 Chinese-Soviet rift	1962 Algeria independent
1962 Chinese-Soviet rift		
1962–1965 Vatican Council II: reforms in Catholic church	1962 Chinese-Indian border war	

WESTERN EUROPE	CENTRAL EUROPE	EASTERN EUROPE
1955 West Germany in NATO	1955 Austrian peace treaty	1955 Warsaw Pact
		1956 Khrushchev denounces Stalin's crimes
		1956 Polish, Hungarian risings crushed
1957 Rome treaties: European Economic Community (EEC, or Common Market): 6 members	1957 Rome treaties: European Economic Community (EEC)	1957 U.S.S.R. launches Sputnik
		1958 U.S.S.R. deploys first intercontinental ballistic missile
1958 Fifth French Republic: de Gaulle first president		1958–1964 Khrushchev in power
1959 British form European Free Trade Association		

WESTERN EUROPE	CENTRAL EUROPE	EASTERN EUROPE
1960 Belgium withdraws from Congo		
1960 France becomes fourth nuclear power		
1960s Spain: industrialization		1960s Liberalization in Soviet satellites
		1960s Industrialization in German Democratic Republic, Poland, Hungary, etc.
	1961 Berlin Wall built	1961 U.S.S.R. launches first man in space
		1961 Soviets test 50-megaton nuclear bomb
1962 French leave Algeria		1962–1963 Chinese Communists split with U.S.S.R.

WORLD AS A WHOLE	ASIA	AFRICA
1963–1978 Pope Paul VI		1963 Organization of African Unity formed: 32 states
1963 Partial nuclear test ban agreement		
1963 U.S.: President Kennedy assassinated		
1963–1969 U.S.: Johnson presidency		
1964 U.S.: Civil Rights Act	1964 Death of Nehru	
1964–1965 Vietnam War: U.S. involvement deepens	1964 Vietnam War: U.S. commits air and ground forces	
	1964 China tests atomic bomb; becomes fifth nuclear power	
	1964 Palestine Liberation Organization (PLO) formed	
1965 United Nations: 110 members		1965 Rhodesia: white minority government proclaims independence from Britain
	1966 Indonesia: Sukarno ousted; Suharto	1966 UN supports Namibia (formerly South African mandate) in independence struggle
	1966–1969 Chinese Cultural Revolution	
	1966–1977 Indira Gandhi: first ministry	1966 Nkrumah overthrown in Ghana
	1967 Arab-Israeli war: Six Day War	1967–1970 Nigeria suppresses Biafra secession
1968 Student demonstrations: U.S., France, Mexico, Japan, etc.	1968 Chinese-Soviet border clashes in Manchuria	1960s– Newly independent states: civil wars, dictatorships, etc.
1968 nonproliferation treaty		
1968 Vietnam War continues; peace talks in Paris		
1969–1974 U.S.: Nixon presidency; détente diplomacy		
1969 American astronauts land on moon	1969 Vietnam: death of Ho Chi Minh	
1970s American and Soviet space explorations, manned and unmanned		
1970s East-West détente		
1970s Voting age lowered to 18: U.S., Britain, France, etc.		
1971 People's Republic of China in UN; replaces Taiwan	1971 Bangladesh: secession from Pakistan	1971–1979 Uganda: repressive regime of Idi Amin
1972 U.S.–Soviet Strategic Arms Limitation Treaty (SALT I)		
1973 U.S. troops leave Vietnam		

WESTERN EUROPE	CENTRAL EUROPE	EASTERN EUROPE
1963 EEC: de Gaulle vetoes British entry	1963–1968 West Germany: Erhard succeeds Adenauer; Christian Democratic coalition continues	
1964–1970 Britain: Labour in office		1964 Khrushchev ousted 1964–1982 Brezhnev in power: military and naval build-up
1965 France: de Gaulle reelected president		
1967 European Community (EC): reorganization 1968 France: near-revolutionary student and labor demonstrations	1967–1974 Greece: military dictatorship	1968 Soviets invade Czecho-slovakia; end liberal Czech regime; Brezhnev Doctrine
1969 France: de Gaulle resigns presidency 1969– Northern Ireland: Catholic-Protestant clashes 1970s Voting age lowered to 18: Britain, France, West Germany, Italy, etc. 1970–1974 Britain: Conservatives in office	1969–1974 West Germany: Brandt chancellor; Social Democratic government; closer relations with Eastern Europe	1970s East-West détente: political, economic ties with West
1973 Britain, Denmark, Ireland join EC: 9 members	1973 German Federal Republic admitted to UN	1973 German Democratic Republic admitted to UN

WORLD AS A WHOLE	ASIA	AFRICA
1973 Chile: military coup ousts leftist government		
1973–1974 Arab oil embargo		1973–1974 Ethiopia: Haile
1974–1982 World economic recession	1974 Turkish invasion of Cyprus	Selassie ousted
1974 U.S.: Nixon resigns; Ford presidency		
1974 India develops atomic bomb		
1975 End of Vietnam War	1975 End of Vietnam War: Communist victories in Vietnam, Laos, Cambodia	1975 End of Portuguese rule in Angola, Mozambique, etc.
1975 End of last European (Portuguese) empire in Africa		
1975 Helsinki Conference	1975–1979 Cambodia: Khmer Rouge dictatorship	

TABLE TEN: 1975–

WORLD AS A WHOLE	ASIA	AFRICA
1975 Helsinki Conference	1975-Civil war in Lebanon	1975– Civil war in Angola
	1976 China: death of Mao	
1977–1981 U.S.: Carter presidency		1977–1978 Somalia and Ethiopia at war
1978– Pope John Paul II	1978– China under Deng: modernization and reform	
1979 Soviets invade Afghanistan	1979 Camp David accords: Israel-Egypt peace treaty	
1979 SALT II treaty	1979–1988 Soviets at war in Afghanistan	
	1979–1988 Vietnam invades, occupies Cambodia	
1980 U.S. embargo on U.S.S.R.	1980–1984 India: Indira Gandhi second ministry	1980s Debt problems; slow economic development, rapid population growth
1980–1981 U.S. hostage crisis in Iran	1980–1988 Iran-Iraq war	1980s Zimbabwe (Rhodesia) independent
1981–1989 U.S.: Reagan presidency	1981 Egypt: assassination of Anwar al-Sadat	
1981– New disease AIDS		
	1982 Israel invades Lebanon; ousts PLO	
	1984 Assassination of Indira Gandhi	1984– South Africa: pressures to end apartheid
1985–1991 Gorbachev reforms in U.S.S.R.: U.S.–Soviet rapprochement		
	1986 Philippines: Marcos dictatorship overthrown	1986 Uganda: 15-year civil war ends

WESTERN EUROPE	CENTRAL EUROPE	EASTERN EUROPE
		1970s Economic difficulties; rising debt
1974–1982 Economic recession	1974–1982 Economic recession	
	1974–1982 Schmidt Social Democratic chancellor	
1974 Portugal: revolution; end of dictatorship		
1975 Spain: death of Franco; constitutional monarchy	1975 Helsinki Accords	1975 Helsinki Accords
1975 Helsinki Accords		

WESTERN EUROPE	CENTRAL EUROPE	EASTERN EUROPE
1975 Helsinki Accords	1975 Helsinki Accords	1975 Helsinki Accords
1979 EC: Greece 10th member		1979 Soviets invade Afghanistan; détente ends
1979 EC: elections for European Parliament		
1979– British Conservatives in office: Thatcher prime minister		
		1980s East European governments: mounting debt problems
		1980 Yugoslavia: death of Tito
		1980–1981 Poland: strikes and unrest; rise of Solidarity
1981– France: Mitterrand Socialist president	1981 Italy: break in Christian Democratic governments after 40 cabinets	
1982 Britain thwarts Argentine takeover of Falklands	1982– Kohl Christian Democratic chancellor	1982 Death of Brezhnev
	1983–1987 Italy: Craxi Socialist premier	
		1985–1991 Gorbachev Soviet leader
1986 Spain and Portugal join EC: 12 members		1986 Chernobyl nuclear disaster

WORLD AS A WHOLE	ASIA	AFRICA
1987 World population reaches 5 billion	1987– Israel: Palestinian uprising begins	
1987–1988 Reagan-Gorbachev arms accord; ending of the Cold War		
	1988 End of Iran-Iraq War	
1989–1993 U.S.: Bush presidency	1989 Vietnam ends occupation of Cambodia	1989–1994 South Africa: de Klerk president, ending of apartheid
1989 End of Communist regimes in Central and Eastern Europe	1989 China suppresses democracy movement	1989 Angola: civil war ends
1989– Latin America: democratic regimes		
1990– Economic recession	1990–1991 Iraq annexes Kuwait; U.S. led coalition forces withdrawal	1990 Namibia independent
1990–1991 Persian Gulf War		
1991 End of Communist regime and dissolution of U.S.S.R.		1991 Ethiopia: revolution
		1992 Somalia: international intervention
1993– U.S.: Clinton presidency	1993 Israel-PLO: peace accord, mutual recognition	1993 Eritrea independent
1993 UN membership: 184	1993 Japan: recession, political scandals, Liberal Democrats lose majority	
1994 World population: 5.6 billion		1994 South Africa: multiracial elections, Mandela president
		1994 Rwanda: civil war

WESTERN EUROPE	CENTRAL EUROPE	EASTERN EUROPE
1987 Single Europe Act 1987 Britain: Conservatives reelected: Thatcher continues in office		1987–1988 Gorbachev-Reagan arms negotiations
1988– France: Mitterrand reelected president 1989 Britain, France, U.S., U.S.S.R. agree to German unification	1989 Fall of Berlin Wall 1989 Fall of Communist regime in East Germany	1988–1989 Soviets withdraw from Afghanistan 1989 Soviets hold multicandidate elections 1989 End of Communist regimes in Eastern Europe
1990 Britain: Major becomes Conservative prime minister 1990– Economic recession, unemployment 1991 EC: Treaty of European Union signed at Maastricht	1990 West Germany and East Germany merge: Federal Republic of Germany 1990– Germany: economic recession, unemployment	1990– East European states: transition to democracy, market economies 1991 Warsaw Pact dissolved 1991 U.S.S.R.: Communist rule ends; U.S.S.R. dissolves into component republics 1991– Russia: Yeltsin president; transition to democracy, market economy 1991– Yugoslavia: disintegration, war, Serb conquests in Bosnia
1992 EC: removal of remaining trade barriers 1993 Maastricht Treaty ratified: EC becomes EU	1993 Czechoslovakia divides: Czech Republic, Slovakia	1993– Russia: instability, president *vs.* legislature
1994 Italy: rightist parties win elections		

APPENDIX II:
RULERS AND REGIMES
In Principal European
Countries since 1500

HOLY ROMAN EMPIRE

Habsburg Line

MAXIMILIAN I	1493–1519
CHARLES V	1519–1556
FERDINAND I	1556–1564
MAXIMILIAN II	1564–1576
RUDOLPH II	1576–1612
MATTHIAS	1612–1619
FERDINAND II	1619–1637
FERDINAND III	1637–1657
LEOPOLD I	1658–1705
JOSEPH I	1705–1711
CHARLES VI	1711–1740

Charles VI was succeeded by a daughter, Maria Theresa, who as a woman could not be elected Holy Roman Emperor. French influence in 1742 secured the election of

Bavarian Line

CHARLES VII	1742–1745

On Charles VII's death the Habsburg control of the Emperorship was resumed.

Lorraine Line

FRANCIS I	1745–1765

(husband of Maria Theresa)

Habsburg-Lorraine Line

JOSEPH II	1765–1790

(son of Francis I and Maria Theresa)

LEOPOLD II	1790–1792
FRANCIS II	1792–1806

The Holy Roman Empire became extinct in 1806.

AUSTRIAN DOMINIONS

The rulers of Austria from 1438 to 1740, and at least titular kings of Hungary from 1526 to 1740, were the same as the Holy Roman Emperors. After 1740:

Habsburg Line (through female heir)

MARIA THERESA	1740–1780
JOSEPH II	1780–1790
LEOPOLD II	1790–1792
FRANCIS II	1792–1835

In 1804 Francis II took the title of Emperor, as Francis I of the Austrian Empire. Austria was declared an "empire" because Napoleon proclaimed France an empire in that year, and because the demise of the Holy Roman Empire could be foreseen.

FERDINAND I	1835–1848
FRANCIS JOSEPH	1848–1916
CHARLES I	1916–1918

The Austrian Empire became extinct in 1918.

BRITISH ISLES

Tudor Line

Kings of England and Ireland

HENRY VII	1485–1509
HENRY VIII	1509–1547
EDWARD VI	1547–1553
MARY I	1553–1558
ELIZABETH I	1558–1603

In 1603 James VI of Scotland, a great-great-grandson of Henry VII, succeeded to the English throne.

Stuart Line

Kings of England and Ireland, and of Scotland

JAMES I	1603–1625
CHARLES I	1625–1649

Republican Interregnum

The Commonwealth 1649–1653
The Protectorate
OLIVER CROMWELL 1653–1658
Lord Protector
RICHARD CROMWELL 1658–1660

Restored Stuart Line

CHARLES II 1660–1685
JAMES II 1685–1688

In 1688 James II was forced out of the country, but Parliament kept the crown in a female branch of the Stuart family, calling in Mary, the daughter of James II, and her husband William III of the Netherlands.

WILLIAM III 1689–1702,
AND MARY II 1689–1694
ANNE 1702–1714

In 1707, through the Union of England and Scotland, the royal title became King (or Queen) of Great Britain and Ireland. The Stuart family having no direct Protestant heirs, the throne passed in 1714 to the German George I, Elector of Hanover, a great-grandson of James I.

Hanoverian Line

Kings of Great Britain and Ireland
GEORGE I 1714–1727
GEORGE II 1727–1760
GEORGE III 1760–1820
GEORGE IV 1820–1830
WILLIAM IV 1830–1837

William IV having no heirs, the British throne passed in 1837 to Victoria, a granddaughter of George III. Though the British family has continued in direct descent from George I, it has dropped the Hanoverian designation and is now known as the House of Windsor. From 1877 to 1947 the British rulers bore the additional title of Emperor (or Empress) of India.

VICTORIA 1837–1901
EDWARD VII 1901–1910
GEORGE V 1910–1936
EDWARD VIII 1936
GEORGE VI 1936–1952
ELIZABETH II 1952–

FRANCE

Valois Line

LOUIS XI 1461–1483
CHARLES VIII 1483–1498
LOUIS XII 1498–1515
FRANCIS I 1515–1547
HENRY II 1547–1559
FRANCIS II 1559–1560
CHARLES IX 1560–1574
HENRY III 1574–1589

In 1589 the Valois line became extinct, and the throne passed to Henry of Bourbon, a remote descendant of French kings of the fourteenth century.

Bourbon Line

HENRY IV 1589–1610
LOUIS XIII 1610–1643
LOUIS XIV 1643–1715
LOUIS XV 1715–1774
LOUIS XVI 1774–1792

The Republic

Convention 1792–1795
Directory 1795–1799
Consulate 1799–1804

The Empire

NAPOLEON I 1804–1814
Emperor of the French
and King of Italy

Restored Bourbon Line

LOUIS XVIII 1814–1824

(Royalists count a Louis XVII, 1793–1795, and date the reign of Louis XVIII from 1795.)

CHARLES X 1824–1830

The Revolution of 1830 gave the throne to the Duke of Orleans, descendant of Louis XIII.

Orleans Line

LOUIS-PHILIPPE 1830–1848

Second Republic

1848–1852

Second Empire

NAPOLEON III   1852–1870
Emperor of the French

Third Republic

1870–1940

Vichy Regime

1940–1944

Provisional Government

1944–1946

Fourth Republic

1946–1958

Fifth Republic

1958–

PRUSSIA (AND GERMANY)

A continuous Hohenzollern line ruled until 1918.

Electors of Brandenburg and Dukes of Prussia

GEORGE WILLIAM	1619–1640
FREDERICK WILLIAM	1640–1688
the "Great Elector"	
FREDERICK III	1688–1713

In 1701 Frederick III was permitted by the Holy Roman Emperor to entitle himself King in Prussia, as Frederick I.

Kings of Prussia

FREDERICK I	1701–1713
FREDERICK WILLIAM I	1713–1740
FREDERICK II, the "Great"	1740–1786
FREDERICK WILLIAM II	1786–1797
FREDERICK WILLIAM III	1797–1840
FREDERICK WILLIAM IV	1840–1861
WILLIAM I	1861–1888

In 1871 William I took the title of German Emperor.

German Emperors

WILLIAM I	1871–1888
FREDERICK III	1888
WILLIAM II	1888–1918

The German Empire became extinct in 1918. It was succeeded by the

Weimar Republic

1919–1933

(an unofficial title for what was still called the Deutsches Reich, a phrase not easy to translate accurately)

The Third Reich

1933–1945

(an unofficial title for the Deutsches Reich under Adolf Hitler)
Allied Military Government in 1945 was followed by

German Federal Republic (West Germany)

1949–1990

German Democratic Republic (East Germany)

1949–1990

The two Germanys were united in 1990.

German Federal Republic

1990–

SARDINIA (AND ITALY)

In 1720 Victor Amadeus II, Duke of Savoy, took the title of King of Sardinia, having acquired the island of that name.

Kings of Sardinia

VICTOR AMADEUS II	1720–1730
CHARLES EMMANUEL III	1730–1773
VICTOR AMADEUS III	1773–1796
CHARLES EMMANUEL IV	1796–1802
VICTOR EMMANUEL I	1802–1821
CHARLES FELIX	1821–1831
CHARLES ALBERT	1831–1849
VICTOR EMMANUEL II	1849–1878

In 1861 Victor Emmanuel II took the title of King of Italy.

Kings of Italy

VICTOR EMMANUEL II	1861–1878
HUMBERT I	1878–1900

VICTOR EMMANUEL III   1900–1946
HUMBERT II   1946

In 1936 Victor Emmanuel III took the title of Emperor of Ethiopia, which became meaningless with British occupation of Ethiopia in 1941. In 1946 the Kingdom of Italy became extinct and was succeeded by the

Italian Republic

1946–

SPAIN

FERDINAND AND ISABELLA   1479–1504/1516

Isabella died in 1504, but Ferdinand lived until 1516, whereupon the Spanish thrones were inherited by their grandson Charles, who became Charles V of the Holy Roman Empire, but was known in Spain as Charles I.

Habsburg Line

CHARLES I   1516–1556
PHILIP II   1556–1598
PHILIP III   1598–1621
PHILIP IV   1621–1665
CHARLES II   1665–1700

With Charles II the Spanish Habsburg line became extinct, and the throne passed to the French Bourbon grandson of Louis XIV of France and great-grandson of Philip IV of Spain.

Bourbon Line

PHILIP V   1700–1746
FERDINAND VI   1746–1759
CHARLES III   1759–1788
CHARLES IV   1788–1808

Bonaparte Line

JOSEPH   1808–1813
(brother of Napoleon)

Restored Bourbon Line

FERDINAND VII   1813–1833
ISABELLA II   1833–1868

In 1868 Isabella abdicated; after a regency, and a brief reign by Amadeus I (Savoy), 1871–1873, there was a short-lived First Republic, 1873–1874, succeeded by

ALFONSO XII   1874–1885
ALFONSO XIII   1885–1931

In 1931 a republican revolution unseated Alfonso XIII.

Second Spanish Republic

1931–1936

Spanish Civil War

1936–1939

Regime of General Francisco Franco

1939–1975

Upon the death of Franco the Bourbon family was restored.

JUAN CARLOS I   1975–

RUSSIA (AND U.S.S.R.)

Grand Dukes of Moscow

IVAN III, the "Great"   1462–1505
BASIL III   1505–1533
IVAN IV, the "Terrible"   1533–1584

In 1547 Ivan IV took the title of Tsar of Russia.

Tsars of Russia

IVAN IV, the "Terrible"   1547–1584
THEODORE I   1584–1598
BORIS GODUNOV   1598–1605

Time of Troubles

1604–1613

Romanov Line

MICHAEL   1613–1645
ALEXIS   1645–1676
THEODORE II   1676–1682
IVAN V AND PETER I   1682–1689
PETER I, the "Great"   1689–1725
CATHERINE I   1725–1727
PETER II   1727–1730
ANNA   1730–1740
IVAN VI   1740–1741
ELIZABETH   1741–1762
PETER III   1762
CATHERINE II, the "Great"   1762–1796
PAUL   1796–1801
ALEXANDER I   1801–1825
NICHOLAS I   1825–1855
ALEXANDER II   1855–1881

Alexander III   1881–1894
Nicholas II   1894–1917

In 1917 the tsardom became extinct.

Provisional Government

1917

Communist Revolution

1917

Union of Soviet Socialist Republics

1922–1991

In 1991 the Communist regime ended and the U.S.S.R. dissolved into its component republics (Russia, Ukraine, etc.), loosely associated with each other in a Commonwealth of Independent States.

APPENDIX III: HISTORICAL POPULATIONS OF VARIOUS COUNTRIES AND CITIES

Figures for dates before the nineteenth century arise from estimates, in some cases subject to a wide margin of error. Those for the nineteenth and twentieth centuries generally reflect census returns, at dates within a few years before or after the round date indicated. For cities, the figures for 1950 and 1990 refer to metropolitan areas without regard to municipal boundaries. Estimates for cities for earlier dates are conveniently assembled in Tertius Chandler and Gerald Fox, *3000 Years of Urban Growth* (New York, 1974) and in Jan De Vries, *Urbanization, 1500–1800* (Cambridge, Mass., 1984).

The rapid growth of European cities in the nineteenth century was made possible by the railroad and was a sign of industrial progress. More recently the populations of the largest European and North American cities have stabilized or even declined. The largest cities are now often found in the less economically developed countries, where urban growth arises more from rural poverty and economic underdevelopment than from industrialization.

For countries, the use of the table is mainly for rough comparisons. It shows, for example, that France was about five times as populous as England in the Middle Ages, and was still more populous than all the German states at the time of the French Revolution, or that Spain declined under the Habsburgs in the seventeenth century, and that Ireland lost population after the famine and ensuing emigration. All countries except Ireland grew rapidly in population in the nineteenth century. For Russia, the figures from 1750 to 1950 reflect territorial expansion as well as internal growth. The figure for the year 2000 represents the territory of the former U.S.S.R. All figures for China are very uncertain, though unquestionably very large. The projected populations of countries for the year 2000 are from *World Population Prospects* (New York: United Nations, 1989). For Nigeria, the 1990 census has been used.

For 1950 and 1990 the figures for Ireland include both the Republic of Ireland and Northern Ireland, and "Germany" includes the former East and West Germany. In 1990 the Irish Republic was about twice as populous as its northern neighbor, and West Germany was almost four times as populous as East Germany, with which it was reunited that year.

CITIES in thousands

	LONDON	MANCHESTER	PARIS	MARSEILLES
14th Century	50	3 –	200	
15th Century				
16th Century	200			
17th Century	575	15 –	450	50 +
18th Century	750		500	90
1800	865	77	600	111
1850	2681	303	1422	195
1900	6581	544	3670	491
1950	8346	2421	4823	655
1990	9400	2580	8707	1110

	FLORENCE	BERLIN	VIENNA	PRAGUE
14th Century	50 +			
15th Century	60	10 –	20	25 +
16th Century	65	12	40 +	40 +
17th Century	75	20	100	40 +
18th Century	75	100	220	75
1800	84	172	247	75
1850	114	500	444	206
1900	206	2712	1675	382
1950	374	3337	1766	922
1990	426	3092	1481	1194

	TOKYO	HONG KONG	JAKARTA	CALCUTTA
1900	1440	284	116	1125
1950	6277	2360	3200	2610
1990	11906	5500	6503	9194

AMSTERDAM	ANTWERP	LISBON	MADRID	ROME
	5	20 +	5 −	30 −
20 −	35			50 −
35	100	100	60	100
100 +	50	73	80	130
150	50	120	120	150
201	62	180	160	153
224	88	240	281	175
511	277	356	540	463
838	584	790	1618	1652
1016	478	808	3183	2815

WARSAW	BUDAPEST	STOCKHOLM	ST. PETERSBURG LENINGRAD	MOSCOW
70		60	100	
100	54 +	76	220	250
150	178	93	485	365
700	732	301	1150	1000
804	1571	744	3182	4847
1649	2089	663	4948	8815

CAIRO	LAGOS	RIO DE JANEIRO	MEXICO CITY	NEW YORK
570	42	750	345	3400
2100	230	2413	2233	12911
6052	1061	5090	14750	18054

COUNTRIES in millions

	ENGLAND AND WALES	SCOTLAND	IRELAND	FRANCE
1300	3.5			15.0
1500	2.8	.8	1.0	16.0
1700	5.5	1.2	2.8	19.0
1800	8.9	1.6	5.2	27.0
1850	17.9	2.9	6.5	34.2
1900	32.5	4.5	4.5	38.5
1950	43.0	5.0	4.3	41.8
1990	50.1	5.4	4.9	56.2
2000 projected	50.6	5.5	5.0	58.2

	SWEDEN	POLAND	RUSSIA- U.S.S.R.	CHINA
1300		1.3		
1500		2.5		
1700	1.6	2.8	12	150
1800	2.3	4.3	30	300
1850	3.5	6.0	62	400
1900	5.1	28.3	104	
1950	7.0	24.8	180 (U.S.S.R.)	547
1990	8.3	38.4	286 (U.S.S.R.)	1,135
2000 projected	8.3	40.4	307	1,289

	BRAZIL	MEXICO	CANADA	U.S.A.
1800		6.0	.4	5.3
1850			2.4	23.2
1900	20.0	13.6	5.4	76.0
1950	52.6	25.7	14.0	152.0
1990	150.3	88.6	26.5	250.1
2000 projected	179.5	107.2	27.6	266.2

BELGIUM	NETHERLANDS	GERMANY	SPAIN	ITALY
.7	.4	7.0		8.0
1.4	1.0	12.0	6.8	10.5
1.6	1.8	15.0	7.5	13.3
3.0	2.0	25.0	10.5	17.2
4.3	3.1	33.8		24.3
6.7	5.1	56.3	19.1	33.6
8.6	10.1	68.3	27.9	46.8
9.9	14.8	77.1	39.3	57.3
10.0	15.2	76.4	40.8	57.9

JAPAN	INDIA PAKISTAN BANGLADESH	INDONESIA	EGYPT	NIGERIA
			2.5	
30.0			5.0	
45.0	294.0	36.0	10.0	
83.2	356.9	60.4	20.0	23.2
123.4	1,092.7	180.5	54.1	90.0
129.1	1,355.6	208.3	66.7	159.1

BIBLIOGRAPHY

The following bibliographical guide is intended for the convenience of students, teachers, and general readers. Although professional students of history may also find it useful, no attempt has been made to provide comprehensive coverage of special areas or topics, or to include many specialized monographs. The aim throughout has been to call attention to the most reliable works, to which the reader may turn for additional bibliographical guidance. Classification follows the plan of chapters in the present book. For reasons of space, untranslated works in foreign languages are excluded, as are general textbooks, articles in periodicals, and (with a few exceptions) primary source materials. When a second date of publication for a book is given without further specification, it is generally the date of reprinting or reissue.

Many of the titles are now or will be available in paperback; up-to-date listings may be found in the *Paperback Book Guide for Colleges*. An asterisk in the reading lists below indicates current availability in a paperback edition.

Introduction

Guides and Reference Works

There are literally hundreds of thousands of books on historical subjects, and it is difficult to find titles and authors on any particular topic. One useful but outdated bibliographical tool has been the American Historical Association's *Guide to Historical Literature* (1931; 2d ed., 1961). A thoroughly revised edition is scheduled for publication in 1995, and new technology, it is hoped, will facilitate future updating. To keep up with the outpouring of historical books, it is important to read the book reviews and listings of new books in the *American Historical Review*, the *Journal of Modern History*, *Foreign Affairs*, and other periodicals.

Detailed chronological listings of events and dates may be found in W. L. Langer, *An Encyclopedia of World History: Ancient, Medieval, and Modern, Chronologically Arranged* (rev. 1972, with plans in progress for a new edition); in S. H. Steinberg, *Historical Tables, 58 B.C.–A.D. 1985* (rev. 1987); and in similar works. Of the many multivolume encyclopedias, the *Encyclopaedia Britannica* (15th ed., 1974, with periodic updates), remains the most valuable. Convenient one-volume reference tools are the *Random House Encyclopedia* (rev. 1990), the *Cambridge Encyclopedia* (1990), the *Concise Columbia Encyclopedia* (rev. 1989), and the *Columbia Encyclopedia* (5th ed., 1993).

Among historical atlases that place European history in its world setting, G. Barraclough (ed.), the (London) *Times Atlas of World History* (rev. 1992), is the most impressive. Also useful, and periodically updated, are the *Rand McNally Atlas of*

World History* (rev. 1993), Hammond's *Historical Atlas of the World** (rev. 1993), and the Penguin Historical Atlas series*. Of many geographical atlases one of the best is the *National Geographic Atlas of the World* (rev. 1992).

Of multivolume historical series, the *New Cambridge Modern History* (14 vols., 1957–1979) is the most useful. The volumes, which will be referred to in the chapters below, contain contributions by specialists from all over the world, but often fail to provide a synthesis for the period covered. Volume 13 (1979), edited by P. Burke, is a welcome collection of thematic essays, and Volume 14 (1975), edited by H. C. Darby and H. Fullard, is an atlas. For European history, *The Rise of Modern Europe* (20 vols., 1936–1985), known as the "Langer series" for its general editor, W. L. Langer, provides three to four volumes (many now outdated) for each of the modern centuries and will be described in the chapters that follow. There are many other series, too numerous to list here, under the auspices of commercial publishers.

Histories in Special Areas

For European economic history, a valuable collaborative work is C. M. Cipolla (ed.), *The Fontana Economic History of Europe** (6 vols., 1972–1976), with chapters contributed by an international roster of experts. Two helpful one-volume syntheses are S. B. Clough and R. T. Rapp, *European Economic History* (rev. 1975), and on a broader time scale, R. Cameron, *A Concise Economic History of the World: From Paleolithic Times to the Present* (rev. 1993). Of special interest are C. P. Kindleberger, *A Financial*

History of Western Europe (rev. 1993), and J. Mokyr, *The Lever of Riches: Technological Creativity and Economic Progress** (1990). On economic thought, one may read R. L. Heilbroner, *The Worldly Philosophers** (1953); E. Whittaker, *Schools and Streams of Economic Thought* (1960); E. Heimann, *History of Economic Doctrines* (1964); and H. W. Spiegel, *The Growth of Economic Thought* (rev. 1983). The best brief introduction to agrarian history is D. Grigg, *The Transformation of Agriculture in the West* (1992).

Geographical influences on European history are discussed in E. A. Freeman and J. B. Bury, *The Historical Geography of Europe* (1974); N. J. G. Pounds, *An Historical Geography of Europe* (3 vols., 1973–1985), ranging from 450 B.C. to 1914; and the essays in E. Genovese and L. Hochberg (eds.), *Geographic Perspectives in History* (1989). J. G. Simmons, *Changing the Face of the Earth: Culture, Environment, and History** (1989), traces the human impact on the planet over the centuries, and E. Le Roy Ladurie examines an important subject in *Times of Feast, Times of Famine: A History of Climate since the Year 1000* (trans. 1971).

For the history of ideas one still reads with profit B. Russell, *A History of Philosophy* (1945); J. H. Randall, Jr., *Making of the Modern Mind** (1926, 1976); and the same author's later work, *The Career of Philosophy* (2 vols., 1962–1965). An impressive comprehensive survey of formal philosophy is F. C. Copleston, *A History of Philosophy* (9 vols., 1946–1975). A thoughtful synthesis for the history of ideas in the modern period is F. L. Baumer, *Modern European Thought: Continuity and Change in Ideas, 1600–1950* (1977). Other useful introductions are R. N. Stromberg's two volumes: *An Intellectual History of Modern Europe* (rev. 1975), and *European Intellectual History since 1789** (rev. 1994).

On political thought, R. Berki, *The History of Political Thought** (1977), is an illuminating brief introduction, and Q. Skinner, *The Foundations of Modern Political Thought* (2 vols., 1978), is a masterful account for the early modern centuries. Two helpful volumes are G. H. Sabine, *A History of Political Theory* (1937; rev. by T. L. Thorson, 1984), and J. H. Burns (ed.), *The Cambridge History of Political Thought, 1450–1700* (1991). On the need to examine political ideas and political vocabulary in

the context of their times, one should read J. G. A. Pocock, *Politics, Language, and Time: Essays on Political Thought and History* (1971).

For demography the reader may turn to D. V. Glass and C. Eversley, *Population in History: Essays in Historical Demography* (1965); E. A. Wrigley, *Population and History** (1969); C. M. Cipolla, *Economic History of World Population** (1974); and T. McKeown, *The Modern Rise of Population* (1977). The pioneering study of A. M. Carr-Saunders, *World Population: Past Growth and Future Trends* (1936), still merits reading. A work of extraordinary scope with broad implications for demographic research is E. A. Wrigley and R. Schofield, *The Population History of England, 1541–1871** (1981). To keep up with current trends, one should consult the *United Nations Demographic Yearbook* and periodical literature.

T. Chandler and G. Fox provide statistical data and other information on the historical growth of the world's cities in *3000 Years of Urban Growth* (1974). A comprehensive history of cities from ancient times to the present in all parts of the globe is P. Bairock, *Cities and Economic Development* (1988), while the history of European urbanization in all its aspects is recounted in P. M. Hohenberg and L. H. Lees, *The Making of Urban Europe, 1000–1950* (1985). B. R. Mitchell, *International Historical Statistics, 1750–1988: Europe* (rev. 1992), is a valuable source for statistical data; two additional volumes are projected for other parts of the world.

For the impact of famine, disease, and the movement of peoples, one may read W. H. McNeill, *Plagues and Peoples* (1976); the same author's *The Global Condition: Conquerors, Catastrophes, and Community** (1993); T. McKeown, *The Origins of Human Disease* (1988); and K. F. Kiple (ed.), *The Cambridge World History of Human Disease* (1992), a valuable reference work.

Of the many books on military history treating war as a social and human phenomenon, three outstanding recent studies ranging from earliest times to the present are A. Jones, *The Art of War in the Western World** (1989); R. L. O'Connell, *Of Arms and Men: A History of War, Weapons, and Aggression** (1990); and J. Keegan, *A History of Warfare* (1993); the latter, like others of Keegan's books, especially noteworthy. To these may be added T. Ropp, *War in the Modern World** (rev. 1962); M. Howard, *War in European History* (1976); and R. A. Preston, S. Wise, and A. Roland, *Men in Arms* (rev. 1991). Of interest in a related category is M. Walzer, *Just and Unjust Wars** (1977). The importance of technology is stressed in B. and F. Brodie, *From Crossbow to H-Bomb* (rev. 1973); W. H. McNeill, *The Pursuit of Power: Technology, Armed Force, and Society since* A.D. *1000** (1982); and M. van Creveld, *Technology and War: From 2000* B.C. *to the Present* (1988). For strategy and the nature of command one turns to P. Paret (ed.), *Makers of Modern Strategy: From Machiavelli to the Nuclear Age* (1986); J. Keegan, *The Mask of Command* (1987); and M. van Creveld, *Command in War** (1985).

A few very different books deserve mention here: W. H. McNeill, *The Rise of the West: A History of the Human Community** (1963), a notable effort to recount the human experience in a global setting; E. R. Wolf, *Europe and the People without History** (1983), by an anthropologist, which portrays Western history as it was seen by societies in Asia, Africa, and the Americas; and P. Kennedy, *The Rise and Fall of the Great Powers: Economic Change and Military Conflict from 1500 to 2000** (1987), which examines the political and economic fortunes of the European nations that at one time played the leading role in world affairs in the modern centuries.

Changing Directions in Historical Writing

Several collections of essays provide insights into contemporary trends in historical writing, among them: M. Kammen (ed.), *The Past before Us: Contemporary Historical Writing in the United States** (1980); C. F. Delzell (ed.), *The Future of History* (1977); G. G. Iggers and H. T. Parker (eds.), *International Handbook of Historical Studies* (1979); and T. K. Rabb and R. I. Rotberg (eds.), *The New History: The 1980s and Beyond** (1982). Two thoughtful volumes, informative on traditional and newer historical writing are P. Burke (ed.), *New Perspectives on Historical Writing** (1992), and J. Appleby, L. Hunt, and M. Jacob, *Telling the Truth about History* (1994).

One of the newer interests of historians has been social history. Stimulated by the *Annales* school of historical writing in

France (the name derived from the French periodical *Annales: Sociétés, Economies, Civilisations*), and by newer kinds of working-class history in England, in which E. P. Thompson, *The Making of the English Working Class** (1963), was a pioneer, historians have concerned themselves increasingly with a social history distinct from older interests in social classes and labor and laboring conditions. They have been examining such subjects as the history of the family, women, sexuality, marriage, the everyday lives and outlook (or *mentalité*) of the urban and rural poor, and popular culture—all studied as history "from the bottom up." Many such works are listed below in the appropriate chapters. An introduction to the newer social history and to popular culture is provided in O. Zung (ed.), *Reliving the Past: The Worlds of Social History* (1985); P. Burke, *Popular Culture in Early Modern Europe** (1978); and C. Mukerjee and M. Schudson (eds.), *Rethinking Popular Culture** (1990).

The history of the family and related subjects has been studied, with divergent conclusions, in P. Ariès, *Centuries of Childhood: A Social History of Family Life** (trans. 1962), a pioneering work; E. Shorter, *The Making of the Modern Family* (1975), whose conclusions have been widely criticized; L. Stone, *The Family, Sex, and Marriage in England, 1500–1800** (1977; abr. 1979); the same author's *Road to Divorce: England, 1530–1987* (1990), and other writings; M. Mitterauer and R. Sieder, *The European Family: Patriarchy to Partnership, 1400 to the Present* (1982); and B. Gottlieb, *The Family in the Western World from the Black Death to the Industrial Age* (1992). Related studies include J. R. Gillis, *Youth and History: Tradition and Change in European Age Relations, 1770 to the Present* (rev., 1981); L. A. Pollock, *Forgotten Children: Parent-Child Relationships from 1500 to 1900** (1984); and R. Phillips, *Untying the Knot: A Short History of Divorce** (1992; abr. ed. of 1988 book).

The diversity of social history is reflected in the series edited by P. Ariès and G. Duby, *A History of Private Life* (5 vols.; trans. 1987–1993), with specialists editing and contributing to each volume. The volumes range from ancient Rome to the contemporary era and provide information on the intimate details of life in the private domain, including, of course, changing definitions of privacy; the contributions, perhaps understandably, are of somewhat uneven quality. Other subjects related to the newer social history are studied in P. Ariès, *The Hour of Our Death** (trans. 1976; 1991), on changing Western attitudes toward death and dying from the Middle Ages to the present; and in various books by M. Foucault, including *Madness and Civilization: A History of Insanity in the Age of Reason* (trans. 1965), *Discipline and Punish: The Birth of the Prison* (trans. 1979), and *A History of Sexuality* (2 vols.; trans. 1978, 1986).

Although the *Annales* historians have contributed a good deal to the newer social history, they have also been important for their emphasis, often quantitative and interdisciplinary, on long-term factors that influence the course of historical change, such as geography, environment, resources, climate, population, diet, and disease, which in their view often merit closer attention than "events." Here F. Braudel, *The Mediterranean and the Mediterranean World in the Age of Philip II* (2 vols., 1949; trans. 1974; rev. and abridged 1 vol. ed., 1992), was a pioneering work.

The *Annales* writers and others may be examined in G. C. Iggers, *New Directions in European Historiography* (1975); T. Stoianovich, *French Historical Method: The Annales Paradigm* (1976); P. Burke, *The French Historical Revolution: The Annales School 1929–1989** (1990); and P. Carrard, *Politics of the New History: French Historical Discourse from Braudel to Chartier* (1992). A cofounder of *Annales* who died in the Resistance during the Second World War is studied with care in C. Fink, *Marc Bloch: A Life in History* (1989). Some of the reflections of the *Annales* school on historical method are to be found in M. Bloch, *The Historian's Craft** (trans. 1953); M. Foucault, *The Order of Things: An Archaeology of the Human Sciences* (trans. 1970); F. Braudel, *On History* (trans. 1980); E. Le Roy Ladurie, *The Territory of the Historian** (trans. 1979) and *The Mind and Method of the Historian* (trans. 1981); F. Furet, *In the Workshop of History** (trans. 1984); and J. Le Goff and P. Nora (eds.), *Constructing the Past: Essays in Historical Methodology* (1985).

There has also been considerable attention in recent decades to the history of women. Many of the writings call for reassessments of various historical eras from the viewpoint of women's status in the era, and for the fuller integration of the history of women into general history. Contributions to the history of women in Europe and the West may be sampled in R. Bridenthal, C. Koonz, and S. Stuard (eds.), *Becoming Visible: Women in European History** (rev. 1987), with essays from ancient times to the twentieth century; M. J. Boxer and J. H. Quataert (eds.), *Connecting Spheres: Women in the Western World, 1500 to the Present** (1986), case studies with informative overview chapters; B. S. Anderson and J. P. Zinsser, *A History of Their Own: Women in Europe from Prehistory to the Present** (2 vols., 1988), thematically organized; and B. G. Smith, *Changing Lives: Women in European History since 1700** (1989), a helpful narrative account. G. Duby and M. Perrot (gen. eds.), *A History of Women in the West* (trans. 1992–94), a multivolume history from ancient times to the present, is less encyclopedic than the title implies but contains interesting chapters. G. Lerner provides many insights into women and history in her two historical studies, *The Creation of Patriarchy** (1986) and *The Creation of Feminist Consciousness: From the Middle Ages to 1870* (1993). Four documentary histories available are J. C. Fout and E. Reimer (eds.), *European Women: A Documentary History, 1789–1945* (1980); J. O'Faolain and L. Martines (eds.), *Not in God's Image: Women in History from the Greeks to the Victorians* (1973); E. O. Hillerstein, L. P. Hume, and K. M. Offen (eds.), *Victorian Women: Women's Lives in England, France, and the United States** (1981); and S. G. Bell and K. M. Offen (eds.), *Women, the Family, and Freedom: The Debate in Documents** (2 vols., 1983).

Illuminating on political thinkers and their treatment of the subject of women from Aristotle on are J. B. Elstain, *Public Man, Private Woman: Women in Social and Political Thought* (1981), and S. M. Okin, *Women in Western Political Thought** (1979, 1992). A vividly written book by A. Fraser, but in the older style of restricting women's history to women of the upper classes, is *The Warrior Queens* (1989), on women since ancient times who led their nations in war. An important monograph is J. W. Scott and L. A. Tilly, *Women, Work, and Family* (1978), focusing on French and English women in the modern centuries. Two provocative, analytical books, stressing gender issues as central to historical understanding, are J. Kelly, *Women, History, and Theory: The Essays of Joan Kelly** (1984, published posthumously), and J. W. Scott, *Gender and the Politics of History* (1988).

Psychological dimensions to the contemporary writing of history may be examined in S. Friedländer, *History and Psychoanalysis** (trans. 1978); P. Loewenberg, *Decoding the Past: The Psychohistorical Approach** (1982); and P. Gay, *Freud for Historians** (1985). For an introduction to the quantitative analysis of historical data one may turn to W. D. Aydelotte and others, *The Dimensions of Quantitative Research in History* (1972); and R. Floud, *An Introduction to Quantitative Methods for Historians** (rev. 1979). Of special interest also is R. G. Hawks, *Economics for Historians** (1980). A good introduction to an important subject is J. L. Reiff, *Structuring the Past: The Use of Computers in History** (1994).

The writing of biography may be examined in J. A. Garraty, *The Nature of Biography* (1957); P. M. Kendall, *The Art of Biography* (1965); C. D. Bowen, *Biography: The Craft and the Calling* (1968); M. Pachter, *Telling Lives* (1979); D. Beales, *History and Biography** (1981); and S. Weinberg, *Telling the Untold Story* (1992). The tapping of neglected sources is examined in P. Thompson, *The Voice of the Past: Oral History* (1978), and D. Henige, *Oral Historiography** (1982). A contemporary medium is explored in P. Sorlin, *The Film in History: Restaging the Past* (1980), and in J. E. O'Connor (ed.), *Image as Artifact: The Historical Analysis of Film and Television** (1990).

Changing reassessments of cultural and intellectual history, borrowing from philosophy, linguistics, anthropology, and literary criticism, much of which may remain elusive for many readers, may be sampled in L. Hunt (ed.), *The New Cultural History** (1989); D. LaCapra, *Rethinking Intellectual History: Texts, Contexts, Language** (1983); D. LaCapra and S. L. Kaplan (eds.), *Modern European Intellectual History: Reappraisals and New Perspectives** (1982); H. White, *The Content of the Form: Narrative Discourse and Historical Representation* (1987); and C. Ginzburg, *Clues, Myths, and the Historical Method** (trans. 1992).

Books critical of the trends in historical writing that emerged in the 1960s and 1970s include J. Barzun, *Clio and the Doctors: Psychohistory, Quantohistory, and History*

(1974); J. H. Hexter, *On Historians: Some of the Makers of Modern History* (1979); T. S. Hamerow, *Reflections on History and Historians* (1987); G. Himmelfarb, *The New History and the Old* (1987) and *On Looking into the Abyss: Untimely Thoughts on Culture and Society* (1994); and G. R. Elton, *Return to Essentials* (1993). Two probing accounts of the historical profession in the United States, with insights into past and present historiographical debates are J. Higham, *History: Professional Scholarship in America** (rev. 1988); and P. Novick, *That Noble Dream: The "Objectivity Question" and the American Historical Profession** (1988).

Historiography, Philosophy of History, Historical Method

A comprehensive introduction to the history of historical writing is E. Breisach, *Historiography: Ancient, Medieval, and Modern** (1983). It may be supplemented by A. D. Momigliano, *The Classical Foundations of Modern Historiography** (1966, 1990). One will wish to read H. Butterfield, *The Origins of History* (1949; rev. 1981); and Butterfield's other writings, of which several have been collected in *Herbert Butterfield on History* (1984). F. Stern (ed.), *The Varieties of History: From Voltaire to the Present** (rev. 1973), is a valuable anthology.

There are many volumes on the philosophy of history written by professional students of philosophy, and sometimes not directly attuned to the needs and interests of practicing historians. The best scholarly introductions are R. E. Atkinson, *Knowledge and Explanation in History** (1978); W. H. Dray's two books, *Philosophy of History** (1964) and *On History and Philosophers of History* (1989); and W. H. Walsh, *An Introduction to the Philosophy of History** (1976). Other recommended studies are R. Aron, *Introduction to the Philosophy of History* (1948, trans. 1961); R. G. Collingwood, *The Idea of History** (1946); A. C. Danto, *Analytical Philosophy of History* (1965); and M. Mandelbaum, *The Anatomy of Historical Knowledge* (1977). Also informative are P. Munz, *The Shapes of Time: A New Look at the Philosophy of History* (1977); and L. Krieger's two books, *Time's Reasons: Philosophies of History Old and New* (1989) and *Ideas and Events: Professing History* (1992). Two convenient introductions are the anthologies edited by H.

Meyerhoff (ed.), *The Philosophy of History in Our Time** (1959), and P. Gardiner (ed.), *Theories of History* (1959).

On the relationship of history to other disciplines and its own distinctive role one may turn to such varied explorations as A. L. Rowse, *The Use of History** (1946), the first volume in the English Teach Yourself History series, a series written for the general reader; C. Gustavson's two books: *A Preface to History** (1955) and *The Mansion of History** (1975); E. H. Carr, *What Is History?* (1962); A. Nevins, *The Gateway to History* (rev. 1962); G. L. Elton, *The Practice of History* (1967); H. S. Hughes, *History as Art and Science** (1957); S. Kent, *Writing History* (rev. 1967); L. Gottschalk, *Understanding History* (rev. 1969); and A. Marwick, *The Nature of History** (rev. 1989). Of special interest for the relationship of the discipline to the social sciences are P. Burke, *History and Social Theory** (1993); J. Elster, *The Cement of Society: A Study of Social Order** (1991) and *Nuts and Bolts from the Social Sciences** (1991); and R. C. Neustadt and E. R. May, *Thinking in Time: The Use of History for Decision Makers* (1986). There is much practical information interestingly presented in J. Barzun and H. F. Graff, *The Modern Researcher** (rev. 1992).

Among thoughtful reflections by historians who have themselves made notable contributions to the writing of history, the following may be suggested: G. S. R. Kitson Clark, *The Critical Historian* (1967); C. V. Wedgwood, *The Sense of the Past* (1960); J. H. Plumb, *The Death of the Past* (1970); B. Lewis, *History Remembered, Recovered, Invented* (1975); F. Gilbert, *History: Choice and Commitment* (1977); W. H. McNeill, *Mythistory and Other Essays* (1986); C. Vann Woodward, *Thinking Back: The Perils of Writing History** (1986) and *The Future of the Past* (1989); L. Stone, *The Past and the Present* (1981) and the *Past and the Present Revisited** (1988); D. Cannadine, *The Pleasures of the Past* (1989); W. J. Bouwsma, *A Usable Past** (1990); and M. Beloff, *An Historian in the Twentieth Century* (1992).

Finally, there are numerous anthologies, historical readings, collections of source materials, and problems series in historical interpretation, of which publishers generally keep readers and teachers well informed. A few titles in these categories will be cited at the end of each chapter.

I. The Rise of Europe

Prehistoric and Ancient Times

For prehistory, the reader may wish to consult J. Hawkes and L. Wooley, *Prehistory and the Beginnings of Civilization* (rev. 1967), the first volume in the *UNESCO History of Mankind;* P. Phillips, *The Prehistory of Europe* (1980); and T. Champion and others, *Prehistoric Europe* (1984).

General accounts for the ancient world would include T. B. Jones, *From the Tigris to the Tiber** (rev. 1978); C. G. Starr, *A History of the Ancient World* (rev. 1991); and H. and R. T. Howe, *The Ancient World** (1987). For Mesopotamia and Egypt one may read J. Hawkes, *The First Great Civilizations** (1973); H. Saggs, *The Greatness That Was Babylon* (1991); and M. A. Murray, *The Splendor That Was Egypt* (rev. 1989).

One of the best summaries of Greek and Roman antiquity, from the eighth century B.C. through the second century A.D., is J. Boardman, J. Griffin, and O. Murray (eds.), *The Oxford History of the Classical World** (1986); one will also wish to read M. Grant, *The Founders of the Western World: A History of Greece and Rome* (1990). There are rewarding insights in M. I. Finley's many writings on Greece and Rome, among them *The Legacy of Greece: A New Appraisal** (1981) and *Politics in the Ancient World** (1983). An outstanding study of women in Greece and Rome is S. B. Pomeroy, *Whores, Wives, and Slaves: Women in Classical Antiquity* (1975).

In addition to numerous surveys of classical Greece, the reader will profit from A. Andrewes, *The Greeks* (1967) and A. H. M. Jones, *Athenian Democracy** (reissued 1986). For Alexander, as an introduction to Hellenistic times, R. L. Fox, *Alexander the Great* (1974) may be compared with P. Green, *Alexander of Macedon, 356–323 B.C.** (1974; rev. 1991). On the rise and fall of the civilization that Alexander helped create, one may read E. S. Gruen, *The Hellenistic World and the Coming of Rome** (2 vols., 1984); P. Green's provocative and critical *Alexander to Actium: The Historical Evolution of the Hellenistic Age* (1991); and G. W. Bowersock, *Hellenism in Late Antiquity* (1992), a more sympathetic brief assessment.

Among many surveys of Rome and Roman civilization, one may suggest H. H. Scullard, *A History of the Roman World* (2 vols.; rev. 1980–1982), and for all aspects of Roman society, K. Christ, *The Romans: An Introduction to Their History and Civilization** (trans. 1984). A superb volume on the end of the Roman Republic, R. Syme, *Roman Revolution** (1939), may be supplemented by A. H. MacDonald, *Republican Rome* (1966), and C. Nicolet, *The World of the Citizen in Republican Rome* (trans. 1980). Books on later Roman history include P. Garnsey and R. Saller, *The Roman Empire: Economy, Society and Culture** (1987); and A. H. M. Jones, *The Later Roman Empire, 284–602** (3 vols., 1964; reissued, 2 vols., 1986).

For the coming of Christianity, N. H. Baynes, *Constantine the Great and the Christian Church* (1931), remains important, but a good, brief account is A. H. M. Jones, *Constantine and the Conversion of Europe** (1948), in the Teach Yourself History series. S. Benko, *Pagan Rome and Early Christians** (1986) and R. A. Markus, *Christianity in the Roman World* (1978) are informative. Efforts to reconstruct the historical Jesus include M. Grant, *Jesus: An Historian's Review of the Gospels* (1977); A. N. Wilson, *Jesus: A Life* (1992); and J. D. Crossan, *Jesus: A Revolutionary Biography* (1993). On St. Augustine and his times, there is a sensitive account by P. R. L. Brown, *Augustine of Hippo** (1967) and another illuminating study by F. Van der Meer, *Augustine the Bishop: Church and Society at the Dawn of the Middle Ages* (1961). For all aspects of theology there is available the magisterial work of J. Pelikan, *The Christian Tradition* (5 vols., 1971–1989), the first three volumes of which relate to the Middle Ages.

The Middle Ages: The Formation of Europe

Among many surveys of the medieval era as a whole, B. Tierney and S. Painter, *Western Europe in the Middle Ages, 300–1475* (rev. 1992), and N. Cantor, *The Civilization of the Middle Ages* (rev. 1993), are outstanding. F. Heer, *The Medieval World* (1963), is a rewarding book. A successful effort emphasizing social history is E. Peters, *Europe and The Middle Ages** (1983). G. Holmes (ed.), *The Oxford Illustrated History of Medieval Europe** (1988), available also in abridged form* (1992) is a collaborative work of distinction and J. Le Goff, *Medieval Civilization, 400–1500* (trans. 1988), a remarkable synthesis by a leading French historian of the *Annales* school, which in recent years has made many imaginative contributions to the reconstruction of the medieval outlook. Historians who have reshaped our understanding of the medieval era are examined in N. Cantor, *Reinventing the Middle Ages* (1992).

Fundamental to the reassessment of Europe's emergence in the early medieval centuries is R. W. Southern, *The Making of the Middle Ages** (1953). Other scholarly books include P. R. L. Brown, *The End of Antiquity** (1971); H. R. Trevor-Roper, *The Rise of Christian Europe** (1965); D. Hay, *Europe: The Emergence of an Idea** (rev. 1968); G. Barraclough, *The Crucible of Europe: The Ninth and Tenth Centuries in European History** (1976); J. M. Wallace-Hadrill, *The Barbarian West, 400–1000** (1952); and A. R. Lewis, *Emerging Medieval Europe, A.D. 400–1000** (1967). Books that carry the story somewhat further in time include C. Brooks, *Europe in the Central Middle Ages, 962–1154** (rev. 1987); G. Duby, *The Making of the Christian West, 980–1140* (trans. 1968); S. R. Packard, *12th Century Europe* (1973); R. H. C. Davis, *A History of Medieval Europe: From Constantine to St. Louis* (rev. 1988); and M. Powicke, *The Thirteenth Century, 1216–1307** (1962, 1991).

For the era of Charlemagne one may read P. Geary, *Before France and Germany: The Creation and Transformation of the Merovingian Empire: The Age of Charlemagne** (1988); H. Fichtenau, *The Carolingian Empire: The Age of Charlemagne** (trans. 1957); A. D. Bullough, *The Age of Charlemagne* (1965); R. Folz, *The Coronation of Charlemagne, 25 December 800* (trans. 1975), covering more than the title implies; and P. Riché, *Daily Life in the World of Charlemagne** (trans. 1978).

The Byzantine Empire and the Islamic World

There are many books on the two civilizations in the Middle East that flourished while Europe in the early medieval centuries was in the so-called "Dark Ages." For the Byzantine, or Eastern Roman, Empire, an older work is G. Ostrogorsky, *History of the Byzantine State* (1950), translated in 1956 by J. M. Hussey, who herself has written a good introduction in briefer compass, *The Byzantine World** (1957) and has also edited *The Byzantine Empire*, Vol. IV (rev. 1966–

1967), in the *Cambridge Medieval History*. Among other narrative and topical accounts are P. Lemerle, *A History of Byzantium* (1964); R. Jenkins, *Byzantium: The Imperial Centuries, A.D. 619–1071* (1966); S. Vryonis, Jr., *Byzantium and Europe** (1967); D. Oblensky, *The Byzantium Commonwealth: Eastern Europe, 500–1453* (1971); D. M. Nicol, *The End of the Byzantine Empire** (1985), on the last two centuries before 1453; and R. Byron, *The Byzantine Achievement* (1988). The end of the empire is graphically described in S. Runciman, *The Fall of Constantinople, 1453** (1965). Valuable for all aspects of Byzantine civilization is A. P. Kazhdan (ed.), *The Oxford Dictionary of Byzantium* (3 vols., 1991).

Good starting points for the study of Islam include H. A. R. Gibb's succinct *Mohammedanism: An Historical Survey* (1949); B. Lewis, *Islam in History: Ideas, People and Events in the Middle East** (rev. 1993), *Islam and the West* (1993), and his many other writings; W. M. Watt, *The Majesty That Was Islam: The Islamic World, 661–1100* (rev. 1990); and M. G. S. Hodgson, *The Venture of Islam: Conscience and History in a World Civilization** (3 vols., 1974), from the beginnings to the mid–twentieth century. Accounts of the founder of Islam include T. Andrae, *Muhammad: The Man and His Faith* (trans. 1936; 1957); W. M. Watt, *Muhammad: Prophet and Statesman** (1961), a condensation of a detailed two-volume study; M. Rodinson, *Muhammad** (rev. 1980); and K. Armstrong, *Muhammad: A Biography of the Prophet** (1993). The best introduction to Arab history is A. Hourani, *A History of the Arab Peoples* (1991); other informative accounts include B. Lewis, *The Arabs in History** (rev. 1964); P. K. Hitti, *The Arabs: A Short History* (rev. 1968); P. Mansfield, *The Arabs* (1976); and M. Rodinson, *The Arabs** (1981). There are many interesting cultural insights in R. Bulliett, *The Camel and the Wheel* (1975), while S. N. Fisher and W. Ochsenwald, *The Middle East: A History* (rev. 1990), studies the region from pre-Islamic times to the twentieth century.

G. E. von Grunebaum in his *Medieval Islam: A Study in Cultural Orientation* (1946) compares Islamic with the Byzantine and Western civilizations of the time, while D. J. Geanakoplos focuses on their interrelationships in *Medieval Western Civilization and the Byzantine and Islamic Worlds: Interaction of Three Cultures* (1979).

The Middle Ages: Economy, Politics, Society

For economic development, the pioneering books by H. Pirenne on the origins of the cities, revival of trade, and other social and economic developments still merit reading, but they have been superseded by more recent research. Among later histories are R. S. Lopez, *The Commercial Revolution of the Middle Ages, 950–1350** (rev. 1976); G. Duby, *The Growth of the European Economy* (1974); and J. L. Bolton, *The Medieval Economy, 1150–1500** (1980). Also informative are N. J. G. Pounds, *An Economic History of Medieval Europe* (1974); C. M. Cipolla (ed.), *The Middle Ages** (rev. 1977), Vol. I of the *Fontana Economic History of Europe;* the same author's *Before the Industrial Revolution: European Society and Economy, 1000–1700** (rev. 1980); and J. Day, the *Medieval Market Economy* (1987). Important too are the appropriate sections of D. C. North and R. P. Thomas, *Rise of the Western World: A New Economic History* (1973), which examines economic growth and other subjects from 900 to 1700. The volumes in the collaborative *Cambridge Economic History of Europe* (1941 ff.) provide authoritative but highly specialized accounts. The second volume, M. M. Postan and E. Miller (eds.), *Trade and Industry in the Middle Ages* (1952, 1987), has been thoroughly revised for its new edition. L. White, Jr., *Medieval Technology and Social Change** (1962) and *Medieval Religion and Technology** (1978) illustrate some of the scholarship which has dispelled the image of the early medieval years as technologically stagnant.

The best introduction to the growth of towns is E. Ennen, *The Medieval Town* (trans. 1979), which incorporates the considerable research since Pirenne. On the complex subjects of feudalism and manorialism, the most informative introduction is F. L. Ganshof, *Feudalism** (rev. 1961). A remarkable effort at comparing ideal models and material realities is G. Duby, *The Three Orders: Feudal Society Imagined* (trans. 1980). M. Bloch's important contributions include *Feudal Society** (1939–1940; trans. 1961) and *Slavery and Serfdom in the Middle Ages* (trans. 1975).

For the emergent nation-states, S. Painter, *Rise of the Feudal Monarchies** (1951) remains a good brief introduction, while S. Reynolds, *Kingdoms and Commu-*

nities in Western Europe, 900–1300 (1984), stresses the bonds of similarity. An important collaborative work is C. Tilly (ed.), *The Formation of National States in Western Europe* (1975). Of the many books available for the national formations the following are a sampling. For Germany: G. Barraclough, *Origins of Modern Germany** (1947), and F. Heer, *The Holy Roman Empire* (trans. 1965). For England: H. Cam, *England before Elizabeth** (1950); B. Lyon, *A Constitutional and Legal History of Medieval England* (1960); and T. Rowley, *The High Middle Ages, 1200–1540* (1988), in the Making of Britain series. For Spain: A. MacKay, *Spain in the Middle Ages: From Frontier to Empire 1000–1500* (1989). For France: J. Dunbabin, *France in the Making, 843–1180** (1985); E. M. Hallam, *Capetian France, 987–1328** (1983); and E. James, *The Origins of France: From Clovis to the Capetians, 500–1000** (1989). For the Italian city-states one may read J. K. Hyde, *Society and Politics in Medieval Italy, 1000–1350** (1973), and D. Waley, *The Italian City Republics** (rev. 1988).

Social History

The first two volumes of *A History of Private Life,* P. Veyne (ed.), *From Pagan Rome to Byzantium* (1987), and G. Duby (ed.), *Revelations of the Medieval World* (1988), explore aspects of social history, as do R. Fossier, *Peasant Life in the Medieval West* (trans. 1988), and H. W. Goetz, *Life in the Middle Ages: From the Seventh to the Thirteenth Century** (1993). For women in the Middle Ages, their constraints and opportunities, one may read the portraits in E. E. Power, *Medieval Women** (M. M. Postan, ed., 1975); A. Lucas, *Women in the Middle Ages: Religion, Marriage, and Letters* (1984); S. Shahar, *The Fourth Estate: A History of Women in the Middle Ages** (1984); D. Herlihy, *Opera Muliebria: Women at Work in Medieval Europe* (1990); and E. Ennen, *The Medieval Woman* (1990). An informative collection of essays is J. M. Bennett and others (eds.), *Sisters and Workers in the Middle Ages** (1989). The transformation of the household is masterfully explored in D. Herlihy, *Medieval Households* (1985), which may be supplemented by B. A. Hanawalt, *The Ties That Bound: Peasant Families in Medieval England* (1986). Special subjects are explored in two impressive studies: C. Brooke, *The*

*Medieval Idea of Marriage** (1989) and J. A. Brundage, *Law, Sex, and Christian Society in Medieval Europe** (1990).

The Middle Ages: Intellect and Piety

Intellectual developments and scholasticism are discussed in many of the books already cited but are also examined with insight in G. Leff, *Medieval Thought* (1958); D. Knowles, *The Evolution of Medieval Thought* (1962); P. Wolff, *The Awakening of Europe** (1968); F. B. Artz, *The Mind of the Middle Ages, 200–1500** (rev. 1980); and J. Pelikan, *The Growth of Medieval Theology, 600–1300** (1981), vol. III of his *The Christian Tradition* referred to earlier. For political thought and philosophy one may also turn to F. C. Copleston, *Medieval Philosophy* (1952) and the same author's *Aquinas* (1955); J. B. Morrall, *Political Thought in Medieval Times** (1965); and W. Ullman, *A History of Political Thought in the Middle Ages** (1965).

For the universities one may read C. H. Haskins, *The Rise of the Universities* (1923, 1959); H. Rashdall's monumental, *The Universities of Europe in the Middle Ages* (3 vols., 1895; revised and reissued 1936, 1987); and G. Leff, *Paris and Oxford Universities in the Thirteenth and Fourteenth Centuries* (1968). For ancient and medieval scientific activities as background to the emergence of modern science, an excellent synthesis is D. C. Lindberg, *The Beginnings of Western Science: The European Scientific Tradition in Philosophical, Religious, and Institutional Context, 600 B.C. to A.D. 1450** (1992).

Valuable introductions to the church as an institution are G. Barraclough, *The Medieval Papacy** (1968); M. Deanesley, *A History of the Medieval Church, 590–1500** (rev. 1969); W. Ullmann, *A Short History of the Papacy in the Middle Ages** (1974); C. Morris, *The Papal Monarchy: The Western Church from 1050 to 1250** (1989); and J. Lynch, *The Medieval Church: A Brief History** (1992). Important also are P. Hughes, *A History of the Church* (3 vols., 1935–1949); R. H. Bainton, *The Penguin History of Christianity** (1960 ff.); and H. Chadwick, *The Pelican History of the Church** (1967 ff.). For the popes from earliest times on, a wealth of information is available in J. N. D. Kelly (ed.), *The Oxford Dictionary of Popes* (1986), and for all aspects of church history J. McManners, *The Oxford Illustrated History of Christianity**

(1990). Of special interest is J. Sayers, *Innocent III: Leader of Europe, 1198–1216** (1994).

For the lives of the saints and the society they lived in one may read D. Weinstein and R. M. Bell, *Saints and Society: The Two Worlds of Western Christendom, 1000–1700** (1983). Other insights into religious life may be obtained from C. Brooke, *The Monastic World, 1000–1300* (1974) and C. H. Laurence, *Medieval Monasticism** (1989).

For the treatment of heresy in medieval society one may read A. S. Turberville, *Medieval Heresy and the Inquisition* (1920, 1932); S. Runciman, *The Medieval Manichee* (1961); E. Le Roy Ladurie, *Montaillou: The Promised Land of Error** (trans. 1978); and E. Peters, *Inquisition** (1988). Peters has also written a broad study, *Torture** (1985), which includes its incorporation into medieval law and practice. A sweeping indictment of medieval intolerance toward "outside" or deviant groups is presented in R. I. Moore, *The Formation of a Persecuting Society: Power and Deviance in Western Europe, 950–1250** (1987), while a scholarly exploration of medieval attitudes toward one such group is J. Boswell, *Christianity, Sexual Tolerance, and Homosexuality: Gay People in Western Europe from the Beginning of the Christian Era to the Fourteenth Century** (1980).

The Crusades

The outthrust of medieval civilization is ably described in J. R. S. Phillips, *The Medieval Expansion of Europe** (1988); and in R. Bartlett, *The Making of Europe: Conquest, Colonization, and Cultural Change, 950–1350* (1993), an important synthesis. The Crusades may be approached through J. R. Smith, *The Crusades: A Short History* (1987); the detailed, colorful S. Runciman, *A History of the Crusades* (3 vols., 1951–1954; reissued 1987); H. E. Mayer, *The Crusades* (rev. and trans. 1988); and the collaborative multivolume *History of the Crusades* (K. M. Setton, gen. ed.; 6 vols., 1955–1990). The assault on Jewish communities in the Rhineland as a consequence of the First Crusade is carefully examined in R. Chazan, *European Jewry and the First Crusade* (1987), while the twelfth-century Muslim foe of the Crusaders is studied in A. S. Ehrenkrentz, *Saladin* (1978).

Problems and Readings*

Several pamphlets in various problems series are relevant to this chapter: D. Kagan (ed.), *The End of the Roman Empire: Decline or Transformation?* (rev. 1991); A. F. Havighurst (ed.), *The Pirenne Thesis* (rev. 1976); J. F. Benton (ed.), *Town Origins: The Evidence from Medieval England* (1968); R. E. Sullivan (ed.), *The Coronation of Charlemagne* (1959); R. S. Lopez (ed.), *The Tenth Century: How Dark the Dark Ages?* (1959); C. W. Hollister (ed.), *The Twelfth-Century Renaissance* (1969); C. R. Young (ed.), *The Renaissance of the Twelfth Century* (1970); S. Williams (ed.), *The Gregorian Epoch* (1966); J. A. Brundage (ed.), *The Crusaders* (1964); J. M. Powell (ed.), *Innocent III* (1963); R. E. Herzstein (ed.), *The Holy Roman Empire in the Middle Ages* (1965); J. L. Abu-Lughod, *The World System in the Thirteenth Century: Dead End or Precursor?* (1994), in the new AHA [American Historical Association] Pamphlets series; R. Eaton, *Islamic History as Global History* (1990), in the same series; and G. P. Bodet (ed.), *Early English Parliaments: High Courts, Royal Councils, or Representative Assemblies?* (1968). In the Anvil series there are P. K. Hitti, *Islam and the West* (1962, 1979), and J. R. Strayer, *Feudalism* (1965, 1979).

II. The Upheaval in Christendom, 1300–1560

Overviews for these years encompassing the later Middle Ages, the Renaissance, and the Reformation include A. G. Dickens, *The Age of Humanism and Reformation: Europe in the Fourteenth to Sixteenth Centuries* (1972); S. E. Ozment, *The Age of Reform, 1250–1550: An Intellectual and Religious History of Late Medieval and Reformation Europe** (1980); and D. Waley, *Later Medieval Europe from Saint Louis to Luther** (rev. 1985). Of many other general accounts one may mention D. Hay, *Europe in the Fourteenth and Fifteenth Centuries** (rev. 1989); H. F. Koenigsberger, *Early Modern Europe, 1500–1789** (1987); G. L. Mosse and G. Q. Bowler, *Europe in the Sixteenth Century** (rev. 1989); and E. F. Rice, Jr., and A. Grafton, *The Foundations of Early Modern Europe** (rev. 1993). Two insightful books are J. R. Hale, *Renaissance and Reformation Thought** (1975) and J. Bossy, *Christianity in the West, 1400–1700** (1985).

There are informative chapters in G. R. Potter (ed.), *The Renaissance, 1493–1520* (rev. 1991) and G. R. Elton (ed.), *The Reformation, 1520–1559* (rev. 1990), Vols. I and II of the *New Cambridge Modern History*. T. K. Rabb, *Renaissance Lives: Portraits of an Age* (1993), provides vivid accounts of notable figures. War and diplomacy are explored in G. Mattingly, *Renaissance Diplomacy* (1971); M. S. Anderson, *The Rise of Modern Diplomacy, 1450–1919* (1993), which begins with this age; and J. R. Hale, *War and Society in Renaissance Europe, 1450–1620** (1986); while E. L. Eisenstein focuses on the printing press as a direct and indirect agent of cultural change in *The Printing Revolution in Early Modern Europe** (1984).

Much newer social history has centered on the early modern centuries. Here P. Burke, *Popular Culture in Early Modern Europe* (1978), mentioned earlier, ranging in time from 1500 to 1800, is fundamental. A few other examples may be cited. C. Ginzburg, *The Cheese and the Worms: The Cosmos of a Sixteenth-Century Miller** (trans. 1980), reconstructs the mentality of an obscure Italian miller of the age. N. Z. Davis, *Society and Culture in Early Modern France* (1975), illuminates the religious and other beliefs of nonliterate peasants, and in *The Return of Martin Guerre** (1983), recounts a fascinating episode in village life. R. Chartier (ed.), *Passions of the Renaissance* (1988), the third volume of the History of Private Life series described earlier, opens the door to aspects of life among all classes in this era. G. Huppert, *After the Black Death: A Social History of Early Modern Europe** (1986) surveys the years from the fourteenth to the eighteenth centuries. Other aspects of social history are examined in L. P. Buck and S. W. Zophy (eds.), *The Social History of the Reformation* (1972); K. von Greyerz (ed.), *Religion and Society in Early Modern Europe, 1500–1800* (1984); and R. Jütte, *Poverty and Deviance in Early Modern Europe** (1994), a volume in the New Approaches to European History series. The ambivalent position of women in the Renaissance is ably conveyed in M. L. King, *Women of the Renaissance** (1991), an outstanding study; I. Maclean, *The Renaissance Notion of Women* (1980); and M. E. Wiesner, *Women and Gender in Early Modern Europe** (1993), also a volume in the New Approaches to European History series, which synthesizes recent scholarship on the subject.

Disasters of the Fourteenth Century

Two brief surveys of the era are R. E. Lerner, *The Age of Adversity: The Fourteenth Century** (1968), and M. McKissack, *The Fourteenth Century, 1307–1399** (1959, 1991). B. W. Tuchman, *A Distant Mirror: The Calamitous Fourteenth Century** (1978) is a vivid account written for the general reader, criticized by some specialists. G. Leff, *The Dissolution of the Medieval Outlook: An Essay on Intellectual Change in the Fourteenth Century* (1976), despite the title, stresses the continuity of medieval thought. The growing restlessness within the church before the Reformation is described in P. Hughes, *The Revolt against the Church: Aquinas to Luther* (1974); E. F. Jacob, *Essays on the Conciliar Epoch* (1953); F. Oakley, *The Western Church in the Later Middle Ages* (1979); and R. N. Swanson, *Church and Society in Late Medieval Europe* (1989). Heresies of the period may be examined in H. Kaminsky, *A History of the Hussite Revolution* (1967); K. B. McFarlane, *John Wycliffe and the Beginnings of English Nonconformity** (1952); and M. Lambert, *Medieval Heresy: From the Gregorian Reform to the Reformation** (1992).

The devastating fourteenth-century plague that swept Europe and other parts of the globe from 1347 to 1351, which historians say cost as many as 28 million lives, is examined in W. H. McNeill, *Plagues and Peoples** (1976), cited earlier; P. Ziegler, *The Black Death* (1969); and R. S. Gottfried, *The Black Death: Natural and Human Disaster in Medieval Europe* (1983). The long war between France and England over the years 1337 to 1453 may be studied in E. Perroy, *The Hundred Years War* (trans. 1965); and in books of the same title by D. Seward (1978) and R. Neillands* (reissued 1991). C. Allmand, *The Hundred Years War: England and France at War, c. 1300–c. 1450** (1988), explores the war's impact on both countries.

For the *jacqueries* and other popular revolts one may read M. Mollat and P. Wolff, *The Popular Revolutions of the Late Middle Ages* (trans. 1972) and G. Fourquin, *The Anatomy of Popular Rebellion in the Middle Ages* (trans. 1978).

The phenomenon of witchcraft in the early modern centuries between 1450 and 1750 has understandably attracted a good deal of attention. During those years more than 100,000 people, mainly women, were prosecuted in secular and ecclesiastical courts, and many put to death. To understand the phenomenon, K. Thomas, *Religion and the Decline of Magic** (1971), is of fundamental importance, but one should also read H. R. Trevor-Roper, *The European Witch-Craze of the Sixteenth and Seventeenth Centuries** (1969); C. Larner, *Witchcraft and Religion: The Politics of Popular Belief** (1985); C. Ginzburg, *Ecstasies: Deciphering the Witches' Sabbath* (1991); B. P. Levack, *The Witch-Hunt in Early Modern Europe** (1987), which synthesizes the literature; and B. Ankerloo and G. Henningsen (eds.), *Early Modern European Witchcraft: Centres and Peripheries** (1990).

The Renaissance in Italy

In addition to the general accounts already cited, one may turn for all aspects of the Renaissance to M. P. Gilmore, *The World of Humanism, 1453–1517** (1952), an older still valuable volume in the Langer series. The concept of the "Renaissance" itself is explored in W. K. Ferguson, *The Renaissance in Historical Thought: Five Centuries of Interpretation* (1948), which examines among other writings the classical accounts of the Italian Renaissance by J. A. Symonds (7 vols., 1875–1886) and J. Burckhardt (1860; reissued 1944).

For the quickening of activities in the Italian city-states one turns to D. Hay, *The Italian Renaissance in Its Historical Background** (rev. 1977); D. Hay and J. Law, *Italy in the Age of the Renaissance, 1380–1630** (1989); P. Burke, *The Italian Renaissance: Culture and Society in Italy** (rev. 1987); F. Braudel, *Out of Italy, 1450–1650* (trans. 1992), by the *Annales* historian; and P. Denley, *The Italian Renaissance** (1993). The revived interest in the classics is studied in R. Weiss, *The Renaissance Discovery of Classical Antiquity** (1969, 1988); and the philosophical debates of the time in B. P. Copenhaver and C. B. Schmitt, *Renaissance Philosophy** (1992). The fusion of politics and humanism (or "civic humanism") is traced in a pioneering work by H. Baron, *The Crisis of the Early Italian Renaissance: Civic Humanism and Republican Liberty in an Age of Classicism and Tyranny** (1955; rev. 1966). The relationship of politics and cultural life is also graphically portrayed in L. Martines, *Power and Imagination: City States in Renaissance Italy** (1979). A famous Renaissance prelate is portrayed in C. Shaw, *Julius II: The Warrior Pope* (1993).

On Machiavelli, there are studies by F. Chabod, *Machiavelli and the Renaissance* (trans. 1958); the brief J. R. Hale, *Machiavelli and Renaissance Italy** (Teach Yourself History series, 1960); and a remarkable intellectual biography, S. de Grazia, *Machiavelli in Hell** (1990), which may be supplemented by A. J. Parel's revisionist *The Machiavellian Cosmos* (1992). A provocative study of political thought and discourse as influenced by the Renaissance from the fifteenth to the eighteenth centuries is J. G. A. Pocock, *The Machiavellian Moment: Florentine Political Thought and the Atlantic Republican Tradition** (1975), while J. R. Hale (ed.), *A Concise Encyclopedia of the Italian Renaissance* (1981) is a convenient reference tool.

Numerous studies focusing on each of the Italian city-states have helped illuminate the world of humanism, of which only a few titles can be cited here. Much of the focus has been on Florence, for which G. Brucker, *Renaissance Florence** (rev. 1983), and G. Holmes, *The Florentine Enlightenment, 1400–1450** (1992), are most helpful. Other informative studies include J. R. Hale, *Florence and the Medici: The Pattern of Control* (1978), an especially insightful account; R. A. Goldthwaite, *The Building of Renaissance Florence: An Economic and Social History* (1980); M. Becker, *Florence in Transition* (2 vols., 1967–1969); D. Weinstein, *Savanorola and Florence* (1970); and C. Fusero, *The Borgias* (trans. 1973). A colorful popular account is C. Hibbert, *Florence: The Biography of a City* (1993).

Outstanding studies of Venice with varying perspectives include: F. C. Lane, *Venice: A Maritime Republic** (1973); W. H. McNeill, *Venice, The Hinge of Europe, 1081–1797* (1974); W. Bouwsma, *Venice and the Defense of Republican Liberty: Renaissance Values in the Age of the Counter Reformation* (1968); B. Pullan, *Rich and Poor in Renaissance Venice* (1971); and J. J. Norwich, *A History of Venice* (1982). For Rome, one may read P. Partner, *The Lands* *of St. Peter: The Papal State in the Middle Ages and the Early Renaissance* (1972); the same author's *Renaissance Rome, 1500–1559: A Portrait of a Society** (1977); and C. L. Stinger, *The Renaissance in Rome* (1985).

The Renaissance outside Italy

The best introduction to the northern Renaissance remains J. Huizinga, *The Waning of the Middle Ages: Life, Thought, and Art in France and the Netherlands in the Fourteenth and Fifteenth Centuries** (1924; reissued 1976); one should also read the same author's *Erasmus and the Age of Reformation** (1924; reissued 1957). For the Dutch humanist one may also read the brief, spirited M. M. Phillips, *Erasmus and the Northern Renaissance** (1950); R. M. Bainton, *Erasmus of Christendom* (1969); J. D. Tracy, *The Politics of Erasmus* (1978); and L. Halkin, *Erasmus: A Critical Biography* (1992). For Christian humanism in general and its contribution to the religious changes of the age one turns to E. H. Harbison, *The Christian Scholar in the Age of the Reformation** (1956); L. W. Spitz, *The Religious Renaissance of the German Humanists* (1963); and J. H. Overfield, *Humanism and Scholasticism in Late Medieval Germany* (1984).

The New Monarchies

For a good overview consult R. Bonney, *The European Dynastic States, 1494–1660* (1991). J. R. Lander, *Government and Community: England, 1450–1509* (1980), describes in detail the curbing of feudal power and the evolution of the modern state in England; while E. F. Jacob, *The Fifteenth Century** (1961, 1993), and A. Goodman, *The New Monarchy: England, 1471–1534* (1988), are also helpful. The first Tudor monarch is examined in S. B. Chrimes, *Henry VII* (1972) and in M. V. C. Alexander, *The First of the Tudors: A Study of Henry VII and His Reign* (1980). All aspects of the age are examined in J. Youings, *Sixteenth-Century England** (1984). For France two books are illuminating: L. Batiffol, *The Century of the Renaissance* (trans. 1961) and L. Febvre, *Life in Renaissance France** (trans. 1977); while two good biographies of "new monarchs" are J. M. Tyrrell, *Louis XI* (1980), and R. J. Knecht, *Francis I** (1982), the latter a biography of distinction.

General Works on the Reformation

The best synthesis for the sixteenth-century upheaval in church and society, providing valuable bibliographic guidance as well, is L. W. Spitz, *The Protestant Reformation, 1517–1559** (1985), in the Langer series. Other informative accounts include G. R. Elton, *Reformation Europe, 1517–1559** (1963); A. G. Dickens, *Reformation and Society in Sixteenth-Century Europe** (1960); O. Chadwick, *The Reformation** (1963); E. H. Harbison, *The Age of the Reformation** (1963); K. Holl, *The Cultural Significance of the Reformation* (1959); H. J. Hillerbrand, *Men and Ideas of the Sixteenth Century** (1969); and E. Cameron, *The European Reformation** (1991). Two studies by eminent Catholic scholars are P. Hughes, *A Popular History of the Reformation** (1957), and J. Lortz, *How the Reformation Came* (1964). A critical guide to the historiography of the Reformation and the key debates relating to it is A. G. Dickens and J. M. Tonkin with K. Powell, *The Reformation in Historical Thought* (1985).

For the political background one may turn to H. Holborn, *A History of Modern Germany: The Reformation* (1959), the first volume of a three-volume history of Germany; and F. L. Carsten, *Princes and Parliaments in Germany* (1959). Two outstanding accounts of the leading ruler of the age are K. Brandi, *The Emperor Charles V** (trans. 1939; 1968), a classic since its publication; and M. Fernández Alvarez, *Charles V: Elected Emperor and Hereditary Ruler* (trans. 1975).

Biographical accounts of Luther include R. H. Bainton, *Here I Stand: A Life of Martin Luther* (1950); V. H. H. Green, *Luther and the Reformation* (1964, 1969); A. G. Dickens, *Martin Luther and the Reformation** (1967); J. Atkinson, *Martin Luther and the Birth of Protestantism** (1968); and R. Marius, *Luther* (1974). E. H. Erikson offers psychoanalytic insights into the religious leader's identity crises in *Young Man Luther: A Study in Psychoanalysis and History** (1962). Among other studies are H. Boehmer, *Martin Luther: Road to Reformation* (1960), on the reformer's formative years; H. G. Haile, *Luther: An Experiment in Biography* (1980); M. U. Edwards, Jr., *Luther's Last Battles: Politics and Polemics, 1531–1546** (1983); and G. Brendler, *Martin Luther: Theology and Revolution* (1989). The appeal of Lutheran ideas is skillfully analyzed in R. W. Scribner, *For the Sake of Simple Folk: Popular Propaganda in the German Reformation* (1981). P. Blickle, *The Revolution of 1525: The German Peasants' War from a New Perspective* (trans. 1981), studies that event and Luther's role comprehensively but may be supplemented by the essays in B. Scribner and G. Benecke (eds.), *The German Peasant War, 1525: New Viewpoints* (1979).

An admirable biography of Calvin, capturing the spirit of the man and his times, is W. J. Bouwsma, *John Calvin: A Sixteenth-Century Portrait** (1987). Studies of the reformer's thought and influence include A. M. Schmidt, *John Calvin and the Calvinist Tradition* (trans. 1960), and F. Wendel, *Calvin: The Origins and Development of His Religious Thought* (trans. 1963). An outstanding biography of another reformer is G. R. Potter, *Zwingli* (1977), on whom W. P. Stephens has also written: *Zwingli: An Introduction to His Thought* (1992). R. H. Bainton, *Hunted Heretic: The Life and Death of Michael Servetus** (1960), may be compared with J. Friedman, *Michael Servetus: A Case Study in Total Heresy* (1978). W. S. Reid has written *Trumpeter of God: A Biography of John Knox* (1975).

The cities in which the major events of the Reformation occurred are examined in G. Strauss, *Nuremberg in the Sixteenth Century** (1966); W. Monter, *Calvin's Geneva** (1967); and S. E. Ozment, *The Reformation in the Cities: The Appeal of Protestantism to Sixteenth Century Germany and Switzerland** (1975). Ozment's *When Fathers Ruled: Family Life in Reformation Europe** (1983) describes the patriarchal household as less tyrannical than traditionally portrayed. R. H. Bainton, *Women of the Reformation* (3 vols., 1971–1977), studies the contributions of women to the religious changes of the era.

The Reformation in England

The course of the Reformation in England may be approached through a number of syntheses: A. G. Dickens, *The English Reformation** (1964); D. H. Pill, *The English Reformation, 1529–1558** (1973); G. R. Elton, *Reform and Reformation in England, 1509–1558** (1977); J. J. Scarisbrick, *The Reformation and the English People** (1986); and R. Rex, *Henry VIII and the English Reformation** (1993). Recent scholarship is also communicated in C. Haigh

(ed.), *The English Reformation Revised** (1987). L. Solt, *Church and State in Early Modern England, 1509–1640* (1990) follows the continuing religious tensions on into the next century.

R. Marius, *Thomas More: A Biography* (1985), the most discerning biography of the scholar, statesman, and martyr, may be supplemented by L. L. Martz, *Thomas More: The Search for the Inner Man** (1990). Admirable on an important subject is D. Knowles, *Bare Ruined Choirs: The Dissolution of the English Monasteries* (1959, 1976), while two other informative accounts are J. Youings, *The Dissolution of the Monasteries* (1971), and E. Duffy, *The Stripping of the Altars* (1992). Additional social and economic facets of these years are examined in W. G. Hoskins, *The Age of Plunder: The England of Henry VIII, 1500–1547** (1976).

Three provocative books dealing with the social implications of the Reformation for the future course of England are R. H. Tawney, *Religion and the Rise of Capitalism** (1926, 1947), insightful even if superseded by later research; C. Hill, *Reformation to Industrial Revolution: The Making of Modern English Society** (1967), also emphasizing class interests; and H. R. Trevor-Roper, *Religion, the Reformation, and Social Change* (1967), which is less persuaded by the connection between religion and class.

A distinguished biography focusing on the king as well as the events of his reign is J. J. Scarisbrick, *Henry VIII** (1968, 1986); also thoughtful is L. B. Smith, *Henry VIII: The Mask of Royalty* (1971). The famous divorce, among other matters, is examined in H. A. Kelly, *The Matrimonial Trials of Henry VIII* (1975), while for Henry's wives, in addition to several individual biographies for each, one may read A. Fraser, *The Wives of Henry VIII* (1992) and A. Weir, *Six Wives of Henry VIII* (1992), both informative. Henry VIII's two immediate successors and their brief reigns are described in W. K. Jordan, *Edward VI* (2 vols., 1968–1970); D. M. Loades, *Mary Tudor* (1989); and C. Erickson, *Bloody Mary: The Life of Mary Tudor** (1993). Books on Elizabeth will be described in the next chapter, but for studies of religion in all or part of her reign one may turn to R. McGrath, *Papists and Puritans under Elizabeth I* (1968); A. Morey, *The Catholic Subjects of Elizabeth I* (1978); and P. Collinson's two books: *The Elizabethan Puritan*

*Movement** (1967; reissued 1990) and *The Religion of Protestants: The Church in English Society, 1559–1625** (1983).

Other Reformation Themes

The various forms of Protestantism are placed in doctrinal perspective in J. S. Whale, *The Protestant Tradition* (1959); E. G. Leonard, *A History of Protestantism* (1965); B. M. G. Reardon, *Religious Thought in the Reformation** (1981); and A. McGrath, *Reformation Thought** (1988); while the radical movements of the era may be studied in G. H. Williams, *The Radical Reformation* (1962); N. Cohn, *The Pursuit of the Millennium: Revolutionary Messianism in Medieval and Reformation Europe* (1957, 1964); and M. A. Mullett, *Radical Religious Movements in Early Modern Europe** (1980). An important subject is explored in H. Kamen, *The Rise of Toleration* (1967).

On the much debated question concerning the relation between economic change and Protestant religious doctrine, especially Calvinism, a debate that was opened by Max Weber in *The Protestant Ethic and the Spirit of Capitalism** (1904, reissued 1955) and further developed by R. H. Tawney in the 1920s, one may read R. M. Mitchell, *Calvin and the Puritan's View of the Protestant Ethic* (1979); G. Marshall, *In Search of the Spirit of Capitalism: An Essay on Max Weber's Protestant Ethic Thesis* (1982), a balanced review of the thesis and the debate; and the contributions in H. Lehmann and G. Roth (eds.), *Weber's Protestant Ethic* (1993), which add many new insights.

The Catholic response to the Reformation is studied in M. R. O'Connell, *The Counter Reformation, 1559–1610** (1974), in the Langer series; in A. G. Dickens, *The Counter Reformation* (1969); and in P. Janelle, *The Catholic Reformation* (1951). N. S. Davidson, *The Counter Reformation** (1987), provides a brief overview. Important for the Catholic response and other matters is J. Pelikan, *Reformation of Church and Dogma, 1300–1700** (1983), Vol. IV of his *The Christian Tradition*. H. Jedin, *The Council of Trent* (2 vols., 1957–1961), presents the fullest account of the important council and its reforms. Introductions to the literature on the Society of Jesus are provided in C. Hollis, *The Jesuits* (1968); M. Foss, *The Founding of the Jesuits, 1540* (1969); and W. B. Bangert, *A History of the*

Society of Jesus (1972). There are biographies of Loyola by J. Brodrick (1956), P. Caramon (1990), and W. Meissner (1992), the latter a psychoanalytical study.

Problems and Readings*

Pamphlets in various problems series include W. M. Bowsky (ed.), *The Black Death: A Turning Point in History?* (1978); K. H. Dannenfeldt (ed.), *The Renaissance* (rev. 1974); D. Hay (ed.), *The Renaissance Debate* (1963); D. L. Jensen (ed.), *Machievalli: Cynic, Patriot, or Political Scientist?* (1960); L. W. Spitz (ed.), *The Reformation* (rev. 1972); K. C. Sessions (ed.), *Reformation and Authority: The Meaning of the Peasants' Revolt* (1968); A. J. Slavin (ed.), *The New Monarchies* (1964) and *Henry VIII and the English Reformation* (1968); R. W. Green, *Protestantism, Capitalism, and Social Sciences: The Weber Thesis Controversy* (rev. 1973); and R. Kingdon, *Calvin and Calvinism: Sources of Democracy?* (1970). Source material and commentary are provided in M. Rady (ed.), *The Emperor Charles V* (1988); M. D. Palmer, *Henry VIII* (rev. 1988); H. J. Hillerbrand (ed.), *The Protestant Reformation: A Narrative History Related by Contemporary Observers and Participants* (1964); L. W. Spitz (ed.), *The Protestant Reformation* (1966); G. R. Elton (ed.), *Renaissance and Reformation, 1300–1648* (1963); and R. H. Bainton, *The Age of the Reformation** (1956, 1984).

III. Economic Renewal and Wars of Religion, 1560–1648

Of general treatments for these years, covering institutional and international developments, the best guides are J. H. Elliott, *Europe Divided, 1559–1598** (rev. 1982); C. Wilson, *The Transformation of Europe, 1558–1648* (1976); G. Parker, *Europe in Crisis, 1598–1648* (1979); H. Kamen, *European Society, 1500–1700* (1984); and V. G. Kiernan, *State and Society in Europe, 1550–1650** (1987). F. Braudel's magisterial work stressing broad geographic, demographic, and economic developments, *The Mediterranean and the Mediterranean World in the Age of Philip II** (rev. and abr. ed., 1992), has been cited in the introductory section.

Analytical treatments focusing on the concept of crisis in the seventeenth century (and useful for this and the following chapter) include T. Aston (ed.), *Crisis in Europe,*

1560–1660: Essays from Past and Present* (1966); G. Parker and L. M. Smith, *The General Crisis of the Seventeenth Century* (1978); T. K. Rabb, *The Struggle for Stability in Early Modern Europe** (1976); and T. Munck, *Seventeenth-Century Europe: State, Conflict, and the Social Order in Europe, 1598–1700** (1990). Agrarian and urban unrest is studied in P. Zagorin, *Rebels and Rulers 1500–1660** (2 vols., 1982); J. A. Goldstone, *Revolution and Rebellion in the Early Modern World** (1991), which is overly schematic; and C. Tilly, *European Revolutions, 1492–1992* (1992). The impact on society of military change is explained and debated in G. Clark, *War and Society in the Seventeenth Century* (1958); G. Parker, *The Military Revolution: Military Innovation and the Rise of the West, 1500–1800** (1988); J. Black, *A Military Revolution? Military Change and European Society, 1550–1800** (1991); and B. M. Downing, *The Military Revolution and Political Change: The Origins of Democracy and Autocracy in Early Modern Europe** (1993). The latter is meant to be compared with B. Moore, *The Social Origins of Dictatorship and Democracy: Lord and Peasant in the Making of the Modern World** (1966).

The Opening of the Atlantic

Good introductions to European exploration and settlement, beginning in the pre-Columbian age, are F. Fernández-Armesto, *Before Columbus: Exploration and Colonization from the Mediterranean to the Atlantic, 1229–1492* (1987); J. H. Parry, *The Age of Reconnaissance: Discovery, Exploration and Settlement, 1450–1650** (rev. 1981); and G. Scammell, *The First Imperial Age: European Overseas Expansion, 1400–1715* (1989). Still valuable is S. E. Morison, *The European Discovery of America* (2 vols., 1971–1974, 1993). C. M. Cipolla stresses the importance of technology for the European explorations in *Guns, Sails, and Empires: 1400–1700** (1965).

The five-hundredth anniversary of Columbus' first voyage stimulated the appearance of many new books, many vehemently critical of the European impact on the New World, and seeing the voyages less as discovery than as intrusion or conquest, or at best as encounter with other peoples. Three examples of this critical literature are K. Sale, *The Conquest of Paradise: Christopher Columbus and the Columbian Legacy* (1990); T. Todorov, *The Conquest of America: The Question of the Other* (trans. 1984); and D. E. Stannard, *American Holocaust: Columbus and the Conquest of the New World* (1993). Two balanced accounts, placing Columbus in the context of his times without overlooking the consequences of the European arrival are W. D. Phillips, Jr., and C. R. Phillips, *The Worlds of Christopher Columbus** (1991), and F. Fernández-Armesto, *Columbus** (1991). A scholarly effort to examine much that remains obscure about the explorer is D. Henige, *In Search of Columbus: The Sources for the First Voyage* (1991). An older study by S. E. Morison, *Admiral of the Ocean Sea* (1942), skillfully reconstructs Columbus' voyages but is now criticized for overestimating his skills and modernity. P. Liss, *Isabel the Queen* (1992), is a thoughtful biography of his patron.

J. A. Levenson (ed.), *Circa 1492: Art in the Age of Exploration** (1991), a splendidly illustrated catalog prepared for an exhibition to commemorate the quincentenary, presents the impressive art and artifacts of people from all over the globe in this age, including the New World. Two thoughtful books by A. W. Crosby demonstrate that European plants, animals, and diseases had as much to do with the success of European expansion, and the consequent devastation for the indigenous peoples, as military conquest: *The Columbian Exchange: Biological and Cultural Consequences of 1492** (1972), and a broader study, *Ecological Imperialism: The Biological Expansion of Europe, 900–1900** (1986). For the impact of the discoveries on European thought, two thoughtful books are W. Brandon, *New Worlds for Old: Reports from the New World and Their Effect on the Development of Social Thought in Europe, 1500–1800* (1986), and A. Pagden, *European Encounters with the New World: From Renaissance to Romanticism* (1992).

Portugal and Spain in Europe and Overseas

The best introduction to the overseas exploits of both countries is L. N. McAlister, *Spain and Portugal in the New World, 1492–1700** (1983). Portuguese maritime and colonial enterprises are recounted in C. R. Boxer, *The Portuguese Seaborne Empire: 1415–1825* (1969); one may also read B. W. Diffie and G. D. Winius, *Founda-*

tions of the Portuguese Empire, 1415–1580 (1977). On Portugal, there are sound histories by H. V. Livermore, *A New History of Portugal** (1977); A. H. De Oliveira Marques, *History of Portugal** (rev. 1976); and on the Iberian peninsula, S. G. Payne, *A History of Spain and Portugal* (2 vols., 1973).

The best accounts for Spain in the early modern centuries are J. H. Elliott, *Imperial Spain, 1469–1714** (1964), which may be supplemented by his *Spain and Its World, 1500–1700** (1986); J. Lynch, *Spain under the Habsburgs 1516–1700** (2 vols.; rev. 1992); and H. Kamen, *Spain, 1469–1714: A Society of Conflict** (rev. 1991). Three illuminating studies of the sixteenth-century Spanish sovereign are C. Petrie, *Philip II of Spain* (1963), as much an account of Spanish affairs as a biography; P. Pierson, *Philip II of Spain* (1976); and G. Parker, *Philip II* (1978), the most informative study. An insightful book on the Spanish arm of the Counter Reformation is H. Kamen, *Inquisition and Society in Spain in the Sixteenth and Seventeenth Centuries** (1985).

Although G. Mattingly, *The Armada** (1959, 1989), remains unsurpassed in placing the dramatic episode in its diplomatic and ideological setting, a few additional books merit mention: R. Whiting, *The Enterprise of England: The Spanish Armada* (1988); C. Martin and G. Parker, *The Spanish Armada* (1989); P. Pierson, *Commander of the Armada: The Seventh Duke of Medina Sidonia** (1990); and F. Fernández-Armesto, *The Spanish Armada: The Experience of War in 1588** (1989).

Books examining Spain after the age of Philip II include R. A. Stradling, *Philip IV and the Government of Spain, 1621–1665* (1988), and two outstanding studies by J. H. Elliott: *The Revolt of the Catalans: A Study in the Decline of Spain, 1598–1640** (1963, 1984) and *The Count-Duke of Olivares: The Statesman in an Age of Decline* (1987), on Philip IV's principal adviser from 1621 to 1643.

For the Spanish empire in the new world, one may read C. Gibson, *Spain in America** (1966, 1990); J. H. Parry, *The Spanish Seaborne Empire** (1966); J. H. Elliott, *The Old World and the New, 1492–1650* (1970, 1992) and *Spain and Its World** (1986), cited earlier; C. O. Sauer, *The Early Spanish Main** (1961, 1990); and C. M. MacLachlan, *Spain's Empire in the New World** (1988). A pioneer inquiry into the impact of the

discovery of silver upon economic changes in Europe was E. J. Hamilton, *American Treasure and the Price Revolution in Spain, 1501–1650* (1934), although some of its conclusions have been modified. The subject also is examined in P. Vila, *A History of Gold and Money, 1450–1920* (trans. 1976), and in J. N. Ball, *Merchants and Merchandise: The Expansion of Trade in Europe, 1500–1630* (1977). For the Spanish conquest two older, vivid accounts are F. A. Kirkpatrick, *The Spanish Conquistadores* (1934, 1949), and J. Hemmings, *The Conquest of the Incas** (1970). Newer scholarship is reflected in R. L. Marks, *Cortés: The Great Adventurer and the Fate of Aztec Mexico* (1993). On attempts by the church and others to mitigate the evils of the conquest one still turns to L. Hanke, *The Struggle for Justice in the Conquest of America* (1949). The best scholarly accounts of the enforced labor and the demographic consequences of the conquest may be found in the chapters contributed to L. Bethell (ed.), *The Cambridge History of Latin America*, Vols. I and II, *Colonial Latin America* (1988). An informative survey for all aspects of Latin America in the colonial era is M. A. Burkholder and L. L. Johnson, *Colonial Latin America** (rev. 1993).

Of the many books on the Atlantic slave trade and slavery, two of the most informative are H. S. Klein, *African Slavery in Latin America and the Caribbean* (1987), and V. B. Thompson, *The Making of the African Diaspora in the Americas, 1441–1900** (1988). The writings of D. B. Davis, *Slavery and Human Progress** (1984), and his other volumes cited in later chapters, offer insights into the phenomenon of slavery. The historical background is presented in W. D. Phillips, *Slavery from Roman Times to the Early Transatlantic Trade* (1985), carrying the story to 1650, and in B. Lewis, *Race and Slavery in the Middle East* (1990). E. Williams, *Capitalism and Slavery** (1944), some of whose conclusions have been modified by later research, early emphasized that the emerging Atlantic economy was supported by African slavery, a theme on which there are informative essays in B. L. Solow (ed.), *Slavery and the Rise of the Atlantic System** (1991). The grim story of the slave trade is recounted in many books, among them, J. Pope-Hennessy, *Sins of the Fathers: A Study of the Atlantic Slave Traders 1441–1807** (1968); D. P. Mannix and M. Cowley, *Black Cargoes* (1962); P.

D. Curtin, *The Atlantic Slave Trade** (1969); H. S. Klein, *The Middle Passage** (1978); and J. A. Rawley, *The Transatlantic Slave Trade* (1981). A valuable synthesis of historical writings on slavery in its North American setting is P. Kolchin, *American Slavery, 1619–1877* (1993).

Changing Social Structures, Early Capitalism, Mercantilism

A key study of early economic history is J. De Vries, *The Economy of Europe in an Age of Crisis, 1600–1750** (1976), but one will wish to consult also R. Davis, *The Rise of the Atlantic Economies** (1973); C. M. Cipolla, *Before the Industrial Revolution: European Society and Economy, 1000–1700* (rev. 1980); P. Kriedte, *Peasants, Landlords, and Merchant Capitalists: Europe and the World Economy, 1500–1800** (1983); and A. K. Smith, *Creating a World Economy: Merchant Capital, Colonialism, and World Trade, 1400–1825** (1991). The reasons why rapid economic change took place in western Europe rather than elsewhere are explored in E. L. Jones, *The European Miracle: Environments, Economics, and Geopolitics in the History of Europe and Asia* (rev. 1987), and in an informative collection of essays, J. Baechler and others (eds.), *Europe and the Rise of Capitalism** (1988).

A remarkable though unsystematic and often impressionistic account of social and economic change, and of life and labor, in the early modern centuries is the three-volume work of F. Braudel, *Civilization and Capitalism, 15th–18th Century** (trans. 1981–1984; reissued 1992): Vol. I, *The Structures of Everyday Life;* Vol. II, *The Wheels of Commerce;* and Vol. III, *The Perspective of the World.* The broad themes of the work are summarized in *Afterthoughts on Material Civilization and Capitalism** (trans. 1977). Another large-scale study, reflecting the influence of Braudel and focusing on the shifting of economic power is I. Wallerstein, *The Modern World-System** (1974 ff.), of which three volumes have appeared to date, analyzing respectively the origins of the world economy, mercantilism from 1600 to 1750, and the expansion of the global economy from 1730 to the 1840s. The development of a capitalist economy is also traced in W. N. Parker, *Essays on the History of Capitalism* (2 vols.): Vol. I, *Europe and the World Economy** (1984);

and Vol. II, *America and the Wider World** (1991); and an important intercultural dimension is added in P. D. Curtin, *Cross-Cultural Trade in World History** (1984).

Much of the debate on the early modern centuries focuses on the continuity of European economic history since the Middle Ages and on early industrialization. The debate on "protoindustrialization" is examined in P. Kriedte (ed.), *Industrialization before Industrialization: Rural Industry and the Genesis of Capitalism* (1981) and in M. P. Gutmann, *Toward the Modern Economy: Early Industry in Europe, 1500–1800** (1988). Additional studies will be cited in Chapter XI.

For the early demography of Europe one may turn to M. W. Flynn, *The European Demographic System, 1500–1820** (1981); and for the growth of cities, to P. M. Hohenberg and L. H. Lees, *The Making of Urban Europe, 1000–1950** (1985), cited earlier; and J. De Vries, *European Urbanization, 1500–1800* (1984). There are valuable chapters in C. M. Cipolla (ed.), *The Fontana Economic History of Europe: The Sixteenth and Seventeenth Centuries** (1974), and in the two volumes edited by E. E. Rich and C. H. Wilson in the *Cambridge Economic History of Europe*, Vol. IV (1976) and Vol. V (1977).

Revolt of the Netherlands

G. Parker, *The Dutch Revolt* (1977), an admirable comprehensive study, may be compared with P. Geyl's masterful older account: *The Revolt of the Netherlands, 1555–1609* (1932; trans. 1958), and *The Netherlands in the Seventeenth Century, 1609–1715* (2 vols; trans. 1961–1964). C. V. Wedgwood, *William the Silent** (1944), is an excellent, laudatory biography. W. S. Maltby, *Alba: A Biography* (1983), studies the Duke of Alba, the Spanish governor sent to suppress the Dutch in the mid–sixteenth century and who thereby helped to create the Dutch nation.

The Tudor Age: Elizabethan England

The best syntheses for the Tudor monarchs, early and later, are G. R. Elton, *England under the Tudors** (rev. 1991); J. A. Williamson, *The Tudor Age, 1485–1603** (rev. 1979); P. Williams, *The Tudor Regime** (1981); and J. Guy, *Tudor England** (1988). Informative for the Tudors and their successors is J.

Guy and J. Morrill, *The Tudors and Stuarts**
(1993), a volume in the *Oxford History of
Britain*. Three general accounts that take
their start in this era and move forward into
the seventeenth century are A. G. R. Smith,
*The Emergence of a Nation State: The
Commonwealth of England, 1529–1660**
(1984); R. H. Silcock, *Revolution, Reaction,
and the Triumph of Conservatism: English
History, 1555–1700** (1984); and M. Reed,
The Age of Exuberance, 1550–1700 (1986).

For the Elizabethan era one may read J.
Hurstfield, *Elizabeth I and the Unity of
England** (1966); and a trilogy of distinction
by W. T. MacCaffrey, *The Shaping of the
Elizabethan Regime** (1968); *Queen Elizabeth and the Making of Policy, 1572–1588**
(1981); and *Elizabeth I: War and Politics,
1588–1603** (1992). Elizabeth's relations
with Parliament are examined in J. E.
Neale's two books: *The Elizabethan House
of Commons* (1949) and *Elizabeth I and Her
Parliaments* (2 vols., 1953–1957); and in G.
R. Elton, *The Parliament of England, 1559–
1581** (1986). For the religious question in
these years one may turn to D. MacCulloch,
*The Later Reformation in England, 1547–
1603* (1990). Focusing on foreign affairs are
R. B. Wernham's *Before the Armada** (1972)
and *After the Armada** (1984). On the naval
and imperial side one may also read D. B.
Quinn and A. N. Ryan, *England's Sea
Empire, 1550–1642* (1984), and K. R. An-
drews, *Trade, Plunder, and Settlement:
Maritime Enterprise and the Genesis of the
British Empire, 1480–1630** (1985).

L. B. Smith, *The Elizabethan World*
(1967) is a colorful account, and A. L.
Rowse crowds many subjects into two of
his many books: *The Elizabethan Age* (2
vols., 1950–1955) and *The Elizabethan Renaissance: The Cultural Achievement*
(1972). Of the numerous biographies of Elizabeth one may still read with profit the
somewhat adulatory older J. E. Neale,
*Queen Elizabeth I** (1934, 1966); and the
more recent, A. Somerset, *Elizabeth I*
(1992), a lively volume which incorporates
some but not all newer scholarship. There
are other commendable studies by N. Williams (1967), L. B. Smith (1976), E. Erickson
(1983), and S. Bassett* (1989), while C.
Haigh, *Elizabeth I* (1988), is perhaps overly
critical. On Elizabeth's rival, A. Fraser,
among her many notable volumes, has written *Mary Queen of Scots** (1969, 1993).

An overview of society and economy is
helpfully presented in D. M. Palliser, *The
Age of Elizabeth: England under the Later
Tudors, 1547–1603** (rev. 1992). Social and
economic changes of the age, or that take
their start in this age, are masterfully explored in L. Stone, *The Crisis of the Aristocracy, 1558–1641** (1965; abr. ed., 1967); and
in L. and J. C. Stone, *An Open Elite?:
England, 1540–1880** (1984; abr. ed., 1986),
which questions upward social mobility in
England. Other important studies are H.
R. Trevor-Roper, *The Gentry, 1540–1640*
(1953); G. E. Mingay, *The Rise and Fall of
a Ruling Class* (1976); and A. Macfarlane,
*The Origins of English Individualism: The
Family, Property, and Social Transition**
(1978).

Historical research to reconstruct the
history of the family is brilliantly exemplified
in L. Stone, *The Family, Sex, and Marriage
in England, 1500–1800** (1977; abr. ed.,
1979) and in *Road to Divorce: England,
1530–1987* (1990), both cited in the introductory section; the latter book is being supplemented by accompanying volumes of revealing case studies, the first of which is
*Uncertain Unions: Marriage in England,
1660–1753* (1992). Other recommended studies are R. A. Houlbrooke, *The English
Family, 1450–1700** (1984); J. R. Gillis, *For
Better, For Worse: British Marriages, 1600
to the Present** (1985); and A. Macfarlane,
*Marriage and Love in England: Modes of
Reproduction, 1300–1840** (1987).

Two important books are P. Laslett, *The
World We Have Lost: England before the
Industrial Age** (1965), a pioneering work
that presents a perhaps overly placid and
stable picture of these years; and E. A.
Wrigley and R. S. Schofield, *The Population
History of England, 1541–1871** (1981), cited
in the introductory section as a model of
new demographic research.

Disintegration and Reconstruction
of France

Informative introductions to the religious
and dynastic turmoil in sixteenth-century
France include R. Briggs, *Early Modern
France, 1560–1715** (1977); H. A. Lloyd,
*The State, France, and the Sixteenth Cen-
tury* (1983); and R. J. Knecht, *French Renaissance Monarchy: Francis I and Henry
II** (1984). J. H. M. Salmon's two books are
of special value: *Society in Crisis: France
in the Sixteenth Century* (rev. 1979) and
*Renaissance and Revolt: Essays in the Intel-
lectual and Social History of Early France*

(1987). Major French works available in translation are R. Mandrou, *Introduction to Modern France, 1500–1640: An Essay in Historical Psychology* (trans. 1976); E. Le Roy Ladurie's two studies: *The French Peasantry, 1450–1660* (rev. and trans. 1986) and *Early Modern France, 1460–1610* (trans. 1993); and R. Mousnier, *The Institutions of France under the Absolute Monarchy, 1598–1789* (2 vols., trans. 1979–1984), which exhaustively studies society and the state.

The religious wars are also explored in N. M. Sutherland's *The Massacre of St. Bartholomew and the European Conflict, 1559–1572* (1973) and *The Huguenot Struggle for Recognition* (1980); B. B. Diefendorf, *Beneath the Cross: Catholics and Huguenots in Sixteenth-Century Paris* (1991); R. M. Kingdon, *Myths about the St. Bartholemew's Day Massacre, 1572–1576* (1988); and H. Heller, *Iron and Blood: Civil Wars in Sixteenth Century France* (1991). The intellectual dimension is examined in D. R. Kelley, *The Beginning of Ideology: Consciousness and Society in the French Reformation** (1981). An illuminating biography of the first Bourbon king, D. Buisseret, *Henry IV* (1984), may be supplemented by M. Greengrass, *France in the Age of Henri IV: The Struggle for Stability** (1984), and R. Mousnier, *The Assassination of Henry IV* (trans. 1973).

Constitutional developments are comprehensively explored in J. R. Major, *Representative Government in Early Modern France* (1980), which stresses the vitality of the early representative bodies; P. Anderson, *Lineages of the Absolutist State* (1974); J. M. Haydon, *France and the Estates General of 1614* (1974); and H. H. Rowen, *The King's State: Proprietary Dynasticism in Early Modern France* (1980), which studies the state as royal property. D. Bitton, *The French Nobility in Crisis, 1560–1640* (1969), describes arguments for and against nobility two centuries before the French Revolution.

For the era of Louis XIII and the minister who overshadowed him one reads V. L. Tapié, *France in the Age of Louis XIII and Richelieu** (trans. 1974, reissued 1984). The king himself is studied in A. Lloyd Moote, *Louis XIII, The Just** (1989). For Richelieu there are C. V. Wedgwood's brief *Richelieu and the French Monarchy** (1949); G. R. R. Treasure, *Cardinal Richelieu and the Development of Absolutism* (1972); W. F. Church, *Richelieu and Reason of State* (1972); J. Bergin, *Cardinal Richelieu: Power*

and the Pursuit of Wealth* (1985) and *The Rise of Richelieu* (1991); and R. J. Knecht, *Richelieu** (1991), in the excellent Profiles in Power series. The strengthening of royal power under Richelieu and his successor is examined in R. Bonney, *Society and Government in France under Richelieu and Mazarin, 1624–1661* (1988); and in J. Bergin and L. Brockless (eds.), *Richelieu and His Age* (1992). A penetrating comparative study of Richelieu and of his Spanish contemporary and rival, the Count-Duke of Olivares, is J. H. Elliott, *Richelieu and Olivares** (1984).

The Thirty Years' War, 1618–1648

The most up-to-date authoritative account is G. Parker, *The Thirty Years' War** (1988). Other accounts are available by C. V. Wedgwood* (1938, 1981), S. H. Steinberg* (1966), G. Pagès* (trans. 1971), and J. V. Polisensky (trans. 1971).* Biographical accounts include G. Mann, *Wallenstein: His Life Narrated* (trans. 1976), a major biographical study; N. Ahnlund, *Gustav Adolf the Great* (1932, 1940); and M. Roberts, *Gustavus Adolphus** (1992), in the Profiles in Power series. A detailed treatment of all aspects of Swedish history is to be found in the books of M. Roberts: *The Early Vasas: A History of Sweden, 1523–1611** (1968, 1986); *Gustavus Adolphus and the Rise of Sweden* (1973); *The Swedish Imperial Experience, 1560–1718* (1979); and *The Age of Liberty: Sweden, 1719–1772* (1986). The conversion to Catholicism of Gustavus Adolphus' daughter and her abdication is told in G. Masson, *Queen Christina* (1968), and in S. Svolpe, *Christina of Sweden* (trans. and abr. 1966), by a Swedish historian.

Problems and Readings*

The following will be found useful: D. L. Jensen (ed.), *The Expansion of Europe* (1967); J. H. Parry (ed.), *The European Reconnaissance* (1968); M. Lunenfeld (ed.), *1492: Discovery, Invasion, Encounter* (1991); A. W. Crosby, *The Columbian Voyages, the Columbian Exchange, and Their Histories* (1987), in the AHA Pamphlets series; W. E. Minchitan (ed.), *Mercantilism: System or Expediency?* (1969); J. M. Levine (ed.), *Elizabeth I* (Great Lives Observed, 1969); R. L. Greaves, *Elizabeth I, Queen of England* (1974); J. C. Rule and J. J. TePaske (eds.), *The Character of Philip II: The Prob-*

lem of Moral Judgments in History (1963); J. J. TePaske (ed.), *Three American Empires* (1967); J. F. Bannon (ed.), *Indian Labor in the Spanish Indies* (1966); J. H. M. Salmon (ed.), *The French Wars of Religion* (1967); and T. K. Rabb (ed.), *The Thirty Years' War* (rev. 1981). Two brief narrative accounts are M. Greengrass, *The French Reformation** (1981) and S. J. Lee, *The Thirty Years War** (1991); narrative and documents are available in R. J. Knecht, *The French Wars of Religion, 1559–1598* (1989), and P. Limm, *The Thirty Years War* (1984).

IV. The Establishment of West-European Leadership

General accounts for the seventeenth century may overlap with books described in the preceding chapter. Informative general works include: M. Ashley, *The Golden Century: Europe, 1598–1715** (1969); R. N. Hatton, *Europe in the Age of Louis XIV** (1969, 1979); and D. H. Pennington, *Europe in the Seventeenth Century** (rev. 1989). Two other general histories that begin with these years are W. Doyle, *The Old European Order, 1660–1800** (rev. 1993), and G. R. R. Treasure, *The Making of Modern Europe, 1648–1780** (1985). For international affairs, diplomacy, and war, two thoughtful accounts are D. McKay and H. M. Scott, *The Rise of the Great Powers, 1648–1815** (1983), and J. Black, *The Rise of the European Powers, 1679–1793** (1990). The diplomatic practices and institutions of the age are described in W. J. Roosen, *The Age of Louis XIV: The Rise of Modern Diplomacy** (1976), while the nature of warfare is examined in J. Childs, *Armies and Warfare in Europe, 1648–1789* (1983), and M. S. Anderson, *War and Society in Europe of the Old Regime, 1618–1789* (1988).

Three older volumes in the Langer series provide coverage: C. J. Friedrich, *The Age of the Baroque, 1610–1660** (1952); F. L. Nussbaum, *The Triumph of Science and Reason, 1660–1685** (1953); and J. B. Wolf, *The Emergence of the Great Powers, 1685–1715** (1951). F. L. Carsten (ed.), *The Ascendancy of France, 1648–1688** (1961), and J. S. Bromley (ed.), *The Rise of Great Britain and Russia, 1688–1715/25** (1970), Vols. V and VI of the *New Cambridge Modern History*, offer informative chapters on many topics.

The Dutch Republic

For the Netherlands in the seventeenth century one may read C. Wilson, *The Dutch Republic and the Civilization of the Seventeenth Century** (1968), an excellent brief introduction; K. H. D. Haley, *The Dutch Republic in the Seventeenth Century* (1972); J. L. Price, *Culture and Society in the Dutch Republic during the Seventeenth Century* (1974); and S. Schama, *The Embarrassment of Riches: An Interpretation of Dutch Culture in the Golden Age** (1988), a skillful synthesis of art history and social history. Colonial expansion is described in C. R. Boxer, *The Dutch Seaborne Empire, 1600–1800* (1965); the Dutch economy in J. A. van Houtte, *An Economic History of the Low Countries, 800–1800* (1977), and J. De Vries, *The Dutch Rural Economy in the Golden Age, 1500–1700* (1974). For the Dutch role on the European and world scene two books by J. I. Israel are important: *The Dutch Republic and the Hispanic World, 1606–1661** (1982) and *Dutch Primacy in World Trade, 1585–1740** (1989).

For William of Orange, the best study is S. B. Baxter, *William III and the Defense of European Liberty, 1650–1702* (1966). N. A. Robb, *William of Orange* (2 vols., 1963–1966), is stronger on biographical than on political details, and D. Ogg, *William III** (1956), is a brief sketch. A comprehensive biography of a leading Dutch statesman is H. H. Rowen, *Jan de Witt: Statesman of "True Freedom"* (1986), an adaptation of the same author's more detailed biography (1978). Rowen also examines all of the stadholders beginning with William I ("the Silent") in *The Princes of Orange: The Stadholders in the Dutch Republic** (1988).

Seventeenth-Century England

Two judicious accounts of the seventeenth-century political and religious conflicts, incorporating recent scholarship and interpretation, are D. Hirst, *Authority and Conflict: England, 1603–1658** (1986), and G. E. Aylmer, *Rebellion or Revolution?: England, 1640–1669** (1986). Other recommended general works include J. P. Kenyon, *Stuart England** (1978); R. Lockyer, *The Early Stuarts: A Political History of England, 1603–1642** (1989); and B. Coward, *The Stuart Age, 1603–1714** (rev. 1994). England's role in international affairs is studied in J. R. Jones, *Britain and Europe in the Seventeenth Century** (1966).

For social and economic developments in this age, illuminating studies include C. Wilson, *England's Apprenticeship, 1603–1763* (rev. 1984); K. Wrightson, *English Society, 1580–1680* (1982); and J. A. Sharpe, *Early Modern England: A Social History, 1550–1760* (1990). Books on the gentry and aristocracy by H. R. Trevor-Roper, L. Stone, and others have been cited in Chapter III. To them should be added J. V. Beckett, *The Aristocracy in England, 1660–1914** (1988).

Few subjects have been as debated as the political and religious conflicts in seventeenth-century England. Some historians stress class and ideological conflict and interpret the events as the first modern European revolution. Others downplay what they see as anachronistic ideological interpretations, emphasize local rivalries, and insist on the importance of day-to-day contingencies. As an introduction to divergent interpretations one may compare L. Stone, *The Causes of the English Revolution, 1629–1642** (1972); C. Russell, *The Causes of the English Civil War** (1990); R. C. Richardson, *The Debate on the English Revolution Revisited* (1989); and A. Hughes, *The Causes of the English Civil War* (1991).

For the general reader, the narrative excitement of the events is captured in C. V. Wedgwood's trilogy: *The King's Peace, 1637–1641** (1955); *The King's War, 1641–1647** (1959); and *A Coffin for King Charles: The Trial and Execution of Charles I** (1964), in which she insists that the "why" (the analysis) must flow from the "how" (the narrative). A recent popular dramatic account, with considerable attention to the military aspects, is C. Hibbert, *Cavaliers and Roundheads: The English Civil War, 1642–1649* (1993). For the opening episodes of these years A. Fletcher, *The Outbreak of the English Civil War* (1981), and K. Sharpe, *The Personal Rule of Charles I* (1992), both of which tend to minimize long-term social and economic causes, may be compared with L. J. Reeve, *Charles I and the Road to Personal Rule* (1989); R. Cust, *The Forced Loan and English Politics* (1986); and R. Brenner, *Merchants and Revolution* (1992). Of special interest is C. Carlton, *Going to the Wars: The Experience of the British Civil Wars, 1638–1651* (1992).

Studies that downplay broader ideologi-

cal interpretations but provide detailed narrative and analysis include C. Russell, *A Crisis of Parliaments** (1971), *Parliaments and English Politics, 1621–1629* (1979), and *The Fall of the British Monarchies, 1637–1642* (1991), which may be read along with J. Morrill, *The Revolt of the Provinces: Conservatism and Revolution in the English Civil War, 1630–1650* (1980) and *The Nature of the English Revolution** (1993), a collection of essays.

D. Willson's biography of the first Stuart monarch, *King James VI and I** (1956), may be compared with the more recent biography by M. Lee, Jr. (1990). Two recent fair-minded assessments of his ill-fated successor are C. Carlton, *Charles I: The Personal Monarch** (1984), and P. Gregg, *King Charles I* (1984). On the prelate who reinforced the king's persecution of the Puritans, H. R. Trevor-Roper's impressive *Archbishop Laud, 1573–1645* (1940), has not been superseded but may be read along with C. Carlton, *Archbishop William Laud* (1988).

For Cromwell many maintain that C. Firth, *Oliver Cromwell and the Rule of the Puritans in England** (1900; reissued many times) remains the best biographical account, but more recent studies include A. Fraser, *Cromwell, The Lord Protector* (1973); C. Hill, *God's Englishman** (1972); J. Morrill's largely unsympathetic *Oliver Cromwell and the English Revolution* (1990); and B. Coward, *Oliver Cromwell** (1991). An impressive study of the Roundhead army is I. Gentles, *The New Model Army in England, Ireland, and Scotland, 1645–1653* (1992). A good introduction to the Cromwellian era and the interregnum is R. Hutton, *The British Republic, 1649–1660* (1990); a more detailed study is A. Woolrych, *Commonwealth to Protectorate** (1982).

Christopher Hill, whose biography of Cromwell has been cited, has done much to influence class and ideological interpretations of seventeenth-century events. His several Marxist-inspired but not dogmatic studies emphasize that the ideas of the age reflected economic class interests and that many contemporary political and social issues first emerged in the radicalism of this period. Among his books are *Puritanism and Revolution** (1958), *A Century of Revolution* (1961), *Intellectual Origins of the English Revolution** (1965), *The World Turned Upside Down: Radical Ideas during the English Revolution** (1972), and *Change and Con-*

*tinuity in Seventeenth-Century England** (rev. 1991). Additional examples of inquiries into the radicalism of the age are M. Walzer, *The Revolution of the Saints: A Study in the Origins of Radical Politics** (1965); P. G. Rogers, *The Fifth Monarchy Men* (1966); G. E. Aylmer, *The Levellers in the English Revolution* (1975); and B. Manning, *The English People and the English Revolution, 1640–1649* (1976). An important assessment is J. O. Appleby, *Economic Thought and Ideology in Seventeenth Century England* (1978); while an intriguing study in social history relating popular culture to the political ferment of the age is D. Underdown, *Revel, Riot, and Rebellion: Popular Politics and Culture in England, 1603–1660** (1985). The same author has also written a political study *Pride's Purge: Politics and the Puritan Revolution** (1971, 1985) and *Fire from Heaven: Life in an English Town in the Seventeenth Century* (1992).

Class and ideological interpretations may also be sampled in R. Cust and A. Hughes (eds.), *Conflict in Early Stuart England: Studies in Religion and Politics, 1603–1642** (1991); J. P. Somerville, *Politics and Ideology in England, 1603–1642* (1986); and T. Cogswell, *The Blessed Revolution: English Politics and the Coming of War, 1621–1624* (1989).

On the Irish question, good introductions are provided in J. C. Beckett, *The Making of Modern Ireland, 1603–1921* (1966), and R. F. Foster, *Modern Ireland, 1600–1972* (1988); and for the Cromwellian age, there are two important studies: P. B. Ellis, *Ireland, 1652–1660* (1975), and T. C. Barnard, *Cromwellian Ireland: English Government and Reform in Ireland, 1649–1660* (1975). Many other aspects of Irish history are explored in R. F. Foster (ed.), *The Oxford Illustrated History of Ireland** (1989).

The Restoration: Charles II; James II; The Revolution of 1688

Two of the best accounts of this and the age that followed are J. R. Jones, *Country and Court: England, 1658–1714** (1978), and G. Holmes, *The Making of a Great Power: Late Stuart and Early Georgian Britain, 1660–1722** (1993). For the end of the Protectorate and the restoration of the monarchy, one also turns to D. Ogg, *England in the Reign of Charles II** (1955, 1985); P. Seaward, *The Restoration, 1660–1688* (1991); and R. Hutton, *The Restoration: A Political*

*and Religious History of England and Wales, 1658–1667** (1985, 1993). The king's abilities are assessed in A. Fraser, *Royal Charles: Charles II and the Restoration** (1971), perhaps the best of her many biographies; in J. R. Jones, *Charles II: Royal Politician* (1987); and in R. Hutton, *Charles II: King of England, Scotland, and Ireland* (1990). For his successor F. C. Turner, *James II* (1945), is fair and factual, as is J. Miller, *James II: A Study in Kingship* (1977), which stresses the monarch's personal integrity but failure as a king.

For the background to the Revolution of 1688 and subsequent events one may read, among other accounts, D. Ogg, *England in the Reign of James II and William III** (1955, 1984); L. Pinkham, *William III and the Respectable Revolution* (1954); M. Ashley, *The Glorious Revolution of 1688* (1967); S. Prall, *The Bloodless Revolution: England, 1688* (1972); J. R. Jones, *The Revolution of 1688 in England* (1972); and J. Childs, *The Army, James II, and the Glorious Revolution* (1980). A special subject is admirably studied in L. G. Schwoerer, *The Declaration of Rights, 1689* (1981). G. M. Trevelyan, *The English Revolution 1688–1689** (1939, 1965), a classic defense of the revolution, argues that the revolution strengthened conservatism for the eighteenth century but that the long-run consequences made the revolution a turning point in history. The Whig historian is himself studied in D. Cannadine, *G. M. Trevelyan: A Life in History* (1993). A newer assessment of the revolution, W. A. Speck, *Reluctant Revolutionaries: Englishmen and the Revolution of 1688** (1988), sees the events as a decisive though not inevitable step toward parliamentary government. These and other interpretations are discussed in J. I. Israel (ed.), *The Anglo-Dutch Movement: Essays on the Glorious Revolution and Its World Impact* (1991), and in L. G. Schwoerer (ed.), *The Revolution of 1688–1689: Changing Perspectives* (1992); and there are additional insights in H. R. Trevor-Roper's essays, *From Counter Reformation to Glorious Revolution* (1992).

For the role played in international affairs by William of Orange after he took the English throne in 1689, one may read the biographies listed earlier in this chapter, along with D. W. Jones, *War and Economy in the Age of William III and Marlborough* (1988). Winston Churchill has written a detailed biography of John Churchill, the military commander who was his ancestor: W. S. Churchill, *Marlborough: His Life and Times* (4 vols., 1933–1938; abr. ed., 1968). G. M. Trevelyan, *England under Queen Anne* (3 vols., 1930–1934), vividly portrays the succeeding age; and on the sovereign herself, E. Gregg, *Queen Anne* (1980), is excellent. The background to the Act of Union of 1707 joining England and Scotland is explored in B. P. Levack, *The Formation of the British State: England, Scotland, and the Union, 1603–1707* (1987).

For women in seventeenth-century England one may turn to A. Fraser, *The Weaker Vessel: Woman's Lot in Seventeenth Century England* (1985), a series of portraits, mostly of upper-class women, written in her usual lively style. The scholarly essays in M. Prior (ed.), *Women in English Society, 1500–1800** (1985), relate to women of all classes. A pioneering work in social history is A. Clark, *Working Life of Women in the Seventeenth Century* (1919, 1993). R. Thompson, *Women in Stuart England and America* (1974), is a successful comparative study. L. G. Schwoerer illuminates the independent life of a seventeenth-century woman in *Lady Rachel Russell: "One of the Best of Women,"* (1987), while S. Rowbotham ranges from the English civil war to the present in *Hidden from History: Rediscovering Women in History, from the 17th Century to the Present* (1974, 1989).

The France of Louis XIV

Many of the general accounts cited at the beginning of this chapter focus on the French predominance in this age. In addition, the following books explore various aspects of Louis XIV and his reign: J. B. Wolf, *Louis XIV** (1968), a comprehensive biography; V. Buranelli, *Louis XIV** (1966), a brief, sympathetic account; M. Ashley, *Louis XIV and the Greatness of France** (Teach Yourself History series, 1948); R. N. Hatton, *Louis XIV and Absolutism* (1976); A. Lossky, *Louis XIV and the Ascendancy of France* (1977); and F. Bluche, *Louis XIV* (1990), a detailed narrative. Available also are the essays in P. Sonnino and others (eds.), *The Reign of Louis XIV** (1991), while P. Burke, *The Fabrication of Louis XIV* (1992) examines the molding of the king's image over his long reign. W. F. Church offers a historiographical assessment in *Louis XIV in Historical Thought: From Voltaire to the Annales School* (1976).

Other interpretive volumes are W. H. Lewis, *The Splendid Century: Life in the France of Louis XIV** (1953); G. R. R. Treasure, *Seventeenth-Century France** (1966); V. L. Tapié, *The Age of Grandeur* (rev. 1966); and O. Ranum, *Paris in the Age of Absolutism** (1969). Three studies by P. Goubert: *Louis XIV and Twenty Million Frenchmen** (trans. 1972); his more detailed *The Ancien Regime: French Society, 1600–1750** (trans. and abr. 1974); and *The French Peasantry in the Seventeenth Century** (trans. 1986), are invaluable studies of French society and the people of the time by an *Annales* historian. C. Tilly, *The Contentious French: Four Centuries of Popular Struggle** (1986), an incisive study of popular restlessness and collective action, begins with these years.

Three books focusing on provincial institutions and other limitations on royal authority, and providing added insights into Louis XIV's rule, are W. Beik, *Absolutism and Society in Seventeenth-Century France: State Power and Provincial Aristocracy in Languedoc** (1985); R. Mettam, *Power and Faction in Louis XIV's France* (1988); and S. Kettering, *Patrons, Brokers, and Clients in Seventeenth-Century France* (1986). Two older books that examine constraints on royal authority are A. L. Moote, *The Revolt of the Judges: The Parlement of Paris and the Fronde, 1643–1652* (1971); and L. Rothkrug, *Opposition to Louis XIV: The Political and Social Origins of the Enlightenment* (1965).

The close regulation of the French economy is described in detail in C. W. Cole, *Colbert and a Century of French Mercantilism* (2 vols., 1939), and a sequel (1943) that carries the story to 1700; and a biography of the French finance minister is available in A. Trout, *Jean-Baptiste Colbert* (1978). Financial matters are examined on a broad scale in J. Dent, *Crisis in France: Crown, Financiers, and Society in Seventeenth-Century France* (1973); and in R. Bonney, *The King's Debts: Finance and Politics in France, 1589–1661* (1981).

Religious matters are explored in E. E. Reynolds, *Bossuet* (1963); E. I. Perry, *From Theology to History: French Religious Controversy and the Revocation of the Edict of Nantes* (1973); A. Sedgwick, *Jansenism in Seventeenth-Century France* (1977); and in a special way in W. Scoville, *The Persecution of the Huguenots and French Economic Development, 1680–1720* (1960). On the colonial empire one may read H. I. Priestley, *France Overseas through the Old Regime: A Study of European Expansion* (1939); and W. J. Eccles, *Canada under Louis XIV, 1663–1701* (1964). P. W. Bamford has written two illuminating books, *Forests and French Sea Power, 1660–1789* (1956) and *Fighting Ships and Prisons: The Mediterranean Galleys of France in the Age of Louis XIV* (1973).

C. C. Lougee, *Le Paradis des Femmes: Women, Salons, and Social Stratification in Seventeenth Century France* (1976), examines the relationship of influential women of the age to seventeenth-century society and culture; a more general work is W. Gibson, *Women in Seventeenth-Century France* (1989); and a special woman of letters is studied in J. A. and W. T. Ojala, *Madame de Sévigné: A Seventeenth-Century Life* (1990).

On Louis XIV's wars one may read C. Ekberg, *The Failure of Louis XIV's Dutch War* (1979); P. Sonnino, *Louis XIV and the Origins of the Dutch War* (1988); the essays in R. N. Hatton (ed.), *Louis XIV and Europe* (1976); and H. Kamen, *The War of Succession in Spain, 1700–1715* (1969). Two books that examine the final stages of Habsburg rule are H. Kamen, *Spain in the Later Seventeenth Century, 1665–1700* (1980), in which he sees revival rather than decline on the eve of the French attack; and R. A. Stradling, *Europe and the Decline of Spain, 1580–1720* (1981). For Spain in the century after the Habsburgs, an outstanding account is J. Lynch, *Bourbon Spain, 1700–1808* (1989).

*Problems and Readings**

For the debate over events in England, see P. A. M. Taylor (ed.), *The Origins of the English Civil War: Conspiracy, Crusade, or Class Conflict* (1960); L. Stone (ed.), *Social Change and Revolution in England, 1540–1640* (1965); R. E. Boyer (ed.), *Oliver Cromwell and the Puritan Revolution: Failure of a Man or Faith?* (1966); J. F. H. New (ed.), *Oliver Cromwell, Pretender, Puritan, Statesman, Paradox?* (1972); R. A. Sharp (ed.), *Political Ideas of the English Civil War, 1641–1649** (1983); G. M. Straka (ed.), *The Revolution of 1688 and the Birth of the English Political Nation* (rev. 1973); and P. Seaver (ed.), *Seventeenth Century England: Society in an Age of Revolution** (1976). For France, one may turn to W. F. Church

(ed.), *The Impact of Absolutism in France: National Experience under Richelieu, Mazarin, and Louis XIV* (1969) and *The Greatness of Louis XIV: Myth or Reality* (rev. 1972); H. G. Judge (ed.), *Louis XIV* (1965); J. C. Rule (ed.), *Louis XIV and the Craft of Kingship* (1969); and R. F. Kierstead (ed.), *State and Society in Seventeenth-Century France** (1975). Brief narrative essays include D. L. Smith, *Oliver Cromwell: Politics and Revolution in the English Revolution, 1640–1658** (1991); T. Bernard, *The English Republic, 1649–1660* (1982); F. D. Dow, *Radicalism in the English Revolution** (1985); K. H. D. Haley, *Politics in the Reign of Charles II** (1985); and D. L. Smith, *Louis XIV** (1992).

V. The Transformation of Eastern Europe, 1648–1740

J. S. Bromley (ed.), *The Rise of Great Britain and Russia, 1688–1725* (1969), Vol. VI of the *New Cambridge Modern History*, mentioned earlier, has informative but highly specialized chapters. J. H. Shennan, *Liberty and Order in Early Modern Europe: The Subject and the State, 1650–1800** (1986), focusing on France and Russia, highlights differences in the development of western and eastern Europe. Informative books that explain the complexities of central and eastern Europe, carrying their accounts toward the present, are L. C. Tihany, *A History of Middle Europe: From the Earliest Times to the Age of the World Wars* (1976); P. Wandycz, *The Price of Freedom: A History of East Central Europe from the Middle Ages to the Present* (1992); and P. D. Longworth, *The Making of Eastern Europe* (1992). Older syntheses by F. Dvornik (1949, 1962) and O. Halecki (1952) are still useful. Of special importance is the multivolume *A History of Central Europe*, in progress. P. R. Magocsi, *Historical Atlas of East Central Europe* (1994), Vol. I of the series, is an impressive work of reference. J. W. Sedlar, *East Central Europe in the Middle Ages, 1000–1500* (1994) synthesizes the medieval period; and A. Maczak and others, *East Central Europe in Transition** (1985) focuses on the fourteenth to the seventeenth centuries. For the Balkans, valuable studies are L. S. Stavrianos, *The Balkans since 1453* (1958); B. and C. Jelavich, *The Balkans* (1965); and R. Ristelhueber, *A History of the Balkan Peoples* (trans. 1971). For the Balkans in this age,

P. F. Sugar, *Southeastern Europe under Ottoman Rule, 1354–1804** (1977), also in the series cited above, is informative. Additional books will be cited in later chapters.

The Ottoman Empire

N. Itzkowitz, *Ottoman Empire and Islamic Tradition** (1972), is a good brief introduction for the years 1300 to the late eighteenth century. J. P. D. Balfour [Lord Kinross], *The Ottoman Centuries: The Rise and Fall of the Turkish Empire* (1977), is a comprehensive narrative, as are S. Shaw, *History of the Ottoman Empire and Modern Turkey** of which Vol. 1 (1976) covers the years 1280–1808, and H. Inalcik, *The Ottoman Empire: The Classical Age, 1300–1600* (1973). A popular but sound account is F. W. Fernau, *Moslems on the March* (trans. 1954). The Turkish role in European affairs is explored in D. M. Vaughan, *Europe and the Turk: A Pattern of Alliances, 1350–1700* (1954); P. Coles, *The Ottoman Impact on Europe, 1350–1699** (1968); and K. M. Setton, *Venice, Austria, and the Turks in the Seventeenth Century* (1991).

Of interest on a special subject is R. Schwoebel, *The Shadow of the Crescent: The Renaissance Image of the Turk, 1453–1517* (1967). For the sixteenth century, R. O. Merriman, *Suleiman the Magnificent, 1520–1566* (1944), remains the best general introduction. B. H. Sumner, *Peter the Great and the Ottoman Empire* (1949), describes relations between Turkey and Russia in a later important period. C. E. Bosworth, *The Islamic Dynasties: A Chronological and Genealogical Handbook* (1976), is a useful reference tool.

Austria and the Habsburgs: To 1740

Basic books for these years are R. A. Kann, *A History of the Habsburg Empire, 1526–1918** (1974); R. J. Evans, *The Making of the Habsburg Empire, 1550–1770** (1979); A. Wandruszka, *The House of Habsburg* (trans. 1964); C. Ingrao, *The Habsburg Monarchy, 1618–1815** (1993), in the New Approaches to European History series; and J. Bérenger, *The History of the Habsburg Empire, 1273–1700** (trans. 1994), the first of two projected volumes. For the early period one may also read H. F. Koenigsberger, *The Habsburgs and Europe, 1516–1660* (1971). J. F. Spielman has written *Leopold I of Austria* (1977), a balanced

treatment of the seventeenth-century emperor; and for Eugene of Savoy, an outstanding biography is D. McKay, *Prince Eugene of Savoy* (Men in Office series, 1977). Two vivid accounts of the Turkish siege of 1683 are J. Stoye, *The Siege of Vienna* (1964), and T. M. Barker, *Double Eagle and Crescent: Vienna's Second Turkish Siege* (1967).

The Holy Roman Empire: The German States

A good introductory survey of all German history is M. Fulbrook, *A Concise History of Germany** (1991). H. Holborn, in his *History of Modern Germany*, Vol. II, *1648–1840* (1975), covers the fluid situation in the Holy Roman Empire after the Thirty Years' War, as does J. Gagliardo, *Germany under the Old Regime, 1600–1790** (1991). One will also wish to read E. Sagorra, *A Social History of Germany, 1648–1914* (1977), with many fascinating insights; and R. Vierhaus, *Germany in the Age of Absolutism** (1989), which studies the years 1618–1763. G. Benecke, *Society and Politics in Germany, 1500–1750* (1974), presents the case for the empire as a viable constitutional entity, while two important contributions to understanding the formation of the German political tradition are F. L. Carsten, *Princes and Parliaments in Germany* (1959), and M. Walker, *German Home Towns: Community, State, and General Estate, 1648–1871* (1971). J. A. Vann thoroughly explores the evolving social structure and institutions of a key principality in *The Making of a State: Württemberg, 1593–1793* (1984).

For Prussia, convenient introductions are F. L. Carsten, *The Origins of Prussia* (1954); S. B. Fay and K. Epstein, *The Rise of Brandenburg-Prussia to 1786* (1937, 1974, 1981); and H. W. Koch, *A History of Prussia** (1978). A thoughtful evocation of the state, dissolved after the Second World War, is T. von Thadden, *Prussia: The History of a Lost State* (1986). An invaluable study going well beyond the scope of this chapter is G. A. Craig, *The Politics of the Prussian Army, 1640–1945** (1956, 1964). Important also is H. Rosenberg, *Bureaucracy, Aristocracy, and Autocracy: The Prussian Experience, 1660–1815** (1958), which may be supplemented by J. A. Armstrong, *The European Administrative Elite** (1973), a comparative study of European bureaucracies during this period. On the early Hohenzollerns, one may read F.

Schevill, *The Great Elector* (1947); R. Ergang, *The Potsdam Führer: Frederick William I, Father of Prussian Militarism* (1941, 1972); and R. A. Derwart, *The Administrative Reforms of Frederick William I of Prussia* (1953). Books on Frederick the Great are cited in Chapter VIII.

Russia: To 1725

There are many excellent narrative accounts of Russian history, with good coverage of the early years, among them M. T. Florinsky, *Russia: A Short History* (2 vols., 1953; abr. ed., 1969). For the early years, and the expansion and transformation of Muscovy, one may read R. O. Crummey, *The Formation of Muscovy, 1304–1613** (1987), while P. Dukes, *The Making of Russian Absolutism, 1613–1801** (1982), traces the tsardom from the beginning of the Romanov dynasty over the next two centuries. The military side to Russian society and the "service state" are ably examined in J. L. H. Keep, *Soldiers of the Tsar: Army and Society in Russia, 1462–1874* (1985), and the rural scene is studied in J. Blum, *Lord and Peasant in Russia from the Ninth to the Nineteenth Century** (1961). P. Avrich examines social upheavals in *Russian Rebels, 1600–1800* (1972), while R. Mousnier treats agrarian unrest comparatively in *Peasant Uprisings in Seventeenth-Century France, Russia, and China* (trans. 1970).

There are vivid popular narratives by H. Lamb, *The March of Muscovy: Ivan the Terrible and the Growth of the Russian Empire, 1400–1648* (1948) and *The City and the Tsar: Peter the Great and the Move to the West, 1648–1762* (1948). On the early rulers, there are available J. Fennell, *Ivan the Great of Moscow* (1961); I. Grey, *Ivan III and the Unification of Russia* (1965); the same author's *Ivan the Terrible* (1964); and P. Yanov, *The Origins of Autocracy: Ivan the Terrible in Russian History* (1980). W. B. Lincoln, *Autocrats of All the Russias* (1981) is a remarkable large-scale study of all the Romanovs, the fifteen tsars and four tsarinas who ruled Russia between 1613 and 1917; and an absorbing impressionistic cultural history is J. H. Billington, *The Icon and the Axe: An Interpretive History of Russian Culture** (1966). Of special interest is a second book by W. B. Lincoln, *The Conquest of a Continent: Siberia and the Russians* (1994), describing Russian expansion across northern Asia since the sixteenth century and the use of the territory for trade, settlement, and penal colonies.

On Peter and the reforms of his reign, an older outstanding biography, M. Klyuchevsky, *Peter the Great* (trans. 1958), may be compared with two excellent briefer accounts: B. H. Sumner, *Peter the Great and the Emergence of Russia** (Teach Yourself History series, 1950), and M. S. Anderson, *Peter the Great* (Men in Office series, 1978). R. K. Massie, *Peter the Great: His Life and World* (1980), is a long, vivid, and colorful popular account, but criticized by specialists. N. Riasanovsky, *The Image of Peter the Great in Russian History and Thought** (1985), examines the ruler's long-range cultural impact, while one aspect of his cultural revolution is examined in J. Cracraft, *The Petrine Revolution in Russian Architecture* (1988). An admirable study in comparative cultural history is D. W. Treadgold, *The West in Russia and China: Religious and Secular Thought in Modern Times** (2 vols., 1973), the first volume covering Russia for the years 1472–1917. For Sweden, and for Peter's great Swedish rival, an outstanding biography is R. N. Hatton, *Charles XII of Sweden* (1969). A number of important studies by M. Roberts and others have been cited in Chapter III; for these years M. Roberts, *The Swedish Imperial Experience, 1560–1718* (1979), deserves mention. The Baltic shore is explored in S. P. Oakley, *War and Peace in the Baltic, 1560–1790* (1993).

Poland: The Partitions

For Poland in these years, one may turn to the first volume of N. Davies, *A History of Poland: God's Playground* (2 vols., 1981): Vol. 1, *The Origins to 1795;* to the same author's *Heart of Europe: A Short History of Poland** (1984); and to O. Halecki, *A History of Poland* (rev. 1961). The quarrel over the succession to the Polish throne is recounted in J. L. Sutton, *The King's Honor and the King's Cardinal [Fleury]: The War of the Polish Succession* (1980). On the eighteenth-century partitions, one may consult H. H. Kaplan, *The First Partition of Poland* (1962); the older R. H. Lord, *The Second Partition of Poland* (1915); and for the years that followed, P. Wandycz, *The Lands of Partitioned Poland, 1795–1918** (1974), Vol. VII of *A History of East Central Europe*. A special subject is treated in B.

D. Weinryb, *The Jews of Poland: A Social and Economic History of the Jewish Community in Poland from 1100 to 1800* (1973), and in the essays in C. Abramsky and others (eds.), *The Jews in Poland** (1988).

Problems and Readings*

Various volumes of readings in Russian history and Russian civilization from earliest times to the present are available, among them those edited by W. B. Walsh (3 vols., rev. 1963), T. Riha (3 vols., rev. 1969), and G. Vernadsky and others (3 vols., 1972). On Peter's innovations, there are M. Raeff (ed.), *Peter the Great Changes Russia* (rev. 1972), and J. Cracraft (ed.), *Peter the Great Transforms Russia* (1991). For the Ottoman Empire there is W. S. Vucinich, *The Ottoman Empire: Its Record and Legacy* (Anvil series, 1965, 1979).

VI. The Struggle for Wealth and Empire

For the years covered in this chapter, 1713–1763, helpful syntheses include P. Langford, *The Eighteenth Century, 1688–1815** (1977); I. Woloch, *Eighteenth Century Europe: Tradition and Progress, 1715–1789** (1982); M. S. Anderson, *Europe in the Eighteenth Century, 1713–1783** (rev. 1987); and J. Black, *Eighteenth-Century Europe, 1700–1789** (1990). In the Langer series there are available P. Roberts, *The Quest for Security, 1715–1740** (1947), and W. L. Dorn, *Competition for Empire, 1740–1763** (1940), the latter particularly good on the relation of the European states to overseas expansion and rivalries. J. O. Lindsay (ed.), *The Old Regime, 1713–1763* (1957), Vol. VII in the *New Cambridge Modern History*, has informative chapters on domestic and international developments. R. S. Browning, *The War of the Austrian Succession* (1993), is an outstanding wide-ranging study of the first phase of the mid–eighteenth century conflict, and there are studies of the Seven Years' War by R. Ravory (1966) and A. H. Kaplan (1968). A useful reference work is J. Black and R. Porter (eds.), *A Dictionary of Eighteenth-Century World History* (1993).

Popular Culture and Everyday Life

The differences between elite and popular culture emerge from three books mentioned earlier: P. Burke, *Popular Culture in Early Modern Europe* (1978); K. Thomas, *Religion and the Decline of Magic* (1971); and F. Braudel, *The Structures of Everyday Life* (trans. 1981, 1991), the first volume of his three-volume study. They may be supplemented by the essays in J. Beauroy and others, *The Wolf and the Lamb: Popular Culture in France from the Old Regime to the Twentieth Century* (1977), and A. Mitchell and I. Deák (eds.), *Everyman in Europe: Essays in Social History* (2 vols., rev. 1981).

The Global Economy and the Colonial Empires

The final two volumes of Braudel's work, *The Wheels of Commerce* (trans. 1983) and *The Perspectives of the World* (both reissued in 1991), offer remarkable insights into the global economy. A far-ranging study relevant for the years after 1650 is S. W. Mintz, *Sweetness and Power: The Place of Sugar in Modern History** (1985). The celebrated speculative ventures of the age are graphically described in J. Carswell, *The South Sea Bubble* (1960); in the relevant chapters of C. P. Kindleberger, *Manias, Panics, and Crashes: A History of Financial Crises* (1978); and in J. K. Galbraith, *A Short History of Financial Euphoria: A Hymn of Caution** (1993).

Several books on European overseas expansion listed for Chapters III and IV also discuss the eighteenth century. To these must be added H. Furber's excellent synthesis, *Rival Empires of Trade in the Orient, 1600–1800* (1976); J. H. Parry, *Trade and Dominion: The European Overseas Empires in the Eighteenth Century* (1971); and G. Williams, *The Expansion of Europe in the Eighteenth Century: Overseas Rivalry, Discovery, and Exploitation* (1960). One may also read the relevant chapters of D. K. Fieldhouse, *The Colonial Empires: A Comparative Survey from the Eighteenth Century* (1966); C. E. Carrington, *The British Overseas: Exploits of a Nation of Shopkeepers* (rev. 1968); and K. M. Pannikar, *Asia and Western Dominance: The Vasco da Gama Epoch of Asian History, 1498–1945** (rev. 1959), by an Indian scholar.

The impact of Asia on Europe in the early modern centuries from the sixteenth century on is studied in great detail in D. F. Lach, *Asia in the Making of Europe* (1965–), now in its third massive volume (1993), of which G. J. Van Kley is coauthor. A useful collaborative work is A. T. Embree and C. Gluck (eds.), *Asia in Western and World History* (1993).

P. Lawson, *The East India Company: A History** (1993) describes the powerful organization and its activities from its beginnings in 1603 to its demise in 1857. The eighteenth-century impact on India is further explored in H. Furber, *John Company at Work: A Study of European Expansion in India in the Late Eighteenth Century* (1948); P. Woodruff [Mason], *The Men Who Ruled India** (2 vols., 1954–1957); and M. Andrewes, *British India* (1964). The case for and against the first British governor general is weighed in P. J. Marshall, *The Impeachment of Warren Hastings* (1965). For India itself the best introductions are P. Spear, *The Oxford History of Modern India, 1740–1975** (rev. 1979), and S. Wolpert, *A New History of India** (rev. 1993). An account by Indian scholars is available in R. C. Majumdar (ed.), *The Struggle for Empire* (1957), the fifth volume of a collaborative work. J. E. Schwartzberg (ed.), *A Historical Atlas of South Asia* (rev. 1992), is a superb atlas.

For the French in North America one may read W. J. Eccles, *France in America* (1972) and *The Canadian Frontier, 1534–1760* (1974); P. Boucher, *Les Nouvelles Frances: France in America, 1500–1815* (1989), a brief illustrated account. The importance of the West Indies for the Atlantic economy emerges from N. F. Crouse, *The French Struggle for the West Indies, 1665–1713* (1944); R. S. Dunn, *Sugar and Slaves** (1972); and S. W. Mintz's *Sweetness and Power** (1985) cited above.

British Politics and Society in the Eighteenth Century

Books on eighteenth-century France are listed below in Chapter VIII, but two works should be mentioned here: J. H. Shannon, *Philippe, Duke of Orleans: Regent of France, 1715–1723* (1979), and R. Butler, *Choiseul: Father and Son* (1980), the first volume of a larger study.

There is a growing literature on eighteenth-century British politics and society after the settlement of 1688–1689. L. B. Namier, who wrote with precision and depth but insisted on narrow political and parliamentary history, long had an enormous influence. His most important books were *The Structure of Politics at the Accession of George III* (2 vols., 1920; reissued 1957)

and *England in the Age of the American Revolution* (1931). He also launched a large-scale collaborative project in prosopography, or collective biography, seeking to reconstruct in minute detail the composition of the modern British parliaments. His approach, adopted by other historians, downplayed the importance of ideology in the seventeenth-century revolutions, as discussed in Chapter IV, and even the triumph of parliament over crown in 1688. His influence is demonstrated in J. P. Kenyon, *Revolution Principles: The Politics of Party, 1689–1720* (1977, 1990), and J. C. D. Clark's two books: *English Society, 1688–1832** (1985) and *Revolution and Rebellion** (1986).

An innovative work widening the political arena is J. Brewer, *Party Ideology and Popular Politics at the Accession of George III* (1976). At the same time E. P. Thompson's interest in social history has influenced eighteenth-century studies. For books affording broad insights into eighteenth-century British politics and society one may turn to G. S. Holmes, *British Politics in the Reign of Queen Anne** (1967; rev. 1987); the same author's *The Age of Oligarchy: Pre-Industrial Britain, 1722–1783** (1993); J. H. Plumb, *The Origins of Political Stability in England, 1675–1725* (1967); G. S. Holmes and W. A. Speck, *The Divided Society: Parties and Politics in England, 1694–1716* (1968); and W. A. Speck, *Stability and Strife: England, 1714–1760** (1977).

For the economy and society one may read N. McKendrick, J. Brewer, and J. H. Plumb, *The Birth of a Consumer Society: The Commercialization of Eighteenth-Century England* (1982), which demonstrates that middle-class material values were shared by the poorer classes; P. Langford, *A Polite and Commercial People: England, 1727–1783** (1989), an insightful inquiry; and R. Porter, *English Society in the Eighteenth Century** (1984), another admirable account. One may also read P. Mathias, *The First Industrial Nation: An Economic History of Britain, 1700–1914** (1983); C. Hill, *British Economic and Social History, 1700–1982** (rev. 1985); and P. Langford and C. Harvie, *The Eighteenth Century and the Age of Industry** (1992), in the *Oxford History of Britain*. F. M. L. Thompson, *The Cambridge Social History of Britain, 1750–1950** (rev. 1993) begins with these years.

Biographical accounts include R. N. Hatton, *George I, Elector and King* (1979); J. H. Plumb, *Sir Robert Walpole* (2 vols.,

1951–1956), a biography of distinction; the same author's *The First Four Georges** (1956); H. T. Dickinson, *Walpole and the Whig Supremacy** (1973); B. Kemp, *Sir Robert Walpole* (1976); and J. Black, *Robert Walpole and the Nature of Politics in Early Eighteenth-Century England* (1990). There are biographies of the elder Pitt by B. Williams (2 vols., 1966), S. Ayling (1976), P. D. Brown (1978), and J. Black (1993). The Jacobite uprisings are discussed in books by B. Lenman (1980), P. K. Monod (1983), and F. McLynn (1981). McLynn has also written a biography of the Young Pretender, *Bonnie Prince Charlie: Charles Edward Stuart* (1991) and *Crime and Punishment in Eighteenth-Century England** (1991), which traces prevailing insecurity to the Jacobite threat. The latter may be supplemented by P. Linebaugh, *The London Hanged: Crime and Punishment in the Eighteenth Century* (1992), an impressive study.

Especially insightful on the formation of the British national identity in these years is L. Colley, *Britons: Forging the Nation, 1707–1837* (1992), which may be supplemented by H. F. Kearney, *The British Isles: A History of Four Nations* (1989). W. A. Speck's informative survey, *A Concise History of Britain, 1707–1975* (1993), begins with these years.

The Great War of the Mid–Eighteenth Century, 1740–1763

J. Brewer, *The Sinews of Power: War, Money, and the English State, 1688–1783** (1990), persuasively demonstrates that it was the fiscal strength and war-making capacities of the British parliamentary government after 1688 that made possible Britain's ascent as a global power in the eighteenth century, a thesis also advanced in P. G. Dickinson, *The Financial Revolution in England, 1688–1756* (1967). For the crisis created by the mid-century wars, in addition to the biographical accounts of Pitt already cited, one may read M. Peters, *Pitt and Popularity: The Patriot Minister and London Opinion during the Seven Years' War* (1980), and R. Middleton, *The Pitt-Newcastle Ministry and the Conduct of the Seven Years' War, 1757–1762* (1985).

A. Sorel, *Europe under the Old Regime** (trans. 1947), the introduction to his untranslated larger study of Europe in the age of the French Revolution (8 vols., 1895–1904), provides valuable insights into the European balance of power. C. Duffy, *The Army of Maria Theresa: The Armed Forces of Imperial Austria, 1740–1780* (1977), ably explores the nature of the Habsburg army, and the same author examines Frederick's skill in statecraft and military prowess in *Frederick the Great: A Military Life** (1988). On the negotiations ending the Seven Years' War, Z. E. Rashed has written *The Peace of Paris, 1763* (1952).

Problems and Readings*

A sampling of recent scholarship on eighteenth-century British politics and society is provided in D. A. Baugh (ed.), *Aristocratic Government and Society in Eighteenth-Century England: The Foundations of Stability* (1975). C. G. Robertson, *Chatham and the British Empire** (1948), is a lively study in the Teach Yourself History series.

VII. *The Scientific View of the World*

Histories of Science

A valuable collaborative survey is L. P. Williams and H. J. Steffens (eds.), *The History of Science in Western Civilization** (3 vols., 1977–1978), from antiquity to the twentieth century. Other excellent historical accounts are A. R. and M. B. Hall, *Brief History of Science* (1961); S. F. Mason, *A History of the Sciences** (1962); R. Taton, *History of Science* (4 vols., trans. 1964–1966); and R. Olson, *Science Deified and Science Defied: The Historical Significance of Science in Western Culture** (2 vols., 1982–1991), a far-reaching study ranging from prehistoric times to 1820. Ancient and medieval science is also explored in D. C. Lindberg, *The Beginnings of Western Science** (1992), cited in Chapter II. For individual scientists one may consult the *Dictionary of Scientific Biography* (8 vols., 1970–1980), and for new works in the history of science, the annual bibliographies published in *Isis*. W. H. Brock, *The Norton History of Chemistry* (1993), is the first volume of a projected ten-volume series devoted to individual scientific disciplines. Useful also is R. C. Olby and others, *Companion to the History of Modern Science* (1990).

The Scientific Revolution

For the fundamental reorientation of thinking about nature and the universe in early modern times three older but still valuable introductions are H. Butterfield, *The Origins of Modern Science** (1949; rev., 1965); A. R. Hall, *The Revolution in Science, 1500–1750: The Formation of the Modern Scientific Attitude** (1954; rev. 1983); and A. Koyré, *From the Closed World to the Infinite Universe** (1957; reissued 1968). Other informative accounts include M. Boas, *The Scientific Renaissance, 1450–1630* (1962); A. G. R. Smith, *Science and Society in the Sixteenth and Seventeenth Centuries* (1972); A. G. Debus, *Man and Nature in the Renaissance** (1978); and R. S. Westfall, *The Construction of Modern Science** (1971). Of special interest are I. B. Cohen's *The Birth of a New Physics* (1960; rev. 1985), which traces changes from Aristotle to Kepler, and *The Newtonian Revolution* (1980). The same author has also written *Revolution in Science** (1985), encyclopedic and detailed, illuminating the transformation of scientific ideas. On the nature of revolutionary breakthroughs in science a highly influential work has been T. S. Kuhn, *The Structure of Scientific Revolution** (1962, 1989), which challenges the belief in progressive and cumulative scientific advance. Kuhn has also written *The Copernican Revolution** (1957, 1985). P. B. Medawar, *Pluto's Republic* (1982), humorously entitled but a serious book, explores the persistence of pseudo- and quasi-scientific thinking from Bacon to the present.

For all aspects of technology and the practical application of science, one may consult C. Singer and others, *A History of Technology* (8 vols., 1954–1984), from prehistory to the mid–twentieth century; T. K. Derry and T. I. Williams, *A Short History of Technology from the Earliest Times to A.D. 1900* (1961); and W. Beranek, Jr., and G. Ranis, *Science, Technology, and Human Development* (1978). Two stimulating books are A. Pacey, *The Maze of Ingenuity** (1976), and S. Shapin and S. Schaffer, *Leviathan and the Air Pump* (1985). Technology as a social force is explored in the classic study of L. Mumford, *Technics and Civilization* (1934), and in O. Mayr, *Authority, Liberty, and Automatic Machinery in Early Modern Europe** (1986).

A number of provocative studies relate the scientific revolution culminating in Newton to the political and social ferment in seventeenth-century England and stress the practical implications for a commercial society. Here an admirable synthesis is M.

C. Jacob, *The Cultural Meaning of the Scientific Revolution** (1988); the same author has also written *The Newtonians and the English Revolution, 1689–1720* (1978). Related studies include J. R. Jacob, *Robert Boyle and the English Revolution* (1978); R. K. Merton, *Science, Technology, and Society in Seventeenth Century England* (1970); C. Webster, *The Great Instauration: Science, Medicine, and Reform, 1626–1660* (1976); and M. Hunter, *Science and Society in Restauration England* (1981). The role played by women in the scientific revolution is skillfully explored in L. Schiebinger, *The Mind Has No Sex? Women and the Origins of Modern Science* (1990), the phrase in the title deriving from Descartes; it may be read along with E. Harth, *Cartesian Women: Versions and Subversions of Rational Discourse in the Old Regime** (1993), which compares the role of women intellectuals in this age and in the century that followed.

Biographically Oriented Accounts

The contributions of the pioneer astronomers are described in many of the books already cited and in A. Armitage, *Copernicus: The Founder of Modern Astronomy* (1938) and *The World of Copernicus* (1947); J. A. Grade, *The Life and Times of Tycho Brahe* (1947); M. Caspar, *Kepler* (trans. 1959); C. Baumgardt, *Johannes Kepler: Life and Letters* (1951); and A. Koestler, *The Watershed: A Biography of Johannes Kepler** (1960, 1985). For Galileo one may read L. Fermi and G. Bernardini, *Galileo and the Scientific Revolution** (1961), and A. Koyré, *Galileo Studies* (1978); while an "internal" study of his scientific activities is available in S. Drake, *Galileo at Work: His Scientific Biography* (1978), in which the author has reconstructed the scientist's instruments and examined his notebooks. The opposition that Galileo aroused from the church and other authorities is described in G. de Santillana, *The Crime of Galileo** (1955), and in J. J. Langford, *Galileo, Science, and the Church** (1992), while M. A. Finocchiaro provides the documentation for the trial of 1633 in *The Galileo Affair: A Documentary History** (1989). P. Redondi, *Galileo: Heretic** (trans. 1987) is a provocative revisionist account, not entirely convincing, arguing that Galileo was prosecuted because his scientific theories undermined church dogma on transubstantiation. For

Newton, R. S. Westfall, *Never at Rest: A Biography of Isaac Newton* (1982, 1993), is a biography of distinction; there are biographies also by G. E. Christianson (1984) and A. R. Hall, (1992), the latter comprehensive but technical.

Science and Thought

Three informative studies of Francis Bacon are C. D. Bowen, *Francis Bacon: The Temper of the Man* (1963); P. Rossi, *Francis Bacon: From Magic to Science* (1968); and J. J. Epstein, *Francis Bacon: A Political Biography* (1977). A major reappraisal exploring his insights into nature and the politics of his age is B. H. G. Wormald, *Francis Bacon: History, Politics, and Science, 1561–1626* (1993). There are other informative studies by F. H. Anderson (1948), B. Farrington (1949), and J. Martin (1991). Descartes and his influence are explored in A. G. Balz, *Descartes and the Modern Mind* (1952, 1967), and in J. R. Vrooman, *René Descartes* (1970).

For Pascal, one may read M. Bishop, *Pascal: The Life of Genius* (1936), and A. Krailsheimer, *Pascal** (1980); and for Pierre Bayle, H. Robinson, *Bayle the Skeptic* (1931). Skepticism is further explored in F. L. Baumer, *Religion and the Rise of Skepticism* (1960), and in R. H. Popkin, *The History of Skepticism from Erasmus to Spinoza** (rev. 1979); Montaigne, its sixteenth-century exemplar, is studied in excellent biographies by D. M. Frame* (1965) and H. Friedrich* (trans. 1991). A provocative book exploring the relationship of rationalism to Western thought from the seventeenth century on is E. Gellner, *Reason and Rationalism* (1990).

For the political thought of the period an overview is provided in F. L. Baumer, *Modern European Thought: Continuity and Change in Ideas, 1600–1950* (1970), cited earlier. On Locke, one may read M. Cranston, *John Locke* (1957), the most informative study; M. Seliger, *The Liberal Politics of John Locke* (1969); J. Dunn, *The Political Thought of John Locke* (1969); and R. Ashcraft, *Locke's Two Treatises of Government* (1986). Hobbes is studied in D. D. Raphael, *Hobbes: Morals and Politics* (1978); and R. Tuck, *Hobbes** (1989), a brief appraisal. Useful for French thinkers in these years is N. O. Keohane, *Philosophy and the State in France: The Renaissance to the Enlightenment** (1980).

Problems and Readings*

Recommended are D. C. Lindberg and R. S. Westman (eds.), *Reappraisals of the Scientific Revolution* (1990); G. Basalla, *The Rise of Modern Science: External or Internal Factors?* (1968); and E. Rosen, *Copernicus and the Scientific Revolution* (Anvil series, 1984). A useful anthology is M. B. Hall (ed.), *Nature and Nature's Laws: Documents of the Scientific Revolution* (1969).

VIII. The Age of Enlightenment

For background, the eighteenth-century accounts listed at the beginning of Chapter VI should be consulted, and to them should be added A. Goodwin (ed.), *The American and French Revolutions, 1763–1793** (1965), Vol. VIII of the *New Cambridge Modern History*. An older account, in the Langer series, L. Gershoy, *From Despotism to Revolution, 1763–1789** (1944), remains illuminating, as does the brief L. Krieger, *Kings and Philosophers, 1689–1789** (1970).

Enlightenment Thought

The most successful effort to interpret the thought of the era on a European-wide scale is P. Gay, *The Enlightenment: An Interpretation* (2 vols., 1966–1969); the author also explores some of his postulates in *The Party of Humanity: Essays on the French Enlightenment* (1964). The older works by the French scholar P. Hazard are still read with profit: *The European Mind: The Critical Years, 1680–1715* (1935; trans. 1953), and *European Thought in the Eighteenth Century: from Montesquieu to Lessing* (1946; trans. 1954). Other important interpretations are to be found in E. Cassirer, *The Philosophy of the Enlightenment* (1932; trans. 1951); A. Cobban, *In Search of Humanity: The Role of the Enlightenment in Modern History* (1960); L. G. Crocker, *An Age of Crisis: Man and World in Eighteenth Century Thought* (1959); N. Hampson, *A Cultural History of the Enlightenment** (1969); and I. O. Wade, *The Structure and Form of the French Enlightenment* (2 vols., 1977). An informative concise introduction is M. Cranston, *Philosophers and Pamphleteers: Political Theorists of the Enlightenment** (1986), while R. Anchor, *The Enlightenment Tradition** (1979), is a useful survey.

On the theme of progress, three older

accounts, J. B. Bury, *The Idea of Progress: An Inquiry into Its Origin and Growth* (1920, 1955); C. Frankel, *The Faith of Reason: The Idea of Progress in the French Enlightenment* (1938); and R. V. Sampson, *Progress in the Age of Reason: The Seventeenth Century to the Present Day* (1956), may be compared with R. Nisbet, *History of the Idea of Progress* (1980), which treats the concept on a broad time scale. On economic thought, M. Beer, *An Inquiry into Physiocracy* (1939), should be supplemented by E. Fox-Genovese, *The Origins of Physiocracy: Economic Revolution and Social Order in Eighteenth-Century France* (1976).

The Philosophes

There are numerous books on the leading thinkers of the Enlightenment. On Voltaire, P. Gay, *Voltaire's Politics: The Poet as Realist** (rev. 1988), reveals Voltaire's pragmatic reactions to the events of his day, while H. Mason, *Voltaire: A Biography* (1981), is a concise authoritative account. There are other studies by H. N. Brailsford (1935, 1963); by A. D. Aldridge (1975), a good overview; by T. Bestermann (1969), the editor of Voltaire's correspondence; and by A. J. Ayer (1986), the English philosopher, which stresses Voltaire as crusader. J. H. Brumfitt, *Voltaire Historian* (1958), assesses Voltaire's pioneer role in his day in the writing of social and cultural history. For Montesquieu there is an outstanding study by R. Shackleton, *Montesquieu: A Critical Biography* (1961), and an illuminating brief examination of his thought in J. N. Shklar, *Montesquieu** (1987). On Diderot, A. M. Wilson's biography (2 vols., 1957, 1972) is superb, and P. N. Furbank, *Diderot: A Critical Biography* (1993), is equally impressive and adds new materials.

For the elusive Rousseau, a good introduction is F. C. Green, *Jean-Jacques Rousseau: A Critical Study of His Life and Writings* (1955, 1970). E. Cassirer, *The Question of Jean-Jacques Rousseau* (trans. 1963) remains fundamental. In addition to many other studies there are available J. Guéhenno, *Jean-Jacques Rousseau* (2 vols., trans. 1966); J. H. Huizinga, *Rousseau: The Self-Made Man* (1975); R. Grimsley, *The Philosophy of Rousseau* (1973); M. Cranston's reassessment, *The Early Life and Works of Jean-Jacques Rousseau, 1712–1754** (1983), with a sequel (1991) for the years 1754–1762; J. Miller, *Rousseau:*

Dreamer of Democracy* (1984); and J. N. Shklar, *Men and Citizens: A Study of Rousseau's Social Theory** (1985). A challenging interpretation, grounded in literary criticism but with little relation to historical context, is J. Starobinski, *Jean-Jacques Rousseau: Transparency and Obstruction** (1958; rev. 1971; trans. 1988).

On Condorcet, K. M. Baker has written the exhaustive *Condorcet: From Natural Philosophy to Social Mathematics* (1975), while J. S. Schapiro, *Condorcet and the Rise of Liberalism* (1934), is a brief, general study. On a lesser known *philosophe*, sympathetic to the poorer classes, an excellent account is D. G. Levy, *The Ideas and Careers of Simon-Nicolas-Henri-Linguet* (1980). H. G. Payne, *The Philosophes and the People* (1971), traces the divergent views of the famous writers toward the lower classes, as does H. Chisick, *The Limits of Reform in the Enlightenment* (1981).

For the connection between the ideas of the Enlightenment and the Revolution one still reads with profit D. Mornet, *Intellectual Origins of the French Revolution* (trans. 1933), which saw a more direct link than most contemporary scholars would concede. Three major reassessments are F. Furet, *Interpreting the French Revolution* (1981); K. M. Baker, *Inventing the French Revolution: Essays in the Political Culture of the Eighteenth Century** (1990); and R. Chartier, *The Cultural Origins of the French Revolution* (trans. 1991). Two books on the use and abuse of the ideas of the *philosophes* by the later revolutionaries are N. Hampson, *Will and Circumstance: Montesquieu, Rousseau, and the French Revolution* (1984), and C. Blum, *Rousseau and the Republic of Virtue: The Language of Politics in the French Revolution** (1986).

Intellectual ties between France and America are discussed in L. Gottschalk and D. F. Lach, *Toward the French Revolution: Europe and America in the Eighteenth-Century World** (1973), and in A. O. Aldridge, *Franklin and His French Contemporaries* (1957, 1965). On Franklin one may also read C. A. Lopez *Mon Cher Papa: Franklin and the Ladies of Paris** (rev. 1990). Books that explore the significance of the Americas for European life and thought include A. Gerbi, *The Dispute of the New World, 1750–1900* (1973); W. Brandon, *New Worlds for Old* (1986), cited in Chapter III; and C. Vann Woodward, *The Old World's New World** (1991), on changing European perceptions of America. An outstanding effort to explore the most important collaborative work of the French Enlightenment is R. Darnton, *The Business of Enlightenment: A Publishing History of the Encyclopédie, 1775–1800** (1979). The same author's other books, among them *Mesmerism and the End of the Enlightenment in France* (1968), *The Literary Underground of the Old Regime** (1985), and *The Great Cat Massacre* (1985) help explain popular culture and radical political thought among ordinary men and women of the age. J. L. Lough, *The Contributors to the Encyclopédie* (1973) is a thoughtful brief study. The growth of literacy is explored, especially for the years after 1680, in F. Furet and J. Ozouf, *Reading and Writing: Literacy in France from Calvin to Jules Ferry** (trans. 1983), and in J. S. Allen, *In the Public Eye: A History of Readership in Modern France, 1800–1940* (1991).

W. Roberts, *Morality and Social Class: Eighteenth-Century French Literature and Painting* (1974), links the creative arts to political and social life, as does A. Boime, *A Social History of Modern Art*: Vol. I, *Art in an Age of Revolution, 1750–1800** (1987), the first volume of a projected larger work.

The Enlightenment: Scotland, England, Italy, Germany

An informative introduction to Scotland in this age is B. Lenman, *Integration, Enlightenment, and Industrialization: Scotland, 1746–1832** (1981). A valuable assessment of the important Scottish thinkers is A. C. Chitnis, *The Scottish Enlightenment: A Social History* (1976), which may be supplemented by K. Haakonssen, *The Science of a Legislator: The Natural Jurisprudence of David Hume and Adam Smith* (1981), and D. Forbes, *Hume's Philosophical Politics* (1984). Additional books on Adam Smith and on the implications of his ideas for later economic thought will be cited in Chapter XI. The essays in two collaborative volumes are rewarding: I. Hont and M. Ignatieff (eds.), *Wealth and Virtue in the Shaping of the Political Economy in the Scottish Enlightenment* (1984), and D. Daiches and others (eds.), *A Hotbed of Genius: The Scottish Enlightenment, 1730–1790** (1987).

For the Enlightenment in its English setting, one may read G. R. Cragg, *Reason and Authority in the Eighteenth Century* (1964), and J. Redwood, *Reason, Radicals,* *and Religion: The Age of Enlightenment in England, 1660–1750* (1976). Cragg also explores the relationship between religion and the Enlightenment in *The Church and the Age of Reason, 1648–1789** (1961), while B. Semmel, *The Methodist Revolution* (1973), sees Wesleyan evangelicalism as the English counterpart to democratic stirrings in Europe and America. J. G. A. Pocock subtly reexamines a number of English thinkers, including Hume, Gibbon, and Burke, and the nature of political discourse in the age, in *Virtue, Commerce, and History: Essays in Political Thought and History** (1985). For Gibbon the brief J. W. Burrow, *Gibbon** (1985), and P. B. Craddock's admirable two-volume biography (1982–1988) are available. For the German poet–philosopher Goethe, the first volume of an outstanding detailed biography has appeared, N. Boyle, *Goethe: The Poet and the Age* (1991).

H. Maestro has written a solid biography of the Italian jurist and reformer who served the Austrian state, *Cesare Beccaria and the Origins of Penal Reform* (1973). For the Italian city-states in this age there are available D. Carpanetto and G. Ricuperati, *Italy in the Age of Reason, 1685–1789** (1987), and F. Venturi, *Italy and the Enlightenment: Studies in a Cosmopolitan Century* (1972). Venturi has also written *The End of the Old Regime in Europe, 1776–1789* (2 vols., trans. 1991), a broad study of the Enlightenment as seen by Italian observers, part of a larger work. The leading Italian philosopher of the Enlightenment, little known in his own time, is studied in L. Pompa, *Vico: A Study of the "New Science"* (1975); G. Tagliocozzo and D. P. Verene (eds.), *Giambattista Vico's Science of Humanity* (1976); P. Burke's brief *Vico** (1985); and M. Lilla, *G. B. Vico: The Making of an Anti-Modern* (1993).

Other Enlightenment Themes

Religion and related themes are examined in R. R. Palmer, *Catholics and Unbelievers in Eighteenth Century France** (1939); in F. E. Manuel, *The Eighteenth Century Confronts the Gods** (1959) and *The Changing of the Gods* (1983); and in J. M. McManners, *Death and Enlightenment: Changing Attitudes to Death among Christians and Unbelievers in Eighteenth Century France** (1982). An important episode is studied in D. D. Bien, *The Calas Affair: Persecution,*

Toleration, and Heresy in Eighteenth Century Toulouse (1960). M. C. Jacob, *The Radical Enlightenment: Pantheists, Freemasons, and Republicans** (1981), explores radical ideas that flourished in Dutch literary circles, and in an impressive broader study, *Living the Enlightenment: Freemasonry and Politics in 18th Century Europe** (1991), she uncovers many of the roots of democratic politics.

For an introduction to the role and status of women in the Enlightenment, their accomplishments and the constraints upon them, one may turn to K. Rogers, *Feminism in Eighteenth-Century England* (1976); the essays in S. I. Spencer (ed.), *French Women and the Age of Enlightenment** (1985); and V. Jones, *Women in the Eighteenth Century: Constructions of Femininity** (1990), an anthology of documents.

On a special subject, A. Hertzberg, *The French Enlightenment and the Jews* (1968), contends that by stressing universal values the *philosophes* contributed to anti-Semitism; also critical of the Enlightenment is J. Katz, *Out of the Ghetto: The Social Background of Jewish Emancipation, 1770–1870* (1973). Jewish integration is explored in R. Mahler, *A History of Modern Jewry, 1780–1815* (1971); J. Israel, *European Jewry in the Age of Mercantilism, 1550–1750** (1985, 1989); and F. Malino and D. Sorkin (eds.), *From East to West: Jews in a Changing Europe* (1990), focusing on the years 1750 to 1870.

France in the Old Regime

Several books on modern France begin with developments in the eighteenth century, among them: A. Cobban, *A History of Modern France** (3 vols., 1957–1965); G. Wright, *France in Modern Times: 1760 to the Present** (rev. 1987); and R. Price, *An Economic History of Modern France 1730–1914* (1981). Price has also written *A Concise History of France** (1993), a useful recent survey, as has J. Popkin* (1993). A. Moulin, *Peasantry and Society in France since 1789** (1991), begins in this age.

Books that study the era for its own sake and not merely as a prologue to the revolution include C. B. Behrens, *The Ancien Regime** (1967); E. N. Williams, *The Ancien Regime in Europe* (1970); J. Lough, *An Introduction to Eighteenth-Century France* (1960); and P. R. Campbell, *The Ancien Regime in France* (1988). The financial crisis is explored in depth in J. F. Bosher, *French Finances, 1770–1795: From Business to Bureaucracy* (1970), and on Turgot, one may read D. Dakin, *Turgot and the Ancien Regime in France* (1965). The attempts at reform are also examined in G. P. Gooch, *Louis XV: The Monarchy in Decline* (1956).

The changing role of the nobility may be studied in F. L. Ford, *Robe and Sword: The Regrouping of the French Aristocracy after Louis XIV** (1953); and in R. Forster, *The Nobility of Toulouse in the Eighteenth Century* (1960), and his other books. G. Chaussinand-Noguret, *The French Nobility in the Eighteenth Century* (1985), portrays the prerevolutionary nobility as socially productive, while A. Goodwin (ed.), *The European Nobility in the Eighteenth Century* (1953), brings together an important collection of essays on that subject. The response to problems of poverty and hunger in eighteenth-century France may be examined in O. Hufton, *The Poor of Eighteenth-Century France, 1750–1789* (1974); in S. L. Kaplan's two books: *Bread, Politics, and Political Economy in the Reign of Louis XV* (2 vols., 1976) and *Provisioning Paris: Merchants and Millers in the Grain and Flour Trade during the Eighteenth Century* (1986); and in S. M. Adams, *Bureaucrats and Beggars: French Social Policy in the Age of Enlightenment* (1990): Parisian life at the time is reconstructed in D. Roche, *The People of Paris** (trans. 1987). The status of domestic servants as a key to broader social relations is examined in S. C. Maza, *Servants and Masters in Eighteenth Century France: The Uses of Loyalty* (1983), and in C. Fairchilds, *Domestic Enemies: Servants and Their Masters in Old Regime France* (1984).

Enlightened Despotism in Europe

A thoughtful brief introduction is J. G. Gagliardo, *Enlightened Despotism** (1967), while L. Krieger, *An Essay on the Theory of Enlightenment and Despotism* (1975), is a difficult but rewarding analysis.

German political fragmentation and cultural stirrings are examined in J. G. Gagliardo's *Reich and Nation: The Holy Roman Empire as Idea and Reality, 1763–1806* (1980) and *Germany under the Old Regime, 1600–1790** (1991). R. Vierhaus, *Germany in the Age of Absolutism** (1989), is a brief survey. J. J. Sheehan, *Germany, 1770–1866* (1989), is an outstanding larger history that begins with this period. Of special interest also for the Enlightenment years is F. Hertz, *The Development of the German Public Mind*, (1962). For Prussia and Frederick the Great, one may turn to C. P. Gooch, *Frederick the Great: The Ruler, the Writer, the Man* (1974); G. Ritter, *Frederick the Great* (1968), a brief sympathetic account; D. B. Horn, *Frederick the Great and the Rise of Prussia* (1969); and R. B. Asprey, *Frederick the Great: The Great Enigma* (1986). His bureaucracy is examined in H. C. Johnson, *Frederick the Great and His Officials* (1975), and in W. Hubatsch, *Frederick the Great of Prussia: Absolutism and Administration* (Men in Office series; trans. 1977).

A concise introduction to eighteenth-century Austria is E. Wangermann, *The Austrian Achievement, 1700–1800* (1973). D. F. Good, *The Economic Rise of the Habsburg Empire, 1750–1914* (1984), begins with these years, while P. G. M. Dickson, *Finance and Government under Maria Theresa, 1740–1780* (2 vols., 1988), is an in-depth economic study. The Habsburg empress may be studied in E. Cruikshank, *Maria Theresa* (1969); her son in S. K. Padover, *The Revolutionary Emperor* (rev. 1967); P. P. Bernard, *Joseph II* (1968), a brief, balanced account; T. C. W. Blanning, *Joseph II* (1994), in the Profiles in Power series; and D. Beales, *Joseph II: Vol. I, In the Shadow of Maria Theresa, 1741–1780* (1987), the first volume of a larger biography in progress, which shows in detail how Joseph attempted to shape policy even before his own reign began in 1780.

Enlightened despotism in Russia is examined in a judicious large-scale study, I. de Madariaga, *Russia in the Age of Catherine the Great* (1981), available in abridged form as *Catherine the Great: A Short History* (1990); for a somewhat different appraisal, one may read J. T. Alexander, *Catherine the Great: Life and Legend** (1988). There are also biographies of Catherine by I. Grey (1962), Z. Oldenbourg (1965), J. Haslip (1977), and V. Cronin (1978). G. S. Thomson, *Catherine the Great and the Expansion of Russia* (Teach Yourself History series, 1947), remains a useful introduction. Other valuable studies of eighteenth-century Russia include H. Rogger, *National Consciousness in Eighteenth-Century Russia* (1960); M. Raeff, *Origins of the Russian Intelligentsia: The Eighteenth-Century Nobility** (1966); and D. Ransel, *The Politics of Cathe-*

rinean Russia (1975). Economic developments are traced in A. Kahan, *The Plow, the Hammer, and the Knout: An Economic History of Eighteenth-Century Russia* (1985). Revolts and social stirrings may be studied in P. Avrich, *Russian Rebels, 1600–1800* (1972), cited earlier, and in two books by J. T. Alexander on the Pugachev uprising: *Autocratic Politics in a National Crisis* (1969) and *Emperor of the Cossacks* (1973).

The American Revolution and Britain

The attempt by R. R. Palmer, J. Godechot, and others to explore the American and French revolutions in a broader eighteenth-century revolutionary setting is described in the next chapter. H. F. May, *The Enlightenment in America* (1976), and H. S. Commager, *The Empire of Reason: How Europe Imagined and America Realized the Enlightenment** (1977), are both challenging books. For background to the revolution one should read B. Bailyn *The Ideological Origins of the American Revolution** (1967; rev. 1992). The link with events and ideas in seventeenth-century England is stressed in E. S. Morgan, *Inventing the People: The Rise of Popular Sovereignty in England and America* (1988). Morgan has also written one of the best overall accounts, *The Birth of the Republic, 1763–89** (rev. 1993), which may be supplemented by G. S. Wood, *The Radicalism of the American Revolution* (1992), a provocative interpretive essay.

For a sampling of interpretive studies one may turn to I. R. Christie and B. W. Labaree, *Empire or Independence, 1760–1776: A British-American Dialogue on the Coming of the American Revolution* (1976); R. B. Morris, *The American Revolution Reconsidered** (1967); J. Greene, *The Ambiguity of the American Revolution** (1968); and R. W. Tucker and D. C. Hendrickson, *The Fall of the First British Empire: Origins of the War of American Independence* (1982). There are many studies of the old colonial system, especially L. H. Gipson's monumental work (13 vols., 1936–1967). The attempt at firmer control after 1763 is studied in K. Perry, *British Politics and the American Revolution* (1990).

There are numerous books on the military aspects of the war, among them, H. R. Peckham, *The War for Independence* (1958); J. R. Alden, *A History of the American Revolution* (1969); P. Mackesy, *The War for America* (1964); and J. Shy, *A People*

Numerous and Armed: Reflections on the Military Struggle for American Independence (1976). The French contribution is examined in J. Dull, *The French Navy and American Independence* (1975), and in L. Kennett, *The French Forces in America, 1780–1783* (1978).

For diplomacy and international affairs there are S. R. Bemis' older *The Diplomacy of the American Revolution* (1935); W. C. Stinchcombe, *The American Revolution and the French Alliance* (1969); H. M. Scott, *British Foreign Policy in the Age of the American Revolution* (1991); and on the peace negotiations, R. B. Morris, *The Peacemakers: The Great Powers and American Independence* (1965), an outstanding study.

For Britain in the eighteenth century one should consult the books described in Chapter VI. In addition, on movements for parliamentary reform informative studies include J. R. Pole, *Political Representation in England and the Origins of the American Revolution* (1967); G. Rudé, *Wilkes and Political Liberty* (1962); I. R. Christie, *Wilkes, Wyvill, and Reform* (1963); C. Cone, *The English Jacobins: Reformers in Late Eighteenth Century England* (1968); and C. Bonwick, *English Radicals and the American Revolution* (1977). Two books by I. R. Christie are rewarding: *Wars and Revolutions: Britain, 1760–1815** (1982) and *Stress and Stability in Late Eighteenth-Century Britain: Reflections on the British Avoidance of Revolution** (1984).

Problems and Readings*

Two useful anthologies are I. Schneider (ed.), *The Enlightenment* (1965), and P. Gay, *The Enlightenment: A Comprehensive Anthology** (1976), while two brief surveys are W. Doyle, *The Ancien Regime** (1987), and R. Porter, *The Enlightenment** (1990). Pamphlets include R. Wines (ed.), *Enlightened Despotism: Reform or Reaction?* (1967); P. Paret (ed.), *Frederick the Great* (1972); T. M. Barker (ed.), *Frederick the Great and the Making of Prussia* (1976); M. Raeff (ed.), *Catherine the Great* (1972); E. A. Reitan (ed.), *George III: Tyrant or Constitutional Monarch?* (1964); and J. K. Martin and K. R. Stubaus (eds.), *American Revolution: Whose Revolution?* (1981). M. Beloff (ed.), *The Debate on the American Revolution, 1761–1783* (1949) provides source materials for the British setting.

There are stimulating comparative interpretations in J. G. A. Pocock (ed.), *Three British Revolutions: 1641, 1688, 1776* (1980).

IX. The French Revolution

A. Goodwin (ed.), *The American and French Revolutions, 1763–1793** (1965), Vol. VIII of the *New Cambridge Modern History*, already cited, and its sequel volume, C. W. Crawley (ed.), *War and Peace in an Age of Upheaval, 1793–1830** (1965), have informative chapters. Surveys encompassing the revolutionary era as a whole include E. J. Hobsbawn, *The Age of Revolution: Europe, 1789–1848** (1962); N. Hampson, *The First European Revolution, 1776–1850** (1969); C. Breunig, *The Age of Revolution and Reaction, 1789–1850** (rev. 1977); and F. L. Ford, *Europe, 1780–1830** (rev. 1989).

The French Revolution

As the bicentennial in 1989 of the French Revolution demonstrated, the French themselves are less divided than formerly over the legacy of 1789, but wide differences in scholarly interpretation, emphasis, and conceptualization persist. The reader may assess current scholarship through F. Furet and M. Ozouf (eds.), *A Critical Dictionary of the French Revolution* (trans. 1989), which consists of 99 encyclopedia-type articles covering events, institutions, persons, and ideas, as well as historians of the Revolution. Another informative compendium is S. F. Scott and B. Rothaus, *Historical Dictionary of the French Revolution, 1787–1799* (2 vols., 1985). Three impressive volumes incorporating the contributions of many international scholars have been published as *The French Revolution and the Creation of Modern Political Culture*: Vol. I, K. M. Baker (ed.), *The Political Culture of the Old Regime* (1987); Vol. II, C. Lucas (ed.), *The Political Culture of the French Revolution* (1989); and Vol. III, F. Furet (ed.), *The Influence of the French Revolution on Nineteenth-Century Europe* (1989). The Revolution is viewed in thoughtful perspective for the general reader by eight scholars in G. Best (ed.), *The Permanent Revolution: The French Revolution and Its Legacy, 1789–1989** (1989); in depth by specialists in C. Lucas (ed.), *Rewriting the French Revolution* (1991); and in E. J. Hobsbawm, *Echoes from the Marseillaise: Two Centuries Look*

Back on the French Revolution (1990), an insightful critique of liberal, Marxist, and revisionist interpretations.

Of narrative histories, S. Schama, *Citizens: A Chronicle of the French Revolution* (1989), carrying the events to 1794, effectively captures the color and drama but overemphasizes the progressiveness of the old regime and the inevitability of the later excesses of the Revolution. Four comprehensive political narratives are W. Doyle, *The Oxford History of the French Revolution** (1989); J. F. Bosher, *The French Revolution* (1988); D. G. M. Sutherland, *France, 1789–1815: Revolution and Counterrevolution** (1986); and A. Forrest, *The French Revolution** (1993). One still reads with profit two older books: J. M. Thompson, *The French Revolution** (1943, 1985) and C. Brinton, *A Decade of Revolution, 1789–1799** (1934; rev. 1962), the latter in the Langer series.

For special aspects the reader may turn to N. Hampson, *A Social History of the French Revolution** (1963); E. Kennedy, *A Cultural History of the French Revolution** (1989), which ably communicates the cultural effervescence of the age; and F. Aftalion, *The French Revolution: An Economic Interpretation** (trans. 1990). The art of the era comes alive in R. Paulson, *Representations of Revolution, 1789–1820** (1983), and in A. Boime, *Art in an Age of Revolution, 1750–1800** (1987), cited in the previous chapter, while architectural design is explored imaginatively in J. A. Leith, *Space and Revolution* (1991). In another area R. R. Palmer, *The Improvement of Humanity: Education and the French Revolution* (1985), examines the educational institutions which sought to disseminate revolutionary ideals.

There are now numerous older volumes more important to historiography than to history, by writers of such vastly differing viewpoints as J. Michelet, J. Jaurès, H. Taine, T. Carlyle, L. Madelin, P. Gaxotte, A. Aulard, and A. Mathiez. Two nineteenth-century accounts, contrasting sharply in interpretation, are available as K. J. Fielding and D. Sorensen (eds.), *Thomas Carlyle, The French Revolution** (1837; edited and reissued 1989); and G. Wright (ed.), *Jules Michelet, History of the French Revolution** (original trans. 1847; abr. and ed. 1967).

Many twentieth-century scholars have emphasized the class basis of the Revolution and see political differences emerging from the economic self-interest of groups and factions. A classical synthesis of this approach, which nonetheless retains a judicious balance, is G. Lefebvre, *The French Revolution** (1951; 2 vols. in trans. 1962–1964). A more extreme example, stressing class struggle, is A. Soboul, *The French Revolution, 1789–1799: From the Storming of the Bastille to Napoleon** (trans. 1977). The class struggle is also highlighted in G. Rudé, *The French Revolution** (1989). Two books by A. Cobban: *The Myth of the French Revolution** (1953) and *The Social Interpretation of The French Revolution** (1964), vigorously reject the notion of a "bourgeois revolution."

New ways to study the Revolution as a cultural phenomenon, minimizing narrative, and borrowing from cultural anthropology and literary criticism, are explored in F. Furet, *Interpreting the French Revolution** (1978; trans. 1981), cited earlier. The new methodology is exemplified in two books by L. Hunt: *Politics, Culture, and Class in the French Revolution** (1984) and *The Family Romance of the French Revolution** (1992), which approaches continuing questions of legitimacy and authority by using family as metaphor; and in M. Ozouf, *Festivals and the French Revolution** (1988).

The Events of the Revolution

For the immediate background of the Revolution, including the financial crisis, one may read M. Vovelle, *The Fall of the French Monarchy, 1787–1792** (trans. 1984), in a French series originally published by Seuil; W. Doyle, *Origins of the French Revolution** (rev. 1988); J. Egret, *The French Pre-Revolution, 1787–1788* (trans. 1977); and the two older volumes by G. Lefebvre: *The Coming of the French Revolution** (trans. 1947) and *The Great Fear of 1789: Rural Panic in Revolutionary France** (trans. 1982). The final effort at financial reconstruction is recounted in R. D. Harris, *Necker: Reform Statesman of the Ancien Regime* (1979), and *Necker and the Revolution of 1789* (1988). J. Hardman, *Louis XVI* (1992) is a thoughtful full-length biography of the monarch.

The reform phase of the Revolution under the first two legislative bodies is studied in N. Hampson, *Prelude to Terror: The Constituent Assembly and the Failure of Consensus, 1789–1791* (1989), and C. J. Mitchell, *The French Legislative Assembly of 1791* (1988). The coming of the war in 1792 and the radicalization of the Revolution may be studied in M. Bouloiseau, *The Jacobin Republic, 1792–1794** (trans. 1984), in the Seuil series; and in two books by M. J. Sydenham: *The Girondins* (1961) and *The First French Republic 1792–1804* (1974).

For the year of the Terror the reader may turn to A. Soboul, *The Parisian Sans-Culottes and the French Revolution, 1793–1794* (trans. 1964); R. R. Palmer, *Twelve Who Ruled: The Year of the Terror in the French Revolution* (1941; reissued 1958, 1989); and C. Lucas, *The Structure of the Terror* (1973). A dramatic episode foreshadowing the Terror is recounted in D. J. Jordan, *The King's Trial: Louis XVI vs. the French Revolution** (1979).

Three different aspects of the revolutionary impact are explored in J. McManners, *The French Revolution and the Church** (1969); P. Higonnet, *Class, Ideology, and the Rights of Nobles during the French Revolution* (1981); and P. Jones, *The Peasantry in the French Revolution** (1988). A. Forrest, *The French Revolution and the Poor* (1981), examines the welfare legislation adopted in the revolutionary decade.

Among R. Cobb's illuminating books about the life and activism of the lower classes are *The Police and the People: French Popular Protest, 1789–1820* (1970); *Paris and Its Provinces, 1792–1802* (1975); and *The People's Armies* (1961, 1987), an impressive study of the armed groups that scoured the countryside for food and other military needs of the revolutionary government. For the counterrevolution one turns to the broader narrative by D. G. M. Sutherland, *France, 1789–1815** (1986), cited above; J. Godechot, *The Counter-Revolution* (trans. 1971); and J. Roberts, *The Counter-Revolution in France, 1787–1830* (1990). Three valuable special studies are C. Tilly, *The Vendée** (1964); M. Hutt, *Chouannerie and the Counter-Revolution* (1984); and T. W. Margadant, *Urban Rivalries in the French Revolution** (1992), which examines tensions between the provincial towns and the central authority in Paris.

For the reaction after Robespierre's downfall and the regime that followed, one may turn to the third of the books on the Revolution in the Seuil series, D. Woronoff, *The Thermidorean Regime and the Directory, 1794–1799** (trans. 1984), and to M. Lyons, *France under the Directory* (1975). The crushing of the Babeuf uprising is described in R. B. Rose, *Gracchus Babeuf: The First Revolutionary Communist* (1978).

War and Diplomacy

On the coming of the war in 1792 and the first two coalitions one may read T. C. W. Blanning, *The Origins of the French Revolutionary Wars** (1989). The war and its various diplomatic aspects are discussed in S. T. Ross, *European Diplomatic History, 1789–1815: France against Europe** (1969), and the same author's *Quest for Victory: French Military Strategy, 1792–1799* (1973). The French army that fought the war is described in impressive detail in J. P. Bertaud, *The Army of the French Revolution: From Citizen-Soldiers to Instrument of Power* (trans. 1988); it may be supplemented by A. Forrest, *Conscripts and Deserters: The Army and French Society during the Revolution and Empire* (1989). Taking its start in this age is G. Best, *War and Society in Revolutionary Europe, 1770–1870** (1986). An informative book on British diplomacy and espionage in these years is H. Mitchell, *The Underground War against Revolutionary France, 1794–1800* (1965). On the emergence of Bonaparte, one may turn to G. Ferrero, *The Gamble: Bonaparte in Italy, 1796–1797* (1939); P. G. Elgood, *Bonaparte's Adventure in Egypt* (1931); and J. C. Herold's vivid *Bonaparte in Egypt* (1962). Additional books on Napoleon are listed in the following chapter.

Biographical Accounts

J. M. Thompson, *Leaders of the French Revolution** (1929; reissued 1988), sketching eleven outstanding personalities, still merits reading. Specific biographical accounts include A. Vallentin, *Mirabeau* (1948); G. C. Van Deusen, *Sieyès: His Life and His Nationalism* (1932), which should be supplemented by M. Forsyth, *Reason and Revolution: The Political Thought of the Abbé Sieyès* (1987); H. Dupré, *Lazare Carnot* (1940), on the "organizer of victory"; and L. Gottschalk, *Jean-Paul Marat: A Study in Radicalism* (1927, 1966). N. Hampson has written the most fair-minded account of a controversial political leader in *Danton** (1978, 1988), while G. May, *Madame Roland and the Age of Revolution* (1970), sympathetically portrays a Girondist leader who fell victim to the Terror.

A balanced biography of the most prominent figure on the Committee of Public Safety is J. M. Thompson, *Robespierre* (1935, 1988), on whom the same author has a brief study in the Teach Yourself History series, *Robespierre and the French Revolution** (1953). One also may read M. Gallo, *Robespierre, the Incorruptible: A Psychobiography* (trans. 1971), provocative but not completely convincing; G. Rudé, *Robespierre: Portrait of a Revolutionary Democrat* (1975), which makes the best possible case for the Jacobin leader; N. Hampson, *The Life and Opinions of Maximilien Robespierre** (1974, 1988), which asks observers to react to the often contradictory evidence; and D. P. Jordan, *The Revolutionary Career of Maximilien Robespierre** (1985). Robespierre's associates are studied in N. Hampson, *Saint-Just** (1991), and in L. Gershoy, *Bertrand Barère: A Reluctant Terrorist* (1962), an impressive portrait.

The Revolution outside France

For the view of the French Revolution as part of a broader European and Atlantic movement one may turn to R. R. Palmer, *The Age of the Democratic Revolution: A Political History of Europe and America, 1760–1800** (2 vols., 1959–1964); the first volume, *The Challenge*, carries the account to 1792, the second, *The Struggle*, to 1800; see also by the same author, *The World of the French Revolution** (1970). The conclusions of the French scholar J. Godechot [*La Grande Nation* (2 vols., 1956), and other works], are available in summary form as *France and the Atlantic Revolution, 1770–1799* (1965). Along related lines P. Higonnet traces the genesis of the republican idea in *Sister Republics: The Origins of French and American Republicanism* (1988). The German states are studied in three older studies: G. P. Gooch, *Germany and the French Revolution* (1920); the same author's *Studies in German History* (1948); and F. Meinecke, *The Age of German Liberation, 1789–1815** (1906; trans. 1957). They may be supplemented by J. M. Diefendorf, *Businessmen and Politics in the Rhineland, 1789–1834* (1980); K. Epstein, *The Genesis of German Conservatism* (1966), a rewarding study; and additional books listed in the following chapter.

Events in the Netherlands are examined in S. Schama, *Patriots and Liberators: Revolution and Government in the Netherlands, 1780–1813* (1977), and in northern Europe

in H. A. Barton, *Scandinavia in the Revolutionary Era, 1760–1815** (1986). The Irish rebellion of 1798 is placed in its European setting in M. Elliott, *Partners in Revolution: The United Irishmen in France** (1982); the same author's, *Wolfe Tone: Prophet of Irish Independence* (1989); and in R. B. McDowell, *Ireland in the Age of Imperialism and Revolution, 1760–1801* (1979).

For repercussions in Haiti and the black world, one may read C. L. R. James, *The Black Jacobins: Toussaint L'Ouverture and the San Domingo Revolution* (1938; rev. 1963), which should be supplemented by D. P. Geggus, *Slavery, War, and Revolution: The British Occupation of Saint Domingue, 1793–1798* (1982), and M. Duffy, *Soldiers, Sugar, and Seapower: The British Expeditions to the West Indies and the War against Revolutionary France* (1987).

An outstanding study of British reaction to the Revolution is A. Goodwin, *The Friends of Liberty: The English Democratic Movement in the Age of the French Revolution* (1979), while an informative brief essay is H. T. Dickinson, *British Radicalism and the French Revolution, 1789–1815* (1985). The debate in the political arena dramatically emerges from the documents presented in M. Butler (ed.), *Burke, Paine, Godwin, and the Revolutionary Controversy** (1984); H. T. Dickinson (ed.), *Britain and the French Revolution* (1989); M. Philip (ed.), *The French Revolution and British Popular Politics* (1991); and S. Prickett (ed.), *England and the French Revolution* (1989). An impressive effort to justify Burke's opposition to the Revolution and to demonstrate his consistent campaign against the abuse of authority is C. Cruise O'Brien, *The Great Melody: A Thematic Biography and Commented Anthology of Edmund Burke* (1990). Fox is studied in L. G. Mitchell, *Charles James Fox* (1992). The British political setting in these years to about 1830 is sketched in J. W. Derry, *Politics in the Age of Fox, Pitt, and Liverpool: Continuity and Transformation* (1990). Books focusing on popular unrest in both France and England are G. Rudé, *The Crowd in History: A Study of Popular Disturbances in France and England, 1730–1848* (1964), and G. A. Williams, *Artisans and Sans-Culottes* (1968).

The revolutionary career in England, America, and France of a leading revolutionist of the age is studied in D. F. Hawke, *Paine* (1974), and in E. Foner, *Tom Paine and the American Revolution* (1976); and

Paine's political thought is examined in A. J. Ayer, *Thomas Paine* (1989), and in M. Philip, *Paine** (1989). For the thought and career of a leading Englishwoman of the age, a pioneer feminist sympathetic to the Revolution, one may read E. Flexner, *Mary Wollstonecraft** (1972); there are other biographical accounts by C. Tomalin (1975), M. Ferguson and J. Todd (1984), and J. Lorch (1990). The role of women in the age is explored in J. B. Landes, *Women and the Public Sphere in the Age of the French Revolution* (1988); L. Kelly, *Women of the French Revolution* (1989); and S. E. Meltzer and L. W. Rabine (eds.), *Rebel Daughters: Women and the French Revolution** (1992). The essays in D. G. Levy and H. B. Applewhite (eds.), *Women and Politics in the Age of the Democratic Revolution* (1990), study women activists in revolutionary Europe and America.

In a comparative study, C. B. A. Behrens, *Society, Government, and the Enlightenment: The Experiences of Eighteenth-Century France and Prussia* (1985), tries to explain the different responses to the challenges of the age, while J. C. Lamberti, *Tocqueville and the Two Democracies* (trans. 1989), grapples with Tocqueville's explanations of why revolution led to an era of instability in France and to stable constitutional government in the United States.

Early efforts to study the phenomenon of revolution on a comparative basis included C. Brinton, *The Anatomy of Revolution** (1935; rev. 1965), and H. Arendt, *On Revolution** (1963). J. Talmon in *The Origins of Totalitarian Democracy* (1952) and his other books saw the roots of twentieth-century dictatorship in the radical phase of the French Revolution. Theories of political and social revolution are explored in two influential books by B. Moore: *Social Origins of Dictatorship and Democracy: Lord and Peasant in the Making of the Modern World* (1966), cited earlier, and *Injustice: The Social Basis of Obedience and Revolt* (1978); and in D. W. Treadgold, *Freedom: A History* (1992).

Problems and Readings*

Relevant studies include W. F. Church (ed.), *The Influence of the Enlightenment on the French Revolution* (rev. 1974); R. W. Greenlaw (ed.), *The Social Origins of the French Revolution: The Debate on the Role*

of the Middle Classes (1975); I. Woloch (ed.), *The Peasantry in the Old Regime: Condition and Protests* (1977); P. Amann (ed.), *The Eighteenth Century Revolution: French or Western?* (1963); R. Bienvenu (ed.), *The Ninth of Thermidor: The Fall of Robespierre* (1968); and S. Ross (ed.), *The French Revolution: Conflict or Continuity?* (1978). Two brief accounts are T. C. W. Blanning, *The French Revolution: Autocrats versus Bourgeois** (1989), and O. Connelly and F. Hembree, *The French Revolution** (1993). A comprehensive volume examining divergent appraisals of the Revolution is F. A. Kafker and J. M. Laux (eds.), *The French Revolution: Conflicting Interpretations* (rev. 1989); and for sociologically oriented analysis there is J. Kaplow (ed.), *New Perspectives on the French Revolution: Readings in Historical Sociology* (1965). Other collections of documents include A. Cobban (ed.), *The Debate on the French Revolution, 1789–1799* (1949); J. H. Stewart (ed.), *A Documentary Survey of the French Revolution* (1951); and R. Cobb, *French Revolution Documents* (1966). The Haitian revolutionary leader may be studied in A. M. Schlesinger, Jr. (ed.), *Toussaint L'Ouverture: Haitian Liberator* (1989), and in J. Borome (ed.), *Toussaint L'Ouverture: A Life with Letters* (1994), both in the Anvil series. Two unique collections of documents on women in the era are D. G. Levy, H. B. Applewhite, and M. D. Johnson (eds. and trans.), *Women in Revolutionary Paris, 1789–1815** (1981), and M. Yalom, *Blood Sisters: The French Revolution in Women's Memory* (1993), accounts by women eyewitnesses and participants. R. Cobb and C. Jones (eds.), *Voices of the French Revolution* (1989), is a large-scale anthology sampling leaders, observers, and victims.

X. Napoleonic Europe

Many of the books on the Revolution cited in the previous chapter continue on into the Napoleonic age. Two general surveys of Europe in the age of Napoleon are G. Bruun, *Europe and the French Imperium, 1799–1814** (rev. 1957) in the Langer series, and O. Connelly, *The Epoch of Napoleon: France and Europe** (1978). J. C. Herold has written a colorful account of the period in *The Age of Napoleon* (1963). Two useful reference works for the age are O. Connelly and others (eds.), *Historical Dictionary of Napoleonic France* (1985), and C. Emsley,

*The Longman Companion to Napoleonic Europe** (1993).

Napoleon and Napoleonic France

For Napoleonic France a valuable synthesis of French society is L. Bergeron, *France under Napoleon** (trans. 1981), while R. Holtman, *The Napoleonic Revolution** (1967), is a brief judicious assessment. A. Boime continues his *Social History of Modern Art* with Vol. II, *Art in the Age of Bonapartism, 1800–1815** (1992).

Of the many biographies and biographically oriented studies of Napoleon, three may be singled out: J. M. Thompson, *Napoleon Bonaparte: His Rise and Fall* (1952); G. Lefebvre, *Napoleon* (2 vols., 1935; trans. 1969), a work of distinction; and F. M. Markham, *Napoleon** (1964). Markham has also written *Napoleon and the Awakening of Europe* (Teach Yourself History series, 1954). Two other recommended accounts are V. Cronin, *Napoleon Bonaparte* (1972), and the concise R. Dufraisse, *Napoleon** (trans. 1990). The empire that Napoleon governed may be studied in O. Connelly, *Napoleon's Satellite Kingdoms* (1965, 1990); G. Ellis, *The Napoleonic Empire** (1991); S. Woolf, *Napoleon's Integration of Europe* (1991); and C. Emsley, *Napoleonic Europe* (1993). Napoleon as a military leader is appraised in G. E. Rothenberg, *The Art of Warfare in the Age of Napoleon* (1978), an excellent overview; O. Connelly, *Blundering to Glory: Napoleon's Military Campaigns* (1987), amusing and insightful; and J. R. Elting, *Swords around a Throne: Napoleon's Grande Armeé* (1988), an impressive account. Other recommended books are D. G. Chandler, *The Campaigns of Napoleon** (1966); the same author's *Napoleon's Marshals* (1987); and M. Glover, *The Napoleonic Wars: An Illustrated History, 1792–1815* (1978). The Continental blockade is studied in an older book by E. F. Hecksher (1922) and in G. Ellis, *Napoleon's Continental Blockade* (1991). Some specific battles are examined in C. Duffy, *Austerlitz, 1805* (1977); H. T. Parker, *Three Napoleonic Battles* (rev. 1983); and A. Schom, *Trafalgar: Countdown to Battle* (1992). The Spanish military effort, along with popular resistance, is studied in books on the Peninsular War by M. Glover (1974), D. Gates (1986), and C. J. Esdaile (1988). On the campaign in Russia, E. Tarlé, *Napoleon's Invasion of Russia, 1812* (trans. 1942),

may be supplemented by N. Nicolson, *Napoleon: 1812* (1986). Napoleon's final battle is described in C. Hibbert, *Waterloo: Napoleon's Last Campaign* (1967). On the final phase of the emperor's career one may read N. MacKenzie, *The Escape from Elba: The Fall and Flight of Napoleon, 1814–1815* (1982), and A. Schom, *One Hundred Days: Napoleon's Road to Waterloo* (1992). B. Weider and D. Hopgood, *The Murder of Napoleon* (1982), tries to unravel the mystery of how Napoleon died on St. Helena.

Biographical studies of Talleyrand have been written by A. Duff Cooper* (1932), C. Brinton* (1936), L. Madelin (1948), and J. Orieux (trans. 1974), while S. Zweig has written *Joseph Fouché: Portrait of a Politician* (1930). Three biographies of women of the era are: E. J. Knapton, *Empress Josephine** (1963); the same author's *The Lady of the Holy Alliance: The Life of Julie de Krüdener* (1939); and J. C. Herold, *Mistress to an Age** (1958), on Mme. de Staël, whose opposition to Napoleon led to her exile. Napoleon's family is studied in O. Connelly, *The Gentle Bonaparte: A Biography of Joseph, Napoleon's Elder Brother* (1968), and in F. Markham, *The Bonapartes* (1975).

Britain in the Time of Napoleon

The volumes of A. Bryant, *The Years of Endurance, 1793–1802* (1942), *The Years of Victory, 1802–1812* (1944), and *The Age of Elegance, 1812–1822* (1950), treat the period in detail from the British point of view. The war era receives special attention in J. Ehrmann, *William Pitt the Younger* (2 vols., 1969–1984), and in P. Mackesy, *War without Victory: The Downfall of Pitt, 1799–1802* (1984). There are biographies of Lord Nelson by C. Oman [Lenanton] (1946), G. M. Bennett (1972), C. Lloyd (1973), and D. and S. Howarth (1989). For Wellington one may turn to studies by C. Petrie (1956), E. Longford (2 vols., 1969–1972), and N. Thompson (1986). The impact of the war and other economic changes of the age are explored in C. Ensley, *British Society and the French Wars, 1793–1814* (1980), and in A. D. Harvey, *Britain in the Early Nineteenth Century* (1978). British expansion overseas is examined in C. A. Bayly, *Imperial Meridian: The British Empire and the World, 1780–1830** (1989). The debate over the end of the transatlantic slave trade in 1810 will be discussed in Chapter XI, but two books should be mentioned here: D. B. Davis, *The Problem of Slavery in the Age of Revolution, 1770–1823* (1975), and R. Anstey, *The Atlantic Slave Trade and British Abolition, 1760–1810* (1975).

Other Countries in Napoleonic Times

For Anglo-American relations in the decades from 1795 to 1823, there are available the three volumes of B. Perkins: *The First Rapprochement* (1955), *Prologue to War* (1961), and *Castlereagh and Adams* (1964), as well as the general diplomatic study of H. C. Allen, *Great Britain and the United States, 1783–1952* (1955). The American domestic scene is presented in M. Smelser, *The Democratic Republic, 1801–1815* (1986). There are accounts of the War of 1812 by H. L. Coles (1965), R. Horsman (1969), and D. R. Hickey (1990).

For the German states, in addition to books cited in the two previous chapters, one may read H. Kohn, *Prelude to Nation-States: The French and German Experience, 1789–1815* (1967), and H. Brunschwig, *Enlightenment and Romanticism in Eighteenth Century Prussia* (1974). For the reactions in Prussia there is the acute assessment of W. M. Simon, *The Failure of the Prussian Reform Movement, 1807–1819* (1955); one may also read G. S. Ford's older account, *Stein and the Era of Reform in Prussia, 1807–1815 (1922); C. de Grunwald, Napoleon's Nemesis: The Life of Baron Stein* (1964); and W. O. Shanahan, *Prussian Military Reforms, 1786–1813* (1954). On the Prussian military theorist, P. Paret has written a comprehensive biography, *Clausewitz: The Man, His Theories, and His Times** (1985), and has edited the famous tract *On War* (1832; ed. 1989).

For Russia in this era one may read A. Lobanov-Rostovsky, *Russia and Europe 1789–1825* (1947); and for Alexander, A. McConnell, *Tsar Alexander I: Paternalistic Reformer* (1970); A. Palmer, *Alexander I, Tsar of War and Peace* (1975); and J. M. Hartley, *Alexander I** (1994), in the Profiles in Power series.

The best account of Spain in the Napoleonic era is G. H. Lovett, *Napoleon and the Birth of Modern Spain* (3 vols., 1965), while R. Carr, *Spain 1808–1975** (rev., 1982) begins his valuable synthesis of modern Spanish history with these years. The revolutionary events in the Western Hemisphere ignited by Napoleon's invasion of Spain are recounted in J. Lynch, *The Spanish American Revolutions, 1808–1820* (rev. 1980), and in the relevant sections of L. Bethell (ed.), *The Cambridge History of Latin America*: Vol. II, *Colonial Latin America* (1988).

Wartime Diplomacy and the Congress of Vienna

Informative guides to the diplomacy of these years and to the Congress of Vienna include C. Buckland, *Metternich and the British Government, 1809–1813* (1932); C. K. Webster's two books: *The Foreign Policy of Castlereagh, 1812–1815* (1913) and *The Congress of Vienna, 1814–1815* (rev. 1934); and E. E. Kraehe, *Metternich's German Policy: Vol. I, The Contest with Napoleon, 1799–1814** (1963) and Vol. II, *The Congress of Vienna, 1814–1815** (1983). Important for this and for the chapter that follows on postwar diplomacy are C. K. Webster, *The Foreign Policy of Castlereagh, 1815–1822* (rev. 1934); H. Nicolson, *The Congress of Vienna: A Study in Allied Unity, 1812–1822** (1946); and H. Kissinger, *A World Restored: Metternich, Castlereagh and the Problem of Peace, 1812–1822* (1957).

Problems and Readings*

P. Geyl, *Napoleon: For and Against* (1949), is an older insightful synthesis of divergent interpretations; to it should be added D. H. Pinkney (ed.), *Napoleon: Historical Enigma* (1969), and F. A. Kafker and J. M. Laux (eds.), *Napoleon and His Times: Selected Interpretations* (rev. 1992), a valuable anthology.

XI. Reaction versus Progress, 1815–1848

The resettling of European institutions after the French Revolution and Napoleon in many ways marked the opening of a new historical era. There are numerous general, national, and topical histories, accordingly, that take their starting point around 1815.

Nineteenth-Century Europe

Helpful guides to all aspects of nineteenth-century history include M. S. Anderson, *The*

Ascendancy of Europe, 1815–1914* (rev. 1986); T. S. Hamerow, *The Birth of a New Europe: State and Society in the Nineteenth Century* (1983); and R. Gildea, *Barricades and Borders: Europe, 1800–1914** (1987). There are informative chapters also in C. Morazé (ed.), *The Nineteenth Century, 1775 to 1905* (1977), Vol. V of the *UNESCO History of Mankind.* Valuable for its tables, charts, and maps is N. J. G. Pounds, *An Historical Geography of Europe, 1800–1914** (1985); and two useful reference tools are G. A. Kertesz (ed.), *Documents in the Political History of the European Continent, 1815–1939* (1969), and C. Cook and J. Stevenson, *The Longman Handbook of Modern European History, 1763–1991** (rev. 1992).

A work in social and cultural history spanning the nineteenth century to 1914 is P. Gay, *The Bourgeois Experience: Victoria to Freud*, of which three of the projected five volumes have appeared: *Education of the Senses** (1984), *The Tender Passion** (1986), and *The Cultivation of Hatred* (1993). The fourth volume of the *History of Private Life* also takes in these years: M. Perrot (ed.), *From the French Revolution to the Great War* (1987). For social classes one may turn to J. Kocka and A. Mitchell (eds.), *Bourgeois Society in Nineteenth-Century Europe* (1993); C. Morazé *The Triumph of the Middle Classes** (trans. 1966); P. M. Pilbeam, *The Middle Classes in Europe, 1789–1914: France, Germany, Italy, and Russia** (1990); and for the upper classes, D. Lieven, *The Aristocracy in Europe, 1815–1914** (1992). For rural change in the late eighteenth and nineteenth centuries, there is J. Blum, *The End of the Old Order in Rural Europe** (1978), and A. Moulin, *Peasantry and Society in France since 1789** (trans. 1991), cited in Chapter VIII. For religion one may read H. Vidler, *The Church in the Age of Revolution: 1789 to the Present Day* (1961); H. McLeod, *Religion and the People of Western Europe, 1789–1970** (1981); and O. Chadwick, *The Secularization of the European Mind in the Nineteenth Century** (1976). On women in the nineteenth century in addition to general works already cited, good introductions are P. Branca, *Women in Europe since 1750* (1978); P. S. Robertson, *An Experience of Women: Patterns and Change in Nineteenth-Century Europe* (1982); and S. Delamont and L. Duffin (eds.), *The Nineteenth-Century Woman: Her Cultural and Physical World* (1978).

Europe, 1815–1848

General guides to the reorientation after 1815 include F. B. Artz, *Reaction and Revolution, 1814–1832** (1934), still useful, and W. L. Langer, *Political and Social Upheaval, 1832–1852** (1969), both in the Langer series; and G. de Bertier de Sauvigny, *Metternich and His Times* (trans. 1967). There are valuable sections by specialists in Vol. IX of the *New Cambridge Modern History*, C. W. Crawley (ed.), *War and Peace in an Age of Upheaval, 1793–1830* (1965), and in Vol. X, J. P. T. Bury (ed.), *The Zenith of European Power, 1830–1870* (1960), with an overview for each volume by the editor. E. J. Hobsbawm has written one of his stimulating books on this era, *The Age of Revolution: Europe, 1789–1848** (1962), already cited, the first of a trilogy on the nineteenth century. For the papacy in the revolutionary ferment of the age, one may read E. E. Y. Hales, *Revolution and Papacy, 1769–1846* (1960), and O. Chadwick, *The Popes and European Revolution* (1981).

Industrial Revolution

Detailed treatment is found in the final three volumes of the collaborative *Cambridge Economic History of Europe*, Vols. VI–VIII (1965–1988), which examine economic history during and since the Industrial Revolution. D. S. Landes' contribution to Vol. VI has been published separately in expanded form as *The Unbound Prometheus: Technological Change and Industrial Development in Western Europe from 1750 to the Present** (1969). Other informative accounts are R. M. Hartwell, *The Industrial Revolution and Economic Growth* (1971); C. M. Cipolla (ed.), *The Emergence of Industrial Societies* (1973), which are Vols. III and IV of the *Fontana Economic History of Europe*; A. S. Milward and S. B. Saul, *The Economic Development of Continental Europe, 1780–1870* (1973); S. Pollard, *Peaceful Conquest: The Industrialization of Europe, 1760–1970** (1981); C. Trebilcock, *The Industrialization of the Continental Powers, 1780–1914** (1981); and T. Kemp, *Industrialization in Nineteenth Century Europe* (rev. 1985). There are thoughtful essays in P. Mathias and J. A. Davis (eds.), *The First Industrial Revolutions* (1990). The social and political implications behind the growth of an industrial civilization are examined in J. McManners, *European History: Men, Machines, and Freedom** (1967); P. N. Stearns, *The Impact of the Industrial Revolution* (1971); and in E. A. Wrigley, *People, Cities, and Wealth: The Transformation of Traditional Society** (1987).

The complexities surrounding the emergence of industrialism in England are examined in numerous books. Brief informative accounts include T. S. Ashton, *The Industrial Revolution 1760–1830** (1948); P. Deane, *The First Industrial Revolution** (rev. 1979); and P. Mathias, *The First Industrial Nation: An Economic History of Britain, 1700–1914* (rev. 1983). A classic study, P. Mantoux, *The Industrial Revolution in the Eighteenth Century* (1906; rev. and trans. 1928; reissued 1983 with forewords by T. S. Ashton and J. K. Galbraith), although modified by subsequent research, may still be read with profit. Recent literature ties economic growth and industrialization more closely to the early modern centuries, sees no clearly defined, straight path to industrial development, and notes that the economic surge in growth in the early nineteenth century even went unnoticed. Such interpretations are offered in M. Berg, *The Age of Manufactures, 1700–1820: Industry, Innovation, and Work in Britain** (1985), and E. A. Wrigley, *Continuity, Chance, and Change: The Character of the Industrial Revolution in England* (1988). However, P. Hudson, in *The Genesis of Industrial Capitalism* (1986) and *The Industrial Revolution** (1992) stresses protoindustrialization but contends that revisionism may have gone too far in denying the fundamental economic changes of the early nineteenth century. A useful reference tool is B. R. Mitchell, *British Historical Statistics* (1988).

Insights into the nineteenth-century manufacturers are provided in A. Howe, *The Cotton Masters, 1830–1860* (1984); F. Crouzet, *The First Industrialists* (1985); L. Davidoff and C. Hall, *Family Fortunes: Men and Women of the English Middle Class, 1780–1850** (1987); and R. S. Fitton, *The Arkwrights: Spinners of Fortune* (1989). Changes in British agriculture and the nature of the enclosure movement may be studied in D. B. Grigg, *English Agriculture* (1989), and J. A. Yelling, *Common Field and Enclo-*

sure in England 1450–1850 (1977). The impact of social and economic change on the countryside is studied in K. D. M. Snell, *Annals of the Labouring Poor: Social Change and Agrarian England 1660–1900** (1985).

Social Consequences of Industrialism

There is a large and controversial literature on the effects of industrial change on the British working classes. F. Engels, *The Condition of the Working Class in England** [1844; reissued, D. McLellan (ed.), 1993], and A. Toynbee, *Lectures on the Industrial Revolution in England* (1884, reissued 1969), were classic descriptions of such exploitation, while J. L. and B. Hammond in several vehement books such as *The Town Labourer, 1760–1832: The New Civilization** (1919), *The Age of the Chartists** (1930), and other works also argued the economic abuse of the common people. For a somewhat revised view one may read J. T. Ward, *The Factory System, 1830–1855* (1962), and M. I. Thomis, *Responses to Industrialization: The British Experience 1780–1850** (1976). The essays in F. A. von Hayek (ed.), *Capitalism and the Historians** (1954), tend to minimize the harmful effects of early industrialism. The debate took a new turn with books such as P. Laslett, *The World We Have Lost: England before the Industrial Age** (1965), cited earlier, which somewhat overemphasizes the stability of the early modern centuries, and E. P. Thompson, *The Making of the English Working Class** (1963), which reinforces the picture of a militant working-class culture emerging to resist industrial society. E. J. Hobsbawm provides considerable empirical data in *Industry and Empire: An Economic History of Britain since 1750* (1968), to support the older picture of exploitation. For a helpful synthesis the reader may turn to two books by J. Rule: *The Experience of Labour in Eighteenth-Century English Industry* (1984) and *The Labouring Classes in Early Industrial England, 1750–1850** (1986).

Two representative studies of labor conditions in this age are E. Gauldie, *Cruel Habitations: A History of Working Class Housing, 1780–1918* (1973), and K. Williams, *From Pauperism to Poverty* (1981), on the poor laws. Working class experiences are depicted in E. R. Pike, *Human Documents of the Industrial Revolution in Britain** (reissued 1988); D. Vincent, *Bread,*

Knowledge and Freedom: A Study of Nineteenth-Century Working Class Autobiography (1981); I. Pinchbeck, *Women Workers and the Industrial Revolution, 1750–1850* (1930, 1969); and the relevant sections of I. Pinchbeck and M. Hewitt, *Children in English Society* (2 vols., 1969–1973). In a very different vein G. Himmelfarb's *The Idea of Poverty: England in the Early Industrial Age (1954)* and *Poverty and Compassion: The Moral Indignation of the Late Victorians** (1991) examine the writings of these years to demonstrate the complexities involved in defining poverty and social responsibilities.

For protest movements of the age, D. G. Wright, *Popular Radicalism: The Working Class Experience, 1780–1880** (1988), is helpful as a summary. Specific studies include M. I. Thomas, *The Luddites: Machine-Breaking in Regency England* (1979); R. J. White, *Waterloo to Peterloo* (1957); D. Rend, *Peterloo: The Massacre and Its Background* (1958); E. J. Hobsbawm and G. Rudé, *Captain Swing* (1969), a study of the rural poor and agrarian unrest; and J. Knott, *Popular Opposition to the 1834 Poor Law* (1986). On an important subject there is G. Rudé, *Criminal and Victim: Crime and Society in Early Nineteenth-Century England* (1985), which may be supplemented by M. Ignatieff, *A Just Measure of Pain: The Penitentiary and the Industrial Revolution, 1750–1850* (1979). For the Chartists older studies have been superseded by J. T. Ward, *Chartism* (1973); D. Jones, *Chartism and the Chartists* (1975); and D. Thompson, *The Chartists: Popular Politics in the Industrial Revolution* (1984). Chartist leaders are vividly portrayed in J. Epstein, *The Lion of Freedom: Feargus O'Connor and the Chartist Movement, 1832–1842* (1982), and in J. Wiener, *William Lovett** (1989). The creation in England and Ireland of a modern police system more to suppress popular protest than to control crime is studied in S. H. Palmer, *Police and Protest in England and Ireland, 1780–1850* (1988).

An overall view of social policy and reform is available in S. G. Checkland, *British Public Policy, 1776–1939: An Economic, Social, and Political Perspective** (1985), while earlier factory reform is discussed in M. W. Thomas, *The Early Factory Legislation* (1948), and J. T. Ward, *The Factory System, 1830–1855* (1962), cited earlier. For the pressures to repeal the tariffs on grain, one may read N. McCord, *The Anti-Corn-Law League, 1838–1846* (1958); and B. Hilton, *Corn, Cash, Commerce: The Economic Policies of the Tory Governments, 1815–1830* (1978). On the Reform Bill of 1832, M. Brock, *The Great Reform Act** (1973), is an outstanding study.

Several books study the antislavery movement as part of this age of protest. Slavery as an institution is explored in D. B. Davis, *The Problem of Slavery in Western Culture* (1966) and *Slavery and Human Progress* (1984); and for these years, *The Problem of Slavery in the Age of Revolution, 1770–1823** (1975), cited in Chapter X. Slavery in the Atlantic world is examined in R. Blackburn, *The Overthrow of Colonial Slavery* (1989), a comprehensive and moving account, and D. Eltis, *Economic Growth and the Ending of the Transatlantic Slave Trade* (1988), equally impressive. How the British in response to secular and religious reformers and populist pressures abolished the slave trade in 1807 and slavery as a colonial institution in 1833, even though it ran counter to their economic self-interest, is studied in R. Anstey, *The Atlantic Slave Trade and British Abolition, 1760–1810* (1975), and S. Drescher, *Econocide: British Slavery in the Era of Abolition* (1977) and *Capitalism and Anti-Slavery: British Mobilization in Comparative Perspective* (1988), focusing on activist pressures in England that set it apart from other countries.

For accounts of Britain in the years after 1815 moving on into the early Victorian age that opened in 1837, the most informative synthesis is N. Gash, *Aristocracy and People: Britain, 1815–1865** (New History of England series, 1979). Other helpful books are A. Wood, *Nineteenth-Century Britain, 1815–1914* (1960); D. Thomson, *England in the Nineteenth Century* (rev., 1964); A. Briggs, *The Age of Improvement, 1783–1867** (rev. 1979), and his other books; and D. Marshall, *Industrial England, 1776–1861* (1973). Of special importance are J. W. Osborne, *The Silent Revolution: The Industrial Revolution in England as a Source of Cultural Change* (1972), and H. Perkin, *The Origins of Modern English Society, 1780–1880** (1969, 1985). The older multivolume works of E. Halévy, translated from French, remain informative for ideas, institutions, and individuals: *The Growth of Philosophic Radicalism* (3 vols., 1901–1904; trans. 1949) and *History of the English People in the Nineteenth Century* (6 vols., 1912–1930; trans. 1949–1952).

Among the many biographies of the political leaders and reformers of the age are G. M. Trevelyan, *Lord Grey of the Reform Bill* (1920, 1937), which may now be compared with E. A. Smith, *Lord Grey, 1764–1845* (1990), and with J. W. Derry, *Charles, Earl Grey: Aristocratic Reformer* (1992); N. Gash's outstanding study of Peel: *Mr. Secretary Peel and Sir Robert Peel** (2 vols.; rev. 1985); C. R. Fay, *Huskisson and His Age* (1951); C. Driver, *Tory Radical: The Life of Richard Oastler* (1946); G. F. A. Best, *Shaftesbury* (1964); and J. Pollock, *Wilberforce* (1978). G. M. Trevelyan's older biography of John Bright (1913) may be compared with K. Robbins, *John Bright* (1979). For Cobbett one may read G. Spater, *William Cobbett: The Poor Man's Friend* (2 vols., 1982), and J. Dyck, *William Cobbett and Rural Popular Protest* (1992). How Richard Cobden dominated the strategies of middle-class radicalism emerges from N. C. Edsall, *Richard Cobden: Independent Radical* (1986), and W. Hinde, *Richard Cobden: A Victorian Outsider* (1987). There are biographies of Robert Owen by G. D. H. Cole (rev. 1966), and M. I. Cole (1953, 1969). Radical social criticism is also studied in W. Stafford, *Socialism, Radicalism, and Nostalgia, 1775–1830** (1986). The Conservative party is studied with care in B. Coleman, *Conservatism and the Conservative Party in Nineteenth-Century Britain* (1988). For women in the era one may turn to J. H. Murray, *Strongminded Women and Other Lost Voices from Nineteenth-Century England** (1982).

France, 1815–1848

As a sequel to the volumes on the Revolution, an eight-volume series on the history of France from 1815 on into the twentieth century, originally published by Seuil, has become available in translation as *The Cambridge History of Modern France*. The first volume, A. Jardin and A.-J. Tudesq, *Restoration and Reaction, 1815–1848** (1973; trans. 1983) is mostly a political narrative. A brief overview of these years is provided in W. Fortescue, *Revolution and Counter-Revolution in France, 1815–1852** (1988), and a helpful work of reference is E. L. Newman (ed.), *Historical Dictionary of France from the 1815 Revolution to the Second Empire* (2 vols., 1987). Among accounts that begin in this era are R. Magraw, *France, 1815–1914: The Bourgeois Century**

(1983); J. P. T. Bury, *France, 1814–1940** (rev. 1986); and R. Price, *A Social History of Nineteenth-Century France** (1988). Of special interest is F. Furet, *Revolutionary France, 1770–1880** (trans. 1992), which describes the struggle in the nineteenth century to absorb the changes introduced by the Revolution. For economic developments one may turn to F. Caron, *An Economic History of Modern France* (trans. 1979); two books by R. Price, *The Economic Modernization of France* (1975) and *An Economic History of Modern France, 1730–1914* (1981); R. E. Cameron, *France and the Economic Development of Europe, 1800–1914* (1961); and P. O. Brien and C. Keyder, *Economic Growth in Britain and France, 1780–1914* (1978). On a special subject J. N. Moody, *French Education since Napoleon* (1978) is rewarding.

For the years 1815–1830 G. de Bertier de Sauvigny, *The Bourbon Restoration* (trans. 1966) remains valuable, while P. Mansel, *The Court of France, 1789–1830** (1989) demonstrates how Louis XVIII and Charles X continued the pre-Revolutionary monarchy. D. Higgs, *Nobles and Nineteenth-Century France: The Practice of Inegalitarianism* (1987) refutes the assumption that the nobility lost its identity after 1789. Conservative ideas and activities are examined in P. Spencer, *Politics of Belief in Nineteenth-Century France* (1954); P. N. Stearns, *Priest and Revolutionary: Lamennais and the Dilemma of French Catholicism* (1967); D. Porch, *Army and Revolution: France, 1815–1848* (1974); and R. Rémond, *The Right Wing in France: From 1815 to de Gaulle* (trans. 1966), useful for this period on into the twentieth century. For religion A. Dansette, *The Religious History of Modern France* (2 vols.; trans. 1961), may be supplemented by R. Gibson, *A Social History of French Catholicism, 1789–1914* (1989); N. Ravitch, *The Catholic Church and the French Nation, 1685–1985* (1990); and A. M. C. Waterman, *Revolution, Economics, and Religion: Christian Political Economy, 1789–1833* (1991). Of special interest is A. B. Spitzer, *The French Generation of 1820* (1987).

The July Monarchy

For the revolutionary events of 1830 one may read D. H. Pinkney, *The French Revolution of 1830* (1972), an admirable account; P. Pilbeam, *The 1830 Revolution in France*

(1991), an insightful analytical study rather than a narrative; and C. H. Church, *Europe in 1830: Revolution and Political Change* (1983), which places the revolution in its European-wide setting. For Louis Philippe's reign, H. A. C. Collingham, *The July Monarchy: A Political History of France 1830–1848** (1988), is a detailed political and diplomatic account, while D. H. Pinkney, *Decisive Years in France, 1840–1847* (1986), presents the years of the July Monarchy as a watershed in French social and economic development. Labor and popular stirrings are ably examined in R. J. Bezucha, *The Lyon Uprising of 1834* (1974), and E. Berenson, *Populist Religion and Left-Wing Politics in France, 1830–1852* (1984).

An impressive study in cultural and social history focusing on the importance of the Revolution in the political culture and lives of the people is M. Agulhon, *The Republic in the Village: The People of the Var from the French Revolution to the Second Republic* (1971; trans. 1982). Newer approaches to social history are found also in W. H. Sewell, Jr., *The Language of Labor from the Old Regime to 1848** (1980), and W. M. Reddy, *The Rise of Market Culture: The Textile Trade and French Society, 1750–1900** (1984), as much a study in cultural anthropology as economic history. P. N. Stearns explores class relationships in *Paths to Authority: The Middle Class and the Industrial Labor Force in France, 1820–1848* (1978). Outstanding studies in urban history are J. M. Merriman, *The Red City: Limoges and the French Nineteenth Century** (1985) and the *Margins of City Life: Explorations of the French Urban Frontier, 1815–1851* (1991); and W. H. Sewell, Jr., *Structure and Mobility: The Men and Women of Marseille, 1820–1870* (1985). L. S. Kramer, *Threshold of a New World: Intellectuals and the Exile Experience in Paris, 1830–1848* (1988), conveys the cultural vitality of the capital as it appeared to exiles like Marx and others. An older study of importance is L. Chevalier, *Laboring Classes and Dangerous Classes in Paris during the First Half of the Nineteenth Century* (trans. 1973).

For women in this age one may read B. G. Smith, *Ladies of the Leisure Class: The Bourgeoises of Northern France in the Nineteenth Century** (1982), and C. G. Moses, *French Feminism in the Nineteenth Century** (1984). An informative comparative study is T. McBride, *The Domestic Revolution: The Modernization of Household Service in England and France, 1820–1920* (1976). An insightful monograph illuminating aspects of early industrialization and the role of women is G. L. Gullickson, *The Spinners and Weavers of Auffay: Rural Industry and the Sexual Division of Labor in a French Village, 1750–1850* (1986), and the impact of rapid change on children is explored in C. Heywood, *Childhood in Nineteenth-Century France: Work, Health, and Education among the Classes Populaires* (1988). A special subject is explored in P. O'Brien, *The Promise of Punishment: Prisons in Nineteenth-Century France* (1981), and G. Wright, *Between the Guillotine and Liberty: Two Centuries of the Crime Problem in France** (1983).

Biographical Accounts

On Thiers, a historian-statesman of this era, one may read J. P. T. Bury and R. P. Tombs, *Thiers, 1797–1877: A Political Life* (1986). For a second statesman-historian, D. Johnson, *Guizot: Aspects of French History, 1787–1874* (1963), illuminates his life and much else. For the last Bourbon king one may read V. D. Beach, *Charles X of France* (1971), and for Louis Philippe, T. Howarth, *Citizen-King* (1961).

Germany, 1815–1848

J. J. Sheehan, *German History, 1770–1866** (1990), cited in Chapter VIII, is invaluable for these years. Also informative are W. Carr, *A History of Germany, 1815–1990** (1991); A. Ramm, *Germany 1789–1919: A Political History* (1967), insightful on political thought; and H. James, *A German Identity, 1770–1990* (1990), perceptive on economic and other matters. Two important inquiries into the failure of German liberal democracy to triumph before time ran out in 1914 are J. J. Sheehan, *German Liberalism in the Nineteenth Century** (1978), and J. L. Snell and H. A. Schmitt, *The Democratic Movement in Germany, 1789–1914* (1976). L. Krieger, *The German Idea of Freedom: History of a Political Tradition* (1957), traces the concept with much subtlety from the eighteenth century onward. Other illuminating books are H. Kohn, *The Mind of Germany: The Education of a Nation* (1960); K. Epstein, *The Genesis of German Conservatism** (1975), cited earlier; and H. Schulze, *The Course of German*

Nationalism: From Frederick the Great to Bismarck, 1763–1867* (1991). There are thoughtful essays in L. E. Jones and K. H. Jarausch (eds.), *In Search of a Liberal Germany: German Liberalism from 1789 to the Present* (1990). Three books offering insights into politics, economics, and national stirrings in these years are T. S. Hamerow, *Restoration, Revolution, and Reaction: Economics and Politics in Germany, 1815–1871** (1958); R. H. Thomas, *Liberalism, Nationalism and the German Intellectuals, 1822–1847* (1952); and M. Kitchen, *The Political Economy of Germany, 1815–1914* (1978). A special subject is explored in W. Laqueur, *Young Germany: A History of the German Youth Movement* (1962). The role of German women in society is examined in R.-E. B. Joeres and M. J. Maynes (eds.), *German Women in the Eighteenth and Nineteenth Centuries: A Social and Literary History* (1986), and J. C. Fout (ed.), *German Women in the Nineteenth Century: A Social History** (1986).

Austria, Russia, Poland, Greece, Spain, Italy, and Other Countries

On the Habsburg monarchy after 1815, C. A. Macartney, *The Habsburg Empire, 1790–1918* (1969), is a masterful survey with full treatment of all the nationalities. Recommended also are A. Wandruszka, *The House of Habsburg* (trans. 1964); R. A. Kann, *A History of the Habsburg Empire, 1526–1918** (1974), both cited in Chapter V; and A. Steed, *The Decline and Fall of the Habsburg Empire 1815–1918** (1989). Foreign affairs are emphasized in A. J. P. Taylor, *The Habsburg Monarchy, 1809–1918** (rev. 1949); B. Jelavich, *The Habsburg Empire in European Affairs, 1814–1918** (1969); and F. R. Bridge, *The Habsburg Monarchy among the Great Powers, 1815–1918* (1991). All aspects of Austrian history on into the twentieth century are ably treated in B. Jelavich, *Modern Austria: Empire and Republic, 1815–1986** (1987).

For Europe from the Baltic to the Aegean, R. Okey, *Eastern Europe, 1740–1985** (rev. 1987), covers these years. Valuable for the Ottoman Empire here and in subsequent chapters are M. S. Anderson, *The Eastern Question, 1774–1923* (1966), and M. E. Yapp, *The Making of the Modern Near East, 1792–1923** (1988).

For Russia, among many histories that begin with Alexander I, two outstanding accounts are D. Saunders, *Russia in the Age of Reaction and Reform, 1801–1881* (1993), and H. Seton-Watson, *The Russian Empire, 1801–1917** (1967). Biographies of Alexander I have been cited in Chapter X. A major study of Alexander's successor is W. B. Lincoln, *Nicholas I: Emperor and Autocrat of All the Russias* (1978). For these years, one may also consult A. G. Mazour, *The First Russian Revolution, 1825: The Decembrist Movement** (1937, 1961); M. Zetling, *The Decembrists* (1985); and M. Raeff, *The Decembrist Movement* (1966), a narrative with documents. For Poland, there are the second volume of N. Davies, *A History of Poland: God's Playground* (2 vols., 1981), which begins in 1795; his briefer *Heart of Europe: A Short History of Poland** (1986); and P. Wandycz, *The Lands of Partitioned Poland 1795–1918** (1974), all cited in Chapter V. R. F. Leslie, *Polish Politics and the Revolution of 1830* (1956), is a key monograph for these years, and there are chapters by specialists for the later years in the volume edited by Leslie, *The History of Poland since 1863* (1980).

For the Balkans, informative volumes are R. L. Wolff, *The Balkans in Our Time** (rev. 1978), and B. Jelavich, *History of the Balkans* (2 vols., 1983), the first volume on the eighteenth and nineteenth centuries, the second on the twentieth. Two brief informative surveys are L. S. Stavrianos, *The Balkans since 1815** (1965), and B. and C. Jelavich, *The Balkans* (1965) and *The Establishment of the Balkan National States, 1804–1920** (1980), Vol. VIII of *A History of East Central Europe*. Serbian history is studied in detail in M. B. Petrovich, *A History of Modern Serbia, 1804–1918* (2 vols., 1976). For Greece, a balanced authoritative study is R. Clogg, *A Concise History of Greece** (rev. 1986). Stirrings in this period are described in C. M. Woodhouse, *The Greek War of Independence* (1952); D. Howarth, *The Greek Adventure* (1976); and R. Clogg (ed.), *The Struggle for Greek Independence* (1973), a collection of essays, and *The Movement for Greek Independence, 1770–1821* (1976), a volume of documents.

For the Risorgimento in Italy and the ferment and frustrations of the movement for unification, good introductions are D. Beales, *The Risorgimento and the Unification of Italy* (1971); H. Hearder, *Italy in the Age of the Risorgimento, 1790–1870** (1983); and S. Woolf, *A History of Italy, 1700–1860** (rev. 1986). These histories may be supplemented by G. T. Romani, *The Neapolitan Revolution of 1820–1821* (1950); C. M. Lovett, *The Democratic Movement in Italy, 1830–1876* (1982), and additional books cited in the following chapter.

For Belgium and the Dutch Netherlands in these and subsequent years, a discerning account by an eminent Dutch historian is E. H. Kossman, *The Low Countries, 1780–1940* (1978). The emerging importance of Belgium in international affairs is traced in J. E. Helmreich, *Belgium and Europe: A Study of Small-Power Diplomacy* (1976). For Spain, a masterful, balanced, and comprehensive account is R. Carr, *Spain, 1808–1975* (rev. 1982), cited in Chapter X.

Nineteenth-Century Thought

One still profits from a remarkable older study, J. T. Merz, *A History of European Thought in the Nineteenth Century* (4 vols., 1896–1914). Two overall surveys carrying cultural and intellectual history forward to the twentieth century are G. L. Mosse, *The Culture of Western Europe: The Nineteenth and Twentieth Centuries* (rev. 1988), and R. N. Stromberg, *European Intellectual History since 1789** (rev. 1994). Useful anthologies are E. C. Black, *The Posture of Europe, 1815–1940: Readings in European Intellectual History** (1964), and E. Weber (ed.), *Paths to the Present: European Thought from Romanticism to Existentialism** (1960).

For the interplay of ideas and politics, one may read D. C. Somervell, *English Thought in the Nineteenth Century** (1929, 1950); and J. Bowle, *Politics and Opinion in the Nineteenth Century** (1954). A special theme is skillfully explored in O. Chadwick, *The Secularization of the European Mind in the Nineteenth Century** (1976), cited earlier. Provocative general books include G. O. Griffith, *Interpreters of Man: A Review of Secular and Religious Thought from Hegel to Barth* (1943); P. Roubiczek, *Misrepresentation of Man: Studies in European Thought in the Nineteenth Century* (1947); and M. Peckham, *Beyond the Tragic Vision: The Quest for Identity in the Nineteenth Century** (1962). Political and other meanings of romanticism are examined in J. Barzun, *Classic, Romantic, and Modern** (rev. 1961) and *Berlioz and the Romantic Century** (1950, 1982); in D. O. Evans, *Social Romanticism in France, 1830–1848* (1951); and in N. V. Riasanovsky, *The Emergence of Romanticism* (1992).

On the nature of ideology, the best introduction is D. McLellan, *Ideology** (1986). Also helpful are G. Rudé, *Ideology and Popular Protest** (1980); and for political alignments, D. Caute, *The Left in Europe since 1789** (1966); and H. Rogger and E. Weber (eds.), *The European Right: A Historical Profile** (1965).

On historians and their contributions to nineteenth-century views of life, one may read, among other books, A. Mitzman, *Michelet, Historian: Rebirth and Romanticism in Nineteenth Century Europe* (1990); L. Krieger, *Ranke, The Meaning of History* (1977); J. Clive, *Macaulay* (1987); J. Hamburger, *Macaulay and the Whig Tradition* (1976); G. C. Iggers, *The German Conception of History: From Herder to the Present* (1968); M. Mandelbaum, *History, Man, and Reason: A Study of Nineteenth-Century Thought* (1971); and H. White, *Metahistory: The Historical Imagination in Nineteenth-Century Europe* (1973), a provocative but complex book. On Hegel one may read S. Hook, *From Hegel to Marx* (1936, 1962); B. T. Wilkins, *Hegel's Philosophy of History* (1975); L. Dickey, *Hegel: Religion, Economics, and the Politics of Spirit, 1770–1807* (1987); and J. E. Toews, *Hegelianism: The Path toward Dialectical Humanism 1805–1841** (1985).

The "Isms": Nationalism, Liberalism, Conservatism, Socialism

The vast literature on nationalism, including the many older studies by C. J. H. Hayes and H. Kohn, may be approached through L. L. Snyder, *Varieties of Nationalism* (1976); B. C. Shafer, *Faces of Nationalism* (1972); E. J. Hobsbawm, *Nations and Nationalism since 1780** (rev. 1992); W. Connor, *Ethnonationalism: The Quest for Understanding** (1994); and A. D. Smith, *The Ethnic Origins of Nations** (1986) and *National Identity** (1991). R. Bendix, *Kings or People: Power and the Mandate to Rule* (1978), is a bold large-scale effort to examine the transition to modern conceptions of legitimacy in government. H. Seton-Watson, *Nations and States: An Enquiry into the Origins of Nations and the Politics of Nationalism* (1977), is another large-scale investigation. Of special importance are the studies undertaken by C. Tilly into national development in *The Formation of National States in Western Europe* (1975), cited in Chapter I, and *Coercion, Capital, and Euro-*

pean States, 990–1990 (1990). An impressive comparative work on nationalism, studying England, the United States, France, Germany, and Russia is L. Greenfeld, *Five Roads to Modernity** (1992).

For the origins, meaning, and evolution of classical liberalism, a good introduction is J. Gray, *Liberalism** (1986), which may be read along with A. Arblaster, *The Rise and Decline of Western Liberalism** (1986), and J. Rawls, *Political Liberalism* (1992), a philosophical inquiry. An influential earlier account, H. J. Laski, *The Rise of European Liberalism** (1936), saw the history of liberalism as the gradual taming in later times of a seventeenth-century revolutionary doctrine. Two useful anthologies are A. Bullock and M. Shock (eds.), *The Liberal Tradition** (1957), and D. Sidorsky (ed.), *The Liberal Tradition in European Thought** (1970).

Among books on the leading exemplar of classical liberalism, one may read R. J. Halliday, *John Stuart Mill* (1976), a brief introductory account; G. Himmelfarb, *On Liberty and Liberalism: The Case of John Stuart Mill* (1974); B. Semmel, *John Stuart Mill and the Pursuit of Virtue* (1984); D. F. Thompson, *John Stuart Mill and Representative Government* (1976); and the vehemently critical M. Cowling, *Mill and Liberalism* (rev. 1990). In an area where Mill and his wife pioneered, A. Rossi has edited John Stuart and Harriet Taylor Mill, *Essays on Sex Equality* (1970). Mill and others are studied in S. R. Letwin, *The Pursuit of Certainty: David Hume, Jeremy Bentham, John Stuart Mill, Beatrice Webb* (1963). Bentham is also studied in a biography by M. Mack (1963) and in a brief appraisal by J. Dinwiddy (1989). For the French setting an admirable study is G. A. Kelly, *The Humane Comedy: Constant, Toqueville, and French Liberalism* (1992), which may be supplemented by B. Fontant, *Benjamin Constant and the Post-Revolutionary Mind* (1991), and R. R. Palmer, *From Jacobin to Liberal: Marc-Antoine Jullien, 1775–1848* (1993).

For the persistence of conservatism one may read P. Viereck, *Conservatism Revisited: The Revolt against Revolt, 1815–1949** (1949, 1965); J. Weiss, *Conservatism in Europe, 1770–1945: Traditionalism, Reaction, and Counter-Revolution* (1977); and R. A. Nisbet, *Conservatism: Dream and Reality** (1986).

Three good starting places for the study of the socialist and revolutionary tradition are F. E. Manuel, *The Prophets of Paris: Turgot, Condorcet, Saint-Simon, Fourier, Comte** (1962), which stresses the link between Enlightenment ideas and nineteenth-century social thought; J. L. Talmon, *Political Messianism: The Romantic Phase* (1960); and J. H. Billington, *Fire in the Minds of Men: Origins of the Revolutionary Faith* (1980), which in colorful detail focuses on the more conspiratorial revolutionaries. F. E. and F. P. Manuel masterfully trace an important theme in *Utopian Thought in the Western World** (1979), which may be supplemented with K. Kumar, *Utopia and Anti-Utopia in Modern Times* (1987).

Books on Marx and Marxism will be cited in the following chapter. The best one-volume introduction to the origins and evolution of socialism is A. S. Lindemann, *A History of European Socialism** (1983). Informative also are N. I. MacKenzie, *Socialism: A Short History* (1949); L. Derfler, *Socialism since Marx: A Century of the European Left** (1973); and W. Lerner, *A History of Socialism and Communism in Modern Times: Theorists, Activists, and Humanists** (rev. 1994). G. Lichtheim, *The Origins of Socialism* (1969), *A Short History of Socialism** (1970), and his other writings are especially stimulating. Two large-scale comprehensive studies, stressing the interaction of individuals, movements, and ideas, are G. D. H. Cole, *A History of Socialist Thought* (4 vols., 1953–1956), covering the years 1789 to 1939, and C. Landauer and others, *European Socialism: A History of Ideas and Movements from the Industrial Revolution to Hitler's Seizure of Power* (2 vols., 1960). A key utopian socialist is studied in J. F. Beecher, *Charles Fourier: The Visionary and His World* (1987), and a second, who attracted a wide following, in F. E. Manuel, *The New World of Henri Saint-Simon* (1956); G. G. Iggers, *The Cult of Authority: The Political Cult of the Saint-Simonians* (1958); and R. B. Carlisle, *The Proffered Crown: Saint Simonianism and the Doctrine of Hope* (1987). On the link between socialism and women activists, one may read M. J. Boxer and J. H. Quataert (eds.), *Socialist Women: European Socialist Feminism in the Nineteenth and Early Twentieth Centuries** (1978), and other books to be cited in Chapter XIV. A. Fried and R. Sanders, *Socialist Thought: A Documentary History** (rev. 1993), and I. Howe (ed.), *Essential Works of Socialism** (1976) are handy anthologies.

Economic Thought

For the development of economic ideas, one may also turn to the histories of economic doctrine and thought mentioned in the introductory section. An innovative and rewarding book is M. Berg, *The Machinery Question and the Making of Political Economy, 1815–1848* (1980). J. K. Galbraith, *The Age of Uncertainty* (1977), is a sprightly series of essays on economic thinkers from Adam Smith to the present, and R. Heilbroner, *The Worldly Philosophers** (1953), is useful on the economic liberals. For Adam Smith's moral and economic ideas, referred to earlier in Chapter VIII, an especially thoughtful overview is J. Z. Muller, *Adam Smith in His Time and Ours: Designing the Decent Society** (1992); informative also are D. A. Riesman, *Adam Smith's Sociological Economics* (1976); D. Winch, *Adam Smith's Politics** (1978); and P. H. Werhane, *Adam Smith and His Legacy for Modern Capitalism* (1991). For Malthus, a biographical account, stronger for his life than his intellectual contributions, is P. James, *Population Malthus: His Life and Times* (1979).

International Affairs after the Congress of Vienna

For diplomacy and international affairs, two valuable surveys are F. R. Bridge and R. Bullen, *The Great Powers and the European States System, 1815–1914** (1980), and N. Rich, *Great Power Diplomacy, 1815–1914** (1980). Books on the Congress of Vienna have been cited at the end of Chapter X. For the post-Napoleonic era the reader may turn to H. G. Schenk, *The Aftermath of the Napoleonic Wars* (1947); E. V. Gulick, *Europe's Classical Balance of Power** (1955); and P. W. Schroeder, *Metternich's Diplomacy at Its Zenith, 1820–1823* (1962), an especially valuable study. H. Kissinger, *A World Restored: Metternich, Castlereagh and the Problems of Peace, 1812–1822* (1957), cited in Chapter X, discusses balance-of-power politics and ideology before the author became a practitioner of the art; he is the author also of *Diplomacy* (1994), which pays special attention to this age. I. C. Nichols, Jr., analyzes the congress system in action in *The European Pentarchy and the Congress of Verona, 1822* (1971). British foreign affairs and diplomatic history in the post-Napoleonic era may also be followed through C. K. Webster: *The Foreign Policy of Castlereagh, 1815–1822* (1925), *Palmerston, Metternich, and the European System, 1830–1841* (1934), and *The Foreign Policy of Palmerston* (2 vols., 1951; reissued 1969). Other accounts of political leaders and events include C. J. Bartlett, *Castlereagh* (1967); J. Derry, *Castlereagh* (1976); W. Hinde, *George Canning* (1989); D. Southgate, *"The Most English Minister": The Policies and Politics of Palmerston* (1966); and K. Bourne, *Palmerston: The Early Years* (1982), with a second volume projected. C. Howard, *Britain and the Casus Belli, 1822–1902* (1974), focuses on British foreign ministers throughout the nineteenth century. American foreign policy in these years is assessed in B. Perkins, *The Creation of a Republican Empire, 1776–1865* (1993), the first of four volumes in the *Cambridge History of American Foreign Relations*.

The involvement of the European powers and the United States in Latin America is studied in C. K. Webster, *Britain and the Independence of Latin America, 1812–1830* (1944); R. Miller, *Britain and Latin America in the Nineteenth and Twentieth Century** (1993); A. P. Whitaker, *The United States and the Independence of Latin America, 1800–1830* (1941); D. Perkins, *A History of the Monroe Doctrine* (1941, 1963); E. R. May, *The Making of the Monroe Doctrine** (1975); and B. Perkins, *Castlereagh and Adams* (1965). A special perspective is provided in J. J. Johnson, *A Hemisphere Apart: The Foundations of United States Policy toward Latin America* (1990), which focuses on the years 1815–1830. For all aspects of the colonial revolutions one may turn to J. Lynch, *The Spanish American Revolutions, 1808–1821* (rev. 1986), and to the appropriate chapters in Vol. III of L. Bethell (ed.), *The Cambridge History of Latin America* (1988), both cited in Chapter X. Two biographical introductions to the subject are J. B. Trend, *Bolivar and the Independence of Spanish America** (Teach Yourself History series, 1948), and J. Kinsbrunner, *Bernardo O'Higgins** (1968). How Spain responded to its colonies is recounted in M. P. Costeloe, *Imperial Spain and the Spanish American Revolutions, 1810–1840* (1986).

Problems and Readings*

P. N. Stearns (ed.), *A Century for Debate: Problems in the Interpretation of European*

History, 1789–1914 (1969), and G. Rudé, *Debate on Europe* (1972), summarize historiographical debate on several issues. A stimulating examination of one such issue in the American and British setting is T. Bender (ed.), *The Antislavery Debate: Capitalism and Abolitionism as a Problem in Historical Interpretation** (1992).

Specialized pamphlets include G. A. Cahill (ed.), *The Great Reform Bill of 1832: Liberal or Conservative?* (1969); J. M. Merriman (ed.), *1830 in France* (1976); J. B. Halsted (ed.), *Romanticism: Definition, Explanation, and Evaluation* (1965); H. F. Schwarz (ed.), *Metternich: The "Coachman of Europe": Statesman or Evil Genius?* (1962); M. Walker (ed.), *Metternich's Europe, 1815–1848* (1986); and E. E. Kraehe (ed.), *The Metternich Controversy* (1971). A brief essay in the British Historical Association series is J. R. Dinwiddy, *From Luddism to the First Reform Bill in England, 1810–1832** (1985).

Social and economic themes are explored in P. A. M. Taylor (ed.), *The Industrial Revolution in Britain: Triumph or Disaster?* (rev. 1970); A. J. Taylor (ed.), *The Standard of Living in Britain in the Industrial Revolution* (1975); L. R. Berlanstein (ed.), *The Industrial Revolution and Work in Nineteenth Century Europe** (1992); M. L. McDougall (ed.), *The Working Class in Modern Europe* (1975); A. and L. Lees (eds.), *The Urbanization of European Society in the Nineteenth Century* (1976); and A. Esler (ed.), *The Youth Revolution: Conflict of Generations in Modern History* (1974). P. N. Stearns, *Interpreting the Industrial Revolution** (1991), in the AHA Pamphlets series helps place the changes in comparative perspective. Many of the edited pamphlets and readings in the Anvil series and their introductory essays remain useful: H. Kohn, *Nationalism: Its Meaning and History* (1965, 1982); P. Viereck, *Conservatism: From John Adams to Churchill* (1956); J. S. Schapiro, *Liberalism: Its Meaning and History* (1958); J. H. Stewart, *The Restoration Era in France, 1814–1830* (1968); and P. Beik, *Louis Philippe and the July Monarchy* (1965). On Latin American subjects, two titles in the same series are R. A. Humphreys and J. Lynch, *The Origins of the Latin American Revolutions, 1808–1826* (1967), and J. J. Johnson, *Simón Bolivar and Spanish-American Independence, 1783–1830* (1968, 1992).

XII. Revolution and the Reimposition of Order 1848–1870

The best synthesis for the background, events, and aftermath of the revolutions of 1848 is W. L. Langer, *Political and Social Upheaval, 1832–1852** (1969), in the series edited by the author, cited in the previous chapter. Other informative studies include P. S. Robertson, *Revolutions of 1848: A Social History** (1952); P. N. Stearns, *1848: The Revolutionary Tide in Europe** (1974); and J. Sigman, *1848: The Romantic and Democratic Revolutions in Europe* (trans. 1973). Of special interest is L. B. Namier, *1848: The Revolution of the Intellectuals** (1946, 1992), which sees the events in central and eastern Europe as ushering in an age of nationalism, not of liberalism. As a sequel to an earlier volume for the years 1789–1848, E. J. Hobsbawm continues his provocative analysis in *The Age of Capital, 1848–1875** (1976), adding a global dimension to the account. An outstanding attempt to view the period 1848–1918 from the point of view of international affairs is A. J. P. Taylor, *The Struggle for Mastery in Europe, 1848–1918* (Oxford History of Modern Europe, 1954).

Revolutions in Various Countries

FRANCE. General histories include G. Duveau, *The Making of a Revolution** (trans. 1968); F. A. De Luna, *France under Cavaignac* (1969); and R. Price, *The French Second Republic: A Social History* (1972). Informative also are the essays edited by R. Price, *Revolution and Reaction: 1848 and the Second French Republic* (1976), while M. Agulhon, *The Republican Experiment, 1848–1852** (1983), Vol. II of the *Cambridge History of Modern France*, subtly examines the assumptions behind formal political positions and analyzes republican and revolutionary symbolism.

Studies offering insights into popular militancy and the reactions it engendered include P. H. Amann, *Revolutions and Mass Democracy: The Paris Club Movement in 1848* (1976); M. Traugott, *The Armies of the Poor: Determinants of Working Class Participation in the Parisian Insurrection of 1848* (1985); J. W. Merriman, *The Agony of the Republic: The Repression of the Left in Revolutionary France, 1848–1851* (1978); and T. W. Margadant, *French Peasants in*

Revolt: The Insurrection of 1851 (1979), a study of the provincial response.

HABSBURG LANDS. For Austria one may read J. Redlich, *Emperor Francis Joseph of Austria* (trans. 1929; reissued 1965), an absorbing older biography, and J. Bled, *Franz Joseph* (1992). For background and revolutionary developments there are J. Blum, *Noble Landowners and Agriculture in Austria, 1815–1848: The Origins of the Peasant Emancipation of 1848* (1948); A. Schwarzenberg, *Prince Felix zu Schwarzenberg: Prime Minister of Austria, 1848–1852* (1947); and R. J. Rath, *The Viennese Revolution of 1848* (1957).

For the other parts of the empire in revolt one may read S. Z. Pech, *The Czech Revolution of 1848–1849* (1979); B. K. Kiraly, *Ferenc Deák* (1975); and I. Deák, *The Lawful Revolution: Louis Kossuth and the Hungarians, 1848–1849* (1979), a vivid account, demonstrating Kossuth's strengths and shortcomings. The end of the revolution is described in A. Sked, *The Survival of the Habsburg Empire: Radetsky, the Imperial Army, and the Class War, 1848* (1979), and in I. W. Roberts, *Nicholas I and the Russian Intervention in Hungary* (1991).

ITALY. Books on the Risorgimento have been cited in Chapter XI; others on unification will be described in the chapter that follows. Studies relevant to 1848 are G. M. Trevelyan's classic account, *Garibaldi's Defense of the Roman Republic, 1848–1849* (1907, 1949); P. Ginsborg, *Daniele Manin and the Venetian Revolution of 1848–49* (1979); and two books by E. E. Y. Hales: *Pio Nono [Pius IX]: European Politics and Religion in the Nineteenth Century* (1954) and *Revolution and Papacy, 1769–1846* (1960).

GERMANY AND THE FRANKFURT ASSEMBLY. In addition to L. B. Namier, *1848: The Revolution of the Intellectuals*, cited earlier in this chapter, which is sharply critical of the Frankfurt Assembly, informative studies include V. Valentin, *1848: Chapters of German History* (trans. 1940), and E. Eyck, *The Frankfurt Parliament, 1848–1849* (1968), a detailed account of the assembly itself. J. Sperber, *Rhineland Radicals: The Democratic Movement and the Revolution of 1848–1849* (1991), focuses on the more radical elements in the revolution.

ENGLAND AND IRELAND. The influence of the events on the Continent and the confrontation with both Chartism and Irish nationalism are recounted in J. Saville, *1848: The British State and the Chartist Movement** (1987). A special subject is graphically treated in C. B. Woodham-Smith, *The Great Hunger: Ireland 1845–1849* (1962).

Marx and Marxism

D. McLellan, *Karl Marx: His Life and Thought** (1973), is an outstanding biography of Marx; other insightful studies include J. Seigel, *Marx's Fate: The Shape of a Life** (1978, 1993); I. Berlin, *Karl Marx: His Life and Environment* (1939, 1966); S. K. Padover, *Karl Marx: An Intimate Biography* (1978); and B. Mazlish, *The Meaning of Karl Marx* (1984). Important for understanding the life and thought of Engels are studies by G. Mayer (1920, 1969), older, but still useful; S. Marcus (1974); D. McLellan* (1978); T. Carver (1990); and J. D. Hunley (1990).

On the theoretical foundations and concrete manifestations of socialism, there is an enormous and highly controversial literature, to which the books cited for the beginnings of socialism in Chapter XI and for the years after 1870 in Chapter XIV may offer some guidance. The relationship between Marx's early writings and his mature thought is much discussed. A perceptive analysis for the general reader is J. Elster, *An Introduction to Karl Marx** (1986), while the same author's *Making Sense of Marx** (1985), a much longer book, subjects Marx's theories to severe critical analysis. E. Fromm, *Marx's Concept of Man* (1969), reprints and comments on the 1844 manuscripts. Other interpretive accounts include R. N. Hunt, *The Political Ideas of Marx and Engels* (2 vols., 1976–1984); R. Tucker's *The Marxian Revolutionary Idea** (1969) and *Philosophy and Myth in Karl Marx* (rev. 1972); A. G. Meyer, *Marxism: Unity of Theory and Practice** (1957); G. Lichtheim, *Marxism: An Historical and Critical Study** (1961); S. Avinieri, *The Social and Political Thought of Karl Marx* (1971); and A. H. Wood, *Karl Marx* (1981), less impressed than others by the importance of the early manuscripts. R. S. Gottlieb, *Marxism, 1844–1990: Origins, Betrayal, Rebirth** (1992), sees a rebirth of the liberating aspects of

Marxism in contemporary activist movements.

A large-scale, critical analysis by a distinguished Polish scholar is L. Kolakowski, *Main Currents of Marxism: Its Rise, Growth, and Dissolution** (3 vols.; trans. 1978). E. Wilson, *To the Finland Station: A Study in the Writing and Acting of History** (1940), is an imaginative discussion of the use of history by socialists and nonsocialists. Insights into the Marxist interpretation of history are provided in G. A. Cohen, *Karl Marx's Theory of History: A Defense* (1978), an especially cogent analysis; W. H. Shaw, *Marx's Theory of History* (1978); and M. Rader, *Marx's Interpretation of History** (1979).

F. Furet, *Marx and the French Revolution* (trans. 1988), brings together and critically assesses Marx's fragmentary writings on that event, and R. Williams, *Marxism and Literature* (1977), demonstrates one aspect of the wider applicability of Marx's theories.

For Auguste Comte and positivism there are available M. Pickering, *Auguste Comte: An Intellectual Biography* (1992), the first volume of a projected two-volume study; M. Simon, *European Positivism in the Nineteenth Century* (1963); D. G. Charlton, *Positivist Thought in France during the Second Empire* (1959); and T. R. Wright, *The Religion of Humanity: The Impact of Comtean Positivism on Victorian Britain* (1986). G. Lenzer has edited *Auguste Comte and Positivism: The Essential Writings** (1975).

Napoleon III and Bonapartism

The best overview, assessing the progress toward modernization, is A. Plessis, *The Rise and Fall of the Second Empire, 1852–1871** (trans. 1985), Vol. III of the *Cambridge History of Modern France*. Other informative accounts are J. M. Thompson, *Louis Napoleon and the Second Empire** (1954, 1967); J. P. T. Bury, *Napoleon III and the Second Empire* (1964); B. D. Gooch, *The Reign of Napoleon III** (1969); and W. H. C. Smith, *Second Empire and Commune: France, 1848–1871** (1985), which focuses on the regime's disastrous foreign policy and collapse. A useful reference tool is W. E. Echard (ed.), *Historical Dictionary of the French Second Empire* (1985).

Biographical treatments include T. A. B. Corley, *Democratic Despot: A Life of* *Napoleon III* (1961); W. H. C. Smith, *Napoleon III* (1973); and J. F. McMillan, *Napoleon III** (Profiles in Power series, 1993). Other studies include T. Zeldin, *The Political System of Napoleon III* (1958); G. P. Gooch, *The Second Empire* (1960), a series of judicious essays; H. C. Payne, *The Police State of Louis Napoleon Bonaparte, 1851–1860* (1966); and D. Kulstein, *Napoleon III and the Working Class* (1969). There are three evocative explorations of the age by R. L. Williams: *The World of Napoleon III** (1957), *The Mortal Napoleon III* (1971), and *Manners and Murders in the World of Louis Napoleon* (1975). Education and social mobility are examined in R. D. Anderson, *Education in France, 1848–1870* (1975), and P. J. Harrigan, *Mobility, Elites, and Education in French Society of the Second Empire* (1980), which finds more mobility than other accounts. On the rebuilding of Paris, one may read D. H. Pinkney, *Napoleon III and the Rebuilding of Paris** (1958), and J. M. and B. Chapman, *The Life and Times of Baron Haussmann* (1957). A scholarly effort to rehabilitate the empress is H. Kurtz, *The Empress Eugénie, 1826–1920* (1964), which may be supplemented by N. N. Barker, *Distaff Diplomacy: The Empress Eugénie and the Foreign Policy of the Second Empire* (1967). Tendencies in later years to praise Napoleon III for presiding over political stability and material progress are explored in S. L. Campbell, *The Second Empire Revisited: A Study in French Historiography* (1978).

Problems and Readings*

Useful booklets include M. Kranzberg (ed.), *1848: A Turning Point?* (1959); S. M. Osgood (ed.), *Napoleon III and the Second Empire* (1973); and D. G. Gooch (ed.), *Napoleon III, Man of Destiny: Enlightened Statesman or Proto-Fascist?* (1963, 1976). In the Anvil and other series, there are G. Bruun, *Revolution and Reaction, 1848–1852* (1958); W. H. C. Smith, *France, 1848–1871* (1985); S. Hook, *Marx and the Marxists: The Ambiguous Legacy* (1955, 1982); G. Fasel, *European Upheaval: The Revolutions of 1848** (1970); and P. Jones, *The 1848 Revolutions* (1992). J. Sperber, *The European Revolutions, 1848–1851* (1993), a volume in the New Approaches to European History series, synthesizes the important themes and problems of interpretation of these years. R. Tucker has edited *The Marx-Engels Reader** (rev. 1978), an anthology with thoughtful introductions, while J. Elster (ed.), *Karl Marx: A Reader** (1986), is organized thematically.

XIII. The Consolidation of Large Nation-States, 1859–1871

J. P. T. Bury (ed.), *The Zenith of European Power, 1830–1871* (1966), cited in Chapter XI, offers many informative chapters, and N. Rich, *The Age of Nationalism and Reform, 1850–1890** (1970), provides a balanced synthesis. Analytical books on nationalism have been cited in Chapter XI. R. C. Binkley, *Realism and Nationalism, 1852–1871** (1935), in the Langer series, is an older effort to clarify the era that followed the revolutions of 1848.

The Crimean War

For the war itself one may read A. Palmer, *The Banner of Battle, The Story of the Crimean War** (1987), and accounts by L. F. V. Blake (1972) and P. Warner (1973). The diplomatic aspects are studied in W. Baumgart: *The Peace of Paris, 1856* (1981); N. Rich, *Why the Crimean War? A Cautionary Tale** (1985); D. Wetzel, *The Crimean War: A Diplomatic History* (1985); and D. M. Goldfrank, *The Origins of the Crimean War** (1993). An impressive book rehabilitating Austrian policy is P. W. Schroeder, *Austria, Great Britain, and the Crimean War: The Destruction of the European Concert* (1972), while J. S. Curtiss, *Russia's Crimean War* (1979), sees the Western powers as more responsible than Russia for the outbreak. The famous "Charge of the Light Brigade" is skillfully recounted in C. B. Woodham-Smith, *The Reason Why** (1953), and the same author has written a biography of Florence Nightingale (1951), as have R. G. Herbert (1981) and F. B. Smith (1982). On the changing nature of warfare emerging in this sera, one may read C. B. Falls, *A Hundred Years of War** (1954).

Unification of Italy

Books on the unification movement have already appeared in Chapters XI and XII; to them should be added F. J. Cappa, *The Origins of the Italian Wars of Independence** (1992). D. Mack Smith has written the most informative studies of the leaders of unification: *Cavour and Garibaldi in 1860: A Study in Political Conflict** (1954, 1985); *Giuseppe Garibaldi: A Brief Life* (1956); *Cavour* (1985), the latter critical of the Piedmontese statesman's opportunism; and *Mazzini* (1994). For the soldier-hero, one may also read C. Hibbert, *Garibaldi and His Enemies* (1966), a vivid popular account, and J. Ridley, *Garibaldi* (1975), a detailed, authoritative study. For Mazzini see also G. O. Griffith, *Mazzini: Prophet of Modern Europe* (1932, 1970), and other biographical studies by S. Barr (1937), G. Salvemini (1957), and E. Holt (1967). An outstanding study of Italy after unification is D. Mack Smith, *Italy: A Modern History* (1959), while the same author's *Italy and Its Monarchy** (1990) is an unflattering portrait of the House of Savoy.

Bismarck and the Founding of the Second Reich

G. A. Craig, *Germany, 1866–1945** (*Oxford History of Modern Europe*, 1978), is a masterful account covering the years from Bismarck to Hitler, with many insights into German society and culture; a companion volume, *The Germans* (1982), equally perceptive, mentioned earlier, is a series of essays on selected themes. The same author's *The Politics of the Prussian Army, 1640–1945** (1956, 1964) cited in Chapter V, is also useful for the nineteenth and twentieth centuries.

For Bismarck the outstanding account is O. Pflanze, *Bismarck and the Development of Germany* (3 vols., 1990) demonstrating in great detail how Bismarck controlled the dynamic social and economic forces of his day; a second commendable large-scale account is L. Gall, *Bismarck: The White Revolutionary* (2 vols., trans. 1986–1987). E. Eyck, *Bismarck and the German Empire** (1950, 1984), summarizes a German historian's larger critical work. Other biographical accounts include A. Palmer, *Bismarck** (1976), a judicious, well-balanced account; A. J. P. Taylor, *Bismarck: The Man and the Statesman** (1955, 1987), less judicious but provocative; and J. E. Rose, *Bismarck* (1987). W. N. Medlicott, *Bismarck and Modern Germany** (Teach Yourself History series, 1965), is an excellent brief introduction, and B. Waller, *Bismarck** (1985), an informative essay. G. O. Kent, *Bismarck and*

His Times* (1978), is especially useful for the historiographical debate on questions relating to Bismarck.

T. S. Hamerow, *The Social Foundations of German Unification, 1858–1871* (2 vols., 1969–1972), is a solid, rewarding study. An interesting account of Bismarck's Jewish financial adviser, illuminating much of German history during these years, is F. Stern, *Gold and Iron: Bismarck, Bleichröder, and the Building of the German Empire* (1977). The contribution of the customs union to unification is described in W. O. Henderson, *The Zollverein* (1939, 1959), and in A. H. Price, *The Evolution of the Zollverein* (1949), while the broad aspects of economic development are examined in Henderson's larger work, *The Rise of German Industrial Power, 1834–1914** (1976).

For the wars of unification and the events of 1870–1871, recommended studies include W. Carr, *The Origins of the Wars of German Unification** (1991); L. D. Steefel, *Bismarck, the Hohenzollern Candidacy, and the Origins of the Franco-German War of 1870* (1962); and W. E. Mosse, *The European Powers and the German Question* (1958). M. Howard, *The Franco-Prussian War: The German Invasion of France, 1870–1871* (1967, 1981), is a major study of the war and related events.

Austria-Hungary

For the Compromise of 1867 and the creation of the Dual Monarchy, the volumes by C. A. Macartney and other studies cited for Chapter XI, will be helpful. W. S. Johnston, *The Austrian Mind: An Intellectual and Social History** (1976), covers broad aspects of Austrian life, while Jewish contributions to the empire are sympathetically assessed in R. S. Wistrich, *The Jews of Vienna in the Age of Franz Joseph* (1989); S. Beller, *Vienna and the Jews** (1989); and W. O. McCagg, Jr., *A History of Habsburg Jews, 1670–1918** (1993). For the military, there are G. E. Rothenberg, *The Army of Francis Joseph* (1976), and I. Deák, *Beyond Nationalism: A Social and Political History of the Habsburg Officer Corps, 1848–1918** (1990), which illuminates the Dual Monarchy in many other ways. For Hungary, G. Szabod, *Hungarian Political Trends between the Revolution and the Compromise, 1849–1867* (1977), provides insights into Magyar politics and society, while J. K. Hoensch, *A*

History of Modern Hungary, 1867–1986* (1988), carries the story forward in time.

The Russia of Alexander II

An authoritative treatment for these years is provided in the histories by D. Saunders (1992) and H. Seton-Watson (1967), both cited in Chapter XI, and in R. Pipes, *Russia under the Old Regime* (1975). On the reign of the last five rulers from Alexander I to Nicholas II, S. Harcave has written *Years of the Golden Cockerel: The Last Romanov Tsars, 1814–1917* (1968), a subject covered also in the latter portions of W. B. Lincoln, *The Romanovs: Autocrats of All the Russias* (1981), cited in Chapter V.

On the reforms of Alexander II, one may turn to W. E. Mosse, *Alexander II and the Modernization of Russia** (1958), and to studies by S. Graham (1935), D. Footman (1974), and D. Lieven (1989). The place of the peasant emancipation in Russian history may be studied in J. Blum: *Lord and Peasant in Russia from the Ninth to the Nineteenth Century** (1961) and *The End of the Old Order in Rural Europe** (1978), both cited in earlier chapters; in G. T. Robinson, *Rural Russia under the Old Regime** (1930, 1980); and in T. Emmons, *The Russian Landed Gentry and the Peasant Emancipation of 1861* (1968).

For the activist world of nineteenth-century Russia and the world of the Russian exiles there is a helpful synthesis: F. Venturi, *A History of the Populist and Socialist Movements in Nineteenth-Century Russia** (trans. 1983), and many special studies, among them: E. H. Carr, *The Romantic Exiles: A Nineteenth Century Portrait Gallery** (1933, 1949) and *Michael Bakunin* (1937); M. A. Miller, *The Russian Revolutionary Emigrés 1825–1870* (1986); A. P. Mendel, *Michael Bakunin: Roots of Apocalypse* (1982); M. E. Malia, *Alexander Herzen and the Birth of Russian Socialism** (1961); E. Acton, *Alexander Herzen and the Role of the Intellectual Revolutionary* (1979); and V. Broido, *Apostles into Terrorists: Women and the Revolutionary Movement in the Russia of Alexander II* (1977). Special subjects are explored in R. F. Leslie, *Reform and Insurrection in Russian Poland, 1856–1865* (1963), and in J. Frankel, *Prophecy and Politics: Socialism, Nationalism, and the Russian Jews, 1862–1917* (1981). Other books on prerevolutionary Russia will be described in Chapter XVII.

United States

The mid-century Civil War and its aftermath of Reconstruction have been the subject of many histories, but two books present each with remarkable narrative skill and analytical insight: J. M. McPherson, *Battle Cry of Freedom: The Civil War Era* (1988), and E. Foner, *Reconstruction: America's Unfinished Revolution, 1863–1877** (1988).

Books by D. B. Davis and others on slavery and the slave trade as a Western institution have been described in Chapters III, X, and XI. To them may be added O. Patterson, *Slavery and Social Death: A Comparative Study* (1982), which examines the institution and practice in various cultures and eras. A large literature has developed on the slave experience and slave culture in North America, which P. Kolchin, *American Slavery, 1619–1877* (1993), cited earlier, skillfully synthesizes; the same author has also written an outstanding comparative study, *Unfree Labor: American Slavery and Russian Serfdom* (1987). Two leading examples of the literature on American slavery are E. D. Genovese, *Roll, Jordan, Roll: The World the Slaves Made* (1974), and H. G. Gutman, *The Black Family in Slavery and Freedom, 1750–1925* (1976). The controversial R. W. Fogel and S. L. Engerman, *Time on the Cross* (2 vols., 1974), which demonstrated the economic profitability of slavery, has been questioned by many historians. Two informative surveys of African-American history are J. H. Franklin (with, in later editions, A. A. Moss, Jr.), *From Slavery to Freedom: A History of African Americans* (rev. 1994), and M. F. Berry and J. Blassingame, *Long Memory: The Black Experience in America* (1982).

Canada

Informative introductions to the history of Canada include M. Conrad, A. Finkel, and others, *History of the Canadian Peoples** (2 vols., 1993), the volumes dividing at 1867; G. Woodcock, *A Social History of Canada* (1988); J. L. Granatstein and others, *Nation: Canada since Confederation* (rev. 1991); and J. L. Finlay and D. N. Sprague, *The Structure of Canadian History* (2 vols., 1992), especially insightful. The growth of Canadian self-government within an imperial framework is described in J. M. Ward, *Colonial Self-Government: The British Experience, 1759–1856* (1976), and the emer-

gence of the dominion idea, beginning in these years, is comprehensively treated in W. D. McIntyre, *The Commonwealth of Nations: Origins and Impact, 1869–1971* (1977). The *Encyclopedia of Canada* (4 vols., 1988) is a valuable reference tool. The Australian story is ably recounted in the collaborative F. K. Crowley (ed.), *A New History of Australia* (1975), and in J. Rickard, *Australia: A Cultural History** (1988); and a valuable reference tool is J. Bassett, *The Oxford Illustrated Dictionary of Australian History* (1993). An excellent introduction to New Zealand is G. W. Rice (ed.), *The Oxford History of New Zealand* (rev. 1992).

Japan and the West

C. Totman, *Japan before Perry: A Short History** (1981) provides a concise overview of the earlier centuries. G. B. Sansom, *Japan: A Short Cultural History* (rev. 1962) and *The Western World and Japan* (1950), describe Japan before and during the nineteenth century, and there are informative chapters for the years 1550–1800 in J. W. Hall (ed.), *The Cambridge History of Japan*, Vol. IV, *Early Modern Japan* (1991). Three books by E. O. Reischauer: *Japan: The Story of a Nation** (rev. 1989), *The United States and Japan** (rev. 1965), and *The Japanese** (1977), are highly recommended, as is W. G. Beasley, *The Rise of Modern Japan** (1991).

The best account of the Meiji era is Beasley's *The Meiji Restoration* (1972), but it may be supplemented by P. Duus, *The Rise of Modern Japan* (1976); T. Nejita, *Japan* (1973); and K. B. Pyle, *The Making of Modern Japan* (1986). Two especially illuminating books are C. Gluck, *Japan's Modern Myths: Ideology in the Late Meiji Period* (1985), and D. E. Westney, *Imitation and Innovation: The Transfer of Western Organizational Patterns to Meiji Japan* (1987).

Problems and Readings*

For an overall perspective: H. Kohn (ed.), *Nationalism and Realism, 1852–1879* (1968), is available in the Anvil series. On the Crimean War: B. D. Gooch (ed.), *The Origins of the Crimean War* (1969). On Italy: C. F. Delzell (ed.), *The Unification of Italy, 1859–1861* (1965); M. Walker (ed.), *Plombières: Secret Diplomacy and the Rebirth of Italy* (1968); and D. Mack Smith (ed.), *The Making of Italy, 1796–1870* (1968). On Germany: T. S. Hamerow (ed.), *Otto von Bismarck: A Historical Assessment* (rev. 1972); O. Pflanze (ed.), *The Unification of Germany, 1848–1871* (1979); F. B. M. Hollyday, *Bismarck* (Great Lives Observed series, 1970); and D. G. Williamson, *Bismarck and Germany, 1862–1890* (1986). On Austria-Hungary: H. J. and N. M. Gordon, *The Austrian Empire: Abortive Federation?* (1975). On Japan: A. Tiedemann, *Modern Japan: A Brief History* (1962, 1980), in the Anvil series.

XIV. European Civilization, 1871–1914

Two volumes in the Langer series examine these years: C. J. H. Hayes, *A Generation of Materialism, 1871–1900** (1941, 1983), portraying the dual nature of the age as climax of enlightenment and seedtime of future turmoil; and O. J. Hale, *The Great Illusion, 1900–1914** (1971), exploring the many accomplishments of the early twentieth-century years and the widespread belief in continuing peace and progress. E. J. Hobsbawm follows his two earlier books, *The Age of Revolution** (1962) and *The Age of Capital** (1975), both cited earlier, with *The Age of Empire, 1875–1914* (1988) to complete a thoughtful trilogy. G. Barraclough, *An Introduction to Contemporary History** (1964), a provocative essay, calls for a global approach to the years since 1890, a theme developed at length in J. Romein, *The Watershed of Two Eras: Europe in 1900* (trans. 1978). Of special interest also is N. Stone, *Europe Transformed, 1878–1919* (1984).

In the *New Cambridge Modern History* there are informative chapters in F. H. Hinsley (ed.), *Material Progress and Worldwide Problems, 1870–1898* (1962), and in C. L. Mowat (ed.), *The Shifting Balance of World Forces, 1898–1945* (rev. 1968). There are numerous general surveys of twentieth-century history that begin with the 1870–1914 era. Two rewarding collaborative volumes are C. Nicholls (ed.), *Power: A Political History of the Twentieth Century* (1990) and S. Pollard (ed.), *An Economic History of the Twentieth Century* (1990). For Europe, economic and social development is studied in F. B. Tipton and R. Aldrich, *An Economic and Social History of Europe, 1890–1939** (1987), with a sequel volume for later years.

A few special books deserve mention.

R. Wohl, *The Generation of 1914* (1979), relates the restlessness of the postwar generation to the pre-1914 ferment; B. W. Tuchman, *The Proud Tower: A Portrait of the World before the War, 1890–1914** (1966), provides selected vignettes for these years; and E. R. Tannenbaum, *1900: The Generation before the Great War* (1976), offers a potpourri of insights into the social history of the times. A. J. Mayer, *The Persistence of the Old Regime: Europe to the Great War* (1981), contends that aristocratic and not democratic values dominated European society down to 1914, while G. M. Luebbert, *Liberalism, Fascism, or Social Democracy: Social Classes and the Political Origins of Regimes in Interwar Europe** (1991) argues that the class alignments of the pre-1914 years determined the course of later developments. A positive assessment of the end-of-the-century era emerges from the essays in M. Teich and R. Porter (eds.), *Fin de Siècle and Its Legacy* (1990).

Women's lives and activities are documented in E. O. Hellerstein, L. P. Hume, and K. M. Offen (eds.), *Victorian Women: A Documentary Account of Women's Lives in Nineteenth Century England, France, and the United States** (1981), and R. J. Evans provides a comparative study in *The Feminists: Women's Emancipation Movements in Europe, America, and Australia, 1840–1920* (1977).

The European and World Economy

For industrial growth on the Continent, in addition to economic histories described in Chapter XI, one may turn to A. S. Milward and S. B. Saul, *The Development of the Economies of Continental Europe, 1850–1914* (1977), a comprehensive treatment for these years, and to C. P. Kindleberger, *Economic Growth in France and Britain, 1851–1950* (1963). For Germany, one may read G. Stolper and others, *The German Economy: 1870 to the Present* (1940; trans. 1967), and W. O. Henderson, *The Rise of German Industrial Power, 1834–1914** (1976), cited in Chapter XIII.

For the global economy useful works include W. Ashworth, *A Short History of the International Economy since 1850* (rev. 1963); W. Woodruff's *The Impact of Western Man: A Study of Europe's Role in the World Economy, 1750–1960* (1966) and *Emergence of an International Economy* (1970); and A. G. Kenwood and A. L.

Longheed, *The Growth of the International Economy, 1820–1980* (1983). W. W. Rostow, *The World Economy: History and Prospect* (1978), is an ambitious effort to study industrial growth from its origins in eighteenth-century Britain to its global diffusion. The nature of late nineteenth-century capitalism is explored in two illuminating books by A. D. Chandler, Jr.: *The Visible Hand* (1977), which stresses the central function of management, and *Scale and Scope, The Dynamics of Industrial Capitalism* (1990), a comparative study of leading corporations in Britain, Germany, and the United States.

International finance is examined in two older studies: L. H. Jenks, *The Migration of British Capital to 1875* (1927, 1938), and H. Feis, *Europe, the World's Banker, 1870–1914** (1930). To these should be added C. P. Kindleberger, *A Financial History of Western Europe** (rev. 1992), cited in the Introduction; M. DeCecco, *Money and Empire: The International Gold Standard, 1890–1914* (1974); R. S. Sayers, *The Bank of England, 1891–1944* (2 vols., 1985); and R. C. Michie, *Capitals of Finance: The London and New York Stock Exchanges, 1850–1914* (1987). The role of foreign capital in the economy of the United States, which made it the world's largest debtor nation in 1914, is clarified in M. Wilkins, *The History of Foreign Investment in the United States to 1914* (1989).

Demography and Migration

Several books on earlier population growth, also useful here, have been cited in the Introduction. C. M. Cipolla, *The Economic History of World Populations* (1962), and T. H. Hollingsworth, *Historical Demography* (1969), are good introductory guides.

T. McKeown, *The Modern Rise of Population* (1977), stresses the importance of food availability rather than medical advances for population growth in the nineteenth century. Other aspects are discussed in E. A. Wrigley, *Industrial Growth and Population Change* (1961); D. Grigg, *Population Growth and Agrarian Change* (1980); and in C. Tilly (ed.), *Historical Studies of Changing Fertility** (1978). Population statistics for the contemporary era of explosive growth may be brought up to date by consulting the *United Nations Statistical Yearbook* (1948 ff.) and *Demographic Yearbook* (1948 ff.). Additional books are cited in Chapter XXIV.

For the movement of peoples, two collections of essays are helpful: W. H. McNeill and R. S. Adams (eds.), *Human Migration; Patterns and Politics* (1978), and I. Glazier and L. deRosa (eds.), *Migration across Time and Nations: Population Mobility in Historical Contexts* (1986). Also available are the earlier volumes by W. F. Willcox and others, *International Migrations* (2 vols., 1929–1931), and D. R. Taft and R. Robbins, *International Migrations: The Immigrant in the Modern World* (1955). Informative works include L. P. Moch, *Moving Europeans: Migration in Western Europe since 1650* (1993); M. L. Hansen, *The Atlantic Migration, 1607–1860* (1940); and P. Taylor, *The Distant Magnet: European Migration to the United States* (1971). A sampling of other migration studies would include M. Walker, *Germany and the Emigration, 1816–1885* (1964); W. Adams, *Ireland and the Irish Emigration to the New World* (reissued 1967); and K. A. Miller, *Emigrants and Exiles: Ireland and the Irish Exodus to North America** (1985). On the absorption of America's immigrants, S. Thernstrom and others (eds.), the *Harvard Encyclopedia of American Ethnic Groups* (1980), is a valuable work of reference.

France, 1871–1914

For all aspects of France in this era the reader might turn first to J. M. Mayeur and M. Rebérioux, *The Third Republic from Its Origins to the Great War, 1871–1914** (trans. 1984), Vol. IV of the *Cambridge History of Modern France*, and to M. Agulhon, *The French Republic, 1879–1992*, which carries the story to the present in the author's own distinctive way. A concise synthesis with a positive assessment of these years is R. D. Anderson, *France, 1870–1914: Politics and Society* (1977). A provocative Marxist analysis of these years is provided in S. Elwitt's two-volume study: *The Making of the Third Republic* (1975) and *The Third Republic Defended* (1988). Two older accounts remain valuable: D. Brogan, *The Development of Modern France, 1870–1939* (rev. 1967), and D. Thomson, *Democracy in France* (rev. 1969). An unorthodox history with absorbing details and insights is T. Zeldin, *France, 1848–1945** (2 vols., 1973–1977, 1992): Vol. I, *Ambition, Love, and Politics*, and Vol. II, *Intellect, Taste and Anxiety.**

An important study arguing that French national unity was accomplished only belatedly by such agencies as the schools and army, with much detail on rural life in France, is E. Weber, *Peasants into Frenchmen: The Modernization of Rural France, 1870–1914* (1976). The same author's *France, Fin de Siècle** (1986) offers fascinating vignettes and anecdotal insights into French society and life. The arts and cultural life are opened up in R. Shattuck, *The Banquet Years: The Arts in France, 1885–1918* (1958); T. J. Clark, *Image of the People* (1973); and J. Seigel, *Bohemian Paris: Culture, Politics, and the Boundaries of Bourgeois Life, 1830–1930* (1986).

A valuable guide to major themes in French history and to writings on France beginning with these years is J. F. McMillan, *Twentieth-Century France: Politics and Society in France, 1898–1991** (1992), while two works of reference are P. Hutton (ed.), *Encyclopedia of the French Third Republic* (2 vols., 1986), and D. Bell and others (eds.), *A Biographical Dictionary of French Political Leaders since 1870* (1990).

Outstanding biographies include J. P. T. Bury's three-volume study (1936–1981) of the republican leader Gambetta; D. R. Watson, *Georges Clemenceau* (1974), on the Radical parliamentarian and premier; and H. Goldberg, *The Life of Jean Jaurès* (1962), on the Socialist tribune. The two best studies of the Dreyfus affair of the many available are D. Johnson, *France and the Dreyfus Affair* (1967), and J.-D. Bredin, *The Affair: the Case of Alfred Dreyfus* (trans. 1986). The history of women in the Third Republic is examined in J. F. McMillan, *Housewife or Harlot: The Place of Women in French Society, 1870–1940* (1981), the title derived from a remark by Proudhon; while S. C. Hause with A. R. Kenney, *Women's Suffrage and Social Politics in the French Third Republic* (1984), explores the failed movement in these years to extend the suffrage to women. Additional works relating to France in this era will be cited later in the chapter.

Great Britain, 1871–1914

E. J. Feuchtwanger, *Democracy and Empire: Britain, 1865–1914** (1985), places the period in broad context, while three useful surveys are R. C. K. Ensor, *England, 1870–1914** (1936, 1986), older but still informative; N. McCord, *British History, 1815–1906** (1991); and D. Read, *The Age of Urban Democracy: England, 1868–1914**

(rev. 1993). The economy is studied in F. Crouzet, *The Victorian Economy** (trans. 1982), and special economic insights are added in A. L. Friedberg, *The Weary Titan: Britain and the Experience of Relative Decline, 1895–1905** (1989), and in S. Pollard, *British Economy, 1870–1914** (1989). Syntheses moving well into the twentieth century are K. Robbins, *The Eclipse of a Great Power: Modern Britain, 1870–1975** (1983); A. Havighurst, *Britain in Transition: The Twentieth Century* (rev. 1985); M. Pugh, *The Making of Modern British Politics, 1867–1939** (rev. 1993); and B. Porter, *Britain, Europe, and the World, 1850–1986: Delusions of Grandeur** (rev. 1987). Two valuable bibliographical guides are H. J. Hanham (ed.), *Bibliography of British History, 1851–1914* (1977), and A. F. Havighurst, *Modern England, 1901–1984* (rev. 1988).

The patterns of urban and rural life are examined in two outstanding collaborative histories: H. J. Dyos and M. Wolff (eds.), *The Victorian City* (2 vols., 1973), and G. E. Mingay (ed.), *The Victorian Countryside* (2 vols., 1981); the shift to an urban society in G. E. Mingay, *The Transformation of Britain, 1830–1939* (1986). The changing fortunes of the landed aristocracy are studied in F. M. L. Thompson, *English Landed Society in the Nineteenth Century* (1963), and in a far-reaching, impressive book, D. Cannadine, *The Decline and Fall of the British Aristocracy* (1990), which focuses with telling detail on the 1870s to the present.

In addition one may read G. M. Young, *Portrait of an Age: Victorian England* (2 vols., 1934; enlarged new ed., 1977); three books by A. Briggs, *Victorian People* (1954), *Victorian Cities* (1963), and *Victorian Things* (1989); and G. S. R. Kitson Clark, *The Making of Victorian England* (1967). For the early twentieth century these books may be supplemented by S. Hynes, *The Edwardian Turn of Mind* (1968), and P. Thompson, *The Edwardians: The Remaking of British Society** (rev. 1992). Of the many biographies of Victoria, one may still turn to L. Strachey's adulatory *Queen Victoria** (1921), but one should also read E. Longford, *Queen Victoria** (1965), a sympathetic yet balanced account, and S. Weintraub, *Victoria: An Intimate Biography* (1987), a reappraisal with interesting insights.

Of the many studies of Gladstone, including J. Morley's three-volume account (1903; reissued 1968), one should read E. J.

Feuchtwanger, *Gladstone* (1975), and P. Stansky, *Gladstone** (1979). Two studies that capture in detail the complexities of Gladstone's private and public life are R. Shannon, *Gladstone:* Vol. I, *1809–1865* (1986), to be followed by a sequel volume; and H. C. G. Matthew, *Gladstone, 1809–1874** (1987), which carries the biography through his first ministry. For Disraeli, older biographies have been superseded by R. Blake, *Disraeli** (1967), a biography of distinction; there are other studies by G. Bradford (1983), J. Vincent* (1990), and S. Weintraub (1993). Joseph Chamberlain is the subject of an exhaustive six-volume biography, *The Life of Joseph Chamberlain* (1932–1969), the first four volumes by J. L. Garvin and the final two by J. Amery. Two briefer accounts are R. Jay, *Joseph Chamberlain* (1981), and M. Balfour, *Britain and Joseph Chamberlain* (1985). Three volumes of a projected four-volume biography of David Lloyd George by J. Grigg (1973, 1978, 1985) have been completed; also available are accounts by B. B. Gilbert (1987), M. Pugh* (1988), S. Constantine (1991), and C. Wrigley (1992). For Asquith one may read S. Koss, *Asquith* (1976); and for Balfour, R. F. Mackay, *Balfour: Intellectual Statesman* (1983).

Political and party issues are examined in depth in M. Cowling, *1867: Disraeli, Gladstone, and Revolution: The Passing of the Second Reform Bill* (1967); and in F. B. Smith, *The Making of the Second Reform Bill* (1966). The Conservative party is studied in P. Smith, *Disraelian Conservatism and Social Reform* (1967); B. Coleman, *Conservatism and the Conservative Party in Nineteenth Century Britain* (1988); R. Stewart, *The Foundation of the Conservative Party, 1832–1867* (1978); and R. Shannon, *The Age of Disraeli, 1868–1881: The Rise of Tory Democracy* (1992). For the party in these years and beyond there is J. Ramaden, *The Age of Balfour and Baldwin, 1902–1940* (1978). The transformation of the Liberals in the early twentieth century is studied in R. Richter, *The Politics of Conscience* (1964); C. Cross, *The Liberals in Power, 1905–1914* (1963); and G. L. Bernstein, *Liberalism and Liberal Politics in Edwardian England* (1986). Especially insightful is G. R. Searle, *The Quest for National Efficiency: A Study in British Politics and British Political Thought, 1899–1914* (1971). An important account of a critical event is B. K. Murray, *The People's*

Budget, 1909–1910: Lloyd George and Liberal Politics (1980). The emergence of the "new liberalism" is clarified in D. Roberts, *Origins of the British Welfare State* (1960); P. Clarke, *Liberals and Social Democrats* (1978); M. Freeden, *The New Liberalism: An Ideology of Social Reform** (1978); and J. Brown, *The Welfare State in Britain** (1993).

The women's rights movement in this era is studied in J. Kamm, *Rapiers and Battleaxes: The Women's Movement and Its Aftermath* (1966); C. Rover, *Women's Suffrage and Party Politics in Britain, 1866–1914* (1967); D. Morgan, *Suffragists and Liberals: The Politics of Woman Suffrage in England* (1975); A. Rosen, *Rise Up Women!: The Women's Social and Political Union, 1903–1914* (1974); and J. Luddington and J. Norris, *One Hand Tied behind Us: The Rise of the Women's Suffrage Movement* (1978). D. Mitchell's popular account, *The Fighting Pankhursts: A Study in Tenacity* (1967), may be supplemented by P. W. Romero, *E. Sylvia Pankhurst: Portrait of a Radical** (1987). In addition, S. Holton, *Feminism and Democracy: Women's Suffrage and Reform Politics in Britain, 1900–1918* (1986), focuses on less known provincial suffragists, and S. K. Kent, *Sex and Suffrage in Britain, 1860–1914** (1990), sees the suffrage campaign as part of a broader movement for a reformed society. Objections to the extension of the suffrage are described in B. H. Harrison, *Separate Spheres: The Opposition to the Woman's Suffrage Movement in Britain* (1978), and the restrictions on male voting before 1918 explained in M. Pugh, *Electoral Reform in War and Peace, 1906–1918* (1978).

Of many studies that examine the status and role of women of various backgrounds in this era a sampling would include M. Vicinus, *Suffer and Be Still: Women in the Victorian Age* (1973), and the volume she has edited, *A Widening Sphere: Changing Roles of Victorian Women* (1977); P. Branca, *Silent Sisterhood: Middle Class Women in the Victorian Home* (1975); E. Longworth, *Eminent Victorian Women* (1981); and B. Caine, *Victorian Feminists* (1992). Working-class women are studied in N. C. Solden, *Women in British Trade Unions, 1874–1976* (1978), and in E. Roberts, *A Woman's Place: An Oral History of Working Class Women** (1985). A key social problem is thoughtfully examined in J. R. Walkowitz, *Prostitution and Victorian Soci-*

ety: Women, Class, and the State (1980), and the same author has also written *City of Dreadful Delight: Narratives of Sexual Danger in Late-Victorian London** (1992). One may also read P. McHugh, *Prostitution and Victorian Social Reform* (1980).

The Irish question is discussed in J. C. Beckett, *The Making of Modern Ireland* (1966), cited in Chapter IV; L. J. McCaffrey, *The Irish Question, 1800–1922** (1968); K. T. Hoppen, *Ireland since 1800: Conflict and Conformity** (1989); and in a remarkable study focusing on the years 1912 to 1921, G. Dangerfield, *The Damnable Question: A Study of Anglo-Irish Relations* (1976). The same author's *The Strange Death of Liberal England** (1935), remains provocative as a searching study of the tensions in English society between 1910 and 1914.

The German Empire

Several important books for Germany in the nineteenth century have been cited in Chapters XI–XIII. To them should be added: A. Rosenberg, *The Birth of the German Republic, 1871–1918* (1931, 1964), older but still insightful; H.-U. Wehler, *The German Empire, 1871–1918** (1973; trans. 1985), a work reflecting the thinking of a new generation of German historians; and V. R. Berghahn, *Modern Germany: Society, Economy, and Politics in the Twentieth Century* (1983), an admirable survey. An important larger study, the last three volumes of which cover the years 1890–1914, is G. Ritter *The Sword and the Scepter: The Problem of Militarism in Germany* (4 vols.; trans. 1969–1973). An older book, A. Gerschenkron, *Bread and Democracy in Germany* (1943, 1989), remains valuable for insights into the pressure from agricultural interests on politics and society.

Examples of newer thinking about the structure of imperial Germany and class relationships include D. Blackbourn and G. Eley, *The Peculiarities of German History: Bourgeois Society and Politics in Nineteenth-Century German History** (1984); G. Eley, *From Unification to Nazism: Reinterpreting the German Past* (1986); D. Blackbourn, *Populists and Patricians: Essays in Modern German History* (1987); R. J. Evans, *Rethinking German History: Nineteenth Century Germany and the Origins of the Third Reich** (1990); and the essays in J. C. Fout (ed.), *Politics, Parties, and the*

Authoritarian State: Imperial Germany, 1871–1918* (2 vols., 1986).

For developments in the immediate post-Bismarckian years one may read J. A. Nichols, *Germany after Bismarck** (1959), on the Caprivi era; and J. C. G. Röhl, *Germany without Bismarck: The Crisis of Government in the Second Reich, 1890–1900* (1968). The best full biography of William II is M. Balfour, *The Kaiser and His Times* (1964), although L. Cecil, *William II: Prince and Emperor, 1859–1900* (1989), is highly recommended for the earlier years. T. A. Kohut, *Wilhelm II and the Germans* (1991) is also an insightful study. There are stimulating essays in J. C. G. Röhl and N. Sombart (eds.), *Kaiser Wilhelm II: New Interpretations* (1982). The universities in this era are examined in K. H. Jarausch, *Students, Society, and Politics in Imperial Germany: The Rise of Academic Illiberalism** (1982); the same author has also written an illuminating biographical study of Bethmann-Hollweg (1973).

Books focusing on specific localities and providing broad insights into politics, society, and class include D. Crew, *Town in the Ruhr: A Social History of Bochum, 1860–1914* (1979); D. Blackbourn, *Class, Religion, and Local Politics in Wilhelmine Germany: The Centre Party in Württemberg before 1914* (1980); M. Nolan, *Social Democracy and Society: Working Class Radicalism in Düsseldorf, 1890–1920* (1980); and S. H. F. Hickey, *Workers in Imperial Germany: The Miners of the Ruhr* (1985). The political and cultural history of the Jewish community before the Third Reich is studied in R. Gay, *The Jews of Germany* (1992), and in P. Pulzer, *Jews and the German State: The Political History of a Minority* (1992), which carries the story forward in time. Women as a pressure group for political change are studied in R. J. Evans, *The Feminist Movement in Germany, 1894–1933** (1976), and in U. Frevert, *Women in Germany History: From Bourgeois Emancipation to Sexual Liberation* (1989).

Austria-Hungary; Italy

To books on Austria-Hungary cited in Chapters XI–XIII should be added C. E. Schorske, *Fin de Siècle Vienna: Politics and Culture** (1980), a remarkable study of political, artistic, and intellectual responses to the failure of bourgeois liberalism. Important also is A. Janik and S. Toulmin,

Wittgenstein's Vienna (1973), while an evocative portrait of life and creativity in the second city of the empire is J. Lukacs, *Budapest 1900* (1989).

The best narrative accounts of Italy since unification are D. Mack Smith, *Italy: A Modern History* (rev. 1969), cited earlier, and M. Clark, *Modern Italy, 1871–1982** (1984). Economic developments are studied in S. B. Clough, *The Economic History of Modern Italy* (1964). For the years immediately after unification, an illuminating account is C. Seton-Watson, *Italy from Liberalism to Fascism, 1870–1925* (1967), which may be supplemented by J. A. Thayer, *Italy and the Great War: Politics and Culture, 1870–1915* (1964); A. W. Salomone, *Italian Democracy in the Making: The Political Scene in the Giolittian Era, 1900–1914* (1949, 1960); S. Saladino, *Italy from Unification to 1919** (1970); and R. A. Webster, *Industrial Imperialism in Italy, 1908–1915* (1976).

Socialist and Labor Movements

To books cited in Chapters XI and XII may be added H. Mitchell and P. N. Stearns, *Workers and Protest: The European Labor Movement, the Working Classes, and the Origins of Social Democracy, 1890–1914** (1971), and A. Przeworski, *Capitalism and Social Democracy** (1985), which explores the strategic choices confronted by socialist movements. There are many specific studies of socialist parties in each country. For Germany, books include C. E. Schorske, *German Social Democracy, 1905–1917** (1955), an especially valuable study; A. J. Berlau, *The German Social Democratic Party, 1914–1921* (1949); P. Gay, *The Dilemma of Democratic Socialism: Eduard Bernstein's Challenge to Marx** (1952), an examination of early revisionism; G. Roth, *The Social Democrats in Imperial Germany* (1963); W. M. Maehl, *August Bebel: Shadow Emperor of the German Workers* (1980); and V. L. Lidtke, *The Outlawed Party: Social Democracy in Germany, 1878–1890* (1966). Lidtke has also written an outstanding study of the working-class culture that developed around the German socialist movement, *The Alternative Culture: Socialist Labor in Imperial Germany* (1985), while the German socialist position on colonialism is probed in R. Fletcher, *Revisionism and Empire: Socialist Imperialism in Germany, 1897–1914* (1984).

For Britain, N. and J. MacKenzie, *The Fabians* (1977), skillfully combines biography and social and intellectual history, while two leading Fabians, Sidney and Beatrice Webb, are studied in M. Cole (ed.), *The Webbs and Their Work* (1949), and in K. Muggeridge and R. Adam, *Beatrice Webb: A Life, 1858–1943* (1948). Of the many studies of George Bernard Shaw, M. Holroyd, *Bernard Shaw* (3 vols., 1981–1992), is an extraordinary work. Of special interest is E. P. Thompson, *William Morris: Romantic or Revolutionary** (rev. 1976). Two volumes by S. Pierson probe the origins of British socialism: *Marxism and the Origins of British Socialism* (1973) and *British Socialists: The Journey from Fantasy to Politics* (1979), which carries the story to 1919. Other recommended books are H. Pelling, *The Origins of the Labour Party, 1880–1900* (1954, 1965); T. Forester, *The British Labour Party and the Working Class* (1976); R. Moore, *The Emergence of the Labour Party, 1880–1924* (1978), a fine synthesis; and D. Tanner, *Political Change and the Labour Party, 1900–1918* (1990). Carrying the story well into the twentieth century are K. Laybourn, *The Rise of Labour: The British Labour Party, 1890–1979** (1989), and K. O. Morgan, *Labour People: Leaders and Lieutenants: Hardie to Kinnock** (1987).

For France, for an overall view with many interesting insights, one may read T. Judt, *Marxism and the French Left: Studies in Labour and Politics in France, 1830–1981* (1986); R. Magraw, *A History of the French Working Class* (2 vols., 1992) the first volume studying the years 1815–1870, the second 1871–1939; and R. Stuart, *Marxism at Work: Ideology, Class, and French Socialism during the Third Republic* (1992). The origins of the Socialist party are recounted in A. Noland, *The Founding of the French Socialist Party, 1893–1905* (1956), and there are informative biographical studies on Socialist leaders, among them: H. Goldberg on Jean Jaurès (1962), cited earlier; L. Derfler (1977) and M. M. Farrar (1991) on Alexandre Millerand; L. Derfler on Paul Lafargue (1991); and K. S. Vincent on Pierre-Joseph Proudhon (1984) and Benoît Malon (1992). The spiritual precursor of Christian social democracy is studied in H. A. Schmitt, *Charles Péguy: The Decline of an Idealist* (1967).

On the Socialist international organization, J. Joll, *The Second International, 1889–1914* (rev. 1974), is a concise survey, and J. Braunthal, *History of the International* (3 vols., trans. 1961–1980), a detailed study. The breakup of the International is described in G. Haupt. *Socialism and the Great War: The Collapse of the Second International* (1972). The most comprehensive introduction to anarchism is G. Woodcock, *Anarchism: A History of Libertarian Ideas and Movements* (1962), but also useful is J. Joll, *The Anarchists** (rev. 1981).

There has been considerable interest in Rosa Luxemburg and her contributions to international socialism. J. P. Nettl, *Rosa Luxemburg** (2 vols., 1966; abr. 1 vol., 1969), is an admirable biography; other studies include books by N. Geras (1976); E. Eltinger (1987), with new material on her political and personal life; R. Abraham (1989), a concise account; and S. E. Bronner (1990).

On the activist role of women in the socialist movement one may turn to R. J. Evans, *Comrades and Sisters: Feminism, Socialism, and Pacifism in Europe, 1870–1945* (1987), and to M. J. Boxer and J. H. Quataert (eds.), *Socialist Women: European Socialist Feminism in the Nineteenth and Early Twentieth Centuries** (1978), cited earlier. For the German socialists there is J. H. Quataert, *Reluctant Feminists in German Social Democracy, 1865–1917* (1979), and for the French, C. Sowerwine, *Sisters or Citizens: Women and Socialism in France since 1876* (1982), and P. Hilden, *Working Class Women and Socialist Politics in France: A Regional Study, 1880–1914* (1986).

Labor History

Recent labor history has attempted to convey the experiences of laboring men and women apart from organized labor movements and to integrate labor protest into a broader cultural context. Here E. P. Thompson, whose works have been cited, has been a pioneer. Another exemplar, E. J. Hobsbawm, has written, among other works, *Primitive Rebels** (1959), *Labouring Men** (1964), and *Workers: Worlds of Labour** (1985). A successful effort for the English experience in these years is S. Meacham, *A Life Apart: The English Working Class, 1890–1914* (1977). Other interesting examples for British labor are D. Kynaston, *The British Working Class, 1850–1914* (1976); J. Benson, *The Working Class in Britain, 1850–1939* (1989); and R. Price,

Labour in British Society* (1990). Traditional trade union history may be studied in H. Pelling, *A History of Trade Unionism* (1963).

For France, examples of the newer labor history would include J. W. Scott, *The Glassmakers of Carmaux: French Craftsmen and Political Action in a Nineteenth-Century City** (1974); B. H. Moss, *The Origins of the French Labor Movement, 1830–1914: The Socialism of Skilled Workers* (1976); L. R. Berlanstein, *The Working People of Paris, 1871–1914* (1984); M. P. Hanagan, *The Logic of Solidarity: Artisans and Workers in Three French Towns, 1871–1914* (1980) and *Nascent Proletarians: Class Formation in Post-Revolutionary France* (1990); and D. Reid, *The Miners of Decazeville: A Genealogy of Deindustrialization* (1986) and *Paris Sewers and Sewermen: Realities and Representations** (1991). A comprehensive study is G. Noiriel, *Workers in French Society in the 19th and 20th Centuries* (trans. 1990); and the strike as a social phenomenon in these years is studied in M. Perrot, *Workers on Strike: France, 1871–1890* (trans. 1987). The importance of syndicalism is examined in several older books and in S. Milner, *French Syndicalism and the International Labor Movement, 1900–1914* (1990).

New Movements in Science

Several histories of science are cited in Chapter VII. Science in the nineteenth and early twentieth centuries is studied in W. P. D. Wightman, *The Growth of Scientific Ideas* (1951), and D. Knight, *The Age of Science* (1986).

On biology, evolution, and Darwinism one may turn to P. B. Sears, *Charles Darwin: The Naturalist as a Cultural Force* (1950); R. W. Clark, *The Survival of Charles Darwin* (1985), by a popular biographer; M. Ruse, *The Darwinian Revolution* (1979); A. Desmond, *The Politics of Evolution* (1989); A. Desmond and J. Moore, *Darwin* (1991); and D. I. Hull, *Darwin and His Critics* (1993). A good introduction is D. Young, *The Discovery of Evolution** (1993). Illuminating for its psychological insights is J. Bowlby, *Charles Darwin: A New Life* (1991). The several books of P. J. Bowler, notably *Charles Darwin: The Man and His Influence* (1990) and *Evolution: The History of an Idea* (rev. 1989), deserve attention. Brief biographical accounts of two other contributors to evolutionary theory and biological sciences in this era are L. J. Jordanova, *Lamarck** (1985), and V. Orel, *Mendel** (1985), both in a British Past Masters series. The breakthrough in geology and its cultural impact may be studied in C. C. Gillispie, *Genesis and Geology* (1951); R. Porter, *The Making of Geology* (1977); R. Laudan, *From Mineralogy to Geology* (1987); D. R. Dean, *James Hutton and the History of Geology* (1992); and S. J. Gould, *Time's Arrow, Time's Cycle: Myth and Metaphor in the Discovery of Geological Time** (1987).

For the impact of these scientific developments on religion, the classic account is A. D. White, *A History of the Warfare of Science and Theology** (1896, many eds.); more recent studies include W. Irvine, *Apes, Angels, and Victorians* (1955, 1983); J. R. Moore, *The Post-Darwinian Controversies: A Study of the Protestant Struggle to Come to Terms with Darwin in Great Britain and America, 1870–1900** (1979); D. C. Lindberg and R. L. Numbers (eds.), *Historical Essays on the Encounter between Christianity and Science** (1986); and J. H. Brooke, *Science and Religion: Some Historical Perspectives** (1991).

On the emergence of modern physics and the transformation of Newtonian concepts one may turn to V. F. Weisskopf, *Physics in the Twentieth Century* (1972), and B. L. Cline, *Men Who Made a New Physics** (1965, 1987). Einstein may best be approached through A. Pais, *"Subtle is the Lord": The Science and the Life of Albert Einstein** (1982), a major work; H. Cuny, *Albert Einstein** (1962), brief and concise; R. W. Clark, *Einstein: The Life and Times** (1971); J. Bernstein, *Einstein** (1973); and M. White and J. Gribbon, *Einstein: A Life in Science* (1994).

For the theoretical foundations of science and the nature of scientific discovery one may read the books by T. S. Kuhn* (1962) and I. B. Cohen* (1985), cited in Chapter VII, and two studies by G. Holton, *The Scientific Imagination: Case Studies** (1978) and *Thematic Origins of Scientific Thought: Kepler to Einstein** (rev. 1988).

For Freud, there is an older biography by E. Jones, an English coworker of Freud (3 vols., 1953–1957; abr. 1 vol., 1974), and an impressive study by P. Gay, *Freud: A Life for Our Time* (1988). A. Storr, *Freud** (1989) is a thoughtful brief assessment. Because many questions arise on the impor-

tance for Freud's theories of his experiences in turn-of-the-century Vienna, the reader may also wish to consult W. J. McGrath, *Freud's Discovery of Psychoanalysis: The Politics of Hysteria* (1986); A. Esterson, *Seductive Mirage: An Exploration of the Work of Sigmund Freud* (1993), highly critical; and various other studies.

Social Thought

Outstanding works are H. S. Hughes, *Consciousness and Society: The Reorientation of European Social Thought, 1890–1930** (1958); G. Masur, *Prophets of Yesterday: Studies in European Culture, 1890–1914** (1961); M. Biddis, *Age of the Masses: Ideas and Society since 1870* (1977); and S. Kern, *The Culture of Time and Space, 1880–1918** (1983). Virtually a history of thought from Herbert Spencer to the present is W. W. Wagar, *Good Tidings: The Belief in Progress from Darwin to Marcuse* (1972); on that theme one may also read M. Ginsberg, *The Idea of Progress* (1953); R. Nisbet, *History of the Idea of Progress* (1980), cited in Chapter VIII; and a thoughtful collaborative volume, G. Almond, M. Chodorow, and R. H. Pierce (eds.), *Progress and Its Discontents* (1982). An informative study of a dominant nineteenth-century thinker is D. Wiltshire, *The Social and Political Thought of Herbert Spencer* (1978).

The best studies of Nietzsche are W. A. Kaufmann, *Nietzsche: Philosopher, Psychologist, Antichrist** (1950, 1968); R. Hayman, *Nietzsche: A Critical Life* (1980); and T. B. Strong, *Friedrich Nietzsche and the Politics of Transfiguration** (rev. 1988). There are other biographical studies by C. Brinton (1941, 1965), J. P. Stern (1979), R. Schacht (1983), and G. Clive (1984). Useful anthologies for these years are R. N. Stromberg (ed.), *Realism, Naturalism, and Symbolism: Modes of Thought and Expression in Europe, 1848–1914** (1968), and E. Weber (ed.), *Movements, Currents, Trends: Aspects of European Thought in the Nineteenth and Twentieth Centuries** (1991).

Religion since 1871

The relationship between secularized European civilization and its Christian origins is ably treated in O. Chadwick, *The Secularization of the European Mind in the Nineteenth Century** (1976), and in H. McLeod,

Religion and the People of Western Europe, 1789–1970* (1981), both cited in Chapter XI. For religious thought, J. Pelikan, *Christian Doctrine and Modern Culture: Since 1700* (1990), the final volume in his *The Christian Tradition,* may be read along with C. Welch, *Protestant Thought in the Nineteenth Century* (2 vols., 1985), the second volume studying the years 1870–1914. Books examining the impact of science on the Protestant churches have been mentioned earlier in this chapter. For the Roman Catholic reaction one may read T. M. Loome, *Liberal Catholicism, Reform Catholicism, and Modernism* (1979); and L. R. Kurtz, *The Politics of Heresy: The Modernist Crisis in Roman Catholicism* (1986).

For Judaism, H. M. Sachar, *The Course of Modern Jewish History** (rev. 1977) and *A History of Israel: From the Rise of Zionism to Our Time* (rev. 1979), incorporate the nineteenth-century background. The fullest account of Zionism as an ideology is the impressive study in three volumes (1975–1987) by D. Vital: *The Origins of Zionism,** *Zionism: The Formative Years,** and *Zionism: the Crucial Phase,** which carries the story to 1919. Another insightful work is S. Avinieri, *The Making of Modern Zionism: The Intellectual Origins of the Jewish State* (1981).

The Assault on Liberalism: Racism, the Cult of Violence

Many of the books cited above examine the undermining of liberal values in the late nineteenth century, with implications for the twentieth. Two key studies are H. Arendt, *The Origins of Totalitarianism** (1951), and J. Barzun, *Darwin, Marx, Wagner: Critique of a Heritage** (rev. 1981), which stresses similarities, as the author sees it, in the way each of these figures undermined classical liberalism.

For racism and anti-Semitism in these years, one may read P. Pulzer, *The Rise of Political Anti-Semitism in Germany and Austria** (rev. 1988); L. Poliakov, *The Aryan Myth: A History of Racist and Nationalist Ideas in Europe* (trans. 1974); J. Katz, *From Prejudice to Destruction: Anti-Semitism, 1700–1933* (1980); G. L. Mosse, *Toward the Final Solution: A History of European Racism* (1978); and two books by P. L. Rose, *Revolutionary Anti-Semitism in Germany from Kant to Wagner* (1991) and *Wagner: Race and Revolution* (1992). Anti-Semitism

is placed in broad historical perspective in R. S. Wistrich, *Anti-Semitism: The Longest Hatred* (1992), a remarkable account ranging from pre-Christian times through the twentieth century, and in two books by G. I. Langmuir: *History, Religion, and Anti-Semitism** (1990) and *Toward A Definition of Anti-Semitism* (1991).

Books on anti-Semitism in France relating to the Dreyfus affair include R. F. Byrnes, *Anti-Semitism in Modern France: Prologue to the Dreyfus Affair* (1950), and S. Wilson, *Ideology and Experience: Anti-Semitism in Modern France at the Time of the Dreyfus Affair* (1982), especially insightful; books on the affair itself have already been cited. A. S. Lindemann, *The Jew Accused: Three Anti-Semitic Affairs: Dreyfus, Beilis, Frank, 1894–1915** (1991) skillfully compares the French affair with episodes in tsarist Russia and the United States. J. J. Roth, *The Cult of Violence: Sorel and the Sorelians* (1980), is illuminating on the founder of syndicalism and his followers. The origins of twentieth-century fascist ideology are studied in Z. Sternhell, *Neither Right Nor Left: Fascist Ideology in France* (1986), a much-debated book, which finds many of the roots of fascist thought in the ideas and ideology of the left; the same author's inquiry into the origins of Italian fascism will be cited later. A precursor of fascism is studied in C. S. Doty, *From Cultural Rebellion to Counterrevolution: The Politics of Maurice Barrès* (1976), and in R. Soucy, *Fascism in France: The Case of Maurice Barrès* (1972).

Problems and Readings*

Pamphlets relating to this chapter include R. L. Williams (ed.), *The Commune of Paris, 1871* (1969); S. Edwards (ed.) *The Dreyfus Affair: Tragedy of Errors?* (1964) and *The Third French Republic, 1870–1940* (Anvil series, 1966, 1982); H. R. Kedward (ed.), *The Dreyfus Affair: Catalyst for Tensions in French Society* (1965); E. C. Helmreich (ed.), *A Free Church in a Free State: The Catholic Church, Italy, Germany, France, 1864–1914* (1964); T. S. Hamerow (ed.), *The Age of Bismarck: Documents and Interpretations* (1974); J. J. Sheehan (ed.), *Imperial Germany* (1976); H. Schultz (ed.), *English Liberalism and the State: Individualism or Collectivism* (1974); E. C. Black (ed.), *Victorian Culture and Society* (1974); and P. Stansky (ed.), *The Victorian Revolu-*

tion: *Government and Society in Victoria's Britain* (1973). Also useful are R. S. Levy (ed.), *Anti-Semitism in Modern Times: An Anthology of Texts** (1991); and two works cited in Chapter XI: M. L. McDougall (ed.), *The Working Class in Modern Europe* (1975), and A. and L. Lees (eds.), *The Urbanization of European Society in the Nineteenth Century* (1975). Materials on science and intellectual developments are available in H. Vanderpool (ed.), *Darwin and Darwinism* (1974), and in L. P. Williams (ed.), *Relativity Theory: Its Origins and Impact on Modern Thought* (1968).

XV. Europe's World Supremacy

Many of the general accounts for the years 1871–1914 cited in the previous chapter will also be helpful here. Other informative introductions, some moving on into the twentieth century, include H. Gollwitzer, *Europe in the Age of Imperialism, 1848–1917* (1974); W. D. Smith, *European Imperialism in the Nineteenth and Twentieth Centuries** (1982); V. G. Kiernan, *From Conquest to Collapse: European Empires from 1815 to 1960* (1982); and J. N. Pieterse, *Empire and Emancipation* (1989). For diplomatic matters W. L. Langer, *The Diplomacy of Imperialism, 1890–1902** (2 vols., 1935; rev. 1965), remains valuable; it may be supplemented by R. Shannon, *The Crisis of Imperialism, 1865–1915* (1974). The role played by Western technology in European expansion is examined in D. R. Headrick, *The Tools of Empire** (1981) and *The Tentacles of Progress** (1988).

Imperialism in General

Continuing debate about the motives of imperialism has in part been stimulated by the seminal study of R. Robinson and J. Gallagher, *Africa and the Victorians: The Official Mind of Imperialism** (1961, 1981). They see no sharp break with the past in the 1870s, stress the importance of economic penetration over annexation, and argue that the European powers were drawn into formal empires in Africa by internal power vacuums. Imperialism, they argue, cannot be understood without a study of the indigenous societies involved. An excellent introduction to the debate is W. R. Louis (ed.), *Imperialism: The Robinson-Gallagher Controversy** (1976). Two books by D. Fieldhouse, *Economics and Empire, 1830–1914*

(1973) and *Colonialism, 1870–1945* (1981), also give a high priority to national prestige and security. On the other hand, P. J. Cain and A. G. Hopkins, *British Imperialism: Innovation and Expansion, 1688–1914** (1993), in an important study argue that "gentlemanly capitalism," i.e., the commercial and financial interests of London's City lay behind the expansion; and a sequel volume maintains that the same interests found a new economic role for themselves after the decline of the empire. Motives and justifications for imperialism are also analyzed in R. Koebner and H. D. Schmidt, *Imperialism: The Story and Significance of a Political Word, 1840–1960* (1964); A. P. Thornton, *Doctrines of Imperialism* (1965); G. Lichtheim, *Imperialism* (1970); C. Reynolds, *Modes of Imperialism* (1981); T. Smith, *The Pattern of Imperialism* (1982); and W. J. Mommsen, *Theories of Imperialism* (trans. 1980).

Provocative discussions of the confrontation between Europeans and non-Europeans include R. Maunier, *The Sociology of Colonies: An Introduction to the Study of Race Contact* (2 vols., 1949); D. Mannoni, *Prospero and Caliban: The Psychology of Colonization** (1956), stressing the psychological impact on both rulers and governed; T. Geiger, *The Conflicted Relationship: The West and the Transformation of Asia, Africa, and Latin America* (1967); G. W. Goug, *The Standards of "Civilization" in International Society* (1984); and V. G. Kiernan, *The Lords of Human Kind: Black Man, Yellow Man, and White Man in the Age of Empire** (1987).

British and European Imperialism

B. Porter, *The Lion's Share: A Short History of British Imperialism, 1850–1983** (rev. 1984), is a lively and informative account; recommended also is R. Hyam, *Britain's Imperial Century, 1815–1914* (1976). The best synthesis for the earlier years is C. A. Bayly, *The Imperial Meridian: The British Empire and the World, 1780–1830** (1989). The impact on the British public is studied in J. McKenzie, *Propaganda and Empire: The Manipulation of British Opinion, 1880–1960* (1988) and in a volume edited by the same author, *Imperialism and Popular Culture* (1989). The opponents of imperialism are described in A. P. Thornton, *The Imperial Idea and Its Enemies* (1959), and in B. Porter, *Critics of Empire: British*

Radical Attitudes to Colonialism in Africa, 1895–1914 (1968).

The imperial activities of the other European powers are described in W. O. Henderson, *Studies in German Colonial History* (1963); W. D. Smith, *The German Colonial Empire* (1978); H. Brunschwig, *French Colonialism, 1871–1914* (1960; trans. 1966); R. A. Webster, *Industrial Imperialism in Italy, 1908–1915* (1975), cited earlier; and M. Kuitenbrouwer, *The Netherlands and the Rise of Modern Imperialism* (trans. 1991). On both the theory and practice of imperialism an important comparative study is W. Baumgart, *Imperialism: The Idea and Reality of British and French Colonial Expansion, 1880–1914* (trans. 1982).

The Americas

For all aspects of relationships with Latin America, the contributed chapters in the first five volumes (1988) of L. Bethell (ed.), *The Cambridge History of Latin America* (9 vols. projected) are valuable: Vols. I and II, *Colonial Latin America*; Vol. III, *From Independence to c. 1870*; and Vols. IV–V, *From 1870 to 1930*. D. Bushnell and N. Macaulay, *The Emergence of Latin America in the Nineteenth Century** (rev. 1993), is an outstanding survey; it may be supplemented by E. B. Burns, *The Poverty of Progress: Latin America in the Nineteenth Century** (1980).

D. Dawson, *The Mexican Adventure* (1935), is a careful account of Napoleon III's fiasco during the 1860s, and may be read along with N. N. Baker, *The French Experience in Mexico, 1821–1861* (1979). The nineteenth-century Mexican rebel leader is studied in B. Hamnett, *Juárez** (1993) in the Profiles in Power series. Going beyond the scope of these years, an older study, F. Tannenbaum, *Mexico: The Struggle for Peace and Bread* (1950), provides a thoughtful narrative of Mexican history, but should be supplemented by such books as R. E. Ruiz, *The Great Rebellion: Mexico, 1905–1924** (1980) and *Triumphs and Tragedy: A History of the Mexican People** (1992); A. Knight, *The Mexican Revolution* (2 vols., 1986); and J. M. Hart, *Revolutionary Mexico* (1987). The Indian revolutionary leader Emiliano Zapata is studied in biographies by J. Womack* (1968) and R. Parkinson (1980).

For the imperialist activities of the United States in these years, one may consult J.

W. Pratt, *Expansionists of 1898** (1936) and *America's Colonial Empire** (1954); W. LaFeber, *The New Empire* (1963); F. Merk, *Manifest Destiny and Mission in American History* (1963); and J. Dobson, *America's Ascent: The United States Becomes a Great Power, 1880–1914* (1978). W. A. Williams, *The Tragedy of American Democracy** (rev. 1972), is highly critical of American imperialism, while a thoughtful assessment of American motives is found in E. R. May, *Imperial Democracy* (1961) and *American Imperialism: A Speculative Essay* (1968).

For the Spanish American War one may read W. Millis, *The Martial Spirit** (1931), an older account; F. Freidel, *The Splendid Little War* (1958); and D. F. Trask, *The War with Spain in 1898* (1981). Other episodes of American expansion are recounted in P. Stanley, *A Nation in the Making: The Philippines and the United States* (1974); M. Tate, *The United States and the Hawaiian Kingdom* (1965); D. McCullough, *The Path between the Seas: The Creation of the Panama Canal, 1870–1914* (1977); and W. LaFeber, *The Panama Canal* (rev. 1989). The second volume of the *Cambridge History of American Foreign Relations*, W. LaFeber, *The American Search for Opportunity, 1865–1913* (1993), will also be useful here.

The Ottoman Empire, the Middle East, and the Balkans

An informative synthesis for the years from the founding of Islam to the present is S. N. Fisher and W. Ochsenwald, *The Middle East: A History** (rev. 1990), cited earlier, while nineteenth-century economic developments are examined in R. Owen, *The Middle East and the World Economy, 1800–1914* (1981), and in C. Issawi, *The Economic History of the Middle East, 1800–1914* (1966). For the role of the Ottoman Empire in European diplomacy and for national stirrings in the Empire, the books cited in Chapter XI by M. S. Anderson (1966) and M. E. Yapp* (1988) are instructive. Older but valuable diplomatic studies include R. W. Seton-Watson, *Disraeli, Gladstone, and the Eastern Question* (1935); W. N. Medlicott, *The Congress of Berlin and After* (1938; 1963); E. M. Earle, *Turkey, the Great Powers, and the Bagdad Railway* (1923); and M. K. Chapman, *Great Britain and the Bagdad Railway* (1948).

Other recommended books are J. Haslip,

The Sultan: The Life of Abdul Hamid II (1958), a vivid scholarly account with insight into the Empire; R. H. Davison, *Reform in the Ottoman Empire, 1856–1876* (1963); and D. Kushner, *The Rise of Turkish Nationalism, 1876–1908* (1977). For Egypt, there are available H. Dodwell, *The Founder of Modern Egypt: A Study of Muhammad Ali [Mehemet Ali]* (1931); D. S. Landes, *Bankers and Pashas: International Finance and Economic Imperialism in Egypt** (1958); P. Grau, *Islamic Roots of Capitalism: Egypt, 1760–1840* (1979); and R. L. Tignor, *Modernization and British Colonial Rule in Egypt, 1882–1914* (1966). Carrying the story toward the present is P. J. Valikiotis, *The History of Modern Egypt: From Muhammad Ali to Mubarek* (rev. 1991). The diplomacy surrounding the construction of the Suez Canal may be studied in J. Marlowe, *World Ditch: The Making of the Suez Canal* (1964); J. Pudney, *Suez: De Lesseps' Canal* (1969); and J. P. D. Balfour [Lord Kinross], *Between Two Seas* (1969). The French experience in Lebanon is examined in J. F. Spagnolo, *French and Ottoman Lebanon, 1861–1914* (1977), which may be supplemented by C. M. Andrew and A. S. Kanya-Forstner, *The Climax of French Imperial Expansion, 1914–1924* (1981). The Italian experience in Libya is studied in C. G. Segrè, *Fourth Shore: The Italian Colonization of Libya* (1975).

For the rivalries in the Balkans and the emergent nationalist movements, in addition to books cited in Chapter XI, one may turn to B. H. Sumner, *Russia and the Balkans, 1870–1880* (1974); B. Jelavich, *Russia's Balkan Entanglements, 1806–1914* (1954); and G. J. Bobango, *The Emergence of the Romanian National State* (1979). A good overall survey for Romania is V. Georgescu, *The Romanians: A History* (1992).

Africa

Perhaps the best introduction to African history is R. Oliver, *The African Experience: Major Themes in African History from Earliest Times to the Present* (1992), by a British historian who has done much to stimulate contemporary African studies. Other valuable introductions include J. D. Fage, *A History of Africa** (rev. 1989); B. Davidson, *Africa in History** (rev. 1974); K. Shillington, *History of Africa** (1989), focusing on sub-Saharan Africa; and P. D. Curtin, S. Feierman, L. Thompson, and J. Vansina, *African History** (1978). A. E. Afigbo, E. A. Ayandele, and other African historians in *The Making of Modern Africa* (2 vols., rev. 1986), study the continent over the past two centuries. Two volumes in the *Cambridge History of Africa*, Vol. V (1977) and Vol. VI (1985) cover the years of colonial domination and the African response, while these years are also studied in J. F. A. Ajayi (ed.), *Africa in the Nineteenth Century until the 1880s* (1989), and A. A. Boahen (ed.), *Africa under Colonial Domination, 1880–1935** (1985; abr. ed. 1990), which comprise Vols. VI and VII, respectively, of the eight-volume *UNESCO General History of Africa*. Additional books on Africa will be cited in Chapter XXII.

Vivid accounts on a grand scale are R. Hallett, *Africa to 1875* (1970) and *Africa since 1875* (1974); in these and his other books, the author examines the inner workings of African society as well as the European impact. Insights are also provided in C. Coquéry-Vidrovitch, *Africa: Endurance and Change South of the Sahara* (1989), and in D. Lamb, *The Africans** (1983). The use of "oral tradition" in the reconstruction of African history is explained in J. Vansina, *Oral Tradition: A Study of Historical Methodology* (1963), and demonstrated by the same author in *Kingdoms of the Savanna** (1966).

P. Duignan and L. H. Gann, *Burden of Empire: An Appraisal of Western Colonialism South of the Sahara* (1967), and their other writings emphasize a "benevolent imperialism" and attempt to demonstrate that the benefits of European expansion outweighed the debits. The same writers have coedited a five-volume collaborative history, *Colonialism in Africa, 1870–1960* (1969–1973). In three additional books they focus on colonial administration by the Germans (1977), the British (1978), and the Belgians (1979); and they have coedited *African Proconsuls: European Governors in Africa* (1978). In the same tradition, T. Pakenham has written a detailed narrative, *The Scramble for Africa: The White Man's Conquest of the Dark Continent from 1870–1912** (1992). It may be compared with A. A. Boahen, *African Perspectives on Colonialism** (1989), and F. McLynn, *Hearts of Darkness: The European Exploration of Africa* (1993).

Available also are H. S. Wilson, *The Imperial Experience in Sub-Saharan Africa since 1870* (1977), a well-balanced synthesis;

and for the French experience, W. B. Cohen, *Rulers of Empire: The French Colonial Service in Africa* (1971) and *The French Encounter with Africans: White Response to Blacks, 1530–1880* (1981). On the slave trade and its abolition, in addition to works cited in Chapters III and XI, one may read B. Davidson, *Black Mother: The Years of the African Slave Trade* (1961), and on the Brussels Conference of 1889, S. Miers, *Britain and the Ending of the Slave Trade* (1975).

There are biographical studies of Livingstone by, among others, J. Simmons* (1955), T. Jeal (1973), and O. Ransford (1978), the last a psychologically oriented study. Other leading figures are examined in R. Hall, *Stanley: An Adventurer Explored* (1976), highly informative; R. Oliver, *Sir Harry Johnston and the Scramble for Africa* (1957); G. Elton, *Gordon of Khartoum* (1954); J. Marlowe, *Mission to Khartoum* (1969); and M. F. Perham, *Lugard: The Years of Adventure, 1858–1898* (1936), an impressive older work. For Kitchener, the somewhat adulatory P. Warner, *Kitchener: The Man behind the Legend* (1986), may be compared with the more critical T. Royle, *The Kitchener Enigma* (1986). The good, brief biography of Cecil Rhodes by J. Flint (1976) still merits reading, but R. I. Rotberg, *The Founder: Cecil Rhodes and the Pursuit of Power** (1988), is an outstanding study enriched by psychological insights. For a biography of the African leader who defeated the Italians at Adowa, one may read H. G. Marcus, *The Life and Times of Menelik II: Ethiopia, 1844–1913* (1975).

The best study of the Congo to 1908 is R. Slade, *King Leopold's Congo* (1962), on which one may also read N. Ascherson, *The King Incorporated* (1963), and R. Anstey, *King Leopold's Legacy* (1966); Anstey has also written *Britain and the Congo in the Nineteenth Century* (1962).

For southern Africa and the emergence of the Union of South Africa, L. Thompson, *A History of South Africa* (1990), is a superb synthesis for later decades as well. The South African War of 1899–1902 is recounted in B. Farwell, *The Great Anglo-Boer War* (1976), and T. Pakenham, *The Boer War* (1979). Two interesting biographical accounts relating to these years are B. Williams, *Botha, Smuts, and South Africa* (Teach Yourself History series, 1948), and K. Ingham, *Jan Christian Smuts: The Conscience of a South African* (1986).

Asia

Among informative general surveys of the European impact on Asia are J. Pratt, *The Expansion of Europe in the Far East* (1947); K. M. Pannikar, *Asia and Western Dominance: The Vasco da Gama Epoch of Asian History, 1498–1945** (rev. 1950), cited in Chapter VI; P. H. Clyde and B. F. Beers, *The Far East: A History of Western Impacts and Eastern Responses* (rev. 1991); E. S. Dodge, *Islands and Empires: Western Impact on the Pacific and East Asia* (1976); and R. Murphey, *The Outsiders: The Western Experience in India and China* (1977). Case studies of European expansion in Asia are provided in I. Copeland, *The Burden of Empire: Perspectives on Imperialism and Colonialism** (1991).

For nineteenth-century developments in India, in addition to books described in Chapter VI, one may read W. Golant, *The Long Afternoon: British India, 1601–1947* (1975); M. E. Chamberlain, *Britain and India: The Interactions of the Peoples* (1974), which shows how little influence the British had over forces shaping Indian society; and two volumes in the *New Cambridge History of India*: P. J. Marshall, *Bengal: The British Bridgehead** (1988), and C. A. Bayly, *Indian Society and the Making of the British Empire** (1990). The revolt of 1857 and its consequences are studied in S. Sen, *Eighteen Fifty Seven* (1957); C. Hibbert, *The Great Mutiny: India 1857** (1980); E. Stokes and C. A. Bayly, *The Peasant Armed: The Indian Rebellion of 1857* (1986); and T. R. Metcalf, *The Aftermath of Revolt: India, 1857–1870* (1964).

One of the best introductions to East Asia is J. K. Fairbank, E. O. Reischauer, and A. M. Craig, *East Asia: Tradition and Transformation** (rev. 1989); and for China, J. K. Fairbank, *China: A New History* (1992). Other overviews of Chinese history include C. O. Hucker, *China's Imperial Past* (1975); N. F. Sizer, *China: A Brief History** (1981); and I. C. Y. Hsu, *The Rise of Modern China* (rev. 1989). The first volumes published (1979) of the collaborative *Cambridge History of China* (D. Twitchett and J. K. Fairbank, gen. eds.), cover the late Ch'ing (or Manchu) period, 1800–1911. The decay of the Ming dynasty, the Manchu conquest, and the consolidation of Manchu rule are recounted in F. Wakeman, Jr., *The Great Enterprise: The Manchu Reconstruction of Imperial Order in Seven-*

teenth Century China (2 vols., 1985). J. Spence, *The Search for Modern China* (1990), goes back over four centuries with perceptive insights into China's relations with the West. The same author's *The Gate of Heavenly Peace: The Chinese and Their Revolution, 1895–1980** (1981) links earlier history to twentieth-century revolution, the subject also of J. K. Fairbank, *The Great Chinese Revolution, 1800–1985** (1986), and of R. A. Scalopino and G. T. Yu, *Modern China and Its Revolutionary Process: Recurrent Challenges to the Traditional Order, 1850–1920* (1988).

A massive authoritative study of the mid-nineteenth century Taiping upheaval is Jen Yu-wen, *The Taiping Revolutionary Movement* (1973), but one may also read S. Y. Teng, *The Taiping Rebellion and the Western Powers* (rev. 1977). European relations with China, including the Opium Wars, are studied in J. K. Fairbank, *Trade and Diplomacy on the China Coast: The Opening of the Treaty Ports, 1842–1854** (2 vols., 1953); in Ssu-yu Teng and J. K. Fairbank, *China's Response to the West: A Documentary Survey, 1839–1923** (1954–1963); and in other books on the Opium Wars by J. Beeching (1976), P. W. Fay (1975), and B. Ingles (1976). The anti-foreign upheaval of 1898–1900 is examined in V. Purcell, *The Boxer Uprising* (1963), and J. W. Esherick, *The Origins of the Boxer Uprising** (1987). On the United States role in the Far East and the Open Door policy one may read M. H. Hunt, *Frontier Defense and the Open Door: Manchuria in Chinese American Relations, 1895–1911* (1973); W. Cohen, *America's Response to China* (rev. 1980); and J. C. Thomsen, Jr., P. W. Stanley, and J. C. Perry, *Sentimental Imperialists: The American Experience in East Asia* (1981). For the confrontation between Russia and Japan, one may read I. Nish, *The Origins of the Russo-Japanese War** (1985), while Russian foreign policy in broader scope is studied in B. H. Sumner, *Tsardom and Imperialism in the Far East and the Middle East, 1880–1914* (1942). For the study of the Russian fleet defeated at Tsushima by the Japanese, one may read A. Nobikov-Privoy, *Tsushima* (trans. 1944); F. Theiss, *The Voyage of Forgotten Men* (1947); and R. Hough, *The Fleet That Had to Die* (1958). The diplomatic history of the war is recounted in J. A. White, *The Diplomacy of the Russo-Japanese War* (1964), and an admirable general narrative is D. Walder, *The Short Victorious*

War: The Russo-Japanese Conflict, 1904–1905 (1975).

Problems and Readings*

Relevant titles include H. M. Wright (ed.), *The "New Imperialism": An Analysis of the Late Nineteenth Century Expansion* (rev. 1975); R. Owen and B. Sutcliffe (eds.), *Studies in the Theory of Imperialism* (1972); R. W. Winks (ed.), *British Imperialism: Gold, God, Glory* (1963); W. R. Louis (ed.), *Imperialism: The Robinson-Gallagher Controversy* (1976), cited earlier in this chapter; R. F. Betts (ed.), *The Scramble for Africa: Causes and Dimensions of Empire* (1966); M. E. Chamberlain (ed.), *The Scramble for Africa* (1974); R. I. Rotberg (ed.), *Africa and Its Explorers* (1970); T. C. Caldwell (ed.), *The Anglo-Boer War* (1965); and R. A. Austen (ed.), *Modern Imperialism: Western Overseas Expansion in the Age of Industrialization* (1969). On India, there are M. D. Lewis (ed.), *The British in India* (1962); P. J. Marshall (ed.), *Problems of Empire: Britain and India, 1757–1813* (1968); and A. T. Embree (ed.), *1857 in India: Mutiny or War of Independence?* (1963). A helpful anthology is G. Nadel and P. Curtis (eds.), *Imperialism and Colonialism* (1964). Two studies exemplifying newer approaches to the study of imperialism, both in the AHA Pamphlets series, are M. Adas, *"High" Imperialism and the "New" History* (1994), and M. Strobel, *Gender, Sex, and Empire* (1994).

XVI. The First World War

Accounts of international relations emphasizing the shift from a European to a global balance of power include G. Ross, *The Great Powers and the Decline of the European States System, 1914–1945** (1983); C. J. Bartlett, *The Global Conflict: The International Rivalry of the Great Powers, 1880–1990** (rev. 1994); J. Joll, *Europe since 1870: An International History** (1973); and W. R. Keylor, *The Twentieth-Century World: An International History** (rev. 1992).

Diplomatic Background, Origins, Responsibilities

The most judicious account of the war's complex origins, assessing both the evidence and divergent interpretations, is J. Joll, *The Origins of the First World War**

(rev. 1992). Two attempts to synthesize the protracted debate over war responsibility are J. W. Langdon, *July 1914: The Long Debate: 1918–1990* (1991), and R. J. W. Evans and H. P. Van Strandmann (eds.), *The Coming of the First World War** (1989).

The war-guilt controversy reopened after 1945 when the West German scholar Fritz Fischer, on the basis of new archival materials, reaffirmed German culpability in *Germany's Aims in the First World War** (1961; trans. 1967). Fischer also presents his interpretations in *War of Illusions: Germany's Policies, 1911–1914* (trans. 1975), *World Power or Decline: The Controversy over Germany's Aims in the First World War* (trans. 1974), and *From Kaiserreich to Third Reich** (trans. 1986). His argument that Germany had to grasp for "world power" or face decline, and that elite groups in Germany pressed this objective to thwart democratization, is reinforced by I. Geiss, *German Foreign Policy, 1871–1914* (1976).

Among older works of continuing value are S. B. Fay, *The Origins of the World War** (1928, 1930); B. E. Schmitt, *The Coming of the War, 1914* (2 vols., 1930); and L. Albertini, *The Origins of the War of 1914* (3 vols., 1942–1943; trans. 1952–1957), an exhaustive account. A. J. P. Taylor, *The Struggle for Mastery in Europe, 1848–1918* (1954), cited in Chapter XII, remains invaluable.

On diplomacy in the decades after 1870, there are the older important studies by W. L. Langer: *European Alliances and Alignments, 1871–1890** (1931, 1950), *The Franco-Russian Alliance, 1880–1894* (1929), and *The Diplomacy of Imperialism, 1890–1902* (2 vols., 1935), the last cited in the previous chapter. A masterful diplomatic account with added insights is the two-volume study by the diplomat-historian G. F. Kennan, *The Decline of Bismarck's European Order: Franco-Russian Relations, 1875–1890** (1979) and *The Fateful Alliance: France, Russia, and the Coming of the First World War** (1984). A colorful reconstruction of the era for the general reader, focusing on monarchs, military leaders, and diplomats is R. K. Massie, *Dreadnought: Britain, Germany, and the Coming of the First World War* (1992).

D. E. Lee's careful study, *Europe's Crucial Years: The Diplomatic Background of World War I, 1902–1914* (1974), reaffirms the argument that each state acted out of desperation in defense of its own presumed interests. Successful efforts in a British series to study domestic and foreign considerations together, in keeping with the newer emphases of diplomatic historians, are V. R. Berghahn, *Germany and the Approach of War in 1914* (rev. 1994); Z. S. Steiner, *Britain and the Origins of the First World War* (1977); R. J. B. Bosworth, *Italy, the Least of the Great Powers: Italian Foreign Policy before the First World War* (1980); J. F. V. Krieger, *France and the Origins of the First World War* (1984); D. C. B. Lieven, *Russia and the Origins of the First World War* (1984); and S. R. Williamson, Jr., *Austria-Hungary and the Origins of the First World War** (1991). Three volumes in another British series on foreign policy are also valuable for these years: J. Néré, *The Foreign Policy of France from 1914 to 1945* (trans. 1975); F. R. Bridge, *From Sadowa to Sarajevo: The Foreign Policy of Austria-Hungary, 1866–1914* (1972); and C. J. Lowe and F. Marzari, *Italian Foreign Policy, 1870–1940* (1975).

Among many specialized studies of pre-war diplomacy and strategic planning, a few stand out: J. A. S. Grenville, *Lord Salisbury and Foreign Policy: The Close of the Nineteenth Century, 1899–1914* (1964); G. Monger, *The End of Isolation: British Foreign Policy, 1900–1907* (1963); C. Andrew, *Théophile Delcassé and the Making of the Entente Cordiale: A Reappraisal of French Foreign Policy, 1898–1905* (1968); S. R. Williamson, Jr., *The Politics of Grand Strategy: Britain and France Prepare for War, 1904–1914* (1969); and M. B. Hayne, *The French Foreign Office and the Origins of the First World War* (1993). In addition one should read P. Kennedy, *The Rise of the Anglo-German Antagonism, 1860–1914** (1980), *Strategy and Diplomacy, 1870–1945** (1984), and a collaborative volume he has edited, *War Plans of the Great Powers, 1880–1914** (1979). The Balkan antecedents of the war are examined in E. C. Helmreich, *The Diplomacy of the Balkan Wars, 1912–1913* (1938, 1969); V. Dedijer, *The Road to Sarajevo* (1966); J. Remak, *Sarajevo: The Story of a Political Murder* (1959); and J. Cameron, *1914* (1959).

The involvement of the United States in the war is studied in E. F. May, *The World War and American Isolation, 1914–1917** (1959), an outstanding study; R. Gregory, *The Origins of American Intervention in the First World War* (1971); P. Devlin, *Too Proud to Fight: Woodrow Wilson's Neutral-*

ity (1974); J. J. Sanford, *Wilsonian Maritime Diplomacy* (1978); and R. H. Ferrell, *Woodrow Wilson and World War I* (1985). On a special subject, there is B. W. Tuchman, *The Zimmermann Telegram** (1985), while T. A. Bailey and P. B. Ryan, *The Lusitania Disaster* (1975), makes a case for the German legal position.

The War

For the war there are informative narrative accounts by B. H. Liddell Hart* (1934), C. R. M. Cruttwell* (1934, 1990), C. B. Falls* (1959), and H. Baldwin* (1962). Two illustrated histories are the *American Heritage History of World War I* (1964), with the narrative by S. L. A. Marshall; and A. J. P. Taylor, *An Illustrated History of the First World War** (1964). More recent accounts examining both military and social aspects and the social impact of the war include M. Ferro, *The Great War, 1914–1918** (trans. 1973); K. Robbins, *The First World War** (1984); B. E. Schmitt and H. C. Vedeler, *The World in the Crucible, 1914–1919** (1984), in the Langer series; and J. M. Winter, *The Experience of World War I* (1989). On the opening phase of the war, B. W. Tuchman, *The Guns of August* (1962), is a vivid account. G. Ritter, *The Schlieffen Plan* (trans. 1958), is a valuable analysis, but L. L. Farrar, *The Short-War Illusion** (1973), also should be consulted. A small sampling of literature on various episodes of the war would include R. Rhodes James, *Gallipoli* (1965); A. Horne, *The Price of Glory: Verdun, 1916** (1963); R. M. Watt, *Dare Call It Treason* (1963), on the French army mutinies of 1917; and J. Terraine, *To Win a War: 1918, The Year of Victory* (1981). The war in eastern Europe is graphically described in N. Stone, *The Eastern Front, 1914–1917* (1976), and the naval war in R. Hough, *The Great War at Sea, 1914–1918** (1984). Strategy and decision making are studied in F. Maurice, *Lessons of Allied Cooperation: Naval, Military and Air, 1914–1918* (1942); M. Hankey, *The Supreme Command, 1914–1918* (2 vols., 1961); and C. Barnett, *The Swordbearers: The Supreme Command in the First World War* (1963).

Books that seek to convey the ordeal of trench warfare on the Western Front include E. J. Leed, *No Man's Land: Combat and Identity in World War I* (1979); T. Ashworth, *Trench Warfare, 1914–1918: The Live and Let-Live System* (1980); and J. Ellis, *Eye-Deep in Hell: Trench Warfare in World War I** (1989). Ellis has also written *The Social History of the Machine Gun** (1986). J. Keegan, *The Face of Battle* (1976), in one memorable chapter evokes the horrors of the Somme. For the American military experience one may read E. M. Coffman, *The War to End All Wars* (1969). A special subject is examined in L. F. Haber, *The Poisonous Cloud: Chemical Warfare in the First World War* (1980), and E. M. Spiers, *Chemical Warfare* (1986).

P. Fussell, *The Great War and Modern Memory** (1975), a moving account of how the miseries of the war became part of contemporary literature and culture, may be read along with S. Hynes, *A War Imagined: The First World War and English Culture* (1992). Two other studies of the intellectual impact of the war are R. N. Stromberg, *Redemption by War: The Intellectuals and 1914* (1982), and M. Ecksteins, *The Rites of Spring: The Great War and the Birth of the Modern Age* (1989), an ambitious inquiry into the shaping of a new cultural consciousness.

The Home Front: Social and Economic Impact of the War

For the impact of war and of preparations for war on European society from the late nineteenth century on, one should read B. Bond, *War and Society in Europe, 1870–1970** (1986). The significance of war for social change is also examined in A. Marwick, *War and Social Change in the Twentieth Century* (1975), a comparative examination of five countries. G. Hardach, *The First World War, 1914–1918* (History of the World Economy in the Twentieth Century series, 1977), focuses on the economic aspects of the war and its consequences. There are many informative studies in the older multivolume Carnegie Endowment *Economic and Social History of the World War* (J. T. Shotwell, gen. ed., 1924–1940), of which over 100 volumes were published.

For the war on the home front one may turn to F. Chambers, *The War behind the War, 1914–1918* (1939), an older but still valuable account; J. Williams, *The Other Battleground: The Home Fronts—Britain, France and Germany, 1914–1918* (1972); and the essays in R. Wall and J. Winter (eds.), *The Upheaval of War: Family, Work, and Welfare in Europe, 1914–1918* (1989). For Britain, one may read J. M. Winter,

The Great War and the British People (1986), an outstanding volume; A. Marwick, *The Deluge: British Society and the First World War* (1965); T. Wilson, *The Myriad Faces of War: Britain and the Great War, 1914–1918* (1986); B. Waites, *A Class Society at War: England, 1914–1918* (1988); and J. Bourne, *Britain and the Great War, 1914–1918** (1989). The domestic front in other countries is studied in J. Kocka, *Facing Total War: German Society, 1914–1918* (trans. 1984); J.-J. Becker, *The Great War and the French People** (trans. 1986); P. J. Flood, *France, 1914–1918: Public Opinion and the War Effort* (1989); and D. M. Kennedy, *Over Here: The First World War and American Society* (1980).

The contributions of women to the war effort are examined in A. Marwick, *Women at War, 1914–1918* (1977); G. Braybon, *Women Workers in the First World War: The British Experience** (1981); and M. W. Greenwald, *Women, War, and Work: The Impact of World War I on Women Workers in the United States* (1980).

Political developments affecting the conduct of the war are examined in E. L. Woodward, *Great Britain and the War of 1914–1918* (1967); P. Guinn, *British Strategy and Policies, 1914–1918* (1965); J. Turner, *British Politics and the Great War: Coalition and Conflict, 1915–1918* (1992); J. C. King, *Generals and Politicians: Conflict between France's High Command, Parliament, and Government, 1914–1918* (1951); G. D. Feldman, *Army, Industry, and Labor in Germany, 1914–1918* (1986); and R. B. Armeson, *Total Warfare and Compulsory Labor* (1964), also on Germany. The final volume of G. Ritter, *The Sword and the Scepter: The Problem of Militarism in Germany*, Vol. IV, *The Reign of German Militarism and the Disaster of 1918* (trans. 1973), describes the misuse of the power that the German generals preempted. The dictatorship of the military leaders is examined with telling detail in M. Kitchen, *The Silent Dictatorship: The Politics of the German High Command under Hindenburg and Ludendorff, 1916–1918* (1976).

The growth of socialist and radical movements opposing the war may be studied in M. Fainsod, *International Socialism and the World War* (1935), and in F. L. Carsten, *War against War: British and German Radical Movements in the First World War* (1982); and the precursors to these movements in S. E. Cooper, *Patriotic Pacifism:*

Waging War on War in Europe, 1815–1914 (1991).

On the human costs of the war, one may consult T. J. Mitchell and G. M. Smith, *Medical Services: Casualties and Medical Statistics of the Great War* (1931); and for the devastating worldwide influenza epidemic that doubled the combat toll, A. W. Crosby, *America's Forgotten Pandemic: The Influenza of 1918** (1976, 1990).

One of the lesser-known tragedies of the war, the forced deportation of the Armenians by the Turkish authorities, and the ensuing mass deaths, is recounted in C. J. Walker, *Armenia: The Survival of a Nation* (rev. 1990); D. M. Lang, *The Armenians: A People in Exile** (1989); and R. Melson, *Revolution and Genocide: On the Origins of the Armenian Genocide and the Holocaust* (1993), which sees the episode as the first chapter in twentieth-century ethnic destruction.

Wartime Diplomacy

For wartime diplomacy one will profit from D. Stevenson, *The First World War and International Politics** (1988), and Z. A. B. Zeman, *The Gentlemen Negotiators: A Diplomatic History of the First World War* (1971). Stevenson also examines the evolution of Allied war objectives in, *French War Aims against Germany* (1982), as does V. H. Rothwell, *British War Aims and Peace Diplomacy, 1914–1918* (1971). Two provocative studies focusing on the diplomatic duel between the United States and Russia are V. S. Mamatey, *The United States and East Central Europe, 1914–1918* (1957), and A. J. Mayer, *Wilson vs. Lenin: The Political Origins of the New Diplomacy** (1959). The fate of the German colonial empire is explored in W. R. Louis, *Great Britain and Germany's Lost Colonies, 1914–1919* (1967).

For Allied activities in the Middle East, and on the revolt of the Arabs against the Turks, one may begin with T. E. Lawrence, *Seven Pillars of Wisdom** (1926, 1935), fascinating but to be read with caution, and J. Wilson, *Lawrence of Arabia: The Authorized Biography of T. E. Lawrence* (1990), now the fullest biography. Focusing on the Middle East and the end of the Ottoman Empire are C. E. Dawn, *From Ottomanism to Arabism* (1973); H. M. Sachar, *The Emergence of the Middle East, 1914–1924* (1969); E. Monroe, *Britain's Moment in the Middle East 1914–1971* (rev. 1981); P. C. Helmreich,

From Paris to Sèvres: The Partition of the Ottoman Empire at the Peace Conference of 1919–1920 (1974); and D. Franklin, *A Peace to End All Peace: Creating the Modern Middle East, 1914–1922* (1989), especially informative.

The emergence of the British mandate for Palestine is studied in impressive detail in L. Stein, *The Balfour Declaration* (1961); in I. Friedman's two books, *The Question of Palestine, 1914–1918: British, Jewish, Arab Relations* (1973) and *Germany, Turkey, and Zionism, 1897–1918* (1977); and in R. Sanders, *The High Walls of Jerusalem: A History of the Balfour Declaration and the Birth of the British Mandate* (1984).

The Peace

For the armistice, one may turn to F. Maurice, *The Armistice of 1918* (1943); H. R. Rudin, *Armistice, 1918* (1944); and S. Weintraub, *A Stillness Heard Round the World: The End of the Great War, November 1918** (1987), a colorful evocation of the war's end. The revolutionary mood of the early postwar era is described in G. Schulz, *Revolution and Peace Treaties, 1917–1920* (trans. 1972); F. L. Carsten, *Revolution in Central Europe, 1918–1919* (1972); and in the essays in C. L. Bertrand (ed.), *Revolutionary Situations in Europe, 1917–1922* (1977). The end of the Habsburg empire is studied in A. J. May, *The Passing of the Hapsburg Monarchy, 1914–1918* (2 vols., 1966), and Z. A. B. Zeman, *The Breakup of the Habsburg Empire, 1914–1918* (1961). The British policy toward the independence movements in central and eastern Europe is explored in K. J. Calder, *Britain and the Origins of the New Europe, 1914–1918* (1976).

On the Paris peace conference, the best introduction is now A. Sharp, *The Versailles Settlement: Peacemaking in Paris** (1991). Valuable older accounts include P. Birdsall, *Versailles Twenty Years After* (1941), sympathetic to Wilson; H. Nicholson, *Peacemaking, 1919* (1933, 1939); and G. B. Noble, *Policies and Opinions at Paris, 1919* (1935). The decision-making process itself is studied in H. Elcock, *Portrait of a Decision: The Council of Four and the Treaty of Versailles* (1972). The debates are available in P. Mantoux (ed.), *The Paris Peace Conference, 1919: Proceedings of the Council of Four* (1955; trans. 1964).

British policy is explored with insight in M. L. Dockrill and J. E. Goold, *Peace without Promise: Britain and the Peace Conferences, 1919–1923* (1981). On Wilson's role, the best study is A. Walworth, *Wilson and His Peacemakers: American Diplomacy at the Paris Peace Conference, 1919* (1987). One should also read K. A. Clements, *The Presidency of Woodrow Wilson** (1992), a concise appraisal; A. Heckscher, *Woodrow Wilson* (1992), a detailed full-length biography but somewhat adulatory; and two studies by Wilson's major biographer, A. S. Link: *Wilson the Diplomatist* (1957) and *Woodrow Wilson: War, Revolution, and Peace* (1979). Link's edition of *The Papers of Woodrow Wilson* (1966–1993), now complete in 69 volumes, is a monumental work of American scholarship. Biographies of Clemenceau by D. R. Watson, and of David Lloyd George by Grigg and others have been cited in Chapter XIV. For Orlando and the Italian role one may read R. Albrecht-Carrié, *Italy at the Paris Peace Conference* (1938), older but still helpful.

A brilliant although not entirely convincing study arguing that the major preoccupation underlying decisions at Versailles was the threat of Bolshevism and domestic radicalism is A. J. Mayer, *Politics and Diplomacy of Peacemaking: Containment and Counter-Revolution at Versailles, 1918–1919* (1967); it may be compared with J. M. Thompson, *Russia, Bolshevism, and the Versailles Peace* (1966), which views the revolutionary threat as important but not dominating.

In addition to S. Bonsal, *Suitors and Suppliants: The Little Nations at Versailles* (1946), there are also monographs on many of the smaller countries: F. Deák on Hungary (1942), D. Perman on Czechoslovakia (1962), D. Spector on Romania (1962), T. Komarnicki on Poland (1957), I. J. Lederer on Yugoslavia (1963), and S. Marks on Belgium (1981). The Polish question is carefully examined by a Danish historian, K. Lundrgreen-Nielsen, *The Polish Problem at the Paris Peace Conference* (trans. 1979). J. C. King explores a special subject in *Foch versus Clemenceau: France and German Dismemberment, 1918–1919* (1960), which may be supplemented by W. A. McDougall, *France's Rhineland Diplomacy, 1914–1924* (1978), a study valuable also for postwar developments. On the hotly disputed issue of reparations, J. M. Keynes, *The Economic Consequences of the Peace* (1920), became the single most influential book, vehemently critical of the entire peace settlement. E.

Mantoux, *The Carthaginian Peace—or the Economic Consequences of Mr. Keynes* (1946), is a vigorous reply to Keynes written many years later. The first volume of what promises to be an outstanding study, R. Skidelsky, *John Maynard Keynes: A Biography*: Vol. I, *Hopes Betrayed, 1883–1920** (1986), carries Keynes through the peace conference. Other books on Keynes will be described in Chapter XIX.

The creation of the League of Nations is explored in H. R. Winkler, *The League of Nations Movement in Great Britain, 1914–1919* (1952), and in G. W. Egerton, *Great Britain and the Creation of the League of Nations* (1978). A useful reference work for this and subsequent chapters is J. A. S. Grenville (ed.), *The Major International Treaties, 1914–1945: A History and Guide with Texts* (1988), and its sequel volume for the years after 1945, edited by J. A. S. Grenville and B. Wasserstein (1988).

Problems and Readings*

Conflicting interpretations of the war's origins are presented in D. E. Lee (ed.), *The Outbreak of the First World War* (rev. 1976); J. Remak (ed.), *The First World War: Causes, Conduct, Consequences* (1971); H. W. Koch (ed.), *The Origins of the First World War: Great Power Rivalry and German War Aims* (rev. 1984); I. Geiss (ed.), *July 1914* (1969); and H. H. Herwig (ed.), *The Outbreak of World War I* (1990). For the peace settlement there are I. J. Lederer (ed.), *The Versailles Settlement: Was It Foredoomed to Failure?* (1960); T. P. Greene (ed.), *Wilson at Versailles* (1957); and R. A. Stone (ed.), *Wilson and the League of Nations: Why America's Rejection* (1967, 1978). The impact of the war is assessed in R. Albrecht-Carrié (ed.), *The Meaning of the First World War* (1965), and J. J. Roth (ed.), *World War I: A Turning Point in Modern History* (1967). Useful for one category of published sources on diplomacy is F. M. Messick (ed.), *Primary Sources in European Diplomacy: A Bibliography of Published Memoirs and Diaries* (1987).

For twentieth-century history in general, two anthologies of interpretive readings on controversial topics are G. Wright and A. Mejia, Jr., *An Age of Controversy* (rev. 1973), and L. Derfler, *An Age of Conflict** (1990).

XVII. The Russian Revolution and the Soviet Union

Russia before 1917: Late Tsarist Russia

A number of books on nineteenth-century Russia have been cited in Chapters XI and XIII. For late tsarist Russia specifically, one should read L. Kochan, *Russia in Revolution, 1890–1918* (1966), and H. Rogger, *Russia in the Age of Modernization and Revolution, 1881–1917** (1983). Economic change and modernization are also discussed in T. H. Von Laue, *Sergei Witte and the Industrialization of Russia** (1963).

Political thought and ferment may be studied in F. Venturi, *Roots of Revolution** (trans. 1983), cited earlier; A. P. Mendel, *Dilemmas of Progress in Tsarist Russia* (1961); A. Vucinich, *Social Thought in Tsarist Russia* (1976); and P. Pomper, *The Revolutionary Intelligentsia** (rev. 1993). The world of labor is examined in V. E. Bonnell, *Roots of Rebellion: Workers' Politics and Organizations in St. Petersburg and Moscow, 1900–1914* (1983), and in the volume she has edited of workers' autobiographical accounts, *The Russian Worker: Life and Labor under the Tsarist Regime** (1983).

Political leaders who served the tsar are studied in R. F. Byrnes, *Pobedonostsev: His Life and Thought* (1968), an exemplar of tsarist obscurantism; and R. Pipes, *Struve* (2 vols., 1970–1980), informative on the fate of liberalism. Right-wing extremism linked to anti-Semitic pogroms is explored in W. Laqueur, *Black Hundred: The Rise of the Extreme Right in Russia* (1993). For the emergent revolutionary leaders, in addition to biographies cited later, one may read D. W. Treadgold, *Lenin and His Rivals: The Struggle for Russia's Future, 1898–1906* (1950); L. Haimson, *The Russian Marxists and the Origins of Bolshevism* (1955), an outstanding study; I. Getzler, *Martov* (1967); S. H. Baron, *Plekhanov: The Father of Russian Marxism** (1963); and A. Ascher, *Pavel Axelrod and the Development of Menshevism* (1972). On the anarchists, there is P. Avrich, *The Russian Anarchists* (1967); and on a leading exemplar, G. Woodcock and I. Avukamovic, *The Anarchist Prince* (1950); M. A. Miller, *Kropotkin* (1976); and C. Cahm, *Peter Kropotkin and the Rise of Revolutionary Anarchism* (1989).

The events of 1905 are narrated and analyzed in a valuable two-volume account by A. Ascher: *The Revolution of 1905:* Vol. I, *Russia in Disarray* (1988), and

Vol. II, *Authority Restored* (1992), carrying the story to 1907. Also informative are W. Sablinsky, *The Road to Bloody Sunday: Father Gapon and the St. Petersburg Massacre of 1905* (1976), and A. M. Verner, *The Crisis of Russian Autocracy: Nicholas II and the 1905 Revolution* (1990).

Explorations of the ill-fated effort to establish a constitutional monarchy after the 1905 upheaval include A. E. Healy, *The Russian Autocracy in Crisis, 1905–1907* (1976); A. Levin's two studies: *The Second Duma* (1940, 1966) and its sequel, *The Third Duma: Election and Profile* (1973); and G. Hosking, *The Russian Constitutional Experiment: Government and Duma, 1906–1914* (1973). The prewar years and the wartime experience are vividly described in W. B. Lincoln, *In War's Dark Shadow** (1983) and *Passage through Armageddon** (1986). The confusion at the court graphically emerges from R. K. Massie's popular account, *Nicholas and Alexandra** (1967, 1985). For the last Romanoff one may also read M. Ferro, *Nicholas II: The Last of the Tsars* (1993), while E. Radzinsky, *The Last Tsar: The Life and Death of Nicholas II* (trans. 1992), dramatically reconstructs the execution of the royal family in 1918.

The Revolutions of 1917

The best account of the February revolution is T. Hasegawa, *The February Revolution: Petrograd, 1917* (1981); other informative studies are G. Katkov, *Russia 1917: The February Revolution* (1967); M. Ferro, *The Russian Revolution of February 1917* (1971); and E. N. Burdzhalov, *Russia's Second Revolution: The February 1917 Uprising in Petrograd** (1987). The ill-fated Kerensky is studied in R. Abraham, *Alexander Kerensky: The First Love of the Revolution (1987).*

For the Bolshevik revolution one may turn to J. M. Thompson, *Revolutionary Russia, 1917** (1981); R. V. Daniels, *Red October: The Bolshevik Revolution of 1917** (rev. 1984); R. Medvedev, *The October Revolution** (trans. 1985); and the fullest and most comprehensive account, R. Pipes, *The Russian Revolution* (1990). There are valuable essays in E. R. and J. Frankel and B. Knei-Paz (eds.), *Revolution in Russia: Reassessments of 1917** (1992). Focusing on the social breadth and depth of the revolution are two books by M. Ferro: *The Fall of Tsarism and the Origins of Bolshevik Power* (trans. 1967) and *October 1917: A*

Social History of the Russian Revolution (trans. 1980). Other informative studies on the social dimensions of the upheaval include J. L. H. Keep, *The Russian Revolution: A Study in Mass Mobilization* (1977); A. Rabinowitch, *Prelude to Revolution: The Petrograd Bolsheviks and the July 1917 Uprising** (1968, 1991); D. Koenker, *Moscow Workers and the 1917 Revolution* (1981); and T. McDaniel, *Autocracy, Capitalism, and Revolution in Russia** (1988). The dissolution of the army and much else is covered in A. K. Wildman, *The End of the Russian Imperial Army* (2 vols., 1980–1987); and the peasants' role is studied in G. J. Gill, *Peasants and Government in the Russian Revolution* (1979).

The best introductions to the civil war, the formation of the Soviet state, and foreign intervention are E. Mawdsley, *The Russian Civil War** (1987), and W. B. Lincoln, *Red Victory: A History of the Russian Civil War* (1990). The reconquest of the Ukraine and of other parts of the tsarist empire that for a time became independent is described in R. Pipes, *The Formation of the Soviet Union: Communism and Nationalism, 1917–1923** (rev. 1964). For the withdrawal from the war and the subsequent Allied intervention there are available G. F. Kennan's admirable *Soviet-American Relations, 1917–1920** (2 vols., 1956–1958), and R. H. Ullman, *Anglo-Soviet Relations, 1917–1921* (3 vols., 1961–1972), a masterful account of the British role in the intervention. The best study of the peace imposed by Germany is J. W. Wheeler-Bennett, *The Forgotten Peace: Brest-Litovsk, March 1918* (1939), and the stormy relations of the Soviets with newly independent Poland are described in P. S. Wandycz, *Soviet-Polish Relations, 1917–1921* (1969). An authoritative reference guide for all these events is H. Shukman (ed.), *The Blackwell Encyclopedia of the Russian Revolution* (1988).

The U.S.S.R.

For the early years one should read R. Pipes, *Russia under the Bolshevik Regime* (1994), which carries the author's history through Lenin's death; L. Schapiro, *The Origins of the Communist Autocracy: Political Opposition in the Soviet State, 1917–1922* (1955), especially insightful; W. G. Rosenberg, *Liberals in the Russian Revolution: The Constitutional Democratic Party, 1917–1921* (1974); and P. Avrich, *Kronstadt,*

1921* (1970, 1991), on the leftist uprising and its suppression by Lenin and Bolsheviks. An institution that was destined to endure is studied in L. D. Gerson, *The Secret Police in Lenin's Russia* (1976), and G. Leggett, *The Cheka: Lenin's Political Police** (1981).

For the years under Lenin and the early years of Stalin's rule one may consult E. H. Carr's massive *A History of Soviet Russia* (14 vols., 1950–1979), with a one-volume synthesis, *The Russian Revolution from Lenin to Stalin* (1979), in which Carr seeks to make the best possible case for the reconstruction of Soviet society in the years 1917 to 1929. Focusing on sociological and cultural change in this period are S. Fitzpatrick, *The Russian Revolution, 1917–1932** (1982), and R. Stites, *Revolutionary Dreams: Utopian Vision and Experimental Life in the Russian Revolution** (1988), while G. Hosking, *The First Socialist Society: A History of the Soviet Union from Within** (rev. 1993), carries a comprehensive social history through to the end of the Soviet experiment. For all aspects of economic developments from 1917 on, one must turn to A. Nove, *An Economic History of the U.S.S.R.** (rev. 1989); for Lenin's New Economic Policy, one may also read A. M. Ball, *Russia's Last Capitalists: The Nepmen, 1921–1929** (1988). Soviet society and the economy before Stalin's tightened grip on the country are described in M. Reiman, *The Birth of Stalinism: The U.S.S.R. on the Eve of the "Second Revolution"* (trans. 1987).

Russian agriculture is examined in perspective in L. Volin, *A Century of Russian Agriculture: From Alexander II to Khrushchev* (1970), and collectivization as a prelude to the First Five-Year Plan is studied in great detail in R. W. Davies, *The Industrialization of Soviet Russia* (3 vols., 1980–1989). Especially insightful is M. Lewin, *Russian Peasants and Soviet Power* (trans. 1975), while R. Conquest, *The Harvest of Sorrow: Soviet Collectivization and the Terror-Famine** (1987), graphically reconstructs the ruthlessness of collectivization and the accompanying famine of 1932, encouraged by Stalin, the author insists, to curb nationalist unrest in the Ukraine and elsewhere. Conquest, one of the earliest critics of the Stalinist terror, has also written *Stalin: Breaker of Nations** (1992).

For the political terror in the Stalin era the most revealing studies are R. Medvedev, *Let History Judge: The Origins and Conse-* *quences of Stalinism* (1971; expanded and trans. 1989), by a Soviet dissident historian; and for the party purges and terror of 1936–1938, stressing the enormity of the blood bath, now officially conceded, R. Conquest, *The Great Terror: A Reassessment** (1968; rev. 1990). Some of the corroborative new evidence surfacing in the years after 1985 is discussed in W. Laqueur, *Stalin: The Glasnost Revelations* (1990). The origins of the party purges are examined in R. Conquest, *Stalin and the Kirov Murder** (1989), and in J. A. Getty, *Origins of the Great Purges: The Soviet Communist Party Reconsidered, 1933–1938** (1986). Three older studies may also be consulted: L. Schapiro, *The Communist Party of the Soviet Union** (1960); J. A. Armstrong, *The Politics of Totalitarianism: The Communist Party of the Soviet Union* (1961); and Z. B. Brzezinski, *The Permanent Purge: Politics in Soviet Totalitarianism* (1956). An insightful general account of the years from the Revolution to Stalin's death is H. Carrère d'Encausse, *A History of the Soviet Union, 1917–1953** (2 vols.; trans. 1982).

Biographical Accounts

Among biographical accounts that further illuminate these years there are B. D. Wolfe, *Three Who Made a Revolution: A Biographical History* [Lenin, Trotsky, Stalin] (1948, 1964); H. Shukman, *Lenin and the Russian Revolution** (1987); A. B. Ulam, *The Bolsheviks: The Intellectual and Political History of the Triumph of Communism in Russia** (1965), reissued as *Lenin and the Bolsheviks** (1969). There are also lives of Lenin by D. Shub* (1948, 1966), L. F. Fischer* (1964), M. C. Morgan (1971), R. Conquest (1972), and R. H. W. Theen (1973). Lenin's wife and her fate in the Stalin years are ably studied in R. H. McNeal, *Bride of the Revolution: Krupskaya and Lenin* (1972). The Bolshevek leader's last years are recounted in M. Lewin, *Lenin's Last Struggle** (1978).

I. Deutscher's overly sympathetic three-volume life of Trotsky (1954–1963), and R. Segal, *Leon Trotsky* (1979), also sympathetic, may be compared with the more balanced appraisals by R. S. Wistrich, *Trotsky: Fate of a Revolutionary* (1979), and I. Howe, *Leon Trotsky* (1979).

An outstanding study of Stalin in the years before the Second World War is R. C. Tucker, *Stalin as Revolutionary, 1879–*

1929* (1973), and *Stalin in Power: The Revolution from Above, 1928–1941** (1990). Another important study, A. B. Ulam, *Stalin: The Man and His Era** (1973), may be compared with the imaginative but uncritical I. Deutscher, *Stalin: A Political Biography** (1949, 1967). One may also read R. H. McNeal, *Stalin: Man and Ruler** (1988), and R. M. Slusser, *Stalin in October: The Man Who Missed the Revolution* (1987), arguing that the dictator compensated in late years for his lesser role in 1917. In a special category is D. Volkogonov, *Stalin: Triumph and Tragedy* (trans. 1992), a detailed biography long in preparation by a Soviet military intelligence officer who from the early 1970s was given unique access to key sources. S. F. Cohen, *Bukharin and the Bolshevik Revolution: A Political Biography, 1888–1938** (1973), is an outstanding study of a leading Old Bolshevik who helped shape Lenin's New Economic Policy and had he prevailed might have averted the Stalinist dictatorship. The career of another Old Bolshevik, a victim also of Stalin's terror, is recounted in W. Lerner, *Karl Radek: The Last Internationalist* (1970). An illuminating study of the opposition within the party is R. V. Daniels, *The Conscience of the Revolution** (1960).

Among thoughtful earlier efforts to assess the Russian experience from the Revolution on into the interwar years and beyond are T. H. Von Laue, *Why Lenin? Why Stalin? A Reappraisal of the Russian Revolution, 1900–1930** (1964); E. Acton, *Rethinking the Russian Revolution** (1990); A. Nove, *Was Stalin Really Necessary?* (1965); S. F. Cohen, *Rethinking the Soviet Experience: Politics and History since 1917** (1985); and two books by M. Lewin: *The Making of the Soviet System: Essays in the Social History of Interwar Russia** (1985) and *The Gorbachev Phenomenon: A Historical Interpretation** (rev. 1991). Books written with the perspective of the regime's collapse in 1991 will be described in later chapters.

Other Themes and Institutions

On other subjects and institutions one may read R. Kolkowitz, *The Soviet Military and the Communist Party* (1967); J. S. Curtiss, *The Russian Church and the Soviet State, 1917–1941* (1953); L. R. Graham, *Science and Philosophy in the Soviet Union* (1972), and other writings; C. V. James, *Soviet Socialist Realism* (1973), on the arts and

literature; and S. P. Ramet (ed.), *Religious Policy in the Soviet Union* (1992). The Jewish question is thoughtfully explored in Z. Gitelman, *The Jews of Russia and the Soviet Union* (1988); S. W. Baron, *The Russian Jew under Tsars and Soviets* (1964); B. Pinkus, *The Jews of the Soviet Union: A History of a National Minority** (1988); and N. Levin, *The Jews in the Soviet Union: Paradox of Survival* (2 vols., 1988).

The role of women in the prerevolutionary and postrevolutionary years may be studied in R. Stites, *The Women's Liberation Movement in Russia: Feminism, Nihilism, and Bolshevism, 1860–1930** (rev. 1991); G. W. Lapidus, *Women in Soviet Society: Equality, Development, and Social Change** (1978); B. E. Clements and others (eds.), *Russia's Women: Accommodation, Resistance, Transformation* (1990); and L. Edmondson (ed.), *Women and Society in Russia and the Soviet Union* (1992).

Soviet Foreign Relations and World Communism

The best introduction to Soviet foreign policy is A. B. Ulam, *Expansion and Coexistence: The History of Soviet Foreign Policy, 1917–1973** (rev. 1974), and other writings by the same author. Still useful are the volumes by L. F. Fischer: *The Soviets in World Affairs, 1917–1929* (rev. 1960) and *Russia's Road from Peace to War: Soviet Foreign Relations, 1917–1941* (1969). A good brief survey is G. F. Kennan, *Soviet Foreign Policy, 1917–1941** (1960, 1979), in the Anvil series, and Stalin's foreign minister is studied in H. D. Phillips, *Between Revolution and the West: A Political Biography of Maxim M. Litvinov* (1992). B. Jelavich, *St. Petersburg and Moscow: Tsarist and Soviet Foreign Policy, 1814–1974** (1974), effectively notes patterns of continuity before and after 1917. Relations with Japan are studied in J. Haslam, *The Soviet Union and the Threat from the East, 1933–1941* (1992).

On the transformation of earlier socialism and Marxism into communism, a number of studies have been described in Chapters XI, XII, and XIV. Recommended also are A. B. Ulam, *The Unfinished Revolution: An Essay on the Sources of Marxism and Communism** (1960); A. G. Meyer's two books, *Leninism* (1957) and *Communism** (1960); and O. A. Narkiewicz, *Marxism and the Reality of Power* (1981). Personal testimonies about the impact of communism may be found in A. Balabanoff, *My Life as a Rebel* (1938), and in R. H. Crossman (ed.), *The God that Failed** (1950), an insightful series of essays on faith and disillusionment. Two biographies of an American participant-observer in Russia in 1917, John Reed, the author of *Ten Days that Shook the World** (1919), are R. Rosenstone, *Romantic Revolutionary** (1975), and E. Hornberger, *John Reed* (1991).

On the Comintern, one may turn to H. Seton-Watson, *From Lenin to Khrushchev: The History of World Communism** (1953, 1960); F. Borkenau, *The Communist International* (1938), as seen by a participant; the same author's *World Communism** (1953); and G. Nollan, *International Communism and World Revolution* (1961). Special studies include J. W. Hulse, *The Forming of the Communist International* (1964); R. Fischer, *Stalin and German Communism* (1948); K. E. McKenzie, *Comintern and World Revolution, 1928–1943* (1964); B. Lazitch and M. M. Drachkovitch, *Lenin and the Comintern* (1972), a detailed account to 1921; and E. H. Carr, *Twilight of the Comintern, 1930–1935* (1982). The impact of Bolshevism on French, Italian, and German socialism is ably explored in A. S. Lindemann, *The "Red Years": European Socialism vs. Bolshevism, 1918–1920* (1974), while R. Wohl examines the French experience with insight and depth in *French Communism in the Making, 1919–1924* (1966).

Problems and Readings*

Available are R. H. McNeal (ed.), *Russia in Transition, 1905–1914: Evolution or Revolution?* (1969); M. McCauley (ed.), *Octobrists to Bolsheviks: Imperial Russia, 1905–1917* (1984); A. E. Adams (ed.), *Imperial Russia after 1861: Peaceful Modernization or Revolution?* (1965); R. G. Suny and A. E. Adams (eds.), *The Russian Revolution and Bolshevik Victory* (rev. 1990); V. D. Medlin (ed.), *The Russian Revolution* (1979); B. M. Unterberger (ed.), *American Intervention in the Russian Civil War* (1969); S. W. Page (ed.), *Lenin: Dedicated Marxist or Pragmatic Revolutionary?* (1969); R. V. Daniels (ed.), *The Stalin Revolution: Foundations of the Totalitarian Era* (1990); and R. C. Tucker and S. F. Cohen (eds.), *The Great Purge Trials* (1965).

XVIII. The Apparent Victory of Democracy

The attempt in the interwar years to put together a shattered polity in Europe is described in R. J. Sontag, *A Broken World, 1919–1939** (1971), a volume in the Langer series, helpful for this and the chapter that follows, while two efforts to examine the pattern of reconstruction in Europe after the war are C. S. Maier, *Recasting Bourgeois Europe: Stabilization in France, Germany and Italy in the Decade after World War I** (1975), stressing the link between interest groups and conservative government, and D. P. Silverman, *Reconstructing Europe after the Great War* (1982).

International Relations in the 1920s

Books placing post-1918 Europe in a global setting have been mentioned in Chapter XVI. A useful reference work for twentieth-century world history is C. Cook and J. Stevenson, *The Longman Handbook of World History since 1918** (1991). Introductions to international affairs in this era focusing on Europe are P. Renouvin, *War and Aftermath, 1914–1929* (1968), and S. Marks, *The Illusion of Peace: International Relations in Europe, 1918–1933** (1976). The high point of reconciliation is ably treated in J. Jacobson, *Locarno Diplomacy: Germany and the West, 1925–1929* (1972). For American foreign policy encompassing the two world wars and the interwar years, A. Iriye, *The Globalizing of America, 1913–1945* (1993), a volume in the *Cambridge History of American Foreign Relations*, is illuminating.

B. Kent, *The Spoils of War: The Politics, Economics, and Diplomacy of Reparations, 1918–1932* (1989), synthesizes the considerable literature on the complex reparations question, on which other studies include M. Trachtenberg, *Reparations in World Politics: France and European Economic Diplomacy, 1916–1923* (1980); S. A. Schuker, *The End of French Predominance in Europe: The Financial Crisis of 1924 and the Adoption of the Dawes Plan* (1976); and M. J. Hogan, *Informal Entente: The Private Structure of Cooperation in Anglo-American Economic Diplomacy, 1918–1928* (1977). The American role in these years in relation to Europe is studied in M. P. Leffler, *The Elusive Quest: America's Pursuit of European Stability and French Security* (1979), and on a broader scale in F. Costigliola, *Awkward Dominion: American Political, Economic, and Cultural Relations with Europe, 1919–1933* (1984). On the British role one may read A. Orde, *British Policy and European Reconstruction after the First World War (1990)*. The response of the United States and Britain to the revolutionary events of the era, and not only to the revolution in Russia, is examined in L. C. Gardner, *Safe for Democracy: The Anglo-American Response to Revolution, 1913–1923** (1984).

The cooperation between the Soviet Union and Weimar Germany is studied in G. Freund, *Unholy Alliance* (1957); K. Rosenbaum, *Community of Fate: German-Soviet Diplomatic Relations, 1922–1928* (1965); and H. L. Dyck, *Weimar Germany and Soviet Russia, 1926–1933* (1966).

For the League of Nations one may read F. P. Walters, *A History of the League of Nations* (2 vols., 1952), and F. S. Northedge, *The League of Nations: Its Life and Times, 1920–1946* (1986), which notes that despite its shortcomings the League helped to transform the older diplomacy. A special problem in which the League played a large role is discussed in a wide-ranging study, M. R. Marrus, *The Unwanted: European Refugees in the Twentieth Century** (1985). Books on efforts at disarmament include J. M. Wheeler-Bennett, *The Pipe Dream of Peace: The Collapse of Disarmament* (1935); R. H. Ferrell, *Peace in Their Time: The Origins of the Kellogg-Briand Pact** (1952); R. Dingman, *Power in the Pacific: The Origins of Naval Arms Limitation, 1914–1922* (1976); and E. W. Bennett, *German Rearmament and the West, 1932–1933* (1979).

Revolt of Asia: East Asia

For China in the early part of the twentieth century, in addition to books cited in Chapter XV, the best introductions are H. Z. Schiffrin, *Sun Yat-sen and the Origins of the 1911 Revolution* (1969); F. Wakeman, *The Fall of Imperial China* (1975); and the essays in M. C. Wright (ed.), *China in Revolution: The First Phase, 1900–1913* (1968). The story of the last Manchu ruler (later appointed by the Japanese to rule in conquered Manchuria) is recounted in B. Power, *The Puppet Emperor: The Life of Pu Yi, Last Emperor of China* (1988).

Biographical studies for Sun include L. Sharman, *Sun Yat-sen and Communism* (1961), and C. M. Wilbur, *Sun Yat-sen: Frustrated Patriot* (1976); his successor is studied in E. P. Young, *The Presidency of Yuan Shih-kai: Liberalism and Dictatorship in Early Republican China* (1978). On the resentments stirred by the Chinese treatment at Versailles, one should read V. Schwarcz, *The Chinese Enlightenment: Intellectuals and the Legacy of the May Fourth Movement of 1919** (1986). The era of Chiang Kai-shek and Kuomintang rule is studied in L. Eastman, *The Abortive Revolution: China under Nationalist Rule, 1927–1937* (1974). Although books on Communist China will be described in Chapter XXI, one should mention here A. Dirlik, *The Origins of Chinese Communism** (1988), and vivid accounts of the Long March of 1934–1935 by D. Wilson (1972), H. Salisbury (1984), and B. Yang (1990).

General books on Japan have been cited in Chapter XIII. On the rise of militarism in Japan one should read J. B. Crowley, *Japan's Quest for Autonomy: National Security and Foreign Policy, 1930–1938* (1966), and two books by A. Iriye: *Pacific Estrangement: Japanese and American Expansion, 1897–1911* (1972) and *After Imperialism: The Search for a New Order in the Far East, 1921–1931* (1965). S. R. Smith, *The Manchurian Crisis, 1931–1932* (1948), recounts the first important break in the League's collective security system. M. and S. Harries, *Soldiers of the Sun: The Rise and Fall of the Japanese Imperial Army* (1992) carries its subject from 1904 to military collapse in 1945.

The Revolt of Asia: The Middle East and South Asia

An introduction to the ferment in Asia is provided in J. and J. E. Romein, *The Asian Century: A History of Modern Nationalism in Asia* (trans. 1962). Two good introductions to developments in the Middle East are P. Mansfield, *The Ottoman Empire and Its Successors** (1973), and A. Hourani, *The Emergence of the Modern Middle East* (1981). For the Turkish Revolution, B. Lewis, *The Emergence of Modern Turkey* (rev. 1969), and S. J. and E. K. Shaw, *History of the Ottoman Empire and Modern Turkey*, Vol. II (1977), a detailed account, are valuable; they may be supplemented by R. D. Robinson, *The First Turkish Republic* (1963); W. F. Weiker, *The Modernization* of Turkey (1981); and F. Ahmad, *The Making of Modern Turkey** (1993). Informative biographical accounts of the Turkish statesman-reformer are J. P. D. Balfour [Lord Kinross], *Atatürk: A Biography of Mustafa Kemal* (1966), V. E. Volkan and N. Itzkowitz, *The Immortal Atatürk: A Psychobiography** (1984); and a biographical study by F. Tachau (1987).

Arab stirrings in the Middle East are discussed in G. Antonius, *The Arab Awakening** (1965); Z. B. Zeine, *Struggle for Arab Independence* (1960); and E. Kedouri, *Islam and the Modern World* (1980). The response of the European powers is described in A. Williams, *Britain and France in the Middle East and North Africa, 1914–1967* (1969), and in other books cited in Chapter XVI.

For the Indian subcontinent, two histories that try to understand developments in Indian terms and not as reactions to the West are P. Spear, *The Oxford History of Modern India* (rev. 1979), and S. Wolpert, *A New History of India** (rev. 1993), cited in Chapter VI. Highly recommended also is S. Sarkar, *Modern India, 1885–1947** (rev. 1989). The origins of Indian nationalism are discussed in A. Seal, *The Emergence of Indian Nationalism* (1968); R. J. Moore, *The Crisis of Indian Unity, 1917–1940* (1974); and A. T. Embree, *India's Search for National Identity** (1972).

There is a large literature on Gandhi. To an older biography by B. R. Nanda (1959) one may add G. Ashe, *Gandhi: A Study in Revolution** (1968); E. H. Erikson, *Gandhi's Truth: On the Origins of Militant Nonviolence** (1969), with interesting psychoanalytical insights; R. N. Iyer, *The Moral and Political Thought of Mahatma Gandhi** (1973), perhaps the best book for grasping the mind of Gandhi; and J. M. Brown's impressive volumes: *Gandhi's Rise to Power in Indian Politics, 1915–1922* (1972), *Gandhi and Civil Disobedience: The Mahatma in Indian Politics, 1928–1934* (1977), and *Gandhi: Prisoner of Hope* (1990). A. Copley, *Gandhi** (1987), is a good brief account. For Nehru there are available S. Gopal, *Jawaharlal Nehru: A Biography** (3 vols., 1976–1984; 1 vol. abr. ed., 1993), informative on the country as well as the man, and biographies by F. Moraes (1957), M. Brecher* (1959), B. R. Nanda (1962), and E. N. Pandy (1976). Nehru's autobiography, *Toward Freedom** (1941), and his other writings are rewarding.

The Depression: Collapse of the World Economy

Books on the impact of the depression on politics and society in various countries will appear in the following chapter.

The economy in the framework of the post-1919 world may be studied in D. N. Aldcroft, *From Versailles to Wall Street: The International Economy in the 1920s** (1977), one of five volumes in the History of the World Economy in the Twentieth Century series; and in G. Ziebura, *World Economy and World Politics* (trans. 1990). For the stock market collapse, J. K. Galbraith, *The Great Crash, 1929* (1955), is unsurpassed, while a comprehensive account of the worldwide depression is C. P. Kindleberger, *The World in Depression, 1929–1939** (rev. 1986), in the series just cited. Informative too is G. Rees, *The Great Slump: Capitalism in Crisis, 1929–1933* (1972). Interesting for different national responses to the crisis is J. A. Garraty, *The Great Depression* (1986), and the same author's *Unemployment in History: Economic Thought and Public Policy* (1978).

Still useful older surveys include H. V. Hodson, *Slump and Recovery, 1929–1937* (1938); H. W. Arndt, *The Economic Lessons of the Nineteen Thirties* (1944), especially insightful; G. Haberler, *Prosperity and Depression* (rev. 1941); and W. A. Lewis, *Economic Survey, 1919–1939* (1948). There are helpful essays in W. Laqueur and G. L. Mosse (eds.), *The Great Depression** (1970), originally a volume of the *Journal of Contemporary History*, and in K. Brunner (ed.), *The Great Depression Revisited* (1981), the latter somewhat technical. A neglected subject is examined in A. J. H. Latham, *The Depression and the Developing World, 1914–1939* (1981), and international economic relations are studied in E. W. Bennett, *Germany and the Diplomacy of the Financial Crisis, 1931* (1962).

M. Friedman and A. J. Schwartz, *The Great Contraction, 1929–1933* (1965), abstracted from a larger study, argues the monetary causes of the depression; it should be read with P. Temin, *Did Monetary Forces Cause the Great Depression?* (1976); P. Fearon, *The Origins and Nature of the Great Slump, 1929–1932* (1979); and C. P. Kindleberger, *Keynesianism vs. Monetarism and Other Essays in Financial History** (1985). An important subject is examined in D. Eichengreen, *Golden Fetters: The Gold

Standard and the Great Depression, 1919–1939 (1992), and the Austrian bank failure in A. Schubert, *The Credit-Anstalt Crisis of 1931* (1992).

For Keynes, there is the illuminating second volume of the three-volume biography in progress by R. Skidelsky cited in Chapter XVI, *John Maynard Keynes: The Economist as Savior, 1920–1937* (1993), informative for his life and ideas; and another detailed study, D. E. Moggridge, *Maynard Keynes: An Economist's Biography* (1992), by the editor of Keynes' papers. For Keynes' ideas one turns also to C. Hession, *John Maynard Keynes: A Personalized Biography of the Man Who Revolutionized Capitalism and the Way We Live* (1984), informative despite its inflated title; P. Clarke, *The Keynesian Revolution in the Making, 1924–1936** (1989); and R. Lekachman, *The Age of Keynes** (1960) which focuses on the post-1945 years when Keynesian influence took hold.

Problems and Readings*

Two titles in the Heath problems series are relevant for this chapter: M. D. Lewis (ed.), *Gandhi: Maker of Modern India?* (1965), and R. F. Himmelberg (ed.), *The Great Depression and American Capitalism* (1968). J. M. Laux, *The Great Depression in Europe* (1974), is a thoughtful essay in the Forums in History series.

XIX. Democracy and Dictatorship

Some general accounts for the interwar years and the Great Depression have been described in the previous chapter, and books on the international crises of the 1930s will appear in the chapter that follows. Studies that focus on the democracies and dictatorships in this era are E. Wiskemann, *Europe of the Dictators, 1919–1945* (1960); M. Kitchen, *Europe between the Wars** (1988); and D. C. Large, *Between Two Fires: Europe's Path in the 1930s* (1990). Helpful as an introduction to the varieties of European dictatorship is S. J. Lee, *The European Dictatorships, 1918–1945** (1987).

The United States and the New Deal

The interwar years, the impact of the depression, and the New Deal may best be approached through W. E. Leuchtenburg: *The Perils of Prosperity, 1914–1932* (rev. 1993)

and *Franklin D. Roosevelt and the New Deal** (1961). Informative also are D. A. Shannon, *Between the Wars: America, 1919–1941** (1965); J. J. Hutmacher, *Trial by War and Depression, 1919–1941** (1973); R. S. McElvaine, *The Great Depression* (1984); P. Conkin, *The New Deal* (1967); A. Romasco, *The Politics of Recovery* (1983); and T. H. Watkins, *The Great Depression: America in the 1930s* (1993), written originally to accompany a television series.

Several biographical accounts of Roosevelt offer insights into the man, his presidency, and the bold but pragmatic efforts to cope with the depression. Among the most illuminating are A. M. Schlesinger, Jr., *The Age of Roosevelt* (3 vols., 1957–1960); J. M. Burns, *Roosevelt: The Lion and the Fox** (1956); F. Freidel's biography (4 vols., 1957–1973), mostly on the earlier years; the same author's synthesis, *A Rendezvous with Destiny* (1990); and K. S. Davis' multivolume *FDR*, of which four of a projected five volumes have appeared (1972–1993), carrying the story through Roosevelt's second term. The effect on those who lived through the economic crisis is vividly portrayed in C. Bird, *The Invisible Scar** (1966); S. Terkel, *Hard Times: An Oral History of the Great Depression* (1970); R. J. Simon (ed.), *As We Saw the Thirties* (1967); and R. S. McElvaine (ed.), *Down and Out in the Great Depression* (1983). The growth of the labor movement in these years may be studied in I. Bernstein, *The Turbulent Years* (1970), and the impact on women in W. D. Wandersee, *Women's Work and Family Values, 1920–1940* (1981). An informative comparative study is S. Salter and J. Stevenson, *The Working Class and Politics in Europe and America, 1929–1945* (1989).

Britain between the Wars

General accounts for Britain, some extending beyond the interwar years, are C. L. Mowat, *Britain between the Wars, 1918–1940* (1955), an older but still valuable synthesis; A. J. P. Taylor, *English History, 1914–1945** (1965), written with the author's usual verve; A. Marwick, *Britain in the Century of Total War: War, Peace, and Social Change, 1900–1967* (1968); W. N. Medlicott, *Contemporary England, 1914–1964* (1967); and M. Beloff, *Wars and Welfare: Britain, 1914–1945** (1984). An overview of the British economic scene is provided in S. Pollard, *The Development of the British Economy, 1914–1980* (rev. 1983); other books on the British economy will be cited in Chapter XXI.

An outstanding account of changes in British life for all classes, and much else, is provided in J. Stevenson, *British Society, 1914–1945* (1984). Other suggested studies include W. McElwee, *Britain's Locust Years, 1918–1940* (1962); S. Glynn and J. Oxborrow, *Interwar Britain: Social and Economic History* (1976); N. Branson and M. Heinemann, *Britain in the Nineteen Thirties* (1971); J. Stevenson and C. Cook, *The Slump: Society and Politics during the Depression* (1978); S. Hynes, *The Auden Generation: Literature and Politics in the 1930s* (1977); and R. Blythe, *The Age of Illusion: Some Glimpses of Britain between the Wars, 1919–1940* * (rev. 1984). The gap between popular hopes at the end of the war and postwar realities in highlighted in P. B. Johnson, *Land Fit for Heroes: The Planning of British Reconstruction, 1916–1919* (1968), and in B. B. Gilbert, *British Social Policy, 1914–1939* (1970). The postwar lot of the British wartime women workers is portrayed in D. Beddoe, *Back to Home and Duty: Women between the Wars, 1919–1939* * (1990), and women activists are described in B. Harrison, *Prudent Revolutionaries: Portraits of British Feminists between the Wars* (1987).

On the decline of the Liberal party and the rise of Labour, one may read W. Wilson, *The Downfall of the Liberal Party, 1914–1935* (1966); M. Freeden, *Liberalism Divided: British Political Thought, 1914–1939* (1986); and R. McKibbin, *The Evolution of the Labour Party, 1910–1924* (1974). The Conservative party in these years is portrayed in J. Ramaden, *The Age of Balfour and Baldwin, 1902–1940* (1978), cited in Chapter XIV.

The general strike of 1926 is studied in books by P. Renshaw (1976) and G. A. Phillips (1976); and the 1931 crisis in R. S. Bassett, *1931: Political Crisis* (1958); R. Skidelsky, *Politicians and the Slump: The Labour Government of 1929–1931* (1967); S. Ball, *Baldwin and the Conservative Party: The Crisis of 1929–1931* (1988); and A. Thorpe, *The British General Elections of 1931* (1991). The best synthesis for these events is P. Williamson, *National Crisis and National Government: British Politics, the Economy, and the Empire, 1926–1932* (1992).

The divisions within the left emerge from B. Pimlott, *Labour and the Left in the 1930s* * (rev. 1986), and the threat of fascism is examined in R. Skidelsky, *Oswald Mosley* (1976), the Labour leader who became Britain's leading fascist of the era, and on a broader scale in R. Thurlow, *Fascism in Britain: A History, 1918–1985* (1987), and D. S. Lewis, *Illusions of Grandeur: Mosley, Fascism and British Society, 1931–1981* (1990).

Among many biographical studies, there are biographies of Ramsay MacDonald by D. Marquand (1977) and by A. Morgan (1987); of Arthur Henderson, MacDonald's rival for Labour party leadership, by F. M. Leventhal* (1989); of Lloyd George in the years 1922–1931 by J. Campbell (1977) and by J. Grigg in the multivolume work cited earlier; and of Stanley Baldwin written jointly by K. Middlemas and J. Barnes (1969). For Neville Chamberlain, the first volume of a large-scale, highly detailed biography has appeared: D. Dilks, *Neville Chamberlain: Pioneering and Reform, 1870–1929* (1989); books on his foreign policy will be described in the next chapter. K. Rose, *King George V* (1984), is a scholarly biography of the monarch.

On British relations with the dominions one may turn to D. Hall, *Commonwealth: History of the British Commonwealth of Nations* (1971), a detailed account, and N. Mansergh, *The Commonwealth Experience* (1969). An outstanding study of Ireland in this era is J. M. Curran, *The Birth of the Irish Free State, 1921–1923* (1980), and an impressive account on a broader time scale is J. J. Lee, *Ireland, 1912–1985: Politics and Society* * (1990). The failure to resolve the question of Northern Ireland is examined in N. Mansergh, *The Unresolved Question: The Anglo-Irish Settlement and Its Undoing, 1912–1972* (1991).

France between the Wars

Two volumes in the *Cambridge History of Modern France* treat these years: P. Bernard and H. Dubief, *The Decline of the Third Republic, 1914–1938* * (trans. 1985), and J. P. Azéma, *From Munich to the Liberation, 1938–1944* * (trans. 1985), the latter somewhat more probing; and there are incisive essays in S. Hoffmann and others, *In Search of France: The Economy, Society, and Political System in the Twentieth Century* *

(1963). Two helpful studies are T. Kemp, *The French Economy, 1913–1939* (1972), and C. Dyer, *Population and Society in Twentieth Century France* (1978). An illuminating study of government planning and economic management, which were less successful in the interwar years than later, is R. F. Kuisel, *Capital and the State in Modern France: Renovation and Economic Management in the Twentieth Century** (1981). The French franc between the wars is studied in books by M. Wolfe (1961) and K. Mouré (1991), and another important subject in G. Wright, *Rural Revolution in France: The Peasantry in the Twentieth Century** (1964). For labor there are available H. W. Ehrmann, *French Labor: From Popular Front to Liberation* (1947), and the relevant chapters in T. Judt, *Marxism and the French Left** (1986), cited in Chapter XIV.

The response to the depression and the threat to the Third Republic are explored in two books by J. Jackson: *The Politics of Depression in France, 1932–1936** (1985) and *The Popular Front in France: Defending Democracy, 1923–1938** (1988). For the Socialist leader of the Popular Front one may read J. Colton, *Léon Blum: Humanist in Politics** (1966, 1987), and J. Lacouture, *Léon Blum* (1977; trans. 1982). Other studies of the political left in the Popular Front era include P. J. Larmour, *The French Radical Party in the 1930s* (1964); J. T. Marcus, *French Socialism in the Crisis Years, 1933–36* (1958); N. Greene, *Crisis and Decline: The French Socialist Party in the Popular Front Era* (1969); H. Gruber, *Léon Blum, French Socialism, and the Popular Front** (1986); D. Caute, *Communism and the French Intellectuals, 1914–1960* (1965); and D. R. Brower, *The New Jacobins: The French Communist Party and the Popular Front* (1968). The right, the extreme right, and fascist-type movements are studied in several of the books cited for the pre-1914 years; to them should be added R. Soucy, *French Fascism: The First Wave, 1924–1933* (1985); H. Lebovics, *True France: The Wars over Cultural Identity, 1900–1945* (1992); and P. Birnbaum, *Anti-Semitism in France: A Political History from Léon Blum to the Present* (1992).

Still valuable for the 1930s are the perceptive journalistic accounts of A. Werth, of which *The Twilight of France, 1933–1940* (1942), is a condensation of his earlier volumes. O. Bernier, *Fireworks at Dusk: Paris in the Thirties* (1993), is a colorful popular portrait of politics and high society for the general reader.

Italy: The Fascist Experience

Introductions to the Italian experience include A. Cassels, *Fascist Italy** (1968); E. Wiskemann, *Fascism in Italy** (1969); F. Chabod, *A History of Italian Fascism* (1963), concise but perceptive; and an impressive book on the early years, A. Lyttelton, *The Seizure of Power: Fascism in Italy, 1919–1929* (1973). The relevant chapters in C. Seton-Watson, *Italy from Liberalism to Fascism, 1870–1925* (1967), cited earlier, are valuable as are those in H. S. Hughes, *The United States and Italy* (rev. 1979).

On the nature of the Fascist state, H. Finer, *Mussolini's Italy** (1933, 1965), and G. Salvemini, *Under the Axe of Fascism* (1936, 1970), remain informative but should be supplemented by R. Sarti, *Fascism and the Industrial Leadership in Italy, 1919–1940* (1971), and M. Gallo, *Mussolini's Italy: Twenty Years of the Fascist Era* (1973). A. J. Gregor, *Italian Fascism and Developmental Dictatorship** (1979), tends somewhat reductively to equate Italian fascism with forced modernization. The impact on Italian society is comprehensively examined in E. R. Tannenbaum, *The Fascist Experience: Italian Society and Culture, 1922–1945* (1972), which may be supplemented by V. de Grazia's two books, *The Culture of Consent: Mass Organization of Leisure in Fascist Italy* (1981), and *How Fascism Ruled Women: Italy, 1922–1945* (1991).

The compromise with the church is explored in R. A. Webster, *The Cross and the Fasces: Christian Democracy in Italy* (1960), and J. F. Pollard, *The Vatican and Italian Fascism, 1929–1932* (1985). Mussolini's racial policy is studied in M. Michaelis, *Mussolini and the Jews: German-Italian Relations and the Jewish Question in Italy, 1922–1945* (1978); S. Zucotti, *The Italians and the Holocaust: Persecution, Rescue, and Survival* (1988), an excellent study; J. Steinberg, *All or Nothing: The Axis and the Holocaust, 1941–1943* (1992); and A. Stille, *Benevolence and Betrayal: Five Italian Jewish Families under Fascism* (1993), a poignant portrayal.

On Il Duce, the best study is D. Mack Smith, *Mussolini* (1982), straightforward and comprehensive, but there is also an informative biography by I. Kirkpatrick, *Mussolini: Study of a Demagogue** (1964). The older G. Megaro, *Mussolini in the Making* (1938), remains useful for the early years but should be supplemented by A. J. Gregor, *Young Mussolini and the Intellectual Origins of Fascism* (1979), and Z. Sternhell, *The Birth of Fascist Ideology: From Cultural Rebellion to Political Revolution* (1993), an outstanding study. The underground struggle against fascism from 1924 to 1943 is thoughtfully analyzed in C. F. Delzell, *Mussolini's Enemies: The Italian Anti-Fascist Resistance* (1961).

Foreign and colonial policy is examined in G. Barclay, *The Rise and Fall of the New Roman Empire: Italy's Bid for World Power, 1890–1943* (1973), emphasizing pre-Fascist expansionism; A. Cassels, *Mussolini's Early Diplomacy* (1970); and D. Mack Smith, *Mussolini's Roman Empire* (1976). Mussolini as a failed military leader is ably explored in M. Knox, *Mussolini Unleashed, 1939–1941: Politics and Strategy in Fascist Italy's Last War** (1982). The last phase of the dictator's career is narrated in detail in F. W. Deakin, *The Brutal Friendship: Mussolini, Hitler, and the Fall of Italian Fascism** (1962), the final portion of which is available as *The Six Hundred Days of Mussolini** (1966). C. G. Segrè, *Italo Balbo: A Fascist Life* (1987), studies Mussolini's one-time heir apparent.

Germany, 1919–1933: The Weimar Republic

For the collapse of the Weimar Republic and the triumph of Hitler, several of the longer-range histories of Germany cited in Chapters XIII and XIV will also be helpful. Narrative accounts of Weimar include A. J. Nicholls, *Weimar and the Rise of Hitler** (rev. 1991); D. Childs, *Germany since 1918* (rev. 1980); S. Taylor, *Revolution and Counter-Revolution in Germany, 1918–1933* (1984); E. Kolb, *The Weimar Republic* (trans. 1988); and H. Heiber, *The Weimar Republic: Germany, 1918–1933** (1986); and from the perspective of recent years, M. Fulbrook, *The Divided Nation: A History of Germany, 1918–1990** (1992). The continuity with imperial foreign policy is thoughtfully studied in M. M. Lee and W. Michalka, *German Foreign Policy, 1917–1933: Continuity or Break?* (1987). Two older detailed political histories, A. Rosenberg, *A History*

of the German Republic* (1936), and E. Eyck, *A History of the Weimar Republic* (2 vols., trans. 1962–1965), and a briefer account, S. W. Halperin, *Germany Tried Democracy: A Political History of the Reich from 1918 to 1933** (1946), remain instructive on parties and personalities. Works on the uneasy early years include R. Watts, *The Kings Depart* (1968); A. J. Ryder, *The German Revolution of 1918: A Study of German Socialism in War and Revolt* (1967); and S. Haffner, *Failure of a Revolution: Germany, 1918–1919* (trans. 1973). The inflation of 1923 is studied in S. B. Webb, *Hyperinflation and Stabilization in Weimar Germany* (1989), and in G. S. Feldman, *The Great Disorder: Politics, Economics, and Society in the German Inflation, 1914–1924* (1992), a far-ranging, exhaustive study.

The most informed inquiry into efforts to cope with the depression is H. James, *The German Slump: Politics and Economics, 1924–1936** (1986). The inability of the political parties and diverse interest groups to cooperate is critically analyzed in D. Abraham, *The Collapse of the Weimar Republic: Political Economy and Crisis** (1981; rev. 1986); and in L. E. Jones, *German Liberalism and the Dissolution of the Weimar Party System, 1918–1933* (1989), a detailed study. W. L. Guttman, *The German Social Democratic Party, 1875–1933* (1981), examines a major party of the left, while the resort to extraparliamentary tactics receives attention in J. M. Riehl, *Paramilitary Politics in Weimar Germany* (1977); P. Fritzsche, *Rehearsals for Fascism: Populism and Political Mobilization in Weimar Germany* (1990); and E. Rosenhaft, *Beating the Fascists? The German Communists and Political Violence, 1929–1933* (1984). The question of army loyalties to the republic is examined in depth in F. L. Carsten, *The Reichswehr and Politics, 1918 to 1933** (trans. 1966); J. W. Wheeler-Bennett, *The Nemesis of Power: The German Army in Politics, 1918–1945** (rev. 1964); and G. A. Craig, *The Politics of the Prussian Army, 1640–1945** (1956, 1964), cited in Chapter V.

Among thoughtful efforts to explore the ideological roots of Weimar's failure are F. Stern, *The Politics of Cultural Despair: A Study in the Use of the Germanic Ideology** (1961) and *The Failure of Illiberalism: Essays on the Political Culture of Germany* (1972), and G. L. Mosse, *The Crisis of German Ideology: Intellectual Origins of the Third Reich** (1964). Cultural history in these years is examined P. Gay, *Weimar Culture: The Outsider as Insider* (1968); W. Laqueur, *Weimar: A Cultural History, 1918–1933* (1974); and D. J. K. Peukert, *The Weimar Republic: The Crisis of Classical Modernity* (trans. 1992). Some political leaders of the republic are studied in H. Kessler, *Walter Rathenau* (1929); K. Epstein, *Matthias Erzberger and the Dilemma of German Democracy* (1959); H. W. Gatzke, *Stresemann and the Rearmament of Germany** (1954); H. A. Turner, *Stresemann and the Politics of the Weimar Republic** (1963); J. W. Wheeler-Bennett, *Wooden Titan: Hindenburg in Twenty Years of German History, 1914–1934* (1936); and A. Dorpalen, *Hindenburg and the Weimar Republic* (1964). Especially helpful is P. Stachura, *Political Leaders in Weimar Germany: A Biographical Study* (1993).

Germany, 1933–1945: The Third Reich

A valuable introduction to the vast literature on the Third Reich is I. Kershaw, *The Nazi Dictatorship: Problems and Perspectives of Interpretation** (rev. 1989), while P. Ayço-berry, *The Nazi Question: An Essay on the Interpretation of National Socialism, 1922–1975** (trans. 1981), is a helpful historiographical study.

On the coming to power of the Nazis one may first turn to M. Broszat, *Hitler and the Collapse of Weimar Germany** (trans. 1987), focusing on the years 1929–1933. There are informative essays in T. Eschenburg and others, *The Path to Dictatorship, 1919–1933* (1966); and P. Stachura (ed.), *The Nazi Machtergreifung* (1983). In a carefully researched book H. A. Turner, *German Big Business and the Rise of Hitler* (1985), refutes the thesis that big business and heavy industry brought Hitler to power even if they did lend support to various antirepublican elements. Two important studies illuminate the Nazi appeal to diverse segments of the population: W. S. Allen, *The Nazi Seizure of Power: The Experience of a Single German Town, 1922–1945** (1965; rev. 1984), on Northeim in northern Germany, and J. H. Grill, *The Nazi Movement in Baden, 1920–1945* (1984). Two extraordinary efforts to assess the Nazi appeal at the polls are R. F. Hamilton, *Who Voted for Hitler?** (1982), and T. Childers, *The Nazi Voter: The Social Foundations of Fascism in Germany, 1919–1933* (1983), which both tend to confirm that Nazi support came from

all segments of the population, and not only from the lower middle class.

M. H. Kater, *The Nazi Party: A Social Profile of Members and Leaders, 1919–1945** (1983), is an exhaustive sociological analysis of those who joined and led the party, while D. Orlow, *The History of the Nazi Party* (2 vols., 1969–1973), is a comprehensive organizational history. For the SS one may read G. Reitlinger, *SS: Alibi of a Nation, 1922–1945** (1956); R. L. Koehl, *The Black Corps: The Structure and Power Struggles of the SS* (1983); and H. F. Ziegler, *Nazi Germany's New Aristocracy: The SS Leadership, 1925–1939* (1990). The Brownshirts are studied in C. Fischer, *Stormtroopers: A Social, Economic and Ideological Analysis, 1929–1935* (1983). Other institutions of the Nazi era are discussed in numerous books, among them, R. Gellately, *The Gestapo and German Society* (1990); T. Taylor, *Sword and Swastika: Generals and Nazis in the Third Reich** (1952); O. Bartov, *Hitler's Army: Soldiers, Nazis, and War in the Third Reich** (1991). P. Seabury, *The Wilhelmstrasse: A Study of German Diplomats under the Nazi Regime* (1955); O. J. Hale, *The Captive Press in the Third Reich* (1964); Z. A. B. Zeman, *Nazi Propaganda* (1964); P. Hayes, *Industry and Ideology: I. G. Farben in the Nazi Era* (1987); and I. Miller, *Hitler's Justice: The Courts of the Third Reich** (1991).

Religion and related matters are examined in E. C. Helmreich, *The German Churches under Hitler* (1979); J. S. Conway, *The Nazi Persecution of the Churches, 1933–1945* (1968); G. Lewy, *The Catholic Church and Nazi Germany* (1964); and S. Friedländer, *Pius XII and the Third Reich: A Documentation* (1966). Books on Hitler's persecution of the Jews, and on the death camps and the Holocaust, will be described in the next chapter, but one should mention here L. S. Dawidowicz, *The War against the Jews, 1933–1945** (1976), and S. Gordon, *Hitler, Germans, and the Jewish Question* (1984).

For all aspects of the Nazi era K. Hildebrand, *The Third Reich** (1984), is valuable, while D. G. Williamson, *The Third Reich** (1982), is a helpful introduction. On the Nazi state three outstanding analyses are K. D. Bracher, *The German Dictatorship** (trans. 1970); M. Broszat, *The Hitler State** (trans. 1981); and M. Burleigh and W. Wippermann, *The Racial State: Germany, 1933–1945* (1992). D. Schoenbaum, *Hitler's Social Rev-*

olution: Class and Status in Nazi Germany, 1933–1939* (1966) sees a leveling effect not accomplished by earlier regimes. Studies exploring new avenues to understanding popular responses include I. Kershaw, *The "Hitler Myth": Image and Reality in the Third Reich** (1987), D. J. K. Peukert, *Inside Nazi Germany: Conformity, Opposition, and Racism in Everyday Life* (trans. 1987); and N. Frei, *National Socialist Rule in Germany: The Führer State, 1933–1945** (trans. 1993). There are perceptive insights into life under the Nazis in R. Bessel (ed.), *Life in the Third Reich** (1987), and in G. L. Mosse, *Nazi Culture: Intellectual, Cultural, and Social Life in the Third Reich* (1966).

The best study of women in the Third Reich, with special attention to those who supported and those who resisted the regime, is C. Koonz, *Mothers in the Fatherland: Women, the Family, and Nazi Politics** (1987). It may be supplemented by J. Stephenson, *Women in Nazi Society* (1976) and *The Nazi Organization of Women* (1981); and the essays in R. Bridenthal and others, *When Biology Became Destiny: Women in Weimar and Nazi Germany** (1989).

That there was no mass resistance but opposition only from resolute individuals and small groups emerges from two comprehensive accounts: P. Hoffmann, *German Resistance to Hitler** (rev. 1988), and M. Balfour, *Withstanding Hitler in Germany, 1933–1945* (1989); they may be supplemented by T. Prittie, *Germans against Hitler* (1964); H. Rothfels, *The German Opposition to Hitler** (rev. 1987); and the essays in D. C. Lodge (ed.), *Contending with Hitler: Varieties of German Resistance in the Third Reich* (1992).

Of the many biographies of Hitler, two stand out: A. Bullock, *Hitler: A Study in Tyranny** (1952; rev. 1964), and J. C. Fest, *Hitler* (trans. 1975, somewhat condensed from the German original). Bullock has also written a remarkable in-depth Plutarchian narrative, *Hitler and Stalin: Parallel Lives* (1992). An insightful brief account is I. Kershaw, *Hitler** (1991), in the Profiles in Power series. R. Binion, *Hitler among the Germans* (1976), uses psychoanalytical methods to explain the inner wellsprings of the obsessed leader, while R. L. Waite, *The Psychopathic God: Adolf Hitler** (1977), effectively combines psychoanalytical and more conventional techniques. Two analyti-

cal interpretive essays that raise pertinent questions are S. Haffner, *The Meaning of Hitler** (trans. 1980), and W. Carr, *Hitler: A Study in Personality and Politics* (1979). N. Stone, *Hitler* (1980) focuses on the war years, while the end of the leader and his regime is vividly recounted in H. R. Trevor-Roper, *The Last Days of Hitler** (rev. 1966).

Some of Hitler's associates are studied in J. C. Fest, *The Face of the Third Reich: Portraits of the Nazi Leadership** (trans. 1977); B. F. Smith, *Heinrich Himmler: A Nazi in the Making, 1900–1926* (1971); R. Smelser, *Robert Ley: Hitler's Labor Front Leader* (1989); R. G. Reuth, *Goebbels* (trans. 1994); and D. Irving, *Göring: A Biography* (1989), which as in this author's other books on the Third Reich makes the best possible case for his subject. Hitler's foreign minister is studied in M. Bloch, *Ribbentrop* (1993), a detailed diplomatic account; and in J. Weitz, *Hitler's Diplomat: The Life and Times of Joachim Ribbentrop* (1992), more biographically oriented. Two convenient handbooks on the institutions and personalities of the regime are R. S. Wistrich, *Who's Who in Nazi Germany* (1982), and C. Zentner and F. Bedürftig, *The Encyclopedia of the Third Reich* (2 vols., 1991).

Defining Totalitarianism and Fascism

The origins and nature of twentieth-century ideologies are explored in many books, notably in K. D. Bracher's comprehensive *A History of Political Thought in the Twentieth Century* (trans. 1984). Among efforts to examine totalitarianism, left and right, are C. J. Friedrich and Z. K. Brzezinski, *Totalitarian Dictatorship and Autocracy** (rev. 1965); H. Arendt, *Origins of Totalitarianism* (rev. 1966), cited in Chapter XIV; H. Bucheim, *Totalitarian Rule* (trans. 1967); A. Perlmutter, *Modern Authoritarianism* (1981); and S. P. Soper, *Totalitarianism: A Conceptual Approach* (1985).

For efforts to arrive at a generic definition of fascism as a phenomenon of the interwar years the best introduction is F. L. Carsten, *The Rise of Fascism** (rev. 1980). Among other thoughtful studies are S. G. Payne, *Fascism: Comparison and Definition* (1980); H. R. Kedward, *Fascism in Western Europe, 1900–1945* (1969); R. De Felice, *Fascism* (1976), by the Italian biographer of Mussolini; J. Weiss, *The Fascist Tradition: Radical Right-Wing Extremism in Modern*

Europe* (1967); A. Cassels, *Fascism** (1975); and A. J. Gregor, *The Ideology of Fascism: The Rationale of Totalitarianism* (1969). Readers will find E. Nolte, *Three Faces of Fascism: Action Française, Italian Fascism, National Socialism** (trans. 1966), provocative but difficult. The intellectual origins of fascism in its Italian setting are traced in Z. Sternhell, *The Birth of Fascist Ideology* (1993), cited earlier in this chapter. Other informative books are H. Rogger and E. Weber (eds.), *The European Right: A Historical Profile** (1965); S. J. Woolf and others, *European Fascism* (1968); and W. Laqueur and G. L. Mosse (eds.), *International Fascism, 1920–1945** (1966). The results of a sociological investigation into the class origins of fascist supporters in twenty-one countries are available in S. U. Larsen and others (eds.), *Who Were the Fascists? Social Roots of European Fascism* (1980), which may be supplemented by D. Muhlberger (ed.), *The Social Basis of European Fascist Movements* (1987).

Other European Developments in the Interwar Years

Spain and the Spanish Civil War are discussed in the following chapter. The most informative volumes on Central and Eastern Europe are H. Seton-Watson, *Eastern Europe between the Wars, 1918–1941* (rev. 1967), J. Rothschild, *East Central Europe between the Two World Wars** (1975); Vol. IX of *A History of East Central Europe*; and the relevant chapters in A. Palmer, *The Lands Between: A History of East-Central Europe since the Congress of Vienna* (1970). An incisive inquiry blaming political and economic problems on the efforts at modernization in these years is I. T. Berend, *The Crisis Zone of Europe: An Interpretation of East-Central European History in the First Half of the Twentieth Century* (1986). A special subject is ably explored in E. Mendelsohn, *The Jews of East Central Europe between the World Wars** (1983). For the Balkans there are available the relevant chapters in R. L. Wolff, *The Balkans in Our Time* (rev. 1978); L. S. Stavrianos, *The Balkans since 1815** (1965); and B. Jelavich, *History of the Balkans: The Twentieth Century** (1983); all cited earlier. R. Kaplan, *Balkan Ghosts: A Journey through Time* (1993), is an interesting impressionistic account illuminating the contemporary era as well.

A few titles may be suggested for some of the successor states. For Austria: C. A. Gulick, *Austria from Habsburg to Hitler* (2 vols., 1948), sympathetic to the Austrian socialists; C. E. Edmondson, *The Heimwehr and Austrian Politics, 1918–1936* (1978); M. Kitchen, *The Coming of Austrian Fascism* (1980); F. L. Carsten, *Fascist Movements in Austria: From Schönerer to Hitler** (1977); and B. F. Pauley, *Hitler and the Forgotten Nazis: A History of Austrian National Socialism* (1981). For Hungary: C. A. Macartney, *October Fifteenth: A History of Modern Hungary, 1929–1945* (2 vols.; rev. 1962); and R. L. Tönes, *Bela Kun and the Hungarian Soviet Republic* (1967), on the short-lived Communist regime of 1919. For Czechoslovakia: J. Kolvoda, *The Genesis of Czechoslovakia* (1985); Z. A. B. Zeman, *The Masaryks: The Making of Czechoslovakia** (1976, 1991); R. W. Seton-Watson, *A History of the Czechs and Slovaks* (1943, 1965); E. Wiskemann, *Czechs and Germans* (rev. 1967); V. Olivova, *The Doomed Democracy: Czechoslovakia in a Disrupted Europe, 1918–1938* (1972); and C. S. Leff, *National Conflict in Czechoslovakia: The Making and Remaking of a State, 1918–1987* (1988), which carries the story toward the present. For Yugoslavia: I. Banac, *The National Question in Jugoslavia* (1985), an outstanding inquiry into the genesis of the multiethnic state, focusing on the years 1918–1921; F. Singleton, *A Short History of the Jugoslav Peoples** (1985); and R. West, *Black Lamb and Grey Falcon* (2 vols., 1941; reissued 1992), a gifted journalist's insightful account that takes on added significance in the 1990s. For Poland: M. K. Dziewanowski, *Poland in the Twentieth Century* (1977); A. Polonsky, *Politics in Independent Poland, 1921–1939* (1972); H. Roos, *A History of Modern Poland* (1966); and the volumes of N. Davies cited in Chapter XI. For Finland and the Baltic states: J. H. Wuorinen, *A History of Finland* (1965); D. G. Kirby, *Finland in the Twentieth Century* (1979); and G. von Rauch, *The Baltic States—Estonia, Latvia, and Lithuania: The Years of Independence, 1917–1940* (1947, 1987).

Problems and Readings*

On the American New Deal, a selection of conflicting interpretations is conveniently presented in E. C. Rozwenc (ed.), *The New Deal: Revolution or Evolution?* (rev. 1959), and in M. Keller (ed.), *The New Deal* (1963). For Britain: J. A. Thompson (ed.), *The Collapse of the British Liberal Party: Fate or Self-Destruction?* (1969), and A. Thorpe, *Britain in the 1930s** (1992), a brief narrative essay. For Italy: S. W. Halperin, *Mussolini and Italian Fascism* (1964), and R. Sarti (ed.), *The Ax Within: Italian Fascism in Action* (1974). For Weimar Germany: R. N. Hunt (ed.), *The Creation of the Weimar Republic: Stillborn Democracy?* (1969); F. K. Ringer (ed.), *The German Inflation of 1923* (1969); I. Kershaw (ed.), *Weimar: Why Did German Democracy Fail?* (1990); and W. O. Simpson *Hitler and Germany,** a brief narrative account of Hitler's coming to power. For the Nazi era: F. Stern (ed.), *The Path to Dictatorship* (1967); H. A. Turner (ed.), *Nazism and the Third Reich* (1972); A. Mitchell (ed.), *Hitler's Dictatorship and the German Nation* (rev. 1990); R. G. L. Waite (ed.), *Hitler and Nazi Germany* (rev. 1969); and J. Noakes and G. Pridham (eds.), *Documents of Nazism, 1919–1945* (1975). On fascism and totalitarianism, there are available P. T. Mason, *Totalitarianism: Temporary Madness or Permanent Danger?* (1967); E. Weber, *Varieties of Fascism: Doctrines of Revolution in the Twentieth Century* (1964, 1982); N. Greene (ed.), *Fascism: An Anthology* (1968); C. F. Delzell (ed.), *Mediterranean Fascism* (1970); W. Laqueur (ed.), *Fascism: A Reader's Guide* (1976); H. A. Turner, Jr., (ed.), *Reappraisals of Fascism* (1975); R. de Felice (ed.), *Interpretations of Fascism* (trans. 1977); and G. L. Mosse (ed.), *International Fascism: New Thoughts and New Appraisals* (1979).

XX. The Second World War

Spain and the Spanish Civil War

The most comprehensive narrative account of the Spanish conflict, including the international ramifications, is H. Thomas, *The Spanish Civil War** (1961; rev. 1977; reissued 1987), in which Franco's skill as a manipulator and survivor clearly emerges. Other recommended accounts are G. Jackson, *The Spanish Republic and the Civil War, 1931–1939** (1965; abr. ed., 1974); B. Bolloten, *The Spanish Civil War: Revolution and Counterrevolution* (1991), incorporating the author's earlier studies of the Communist role in the war; and P. Broué and E. Témime, *The Revolution and the Civil War in Spain* (trans. 1972). There are histories

also by P. Wyden (1983), A. Beevor (1983), and S. M. Ellwood* (1991). H. Browne, *Spain's Civil War** (1983), provides a brief overview, and R. Carr, *The Spanish Tragedy: The Civil War in Perspective* (1977), adds analytical insights. The turbulent background is ably conveyed in G. Brenan, *The Spanish Labyrinth** (1943); R. A. H. Robinson, *The Origins of Franco Spain: The Right, the Republic, and the Revolution, 1931–1936* (1971); E. E. Malefakis, *Agrarian Reform and Peasant Revolution in Spain: Origins of the Civil War* (1970), an impressive study; and P. Preston, *The Coming of the Spanish Civil War: Reform, Reaction, and Revolution in the Second Republic, 1931–1936* (1978). The Spanish Socialist party is studied in H. Graham, *Socialism and War: The Spanish Socialist Party in Power and Crisis, 1930–1939* (1991). There are informative essays in three collaborative volumes: M. S. Alexander and H. Graham (eds.), *The French and Spanish Popular Fronts: Comparative Perspectives* (1989); P. Preston (ed.), *Revolution and War in Spain, 1931–1939** (1985); and M. Blinkhorn (ed.), *Spain in Conflict, 1931–1939* (1986).

Three studies of the American response to the war are F. J. Taylor, *The United States and the Spanish Civil War* (1956); A. Guttmann, *The Wound in the Heart: America and the Spanish Civil War* (1962); and R. P. Traina, *American Diplomacy and the Spanish Civil War* (1968). Other memorable aspects are touched upon in P. Stansky and W. Abrahams, *Journey to the Frontier: Julian Bell and John Cornford: Their Lives and the 1930s** (1966), on two young English poets who fought for the Republic; the same authors' *George Orwell* (2 vols., 1972–1980); Orwell's own *Homage to Catalonia** (1938), by one who became disillusioned; and S. Weintraub, *The Last Great Cause: The Intellectuals and the Spanish Civil War* (1968). There are also biographies of Orwell by B. Crick (1980) and M. Shelden (1991). The volunteers who out of idealism fought for the Republic are studied in V. Brome, *The International Brigades* (1966), and in R. D. Richardson, *Comintern Army: The International Brigades and the Spanish Civil War* (1982), which stresses the Stalinist discipline imposed. Two balanced studies of Franco are J. J. W. Trythall, *El Caudillo* (1970), and S. Ellwood, *Franco* (Profiles in Power series, 1994). S. G. Payne has written a comprehensive monograph, *Falange: A History of Spanish Fascism** (1961), and on Franco's years in power, *The Franco Regime, 1936–1975* (1987).

Background to the Second World War

Although there is no one comprehensive treatment taking into account the sources now available for the diplomacy of the interwar years and the background to the Second World War, there are a number of important books on the subject. An excellent European Diplomatic History series providing bibliographical and archival guidance was inaugurated with C. M. Kimmich (ed.), *German Foreign Policy, 1918–1945: Guide to Research and Research Materials* (1981); and updated volumes (1992) for it and for the foreign policy of the other major European powers are now available: R. J. Young (ed.), for France; A. Cassels (ed.), for Italy; S. Aster (ed.), for Britain; R. H. Johnston (ed.), for the Soviet Union; as well as volumes for the League and related international organizations, and for international economic relations. The opening of the British and French archives and the availability of the German archives have made many earlier works obsolete or at least incomplete.

Among the most informative general inquiries into the coming of the Second World War are P. Renouvin, *World War II and Its Origins: International Relations 1929–1945* (trans. 1969); M. Baumont, *The Origins of the Second World War* (trans. 1978); A. Adamthwaite, *The Making of the Second World War* (rev. 1993); and P. M. H. Bell, *The Origins of the Second World War in Europe* (1986). Many of the books on the diplomacy of the interwar years cited at the beginning of Chapter XVIII should also be consulted.

On the eleven months between Munich and the outbreak of the war, D. C. Watt, *How War Came: The Immediate Origins of the Second World War, 1938–1939* (1989), is a masterful study. The conclusions tend to refute A. J. P. Taylor's *The Origins of the Second World War* (1961), which depicts Hitler as one who did not desire war but merely took advantage of his opponents' uncertainty. On the Taylor thesis one may also read the evaluations in G. Martel (ed.), *"The Origins of the Second World War" Reconsidered: The A. J. P. Taylor Debate after Twenty-Five Years* (1986), and R. Boyce and E. M. Robertson (eds.), *Paths to War: New Essays on the Origins of the Second World War* (1989).

A major study of German foreign policy based on exhaustive use of the documents and strongly emphasizing Hitler's responsibilities and initiatives is G. L. Weinberg, *The Foreign Policy of Hitler's Germany:* Vol. I, *Diplomatic Revolution in Europe, 1933–1936* (1970), and Vol. II, *Starting World War II, 1937–1939* (1980). A second study with similar conclusions is N. Rich, *Hitler's War Aims* (2 vols., 1973–1974). For assessments of German foreign policy, one may also read E. M. Robertson, *Hitler's Pre-War Policies and Military Planning, 1933–1939* (1967); K. Hildebrand, *The Foreign Policy of the Third Reich** (1974); J. Hiden, *Germany and Europe, 1919–1939** (rev. 1993); and E. Jäckel, *Hitler's World View** (1981). Attempts to examine German foreign policy in broad perspective include A. Hillgruber, *Germany and the Two World Wars** (trans. 1981); W. D. Smith, *The Ideological Origins of Nazi Imperialism** (1986); K. Hildebrand, *German Foreign Policy from Bismarck to Adenauer* (trans. 1989); F. Fischer, *From Kaiserreich to Third Reich** (trans. 1986), cited earlier; and the essays in V. R. Berghahn and M. Kitchen (eds.), *Germany and the Age of Total War* (1981).

British policy in the 1930s, including the economic constraints on a more assertive policy, is examined in M. Cowling, *The Impact of Hitler: British Politics and British Policy, 1933–1940** (1975); R. P. Shay, Jr., *British Rearmament in the Thirties: Politics and Profits* (1977); G. C. Peden, *British Rearmament and the Treasury, 1932–1939* (1979); and R. Douglas, *In the Year of Munich* (1978). Highly critical of appeasement are A. L. Rowse, *Appeasement: A Study in Political Decline, 1933–1939** (1961); M. Gilbert and R. Gott, *The Appeasers* (1963); M. Gilbert, *The Roots of Appeasement* (1966); and M. George, *The Warped Vision: British Foreign Policy, 1933–1939* (1965). The opposition to appeasement is also examined in W. R. Rock, *Appeasement on Trial: British Foreign Policy and Its Critics, 1938–1939* (1966); N. Thompson, *The Anti-Appeasers* (1971); and R. A. C. Parker, *Chamberlain and Appeasement** (1993). There are informative essays in W. Mommsen and L. Kettenacker (eds.), *The Fascist Challenge and the Policy of Appeasement* (1983), while K. Robbins, *Appeasement** (1988), provides a brief overview of the debate.

In connection with the 1930s, W. S.

Churchill, *The Gathering Storm** (1948), covering his years in the opposition, the first volume of his *The Second World War** (6 vols., 1948–1953), is indispensable, even if it should be read along with other books on the subject. The fifth volume of M. Gilbert's massive biography of Churchill, to be described below, also deals with these years: *Winston S. Churchill*: Vol. V, *The Prophet of Truth, 1922–1939* (1977).

Biographical studies focusing on British foreign policy include two studies of Anthony Eden, one highly critical, by D. Carlton (1981), the second more defensive, by R. Rhodes James (1987); and a study of Sir Samuel Hoare by J. A. Cross (1977). For Neville Chamberlain there are studies by K. Feiling (1946), I. MacLeod (1961), and J. Charmley (1990), all somewhat defensive, and a balanced assessment by W. R. Rock (1969).

Several impressive studies examine British foreign policy in long-range perspective, among them: F. S. Northedge, *The Troubled Giant: Britain among the Great Powers, 1916–1939* (1966); W. N. Medlicott, *British Foreign Policy since Versailles, 1919–1963* (rev. 1968); C. Barnett, *The Collapse of British Power* (1972); P. Kennedy, *The Realities behind Diplomacy: Background Influences on British External Policy, 1865–1980** (1983); C. J. Bartlett, *British Foreign Policy in the Twentieth Century** (1989); and the essays in D. Dilks (ed.), *Retreat from Power: Studies in Britain's Foreign Policy of the Twentieth Century* (2 vols., 1989), the first volume covering the years 1906–1939.

For French foreign policy in these years the fullest accounts are by A. Adamthwaite, *France and the Coming of the Second World War, 1936–1939* (1977) and *Grandeur and Decline: France, 1914–1940** (1991). They may be supplemented by W. E. Scott, *Alliance against Hitler: The Origins of the Franco-Soviet Pact* (1962); H. Shamir, *Economic Crises and French Foreign Policy, 1930–1936* (1989); and A. H. Furnia, *The Diplomacy of Appeasement* (1966). Two French foreign ministers are studied in R. J. Young, *Power and Pleasure: Louis Barthou and the Third French Republic* (1991), on the diplomat-minister assassinated in 1934; and in J. E. Dreifort, *Yvon Delbos at the Quai d'Orsay: French Foreign Policy during the Popular Front, 1936–1938* (1974). The limited options of the Popular Front are carefully examined in N. Jordan, *The Popular Front and Central Europe: The Dilem-mas of French Impotence, 1918–1940* (1992). A special subject is explored in N. Ingram, *The Politics of Dissent: Pacifism in France, 1919–1939* (1991).

There are many books on specific episodes and subjects. The Ethiopian conquest is studied in two books by G. W. Baer: *The Coming of the Italo-Ethiopian War* (1967) and *Test Case: Italy, Ethiopia, and the League of Nations* (1976); E. M. Robertson, *Mussolini as Empire-Builder: Europe and Africa, 1932–1936* (1977); F. Hardie, *The Abyssinian Crisis* (1974); and A. del Boca, *The Ethiopian War, 1935–1941* (1969). The Rhineland episode is examined in J. T. Emerson, *The Rhineland Crisis, 7 March 1936* (1977). On the annexation of Austria, one may read G. Brook-Shepherd, *Anschluss: The Rape of Austria* (1963) and *Dollfuss* (1961); J. Gehl, *Austria, Germany and the Anschluss, 1931–1938* (1963); and D. Wagner and G. Tomkowitz, *Anschluss: The Week Hitler Seized Vienna* (1971). For Munich, the best detailed account is T. Taylor, *Munich: The Price of Peace** (1980), but also informative are J. W. Wheeler-Bennett, *Munich: Prologue to Tragedy** (1948, 1963); K. Eubank, *Munich* (1963); H. Noguères, *Munich: "Peace for Our Time"* (trans. 1963); and K. Robbins, *Munich 1938* (1963). F. Gilbert and G. A. Craig (eds.), *The Diplomats, 1919–1939** (1953), include valuable chapters on the individuals who helped make foreign policy in the era.

Studies focusing on eastern Europe include D. E. Kaiser, *Economic Diplomacy and the Origins of the Second World War: Germany, Britain, France, and Eastern Europe, 1930–1939* (1980); A. Cienciala, *Poland and the Western Powers, 1938–1939* (1968); S. Newman, *March 1939: The British Guarantee to Poland* (1976); and A. J. Prazmowska, *Britain, Poland, and the Eastern Front, 1939* (1987). The origins and subsequent history of the German-Soviet Pact of August 23, 1939, are recounted in G. L. Weinberg, *Germany and the Soviet Union, 1939–1941* (1954), and in A. Read and D. Fisher, *The Deadly Embrace: Hitler, Stalin and the Nazi-Soviet Pact, 1939–1941* (1989); valuable also is J. E. McSherry, *Stalin, Hitler, and Europe* (2 vols., 1968–1972).

The role of the United States in these years is traced in two comprehensive volumes by W. L. Langer and S. E. Gleason, *The Challenge to Isolation, 1937–1940* (1952) and *The Undeclared War, 1940–1941* (1953). Other important studies include R.

Ferrell, *American Diplomacy in the Great Depression* (1957); C. A. MacDonald, *The United States, Britain, and Appeasement, 1930–1939* (1981); D. Reynolds, *The Creation of the Anglo-American Alliance, 1937–1941* (1982); and W. R. Rock, *Chamberlain and Roosevelt: British Foreign Policy and the United States, 1937–1940* (1989). The most informative study of Roosevelt's foreign policy, sympathetic yet critical, is R. Dallek, *Franklin D. Roosevelt and American Foreign Policy, 1932–1945** (1979). For the war years it may be supplemented by J. M. Burns, *Roosevelt: The Soldier of Freedom** (1970); F. Marks, *Wind over Sand: The Diplomacy of Franklin Roosevelt* (1988); and W. F. Kimball, *The Juggler: Franklin Roosevelt as Wartime Statesman* (1991).

The expansion of the European conflict into a global war is related in W. Carr, *Poland to Pearl Harbor: The Making of the Second World War** (1985). The events in East Asia may also be studied through A. Iriye, *The Origins of the Second World War in Asia and the Pacific** (1987); D. J. Lu, *From the Marco Polo Bridge to Pearl Harbor* (1961); R. Butow, *Tojo and the Coming of the War* (1961); and P. W. Schroeder, *The Axis Alliance and Japanese-American Relations, 1941* (1963). The attack of December 7, 1941, is studied in R. Wohlstetter, *Pearl Harbor: Warning and Decision** (1962); G. W. Prange, *At Dawn We Slept: The Untold Story of Pearl Harbor** (1981); and H. C. Clausen and B. Lee, *Pearl Harbor: Final Judgment* (1992), an updating of an official inquiry first published in 1946.

Hitler's relations with Italy are discussed in F. W. Deakin's detailed *The Brutal Friendship,** cited in Chapter XIX; and with Japan, in J. Menzel, *Hitler and Japan: The Hollow Alliance* (1966), and J. P. Fox, *Germany and the Far Eastern Crisis: A Study in Diplomacy and Ideology* (1982).

The War: Military Aspects

Of the numerous narrative histories of the war, the most comprehensive and up-to-date syntheses are M. Gilbert, *The Second World War* (rev. 1991); J. Keegan, *The Second World War* (1989); H. P. Willmott, *The Great Crusade* (1990); R. A. C. Parker, *Struggle for Survival** (1990); and G. L. Weinberg, *A World at Arms: A Global History of World War II* (1993). Keegan has also edited the superb *Times Atlas of the*

Second World War (1989). An impressive collaborative volume is J. Campbell (ed.), *The Experience of World War II* (1989). Two outstanding older accounts are P. Calvocoressi and G. Wint, *Total War: Causes and Courses of the Second World War** (1972; rev. 1990), and G. Wright, *The Ordeal of Total War, 1939–1945** (1968), focusing on Europe, in the Langer series. There are many narrative histories and accounts of specific campaigns and battles. W. S. Churchill, *The Second World War** (6 vols., 1948–1953; 1 vol. abr., 1959), already mentioned, in an indispensable, full-dress history by the historian-statesman, written in the grand style, but it should be read in conjunction with other studies now available.

Many volumes of the detailed official histories of the United Kingdom, Canada, and the United States have appeared. Of special note is the official U.S. Navy history in fifteen volumes prepared by S. E. Morison (1947 ff.) and published in a one-volume abridgement as *The Two-Ocean War: A Short History of the United States Navy in the Second World War* (1963). On naval warfare, there also are available R. Hough, *The Longest Battle: The War at Sea, 1939–1945* (1986), and J. Creswell, *Sea Warfare, 1939–1945* (1967). The air war as fought by each of the major powers is examined in R. J. Overy, *The Air War, 1939–1945* (1980), and the great air battle of the war in R. Hough and D. Richards, *The Battle of Britain* (1989). C. K. Webster and N. N. Frankland, *Strategic Air Offensive against Germany, 1939–1945* (1961), official postwar surveys, and a number of other books demonstrate that Allied strategic bombing was less effective than thought at the time.

The war of intelligence is assessed in detail in F. H. Hinsley and others, *British Intelligence in the Second World War* (5 vols., 1979–1991). The Allied penetration and use of the highest German military code in Operation Ultra, not revealed or utilized in writing the history of the war until the 1970s, is recounted in F. Winterbotham, *The Ultra Secret* (1974); R. Bennett, *Ultra in the West* (1979); P. Calvocoressi, *Top Secret Ultra* (1980); and R. Lewin, *Ultra Goes to War* (1979). Lewin has also described the American breaking of the Japanese codes in *The American Magic** (1982), also studied at length in J. Drea, *MacArthur's Ultra: Codebreaking and the War against Japan, 1942–1945* (1992).

Strategy and high-level decisions, Allied and Axis, are discussed in K. R. Greenfield (ed.), *Command Decisions* (1959); B. H. Liddell Hart, *The Other Side of the Hill** (rev. 1951); H.-A. Jacobsen and J. Rohwer (eds.), *Decisive Battles of World War II: The German View* (1965); H. Trevor-Roper (ed.), *From Blitzkrieg to Defeat* (1965); and D. Downing, *The Devil's Virtuosos: German Generals at War, 1940–1945* (1977). Useful also is H.-A. Jacobsen and A. L. Smith, Jr., (eds.), *World War II: Policy and Strategy* (1979), a selection of documents and commentary.

The military aspects of France's defeat in 1940 may be approached through A. Horne, *To Lose a Battle: France, 1940* (1969), the most detailed account; G. Chapman, *Why France Fell: The Defeat of the French Army in 1940* (1969); A. Beaufre, *1940: The Fall of France* (trans. 1968); and J. A. Gunsberg, *Divided and Conquered: The French High Command and the Defeat of the West, 1940* (1979). The background to the defeat is explored in P. C. F. Bankwitz, *Maxime Weygand and Civil-Military Relations in Modern France* (1967); J. M. Hughes, *To the Maginot Line: The Politics of French Military Preparation in the 1920s* (1971); R. F. Young, *In Command of France: French Foreign Policy and Military Planning, 1933–1940* (1978); and M. S. Alexander, *The Republic in Danger: General Maurice Gamelin and the Politics of French Defence, 1938–1940* (1993). The relationship with Britain is studied in E. M. Gates, *End of the Affair: The Collapse of the Anglo-French Alliance, 1939–1940* (1981), and P. H. M. Bell, *A Certain Eventuality: Britain and the Fall of France* (1975). W. L. Shirer, *The Collapse of the Third Republic: An Inquiry into the Fall of France in 1940** (1969), is a thoughtful account by a reflective journalist, and M. Bloch, *Strange Defeat** (1940), a moving memoir by the eminent medievalist executed as a member of the Resistance. His biography by C. Fink (1989) has been cited in the introduction.

The Russo-Finnish conflict of 1939–1940 is narrated in R. W. Condon, *The Winter War* (1972); F. Chew, *The White Death* (1971); and M. Jacobson, *The Diplomacy of the Winter War* (1961). For the war in eastern Europe after the German invasion one may read A. Werth, *Russia at War, 1941–1945** (1964); A. Clark, *Barbarossa: The Russian-German Conflict, 1941–1945*

(1965); A. Seaton, *The Russo-German War* (1971); E. F. Ziemke and M. E. Bauer, *Moscow to Stalingrad: Decision in the East* (1987); and two impressive military narratives of Stalin's war with Germany by J. Erickson: *The Road to Stalingrad* (1975, 1984) and *The Road to Berlin* (1984), along with the same author's *The Soviet High Command, 1918–1941* (1962). A. Seaton, *Stalin as Military Commander* (1976), is a careful study. A. Paul, *Katyn: The Untold Story of Stalin's Polish Massacre* (1991), recounts the early episode of the war in which thousands of Polish officers and soldiers captured in 1939 lost their lives at Soviet hands, as confirmed by newly opened archives.

The war in the Pacific is ably presented in C. Bateson, *The War with Japan* (1968); S. Ienaga, *The Pacific War: World War II and the Japanese, 1931–1945* (trans. 1978), by a distinguished Japanese historian; and in A. Iriye, *Power and Culture: The Japanese-American War, 1941–1945** (1981), offering some new insights. M. and S. Harries, *Soldiers of the Sun* (1992), cited in Chapter XVIII, recounts the story of the imperial army in conquest and collapse, while H. T. and T. F. Cooke, *Japan at War: An Oral History* (1992) provides unusual eyewitness testimony to Japanese military conduct. A far-reaching study examining the impact of the war on Asia is C. Thorne, *The Far Eastern War: States and Societies, 1941–1945** (1985; reissued with this title, 1988), while the same author examines the coalition that fought the war in *Allies of a Kind: The United States, Britain, and the War against Japan, 1941–1945** (1979). On the last phase in the Pacific, R. Butow, *Japan's Decision to Surrender** (1954), and W. Craig, *The Fall of Japan* (1968), help illuminate controversies over how inevitable or imminent Japan's surrender was. On the development of the atomic bomb and its first use, one may read W. L. Laurence, *Dawn over Zero* (1946), and R. Rhodes, *The Making of the Atomic Bomb* (1986), a remarkably comprehensive account; and on the German effort to create the bomb, M. Walker, *German National Socialism and the Quest for Nuclear Power, 1939–1949** (1990).

Biographical Accounts

M. Gilbert has completed a monumental official biography, *Winston S. Churchill*

(8 vols., 1966–1989), already mentioned; the first two volumes, for the years before 1914, were prepared by Churchill's son, Randolph Churchill. Accompanying each volume are companion volumes reproducing the sources. The war years are studied in Vol. VI, *First Hour, 1939–1941** (1983), and Vol. VII, *Road to Victory, 1941–1945** (1986), and the postwar years in *Never Despair, 1945–1965* (1989). The biography is written with clarity and extraordinary chronological detail but falls short in analysis, comment, or reference to divergent interpretations. Gilbert has also written a one-volume synthesis along much the same lines, *Churchill: A Life** (1992). Another large-scale biography in progress, W. Manchester, *The Last Lion*, of which Vol. II, *Alone, 1932–1940* (1989), describes the prewar years, is excessively adulatory; while J. Charmley, *Churchill: The End of Glory* (1993) unconvincingly argues that Churchill waged an unnecessary war, disastrous for Britain's future. A balanced brief study is K. Robbins, *Churchill** (1992), in the Profiles in Power series. For the early years, focusing on miscalculations and mistakes, R. Rhodes James has written *Churchill: A Study in Failure, 1900–1939* (1970). Churchill's role as wartime leader is scrutinized in T. Ben-Moshe, *Churchill: Strategy and History* (1993), and in essays in two collaborative volumes edited by A. J. P. Taylor and others (1969), and by R. Blake and W. R. Louis (1993). Although demythologizing Churchill may be necessary, D. Irving, *Churchill's War: The Struggle for Power* (1989), the first volume of a projected larger work, is unpersuasively hostile. Irving, an Australian historian, sometimes offers new materials or new ways of looking at older materials but strains credulity; in *Hitler's War** (1977), he absolves Hitler of any direct responsibility for the war or for the Nazi atrocities. His biography of Rommel, *The Trail of the Fox* (1977), however, is more balanced.

Even a limited listing of studies relating to Allied military leaders would have to include F. C. Pogue on George C. Marshall (4 vols., 1963–1987), and M. Stoler on the same subject (1989); S. E. Ambrose on Dwight D. Eisenhower (2 vols.; 1 vol. abr., 1990); M. Schaller on Douglas MacArthur (1989); A. Bryant on Field Marshal Sir Alan Brooke (2 vols., 1957–1959); R. Lamb (1984); N. Hamilton (1985) on Montgomery; and P. Ziegler on Mountbatten (1985).

The War: Social and Economic Impact

For the social and economic impact of the war the best one-volume synthesis is A. S. Milward, *War, Economy, and Society, 1939–1945** (History of the World Economy in the Twentieth Century series, 1977). For the British wartime scene, A. Calder, *The People's War: Britain, 1939–1945* (1969), is highly informative, and there are excellent volumes in the U.K. official history, among them W. C. Hancock and M. M. Gowing, *British War Economy* (1949); R. M. Titmuss, *Problems of Social Policy* (1950); and M. M. Postan, *British War Production* (1950). A graphic documentary and photographic account is A. Marwick, *The Home Front: The British and the Second World War* (1977). E. S. Beck, *The European Home Fronts, 1939–1945** (1993) is a useful brief synthesis. The wartime Soviet scene is studied in detail in J. Barber and M. Harrison, *The Soviet Home Front, 1941–1945: A Social and Economic History of the U.S.S.R. in World War II** (1992). Various phases of the American domestic scene are treated in A. R. Buchanan, *The United States and World War II** (2 vols., 1964); J. M. Blum, *V for Victory: Politics and American Culture during World War II* (1976); and A. M. Winkler, *Home Front U.S.A.** (1986). Both W. L. O'Neill, *America's Fight at Home and Abroad in World War II* (1993), and M. C. C. Adams, *The Best War Ever: America and World War II** (1994) deflate military and civilian leadership. Similarly, on a broader scale, P. Fussell, *Wartime: Understanding and Behavior in the Second World War** (1989), ironically contrasts government rhetoric and government shortcomings.

The entry of women into the wartime labor force is examined in K. Anderson, *Wartime Women: Sex Roles, Family Relations, and the Status of Women during World War II* (1981); L. J. Rupp, *Mobilizing Women for War: German and American Propaganda, 1939–1945* (1978); and in essays in M. R. Higonnet and others, *Behind the Lines: Gender and the Two World Wars** (1987).

That Hitler did not prepare for war in depth because he expected a quick victory emerges clearly from B. H. Klein, *Germany's Economic Preparations for War* (1959); B. A. Carroll, *Design for Total War: Arms and Economics in the Third Reich*

(1968); and A. S. Milward, *The German Economy at War* (1965). In this connection Albert Speer's memoirs, *Inside the Third Reich* (1974), are revealing if read critically.

Hitler's New Order: Collaboration and Resistance

The first attempt to study the German occupation of Europe as a whole was a *Survey of International Affairs* volume covering the years 1939–1946, *Hitler's Europe* (1954). Numerous studies have since appeared on individual countries, many on the French experience.

For Vichy the best study is R. O. Paxton, *Vichy France: Old Guard and New Order, 1940–1944** (1972); the same author also has written *Parades and Politics at Vichy* (1966), and with M. R. Marrus, *Vichy France and the Jews* (1981), which shows French culpability for many acts during the German occupation. The latter volume may be compared with S. Zucotti, *The Holocaust, the French, and the Jews* (1993), a valuable study but perhaps insufficiently critical of the French. A good brief introduction is H. R. Kedward, *Occupied France: Collaboration and Resistance** (1985). On collaboration, one may study B. M. Gordon, *Collaborationism in France during the Second World War* (1980), while J. F. Sweets, *Choices in Vichy France: The French under Nazi Occupation* (1986), poignantly demonstrates the complexities of collaboration and resistance. A. S. Milward, *The New Order and the French Economy* (1970), surveys the economic aspects of the regime, while cultural aspects may be approached through A. Y. Kaplan, *Fascism, Literature, and French Intellectual Life* (1986); G. Hirshfeld and P. Marsh (eds.), *Collaboration in France: Politics and Culture during the Nazi Occupation, 1940–1944* (1989); and M. C. Cone, *Artists under Vichy* (1992). A thoughtful study, H. Rousso, *The Vichy Syndrome: History and Memory in France since 1944** (trans. 1991), explores French attitudes toward the Vichy trauma.

American relations with Vichy are studied in W. L. Langer, *Our Vichy Gamble** (1947), a somewhat defensive account, and British relations in R. T. Thomas, *Britain and Vichy: The Dilemma of Anglo-French Relations, 1940–1942* (1979). There is a biography of Laval by H. Cole (1963), and a detailed study focusing on diplomatic events by G. Warner, *Pierre Laval and the Eclipse*

of France, 1931–1945 (1968), while H. R. Lottman, *Petain, Hero or Traitor* (1985), highlights but does not resolve the ambivalent role played by the Marshal.

The Resistance in France may be studied in D. Schoenbrun, *Soldiers of the Night: The Story of the French Resistance* (1980); M. R. D. Foot, *SOE in France* (1966); J. F. Sweets, *The Politics of Resistance in France, 1940–1944* (1976); H. R. Kedward, *Resistance in Vichy France: Ideas and Motivation in the Southern Zone, 1940–1942** (1978); and M. L. Rossiter, *Women in the Resistance** (1985). The liberation is dramatically described in R. Aron, *France Reborn* (trans. 1964); and related events in P. Novick, *The Resistance versus Vichy: The Purge of Collaborators in Liberated France* (1969), and in H. R. Lottman, *The Purge* (1986). For the years from the 1930s to liberation, Charles de Gaulle's *War Memoirs** (3 vols.; trans. 1958–1960), are indispensable. De Gaulle's wartime difficulties with London and Washington are described in A. L. Funk, *Charles de Gaulle: The Crucial Years, 1943–1944* (1959); M. Viorst, *Hostile Allies: FDR and Charles de Gaulle* (1965); F. Kersaudy, *Churchill and de Gaulle* (1982); and R. Aglion, *Roosevelt and de Gaulle: Allies in Conflict* (trans. 1988), written by one of de Gaulle's diplomats. For de Gaulle, J. Lacouture's biography (2 vols., trans. 1992; 3 vols. in the French original) is the outstanding account: Vol. I, *The Rebel, 1890–1944,** and Vol. II, *The Ruler, 1945–1970.**

Studies of other countries under the German occupation include W. Warmbrunn, *The Dutch under German Occupation, 1940–1945* (1963); G. Hirschfeld, *Nazi Rule and Dutch Collaboration, 1940–1945* (trans. 1988); A. S. Milward, *The Fascist Economy in Norway* (1972); R. L. Braham, *The Hungarian Labor Service System, 1939–1945* (1977); J. Gillingham, *Belgian Business and the Nazi New Order* (1977); and M. Mazower, *Inside Hitler's Greece: The Experience of Occupation, 1941–1944* (1993). The Polish experience is recounted in J. T. Gross, *Polish Society under German Occupation: The Generalgouvernement, 1939–1944* (1979), and in R. C. Lukas, *The Forgotten Holocaust: The Poles under German Occupation, 1939–1944* (1986). In its Norwegian setting, collaborationism is illuminated in detail in O. K. Hoidal, *Quisling: A Study in Treason* (1989). For the Soviet Union, two studies demonstrating, among other things, the ineptitude of the Germans in exploiting existing discontent are A. Dallin, *German Rule in Russia, 1941–1945* (rev. 1981), and T. Schulte, *The German Army and Nazi Policies in Occupied Russia, 1941–1945* (1989). Also illuminating are J. A. Armstrong, *Ukrainian Nationalism, 1939–1945* (1955), and C. Andrew, *Vlasov and the Russian Liberation Movement, 1941–1945* (1986), on the collaborationist general.

For the Europe-wide Resistance, there is the informative study by H. Michel, *The Shadow War: The European Resistance, 1939–1945* (trans. 1972); the useful though somewhat anecdotal M. R. D. Foot, *Resistance: European Resistance to Nazism, 1940–1945* (1977); and J. Haestrup, *European Resistance Movements, 1939–1945* (rev. 1981), a comprehensive account. The renovative spirit of the Resistance and its message for the postwar world are captured in J. D. Wilkinson, *The Intellectual Resistance in Europe* (1981). Books on the German Resistance have been cited in Chapter XIX.

The Holocaust

There is a large literature on the grim subject of the systematic mass slaughter by the Nazis of the European Jews during the war years. The most informative and comprehensive study is R. Hilberg, *The Destruction of the European Jews** (3 vols., rev. 1983; 1 vol. abr., 1985), which may be supplemented by the same author's *Perpetrators, Victims, Bystanders: The Jewish Catastrophe, 1933–1945* (1992), adding additional insights. Other important studies are M. Gilbert, *The Holocaust: The History of the Jews of Europe during the Second World War** (1986); L. S. Dawidowicz, *The War against the Jews, 1933–1945** (1976), cited earlier; Y. Bauer, *A History of the Holocaust** (1982); and L. Yahil, *The Holocaust: The Fate of European Jewry, 1932–1945** (1987, trans. 1990). A provocative interpretive account is A. J. Mayer, *Why Did the Heavens Not Darken? The "Final Solution" in History* (1989), which sees the root cause in earlier twentieth-century destructiveness. An exhaustive reference work, with contributions by many scholars and with bibliographies in many languages, is I. Gutman (ed.), *Encyclopedia of the Holocaust* (4 vols., 1990), while M. Gilbert has edited an *Atlas of the Holocaust* (1993).

H. Fein, *Accounting for Genocide: National Responses and Jewish Victimization during the Holocaust* (1979), examines the diversity of the experience in different countries, while R. L. Braham, *The Politics of Genocide: The Holocaust in Hungary* (2 vols., 1981), is an outstanding study of one country. A key episode of Jewish resistance is recounted in I. Gutman, *The Jews of Warsaw, 1939–1943: Ghetto, Underground, Revolt* (trans. 1982).

Among many studies of the concentration and death camps are E. Kogon, *The Theory and Practice of Hell** (1950), one of the earliest books by a survivor; T. Des Pres, *The Survivor: An Anatomy of Life in the Death Camps** (1976); T. Segev, *Soldiers of Evil: The Commandants of the Nazi Concentration Camps* (trans. 1989); and R. J. Lifton, *The Death Doctors: Medical Killing and the Psychology of Genocide* (1987). For the debate over the origin of the Holocaust, i.e., between "intentionalists," who see the genocidal destruction as motivated from the beginning by Hitler and his ideology, and "functionalists," who see it as developing incrementally once the Nazis controlled Eastern Europe, the best synthesis is C. Browning, *The Path to Genocide: Essays on Launching the Final Solution** (1993). Hitler's fundamental responsibility is described in G. Fleming, *Hitler and the Final Solution** (1984), and R. Breitman, *The Architect of Genocide: The Final Solution* (1991). That some issues remain unresolved emerges from the essays in F. Furet (ed.), *Unanswered Questions: Nazi Germany and the Genocide of the Jews** (1989).

How historians have written about the subject is explored in L. S. Dawidowicz, *The Holocaust and the Historians** (1981), and in M. R. Marrus, *The Holocaust in History* (1987), a highly rewarding study. A much discussed essay on the question of responsibility and guilt is H. Arendt, *Eichmann in Jerusalem: A Report on the Banality of Evil** (1963), written at the time of the trial of the high-ranking bureaucrat who carried out the operation. Y. Bauer, *The Holocaust in Historical Perspective* (1978), argues the uniqueness of the episode and disputes later misuses of the word "genocide"; on this, one may also read L. Kuper, *Genocide: Its Political Use in the Twentieth Century* (1982). The acrimonious debate among German historians in the mid-1980s, in which E. Nolte and others sought to mitigate the evils of the Holocaust by comparing it to other twentieth-century atrocities such as those of Stalin, is thoughtfully explored in C. S. Maier, *The Unmasterable Past: History, Holocaust, and German National Identity* (1988), and in R. J. Evans, *In Hitler's Shadow: West German Historians and the Attempt to Escape from the Nazi Past* (1989). Broader efforts to deny or minimize the Holocaust are critically scrutinized in two persuasive books: D. E. Lipstadt, *The Growing Assault on Truth and Memory* (1993), and P. Vidal-Naquet, *Assassins of Memory: Essays on the Denial of the Holocaust** (trans. 1993).

There is a large literature on the failure of the authorities in the United States, Britain, and the Vatican to rescue the doomed European Jews; among the more searching inquiries are B. Wasserstein, *Britain and the Jews of Europe, 1939–1945* (1979); M. Gilbert, *Auschwitz and the Allies* (1981); W. Laqueur, *The Terrible Secret** (1980); S. Friedländer, *Pius XII and the Third Reich* (1966); and J. F. Morley, *Vatican Diplomacy and the Jews during the Holocaust, 1939–1945* (1980). For the United States, A. D. Morse, *While Six Million Died* (1968), may be supplemented with books, among others, by D. S. Wyman (1968, 1984), S. M. Finger (1980), Y. Bauer (1981), and D. E. Lipstadt (1986). For the Nazi atrocities against other ethnic groups in Europe, including Russians, Poles, Gypsies, and others, one may read B. Wytwycky, *The Other Holocaust: Many Circles of Hell* (1986), a brief introduction; M. Burleigh and W. Wippermann, *The Racial State in Germany, 1933–1945* (1992), cited in Chapter XIX; and the essays in M. Berenbaum (ed.), *A Mosaic of Victims: Non-Jews Persecuted and Murdered by the Nazis* (1992).

The proceedings of the Nuremberg trials have been published as International Military Tribunal, *Trial of the Major War Criminals before the International Military Tribunal, 1945–1946* (42 vols., 1947–1949), and as *Nazi Conspiracy and Aggression* (8 vols., 2 supplements, 1946–1958). Two informative books on the origin and nature of the trials by B. F. Smith, *Reaching Judgment at Nuremberg* (1977) and *The Road to Nuremberg* (1981) argue that the trials prevented an anarchic bloodbath and should not be dismissed as merely "victor's justice". Other thoughtful discussions are found in P. Calvocoressi, *Nuremberg: The Facts, the Law, and the Consequences* (1948); E. Davidson, *The Trial of the Germans: Nuremberg, 1945–1946* (1966); W. Maser, *Nuremberg: A Nation on Trial* (1979); R. E. Conot,

Justice at Nuremberg* (1983); and T. Taylor *The Anatomy of the Nuremberg Trials: A Personal Memoir* (1993), by a chief prosecutor who analyzes deficiencies in the procedures and questions the effectiveness of the trials as a deterrent to later wrongdoing. The trials of the Japanese war leaders are critically analyzed in R. Minear, *Victor's Justice: The Tokyo War Crimes Trial* (1979), which should be supplemented by P. R. Piccigallo, *The Japanese on Trial: Allied War Crimes Operations in the East, 1945–1951* (1979), and A. C. Brackman, *The Other Nuremberg: The Untold Story of the Tokyo War Crimes Trials** (1987).

Wartime Diplomacy and Origins of the Cold War

A large literature has emerged stressing the origins of the Cold War in Soviet-American wartime relations. Wartime diplomacy may be approached through the latter volumes of Churchill's history and through Vols. VI and VII of M. Gilbert's biography of Churchill, described earlier. E. L. Woodward, *British Foreign Policy in the Second World War* (5 vols., 1962–1977), is based on the Foreign Office archives, to which the author was given early access. The volumes of H. Feis, sympathetic to the Western leaders, are indispensable as an introduction: *Churchill, Roosevelt, Stalin: The War They Waged and the Peace They Sought** (1957), covering the years from 1941 to the collapse of Germany; *Between War and Peace: The Potsdam Conference** (1960); and on the last phase, *The Atomic Bomb and the End of the War in the Pacific** (1961, 1966). Of special value are G. Smith, *American Diplomacy during the Second World War, 1941–1945** (1965), and the volume on Roosevelt's foreign policy by R. Dallek (1979), cited earlier. Among other studies are V. Mastny, *Russia's Road to the Cold War: Diplomacy, Warfare, and the Politics of Communism, 1941–1945* (1979), projecting a case for the logic of Soviet policy-making, and R. V. Daniels, *Russia: The Roots of Confrontation** (1985).

The rift over the opening of a second front is thoughtfully examined in M. Stoler, *The Politics of the Second Front* (1977). Other key studies are G. C. Herring, *Aid to Russia, 1941–1946: Strategy, Diplomacy and the Origins of the Cold War* (1973); M. Kitchen, *British Policy toward the Soviet Union during the Second World War* (1987);

S. M. Miner, *Between Churchill and Stalin: The Soviet Union, Great Britain, and the Origins of the Grand Alliance* (1989); and K. Saintsbury, *The Turning Point* (1985), which sees the wartime conferences in 1943 and not Yalta as pivotal for future troubles. For the Yalta Conference one should read among other accounts, R. D. Buhite, *Decision at Yalta* (1986), and L. C. Gardner, *Spheres of Influence: The Great Powers Partition Europe: From Munich to Yalta* (1993).

On the American use of the atomic bomb, one may read M. J. Sherwin, *A World Destroyed: The Atomic Bomb and the Grand Alliance* (1975), an impressive, balanced study and G. Herken, *The Winning Weapon: The Atomic Bomb in the Cold War, 1945–1950.* Two of several books criticizing the use of the bomb are G. Alperowitz, *Atomic Diplomacy: Hiroshima and Potsdam** (rev. 1985), and B. J. Bernstein, *The Atomic Bomb: The Critical Issues** (1975).

On population movements during and following the war there are available J. B. Schechtman, *European Population Transfer, 1939–1945* (1946); E. M. Kulischer, *Europeans on the Move: War and Population Changes, 1917–1947* (1948); M. J. Proudfoot, *European Refugees, 1939–1952* (1957); and M. R. Marrus, *The Unwanted: European Refugees in the Twentieth Century** (1985), cited in Chapter XVIII.

Problems and Readings*

For prewar diplomacy and the war there are available: H. W. Gatzke (ed.), *European Diplomacy between Two Wars, 1919–1939* (1972); L. F. Schaefer (ed.), *The Ethiopian Crisis: Touchstone of Appeasement?* (1961); G. Jackson (ed.), *The Spanish Civil War: Domestic Crisis or International Conspiracy?* (1967); A. Guttmann (ed.), *American Neutrality and the Spanish Civil War* (1963); F. L. Loewenheim (ed.), *Peace or Appeasement: Hitler, Chamberlain, and the Munich Crisis* (1965); D. E. Lee (ed.), *Munich: Blunder, Plot, or Tragic Necessity?* (1969); S. M. Osgood (ed.), *The Fall of France, 1940* (rev. 1972); I. Morris (ed.), *Japan, 1931–1945: Militarism, Fascism, Japanism?* (1963); H. L. Trefousse, *Pearl Harbor: The Continuing Controversy* (1982); K. W. Eubank (ed.), *World War II: Roots and Causes* (rev. 1991); L. S. Dawidowicz (ed.), *A Holocaust Reader* (1976); and D. Niewyk (ed.), *The Holocaust* (1991). Available in

the Anvil series in N. Levin *The Holocaust Years* (1990). The debate among German historians over the uniqueness of the Holocaust may be sampled in G. Thomas (ed.), *The Unresolved Past: A Debate in German History* (1991).

XXI. The Postwar Era: The Age of the Superpowers

The Cold War: The Opening Decade

Several books on the wartime origins of the Soviet-Western rift have been described at the end of the previous chapter. Among the many books that examine Soviet behavior and American perceptions and misperceptions in the early postwar years are J. L. Gaddis, *The United States and the Origins of the Cold War, 1941–1947** (1972); D. Yergin, *Shattered Peace: The Origins of the Cold War and the National Security State* (1977); D. Sharnik, *Inside the Cold War* (1987); R. B. Woods and H. Jones, *Dawning of the Cold War* (1991); and W. LaFeber, *America, Russia, and the Cold War 1945–1990** (rev. 1991). Especially informative are A. B. Ulam's *The Rivals: American and Russia since World War II* (1971) and *Dangerous Relations: The Soviet Union in World Politics, 1970–1982* (1983). Valuable also is W. I. Cohen, *America in the Age of Soviet Power, 1945–1991* (1993), the fourth volume in the *Cambridge History of American Foreign Relations.* Two early efforts to examine the tensions in historical perspective, i.e., going back to 1917, are L. Halle, *The Cold War as History* (1967), and A. Fontaine, *History of the Cold War* (2 vols.; trans. 1968–1969). H. Feis, *From Trust to Terror: The Onset of the Cold War, 1945–1950** (1970), completes his series of wartime diplomatic histories. A large revisionist literature blames American postwar political and economic ambitions or miscalculations for the Cold War. A sampling would include books by W. A. Williams (1952, 1959), K. Ingram (1955), D. F. Fleming (1961), G. Kolko (1969, 1972), L. C. Gardner (1970), and T. G. Paterson (1973, 1979). For guidance to the literature as a whole one may turn to J. L. Black, *Origins, Evolution, and Nature of the Cold War: An Annotated Bibliography* (1985), and J. W. Young, *The Longman Companion to Cold War and Détente, 1941–1991** (1993).

The transition from war to postwar is explored in R. Douglas, *From War to Cold*

War, 1942–1948 (1981); D. Reynolds (ed.), *The Origins of the Cold War in Europe* (1994), with thoughtful essays; and J. L. Gormby, *The Collapse of the Grand Alliance, 1945–1948* (1987). An impressive first volume of a projected large-scale history of the early postwar years has appeared: H. Thomas, *The Beginnings of the Cold War, 1945–1946* (1987), with perceptive insights into the protagonists; and a second detailed account, emphasizing Churchill's role, F. J. Harbutt, *The Iron Curtain: Churchill, America, and the Origins of the Cold War** (1986). The evolution of the Truman Doctrine is studied in T. A. Couloubis, *The U.S., Greece, and Turkey* (1983), and the military and economic assumptions behind Truman's policies in M. P. Leffler, *A Preponderance of Power: National Security, the Truman Administration, and the Cold War* (1992). The president is himself studied in D. McCullough, *Truman** (1992), a colorful biography which, however, ignores scholarly controversies over the origins of the Cold War and related matters. On the diplomat who helped shape the American containment policy and later regretted the military form that it came to assume, one should read G. F. Kennan, *American Diplomacy** (1951; rev. 1985), and his several other books, along with analyses of his thought and career such as A. D. Mayers, *George Kennan and the Dilemmas of U.S. Foreign Policy** (1988). Kennan, Acheson, and other key American foreign policy figures are also studied in W. Isaacson and E. Thomas, *The Wise Men* (1986). On the "Munich syndrome," or the resolve by Truman and others not to repeat the appeasement of the 1930s, one may read G. Rystad, *Prisoners of the Past* (1982); E. R. May, *The Lessons of the Past: The Use and Misuse of History in American Foreign Policy* (1973); and D. Halberstam, *The Best and the Brightest** (1972), the latter principally on the war in Vietnam. R. Dallek, *The American Style of Foreign Policy: Cultural Politics and Foreign Affairs** (1990), assesses the continuing impact of domestic pressures on American foreign policy.

The revolutionary implications of nuclear weapons for the post-1945 world are discussed in M. Mandelbaum's *The United States and Nuclear Weapons, 1946–1976* (1979) and *The Nuclear Revolution: International Politics before and after Hiroshima** (1981). Efforts at disarmament and arms control are examined in R. E. Powaski,

March to Armageddon: The United States and the Nuclear Arms Race, 1939 to the Present (1987). Additional books on nuclear arms and disarmament will be suggested in later chapters.

The origins and founding of the United Nations are studied in R. B. Russell, *A History of the United Nations, 1940–1945* (1958); F. P. King, *The New Internationalism: Allied Policy and the European Peace, 1939–1945* (1973); and R. C. Hildebrand, *Dumbarton Oaks: The Origins of the United Nations and the Search for Postwar Security* (1990). Its subsequent history may be traced in C. M. Eichelberger, *The UN: The First Twenty Years* (1965), and in E. Luard, *A History of the United Nations*, (2 vols., 1982–1989). The limitations of international cooperation are assessed in T. M. Franck, *Nation against Nation* (1985), and A. Roberts, *United Nations, Divided World* (1988). Books that examine Western Europe's role in the postwar setting include A. W. DePorte, *Europe between the Superpowers: The Enduring Alliance* (rev. 1986), and A. Grosser, *The Western Alliance: European-American Relations since 1945* (trans. 1980). The origins of the North Atlantic Treaty Organization may be studied in T. P. Ireland, *Creating the Entangling Alliance: The Origins of the North Atlantic Treaty Organization* (1981).

Economic Reconstruction and the Reshaping of the World Economy

The most informative studies of postwar economic reconstruction and of the economic growth that followed for close to three decades are H. Van der Wee, *Prosperity and Upheaval: The World Economy, 1945–1980** (History of the World Economy in the Twentieth Century series, 1986), and P. Armstrong, A. Glyn, and J. Harrison, *Capitalism since World War II: The Making and Breakup of the Great Boom* (1984). They may be supplemented by the essays in S. A. Marglin and J. B. Schor (eds.), *The Golden Age of Capitalism: Reinterpreting the Postwar Experience** (1990).

The Bretton Woods monetary arrangements are examined in A. E. Ecks, Jr., *A Search for Solvency: Bretton Woods and the International Monetary System, 1941–1971* (1975); R. Solomon, *The International Monetary System, 1945–1976* (1977); and B. Tew, *The Evolution of the International Monetary System, 1945–1981* (1981). The arrangements for Western Europe are studied in P. Ludlow, *The Making of the European Monetary System* (1982).

For European economic developments one may turn also to C. M. Cipolla (ed.), *The Fontana Economic History of Europe*, Vols. V and VI (1976). Thoughtful surveys of Europe in the postwar era include W. Laqueur, *Europe in Our Time: A History, 1945–1992** (rev. 1992); F. Tipton and R. Aldrich, *An Economic and Social History of Europe, 1939 to the Present** (1987), the sequel to a volume cited in Chapter XIV; and D. Urwin, *Western Europe since 1945** (rev. 1989).

For the immediate postwar years and the American role in reconstruction, M. J. Hogan, *The Marshall Plan: America, Britain, and the Reconstruction of Western Europe, 1947–1952** (1987), is an outstanding account. Other books that merit attention are A. S. Milward, *The Reconstruction of Western Europe, 1945–1951* (1984), which credits European initiative and skills as much as American aid; J. Gimbel, *The Origins of the Marshall Plan* (1976); C. L. Mee, *The Marshall Plan and the Launching of the Pax Americana* (1989); and D. W. Ellwood, *Rebuilding Europe: Western Europe, America, and Postwar Reconstruction, 1945–1955** (1992).

An impressive synthesis on postwar reconstruction in all aspects is P. Duignan and L. H. Gann, *The Rebirth of the West: Culture, Politics, and Society, 1945–1958* (1990). Some of the social consequences of the economic changes in Europe are also explored in S. Rothman, *European Society and Politics: Britain, France, and Germany** (1976), and A. Sampson, *The New Europeans* (rev. 1971). A special subject receives attention in two books by S. Castles: *Here for Good: Western Europe's New Ethnic Minorities (1984)* and *Migrant Workers in European Societies** (1989).

The postwar welfare state is carefully examined by the British study group, Political and Economic Planning, in *Economic Planning and Policies in Britain, France, and Germany* (1968); and in D. E. Ashford, *The Emergence of the Welfare States* (1987). Detailed analyses are available in P. Flora (ed.), *Growth to Limits: The Western European Welfare States since World War II* (5 vols., 1986–1988). On Keynes and Keynesianism, highly influential in the managed economies of the early postwar decades, one may read R. Lekachman, *The Age of Keynes** (1966), and books on Keynes cited in Chapter XIX. On the role of government one may also read A. Shonfield, *Modern Capitalism: The Changing Balance of Public and Private Power* (1969); S. Lieberman, *The Growth of the European Mixed Economies, 1945–1970* (1977); P. A. Hall, *Governing the Economy: The Politics of State Intervention in Britain and France** (1986); and the essays in A. Graham with A. Seldon (eds.), *Government and Economies in the Postwar World (1990)*.

On Western European economic integration, A. S. Milward, *The European Rescue of the Nation-State* (1992), an outstanding study, explores the origins of the European Community and argues that the intention was not to supersede but to salvage the European nation-state. Highly informative for these years is J. Gillingham, *Coal, Steel, and the Rebirth of Europe, 1945–1955: The Germans and the French from Ruhr Conflict to Economic Community* (1991). Available also are D. W. Urwin, *The Community of Europe: A History of European Integration since 1945** (1991), and two volumes of a detailed study, W. Lipgens, *A History of European Integration* (trans. 1982), for the years 1945–1947 and a sequel volume by M. Jansen (trans. 1975) for the years 1947–1975. The historical background to unification is sketched in J. Lukacs, *Decline and Rise of Europe** (1965). A good brief introduction carrying the story toward the present is F. Lewis, *Europe's Road to Unity** (1992), while a comprehensive treatment is available in D. W. P. Lewis, *The Road to Europe: History, Institutions, and Prospects of European Integration, 1949–1993** (1993). For a key architect of European unity, one may turn to M. and S. Bromberger, *Jean Monnet and the United States of Europe* (trans. 1969), and to D. Brinkley and C. Hackett (ed.), *Jean Monnet: The Path to European Unity* (1991). Additional books on the evolution of the European Community will be cited in Chapter XXIII.

The Western Countries (and Japan) after 1945

For the Western countries many of the books cited for Chapter XIX will also be helpful.

BRITAIN. K. O. Morgan, *The People's Peace: British History, 1945–1990** (1991), and D. Childs, *Britain since 1945* (rev. 1992) provide good overviews, while A. Cairn-cross, *The British Economy since 1945: Economic Policy and Performance, 1945–1990** (1992) analyzes economic developments. Britain's loss of primacy and world power beginning with its "relative decline" in the late nineteenth century is discussed in a number of books, among them: M. W. Kirby, *The Decline of British Power since 1870* (1981); R. Blake, *The Decline of Power, 1915–1964** (1985); B. Porter, *Britain, Europe, and the World, 1850–1986: Delusion of Grandeur** (1987); and two incisive analyses by C. Barnett: *The collapse of British Power* (1986) and *The Pride and the Fall: The Dream and Illusion of Britain as a Great Nation* (1988). An influential study tracing the loss of leadership to a social and educational system that failed to prize entrepreneurship is M. Wiener, *English Culture and the Decline of the Industrial Spirit, 1850–1980* (1981), which may be supplemented by W. D. Rubenstein, *Capitalism, Culture, and Decline in Britain, 1750–1990** (1993). That the reasons for decline remain controversial, however, emerges from the debate and discussion in A. Sked, *Britain's Decline: Problems and Perspectives** (1987), and from the essays in B. Collins and K. Robbins (eds.), *British Culture and Economic Decline* (1990).

The best account of the postwar Labour governments and the emergence of the welfare state is K. O. Morgan, *Labour in Power, 1945–1951** (1984), a balanced study with in-depth portraits of Attlee and other key figures; informative also is H. Pelling, *The Labour Governments, 1945–1951* (1984). The creation and consolidation of the welfare state is studied in P. Gregg, *The Welfare State: An Economic and Social History of Great Britain from 1945 to the Present Day* (1969); S. H. Beer, *British Politics in the Collectivist Age* (1965); and T. O. Lloyd, *Empire to Welfare State, 1906–1985** (rev. 1986). For the social impact one may read A. Marwick, *British Society since 1945** (1982), and A. Sampson, *The New Anatomy of Britain** (rev. 1983). A biographical study of distinction is A. Bullock, *The Life and Times of Ernest Bevin* (3 vols., 1960–1983), and a special subject is explored in Z. A. Layton-Henry, *The Politics of Race in Britain* (1984).

To studies of the Irish question cited in Chapters XIV and XIX and the troubles in Northern Ireland may be added T. Brown, *Ireland: A Social and Cultural History, 1922 to the Present** (1985); O. MacDonagh, *States of Mind: A Study of Anglo-Irish Conflict, 1780–1980** (1983); and P. Arthur and K. Jeffery, *Northern Ireland since 1968** (1988).

FRANCE. Fourth and Fifth Republics. A useful reference tool is W. Northcutt (ed.), *Historical Dictionary of the French Fourth and Fifth Republics, 1946–1991* (1991). The best synthesis for the short-lived Fourth Republic is J.-P. Rioux, *The Fourth Republic, 1944–1958** (trans. 1987), a volume in the *Cambridge History of Modern France*. The formative early years are studied in H. Footitt and J. Simmonds, *France, 1943–1945: The Politics of Liberation* (1988); and A. Shennan, *Rethinking France: Plans for Renewal, 1940–1946* (1989). I. M. Wall, *The United States and the Making of Postwar France, 1945–1954* (1991), and R. Kuisel, *Seducing the French: The Dilemma of Americanization* (1993), are insightful on American political and cultural influences, and Kuisel, *Capitalism and the State in Modern France* (1981), cited in Chapter XIX, places governmental direction of the economy in historical perspective. Mendès-France's reform efforts in the early 1950s are sympathetically portrayed in J. Lacouture, *Pierre Mendès-France* (trans. 1984).

Of the colonial wars that helped bring down the Fourth Republic, the war in Indochina is graphically portrayed in B. B. Fall, *Street without Joy: Indochina at War, 1946–1954* (rev. 1964), and in the same author's *Hell in a Very Small Place: The Siege of Dien Bien Phu* (1967). Other books on Indochina will be cited in Chapter XXIII. The ill-fated effort to retain Algeria is described in A. Horne, *A Savage War of Peace: Algeria, 1954–1962* (1978), a comprehensive account, and J. Talbott, *The War without a Name: France in Algeria, 1954–1962* (1980). Subsequent relationships with Algeria are traced in J. Reudy, *Modern Algeria: The Origins and Development of a Nation* (1983). For the Fifth Republic the best synthesis is S. Berstein, *The Republic of de Gaulle, 1958–1969* (trans. 1993), the eighth volume of the *Cambridge History of Modern France*. One may also read S. Hoffmann's informative *Decline or Renewal? France since the Popular Front: Government and People, 1936–1986** (1988); J. Ardagh, *The New France, De Gaulle and After* (rev. 1977); and M. Larkin, *France since the Popular Front: Government and*

People, 1936–1986* (1988). C. Tilley, *The Contentious French** (1986), cited earlier, puts much of contemporary France in perspective. J. Lacouture's biography of de Gaulle (2 vols., trans. 1992) has been mentioned in Chapter XX; there are also biographical accounts among others, by B. Crozier (1973), B. Ledwidge (1983), D. Cook (1984), and A. Shennan* (1993).

GERMANY. For West Germany during the years of partition an impressive comprehensive narrative is D. L. Bark and D. R. Gress, *A History of West Germany* (2 vols., rev. 1993). A briefer account is M. Balfour, *West Germany: A Contemporary History* (rev. 1982). For the German "economic miracle" one may read H. C. Wallich, *Mainsprings of the German Revival* (1955), and A. Kramer, *The West German Economy, 1945–1955* (1990); and for the powerful economy that later emerged, E. Hartrich, *The Fourth and Richest Reich* (1980), and E. O. Smith, *The West German Economy* (1983). A later assessment is provided in H. Giersch and others, *The Fading Miracle: Four Decades of Market Economy in Germany* (1992). The American role in the early years is studied in G. M. Diefendorf and others (eds.), *American Policy and the Reconstruction of West Germany, 1945–1955* (1993); and of special interest is V. R. Berghahn, *The Americanization of West German Industry, 1945–1973* (1986). For the early years one may also read F. Golay, *The Founding of the Federal Republic of Germany (1955)*, and R. Hiscocks, *The Adenauer Era** (1966). T. Prittie has written biographies of Konrad Adenauer (1972) and of Willy Brandt (1974).

For West and East Germany, including the relationship of the two states over the four postwar decades of partition, two highly informative accounts are H. A. Turner, Jr., *Germany from Partition to Reunification** (rev. 1992), and M. Fulbrook, *The Divided Nation: A History of Germany, 1918–1990** (1992), cited in Chapter XIX. T. Garton Ash, *In Europe's Name: Germany and the Divided Continent* (1993), incisively reassesses Willy Brandt's efforts to improve East-West relations and many other matters. The East German Communist leadership is examined in C. Stern, *Ulbrecht: A Political Biography* (1965), and the effort to prevent the flight of the East Germans after 1961 is studied in P. Galante and P. Miller, *The Berlin Wall* (1965). There are provocative insights into the German search for self-understanding in R. Dahrendorf, *Society and Democracy in Germany* (1967); G. A. Craig, *The Germans** (1982), cited in Chapter XIII; F. Stern, *Dreams and Delusions: The Drama of German History* (1987); and H. James, *A German Identity, 1770–1990* (1990), also cited earlier.

ITALY. Three insightful studies of Italian political life are F. Spotts and T. Wieser, *Italy: A Difficult Democracy** (1986); J. LaPalombara, *Democracy, Italian Style* (1987); and R. Putman, *Making Democracy Work: Civic Traditions in Modern Italy* (1993). All three describe the paradox whereby the country has known remarkable social and economic progress despite political difficulties. For the postwar years one may also read D. W. Ellwood, *Italy, 1943–1945* (1985); N. Kogan, *A Political History of Postwar Italy* (2 vols., 1966–1981); and P. Ginsborg, *A History of Contemporary Italy: Society and Politics, 1943–1988* (1990). The American role in the early years is assessed in J. L. Harper, *America and the Reconstruction of Italy, 1945–1948* (1986). The special role of the Italian Communist party from liberation to the mid-1980s is examined in J. B. Urban, *Moscow and the Italian Communist Party: From Togliatti to Berlinguer* (1986), and in A. De Grand, *The Italian Left in the Twentieth Century: A History of the Socialist and Communist Parties* (1989).

JAPAN. Books that help explain how much and how little Japan was changed by wartime defeat and occupation include W. G. Beasley, *The Rise of Modern Japan** (1991); E. O. Reischauer, *The Japanese Today: Change and Continuity** (1988), and J. W. Dower, *Japan in War and Peace* (1993). For the postwar years one may also turn to A. Gordon (ed.), *Postwar Japan as History** (1993), and P. Bailey, *Japan since 1945** (1993), a brief narrative account. Studies of the occupation include M. Schaller, *The American Occupation of Japan* (1985); H. B. Schonberger, *Aftermath of War* (1989); and R. E. Ward and Y. Sakamoto (eds.), *Democratizing Japan: The Allied Occupation* (1987). Among studies of the economy are J. B. Cohen, *Japan's Post-War Economy* (1958); G. C. Allen, *Japan's Economic Recovery* (1958); and for the later expansion, H. Patrick and H. Rosovsky (eds.), *Asia's New Giant: How the Japanese Economy Works* (1976). Of special interest are C.

Johnson, *MITI and the Japanese Miracle: The Growth of Industrial Policy, 1925–1974* (1982), on the government research and development agency, and W. W. Lockwood, *State and Economic Enterprise in Japan* (1986). A critical assessment in the mid-1990s is C. Wood, *The Bubble Economy* (1993). There are valuable insights into the Japanese political culture in M. Masao, *Thought and Behavior in Modern Japanese Politics* (1963); K. van Wolferen, *The Enigma of Japanese Power: People and Politics in a Stateless Nation* (1989); and C. Gluck and S. R. Graubard (eds.), *Showa: The Japan of Hirohito* (1993).

THE UNITED STATES. Although no listing on domestic developments in the contemporary United States is possible here, an introduction to the postwar years is provided in G. Hodgson, *America in Our Time* (1976); W. E. Leuchtenburg, *A Troubled Feast: American Society since 1945** (rev. 1979); and W. H. Chafe, *The Unfinished Journey: America since World War II* (rev. 1991). Perspectives on contemporary social and economic problems are offered in J. T. Patterson, *America's Struggle against Poverty, 1900–1980* (1981); R. Polenberg, *One Nation Divisible: Class, Race, and Ethnicity in the United States since 1938* (1980); A. Hacker, *Two Nations: Black and White, Separate, Hostile, Unequal* (1992); and G. J. Jaynes and R. M. Williams (eds.), *A Common Destiny: Blacks and American Society* (1989).

The Soviet Union: From Stalin to Brezhnev

Of the many volumes for the Stalin years listed in Chapter XVII, one of the best assessments is A. B. Ulam, *Stalin: The Man and His Era* (1987). The postwar years and the evolution of the Soviet system after 1953 are explored in A. Nove, *Stalinism and After: The Road to Gorbachev** (rev. 1989); and in S. Bialer's three books: *Stalin's Successors: Leadership, Stability, and Change in the Soviet Union* (1980), *The Domestic Context of Soviet Foreign Policy* (1981), and *The Soviet Paradox: External Expansion, Internal Decline* (1986). The Soviet economy in the early 1980s is assessed in M. I. Goldman, *The U.S.S.R. in Crisis: The Failure of an Economic System* (1983), and A. Nove, *The Soviet Economic System* (rev. 1986). Foreign policy is studied in R. Edmonds, *Soviet Foreign Policy: The Brezhnev Years** (1983); and the origins and nature of the involvement in Afghanistan in M. Urban, *War in Afghanistan* (rev. 1991).

For the Soviet dissenters one may turn to R. Conquest, *The Politics of Ideas in the U.S.S.R.* (1967); P. Reddaway, *Russia's Underground Intellectuals* (1970); A. Rothberg, *The Heirs of Stalin: Dissidence and the Soviet Regime, 1953–1970* (1972); and R. T. Tökes (ed.), *Dissent in the U.S.S.R.: Politics, Ideology, and People* (1975). M. Scammell, *Solzhenitzyn* (1984), provides a balanced assessment of the at times controversial novelist. A. Knight, *The KGB: Police and Politics in the Soviet Union** (1988), carries the story of the secret police to the mid-1980s, and has also written on its chief from 1938 to 1953, *Beria: Stalin's First Lieutenant* (1993). Anti-Semitism may be studied in L. Rapoport, *Stalin's War against the Jews: The Doctors' Plot and the Soviet Solution* (1990); B. Pinkus, *The Soviet Government and the Jews, 1948–1967** (1985), cited earlier; and R. O. Freedman (ed.), *Soviet Jewry in the Decisive Decade, 1971–1980* (1987).

For the Communist movement in the postwar years, A. Westoby, *Communism since World War II* (rev. 1989), provides encyclopedic coverage, while J. Braunthal examines the 25 years after the dissolution of the Comintern in *History of the International: Vol. III, World Socialism, 1943–1968* (trans. 1980). The break from Moscow control and the phenomenon of Eurocommunism may be studied in G. R. Urban, *Eurocommunism* (1978); A. Kriegel, *Eurocommunism* (trans. 1978); and C. Boggs, *The Impasse of European Communism* (1982).

Eastern Europe under Soviet Domination

How communism was imposed on Eastern Europe is explored in H. Seton-Watson, *The East European Revolution* (rev. 1956). The years of Communist domination and the mounting restiveness in Eastern Europe are studied in J. Rothschild, *Return to Diversity: A Political History of East Central Europe since World War II** (rev. 1993), and in G. Schöpflin, *Politics in Eastern Europe, 1945–1992** (1993).

For Hungary and the uprising of 1956 one may read P. C. Zinner, *Revolution in Hungary* (1962); B. Kovrig, *Communism in Hungary from Kun to Kádár* (1979); and C. Gati, *Hungary and the Soviet Bloc* (1988).

Czechoslovakia as victim, first of Hitler then of Stalin, is examined in E. Toborsky, *President Eduard Beneš: Between East and West, 1938–1948* (1981). The crisis of 1968 is studied in G. Golan, *The Czechoslovak Reform Movement: Communism in Crisis, 1962–1968* (1971); and in books by V. Kusin (1971), Z. A. B. Zeman (1969), and K. Dawisha (1984).

For the emergence of communism in Yugoslavia, A. Dijilas, *The Contested Country: Yugoslav Unity and Communist Revolution, 1919–1953* (1991), is an outstanding study. Informative on Tito's efforts to govern the multinational state are D. Rusinow, *The Yugoslav Experiment, 1948–1974** (1977); D. Wilson, *Tito's Yugoslavia* (1979); and H. Lydall, *Yugoslavia in Crisis* (1989). Additional books for the former Yugoslavia and books for Poland and other East-European countries will be described in Chapter XXIV.

China under Mao

As background to the emergence of communism, and for a sense of the continuing revolution in China in modern times, books cited in Chapters XV and XVIII, especially those by J. D. Spence and J. K. Fairbank, should be consulted. For the years after 1949 the best overviews are M. Meisner, *Mao's China and After: A History of the People's Republic** (rev. 1986), and L. Dittmer, *China's Continuous Revolution: The Post-Liberation Era, 1949–1981* (1987).

There are authoritative detailed chapters in the collaborative *Cambridge History of China,* Volume XV (R. MacFarquhar and J. K. Fairbank, eds.), published in two separate parts: Part I, *The People's Republic: The Emergence of Revolutionary China, 1949–1965* (1987), and Part II, *The People's Republic: Revolutions within the Chinese Revolution, 1966–1982* (1992). S. Schram, *The Political Thought of Mao Tse-tung* (rev. 1969), is a rewarding study.

The Korean War

For background and an introduction to Asia's role in world politics, one may consult D. F. Lach and E. S. Wehrle, *International Politics in East Asia since World War II* (1975). For American relations with the Asian countries in the early postwar years, W. Borden, *The Pacific Alliance* (1984), and J. Matray, *The Reluctant Crusade: Ameri-*

can Foreign Policy in Korea, 1941–1950 (1980), are especially helpful. The fullest inquiry into the origins of the Korean War, openly revisionist, is B. Cumings, *The Origins of the Korean War* (2 vols., 1981–1990); it may be compared with P. Lowe, *The Origins of the Korean War** (1986). There are narrative accounts by B. I. Kaufman (1986), M. Hastings (1987), C. Blair (1989), and J. Merrill (1989). The military aspects are emphasized in A. Bevin, *Korea* (1987), and in J. B. Toland, *In Mortal Combat: Korea, 1950–1953* (1992), while the long career of the Communist leader is studied in D. S. Suh, *Kim Il Sung: The North Korean Leader* (1988).

Problems and Readings*

The background to the Cold War may be examined in N. A. Graebner (ed.), *The Cold War: A Conflict of Ideology and Power* (rev. 1976); T. G. Paterson and R. J. McMahon (eds.), *The Origins of the Cold War* (rev. 1991); E. R. May (ed.), *American Cold War Strategy: Interpreting NSC 68* (1994); L. C. Gardner (ed.), *Origins of the Cold War* (1970); R. H. Miller (ed.), *The Evolution of the Cold War: From Confrontation to Containment** (1979); and C. S. Maier (ed.), *The Cold War in Europe: Its Origins and Consequences** (rev. 1990). The movement toward European unity is examined in H. A. Schmitt (ed.), *European Union: From Hitler to de Gaulle* (Anvil series, 1969) and in F. R. Willis (ed.), *European Integration* (1975). For the Communist triumph in China there is P. P. Y. Loh, *The Kuomintang Debacle of 1949: Conquest or Collapse?* (1965).

XXII. Empires into Nations: The Developing World

End of the European Empires

Many of the books mentioned in Chapters XV and XVIII also should be consulted. For the background to the post-1945 colonial revolutions, two of the best introductions are R. Emerson, *From Empire to Nation: The Rise to Self-Assertion of Asian and African Peoples** (1960), and T. Hodgkin, *Nationalism in Colonial Africa* (1956). A comprehensive account of the end of empire is offered in F. Ansprenger, *The Dissolution of Colonial Empires** (1989), while M. E. Chamberlain, *Decolonization: The Fall of* *the European Empires* (1985) is an informative brief synthesis. Books that examine colonial administration in the final phases before independence include M. Perham, *Colonial Sequence, 1930–1949* (1976); R. F. Betts, *Uncertain Dimensions: Western Overseas Empires in the Twentieth Century* (1985); and R. F. Holland, *European Decolonization, 1918–1981* (1985). There are vignettes of selected Asian and African nationalist leaders in H. Tinker, *Men Who Overturned Empires: Fighters, Dreamers, and Schemers* (1987).

On nationalism and the emergent nations, many of the books cited in Chapter XI on the older nationalism should also be consulted. Especially informative are E. Kedourie, *Nationalism in Asia and Africa* (1971); A. D. S. Smith, *Nationalism in the Twentieth Century* (1979) and *The Ethnic Origins of Nations* (1986); E. J. Hobsbawm, *Nations and Nationalism since 1780* (1990); and B. Anderson, *Imagined Communities: Reflections on the Origin and Spread of Nationalism* (rev. 1991).

End of the British Empire

The disintegration of the British empire is studied in J. Darwin, *Britain and Decolonisation: The Retreat from Empire in the Post-War World* (1988) and in a briefer account, *End of Empire* (1990); and in D. A. Low, *Eclipse of Empire* (1991). Wartime controversies between Churchill and Roosevelt are skillfully analyzed in W. R. Louis, *Imperialism at Bay: The United States and the Decolonization of the British Empire 1941–1945* (1978), while the same author examines the British effort to retain its influence in the Middle East in *The British Empire in the Middle East, 1945–1951: Arab Nationalism, the United States, and Postwar Imperialism* (1984). Of special interest for Britain's continuing global role is P. J. Cain and A. G. Hopkins, *British Imperialism: Crisis and Deconstruction, 1914–1990* (1993), a sequel to the volume cited in Chapter XV. British and French reactions to the loss of empire are compared in M. Kahler, *Decolonization in Britain and France* (1984).

The British withdrawal from the Indian subcontinent and the early years of independence are examined in H. V. Hodson, *The Great Divide: Britain-India-Pakistan* (rev. 1985), and in S. Sarkar, *Modern India, 1885–1947* (rev. 1989), cited in Chapter XVIII. For India, and the politics and culture of

South Asia in general, one may turn for guidance to S. Wolpert, *A New History of India* (rev. 1993), cited earlier. The Indian experiment in economic planning and parliamentary democracy is assessed in L. I. and S. H. Rudolph, *In Pursuit of Lakshmi [the Indian Goddess of Fortune]: The Political Economy of the Indian State* (1987). Biographies of Gandhi and Nehru have been mentioned in Chapter XVIII. For the Congress party, Nehru's leadership, and Indira Gandhi, one may turn to P. Brass, *The Politics of India since Independence* (1990). Three thoughtful assessments of key forces at work in contemporary India are A. T. Embree, *Utopias in Conflict: Religion and Nationalism in Modern India* (1990); B. Crossette, *India: Facing the Twenty-First Century* (1993); and V. S. Naipaul, *India: A Million Mutinies Now* (1992). The inability of Pakistan to integrate East Pakistan and the emergence of Bangladesh is studied in R. Jahan, *Pakistan: Failure in National Integration* (1972). On the founder of the Muslim state, informative studies are A. Jalal, *The Sole Spokesman: Jinnah, the Muslim League, and the Demand for Pakistan* (1985), and S. Wolpert; *Jinnah of Pakistan* (1984).

For developments in Southeast Asia, two good introductions are D. R. SarDesai, *Southeast Asia: Past and Present* (1988), and J. Pluvier, *Southeast Asia: From Colonialism to Independence* (1974). The war fought by the British in the Malay peninsula is described in R. Jackson, *The Malayan Emergency: The Commonwealth Wars, 1948–1966* (1990). For the British success in attracting the newly independent states to membership in the transformed Commonwealth of Nations one may read R. J. Moore, *Making the New Commonwealth* (1987).

The struggle against the Dutch in Indonesia and the years of independence may be approached through two biographical accounts: J. D. Legge, *Sukarno* (1972), and D. Jenkins, *Suharto and His Generals* (1984).

For Africa, two indispensable volumes are P. Gifford and W. R. Louis (eds.), *The Transfer of Power in Africa: Decolonization, 1940–1960* (1982) and *Decolonization and African Independence: The Transfers of Power, 1960–1980* (1988). A good overview is provided in J. D. Hargeaves, *Decolonization in Africa* (1988) and an insightful survey for the years 1914 to the present is available in B. Davidson, *Modern Africa: A*

*Social and Political History** (rev. 1994). Important additional perspectives by African historians are provided in A. A. Mazrui (ed.), *Africa since 1935 (1993)*, Vol VIII of the *UNESCO General History of Africa*. Books examining problems after independence include B. Davidson, *The Black Man's Burden: Africa and the Curse of the Nation-State* (1992), which sees the nation-state as an artificial importation into the continent, and J. Harding, *The Fate of Africa: Continent on the Brink of Ruin* (1993), which graphically portrays the ethnic conflicts. An introduction to francophone Africa is provided in E. Mortimer, *France and the Africans, 1944–1960* (1969), while the career of the poet-statesman of Senegal is portrayed in J. G. Vaillant, *Black, French, and African: A Life of Léopold Sédar Senghor* (1990).

The best historical account of South Africa and its peoples is L. Thompson, *A History of South Africa* (1990), cited in Chapter XV, while a good brief introduction is N. Worden, *The Making of Modern South Africa** (1993). Among the many assessments of the country's contemporary difficulties are J. Lelyveld, *Move Your Shadow: South Africa Black and White** (1986); D. Ottoway, *Chained Together* (1992); M. Meredith, *In the Name of Apartheid: South Africa in the Postwar Period* (1989); A. Sparks, *The Mind of South Africa* (1990); J. Brewer (ed.), *Can South Africa Survive?* (1989); and H. Adam and K. Moodley, *The Opening of the Apartheid Mind: Options for the New South Africa* (1993). Two illuminating comparative studies are G. M. Fredrickson, *White Supremacy: A Comparative Study in American and South African History* (1981), and J. W. Cell, *The Highest Stage of White Supremacy: The Origins of Segregation in South Africa and the American South* (1982).

The Middle East

For the Middle East, balanced overviews for the postwar years include L. A. Aroian and R. P. Mitchell, *The Modern Middle East and North Africa* (1984); A. Goldschmidt, Jr., *A Concise History of the Middle East** (rev. 1987); W. L. Cleveland, *A History of the Modern Middle East** (1993); G. Corm, *Fragmentation in the Middle East: The Last 30 Years** (1988); and B. Lewis, *The Shaping of the Modern Middle East** (rev. 1993). A useful reference work is R.

Ovendale, *The Longman Companion to the Middle East since 1914** (1992), cited earlier.

Books that thoughtfully examine the significance of the Islamic legacy for the contemporary world include J. O. Voll, *Islam: Continuity and Change in the Modern World** (1982); H. Munson, Jr., *Islam and Revolution in the Middle East* (1988); E. Swan, *Radical Islam: Medieval Theology and Modern Politics* (1985) and *Interpretations of Islam* (1988); B. Lewis, *The Political Language of Islam* (1988), *Islam and the West* (1993), and other writings; and J. I. Esposito, *The Islamic Threat: Myth or Reality?* (1992).

Books that examine the Western involvement in the Middle East have been cited in Chapters XV, XVI, and XVIII. To them may be added A. Roshwald, *Estranged Bedfellows: Britain and France in the Middle East during World War II* (1990); and H. M. Sachar, *Europe Leaves the Middle East, 1936–1954* (1976). An indispensable study of American involvement is S. P. Tillman, *The U.S. and the Middle East* (1982).

Books that illuminate the tragedy of Lebanon include I. Rabinovich, *The War for Lebanon, 1970–1983* (1984); Y. Evron, *War and Intervention in Lebanon* (1987); T. Petran, *The Struggle over Lebanon* (1987); S. Khalaf, *Lebanon's Predicament** (1988); and S. Mackey, *Lebanon* (1989).

For internal developments in Iraq informative studies include P. Marr, *The Modern History of Iraq* (1985); M. F. and P. Sluglett, *Iraq since 1958: From Revolution to Dictatorship** (1991), and S. al-Khalil [pseud.], *Republic of Fear: The Politics of Modern Iraq* (1989), which may be supplemented by the same author's later book published under his own name, K. Makiya, *Cruelty and Silence: War, Tyranny, Uprising, and the Arab World* (1993). The Iraqi dictator and the Baath party dictatorship are also studied in E. Karsh and I. Rautsi, *Saddam Hussein: A Political Biography* (1991).

One of the best introductions to the history of modern Israel is H. M. Sachar, *A History of Israel,* (2 vols; rev. 1979, 1987). Two biographies that help understand the early idealism of Zionism are J. Reinharz, *Chaim Weizmann* (2 vols., 1985–1993, with a third vol. projected), and S. Teveth, *Ben-Gurion: The Burning Ground, 1866–1948* (1987); there are studies also of Golda Meir by E. Ayres (1969) and P. Mann (1971). M. Cohen, *Zion and State: Nation, Class, and the Shaping of Modern Israel* (1987), explores the divisions between labor Zionism and conservative nationalism.

For the clash of Arab and Jewish interests from 1920 to 1948 under the British mandate, and the recognition of Israel in 1948, one may read M. J. Cohen, *The Origins and Evolution of the Arab-Zionist Conflict** (1987), and the same author's *Truman and Israel* (1990). An overview of the four Arab-Israeli wars from 1948 to 1973 and the entanglement in Lebanon is provided in R. Ovendale, *The Origins of the Arab-Israeli Wars** (rev. 1992), and S. D. Bailey, *Four Arab-Israeli Wars and the Peace Process* (1990). Two moving accounts of Israeli-Palestinian tensions are T. L. Friedman, *From Beirut to Jerusalem* (1989), and D. K. Shipler, *Arab and Jew: Wounded Spirits in a Promised Land* (1989). Thoughtful studies focusing on the Palestinians are B. Kimmerling and J. S. Migdal, *Palestinians: The Making of a People* (1992); C. P. Smith, *Palestine and the Arab-Israeli Conflict* (rev. 1992); and B. Morris, *The Birth of the Palestinian Refugee Problem, 1947–1948* (1987) and *1948 and After: Israel and the Palestinians* (1990).

The international crisis in 1956 over Egypt's closing of the Suez Canal is examined in H. Thomas, *The Suez Affair* (1966); D. Carlton, *Britain and the Suez Crisis* (1988); and W. R. Louis and R. Owen (eds.), *Suez 1956: The Crisis and Its Consequences* (1989).

The Revolution in Iran

The background and course of the revolutionary events in Iran may be studied in N. R. Keddie, *Roots of Revolution: An Interpretive History of Modern Iran** (1981); D. Wilber, *Iran Past and Present: From Monarchy to Islamic Republic* (1982); S. Bakhash, *The Reign of the Ayotollahs: Iran and the Islamic Revolution** (1983); S. A. Arjomand, *The Turban for the Crown: The Islamic Revolution in Iran** (1989); and R. Wright, *In the Name of God: The Khomeini Decade* (1989) and *Sacred Rage: The Wrath of Militant Islam* (1989). For the American ties with the shah, the impact of the revolution, and the Teheran hostage crisis, one may read J. A. Bill, *The Eagle and the Lion: The Tragedy of American-Iranian Relations* (1988). The eight-year war between Iran and Iraq is described in D. Hiro, *The Longest War: The Iran-Iraq Military Conflict**

(1991), and in E. Karsh (ed.), *Iran-Iraq War: Impact and Implications* (1990). Books on Iraq and the Persian Gulf War of 1990–1991 will be cited in Chapter XXIV.

Changing Latin America

For an introduction to twentieth-century changes in Latin America one may turn to T. E. Skidmore and P. H. Smith, *Modern Latin America** (rev. 1992), and to L. Bethell (ed.), *The Cambridge History of Latin America;* Vol. VIII, *Latin America since 1930: Spanish South America* (1991). General works cited in Chapters X, XI, and XV will also be helpful. Of special interest is R. L. Harris, *Marxism, Socialism, and Democracy in Latin America** (1992). A valuable reference work is S. Collier and others, *The Cambridge Encyclopedia of Latin America and the Caribbean* (rev. 1992).

The vicissitudes of American policies toward Latin America are explored in L. Langley, *America and the Americas* (1989); R. A. Pastor, *Whirlpool: United States Foreign Policy toward Latin America and the Caribbean* (1992); and W. LaFeber, *Inevitable Revolutions: The United States in Central America* (rev. 1993). D. B. Davis, *Revolutions: Reflections on American Equality and Foreign Liberation (1990)*, thoughtfully compares past and present American attitudes toward revolutionary change. Books on Cuba will be cited in the chapter that follows.

Modernization and Development in the Third World

The impact of modernization is examined historically and comparatively in C. E. Black, *The Dynamics of Modernization** (1966); and in I. R. Sinai, *The Challenge of Modernization** (1964) and *In Search of the Modern World* (1968). Of special interest are L. S. Stavrianos, *Global Rift: The Third World Comes of Age* (1981); T. H. Von Laue, *The World Revolution of Westernization: The Twentieth Century in Global Perspective** (1987), which stresses the destabilizing effects of modernization; and M. Adas, *Machines the Measure of Men: Science, Technology and Ideologies of Western Dominance* (1988).

For the economics of development, theories of growth, and development models followed in the post-1945 years, one may read A. Bagchi, *The Political Economy of*

Underdevelopment (1982), an outstanding study; H. W. Arndt, *Economic Development: The History of an Idea** (1987); I. M. D. Little, *Economic Development: Theory, Policy, and International Relations* (1984), unsympathetic to planned development; W. W. Rostow, *Theorists of Economic Growth from David Hume to the Present** (1990); L. E. Harrison, *Underdevelopment Is a State of Mind* (1985); and R. D. Stone, *The Nature of Development* (1992), also critical of the effort to introduce Western-style development without adequate preparation.

For the development experience in various parts of the world one may turn to C. Young, *Ideology and Development in Africa* (1982); D. K. Fieldhouse, *Black Africa, 1945–1980: Economic Decolonization and Arrested Development** (1986), which studies both British and French former colonies; L. Cockcroft, *Africa's Way: A Journey from the Past* (1990); J. Iliffe, *The African Poor: A History** (1987); R. A. Scalapino, *The Politics of Development: Perspectives on Twentieth-Century Asia* (1989), an insightful small book; and A. Richards and J. Waterbury, *A Political Economy of the Middle East** (1988). Available also are J. Mayall and A. Payne (eds.), *The Fallacies of Hope: the Post-Colonial Record of the Commonwealth Third World* (1991); and T. Kemp, *Industrialization in the Non-Western World** (1989), with analyses of India, Brazil, and Nigeria. A knowledgeable, if overdrawn, indictment of the international aid bureaucracy is to be found in G. Hancock, *Lords of Poverty: The Power, Prestige, and Corruption of the International Aid Business* (1989).

The best introduction to the north-south debate over a new international economic order is the report by the Independent Commission on International Development, chaired by Willy Brandt: *North-South: A Program for Survival* (1980). It may be supplemented by W. A. Lewis, *The Evolution of the International Economic Order** (1978); A. Fishlow and others, *Rich and Poor Nations in the World Economy* (1978); and B. Nossiter, *The Global Struggle for More: Third World Conflicts with the Rich Nations** (1986). The burden of debt in the Third World is explored in J. D. Sachs (ed.), *Developing Country Debt and the World Economy** (1989). Of special interest is J. W. Warnock, *Politics of Hunger: The Global Food System** (1987). Books on population will be cited in Chapter XXIV.

Problems and Readings*

For background there is a helpful anthology, G. Nadel and P. Curtis (eds.), *Imperialism and Colonialism* (1964), cited earlier. Two relevant pamphlets are J. Baird (ed.), *The End of the European Empires: Decolonization after World War II* (1975), and T. W. Wallbank (ed.), *The Partition of India: Causes and Responsibilities* (1960). For the Middle East one may turn to T. E. Farah (ed.), *Pan-Arabism and Arab Nationalism: The Continuing Debate* (1987), and A. Hourani, P. S. Khouri, and M. C. Wilson (eds.), *The Modern Middle East: A Reader* (1994). For Latin America there is D. Rock (ed.), *Latin America in the 1940s: War and Postwar Transitions* (1994). Two titles in the Anvil series will be illuminating for different parts of the world: L. L. Snyder (ed.), *Contemporary Nationalisms* (1992), and W. Connor, *Ethnicity, Ethnocentrism, and Ethnonationalism* (1993).

XXIII. A World Endangered: The Cold War

International Relations: Confrontation and Détente

Books described in Chapters XX and XXI focus on the first postwar decade of Soviet-American relations: to them may be added R. Levering, *The Cold War, 1945–1987** (rev. 1988); S. R. Ashton, *In Search of Détente: The Politics of East-West Relations since 1945* (1989); S. Brown, *The Faces of Power: United States Foreign Policy from Truman to Clinton** (rev. 1994); and G. A. Craig and F. Loewenheim (eds.), *The Diplomats, 1939–1979* (1994), a valuable set of essays. For the Kennedy years, the best introduction is M. R. Beschloss, *The Crisis Years: Kennedy and Khrushchev, 1960–1963* (1992).

How the developing world became involved in the Soviet-Western confrontation is explored in R. J. Barnet, *Intervention and Revolution: The United States in the Third World* (1968); G. Kolko, *Confronting the Third World: U.S. Foreign Policy, 1945–1980* (1988), critical of U.S. policies; B. D. Porter, *The U.S.S.R. in Third World Conflicts: Soviet Arms and Diplomacy in Local Wars, 1945–1980** (1984), which focuses on the Middle East and Africa; and G. Lundestad, *East, West, North, South: Major Developments in International Poli-*

tics, 1945–1990* (1991) by a Norwegian historian.

For U.S.-Cuban relations in historical perspective and for the background and nature of Castro's revolution, one may read J. R. Benjamin, *The United States and the Origins of the Cuban Revolution* (1990); L. A. Perez, Jr., *Between Reform and Revolution** (1988); J. M. del Aquila, *Cuba: Dilemmas of a Revolution** (1988), which includes an account of Castro's military activities in Africa; and M. Merez-Stable, *The Cuban Revolution: Origins, Course, Legacy** (1993). R. E. Quirk, *Fidel Castro* (1993), is a critical biographical assessment. The Bay of Pigs episode is described in T. Higgins, *The Perfect Failure* (1987), and the missile crisis of 1962 is studied in perspective in L. Brune, *The Missile Crisis* (1985), and R. A. Divine (ed.), *The Cuban Missile Crisis** (rev. 1990).

On the United States relationship with its NATO allies in the Cold War years, one may read R. J. Barnet, *The Alliance* (1983); D. P. Calleo, *Beyond American Hegemony* (1987); L. S. Kaplan, *NATO and the United States* (1988); J. H. Wyllie, *European Security in the Nuclear Age* (1986); and the essays in L. S. Kaplan and R. W. Clawson (eds.), *NATO after Thirty Years* (1985).

The Vietnam War

Efforts to explore Vietnamese history and to place post-1945 events in historical perspective include A. B. Woodside, *Community and Revolution in Modern Vietnam* (1976); W. J. Duiker, *The Rise of Nationalism in Vietnam, 1900–1941* (1976); J. P. Harrison, *The Endless War: Vietnam's Struggle for Independence** (1989); A. Short, *The Origins of the Vietnam War** (1989); D. R. SarDesai, *Vietnam: The Struggle for National Identity** (rev. 1992); and M. B. Young, *The Vietnam Wars, 1945–1990** (1991), a valuable synthesis.

The American involvement is skillfully explained in G. McT. Kahin, *Intervention: How America Became Involved in Vietnam* (1986), which perceives the United States as ignoring the nationalist aspects of the war and seeing it as Communist aggression only. American miscalculations are heavily emphasized in D. Halberstam, *The Best and the Brightest** (1972), cited earlier, and in G. Kolko, *Anatomy of a War: Vietnam, the United States, and the Modern Historical*

Experience (1985), while G. Lewy, *America in Vietnam** (1978), defends United States policies.

The war itself is studied in G. Herring, *America's Longest War: The United States and Vietnam, 1950–1975** (1979), an outstanding account; S. Karnow, *Vietnam: A History** (1985), helpful on decision making and strategy; L. Berman, *Lyndon Johnson's War* (1989); and S. Hersh, *The Price of Power* (1983), on the extension of the war under Nixon and Kissinger.

The aftermath of the war receives a grim assessment in N. Van Canh with E. Cooper, *Vietnam under Communism, 1975–1982* (1983). For Cambodia, there are two valuable studies by D. P. Chandler, *The Tragedy of Cambodian History: Power, War, and Revolution since 1945* (1992) and *Brother Number One: Pol Pot* (1992), a biographical account.

On guerrilla warfare in Vietnam and elsewhere, informative books are W. Laqueur, *Guerrilla: A Historical and Critical Study* (1977); R. Asprey, *War in Shadows: The Guerrilla in History* (1976); E. E. Rice, *Wars of the Third Kind: Conflict in the Underdeveloped Countries* (1988); and M. van Creveld, *The Transformation of War* (1991), a searching reassessment of the pattern of modern conflict.

The Nuclear Arms Build-Up

There are numerous books on the nuclear arms build-up, the apocalyptic dangers the world has learned to live with, and the contributions of strategic deterrence to the armed peace in the Cold War years. An outstanding exhaustive study is McG. Bundy, *Danger and Survival: Choices about the Bomb in the First Fifty Years* (1988); only gradually, the author demonstrates, was it recognized that the bomb could not be thought of as an instrument of war like other weapons; the book also includes an informative account of the Cuban missile crisis. Other counsels of strategy accepting deterrence but calling for continuing efforts at nuclear arms control, are R. McNamara, *Blundering into Disaster: Surviving the First Century of the Nuclear Age* (1987); G. F. Kennan, *The Nuclear Delusion: Soviet-American Relations in the Atomic Age** (1983); S. Zuckerman, *Nuclear Illusion and Reality* (1982); G. Gasteyer, *Searching for World Security* (1987); M. Mandelbaum, *The*

Fate of Nations: The Search for National Security in the Nineteenth and Twentieth Centuries (1988); and J. Newhouse, *War and Peace in the Nuclear Age* (1989). Another kind of literature has called for a fundamental rethinking about nuclear arms. Representative are J. Schell's two books: *The Fate of the Earth* (1982) and *The Abolition* (1984); and F. Dyson, *Weapons and Hope* (1984); by an eminent physicist. A thoughtful contribution to the discussion is J. Finnis, J. M. Boyle, Jr., and G. Grisez, *Nuclear Deterrence, Morality, and Realism* (1987). The worldwide movement for nuclear disarmament is examined in A. Carter, *Peace Movements: International Protest and World Politics since 1945* (1992).

Books that illuminate the successes and failures of détente under Nixon and Kissinger and their successors include R. L. Garthoff, *Détente and Confrontation* (1985); R. W. Stevenson, *The Rise and Fall of Détente* (1985); and T. G. Paterson, *Meeting the Communist Threat: Truman to Reagan** (1989). Also available are R. D. Schulzinger, *Henry Kissinger: Doctor of Diplomacy* (1989); W. Isaacson, *Kissinger: A Biography* (1992); and R. C. Thornton, *The Carter Years: Toward a New Global Order* (1991). For assessments of American foreign policy and the search for security in the perspective of over four decades one should read J. L. Gaddis, *The Long Peace: Inquiries into the History of the Cold War* (1987), a thoughtful appraisal; and T. J. McCormick, *America: A Half-Century of United States Foreign Policy in the Cold War** (1989). The collapse of the Soviet Union in 1991 and the altered international scene have brought additional books, cited in the final chapter.

The World Economy: Economic Slowdown

Informative introductions to the global economy as it developed in the post-1945 years are W. W. Rostow, *The World Economy: History and Prospect* (1977); W. M. Scammell, *The International Economy since 1945* (1980); and A. G. Kenwood and A. I. Lougheed, *The Growth of the International Economy, 1820–1980* (1983). Two volumes by I. Wallerstein, *The Capitalist World Economy* (1979) and *The Politics of the World Economy* (1984), following upon his earlier studies, provide provocative economic and historical analysis. The nature of the new information technology that has

helped to create a "postindustrial" society is described in P. F. Drucker, *Post-Capitalist Society* (1993), while R. B. Reich, *The Work of Nations: Preparing Ourselves for Twenty-First Century Capitalism* (1991), thoughtfully explains how globalism and other changes have transformed older industrial capitalism.

The role of oil in the economy and in global politics is admirably described in D. Yergin, *The Prize: The Epic Quest for Oil, Money, and Power** (1990); and P. R. Odell, *Oil and World Power** (rev. 1987). The impact of the oil embargo of 1973–1974 on Europe is studied in R. Lieber, *Oil and the Middle East: Europe in the Energy Crisis* (1976). For the multinational corporations one may turn to M. Wilkin, *The Maturing of Multinational Enterprise* (1974); R. Vernon, *Storm over the Multinationals* (1977); and R. J. Barnet and J. Cavanagh, *Global Dreams: Imperial Corporations and the New World Order* (1994).

The historic link between economic strength and political and military hegemony is traced masterfully in P. Kennedy, *The Rise and Fall of the Great Powers: Economic Change and Military Conflict from 1500 to 2000** (1987), cited in the Introduction; it may be read along with M. Olson, *The Rise and Decline of Nations* (1982). Kennedy's volume and his other writings raise the question of America's relative decline in economic leadership, a subject on which there have been many jeremiads. The Japanese challenge, in particular, is described in E. F. Vogel, *Japan as Number One: Lessons for America** (1979); C. V. Prestowitz, Jr., *Trading Places: How We Allowed Japan to Take the Lead* (1988); and G. Friedman and M. LeBard, *The Coming War with Japan* (1991), informative despite the alarmist title. On the threat from more than one source, one may read L. Thurow, *Head to Head: The Coming Economic Battle among Japan, Europe, and America* (1992), and E. N. Luttwak, *The Endangered American Dream* (1993), which describes the "geo-economic" struggle. The phenomenal economic growth of Hong Kong, Taiwan, Singapore, and South Korea is described in E. F. Vogel, *The Four Little Dragons** (1992). The decline of older American industry is described in B. Bluestone and B. Harrison, *The Deindustrialization of America* (1982), but the continuing importance of the American economy emerges from M. Feldstein (ed.), *The United States in the World Economy** (1988). H. R. Nye, *The Myth of American Decline* (1990); and J. S. Nye, *Bound to Lead: The Changing Nature of American Power* (1990).

The impact of the global recession that began in 1974 and the dilemmas it has posed for policymakers are studied in several of the books on the global economy cited in Chapter XXI; to them should be added L. Anel, *Recession, the Western Economies, and the Changing World Order* (1981); E. S. Einhorn and J. Logue, *Welfare States in Hard Times* (1982); R. Skidelsky (ed.), *The End of the Keynesian Era* (1977); A. Cox (ed.), *Politics, Policy and the European Recession* (1982); and J. H. Hollifield, *Immigrants, Markets, and States: the Political Economy of Postwar Europe* (1992).

In addition to books cited in Chapter XXI, the operations, accomplishments, and problems of the European Community may be studied in D. Swann, *The Economics of the Common Market* (rev. 1984); E. Neville-Rolf, *The Politics of Agriculture in the European Community* (1984); S. Bulmer and W. E. Paterson, *The Federal Republic of Germany and the European Community* (1987); and S. George, *Britain and European Integration since 1945** (1991). There are thoughtful essays assessing the first thirty years of the Rome treaties and plans for closer economic integration in H. Brugmans (ed.), *Europe: Dream, Adventure, Reality* (1987). On progress toward closer unity and the transformation of the EC into the European Union (EU) under the Maastricht treaty, a good guide is J. Pinder, *European Community: The Building of a Union** (1992).

Western Europe: Politics and Society since 1974

The books on Western Europe described in Chapter XXI are almost all relevant here. To them one may add D. W. Urwin and W. E. Paterson (eds.), *Politics in Western Europe Today: Perspectives, Policies, and Issues since 1980** (1991).

BRITAIN. For Britain, Margaret Thatcher's conservative leadership and the changes in Britain in the decade after 1979 are assessed in P. Jenkins, *Mrs. Thatcher's Revolution: The Ending of the Socialist Era* (1988), a perceptive account, and in P. Riddell, *The Thatcher Era and Its Legacy** (1991). One

may also read L. Freedman, *Britain and the Falklands War** (1988), and an informative biographical account, H. Young, *The Iron Lady: A Biography of Margaret Thatcher* (1989). Two comparative studies of the conservative efforts in the United States and Britain in the 1980s to curb the welfare state, encourage entrepreneurial spirit, and revive national pride are J. Krieger, *Reagan, Thatcher, and the Politics of Decline** (1986), and A. Gamble, *The Free Economy and the Strong State* (1988). Divergent interpretations of these efforts are provided in R. Skidelsky (ed.), *Thatcherism* (1987), and in J. K. Galbraith: *The Voice of the Poor* (1983) and *The Culture of Contentment* (1992).

FRANCE. The Mitterrand experience that began in 1981 is examined in D. S. Bell and B. Criddle, *The French Socialist Party: The Emergence of a Party of Government** (rev. 1988); G. Ross, S. Hoffman, and S. Malzacher, *The Mitterrand Experiment** (1987); J. W. Friend, *Seven Years in France: François Mitterrand and the Unintended Revolution, 1981–1988* (1989); and D. Singer, *Is Socialism Doomed? The Meaning of Mitterrand* (1988). W. Northcutt, *Mitterrand: A Political Biography* (1992), a preliminary assessment, may be read along with the same author's *The French Socialist and Communist Parties under the Fifth Republic, 1958–1981* (1985).

For the evolution of socialism one may read M. Harrington, *Socialism Past and Future* (1989); W. E. Paterson and A. H. Thomas (eds.), *The Future of Social Democracy* (1986); and C. Lemke and G. Marles (eds.), *The Crisis of Socialism in Europe** (1992). The collapse of Soviet communism is bringing reassessments of socialism and communism in Europe and elsewhere.

SPAIN AND PORTUGAL. On developments in Spain one may read M. Gallo, *Spain under Franco* (1976); R. Carr and J. P. Fusi-Azpurúa, *Spain: Dictatorship to Democracy* (rev. 1981); P. Preston, *The Triumph of Democracy in Spain** (1986); and K. Maxwell and S. Spiegel, *The New Spain: From Isolation to Influence** (1994).

For Portugal, the revolution of 1974 and the gradual emergence of political stability are studied in H. Kay, *Salazar and Modern Portugal* (1970); A DeFigueredo, *Portugal: Fifty Years of Dictatorship* (1976); H. G. Ferreira and M. W. Marshall, *Portugal's*

Revolution: Ten Years On (1986); and T. Gallagher, *Portugal: A Twentieth Century Interpretation* (1983).

The Communist World: China after Mao

Several of the volumes cited in Chapter XXI for the Mao era also describe Deng's program of modernization and liberalization. To these may be added H. E. Salisbury, *The New Emperors: China in the Era of Mao and Deng* (1992), by an insightful journalist; and W. H. Overholt, *The Rise of China: How Economic Reform Is Creating a Superpower* (1993), a positive assessment of China's economic advances. Informative for the Deng reforms are R. P. Suttmeier, *Science, Technology, and China's Drive for Modernization* (1980); H. Harding, *China's Second Revolution: Reformation after Mao* (1987); and D. W.-W. Chang, *China under Deng Xiaoping* (1991), which is optimistic about economic reform despite political repression and factional struggles. An important subject is thoughtfully explored in H. Harding, *A Fragile Relationship: The United States and China since 1972** (1992). On the population question, one may read J. Banister, *China's Changing Population* (1987), and H. Yuan Ten and others, *China's Demographic Dilemma** (1992).

Problems and Readings*

For the confrontation over Cuba and other subjects, one may turn to D. B. Kunz (ed.), *The Diplomacy of the Crucial Decade: American Foreign Relations during the 1960s* (1994); and to R. A. Divine (ed.), *The Cuban Missile Crisis* (rev. 1990), cited earlier. For Vietnam there are J. P. Kimball (ed.), *The Reason Why: The Debate about the Causes of American Involvement in the Vietnam War* (1991), and D. W. Levy, *The Debate over Vietnam* (1993). For the youth movement in the United States sparked by opposition to the Vietnam War, there is A. J. Esler (ed.), *The Youth Revolution: The Conflict of Generations in Modern History* (1974). The origins of nuclear arms and efforts at arms control are examined in K. Eubank, *The Bomb* (1991), in the Anvil series.

XXIV. A World Transformed

It is difficult to assess the durable value of the literature dealing with the events and developments of recent years. For new books the reviews and bibliographies published in *Foreign Affairs* and in the professional and other journals should be consulted.

The Crisis in the Soviet Union: The Gorbachev Reforms, 1985–1991

Efforts to assess the Gorbachev reforms in their historical context include Z. A. Medvedev, *Gorbachev** (1986); A. Nove, *Glasnost in Action: Cultural Renaissance in Russia** (1989); M. Lewin, *The Gorbachev Phenomenon** (rev. 1991), cited in Chapter XXI; B. Kerblay, *Gorbachev's Russia* (1989); R. C. Tucker, *Political Culture and Leadership: Soviet Russia from Lenin to Gorbachev* (1987); and G. Hosking, *The Awakening of the Soviet Union** (1991). Especially valuable for the Gorbachev era, his fall from power, and the dissolution of the Soviet Union is J. B. Dunlop, *The Rise of Russia and the Fall of the Soviet Empire* (1993), while M. E. Malia, *The Soviet Tragedy: A History of Socialism in Russia, 1917–1991* (1993), perceptively evaluates these events in historical perspective. M. McCauley, *The Soviet Union: 1917–1991** (rev. 1993), provides a good overview. Specifically on the economy, one may read E. A. Hewett, *Reforming the Soviet Economy: Equality versus Efficiency** (1988); A. Aslund, *Gorbachev's Struggle for Economic Reform** (1989); and M. I. Goldman, *What Went Wrong with Perestroika* (1991). For the ferment in the nationalities, informative accounts are J. E. Mace, *Communism and the Dilemmas of National Liberation* (1993), and B. Nahaylo and V. Swoboda, *Soviet Disunion: A History of the Nationalities Problem in the Soviet Union* (1990), detailed and comprehensive. H. R. Huttenbach (ed.), *Nationalities in the Soviet Union** (1993), is a brief study in the Anvil series.

The Transformation of Central and Eastern Europe: 1989

Several books have already been cited in Chapter XXI for Central and Eastern Europe in the post-1945 years. The growing restiveness under Soviet domination also emerges from M. Charlton, *The Eagle and the Small Birds: Crisis in the Soviet Union from Yalta to Solidarity* (1987), and from G. Schöpflin and N. Woods (eds.), *In Search of Central Europe* (1989).

T. Garton Ash, a British journalist-historian, vividly describes the rising ferment and the collapse of the Communist regimes in Central and Eastern Europe in 1989 in *The Polish Revolution: Solidarity, 1980–1982* (1983); *The Uses of Adversity: Essays on the Fate of Central Europe* (1989); and *The Magic Lantern* [a theater in Prague]: *The Revolution of '89 Witnessed in Warsaw, Budapest, Berlin, and Prague** (1990). Other informative studies include J. F. Brown, *Surge to Freedom: The End of Communist Rule in Eastern Europe** (1991); Z. A. B. Zeman, *The Making and Breaking of Communist Europe** (1991); G. Weigel, *The Final Revolution: The Breaking of. Communist Europe** (1992); and G. Stokes, *The Walls Came Tumbling Down: The Collapse of Communism in Eastern Europe** (1993).

Careful assessments of the events leading to German reunification are to be found in four informative books: T. Garton Ash, *In Europe's Name: Germany and the Divided Continent* (1993), cited in Chapter XXI; K. H. Jarausch, *The Rush to German Unity** (1993); E. Pond, *Beyond the Wall: Germany's Road to Unification* (1993); and P. H. Merkl, *German Unification in the European Context** (1993).

A few additional books on the background, nature, and preliminary consequences of the Revolution of 1989 in the Central and Eastern European countries merit citing.

POLAND: A. Kemp-Welch, *The Birth of Solidarity* (1991); R. Laba, *The Roots of Solidarity: A Political Sociology of Poland's Working Class Democratization* (1991), more informative than its title might indicate; L. Goodwyn, *Breaking the Barrier: The Rise of Solidarity in Poland* (1991), by a student of American populism; and J. Harrison, *The Solidarity Decade: Poland, 1980–1991* (1993).

CZECHOSLOVAKIA: B. Wheaton and Z. Kavan, *The Velvet Revolution* (1992), and E. Kriscova, *Vaclav Havel: The Authorized Biography* (1993), an uncritical book, which helps, however, to communicate the playwright-statesman's thought and influence. The background that led to partition in 1993 is described in books cited in Chapter XIX, especially J. Kolvoda, *The Genesis of Czechoslovakia* (1986), and C. S. Leff, *National Conflict in Czechoslovakia: The Making and Remaking of a State, 1919–1987* (1988).

ROMANIA: N. Ratesh, *Romania: The Entangled Revolution** (1992), the best brief account; V. Georgescu, *The Romanians: A History* (1992) cited in Chapter XIII, excellent for the long-range historical background; E. Behr, *"Kiss The Hand You Cannot Bite": The Rise and Fall of the Ceausescus* (1992); and T. Gilberg, *Nationalism and Communism in Romania: The Rise and Fall of Ceausescu's Personal Dictatorship* (1990).

ESTONIA, LATVIA, LITHUANIA. For the Baltic states, where the independence movements helped catalyze the dissolution of the U.S.S.R. itself: A. Lieven, *The Baltic Revolution: Estonia, Latvia, Lithuania and the Path to Independence* (1993), an excellent book, illuminating also on the long-range history of the region; and R. J. Misiunas and R. Taagepera, *The Baltic States: Years of Dependence, 1940–1991** (1993), a detailed account of the years under Soviet rule.

The Disintegration of Yugoslavia

For the historical background one should consult two books cited earlier: I. Banac, *The National Question in Yugoslavia* (1984), for the years 1918–1921; and A. Dijilas, *The Contested Country: Yugoslav Unity and Communist Revolution, 1919–1953* (1991), for the civil war and the emergence of Tito. See also S. K. Pavlowitch, *The Improbable Survivor: Yugoslavia and Its Problems, 1918–1988* (1990), excellent for the system imposed by Tito; and S. P. Ramet, *Nationalism and Federalism in Yugoslavia, 1962–1991** (rev. 1992). Highly informative for Bosnia is N. Malcolm, *Bosnia: A Short History** (1994). The events of the 1990s may be followed in B. Magüs, *The Destruction of Yugoslavia: Tracking the Break-Up, 1980–1992* (1993), and M. Glenny, *The Fall of Yugoslavia: The Third Balkan War** (rev. 1994), an example of outstanding reportage.

The Collapse of Communism and the Dissolution of the Soviet Union

For the events of 1991, and the dissolution of the U.S.S.R., one may turn to the books by J. B. Dunlop and and by M. E. Malia cited earlier in this chapter; D. Remnick, *Lenin's Tomb: The Last Days of the Soviet Empire* (1993), by a perceptive journalist-observer; and R. V. Daniels, *The End of the Communist Revolution* (1993). On the ethnic and national tensions that led to the dissolution of the union and subsequent events one may also read H. Carrère d'Encausse, *The End of the Soviet Empire: The Triumph of the Nations** (trans. 1993); G. Lapidus and others (eds.), *From Union to Commonwealth: Nationalism and Separatism in the Soviet Republics* (1992); and I. Bremmer and R. Taras (eds.), *Nations and Politics in the Soviet Successor States** (1993).

After Communism

D. Yergin and T. Gustafson, *Russia 2010 and What It Means for the World* (1993), presents thoughtful scenarios for the future. Prospects for Central and Eastern Europe are also assessed in E. Hankiss, *East European Alternatives* (1990); V. Tismaneanu, *Eastern Europe after Communism: Reinventing Politics* (1991); R. Dahrendorf, *Reflections on the Revolution in Europe** (1991); J. C. Goldfarb, *After the Fall: The Pursuit of Democracy in Central Europe* (1992); J. F. Brown, *Hopes and Shadows: Eastern Europe after Communism** (1993); and P. Hockenos, *Free to Hate: The Rise of the Right in Post-Communist Eastern Europe* (1993), which describes some unsavory aspects of the postliberation era. The challenges to Europe as whole are examined in J. Nye, R. Keohane, and S. Hoffmann, *Europe after the Cold War* (1993).

Culture, Science, and Thought

Many of the books described in Chapter XIV should be consulted, especially H. S. Hughes, *Consciousness, and Society: The Reorientation of European Social Thought, 1890–1930* (1958), which examines post-Enlightenment ways of looking at positivism, science, and the social sciences. A useful anthology for many aspects of twentieth-century thought is W. W. Wagar (ed.), *Science, Faith, and Man: European Thought since 1914** (1968).

For distinctions between "modernism" and "postmodernism" in various contexts, one may read S. Toulmin, *Cosmopolis: The Hidden Agenda of Modernity* (1989), and M. Sarup, *An Introductory Guide to Poststructuralism and Postmodernism** (rev. 1993). Newer trends in historical writing relating to postmodernism are thoughtfully assessed in J. Appleby, L. Hunt, and M. Jacob, *Telling the Truth about History* (1994), cited in the Introduction.

Books that examine the impact of electronic technology on the arts and society include M. Poster, *The Mode of Information: Poststructuralism and Social Context** (1990); M. A. Rose, *The Post-Modern and the Post-Industrial** (1991); and R. A. Lanham, *The Electronic Word: Democracy, Technology, and the Arts* (1993).

A helpful introduction to contemporary intellectual trends is R. N. Stromberg, *After Everything: Western Intellectual History since 1945** (1975); the same author has written *Makers of Modern Culture: Five Twentieth-Century Thinkers** (1991), exploring Freud, Einstein, Wittgenstein, Joyce, and Sartre. N. Cantor, *Twentieth-Century Culture: Modernism to Deconstruction* (1988), critically assesses major artistic and cultural movements, while a favorable Marxist analysis may be found in F. Jameson, *Postmodernism, or the Cultural Logic of Late Capitalism* (1991).

Useful introductions to the professional philosophers are available in J. Passmore, *A Hundred Years of Philosophy* (1968); O. Hanfling, *Logical Postivism* (1981); and A. J. Ayer, *Philosophy in the Twentieth Century* (1982). Two recommended biographical accounts of twentieth-century philosophers are C. Moorehead, *Bertrand Russell: A Life* (1993), and R. Monk, *Ludwig Wittgenstein: The Duty of Genius* (1990). The origins and nature of existentialism may be studied in M. Warnock, *Existentialism* (1970); G. Brée, *Camus and Sartre* (1972); A. Cohen-Salal, *Sartre* (trans. 1987); and T. R. Koenig, *Existentialism and Human Existence** (1992). T. Judt, *Past Imperfect: French Intellectuals, 1944–1956** (1993) stresses the excessive domination by Sartre and other writers of French intellectual life in the early post-1945 years. For Michel Foucault, several of whose influential historical works have been cited in the Introduction, an unflattering personal portrait emerges from D. Eribon, *Michel Foucault* (trans. 1991), and J. Miller, *The Passion of Michel Foucault* (1993). The debate on Freud, referred to in Chapter XIV, continues with numerous books, among them, P. Robinson, *Freud and His Critics* (1993), which defends Freud but discusses the challenges to his influence.

Introductions to the complexities of contemporary art are provided in A. Neumeyer, *The Search for Meaning in Modern Art* (trans. 1964); G. Woods, *Art without Boundaries, 1950–1970* (1972); and S. Hunter, *Modern Art from Post-Impressionism to the*

Present (rev. 1985). A. Appel, Jr., *The Art of Celebration: Twentieth-Century Painting, Literature, Sculpture, Photography, and Jazz* (1982), stresses the vitality of contemporary culture, including popular culture; while R. Templin (ed.), *The Arts: A History of Expression in the Twentieth Century* (1991), is informative on both the visual arts and literature.

Western religious thought is explored in J. Macquarrie, *Twentieth-Century Religious Thought: The Frontiers of Philosophy and Theology, 1900–1960* (1963), and J. C. Livingston, *Modern Christian Thought: From the Enlightenment to Vatican II* (1971). R. N. Bellah, *Beyond Belief: Essays on Religion in a Post-Traditional World** (1991), explores religion and society in diverse cultural contexts. The continuing debate between science and religion is studied in E. L. Mascall, *Christian Theology and Natural Science* (1965); in S. L. Jaki, *The Road of Science and the Ways to God* (1978); and in J. H. Brooke, *Science and Religion: Some Historical Perspectives** (1991), cited in Chapter XIV. For the profound doctrinal and social changes in contemporary Roman Catholicism one may turn to L. Gilkey, *Catholicism Confronts Modernity* (1975); J. D. Holmes, *The Papacy in the Modern World, 1914–1978* (1981); and E. O. Hanson, *The Catholic Church in World Politics* (1987). For the recent popes there are biographies of John XXIII by M. Trevor (1967) and L. Elliott (1973); of Paul VI by P. Hebblethwaite (1993), a thoroughly detailed and documented account; and a tentative assessment of John Paul II's political activities by D. Wiley (1993).

Books on Einstein and early twentieth-century physics have been cited in Chapter XIV. The best introduction is B. L. Cline, *Men Who Made a New Physics** (1965, 1987), cited earlier. A. Pais has followed up his biography of Einstein (1982) with *Niels Bohr's Times: In Physics, Philosophy, and Polity* (1992). Biographies of twentieth-century physicists include studies of Leo Szilard by U. Lanouette (with B. Silara, 1993); Max Planck by J. Heilbron (1986); Werner Heisenberg by D. C. Cassidy (1991); Erwin Schrödinger* by W. Moore (1993); and Richard Feynman by J. Gleick (1992). For contemporary physics one may turn to H. C. Von Baeyer, *The Taming of the Atom: The Emergence of the Visible Microworld* (1992); J. Bernstein's *Quantum Profiles* (1991) and *Cranks, Quarks, and the Cosmos*

(1993); and L. M. Krauss, *Fear of Physics: A Guide for the Perplexed* (1993).

On the biological revolution, one may read R. Clowes, *The Structure of Life* (1967); R. Olby, *The Path to the Double Helix* (1974); H. F. Judson, *The Eighth Day of Creation: The Makers of the Revolution in Biology* (1979); and B. Wallace, *The Search for the Gene** (1993). In J. Watson, *The Double Helix: A Personal Account of the Discovery of the Structure of DNA* (rev. 1979), a scientist describes himself and other biologists at work. On the need for communication between scientists and nonscientists, an indispensable book is C. P. Snow, *The Two Cultures and the Scientific Revolution** (1959, rev. 1965; new critical ed., with introd. by S. Collini, 1993). It may be supplemented by B. Appleyard, *Understanding the Present* (1993), on the links of science, philosophy, and society.

The setback to medical science and the challenges to society posed by the appearance of AIDs are studied in M. D. Grmek, *History of AIDs: Emergence and Origin of a Modern Pandemic* (trans. 1990); in E. Fee and D. Fox (eds.), *AIDS: The Making of a Chronic Disease* (1991); and V. Berridge and P. Strong (eds.), *AIDS and Contemporary History* (1993).

For space exploration in all its aspects, one should read W. A. McDougall, *. . . the Heavens and the Earth: A Political History of the Space Age** (1985) and W. J. Walter, *Space Age* (1992). Special dimensions are added in V. Cronin, *The View from Planet Earth: Man Looks at the Cosmos* (1981), and J. S. and R. A. Lewis, *Space Resources: Breaking the Bonds of Earth* (1987).

Activist Movements: 1968

The most complete account of the student upheaval of 1968 as a worldwide phenomenon is D. Caute, *The Year of the Barricades: A Journey through 1968** (1989); it may be supplemented by G. Katsiafacis, *The Imagination of the New Left: A Global Analysis of 1968** (1987). One may also read L. S. Feuer, *The Conflict of Generations* (1969); A. J. Esler, *Bombs, Beards, and Barricades* (1971); and G. Stotera, *Death of a Utopia: The Development and Decline of Student Movements in Europe* (1975). The turbulent French scene is studied in R. Aron, *The Elusive Revolution* (trans. 1969); B. E. Brown, *Protest in Paris: Anatomy of a Revolt** (1974); and A. Touraine, *The*

May Movement: Revolt and Reform* (trans. 1979).

For insight into the emergence of youth and youth culture as a contemporary phenomenon one should read J. R. Gillis, *Youth and History: Tradition and Change in European Age Relations: 1770 to the Present* (rev. 1981), and the essays in A. J. Esler (ed.), *The Youth Revolution: The Conflict of Generations in Modern History* (1974), both cited earlier. For the "New Left" in the United States and elsewhere one may read J. P. Diggins, *The American Left in the Twentieth Century* (1973); I. Unger, *The Movement: A History of the American New Left, 1959–1972* (1974); T. Gitlin, *The Sixties: Years of Hope, Days of Rage* (1987), mostly a personal testament; M. Cranston (ed.), *The New Left* (1971); and K. Mehnert, *Moscow and the New Left* (1976).

The Women's Liberation Movement

For the background to the women's liberation movement, the books on the history of women described in the introduction will also serve as a guide. A thoughtful survey is O. Banks, *Faces of Feminism: A Study of Feminism as a Social Movement** (1981, 1986), which shows the link between the women's movements of 1850 in the United States and England to the present. One may also read W. O. O'Neill, *The Women's Movement: Feminism in the United States and England* (1969); J. S. Chafetz and A. G. Dworkin, *Female Revolt: The Rise of Women's Movements in World and Historical Perspective** (1986); and S. E. Cooper, *Western Feminism in the Twentieth Century** (Anvil Series, 1993). An anthology of emergent feminism is A. S. Rossi (ed.), *The Feminist Papers: From [Abigail] Adams to [Simone] de Beauvoir** (1974). The link in the United States between feminism and the civil rights movement and the changing status of American women are studied in W. R. Chafe, *The Paradox of Change: American Women in the 20th Century* (rev. 1992). For contemporary Europe, good introductions are J. Lovenduski, *Women and European Politics: Contemporary Feminism and Public Policy* (1986), and G. Kaplan, *Contemporary Western European Feminism** (1993), while J. Gelb, *Feminism and Politics** (1990), compares American and European experiences. The British scene is studied in S. Rowbotham, *The Past Is before Us: Feminism in Action since the 1960s*

(1989). For France one may turn to C. Duchen, *Feminism in France: From May '68 to Mitterrand** (1986), and D. M. Stetson, *Women's Rights in France* (1987), along with a selection of readings in E. Marks and I. de Courtivron (eds.), *New French Feminism: An Anthology* (1980). A convenient anthology for the German scene is H. Altbach and others (eds.), *German Feminism: Readings in Politics and Literature* (1984), while for Italy one may read L. C. Birnbaum, *Liberazione della Donna: Feminism in Italy* (1986).

On women's changing role in various settings and cultures a sampling of books would include N. J. Hafkin and E. C. Bay (eds.), *Women in Africa: Studies in Social and Economic Change* (1976); N. R. Keddie and B. Baron (eds), *Women in Middle Eastern History: Shifting Boundaries in Sex and Gender** (1991); J. Nash and H. I. Safa (eds.), *Women and Change in Latin America* (1986); and F. Miller, *Latin America: Women and the Search for Social Justice** (1991), an impressive study. Two valuable comparative assessments are I. Tinker (ed.), *Persistent Inequalities: Women and World Development* (1990), and D. Anderson, *The Unfinished Revolution: The Status of Women in Twelve Countries* (1992). The failure to achieve promised equality in socialist societies is examined in books on the Soviet Union cited in Chapter XVII; to them may be added T. Yedlin (ed.), *Women in Eastern Europe and the Soviet Union* (1980), and F. du P. Gray, *Soviet Women: Walking the Tight Rope** (1990). For China one may read D. Davin, *Womanwork: Women and the Party in Revolutionary China* (1976); E. Croll, *Feminism and Socialism in China** (1978); J. Stacey, *Patriarchy and Socialist Revolution in China** (1983); and R. S. Watson and P. B. Edbrey (eds.), *Marriage and Inequality in Chinese Society** (1990).

Terrorism

For terrorism as a twentieth-century political weapon and its implications for contemporary society one may turn to J. B. Bell, *On Revolt: Strategies of National Liberation* (1976); A. Parry, *Terrorism* (1976); W. Laqueur, *The Age of Terrorism* (1987); R. E. Rubinstein, *Alchemists of Revolution: Terrorism in the Modern World** (1987); and P. Wilkinson, *Terrorism** (1990). There are insightful essays in W. Gutteridge (ed.), *The*

New Terrorism (1986), and in W. Reich (ed.), *Origins of Terrorism: Psychologies, Ideologies, Theologies, States of Mind** (1990).

Population, Resources, Environment

Many of the books described in Chapter XXII on economic development will be helpful here. To follow the global demographic explosion of our times and the pressure on natural resources one should read the Worldwatch Institute annual report, *State of the World*, prepared since 1984 by L. R. Brown and others. For statistical projections, the UN's annual reports are invaluable, as are its special reports, such as *World Demographic Estimates and Projections, 1950–2025* (1988). The publications of the Population Reference Bureau are also indispensable, in particular its annual *World Population Data Sheet*. Present population trends are placed in historical perspective in M. Livi-Bacci, *A Concise History of World Population* (trans. 1992). Of special importance is P. Gupte, *The Crowded Earth: People and the Politics of Population* (1984). The concern over "fertility collapse" in the West and over the declining proportion of Europeans to world population is studied in M. Teitelbaum and J. M. Winter, *The Fear of Population Decline* (1985); B. Wattenberg, *Birth Dearth* (1987); D. J. van de Kaa, *Europe's Second Demographic Transition** (1987); and D. Noin and R. Woods (eds.), *The Changing Population of Europe** (1993).

Good introductions to environmental issues are B. Commoner, *The Closing Circle: Nature, Man and Technology* (1971); J. T. Hardy, *Science, Technology, and the Environment* (1975); and D. Worster (ed.), *The Ends of the Earth: Perspectives on Modern Environmental History** (1988). A. Gore, *Earth in the Balance: Ecology and the Human Spirit** (1992), is an eloquent statement by an American political leader. Environmentalism as ideology is examined in R. C. Paehlke, *Environmentalism and the Future of Progressive Politics** (1989). The wholesale environmental destruction in the former U.S.S.R. is examined in M. Feshbach and A. Friendly, Jr., *Ecocide in the U.S.S.R.* (1992). Two books of special interest are C. O. Paepke, *The Evolution of Progress: The End of Economic Growth and the Beginning of Human Transformation* (1993), and C. Ponting, *A Green History of the World: The Environment and the Collapse of Great Civilizations** (1992).

A New Era

The Persian Gulf War of 1990–1991 was the first serious crisis of the post–Cold War era. Several books on Iraq and the Middle East have been cited in Chapter XXII. For the Persian Gulf crisis, one may read E. Sciolino, *The Outlaw State: Saddam Hussein's Quest for Power and the Gulf Crisis* (1992); J. E. Smith, *George Bush's War* (1992), a balanced study despite the title; D. Hiro, *Desert Shield to Desert Storm: The Second Gulf War** (1992), on the military aspects; and L. Freedman and E. Karsh, *The Gulf Conflict, 1990–1991: Diplomacy and War in the New World Order* (1993), a remarkably comprehensive account. The background is ably traced in J. Crystal, *Oil and Politics in the Gulf* (1990) and *Kuwait: The Transformation of an Oil State* (1992).

The end of the Cold War has brought a number of thoughtful studies on the changing international scene, among them: W. G. Hyland, *The Cold War Is Over* (1992); M. J. Hogan (ed.), *The End of the Cold War** (1992); M. R. Beschloss and S. Talbott, *At the Highest Levels: The Inside Story of the End of the Cold War* (1993); J. L. Gaddis, *The United States and the End of the Cold War* (1992); G. Lundstad and O. A. Westad (eds.), *Beyond the Cold War: Future Dimensions in International Relations* (1993); J. Chace, *The Consequences of the Peace: The New Internationalism and American Foreign Policy** (1992); McG. Bundy, W. J. Crowe, Jr., and S. D. Drell, *Reducing Nuclear Danger: The Road Away from the Brink** (1993); M. van Creveld, *Nuclear Proliferation and the Future of Conflict** (1993); and W. E. Burrows and R. Windrem, *The Dangerous Race for Superweapons in a Fragmenting World* (1994).

The explosive ethnic tensions in the contemporary world are thoughtfully examined in D. P. Moynihan, *Pandaemonium: Ethnicity in International Politics* (1993); W. Pfaff, *The Wrath of Nations: Civilization and the Furies of Nationalism* (1993); and Z. Brzezenski, *Out of Control: Global Turmoil on the Eve of the Twenty-First Century* (1993). Of interest also are M. Juergensmeyer, *The New Cold War? Religious Nationalism Confronts the Secular State* (1993); J. Kristeva, *Nations without Nationalism** (1993); and M. Ignatieff, *Blood and*

Belongings: Journeys into the New Nationalism (1994).

Past, Present, and Future

The last decade of the century has brought an initial series of books linking past, present and future, among them: P. Kennedy, *Preparing for the Twenty-First Century* (1993), an insightful sober extrapolation of present trends; F. Fukuyama, *The End of History and the Last Man** (1992), a speculative essay, overly optimistic about the triumph of liberal democracy after the fall of communism; J. F. Revel, *Democracy against Itself: The Future of the Democratic Impulse* (1993), guardedly critical of emergent democracy; J. Lukacs, *The End of the Twentieth Century and the End of the Modern Age* (1992), which sees resurgent nationalism as overshadowing liberal democracy and rational humanism; R. Heilbroner, *21st Century Capitalism* (1993), which predicts expanding market economies, but with public investment in social needs; H. Kissinger, *Diplomacy* (1994), assessing the emergent pattern of global international relations in the perspective of the past few centuries; and W. W. Wagar, *A Short History of the Future* (rev. 1992), reflecting a measured optimism about the new century.

ILLUSTRATION SOURCES

Dates given after names of rulers and popes are the years of reigns or pontificates; those given for all others are the years of birth and death.

Pronunciation is indicated where it is not obvious. With foreign words the purpose is not to show their exact pronunciation in their own language but to suggest how they may be acceptably pronounced in English. Fully Anglicized pronunciations are indicated by the abbreviation *Angl.* Pronunciation is shown by respelling, not by symbols, except that the following symbols are used for vowel sounds not found in English:

ø indicates the sound of ö as in Göttingen. To form this sound, purse the lips as if to say *o*, and then say *ay* as in *ate*.

U indicates the sound of the French *u*, or of German *ü*. To form this sound, purse the lips as if to say *oo*, and then say *ee* as in *eat*.

aN, oN, uN, iN indicate the sounds of the French nasal vowels. Once learned, these are easily pronounced, roughly as follows: For aN, begin to pronounce the English word *on*, but avoid saying the consonant *n* and "nasalize" the *ah* sound instead. For oN do the same with the English *own*; for uN, with the English prefix *un-*; for iN, with the English word *an*.

The sound of *s* as in the word *treasure* is indicated by *zh*. This sound is common in English, though never found at the beginning or end of a word. *igh* always indicates the so-called long *i* as in *high*. The vowel sound of *hoot* is indicated by *oo*, that of *hood* by o̯o.

Compared with English, the European languages are highly regular in their spelling, in that the same letters or combinations of letters are generally pronounced in the same way.

INDEX

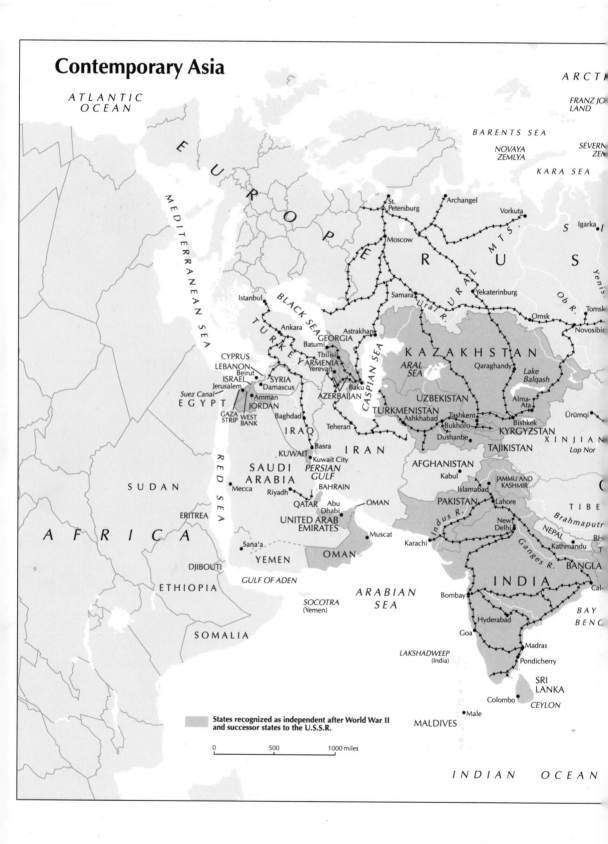

Contemporary Asia

ATLANTIC
OCEAN

MEDITERRANEAN SEA

E U R O P E

ARCTI

FRANZ JO
LAND

BARENTS SEA

NOVAYA
ZEMLYA

KARA SEA

SEVERN
ZEN

St.
Petersburg
Archangel

Vorkuta

Igarka

S

I

Moscow

R

U

S

S

Samara

Yekaterinburg

Omsk

Novosibir

Tomsk

U R A L   M T S.

Ural R.

Ob R.

Yenis

Istanbul

BLACK SEA

Ankara

T U R K E Y

Astrakhan

GEORGIA

Batumi

Tbilisi

ARMENIA

Yerevan

Baku

CASPIAN SEA

K A Z A K H S T A N

ARAL
SEA

Qaraghandy

Lake
Balqash

Alma-
Ata

Ürümqi

CYPRUS

LEBANON

Beirut

ISRAEL

Jerusalem

SYRIA

Damascus

AZERBAIJAN

UZBEKISTAN

Tashkent

Bishkek

KYRGYZSTAN

X I N J I A N

Suez Canal

EGYPT

GAZA
STRIP

WEST
BANK

Amman

JORDAN

Baghdad

TURKMENISTAN

Ashkhabad

Bukhoro

Lop Nor

I R A Q

Teheran

Dushanbe

TAJIKISTAN

SUDAN

RED SEA

KUWAIT

Basra

Kuwait City

I R A N

AFGHANISTAN

Kabul

JAMMU AND
KASHMIR

C

SAUDI
ARABIA

PERSIAN
GULF

Islamabad

TIBE

Mecca

Riyadh

BAHRAIN

QATAR

Abu
Dhabi

OMAN

PAKISTAN

Lahore

Brahmaputr

ERITREA

UNITED ARAB
EMIRATES

Muscat

Karachi

Indus R.

New
Delhi

NEPAL

Kathmandu

BH

T

AFRICA

Sana'a

YEMEN

OMAN

Ganges R.

BANGLA

DJIBOUTI

GULF OF ADEN

SOCOTRA
(Yemen)

ARABIAN
SEA

Bombay

I N D I A

Cal

BAY
BENC

ETHIOPIA

Hyderabad

Goa

Madras

Pondicherry

LAKSHADWEEP
(India)

SOMALIA

SRI
LANKA

Colombo

CEYLON

Male

MALDIVES

States recognized as independent after World War II
and successor states to the U.S.S.R.

0   500   1000 miles

INDIAN   OCEAN